Canada's First Nations

A History of Founding Peoples from Earliest Times

Fourth Edition

Olive Patricia Dickason
with **David T. McNab**

OXFORD
UNIVERSITY PRESS

OXFORD
UNIVERSITY PRESS

8 Sampson Mews, Suite 204, Don Mills, Ontario, M3C 0H5
www.oupcanada.com

Oxford University Press is a department of the University of Oxford.
It furthers the University's objective of excellence in research, scholarship,
and education by publishing worldwide in

Oxford   New York

Auckland   Cape Town   Dar es Salaam   Hong Kong   Karachi
Kuala Lumpur   Madrid   Melbourne   Mexico City   Nairobi
New Delhi   Shanghai   Taipei   Toronto

With offices in

Argentina   Austria   Brazil   Chile   Czech Republic   France   Greece
Guatemala   Hungary   Italy   Japan   Poland   Portugal   Singapore
South Korea   Switzerland   Thailand   Turkey   Ukraine   Vietnam

Oxford is a trade mark of Oxford University Press
in the UK and in certain other countries

Published in Canada by Oxford University Press

Library and Archives Canada Cataloguing in Publication

Dickason, Olive Patricia, 1920–

Canada's first nations : a history of founding peoples from earliest times / Olive Patricia Dickason,
David T. McNab. — 4th ed.

Includes bibliographical references and index.
ISBN 978-0-19-542892-6

1. Native peoples—Canada--History. I. McNab, David, 1947– II. Title.

E78.C2D535 2008   971'.00497   C2008-904713-3

This book is printed on permanent acid-free paper ∞.
Printed and bound in Canada.

2 3 4 — 13 12 11

Contents

List of Maps

'I am an Indian. I am proud to know who I am and where I originated. I am proud to be a unique creation of the Great Spirit. We are part of Mother Earth. . . .

'We have survived, but survival by itself is not enough. A people must also grow and flourish.'

Chief John Snow, *These Mountains Are Our Sacred Places*
(Toronto: Samuel Stevens, 1977).

Acknowledgements

A Senior Rockefeller Fellowship, which allowed me to spend a year at The Newberry Library in Chicago, made it possible to intensify the research and undertake the writing of this book. For this I owe a very special debt to Frederick Hoxie, at that time director of the library's D'Arcy McNickle Center for the History of the American Indian. The Center's associate director, Jay Miller, was unstintingly generous in sharing his knowledge of Amerindians, putting me on to tracks that I would otherwise have missed and coming to my rescue in my frequent confrontations with the computer. The Newberry Library's staff was a joy to work with, particularly John Aubrey, who always knew the answers when it came to the library's extraordinary collections. Francis Jennings and Helen Hornbeck Tanner provided invaluable guidance through the mazeways of Amerindian history. An eye-opening experience was participating in the Transatlantic Encounters Program, organized by David Buisseret of the library's Hermon Dunlap Smith Center for the History of Cartography.

Similarly, the library staff of the University of Alberta has been unfailingly co-operative in the seemingly endless search for detail that this project entailed, as were those of the National Archives and National Library of Canada, Metropolitan Toronto Reference Library, Royal Ontario Museum, Woodland Indian Cultural Education Centre, Hudson's Bay Company Archives in Winnipeg, Alberta Provincial Archives, the Glenbow Museum, the Royal British Columbia Museum, and the BC Provincial Archives. Back at home base, throughout all this, my thesis director, Professor Cornelius Jaenen of the University of Ottawa's History Department, was a wise and supportive guide through the mazeways of history. Three particularly useful conferences were the Self-Determination Symposium organized by the Assembly of First Nations and University of Toronto, 1990; the First Nations Conference on Self Government at Nakoda Lodge, Morley, Alberta, 1991; and the Native Justice Symposium, an all-Native event held in Edmonton, 1991.

Many individuals have responded to my frequent calls for help, opening up more avenues for exploration than I had time to take advantage of. I owe special debts to Alice B. Kehoe, Catharine McClellan, Joseph L. Peyser, Frank

Lestringant, Vicente Cortés Alonso, Philippe Jacquin, Charles Schweger, Milton Freeman, Gurston Dacks, Denys Delâge, Walter Moser, Ron Whistance-Smith, William Phipps, Tom Hill, Sam and Linda Bull, John David Hamilton, John S. Long, Malcolm Davidson, Trudy Nicks, Margaret Carter, Nancy Gibson, Marge Friedel, Muriel Stanley-Venne, Angelina Pratt, George Lang, Desmond Brown, Rod Macleod, Bob Beal, Sheila (Hayes) Genaille, Doreen (L'Hirondelle) Richardson, Eugene Olson, Edward Trzeciak, Jack Douglas, John and Leni Honsaker, and John F. Leslie. When the size of the manuscript taxed the capacities of my computer, Fern Ness, University of Alberta Computing Systems, provided the answer; when the complexities of a new computer challenged too vigorously, which it did all too frequently, Robert J. Burns lent a reassuring and very helpful hand, as did Miriam Smith.

Several people took the time to read all or part of the manuscript with critical eyes, adding much to its breadth and scope, not to mention accuracy. These included Donald B. Smith, Jennifer S.H. Brown, Alan Bryan, Ruth Gruhn, Stuart Mackinnon, Clifford Hickey, Carl Urion, Jay Miller, Nicholas Wickenden, and Anita Harper. I owe a special thanks to Professor Smith for opening up his picture files to me. Finally, the careful editing of Richard Tallman, of both this edition and the first three editions, was particularly helpful.

In acknowledging the help of all those named and unnamed who have contributed so much, I should still point out that the responsibility for the contents and orientation of this book is mine alone.

Further Acknowledgements

I would like to thank Olive Dickason for inviting me to undertake the fourth edition of this book. It has been a fascinating experience for a Métis historian. I would also like to thank Paul-Emile McNab, currently a Master of Environmental Studies graduate student at York University, for agreeing to act as my research assistant for this edition. His research made my work possible.

David T. McNab
June 2008

Introduction

Canada, it used to be said by non-Aboriginals with more or less conviction, is a country of much geography and little history.[1] The ethnocentricity of that position at first puzzled, and even confused, Amerindians, but it has lately begun to anger them. How could such a thing be said, much less believed, when their people have been living here for thousands of years? As they see it, Canada has about 58 founding nations (depending on how they are counted) rather than just the two that have been officially acknowledged. Even Amerindian studies in the Western sense are not new; an early post-contact scholar was the Amerindian Huaman Poma (Felipe de Ayala), who in 1613 wrote a history of the Inca of Peru, *Nueva Crónica y Buen Gobierno*.

History, for its part, has been described as a document-bound discipline. If something was not written, preferably in an official document, it was not historical. Thus were pre-literate societies excluded from history and labelled prehistoric, or perhaps proto-historic. The best they could hope for was to become historic by extension, when they came into contact with literate societies. In other words, Canada's history began with the arrival of Europeans.

As if that were not restrictive enough, another limitation was added: Canada's history has been usually presented not as beginning with the first Europeans, the Norse, who arrived here about AD 1000, but with the French, who came first as fishermen and later as explorers in the sixteenth century, and stayed to settle in the seventeenth. The arbitrariness of this is evident when it is realized that the English were hard on the heels of the French and even preceded them in exploratory voyages, at least one of which, that of John Cabot (d. 1498?), or rather, to use his Italian name, Giovanni Caboto, sailing under the English flag, dated back to 1497. Pushed into the background were the Portuguese, who were also here before the French, exploiting the rich fisheries off the North Atlantic coast, as well as the Basques (usually referred to as Spanish), who may have preceded all the other Europeans of this period in their pursuit of whales. In the sixteenth century the Basques transformed the whale runs of the Strait of Belle Isle into a highly profitable industry, providing oil for European energy needs, and they penetrated as far north as Davis Strait. When Jacques Cartier visited Hochelaga in 1535, he recorded words being used by the Iroquoians that appear to be Basque in origin. The list of Europeans does not end there: the Dutch, leading entrepreneurs, were financing both trading and whaling expeditions, if not always taking part in them; later, they would be associated with Champlain. By the turn of the fifteenth century into the sixteenth, the waters off Canada's North Atlantic coast were the scene of intense international activity, and Cartier's voyages were in the nature of official confirmation of what was already well known.

What was the role of Amerindians and Inuit in all this? Far from being passive partners in European enterprises, as so often portrayed, they were active participants. Indeed, that participation was essential to European success: Basque whalers availed themselves of Inuit harpooning technology to improve greatly the efficiency of their own techniques; Mi'kmaq (Micmac) sea hunters put their expertise at the service of Europeans to pursue walrus for ivory, hides, and train oil, all much in demand by the latter; and later Amerindians did the same thing in the production of furs, so much sought after for the luxury trade, as status-conscious Europeans used furs (among other items) as symbols of rank. It has been estimated that by 1600 there may have been up to a thousand European ships a year engaged in commercial activities in Canada's northeastern coastal waters. Such activity would not have been possible without the co-operation and participation of the first nations of the land. When it came to penetrating the interior of the continent, Amerindians and Inuit guided the way for the European 'explorers', equipped them with the clothing and transportation facilities they needed, and provided them with food. Their contributions in economic terms alone were substantial and can probably never be properly assessed. As political economist Harold Innis (1894–1952) expressed it, 'the Indian and his culture were fundamental to the growth of Canadian institutions.'[2] In the most profound sense of the term, they are Canada's founding peoples.

Because they were oral, rather than literate, peoples (even those who did possess a form of writing had not developed it into a widely shared form of communication), reconstructing their pre-contact history in the Western sense of the term is a daunting task. Canadian historians have, in the past, found it much easier to ignore the earlier period; hence the blinkered view of Canada as a 'young' country.

Europeans found the Americas populated by a variety of peoples who, in broad terms, shared a general civilization, somewhat as the newcomers did themselves in their own homelands. Within that general New World framework was a rich variety of cultural manifestations: the centralized empire of the Peruvian Inca; the decentralized 'empire' of the Mexica; the independent Mayan city-states of Mesoamerica; the city-state of Cahokia on the upper Mississippi, the largest centre of population north of the Rio Grande; a variety of confederacies such as those of Powhatan in present-day Virginia, the Five Nations in northern New York state, and the Huron in southern Ontario; a collection of chiefdoms of various characteristics, including those of the Timucuans of today's Florida, the Natchez, Creeks, Cherokees, and others of the southern United States, the Haida, Kwagiulth (Kwakwaka'wakw, Kwakiutl), and others of the northern Pacific coast; and the comparatively simple band communities of mobile hunters and gatherers. This dazzling variety of cultural particularities has tended to obscure the underlying unity of the Amerindian world view, which saw humans as part of a cosmological order depending on a balance of reciprocating forces to keep the universe functioning in harmony. This contrasts with the Judeo-Christian view of a cosmos dominated by a God in the image of man. In this perspective man is in a privileged position, as up to a certain point he can control nature for his own benefit. These ideological approaches were reflected in their respective technologies: where Europeans used metals for tools and weaponry, Amerindians used them mainly to express their sense of cosmological order. Workaday materials in the Americas were stone, bone, wood, and fibre, although copper and copper alloys were also in use in certain areas.[3] All were crafted with a high degree of sophistication.

In telling the story of the meeting of these disparate civilizations, this book begins with the first appearance of humans in the Americas. Since little is positively known about those distant events, various theories are described without attempting to nail down the 'truth'. This applies also to the development of agriculture and the rise of city-states, the subjects of Chapters 2 and 3. As British archaeologist Ian Hodder has observed, without certainty 'we do not have the right to impose our own universals on the data and to present them as truth.'[4] A challenging aspect of our very early history is that so much remains to be found out.

Chapter 4 looks at Canada's First Nations as Europeans first found them, setting the scene (at least in part) for the story of the interactions that followed, which comprises the bulk of the work.

The early contact period (Chapters 5 through 11) begins with the brief presence of the Norse but is concerned mainly with interactions of Amerindians and French and with how the two peoples set about developing working relationships. The initial reaction of establishing trade was soon complicated by the French drive to evangelize and to remould Amerindians into the European cultural pattern, characteristics that were shared with other colonial powers. Europeans generally did not recognize the validity of Amerindian civilizations, classed them as 'savage', and denied their right to sovereignty and even to landed property rights for those peoples living in non-state societies, which was

the case in Canada. Ambiguities soon developed on the latter point, however, even as it was consistently maintained that Christians had prior rights over non-Christians, whether organized into states or not. Because of the smallness of the populations and the importance of the fur trade, land did not become an issue between French and Amerindians in the north as it did with the English and Spanish to the south. The French never recognized Aboriginal right, however, and when they sought to establish in southern latitudes they encountered the same problems in this regard as other colonizing powers. Even in the north there were violent confrontations: the French–Iroquois War was one of the most prolonged north of the Rio Grande, matched in length only by the British–Mi'kmaq–Abenaki conflict on the east coast.

The British takeover in 1763, which soon led to the opening of the West to the fur trade and later to non-Aboriginal settlement (Chapters 12–14), was the beginning of a difficult period for the Amerindians, as their traditional world became steadily less secure under advancing colonial pressures. Attempts to counter this movement with pan-Amerindian alliances (which had begun during the French regime and had been vigorously suppressed) met with failure on the battlefield. The turning point was the War of 1812, the last of the colonial wars, which ushered in a new way of life for Amerindians as British imperial power became firmly established (Chapters 15–19). The drive to assimilate Amerindians took on a new intensity; this period saw the beginning of the great land-cession treaties, by which the British sought to extinguish what limited land rights they recognized for Amerindians, and Indians sought to work out as congenial arrangements as they could for accommodating themselves to the new order of things. This was also the period that saw the rise of the Métis, the 'New Nation' born of Indians and Euro-Canadians, who in 1869–70 would make

Canadian artist William George Richardson Hind (1833–89) entitled this painting 'Civilization and Barbarism'.
(Metropolitan Toronto Reference Library, J. Ross Robertson Collection, T-33320)

their first stand for their place in the British imperial order.

The rapid disappearance of the buffalo herds of the western Plains under the onslaught of commercial hunters (the animal had long since been exterminated by European settlers east of the Mississippi) precipitated an even more desperate resistance on the part of the Métis, as well as Cree to a lesser extent. This led Canada to inaugurate a campaign of legislating Native cultures out of existence (Chapters 20–7). The Far North, which until this point had been the purview of whalers and trappers, neither of whom directly attacked the Native way of life, suddenly attracted the attention of southerners when its placer gold was discovered. The Klondike gold rush became a Canadian legend, and the isolation that had protected traditional lifestyles was severely cracked. It was not shattered, however, until after World War II when new technology made exploitation of northern resources economically feasible. The Electronic Age also gave a new meaning to oral traditions, and Canada's original peoples— both Amerindian and Inuit, as well as Métis— began to campaign for their rights. No longer was industrial development allowed to ride roughshod over Native rights, at least not without a protest. The Mackenzie Valley Pipeline Inquiry heralded a change in attitudes, and the James Bay Agreement marked a modification in procedures. But established ways of doing and thinking can die hard, as the 'Indian Summer' of 1990, the Wet'suwet'en decision of 1991, and the postponement of the second phase of the James Bay project at Great Whale River so dramatically illustrate. These and other developments led Ottawa to launch its first major official inquiry in co-operation with First Nations into the situation and the concerns of its Aboriginal citizens. As the five-volume report of the Royal Commission on Aboriginal Peoples makes clear, what they are asking for is full and equal partnership in the Canadian federation (Chapter 28).

Natives have become politically sophisticated in their campaigns to salvage what they can of their territories and traditional values; the term 'Aboriginal right', originally applied only to land, has now come to include self-government. Canada has been slow to acknowledge the Native right to an ongoing interest in their lands and has continued to insist on extinguishment of Aboriginal right in return for specified benefits, mostly of an economic nature but also including political concessions. Both Indians and Inuit have become steadily less inclined to accept such arrangements, and in some cases (such as the Mohawk and Dene) they flatly reject them as violations of their basic rights. Unless the government negotiates self-determination, Amerindians could become a permanently disaffected group, as happened with the Irish in Great Britain. Anthropologist Michael Asch made that point when he observed that denying minorities the right to negotiate their concerns with those in power virtually assures resort to violence.[5] Canada once made a reputation for itself as a peacekeeper on the international scene, a reputation it is having difficulty in maintaining, if it has not already lost it, within its own borders.

The Problem of Interpretation

A word about Amerindian tribal classifications is necessary. Labels such as 'Cree', 'Huron', 'Beaver', 'Haida' were imposed by Europeans and do not represent how the people termed themselves, at least aboriginally. In some cases a single label, such as 'Cree', 'Abenaki', or 'Odawa', included a number of distinct groups, more or less closely related by language. These three all belong to the Algonkian language group. The term 'Algonkian' or 'Algonkin' as used in this work refers to language; 'Algonquin' or 'Algonquian' refers to a particular people living in the Eastern Woodlands who are Algonkian speakers and who on first contact were allied to the Hurons. While many of the Europeanized labels have come to be accepted by the Aboriginal peoples, some have not; for instance, the tundra-dwellers of the Arctic objected to 'Eskimo' on the grounds that it was pejorative as it had come to be popularly believed that it came from an Ojibwa term that translated as 'eaters of raw meat', despite the opinion of linguists that it actually derived from a Montagnais term meaning 'she nets a snowshoe'.[6] The tundra-dwellers won their point, and their term for themselves, 'Inuit' ('the people', 'Inuk' in the singular), has been officially accepted. Similarly, the Nootka of the west coast prefer 'Nuu'chah'nulth' ('all along the mountains'), and the Kwakiutl, who had compromised with 'Kwagiulth', have now settled on 'Kwakwaka'wakw' as a more accurate rendition of their tribal name. The Maliseet prefer their own term for themselves, 'Wuastu-kwiuk', rather than 'Maliseet', which is a Mi'kmaq term that translates as 'broken (or lazy) talkers'. Others include 'Mi'kmaq' for Micmac, 'Nisga'a' for Nishga, 'Gwich'in' for Kutchin, 'Wet'suwet'en' for Carrier, and 'Tsuu T'ina' for Sarcee. The Montagnais and Naskapi, referred to as two separate (although closely allied) people in early documentation, today consider themselves to be one, 'Innu'. However, since the terms 'Montagnais' and 'Naskapi' are solidly entrenched in the literature, these names will be retained for the sake of clarity, particularly when citing early documentation. When the context is modern-day, 'Innu' will be used.

This leads to the problem of a general name for New World peoples. Although the term 'Indian' is recognized as originating in a case of mistaken identity, it has come to be widely accepted, particularly by the Aboriginal peoples themselves. The trouble with that term, of course, is that it is also used for the people of India, who with some justification claim prior right. In Canada, with its substantial population from India, this ambiguity is particularly obvious. Francophones have solved the problem by using 'amérindien', which is specific to the Americas, or 'autochtone', which translates as Aboriginal. Anglophones have not reached such an accord; in Canada, 'Native' has come to be widely used, but it is not accepted in the United States on the grounds that anyone born in that country is a native, regardless of racial origin; their accepted form is 'native American'. In Canada, 'Aboriginal' is becoming widely used by Indians as well as non-Indians. 'Amerindian' has not received popular acceptance in English-language Canada and has even less in the United States. However, as it avoids the ambiguities of 'Indian' and 'Native', and is more specific than 'Aboriginal', it is my term of preference.

Problems of translating concepts and even words from one language to another are notorious for misleading the unwary. The word 'father' is a good example of this. For sixteenth- and seventeenth-century Europeans, the connotations of the term included authority and control of the family. In Amerindian languages, the term implied a protector and provider, who could be influential but who lacked authority in the European sense, particularly among matrilineal societies, where mothers had the say over children. The authority figure in such societies was the maternal uncle; when the Iroquois, for instance, referred to the French king as 'father', they were not placing themselves under his authority. If that had been their intention, they would have used the term 'uncle', which they never did.[7]

Amerindian personal names can present difficulties for non-Indians. Since spellings have not, for the most part, been standardized, there is a great variety to choose from. I have mentioned some of these choices, but it was not possible—or even desirable—to try and list them all. What I have done instead has been to indicate some of the variations to expect. The English versions of these names present another problem; for the most part, the best that can be hoped for is an approximation that touches on only a limited aspect of a range of possible meanings. The circumlocutions that can result are hinted at in the attempt to transliterate Nescambiouit's name (Chapter 7). In another case, that of Neolin (Chapter 12), the English version 'One That Is Four' is given without explanation. The reference is to spiritual power and knowledge, as four is a sacred number for Amerindians and also refers to the four directions. A usual English rendering is 'The Enlightened', a partial approximation at best. In many cases names have been so altered by transliterations that their original meanings are obscured.

Place names, on the other hand, are in a separate category. In Amerindian practice, they indicate geographical or ecological characteristics, or else recall a historic event that happened on the spot. Unlike Europeans, and with one major exception, Amerindians do not name places or geographical features after persons or tribes. The exception concerns reserves, sometimes named after individuals, such as Ahtahkakoop, Poundmaker, and Mistawassis. Arctic Quebec (Nunavik) has switched to Inuktitut for its place names.

Problems of interpretation take on a totally different aspect when considering early European accounts of the Americas. For one thing, as English literary scholar Ian S. MacLaren, a specialist in exploration accounts, has pointed out, there can be variation in connotations of words as used in the sixteenth or eighteenth centuries and today. For another, in the case of published accounts, what appeared in print could differ markedly from what the author had written; publishers were sometimes more concerned about saleability than about veracity. Where the original manuscript has survived, this can be checked, but that is rare with early imprints.[8] Since the printed word should not be taken automatically at face value, the researcher is left with the necessity of cross-checking with whatever other sources are available. These are usually few, and sometimes non-existent.

Another area that calls for caution is that of dating. Two systems are used in this work: the standard Gregorian calendar with which we are all familiar for the historic period, which uses the abbreviations BC (before Christ) and AD (anno domini, 'year of our Lord'); and the scientific calendar based on radiocarbon dating for the prehistoric period, which refers to dates in years BP (before present). Where the Gregorian calendar uses the birth of Christ as a pivotal point, radiocarbon dating uses the year 1950. Radiocarbon dating is based on the physical fact that the radioactive carbon isotope 14C decays to the stable isotope 12C at a known and constant rate; therefore, measurement of the residual 14C in organic remains indicates years elapsed since the death of the organism. However, the radiocarbon year does not necessarily correspond to the calendar year, due to the changing 14C content of the atmosphere. In technical publications, this statistical variation is usually included with the date.

A final reminder: the Indian Act applies only to 'status' Indians, that is, those who are registered and listed in the official band rolls. Non-status Indians and Métis are legally classed as ordinary citizens. In the interests of simplicity and readability, the distinction is usually not referred to in the text, except in some specific instances where clarity calls for it. The term 'Métis' is used in its French sense, mixture, usually applied to the crossing of human races, without specifying which ones. On the Labrador coast, mixed-bloods are known to the Inuit as 'Kablunangajuit' and to non-Aboriginals as 'liveyeres', 'settlers', or perhaps 'Labradorians'.

Part I

At the Beginning

Chapter 1

And the People Came

That people were living in the Americas during the later Ice Ages is no longer debated; what is not agreed on is when the movement from the Old World to the New began. When modern humans (*Homo sapiens sapiens*, 'man doubly wise') appeared on the world scene early during the Wisconsin glaciation, 50,000–10,000 BP,[1] their cultural development was comparatively rapid, blossoming in an ever-increasing variety through Europe and across Asia.[2] Their appearance in the New World is more problematic, as bones have not preserved well in its soils, and identifying early campsites and tools can be difficult. The two Americas are the world's only continents where the evidence of early human presence has been based on artifacts, not skeletal remains.[3] As matters stand at present, the oldest dates for human habitation have come out of unglaciated South America, and the most recent ones for pre-contact migration have come from the ice-bound Arctic. When Europeans stumbled on the Caribbean islands in the late fifteenth century, they found Amerindians in what they considered to be their cultural infancy and assumed they were a young people who could have been

here only for a few hundred years. An observant few, among them the Dominican Bartolomé de Las Casas (1484–1566), recognized traces of early habitation that had become grown over and realized that this could only have happened over long periods of time.[4] Majority first impressions, however, proved to be persistent, and only comparatively recently has a long occupation time depth been accepted for the Americas. This raises the question of the place of origin for *Homo sapiens sapiens*. Impassioned attempts to prove an American genesis for modern Indians have not made a convincing case.[5] The identification by archaeologist Louis Leakey (1903–72) of fractured pebbles found at Calico Hills, California, as 100,000- to 200,000-year-old tools would establish the presence of pre-modern humans —possibly even of *Homo erectus*—if he could have substantiated his argument, which neither he nor others have been able to do.

Many Indians believe this is the land of their origin, and their myths, with their metaphoric descriptions of the genesis of humans and the present world, are many and varied; their different perceptions of time and nature

TIMELINE

75,000–15,000 BP	Ice Ages (Wisconsin glaciation), when Bering Strait land bridge was accessible for migration from Asia.	8500 BC	and caribou hunting, spread across Canada.
50,000 BP	Human capability of traversing vast stretches of open ocean, evidenced by peopling of Australia.	9000 BC	Northwest Coast culture established, based on salmon fishing and sea hunting—a sedentary culture with permanent settlements due to rich land and sea resources.
11,000 BP	Bifacially flaked (fluted) stone points and knives dated to 11,000 years ago have been found and identified by archaeologists at both the Asian and North American sides of Beringia. Campsites of peoples of different cultural traditions scattered throughout North and South America.	8000–6000 BC	Hunting of bison by means of drives and jumps begins.
		6500 BC	Domestication of dogs as pack and sled animals and for hunting.
9200–	Fluted spear points, used in bison	6000 BC	Migration of eastern Early Archaic peoples to westerns Plains and mixing with Plano (rippled flaking of spear and knife points) peoples creates Plains culture.

place these tales at another level of reality than that of this work.[6] The myths emphasize and confirm the peoples' fundamental attachment to the land. The Gitksan of northern British Columbia maintain that the Upper Skeena River Valley is their Garden of Eden; several groups, such as the Salish Thompson River people and the Ojibwa, believe that their first ancestors were born of the earth;[7] the Athapaskan Beaver hold that humans crawled through a hollow log in order to reach earth, an obvious birth analogy;[8] the Iroquoians (including the Huron), that the mother of mankind, Aataentsic, fell through a hole in the sky and landed on a tortoise with earth piled on its back.[9] On another plane, the Tsimshian have legends in which migration is a theme.[10]

The most generally held anthropological theory, based on observable data, that *Homo sapiens sapiens* came from Asia via the Bering Strait, was first proposed by Jesuit José de Acosta (*c.* 1539–1600) in *Historia Natural y Moral de las Indias*, published in 1590.[11] Today it is widely accepted by anthropologists and archaeologists that Indians made the crossing on foot during periods when intensification of the Ice Ages lowered the sea level, transforming Bering Strait into a land bridge called Beringia. Once believed to have been a grassy and often boggy steppe, it has been revealed by recent studies to have been covered with birch, heath, and shrub willow.[12] Geologists inform us that there were several periods during the late Pleistocene geological age (the Wisconsin stage) when the land bridge called Beringia emerged, the first identifiable one dating back to about 75,000 BP and the last one ending about 14,000 years ago.[13] This expanse of open grassland and tundra at one point was more than 2,000 kilometres wide, more like a continent than a bridge. It provided forage for such animals as mammoth, mastodon, giant bison, saiga antelope, and the predators that preyed on them. That human hunters followed the herds is a reasonable assumption supported by archaeological evidence from both sides of the Bering Strait, including 11,000-year-old bifacially flaked stone points and knives, and, on

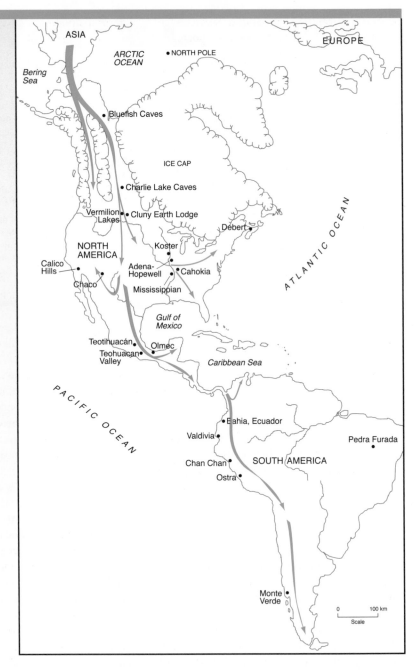

1.1

Possible land route for first human entry into the Americas, as well as some archaeological sites

Source: Alvin M. Josephy, Jr, *The Indian Heritage of America* (New York: Knopf, 1969), 36.

occasion, microblades—small, thin, very sharp stone flakes that were being made 15,000 to 4,500 years ago. Their production required considerable skill. If this was the route, then Siberia must have been inhabited first. Russian archaeologists have reported evidence for the peopling of Yakuktia in central Siberia some 300,000 years ago, long before the appearance of *Homo sapiens sapiens*;[14] Chukotka, on the northeastern tip of Siberia, has yielded a date of 35,000 BP, which is within the range of modern humans.[15]

Since game abounded, should we then assume that the first *Homo sapiens* in the Americas were principally big-game hunters? Yes, as far as Canada is concerned; but for the New World as a whole, that may not have been the case. As archaeological techniques become more sophisticated and research expands, evidence is turning up in South America to suggest that the first humans in those regions may have been primarily foragers (fishing being a form of gathering) and hunters of small game.[16] What is more, the indications are that they were inclined to stay where their food resources were, usually by the shores of sea, lake, or river. They exploited those resources on water as well as on land, which suggests that they used watercraft.[17] Archaeologist Peter Schledermann, working in the eastern Arctic, has concluded that sea mammals were the principal source of food for the people of the Arctic Small Tool Tradition (3000 BC–1200 BC).[18] Even the later, more mobile hunters who pursued big game inland preferred to camp by water, and probably for at least one of the same reasons—the facility of water travel.

Option of the Sea

To return to the means by which people arrived in the Americas: there is no reason to conclude that because Beringia offered a convenient pedestrian route, it was therefore the only one available or used. Nor is there any reason to believe that Beringia's inhabitants were landbound, ignoring the rich marine life on and off its coasts. The sea also offered options; in the Pacific, the Japanese current sweeping from the Asiatic coast eastward to the Americas provided a natural aquatic highway that would not have presented insuperable challenges. The argument that humans at this early stage had not yet developed the skills to undertake travel by water under dangerous Arctic conditions is tenuous at best, particularly in view of the sea voyages that occurred at other latitudes. One could even argue that deep-sea sailing in some respects is not as hazardous as coasting, and that both are easier than walking. That travel by water could have been more practical than travelling by land has long been maintained by archaeologist Knut Fladmark.[19] As he has pointed out, humans have been capable of traversing stretches of water at least as wide as the Bering Strait for 30,000 years or more; there is also the fact that the west coast was largely unglaciated during a temperate period about 60,000 to 25,000 years ago in the late Pleistocene. This may have been the case in southwestern Alberta as well.[20] Australia was peopled about 50,000 BP, and that could only have been by boat, although admittedly not under Arctic conditions, and involving no enormous distances, as at that period sea levels would have been lower than they are today. Island hopping from the Malaysian archipelago to Australia would have faced reduced—but still formidable—sea barriers.[21]

Languages

In North America, the coastal route may have been a factor in producing the abundance of languages along the Pacific coasts of the two Americas, one of the most complex linguistic regions in the world. (In the sixteenth century, the New World had an estimated 2,200 languages.) Studies by anthropologist Richard A. Rogers have shown that in North America, unglaciated areas contained by far the greatest number of languages, 93 per cent, along with a higher degree of differentiation from those that had been glaciated. It is an accepted principle

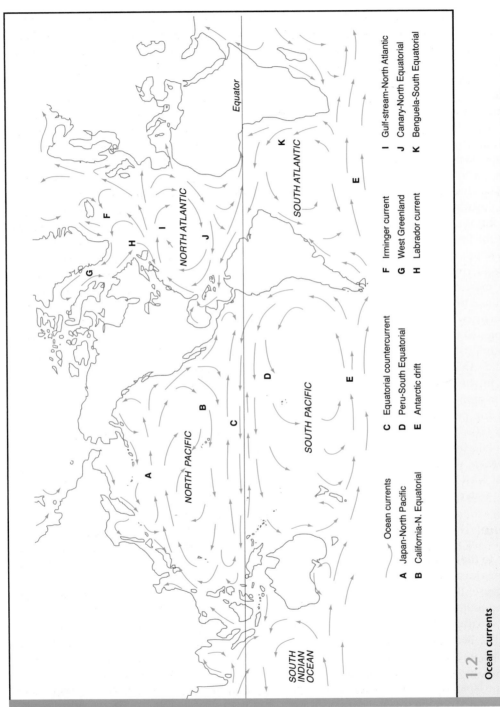

1.2

Ocean currents

Sources: Jessie D. Jennings, ed., *Ancient Native Americans* (San Francisco: Freeman, 1978); *The Rand-McNally Atlas of the Oceans* (New York, Chicago, San Francisco, 1979), 33.

in linguistics that language diversification proceeds very slowly and is proportional to the length of human occupation; where diversification has reached the point of obscuring original linguistic relationships, then substantial time depth is indicated. Archaeologist Ruth Gruhn has called attention to the fact that North America's greatest diversification of language stocks is in California and on the Gulf coast, while in South America more than 1,500 languages were spoken, differing widely in their grammatical constructions and vocabularies. In Gruhn's view all of these languages from both continents are ultimately related in three major stocks. She believes their proliferation to be too great to be explained solely by a series of migrations, but rather that the languages evolved locally over a very long span of time, perhaps close to 50,000 years.[22] She is in accord with anthropologist Joseph H. Greenberg, who sees a possibility that all Indian languages, except for Na-Dene (Athapaskan) and Eskimo-Aleut, developed from a single prototype called Amerind. This highly controversial theory postulates a minimum of three founding migrations, the first of which brought Amerind, by far the largest, most widespread, and most diversified of the three proposed basic groups.[23]

Linguistic evidence suggesting that South America was settled early has been supported by recent archaeological discoveries at Monte Verde in Chile and at Tocado Boqueir'ao do Pedra Furada in Brazil, which indicate that people may have been present in the Americas as early as 32,000 years ago.[24] There are also tantalizing suggestions of extreme antiquity for humans in North America, perhaps early as 22,000 BC.[25] Sites in Pennsylvania, California, Texas, and Mexico have all hinted at a presence that is dated earlier as one proceeds south; finds in south-central New Mexico, announced by archaeologist Richard MacNeish (1918–2001), are of campsites that have been radiocarbon-dated to 36,000 years ago.[26] The one possible exception to this is the unglaciated Yukon, where human occupation dating back to 40,000 years has been argued by archaeologist William N. Irving. If established, this would support the primacy of the Beringia route.[27] The best evidence so far for early humans in the Yukon has come from Bluefish Caves, south of Old Crow. There, debris has been found that was left behind by hunters of about 24,000 to 12,000 years ago. Most of the butchered bones are of land mammals. However, no hearths or human remains have been found on the location.[28] That famous caribou-bone flesher discovered by Gwich'in Peter Lord near Old Crow in 1966, and once dated to 27,000 BP, is now believed to be only 1,000 years old.[29] Even if the more secure dates of 18,000 to 15,000 years ago are preferred for the arrival of humans in North America, there was still plenty of time for the plenitude of languages to have developed on the Pacific coast. That pattern of settlement can best by explained by coastal travel.

Ice-free Corridor

Such a route could also provide an explanation as to why the ice-free corridor along the eastern slopes of the Rockies, which has been hypothesized as the most likely migration path, has not yielded the expected archaeological sites, or even artifacts, unlike the well-documented route between the Andes and the Pacific in South America.[30] Geological data indicate the Canadian corridor was a forbidding region of loose rock, shifting shorelines of glacial lakes, and rugged slopes: no significant faunal remains dating to the period of the late Wisconsin glaciation have been found in the central and northern portions. It is possible that the interior Plateau was used, but there is no evidence there either. As far as interior land travel is concerned, most movements seem to have been from south to north; for example, the Algonkian speakers who occupy so much of Canada's Subarctic forest, the taiga, fanned northward from the Great Lakes, and the buffalo hunters of the northwestern Plains came from two directions, south and east. Exceptions are the Athapaskans (Dene), who, after living in the Far North since about 9,000 years ago, began to move south following a volcanic eruption near White River,[31] and the Inuit, who spread eastward across the Arctic from Siberia. For the rest, as our information stands at present, people somehow looped south of the glaciers, then headed north again as the ice retreated.

The lack of visible archaeological sites on the Pacific Northwest Coast is easier to explain: they were drowned as the ocean rose with the melting of the glaciers. Whether on foot or on water, or a combination of both, Indians reached the southern tip of South America by at least 11,000 BP. Canada's High Arctic was the last region to be populated, after 3000 BC, following some movement into lower Arctic regions a little earlier. Human entry into the Americas seems to have been in the form of a filtering action, perhaps in waves—three, perhaps four, main ones are currently being hypothesized—stretching over long periods of time. While such movements are nearly always considered in connection with Beringia and the Pacific, at certain epochs they would also have been possible along the discontinuous glacial front across the Atlantic into eastern North America. Although the biological evidence indicating Asiatic origins for Indians appears to be secure,[32] there has been speculation, based on fragmentary evidence, that some early humans in the Americas may have come from Europe.[33]

Population Densities

As with languages, the greatest density of pre-contact populations was on the Pacific coast, thought to be about 10 per cent of the total for the two continents. Estimates for the hemispheric population have been going steadily upward in recent years, and have reached a very high 112.5 million for the fifteenth century on the eve of European arrival.[34] In that case, the population for the Americas would have been higher than the 70 million estimated for Europe (excluding Russia) for the beginning of the sixteenth century.[35] For North America north of the Rio Grande in the early sixteenth century, estimates range up to an unlikely 18 million and even higher.[36] They have increased with better understanding of Native subsistence bases and with greater awareness of the effect of imported diseases in the sixteenth century; in some cases these spread far ahead of the actual presence of Europeans, decimating up to 93 per cent of Native populations. The earliest European accounts of the New World all spoke of the 'great multitudes' of people; it was later, when colonization was gaining momentum, that large stretches of territory were found unoccupied and the notion of an 'empty continent' gained currency.[37] Archaeological evidence is mounting to the point where it can now be argued with growing conviction, if not absolute proof, that the pre-Columbian Americas were inhabited in large part to the carrying capacities of the land for the ways of life that were being followed and the types of food preferred. This is being revealed particularly in glaciated areas, where artifacts are emerging out of melting ice in regions previously not thought to have been inhabited.[38]

Original migrations probably involved very small groups. Recent genetic studies suggest that Indians have all descended from four primary maternal lineages, although this is vigorously disputed by advocates of a multiplicity of migrations.[39] Research techniques have now developed to the point where it is considered possible to reconstruct migrations by means of genetic evidence, particularly when it can be related to dental traits and linguistic affiliations.[40] It has been calculated that 25 individuals could have increased in 500 years to a population of 10 million, if it had doubled every generation (about 30 years). That was the rate of growth in European colonies during their early years in North America (the colonists, however, had far more children than their contemporary tribal peoples, and were reinforced by a steady stream of immigration from Europe). In any event, that rate would have been even faster if a generation is reckoned at 20 years, in which case the saturation point for hunting and gathering populations could have been reached in less than 1,000 years, but this did not likely actually happen.[41]

By 11,000 years ago, about the time of the last known mammoth and mastodon kills, campsites of peoples with different economic adaptations and cultural traditions were scattered the length and breadth of the two continents. In that period, and during the next 3,000 years or so, some 200 species representing 60 or more genera of major animals disappeared from the Americas. We do not know what caused these extinctions any more than we know what caused that of the dinosaurs; however, there is speculation that in the former case big-game hunters could have tipped the balance as their population expanded in consequence of the plentifulness of game. Recent work by Schledermann has demonstrated the ease with which a small group of hunters could reduce muskox and caribou to near extinction in the Arctic.[42] Paleontologist Paul S. Martin has pointed to the analogy of the Polynesian arrival in New Zealand and the consequent extinction of the moa bird.[43] In North America, the great auk and the passenger pigeon suffered similar fates when Europeans arrived. On the other hand, there are those who hold that mammoth kills were probably rare;[44] archaeological evidence so far has revealed only about a dozen known kill sites, all west of the Mississippi. About 8,000–5,000 years ago, when climate, sea levels, and land stabilized into configurations that approximate those of today, humans crossed a population and cultural threshold, if one is to judge by the increase in numbers and complexity of archaeological sites.

The megafaunal disappearances do not appear to have involved a radical change in hunting patterns, as such game as bison and caribou was always important. If there was a population drop, as the scarcity of sites from this period has led some archaeologists to believe, it did not last long. People survived for the same reason then as later: by being adaptable. The way of life that developed, based on the exploitation of a wide variety of food sources, called Archaic, was destined to last in some parts of Canada until long after the arrival of Europeans. Around 9200–8500 BC, the making of fluted points displaced earlier forms of manufacture and spread across Canada with extraordinary speed, a phenomenon that remains without parallel in the country's early development. Fluted points have been found from Alaska to northern Mexico, and were once thought to have been a North American development. However, a similar point has been found in northeastern Siberia, 1,770 kilometres from the Bering Strait, which raises questions about migratory movements.[45] In Canada, these points have been found at Debert, Nova Scotia, Charlie Lake Cave in British Columbia, and at the Vermilion Lakes in Alberta. The hunters who made these implements concentrated on bison or caribou, depending on the region; later, from about 8000 to 6000 BC, their descendants on the western Plains, who had abandoned the fluted point for the Plano with its distinctive rippled flaking, were hunting bison by means of drives. That practice became common in Canada around 3000 BC. Contemporary with Plano, Early Archaic developed in the Eastern

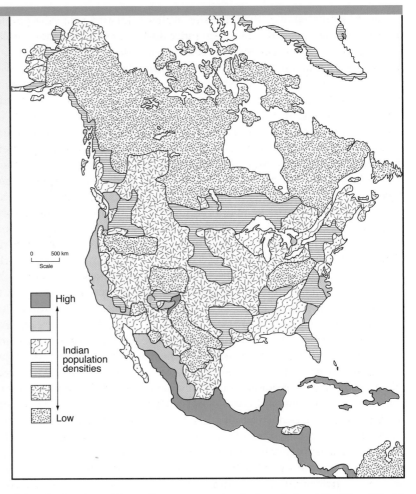

1.3

Aboriginal population densities

Source: Carl Waldman, *Atlas of the North American Indian* (New York: Facts on File, 1985).

Scale: 0 500 km

High

Indian population densities

Low

Woodlands, characterized by distinctive side-notching of points for hafting. Archaeologist James V. Wright says that about 6000 BC eastern Early Archaic peoples migrated to the western Plains, where they came in contact with Plano peoples. Out of this interaction the Plains culture developed.[46] Still another lifestyle had already appeared on the Northwest Coast (beginning about 9000 BC), centred on salmon fishing and sea hunting, also with its distinctive lithic tradition of leaf-shaped projectile points. Receptivity to new ideas and willingness to experiment characterized these Stone Age craftsmen. When Europeans arrived, the whole of the New World was populated not only in all its different landscape and with varying degrees of density, but also with a rich cultural kaleidoscope of something like 2,000 or more different societies.[47]

Physical Characteristics

Even as they widely share certain physical characteristics, such as having little or no body hair (and what they have is usually black), Amerindians are biologically diverse. For example, some groups, particularly on the Pacific coast and in the Great Basin, have facial hair, sometimes heavy. Like the Filipinos, Amerindians are almost universally lacking in A and B blood types, but there are some striking exceptions. A is found among the peoples of the Northwest Coast (in similar frequencies to Hawaiians), as well as among the Beaver, Slavey, and Assiniboine in the interior; most striking of all is the fact that the Blackfoot, Blood, and Peigan of the northwestern Plains have the highest known percentages of A in the world. B is found in highland Peru and in very high percentages among the Carayá of the Brazil interior; early reports of a concentration of B among the Yahgan of Tierra del Fuego, however, have not been confirmed.[48] In Central and South America, the preponderance of Amerindians belong to the O class, with the proportion being somewhat less in North America. This concentration exceeds anything known in the Old World, including the peoples of northern Siberia who are believed to be the source for the Beringian migrations, and indeed genetic studies have indicated that Amerindians are not as closely connected to modern Mongoloids as has been generally believed.[49] These biological data have led to speculation that Indians might be of ancient racial stocks predating contemporary Siberian peoples.[50] Dental studies, which indicated an original stock living 20,000 years ago, support such a hypothesis.[51] On the basis of this evidence, anthropologist Christy G. Turner II theorizes that most Indians are descended from the mammoth hunters of the Clovis culture. Inuit, on the other hand, are genetically distinct from most Indians, except for the Athapaskan speakers of the Northwest.[52] All of these peoples had an average life expectancy of between 20 and 25 years, a figure comparable with that for Europeans of the same period.

Technological Developments[53]

Stone Age technology reached its highest point of development in the Americas, in delicately crafted projectile points and later in the massive constructions of the Maya, Mexica, and Inca; the Inca created the largest Stone Age empire in the world,[54] the 'realm of the Four Quarters' that incorporated more than 200 ethnic groups. Archaeologist Alan Bryan maintains that several different early lithic traditions developed in various parts of the Americas, a range that includes 11,000-year-old 'fish-tail' points near the Straits of Magellan, 13,000-year-old willow-leaf-shaped El Jobo points in northern Venezuela, and the 11,000-year-old Clovis fluted points that spread throughout unglaciated North America.[55] The tools used in making these elegant points have been identified; a modern attempt to make one using such tools succeeded in about two hours, and subsequent stone-knappers have shortened that time to 40 minutes. Stone chipping, incidentally, is one of the world's most difficult crafts. The rate of spoilage was high, about 10 per cent; one of the reasons we have been able to rediscover so much about Stone Age technology is because it left so much debris.

Development of stone and bone tools represented one of humanity's great strides forward into technological sophistication; and while such technology can in a way be regarded as 'simple', it was viable only because of acute and careful observation of nature—still a basic requirement today. Stone Age technology was effective insofar as it was based on detailed and accurate observation, on the one hand, and supported by a workable social organization, on the other. Technology, Stone Age or otherwise, is the product of an accumulated fund of knowledge and is an indicator of peoples' approach to the world and to their own societies. Symbolic logic appears to have influenced tool design from very early; for instance, some speculate that the biface hand axe was based on the human hand as model.[56] The intelligent manipulation of nature backed by supportive social

These finely crafted tools are from the High Plains and date to about 11,000 years ago. Shown are stone knives of various sizes and, in the left foreground, a dark projectile point made by the people of the Clovis cultural complex. Its diagnostic feature is the concave 'fluting' at the base. The dowel-like objects are casts of spear foreshafts that had been made of bone.
(David Arnold/National Geographic Image Collection)

structures made survival possible under extremely difficult conditions. The process is a dynamic one; although rates of change can and do vary, even between the different components of a given society, no living culture is static. Technologies, including that of the

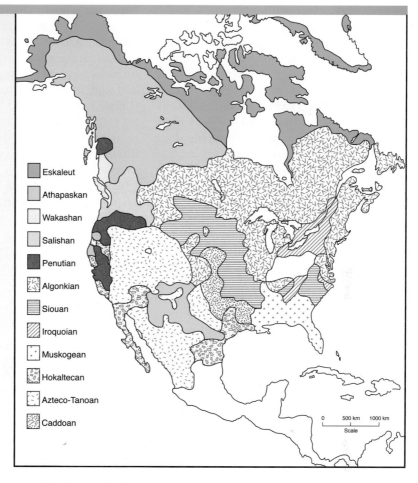

1.4

Aboriginal language groups

Source: Waldman, *Atlas of the North American Indian.*

- Eskaleut
- Athapaskan
- Wakashan
- Salishan
- Penutian
- Algonkian
- Siouan
- Iroquoian
- Muskogean
- Hokaltecan
- Azteco-Tanoan
- Caddoan

0   500 km   1000 km
Scale

Stone Age, change more readily than ideologies. A successful Stone Age technician had to know his materials, where they could be found, how they could be worked, how they would behave under different conditions, and to what uses they could be put. Many of the construction and sculpture achievements of the pre-contact Americas, once thought to be impossible with a Stone Age technology and therefore attributed to vanished races and even to creatures from outer space, are now known to have been within its capabilities. For example, how could jade, the hardest of stone, be carved with Stone Age tools? The answer has been found in the use of abrasives and water. Such a process, of course, was laborious and slow; Stone Age technology was labour- and time-intensive. It could also be material-intensive: its huge structures yielded comparatively little usable space, a result, however, more attributable to ideology than technology.

Archaic Efficiency

In some aspects, this early technology was very efficient indeed. Cutting edges, for example, could be sharper than those achievable with metal. The war club of the Mexica, with its serrated edges made with a row of obsidian blades inserted into a wooden base, was a deadly weapon capable of decapitating a man with one blow. A latter-day stone-knapper, Don E. Crabtree, when faced with the necessity for heart surgery, insisted on making the required tools from obsidian. The result was faster healing and less scarring than would have been the case with steel instruments. Even simple stone fleshing blades were very suitable for the job. Metal's big advantage was durability; stone was easily broken, so that early tool and weapon makers were perpetually busy keeping themselves equipped. One of the results of this incessant activity was the great variety of artifacts and styles that proliferated; in some cases, even the work of individuals can be ascertained. 'Style', however, can simply be the result of resharpening and consequent reshaping, which could and did result in such modifications as shortening a blade or transforming it from one form into another, such as a spear point into a knife. Not all peoples everywhere had the same type of tool kit, even when following similar ways of life; for example, artifacts associated with seed grinding have restricted distribution in South America but are widespread in southern and western North America. Similarly, the hafting of stone points to bone or wooden bases was not universally adopted. The bow and arrow were once thought to have appeared in the Americas about AD 250[57] but are now believed to have been brought over much earlier by Paleo-Eskimos of the Arctic Small Tool Tradition.[58] The bow and arrow were much more efficient than the atlatl (spear thrower), which they superseded, having more firepower as well as greater range and accuracy. They were also easier to manufacture.[59] Ropemaking, netting, and basketmaking appeared very early, during the late Pleistocene.[60]

Questions are now being raised as to the uses to which early tools were put. Archaeologists have concentrated on the hunting aspect;

but what about gathering and processing? Geographer Carl Sauer (1889–1975) noted that the Stone Age tool kit was as useful for cutting and preparing wood, bark, and bast, as well as for gathering and preparing foods such as roots and fruit, as it was for dressing meat and hides. If little is known about these early tools used for collecting and grinding, it is largely because their products were perishable and tended to disappear without a trace, causing them to be overlooked as attention focused on hunting, which left recognizable debris. The development of grinding tools made a wider variety of seeds available for food, such as the small seeds of grasses and amaranths. Peoples who depended on such resources tended to remain in one place, where their supplies were readily at hand. In other words, the mobile lifestyle in pursuit of different food resources cannot be assumed to have been universal at any period; and even when it was practised, it followed a seasonal pattern within a known area. The vision of early humans as aimless wanderers in search of food does not equate with the evidence at hand; in fact, the contrary is strongly indicated, that they have always lived in communities that were as stable as food resources permitted.[61] This was strikingly reinforced during the 'wildfire summer' of 2000, when naturally sparked forest fires ravaged the western United States, revealing scores of previously unknown archaeological sites giving witness to past human life in villages and kivas, among numerous other relics of settled life.[62]

In conclusion, there is now general agreement that humans were present in the Americas at least by 15,000 BC, a date that some would push back to 50,000 BC; environmentally, this would have been possible at an even earlier date.[63] That at least part of the earlier migrations were on land via Beringia seems reasonably clear;[64] more controversial is the question of migration by sea. As evidence slowly accumulates about the earliest patterns of

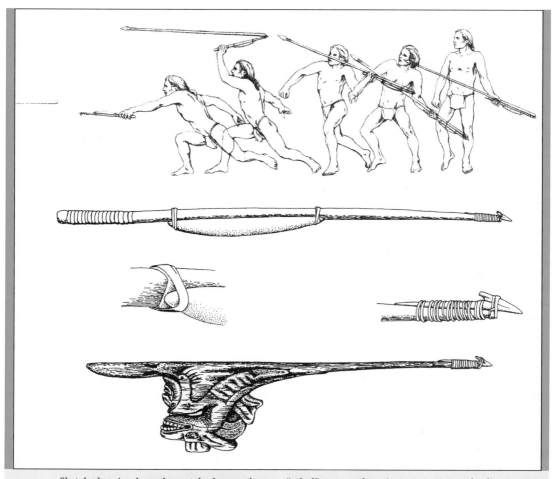

Sketch showing how the notched spear thrower ('atlatl') was used to give extra power to hurling a spear. A weight attached to the underside of the atlatl added to its effectiveness. An unusually elaborate weight, in the form of a plumed serpent holding a human head, is shown at bottom. Carved out of yew-wood with inlaid white-shell eyes, it has been radiocarbon-dated to 1,700 years ago. It was dredged up from the Skagit River, about 50 kilometres south of the Canada–US border, in Washington state.
(University of British Columbia Museum of Anthropology Collection; sketch reproduced with permission from Knut R. Fladmark, Simon Fraser University)

human residence on the two continents, it appears more and more likely that water was at least as important as land for getting about, and perhaps even more so. By about 11,000 BP humans were inhabiting the length and breadth of the Americas, with the greatest concentration of population being along the Pacific coast of the two continents. A thousand or so years later many animal species had disappeared from the American scene, a phenomenon that has not been satisfactorily explained. If an analogy were to be drawn with the faunal exterminations that occurred in the wake of the arrival of Europeans in the Americas, then humans were a factor. In any event, people were firmly established through-out the hemisphere, and in some parts of Central and South America they began experimenting with domesticating plants perhaps as early as 9,000 years ago.

Chapter 2

Settling In

Agriculture appears to have developed independently, within a span of a few thousand years at the end of the last Pleistocene glaciation, in several widely separated regions of the globe: the Near East, the monsoon lands of Southeast Asia, China, Mesoamerica, Peru, and the Amazon. These regions have all been linked in other contexts by proponents of cultural diffusion; however, the once widely held belief that agriculture diffused around the globe from a single point of origin today has few advocates. Another once-popular hypothesis, that agriculture in the Americas developed in arid regions with the help of irrigation, has been even more firmly rejected, as it has been demonstrated that with perhaps one or two exceptions, all of the earliest known cultigens have been developed from prototypes that needed seasonal rainfall. In current thinking, such a global phenomenon must have had a global cause, such as a warming of the world's climate. Botany professor Rowan Sage of the University of Toronto proposes that a sudden and unexplained jump in the atmosphere's carbon dioxide, which occurred about 15,000 years ago, may provide the explanation. Ac-

cording to Sage, carbon dioxide enriched plants by making photosynthesis—the process by which plants convert sunlight into energy—more efficient, increasing their growth rate and size. That triggered their domestication and the emergence of man-the-farmer. Squash seeds found in a Mexican cave near Oaxaca have been dated to 10,000 years ago.[1]

While there are no definite answers as yet as to why humans turned from collecting to cultivating plants in certain areas but not in others that appear equally suitable, it is now accepted that the switch in lifestyle was not as sudden or as complete as once thought; the 'Neolithic Revolution' suggested by Australian archaeologist V. Gordon Childe (1892–1957) appears to have been a gradual, and by no means uniform, process. There is no evidence that pressures of growing populations caused big-game hunters to turn to farming, although the hypothesis is frequently put forward as the most likely explanation. Dependence on collecting rather than hunting may have encouraged a cultural predisposition to experiment with domesticating plants; as Carl Sauer has observed, digging for roots can be viewed as a

TIMELINE

8600–6700 BC	Domesticated plants in Central and South America: gourds, avocados, beans, squash.	AD 1050 –1250	Cahokia (in Illinois) had an estimated population of 30,000–40,000 and, covering 13 square kilometres, was larger than London, England.
5000 BC	Earliest known domestication of corn, in central Mexico.		
2300 BC	Agriculture introduced in Northeast Woodlands: squash.	1200s	Squash (and sunflowers) first grown domestically in Ontario, thus completing triad of the famous 'three sisters'—corn, beans, squash.
1000 BC	First local cultivated plant in Northeast: sunflower.		
700–220 BC	Possible contact between China and Northwest Coast.	15th century	Population estimates of Americas as high as 112.5 million.
AD 500	Corn first cultivated in Canada, in present-day Ontario.	16th century	Estimated 2,200 languages in New World.
AD 1000	Tobacco cultivated in Ontario; beans soon followed.		
	Norse landing and brief settlement on northern tip of Newfoundland.		

sort of unplanned tillage.[2] Fishing, a form of collecting, appears to have played a part in these early attempts at resource management; Classic Mayan agriculturalists, for instance, were also fish farmers, as were the Mississippian Mound Builders and Andean villagers in the Inca empire. Even non-agriculturalists such as hunters of the northwestern Plains had to observe carefully the plants they harvested, such as the prairie turnip (*Psoralea esculenta*, also known as 'white apple'), to determine the appropriate time to gather it for drying and pulverizing for winter use;[3] there is also some evidence that they moved plant stocks from one location to another.

The farmers of the pueblos in what is today the southwestern United States returned to gathering wild foods during times of natural disasters, such as floods and drought. In the latter case, this could last for years. New World farmers and hunters controlled game to a surprising extent through the use of fire. Not only was fire used to control directly the movements of animals, such as those of the buffalo on the Plains, it was also used to modify vegetation, which in turn influenced the animals' feeding patterns; for instance, by the sixteenth century, the farming peoples of the Northeastern Woodlands of North America had transformed their habitat into an ambience particularly suitable for deer—the so-called 'deer parks'.[4] Non-agricultural Californians used the same technique for the same purpose: to have deer on hand when needed for the larder.

Early Crops

Bottle gourds (*Lagenaria siceraria*) may have been among the first domesticated crops in the Americas; in Mexico they were being grown by 7000 BC, and in coastal Peru by 6000 BC.[5] They pose a problem, as they are believed to be native of the Old World; if there was a wild variety of gourds native to the Americas, it has been long extinct. Similarly, cotton, which was being grown in Mexico and in Peru before 2500 BC,

'A Prairie on Fire', near Fort Edmonton, as seen by Paul Kane (1810–71). Fire was extensively used by Amerindians to modify plant growth and the movement of game, as well as to clear land in forested areas.
(With permission of the Royal Ontario Museum © ROM, 912.1.39)

also appears to have Old World connections. The Mexican and Peruvian varieties are separate species (*Gossypium hirsutum*, 'American Upland', and *G. barbadense*, 'Sea Island', respectively), but both have genetic structures that seem to be explainable only through hybridization with Old World cotton, originally domesticated in India. While some argue that this could have occurred by natural processes, botanists see this as highly unlikely and explain the 'wild' hybrids found from the Yucatan to the Galapagos Islands as escaped domesticates.[6] The most authoritative study so far on the evolution of cotton holds that people were involved in the hybridization and that cultivation of the domesticated plant in the New World began in northwestern South America, probably Peru.[7] Not surprisingly, these two cases have been eagerly

picked up by proponents of ancient contact between the New and Old Worlds. Since there is considerable resistance to that hypothesis, mainly on the grounds of insufficient seagoing technology at that early epoch, and since there is little accord on alternative explanations, the origin and development of gourds and cotton as crops are unsolved problems. Coconuts and some varieties of yams were also shared by both New and Old Worlds.

Apart from the exceptions just noted, the New World domesticated plants that made such a contribution to world agriculture were all of undisputed American origin and were developed by Amerindian farmers. The two best-known of these are corn (maize, *Zea mays*) and potatoes (*Solanum tuberosum*), although such items as tomatoes (*Lycopersicon esculentum*),

Problematic Maize and Other Cultigens

As with gourds and cotton, corn presents a problem in tracing New World man's primeval essays into agriculture; in this instance, the resistance concerns the human role in developing the crop. By the sixteenth century, at least 150 varieties of corn, adapted to a wide array of different conditions, were being grown throughout agricultural America, except in the Andes above 3,900 metres, where it was replaced by quinoa (*Chenopodium quinoa*).[10] The difficulty arises from the fact that if a wild corn once flourished, it has not been found; two wild grasses related to corn still grow in the highlands of Mexico—teosinte and tripsacum. Teosinte (the name is Mexican, meaning 'mother of corn') is genetically closely related to the domesticated plant and can be cross-bred with it. Teosinte is demanding in its requirements, wanting equal hours of daylight and darkness and warm temperatures, which effectively restricts its range; corn, in contrast, was being grown from Huronia in the Ontario midlands of Canada all the way through to southern Chile when Europeans arrived. The oldest site known where it may have been developed as a crop is the Tehuacan Valley of central Mexico, near the modern city of Puebla, where cobs the size of cigarette filters were found by MacNeish; they have been dated to 5000 BC. Stone tools for grinding corn (metate, a Nahuatl word for a slightly concave nether milling stone, and mano, a stone roller), perhaps an adaptation from earlier seed-grinders, appeared about 5,000 years ago and are still used today. The mortar and pestle also served the same purpose. It has been estimated that about a thousand years of selective breeding were needed to produce corn in all the many varieties first encountered by Europeans; the principal modification since has been for the cobs to become larger. Corn cannot survive without human

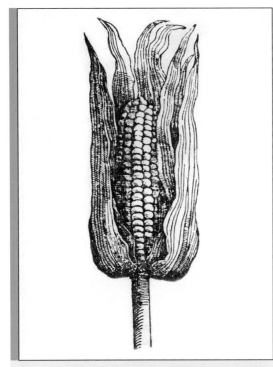

One of the earliest known illustrations of corn to appear in print was in Oviedo's *Historia General de las Indias,* Seville, 1535.

peanuts (*Arachis hypogaea*), pineapples (*Ananas comosus*), and cacao (*Theobroma cacao*, from which chocolate is made) are not far behind. More than 100 species of plants routinely farmed today were originally grown by Amerindians. Maize and potatoes are two of the world's four basic food crops; the other two are wheat (*Triticum vulgare*), developed in Mesopotamia, and rice (*Oryza sativa*), domesticated in the Indus Valley.[8] The most famous of all Amerindian crops, tobacco (*Nicotiana*), was grown for diplomatic, ritual, and some medical uses. In all, it has been estimated that the Huron grew up to 17 varieties of maize and eight types of squash. As well, it is thought that they gathered 34 varieties of wild fruit and 11 kinds of nuts, besides other varieties of wild foods.[9]

2.1

Distribution of maize and cotton in North and Central America

Source: Waldman, *Atlas of the North American Indian.*

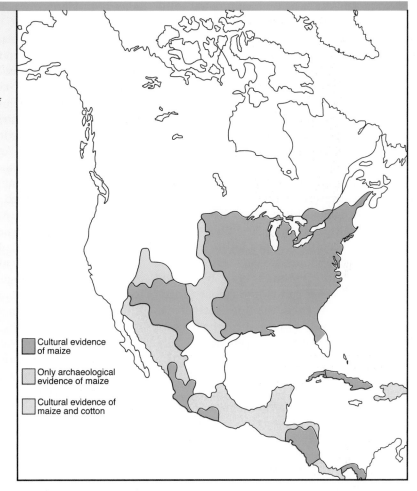

Cultural evidence of maize

Only archaeological evidence of maize

Cultural evidence of maize and cotton

intervention, lacking as it does the capacity to reproduce itself. As a crop, it is among the most efficient in the world in terms of yield.[11] Its development has been ranked as one of the world's great achievements in plant science.[12] To Amerindian farmers, corn is a sentient being that has feelings and can cry.

As we have already seen, gourds were domesticated before corn, and so were squash (*Cucurbita*) and avocados (*Persea americana*), the latter two dating to about 6700 BC. Various beans (*Phaseolus*), chili peppers (*Capsicum*

frutescens),[13] and amaranth (*Amaranthus hypochondriacus*) are at least as ancient; indeed, there is a possibility that the first two were being cultivated before 8600 BC in the Andean region. If that turns out to be the case, then the first attempts at agriculture in the Americas occurred in those mesophytic forests (Colombia and the Upper Amazon have been the locations of recent attention in this regard). It is appearing more and more likely that plant domestication began in several different places with various plants. In the Northeastern Woodlands of North America, where agriculture was introduced with the cultivation of squash, *c.* 2300 BC, probably via southern trade, it was not until about 1000 BC that the first local plant, the sunflower (*Helianthus annus*), was domesticated. Wright points to a different pattern for southern Ontario: corn was the first cultivated food crop to reach that region, and that not until after AD 500, and remained the sole crop for five centuries. Tobacco appeared about AD 1000, with beans following somewhat later. Squash (with sunflowers) did not reach the area until the thirteenth century, finally completing the triad of the famous 'three sisters' in the northernmost limits of its range. The time this took could have been that needed for the plants to be adapted to a shorter growing season. By the sixteenth century, the triad—corn, beans, and squash—was being grown throughout agricultural America. As crops, the three sisters benefited the soil when sown together, which meant they had a sustainability and permanence lacking in modern agriculture.[14] As food they reinforced each other nutritionally when combined in diets.

Both wetlands and drylands were used by early agriculturalists; this was exemplified by the Maya in the lowlands of Mexico and Guatemala, by the Wari of the highlands of Peru, and by the Hohokam of the deserts of southwestern US. By 850 BC ditch irrigation was practised, which in the case of wetlands meant mounding soil and vegetation to above the water level and planting seeds in the top of each mound. The Wari and the later Inca had not only dry conditions to contend with but also mountainous terrains; their methods of piping and controlling water flow to different levels are still in use.

Early Experimentation

Plant domestication could not have occurred without an extensive botanical knowledge already in place; it was no accident that agriculture developed first in warm, moderately rainy latitudes, where plant diversity was greatest and ecological conditions were such as to allow the necessary freedom for experimentation with a comparatively simple technology. Northerners were no less skilful and experimental in exploiting their resources, but the restrictions of their environment in combination with their Stone Age technology, ingenious as it was, meant that their options were more limited. The changeover to agriculture was not an unmitigated blessing, if we are to judge by present archaeological evidence. For one thing, its higher reliance on starchy foods meant an increase in dental problems. For another, if corn was relied on too heavily in the diet, without adequate protein supplements, it could result in a population smaller in stature than ancestral hunters/gatherers and with shorter lifespans. This happened with the Mississippian Mound Builders and may have been a factor in the decline of Cahokia. In the southeast, skeletal remains point to maize agriculture being physically more demanding than the hunting and gathering way of life.[15]

In the past, North American historians have tended to underplay and even disregard Amerindian plant expertise in their concentration on the pre-Columbian absence of farm animals and consequent dependence on hunting for meat. Farming developed in conjunction with hunting: in Canada, this was the case among the Iroquoian farmers of southern Ontario and also occurred in the boreal forest;[16] in the Great Basin of the southwestern US, Numic-speakers camped where they could hunt as well as harvest; in South America, by far the greatest majority of the people combined both activities, making use of a wide variety of natural resources in their seasonal rounds so that they always had something to fall back on. Amerindian agriculture did not require that fields be entirely cleared of trees:

those that yielded useful nuts and fruits were left standing.[17] Neither did they develop the practice of fencing in their fields, since their lands were held in common. If one considers the two continents together, most Amerindians were farmers/hunters at the time Europeans arrived. The lands that appeared 'vacant' to the new arrivals were either hunting areas or else had been recently depopulated because of introduced epidemics. At the other end of the spectrum, the great botanical gardens of Mexico were centres of learning and experimentation, and easily surpassed anything comparable in Europe during the fifteenth and sixteenth centuries.

Amerindian Animal Domestication

While it is undeniable that Amerindian agriculture concentrated on plants rather than animals, in contrast to the European practice, the latter were not ignored. In the New World, however, there were few candidates for the farmyard. The Peruvians domesticated the llama and the guinea pig; the former was used principally as a beast of burden but also provided hides and wool, as well as meat. Dogs were widely (but not universally) present and in North America have been dated to 6500 BC. (Incidentally, it has been theorized that the absence of the dog among some Brazilian tribes indicates peopling of those regions before its domestication.)[18] Some peoples, such as Iroquoians, sacrificed dogs in rituals and ate them as ceremonial food. Others used them as work animals; in the Arctic they pulled sleds for the Inuit (at Iqaluit, however, a secondary breed of dog was raised for food),[19] and on the Plains they were used as pack animals and also for hauling the products of the hunt and camp equipment by means of the travois. On the Northwest Coast, Amerindians had a variety with a white woolly coat that provided fibres for weaving. Although dogs were not universal-

Huron women preparing corn. Father François Du Creux, *Historiae Canadensis*, 1664.
(Library and Archives Canada)

ly used for hunting, in the northern forests they were trained for the purpose, and for the Coast Salish and Tsimshian, owning hunting dogs was a jealously guarded privilege of the higher orders. Turkeys were domesticated (or, as one observer remarked, they domesticated themselves, as they appreciated the food available in settlements). So were other types of fowl and birds. On the whole, Indians depended on hunting and fishing for their protein even as they became sedentary.

By the proto-contact period, plants were, in general, and in spite of regional exceptions, the most important source of nourishment. When it came to medicines, however, the botanical world always had been, and remained, the major source (according to the Cherokee, animals brought diseases and plants provided the cures). Recollect missionary Chrestien Le Clercq (*c.* 1641–after 1700) would report from Acadia, where he was from 1675 to 1686: 'Amerindians are all by nature physicians, apothecaries, and doctors, by virtue of the knowledge and experience they have of certain herbs, which they use successfully to cure ills that seem to us incurable.'[20] That this knowledge had roots that went deep into the past is not questioned. The process by which the Amerindians acquired their herbal lore is not clearly understood, but there is no doubt about the results. More than 500 drugs in the medical pharmacopoeia today were originally used by Amerindians.[21]

Permanent Settlement

Even though agriculture was closely associated with the development of permanent settlement, particularly as populations grew, it was not an essential requirement for the process to begin. Not only did permanent settlements in some cases long predate agriculture, in others the reverse occurred, and agricultural experimentation began long before the adoption of a sedentary lifestyle. Present archaeological evidence indicates that permanent villages in the Americas date back to 13,000–15,000 years ago, before the domestication of plants. Those dates have been recorded for Monte Verde, in southern Chile. In Canada also, archaeology has revealed that permanent settlement was much older than previously thought; a longhouse unearthed near Mission, BC, has been dated to 9,000 years ago.[22] Determining when humans began to experiment with plants is much more difficult than establishing the presence of domestication. What is essential for a sedentary way of living is an assured supply of food in one place, a situation not necessarily dependent on agriculture, at least in the dis-

tant period we are considering, when populations were usually small.

Dependence on wild foods limited the size of permanent settlement rather than preventing it. The residents of Koster, on the upper Mississippi (*c.* 4000 BC, although it was inhabited seasonally for several thousand years before that), never did find it necessary to turn from wild to domesticated food resources, except to a limited extent; the region was so rich in plant and animal life, both on land and in water, that there was little need to undertake cultivation. Similarly, the burial mound builders of Ohio's Adena culture (*c.* 600 BC–100 BC) and those of the later but closely related and much more widespread Hopewell (*c.* 300 BC–AD 400) elaborated complex sedentary chiefdoms in rich self-renewing flood plain environments with comparatively minor assistance from agriculture. The silt deposited in the spring by the Mississippi and its tributaries ensured abundance, so it was not necessary to change village sites from time to time because of resource depletion.

Both of these cultures practised elaborate funerary ceremonies. According to Wright, aspects of these cultures spread northward into Ontario and down the St Lawrence River as far as New Brunswick.[23] In attenuated form, they also spread westward into Manitoba and Saskatchewan; Hopewell-influenced ceramics have been found in Alberta.[24] Such cultural factors may have encouraged village life on the Plains, of which Cluny Earth Lodge at Blackfoot Crossing, 113 kilometres east of Calgary, may have been a northernmost manifestation. According to Blackfoot legend it was built by the Crow, in which case it would be proto-contact.[25] Plains villages were discouraged by recurrent drought, particularly severe between AD 500 and AD 1300, to the point where they disappeared during the fifteenth century, except for those along the Missouri system (Mandan, Hidatsa, Arikara, etc.). Bison populations recovered more rapidly than the human, and the growing presence of the herds prevented the return of farming to the High Plains.

Along the Pacific coast stable communities developed in a number of locations largely because of the resources of the sea, with land providing supplementary foods. Canada's Northwest Coast villages illustrate this; and on the Ecuadorean coast of South America, rich, elegant Chan Chan, seat of the divine kings of the Chimor empire who fell to the Incas during the thirteenth century, became wealthy because of its sea resources. In their case, however, these were backed up with produce from the fertile river valleys that periodically cut through the coastal desert. Ostra, a pre-agricultural 5,000-year-old defensive site on the north-central coast of Peru, indicates a role for warfare in these early societies; war and civilization have so far always gone hand in hand.[26] Once permanence was established, the way was open for the elaboration of social complexities.

Egalitarianism and Hierarchy

The shift from the egalitarian societies of mobile peoples to hierarchical sedentary or semi-sedentary chiefdoms, and eventually to the social complexities of city-states, poses an intriguing problem for historians.[27] Egalitarian societies did not separate authority from the group as a whole, and in some cases they went to considerable lengths to ensure that such a separation did not occur. In those societies, available resources were open to all, and personal abilities translated into influence rather than coercive authority.[28] Free sharing ensured that the superior skills of, say, a hunter benefited the group rather than an individual. The power of chiefs depended on their capacity to provide for their followers, as well as their powers of persuasion; perhaps most importantly of all, they were expected to set an example for

their people. Chiefs, instead of gaining wealth through their positions, could end up the poorest of the group because of the continual demands made on their resources.[29] As Le Clercq described the situation among the Mi'kmaq, a chief could attract followers, but they did what they pleased and were not subordinated to their leader's will,[30] except perhaps to a limited extent in time of war.

The general lack of quarrelling or interpersonal conflict in Amerindian communities impressed Europeans, who wondered how peaceful relations could prevail without the threat of force in the background. Amerindians for their part were not impressed when they saw Europeans being afraid of their captains, 'while they laugh at and make sport of theirs.'[31] Such observations indicate how easy it was for Europeans to miss the subtleties of Amerindian social controls; respect was exceedingly important, and within their spheres of competence, the chiefs did have authority.[32] Thomas Jefferys (d. 1771), geographer to the Prince of Wales (later George III), reported that some chiefs were skilful in eliciting obedience as they knew 'how to confine their commands within the limits of their power'.[33] The situation was quite different in chiefdoms (in Canada, found on the Northwest Coast), where the chiefs did have power, up to and including that of life and death in certain cases. All of these societies placed a high value on personal liberty and freedom.

Neither did all egalitarian societies organize power in the same way; those on the Plains, for example, placed more emphasis on co-ordinated strategies for the hunt and for war than did those of the Eastern Woodlands. In general, selection of the leader was on the basis of qualification, although the sons of chiefs were in a favourable position to succeed their fathers. Besides the established leader, individuals could be chosen by a process of social consensus because of their particular skills and spiritual powers to organize group activities, such as the buffalo hunt, a raid, or a seasonal transfer in the pursuit of food. The authority involved in such positions lasted only as long as the task or project at hand. Should a rival chief appear or factionalism result in a split, the dissident group could always break away and establish itself elsewhere. The difference between egalitarian and state societies can be symbolized by the warrior and the soldier. In the Eastern Woodlands, the warrior—in Iroquoian terms, the bearer of the bones of the nation, a responsibility that included the duty to fight for it—was his own man, to the point of being able to quit a war party without losing face should he feel called on to do so.[34] Younger warriors, out to prove themselves, were under more pressure to stay with the group and obey the leader.[35] A soldier, however, under the command of his superior officer, could be shot for such behaviour, or at the very least court-martialled; in any case he would be disgraced. For the European, discipline had come to mean acceptance of a superior authority and the ability to act in close co-operation with others; for the Amerindian, discipline was for the most part an individual matter, although there were exceptions to this.[36] It included the ability to go for long periods with little or no food; calm endurance of inconveniences, hardships, and suffering; capacity to resist fatigue; and the ability to think for oneself in battle. The Amerindian code of bravery in warfare was not so likely to call for dying while trying to maintain an untenable position, as that of the Europeans so often did; what it did call for (at least in the Northeastern Woodlands) was the proper behaviour under torture, not a quality the latter expected to have to demonstrate.[37] It should be pointed out, however, that torture as a part of warfare was by no means universally practised among Amerindians.

The difference can be looked at another way: the role of authority in setting up camp or in building a movable village, as compared to the type of control needed to build the great constructions of the ceremonial centres and city-states of Mexico and Peru. While co-operative effort was required in both cases, the degree of centralized authority was of necessity much higher in the latter. One point about the process by which such authority was accepted seems clear: in the case of the Americas at least, authority preceded the use of force[38] and was connected with the perceived need to maintain harmony with the cosmos. In other words, the temple mounds and pueblos of North America, the stepped pyramids of Mesoamerica, the megalithic constructions of the Andes, at least in their earlier manifestations, were built by peoples with either a sense of mission or a sense of obligation. By whatever means, they were persuaded to give freely a great deal of time and effort for such projects. A similar phenomenon was witnessed in Europe with the construction of its cathedrals in the Middle Ages. As societies developed, so did the use of compulsion; the Inca, for instance, devised the *mit'a*, a labour tax, to meet the manpower needs of their imperial works projects. The process was obviously a complex one, and whatever its particularities, by the beginning of the Christian era in the Old World, cities or ceremonial centres, with their surrounding farms, dotted the American landscape from the Mississippi Valley to the Gulf of Mexico, across to the Pacific coast, and south to the highlands of Bolivia. In their social organization, Amerindians had achieved a blend of collective motivation, consensual command, and individual achievement that was distinctively their own.

Cosmic Relationships

Concern about keeping on good terms with the cosmos seems to have taken on a new edge with the development of agriculture and the need for planting and seeding to be done at correct times for the crops to flourish. Crops needed sun and water; the farming Mississippian Mound Builders (AD 500–1500), whose domain stretched from Aztalan (Lake Mills, Wisconsin) to Ocmulgee (Georgia), placed great importance on the sun, elevating it to the level of a deity, a trait noticeably lacking in the earlier non-agricultural Hopewellians. So did the Hurons—and the Mi'kmaq on the Atlantic coast, who in the sixteenth century were hunters and gatherers on land and sea but who had a tradition of once being an agricultural people. Rain gods received much attention in Mesoamerica: for the Mexica he was the goggle-eyed, long-toothed Tlaloc; for the Maya, the long-nosed Chac. The personage in Olmec art previously thought to represent only the jaguar earth god is now thought also to have the characteristics of a rain god who came to be honoured throughout South America and Mesoamerica. According to this identification, the 'jaguar' face of the personage is formed by the convergence of two serpents, their bodies joining to form the nose; while its eyes and fangs remain those of the serpent.[39] This combination would have meant that the deity was supremely powerful. The variety of societies that developed reflected the complexities of relationships to the cosmos and to the land.

Patterns of Development

It is apparent that not all societies everywhere go through exactly the same stages of development. In broad terms in the Americas, however, it is generally agreed that permanent settlement has been a necessary preliminary for the development of chiefdoms, which in turn, in a few cases, became states. The old idea that hunters/gatherers were kept so busy finding food that they had no leisure to devote to cultural matters is demonstrably not valid. Chiefdoms did develop in non-agricultural societies, such as those of the Northwest Coast,

as well as in agricultural societies, such as the Mississippian Mound Builders, the Natchez and other agricultural peoples of the Gulf of Mexico, the southern Atlantic coast, and in some regions in between. These chiefdoms varied considerably in their social complexities and centralization of authority; what they had in common was concern with rank based on lineage, through which their redistributive economies functioned. As well, they developed sophisticated artistic traditions, each in a different sphere (the Californians in basketry, the Northwest Coasters in woodwork, the Ohioans and Mississippians in stone sculpture and shell and copperwork, the east coasters in feather work and hide painting).

As Stuart J. Fiedel has pointed out, the Adena-Hopewell-Mississippian chiefdoms were active builders of monumental earthworks, which can still be seen in Ohio, along the Mississippi, and eastward, with some modest manifestations northward into Ontario. The Adena and Hopewell mound builders had been concerned with death, the Mississippians with maintaining the cosmic order via social rank, the Northwest Coast peoples with initiation and validation of rank. The term that Fiedel uses for non-agricultural chiefdoms is 'Developed Archaic'.[40] Some of these lasted until the arrival of Europeans. Those with an agricultural base could support denser populations; where they reached comparatively large proportions, such as at Cahokia in Illinois, which during its peak (AD 1050–1250, although it lasted for about 500 years) had a population estimated at 30,000 to 40,000, the distinction between chiefdom and state becomes blurred. Cahokia had the largest and densest pre-contact population north of the Rio Grande and was bigger than contemporaneous London, England, covering as it did 13 square kilometres of Mississippi River bottom lands. With the exception of writing, it had all the characteristics of a city-state.[41]

The person who fell to earth from heaven is a common theme in Amerindian myth. Sometimes he allegedly left his impression on a rock, as in this case near Prince Rupert, BC.
(Photo © Canadian National Museum of Civilization, photo Harlan I. Smith, 1927, 70401)

For a variety of reasons, some of which are not at all clearly understood, social development was far from being consistent through the Americas, so that some hunting and gathering societies continued in their traditional pattern while others picked up aspects of agricultural cultures. This could happen even when peoples associated with each other in trade or war; for example, the buffalo hunters of the northern Plains traded with the farming Mandans, while those of the southern Plains carried on an active commerce with the agricultural pueblos.

The way of life of each was richer for their interchange, yet each retained its specific character. Similarly, there were farming peoples who retained the Archaic mode even as some of their neighbours developed into city-states and, in one or two cases, empires.

An intriguing mystery is that of three ritual burial mounds dating back to 7,000 years ago that have been found on the southern coast of Labrador, a region where hunters and gatherers have lived for 9,000 years. These elaborate constructions are the oldest known of their scale and complexity anywhere in the world. Ritual burials are normally associated with stable agricultural populations with the resources and the manpower available to invest the time and effort required. In this case it has been estimated that the most elaborate of the burials must have taken a group of 20 individuals about a week to complete; compounding the mystery is the fact that it was the grave of an adolescent, too young for such honours in the usual practice. One can only speculate that some unusual event of extraordinary spiritual significance precipitated such an outpouring of activity.[42] The presence of these mounds in such an unlikely location is a reminder of how sketchy our knowledge is of prehistoric religious practices and their effect on cultural manifestations.

In sum, from the first arrival of humans, the Americas were the scene of a richly diversified budding of cultures. Very early, Indians excelled in the plant sciences; a remarkable achievement was the development of corn, one of the world's most efficient and versatile crops. It has been called the 'collective invention' of innumerable people over thousands of years.[43] Agriculture provided the basis for the rise of city-states and empires in a cultural flowering that was distinctively its own.

Chapter 3

Metropolises and Intercultural Contacts

If there is debate as to how humans arrived in the Americas, there is impassioned argument as to how they became urbanized. What were the factors that led to the rise of city-states? Were the great metropolises of Central and South America completely autonomous developments, or were they influenced along the way by other cultures? If the latter was the case, what other cultures were involved, and when were the contacts made? Thus baldly stated, the question assumes an either/or characteristic that probably does not equate with reality. There is no serious argument against contacts and diffusion between various New World centres; in fact, so many of these have been traced (such as the spread of the use of tobacco, for instance, or the cultivation of corn) that the operation of these processes is accepted as indisputable. In at least one instance, in Canada from about 1000 BC to AD 500, the diffusion of ideas is seen as more important for cultural change than actual migrations. Archaeologist James V. Wright makes that comment in connection with the spread of pottery-making and the bow and arrow.[1] Even so, certain questions about intercultural con-

tacts need to be kept in mind. What was their nature and how important were they? How did they interact with indigenous cultures already in place? The questions take on another character (and become heated) when the possibility of overseas contact between the Americas and the Old World is raised. Answers arrived at in the present state of our knowledge must be considered as tentative, a pushing back of frontiers perhaps, but not final solutions.

Much of the difficulty arises from our imperfect understanding of how civilizations arise in the first place.[2] In the Old World, the process is generally believed to have begun in the Middle East, but it was not long (in archaeological terms) before it was evident in other locations, including the Far East. That there was exchange, not only between related peoples but with other races and cultures, and that this stimulated widely varying developments is not only beyond question, it is not seen as detracting from the originality of particular cultural achievements. That these interactions could take place over long distances involving travel by both land and water is also acknowledged. No one argues that Old World civilizations

TIMELINE

3600 BC	Ceramics dated to this time have been discovered in Americas.	1500 BC– AD 30	Olmec, the 'mother' of American civilizations, in Gulf of Mexico region.
3300 BC– AD 500	Archaeological evidence suggests Chinese contact in Americas.	AD 458	Chinese monk Hwui Shan sails east to land of Fu-Sang (Americas), stays 40 years.
3000– 1200 BC	Possible contact between Mediterranean civilizations and those of New World.	AD 499	Hwui Shan returns to China.

were totally individual autonomous phenomena. In fact, the evidence at hand indicates that uninterrupted isolation is not conducive to innovation. On the contrary, it encourages conservatism; adherence to tradition provides security, whereas innovation can appear threatening. It matters very little whether the new ideas were internally or externally generated—a threat is a threat from any quarter. It is by no means clear, for example, what circumstances will induce a people to allow the security of kinship to be modified by centralized control. Not taking that step, for whatever reason, can preserve the status quo of a culture in a stable adaptation, as illustrated by the Aborigines of Australia and Papua New Guinea; in the Americas, there are the examples of the peoples of Patagonia, Lower California, and the highlands of Brazil. All of these peoples lived in regions where communication with the outside world was so difficult as to be in effect cut off. In the well-documented case of Papua New Guinea the immediate reaction to first meetings with the outside world in the 1930s was a strengthening and efflorescence of the indigenous culture.[3]

The problem with the possibilities of interaction between New and Old World civilizations begins with distance and difficulties of communication. While it is easy to argue that the New World was peopled on foot, as we have seen, that argument can hardly be extended to the importation of the engineering concepts used in constructing Andean roads and waterworks, or the astronomical orientations of stepped pyramids in Mesoamerica, or the alignments of the pueblos of Chaco with their outlying villages.[4] If there were non-Amerindian influences at work in these developments, they most likely came by the easiest and quickest route available—the sea.

Deep-sea Sailing

Deep-sea sailing developed thousands of years ago, an event that is usually assigned to Southeast Asia. Archaeologist Thor Heyerdahl adds another location and advocates the eastern Mediterranean as a candidate for such a development. He holds that the earliest seagoing vessels were rafts with sails and movable centreboards (a Southeast Asian development) and reed ships (eastern Mediterranean).[5] Neither of these have hulls that keep the water out; a raised deck with cabin atop provided dry quarters for those aboard. Their deep-sea capacities, even to the point of going against wind and current, have been established by Heyerdahl as well as by others; in fact, in some respects they are safer than hulled vessels and are virtually unsinkable. Both of these types were still being used in historic times, the former in the Orient and off the Ecuadorean and Peruvian coasts, and the latter in the eastern Mediterranean, parts of Africa, in Lower California and South America, and at Easter Island.

Heyerdahl goes one step further, claiming that the ribbed, planked hull evolved out of the reed ship, also in the eastern Mediterranean, and for one of the same reasons that reed ships developed there in the first place: availability of building supplies. The types of reeds needed (papyrus in Egypt, totora in America, among others) were available locally, as was cedar for splitting into planks. Despite their seaworthiness and carrying capacity (proportionately better than that of hulled vessels), reed ships were not durable; it has been estimated that their life was about two years. They gave way to wooden ships for the same reason that stone gave way to metal: ability to stand up under the stress of usage. Wrecks of frame hulls in the Mediterranean have been dated to 1200 BC; the junks of southeastern China, classed by some as the most efficient ship in the history of sail,[6] are even earlier examples of this type of craft. In Bronze Age Europe the frame hull took the form of the 'nao', the one type of ocean-going craft to be developed in the West. Heyerdahl does not see the dugout canoe, which reached its largest size on Canada's Northwest Coast, as being ancestral to frame hulls but rather as a separate development, as were the ocean-going outrigger canoes of Indonesia. The Beothuk of Newfoundland modified the design of their canoes for ocean or river travel.[7] Both variants had V-shaped cross-sections, the river version having a straight keel-line while that of the ocean-going version was curved or 'rockered'; both needed rock ballast to stay upright in the water.[8] According to archaeologist Ingeborg Marshall, Beothuk canoes relate more closely to those of Athapaskans in the Northwest than they do to canoes of the regions in between, and they incorporate Inuit kayak features as well.[9] It has also been suggested that the design of its frame allowed for a removable skin covering to be placed over the forward part, providing shelter for those aboard. In its ocean-going form, it was a craft well suited for travel among ice floes.[10] Whatever the type of vessel, people 'could have made the trip anytime in the past 40,000 years', according to archaeologist David Kelley. 'They could have made it intentionally and got back again any time in the last 5000.'[11] In his opinion, the 'shipping problem is a straw man.'

Long before the Christian era, the people of ancient southeastern China became known as Pai-Yueh, the Navigators. One can only speculate as to where these early sailors went; however, the peanut, an American plant, has been reported from two coastal Chinese sites dating to about 3300–2800 BC,[12] and two varieties of chickens considered to be native to the Orient were happily at home in America when the Spanish arrived.[13] Chinese records tell of a search for islands in the Eastern (Pacific) Ocean where drugs for longevity were to be found, as well as 'magical beings and strange things'; one such expedition, in 219 BC, resulted in 3,000 young men and women being sent a few years later. Their mission was to establish a trade in the drug, but they were never heard from again. The mention of magical drugs, of course, brings South America to mind, but it is not a connection that is ever likely to be made with any certainty. In AD 458, Chinese records tell us, the monk Hwui Shan, with four companions, sailed to the east and reached the land of Fu-Sang, where he stayed for 40 years, returning to China in 499.[14] He reported that the people of that distant region lived in unfortified houses, did not esteem gold or silver, and drank deer milk, a description that suggests reindeer-herding peoples in Siberia, who could have been reached by sea via Kamchatka Peninsula. Oddly enough, Pietro Martire d'Anghiera (1455–1526), an Italian living at the court of Ferdinand and Isabella whose *Decades* is an early account of Columbus's voyages, wrote that Amerindians did not esteem gold and silver, kept herds of deer, drank their milk, and made cheese.[15] (Milk is not known to

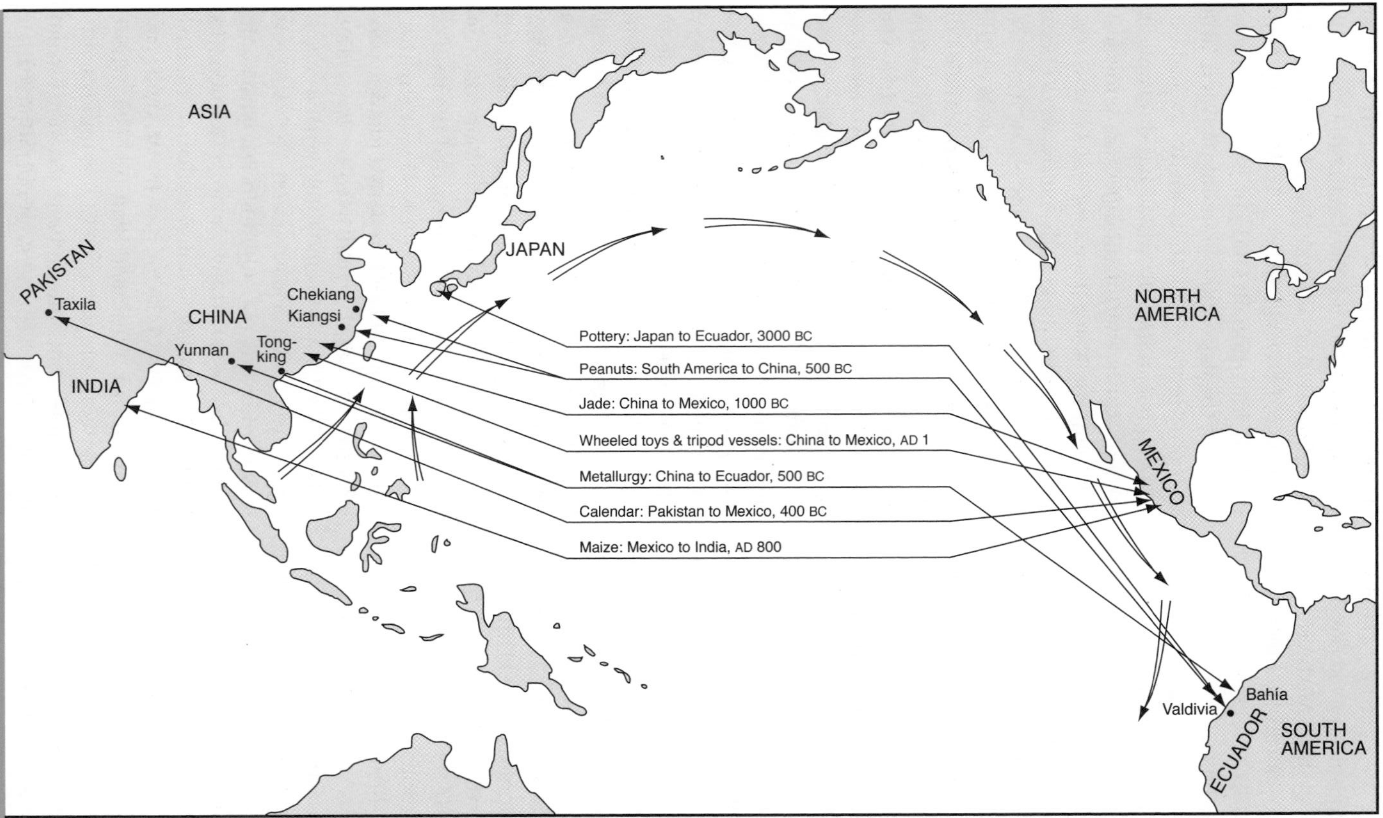
ASIA
PAKISTAN
Taxila
CHINA
Chekiang
Kiangsi
Yunnan
Tong-king
INDIA
JAPAN
Pottery: Japan to Ecuador, 3000 BC
Peanuts: South America to China, 500 BC
Jade: China to Mexico, 1000 BC
Wheeled toys & tripod vessels: China to Mexico, AD 1
Metallurgy: China to Ecuador, 500 BC
Calendar: Pakistan to Mexico, 400 BC
Maize: Mexico to India, AD 800
NORTH AMERICA
MEXICO
Bahía
Valdivia
ECUADOR
SOUTH AMERICA

3.1

Transoceanic exchanges for which there is some evidence

Source: John Barber, 'Oriental Enigma', *Equinox 49* (Jan.–Feb. 1990): 83–95.

be an item in the Amerindian diet, and some New World peoples lack the enzyme needed to digest it.) In AD 507, a Fukienese ship was blown out into the Pacific by a storm and found itself in the midst of strange islands. There does not seem to have been a follow-up voyage.

Transoceanic Technologies

In 1956, ceramics were discovered at Valdivia in southwestern Ecuador, dated to 3200–2800 BC, at that time by far the oldest known of such artifacts in the Americas. Their striking resemblance to pottery of the Middle Jomon period of Japan set off a wave of speculation that the Japanese had introduced pottery-making to the Americas. However, other contemporary New World pottery was soon found that did not always share Jomon's characteristics, and eventually the discovery of even older ceramics that had no resemblance to Valdivia ware ended that particular debate. But it did not resolve the question of the origin of New World pottery, as the oldest finds, now dated to before 3600 BC— unrelated to Valdivia as they are—still indicate a fully formed craft that appears to have been introduced from somewhere.[16] If the weaving of basketry is preliminary to the making of pottery, then one could expect that those areas where basketry became a high art, as in California and the Northwest Coast, would yield indications as to the development of pottery. Such has not been the case; in fact, ceramics were notably absent from both those areas. In northeastern North America, a fully developed type of pottery called Vinette I appeared about 1000 BC, without antecedents. The resemblance of these grit-tempered, cord-marked pots with convoidal bottoms to Old World ceramics has been remarked upon by anthropologist Alice B. Kehoe.[17] Fiedel, on the other hand, holds they could have resulted from local experimentations following exposure to the steatite-tempered pottery of the mid-Atlantic region. Otherwise, two sources are hypothesized for the introduction of pottery into Canada: from Asia via Alaska and the Yukon, or from the south into the east, both before 3,000 years ago.[18]

The pottery problem has, if anything, fuelled the controversy over transoceanic contacts in general, and their role in cultural diffusion, in particular. The issue of the Japanese connection is far from dead, as a particular type of mace considered to be peculiar to Japan has surfaced in Ecuador, dated sometime before AD 500 (interestingly enough, in the Far North the bow and arrow appeared about this time, or shortly before, and spread rapidly southward). Japanese and Amerindians are the only peoples to sing death songs. Those who argue in favour of cultural influences from across the seas point to technologies that were found on both sides of the Pacific, such as suspension bridges, hydraulic works, and blow guns, to name only a few.[19]

Cultural resemblances that appear to stretch the probability of coincidence too far for credibility have been compiled by geographer Stephen Jett (as well as others, such as Paul Shao and R.A. Jairazbhoy). He has listed concordances with China from the Shang dynasty (sixteenth century BC) through to the Han (206 BC–AD 220). Both the Shang Chinese and the Olmec of Central America (c. 1200 BC–BC/AD) made much of the feline motif (sometimes without the lower jaw), dragons, and serpents, and placed special emphasis on mountains. Both erected platform buildings with a north/south orientation, placed jade pieces in the mouths of the dead, and knew about magnetism. By late Shang times the toy dog was to be found in China and the Americas (Peru and Mexico), and dog flesh was eaten on ceremonial occasions on both sides of the ocean. Spreading from late Shang into Chou and Ch'in (700–220 BC), double-headed dragons and sisiutls are found on both sides of the Pacific, particularly on the Canadian

One of the oldest dated art objects from the Northwest Coast, this carved antler tool-haft is about 4,500 years old. It comes from the Glenrose Cannery site on the Fraser River and is 10.7 centimetres long.
(Courtesy Laboratory of Archaeology, University of British Columbia Museum of Anthropology, Vancouver. Cat. no. DgRr 6:2687)

Seated human figure bowls carved out of steatite have been found throughout the southern section of the Northwest Coast, as well as up the Fraser and Thompson rivers, and are believed to date to about 2,500–1,500 years ago. This one came from the Lower Fraser Valley and is 11.5 centimetres high. Similar, life-size figures are found in Mesoamerica.
(Courtesy University of British Columbia Museum of Anthropology, Vancouver, on loan from Jack Yoshioka. Cat. no. A6009)

North-west Coast. During late Chou and Dong-son (early Christian era) metallurgy appeared in the central Andean region and along the Ecuador coast to Costa Rica, but principally in the Ecuadorean Bahía area, generally believed to be the scene of the oldest New World metallurgical work (*c.* 500 BC–AD 500). In style, it is strikingly similar to the Chinese of this period.

If there was a connection, Amerindians were soon experimenting on their own, as they were the first masters of platinum metallurgy; Andean metal workers made skilful use of alloys. Peruvians liked to work with gold, 'the sweat of the Sun', and silver, 'tears of the Moon', in sheets, which they manipulated into desired forms, with particular attention to surfaces and colour. Their style of metallurgy has been described as one of surface transformation.[20] Beaten metal work, however, is far older in the Americas; the Old Copper Culture, in the Lake Superior region and to the south, dates to 4000 BC. (Later cultures, such as Adena, Hopewell, and Mississippian, would develop beaten copper work into a high artistic form.) Interestingly enough, people of the Aishihik culture (AD 750–1800) in southwestern Yukon worked copper they had obtained at the headwaters of the White River into points, awls, and dangles (cones). Their descendants today, the southern Tutchone, have a tradition of their ancestors heat-treating the copper and dipping it in cold water before hammering it.[21] Han China (206 BC–AD 220) and Mexico shared tripod vessels, wheeled toys, and lacquer. Efforts to establish linguistic connections between China and America have gone nowhere, except with place names; according to Jett, 130 Peruvian place names, mainly from Lima northward, correspond to Chinese names, and 95 Peruvian place names have meanings in Chinese but not in the New World regions where they are found. After Han, evidences of Chinese cultural influences become even more tenuous; there is no argument for post-Han contact with the New World.[22]

Transoceanic Exchange

The scene now shifts to Southeast Asia, principally Cambodia, southern India, and the Maldive Islands.[23] The argument here is for a trade contact, mainly with Cambodian Khmers, around AD 400–1000. It has been pointed out that prevailing winds and currents made such commerce possible; but even its most enthusiastic proponents agree that it could not have lasted past the thirteenth century. Botanical evidence indicates an early India–America connection: the hybrid New World cotton, discussed in the previous chapter, suggests as much, particularly as spinning and weaving equipment is the same on both sides of the Pacific.[24] Maize has added to this botanical puzzle, as it seems to have appeared with extraordinary rapidity in the Middle East and Southeast Asia, if indeed it was introduced after Columbus. There is abundant linguistic evidence to this effect: sixteenth-century accounts refer to it by such names as Roman corn, Turkish wheat, Sicilian corn, Guinea corn, Egyptian corn, and Syrian doura, among others. This, of course, does not tell us when it was introduced into those regions; however, the Jesuit Joseph François Lafitau (1681–1746) wrote that Pliny (AD 23/24–79) had mentioned maize being introduced to Rome, but that it was not well received and so disappeared until reintroduced in the sixteenth century. A twelfth-century Indian carving at Halebid, Mysore, India, is of a figure holding a cob of corn.[25] Other New World plants that have appeared in pre-Columbian transpacific contexts include grain amaranth, which may have made the voyage before corn (it was referred to in a tenth-century Chinese document as a crop of Szechwan),[26] the sweet potato (*Ipomoaea batatas*), peanuts (*Arachis hypogaea*), and the coconut palm (*Cocos nucifera*). The reverse seems to be the case with an Asiatic type of rice, *Oryza latifolia*, widely grown in South America.

Kelley has detailed a partial correlation between the calendar of the Mexica and an ancient Hindu zodiac, as well as between the Mayan calendar and the alphabet. He considers these too close to be the result of chance; he also suggests that the ideas underlying the Mayan calendar originated in Taxila, in modern Pakistan, once a centre of learning that attracted scholars from great distances. The calendrical/zodiac correlations involve a sequence of four of the 20 Mexica day names, which correspond to deities in the Hindu zodiac. When the two sequences are placed side by side and co-ordinated with each other, the Mexica day Death corresponds to the Hindu god of death, Yama; the Mexica day Deer to Prajapati, the Hindu god in deer shape; the Mexica day Rabbit (associated in Mexico with the moon and drunkenness) to Soma, the Hindu god of drunkenness who also rules the moon; and finally, the Mexica day Water to the Hindu storm god Rudra.[27]

North African Connections

Further west, we find Egypt and Phoenicia both being advocated for the honour of having reached the New World. Thor Heyerdahl argues that both of these peoples built ocean-going reed ships; when he looked for men who could re-create this ancient craft, he found them at Lake Chad in North Africa and Lake Titicaca in the Andean highlands. It was the latter who built *Ra II*, in which Heyerdahl successfully crossed the Atlantic in 1970, following an unsuccessful attempt the previous year. Not only is the distance much less than across the Pacific, the westward-sweeping Canary Current is stronger than the Japanese Current. Heyerdahl argues for contact between the Mediterranean and the New World, possibly as early as 3000 BC and certainly by 1200 BC, when the Minoan civilization disappeared in what appears to have been a natural disaster and Phoenician cities were rocked by disturbances

of an unspecified nature. His reasoning is that of a seaman; man was no less venturesome in those ancient times than in the fifteenth and sixteenth centuries, and technological limitations were not essentially that different between the two periods. In both eras sailors, highly skilled as they were, had to operate within the framework of natural forces such as winds and currents; as Heyerdahl sees it, what was achievable by the Spaniards was also achievable by the Phoenicians.[28]

North African and European connections have another champion in the highly controversial Barry Fell, zoologist and amateur linguist, who argues from markings and inscriptions on stones found in New England, Iowa, and Oklahoma, which he claims are Iberian Punic. He carries this to the point of proposing that the Zuni are descended from Libyans (related to ancient Egyptians); that Mi'kmaq ideograms are a modified form of Egyptian hieroglyphs; and that the language of the Arizona Pima's creation chant is Semitic.[29] Connections have even been perceived with ancient Greece and Rome, particularly with the Tiwanaku (Tiahuanaco) region of Bolivia and in the Peruvian Andean highlands, with their geometrically designed cities, waterworks, and road systems. These speculations have been reinforced by the prevalence of the 'Greek key' motif in the art of those areas; in the coastal desert, stylistic resemblances have been noted between the pottery of the Peruvian Mochica and that of Greek Attica and Corinth. Perhaps most intriguing of all have been plants painted in a Pompeiian mosaic that have been identified as pineapples and soursops (guanábana, *Annona muricata*); the volcanic eruption that preserved the mural occurred in AD 79.

How Is a Civilization Born?

All of these are suggestive rather than proof. Behind the arguments are two principal views of the rise and development of civilizations: one that accords primacy to internal motivations, the other that sees external stimulation as being essential. Most authorities agree that it is highly unlikely 'civilization' was brought over whole to a welcoming population waiting to be enlightened. The evidence accumulated so far indicates that the civilizations of the New World basically developed in the New World. If they had the benefit of cross-fertilization, which is well within the realm of possibility and in some cases even of probability, this would have encouraged already established processes. For instance, as Kelley says, those correspondences between the Mexican calendar and Hindu zodiac and between the Mayan calendar and the Middle Eastern alphabet could have resulted from contacts after the New World systems of recording time were in use. Given the right conditions, imported ideas could well lead to a new sense of direction,[30] as is also implied by the stories of Quetzalcoatl inherited by both the Mexica and the Maya from the Toltecs, and of Viracocha of the Peruvians. In both of these stories, heroes who brought civilization to the people were prophesied to return one day.

Such a compromise position is not universally accepted, however, and there are those, such as British author Nigel Davies, who deny the likelihood of any external factors powerful enough to have had an important impact.[31] Although forced to admit the profound importance of the Columbian contact, he flatly denies that possibility for earlier experiences. In too many instances, he says, chronologies are so far out of synchronization that apparent correlations between Old World and New World cultural phenomena must be accidental. He belongs to the group that argues instead for the pre-eminence of the subconscious in human development, and cites Carl Jung (1875–1961) to the effect that the near-identical forms of many religions were never 'invent-ed' but were 'born' of a common heritage of the human mind. Davies extends this to art and other creative aspects of cultures. For example, there is the extraordinary resemblance between the complex tattooing and body-painting patterns of the Maori of New Zealand and the Caduveo, tucked away in the Brazilian interior near the Paraguayan border. Anthropologist Claude Lévi-Strauss, in pointing out this phenomenon, also noted that since contact appears to be out of the question, one could only ask if 'internal connections of a psychological nature' were not operating to make possible such coincidences, well beyond the likelihood of mere chance.[32] It has also been argued that single instances such as this one, or that of the Jomon pottery, by themselves have little significance one way or the other; more important is the pattern of cultural complexes as a whole. Archaeologist John Howland Rowe compiled a list of 60 specific features of limited distribution shared by the Andean region and the Mediterranean world before the Middle Ages.[33] A strong opponent of diffusionism, he sought to demonstrate the extent to which independent parallel development was possible. It has been easy, of course, for his evidence to be used in support of the contrary view.

There is also the answer advocated by Heyerdahl, which stretches present understandings of the technological capabilities of early man. He points out that Columbus reached America by taking the ocean highway that is the Canary Current, which with prevailing winds swept him due west into the Caribbean. Carrying on a little further west, Spaniards subsequently reached the Gulf of Mexico, where complex civilizations were flourishing. In this region the 'mother' of American civilizations arose, which we call Olmec, after the natives of Olman, 'Rubber Land' (we do not know what they called themselves or even what language they spoke). This civilization appeared suddenly in a well-settled area about 1500 BC and, so far as is known, without a preceding period of development, during a time of natural disasters in the Old World. It lasted until about the time of Christ, although it was in decline from about 650 BC. The Olmec influenced subsequent city-states such as Teotihuacán (AD 150–700, outside of today's Mexico City), the whole complex of Mayan city-states, the Zapotec-Mixtec of Oaxaca, whose major city was Monte Albán (400 BC–AD 900), and Tajín on the Gulf coast. One of the difficulties with this scenario is that it is not always clear in which direction the influences went; for instance, glyphic writing, once assumed to have been first practised by the Olmec in the New World, has been found to have been present centuries earlier, before 600 BC, at Monte Albán, in the land of the Zapotecs. This was one of the only two sites of the world where writing was indisputably invented (the other was Mesopotamia, before 3000 BC).[34] Heyerdahl, in his comparisons with the Mediterranean world, includes all Amerindian civilizations rather than restricting himself to the Andean, as Rowe does; his list, however, is somewhat shorter.[35] He correlates the beginning of the Olmec with a period of Phoenician emigration; he also relates the beginning date of the Mayan calendar, 4 Ahau 8 Cumhu (3113 BC), to a time of natural disasters and social upheavals in the Mediterranean world.

Botanical and Other Evidence

As matters stand at the present, plants offer the strongest evidence of overseas connections between New and Old Worlds. The proof positive for such a connection that is demanded by the hardliners would be the discovery of Old World artifacts within a dated New World context, or perhaps the reverse. So far that has not happened, despite numerous claims to the contrary.[36] In the meantime, there is such evidence as the Chinese junk cast up on the northwest Pacific coast, reported in the eighteenth century, not to mention the ubiquitous Japanese fishing-net floats, so much sought after by souvenir hunters. There is also the resemblance between the Hindu game of pachesi and the Mexica patolli, so close as to be virtually identical. Myths add to the conundrum: according to one survey, they reveal a relationship between Mesoamerica and the Pacific islands and East and South Asia, on the one hand, and between North America and East and North Asia, on the other, 'thus showing two channels of cultural contact between Eurasia and America'.[37]

Heyerdahl has extended the puzzle further. He sees no reason why early travellers across the Atlantic, like the Spaniards at a later date, did not cross the isthmus and sail down the Pacific coast on sea-going rafts, built with balsa logs from Ecuador and equipped with sails. The Spaniards found a busy coastal traffic of such rafts upon their first arrival; the directions they obtained from Peruvian sailors aided them in their rapid descent down the coast. As Heyerdahl demonstrated with his voyage on the raft *Kon-Tiki* in 1947, such vessels were fully capable of sea-going voyages, not only with prevailing winds and currents but also tacking into the wind. This and other voyages confirmed Acosta's report that the people of Ica and Arica, on the Peruvian coast, 'were wont to saile farre to the Islands of the West'. Heyerdahl sees the settlement of Easter Island with its mysterious giant sculptured heads (some with bodies that were carefully buried), so different from the giant heads of the Olmec, as originating in the Americas. As well, the peopling of Polynesia (including New Zealand), even if largely originating in Southeast Asia as generally accepted, would have had to come via the Americas along the only route available with their sailing technology—the Japanese Current. The sweet potato, the cultivation of which is widespread throughout the Pacific, is an American crop. Among other things, Polynesia and the Americas share bark beaters, the manufacture of bark cloth, the blowgun complex, longhouses, and head-hunting. As Heyerdahl sees it, Polynesia was the last region of the world to be populated by humans, and it was by way of the Americas. Genetic studies have revealed a close relationship between South American Amerindians and Polynesians.[38]

Whatever the outcome of these debates, one point is becoming increasingly clear: New World prehistory was as filled with significant developments as that of the Old World in the fascinating story of man's cultural evolution. Whatever the degree of overseas influence, the civilizations that evolved in the New World were distinctively their own; American Olmec and Chinese Shang each had their dragons, but they are not easily confused, any more than the split animal motif of the Northwest Coast could be with that of the Chou or Ch'in dynasties. What is more, varied as New World cultures were, they fit into a hemisphere-wide pattern; like Europeans on the other side of the Atlantic, they shared a basic civilization. Their 'formidable originality' has led Joseph Needham, director of the East Asian History of Science Library, Cambridge, and Lu Gwei-Djen, associate director, to place Amerindian civilizations on a par with those of the Old World: the Han, the Gupta, and the Hellenistic Age.[39]

Chapter 4

Canada When Europeans Arrived

At the time of the first certainly known European contact with North America, that of the Norse in about AD 1000, by far the majority of Canada's original peoples were hunters and gatherers, as could be expected from the country's northern location.[1] This way of life, based on regulated patterns that had evolved over thousands of years, grew out of an intimate knowledge of resources and the best way of exploiting them. Anthropologist Robin Ridington has made the point that their technology consisted of knowledge rather than tools.[2] It was by means of this knowledge of their ecosystems, and their ingenuity in using them to their own advantage, that Amerindians had been able to survive as well as they did with a comparatively simple tool kit.

Because of Canada's extended coastline (the longest of any nation in the world), many of the Aboriginal peoples were sea-oriented; however, the great variety in the country's geographical regions (Arctic, Subarctic, Northeastern Woodlands, Great Plains, Plateau, and Northwest Coast) ensured many variations on fundamentally similar ways of life.[3] For the most part, the population was thinly scattered, as the prevalent hunting and gathering mode of subsistence is land-intensive; the most widely accepted estimate is about 500,000, although recent demographic studies have pushed the possible figure to well over 2 million.[4] The principal population concentrations were on the Northwest Coast, where abundant and easily available resources had allowed for a sedentary life, and in what is today's southern Ontario, where various branches of Iroquoians practised farming. The Iroquoian groups may have totalled about 60,000 if not more, and the Northwest Coast could have counted as many as 200,000 souls, making it 'one of the most densely populated nonagricultural regions in the world'.[5] Most of these people had been in their locations for thousands of years; as archaeologist James V. Wright has pointed out, only in the Arctic and the interior of British Columbia had there been comparatively recent migrations (AD 1000 and AD 700 respectively).[6]

These people spoke about 50 languages that have been classified into 12 families, of which six were exclusive to present-day British Columbia. By far the most widespread geographically were those within the Algonkian

TIMELINE

3000 BC	Head-Smashed-In Jump in southern Alberta, used for hunting of bison until 1870s, had 30 different mazeways, as many as 20,000 cairns to direct stampeding herds.	800 AD	Iroquoian (Five Nations, Odawa, Huron, etc.) farmer-hunters living in palisaded villages.
2000 BC– AD 1000	Dorset culture thrives in Far North.	1500s or earlier	Iroquoians form confederacies (Huron Confederacy, League of Five Nations) that have major impact on subsequent inter-tribal and Indian–European relations.
1000–500 BC	Hierarchical chiefdoms among sedentary Northwest Coast groups (e.g., Haida, Kwakwaka'wakw, Nuu'chah'nulth, Tsimshian) well established.		

4.1

Aboriginal culture areas

Sources: Waldman, *Atlas of the North American Indian*; R. Bruce Morrison and C. Roderick Wilson, eds, *Native Peoples: The Canadian Experience* (Toronto: McClelland & Stewart, 1986).

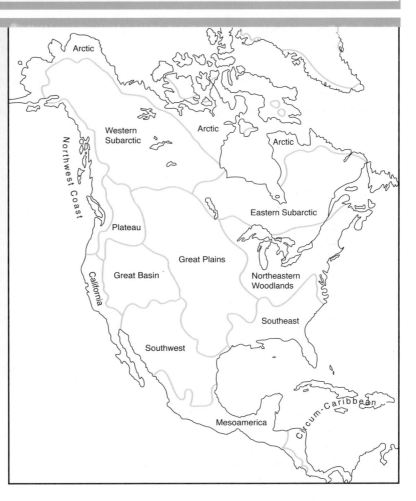

group, spread from the Rocky Mountains to the Atlantic and along the coast from the Arctic to Cape Fear; Cree and Inuktitut had the widest geographical ranges. This accords with anthropologist Richard A. Rogers's hypothesis, that by the proto-historic period areas that were once glaciated (most of Canada and a portion of the northern United States) had fewer languages than areas that had been unglaciated. While Canada was completely covered with ice during the last glaciation, except for parts of the Yukon and some adjacent regions, the strip along the Pacific coast was freed very early. According to Rogers's calculations, once-glaciated areas averaged 18 languages per million square miles and unglaciated regions 52.4 languages per million square miles (2,590,000 square kilometres).[7] Following the rule of thumb of linguistics that greater diversity of language indicates longer occupation, then the settlement of Canada can be judged to be comparatively recent—for the most part, dating to no more than about 15,000 years ago. In any event, the Athapaskan languages spoken in the unglaciated Northwest are more diversified than the Algonkian spoken in the once-glaciated taiga that stretches from the Rockies to the Atlantic coast. Intrusive Iroquoian-Siouan languages have been aptly described as islands in an Algonkian sea. In Canada, as in the two Americas generally, the greater language diversity of the Pacific coast indicates settlement prior to the rest of the country, although this has not so far been backed up archaeologically.[8] At the present, one can only speculate about the villages and campsites that have been drowned by rising sea levels following the retreat of the glaciers.

All of these peoples, whether mobile or sedentary, lived within cultural frameworks that met social and individual needs by emphasizing the group as well as the self. This was true even among those peoples, particularly in the Far North, whose groupings were fluid, depending on the season and availability of food. Land, like air and water, was for the benefit of everyone, and so was communally owned. On the other hand, cultural knowledge was the property of those 'in the know', a jealously guarded privilege, and was selectively passed on through the generations.[9] The social organization of Amerindians, like their languages, displayed a wider variety than was the case in Europe. However, with the exception of some aspects of the chiefdoms of the Northwest Coast, the only area in Canada where that type of social organization developed,[10] Amerindians shared the general characteristics of pre-state societies in that they were egalitarian to the extent that their sexual division of labour and responsibility allowed,[11] and they were regulated by consensus. The leaders' role was to represent the common will; not only were they not equipped to use force, they would have quickly lost their positions if they had tried. This lent extreme importance to eloquence, the power to persuade; a chief's authority was 'in his tongue's end; for he is as powerful in so far as he is eloquent'. Failure in this regard meant loss of position.[12] The Mexica word for ruler translates as 'one who possesses speech'; the centrality of the 'word' was signalled by the importance of keeping it, once given. This characteristic would later be of major importance in the conduct of the fur trade. Anthropologist Miguel León-Portilla has stressed the centrality of poetry—'flower and song'—for the Mexica, who saw it as arising from the divine, the means for expressing the truth;[13] in the seventeenth century, the Jesuits noted the power of the word and song among the peoples of the St Lawrence Valley.[14] This can be extended to Amerindians generally. The Amassalik Inuit of East Greenland use the same word for 'to breathe' and 'to make poetry'; its root means 'life force'. Among the Salish, the loss of a power song was tantamount to losing one's soul.

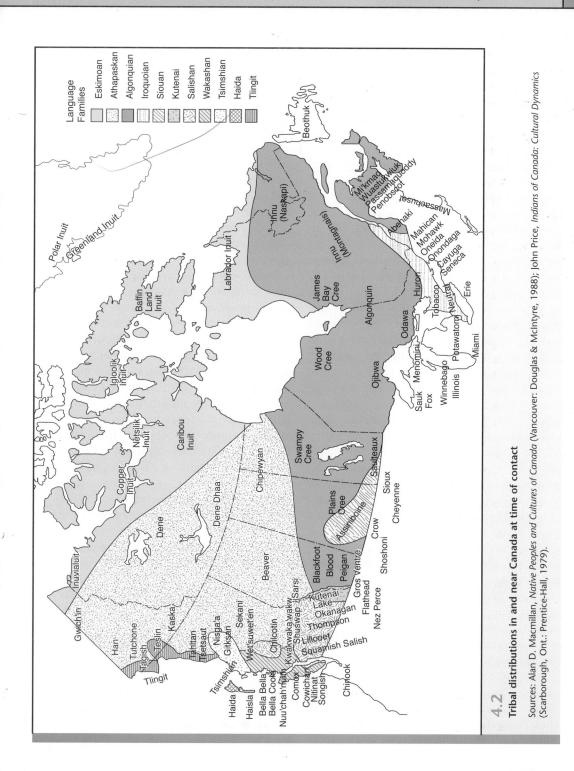

4.2

Tribal distributions in and near Canada at time of contact

Sources: Alan D. Macmillan, *Native Peoples and Cultures of Canada* (Vancouver: Douglas & McIntyre, 1988); John Price, *Indians of Canada: Cultural Dynamics* (Scarborough, Ont.: Prentice-Hall, 1979).

Northwest Coast

Since Canada's west coast pre-contact peoples largely depended on the sea for subsistence, many of them were semi-sedentary; the most mobile were the Kwakwaka'wakw (Kwagiulth). Sometimes sites were occupied by more than one tribal nation, either sequentially or concurrently. The Nuu'chah'nulth (Nootka) of Vancouver Island (along with the Quileute and Quinault, and the Nuu'chah'nulth's relatives, the Makah of the Olympic Peninsula in Washington state) were the whalers of the region, using a technology that had originated with the Aleuts and Inuit to the north. The chiefdoms (such as those of the Haida, Nuu'chah'nulth, Kwakwaka'wakw, and Tsimshian) were hierarchical, with clearly marked class divisions between chiefs, nobles, and commoners based on wealth and heredity; there was also grading within each class. Present archaeological evidence indicates that this stratification developed between 3,000 and 2,500 years ago.[15] Outside and below these classes were slaves, in some villages making up a third of the population. These were usually prisoners of war, but sometimes individuals who had lost status because of debt; one could also be born into slavery, one of the few regions in North America where this happened. In any event, slaves had no rights of any kind and could be put to death at the will of their masters. Overriding class and even tribal distinctions among the northern tribes (Tlingit, Haida, and Tsimshian) was the division of each of these groups into two exogamous moieties,[16] in turn subdivided into clans, which recognized descent only through the female line. Farther south, the Kwakwaka'wakw, Bella Coola, and Nuu'chah'nulth had no moieties, reckoned descent ambilaterally, and practised a ritual life that was dominated by secret societies. These characteristics were less in evidence among the most southern of the Canadian west coast tribes, the Coast Salish, although there were considerable differences among their various groups. In general, their chiefs also had less power; the Salish word for chief translates best as 'leader'.

Overall, social divisions interlocked and sometimes overlapped each other, so that an individual lived in a web of obligations and privileges that operated on the basis of reciprocity. This reciprocity was particularly operative where production and economic matters were concerned; its aim was to reinforce the community. In spiritual matters, individualism prevailed, although even here selfhood was not necessarily perceived as being separate and distinct from others within the group. Identity was acquired as one progressed through life. The elaborate giveaway feasts known as potlatches could be used for various purposes, one of which was to provide the mechanism for ambitious persons to rise in the social scale, and another was to distribute wealth.[17] Originally they had a subsistence function, facilitating food exchanges between those groups with surpluses and those with shortages. Property by which wealth was measured could be either in material goods (especially among the northerners) or in immaterial (cultural) rights such as those to certain songs, dances, or rituals (particularly among the Salish). Despite the emphasis on rank and material goods, more pronounced in the north, the principle of sharing prevailed as far as the basic necessities of life were concerned; a village's hunting, fishing, and gathering territories were divided among its kinship groups and exploited accordingly. Some fishing sites have been in use for thousands of years, such as the one at Kitselas Canyon on the Skeena, 'the river of mists', which dates back for at least 5,000 years.

Warfare along the Northwest Coast appears to have been more widespread before and during early contact with Europeans than it later became, particularly after depopulation as a

Indian cemetery, near Skuzzy Creek,
five miles below North Bend, BC,
northeast of Chilliwack. The people
of the region are the Salishan-speaking
Lower Thompson (Nlaka'pamus).
(Library and Archives Canada, PA-1201111)

An eighteenth-century Tlingit warrior
wearing cedar slat armour. Details at right
show helmet and jaw protector. From
Justino Fernandez, *Tomás de Suría y
su via con Malaspina*, 1791.
Drawn by Alessandro Malaspina.
*(Photo courtesy The Newberry
Library, Chicago)*

result of epidemics. In the Far North its principal purpose appears to have been to kill the enemy, but to the south the objective was the acquisition of slaves and booty, especially canoes (those of the west coast were dugouts, the manufacture of which was long and laborious);[18] the Haida were feared slavers, frequently raiding the Salish of southern Vancouver Island and the mouth of the Fraser River. According to archaeologist Gary Coupland, among such people as the Tlingit, Tsimshian, and Haida, warfare was aggressive and associated with the origins of ranked society, whereas to the south, among the Coast Salish, it was largely defensive.[19] The Tlingit were the only people of the Northwest Coast to practise scalping.

Farmer/Traders of the Boreal Forest

Other sedentary groups were the Iroquoians as well as some Odawa (Ottawa) of the St Lawrence River and Great Lakes—land of the white pine—who had adopted agriculture. In the Great Lakes region at the time of first European contact during the seventeenth century, there were at least 34 First Nations,[20] representing a kaleidoscope of cultures ranging from hunter/gatherers to agriculturalists with variations in between. The farming Iroquoians included the Huron and the Five Nations (later Six Nations, usually referred to simply as Iroquois), who became among the best-known of Canada's Aboriginal societies. These people, as well as the Iroquoians in general, all were farmer-hunters, practised slash-and-burn agriculture, and spoke related languages (apart from the Algonkian-speaking Odawa).[21] They lived in longhouses clustered in palisaded villages that counted up to 1,500 inhabitants each, and occasionally considerably more. This pattern of settlement appears to have developed with the adoption of agriculture and was well in place by AD 800.[22] Villages were moved to new sites when local

resources, such as land and firewood, became exhausted. This could happen anywhere from within 10 to 50 years. For these people, the fourteenth into the fifteenth centuries was a period of population expansion during which some villages expanded and others disappeared, and the 'three sisters'—corn, beans, and squash, each introduced at different times—eventually dominated the regional agricultural scene.[23] All of these factors contributed to rapid social transformation. Although the Iroquoians had earlier experienced intrusions from the burial mound peoples to the south, their cultures appear to have been indigenous developments, even as they adopted and absorbed traits from others. As we have already seen, agriculture and pottery were both introduced, so that ideas and techniques from others certainly contributed to the characteristics of the flourishing societies that Europeans encountered.[24]

Sometime during the sixteenth century, or perhaps earlier, groups of Iroquoians organized into confederacies that were to have powerful impacts in regional politics.[25] The northernmost was that of the Hurons,[26] an alliance of four nations (with a possible fifth) that clustered around the southern end of Georgian Bay; to the south on the Ontario peninsula was that of the Neutrals, about which even less is known than about the Huron; and in today's United States, in the Finger Lakes region of central New York state, was the Five Nations. The Huron Confederacy was concentrated between Lake Simcoe and the southeastern corner of Georgian Bay, an area of about 2,331 square kilometres; as far north as agriculture was practicable with a Stone Age technology, it enjoyed 135–42 frost-free days a year and about 190 growing days. By the early seventeenth century, the Huron had about 2,833 hectares (7,000 acres) under cultivation, and it was reported of Huronia that 'it was easier to get lost in a cornfield than in a forest.'[27] It was the granary for the northern tribes with which they traded,

'Battle on the Northwest Coast', by Paul Kane.
(*With permission of the Royal Ontario Museum © ROM, 912.1.84*)

supplying them with such crops as corn, beans, squash, and tobacco, as well as twine for fish nets, in return for products of the hunt, such as meat, hides, and furs. Huron pottery has been found as far north as James Bay. The beauty and bounty of the land were such that when the French first came to their country, the Huron assumed it was because France was poor by comparison.[28]

By the end of the sixteenth century, Huronia counted a larger population than that of the Five Nations, an estimated 30,000 compared to 16,000.[29] The Huron lived in up to 25 villages, the largest of which, Cahiagué, belonged to the Arendarhonon (Rock) nation[30] and may have had a population of 5,000. These villages were concentrated close to each other at the centre of Huronia, with their cornfields forming a surrounding belt. This allowed for a certain homogeneity in the languages of the confederacy; all

Hurons could understand each other, and their language was the lingua franca of the northern trade networks. The unity of the confederacy was further cemented by the Feast of the Dead, in which the bodies of those who had died (but not violently) were disinterred and prepared for reburial with much ceremony in a common ossuary, in which their bones were mingled. This feast was held at established intervals and also whenever a large village moved, necessitating leaving the dead behind.[31]

Situated as it was at a crossroads in the trading networks that criss-crossed North America, Huronia dominated regional trade routes. It also dominated the political scene and had surrounded the rival Five Nations with a system of alliances that extended as far as the Susquehannocks (Andastes, Conastogas), about 805 kilometres to the south. Huronia apparently absorbed at least some of the St Lawrence

Dekanawidah and Hiawatha meeting Atotarho. From Francis Drake,
The Indian Tribes of the United States, 2 vols, 1884.
(Photo courtesy The Newberry Library, Chicago)

Iroquoians who were dispersed during the sixteenth century, an event in which the Mohawk of the Five Nations appear to have had a hand.[32] Despite this initial position of strength, Huronia would rapidly disintegrate before the realignment of forces brought about by the intrusion of European trade, and the old dominance of the north/south axis would give way to the east/west axis because of the influx of European trade goods from the Atlantic coast.

League of Five Nations

The territory of the League of Ho-de'-no-sau-nee (People of the Longhouse), as the Five Na-tions also called themselves, was more extensive than the lands of the Huron, although their population was less. The league's territory stretched from the Mohawk River on the east to the Genesee River on the west, a distance of about 180 kilometres. It was a geographic position that would come into its own after the establishment of European colonies on the east coast, as it controlled the major routes from the coast to the interior. The Iroquois villages were much more scattered than those of Huronia, as each was surrounded by its own cornfields, and each maintained its own language; the languages of the Five Nations (from east to west, Mohawk, Oneida, Onondaga,

A nineteenth-century depiction of Ojibwa harvesting wild rice. Amerindian care of the stands of wild rice came close to farming. Drawing by Seth Eastman (1808–75).
(Photo courtesy The Newberry Library, Chicago)

Cayuga, and Seneca)[33] were more distinct from each other than those of the Huron. Each of the member nations occupied its own villages, usually two or more; each had its own council, as did each tribe, whose council usually met in the group's largest village.

The 'Great League of Peace', another of the appellations for the Iroquois confederacy, was governed by a council of 50 chiefs representing participant tribes, although not equally; despite that fact, each tribe had one vote. The aim was to keep peace between them and to co-ordinate their external relations, which had to be by unanimous decision. The system would later be described as a 'marvel, only to be accounted for by the fact that the wills of this stubborn people were bent and moulded by the all-controlling influence of patriotism.'[34] Centralization was by no means complete, and member tribes maintained a considerable degree of autonomy, above all in internal affairs. The league had been founded by Dekanawidah, 'Heavenly Messenger', said to have suffered from a speech impediment, and his disciple, Hiawatha (Hionwatha), 'One Who Combs';[35] its symbol was the White Tree of Peace, above which hovered an eagle, a very wise bird 'who sees afar', indicating preparedness for all exigencies. Hiawatha was said to have dedicated himself to peace when he lost his family in an inter-tribal

Baffin Island Inuk woman and baby, taken prisoner by Martin Frobisher in 1577 during his second Arctic voyage. This depiction is by John White, who accompanied the expedition and was the first European artist to portray Inuit.
(Library and Archives Canada, ECM-64-31125)

Northwest Coast. Although the men cleared the fields, the women did the farming. Women exercised considerable influence and had the right to choose sachems (who, however, were selected from within certain families or clans);[38] they also had the right to order the removal of one who proved to be unsatisfactory. All Iroquoians practised torture and cannibalism within a war context, both of which appear to have been introduced from the south comparatively late.[39]

Hunters of Taiga and Tundra

All the other peoples of Canada were hunters and gatherers, although there were several who were at least partly agricultural and others who had been influenced by farming cultures. The Odawa, who relied largely on fish for their subsistence, in certain areas depended quite heavily on their planted crops, and the closely related Ojibwa (Anishinabe)[40] relied on an uncultivated one, wild rice (*Zizania aquatica*). Their care of wild rice stands bordered on farming, to the point where they appear to have been responsible for the spread of the plant beyond areas where it was found naturally. While their dependence on wild rice was much less than that of farmers on their crops—it has been estimated that Iroquoians grew 80 per cent of their food requirements—this is still one more illustration of the large 'grey' area between hunting and farming.[41] The Nipissings and Algonquins, both allies of the Huron, did some planting, but they were too far north for this to be other than marginal for their subsistence. The Montagnais of the northeastern boreal forest also appear to have practised some swidden (slash and burn) agriculture.[42] The Gwich'in (Kutchin, Loucheux) and related Han and Tutchone of the Yukon, in common with other hunting peoples, 'encouraged' the growth of plants near their encampments, particularly those used for medicinal purposes.[43]

feud. The chairman of the Great Council bore the title Thadodaho (Atotarho), after the warlike chief whom Dekanawidah and Hiawatha had converted to peaceful ways.[36] The Great Peace was not an overriding authority, but a 'jural community' charged with maintaining the peace through ceremonial words of condolence and ritual gifts of exchange.[37] The founding of the league has been linked with an eclipse of the sun that was seen in Iroquoia in 1451.

Iroquois social organization included division into phratries and clans, as on the

Ball game on ice in the Northeastern Woodlands, from a drawing by Seth Eastman.
(Photo courtesy The Newberry Library, Chicago)

In the cultural domain, the Nipissings and Odawa practised the Huron custom of the Feast of the Dead, a far more elaborate ceremonial than was usually found among northern hunting societies. The Mi'kmaq and Wuastukwiuk (Maliseet) of the Atlantic coast, specifically today's Nova Scotia, illustrate another type of cultural adaptation: that of an agricultural people reverting to hunting and gathering. According to their traditions, they were descended from a people who had migrated from the south and west; as we have seen in a previous chapter, archaeology has confirmed a connection with the Adena and Hopewellian mound builders of the Ohio Valley. Mi'kmaq social organization was more complex than that of

their northern hunting and gathering neighbours. They called their land Megumaage and divided it into seven districts under a hierarchy of chiefs. The district where Halifax would be established, for instance, was called Gespogoitg, and Cape Breton Island, Oonamag.[44] Another hunting and gathering people, the Siouan Assiniboine (Stoneys), neighbours and allies of the Cree, had also migrated from the south, where their ancestors had once been farmers on the fringes of the Mississippian mound-building complex. Cultural evolution and diffusion are by no means one-way processes involving a fixed sequence of stages.

During this period the ancestors of the modern Inuit, called Thule, were moving steadily

An Arctic version of a ball game, using a stuffed sealskin. Woodcut from a drawing by a nineteenth-century Inuk known only by his baptismal name, Aaron.
(Photo courtesy The Newberry Library, Chicago)

eastward across the Arctic, displacing earlier Dorset (whose culture had evolved from the original Paleo-Eskimo), and reached the Atlantic coast sometime during the fifteenth century. Dorset lingered in the northern Ungava until the fifteenth century; they also held out until about the same time in Newfoundland before giving way to the Beothuk, a proto-Algonkian people who followed an Archaic way of life, based on the winter caribou hunt and the summer exploitation of sea and river resources. Some pockets of Dorset may have continued until the twentieth century on Hudson Bay.[45] The Thule, like the modern Inuit but unlike the Dorset, possessed the bow and arrow, spear thrower, and sealskin-covered kayaks and umiaks, and they used dogs as draft animals. They were the unchallenged masters of the tundra lands beyond the tree line, recog-

nized as such by the Amerindians, who seldom encroached on the Inuit domain. This was made abundantly clear to Samuel Hearne in 1771 as his party made its way towards the Arctic Ocean. As they approached Inuit territory, the Chipewyans deserted, saying that 'the journey seemed likely to be attended with more trouble than would counterbalance the pleasure they could promise themselves by going to war with the Esquimaux.'[46] Sixteenth-century reports that Inuit ranged as far south as Anticosti Island in the Gulf of St Lawrence may have been based on mistaken identity, resulting from linguistic confusion.[47]

Northwestern Plains

On the northwestern Plains, 'where the sky takes care of the earth and the earth takes care of the sky',[48] the population at the beginning of the historic period has been estimated to have averaged less than one person per 10 square miles (26 square kilometres). However, there were wide fluctuations, with considerable influxes from surrounding areas during seasonal hunts. The bison hunt provided the basis for cultural patterns.[49] From about 5000 BC to 2500 BC, during a period called Altithermal, higher temperatures and greater aridity decimated the herds of giant bison by cutting down on their food supply. Before the Altithermal, hunters pursued giant bison; afterward, the bison were of the smaller variety with which we are familiar. Both drives and jumps were practised, depending on the conformation of the land; the greatest number of jump sites have been found in the foothills of the Rocky Mountains, whereas pounds were more commonly used on the Plains, particularly along the continental escarpment known as the Missouri Coteau, where sites have been found at Oxbow and Long Creek in Saskatchewan. In Canada, most drive sites have been found in that province, as well as in Alberta.

These forms of hunting called for a high degree of co-operation and organization, not only within bands but also between them and sometimes inter-tribally. Impounding, or corralling, was the more complex method, and has been described by archaeologist Thomas F. Kehoe as a form of food production rather than hunting—a precursor, if not an early form, of domestication.[50] One of the earliest of the jump sites was Head-Smashed-In in southern Alberta, more than 5,000 years old; it would continue to be used until the 1870s. This was an enormous site, so big that its use was an inter-tribal affair. Recent archaeology has revealed 30 different mazeways along which the buffalo were driven and up to 20,000 cairns that guided the direction of the stampeding herds.[51] Whatever the type of communal hunting, strict regulation was involved; when several tribal nations congregated for such a hunt, rules were enforced by organized camp police. Penalties could include the destruction of the offender's dwelling and personal belongings.[52] In contrast, when herds were small and scattered, individuals could hunt as they pleased. In general, campsites were located on lookouts; some of them found in Alberta include several hundred tipi rings, indicating use over a considerable length of time. It has been estimated that there may be more than a million such rings scattered throughout Alberta.[53] Medicine wheels, important for hunting rites, ringed the bison's northern summer range; some were in use for at least 5,000 years.[54] At the time of European arrival on the east coast, the use of bison jumps and drives was, if anything, increasing.

It has been suggested that Head-Smashed-In was a trading centre, perhaps connected with Cahokia networks, providing bison materials such as pemmican and hides in return for dried maize, artifacts, and possibly tobacco.[55]

Trade and Gift Diplomacy

Uneven distribution of resources ensured that all of these people traded; indeed, the rich kaleidoscope of Amerindian cultures could hardly have been possible without such an integrative institution. Good relations, alliances, and the transfer of spiritual powers were important in these exchanges, rather than economic considerations; however, there could be trade with an enemy if a truce could be agreed upon. As Jesuit Paul Le Jeune (1591–1664) would observe in the St Lawrence Valley:

> Besides having some kind of Laws maintained among themselves, there is also a certain order established as regards foreign nations. Concerning commerce, he is Master of one line of trade who was first to discover it. . . . if any

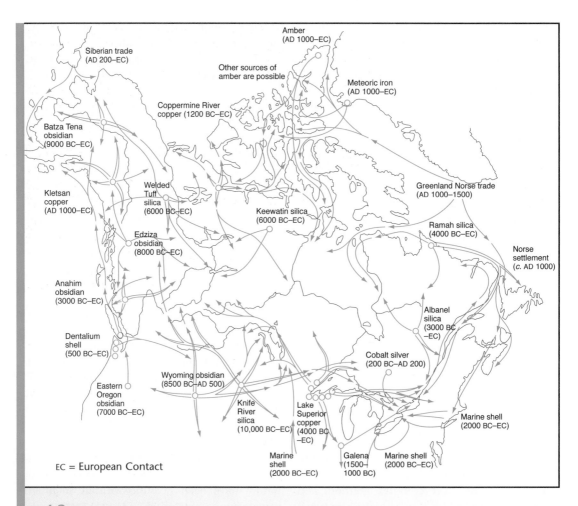

Siberian trade
(AD 200–EC)

Amber
(AD 1000–EC)

Other sources of
amber are possible

Meteoric iron
(AD 1000–EC)

Coppermine River
copper (1200 BC–EC)

Batza Tena
obsidian
(9000 BC–EC)

Kletsan
copper
(AD 1000–EC)

Welded
Tuff
silica
(6000 BC–EC)

Keewatin silica
(6000 BC–EC)

Greenland Norse trade
(AD 1000–1500)

Edziza
obsidian
(8000 BC–EC)

Ramah silica
(4000 BC–EC)

Norse
settlement
(c. AD 1000)

Anahim
obsidian
(3000 BC–EC)

Albanel
silica
(3000 BC
–EC)

Dentalium
shell
(500 BC–EC)

Cobalt silver
(200 BC–AD 200)

Wyoming obsidian
(8500 BC–AD 500)

Eastern
Oregon
obsidian
(7000 BC–EC)

Knife
River
silica
(10,000 BC–EC)

Lake
Superior
copper
(4000 BC
–EC)

Marine shell
(2000 BC–EC)

Marine
shell
(2000 BC–EC)

Galena
(1500–
1000 BC)

Marine shell
(2000 BC–EC)

EC = European Contact

4.3

Some prehistoric trade patterns

Source: R. Cole Harris, ed., *Historical Atlas of Canada*, vol. 1, *From the Beginning to 1800* (Toronto: University of Toronto Press, 1987), plate 14.

one should be bold enough to engage in a trade without permission from him who is Master, he may do a good business in secret and concealment, but if he is surprised by the way he will not be better treated than a thief.[56]

The consequence of alliances is clearer in regions where warfare was practised than in the Far North, where hostilities were expressed in chance killings or raids rather than on an organized basis. Agreements were customarily sealed by an exchange of gifts as well as hostages, which led to the formation of blood ties.

While the value of goods certainly was appreciated, and Amerindians had a good eye for quality, as European traders later would find

The rich variety of regional headdresses. From left: Northwest Coast; Northern (NWT) *(Library and Archives Canada, PA-42064)*; Plains: Stoney *(Library and Archives Canada, NA-667-868)*; Eastern Woodlands (detail from Benjamin West's 'Death of Wolfe') *(Library and Archives Canada, Ottawa/Transfer from the Canadian War Memorial, 1921. Gift of the 2nd Duke of Westminster, Eaton Hall, Cheshire, 1918)*

out, prestige was more important than the accumulation of wealth as such. Acquiring prestige called for generosity, among other virtues. Goods were accumulated to be given away on ceremonial occasions, such as the potlatch on the west coast; trade was a principal means of acquiring the needed goods. Gift exchanges—'I give to you that you may give to me'[57]—were a social and diplomatic obligation; gifts were presented when people visited each other, on special occasions, such as marriage and name-giving, or for obtaining the return of prisoners of war. Status was important in these exchanges; the higher the rank of the recipients, the greater the value of the gifts. Above all, gifts were essential for sealing agreements and alliances with other peoples. Without gifts, negotiations were not even possible; among other things they wiped away tears, appeased anger, aroused nations to war, concluded peace treaties, delivered prisoners, raised the dead.[58] Gifts were metaphors for words; and treaties, once agreed on, were not regarded as self-sustaining. To be kept alive,

they needed to be fed every once in a while by ceremonial exchanges. Later, during the colonial wars, periodic gift distributions would be essential in maintaining the alliances that proved so useful to the colonizing powers; this would be the only pay the allies received for their services as guerrillas.

Trade goods could travel long distances; for instance, obsidian, valued for tools because of its keen cutting edge and also for ceremonial purposes because of its beauty, has been found on archaeological sites far from its place of origin. There are several quarries in British Columbia; the oldest, at Edziza, was in use from 8000 BC until European contact.[59] The copper trade was also active, with the principal source being the surface copper from the western end of Lake Superior, although deposits on the Coppermine River were being worked 3,000 years ago.[60] Cartier's men would become excited when they observed copper knives among Amerindians near the Saguenay, mistaking them for gold. Out of that misconception was born the legend of the Golden Kingdom of the

Saguenay, which would inspire northern exploration by Europeans. Most intriguing of all has been the discovery of steel blades at Ozette, a Makah village on the Olympic Peninsula in the state of Washington that had been buried by a mudslide over 500 years ago, before Columbus. It has been speculated that the blades are of Oriental origin.

Most frequently traded were cherts and flints (silicas) for arrowheads and other tools; various kinds of shells, depending on the region, were also much in demand as they had commercial, diplomatic, and ceremonial roles, as well as being used for personal adornment. In the Northeastern Woodlands and along the Atlantic coast laboriously manufactured shell beads known as wampum came in two colours, white and purple (also called black). The small northern whelks were the most common source for the white, while the quahog clam was the sole source for the purple. On the west coast, abalone—from as far away as California—and dentalium were the stock-in-trade. The Iroquois believed that wampum possessed spiritual power; the two colours, strung or woven into patterned collars and belts, also provided mnemonic devices that recorded transactions such as alliances.[61] As Wright has pointed out, there is no way of knowing what the trade in perishable items was.[62] If we are to judge by the situation at the time of European contact, it could have been considerable. We know that oolachon oil (derived from candlefish) was extensively traded from the Pacific coast into the interior along established routes that came to be known as 'grease trails'. In eastern Canada, trade dates back to at least 4000 BC.

Such widespread trade raises the question of language. Although barter can be conducted with a minimal use of the spoken word, trading languages appear to have a venerable history in the Americas. On the west coast there was Chinook jargon; similarly on the east coast, the Delaware were among those who had a trade language, as did the Inuit in the Arctic. According to popular rumour, Basque whalers had been operating off the North Atlantic coast for so long that by the time French merchants arrived in the seventeenth century, they found the Amerindians and Inuit using Basque words, and Spaniards reported that Montagnais and Basques were able to converse with each other.[63] Linguist Peter Bakker holds that the expression 'adesquidex' with which the Mi'kmaq greeted the French early in the seventeenth century was of Basque origin.[64] Facility in more than one tongue for trade and diplomacy appears to have been common among Amerindians; in the western interior sign language was widely used, and conferences have been reported during which not a word was spoken.[65] Contact languages, combining features of several tongues, served an important need as the multiplicity of Native languages would have otherwise made communication difficult. Chinook jargon (not to be confused with the Chinook language, although based on it) is one of the best known; consisting of Chinook, Sahaptin, and Nuu'chah'nulth, it was already flourishing on the west coast when whites arrived.[66] Later, French and English would contribute to this rich brew. Michif, which developed after the arrival of Europeans, will be discussed in Chapter 11.

World Views

Although local conditions and subsistence bases ensured that the peoples spread across Canada led different lives within distinctive cultural frameworks at various levels of complexity, yet they all practised severe self-discipline to stand alone against an uncertain world, along with the acquisition of as much personal power as possible.[67] Humour was highly valued, and they thoroughly approved of anything that provoked laughter. This characteristic was one of the first to be reported of

New World peoples. In the fifth century Hwui Shan told the Chinese court: 'The People of the land [presumed to be Aleuts] are of a merry nature, and they rejoice when they have an abundance, even of articles that are of little value.'[68] They also knew how to keep their spirits up in the face of starvation. As his Montagnais hosts told Le Jeune, 'keep thy soul from being sad, otherwise thou wilt be sick; see how we do not cease to laugh, although we have little to eat.'[69]

They all observed the law of hospitality, the violation of which was considered a crime;[70] and they all shared the concept of the unity of the universe, although filled with powers of various types and importance. Hospitality could be carried to the point of self-impoverishment, which did not strike Europeans as a virtue when they encountered it. This was observed very early among the Mi'kmaq:

> It is neither gaming nor debauchery that disable them from the payment of their debts, but their vanity, which is excessive, in the presents of peltry to other savages, who come in quality of envoys from one country to another, or as friends and relations upon a visit to one another. Then it is, that a village is sure to exhaust itself in presents; it being a standing rule with them, on the arrival of such persons, to bring out everything they have acquired, during the winter and spring season, in order to give the best and most advantageous idea of themselves.[71]

The unity of the universe meant that all living beings were related—indeed, were 'people', some of whom were human—and had minds, as anthropologist Jay Miller put it.[72] So did some objects that the Western world considers to be inanimate; for instance, certain stones, under certain conditions, could be alive or inhabited by minds in an ongoing dialectical process.[73] This belief in the unity of all living things is central to Amerindian and Inuit myths, despite a large and complicated cast of characters who experience an endless series of adventures.[74] Of utmost importance was harmony, the maintenance of which was by no means automatic, as the demands of life could make it necessary to break the rules; hence the importance in Native legend and myth of the trickster, who could be an individual but who could also be an aspect of the Creator or world force. As well, peaceful co-operation could be shattered by violent confrontations with malevolent, destructive powers.

Recent studies have emphasized the solid basis of these mythologies in natural phenomena. Amerindians and Inuit perceived the universe as an intricate meshing of personalized powers great and small, beneficial and dangerous, whose equilibrium was based on reciprocity. While humans could not control the system, they could influence particular manifestations through alliances with spiritual powers, combined with their knowledge of how these powers worked. Such alliances had to be approached judiciously, as some spirits were more powerful than others, just as some were beneficent and others malevolent; every force had a counterforce. Things were not always what they seemed at first sight; as with stones, even apparently inanimate objects could have unexpected hidden attributes. Keeping the cosmos in tune and staying in tune with the cosmos called for ceremonials, rituals, and taboos that had to be properly observed or performed if they were to be effective. Attention to detail could be so close that a missed step in a dance would result in chastisement. Even the construction of dwellings and the layout of villages and encampments (not to mention the cities and temple complexes to the south) reflected this sense of spiritual order, with its emphasis on centres rather than boundaries.

Some (but not all) tribes recognized an all-powerful spirit, but the important ones to deal

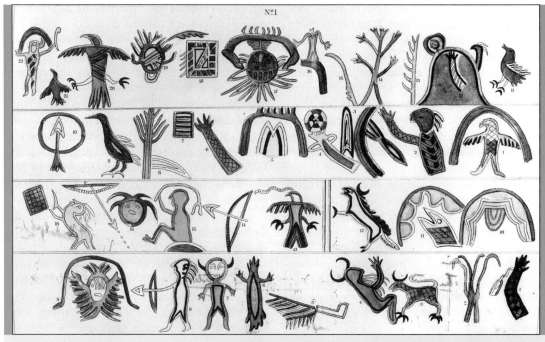

Ojibwa pictographs indicating the sequence for invocations, offerings, songs, for a particular ritual. After Henry Schoolcraft (1793–1864).
(Photo courtesy The Newberry Library, Chicago)

with were those who were directly connected with needs such as food, health, and fertility; also important were those connected with warfare. A person's lot in life was determined by the spirits—or animal powers—who volunteered to be his helpers, which he acquired during a vision quest. This was undertaken at puberty, with attendant purification rites involving prayer and fasting, among other things. Purification to gain spirit power (but not actual helpers) could be undertaken at other times as well; it is thought that much of the rock art that is found across Canada is associated with these occasions. Not surprisingly, the most respected leaders were also shamans (medicine men, sometimes women), individuals who had special abilities for communicating with the non-material world and whose

principal duties were to prevent and cure disease. According to anthropologist Diamond Jenness (1886–1969), the two regions in Canada where human sacrifice was practised were those with the most complex societies—the Iroquoians and the peoples of the Northwest Coast.[75] Whatever the form of their particular societies, Amerindians led full and satisfying social lives within the framework of complex cosmologies, despite the simplicity of their tools. As Le Clercq saw the Mi'kmaq, they lived like 'the first kings of the earth', as in biblical times.[76]

Although inter-tribal hostilities were endemic in the Americas, organized warfare was a characteristic of more complex sedentary societies.[77] Amerindians did not fight for acquisition of land as such, although on the west coast they appear to have done so for the possession of resources, but for blood revenge (which tended to become self-perpetuating feuds), individual prestige, and above all for the acquisition of prisoners, either for adoption or for sacrifice. Apart from the west coast, booty was of less importance.[78] Historian Daniel K. Richter has stressed the importance for the Iroquois of the acquisition of prisoners for mourning and condolence rituals, including adoptions, that helped the Iroquois to deal with death in their ranks.[79] Reparations were a means of controlling feud killings, which among traders such as the Huron were developed into an elaborate system.

Hemispheric Civilization

Canada was in the northern zone of a hemispheric-wide civilization that shared many underlying assumptions, even as it divided into regional manifestations. This, combined with a shared technology, encouraged similar responses to similar needs, despite varying conditions. Jacques Cartier (1491–1557), when he visited the St Lawrence Iroquois in 1535–6, was struck by the basic resemblance of their way of life with that of the Tupinambá of coastal Brazil—both peoples were farmer/hunters in forest habitats, albeit in very different settings. In this, Cartier was in agreement with most sixteenth-century European observers, who frequently commented on the underlying similarity of Amerindian lifeways wherever they visited in the Americas.[80] This is illustrated by cultural elements that occur in North America north of the Rio Grande and in southern South America, with little resembling them in the huge distances in between.[81] The number and complexity of these elements are such that archaeologist Erland Nordenskiöld (1877–1932) ruled out independent adaptations to similar environments—for one thing, many of the elements in question, such as stone boiling

and the frame baby carrier, did not depend on environment. More likely, these reflect the cultures the Amerindians brought with them. In other words, in spite of regional differences, one can speak of an American civilization in the same sense that one can speak of a European civilization. The Amerindians of Canada were on the outskirts of American civilization just as later colonizing settlers were on the frontiers of European civilization.

Much has been made of the differences between the American ethos, with its preponderance of egalitarian societies and view of humans as part of a transcendent universal system, with that of Europe and its rising nation-states, developing capitalism, and firm conviction that humans were not only the centre of the universe but its controlling force.[82] Differences were particularly evident in attitudes towards land, which for Amerindians was common property as it was for the benefit of all, and for Europeans was private property, individually owned. On the other hand, for Amerindians cultural knowledge was a carefully guarded individual privilege that was selectively passed on through the generations, as already noted, in contrast to Europeans, for whom it was generally publicly available. At the time of first contact, however, differences were not as great as they would later become. There were affinities between the societies of the Middle Ages, from which Europe was emerging on its way to industrialization, and the neolithic societies of America, among whom the use of metal was spreading. This is attested to by the ease—indeed, at times the willingness—with which some Europeans could and did adapt to Amerindian life, a tendency that would be vigorously fought by colonial officials.

Even so, the differences struck Europeans upon first arrival; they did not see any resemblances to their own way of life.[83] As late as the end of the seventeenth century, Le Clercq could repeat in all earnestness the old saw that had been around since the days of Columbus, that Amerindians had neither faith, nor king, nor law.[84] How could they, since they were not dominated by chiefs or captains with the power to command? How could they combine to present a united front? Jesuit Pierre Biard (1567–1622), also in Acadia, did not see that the people among whom he found himself were capable of reaching the decisions that would allow for such a course of action.[85]

What was clear to Europeans from the start was that Amerindians did not have the cohesion to prevent the invasion and takeover of their lands. The tendency towards fragmentation, which had been so effective as a technique for survival of independent neolithic societies before contact, with the arrival of Europeans became an instrument for their domination.

The first expression of that domination was the European habit of naming the places they visited without regard for Native usage. This was extended to the people themselves—Amerindians were tagged with labels they never used for themselves, and which were at times unknown to them, and even pejorative, in cases where they had originated with their enemies. Columbus started things off by calling the New World people 'Indians' because he thought he had landed in the Indies; a current Amerindian joke has it that the people should be thankful that he hadn't expected to arrive in Turkey.[86]

Part II

The Outside World Intrudes

Chapter 5

Inuit and Beothuk

First contacts between Europeans and New World peoples occurred over a much longer period than is usually realized.[1] Far from being confined to the dim and distant past, first encounters have been continuing into the historical present in the interior of Brazil and in the historical near-present in the Arctic, as well as in Papua New Guinea. In what is now Canada, first meetings for which there is a reasonably acceptable record began with the Norse about AD 1000 and continued as late as the second decade of the twentieth century, when members of the Canadian Arctic Expedition met isolated bands of Copper and Netsilik Inuit who were completely unknown to the Canadian government.[2] In contrast, these Inuit knew of non-Aboriginals, as their ancestors had had encounters with them. Three years later, in 1918, Royal North-West Mounted Police, while on a search for an Inuk wanted for murder, were still meeting people who had never seen a non-Aboriginal.[3] In other words, first meetings with Inuit occurred, off and on, over a period of more than 900 years. The Amerindian time span for such encounters was about 400 years, with some

Athapaskans of the far Northwest being among the last to meet Euro-Canadians early in the twentieth century.

What Is a First Meeting?

'First meetings' can, of course, be defined in a number of different ways. Historian Urs Bitterli has defined three basic types: contacts, collisions, and relationships, all three of which he admits rarely occur in a pure form.[4] 'Contacts' were encounters, for the most part short-lived, between Europeans and members of a non-European culture, and were usually peaceful, although they often involved ritual displays, such as flag- or cross-planting ceremonies, that could be interpreted as threats and could lead to eventual collisions. 'Collisions' tended to develop in subsequent meetings; Bitterli includes the transmission of disease, the slave trade, and the Spanish *repartimiento* and *encomienda* systems under this heading. Trade, evangelization, and colonial administration characterized the third type, 'relationships'. Returning to the first category, 'contacts' can be further subdivided into pristine encounters, in which one or both

TIMELINE

AD 1000	Thule culture begins to supersede earlier Dorset in North. Norse accounts of 'Skraelings'—probably Dorset people, but may have been Beothuk.
1497	Giovanni Caboto (John Cabot) makes landfall on east coast of Newfoundland.
1524	Giovanni da Verrazzano explores Atlantic coast from Florida to Newfoundland.
1576–8	Arctic voyages of Sir Martin Frobisher, by which time Thule culture has developed into Inuit. Like other explorers, he returns to Europe with an Aboriginal, an Inuk hunter, as a 'token of possession'. The Inuk soon dies in captivity.
1600	Inuit range extends down Labrador coast.
1610–14	John Guy, one of few Europeans to do so, seeks to establish relationship with Beothuks in Newfoundland. In the next two centuries they would be hunted to extermination.
1611	Henry Hudson makes first European contact with Subarctic Indians in James Bay.
1829	Shawnadithit, a woman who was the last known Beothuk, dies.

sides had no previous knowledge of the other, and first encounters preceded by hearsay, the appearance of new trade goods through Native networks, the spread of a new disease, or other evidence such as the debris left behind by explorers. It is with these subtleties in mind that 'first contacts' are considered here.

The first recorded encounters with Europeans in the New World took place in the eastern Arctic, perhaps some of them on Baffin Island, and along the North Atlantic coast of what is now Canada. Two of the peoples most likely to have been involved, Dorset and Beothuk, have since disappeared.

The 'Skraelings' (from 'skraelingjar', meaning small, withered) whom the Norse reported were probably Dorset,[5] but the term could have been used for the Beothuk, proto-Algonkians living in Newfoundland and perhaps also on the Labrador coast. When the Norse arrived, the Dorset, who had been in the region since before 2000 BC, were giving way to the recently appeared Thule. The Norse thought of the Skraelings as beings apart, possibly placing them in a category similar to the folkloric creatures with which they had populated their Old World northern forests. They referred to them as 'trolls' and described them as 'very little people', lacking in iron, who 'use whale teeth for arrowheads and sharp stones for knives'.[6] Another description refers to them as 'small ill-favored men' with 'ugly hair on their heads. They had big eyes and were broad in the cheeks.'[7]

The first illustration known of these 'little people' appeared centuries after first contact, in a 1539 map by Swedish geographer Olaus Magnus (Olaf Mansson, 1490–1557, in 1544 Archbishop of Sweden). The artist followed what seems to have been the popular belief as to how these people looked: pygmy in size, 'hayrie to the outermost joynts of the finger; and that the males have beards down to the knees, but, although they have the shape of man, yet they have little sense or understanding, or distinct speech, but make a shew of a kind of hissing, after the manner of Geese.'[8] This reported short stature is something of a puzzle, as archaeological evidence has not supported the notion that the Dorset were smaller than the Thule. A few years ago, reports of sightings of 'little people' resurfaced in the Cambridge Bay area, as well as around Yellowknife. These mini-hunters, strong and fleet of foot, were reported to shun civilization. There is even an estimate of their numbers: about 60 or 70.[9]

Some First Reactions

Early European records give us no hint as to what the Skraelings thought of the Europeans. We have some idea of what those thoughts might have been from reported Amerindian reactions to first meetings with the Spaniards in the Caribbean in the late fifteenth and early sixteenth centuries, where the people wondered if the Spaniards were spirits, perhaps even 'sons of heaven' or 'Sons of the Sun'.[10] The French would later speculate that the Spanish custom of going about armoured had given Amerindians that impression.[11] In Mexico, the identification was with the culture hero Quetzalcoatl, who long ago had sailed off to the East with the promise to return; in Peru, it was the ancestral deity Viracocha, the eighth Inca who had disappeared walking over the waters of the western sea; in both cases, however, there were doubts that soon grew into the realization that Spaniards were indeed mortal humans.[12] A first meeting of which we have a detailed account that occurred in the 1930s in the highlands of Papua, New Guinea, aroused a highly emotional response as the highlanders presumed at first that the invading Australians were ancestor spirits coming back to their relatives. This reaction reached the point of identifying individuals with deceased loved ones and joyously welcoming them back. This first impression took a while to dispel; even after things had calmed down a bit and the impulse to trade had asserted itself, doubts lingered as to the nature of the Australians.[13] An incident in which

Amerindians thought they were seeing a man returned from the dead occurred in Ajacán (Chesapeake Bay) in 1570. The Jesuits had brought with them Don Luis de Velasco, as they had christened a local cacique's son whom they had captured and taken to New Spain several years before. The first reactions of Don Luis's relatives was to think that the Jesuits had brought their kinsman back from the dead.[14]

The Norse accounts are too sparse to make any such inferences as to first impressions on the part of the Skraelings, but they do tell us that they were eager to trade the products of the hunt for weapons. This contrasts with the Papuans, who were far more interested in acquiring certain types of shells, which were highly prized as status symbols and represented wealth. In both cases, however, trade was the basis for the relationship between whites and Natives, especially during the days of early contact, and would remain important throughout the colonial period.[15] That the Norse traded with the Skraelings has been inferred from the presence of European artifacts in Arctic archaeological sites, particularly burials. Even more intriguing was the discovery in Bergen, in a thirteenth-century context, of a walrus figurine of Inuit workmanship. Bergen was the Norwegian port for traffic with Iceland and Greenland.

That the men of stone and bone were capable of holding their own against the men of iron in pre-fireweapon days is evidenced by the short duration of Norse attempts to settle on northern Newfoundland and mainland coasts. The slim record we have of these events indicates that there were four expeditions to Leifsbudir (Leif's booths, now thought to be the site near L'Anse aux Meadows) at the northern tip of Newfoundland, and that hostilities preceded the abandonment of the colonies.[16] The deterioration of the climate about this time, heralding the 'Little Ice Age' of *c.* 1450–1850,[17] meant that the Greenlanders found it steadily more

Detail of Olaus Magnus map, 1539, showing a Norseman encountering a Norse version of an Inuk.
(Photo courtesy The Newberry Library, Chicago)

difficult to practise their traditional type of farming; by mid-fifteenth century, their skeletal remains show diminishing stature, indicating endemic malnutrition. At sea, the thickening ice pack interfered with shipping, which in any event had been irregular and was decreasing due to conditions in Europe. It eventually stopped, cutting off supplies from Norway upon which the people's lifestyle (including diet) depended.[18] The changing climate favoured instead the sea mammal-hunting activities of the Thule, who were advancing eastward as well as southward down the North

Atlantic coast. By the time Sir Martin Frobisher (?1539–94) undertook his Arctic voyages in 1576, 1577, and 1578, the Thule culture had developed into that of the Inuit. When they met Frobisher, they were already familiar with Europeans and their ships. There was no hint about wondering if Europeans were supernatural beings, any more than there had been on the North Atlantic coast when Giovanni Caboto had made his landfall in 1497. The shock of first encounter appears to have been dissipated very early in those northern regions, perhaps with the Norse, perhaps with later unrecorded meetings. Neither did Giovanni da Verrazzano (*c.* 1485–1528), on his voyage of discovery along the Atlantic coast from Florida to Newfoundland in 1524, encounter the stunned reaction that had greeted the Spaniards in the Caribbean; quite the reverse, in fact, as the people seemed to know what to expect. Either there were more, and earlier, voyages than the record tells us about or there was good communication between coastal Amerindian groups, perhaps along north/south trade routes.

Involuntary Visits

A custom that arose very quickly from these early voyages, and which continued throughout the period of European exploration, was to kidnap Natives and take them back to Europe.[19] Not only was this the best possible proof that the explorer had actually reached the lands he claimed, but there was also the idea that the Natives could be taught the language of their captors and be used as interpreters and guides for future explorations. However, it was costly in terms of human life: if the Natives survived the voyage across the Atlantic, they usually quickly succumbed in Europe to unfamiliar living conditions and diet. Frobisher brought back an Inuk hunter to England, where he was displayed as a 'token of possession', indisputable proof that the explorer had found and claimed new lands for Her Britannic Majesty.[20] The Inuk soon died, but others followed. They were frequently called upon to display their skill in archery, all the more because of the English pride in their reputation as the best archers in Europe. However, the tale that Queen Elizabeth I granted one of these Inuit visitors the unheard-of privilege of shooting some royal swans has been dismissed as a misinterpretation in the retelling.[21] The Inuit back in the Arctic, for their part, maintained an oral tradition of the time when they were visited by the kodlunas (today's kabloonas or Qallu-

naat),[22] which was recorded by a visiting expedition three centuries later, in 1861; as well, they had carefully preserved 'sundry odds and ends' from Frobisher's visit, such as pieces of red brick and brass rings.[23]

Frobisher's captured Inuk did not live long to enjoy his new life in England. Europeans left to stay in the New World appear, on the whole, to have enjoyed a happier fate, so much so that it was not long before individuals were choosing to stay over. For obvious reasons, the record of what happened to them is even scantier than it is for New World people in Europe. The persons selected for this service were convicts, perhaps condemned criminals. If they were not simply being left for punishment but were being offered a chance to redeem themselves, their function was to learn the language and way of life of the people among whom they were to live, as well as something about their land. The idea was for these 'interpreters' to report back to officials of their mother country when they were picked up several years later, if anyone remembered, or cared enough, to do so. The Portuguese did this in Brazil, beginning with Pedro Cabral (*c.* 1460–1526) in 1500 (the men he left behind were never seen by the Portuguese again). The French were particularly successful with this practice in Brazil, creating a cadre of on-the-scene 'truchements' (interpreters) who became key factors in the highly profitable dyewood trade of the sixteenth century; in the Caribbean such men came to be known as *coureurs des isles* and in Canada, *coureurs de bois*. The Danes also did this in Greenland, as described by James Hall (d. 1612) on his voyage of 1605: 'He [the Danish Commander] sets on land one young man to be left in the Countrey, to his cruell fortune, this was done by expresse command of the *State-holder* of *Denmarke*, before his coming forth; they also in the Pinnace set another on land, both being malefactors, giving of them small necessaries. (*It may be those people lived a*

Inuit as they appeared to a sixteenth-century English draughtsman. Note the swaddled baby behind the woman and the depiction of the atlatl with three-pronged spearhead in the hand of the hunter in the kayak.
(Library and Archives Canada)

long time after, and may bee yet living, if the Salvages have not devoured them.)'[24] Hall did not state what the Danish Stadtholder had expected to achieve by this action.

English Impressions

These early English explorers customarily referred to Inuit as 'salvages' but also as 'Indians'—in the eighteenth century, 'Esquimaux Indians' was frequently used. They were reported to 'eate their meate raw' and also to 'eate grasse like bruit beasts, without table or stoole, and when their hands are imbued in blood they lick them clean with their tongues.' Although they were judged to be 'very trac-

table' and 'easie to be brought to civility', they were also taken to be 'Idolaters and witches', serious charges in an age when Europeans burned witches alive at the stake and when Christians tended to consider non-Christians to be *ipso facto* enemies. The English also appear to have shared with Europeans in general the belief that all New World peoples were cannibals, a too-readily accepted generalization from early reports of cannibalistic practices in the West Indies, Mexico, and Brazil. Later, reports became more colourful: to quote Canadian-born interpreter and trading-post clerk Nicolas Jérémie (1669–1732), 'when they kill or capture any of their enemies, they eat them raw and drink their blood. They even

A Greenland Inuit family portrayed during a visit to Bergen, Norway, in 1654.
(National Museum of Denmark, Department of Ethnography)

time Europeans appeared on the scene, an isolated group of Polar Inuit in far northwestern Greenland already possessed iron, and were working it into tools such as knives and weapons such as arrowheads. The source of the metal was a collection of meteorites found in a valley near Cape York. However, while meteoritic iron spread across the Arctic as a valuable trade item,[27] its use for tools and weaponry was restricted by the fact that it is very hard and difficult to work. Even so, Frobisher was struck by an arrow with an iron tip in one of his several mêlées with the Natives.

Initially, Inuit–European encounters followed the pattern of trading and raiding. It is not known if this behaviour extended to Davis Strait, where Dutch, Danish, Norwegian, and Scottish whalers were operating irregularly off the Greenland coast; but by the first half of the eighteenth century, Inuit were occasionally working with Europeans as the latter intensified their whaling activities. It was a co-operation that would reach its fullest development during the nineteenth century, after operations had moved to northwestern Hudson Bay and Americans had become major participants; Arctic whaling would last until the first decade of the twentieth century. The consequent reduction of whale stocks severely affected Inuit domestic offshore whaling and led to changes in hunting patterns. On the positive side, Inuit territory was protected by its Arctic environment, which Europeans found unattractive in the extreme; it would be the second half of the twentieth century before there would be a serious intrusion of Canada's northernmost lands and its people.

Infrequent Trading Encounters

Norse encounters with Skraelings aside, almost all of these early contacts appear to have been with Inuit. Since voyage chroniclers did not differentiate when writing about 'salvages', this is

make infants at the breast drink it, so as to instil in them the barbarian ardour of war from their tenderest years.'[25]

The closest to sustained contact that developed between Natives of the eastern Arctic and Europeans during this period was through whaling. This began along the Labrador coast and the Strait of Belle Isle, where Inuit met with Basque whalers, and later with French. These encounters introduced Europeans to Inuit technology for deep-sea whaling, which during the seventh to the thirteenth centuries was the most advanced in the world. Combined with European deep-sea ships, that technology led to the efflorescence of worldwide whaling.[26] An intriguing sidelight was the fact that by the an inference based on the location of contact but also drawn from the skimpy ethnographic descriptions. The first contact with Subarctic Amerindians appears to have been that of Henry Hudson (*fl.* 1607–11) in James Bay in 1611, more than a century after encounters had become sustained for the Natives of the North Atlantic coast. It was a brief meeting: a lone Cree presented himself, and upon being given some tokens of friendship, left to return with the skins of two deer and two beaver that he offered in trade. The English obliged, and when they showed an inclination to bargain the Cree accepted the offer but indicated he did not like it; picking up his goods, he departed, never to be seen by the English again. Such behaviour suggests that the Cree had a clear idea of the exchange rate he expected, as well as of the trading protocol to be followed, perhaps that of the north/south Native networks, which at that time operated as far north as James Bay. HBC chief factor Andrew Graham (*c.* 1733–1815) reported that the first Amerindians to trade with Europeans in Hudson Bay were an eastern branch of the Cree called Oupeeshepow.[28] He added that 'they relate the arrival and wintering of the unfortunate Captain Henry Hudson, as handed down to them by the tradition of their ancestors.'[29] The Cree, for their part, have a startlingly different remembrance of their first trade with the English. In an episode that appears to have occurred somewhat later and to have involved a group rather than just an individual, they recall that the English wanted the fur clothing they were wearing and persuaded them to trade the clothes off their backs in exchange for European garments.[30] Similar incidents were reported by explorers John Davis (?1550–1605) and Jacques Cartier, although in both these cases they reversed the perspective: as they saw it, the Amerindians were so eager for trade they willingly parted with the clothes they were wearing, and not necessarily for European clothing.

Hudson appears to have been more eager to meet with Amerindians than the latter were to meet the English following the encounter with the lone Cree. His motives were simple, 'for hee was perswaded that if he met with the Salvages, hee should have refreshing of fresh meat, and that good store.' He was disappointed, for 'though the Inhabitants set the woods on fire before him, yet they would not come to him.'[31] Sporadic trade did not develop into a continuing relationship at this time, and violence all too often marked what contact there was, although initial contacts were usually peaceful, as John S. Long has reminded us. He reports an oral tradition of the Cree at the mouth of the Churchill River, who saw strange signs and then encountered Europeans, who invited them aboard their ship. They were not afraid to accept, because from 'the expression on the strangers' faces, they could tell they were welcome aboard.'[32]

The presence of non-Aboriginals in the Arctic and Subarctic may have had more effect on the Natives than the incidence of direct contact would suggest, as the consequences of inshore whaling indicate. From the time of their first appearance in the region, Europeans had frequently encountered disasters that had forced them to abandon supplies and equipment, and sometimes even their ships. For Inuit and Amerindians, this could mean rich benefits as sources for scarce items such as wood and iron. The effects of this availability on Native groups are not known for the early period; but a study by anthropologist Clifford G. Hickey of a similar situation arising from the abandonment in 1853 of the British Royal Navy's *Investigator* on northern Banks Island suggests that this could have been considerable, both socially and economically. In that case, sudden access to wealth changed social alignments and patterns of reciprocity, which in turn influenced those of hunting.[33] Similarly, in twentieth-century Papua, New Guinea, sudden access to wealth in the form of imported shells had profound political and social consequences.

Apart from the Inuit, mainland native North Americans who have the longest history of contact with Europeans are the Amerindians of the North Atlantic coast. This can be dated from Cabot's visit, at a time when Christopher Columbus was between his second and third voyages and Spanish colonization of the West Indies was just beginning. It was a contact that can best be described as casual, at least at first, because Europeans had not come to colonize in those northern regions (which they found only marginally less unattractive than the Arctic), but to exploit the enormously rich fishing grounds, the whale runs up the Strait of Belle Isle, and the walrus rookeries of the Magdeleine Islands in the Gulf of St Lawrence. Then as now, oil was big business, and with the adoption of Inuit hunting techniques, whales became the principal source of supply, along with walrus. Fish was in demand because the European religious calendar counted 153 meatless days a year.

Exploiting sea resources, especially the cod fisheries, did not involve the type of close or sustained contact with the Native population that the fur trade would later; neither did it infringe on Native land usage to the same extent as settlement, although, as we have seen, problems did develop in this regard. Until the fur trade began in earnest and European settlement got underway, the comings and goings entailed in the fisheries (a term that included whaling and walrus hunting) allowed both Amerindians and Europeans to pursue their separate lifestyles without much consideration for each other. By 1600, Inuit had expanded down the Labrador coast, occasioning sporadic hostilities throughout the French régime. By the last decade of the seventeenth century, most French settlers were on the south shore, numbering about 40 families, while the English spread along the east coast into about 30 har-

bours and coves, some counting only one family each.[34] By the second half of the eighteenth century, under the British, not only was settlement expanding even more, but Euro-Canadian trappers were competing with Inuit for fur and game resources. Hostilities increased, with each side raiding and killing as opportunities presented themselves. The Inuit had the advantage of a huge hinterland, inhospitable to Europeans, to which they could retreat. The situation was such that Sir Hugh Palliser, governor of Newfoundland from 1764 to 1768, issued a proclamation in 1764 urging that the 'Eskimo Indians' be treated as friends.[35]

The Beothuk Experience

Less fortunate in this regard were the Beothuk. Very little is known about these people, Archaic hunters on land and sea; not even their language is certain. It may have been a variant of proto-Algonkian. They appear to have had an association with the Inuit, as a burial ground in northeastern Newfoundland is shared by the two peoples. Considering the traditional hostility between the Inuit of the tundra and the Amerindians of the boreal forest in historic times, these burials offer much for speculation, but as yet no answers.

From earliest encounters, Europeans described the Beothuk as 'inhuman and wild'. At first, however, mutual tolerance—or perhaps a mutual distance—operated, and Basques left fishing gear and boats in whaling ports over the winter without loss or damage. In contrast to the Arctic, where whaling had provided a limited basis for co-operation between Europeans and Inuit, no common interest developed between Europeans and Beothuks. Early attempts to establish trade aborted in misunderstanding and violence. Hostile incidents accumulated into a feud that embittered both sides as the development of the dry fishery meant that fishermen needed shore space for their drying racks ('flakes'); often they erected them on sites favoured by the Natives for summer fishing. Mounting irritation between Beothuk and European is only too evident in the references that have come down to us. According to Jean Fonteneau *dit* Alfonce (1483?–1557?), France's top navigator who sailed with Cartier, the Beothuk had 'no more God than beasts, and are bad people'. The poet Pierre Crignon (*c.* 1464–1540) was no more complimentary: 'Between Cape Race and Cape Breton live a cruel and rude people with whom we can neither deal nor converse.'[36]

The Beothuk retreated as far as they could into the interior of the island, occasionally emerging in their cyclical rounds to attempt their traditional exploitation of the sea, if they were not frustrated by the European presence; alternatively, they raided any European gear they could find. Archaeologist Laurie MacLean has reported evidence that Beothuk heat-treated iron they obtained from Europeans.[37] Early in the seventeenth century, Sir Richard Whitbourne (*c.* 1579–1626), one of the best known of the 'fishing admirals' of the Grand Banks, reported that operations were being hampered 'because the Savages of that country . . . secretly every year come into Trinity Bay and Harbor, in the nightime, purposely to steale Sailes, Lines, Hatchets, Hookes, Knives, and such like.' Noting that the Natives were few in number (their aboriginal population has been variously estimated from 500 to 1,000), he wondered if missionaries would not help to bring them into line with the European concept of civility.[38] But none was ever sent; one of the few early colonizers who attempted to establish a working relationship, John Guy (d. *c.* 1629), was in Newfoundland intermittently for only a few years, 1610–14.

Once settlement began, the feuding turned into an open hunting season against the Beothuk. The situation was not helped by the fact that after the first half of the seventeenth century, anti-colonizing English West Country fishing interests were able to influence Parliament to legislate against settlement, which was restricted if not actually placed outside of the law. Official control was not only sporadic, it was exercised for the benefit of the fishing industry; Newfoundland was not declared a colony until 1824. By that time, there were practically no Beothuk left; the last known one, a woman named Shawnadithit, died in 1829.[39]

It could be argued that it was not surprising that events unfolded as they did, since the island's administration had been so haphazard during the 300 or so years when the Beothuk were being hunted down; but in the case of another island colony, that of Tasmania, which began in 1803 as a penal settlement, the extermination of the Natives had proceeded even more rapidly—the last full-blood Tasmanian, also a woman, died in 1876, less than a century later.

In both cases the people lived on islands, limiting their area for retreat, which meant that there were practically no alternatives when traditional subsistence patterns were disrupted. In both cases these problems were compounded by disease; for the Beothuk it was tuberculosis. In both cases the interests of the settlers had been in competition with those of the Natives, leading to open conflict. In both cases Native rights had been seen as being secondary to those of settlers, even when the settlers themselves did not have a clearly established legal position, as in Newfoundland. Later, on the Northwest Coast, band disappearances would take another form, that of smaller groups merging with larger ones. At least five bands disappeared in this way during the nineteenth century. Interestingly enough, in the case of Newfoundland, the oral history of the Mi'kmaq asserts that at the time of the European arrival, they were cohabiting the island with the Beothuk and were intermarrying with them. Consequently, there are Mi'kmaq today who claim Beothuk ancestry.

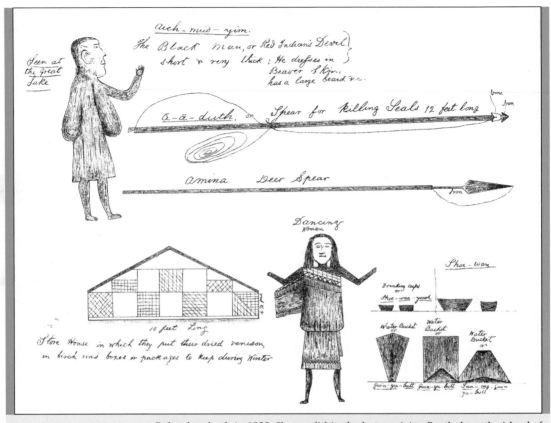

Before her death in 1829, Shawnadithit, the last surviving Beothuk on the island of Newfoundland, drew these images depicting aspects of her culture.
(Library and Archives Canada, C-28594)

First contacts were an ongoing process that continued in varying parts of the country until mid-nineteenth century, and in isolated cases, such as those of the Inuit of Pond Inlet and some Dene, even into the twentieth century. In no instance in Canada do we have records of Native reactions paralleling those of the Caribbean Indians and Mexicans, who wondered if Europeans were returning spirits. The closest to such a reaction was experienced by Cartier when he sailed up the St Lawrence in violation of Stadacona's rights over upriver traffic. In their joy at this breach of Stadacona's trade monopoly, the upriver people welcomed Cartier as a shaman, and brought their sick for his healing touch.[40] Otherwise the documentation that has survived for Canada is silent on the subject.

What is clear, at least at our present level of knowledge, is that first contacts between mainland North America and Europe occurred in the Arctic and along the North Atlantic coast. While the details of these occasions will probably never be known, the consequences, such as the disappearance of the Beothuk, are interwoven into the fabric of Canada's history.

Chapter 6

On the Eastern Edge of the Mainland

St Lawrence Iroquoians

The Iroquoians of the St Lawrence Valley were somewhat later than the Beothuk in meeting Europeans, but they appear to have suffered the consequences even more quickly. However, in this case Europeans not only did not have a direct hand in what happened, it is not even clear that they were a factor at all, as the events are not known with certainty.

The earliest mention we have of St Lawrence Iroquoians is that of Cartier, who while coasting along the Gaspé during his first voyage to Canada (1534) encountered a group presumed to have come from Stadacona (Stadakoh-na), a village on the present site of Quebec City.

> They numbered, as well [as] men, women and children, more than 300 persons, with some forty canoes. When they had mixed with us a little on shore, they came freely in their canoes to the sides of our vessels. . . . They go quite naked, except for a small skin, with which they cover their privy parts, and for a few old furs which they throw over their shoulders. . . . They have their heads shaved all around in circles, except for a tuft on the top of the head, which they have long like a horse's tail. This they do up upon their heads and tie in a knot with leather thongs.

Although these men showed great pleasure at meeting the French, 'they had made all the young women retire into the woods, except two or three who remained, to whom we gave each a comb and a little tin bell, at which they showed great pleasure, thanking the captain by rubbing his arms and his breast with their hands.'[1]

Upon this display of friendship on the part of the French, the Iroquoian leader called the other women from hiding so that they, too, could receive gifts. In this auspicious beginning, the friendliness displayed on both sides followed the general pattern of first encounters between Amerindians and Europeans. It was not a quality of relationship that either side would be able to sustain, particularly after Cartier persuaded Chief Donnacona (Donnakoh-Noh, d. 1539) to allow his two sons, Taignoagny (Tayagnoagny) and Domagaya, to go with him to France on his return voyage.

TIMELINE

1534	Jacques Cartier's first voyage to Canada, where he encounters the Iroquoian village, Stadacona, at present site of Quebec City. Cartier returns to France with two sons of Chief Donnacona.
1535–6	Cartier returns to Stadacona bringing with him Donnacona's sons. He then kidnaps the pair plus Donnacona and other headmen and takes them back to Europe. They all die in France.
1541	Cartier's last voyage, with settlers to establish a colony. This attempted settlement lasts only two years. Hochelaga, at site of present-day Montreal, is largest Iroquoian settlement.
1603	Samuel de Champlain meets Montagnais (Innu) at Tadoussac, at mouth of Saguenay River, joins in celebration of Montagnais victory over Iroquois. Montagnais Chief Anadabijou seals friendship pact with Champlain and French.
1608	Champlain founds Quebec on Stadacona site; all the St Lawrence Iroquoians have gone, driven away and killed in long war with Mohawks and likely, too, in battles with Mi'kmaq.

1610	French re-establish Port Royal (Annapolis Royal) in present-day Nova Scotia. Mi'kmaq Chief Membertou greets them.
1623	Dutch purchase Manhattan Island for 60 guilders ($24).
1627	Charter of La Compagnie des Cent Associés.
1629–32	English gain control of Quebec with help of Montagnais, who were in dispute with French.
1642	French establishment of Montreal; importance of Tadoussac as trading centre begins to wane, as does Montagnais hegemony in region.
1671	Mi'kmaq raid fishing vessel, kill 16.
1710	Defeat of Acadians by British.
1713	Treaty of Utrecht cedes Acadia to British, who assume France must have extinguished Aboriginal title. Mi'kmaq and Wuastukwiuk (Maliseet) caught in middle of European legal concepts but believe land is theirs—they were friends of French, not subjects.

Cartier's purpose was to train them as interpreters, in which he was successful. However, he apparently also expected them to act in the French interest when he brought them back to Stadacona on his second voyage (1535–6). In this he was disappointed, as the pair would prove to be true to their own. In Cartier's eyes, they were not only unappreciative of the hospitality they had received in France, they were even treacherous.

Cartier was a better sailor than diplomat, as his relations with the Stadaconans make clear. The explorer had no doubt that he had 'discovered' Canada,[2] as the north shore of the Gulf of St Lawrence was called, and on his first visit he had erected crosses of possession on the Gaspé and at Stadacona. In doing this, he was acting under official instructions; in Europe's view, Amerindians who were not organized into states could not be classed as inhabitants with a recognizable title to the land.[3] Ironically, accounts published later in France would describe Stadacona as a seat of royal residence.[4] Cartier's attitude towards the Stadaconans was further illustrated during his second voyage, when he sailed up the river against their wishes and in violation of their customary right to a monopoly of upriver

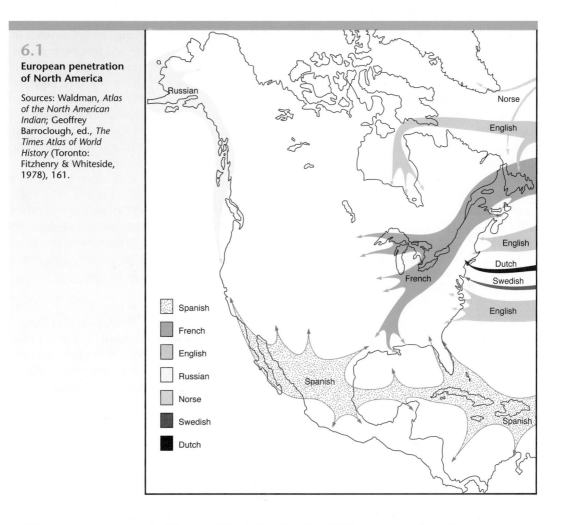

6.1

European penetration of North America

Sources: Waldman, *Atlas of the North American Indian*; Geoffrey Barroclough, ed., *The Times Atlas of World History* (Toronto: Fitzhenry & Whiteside, 1978), 161.

Spanish
French
English
Russian
Norse
Swedish
Dutch

traffic; he then compounded the insult by kidnapping Donnacona, his two sons, and other headmen, and taking them back with him to France. None of them would ever return to their homeland. Cartier's third and last voyage to Canada was in 1541, when he brought settlers for a colony that was to be established under Lieutenant-General Jean-François de La Rocque de Roberval (*c.* 1500–60), who, however, did not arrive until the following year. In the meantime, Cartier reaped the consequences of his previous visits: the Stadaconans were now hostile, 'going about daily to annoy him' and killing his men.[5] Cartier gave up after 10 months and returned home with his famous load of iron pyrites, 'fool's gold', and other ores thought to be precious. They would give rise to the saying, 'False as diamonds from Canada'. Roberval did not fare any better. Overly severe with his colonists, he compounded his problems by mistreating the Amerindians; when he ran out of supplies, he had no recourse but to do as Cartier did and return within the year.[6] France's first attempt at colonizing in the New World had lasted less than two years, 1541–3.

The St Lawrence Iroquoians were a farming people who, according to their location on the river, depended in varying degrees on hunting and fishing as well as on agriculture for their food supply. Their lifestyle came somewhere between that of the northern hunting Algonkians and that of the Huron or Five Nations; the Stadaconans, for instance, geographically less favoured for agriculture, veered towards the former while the Hochelagans, on the site of today's Montreal, were more developed agriculturally and consequently closer to the latter.[7] That they all lived well, storing quantities of food for lean seasons, is attested to by Cartier, who, after commenting on the Hochelagans' store of corn, beans, large cucumbers, and other fruits, observed:

> They have in their houses also large vessels like puncheons, in which they place their fish, such as eels and others, that are smoked during the summer, and on these they live during the winter. They make great store of these as we ourselves saw. All their food is eaten without salt.[8]

Cartier counted 14 villages on the north shore of the river, of which Hochelaga appears to have been the largest, with an estimated 50 longhouses and a population of 1,500. As with Stadacona, Hochelaga would later be described in grandiose terms: in the account of historian François de Belleforest (1530–83), its longhouses became wooden palaces and the village a city that rivalled Moscow in magnificence.[9]

By the time Samuel de Champlain (c. 1570–1635) founded Quebec in 1608 on the site of Stadacona, not one of these villages remained, and instead of St Lawrence Iroquoians he found only the occasional Montagnais hunting band. As the Jesuits would later report, the language that had been spoken at Quebec during the time of Cartier was 'no longer heard in that region'.[10] Champlain heard tales of warfare along the St Lawrence in which the Mohawk were said to have been the aggressors. This was corroborated, at least in part, by a delegation from the Five Nations, who told Champlain they were tired of the war that had been going on for more than 50 years.[11] That would place its beginning at about 1570. Presuming that this war had caused the disappearance of the Laurentian villages, these reports would accord with that of Cartier's nephew, Jacques Noël (fl. 1541–85), who visited Montreal Island in 1585 and had climbed Mount Royal even as his uncle had done 50 years earlier, but who had nothing to say about any Amerindian village on the site, such as the one where Cartier had been welcomed so rapturously.[12]

Stadacona must have played a key role in the war. According to a custom that Amerindians shared with Europeans and other peoples around the world, its location at the mouth of the St Lawrence gave it the right to control upriver traffic. Cartier's attempt during his second voyage to break this control had severely strained his relations with the Stadaconans, who in the end successfully protected their position, and Europeans found themselves barred from the river.[13] Apparently some European goods filtered into the interior through Native networks, but not in sufficient quantities to meet growing demands. This could have been particularly the case with iron axes, held in such high regard and so scarce that they were laboriously sliced with sandstone into narrow chisel-like blades.[14] Anthropologist Bruce G. Trigger has theorized that the difficulty in obtaining such items could have been galling to the Five Nations, especially the Mohawk, who during the sixteenth century did not have direct access to European trade but who were keenly aware of neighbours who did. Resorting to warfare to obtain what they could not get by peaceful means, they attacked the villages controlling the St Lawrence River, particularly Stadacona. The Mohawk success is attested to by the fact that by 1581 Europeans were once more able to enter the river and Stadacona was not being mentioned. By the time Champlain arrived on the scene, the river was deserted except for roving Mohawk war parties, who had spread such terror that Algonquins and Montagnais hardly dared to exploit the region's abundant game. Even at that date, the Mohawks were still relying on war to obtain axes; in 1609, Champlain noted that an Iroquois war party was equipped with 'the poor axes which they sometimes win in war'; otherwise, they had stone axes.[15]

To those who would argue that warfare on such a scale was not likely at that early period, archaeological evidence suggests otherwise; the late prehistoric period appears to have seen warfare escalate to major proportions.[16] Cartier, in his account of his second voyage, reported that 200 Stadaconans had been killed in an encounter with the Mi'kmaq two years previously.[17] As the Stadaconans habitually resorted to the Gaspé for summer fishing, there may have been rivalry over access to ocean resources; trade may also have been a factor. Traditional hostilities with the Mi'kmaq, coupled with climatic changes caused by the Little Ice Age, which would have been disastrous for agriculture so far north, could have compounded the difficulties for the Stadaconans to the point where they were no longer able to resist the attacks of the Mohawks. There is also the likelihood of European-introduced epidemics, which could have caused social dislocation as far into the interior as Hochelaga. As Trigger observes, however, accumulating archaeological data point more securely all the time to the dynamism of Iroquoians in late precontact times. Profound large-scale social and cultural changes had been underway long before the arrival of the Europeans; what happened afterward may well have been a continuation of these processes and developments, in which European-related factors would have had a modest role at best.[18] What evidence exists points to the withdrawal of the St Lawrence Iroquoians westward, to join the Wendat (Huron Confederacy).[19]

Montagnais-Naskapi (Innu)

In contrast to the Beothuks and Stadaconans, Algonkian-speaking Innu (the collective name for the Montagnais-Naskapi) and Mi'kmaq accommodated themselves comparatively successfully to Europeans. It may have been the Montagnais who smoke-signalled Cartier at the mouth of the Strait of Belle Isle north of the Gulf of St Lawrence. The incident occurred during his first voyage (1534):

> We saw smoke rising from fires that the inhabitants of the coast were making on the spot. But because the wind blew towards the shore, we did not approach it; and seeing we kept away, some twelve Indians set off in two canoes, and came freely on board our vessels as if they had been Frenchmen.[20]

The prospect of European trade had lured these hunters of the northern interior to the coast. According to their own traditions, particularly those of the Montagnais, the Innu had been pushed into the Subarctic by the Iroquois before the arrival of Europeans. Theirs was an Archaic culture based on the taiga economy. The Naskapi of Labrador exploited maritime resources as well as caribou; the Montagnais, in the heavily forested interior, depended principally on moose in winter and freshwater fish in summer. However, there was considerable fluidity of movement, and the Montagnais roamed as far as Newfoundland.[21] When a Montagnais band agreed to let Paul Le Jeune, superior of the Jesuits of Quebec, 1632–9, winter with them in 1633–4, they warned him that 'we shall be sometimes two days, sometimes three, without eating, for lack of food; take courage, chihiné, let thy soul be strong to endure suffering and hardship'.[22]

The Naskapi fought the Inuit; the Montagnais fought the Iroquois. When Champlain first met the Montagnais at Tadoussac in 1603, they were celebrating a victory over the Iroquois with their allies, the Algonquin and Maliseet. These raids and counter-raids continued until mid-seventeenth century. In the meantime, Champlain joined in the victory celebrations at the invitation of Montagnais chief Anadabijou (*fl.* 1611) and sealed a pact of friendship with him and his people, which allowed the French to establish on Montagnais territory but which did not involve land title.[23] It was a relationship that would be developed by Anadabijou's son and heir, Miristou, later known as Mahigan Aticq Ouche ('Wolf' and 'Stag', indicating both cruelty and gentleness, d. 1628).

In entering into an alliance according to Amerindian ritual—by which, in effect, the council was the treaty—Champlain was following a practice the French had developed a century earlier in Brazil that had brought them rich rewards in the dyewood trade. In Canada, they would similarly benefit from the fur trade; Canadian furs had taken on a new importance following the Swedish capture in 1583 of Narva, the Baltic port through which Western Europe had obtained furs from the Russians. The French were as quick to take advantage of the new source for furs offered by Canada as they had been previously with the dyewood in Brazil, and they did so by the same technique: alliances with the Amerindians who controlled the source of supply. As in Brazil, they adopted Amerindian diplomatic protocol and negotiated these accords by means of gift distributions accompanied by feasting and speeches. Maintaining the agreements meant repeating these occasions, which came to be annual events. In the reasoning of the French, an alliance was

effective only insofar as it was understood and honoured by both parties; the European practice of written contracts would have been meaningless to the Amerindians. The written agreements between French and Amerindians that have survived have all been with enemies, usually with allies of the English.

The Montagnais had a particular interest in cultivating relations with the Europeans, as Tadoussac, at the mouth of the Saguenay River on the Gulf of St Lawrence, was within their territory. Its location on the southern edge of the taiga and beyond the northern edge of agriculture, and its ease of access, had made it a favourite gathering place from time immemorial for northern hunters and southern agriculturalists to exchange goods. As with the Stadaconans on the St Lawrence, the Montagnais, in controlling the river mouth, controlled the trade up the Saguenay. Since the northern forests held very little attraction for Europeans of the period, even as they recognized that they produced the best furs, and as the Stadaconans had been barring the St Lawrence since 1543, the Montagnais at Tadoussac found themselves in a lucrative position as more and more European ships came to trade. Tadoussac was an outlet for interior trading networks that extended as far north as James Bay and as far west as the Great Lakes.[24] It was a position they were to enjoy for more than half a century, until they were bypassed by the establishment of Quebec in 1608 nearly three decades after the St Lawrence had been reopened. In its heyday, Tadoussac counted as many as 50 ships at one time in its harbour during the summer trading season. By the second decade of the seventeenth century, as many as 1,000 ships annually are estimated to have been trading and fishing along the North Atlantic coasts and in the Gulf of St Lawrence.[25] For the northern Amerindians it was a bonanza as Frenchmen vied with Frenchmen (merchants of La Rochelle, Dieppe, and St Malo competed so

Portage on the Moisie River, Labrador, as painted by William George Richardson Hind.
(Metropolitan Toronto Reference Library, J. Ross Robertson Collection, T-31960)

enthusiastically that the situation verged on civil war), and they all tried to outdo the Dutch.[26] At that time Amsterdam was the leading financial centre of Europe and the centre for transshipment of beaver to Russia for processing. Despite the importance of Tadoussac in the growing trade, the French did not establish a permanent post there until 1599.

Not only did Europeans realize handsome benefits from this trade. Two centuries later, in the Far Northwest of 1787, geographer and surveyor David Thompson (1770–1857) observed that European trade goods:

> were of small value in money but of great utility to the Indians; everything is carried on by barter profitable to both parties but more so to the Indians than to us. We took from them

furrs of no use to them and which had to pass through an immense distance of freight and risques before they could be sold in the market of London. See the wife of an Indian sewing their leather clothing with a pointed brittle bone or sharp thorn and the time and trouble it takes. Show them an awl or a strong needle and they will gladly give the finest Beaver or Wolf skin they have to purchase it.[27]

This should not be taken to mean that there was an instant abandonment of traditional ways of doing things or that Aboriginal life was totally transformed within a generation or so, as has so often been stated; change of itself does not automatically alter identity. Just as Europeans benefited from Amerindian technology (toggling harpoons for whaling, moccasins for footwear, maize as a food crop), so did Amerindians from that of Europeans. In both cases, adaptations were selective and within established cultural patterns. One item that retained undiminished popularity since the days of trading with the Basques was the copper kettle; by the first decade of the seventeenth century, bark vessels were no longer in general use among the Montagnais.[28] The gun, on the other hand, was not widely used by Indians for hunting in the Northeast until the end of the seventeenth century, although it had been adopted for warfare long before that. The guns of this period were not only unreliable, they were not readily available to Aboriginals.

That the Montagnais prospered from this early access to a wide variety of trade goods is indicated by the quantity of presents received from chiefs of different nations at the installation in 1643 of Georges Etouat (d. 1648, a Christian convert, as his given name indicates) as 'Captain' at Tadoussac. Trade had brought such prestige to the post that its holder considered himself the equal of the French governor-general at Quebec City and 'acted the Sovereign', as the Jesuits remarked sourly. The importance of the French in trade was indicated by their influence on the installation ceremonies: Etouat wore a white linen shirt, lace neckband, and scarlet cloak.[29] The name 'Etouat' was that of the position, as well as of the person holding it.

There were also problems connected with the fur trade, for Amerindians as well as for traders. Sometimes this erupted into violence and people were killed, both Amerindians and Frenchmen.[30] Such incidents put strains on the alliance; Champlain's insistence on European-style punishment rather than Amerindian-style reparations when Frenchmen were the victims did nothing to ease the tensions. When the French leader arrested an Algonquin on suspicion of murder, a displeased Tessouat

threatened reprisals.[31] The Montagnais were so annoyed when the French established a trading monopoly and then raised prices[32] that Champlain refused to hold public baptisms for some Montagnais for fear that they would take advantage of the occasion to attack the French.[33] The Montagnais vented their spleen by guiding the English up the river and joining in their attack on Quebec, which resulted in its occupation by the English for three years, 1629–32. In other cases, cultural misunderstandings led to unintended insults. Recollect friar Gabriel 'Theodat' Sagard (fl. 1614–36) tells of an incident at Tadoussac in which a chief, offended with the inappropriate gift he had received from a French captain during pre-trade ceremonies, told his people to come aboard the ship and help themselves to what they wanted, paying what they wished. The French were too few to resist, but even so the Amerindians later had second thoughts and brought extra furs to make up the value of what had been taken. Both sides agreed to forget and forgive, and 'to continue always in their old friendship'. According to Sagard, the French were so concerned about maintaining the trade that they were in greater fear of offending the Amerindians than the Amerindians were of offending the French. In any event, the traders were careful henceforth to ensure that trading rituals were properly observed, not the least element of which was appropriate gifts. They were not so compliant, however, when the Montagnais sought to collect tolls for rights of passage on the St Lawrence, and they quickly moved to curb such 'insolence'.[34]

Another problem area was the exchange rate: the flexibility of the French in this regard did not go down well. Once a rate had been agreed on, the Amerindians expected it to be maintained across the board; one chief, being offered a special deal for himself but excluding his people, indignantly turned it down with the words, 'I am a chief; I do not speak for myself; I speak for my people.'[35] Neither did they have the concept of fluctuating prices according to supply and demand. Perhaps the most serious problem of all, at least from a long-range point of view, was the overexploitation of resources encouraged by the trade. There were those, such as Jesuit historian Pierre-François de Charlevoix (1682–1761), who were appalled at the destruction: a 'handful' of French had arrived, he said, in a land abounding with wildlife; less than a century later, it was already noticeably diminished.[36] Later David Thompson would observe that in the West 'Every intelligent Man saw the poverty that would follow the destruction of the Beaver, but there were no Chiefs to control it; all was perfect liberty and equality.'[37] Some Indians were reported to have joined in the slaughter, killing even the breeding stock.[38]

Despite their initially favourable trading position and the protection their Subarctic habitat afforded for their way of life, the Innu shared in the population decline that was the general Amerindian experience after the arrival of Europeans. Their numbers at the time of contact have been estimated at 5,000, but authorities consider that to be far too conservative, as today they number about 12,000. With the founding of Quebec, it was not long before the Montagnais found themselves replaced by the Huron as principal trading partners of the French. Tadoussac, once the hub of the Canadian fur trade, receded in importance as the French penetrated further and further up the St Lawrence, finally establishing Montreal in 1642.

Outside the mainstream of colonial activity, the Innu pursued their traditional way of life with little modification or interference. They shared with the Inuit the advantage of a hinterland that was both very large and very forbidding to Europeans. It would be centuries before Western technology would be capable of exploiting economically the mineral and hydro-electric potentialities of this huge area; in the interim, the Innu were able to control, at least to a certain extent, the terms of their contact.

Mi'kmaq and Wuastukwiuk (Maliseet)

The coastal Mi'kmaq, like the Innu, quickly found advantage in the European presence. As Charlevoix reported, 'The Acadians have always been on good terms with the French.'[39] This relationship began with the fisheries, which had first attracted European attention to the region. With their close relatives, the Maliseet, the Mi'kmaq willingly entered into the service of Europeans for a few goods or a little pay, doing 'all kinds of work, such as cleaning and butchering whales'.[40] They were above all hunters for marine mammals such as walrus, seal, and small whales, and before the arrival of Europeans they had depended primarily on marine resources, including cod and bass, as well as the deep-sea swordfish, and secondarily on those of the forests.[41] This pattern soon reversed itself as the Mi'kmaq adapted to the fur trade. Their distinctive sea-going canoes, with gunwales swelling upward at the centre, were well adapted to coastal travel as well as for crossing the Gulf of St Lawrence and going to Newfoundland; by the beginning of the seventeenth century, Mi'kmaq were sailing European shallops (keel boats pointed at both ends).[42] They also continued their pre-contact role as middlemen between the hunters of the north and the agriculturalists of the south: one of the names by which the Mi'kmaq were known, 'Taranteens', was said to mean traders.[43] The quality of their early relationship with the French is illustrated by the experience of Pierre du Gua de Monts (1558?–1628) when he established a group of 79 men on the island of Sainte-Croix in 1604–5, then moved to Port Royal (later known as Annapolis Royal) in 1605–7. When the French returned to Port

The 'lauburu' motif is popular with the Mi'kmaq and other Amerindian peoples. Here shown in Mi'kmaq porcupine quillwork, the motif is believed to have originated with the Basques, who regard it as a sort of national symbol. The design is also called a fylfot, because of its use at the bottom of stained glass windows.
(Photo courtesy Ruth Holmes Whitehead, Micmaq Quillwork, Nova Scotia Museum, 1982/ Penn Museum, Image #100575 and A7789)

Royal three years later they found that the Amerindians had touched nothing.[44] An Amerindian custom that surprised early Europeans was that of respecting food caches and supply depots of others, even though unguarded. When the French returned in 1610 to re-establish Port Royal, the paramount Mi'kmaq chief Membertou (d. 1611) was there to greet them.[45]

Trade flourished. For Europeans the profits were great, as the Amerindians, while they did not want to be deceived, responded 'liberally to the presents that they [the French traders] make, without exacting any, since it is certain that they are well content if they get only half the value of what is received from them.'[46] Still, in trading,

the Mi'kmaq were in their element; Nicolas Denys (1598–1688), fur trader and landowner, tells how they soon developed protective mechanisms in dealing with Europeans.[47] Both he and Charlevoix reported that some sagamores took a haughty tone; in the words of the latter, making it clear 'they were honoring the Great Sagamo of the French by treating him as an equal.'[48] That relations were not always peaceful is evident in the record: in 1671, an Amerindian raid on a fishing vessel, killing 16 men, caused so much alarm that the fishermen thereafter kept watch instead of fishing.[49]

The adaptability of the Mi'kmaq to this new situation reflected, at least in part, their social organization, more complex than was to be expected from their hunting economy; it was 'midway between the levels of tribe and chiefdom', as anthropologist Virginia Miller expressed it.[50] It was a cultural conformity that aided them in taking advantage of their geographical position, both economically and politically. Their incorporation into European maritime enterprises also reflected the fact that they were superb seamen. During the eighteenth century, in their war against Britain, they were taking and sailing schooners as large as 70 tons;[51] by the nineteenth century, they were operating as commercial fishermen with their own vessels.[52]

While Mi'kmaq and Wuastukwiuk successfully interacted with Europeans in both fisheries and fur trade, it was their role as guerrillas in the colonial wars that ensured their survival in their ancestral lands until the final defeat of the French in 1760. English slave raids along the Atlantic coast had early aroused the hostility of the Mi'kmaq and pushed them into their alliance with the French. At the beginning they fought for the traditional reasons of prestige and booty, as well as to help their allies. However, the defeat of Acadia in 1710 and the advent of British settlement put another cast on the conflict, which by that time was already a century old.

Consistent with the European view that conquest was primarily concerned with territorial right, Britain saw the Treaty of Utrecht of 1713 as giving her clear sovereign title to Acadia.[53] From this perspective, since Acadia had been a French possession, France must have extinguished Aboriginal title so Britain did not have to repeat the process. From France's point of view, there had been no need to extinguish title, as New France and Acadia were hers by right of 'discovery'.[54] The only Amerindian title she had recognized was a usufructuary one at the pleasure of her monarch, not a proprietary one. The French had been making grants of land to her subjects in Acadia at least since the

beginning of the seventeenth century (earlier trading licences had also included land rights); in New France that process had begun in 1623. In the charter for La Compagnie des Cent Associés (1627), Article 17 had provided for an Amerindian who became Christian to be considered in all respects French, including proprietary and inheritance rights. Any property he acquired, however, came by right of the French Crown, not by Aboriginal right.[55] The subject had never become an issue because of the care the French took to respect the territorial integrity of Amerindian villages and encampments; in Acadia, colonists had brought a highly specialized form of tideland agriculture that used areas of little interest to the Natives. Although the French had avoided raising the issues of land rights and sovereignty, that did not prevent them from considering that France had sovereign rights in both Acadia and New France, as she demonstrated in the Treaty of Utrecht and later treaties.

This was not a belief shared by the original inhabitants. Far from having been subjects of the French, the Mi'kmaq and Wuastukwiuk had welcomed them as friends and allies. They had accepted the French King as their father because he had sent missionaries to teach them their new religion, but the idea that he had any claim on their lands, or that they owed him any more allegiance than they owed to their own chiefs, did not make sense to them. Periodically they reminded the French that they had only granted usage and usufruct of their lands, which still belonged to the Mi'kmaq.[56] In Acadia, France remained too dependent on her allies, for reasons of trade and war, ever to make an issue of these points; rather, colonial officials were carefully instructed to make sure that Amerindians were not disturbed on lands they occupied or otherwise used 'on the pretext they would be improved by the French'.[57] That this had not extended to international recognition of Amerindian sovereignty was only too clear in the Treaty of Utrecht, when the French ceded Acadia to the English without mentioning their Aboriginal allies.

The Mi'kmaq did not consider that their alliance with the French automatically implied their subjugation to the British; and even if they had been conquered, in the Amerindian view that would have involved a web of rights and obligations that related principally to persons and only secondarily, if at all, to territories.[58] As the Mi'kmaq saw it, the only right involving land that the British had acquired through their conquest was that of purchase from the Amerindians. The British were equally firm that whatever title the Mi'kmaq (or any other Acadian Amerindians) might have had had been lost in the twofold process of French colonization followed by French defeat. Fundamentally, the British thought the issue was irrelevant, as in their view the Mi'kmaq and their Aboriginal neighbours had never possessed sovereignty anyway, being mobile or semi-sedentary peoples who had not organized into states. The irony of the British position lay in the fact that in the Thirteen Colonies they had long since recognized a limited form of Aboriginal proprietary rights, in contrast to the French, who had never formally made such an acknowledgement except when it was useful for annoying the British.

Both British and French, as Christian powers, considered that their claims to sovereignty were superior to those of non-Christian peoples. In principle, the French had not found it necessary to modify this position, although, as we have seen, in practice they took care to respect the territories of their allies. The fur trade, important to the colony's economy, capitalized on the hunting skills of the indigenous population rather than competing over territorial rights, which, coupled with the smallness of the French population, meant that land had never become an issue in New France.

The English, however, had first colonized in territories where Amerindians farmed, very much as the English did themselves; consequently, they soon became entangled in the legal absurdity of claiming one set of landownership principles for themselves and a different set for Amerindians. The Dutch had pointed to a solution when they purchased Manhattan Island in 1626,[59] a move that dealt with proprietary right while sidestepping that of sovereignty. The English, after first ridiculing the idea, quickly adopted it; after all, it accorded with a traditional principle of their common law, that there should be no expropriation without compensation. In 1629, John Endecott, governor of Massachusetts Bay Colony from 1628 to 1630, was instructed to purchase title to desired land. The principle of compensation was honoured more in the breach than in the observance, and it became ensnarled in a morass of fraudulent dealings, some of which were difficult to distinguish from outright theft. That the resultant confrontations erupted into wars was not surprising; by the time the British took permanent possession of Acadia, they had already experienced several. The reasons for these troubles were appreciated even at the time.[60]

The British did not at first consider that the principle of compensation applied in Acadia. They appear to have taken for granted that their defeat of France, besides winning them sovereignty, also had absolved them from the necessity of compensating the local Natives for lands. According to British legal thinking of the day, defeated non-Christians had no rights and settlement was a form of conquest, as English settlers brought their laws with them.[61] The French, by settling in Acadia before the conversion of the Natives, had, by that very fact, wiped out whatever rights the Amerindians might have had. On the other hand, their experiences in the Thirteen Colonies to the south had made the English well aware of the wisdom of maintaining good relations. It was not the Amerindians' importance as allies that mattered so much as the difficulties they could cause if they were not.[62] Proclaiming George I as King of Acadia, the British asked the Natives for an oath of fidelity and to share their lands peacefully with the settlers they hoped would soon be coming. In return, they promised more generous annual gifts than the French had been giving, but they relied mainly on offering better trade values at 'truck houses' (trading posts run under government auspices). They also promised not to interfere with the Indians' religion—by that time, many of them, particularly among the Mi'kmaq, were Catholic.

The Amerindians replied that they were pleased to have religious liberty but did not see why they had to have truck houses on their lands; they thought that trade could continue as it had in the past, mostly from shipboard. As for the oath of allegiance, they had never taken one to the French King and did not see why they should do so for the British. As far as the Mi'kmaq were concerned, Acadia was their land, which they called Megumaage and which they had divided into seven districts under a system of chiefs and a paramount chief. They only wanted to continue living in their territories without fear of English encroachment.

The French held a trump card in this contest to win Amerindian loyalties: their missionaries. Of the approximately 100 who worked in Acadia during the French regime, three who had been sent by the Missions Étrangères to the Mi'kmaq stand out: Canadian-born Antoine Gaulin (1674–1740) served from 1698 until 1731, when he retired because of ill health; Spiritan Pierre-Antoine-Simon Maillard (c. 1710–62) was in Acadia from 1735 until his death in 1762; and Spiritan Jean-Louis Le Loutre (1709–72), whose missions from 1737 until 1755 included Acadians as well as Mi'kmaqs. The effectiveness of these missionaries stemmed at least in part from the fact that, traditionally among Amerindians, the

most highly respected leaders were also shamans. Their identification of the centrality of religion in Amerindian leadership and their enlistment of these sentiments in their favour were major factors in the success of the French with their Amerindian alliances. As Joseph de Montbeton de Brouillan *dit* Saint-Ovide, governor of Ile Royale, 1718–39, saw it, 'It is only these men [the missionaries] who can control the Savages in their duty to God and the King.'[63] Maillard put it another way: only through religion, he wrote, could Amerindians be rendered docile.[64] Ritual was traditionally very important in Amerindian lives; in modifying its orientation, the missionaries did not entirely change Amerindian taste in these matters.[65] In this, as well as in using their positions for political ends, French missionaries were so effective that in 1749 the exasperated English put a price on the head of one of the more successful, Le Loutre.[66] In their turn, the British would adopt the French practice of using missionaries as agents of the state, particularly during the negotiations for the numbered treaties during the last part of the nineteenth century and the first part of the twentieth. Missionaries would also act as mediators in other areas, as well, until about mid-twentieth century.

The Mi'kmaq were far from being passive in this struggle for their control. They soon learned to play the English off against the French, and eventually to force the French to reorganize and increase their 'gift' distributions (tools and equipment, guns, weapons and ammunition, food, clothing). For example, in 1751 the Mi'kmaq successfully demanded that special gift distributions to meet their needs be incorporated into the regular ones; the French looked upon this practice as the necessary price of the alliances, as well as reimbursement for services rendered.[67] The distributions, essentially Amerindian in their ritual character, came to be combined with the European custom of awarding titles and medals; Indians had as much of a penchant for honours and prestige as Europeans. It would be difficult to overrate the importance both Natives and French attached to these ceremonies. Even the English, who had initiated the awarding of medals but who still looked upon the annual gift distributions as a form of bribery, were drawn reluctantly into this form of diplomacy.[68]

Thus, although their traditional subsistence base was very quickly overexploited through the activities of the fisheries and fur trade, the Mi'kmaq and Wuastukwiuk were able to substitute the goods and food they received from their allies to maintain their traditional style of life as long as the colonial wars, and consequently their own war, lasted. They were, however, severely reduced in numbers; the Mi'kmaq, the more numerous of the two, dropped to 3,000, and the Wuastukwiuk to 800. There has been much discussion as to the extent of the pre-contact population of the Mi'kmaq; some recent estimates place it as high as 35,000. Membertou, the Mi'kmaq chief reported to have memories of Cartier, in 1610 said that in former times his people had been 'as thickly planted as the hairs upon his head', but that after the arrival of the French they had developed bad habits in respect to food and drink, which had greatly diminished their numbers.[69] In 1617, an especially severe epidemic wreaked havoc among them as well as on other coastal peoples. By 1705, some French were of the opinion that it was hardly worthwhile learning about Amerindian nations, who, although once numerous, were now reduced to 'almost nothing'. It was reported that in 1,500 leagues of New France, there was only one Amerindian for every two Frenchmen.[70]

The Wuastukwiuk, also known as the St John River Indians, shared a similar lifestyle with the Mi'kmaq. According to Maillard, the 'Mickmakis and Mariquets, who, though different in language, have the same customs and manners . . . are of the same way of thinking and acting.' This close relationship had not prevented the Wuastukwiuk and Mi'kmaq from being on hostile terms with each other as well as with branches of the Abenaki when the Europeans arrived. Their differences appear to have been smoothed over, however, as they both became allies of the French, fought together during the colonial wars, and in general shared the same fate afterward. But they maintained a separate identity and sometimes acted separately. For example, the Wuastukwiuk did not join in the Mi'kmaq raid against Canso in 1720 and even disassociated themselves from it before the British authorities. The Mi'kmaq War would continue for nearly half a century; it will be dealt with in Chapter 11.

The Innu (particularly the Montagnais), Mi'kmaq, and Wuastukwiuk were the first to come into lasting relationships with the French. But the Abenaki would become the most important of the French military allies, and would make the phrase 'French and Indians' infamous in the colonial wars.

Chapter 7

People of the Sunrise

The southernmost of the Atlantic coast peoples we are considering here are the Abenaki (Wabanaki), 'those living at the sunrise' (or 'dawnland people', among other variations),[1] closely related to the Mi'kmaq and Wuastukwiuk as well as to other Algonkian speakers to the south.[2] Although their homeland is south of the present Canada–US border, the dislocations caused by colonial wars and European settlement meant that many Abenaki eventually found their home in Canada. Also, their alliance with the French was largely responsible for the connotations that the phrase 'French and Indians' came to assume in colonial history, especially in the United States.

The first of these people known to have come into contact with Europeans, in this case the French, were the Eastern Abenaki. The best early account we have of their land, however, is that of an Englishman, Samuel Purchas, whose 'The Description of the Country of Mawooshen' was published in 1613. 'Norumbega' was to become a better-known name for the region. According to Purchas, it counted

10,000 to 14,000 souls living in semi-permanent villages under the paramount Eastern Abenaki chief, Bashabes (Betsabes, Bessabes, among other variations; d. 1616?). Bashabes was the top man of 23 sagamores and 21 villages along 11 rivers in the region now known as Maine and New Hampshire; because of the nature of the soil and climate, and also the availability of sea resources, the Eastern Abenaki farmed less intensively than Iroquoians. According to at least one historian, however, they were the most culturally advanced of the northern east coast peoples.[3] Although some authorities would not place the population of Mawooshen above 10,000, others believe Purchas's estimate to be conservative, as his account itself suggests. Recently, a population of 11,900 was proposed for 1605; but even then it appears to have been in decline, as by 1616 Father Biard reported that there were no more than 3,000 souls in the region.[4] European diseases soon took their toll here as elsewhere, and villages were wiped out or drastically reduced from a very early date.

The influx of new trade goods also caused

TIMELINE

1607	Mi'kmaq victory over Abenaki at Chouacoet, at mouth of Saco River.	1713	Treaty of Portsmouth encourages some refugee Abenaki, led by Atecouando, to return to New England.
1629	Abenaki envoy sent to Quebec to seek closer ties with French in trade and in their battles with Iroquois.	1716	Nescambiouit, Pigwacket (Abenaki) chief, returns from being feted in France, goes to Fox to seek pan-Indian alliance.
1635	Death of Champlain ends, for a time, the alliance between Eastern Abenaki and French.	1720	French undercut peace negotiations between Abenaki and Iroquois.
1670s	Marriage of French officer to Pidianske, daughter of Penobscot sagamore, ends traditional hostility between Eastern Abenaki and Mi'kmaq: both groups now allied with French.	1722–4	English–Indian War, after Abenaki declare sovereignty over their ancestral lands.
1675–6	King Philip's War in New England results in exodus of Western Abenaki to Canada.	1725	Treaty of Boston signals end to English–Indian War.
early 1700s	Odanak (near Sorel, Que.) largest Abenaki settlement in New France.	1759	Robert Rogers and his Rangers attack, destroy Odanak, but it is soon re-established.

important social and political reverberations. The availability of iron tools and weapons, for instance, inflamed long-standing rivalries; the first decades of the seventeenth century saw the Abenaki, Mi'kmaq, and Wuastukwiuk all fighting each other. Paris lawyer turned historian Marc Lescarbot (*c.* 1570–1642) attributed the 1607 victory of the Mi'kmaq over the Abenaki at Chouacoet, at the mouth of the Saco River, to the French arming the former with metal points for spears and arrows, but above all with swords and cutlasses and even with muskets. He wrote that the cutlasses and swords were devastatingly effective, with muskets providing the *coup de grâce*. This points to the fact that despite declarations of intention to evangelize, France had not yet begun to use missionaries as an official arm of colonization (that would not develop until the second decade of the seventeenth century) and so were not as scrupulous about observing the European ban against supply-ing arms to non-Christians as they would be later with the Huron.[5]

Initial Suspicions

The Abenaki did not develop an association with the French in the fisheries and fur trade as quickly as the Mi'kmaq and Wuastukwiuk, a situation that would have been at least partly dictated by geography. In fact, the French at first shared the Mi'kmaq antipathy for the Abenaki, whom they labelled 'Armouchiquois', a term applied to several of the peoples in the general region. They described the Armouchiquois as being deformed, with small heads and short bodies, whose knees, when they squatted on their heels, passed their heads by more than a foot.[6] Champlain, who actually visited them, reported that they had well-proportioned bodies and even found them to be of 'good disposition', although he said they were inveterate thieves who could not be trusted. The French

figures des montaignais   figure des sauuages almouchicois

David pelleton fecit

Champlain's Engraved Map of 1612: two couples, one identified as Almouchiquois (Abenaki), on the right, the other as Montagnais. The French called the latter by this name because the people told the French that they were descended from a people who had migrated from a mountainous region.
(Library and Archives Canada, C-118494)

even suspected them of cannibalism.[7] These impressions could have been the result of the influence of unfriendly Mi'kmaq, or perhaps Wuastukwiuk, who were guiding the French.[8]

Despite such attitudes, the French appeared promising to the Abenaki as trading partners and as allies, both in their traditional war against the Iroquois[9] and against the slave-raiding English. In 1613, when the English raided the French settlement of St Sauveur on the Penobscot River, they offered to help the beleaguered survivors. In the words of Father Biard:

For, as soon as they heard about it, they came to us at night, and consoled us as best they could, offering us their canoes and their help to take us anywhere we wished to go. They also made the proposition, that if we wanted to live with them, there were three Captains— Betsabes, Aguigueou and Asticou,[10] each one of whom, for his share, would take ten of our band (since there were thirty of us left), and

would take care of us until the following year, when the French ships would arrive upon the coast; and that in this way we should be able to go back to our country without falling into the hands of the wicked Ingrés, as they call the English.[11]

The Abenaki followed this up in 1629 by sending an envoy to Quebec to sound out the possibilities of developing these ties. Champlain was immediately interested, not so much to take up the fight against the Iroquois (with whom, in any event, he was already on hostile terms as a consequence of his trading ties with the Montagnais, Algonquins, and Hurons), but because the Abenaki south of the Saco River were farmers and could possibly help provision his fledgling colony, which was not yet capable of feeding itself. Unable to assist in the war against the Iroquois immediately, he promised to do so as soon as possible; in the meantime, he proposed a mutual assistance program involving food supplies and trade goods.[12] The alliance proposal did not survive Champlain's death in 1635, as the Abenaki quickly demonstrated that they were as commercially minded as the French and took advantage of their access to European goods to develop their own trading networks. The French were annoyed enough to restrict Abenaki visits to Quebec, and finally, in 1649, to warn them to stay away.[13] From this inauspicious beginning developed what was to become one of the most effective and long-lasting alliances in North American colonial history.

Although the French did not meet Western Abenaki until 1642, when their Algonquin allies brought a Sokoki prisoner to Trois-Rivières under the impression he was an Iroquois,[14] they moved much faster to consolidate this new relationship than they had previously done with the Eastern Abenaki. In 1651 Jesuit Gabriel Druillettes (1610–81) was able to bring together various groups, including the Mahican (not usually included with the Abenaki but related), to form a solid front against their traditional enemies the Iroquois, who at that point were being particularly annoying to the French. The Iroquois responded by intensifying their attacks.

The English taking of Acadia in 1654 and the growing intensity of the French–Iroquois War severely restricted communication between French and Abenaki. It was not until France's re-establishment in Acadia in 1670 that the French–Abenaki alliance fully developed. The strategic importance of the Abenaki to the political interests of the French, English, and Iroquois grew as colonial rivalries escalated. Observing this, the French put aside their old reservations about the Abenaki and moved to strengthen their alliance.

Attractions of the French

On the other side of the picture, the French were looking more and more attractive to the Abenaki as English settlement pressures from the south increased, pushing many of them into the French orbit. This was consolidated during the 1670s with the Eastern Abenaki when French officer Jean-Vincent d'Abbadie de Saint-Castin (1652–1707) married Pidianske (or Pidiwamiska), the daughter of Madockawando (d. 1698), sagamore of the Penobscots, 'people of the white rocks country', reputedly the most powerful of the Abenaki tribes. This had the effect of winding down the traditional hostility between the Eastern Abenaki and the Mi'kmaq, as both were now allies of the French. The new situation did not produce unanimity within Abenaki communities, however, as splits developed between pro-French and pro-English factions, leading to a new set of internal tensions that would increase with the quickening tempo of frontier warfare.

The exodus of the Western Abenaki to Canada began as a trickle about this time.[15] It swelled into a major movement as a consequence of King Philip's War, 1675–6, 'that cataclysm in New England history'[16] that destroyed the Amerindian presence in southern New England (the war was fought principally in Massachusetts and Connecticut) and helped to ignite the simultaneous Maine War between the English and the Abenaki, despite the efforts of the latter to prevent it. The Abenaki were in a difficult position: faced with English intransigence, particularly in regard to settler encroachments on their lands, and the steady attrition of their subsistence base, they were forced to take sides. They did not fight solely, or even principally, as allies of the French, but for their own lands. They were pushed back sporadically until the final defeat of New France in 1760; the flow of refugees was particularly heavy in 1722–4 (English–Indian War) and 1744–8 (King George's War). Early in the eighteenth century, Odanak on the St François River near Sorel, Quebec, became the largest Abenaki settlement in New

France. As border raids increased during the 1740s and 1750s, Odanak became the principal source for Abenaki warriors, a situation that resulted in one of the most famous episodes in the annals of colonial warfare, the raid of Robert Rogers and his Rangers in 1759, in which the village was destroyed. It was, however, soon re-established.

In encouraging this influx of refugees, the French were inspired by more than humanitarian or evangelical considerations; they carefully saw to it that the new arrivals were settled in villages situated to act as buffers against invading Iroquois and English, and so strengthened the defences of New France. An inadvertent side effect of this policy was to facilitate the growing contraband fur trade between the French and English colonies, in which both the Abenaki and the Iroquois were active participants.[17] However, the old objections that the Abenakis competed with the French in the fur trade and even deflected furs to the English were no longer seen as important. Instead, Versailles was now urging the colony to make every effort by whatever means necessary to lure the Abenaki away from the English and to encourage raids against the latter.

Some of the practical exigencies of maintaining alliances aroused concern. Particularly contentious was the extent to which the French should adapt to Amerindian ways of doing things. According to an eighteenth-century observer, 'what has, at least, an equal share in attaching the savages to our party, is the connivance, or rather the encouragement the French government has given to the natives of New France, to fall into the savage-way of life, to spread themselves through the savage nations, where they adopt their manners, range the woods with them, and become as keen hunters as themselves.'[18] Such adaptability caused concern in some circles about losing sight of *la mission civilisatrice*, particularly during the early days of the colony when

intermarriage between French and Amerindian was most frequent.[19]

English Countermeasures

The French were successful enough in luring Amerindians to their side that the English began a counter-campaign. They had two effective weapons in their diplomatic armoury: the promise of better deals in trade than the French could provide and, of more importance, the fact that the French had ceded Amerindian lands in the Treaty of Utrecht without consulting or even informing their Native allies. Spreading the word about the treaty's terms as much as they could, the English invited Abenaki who had migrated to New France to return to their ancestral lands. For example, in 1713, at a conference with delegates from the Penobscot and Kennebec rivers, the English told the Amerindians that they expected them, upon their return home, to let their fellow tribesmen know 'how kindly you have been received'. Further, 'we expect you will Draw your remaining Indians from Canada into their Own places upon English Grounds', where they would be expected to abandon their French alliance. If they showed themselves Englishmen, they would be treated as such.[20] Such appeals fell on receptive ears, as the Abenaki shared with the Mi'kmaq a stunned disbelief at the actions of their French allies. In words that would become all too familiar in later confrontations, the Amerindians asked, 'by what right did the French give away a country that did not belong to them' and which the Amerindians had no intention of quitting?[21] The English were thus able to persuade some refugees to return, particularly those who hoped that accommodation was possible, or at least worth a try. Among these were the Eastern Abenaki chiefs Mog (Heracouansit, 'One with Small Handsome Heels', *c.* 1663–1724) of Norridgewock and Atecouando ('Deer Spirit-

Power', *fl.* 1701–26); their efforts led to the Treaty of Portsmouth in 1713 and the beginnings of the counter-migratory movement from Canada. Atecouando set an example, bringing his people back to Pigwacket a decade after they had left for the St François River. Some Abenaki even joined the English in fighting the Mi'kmaqs of Nova Scotia. The Abenaki had been sent in response to a request from Nova Scotia officials, who were being pressed hard by Mi'kmaq attacks. The request had been for '20 or 30 warlike Indians . . . to keep in awe the Indians of this peninsula who believe that all Indians from New England are Mohawks of whom they stand in great fear.'[22]

French colonial officials, for their part, regretted the Treaty of Utrecht; in the words of Philippe de Vaudreuil (*c.* 1643–1725), governor-general of New France, 1703–25, 'war with England was more favourable to us than the peace.'[23] They tried to recoup lost ground by arguing that the English in New England were 'encroaching on their [Abenaki] territory and establishing themselves contrary to the Law of Nations, in a country of which the said Indians have been from all time in possession.'[24] As for their own presence in Amerindian territories, the French pointed to their alliances to claim that they were there with the permission of the Natives. This was an argument they had once used to justify their presence in Brazil, which Portugal claimed by right of the papal bulls of 1493 and the Treaty of Tordesillas, 1494. With this encouragement, chiefs such as Wowurna ('Captain Joseph', *fl.* 1670–1738) of Norridgewock rejected the British claim to sovereignty over his people; others who had gone to Canada reacted by returning to their ancestral homes and reasserting their sovereignty, even in the midst of growing English settlement. This was at least partly what the British were working for, although they never accepted Amerindian claims to sovereignty, as they considered the Abenaki to be subjects. It was certainly not what the French were aiming at: they would have preferred to keep the Abenaki as a fighting force within their colony, where they would be easier to control.

Diplomatic Manoeuvres

The French, with strategic reasons in mind and also concerned with countering English manoeuvres, tried to attract Mi'kmaq and Eastern Abenaki to settle at Ile Royale (Cape Breton; Oonumaghee to the Mi'kmaq). They had no success, however, despite the lavish use of gifts by the missionary Gaulin and the younger Saint-Castin, Bernard-Anselme (1689–1720), the half-Abenaki son of Jean-Vincent. Quite apart from the fact that the Amerindians did not consider the island to be good hunting territory, the Abenaki as well as the Mi'kmaq took strong exception to the proposal that they be dislocated for the political expediency of their allies.[25] It would be 1723 before the Mi'kmaqs, harassed by the English–Indian War, finally agreed to establish at Mirliguèche on Ile Royale if a church were built for them; since that took time to arrange, it was several years before any settled there.[26] The settlement did not last past 1750, when the mission moved to Sainte-Famille on Bras d'Or Lake, where it still is. In another instance the French sought to play on the Abenaki desire for vengeance to get them to establish on the Nicholas River, in Canada but within easy striking distance of the English. The Abenaki answer was a firm rejection, on the grounds that they had already been hit hard by the English and that if vengeance were to be sought it would be from their traditional villages.[27] From all this it is evident that although the French did their best to transform the Abenaki into agents for their imperial interests, the Amerindians were far from being mere pawns in their hands. So true was this that the French complained that their allies insulted them almost as much as they did the English.[28]

The French also intensified their efforts to neutralize English commercial superiority. Their most effective means for achieving this was by carefully observing the annual feasting, speech-making, and gift distribution by which their alliances were maintained; according to Vaudreuil, 'we treat our Indians as Allies, and not as Subjects.'[29] In 1725 they budgeted 4,000 *livres* for this purpose, and the figure grew steadily each year until the final defeat of France in North America. As with the Mi'kmaq and allies generally, the awarding of medals and honours came to be an important element of these occasions; however, reports of French ennoblement of Amerindians are apparently more legendary than factual.[30] Vaudreuil had no doubt that France's ability to maintain a presence in the Northeast was due to the Abenaki, and Versailles agreed; as one missionary observed, 'of all the savages of New France, [the Abenaki are] those who have rendered, and who are in a condition to render, the greatest service.'[31] Vaudreuil was even more categoric: 'By uniting with the Abenakis and the Micmaks, we should be in a position to recover . . . all we have lost in the East by the Treaty of Utrecht.' Further, by winning the co-operation of the Abenaki, the French 'shall have completely provided for the security of Canada'.[32] What had started out as a commercial venture for the French had ended up as the most politically important of all their Amerindian alliances in New France.[33]

Some of the Abenaki battles against the British concerned the French only in a general way. We have already seen that this was the case of the Maine War, 1675–6; the situation was repeated during the virulent three-year struggle that preceded the English destruction of the Eastern Abenaki town of Norridgewock (Narantsouak) in 1724[34] and the defeat of the Pigwacket in 1725. This is the English–Indian War, the opening of which can be dated to an ultimatum issued in 1721 by the Abenaki to Samuel Shute, governor of Massachusetts from 1716 to 1727, in which the Amerindians asserted their sovereignty over the territories east of the Connecticut River but said the English who were there could remain, provided no more came.[35] Rather than seeing this as an effort at compromise, the English regarded it as insolence that had been encouraged by French missionaries, especially Jesuit Sebastian Rale (Râle, Rasle, etc., 1657–1724); the response of Massachusetts was to declare war in 1722.[36] The war ended with the signing of the Treaty of Boston in 1725 and its ratification at Falmouth (Portsmouth, New Hampshire) in 1727, despite belated French attempts to prevent it. Other ratifications soon followed in Nova Scotia. However, neither treaties nor ratifications ensured peace until the final defeat of New France, a situation the English tried to deal with by calling the Amerindians rebels.[37]

Bitter Taste of Defeat

Their defeat had been a bitter pill for the Abenaki to swallow, particularly as they felt that their French allies had let them down; since Utrecht they had been effectively on their own. When they sought help in 1720 from Vaudreuil, the French governor had been constrained by his instructions (England and France being officially at peace) from responding with the wholeheartedness that the Abenaki expected, causing them seriously to doubt his good faith.[38] The French had sent guns and ammunition, as well as Amerindian allies, but not troops, as the Abenaki had requested. Neither were the French always considerate in their treatment of their allies.[39] Under the circumstances, the Abenaki had no choice but to wind down their hostilities against the English, even though they were as convinced as ever of their rights. When it came to land, they saw this not in the terms of absolute ownership but as the right to control its usage and products.

Atecouando (*fl.* 1749–57) of Odanak, for example, in 1752 challenged the authority of the British to survey Abenaki lands without the Natives' permission, adding: 'We forbid you very expressly to kill a single beaver or to take a single stick of wood on the lands we live on. If you want wood, we will sell it to you, but you shall not have it without our permission.'[40] But the direction of events was clear, and ratifications to the 1725 peace had continued as one group after another laid down arms despite continuing violations of their lands. Such an act did not guarantee that the violations would cease, or even that the Abenakis' persons would be respected; Nodogawerrimet, the Norridgewock sachem (d. 1765), for instance, was killed and robbed by English hunters who were never apprehended, despite the fact that he had persistently worked for peaceful coexistence.[41]

Outstanding among the Abenaki who realized that neither warfare nor taking sides with one colonial power against the other was the answer to their difficulties was Wenemouet ('Weak War Chief', d. 1730). A Penobscot chief, he sought to avoid special arrangements with either of the colonizing powers and to negotiate working relationships with both. Unfortunately, such efforts were undermined by continuing settler encroachments, which played into the hands of the French working to maintain their alliance on a war footing. Because of such goals the French reacted violently to an Abenaki initiative to establish relations with the Fox of the Great Lakes area. The Pigwacket chief Nescambiouit ('He who is so important and so highly placed because of his merit that his greatness cannot be attained, even in thought', *c.* 1660–1722), who had been taken to France and honoured by Louis XIV for his efforts in the French cause, in 1716 went to live with the Fox, whose recent defeat had not reconciled them to French penetration into the West. Nescambiouit was one of several Abenaki chiefs who had realized that the Amerindians'

only hope of curbing European expansion lay in united action—a conclusion that would later be arrived at by such leaders as Pontiac of the Odawa and Tecumseh of the Shawnee (a southern branch of the Anishinabeg). The French were able to abort Nescambiouit's initiative, as well as those of his associates, but were so worried by them that they curtailed Abenaki travel into the *pays d'en haut* unless accompanied by French. The Abenaki had played important roles in voyages of exploration, such as those of René Robert Cavelier de La Salle (1643–87) on the Mississippi in the 1670s and 1680s, and in military expeditions such as those of Governor-General Joseph-Antoine Le Febvre de La Barre (1622–88) in 1684 and Jacques-René de Brisay de Denonville (1637–1710) in 1687, both in the region of the Great Lakes.[42] In fact, it appears that the Abenaki were almost as active in the colonial wars of the old Northwest as they were in the Northeast. In 1720, when the Abenaki and the Iroquois exchanged wampum belts, the French moved quickly to stop the peace negotiations, as they believed that otherwise 'the colony would be lost',[43] even though they themselves had signed a peace with the Iroquois in Montreal in 1701. A pan-Amerindian alliance could only have worked against French interests, as indeed it would have done against those of any European colonizer.

For the Abenaki, the French connection meant making the best of a bad predicament. Caught as they were in circumstances that defied their most creative efforts in war and peace, it is not surprising that they were eventually overwhelmed. Until recently, it was believed that the only Eastern Abenaki to survive in their traditional territories was a remnant of the Penobscot, and that Western Abenaki had all but disappeared. It has become apparent, however, that not all Abenaki withdrew into the interior or north into Canada as English settlers pre-empted their lands; some chose to remain. But the cost was high, as they could only do so through an anonymity that amounted to a loss of public identity. Not until the 1970s did they come back into the open and begin their ongoing campaign for US federal recognition as a tribe.[44] In Canada, outside of their ancestral lands, where they were drawn by their French alliance, most Abenaki were able to maintain their public identity, and these survive as a people today.

Chapter 8

Hurons, Five Nations, and Europeans

The French establishment of Quebec in 1608 as the centre for the growing fur trade quickly attracted the attention of the Huron, nearly 1,300 kilometres in the interior and leading traders in their region.[1] With as sharp an eye as Europeans for economic advantage, even if it was within a different social framework, Ochasteguin (*fl.* 1609) of the Hurons negotiated with allied Algonquins, whose territory lay between Huronia and Quebec, for permission to join an Algonquin delegation that was teaming up with the Montagnais to go and meet the French.[2] The Algonquins, with their leader Iroquet (*fl.* 1609–15), were agreeable, and the result was the meeting with Champlain at Quebec in 1609, an event that changed the course of Canada's history.

Ochasteguin's people were the Arendarhonon, 'the People of the Rock', occupying easternmost Huronia. The third newest members of the confederacy, which they are believed to have joined about 1590 (well after European trade goods had begun filtering into the interior; archaeology has turned up European items in Huron graves dating to mid-sixteenth century), they also were the sec-ond largest in population.[3] They may well have been St Lawrence Iroquoians, refugees from the wars that swept through the St Lawrence Valley during the preceding century;[4] in that case, they could also have had memories of earlier contact with Europeans. Be that as it may, according to Amerindian custom, Ochasteguin and members of his clan segment had the right, as the initiators, to monopolize the new Huron trade. Its scale was such, however, that it was politic to allow all the confederates to be involved, which took place before 1615.

The Arendarhonon's initiative in regard to trade did not extend to religion, and they would retain their traditional beliefs despite the best efforts of the Jesuits. The largest tribe in the Huron confederacy was the Attigna-wantan, 'People of the Bear', a founding member. They would play host to the Jesuits and would prove to be the most amenable to Christianity. Another founding tribe that was also amenable to Christianity was the Attignee-nongnahac, 'Barking Dogs' or 'People of the Cord'. Most recent arrivals were the Tahon-taenrat, 'People of the Deer', who joined about 1610.[5] Like the Arendarhonons they also

TIMELINE

1609	Huron leader Ochasteguin of the Arendarhonon and Algonquin leader Iroquet join forces to establish trade in meeting at Quebec with Champlain. Dutch established on Hudson River.
1615	Champlain visits Huronia in response to 1609 invitation of Atironta, principal chief of the Arendarhonon. He winters there after being wounded in battle between Huron and Iroquois that he joined to confirm alliance.
1615–49	Annual Huron trading parties of about 60 canoes, 200 men travel to Quebec (except during English interlude of 1629–32, when Recollect missionaries leave New France).
1623	Dutch establish Fort Orange (Albany, NY).
1624	Iroquois make peace with Hurons, Algonquins to gain access to southern part of trade with French and to begin trade with Dutch.
1633	*Coureur de bois* Étienne Brûlé executed by Huron for dealing with their enemy, the Seneca.
1634	Jesuit missions in New France replace Recollects.
	Smallpox epidemics begin to decimate Algonquins and Huron.
1640s–50s	Iroquois attacks bring end to Algonquin control of Ottawa River, the route from Huronia to Quebec.
1642	Iroquois begin river blockades to disrupt trade from Huronia to Quebec.
1649	Iroquois attack and route Huronia: two Jesuit missionaries burned at stake; Hurons burn their own villages as they flee. Some Huron move close to Quebec; others go south and west to Ohio and Michigan and become known as Wyandots; still others captured and become Iroquois.

resisted Christianity. The possible fifth member, Ataronchronon, 'People of the Marshes', in the lower Wye Valley, does not appear to have had a formal role in the confederacy and may have been a subsidiary group.[6]

Dominant Traders

The political and economic dominance of the Huron at first appears to have been strengthened by the influx of European goods, which by late in the sixteenth century had penetrated as far west as the Seneca by means of war, diplomatic exchanges, and trade.[7] That the Huron prospered is evident in the increasing lavishness of the ritual reburials of the Feast of the Dead, which elaborated as trade developed. The Huron continued to be self-reliant in their manufacture of weapons, maintaining their Stone Age technology until their dispersal. This had not been a matter of choice—according to Sagard, they wanted guns more than anything else[8]—but because of initial French reluctance to trade guns to them as long as they were not converted. As a contemporary observer reported:

> The use of arquebuses, refused to the Infidels by Monsieur the Governor, and granted to the Christian Neophytes, is a powerful attraction to win them: it seems that our Lord intends to use this means in order to render Christianity acceptable in these regions.[9]

This mixing of religious and economic considerations meant that the first Huron Christian to obtain a firearm was Charles Tsondatsaa in 1641.[10] Jesuit Jean de Brébeuf (1593–1649) had recommended him for baptism, after which he

The French fanned the flames of rivalry among the First Nations, solidifying relations with the Huron and Algonquin through military alliances against the Iroquois. This 1632 engraving represents a 1615 attack on an Iroquois village. French infantry, to the left, are shown firing muskets in support of Huron, who are attacking with bows and arrows and fire. At this time, the French did not provide firearms to their hosts.

(Library and Archives Canada, C-005749)

was presented with the musket by Charles Huault de Montmagny, first titular governor of New France, 1636–48.[11]

That year, the Iroquois were reported to have 39 muskets, received in trade with the Dutch and the English; by 1643, the number had risen to 300. The French appear to have underestimated the military importance of the Huron on two counts: lulled by the remoteness of Huronia from both the English and themselves, they did not deem it necessary to arm them as they were doing at that very time with the Abenaki, whether they were Christian or not. Nor did they properly assess the role of

Huronia in keeping the Five Nations in check. The consequences of these misjudgments would become only too evident by mid-seventeenth century, when the Iroquois threatened the very existence of New France.

During the Quebec meeting of 1609, Atironta (*fl.* 1609–15), principal chief of the Arendarhonons,[12] had invited Champlain to visit Huronia and thus seal the trading alliance. This pleased neither the Algonquins nor the Montagnais, both of whom were in direct trading relationships with the French, and both of whom saw this as an attempt to circumvent their positions. Since the Kichesipirini (Algonquins) of Allumette Island[13] in the Ottawa River were on the route between Huronia and Quebec, they took action. By a series of ruses and fostered misunderstandings, their leader, Tessouat (Besouat, *fl.* 1603–13),[14] also known as Le Borgne de l'Isle as he had only one eye, was able to delay this event until the summer of 1615, despite another trip by the Huron to Quebec in 1612 to confirm the invitation (Champlain was in Europe at the time, another reason why there was no immediate result).[15] When the French leader finally visited Huronia, in 1615, he confirmed French desire for an alliance by joining with the Huron in an expedition against an Iroquois village, probably that of the Oneida.[16] Champlain was wounded in the knee and had to be carried back to Huronia, where he recuperated over the winter as the guest of Atironta at Cahiagué.

The alliance was formally concluded the following year at Quebec, with Atironta leading the Huron delegation. When the French presumed too much on this, and in 1626 sent Recollect Joseph de La Roche Daillon (d. 1656) to the neighbouring Neutrals (known to the Huron as Attiwandaron, 'people who speak a slightly different language', and to the French as Neutrals because they managed to stay on peaceful terms with both Huron and Five Nations), the Huron saw to it that he did not stay

long. They had seen the move as being inimical to their trading position.[17] On the other hand, when it suited their trading interests, they facilitated the movements of the Jesuits.[18] This was not the first time the Huron had demonstrated their priorities when it came to trading: in 1633 they had executed *coureur de bois* Étienne Brûlé (*c.* 1592–1633) on the charge of dealing with their enemies, specifically the Seneca.[19]

Shifting Trade Patterns

The Hurons' entente with the French confirmed the shift in importance of trade routes from north/south, as it had been before contact, to east/west, as it became with the presence of Europeans on the Atlantic coast and St Lawrence River. It also confirmed the hostility between the French and the Iroquois, which had begun with the development of the fur trade with the Montagnais, Algonquins, and Mi'kmaq early in the sixteenth century. All of these tribes, along with the Huron, had been fighting the Five Nations long before the arrival of Europeans; in trading with them, the French stepped into a ready-made situation. This had become evident in 1609, the year the Hurons called on Champlain, when the French leader had found it necessary to confirm his intentions to ally with the Algonquin and Montagnais by marching with them against the Five Nations. They had met the enemy, who had not yet been introduced to firearms, towards the southern end of Lake Champlain, near Lake George, where Champlain claimed to have fired his famous shot that brought down two chiefs.[20] It is a claim that today is seriously disputed on the grounds that the firearms of the period did not have such capability.[21] If that was the case, then Champlain's claim would appear to be a ploy in the complicated French court politics of the period, in which his colonization plans could not help but be involved.

A seventeenth-century European view of some Natives of New France. From Joannis de Laet, *Americae utriusque Descriptio*, 1633. Samuel de Champlain described the large round shield being carried by the man in the centre as being made of boiled leather. The Huron warrior on the right is wearing armour made of wooden slats laced together with fibre. The warrior at the left is supposed to be a Montagnais.
(Photo courtesy The Newberry Library, Chicago)

In any event, what is beyond dispute is that Iroquois–French hostility was formally launched; this was reconfirmed in 1610 when Champlain joined Algonquins and Montagnais in repulsing an Iroquois raiding party below Sorel.[22] With the sealing of the Huron–French alliance in 1616, the war would escalate into the most famous Amerindian–European confrontation in Canada's history. According to Charlevoix, Champlain had assumed that because his Indian allies were so firm in their attachment to the French, and because they so heavily outnumbered the Iroquois, he did not think it would be difficult to defeat them. 'He had not foreseen that the Iroquois, who for so long had been at odds with the Savages for a hundred leagues around them, would soon become allies with their neighbours who opposed France, and become the most powerful in this part of America.'[23]

The immediate result, however, was an efflorescence of the fur trade.[24] By plugging into the network of the Huron and convincing them to emphasize furs, the French developed the trade into the principal economic activity of the north. Between 1615 and 1649, the usual flotilla coming down annually from Huronia to Quebec consisted of about 60 canoes and 200 men. The canoes used by the Huron for these brigades averaged six to eight metres in length and held four to five men along with about 90 kilograms of goods. Under good conditions, a canoe could travel close to 100 kilometres a day, but the average was well below that; the round trip took about four weeks. The scale of the trade is indicated by the number of furs at Quebec when it fell to the English in 1629: between 3,000 and 4,000 pelts in storage, and that following a poor trading year. The usual year during this decade saw about 12,000 to 15,000 pelts traded from Huronia, a substantial proportion of the furs exported from Quebec during those years.[25] The departure of the English in 1632 led the Huron the following year to organize the largest of all their flotillas, 140 to 150 canoes, carrying an estimated 500 to 700 men with about 15,000 kilograms of pelts, a volume that would not be matched again until 1646.[26] In an attempt to curb Iroquois attacks, which were stepped up during the 1640s, French soldiers sometimes reinforced the warriors accompanying the flotillas. This was done in 1644 and again in 1645, when 60 canoes and 300 Huron came to Trois-Rivières.[27] Such commerce brought prosperity to everyone involved; at its height, the Huron were reported to account for 50 per cent of the French fur trade.[28] Despite the Iroquois blockade, furs valued at 200,000 to 300,000 *livres* were shipped to France.[29]

Amerindian Trade Protocol

The rapidity with which the Huron developed this trade indicates they already possessed the infrastructure to accommodate it. Order and a certain formality characterized the trading sessions, which were 'a pleasure to watch'.[30] Trading delegations had to obtain permission to cross another's territory. Some groups charged fees (which could be viewed as a form of enforced gift exchange) for the privilege; the best-known example of this in Canadian history was the Kichesipirini (also known as Ehonkehronons) of Allumette Island in the Ottawa River, the main route between Huronia and Montreal. As the traffic increased, the Kichesipirini raised their tolls; the Huron complained loudly but paid. In enforcing these rules, chief Tessouat claimed he was keeping the French trade for the Huron; he also claimed he could force the French back across the sea.[31] As if that were not irritating enough for the French, he saw no reason why they should not pay his tolls, along with everyone else. Outsiders could buy their way into a trade route; or it could be offered as a gesture of friendship or alliance, as the Arendarhonon did with their fellow tribes in the Huron confederacy in connection with the French trade. Although there was no means of enforcing rules, they were respected, as indeed they had to be for the system to work. Increasing Iroquois attacks eroded Tessouat's position in the late 1640s and early 1650s. In spite of their complaints against the Algonquin chief and his people, the Huron fur brigades were the first to suffer the consequences as the Iroquois reduced and eventually eliminated his control of the river.

French Insist on Missionaries

Where the Huron had been eager to expand their trading operations to include the French, they were not nearly so amenable about accepting missionaries. The traders were not that enthusiastic either, as they regarded the clerics as interfering busybodies.[32] But Champlain had insisted: without missionaries, no trade. He arranged for Recollects to come to New France in 1615, and that same year Father Joseph Le Caron (*c.* 1586–1632) was accepted at Carhagouha, among the Attignawantans, the first missionary to Huronia,[33] soon to be joined by the Jesuits. The Recollects did not survive the English occupation of New France

(1629–32), and when France resumed control of her colony in 1633 it was the Jesuits who returned.[34] However, the Recollects continued in Acadia, where they were joined by another branch of the Franciscans, the Capuchins, and eventually, in 1670, they were back in New France. Among the returning Jesuits was Brébeuf, who in 1626 had been selected to go to Huronia because of his facility with languages. The Jesuits had high hopes of evangelizing the Amerindians within a generation, or perhaps as quickly as in six or seven years.[35] Le Jeune in an exuberant moment had written in 1634, 'If our Fathers had gone among the Hurons this year, I expected to write to Your Reverence next year . . . that these barbarians had received the faith.'[36] Instead, it would take Brébeuf nine years to master the Huron language and compile a grammar, building on the pioneer work of Le Caron and Sagard, who had begun the task of compiling a dictionary.[37]

The evangelization of Huronia was destined never to be completed. This mirrored the general picture in New France: evangelism produced a few religious vocations among Amerindian women but not a single priest among the men.[38] The mobile lifestyle was seen as inimical to Christianity, in itself an impediment to virtue:[39] 'if once they can be made to settle down, they are ours.'[40] Such a goal was directly opposed to powerful trading interests, which wanted to keep the Amerindians in the bush harvesting furs; from the first, missionaries felt that the French were more interested in collecting beaver than in saving souls.[41] The Jesuits, deeply committed to their evangelical mission as they were, realized only too well their dependence on the trade and so collaborated with it, but the tension remained unresolved.[42] The French experiences at Huronia, and to some extent with the Montagnais, Mi'kmaq, and Abenaki, have provided us with most of the details that we have about early relationships between Europeans and Amerindians in Canada.

Huron Reaction to Europeans

While each side was curious about the other, this seems to have been more actively expressed by the Amerindians than by Europeans. The Huron, for example, continually tested the French, examining their reactions; in particular, they were curious about the priests' claimed powers, which they judged in comparison with those of their shamans. They were surprised and even nonplussed when missionaries took exception to this and did not want to work with medicine men.[43] Puzzlement turned into hostility, especially when missionaries refused to participate and reciprocate in festivals, and they began to be accused of causing deaths of individuals who resisted them.[44] On the lighter side, objects the French brought with them, such as the animals (dogs with floppy ears, and cats), were subjects of endless interest; indeed, we are informed that cats became most acceptable for gift exchanges.[45] Indians were intrigued with European-style doors, a grinding mill, and clocks. The sounding of the hours seemed to them to be a form of speech, indicating that the clock was alive; the Jesuits took advantage of this to tell the Hurons that when it sounded four times, it was telling them to leave, thus providing themselves with free time after four o'clock.[46] Hurons (in common with Amerindians generally) did not like salt; in fact, they considered it to be poison (with some reason, the way Europeans were using it at the time) and refused to let their children touch it.[47]

At first, of course, neither Huron nor Montagnais had any means of assessing the societies from which the French came; later, they would have reports of their fellows who had visited Europe. These must have been impressionistic and fragmentary, and probably aroused more disbelief than wonder. In any event, the evidence at hand was not sufficient to shake Amerindian cultural self-confidence. 'We have our way of doing things, and you

The tercentenary of Champlain's visit to Huronia in 1615 was celebrated in Penetanguishene, Ont., in 1921. Huron chief Ovide Sioui is shown at left accepting a peace pipe from Iroquois chief Andrew Staat in centre.
(Metropolitan Toronto Reference Library)

have yours, as well as other nations', the Huron repeated time and again to the French.[48] If new dangers such as strange diseases were appearing in encampments, often without Europeans having ever been seen, the connection had not yet been made with these odd visitors with their ugly beards and peculiar social habits.[49] Faced with Champlain's intransigence on the matter of missionaries, the Hurons 'gazed attentively at the Fathers, measured them with their eyes, asked if they were ill-natured, if they paddled well; then took them by the hands, and made signs to them that it would be necessary to handle the paddles well.'[50]

Epidemics Invade

Hardly two years had passed after the Jesuits' return in 1634 when smallpox appeared among the Montagnais, soon to appear among the Hurons; within four years up to two-thirds of the latter were gone. To the disheartened Jesuits, the epidemics seemed to have 'singled out the Christians more than the Infidels, cruelly decimating their families and more frequently sparing those who had refused baptism.'[51] In the Amerindian view, such disasters were neither impersonal nor random; somebody or something must be the cause.

The Jesuits were the obvious suspects, particularly as they did not die of the contagion.[52] The Algonquins of Allumette Island drew the obvious conclusions, tried to scare the French away, and encouraged their Huron allies in their attempts to get the French out of their country, claiming that Champlain had died with the determination to ruin them.[53] The Jesuits sadly observed that Algonquins and Hurons had 'a hatred and an extreme horror of our doctrine. They say that it causes them to die, and that it contains spells and charms which effect the destruction of their corn' besides engendering contagious diseases.[54] The French threatened to withhold trade, a serious matter for the Hurons as the French were their only source for European goods. As if disease were not enough, drought and forest fires added to their troubles. The opportunity was obvious for the Iroquois to escalate their attacks, although they, too, were suffering severely from the epidemics.[55] A not particularly effective counterbalance to the Five Nations was the Council of Three Fires, in which the Potawatomi served as the Fire Keepers, the Odawa as the Trader Nation, and the Ojibwa as the Faith Keepers. The Council was disadvantaged by being geographically far-flung—the Potawatomi were south of Lake Erie, the Odawa on Manitoulin Island, and the Ojibwa on the north shores of Lakes Huron and Superior.

Situation of Five Nations

Where the new trade had provided an opportunity for the Hurons, for the Five Nations it had posed problems. For one thing, the Iroquois did not have allies with whom they could negotiate to gain access to the French, as the Huron had been able to do with the Algonquin. Even when the Dutch established themselves on the Hudson River in 1609, then moved upriver to set up Fort Orange (Albany) in 1623, bringing them much closer, the

Iroquois were barred by the Mahicans. The Dutch, for their part, would have liked to tap into the northern trade, where the best furs were to be had, but were blocked by the Iroquois and Mahicans. The Iroquois decided to try for the Dutch trade, which meant removing the Mahican barrier; it also meant diverting their raiding activities from the St Lawrence Valley.[56] Accordingly, they made peace with the Algonquin and Huron in 1624 (which the French tried to prevent), removing the danger of enemy action from the rear and freeing themselves to attack the Mahicans, whom they finally defeated four years later. The Dutch, at first alarmed and uneasy, accepted what had happened and opened trade relations with the Mohawk. On their eastern front, the Iroquois, pursuing their traditional hostilities against the Abenaki, courted trade relations with the English. From being initially at a disadvantage as far as European trade was concerned, the Iroquois now had an advantage, with two sources of European goods, the English and the Dutch, as well as shorter lines of communication, compared with the Huron, deep in the interior, who only had access to the French. The Iroquois were able to play off the English against the Dutch, to the point where the latter, feeling threatened by both English and French, began to trade arms to the Iroquois. In 1636, when some Algonquins tried to cross Five Nations territory on their way to trade with the Dutch, they were killed by the Mohawk. The Algonquins of Allumette Island, led by Oumasasikweie (La Grenouille, 'The Frog', *fl.* 1633–6), had been trying to turn French–Iroquois differences to their own advantage, but their efforts had backfired.[57] So ended the Mohawk-Algonquin-Huron agreement of 1624.

Sporadic attempts on the part of the French to neutralize the Iroquois by establishing trade with them thus came to nought, and Champlain moved to strengthen his colony's defences. In 1633 he wrote to Armand-Jean du Plessis, Cardinal and Duc de Richelieu, principal minister to Louis XIII of France, 1624–42, requesting 120 men to subdue the Iroquois.[58] He established Trois-Rivières as a buffer for Quebec in 1634 and began to fortify the St Lawrence before his death the following year; the Iroquois responded by building forts on the river from which to harass the fur brigades. Montreal was founded as a religious enterprise in 1642 but quickly became a strategic outpost in the midst of the intensifying Iroquois raids. The die was cast: the French were committed to the fur-producing nations of the north for obvious commercial reasons, and the Five Nations were committed to disrupting the northern trading networks for a combination of reasons, not the least of which was to keep threatened settler encroachment at bay. The war that would dominate the history of New France for a century was well on its way.

The Iroquois (specifically, Mohawk and Seneca) began their blockades of the St Lawrence, Ottawa, and Richelieu rivers in 1642. These were successful enough that in 1644 and 1645 only one brigade in four made it to its destination, in spite of the fact that 22 French soldiers were sent to Huronia in 1644.[59] In two years during that decade, no brigades at all got through. That year the French and some Mohawk negotiated a peace, each side acting independent of its allies—the Algonquin in the case of the French; the four other members of the Five Nations, as well as some of their own nation, in the case of the Mohawk.[60] It brought the short-term benefit of the second largest flotilla, 80 canoes, getting through in 1646. But the cost was the killing of Jesuit Isaac Jogues (1607–46) by holdout Mohawks of the Bear clan,[61] who along with the excluded members of the league were prepared to openly defy the French. Two years later, in 1648, the Huron rallied sufficiently to send down 60 canoes, which picked up French reinforcements at

Trois-Rivières.[62] It proved to be a hollow achievement as the brigade returned home to find three of Huronia's villages destroyed.

The Iroquois had changed their tactics and now were attacking settlements instead of just the convoys. Where previously competition in the beaver trade had been a major motive in the hostilities, it was now the acquisition of captives for adoption to replace Iroquoian population losses from war and disease. On top of that, the French were building fortifications in Iroquois territory.[63] The next year, 1649, when the Five Nations warriors returned in force, the Huron gave up, burned their 15 remaining villages, and dispersed. The French followed their example with their mission, sending up in smoke their dream of a new kind of Christian community in North America blending the two cultures. They also lost two of their missionaries to the fires of the stake, a common lot for captured enemies if they were not adopted. They were the only missionaries to meet this fate, although others were killed.[64] According to the Huron historian Margaret Vincent Tehariolina, the French burned the mission because its reason for existence had disappeared when the Huron lost control of the fur trade.[65] Tehariolina sees this act, and the retreat of the French to Quebec, as the breaking of their promise to protect their allies.

For the Huron, the greatest death toll came from starvation the following winter among those who had fled to Christian Island in Georgian Bay, which did not have the resources to feed them. An estimated 5,000 died there that winter. Of those who survived to the spring, some joined with neighbouring Tionontati (Petun, Khionontateronon) and scattered in various groups to Detroit and northern Ohio, where they shed the French appellation 'Huron' and became known as Wyandots, a variation of their traditional name for themselves. Several of their chiefs, among them Orontony (fl. 1739–50), entered into a trading relationship with the English.[66] Of those who remained with the French alliance and continued to be known as Huron, about 600 went east in a return to their ancient territories along the north shore of the St Lawrence. After several moves and many vicissitudes they established Loretteville outside of Quebec (their ancient Stadacona); it is still the home of their descendants today. Others fled to the Erie and Neutrals, only to be defeated a second time by the Iroquois. The majority, however, went south to join the Iroquois; of those we know about, the Seneca took in the Tahontaenrat (Deer), as well as some Arendarhonon (People of the Rock), although most of the latter went to the Onondaga; and the surviving Attignawantan (Bear) became Mohawk. A few got as far as Oklahoma. In later confrontations with the Iroquois, the French would occasionally have the odd experience of fighting warriors who had once been their Huron allies but who were now confirmed members of the Five Nations.

By 1657, the Five Nations had absorbed so many captives that Le Jeune observed that the league now counted 'more Foreigners than natives of the country'.[67] Perhaps more importantly, the fact that many of the Hurons-turned-Iroquois had been previously exposed to Christian teaching provided the Jesuits with a lever to intensify their evangelical campaign among the Five Nations, a campaign that would eventuate in an out-migration from Iroquoia to settlements around Montreal as converts sought to be near their co-religionists.[68] Although all of the Five Nations lost people in this movement, by far the largest contingent came from Mohawk villages. In 1679, the Mohawk would lose an estimated two-thirds of their people in this way.[69] In the meantime, to the west, the Wyandots of Michilimackinac would give rise to one of the most famous leaders of the Iroquois war, Kondiaronk (Gaspar Soiaga, Souoias, Sastaretsi, known to the French as 'Le Rat', c. 1649–1701).

He would be one of the principal promoters of the peace of 1701 that would be signed at Montreal.[70]

A postscript to the saga of the Huron refugees in the St Lawrence Valley was written in a Quebec court decision in 1990 recognizing their rights to vast territories in the province. Those rights had been guaranteed in a safe-conduct issued to the Hurons by the British three days before the final fall of New France in 1760.[71] The Supreme Court of Canada ruled in *R. v. Sioui* that the safe-conduct was the equivalent of a treaty and was still valid; its terms allowed Hurons 'the free Exercise of their Religion, their Customs and Liberty of trading with the English'. The territory involved stretches from the St Lawrence River to James Bay and from the St Maurice River at Trois-Rivières to the Saguenay River at Tadoussac.[72]

Huronia Dispersed

The dispersal of Huronia occurred 34 years after Champlain's visit and the arrival of the first missionary. From being the most powerful confederacy in the region, demographically, commercially, and militarily, in a little more than a generation Huronia was scattered far and wide, its villages destroyed, its cornfields reverting back to forest. It was far more than simply a defeat of a people: a complex commercial system had been brought down, the consequences of which would reverberate in the interior of the continent, reaching as far as James Bay in the Far North.

What were the factors that caused this to happen? Commanding the crossroads of the northern interior, the Huron had dominated trade in two eras, proto-historic and early historic. Although initially they had prospered, the rise of the east/west route inevitably worked against them, blocked off as they were from alternative European trading partners. Without the capacity to bargain, they soon were dominated by the French, even as they benefited economically, and their trade assured the existence of New France. As the paradox inherent in that situation emerged, a series of events unfolded that proved disastrous not only to the Huron but also to the French. The ruin of their allies brought to an end the Jesuit dream of establishing a New Jerusalem in the heart of North America.[73]

First of all, in a society where spiritual matters had been a matter of individual, personal accommodation, the intense campaign of the Jesuits to get all to conform to the Christian norm had caused tensions as some Huron converted and others resisted.[74] Recognizing the problem, the Jesuits sought to ease the way to conversion by not interfering with Native custom where there was no opposition to Christian values, a compromise that brought them into conflict with officialdom and was only partially successful in the field. Motives for conversion could be more related to preferential treatment in the fur trade than to religious conviction. In 1648, when only an estimated 15 per cent of the Huron were Christian, it was reported that half of those who were in the fur fleet had either converted or were preparing for it.[75] Commercial incentives were considerable, since converts were considered to be French and so entitled to the same prices for their furs as Frenchmen, much higher than those paid to non-Christians. In gift distributions, Christians would be favoured, and in their councils with the Amerindians, the French honoured the Christians above the others.[76] On the other hand, as historian John Webster Grant has reminded us, there were those, such as Joseph Chihwatenha (Chihouatenhoua, Chiohoarehra, 1602?–40), who considered that the French way was that of the future, so it was only sensible to go along with it.[77]

There was always the danger, of course, that such incentives would backfire. An observer in 1750 wrote:

there is reason to believe that they [the Amerindians] only embrace the Catholic faith when they have a reason to do so . . . they practise it in appearance, do what is required, even go to confession, but their shame in avowing their turpitude is false, so that it is apparent they leave without repenting their faults.[78]

In other words, Amerindians were seen as being quite capable of feigning acceptance of Christianity if they thought it was in their interest to do so. Another explanation for such behaviour would be that the Amerindians saw nothing wrong in following the new practices when with whites, and then reverting to their own when in their own encampments. In other cases, evangelization had the effect of giving new life and new strength to Native religions.[79] Even as the missionaries saw elements in Native spiritual beliefs that were similar to their own, so Amerindians identified Christian spiritual beings with those of their own beliefs. For the Montagnais, the Christian God resembled their Atahocan.[80] In their view, there was plenty of room in the cosmos for both sets of spiritual beings, each with its own requirements at the appropriate times and places.[81] This twist to their policy of accommodation to other cultural values aroused the Jesuits to a vigorous counter campaign, using such means as searching dwellings for idols, thus increasing tensions and encouraging factionalism.[82]

In spite of these ambiguities, priests were beginning to replace shamans as intermediaries with the spiritual realm. In the traditional way, chiefs and men in public office also officiated at religious ceremonies, very important in maintaining community cohesion; when they converted, they could no longer participate and instead appointed deputies to carry out the required religious duties.[83] This was aggravated by the high cost of holding traditional feasts, a situation that in turn may have been accentuated by the growing Huron dependency on trade goods. The cumulative effects were the reduction and, in some cases, even the elimination of traditional ceremonies. At Ossossané (an Attignawantan village) in 1648, a Jesuit was named paramount chief to oversee the elimination of customs that were contrary to Christianity.[84] Converts refused to be buried in ossuaries, in effect denying their membership in the tribe. In some cases, Christianized Huron even refused to fight alongside their traditionalist fellow tribesmen.

The French policy of only supplying guns to converts did not help matters; even the missionaries saw the danger of this and did their best to get officials to change their minds, to little or no effect. In the meantime, the growing firepower of the Iroquois, reported to have more than 500 guns, was having a demoralizing effect on the Huron, who had only about 120.[85] Jesuit historian Lucien Campeau sees this disparity in arms as the basic cause of the dispersion, rather than factionalism arising out of missionary activity; as he points out, the Tionontati, Neutrals, and Erie also went down to defeat, and they had been little touched, if at all, by missionary teaching.[86] On the other hand, neither had they been much affected by European trade, certainly not enough to acquire guns. Everyone agrees that the epidemics of 1639–40 contributed to Huron difficulties by taking a particularly heavy toll among the very young and the elderly, leading to social and cultural imbalances and discontinuity. When the Iroquois switched their tactics in 1648 and 1649 to attacking villages instead of fur brigades, the once culturally confident Huron simply disintegrated as a confederation.

Far-flung Consequences

The consequences of this were far-flung, for Amerindians as well as for Frenchmen. The first to be noticed by everyone was the loss of a major food source: Huronia had been a breadbasket not only for Amerindians but also for colonists. In New France, this led to an increase in land-clearing and in agriculture, much to the joy of officials who had been having considerable difficulty in distracting the people from the immediate profits of the fur trade to take up the back-breaking work of establishing farms. Politically, the dispersal of Huronia signalled a development that had been underway for some time: the French had started off as allies of the Amerindians; now it was the Indians who were allies of the French.

The pattern of the fur trade was radically changed, as Montreal picked up where Huronia left off.[87] The annual brigades to Montreal, continued by the Odawa along with remnants of the Huron, diminished and eventually ceased during the 1680s. The Odawa did not have the infrastructure needed to maintain the system or, after 1670, to face the competition of the English newly established on Hudson Bay. Instead, the *coureurs de bois* fanned out from Montreal into the interior: the brigades were now going the other way. Despite the difficulties of inland travel—there were 38 portages between Montreal and Grand Portage, a distance of 1,000 miles—it was an opportunity that was eagerly seized by the colony. The Jesuits reported that 'all our young Frenchmen are planning to go on a trading expedition, to find the Nations that are scattered here and there; and they hope to come back laden with the Beaver-skins of several years' accumulation.'[88] The east/west axis, fuelled with merchandise coming from across the Atlantic, now prevailed. It was as part of this movement that Pierre Esprit Radisson (*c.* 1640–1710) and his brother-in-law, Médard Chouart des Groseilliers (1618–96?), penetrated north of Lake Superior during the 1650s with the indispensable aid of Indian guides and became aware of the rich fur resources that had once been so successfully exploited by the Huron. The way was being prepared for the entrance of the Hudson's Bay Company, a quasi-governmental institution that would play a major role in the Canadian fur trade for two centuries.

In the meantime, the Council of Three Fires undertook a counter-offensive, and by the end of the seventeenth century had driven the Five Nations out of Huronia and the lands of its allies, the Tionontati and Attiwondaronk. This led to the Five Nations agreeing to the Montreal peace of 1701.[89]

Chapter 9

Huronia's Loss Is the Bay's Gain

While Europeans concentrated on developing the fur trade along the St Lawrence–Great Lakes systems, Amerindians were similarly engaged with their networks that stretched northward to the Arctic and southward to the Gulf of Mexico.[1] When the French finally reached Lake Mistassini in 1663, after several unsuccessful attempts, they became aware that enough trade goods were filtering through from the south to satisfy the needs of the northerners. This does much to explain why Henry Hudson's trading episode remained the only one with Amerindians during English explorations of the Bay. It also explains why the French were not able to penetrate overland to the east side of James Bay until 1670. Amerindian networks were coping with the increased volume brought about by the European trade,[2] and the people saw no reason why the French should be encouraged to come in and disturb the equilibrium. Consequently, French attempts to penetrate the region met with repeated failures.[3]

Northern Trade Routes

Four main routes stretched from the St Lawrence Valley to the north: from Tadoussac, in the land of the Montagnais, via the Saguenay River; from Trois-Rivières in the land of the Attikamègues via the St Maurice and Nottaway rivers; and two routes from Huronia to James Bay, the easternmost via the Ottawa, Temiskaming, and Abitibi rivers and the westernmost via the Spanish and Mattagami rivers.[4] The Huron were also able to tap into the Trois-Rivières and Tadoussac systems by means of east–west connectors, part of a network that stretched westward deep into the interior. The copper knives that Cartier's men had seen at Tadoussac had come from Lake Superior.

The decline of Tadoussac at the mouth of the Saguenay after the establishment of Quebec in 1608, and the French penetration into the Great Lakes region to establish direct contact with the Huron a few years later, meant that the focus of the northern trade also shifted west. The result was that the two routes from Huronia to James Bay rose in importance. Until it was destroyed in 1649, Huronia remained the hub of the north/south networks for 30 years. Iroquois raiding parties then went on a rampage seeking to destroy Huron hegemony, reaching as far as James Bay until they were distracted by their league's invasion of the

TIMELINE

c. 1600	Assiniboines break off from Yanktonai Dakota, some going northeast, others northwest.	1690–2	Explorer Henry Kelsey, led by his Cree family and kin, reaches northeast edge of Great Plains.
1668	English expedition to Hudson Bay.	1717	Death of Thanadelthur, Chipewyan woman who had been instrumental in York Factory trade.
1670	Hudson's Bay Company chartered, with monopoly trading rights over all lands (Rupert's Land) draining into Bay.	1724	Master of HBC's Albany Fort censured for teaching Native children to read and write.
1670s	Ojibwa move south into former Iroquoian territories; Cree expand further to north and west.	1754	Henley House massacre of English by Cree.
1671	French move into the West.	1772	Samuel Hearne, with Chipewyan guide Matonabbee and other Amerindians, is first white man to reach Arctic Ocean by overland route.
1680	League of Five Nations invades the Illinois.		
1685–1713	English and French fight for dominance in the Bay, but without Amerindian allies.	1807	HBC opens schools for Native children at principal posts.

Illinois in 1680. The northern networks that had operated so satisfactorily from distant pre-historic times were left in disarray, cut off from access to trading goods from the south.

In this realignment of forces, the Five Nations became the dominant Amerindian factor, as they now controlled the principal routes between the English colonies and the interior. In the words of ethnohistorian Alice Kehoe, the Iroquois could now act 'as gatekeepers and toll-takers in international trade'.[5] It was a position that would be strengthened with the defeat of France in North America in 1760. For most of the eighteenth century, the Iroquois would be the principal Amerindian players in the Northeast.

When the English were spurred by Radisson and Groseilliers to send a trading expedition to the Bay in 1668, they found that Amerindians who had once avoided contact were now eager to trade. The English organized the Hudson's Bay Company, which received its charter in 1670 granting it monopoly trading rights in those regions where the waters drained into the

Bay. There was no question of consulting the Amerindians involved, nor was there any question of the English right to such a unilateral action. That same year the Company established Fort Charles on Rupert River, to the contentment of the local Cree, who were missing the supplies they had once received via the now-disrupted Native networks. A more fortuitous time for the reappearance of the English could hardly be imagined; the instant success of Fort Charles resulted in the rapid spread of HBC forts around the Bay. By 1685 the English system was essentially in place. The French countered with forts of their own in the interior (for instance, in 1684 they built a post on Lake Nipigon) but were finding that the *coureurs de bois* were their most effective weapon in the trade war.

The Amerindians who had been invisible to English explorers hunting for the Northwest Passage, and who had done their best to discourage French penetration of the North, now became partners in the European enterprises. Almost overnight homeguard bands were an

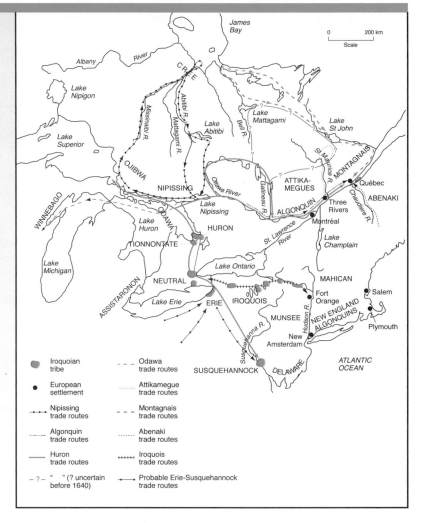

9.1

Major central and eastern trade routes, first half of 17th century

Source: Bruce G. Trigger, *Children of Aataentsic*, vol. 1 (Montreal and Kingston: McGill-Queen's University Press, 1976).

established feature of both English and French posts, following a pattern of behaviour that had been experienced by the French when they had first entered the trade. It was a consequence of the shift in subsistence strategies brought about by the fur trade as prehistoric exploitation of the total environment gave way to the specialized pursuit of fur-bearing animals. The Amerindians turned to the posts to offset the increased danger of famine that this switch in emphasis entailed.[6] Both French and English encouraged the presence of Natives around their establishments in order to have hunters on hand to supply them with fresh meat.

The two trade items that Amerindians had quickly adopted, the metal axe and cooking pot, continued to be much in demand; in the eyes of coastal Indians, the copper kettle was the most valuable of European trade items.[7] This the Europeans understood, as it meshed with their notion of what was practical and useful. They soon assessed Indian preferences shrewdly enough to evolve the tomahawk, one of the first items developed by Europeans specifically for the Indian trade. Combining as it did the war axe with the peace pipe, it had connotations beyond the 'practical' and accorded with the Amerindian concept of the duality of nature, the dichotomy and interaction of life and death. Another successful item was Brazil tobacco; even in the North, where tobacco could only be obtained through trade, smoking was ritually important.[8] Northern Aboriginals quickly learned to esteem tobacco of this grade.

Trade Adaptations

Europeans had more difficulty in understanding Amerindian preferences for other items, such as mirrors, and beads of certain types and colours. These objects substituted for traditional shiny metals, crystals, quartzite, and certain types of shells, all believed to possess qualities relating to the fundamental nature of the universe in both its physical and spiritual aspects. The desire of Indians for these items related to their mystical view of the operation of the cosmos, which to them was just as 'practical' as its material aspect. Beads had the added advantage of being in the form of berries, reputed to have extraordinary curative powers.[9] Crystal, mirrors, copper all had particular associations that made them highly prized. Whether or not Europeans understood this 'otherworldly' aspect of the trade, they soon learned what type of goods would induce Amerindians to trade with them.

They had also quickly learned to appreciate certain aspects of Amerindian technology, such as the canoe, snowshoes, toboggan, and moccasins, to mention the best-known items. Sulpician René de Bréhant de Galinée (c. 1645–78), on a western voyage in 1669–70 to establish missions with Sulpician François Dollier de Casson (1636–1701), had good reason to be

Indians of Nottaway River, Quebec, enlarge a break in a beaver dam before setting a trap in shallow water *(Stephen Greenlees; Library and Archives Canada, PA-151364)*

impressed with the adaptability of these pieces of equipment to the exigencies of travel. When he returned to France, he wrote, he would like to take a canoe with him to demonstrate its virtues to his countrymen. Along with snowshoes, he considered it to be the masterpiece of Amerindian inventiveness.[10] The French were not always so appreciative: trader/explorer Pierre Mallet (1700–after 1751), on a western voyage in the 1740s, complained that birchbark canoes demanded a great deal of care, that they deteriorated if left in the sun, and that they easily became damaged if dragged over sand; in inexperienced hands bark canoes soon fell apart, and even with care they did not last long, a serious handicap on long voyages that went beyond the limits of the birch tree.[11] Galinée, on the contrary, claimed that with proper care they could last up to six years.[12]

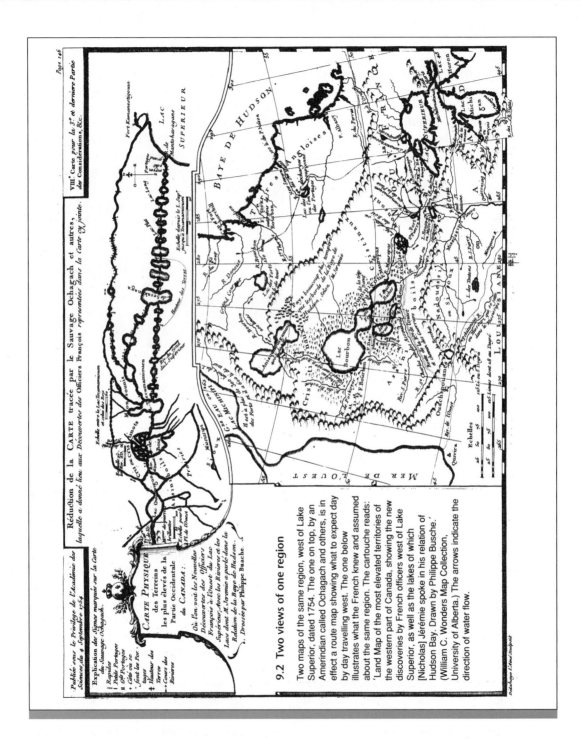

9.2 Two views of one region

Two maps of the same region, west of Lake Superior, dated 1754. The one on top, by an Amerindian called Ochagach and others, is in effect a route map showing what to expect day by day travelling west. The one below illustrates what the French knew and assumed about the same region. The cartouche reads: 'Land Map of the most elevated territories of the western part of Canada, showing the new discoveries by French officers west of Lake Superior, as well as the lakes of which [Nicholas] Jérémie spoke in his relation of Hudson Bay. Drawn by Philippe Busche.' (William C. Wonders Map Collection, University of Alberta.) The arrows indicate the direction of water flow.

It was no accident that Canada's stereotypical fur trade developed in the northern forests. Apart from the availability of the highest-quality furs, the generalized nature of the hunting demanded by boreal forest ecology was the most adaptable to the needs of the trade. More specialized hunters, such as those who harvested the bison herds of the Plains or the caribou herds of the Arctic, had much less incentive to participate because of the difference between their type of hunting and that required for furs. In the seventeenth and eighteenth centuries, the gun was of more use to the boreal forest hunter than it was to hunters of the Plains bison or the barren ground caribou. Much depended on particular circumstances and the quality of guns and ammunition.[13] Samuel Hearne (1745–92) found northern Amerindians using guns in combination with bows and arrows in communal deer hunts.[14] Limitations of the gun curtailed its early acceptance: its uncertain performance in damp or cold weather, its noisiness when it did perform, its weight, insecure supply of ammunition, and the difficulties of maintenance and repair. Similarly, metal traps were not initially seen as particularly useful, as traditional hunting methods easily procured all that was needed.[15] Both guns and metal traps had added handicaps—cost and foreign production. Still, the restricted herding or solitary habits of boreal forest big game favoured the use of the gun, particularly as the weapon itself was improved. Guns were adopted faster than steel traps, which Natives at first tended to acquire for the metal, which they reshaped into useful objects such as chisels and blades of various types.[16] Eventually, however, as the fur trade expanded, steel traps took over. One item that was rapidly adopted was twine; ethnohistorian Toby Morantz has pointed out that it very quickly replaced traditional materials for making fish nets.[17]

Cree as Trading Partners

The Cree (Cristinaux, Christino, Kristinaux, Killistinaux), among whom the English found themselves, were already the largest single group of Canadian Amerindians and were destined to become even more numerous and widespread as they prospered through the fur trade. The English, appreciating their hunting capabilities, found the Cree to be 'of a humane Disposition', capable of soon becoming civilized.[18] Although 'civilizing' Amerindians was not on the English program in the Far North as it was in New England, good relations were essential. It is noteworthy that the Hudson's Bay Company post journals made little use of 'savage', a term so prevalent in the settlements when referring to the Natives. The Cree were in alliance with Assiniboine (Assinipour, Assinipoël, Assinipoualak, 'Warriors of the Rock', later referred to as 'Stoneys' in the West). A Siouan-speaking people, the Assiniboine apparently broke off from the Yanktonai Dakota sometime around 1600, some going northwest, others northeast, into parklands and boreal forest. According to David Thompson, the rupture had not been peaceful.[19]

The English sought to secure their position by entering into alliances or 'agreements', the records of which have not survived, although there are references to them. Bostonian Zachariah Gillam (1636–82), captain of the 1668 expedition, is reported to have negotiated the first of these 'treaties', as they were called at the time.[20] In 1680, the bayside governor, John Nixon (*c.* 1623–92), was instructed to take possession of the territory surrounding the fort by whatever arrangements would be necessary with the Amerindians and to make sure they understood that the English were acquiring 'absolute propriety'.[21] As a contemporary observer put it in 1708, the HBC made 'compacts' with 'the captains or Kings of the Rivers and Territories where they had settlements, for the

Freedom of Trade there, exclusive of all others', so that the Amerindians could not complain they were being encroached upon. These appear to have been oral agreements on the French/Indian model. They were probably entered into on the advice of Groseilliers, drawing on techniques the French had worked out in Brazil and then had developed along the St Lawrence. In the words of English historian John Oldmixon (1673–1742), who never visited the Americas, 'Compacts were render'd as firm as the Indians could make them, by such Ceremonies as were most Sacred and Obligatory among them.'[22] The Indians would have been negotiating for an alliance, without which trade would have been insecure; but 'absolute propriety' was a concept they would not have understood, as it was completely foreign to them.

That some sort of agreement was reached can also be inferred from the fact that Amerindians felt free to come to the posts, as well as from the impression of one observer at least that the HBC was paying them 'rent'.[23] This is probably a reference to the ceremonial gift exchanges and other rituals that accompanied trading, which would have been necessary to keep the alliance functioning. A striking characteristic of the speeches that were a feature of these occasions (at least to Europeans) was the custom of Amerindians to ask the traders to 'pity' them. This has been interpreted as asking for 'needed articles or benefits' or, alternatively, that the Natives were expressing their expectation that those more powerful than they would help them in their hour of need.[24] Trading alliances in the North did not imply military service, as did those in the woodlands of the Northeast. Living conditions in the North did not allow for wars: Amerindians and Inuit may have killed each other on sight (if they could), or even raided each other, but this never led to military campaigns as such. When the English and the French fought it out for dominance in the Bay,

1685–1713, they were not joined by Amerindian allies as they were along the St Lawrence.

When their own supplies ran out, a frequent occurrence because of the uncertainties of shipping schedules, the English depended on the homeguards for food. They sought to correct this situation by training their own men to hunt, but at first with indifferent success.[25] Here, too, feasts and gifts were necessary to keep the relationship with the homeguard functioning; even so, it could vacillate between congeniality and sullen tolerance.[26] Maintenance of the posts plus the demands of the fur trade eventually resulted in the depletion of game, although this did not happen everywhere to the same extent or at the same time. Natural cycles of plenty and scarcity were intensified, making glaringly evident the fundamental conflict between the requirements of the fur trade and the needs for subsistence. Faced with starvation, Indians turned to the posts for help. If such help was not forthcoming, as sometimes happened, ugly incidents could result, although these were rare in the North. One occurred in 1832 at Hannah Bay, an outpost of Moose Factory, when it was raided and its personnel killed by starving Cree.[27]

Neither side was impressed with the other's food; according to Hearne, Indians did not even like bread, 'for though some of them would put a bit of it into their mouths, they soon spit it out again with evident marks of dislike; so that they had no greater relish for our food than we had for theirs.'[28] Some individuals used this reaction to demonstrate their cultural superiority. Esquawino (Esqua:wee:-Noa, *fl.* mid-eighteenth century), known for obvious reasons to the English at Moose Fort as Snuff the Blanket, developed the technique 'of holding his garment to his Nose when [he] enters ye Factory to avoid ye ill scent & from his refusing to eat any Victuals dressed in any Utensil of ours.'[29] On the other side of the picture, Hearne learned to appreciate some (though not all) dishes 'that were it not for prejudice . . . might be eaten by those who have the nicest palates'.[30] Amerindians also eventually demonstrated dietary adaptability; they became so fond of prunes and raisins that they would 'give a Beaver Skin for twelve of them to carry to their Children'. But they continued to disdain cheese, 'having taken up an Opinion that it is made of dead Mens Fat'.[31] The persistent belief on the part of Europeans that Inuit and Amerindians of the Far North were cannibals from force of circumstance was categorically dismissed by Hearne.[32]

Fraternization Disapproved

The HBC sought at first to keep contacts between company 'servants' and Amerindians to a minimum, only to what was absolutely needed for trade. This, of course, turned out to be impossible; for one thing, women played a pivotal role in both trade and Amerindian society generally. This is illustrated by the story of Thanadelthur (d. 1717), a remarkable Chipewyan woman who had been captured by the Cree, escaped with another woman, and survived a year in the bush searching for York Factory, which she had heard about but had only a vague idea as to its location. Her companion died, and shortly afterward Thanadelthur was found by a party from the factory. Taken to the post, she soon became invaluable as an interpreter and in persuading her fellow tribesmen to come to the fort to trade, despite the presence of their traditional enemies, the Cree.[33]

An unexpected side effect of the Company's minimum contact policy was the restriction of its access to the interior because its men were inexperienced in this type of travel. No European at that time could make such a journey without Amerindians acting as guides and hunters.[34] Not until the HBC relaxed its rule, at least tacitly, did exploration of the interior become feasible. Thompson admired the skill of

the Indian 'in being able to guide himself through the darkest pine forests to exactly the place he intended to go, his keen, constant attention on everything; the removal of the smallest stone, the bent or broken twig; a slight mark on the ground, all spoke plain language to him.'[35] The need for new sources of furs, particularly the aggressive expansion of the French, was making such exploration mandatory. The first to undertake an extended voyage, Henry Kelsey (c. 1667–1724), had prepared for it by living with Indians to the extent of becoming 'indianized'; during 1690–2 he was guided by his Cree family and their kin to the northeastern edge of the Great Plains and there saw a northern fringe of the great bison herds the Spaniards had encountered on the southern edge of the Plains in 1541 and the French had reported from the Great Lakes in 1654.[36] Samuel Hearne only encountered failure in his attempts at northern travel until he accepted the advice of his Chipewyan guide Matonabbee (c. 1737–82) and travelled with him 'en famille', allowing the Amerindians to pursue their own way so long as the ultimate objective of the voyage remained in sight. Thus, Hearne became the first white man to reach the Arctic Ocean overland, in 1772.[37] Occasionally, the HBC used Amerindians to extend its sphere of trade; for example, in 1715 a Cree named Swan journeyed up the Churchill River for the Company.[38]

Amerindian Counter-techniques

Even in trade, the HBC did not enjoy the control it would have liked. The Natives were not slow in playing off the English against the French, and they were quite as adept as Europeans in recognizing a better deal, but the goods they accumulated were for redistribution to satisfy social obligations and to acquire prestige rather than for exclusive personal use. They were not businessmen in the same sense as Europeans; for one thing, they were not

Amerindian guide drawing a map on birchbark for the Labrador Peninsula expedition of 1861, as painted by William George Richardson Hind.
(Metropolitan Toronto Reference Library, J. Ross Robertson Collection, T-31956)

guided to the same extent by supply and demand in setting their prices.[39] The English soon discovered, in the wake of the French, that such attitudes indicated neither a lack of a sense of value nor of entrepreneurial enterprise; Indian traders were as eager as anyone to set themselves up in business. They were not deterred by distance, and thought nothing of undertaking long journeys to obtain better prices.[40] Capitalizing on English/French rivalry, they would persuade hunters on their way to bayside posts to part with their best furs and then shop around for the best deal available. The entrepreneur Esquawino was described by a disgruntled trader at Moose Fort as 'ye grand politician of all being a free Agent travelling about, sometimes to ye French, at others to Albany & this Fort, never drinks but has always his scences about him & makes ye best of his Markett at all places.'[41] The English jailed the enterprising Captain Snuff on the charge of interfering with trade and stirring rebellion among the homeguard; Esquawino hanged himself because of loss of face.[42]

Similarly, HBC officials did not at first look kindly upon a tendency displayed by some HBC men to teach Native children to read and write. When the master at Albany Fort did that in 1724, he was censured by his superiors. London complained: 'The Company are very much

The seventeenth-century Ojibwa defeat of the Iroquois as depicted around 1900 with porcupine quills on birchbark by Mesquab (Jonathan Yorke), from the Rama Reserve, Lake Simcoe. Mesquab took the design from a rock painting that once stood at Quarry Point, Lake Couchiching. Working from memory, Mesquab showed two Ojibwa warriors dominating the Mohawk in the centre. According to this presentation, the Ojibwa had firearms while the Iroquois did not.
(Ontario Provincial Museum [now the Royal Ontario Museum], Archaeological Report for 1904.
With permission of the Royal Ontario Museum © ROM)

displeas'd to hear that any Indian is taught to Write & Read or admitted into ye Trading Room to prye into ye Secrets of their affairs in any nature whatsoever without our order & charge you strickly not to continue that nor suffer any such Practices for ye future.'[43] The Cree may have associated the written word with power, very important in a land where survival was not to be taken for granted.[44] It would take a century and the manpower shortage created by the Napoleonic Wars before the HBC would recognize the value of Natives (particularly those born to its own employees) to the trade and

launch a program of training them for service in the Company. In response to the wishes of the parents, the Company opened schools in 1807 at its principal posts.[45] An early problem was keeping the schoolmaster at his job, as the fur trade was so much more lucrative.

Even though socially Amerindians and traders mixed 'unexpectedly well',[46] they continued in their separate ways despite the close co-operation needed for the trade and the prosperity it brought to both sides. Trader Daniel Harmon (1778–1843) sadly observed that the only basis for friendship in the Northwest was the desire of Indians for European goods and the whites' eagerness for the Natives' furs.[47] A particular area of difficulty was reciprocity and the obligations it entailed. Ignoring accepted standards of behaviour could cause resentment and lead to trouble, as happened at Henley House in 1754. When the postmaster did not honour the expected obligation for subsistence to relatives of women who were being kept in the post, the Cree turned on the English, killed them, and looted the establishment.[48]

The expanding presence of the English in North America was deeply disturbing to the French at Quebec, and they launched two encircling movements, the first one in 1671 from the Great Lakes to the west aimed at cutting off the English at the Bay from the interior, and in 1699 to the south down the Mississippi, surrounding the Thirteen Colonies. The Iroquois became alarmed, particularly with the first move, as they saw it as an attempt to cut them off from the fur resources of the North. They responded by attacking the Illinois in 1680 and stepping up their war against New France.

French Expansion

The French move into the West in 1671 was 'to cause the name and the sovereignty of our invincible Monarch to be acknowledged by even the least known and the most remote Nations' in order 'to take possession, in his place and in his Majesty's name, of the territories lying between the East and the West, from Montreal as far as the South Sea, covering the utmost extent and range possible.' Fourteen Amerindian tribal nations were assembled at the Jesuit mission at Sault Ste Marie to witness the ceremonies of possession—the raising of a cross and a post bearing the arms of France;[49] the French formally asked for permission to trade and for free passage, and also 'that the fires of the Ojibwa and the French be made one, and everlasting'.[50]

The French had mastered the Native figurative manner of speech and were careful to tailor their proposal for their audience and to use terms to which each group could relate. Thus, they addressed members of the Ojibwa Crane clan in these words:

> Every morning you will look towards the rising of the sun and you shall see the fire of your French father reflecting toward you, to warm you and your people. If you are in trouble, you, the Crane, must arise in the skies and cry with your 'far sounding' voice, and I will hear you. The fire of your French father will last forever, and warm his children.[51]

Although the Amerindians were far from being oblivious to European interest in their lands, it is very doubtful that they understood the full import of what the French were up to. From their perspective, they had gained a powerful new ally, one who would bring desired trade goods and who had promised to protect them from their enemies. They had no reason but to think that they had just concluded a good deal. The French had learned, however, that the Iroquois, whenever they came across a French metal plaque attached to a tree, tore it off and took it to the English. Thus, Jean Talon (1626–94), intendant of New France for two terms, 1665–8 and 1670–2, admitted the Iroquois were probably aware that the French were claiming the West as theirs.[52] On top of that, this huge expansion was presenting the French with problems of control: their people in the *pays d'en haut*, as the Great Lakes region was referred to, did not always behave well. Whatever the goals of Versailles, the *coureurs de bois* had the acquisition of furs on their minds; as one observer put it, Canadians were 'looking not for The western sea, but The sea of beaver'. Officials, realizing the importance of the friendship of the local Amerindians if they were to maintain a presence, went to some trouble to defuse disturbances.[53]

In the 1670s, the French and the English were not the only ones who were expanding their territories. Two major indigenous expansions originated in the North, armed with guns obtained in the HBC trade. Ojibwa moved south from the north shore of Lake Huron into lands that had once been occupied by such Iroquoians as the Huron, Petun (Tionontati), and Neutrals, all of whom had been dispersed by the Five Nations during the preceding decades, and pushed west, eventually moving onto the Plains. They defeated the Iroquois in skirmishes throughout the last decade of the seventeenth century.[54] The Cree also expanded, which may have been a continuation of a long-standing movement, as they appear to have been established as far west as the Peace River well before the advent of Euro-Canadians.[55] In any event, they were raiding in the Mackenzie basin by 1820; to the north, they were contained by the Chipewyan. To the south, they followed their Assiniboine allies to take up life as buffalo hunters on the northern Plains. When French explorer and fur trader Pierre Gaultier de Varennes et de La Vérendrye (1685–1749) reached the Plains in the 1730s, he encountered a group of Cree south of the Saskatchewan River.[56] This movement was stopped by the Blackfoot and their confederates, who controlled the central and southern Alberta Plains. There is some speculation that the Cree/Assiniboine movement was partly linked to trade, at least in its later phase.[57] In the Maritimes, the Mi'kmaq were not so fortunate: encroached upon by advancing settlement, they were in the throes of a war against the English, a confrontation that had begun early in the seventeenth century and would not end until the final defeat of France in 1760. Add to all this the century-long Iroquois War against New France (which had ended in 1701) and Canada's 'peaceful' frontier takes on the aspect of a wishful myth.

Chapter 10

Some Amerindian–Colonial Wars

Canada prides herself on her peaceful dealings with the Amerindians whose lands she took over during the process of colonization. Yet two of the longest wars in the colonial history of North America took place in Canada. The first is by far the best known: the Iroquois War, fought by the Five Nations and New France from 1609 until 1701. The longest of all Amerindian conflicts in North America was the Mi'kmaq War, fought with the British from about 1613 until 1761; it can be regarded as the northern manifestation of the Abenaki wars, touched upon in Chapter 7. All of these wars were fought intermittently, sometimes with pauses that extended for years between active hostilities. For instance, some historians divide the Iroquois War in two, others into four; as for the Mi'kmaq War, they view it as a series of raids, of which the hostilities called the English–Indian War of 1722–4 were the most important. Equalling or perhaps even surpassing the Iroquois War in the intensity of emotion aroused was the Fox War, a series of engagements between 1710 and 1738, which carried on the Iroquois conflict into the Middle West after the Five Nations had come to terms

with the French in Montreal. Although the Fox War was fought in territory that is now part of the United States, it involved New France almost as deeply as had the Iroquoian conflict and so will be considered here.

The Iroquois War (1609–1701)

The intensity of this conflict was hard on both sides, but neither seemed capable of stopping it despite sporadic efforts. The brief peace of 1645, already noted in connection with the raids on the fur brigades, illustrates some of the difficulties.[1] When the Algonquin war chief Pieskaret (d. 1647) killed 13 Mohawk warriors in one engagement that year,[2] the Mohawk were ready to sue for peace, and the French, feeling the effects of economic strangulation, were only too willing to join. The maladroit negotiations that followed have already been alluded to in Chapter 8: not only were the meetings held behind closed doors without the knowledge of allies and associates, but the peace agreement excluded the non-Christian allies of the French as well; the effect on them when they learned what had happened can

TIMELINE

1609–1701	The Iroquois War.
1650	Mohawk and Seneca join forces to defeat and disperse Neutrals.
1665	French sign peace treaty with League of Five Nations, except for Mohawk, whose raids on French settlements have been especially unsettling.
1675	Seneca defeat the Susquehannocks.
1687	Denonville sends dozens of captive Iroquois to France for service in galleys; 13 survivors eventually returned.
1689	Frontenac, on return to Quebec for second term as governor, brings three of Denonville's captured Seneca with him.
1693	French and Canadiens invade Mohawk territory.
1710–38	Fox War, involving attacks on French traders and blockading of river systems needed for French trade in Upper Midwest.
1713–61	Mi'kmaq War, the last phase.
1716	French besiege Fox village, killing an estimated 1,000 Amerindians.
c. 1720	Tuscarora migrate north to join Iroquois, who become League of Six Nations.
1720s	Fox war chief Kiala seeks alliance with Abenaki (and Chief Nescambiouit), Iroquois, and Chickasaw.
1725	Mascarene's Treaty (Treaty No. 239) with Abenaki after fall of Norridgewock, which details how Amerindians must behave as British subjects.
1734	Kiala and three other Fox leaders travel to Montreal to sue for peace: one chief pressed into galley service; Kiala sent as slave to Martinique, ends up abandoned on Guyana coast.
1749	Halifax established by English. Abenaki and Wuastukwiuk of St John River ratify Mascarene's Treaty.
1752	Mi'kmaq chief from Shubenacadie signs peace treaty with English in Halifax.
1755	Expulsion of Acadians from Nova Scotia.
1758	Louisbourg falls to British, who refuse to include Amerindians in terms of surrender because of earlier massacre of British prisoners at Fort William Henry in New York.
1782	French destroy Fort Prince of Wales on Hudson Bay; outbreak of disease leads Chipewyan to abandon area.

easily be imagined. Similarly, the excluded members of the Iroquois league were so displeased that it took all of the celebrated eloquence of a leading Mohawk negotiator, Kiotseaeton ('The Hook', *fl.* 1645–6), with 17 wampum belts, to persuade even some of them to go along with its terms, at least for a while.[3] Principal among the holdouts were the 'nephews' of the Mohawk, the Oneida. Not surprisingly, it did not take long for hostilities to resume, more intensely than ever. The century of warfare was interwoven with attempts at peace; a major effort occurred in 1653 when all the Iroquois joined with each other to negoti-

ate an accord the French were only too willing to accept, even though their allies were once more excluded. In the breathing space of a few years that followed, the Jesuits were able to establish a mission at Onondaga that would have important consequences in the future. In the meantime, the French allies were allowed no respite, which meant that inevitably the peace collapsed. In the view of the French, the Iroquois were not interested in peace until they obtained control of the flow of beaver from the Old Northwest, deflecting it to the Dutch and then the English.[4]

Except for the interlude of the mid-fifties,

the four decades that followed the 'patched-up peace' of 1645[5] saw the outlying areas of the colony, especially those around Montreal, become nearly impossible to farm. Dollier de Casson described the 'enemy all around us . . . [they] approach like foxes, fight like lions, fly away like birds.' Iroquois warriors, he wrote, thought nothing of passing a 'whole day without moving, and hidden behind a stump' in order to dispatch a colonist.[6] How could one fight a war against an invisible enemy, Jesuit Georges d'Endemare complained, adding that unless all the forests were cut down it would be impossible to stop the raids.[7] The exasperation this type of warfare aroused in the French was illustrated by a proposal that the Iroquois be exterminated.[8]

By 1646 some Hurons, who had not been shaken from their French alliance by the epidemics of the previous decade despite their conviction that the French were responsible, were now reported to be hesitating. The benefits of the trade were great, but there were now some who found 'that it costs them too dear, and they prefer to do without European goods rather than to expose themselves every year.'[9] The aim of the raids was to spread terror, and in this the Iroquois were extremely effective. Jesuit missionary Rale, observing these same techniques among the Abenaki, said they made 'a handfull of warriors more formidable than would a body of two or three thousand European soldiers'.[10] The Iroquois attacks fuelled the anti-French faction among the Huron, and in 1648 they killed a young missionary assistant in the hope of terminating the alliance and getting both French and Christianized Hurons expelled from Huronia. The pro-French faction prevailed, however, and the Jesuits were offered, and accepted, a reparations payment said to have been the largest ever made by the confederacy.[11] That action did not save Wendat (as the Huron referred to their confederacy) from dispersal the following year, a fate shared with their neigh-bours, the Tionontati (Tobacco People, Petun), specialists in growing tobacco. That was only the beginning of the celebrated Iroquoian series of victories.

In 1650 the Mohawk and Seneca joined forces to disperse the Attiwandaron (Neutrals), who in keeping with their geographical position between the Huron and Iroquois confederacies had tried to maintain relations with both sides, but had been more successful with the Huron. They now found themselves in effect swallowed whole by the Iroquois, incorporated into the league. The Erie, who had taken in large numbers of Huron refugees, became the next targets; during 1654–6 they were defeated in a series of attacks. With the Seneca defeat of the Susquehannocks in 1675 after 20 years of hostilities, the Iroquois finally smashed the ring of Huron allies by which they had been encircled during the heyday of Huron power. Not only that, they had spread their terror to Wisconsin and Michigan tribal nations and would soon erupt into Illinois.

For the French, the guerrilla tactics of the Iroquois were harder on nerves than on the lives of the colonists; Dollier de Casson alluded to this when he mentioned frequent skirmishes that wounded many but killed few. At another point he wrote of the many attacks 'in which God was uniformly merciful to Montrealers'. He was of the opinion that the Iroquois lost many more lives than the French.[12] Research appears to support this; it has been estimated that the Iroquois may have lost as many as half their warriors to war and disease during the last two decades of the seventeenth century. The French lost about 200 souls.[13]

The guerrilla type of warfare waged by the Iroquois, based on surprise and speed of movement, was their preferred technique, particularly after they encountered firearms. The only time the French faced an Iroquois army on an open field was in 1609, when Champlain claimed deadly results from his one shot.

Whether or not that story is true, the Iroquois saw no virtue in exposing themselves to fire they could not match, and they resorted to the hunting tactics in which they were highly skilled. Throughout the century of warfare that followed, the French never met the Iroquois in open battle. To the seventeenth-century French —indeed, to Europeans in general—this was a disgraceful way of conducting a war; it was much less wasteful of human life than the European model, but it did not follow rules the Europeans considered acceptable. The northern forests, however, proved not to be suitable for the style of the conquistador, and Europeans did not prevail militarily against boreal Amerindians until they adopted some of their tactics. A proposal to organize Amerindian allies into companies on the same basis as French soldiers met with a cool response, as officials did not think that such a measure would make the Amerindians any more formidable as fighters than they already were. Individual Amerindians who distinguished themselves in the French service were given quasi-military rank; several chiefs received the title of 'major'.[14]

At first, the French sought to make a show of force in the European way. In 1665 they sent out the crack Carignan-Salières regiment, the pride of the French military estalishment, soon followed by Alexandre Prouville de Tracy, lieutenant-general of America from 1663 to 1667, who came up from the Caribbean to set things aright in the northern colony. During the last month of 1665, 13 December to be exact, the French signed a peace treaty at Quebec with four members of the League of Five Nations, excluding the Mohawk, who had been particularly effective harassing French settlements.[15] Later that winter the astonished Mohawk (winter was not their time for fighting) witnessed the regiment's march towards their territory, which in the absence of Algonquin guides, who had failed to show, got lost and wound up near Schenectady, about three days' march from Mohawk villages. The Mohawk advised the English in Albany of the presence of the French force, and the English sent a delegation to ask what the French were doing on English territory (apparently neither side knew that England and France had been at war for the past fortnight). The French, surprised to learn that England claimed title to the region by virtue of having driven out the Dutch two years previously (1664), negotiated for supplies and returned home. The expedition had lost about 400 men from frostbite, exhaustion, and hunger.

Still determined to teach the Mohawk a lesson, the French returned the following September with a much larger expedition, this time accompanied by Huron and Algonquin auxiliaries to show the way, and with a third party bringing up the rear. Again, they did not meet any Iroquois, but they put four Mohawk villages to the torch and destroyed food stores. The French lost 10 men in a storm. The destruction of their supplies apparently hit the Mohawk hard; a few years later La Salle, with Dollier de Casson and Galinée, passing through the land of the Seneca, was presented with 15 tanned deerskins in token of welcome; in the accompanying speech, the Seneca expressed the hope that the French would not burn their villages as they had done those of the Mohawk a few years earlier.[16]

There was a positive outcome to Tracy's enterprise, however, as the Mohawk sued for peace the following spring, in 1667. This time the agreement held, at least for a while. The Iroquois, who at that time were involved in tribal wars from Virginia to Lac Saint Jean as well as in the West, needed time to digest and come to terms with this change in conducting international relations. The French also worked at coming to terms: in 1669, three Frenchmen were executed for killing a Seneca chief. The Seneca were on the leading edge of western expansion, and many of them were trading with the English; in 1670, a worried intendant Talon estimated that the Iroquois had diverted 1.2 million *livres*' worth of beaver. Therefore, it was important that the Seneca not be antagonized. The French decided that the Sault Ste Marie ceremony of 1671 needed to be followed up; accordingly, in 1673 Louis de Buade, Comte de Palluau et de Frontenac, governor-general of New France, 1672–82 and 1689–98, enthroned in a sedan chair, headed up the St Lawrence to found a fort at Cataracoui, now Kingston. There he met delegates from the Five Nations, much disturbed because French were now in Iroquois territory. Not only were Iroquois–Odawa negotiations for a separate peace aborted, but as the French pushed westward the Five Nations became convinced that they were being outflanked, all the more so because the Illinois had joined the French. That same year, 1673, the Iroquois negotiated a treaty with the Odawa by which they promised to provide the latter with trade goods in return for pelts.[17] It did not last past 1700, when the Iroquois violated the treaty's terms by hunting in Odawa territory. In the meantime, in 1680, the league's warriors invaded Illinois country.

The French, for their part, again tried a European-style invasion of Iroquois territory, this one organized by a new governor-general, Joseph-Antoine Le Febvre de La Barre (in office, 1682–5), and aimed at the Seneca (1684).[18] Illness broke out among the troops (New France at that time was suffering an epidemic, possibly cholera, that had killed more than 1,400 out of a population of 11,000), and the army was forced to encamp at a bay in Lake Ontario that became known as Anse de la Famine. There the Iroquois found the French, disease-ridden and running out of food. Otreouti (Hateouati, among other variations, 'Big Mouth', *fl.* 1659–88), Onondaga orator and chief, presented the Iroquois terms: they would pay 1,000 beaver in recompense for damages from their raids, but they were not prepared to accept

peace in Illinois country, nor would they guarantee protection for French traders in the region. The French had no option but to accept, a turn of events that caused shock waves all the way to Versailles. Le Febvre de La Barre was quickly recalled and Jacques-René de Brisay de Denonville (governor-general, 1685–9), a professional soldier, was sent out to recoup what was seen as a loss of French honour.

While Denonville's expedition against the Seneca (1687) had more casualties from disease than from fighting, it did have one skirmish. Admittedly it was an inconclusive ambush, but at least Denonville had engaged the enemy. He had achieved this by adopting the Iroquoian tactics of surprise, surround, give way when pressed, and speed (a quick blow and rapid withdrawal).[19] The *raid-éclair* became one of the elements that would contribute to the reputation of *Canadiens* as feared forest fighters in the cycle of French–English wars that began in 1689. In 1747, for example, Nicolas-Antoine Coulon de Villiers (1708–50), in a rapid winter raid, caught the English troops at Grand Pré totally unaware and overwhelmed them. It had taken a century of warfare, but the French had learned, at least for North America; the English, too, would follow suit.

Denonville's campaign, like Tracy's in 1666 against the Mohawk, destroyed Seneca villages and food stores. He also captured a group of Iroquois, variously estimated at numbering about 36 to 60, and sent them to France for service in the galleys.[20] The coup aroused a frightful row; the Jesuits were especially angry, as they saw it as destroying their years of difficult missionary work among the Five Nations. Army officer Louis-Armand de Lom d'Arce de Lahontan (1666–before 1716), a caustic observer of the colonial scene, claimed that the prisoners had been taken from friendly groups who had come to settle around Fort Cataracoui. Denonville had acted under orders; Versailles had entertained the idea for a long time, not just for New France but for the Caribbean also. In the end, Versailles backed down and returned the 13 survivors. Frontenac brought three back with him when he took up his second term as governor in 1689.

The Seneca, who had suffered severely from the destruction of their stores by Denonville's troops, were not long in taking revenge, in what has gone down in Canadian history as a classic example of Amerindian warfare. Their raid on Lachine on an August dawn of 1689 caught the French completely by surprise. Fifty-six of 77 habitations went up in flames. The casualty rate has been given at anywhere between 24 (by the French) and 200 (by the English); the latter figure, however, included those taken prisoners. The psychological effect was more important; the colony was stunned. For the next few years New France was practically in a state of siege, with Montreal taking the brunt. In 1691, about 30 farms at Pointe-aux-Trembles, outside of Montreal, were burned. When the *habitants* captured some Iroquois, they publicly burned three of them to death. The lessons of warfare worked both ways.

When Frontenac, during the 1690s, was able finally to move the scene of war into the lands of the Mohawk and Onondaga (with few exceptions, most of the earlier fighting had occurred either in New France or in the territories of its allies), inflicting heavy losses, the Iroquois began seriously to consider peace.[21] Their fear of being encircled by the French was becoming a reality as the latter moved down the Mississippi and founded Louisiana in 1699. The French were also encircling them with alliances with western Amerindians, particularly the Odawa and Miami, who had fought very effectively for the French against the Iroquois.[22] The response of their English allies to the league's requests for help had not been adequate, either with supplies of guns and ammunition or otherwise. For example, when the French and Canadiens invaded Mohawk lands

in 1693, the forewarned English had prepared for their own defence but had neglected to inform the Mohawk. The latter suffered much damage and severe losses.[23]

On top of that, the English and the French signed one of their periodic peace treaties in 1697 but did not include the Five Nations in its terms, as they could not agree on the status of the Iroquois; both claimed them as subjects. The Iroquois, of course, did not see themselves as being subject to anyone. Teganissorens (Decanasora, *fl.* last quarter, seventeenth century, and first quarter, eighteenth century), Onondaga chief and leader of the faction that favoured dealing with the French, became a central figure in the negotiations, dominating them for 30 years. Artful to the end, the Five Nations signed a peace with the French in Montreal in 1701 in the face of English objections, then that same year they cemented their alliance with the English in Albany by ceding them lands in southern Ontario that had once been occupied by the Iroquoian Tionontati and Neutrals until their dispersal by the league during the 1650s. The joker was that although the Five Nations claimed the territory, in the meantime it had been effectively occupied by the Ojibwa, whose defeat of the Iroquois in the region during the 1690s has already been noted. Not only were the English apparently unaware of the situation, they also did not know that the Iroquois, in a double twist, had negotiated with the French for their guarantee of hunting and fishing rights to that same region. Further, they assured the French of their neutrality in future wars but made no mention of this to the English. The Iroquois were playing both ends against the middle with great skill.[24]

They had another ace in the hole—their access to English markets in Albany. During their hostilities against the French, they had been careful to protect their position as middlemen in the English trading system. When in

1696 the French market collapsed because of oversupply, the Iroquois offered Amerindian allies of the French safe conduct through Iroquois territories to New York markets. Their purpose was to win the westerners into the Iroquois–English network—a brilliant move that deepened the crisis for the French in the West on both the diplomatic and economic fronts.[25]

What had been achieved by the century of war? It had shifted the balance of Amerindian regional power from Huronia to Iroquoia; the Five Nations emerged with expanded territory, although not so much as they claimed.[26] Despite extensive adoptions of war captives, the league had suffered severe population losses, particularly between 1689 and 1698, when it has been estimated it may have lost as much as half of its fighting forces. Desertions of converts to the Montreal settlements contributed to this.[27] Amazingly enough, the Iroquois had managed to keep their confederacy intact in the face of these disasters and despite the relentless pressures of European settlement. The combination of these factors was changing Iroquois society, one manifestation of which was the abandonment of longhouses in favour of single-family living units. Nevertheless, the Iroquois identity remained strong.

Paradoxically, the Five Nations had also assured the existence of New France, giving the colonists and their allies cohesion and a common purpose in the face of a common enemy. For the colony itself, the enemy had been a source of vitality as the fighting opened military careers and military campaigns provided opportunities for advancement. Indirectly, by knocking out Huronia and its northern trading networks, the Five Nations had facilitated the establishment of the English on Hudson Bay and had precipitated the westward expansion of the French. As Lahontan saw it, the French could have prevented that happening if they had worked at gaining Iroquois friendship while curbing their power. He held that it had

never been in the interest of New France, either economically or politically, to eliminate the Iroquois, despite all the overheated rhetoric to that effect. In fact, by trying to destroy them, the French had played into the hands of the English.[28] Latter-day historians tend to agree that the French failure to form a stable alliance with the Iroquois was a major factor in their 1760 defeat by the British. There is no way of knowing the war's toll for the Five Nations. Hit by epidemics, particularly during the 1640s, they had compensated for their losses by adopting and incorporating defeated peoples. This was a technique the Iroquois used very skilfully, but which the Jesuits would be able to use later to polarize Iroquois society.[29]

The death toll eventually outran replacements, especially when the Five Nations suffered mass defections as a result of the Jesuit missionary efforts. During the 1690s, for example, fully two-thirds of the Mohawk decamped for the two French missions around Montreal. Two factors were involved: the mass absorption of conquered peoples that had followed the dispersion of Huronia; and the evangelization by the Jesuits, which had found fertile ground among the not yet integrated captives. When the missionaries began to have success among the Iroquois themselves, such as when the influential Onondaga chief Garakontié (Harakontié, d. 1677/8) accepted to be baptized and then refused to participate in traditional ceremonies considered essential for the unity of the Great League of Peace, divisions within the Iroquois communities became embittered. Accusing the Jesuits of working for their destruction, traditionalists began a successful campaign to drive them out of Iroquoia. The Jesuits for their part encouraged converts to emigrate to such missionary villages as Sault St Louis (Caughnawaga, today's Kahnawake) and Prairie de la Madeleine (Kentake); the new arrivals were described as a sixth nation, long before the league actually became the League of

Six Nations.[30] The importance the French attached to these new allies is illustrated by their action in sending an eminent convert, the Onondaga orator Aradgi (Arratio, Ateriata, Haratsion, *fl.* 1690–1702), to France to be baptized in the presence of the King and to receive his name, Louis. Aradgi received a silver medal for his role in the negotiations that began in 1697 and would culminate in the peace of 1701. He was retained in Quebec by Frontenac as a guarantor of the agreement.[31] Back in Iroquoia, although the traditionalists had won the day, factionalism had not been rooted out.[32]

Within a couple of decades after the end of the conflict, the League of Five Nations became the League of Six Nations when it was joined by the Tuscarora, fleeing from hostilities with settlers in the Carolinas.

Fox War (1710–38)

As the Iroquois laid down the gauntlet, their allies the Fox (Mesquakie, as they referred to themselves; also known as Outagami), one of the more populous Algonkian peoples of present-day Wisconsin, picked it up. The Fox were trading partners with the Iroquois and so were becoming involved in the English network; they were the only Algonkians of the upper Great Lakes who opposed the French. Although the scene of their war was far from the St Lawrence, in the *pays d'en haut*, it would become bitter, with the French seeking the extermination of the enemy.

When Antoine Laumet *dit* Lamothe Cadillac (1658–1730) established a fort at Detroit (which he called Pontchartrain) the same year that the Five Nations and the French signed their peace in Montreal, he foresaw the fort becoming the hub of the western trade. Already, the French were developing trade with the Sioux, which had deeply disturbed their enemies the Iroquois and was having similar effects on the equally hostile Fox. Although

Cadillac must have been aware of this, as well as other inter-tribal hostilities, he optimistically invited everyone to come and establish around his fort. Some Fox accepted the invitation in 1710, but the French were suspicious and watchful; this turned into anger as the 'cunning and malignant' Fox began to attack French traders.[33]

When the Fox attempted to leave the Green Bay area to join the Iroquois, the French moved to prevent it. The Fox responded in 1711 by blocking the Fox–Wisconsin river system, the main route from the East to the Mississippi and the Sioux. They did this by charging heavy tolls, as well as by plundering trading parties. Not only did they cut the French off from access to the southwest, but the Fox also harassed French allies on their hunting grounds. The French besieged a Fox village for 19 days, killing an estimated 1,000 men, women, and children. Instead of cooling the situation, this had the reverse effect; in 1716, an army was sent out under Louis de La Porte de Louvigny (*c.* 1662–1725), the first French military expedition to penetrate so far west. According to historian Louise Phelps Kellogg (d. 1942), it came out disguised as a trading delegation. Once more the Fox fortified themselves in a village, which the French annihilated; this defeat reopened the Fox–Wisconsin river system for traders.

Peace negotiations were undertaken by Ouchala (*fl.* 1716–27), the Fox peace chief who led a pro-French faction. Among other terms such as the release of prisoners, the Fox agreed to hunt to pay the costs of the war. To ensure that the terms would be carried out, the French took six hostages to Montreal, where two of them fell victim to smallpox. This caused Ouchala to delay going there to ratify the agreement; by the time he eventually did so, he was not able to prevail against the mutual recriminations that were being bandied about concerning breaking the agreement. In 1717 the war was rekindled, not only between the

Fox and the French but also into a complex of feuds between the Fox and other tribes; as well, it raised tensions between New France and Louisiana, as the latter felt that its trading interests were being sacrificed.

A new governor-general, Charles de Beauharnois de la Boische, in office from 1726 to 1747, set out to re-establish French hegemony in the West. Two years later (1728), Paul Marin de la Malgue (1692–1753) became the French leader on the scene, which he would dominate for the next quarter of a century. In the midst of the bitter campaigns that followed, the Fox moved to reaffirm their alliance with the Iroquois. These overtures were carried on by Kiala (Quiala, *fl.* 1733–4), a war chief who headed the anti-French faction and who recognized the need for Amerindians to make a united stand against the European invasion. During the 1720s, besides the Iroquois, he negotiated with the Chickasaw and Abenaki, confirming old alliances and building new ones. Nescambiouit, the Abenaki chief, was involved in these discussions (Chapter 7). This greatly upset the French, who saw it as an attempt to encircle them, cutting them off from their allies and separating New France from Louisiana. In 1730 the Fox, harassed on all sides, sent two redstone axes to the Seneca, asking for permission to come and live with them. In spite of the attempts of the French envoy, Chabert de Joncaire (Sononchiez to the Seneca),[34] to prevent it, the Seneca agreed, and the Fox began their migration. Cornered in 1730 by the pursuing French under Nicolas-Antoine Coulon de Villiers (1683–1733),[35] they held out for 23 days before attempting a sortie. Only a few hundred survived of the 1,300 Fox of a year earlier.[36] The French with their allies set about tracking down the remnants; some groups were able to flee west of the Mississippi. Villiers, one of his sons, and a son-in-law were killed, setting off yet another punitive French expedition (1734); this time, however, the French allies decided that matters had gone far enough, and they refused to go along with the campaign, which consequently came to naught.

In the meantime, in 1733, the remaining Fox had sued for peace; the following year Kiala and three other Fox leaders voluntarily went to Montreal to give themselves up. One of the chiefs was sent to France for service in the galleys. Kiala was sent as a slave to Martinique, but instead was abandoned on the Guyana coast; his wife was adopted by the Hurons of Lorette. Other Fox prisoners were scattered among the missions. Thus ended Kiala's dream of uniting Amerindians from the Atlantic to the Ohio Valley.

Some French allies went to Montreal to plead for their erstwhile enemies. They had begun to have second thoughts: what was happening to the Fox could presage their own doom. During this period the Sauk reconsidered their position and became such firm allies of the Fox that the two peoples ever since have been referred to together. In the final campaigns of the French, more of their allies sided with the Fox and the Sauk. As Beauharnois expressed it, 'You may imagine, Monseigneur, that the Savages have their policy as we have Ours, and they are not greatly pleased at seeing a nation destroyed, for Fear that their turn may come. . . . The Savages as a rule greatly fear the French, but they do not love them.'[37]

Peace was finally achieved in 1738, which was confirmed five years later when Marin de la Malgue, who had stayed with the Fox in the West, led another delegation to Montreal. The Fox were no longer the enemy; from a nation that had once counted at least 1,000 warriors, they could now barely muster 250. In an ironic postscript, some Fox later joined the French and fought with them against the English, including the 1755 attack that annihilated the British army led by General Edward Braddock (1695–1755) and in the Battle of the Plains of Abraham in 1759.

Several points emerge from an assessment of these two conflicts. Militarily, the French were more effective against the Fox than they had been for most of the war against the Iroquois; they had adapted to forest-fighting techniques. Their system of Native alliances was much less stable in the *pays d'en haut* than it was eastward to the Atlantic coast; in this case, it was the English who had made the necessary adaptations to develop and hold Native alliances. On the Atlantic coast the French had had a head start and were able to forge firm alliances before the English realized the importance of this form of diplomacy, but in the Great Lakes area the latter were able to offer stiff competition. Amerindians, on the other hand, were beginning to realize the importance of allying with each other instead of with the invading Europeans. Although pan-Amerindianism barely got a hesitant start, it was sufficient to give the French a severe fright and at least partly accounts for their violent reaction to Fox intransigence.

Mi'kmaq War (1613–1761): The Last Phase, 1713–61

As the final round of the North American colonial wars got underway, the Mi'kmaq pitched into the fray on land and sea, asserting their right to make war or peace as they willed and reaffirming their sovereignty over Megumaage. Between 1713 and 1760, Louisbourg correspondence refers to well over 100 captures of vessels by Amerindians. The Amerindians liked to cruise in their captured ships before abandoning them, forcing their prisoners to serve as crew. At that time they had no use for ships of that size, just as they had no use for artillery. This activity peaked in 1722, the year the English–Indian War broke out. Revivals of lesser proportions in the fifties followed the establishment of Halifax in 1749 and the expulsion in 1755 of the Acadians, many of whom had blood ties with Amerindians.[38]

The turning point came in 1725, when the Abenaki sued for peace following the destruction of Norridgewock. The British took advantage of the situation to negotiate not only for peace (the Treaty of Boston), but also for a second agreement, Treaty No. 239 (also called Mascarene's Treaty), detailing how Amerindians were expected to behave as British subjects.[39]

The peace treaty was a blow to the French, and their immediate reaction was to disclaim that the English–Indian War had been of any concern to them. However, an apparently unfounded report that the missionary Antoine Gaulin was encouraging his Mi'kmaq to sign so annoyed Versailles that Ile Royale's governor, Saint-Ovide, had to come to the missionary's defence.[40] The treaties called for countermeasures, especially as the allies were complaining that the all-important gift distributions often did not have enough goods to go around. The budget for this purpose was steadily increased; by 1756 it had reached 37,000 *livres*, a figure that did not include 'extra-ordinary expenses' entailed when employing Amerindians.[41] Promises of gifts to come were no longer acceptable; the allies would be led only when they had goods in hand. What had started as a matter of protocol to cement alliances and trade agreements had ended as a means of subsistence for Amerindians and a form of protection for the French.

Even as the French spared no effort to engage their allies against the English, they did pause from time to time at the 'férocité inutile' of some of their attacks and on occasion sought to curb them. In 1739, Saint-Ovide, seeking to calm the Amerindians' fears, asked them, for the sake of the French King and themselves, to keep the peace. The Amerindians worried that the French and English would unite to destroy them; they observed that if they had listened less to the French, they would be having less trouble with the English, who were not only taking their lands but also destroying their fishing. They promised to be quiet for the present but warned that they would protect themselves against those who sought to destroy them.[42]

When the British founded Halifax in 1749 in Mi'kmaq territory (in a district the latter called Segepenegatig), they once more failed to consult the Natives. Asking 'Where can we go, if we are to be deprived of our lands?' the Mi'kmaq adopted a European custom and formally declared war.[43] This confirmed the English in their already established conviction that the Mi'kmaq were simply rebels.[44] Mi'kmaq raids were effective enough for Governor Edward Cornwallis (1713–76) to request more arms for the colonists, as 'at present above ten thousand people are awed by two hundred savages.' As the raids intensified, he issued a proclamation commanding the settlers 'to Annoy, distress, take or destroy the Savages commonly called Mic-macks, wherever they are found'.[45] During this period both French and English paid bounties for scalps at escalating rates, no questions asked.[46] In the midst of all this, the British officially encouraged marriages to Amerindian women for a brief period.[47] The British also bowed to the inevitable and began to be more generous in their gift distributions. This influenced the Wuastukwiuk and Abenaki of the St John River, in 1749, to sign ratifications of Mascarene's Treaty. The French sought to counter this by sending René, a chief from Naltigonish, to act as a counteragent, but without success.[48]

More ominous for the French was the news in 1752 that a ranking chief from Shubenacadie had signed a peace treaty in Halifax.[49] This treaty was a major breakthrough, not only in its effect on the course of the Mi'kmaq War but also in the terms of the treaty itself. It guaranteed hunting and fishing rights for the Amerindians, and also regular gift distributions, which would later be transformed into annuity payments for surrendered lands.

The fall of Fort William Henry (at Lake George, New York) in 1757 and the subsequent massacre of English prisoners by French allies raised settler hysteria against Amerindians to such a pitch that when Louisbourg fell to the British in 1758, the victors refused to include Amerindians in the terms of surrender. This was correctly seen as not boding well for them, and when the British formally took over the fortress not an Amerindian was present.

If the Amerindian factor had simply faded at Louisbourg, this was not true for Acadia generally. The British now had the task of ensuring that all chiefs and their people were included in the peace agreement, if a general peace were to be achieved. It took the final defeat of the French in 1760 to accomplish this; a year later, the peace was signed. The Mi'kmaq, Wuastukwiuk, and Abenaki of Acadia finally acknowledged British sovereignty, in return for which they were assured that they would have the full protection of British laws just as any other subject 'as long as the sun and the moon shall endure'.[50]

Several characteristics distinguish the Mi'kmaq War. It was fought largely at sea; that part of it that was fought on land was the only case in Canada where Amerindians fought on their own lands for their own lands. In this aspect, the war in its later phases came to resemble the frontier wars in US. Despite the fact that the Mi'kmaq and Wuastukwiuk have had one of the longest contacts with Europeans, and despite the protracted hostilities, they are still to be found on their ancestral lands, although only on a tiny fraction of what was once theirs.

In this long struggle, Mi'kmaq, Wuastukwiuk, and Abenaki had shown themselves astute in turning imperial rivalries to their own advantage. When it came to self-interest, there was not much to choose between Amerindians and the colonial powers. The difference lay in the fact that both France and Britain were building empires, whereas Amerindians, after a brief initial period when some attempted to use European alliances to expand their own hegemonies, had soon found themselves struggling to survive. Their capacity to keep the colonial powers off balance became their most formidable weapon. Louisbourg's role was vital: for the French, whatever their original intentions for building the fortress, its greatest military usefulness turned out to be as a headquarters for the maintenance of Amerindian alliances and the encouragement of their guerrilla warfare; for the Mi'kmaq and Maliseet it represented a reprieve from European economic and cultural domination, because as guerrillas they were able to dictate to a surprising extent their own terms as allies, particularly with the French.

The spectre of French return to Canada continued to haunt the British until the defeat of Napoleon at Waterloo in 1815. An episode in 1762 had done much to keep this fear alive, when the French invested St John's, Newfoundland, for a couple of months. Hearing this news, the Mi'kmaq became restive, giving settlers a severe fright. Such fears were also fuelled by reports that the Mi'kmaq were being secretly supplied by the French from St Pierre and Miquelon, but those reports were never substantiated. It appears that the Mi'kmaq had gone to the islands, which remained under French control, looking for priests and supplies. The French were under orders to discourage such visits, on the ground that they would only annoy the British and would serve no purpose;[51] however, they appear to have helped the Mi'kmaq anyway. Thrown back on their own resources when traditional territories had long since been overhunted, and with gift distributions cut off, the Mi'kmaq were now desperately searching for a means of subsistence. Groups went to southern Newfoundland, alarming settlers and authorities alike. In spite of official attempts to dislodge them, they had come to stay.[52]

This once assertive, far-ranging people on sea and land now had to take what they could get, and that was not very much; in fact, the process was in reverse, as lands were taken from them as settlers began streaming into the homelands they had fought so hard to protect.

The War in the Bay (1685–1782)

The struggle between the French and English in Hudson Bay, like the Mi'kmaq War, was a series of disconnected raids, sometimes widely spaced in time and place, rather than a sustained conflict. These did not involve Amerindians as allies, as did the conflicts to the south. However, the French–English struggle did affect the Natives when posts were destroyed or were unable to meet their trade requirements; this happened in 1686, when the French took three posts at the bottom of Hudson Bay.[53] The destruction of Fort Prince of Wales in 1782 and the outbreak of disease led to the Chipewyan abandoning the area and moving southward to Athapaskan country. Eventually Inuit filtered into the deserted region, which Samuel Hearne called the 'land of little sticks' and later administrators would label the Keewatin District. Migrating herds of caribou provided the Inuit with a subsistence base; when they began trading with the British and Canadians at interior posts, they became known as Caribou Inuit.[54]

Chapter 11

Amerindians in the French New World

Early Attempts at Social Engineering

Throughout the history of New France, the French policy towards Amerindians was consistent: treat them with every consideration, avoid violence (this was not always successful), and transform them into Frenchmen.[1] The techniques by which these goals were to be reached were established early, in Brazil, where the French had developed their skills in Amerindian diplomacy for a century before they successfully colonized New France.[2] They were listed by Thomas Nelson (1738–89), signer of the Declaration of Independence and briefly governor of Virginia in 1781:

> First, by reasonable presents, secondly by choosing some of the more notable amongst them, to whom is given a constant pay as Lieutenant or Ensigne & thirdly by rewards upon all executions, either upon us or our Indians, giving a certain sume per head, for as many Scalps as shall be brought them. Fourthly by encouraging the youth of the Countrey in accompanying the Indians in all their expeditions.[3]

These four techniques were used by the French throughout the period of New France. A fifth, tried early and later discarded, was to send 'eminent and enterprizing' Amerindians to France 'to amaze and dazzle them with the greatness and splendour of the French Court and Armie'.[4] Amerindians were even reported to have been sent down to Flanders where French armies were mustered expressly to impress them. This was regarded by Nelson as the best means of all of ensuring their loyalty, particularly when the French gave the same treatment to Amerindians taken prisoner from the British colonies. However, it was discontinued as too expensive in relation to the results achieved.[5] Amerindians proved not to be so easily impressed, and they soon learned to take advantage of these occasions to lobby in their own interests. Nelson tells of six sagamores at Versailles at the same time, all soliciting aid from the French against the English.[6] A sixth technique was ceremonial recognition, including presentation of appropriate gifts. For example, a gun or even a cannon salute for a visiting delegation, and the gifts proffered, were important influences on subsequent negotiations.

TIMELINE

1740	Presentation to Amerindians of ceremonial medals begun by French.	1755	The Acadians are expelled from their homeland by the English.
1753	Father Maillard, 'Apostle to the Micmacs', anticipates that within 50 years the Acadians would be so mixed with Mi'kmaq and Wuastukwiuk as to form 'one race'.		

Most successful of all, however, were military commissions and, above all, medals. The presentation of medals was first proposed in 1739 and was implemented the following year. The ceremony quickly became essential for maintaining alliances.

The French were never as comfortable with their wilderness allies as Nelson and popular legend would have us believe. The Amerindians' concept of personal liberty made them uncertain allies at best. The fact that 'le sauvage n'a point de maître' ('the savage has no master')[7] meant that no single technique could be guaranteed to assure control. Abbé Maillard, after 14 years with the Amerindians, observed that he still did not know how to get them to behave as he would have liked.[8] Fur trader and explorer Nicholas Perrot (c. 1644–1717) put it another way: 'Le sauvage ne sçait ce c'est d'obéir: il faut plustost le prier que de le commander.' ('The savage does not know what it is to obey; one must request rather than command.')[9]

The King of France spent a good deal of time and energy, not to mention money, maintaining alliances with these people whose ideas of equality and individual freedom he would not have tolerated for an instant in his own subjects. He recognized, however, that if he were to realize France's colonial ambitions in Canada, it would be necessary to understand the Amerindians in order to Christianize them, to cooperate with them in order to provide an economic base through trade, and to cultivate

them in order to win their support as allies in war. New France's dependence on its Amerindians, both economically and militarily, forced the absolute monarchy of France to compromise some of its most cherished principles.

Historian Thomas C. Haliburton (1796–1865) expressed it differently: he said the French used the Amerindians for the front ranks of their defence, an innovation as useful in its own way as the traditional military posts.[10] Governor-General Beauharnois and Gilles Hocquart, intendant from 1729 to 1748, seemed to have such an idea in mind when they wrote to Jean-Frédéric Phélypeaux, Comte de Maurepas (1701–81, long-time minister to the King):

> It is highly important to preserve the Indians attached as they have always been to France; the English have been deterred from forming any settlement in Acadia solely to the dread of these Indians; and though the latter do in one respect embarrass the French, whose cattle they from time to time even publicly carry off for their support, the French are not sorry to see them residing in the Province, and themselves, as it were, under their protection.[11]

If the French cherished the Amerindians, as historian Francis Parkman (1823–93) wrote,[12] they did so no more than they thought necessary, and for solidly practical reasons. For their part, the Amerindians, unable to control French policy or the course of the Anglo–French conflict any more than they could that of the fur trade, nevertheless influenced the character of all three. France's Amerindian policy emerges as a blend of give-and-take, of giving when necessary to ensure alliance in trade and war, of taking when reaping the profits of the fur trade and the benefits of military actions.

In their campaign to win the hearts and minds of the Amerindians, officials pinned their faith on the women and children, the former because they were seen as hard-working, particularly in the case of the Huron, as they were the ones who tended the crops.[13] In the case of children, a program of sending selected ones to France was begun by the Recollects in 1620 and continued by the Jesuits in 1634.[14] The idea was that after a few years in France, the children would have become proficient in French and familiar enough with French ways that they would retain them upon their return to their native land. Not only that, but they would influence their countrymen to adopt French culture.[15] When the program did not achieve the expected results, it was discontinued amid recriminations about the perverse character of Amerindians.[16]

Attempts at establishing schools for Amerindian children within the colony also met with limited success. Neither day schools nor boarding schools worked out at first, perhaps because the curriculum the French thought appropriate had little relevance to the Amerindian way of life.[17] Another problem was the reluctance of the parents to part with their children, particularly for boarding school. Not only was French discipline foreign to the Amerindian way, but the diet and general regime all too often affected the children's health, to the point of death in some cases.[18] Accommodations were slowly worked out, but the situation remained far from satisfactory. The view that Amerindians were 'simple savages' in an unformed state of nature waiting to be moulded by a civilizing hand was proving to be wide of the mark.

French Law and Amerindians

A thorny question that was never fully resolved during the French regime concerned whether Amerindians were to be treated as allies or as subjects of the French monarch. Did French law apply to Amerindians in the colonies? Here the ambiguities of French policy towards Amerindians came into play: on the international level, and especially when dealing with colonial rivals, particularly the English, the French consistently disclaimed responsibility for the behaviour of their allies on the grounds that they were sovereign. When it came to dealing with Amerindians within their own settlements, however, officials were not always so clear as to which course to follow, although as the colony became more secure, a consensus developed favouring the enforcement of French law.

Champlain, for one, had no doubts as to his stand when two Frenchmen were killed by the Montagnais in 1617.[19] He waited until 1622 when the murderer, believed to have been Cherououny ('The Murderer', 'The Reconciled', d. 1627, a Montagnais chief), came to attend a banquet in honour of some Iroquois ambassadors. Champlain insisted on his expulsion and the following morning the Montagnais presented Champlain with 100 beaver skins to forget the incident. The French leader agreed to forgive the guilty man on the condition that he and his accomplice avow their crime before a meeting of the nations. This was done with considerable pomp on 31 July 1623 at Trois-Rivières and the Montagnais declared his allegiance to the French.[20]

A more clear-cut case occurred in 1664. It involved Robert Hache, an Algonquin who, while drunk, had raped the wife of an inhabitant of Ile d'Orléans. Hache's defence was that not only was he under the influence of the

white man's 'firewater', but he had also committed a white man's crime (rape seldom
occurred among Amerindians). When he
escaped during the trial, the attorney general
asked the colony's Sovereign Council for
advice. They in turn consulted with Algonquin, Montagnais, and Abenaki chiefs, who
pointed out that if the behaviour of their
young men sometimes gave grounds for complaint, the same could be said for that of young
Frenchmen among Amerindians. A Christian
Montagnais from Quebec, Noël Negabamat
(Tekouerimat, *c.* 1600–66), asked that the death
penalty not be invoked as his people had not
been aware of this penalty for rape; however, in
view of their long-standing friendship for the
French, his people would accept this law for
rape as well as for murder in the future. He also
asked that the French stop seizing an Indian
debtor's goods during war, when hunters were
away and could not provide for their families.
The council agreed that such cases deserved
special consideration. So, as far as murder and
rape were concerned, Montagnais and Abenaki
allies had agreed to accept French law.[21] At
Louisbourg also, Indians agreed to accept
French regulations and to follow them as carefully as they did their own customs. These rules
had been drawn up following complaints from
missionaries that their work was nullified
because chiefs would not punish their people.[22]

The question of imposing French law on the
Indians was extremely delicate, as the King
observed. The Amerindians regarded themselves as free and sovereign and did not take
kindly to being put into French prisons for
infractions of laws they knew nothing about
and would not have accepted if they had. As an
eighteenth-century Spanish visitor to Louisbourg saw the situation:

> These natives, whom the French term savages,
> were not absolutely subjects of the King of
> France, nor entirely independent of him. They

acknowledged him lord of the country, but
without any alteration in their way of living; or
submitting themselves to his laws; and so far
were they from paying any tribute, that they
received annually from France a quantity of
apparel, gunpowder and muskets, brandy and
several kinds of tools, in order to keep them
quiet and attached to the French interest; and
this has also been the political practice of that
crown with regard to the savages of Canada.[23]

In other words, as historian W.J. Eccles says,
the French had tacitly granted the Amerindians in the colony something akin to a special status. The French needed the Indians both
in their struggle against the British and in the
fur trade, and they could not risk alienating
them by a vigorous enforcement of French
laws.[24] Sociologist Denys Delâge has drawn
attention to the fact that lands set aside for
Indian villages were never subjected to
seigneurial dues as was otherwise the rule in
New France; neither were Indians living within
the colony subject to conscription in the militia.[25] Some of the allies, especially the Christianized Iroquois around Montreal, maintained
an active trade with the English despite French
disapproval.[26] Particularly after the outbreak of
colonial wars, the French were circumspect in
their treatment of their Indian allies, although
there were some exceptions. Shortly before the
end of the French regime, a contemporary
observer found that they:

> are assiduously caressing and courting them.
> Their missionaries are dispersed up and down
> their several cantonments, where they exercise
> every talent of insinuation, study their man-
> ners, nature and weaknesses, to which they
> flexibly accommodate themselves, and carry
> their points by these arts.[27]

That may be something of an overstate-
ment, but it does indicate the keen French

awareness of the importance of the alliances. Whenever the opportunity presented itself, however, the French imposed their laws as much as they could; as far as they were concerned, whether the Indians wanted it or not, the process of transforming them into subjects had been underway from the moment the colony was established, although this transformation was not fully realized during the French regime.

Personal Aspect: Kinship Underpinnings

The fundamental importance of kinship for Amerindians meant that even political and economic alliances had personal and social aspects. Kinship was more than biological; it could also be established by means of networks of names and affiliations, such as membership in clans. While intermixing and intermarriage occurred independently of such formal arrangements, they were nevertheless closely intertwined. In Canada, the mixing of the races began long before settlement as a consequence of the fishing industries, particularly sea mammal hunting (classed as 'fishing'), where Amerindian expertise was much in demand with consequent personal associations.[28]

Once permanent European settlement had begun early in the seventeenth century, it was at first characterized by a shortage of women. Europe had barely recovered from the demographic disaster of the Black Death, and there was reluctance on the part of land-based powers such as France to encourage emigration on any scale. The first groups that came out were largely male, sometimes selected for their particular trades skills; the official idea was that they would intermarry with the indigenous population, producing a French population overseas. In the words of Champlain to the Huron, 'Our young men will marry your daughters, and we shall be one people.'[29] It was

a policy approved by the Church as long as the brides were first converted to Catholicism.[30]

Such a course was also dictated by climate. At this time the Western world was in the throes of the Little Ice Age; the resultant drop in temperatures had been a factor in the disappearance of the Greenland colonies in the fifteenth century and was causing widespread hardship in Europe.[31] Some alpine villages even disappeared under advancing glaciers. Appropriately enough, during this period the stove with chimney was developed. In Canada, the rigours of the climate were more severe than those of Europe, even at the same latitude, a situation that aroused much speculation.[32] The problem was as fundamental as survival: too heavy a reliance on salted foods and lack of fresh provisions during the long winters meant that scurvy took a high toll.[33] Although Amerindians had shown Cartier how to cope with the problem of scurvy during the winter of 1535–6, the knowledge does not appear to have been passed on, and subsequent colonial attempts, such as those of Champlain, at first suffered severely. Such experiences led to the popular view in France of Canada as 'un lieu de horreur'.[34] In short, co-operation with Amerindians was necessary for Europeans to establish a viable colony, and when it came to selecting a mate, an Amerindian or, later, a Métis had obvious advantages over her European counterpart. Despite determined efforts from London to prevent it, this pattern of intermarriage was repeated among the English when they established themselves on Hudson Bay.[35] Among the French, white women occasionally married Amerindian men. One such case came to official attention when the husband, an Iroquois of Sault St Louis in the service of the French as a courier, requested a donkey to bring in family firewood, as his French wife was not accustomed to such work as Indian women were. The request was granted.[36] If the mixed-blood children were baptized they were accepted into the French community. An odd aside to this was the practice, particularly prevalent towards the end of the French regime, of giving illegitimate children to Amerindians. These children, as well as those taken captive from the English colonies, were raised and lived as Indians.[37]

Intermarriage was not a policy that had originated in Canada. A century earlier, in connection with the dyewood trade in Brazil, French had integrated into Amerindian communities and intermarried with their women.[38] Now, with colonization in view, officials wishing to avoid such 'Indianization' proposed sending French families to live among the Huron. The latter, seeing this as a form of exchange, thought it might be a good idea;[39] they did not at first perceive its purpose, which was to lead them into the French way of life. Intermixing was eased for the French by the widespread and persistent belief that Amerindians were really white, turning brown because of certain practices.[40]

The seriousness with which the French pursued the goal of 'one nation' is witnessed by their complaints to the Huron that 'you have not allied yourselves up to the present with our French people. Your daughters have married with all neighbouring nations but not with ours. . . . Not that we have need of your daughters. . . . But we would like to see only one people in all the land.'[41] The 'one people' they had in mind would, of course, be culturally French; a requirement for such intermarriage would be the conversion of the wives. As Paul Le Jeune observed, the aim was 'to make them like us'. To this end the Ursuline nuns came to the colony in 1639 for the express purpose of educating Amerindian girls in French ways. This would apply not only to religion but also in mundane matters such as running households. Similarly, the Jesuits had a program for teaching boys 'to make hatchets, knives, and other things which are very necessary to them'.[42]

Everything depended on getting the mobile hunters to settle down, to start clearing the land and farming after the French model; this was so firmly believed that the missionaries were prepared to have the necessary preparatory work done at their own expense.[43] Above all, Amerindians must learn to accept centralized authority, to which all would be subordinated.[44] In New France and Acadia, however, the opposite was happening, and many of the French who acquired Amerindian families were content 'to become barbarians, and to render themselves exactly like them'.[45] Indian self-confidence was such that on one occasion, Iroquois told the French 'we have learned to change Frenchmen into Hiroquois', but added diplomatically, 'let us rather say that they will become French and Hiroquois at the same time.'[46] The French were only too well aware of this possibility. Sagard had observed that the French, even though 'better instructed and raised in the school of the faith, become Savages simply by living with the Savages, and lose even the appearance of Christianity.'[47] This was happening at a time when missionaries were doing their best to get migratory hunters to settle into villages. Sagard told of Étienne Brûlé making a tobacco offering at the beginning of a voyage, which was one of the most successful he had ever made.[48] The well-known arrow sash, which would become a symbol of the voyageur and later of the Métis, was an adaptation of an Iroquoian burden-strap design.

The Huron had concerns about the terms the French would offer for a mixed marriage. First, what would be given for a wife? 'Among the Hurons, the custom was to give a great deal . . . a beaver robe and perhaps a porcelain collar.' Second, would the wife have all the couple's possessions at her disposal? Third, should the husband return to France, would he take his wife with him? If she remained, what would he leave her? Fourth, if the wife failed in her duty and her husband drove her away, what could she take with her? Or if she just wanted to return to her relatives? As the Jesuits observed, there were indeed many things to be considered.[49] As these questions make evident, the Huron, and other Indians as well, were concerned about the treatment of their women. In fact, they could be 'very much insulted when some foolish Frenchman dares to meddle with their women. Once, when a certain madcap took some liberties, they came and told our Captain that he should look out for his men, informing him that anyone who attempted to do that again would not stand much of a chance, that they would kill him on the spot.'[50]

Extent of Intermarriage

The extent to which intermarriage occurred will probably never be known because of the inadequacy of the record; officially, there were 120 mixed marriages during the French regime. Unofficially, unions often occurred according to the 'custom of the country', which the missionaries regarded as a form of concubinage.[51] Hints as to its prevalence are found in indirect evidence. Colonel Samuel Vetch, second English commander at Port Royal, 1710–13, noted that as the Acadians had contracted marriages with Amerindians who had converted, they had a strong influence over them.[52] A letter published in London in 1758 from a certain 'Monsieur de Varennes' claimed:

> We employ besides a much more effectual method of uniting them to us, and that is, by the intermarriage of our people with the savage women, which is a circumstance which draws the ties of alliance closer. The children produced by these are generally hardy, inured to the fatigues of the chace [sic] and war, and turn out very serviceable subjects in their way.[53]

Later in the same letter there is a description of Acadians, who had been dispersed by the English in 1755: 'They were a mixed breed, that is to say, most of them proceeded from marriages or concubinage of the savage women with the first settlers, who were of various nations, but chiefly French.'[54] That point had already been made by Maillard, 'Apostle to the Micmacs', who had written in 1753 that he did not expect more than 50 years to elapse before the French colonists were so mixed with the Mi'kmaq and Wuastukwiuk that it would be impossible to distinguish them.[55] Acadians appear to have been well on the way towards realizing the official goal of 'one race'. Indeed, some have recently rediscovered this heritage and are claiming Aboriginal status.[56]

Such mixing would have been encouraged by the exigencies of the fur trade, which was the economic reason for the colony in the first place. The trade remained the principal economic activity of the colony throughout the French regime and functioned best when certain formalities were observed. Not the least of these was intermarriage; Amerindian society, with its stress on kinship, much preferred this type of relationship as a basis for its trading alliances. Because of this approach, such marriages were usually seen by the Amerindians as bringing honour to their people. One enthusiastic report even had this reaching the point of the children speaking French rather than the language of their mothers.[57]

> When a Frenchman trades with them [Amerindians], he takes into his services one of their Daughters, the one, presumably, who is most to his taste; he asks the Father for her, & under certain conditions, it is arranged; he promises to give the Father some blankets, a few shirts, a Musket, Powder & Shot, Tobacco & Tool; they come to an agreement at last, & the exchange is made. The Girl, who is familiar with the Country, undertakes, on her part, to serve the Frenchman in every way, to dress his pelts, to sell his Merchandise for a specified

length of time; the bargain is faithfully carried out on both sides.[58]

Historians of the fur trade in the Northwest will recognize this description, as it so closely parallels what happened in that region at a later date. In the eastern trade, no less than in that of the Northwest, women played a vital role, both because of their family connections and because of their particular skills. Only recently have historians begun to pay attention to this fundamental aspect of our early history, mainly in connection with the much better documented Northwest.[59]

Such an arrangement for accommodating fur traders was facilitated by Amerindian attitudes towards marriage. While kinship was all-important to them, they did not consider marriage to be necessarily permanent, particularly if no children were involved; among some peoples, such as the Iroquoians, the women had as much liberty in this regard as the men.[60] Besides, polygyny was an integral part of their social and economic frameworks. As far as they were concerned, it was perfectly acceptable for a European trader to take one of their women to wife even if he were known to have another back in his own community. Inevitably, such arrangements developed, not only within the framework of the fur trade but also within that of military alliances. Two outstanding French envoys who had concurrent French and Indian wives were Paul Le Moyne de Maricourt (1663–1704) with the Onondaga and Louis-Thomas Chabert de Joncaire (*c.* 1670–1739) with the Seneca.[61] This was one of the principal aspects of the 'disorderliness' and 'libertinage' of the frontier that aroused the condemnation of the missionaries. In general they supported intermarriage as long as their rules were obeyed; they also wanted to see those rules extended into Amerindian societies. On the western frontier, however, they were even less in control of the situation than they were at Quebec and

Montreal; not only were Frenchmen living in Amerindian villages, many of them were trading with the English.[62] Missionaries, particularly the Jesuits, became convinced that the best way to regularize and stabilize marriages according to European Christian practice would be to offer official incentives.[63] Persistent lobbying on their part bore fruit in 1680, when Versailles budgeted 3,000 *livres* for dowries of 50 *livres* each for French and Indian girls who married Frenchmen; later, 1,000 *livres* were budgeted for Indian girls to be taught French housekeeping skills with a view to making 'marriages customary between these girls and the French'. But support, even when official, did not produce the results the Jesuits had confidently expected. Few claimed the dowry, and officials were soon complaining that Indian girls were not marrying into the colony.[64] The dowries remained in the budget until 1702; the provision for the education of Amerindian girls continued.

In the meantime, on the frontier mixed marriages 'according to the custom of the country' were common.[65] Missionaries occasionally paused in their condemnations to see a positive side to the situation. Jesuit Julien Bineteau (1660–99) wrote from the Illinois country in 1699: 'There are also some women married to some of our Frenchmen who would be a good example to the best regulated households in France. Some of those who are married to Savages manifest extraordinary care in maintaining piety in their families.'[66]

Colonial Opposition to Intermarriage

By early in the eighteenth century, colonial opposition to intermarriage was growing.[67] On the official level, this reflected the difficulties the French were having in maintaining alliances in the Old Northwest; in that region at least, 'one race' was proving to be of doubtful value as a political instrument.[68] The French never developed as secure alliances in the Great Lakes region as they had been able to do in the Maritimes. For one thing, the English by then were actively competing for Amerindian loyalty, which put the Natives in a good bargaining position. For the Métis, with a foot in both European and Amerindian camps (more often the latter), it placed a premium on their services as interpreters and go-betweens.[69] These political factors, coupled with the economic importance of the fur trade for which the Métis were especially well-qualified and the remoteness of the Old Northwest from centres of official control, meant that a Métis sense of separate identity began to emerge. It was a trend that alarmed French officialdom, contrary as it was to its purpose of 'one race'. Maurepas was among those who thought that the missionaries were too liberal in this regard and observed that they should not be so casual about marrying Frenchmen to Amerindian women.[70] This was initially expressed in the Old Northwest, where such marriages predominated. First of all, restrictions were placed on the right of Amerindian women to inherit their French husbands' property, a measure contrary to the provisions of Article 17 of the charter of the Company of New France. This was followed in 1735 by an edict requiring the consent of the governor or commanding officer for all mixed marriages.[71] As the goal of 'one nation' faded in the face of the emerging reality of a people who would eventually consider themselves a 'new nation', a new political dimension was forming that would be far removed from the original colonial purpose of forging a New France overseas. Its consequences in the later history of Canada would be profound, as shall be seen.

An intriguing aspect of this intermixing is that a pidgin or creole language did not develop within the general context of the fur trade; French was the operative means of communication, although English was also in use.[72]

Pidgin (or perhaps pre-pidgin) did develop on the North Atlantic coast between the Basques and Algonkians; and on the Northwest Coast, fur traders would later adapt the pre-existing Chinook jargon to their needs.[73] The large number of French words it incorporated points to the predominance of that language in the trade. Linguist George Lang theorizes that the absence of a general fur-trade pidgin was due to the language skills of the voyageur, whose bilingualism (or perhaps multilingualism) precluded the development of a creole language.[74] What did appear among Métis of Plains and parklands was Michif, a fully developed language that combines French nouns and noun phrases with the Plains Cree verbal system; Bakker says that it is neither a pidgin nor an interlanguage but must be considered a mixed language, a rare phenomenon.[75] Its Cree and French components are correctly used, which means that those who created it must have been fully bilingual.[76] Michif has been called the 'nec plus ultra' of contact languages.[77] Once believed to have been restricted to the southeastern parklands in the Turtle Mountain region of Manitoba and North Dakota, it has been revealed to be much more widespread, reaching into northwestern Alberta, where it is called 'Métis Cree'; in parts of its more easterly range, it incorporates Ojibwa as well. The Manitoba Métis Federation was surprised to discover some of this while conducting a project of recording elders' recollections. Serious study of this phenomenon has only just begun.[78]

Amerindian societies had displayed far more strength than the French had expected in their colonization of New France. Other colonizing powers had similar experiences, varying in contexts and policies but all delivering a similar message. In Charlevoix's view, Amerindians were 'true philosophers', as they had their priorities straight. He illustrated this by telling of a group of Iroquois who had visited Paris in

1666, and who had been shown royal residences 'and all the beauties of our great city, but who still preferred their home villages'.[79]

French officialdom tended to be baffled by such cultural resistance, genuinely puzzled at the 'blindness' of the Amerindians to the benefits of French civilization. Some individuals showed insight; for instance, Lescarbot wrote that 'one cannot root out all at once customs and habitual ways of doing things from a people, whoever they are.'[80] Such perceptions seldom penetrated to official levels, however.

Part III

Spread Across the Continent

Chapter 12

Amerindians in a Shifting World

Treaties and Alliances

Alliances and treaties are concomitant with trade and war, and the situation in Acadia and New France was no exception. Although the French had learned in Brazil how useful and profitable alliances with Amerindians could be in matters of trade, when it came to their first attempt to colonize in the New World, at Charlesbourg-Royal near the St Lawrence Iroquoian village of Stadacona (today's Quebec) in 1541–3, they proceeded on the basis that this region was *terra nullius*, uninhabited land.[1] The argument was not original with them (it had been used by Spaniards and Portuguese, and would also be used by the English); its gist was that since the Amerindians led a mobile life without settled abode, 'ranging' the land 'like beasts in the woods', they could not be classed as inhabitants according to European law. Further, since Europeans believed that Christian rights prevailed over those of non-Christians, the French had no qualms about claiming possession and attempting to establish a colony without the Indians' permission. They never recognized Aboriginal right; for

instance, the French monarch never expressed any doubt about his right to dispose of Amerindian lands to French subjects, as he did in 1627 with the grant of all of North America that was not already occupied by a Christian prince to the Company of One Hundred Associates (also known as the Company of New France). Similarly, in 1651 he granted letters patent to the Jesuits 'giving them rights of fishery in all lands acquired by them in both North and South America, and permission to establish themselves in all Islands, or places on the mainland, wherever it shall seem good to them, in America.'[2] Assumption of sovereignty was one thing; realizing it with settlement would prove to be something else again. Charlesbourg-Royal's failure pointed to the need for Amerindian co-operation if colonization was to be successful in those northern regions, where ecological conditions were not within the range of the experience of French settlers.

As we have already seen, the French had had little difficulty in working out agreements for establishing trade, as in Brazil for dyewood. They had done this by negotiating

TIMELINE

1760	Fall of Montreal to British. British Commander-in-Chief Jeffrey Amherst ends 'gift' distributions to Amerindians.	1766	Ratification of agreements at Fort Ontario, at which Pontiac dominates.
1760s–70s	Pan-Indian alliance, the Federation of Seven Fires, forms to resist loss of lands to settlers, but doesn't survive colonial distrust and US War of Independence.	1769	Pontiac murdered by Illinois tribesman.
		1774	Quebec Act brings Ohio Valley and Great Lakes region under Quebec jurisdiction; Americans object that their legitimate expansion is being thwarted.
1762	Amerindian alliance, led by Pontiac, Odawa war chief, lays siege to Fort Detroit for five months.	1775	American invasion of eastern Canada repulsed for two weeks by Iroquois.
1763	Treaty of Paris effectively ends French presence in North America. Proclamation of 1763 at least partially acknowledges Amerindian territorial rights. Nine British forts, including Fort Michilimackinac, fall to Amerindians in May–June. Neolin, 'The Delaware Prophet', calls to drive Europeans back into the sea. Amherst proposes giving Indians smallpox-infested blankets.	1776–83	Amerindians caught up on both sides of US War of Independence.
		1783	Peace of Paris to end conflict between Britain and Thirteen Colonies completely ignores Amerindians.
		1784	Loyalist Iroquois granted Six Nations Reserve (Haldimand Grant) on Grand River in Upper Canada after cession of 3 million acres on Niagara Peninsula.
1764	Peace conference at Fort Niagara formed by Sir William Johnson: 2,000 Amerindians from 19 tribes respond, but Pontiac does not go.	late 1700s– early 1800s	Millions of acres in present-day southern and central Ontario ceded by Ojibwa and Odawa.
1765	Pontiac signs separate agreement, but does not give up Indian lands.		

and establishing ongoing relations within the framework of Amerindian custom. While such give-and-take was tolerated in the realm of trade, it was not at first seen as appropriate where permanent settlement under the French flag was concerned. It took the failures of the colonization attempts on the St Lawrence, in Brazil (1555–60), and in Florida (including parts of today's South Carolina, 1562–5) to spur France into serious reconsideration of her policies. One of the more widespread criticisms that emerged out of these disasters was that the French had not given proper consideration to their indigenous allies when they had attempted colonization and had even antagonized them by being 'rude and tyrannical'.[3] There were others who thought that co-operation in itself was not enough; strong leadership backed by military and naval force was needed.[4] France would use a combination of both in her colonial enterprises, but her flexibility in dealing with Indians on their own terms made her reputation as the most successful of all the colonizers in the New World in establishing a rapport with its Aboriginal inhabitants. This flexibility, it should be emphasized again, was more evident in trade than in matters relating to colonization.

The English, not trusting oral agreements, insisted on European-style written treaties; in relying on European traditions, they assumed the presence of hierarchy and centralized authority in Amerindian societies.[5] As this usually did not equate with the political realities of the communities they encountered (in Canada, the possible exceptions would have been some of the chiefdoms of the Northwest Coast), they, too, had to adapt and on occasion entered into unwritten agreements, but they resisted such expedients. Even with the written treaties, it is not clear what legal status the English accorded to them, even at the time; since no colonizing power considered Amerindians to be sovereign, they could not have been considered to be international agreements, although the rhetoric they evoked easily gave that impression. So far as is known, none of these treaties were put through the procedure in the British Parliament that would have been necessary for such a status to have been recognized, nor have Canadian courts made such an acknowledgement. Where 'Indian title' was admitted, there was no agreement among colonizers as to what it included. What was agreed was that a 'savage' could never validly exercise sovereignty, which was a power recognized only for peoples living within organized states. Some further specified that the states had to be Christian. The legal nature of the treaties has never been fully clarified.[6]

The first of the British treaties that included Indians in what is now Canada was the Treaty of Portsmouth, New Hampshire, signed in 1713. The Canadian Amerindians involved were those of the St John River, largely Wuastukwiuk but perhaps including some Mi'kmaq and Abenaki. The treaty was for peace and friendship, similar to previous agreements, but broke new ground by adding that Amerindians were not to be molested in the territories where they lived, and they were to enjoy 'free liberty for Hunting, Fishing, Fowling, and all other [of]

their Lawful Liberties & Privileges'.[7] These provisions were repeated in the Treaty of Boston, 1725 (Chapter 7). This treaty included Mi'kmaq of Cape Sable and other areas, as well as Wuastukwiuk. At the same time the British took advantage of the disarray of Indians following the defeat at Norridgewock to insist on another agreement, Treaty No. 239, sometimes called Mascarene's Treaty after its principal British negotiator.[8] Its purpose was to get Mi'kmaq, Wuastukwiuk, and Abenaki to agree that the Treaty of Utrecht had made the British Crown 'the rightful possessor of the Province of Nova Scotia or Acadia according to ancient boundaries'.[9] That the British took such measures to get the Amerindians to 'acknowledge His said Majesty King George's jurisdiction and dominion over the territories of the said Province of Nova Scotia or Acadia' and to make their submission to him indicates the troubles they were having in this regard.

A principal problem was getting the signatures of all those affected, as Amerindians did not accept that one could sign for all; at most a chief could sign for his immediate band, and then only if its members had been consulted and were in agreement. In the case of the two treaties signed at Boston, this meant arranging ratifications and confirmations because, unless all the chiefs and groups considered themselves included, agreements of any kind were at best only partially effective. Tracking down the chiefs and their bands was a slow process that at first did not much influence the course of the Mi'kmaq War.

Another problem was that of language. Negotiations had to be conducted through interpreters, who apparently were not always scrupulous with their renditions of proposed terms or points made in discussion.[10] As Recollect missionary Sagard observed, interpreters often missed the point either from 'ignorance or contempt, which is a very dangerous thing as it has often led to big accidents'.[11] Even if honest attempts were made, direct translations could be difficult if not impossible, as missionary Maillard experienced with the Mi'kmaq.[12] The British sought to deal with this by including statements in the final draft that its terms had been carefully read and interpreted, and the Indians agreed they understood what was involved. With the Boston treaty, it was noted that its terms had been 'read distinctly' by 'Sworn Interpreters'. In 1749, a ratification of Treaty No. 239 by the Amerindians of St John River included the acknowledgement that its terms had been 'faithfully interpreted to us [the native signers] by Madame de Bellisle, inhabitant of this river, nominated by us for that purpose'.[13] The problems, however, continued; for one, the two 1725 treaties were not always clearly distinguished. Compounding the problems were grave difficulties in translating concepts, such as that of exclusive landownership, which had no counterpart in Native languages. This situation was never satisfactorily resolved throughout the treaty-making period, up to and including the last of the numbered treaties in western Canada, Treaty Eleven, signed in 1921. As confusions and even deceptions proliferated, so did suspicion and distrust on both sides.

Annuities first appeared in the Halifax Treaty of 1752, signed with the Shubenacadie band of Mi'kmaq. It took the form of promising regular gift distributions, probably an indication of the importance the British attached to this treaty, which was a major break in the prolonged hostilities with the Mi'kmaq. It also acknowledged the Mi'kmaq's right to 'free liberty of Hunting and Fishing as usual' and 'to trade to the best Advantage'.[14] During negotiations, the Mi'kmaq chief, Major Jean-Baptiste (Joseph) Cope (Coppe, d. 1758/60), held that 'the Indians should be paid for the land the English had settled upon in this country.'[15] This was not a point the British were yet ready to agree to, at least in Nova Scotia, for reasons already noted. The peace established by the treaty was soon broken when Mi'kmaq killed two Englishmen.

The 1763 Treaty of Paris formally ended the presence of the French in continental North America when, according to historian Max Savelle, they handed over the largest extent of territory ever covered 'by any treaty dealing with the American hemisphere before or since'.[16]

A Difficult New World

If the defeat of France in the New World was a bitter blow to French Canada, it was a disaster for many Amerindians, from the east coast to the Great Lakes and even westward. Besides depriving them of their bargaining position between two rival powers, it also cut them off with brutal suddenness from their 'presents'. To make matters worse, although Article 40 of the capitulation of the French at Montreal in 1760 guaranteed Amerindians (particularly Britain's allies) protection for the lands they inhabited, it quickly proved to be difficult to enforce.[17] Colonial governments displayed little, if any, will to evict squatting settlers.

British Commander-in-Chief Jeffrey Amherst (1717–97) lost no time introducing economies after the fall of Montreal. Among the first items to be cut were the 'gift' distributions; now that the French were gone, the British did not see the necessity of maintaining a custom that in their eyes was little better than bribery. Amherst, for his part, was adamant against 'purchasing the good behavior, either of Indians, or of any others'. In Amerindian eyes, the annual gift-giving ceremonies not only symbolized the renewal of English/Amerindian alliances, they were also the agreed-upon price by which the Indians allowed the English to use their lands. To complicate matters, Amerindians had come to depend on such items as guns and ammunition. Sir William Johnson (Warraghiyagey, 'He Who Does Much Business'), northern superintendent for

12.1

Proclamation line of 1763

Source: Waldman, *Atlas of the North American Indian.*

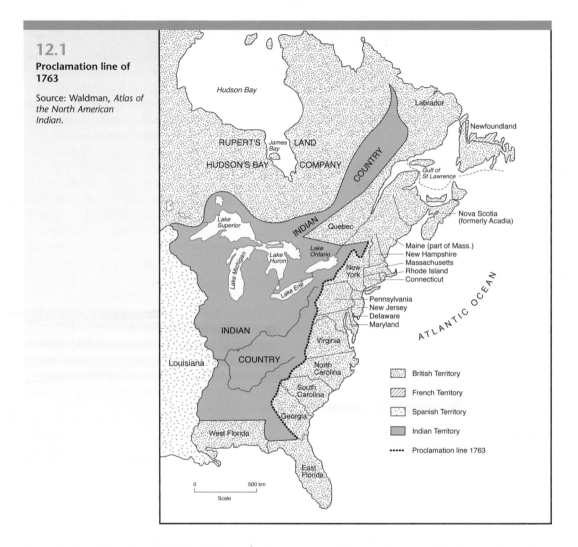

Hudson Bay

Labrador

Newfoundland

RUPERT'S   James   LAND
            Bay

HUDSON'S BAY   COMPANY

INDIAN   COUNTRY

Gulf of St Lawrence

Lake Superior

Lake Michigan

Lake Huron

Lake Ontario

Quebec

Nova Scotia (formerly Acadia)

Maine (part of Mass.)
New Hampshire
Massachusetts
Rhode Island
Connecticut

New York

Lake Erie

Pennsylvania
New Jersey
Delaware
Maryland

INDIAN

Virginia

COUNTRY

Louisiana

North Carolina

South Carolina

Georgia

West Florida

East Florida

ATLANTIC OCEAN

	British Territory
	French Territory
	Spanish Territory
	Indian Territory
•••••	Proclamation line 1763

0   500 km
Scale

Amerindian affairs from 1755 to 1774, strongly advised Amherst against the cutback, observing that 'the Indians grow more & more convinced that we are trifling with them & neither mean to regulate Trade or prevent Any of the abuses they daily complain of.'[18] He was not heeded. In coastal regions, the situation was further complicated by the continuing activities of French trading ships.[19]

Britain's Amerindian allies had been led to believe that once the French were driven out, encroaching settlers would also go; but when the French left, more settlers than ever moved into their territories.[20] The allies had been promised that with peace they would be getting better deals in trade; instead, British traders raised their prices, claiming that they had had to sell unprofitably low during the war. During hostilities the British had co-operated with Amerindian leaders to limit the liquor trade in order to preserve them as allies, but with peace they displayed much less interest in protecting the Natives from the traffic that was so deleterious to them yet highly profitable to the settlers.[21] Traders swarmed into Amerindian territory, where they all too often behaved badly; the Amerindians were powerless to control them, and colonial governments found it inexpedient to do so. The British were aware that such behaviour and malpractices were causing the Amerindians to desert from their alliances.[22] Even though, in the words of Peter Wraxall, New York's secretary for Indian Affairs, 1750–9, trade was 'the chief Cement which binds us together', it had its perils for both Amerindians and whites. Nonetheless, trade was the 'first Principle of our whole System of Indian politics'.[23]

The Amerindians, on whichever side they found themselves, had seen the struggle between the French and English as the concern of the combatants, in which they (the Aboriginals) were involved only as fighting allies; they had no conception that their lands were at stake. As more than one chief remarked, it had not been the Indians who had been conquered. This land was their land, and they had allowed the Europeans to come and settle on it under certain conditions, such as the gift distributions. Ojibwa chief Minweweh (Minavavana, c. 1710–70), 'The one of the silver tongue' also known as 'Le Grand Sauteur', who had fought with the French and who allied with Pontiac, voiced a general sentiment when he told the British: 'Although you have conquered the French, you have not conquered us. We are not your slaves. These lakes, these woods and mountains were left us by our ancestors. They are our inheritance, and we will part with them to none.'[24] The British, uneasily aware of Amerindian fears about losing their lands, would move eventually to reassure them by at least partially acknowledging their territorial rights in the Proclamation of 1763.

In the meantime, discontent spread and rumours flew. Why were the British denying Amerindians the guns and ammunition they needed for the hunt, if not to wipe them out? Why were settlers being allowed to take over Amerindian lands? Even worse were the techniques being used by the newcomers to 'purchase' Amerindian lands and the extent of the lands involved. In 1756, Johnson had warned about the effects of such practices. As the Amerindians observed to George Croghan (d. 1782), a successful trader who for 15 years was Johnson's right-hand man, 'in either case they would lose their Lands, & the consideration they got was soon spent, altho' the Lands remained', but in the hands of the non-Aboriginals.[25] An Indian resistance loomed alarmingly close as councils were held and tribal nations met to share their grievances; out of this coalesced the Federation of Seven Fires (also called the Seven Nations of Canada), which has been described as an alliance network linking French mission Indians.[26] According to Delâge the central fire was maintained at Kahnawake, where the members gathered every three years. The confederacy did not survive the dislocations of the US War of Independence, or colonial distrust of anything that smacked of pan-Indianism.[27] Colonial officials were not unaware of the causes of Native unrest. In Croghan's view:

> The Indians are a very jealous people, and they had great expectations of being very generally supplied by us, and from their poverty and mercenary disposition they can't bear such disappointment. . . . if the Senecas, Delawares and Shawnees should break with us, it will end in a general war with all the western nations, though they at present seem jealous of each other.[28]

A British plan to control the traders by restricting trade to the posts and to eliminate rum failed, and Native resentment reached the boiling point. Johnson, in alarm, called a general peace conference at Detroit in 1761. Just before it opened, he received a letter from Amherst forbidding the issuance of gifts. Johnson considered the decision so unwise he ignored it for the moment; but the truth was not long in coming out, as other expected distributions did not take place. By the spring of 1762, Amerindians experienced a scarcity of goods, particularly of ammunition.

Into this troubled situation emerged a remarkable man, Pontiac (Ponteack, Pontiague, Obwandiyag, 1712/1725–69), an Odawa war chief. His origins are obscure, and we have only a vague idea of what he looked like.[29] His personality gave rise to contradictory reports: he was said to be imperious of manner, 'proud, vindictive, warlike, and very easily offended';[30] however, Major Robert Rogers (1731–95), who had gone to Detroit in the fall of 1760 with 200 of his famous Rangers, and who had reason to be grateful to Pontiac for having prevented his warriors from attacking the British contingent, found him to be a man of 'great strength of judgment and a thirst after knowledge'. According to Major Rogers, Pontiac was not only prepared to accept British settlement but even to encourage it, but he expected to be treated with respect and honour.[31] A British officer was also impressed: 'He is in a manner Ador'd by all the Nations hereabouts, and He is more remarkable for His integrity & humanity than either French Man or Indian in the Colony.' Although he had fought on the side of the French, when Montreal fell he had quickly moved to establish good relations with the British, on the strength of the latter's promises of more liberal treatment in trade. When that did not produce the desired results he again turned to the French, this time those who had remained in the Old Northwest, but they refused to co-operate with their erstwhile ally.

Pontiac appears to have supported a movement among the Amerindians that claimed a spiritual vision had called for the return to the ways of their ancestors. This was an early manifestation of nativistic movements by which Amerindians sought to cope with the invasion of their lands and missionary pressures against their way of life. Neolin ('One That Is Four', *fl.* 1760s), one of two known as 'The Delaware Prophet', urged his people to abstain completely from contact with whites: 'I warn you, that if you allow the English among you, you are dead, maladies, smallpox, and their poison will destroy you totally, you must pray to me and do only my will.'[32]

During the summer of 1762, a war belt and hatchet circulated through the Old Northwest. Resentment had been building for well over a year, encouraged by the French residents still in the area. That fall, the Seneca struck the first blow by killing two traders; a month later, two British soldiers were killed in the Ohio Valley. Pontiac, after a series of successful engagements against the English, sought to take Fort Detroit by a ruse. His plan betrayed, Pontiac laid siege instead, an unusual action for Amerindians, who in general did not like attacking fortifications. Tecumseh would later express Amerindian feelings about this type of warfare: 'It is hard to attack people who live like groundhogs.'[33] The siege lasted for five months. Minweweh and Madjeckewiss (Machiquawish, among other variations, *c.* 1735–*c.*1805) had better luck with a similar ruse against Fort Michilimackinac, when they organized the well-known lacrosse game that allowed their warriors to gain entrance to the fort and overwhelm its garrison. Between 16 May and 20 June 1763, nine British forts fell. The only posts in the war zone that remained in British hands were those at Detroit (Pontiac's men had given up by the end of October), Niagara, and Fort Pitt. Fort Pitt had been rescued by an expeditionary force under Colonel Henry Bouquet (1719–65), a Swiss-born officer who had learned something from Indian tactics. He taught his troops to move while firing, to form a circle when pressed, and to use the bayonet. The bayonet, like the sword, was not generally adopted by Amerindians. Despite the British success in this hard-fought engagement, by the end of the summer the Indians were in control of most of the Old Northwest. The system of garrisoned forts had not proven effective against Amerindians.

Neolin's call to drive the Europeans back into the sea seemed to be on its way to success. In his exhortations, he used a diagram painted on deerskin to illustrate how non-Aboriginals were blocking Indians from the enjoyment of their lands.[34] As his influence increased, so did that of Pontiac, despite the failure at Detroit. Prominent as he was, Pontiac does not appear to have been the originator of the troubles, which were more in the nature of a spontaneous combustion.[35] It was the most formidable Native uprising faced by the British during the eighteenth century.

Amherst's immediate reaction was to underestimate both its scope and importance. Not having much regard for Amerindians, he at first did not believe they were capable of such feats. When he was finally convinced, he urged that every method be used against them, including that notorious recommendation about distributing smallpox-infected blankets in their encampments; he also advocated the use of drugs. Those who were wise in the ways of Amerindians counselled patience, as the fire would burn itself out. The Amerindians had no use for the forts they were taking; they were after the supplies.

Indeed, the winter of 1763–4 passed without serious incident, as the Indians dispersed to their hunting grounds equipped with pillaged goods. When they began to run short, especially of ammunition, some voluntarily brought back prisoners in a gesture for peace and others returned to their British alliance. The British had reprisals on their minds, however, and insisted on sending out retaliatory expeditions. One of these, under the command of Colonel Bouquet, succeeded in obtaining the release of 200 prisoners and the promise of release for 100 more. The British soon learned that retribution was not a realistic policy, not only because Amerindians were so hard to find but because even when they were located, the only punishment that could be meted out was either to kill them or to deprive them of their horses and possessions, neither of which served the purpose.

Sir William Johnson sought to resolve the situation by convoking a peace conference at Fort Niagara in 1764. About 2,000 Amerindians from 19 tribes responded to his call, but Pontiac was not among them. Johnson's technique was that of divide and conquer, dealing with each tribe separately. Among other items, they were asked to return all prisoners immediately, compensate traders for their losses, and break off relations with enemies of the British. Future grievances were to be submitted to the commandant at Detroit. An important item was an agreed-upon schedule of values for trade goods. The following year, 1765, Pontiac signed a separate agreement, in which he stipulated that France's surrender of its forts to the English did not mean that the latter could automatically take over the Indians' land, as the French had been only tenants of the Natives. He agreed that the British could reoccupy their forts, but hunting grounds must remain undisturbed.

When the final ratification of the agreements took place at a general gathering at Fort Ontario in 1766, Pontiac was a dominant figure and was allowed by Johnson to speak on behalf of all. That did not sit well with the other chiefs, and from then on his influence rapidly diminished. Three years later Pontiac was murdered by an Illinois tribesman, said to have been bribed by an English trader. Contrary to expectations, apart from some isolated killings, Pontiac's death did not ignite general inter-tribal warfare.[36] Still, the quiet that settled over the frontier was not a reconciled one, neither for the Amerindians nor for the frontiersmen.

Although figures are not available, Amerindian losses during the resistance appear to have been negligible. In contrast, the settlers counted about 2,000 killed or captured and tremendous property damage. Despite the toll, European settlement had not been seriously deterred, and the fur trade had been affected hardly at all. Pontiac, like Nescambiouit of the Abenaki and Kiala of the Fox before him, had perceived the need for united action against the Europeans but had not been able to achieve it on a scale sufficient to change the course of events.

Worsening Position

Instead of holding the balance of power between two imperial rivals as they had when France was present, Indians now found themselves jockeying for position between an imperial power, Great Britain, and her restive Thirteen Colonies, who would soon gain their independence as the United States of America. Under the earlier arrangement, both Britain and France had something to gain from Amerindian alliances; in the new situation, only Britain at first found it expedient to court such arrangements. In this regard, she had stepped into France's shoes, a not always comfortable fit.

The Quebec Act of 1774 brought the Ohio Valley and Great Lakes region under the jurisdiction of Quebec, one of the results of which was the transfer of the headquarters of the fur trade from Albany to Montreal. This shift in colonial administration superseded the arrangement made by the Proclamation of 1763; later, the argument would be made that it also abrogated the Proclamation's measures in respect to Indian lands. It has not been sustained, and today the Proclamation remains embedded in the Canadian Constitution. At the time, the British assured the Amerindians that they were protecting their territory against the illegal encroachments of settlers. The Thirteen Colonies had a different view: they felt that they were being deliberately thwarted in what they saw as a legitimate expansion. For them, the Act was provocation enough to launch their War of Independence. In 1775, Massachusetts entered into negotiations with the Mi'kmaq and Penobscots, and the following year a group of Mi'kmaq signed a treaty at Watertown, by which they agreed to send men to the American army. But most of the people were opposed, and the treaty was quickly disavowed.

Using the American precedent as an excuse, General Thomas Gage, commander-in-chief of the British forces from 1763 to 1775, issued an order to Guy Carleton, governor of Quebec, 1766–77, to use Amerindians on the frontier. Carleton delayed implementing the order; for one thing, the fur trade was booming, and Britain was building trading posts in the West (Fort Mackinac, on Mackinac Island, was built in 1780).[37] In eastern Canada, however, the story was different as Americans invaded in 1775, an action that brought the Iroquois of Kahnawake into the conflict. The Amerindians repulsed two assaults but became convinced that they were being sacrificed to protect British troops and went home. Their action had delayed the American invasion by nearly two weeks.

Amerindians, particularly the Iroquois, were by now deeply involved in the conflict, despite efforts to maintain the neutrality they had decided on after the Treaty of Montreal at the beginning of the century. It split the League of Six Nations: the Mohawks, guided by the influential Mary Brant (Konwatsi?tsiaié'nni, c. 1736–96) and her younger brother, the war chief Joseph (Thayendanegea, 1743–1807), were pro-British.[38] (Joseph had made a trip to England in 1775, during which he had been lionized by British society.) So were the Cayugas. The Mohawks' 'little brothers', the Oneidas, and the

Tuscaroras favoured the Americans. The Oneida had been influenced by the New England missionary Rev. Samuel Kirkland (1741–1808) as well as the 'matchless' oratory of the Seneca Red Jacket (Otatiani, Sagoyewotha, 'He Keeps Them Awake', *c.* 1750–1830), Brant's opponent.[39] The Seneca and Onondaga were split. Lines were fluid as inner dissensions increased; external relations also suffered, and attempts to form a united Amerindian front got nowhere. For one example, when the Cherokee went on the warpath in 1776, they went alone. As the Iroquois phrased it, the White Tree of Peace had been uprooted.[40]

The peace that was signed between Great Britain and the US in Paris in 1783 completely ignored the Amerindians. No provisions were made for their lands in the transfer of territory to the Americans; in particular, the cession of the Ohio Valley aroused a violent reaction on the part of British allies. Once more, Indians had to face the unpleasant fact that siding with the losing side in a European-style war meant loss of lands, even if they themselves had not been defeated. As the Iroquois bitterly observed, they had not been defeated in the war, but they certainly were by the peace; Americans flatly rejected proposals for the establishment of a separate indigenous state. The British, in an effort to placate their allies, did not evacuate the western posts as provided for in the treaty, a stance that would lead to prolonged wrangling with the Americans.[41] For Indians dislodged by the war, the posts became a refuge as 2,000 fled during the winter of 1784.[42] For the 5,000 or so Iroquois refugees who congregated between the Genesee River and Niagara, the British negotiated with the Mississauga, as they called the Ojibwa on the north shore of Lake Ontario, and purchased land along the Grand River in Upper Canada. Although the original grant of 1784 has been much reduced since, the Six Nations are still there.

American pressure eventually forced the British to vacate the western posts, which they

Joseph Brant, Mohawk war chief, as portrayed during a visit to England, 1775–6. This portrait was published in *The London Magazine*, July 1776. *(Metropolitan Toronto Reference Library, J. Ross Robertson Collection, T-15494)*

agreed to by the Jay Treaty of 1794 and put into effect two years later. For the Amerindians, this meant the loss of a buffer against the steadily increasing pressures from the east. On the positive side, the treaty provided for unhindered passage for Indians over the border between Canada and the United States, and exempted them from levies on personal goods. These have not been provisions that either side has been careful about honouring. The treaty did not apply to the Amerindians of Rupert's Land.[43]

Proclamations

Long before the uprising, the British had recognized that pressures on land as well as 'the shameful manner' in which trade was conducted in Amerindian territory were inciting Native restiveness. Following the defeat of France, even before the terms of the Peace of Paris were concluded in 1763, officials moved to correct the situation by means of a series of proclamations.[44]

The first one, in 1761, issued to the governors of Nova Scotia, New Hampshire, New York, North and South Carolina, and Georgia, forbade them to grant lands or make settlements that would interfere with Amerindians bordering on those colonies. Any settlers found to be unlawfully established upon Amerindian lands were to be evicted. There were to be no more sales of Amerindian lands without official authorization—in other words, a licence, which was to be issued only after the application had been approved by the Commissioners for Trade and Plantations in London.

When Jonathan Belcher, lieutenant-governor of Nova Scotia, 1761–3, inquired about land claims in the colony, he was told that the Mi'kmaq had a right to use the sea coast from Cape Fronsac 'onwards'. Belcher had sought London's position because of what he considered to be the 'extravagant and unwarrantable demands' of the Mi'kmaq. He also worried about the Acadians remaining in the colony after their expulsion of 1755, as he felt they were working to incite the Amerindians against the British.

A wave of Amerindian complaints that these instructions were not being honoured led to their reassertion and clarification in 1762. The south coast of Nova Scotia from Chaleur Bay to Canso to Musquodoboit Bay, about 35 kilometres east of Halifax, was to be reserved for the Mi'kmaq. Hardly had this proclamation been issued, however, than the French investment of St John's during the summer of 1762 made the reservation of coastal territories for the Mi'kmaq a dead letter.

The Proclamation of 1763, following hard on the heels of the Peace of Paris of that same year, was concerned with more than Amer-

indian affairs; for example, there were the forms of government to be established in newly acquired territories (a thorny issue in Quebec) and the management of frontier settlements to be worked out.[45] The Proclamation had been a long time in the making as a consequence of such continuing confrontations as the Mi'kmaq War; however, its issuance was precipitated by the troubles in the Far Northwest. Even though it was originally conceived as a temporary measure, to make it operative agreements had to be worked out as to where the boundaries lay between Indian territory and the colonies. The process took five years and involved 10 treaties.[46] Although the Proclamation appears to have been intended to apply to the Maritime colonies, it was not acted upon by their governments and so became a dead letter in those regions.[47]

The Proclamation is best known for its provision that all lands that had not been ceded to or purchased by Britain and that formed part of British North America were to be considered 'reserved lands' for the indigenes. In practice this meant lands beyond the Appalachian Mountains and the western borders of Quebec, about a third of the North American interior, but its western boundaries were not defined. In its words, it applied to those lands 'to the Westward of the sources of the Rivers which fall into the Sea from the West and Northwest', which hardly clarifies the situation. Although it was not applied in Quebec or British Columbia, it included lands within established colonies that had not yet been ceded or purchased or set aside for Amerindians. It did not apply to Rupert's Land, whatever its boundaries were, deemed to be under the jurisdiction of the HBC; neither was it operative in the Arctic, which in any event had a different land-use pattern. The Crown reserved to itself the right to extinguish 'Indian title', resurrecting a policy legislated in Virginia in 1655 but which had fallen into disuse. In the legal terminology of the day, 'Indian title' meant rights of occupancy and use, not ownership in fee simple. It was assumed that Britain held underlying sovereign title, as the Proclamation's wording indicates: it was 'our' lands that were being reserved for Amerindians and to which the Crown was extending its protection. The areas that interested the Crown specifically were those that had potential for settlement, but it wanted to prevent 'unjust Settlement and fraudulent Purchase' of Indian lands, thus slowing down the pace of colonization in order to keep the peace on the frontier. This protection was not seen as extending to unceded Mi'kmaq and Wuastukwiuk lands because the British were still persisting in their view, dealt with in Chapter 6, that their title had already been extinguished twice over—first by French occupation and then by the Treaty of Utrecht.[48]

A question still being argued is whether the Proclamation recognized a pre-existing title or created it.[49] A movement in the courts towards the position that Amerindian title preceded colonization has been reversed by recent decisions that see Native rights as arising out of the Proclamation. This will be discussed in Chapter 23.

Effects on Treaties

After the 1763 Proclamation, treaties and administration took on a different character, a development that would find its continuity in Upper Canada. Priorities changed—instead of being primarily concerned with peace and secondarily (if at all) with land issues, treaties now focused primarily on land, secondarily on peace and friendship. This was a direct consequence of the Proclamation's reservation to the Crown of the right to acquire Indian lands, which henceforth was to be done only by a treaty negotiated at a public meeting. Land-cession treaties would be signed with the Aboriginal peoples of central and western

Canada (except for the Sioux who, apart from the Assiniboine, were late arrivals in the Canadian West and so had no traditional land base there) but not with those of the east or west coasts, the Maritimes, Lower Canada, or the Arctic; about one-half of Canada's lands have been formally ceded by Amerindians to the government.[50]

The year following the Proclamation saw two treaties negotiated in Upper Canada that permitted British use of the portage at Niagara Falls in return for a trade agreement. Other provisions were similar to those of earlier treaties in other areas: the Amerindians were to keep the peace with the British, avoid helping the enemy, assist in the defence of British posts and supply routes, and return prisoners of war. The first was with the Huron/Wyandot of the Detroit/Windsor region, the other with the Seneca.[51] The second treaty was renegotiated with the Mississauga in 1781, whom the British now recognized as the rightful owners of the land in question, a strip six kilometres wide along the west bank of the Niagara River. The price agreed on by Wabakinine (Wabacoming, d. 1796) and other chiefs was 'three hundred suits of clothing'.[52] Other surrenders quickly followed; between 1815 and 1825 Indians signed nine treaties, giving up almost the entire peninsula between Lakes Ontario, Erie, and Huron.[53] At first these treaties were for parcels of land for specific projects. Until 1798, the government had no problem in obtaining surrenders for about three pence an acre in either cash or goods, although the value of 'wild' land was estimated at from six to 15 pence an acre.[54] At that time Upper Canada was the western frontier; some of the transactions were not properly recorded and many were imprecise in their terms or in regard to boundaries, giving rise to later disputes. They soon formed the vast majority of the 483 treaties listed for Canada in 1912, although a little more than 20 of the 30 or so major ones account for most of Ontario's geographical area. By this time the change in the character of treaties was complete. Although peace and friendship continued to be mentioned, the agreements had become essentially land transfers. This would be the nature of the treaties that would be signed in the West.

A harbinger of the huge land-cession treaties that would begin with the Robinson agreements of 1850 was the accord reached for the Niagara Peninsula in 1784 by Wabakinine and other chiefs with Frederick Haldimand, governor of Quebec, 1778–86, by which the Amerindians 'sold' 3 million acres of land (1,214,057 hectares) to the Crown for £1,180 in goods. The purpose was to provide land for the Iroquois loyalists who had been dispossessed in the United States as a consequence of their siding with the British during the American War of Independence. Worried at the anger of their Native allies over this development and haunted by the fear of an Amerindian war, the British had moved quickly to reassure Iroquois loyalists that they had not been abandoned by Britain.[55] By far the largest portion of the territory acquired from the Mississaugas went to Joseph Brant and his followers, when the Iroquois received a tract six miles deep on either side of the Grand River beginning at its mouth—a total of 2,842,480 acres (1,150,311 hectares), 'which them and their posterity are to enjoy forever'. Known as the Haldimand Grant, it provided the land base for the Six Nations Reserve.[56] A 1785 reserve census enumerated a population of 1,843; Mohawks were in the majority, with 448 persons counted; Onondagas accounted for 245, Oneidas for 162, Tuscaroras, 129, and Senecas, 78. The rest were made up by various tribes, such as Delawares and Creeks, among others.[57]

There followed a long struggle between the government and Brant as to land policies: Brant held that the Iroquois had a fee simple title, which included the right of selling and leasing to private individuals. He argued that the hunting way of life was no longer sustainable in that region, and that the only source of income available to the Iroquois was from the sale of parts of their grant. He also sought the establishment of non-Amerindian farmers amid his people to teach them the settlers' agricultural techniques. Brant eventually won his argument, the consequence of which was a severe erosion of the original grant; eventually the sale of 381,480 acres (154,379 hectares) for prices ranging from three to six shillings an acre was confirmed.[58] He lost considerably on all counts, as many of his transactions were never regularized; besides, it was one thing to sell to private purchasers at high prices but quite another to collect from them.[59] One effect of his dealings was to increase substantially the price of land.[60] The government, alarmed, reverted to its former policy of curtailing Amerindian rights to alienate their lands. On top of all that, a government survey of the reserve in 1791 ruled that it was much smaller than that described by the Haldimand Grant, stopping far short of the river's source; documents delineating the original grant had gone missing.[61] What remained was confirmed by the Simcoe Deed of 1793. Other Iroquois leaders, with fewer followers, received more modest grants, such as that of Tyendinaga Reserve at the Bay of Quinte to Mohawk Captain John Deserontyon (Deseronto, Odeserundiye, c. 1740s–1811) and his band of 200. Thus the Iroquois returned to the lands that had once been occupied by other branches of their people.

In 2001, the Six Nations Reserve counted the largest population—21,474—of any of Canada's reserves; however, about half of the band's members live off-reserve. The next largest is that of the Mohawks of Akwesasne, Ontario, with approximately 12,000. The smallest band, consisting of one member living on the reserve and a few others off-reserve, is the Salishan-speaking New Westminster band in BC, the Qayqayt First Nation. It once had three tiny locations on the Fraser River and 170 members, but the reserve was returned to the province in 1913 when the people were decimated by smallpox and the survivors were moved to another reserve. In the hope of re-establishing the band, Chief Rhonda Larrabee filed a land claim. The band's present assets consist of a computer, a fax machine, and a telephone.[62]

Large-scale land cessions had become the order of the day for the Ojibwa and the closely related Odawa between Lake Erie and the Thames River in Upper Canada. For example, in 1790, 2 million acres (809,371 hectares) were surrendered for £1,200, and two years later 3 million acres (1,214,057 hectares) were ceded for the same amount.[63] In the second decade of the nineteenth century, cash payments gave way to annuities, which the administration considered to be more economical. As already noted, this principle of annual payments had been introduced in the 1752 treaty with the Mi'kmaq as a variation of gift distributions. Now it underwent another transformation, and annuities were substituted for cash payments for land. Its first use in this new incarnation was by Thomas Douglas, Earl of Selkirk (1771–1820), at Red River in 1817; the following year, 1818, it was used in the Collingwood Treaty to settle for 1,592,000 acres (644,259 hectares) ceded in return for a 'perpetual' annuity of £1,200. The Ojibwa chief Musquakie (Mayawassino, William Yellowhead, d. 1864) was one of the principal negotiating chiefs.[64] His father had previously surrendered 250,000 acres (101,171 hectares) in present-day Simcoe County. Following a suggestion in 1829 of Sir John Colborne, lieutenant-governor for Upper Canada from 1828 to 1836, annuities could be paid in the form of housing, equipment, and/or provisions instead of cash, which was done in 1822 when the Mississauga surrendered 2,748,000 acres (1,112,096 hectares). In that case, it was further agreed that payments were to be made to each individual member of the band, a total of 257 souls. Annuities indeed were more economical for the administration as they were financed from funds established with the proceeds of subsequent sales of surrendered lands.

Effects on Administration

Regulation of trade was another principal concern of Amerindian administration at this time. In the past, government monopoly had been exercised through a system of government 'truck' houses, which in Nova Scotia had been established in 1760; it did not pay for itself. In 1764 a plan was adopted to implement a provision in the Proclamation of 1763 for the opening of trade to all. However, it was restricted to designated locations, which in the North meant military posts.[65] Anyone who wanted to trade had to obtain a licence and post bond for good behaviour. These requirements proved to be highly unpopular with traders, who launched a vigorous, and ultimately successful, campaign against them.

Chapter 13

On the Great Plains

The use of horses for hunting bison on the Plains, which today is considered traditional, crystallized in Canada between 1600 and 1750, depending on locality; in southern Alberta, Saskatchewan, and Manitoba it seems to have developed during the first half of the eighteenth century.[1] Horses not only altered the hunt, transportation, and warfare, but also, and perhaps most importantly, trade routes. Interestingly, horses did not generally become a source of subsistence in themselves, as they had in Asia.[2] However, to view the changes that did occur as simply superficial, as some have done, is to misunderstand the process of cultural evolution. Technologies change faster than institutions, and institutions change faster than ideologies. In less than two centuries on the northwestern Plains, the horse, in conjunction with the fur trade, had markedly influenced the principal institutions of Plains Amerindian society; given more time, more profound ideological modifications would probably have been effected as well.[3]

Introduction of Horses

There is considerable question as to when Amerindians began to own and ride horses after they had been reintroduced into the Americas by the Spaniards. However, Amerindians had their own wild ponies before Europeans came, and these ponies have survived.[4] In 1541 Antonio de Mendoza, first viceroy of New Spain from 1535 to 1550, provided mounts for his Mexican allies during a campaign in central Mexico; about 1567, the Indians of Sonora rode horses and used them for food.[5] Spanish stock-raising settlements in the Southwest, particularly in the neighbourhood of Santa Fe, were apparently points of diffusion;[6] as for the Atlantic seaboard, where horses had been present since early in the seventeenth century, they do not seem to have crossed the Alleghenies until later. On the southern Plains, Indians owned horses by 1630 and may well have had some as early as 1600. Athapaskan-speaking Apache were raiding on horseback by mid-seventeenth century;[7] indeed,

TIMELINE

1600–1870	Development and flourishing of bison-hunting way of life.
1630	Indians on southern Plains own horses, after Spanish introduced horses a century earlier in Mexico.
1730s	Shoshoni using horses for raiding.
mid-1700s	Cree who had traded with HBC on the Bay, and with French now established on Saskatchewan River, introduce guns to Plains culture.
1752–63	French–Indian War disrupts trade in the West.
1770	British traders back on Upper Mississippi and Saskatchewan after French–Indian War.
1774	HBC inland post of Cumberland House (near The Pas, Manitoba).
1779	HBC Hudson House post (west of Prince Albert, Sask.).
	Cree attack independent traders at Eagle Hills Fort on the Saskatchewan.
1781–2	Epidemic takes heavy toll on Shoshoni, and Blackfoot Confederacy—now armed and on horseback—forces Shoshoni off northern Plains. Gros Ventre, weakened by epidemic, pushed south and east by Assiniboine and Cree.
1793	Cree wipe out a Gros Ventre band near South Branch House.
1793–4	Gros Ventre retaliate against Cree by looting HBC's Manchester House and by destroying South Branch House.
1799	North West Company post at Rocky Mountain House the first in Blackfoot territory.
c. 1800	Fur traders bring Iroquois, Nipissings, Algonquins to the West to trap for them, causing considerable resentment among the Blackfoot and Peigan.
1807	Nor'Wester David Thompson establishes post in Kutenai territory.
1818	International border between Canada and the US is established.
1830s	Thriving buffalo robe and pemmican trade such that tipis are large enough to accommodate 100 people.
1833	Peigan chief, Sackomaph, reportedly owned 4,000–5,000 horses.

they evolved Amerindian techniques for mounted warfare and also had become the prototype of the mounted buffalo hunter. The new character of the buffalo hunt influenced some parklands farming peoples, such as the Cheyenne and some branches of the Sioux, to abandon agriculture for the excitement of the chase. Horse stealing became a favourite activity and was an accepted way of acquiring animals; around 1800, some Blackfoot, raiding on the northern Plains, were reported to be riding horses with Spanish brands.[8] Bison herds appear to have reached their great numbers not long before the arrival of Europeans. These were reported by Francisco Vasquez Coronado (1510–54) in the south (1541), by Jesuit Simon Le Moyne (1604–65) in the Great Lakes region (1654), and, as previously noted, by Henry Kelsey on the Saskatchewan River (1690). These herds could well have prevented the return of village farmers to the Plains following the droughts.[9] Hernando de Soto (c. 1500–42) in 1541 reported 'that cattle were in such plenty' in north-central Arkansas, 'no maize-field could be protected from them, and the inhabitants lived upon the meat.'[10]

With horses, running buffalo became universally favoured as a hunting technique, although surrounds also increased, as they were now more efficient. The earliest description we have of a surround is from Henry Kelsey in 1691:

> The Instant ye Indians going a hunting Kill'd great store of Buffilo Now ye manner of their hunting these Beasts on ye Barren ground is when they see a great parcel of them together they surround them with men wch done they gather themselves into a smaller Compose Keeping ye Beast still in ye middle & so shooting yon till they break out at some place or other & so gett away from yon.[11]

Jumps began to fall into disuse between 1840 and 1850; the last known use was by the Blackfoot in 1873.[12] Pounds were the preferred method, especially for fall and winter; they continued to be used until the end of the herds. Another effect of the horse was to eliminate women from direct participation in buffalo drives, turning their attention exclusively to the preparation of hides and meat. The robe trade placed a premium on their services, greatly encouraging polygyny.[13] This rise in women's economic importance was not paralleled in the political realm.

Apart from its usefulness for hunting and transport, the horse both extended and altered trade routes. Consequently, it became a symbol of wealth in its own right and, as always with the growth of affluence, polarized economic status both between individuals and between tribes. For example, in 1833 a Peigan chief, Sackomaph, was reported to own between 4,000 and 5,000 horses, 150 of which were sacrificed upon his death. On a more modest scale, trader Alexander Henry the Younger (*fl.* 1791–1814) reported in 1809 that individual Siksika of Painted Feather's band owned as many as 50 horses and that among the Peigan the number belonging to an individual could reach 300.[14] Prices apparently varied considerably. Henry at one point observed that a common pack horse could not be obtained from the Gros Ventres for less than a gun, a fathom of HBC stroud (a kind of cloth), and 200 balls and powder; among the Siksika, however, such a horse could be obtained for a 'carrot' of tobacco, about three pounds.[15] Among tribes, the Assiniboine and Plains Cree had fewer horses than the Blackfoot. That may have encouraged them to develop their skills as horse raiders; David Thompson described a spectacular raid in which a band of Assiniboines disguised as antelopes made off with 50 horses from Rocky Mountain House.[16] Such raids were carried out against the enemy and thus were acts of war, not theft.[17]

The Shoshoni (Snake, Gens du Serpent), seasonal residents of grasslands and Plateau, are generally believed to have been the first to acquire horses on the northwestern Plains.[18] Their sources were their relatives to the south, the Comanche, as well as neighbours, such as the Coeur d'Alene and Flathead from the western Plateau and Columbia River, who were early large-scale herders.[19] The Shoshoni may have employed their horses at first principally for the hunt, presaging, as the Apache had done earlier in the south, the emergence of buffalo-based 'horse cultures' in the north. By the 1730s the Shoshoni were using horses for raiding, and during the following decades they were feared mounted warriors of the Plains.[20] Word quickly spread of the strange animal, 'swift as deer', which would become known to the Cree as Misstutim, 'big dog'. A Cree who had been adopted by the Peigans, Saukamapee, described to Thompson his first encounter with the new arrival, which occurred while he and some fellow tribesmen were hunting. Attacking a lone Shoshoni, the Peigans succeeded in killing his mount and crowded in wonder about the fallen animal which, like the dog, was a slave to man and carried his burdens.[21] The Blackfoot called it 'Ponokamita', 'elk dog', in recognition of its size and usefulness.

Tribal Distribution

At this time, all of the year-round residents of the northwestern Plains were Algonkian or Siouan speakers except the Tsuu T'ina, who spoke an Athapaskan language and who had broken away from the northern Beaver, apparently not long before the arrival of Europeans. Eventually, the Tsuu T'ina became part of the Blackfoot Confederacy, along with the Siksika (Blackfoot proper), Kainah (Blood), and Peigan (Peeagan, Peekanow), the most westerly and southerly of the confederates.[22] Linguistic evidence indicates a great time span of occupation for the Algonkian-speaking Blackfoot, much of it in isolation from their own language group. Speech similarities between the Blackfoot and the Kutenai of the Plateau may hark back to the time when the latter resorted seasonally to the Plains. Of the historic Plains people, the Blackfoot were probably the first to arrive; cultural indications are that they came from the Eastern Woodlands.[23] Directly to the east of the confederacy were the allied Algonkian-speaking Gros Ventre (Atsina, originally a division of the Arapaho; also known as Fall or Rapids Amerindians),[24] who may have been the second to arrive in the region.[25] They share with the Blackfoot the probability of being the 'Archithinue' or 'Archithine' reported by Anthony Henday (fl. 1750–62) in 1754.[26] Along with the Blackfoot, they were the only northern Plains Amerindians with graded men's societies (to the south, such societies were found among the Mandan, Hidatsa, and Arapaho).[27] Later Matthew Cocking (1743–99) would be impressed with Gros Ventre customs and manners, which he found more like those of Europeans.[28] If we except the Plains Ojibwa (Saulteaux, Bungi), who reached Saskatchewan by the late eighteenth century but who did not establish a major presence on the high Plains,[29] the newest arrivals in this northwestern region are the Plains Cree. Their arrival dates from the early eighteenth century and may have been in association with their close allies, the Siouan Assiniboine, who preceded them.

Power Balances

The early historic period saw the southwestern parts of the region being dominated by the raiding mounted Shoshoni; the Kutenai, who also had horses by that time, appear to have used them for trading rather than raiding. The Shoshoni wore six-ply quilted armour and carried shields, but as yet they did not have firearms. What European trading connections they had were to the south, and the Spaniards did not trade in arms with Amerindians. The sinew-backed bow was an efficient weapon, particularly when used with metal-tipped arrows, and was both more accurate and more reliable than guns until about the middle of the nineteenth century. Those of the Shoshoni were particularly prized. With the exception of the late-arriving Cree, Assiniboine, and Saulteaux, all of whom had earlier associations with the fur trade, it was the preferred weapon of traditional Plains buffalo hunters. In 1811, the younger Henry reported that Peigans would trade a horse or a gun for such a bow.[30] The principal economic purpose of the Shoshoni raids seems to have been the acquisition of captives, who as slaves were useful to Amerindians, Spaniards, and French, and so had high trading value.

The appearance of the gun heralded the final phase of shifting Amerindian power balances on the northern Plains before the advent of settlement. The Shoshoni first encountered guns in the hands of their enemy, the Cree.[31] The Cree, trading with the English on Hudson Bay and with the French, by mid-eighteenth century were established on the Saskatchewan River and had been armed for some time. The Shoshoni quickly discovered that this new weaponry seriously diminished the advantage they had gained with the horse.[32] While there is argument as to the extent of the influence of the early smooth-bore gun on Plains warfare patterns,[33] there seems little reason to doubt that it had at the very least considerable psychological impact. For one thing, a musket ball was harder to dodge than an arrow or a spear; for another, when it hit, it rendered traditional armour obsolete. (Eastern Indians, such as the Iroquois and Abenaki, had earlier experienced this; despite the inadequacies of such weaponry, they had adopted guns as fast as they could acquire them.) In the hands of a mounted warrior, as happened on the Plains, even the smooth-bore musket, unreliable as it was, could be overpowering.[34] As David Thompson observed, war on the Plains was not fought in the same manner as war in the woods. On the Plains 'they act as a body in concert in all their movements, in the woods it is always Man to Man.'[35]

Before the Shoshoni were able to obtain regular access to firearms, the French and Indian War (1754–63)—the New World aspect of the Seven Years' War in Europe—was seriously interrupting trade in the West. By 1770, British traders were back on the Upper Mississippi and the Saskatchewan and were beginning to penetrate into the Far Northwest; but France as a power had all but disappeared from North America, and her jurisdiction over Louisiana had been transferred to Spain. This dealt a severe blow to whatever hopes the Shoshoni might have had of obtaining enough guns to face their enemies. As the Blackfoot confederates, now mounted, already had access to British firearms, the Shoshoni were pushed off the northern Plains by the end of the eighteenth century.[36] In achieving this, the Blackfoot were powerfully aided by epidemics, especially that of 1781–2, which took a heavy toll on the Shoshoni.[37] By the turn of the century, the victorious Peigans, who had been the confederates mainly involved in the struggle, were referring to the once-dreaded Shoshoni as miserable old women, whom they could defeat with sticks and stones.[38] With the removal of the Shoshoni threat, the fragile alliance of the confederacy with Assiniboine and Cree lost its principal motivation and the two expanding power groups came into collision.

Trading Patterns

Before this happened, and while they were still allies, the Blackfoot had obtained their first European trade items through the Assiniboine and Cree network rather than directly from Europeans. Linguistic evidence hints that the first Europeans they met were French, as they designated them as 'Real (or Original) Old Man People'; their term for non-Aboriginals in general was 'Napikawan', a term of considerable respect, as the Blackfoot term for the Creator was 'Napi'. That the French were the first to be encountered is confirmed by Peter Fidler (1769–1822).[39] However, the first identifiable meeting is the well-known encounter with Henday, who had been led to them by Attikarish in 1754–5.[40] It is thought that the Blackfoot were all mounted, although at the time Henday's report that they had horses was greeted with disbelief by the English on the Bay.[41] By then, the Blackfoot were well into their period of expansion; as the Peigan pushed the Shoshoni south and west, the Tsuu T'ina moved into the North Saskatchewan basin and the allied Gros Ventre occupied territories vacated by the Blackfoot around the Eagle Hills. By 1770, the area along the eastern Rockies north of Yellowstone to the boreal forest was controlled by the Blackfoot Confederacy and its allies.

The Blackfoot never took to trading with Europeans as had the Cree and Assiniboine; neither Henday nor Cocking, later, had been able to persuade them or the Gros Ventre to make the arduous journey to the Bay. Not only were their needs being served adequately through the Native networks, but they would have faced opposition if they had tried to penetrate Cree and Assiniboine hunting territory that lay athwart the route to the Bay. Both Cree and Assiniboine vigorously protected their trading positions as middlemen between the posts on the Bay and peoples of the interior, particularly those of the northwestern Plains. What they were unable to prevent was the arrival of European traders. There was also the fact that the demands of the fur trade conflicted with those of buffalo hunting. Late fall and early winter was the best season for trapping furs, as pelts were then in their prime; it was also the best time for killing bison and preparing winter provisions. From the social aspect, trapping was a family affair, whereas buffalo hunting involved the whole community. Of the Blackfoot confederates, the Peigan had the most beaver in their territory and consequently became the most active as trappers; the others, as well as the allies, became provisioners for the trade rather than trappers for furs. This independence of the Blackfoot and Gros Ventre spurred the Hudson's Bay Company to establish the inland posts of Cumberland House (near The Pas, Manitoba) in 1774 and Hudson House (west of Prince Albert) in 1779. By the time the Nor'Westers built Fort Augustus on the North Saskatchewan in 1795 and the Hudson's Bay Company countered with Fort Edmonton that same year, Blackfoot territory was ringed with trading posts.[42] It was not until 1799, when Nor'Westers built the first Rocky Mountain House, that a post was established within the Blackfoot sphere of control.

Shifting Trade Focus

The establishment of the international border between Canada and the United States in 1818 further complicated what had become a complex situation. Despite their unwillingness to meet the fur trade on its terms, the Blackfoot and Gros Ventre felt that they were not being treated in trade as well as their enemies, the Cree, particularly in the case of firearms.[43] The traders, especially the independents, did not help when they treated Amerindians badly, as happened all too frequently. The resultant tensions sometimes erupted into violence, as in 1781 when Amerindians burned the prairie around the posts, which the traders believed was done to scare game away.[44] When the Nor'Westers sought to cross the mountains to make contact with the Kutenai and other Plateau peoples, the Peigan became seriously alarmed, 'for they dreaded the western Indians being furnished with Arms and Amunition'.[45] David Thompson finally succeeded in building a post in Kutenai territory in 1807, which moved the Peigans, already disturbed by the killing of two of their tribesmen by members of the Lewis and Clark expedition shortly before, to raise a war party. Although Thompson was able to negotiate a peaceful settlement, the unfortunate result for him was the famous delay that cost the Nor'Westers the right to claim the mouth of the Columbia River for Britain.[46] That same year a band of Blood and Gros Ventre pillaged Fort Augustus, and when the Hudson's Bay Company built Peigan Post (Old Bow Fort) in 1832 in territory controlled by the Kainah, the latter refused to allow their allies to trade there, forcing the closing of the post two years later.[47]

Nor did it take long for the Blackfoot to take advantage of the new international boundary; they became adept at raiding posts built in that part of their territory claimed by the United States and then selling the proceeds north of the border.[48] The situation was aggravated when Euro-Americans—the 'Mountain Men' of American western folklore—began trapping in Indian territory, an act the Blackfoot considered trespassing. Canadian traders had already, at the end of the eighteenth century, 'brought in a great number of Iroquois, Nepissings, and

Plains Amerindians negotiating a trade with an HBC factor in the mid-1800s. The travois of both horse and dog are loaded with trade goods. From *Harper's Monthly*, June 1879.
(Glenbow Archives, NA-1406-40)

Algonquins' to act as trappers for them, men who 'with their steel traps had destroyed the Beaver on their own lands in Canada and New Brunswick'.[49] Since the Blackfoot would not allow them on their lands, the newcomers went north and west, some going to the Upper Columbia, later moving down to the Lower Columbia and the Snake. If they encroached upon Peigan lands, they were driven off in attacks that could be bloody. Thompson reported that several hundred had been killed for that reason, perhaps an exaggeration.[50]

Expansion, Prosperity

In Canada, the opening of the rich fur resources of the Far Northwest—the Athabasca region—and the growing market for buffalo robes shifted the trade's focus and brought about better relations between the Blackfoot and traders. The need for provisions for the Athabasca trade greatly increased the demand for pemmican, a product of the buffalo hunt. Pemmican, a highly concentrated food that could be kept indefinitely, had the added advantage of being well suited for transport in small northern canoes.[51] As this new trade boomed in the North, buffalo robes were finding widening markets in the south, for industry as well as for domestic use. Transportation was the key here also, in this case the building of railroads, which made it practicable to get the bulky, heavy hides to market. Buffalo hunters flourished; the northern Plains, where affluence was traditionally manifested in the size of tipis, by the 1830s saw them becoming large enough to accommodate as many as 100 persons.[52] The new commerce placed a premium on the services of women. Where Plains Indian women had usually married in their late teens, girls as young as 12 now did so; on the other hand, rarely could a man afford to buy a wife before he was in his mid-thirties. As polygyny developed, so did a hierarchy among wives, with the senior wife usually directing the others.[53] Women taken in raids now tended to be retained by their captors rather than sold, a trend that accelerated after the first third of the nineteenth century.

Commercialism and its concomitant emphasis on wealth affected other social institutions as well. Special-interest societies multiplied, of which the best known were connected with war and the maintenance of camp and hunt discipline. War as a way of life was a comparatively recent development; for the Blackfoot it became a means of accumulating wealth, making possible the elaboration of ceremonials that were the route to prestige. Still, something of the old ways persisted, for although the Blackfoot were a major military power on the northwestern Plains for more than a century, it remained possible in their society to become a chief without going on the warpath.[54] Even if the path of war was chosen, counting coups was esteemed a braver act than killing, as touching the enemy and escaping was an action that took power. Bravery and generosity were the requisites, as they were among the Plains Cree and others.

Warfare intensified, however. The Gros Ventre, weakened by the ravages of the 1781–2 epidemic, were pushed south and east by the Assiniboine and Cree. In 1793, Cree wiped out a Gros Ventre band near South Branch House. Such incidents greatly exacerbated the resentment shared by the Gros Ventre and the Blackfoot towards the trading success of the Cree and the Assiniboine, which made possible the latter's superiority in arms.[55] In the eyes of the Gros Ventre, HBC traders were in effect allies of their enemies, so they responded to the Cree raid by attacking the Company's Manchester House (on Pine Island, Saskatchewan River), which they looted that same year, and by destroying South Branch House the following year. Eventually, like the Shoshoni, they were pushed south of the international border.[56]

In contrast to the Gros Ventre, the Cree and Assiniboine were still expanding since their arrival on the Plains near the end of the seventeenth century. Although they also had suffered severely from the epidemics (1776–7 had been particularly hard on them), their numbers were such that they were able to recover and continue their expansion.[57] In the southwest, they were stopped by the Blackfoot, their erstwhile allies when the Shoshoni were a common enemy. Cree and Blackfoot now considered each other their worst foe.

Neither Cree nor Assiniboine had difficulty

in adapting to Plains life. By 1772, Cree were impounding bison, but they preferred the gun to the bow for the hunt, in contrast to peoples longer established on the grasslands. However, buffalo hunting lessened dependence on the fur trade; the phenomenon of the 'homeguard', so characteristic of the trading posts of the northern forests, was less apparent on the Plains, although it was present on a reduced scale, as at Fort Pembina.[58] Instead, buffalo hunters became provisioners for the trade, particularly after the opening up of the Athabasca region, where the posts could not sustain themselves.

Trading Scene Turns Violent

Reduced dependence on the fur trade affected relationships with traders, and the Plains Cree were involved in one of the most widely remembered confrontations. It occurred in 1779 in reaction to the callous behaviour of a group of independent traders at Fort Montagne d'Aigle (Eagle Hills Fort), on the Saskatchewan between Eagle Hills Creek and Battle River. Two traders were killed and the rest were forced to flee; the post was abandoned and apparently was never permanently reoccupied. The incident also caused the abandonment that same year of the Nor'Wester Fort du Milieu and the HBC's Hudson House. Nor was this an isolated occurrence. The Cree, for example, were participants in a mêlée in 1781 at Fort des Trembles on the Assiniboine that resulted in the death of three traders and up to 30 Amerindians. Only the outbreak of the 1781–2 smallpox epidemic prevented large-scale retaliations against traders.[59] The much vaunted peaceful co-operation that was characteristic of the fur trade in the northern forests was not so evident on the Plains.

Golden Years

In spite of this, the converging influences of the horse and the fur trade fostered a florescence of Plains cultures, whose golden years in the Northwest are usually dated from 1750 to 1880. The horse facilitated the exploitation of the buffalo herds and the extension of overland routes; the fur trade made available a new range of goods and, more importantly, provided new markets for products of the hunt. This meant that as long as the herds lasted, Plains Amerindians were able to hold their own and indeed to reach new heights of cultural expression as their societies became increasingly complex. They were even able to overcome to a large extent the demographic disasters precipitated by introduced diseases. But they did not have time to make their own accommodations to the disappearance of the herds upon which all this was based. The dramatic suddenness of that occurrence catapulted events beyond their control.

This flourishing of a culture soon to be transformed was not unique to the Plains. It had previously occurred in the Eastern Woodlands, for example, among the Ojibwa, Woods Cree, and Iroquois; and it occurred simultaneously and continued somewhat later on the west coast, where one of its more spectacular manifestations was the burgeoning of totem poles, not to mention the appearance of button blankets and argillite carving. But in sheer artistry of dress, the mounted plainsman achieved an elegance never surpassed; as an expression of the mobile, buffalo-hunting way of life, he was his own *pièce de résistance*.

Chapter 14

Westward and Northward

The invasion of the fur trade into the Far Northwest, today's Northwest Territories and British Columbia, received an enormous impetus when the British eased restrictions at the interior posts in 1768. The invasion came as a giant pincer movement, following pre-existing Amerindian trade patterns, expanding westward by land from Hudson Bay and the northern Plains and by sea along the Pacific coast until turning eastward by land into the interior. The westward movement can be dated from the seventeenth-century expansion of the Cree and Assiniboine, which brought the fur trade with it. It culminated in the voyage of Alexander Mackenzie (1764–1820) of the North West Company, which followed Amerindian trading routes from the Peace River down the Parsnip and Liard rivers to the Bella Coola River, reaching the ocean at Bentinck Arm in 1793. The coastal movement has been usually dated from the visit of Captain James Cook (1728–79) to Nootka Sound in 1778; however, recent scholarship makes a strong case that Sir Francis Drake (1541?–1596) visited the Northwest Coast in 1579.[1] He was followed a century and a half later by Vitus Bering (1681–1741), who claimed

Alaska for Russia in 1741. Spaniards arrived offshore in 1774, returning in 1789 to build a fort to protect their claims. They remained until both Britain and Spain agreed to vacate the region in 1794. The British would soon come back, but not the Spanish. Spearheading the Canadian involvement in both land and sea movements was the North West Company, a group of floating fur trade partnerships that coalesced into 'companies', the first in 1779 and the second in 1783.[2] The Hudson's Bay Company became active on the Pacific coast after its amalgamation with the North West Company in 1821; its ship, *Beaver,* arrived in Vancouver in 1836, the first steamer to ply those coastal waters. In the meantime, Amerindian coastal trade networks flourished as Native entrepreneurs capitalized on European initiatives.

The headstart of the Cree in gaining access to European trade goods was a substantial one. Earliest mention of the 'Kristinaux' is in the *Jesuit Relations* of the 1640s. It was 30 years before the English established on the Bay, another 20 years after that before they began to probe into the western interior, and still another 20 years before some Chipewyan were

TIMELINE

1778	Captain James Cook sails into Nootka Sound on British Columbia coast. Amerindian guides take Peter Pond to west via Methye Portage, the third great route for fur resources (after St Lawrence and Hudson Bay).
1785	First trading ship—British—arrives on Northwest Coast.
1788	Pond establishes Fort Chipewyan for North West Company.
1791	A Haida chief, Koyah, disgraced by British, becomes enemy of fur trade and attacks ships and traders.
1793	Alexander Mackenzie reaches Pacific coast overland after following Amerindian trade routes.
1799	Dene Dháa (Beaver) seek fur-trading post for their territory.
1800–4	Iroquois trappers famed as rivermen, from Kahnawake, Kanesatake, and Akwesasne, most under contract to North West Company, move west, eventually settle in Athabasca and Peace River regions.

1803	Muquinna, a Nuu'chah'nulth chief, attacks the *Boston*—only two crew survive; Muquinna subsequently has elaborate potlatch.
1811	David Thompson gains access to Athabasca Pass through negotiation with Tsuu T'ina, which becomes the route to the Plateau and Pacific coast until 1841.
	Trade ship *Tonquin* blown up by Amerindians on BC coast, no survivors.
1821	Hudson's Bay Company and North West Company amalgamate.
1827	Fort Langley established on Fraser River.
1834	Fort Simpson moved to Tsimshian Peninsula; nine bands of Tsimshian encamp nearby to control and profit from trade.
1847	Fort Rupert established on north end of Vancouver Island; four Kwakwaka'wakw bands move to area for trade.

persuaded to visit a post, in this case York Factory. Thus the Cree bands of Hudson Bay had a century to develop this new connection before the people of the Far Northwest made their first tenuous contact. Throughout all this time, Native trade networks were operating, and it is likely that even at that early date European merchandise worked its way deep into the interior long before traders did. Certainly this was the case in the Great Lakes region, where archaeologists have found trade goods, and even ship's fittings, in burials dating back to the middle of the sixteenth century, which was 70 years before Europeans are known to have made it into that region in person.[3] Samuel Hearne, on his voyage to the Arctic, found beads of a type not traded by the HBC in an Inuit camp at the mouth of the Coppermine River.[4]

Even though contact between Europeans and Amerindians was low-key during this period, it affected Native relationships. Integration into an economy based on production for exchange rather than for use, instead of providing for greater security, introduced new variables that had a destabilizing effect on Amerindian ways of life. We have seen that the Cree, with their early acquisition of arms, expanded in two arenas—from already established positions in the Northwest and southward to erupt onto the northern Plains. As the tribes readjusted their territories and sought to get control of a larger share of the fur trade, Athapaskans not only fought Cree, they also came into conflict with other Athapaskans. Thus, the Chipewyans contended with Yellowknives and Dogribs to keep them from direct

Caribou Inuit moving camp near Yathkyet Lake, Keewatin District, July 1922.
The women and children move first, followed by the men and dogs.
(National Museum of Denmark, Department of Ethnography)

access to the Hudson Bay posts.[5] Once the HBC posts moved inland, these hostilities lost their reason for being and stopped. The traditional enmity between the woodland Indians and the people of the tundra—the Inuit—was more deeply rooted and continued far longer.

Another element adding to the complexity of this picture was the arrival of Iroquois trappers, famed as rivermen, at the end of the eighteenth century (already referred to in the previous chapter). Mostly from Caughnawaga (Kahnawake) but also from Oka (Kanesatake) and St Regis (Akwesasne), the majority came under contract with the North West Company, with a few coming on their own.[6] The greatest number, more than 300, came between 1800 and 1804. By 1810 they had concentrated along the eastern slopes of the Rockies in the Athabasca and Peace River regions; by 1821 the movement was tapering off, and most of the newcomers had completed their contracts and were now 'freemen'. Efficient fur hunters, the Iroquois used the latest technology, metal traps. One report has it that in 1819 the North West Company was obtaining nearly two-fifths of its fur returns from Canadian and Iroquois free trappers.[7] After the amalgamation of the NWC with the Hudson's Bay Company in 1821, the Lesser Slave Lake post accounted for more than one-twelfth of the total returns for the Company that year, by far the largest quantity for a single post.[8] Small wonder that the freemen were accused of overtrapping to the point of stripping the region of its fur resources. They intermarried locally, which usually meant with Cree or Métis, but later with non-Aboriginals; their descendants in Alberta today are found principally at Grand Cache, Lac Ste Anne, and Lesser Slave Lake.[9]

Into the 'New Peru' of Athabasca Country

When his Amerindian guides took Peter Pond (1739/40–1807) to Methye Portage in 1778,[10] the third great route into Canada's fur resources was opened up (the others were the St Lawrence and Hudson Bay). The new route over the height of land that connected Hudson Bay and Arctic drainages meant that in 1788 Peter Pond could establish Fort Chipewyan, which would become the most important North West Company post in the North. Within four years, the NWC also had established posts near the present sites of Fort McMurray and Peace River, and by 1805 it had important posts at Dunvegan and Fort St John, both on the Peace River, and at Lesser Slave Lake. Rivalry between the Hudson's Bay Company and the North West Company intensified, which meant that for the people, credit became easy to obtain and liquor flowed. The spread of posts also meant that more tribes gained direct access to white traders, and the Cree lost out as middlemen. When the HBC gained control of the trade with the 1821 merger, it began to curb the use of alcohol and to change the terms of trade, to the disadvantage of the Amerindians. Montreal lost out to London as the headquarters for the trade, which meant that canoe brigades no longer left Lachine for Fort William each spring. Instead, York Factory on Hudson Bay, at the mouths of the Nelson and Hayes rivers, became the principal entrepôt. The HBC's position of exclusive dominance lasted for the better part of half a century. It was during this time that missionaries became a presence in the Northwest.

Breaking the mountain barrier into central British Columbia presented a particular problem for Europeans, as this move on their part was seen as a threat by established Amerindian interests—hardly a new experience, as Cartier had encountered the same situation at Stadacona in the early sixteenth century (Chapter 6).[11] According to historian W.A. Sloan, the Blackfoot Confederacy controlled the more easily traversed passes to the south, and they were apprehensive that their enemies would obtain European firearms. It was not until the Confederacy was distracted by the killing of some of their tribesmen by the American Lewis and Clark expedition (1804–6) that David Thompson was able to push through Howse Pass.[12] That was a temporary breakthrough, as the pass originated in Peigan territory and so was under their control. Finally, in 1811, Thompson was able to negotiate with the Tsuu T'ina for the use of the more northerly, longer, and more difficult Athabasca Pass. That would be the route for the European traders until 1841. By mid-century the decline of the buffalo herds was becoming evident, influencing the Blackfoot to reconsider their position in regard to trade.[13]

The traders were aided in their efforts by the Kutenai of the Plateau, anxious to get direct access to trade goods, particularly guns. This was a new expression of an old rivalry with the Blackfoot Confederacy, which long predated the arrival of European trade; in pre-contact days it had been expressed over rights to hunt buffalo on the Plains. According to Fidler, the Kutenai were being charged exorbitant prices by the networks controlled by the Blackfoot Confederacy—as much as 10 skins for an item they could obtain for one at a post. Horses were the Kutenai's principal stock-in-trade, much desired by the Peigan and other Plains peoples, who consequently took all the more care to see that the Kutenai did not gain access to European traders. Nor'Wester Duncan M'Gillivray (early 1770s–1808), at Fort George on the

Indian boys on the trail with pack dogs. *(Reproduced with permission of Natural Resources Canada 2008, courtesy of the Geological Survey of Canada, H.S. Bostock #96558)*

Saskatchewan, noted in his journal that 'the Coutonées [Kutenai] a tribe from the Southwest are determined to force their way this year [1795] to the Fort or perish in the attempt.'[14] They pinned their faith for 'obtaining a safe passage hither by bribing their enemies with Bands of Horses'. As the Peigan and their associates anxiously watched, and despite their best efforts to prevent it, the Kutenai and other interior tribes slowly acquired arms. Once Thompson succeeded in establishing a post on the border between the Kutenai and the Flatheads, other traders quickly followed. Eventually, the Flatheads were in a position to face the Peigans, and in 1810 and again in 1812 they defeated them. The Peigans blamed this on the white men and vowed vengeance.[15] As on the Plains, the fur trade in its westward movement was not always peaceful as it encroached on established Amerindian trade networks.

To the north, entrenched interests were less in evidence as European traders pushed westward. Quite the contrary, in fact, as far as the Dene Dháa Beaver, an Athapaskan people, were concerned; they sought out a fur-trading post on their own initiative in 1799. They were led by an unusual chief, Makenunatane (Swan Chief, so-called because his soul could fly high like a swan), who appears to have realized that the new trade meant a shift in lifeways—for one thing, it called for individualized trapping rather than communal hunting for subsistence. This would obviously call for new rituals; thus he and his people were interested in learning about Christianity.[16] It is perhaps not surprising that the Dene Dháa still have a living prophet tradition.

On the Northwest Coast

The sea otter motivated the opening of the fur trade of the Pacific coast, recapitulating and

Amerindian suspension bridge at Hagwilget, BC, built in the 1880s on the Upper Skeena River.
(Photo © Canadian Museum of Civilization, photo Edward Sapie, c. 1920, 61131)

condensing what had happened on the Atlantic coast nearly 300 years earlier with beaver.[17] But where shipboard trade had continued for more than a century in Acadia and the Gulf of St Lawrence after beginning as an almost incidental spinoff from the more profitable fisheries, on the Northwest Coast it was the main economic activity for a short but intense period, less than half a century. In both regions, the trade depended on Amerindian middlemen, which meant that it was conducted according to Amerindian protocol. When European colonization took over, as it did in both cases, it occurred more quickly and for the most part more peacefully on the Northwest Coast than it had done in the East. In the East, settlement was preceded by almost a century of trading and then was launched in the midst of colonial power struggles that continued for a century and a half. Contact on the west coast, despite its comparatively peaceful character, resulted in an 80 per cent drop of the Aboriginal population within a century.[18]

The sea otter trade began as a consequence of the activities of Captain Cook's crew, who had acquired sea otter among other furs during their visit at Nootka Sound.[19] The ship went on to China (without Cook, who had been killed during a stopover in the Hawaiian Islands), and there the British discovered the Chinese

Nineteenth-century chiefs of the Wolf Crest of Git-lak-damaks, Nass River, surrounded by wealth acquired in trade and warfare. Standing, beginning fourth from left, Andrew Nash, John Nash, James Percival, Philip Nash, and Charlie Brown (right rear). Seated, second from right, Mrs Eliza Woods and Matilda Peal, née Brown, aunt of the chiefs.
(Library and Archives Canada, PA-95524)

passion for sea otter fur and the high prices they were willing to pay for it. It was a market the Russians had been exploiting since mid-eighteenth century in their advance through the Aleutian Islands to the Alaskan mainland. The news that the Russians had arrived in America had disturbed the Spaniards in California sufficiently that they had sent expeditions northward, but after a few years at Nootka Sound they withdrew. Not only was the outpost far distant from the now-declining Spanish empire, but the Spaniards do not appear to have appreciated the full potential of its marine fur-bearers. The sea otter gave rise to the China clipper trade between Europe (or New England), the Northwest Coast, and China. Sea otter pelts were traded in China for silks, porcelains, and spices, as well as other items commanding high prices in Europe and in eastern North America. A single round trip could take more than three years, but if all went well it could realize a fortune.

The first trading ship arrived on the Northwest Coast in 1785; it was British. However, Americans ('Boston men') were soon dominant. During the following 40 years, until 1825, about 330 vessels flying a variety of national flags came into the region to trade. Of these, 60 per cent made only one visit; 23 per cent are recorded as having made three or more visits. The peak trading years were between 1792 and 1812; by about 1825 the sea otter had been decimated and traders were casting about for other resources to exploit. The fur seal of the Pribilof Islands suffered a similar fate.

James Hanna (d. 1787), captain of that first British trading ship, obtained 560 otter skins on which he realized $20,000, a fortune in those days. John Kendrick (c. 1740–94), commander of the expedition of the *Columbia* and *Lady Washington*, the first vessels from Boston to join the fur rush, made a deal that became legendary when he got 200 sea otter pelts, valued at $8,000, for an equal number of iron chisels, valued at $100.[20] A trade matching that in values exchanged, if not in volume, was made by a Russian who obtained 60 pelts for a handful of nails. When an enterprising American trader persuaded his ship's blacksmith to replicate the Amerindians' ceremonial cedar collars in iron, he traded them at the rate of three sea otter skins for one collar. That lasted for about a year, when the region became saturated with iron collars. Incidentally, the Natives of the Northwest Coast, so fond of abalone shell that they traded all the way down to California for it, flatly refused to accept artificial shell. While the differences in the scale of values between Amerindians and Europeans had made huge profits possible for the latter, the benefits were not entirely one-sided. In terms of their own priorities, Amerindians also acquired substantial wealth, as we have seen happened in other parts of Canada.

As on the east coast nearly three centuries earlier, shipboard trade resulted in limited contact with Amerindians and thus at first intensified existing cultural patterns rather than causing a major reorientation in their way of life.[21] Changes in tool kits and equipment resulted in an efflorescence of the arts: for example, the acquisition of iron tools meant that totem poles became taller and more elaborate. More slowly, dress shifted from buckskin to cloth, and capes that had once been woven of cedarbark and mountain goat wool (or dog hair) came to be made of navy blue and red blanket cloth, trimmed with buttons and thimbles. Blankets became the unit of trade, as Made Beaver had been for the rest of Canada.[22] It would be little more than half a century before non-Native settlement would begin, in mid-nineteenth century, much less than the century or so enjoyed by the Mi'kmaq and Wuastukwiuk on the east coast, but still time to make adjustments. British Columbia remained predominantly Amerindian until the 1880s.

Still, all was not as before. More wealth meant more power for chiefs; those who were in a position to do so quickly claimed monopolies and took over middlemen roles in the brief but highly profitable trade. Some of these chiefs became wealthy, which resulted in an increase in potlatches. One of the better known was Muquinna ('Possessor of Pebbles', *fl.* 1786–1817)[23] at Nootka Sound, who in 1803 gave a famous potlatch during which he dispensed 200 muskets, 200 yards of cloth, 100 chemises, 100 looking glasses, and seven barrels of gunpowder. Two principal factors ensured that this prosperity would be ephemeral for Muquinna as well as for other chiefs in a similar position: the near-extermination of the sea otter and the fact that the coastal regions, limited in extent as they were, quickly became glutted with trade goods. Even supplies of highly prized copper reached the saturation point around 1800. A third factor was the introduction of the HBC steamer *Beaver*, which, while facilitating trade, also shifted much of its activity to the inside passage.

In the meantime, during those heady early days of the trade, Amerindians soon learned to temper their eagerness to do business, and they became skilled in playing off trading ships, and even nations, against each other. For a short period Yankees and Russians managed to cooperate in the fiercely competitive situation, with the Americans providing the ships and food and the Russians the Aleut hunters whom they had forced into service.[24] This arrangement was for harvesting sea otters off the California coast; it lasted from 1803 until 1813, by which time the animals were so scarce in those southern waters the deal was no longer profitable. Canadians did not appear on the scene until 1811, when Nor'Wester David Thompson arrived at the mouth of the Columbia to find Americans (largely former Nor'Westers) already building a post there. Eventually, as one competitor after another was knocked out, the HBC dominated the scene. By agreeing to supply the Russian posts with food, the HBC undercut the Americans. For the most part, these rivalries were of short duration, in contrast to the prolonged confrontations in the *petit nord* and on the Plains.

Incidence of Violence

As elsewhere in Canada, the European presence had the immediate effect of increasing tribal warfare, the principal purposes of which on the Northwest Coast were to acquire slaves and canoes. This, however, appears to have been short term, and in the maritime trade itself there were comparatively few incidents. Those that did occur included a number of retaliations on the part of Indians against outrages that had been committed against them; but as historian Robin Fisher has pointed out, there were a wide variety of causes, most of which are now difficult to determine, if indeed they can be determined at all.[25] One of the best-known incidents involved Koyah (Coya, Kouyer, 'Raven', d. 1795?), a ranking Haida chief, and Captain Kendrick. Kendrick allowed too many Indians aboard the *Lady Washington*, and some minor items, including some of his personal linen, were pilfered. Kendrick seized Koyah and another chief, bolted each by a leg to a gun carriage, and threatened them with death until amends were made, which in Kendrick's ultimatum included trading all the furs in the village. Not

Portrait of Muquinna. In 1803, Muquinna held a potlatch at Nootka Sound at which he gave away 200 muskets and seven barrels of gunpowder. Already, however, overhunting of the sea otter on the west coast was taking its toll, and Muquinna's prosperity would be short-lived.
(Image A-02678, courtesy of Royal BC Museum, BC Archives)

satisfied when his terms were met, Kendrick further disgraced Koyah by whipping him and cutting off his hair, among other indignities.[26] Such a disgrace ruined Koyah's standing as a chief and turned him into an enemy of the fur trade; from then on, he attacked ships and traders whenever he could, including the *Lady Washington* in 1791. He lost his wife and two of his children in one of these episodes.[27]

Muquinna was more successful than Koyah when he overwhelmed the crew of the *Boston* in 1803, only two of whom were allowed to survive.[28] In this case, there seems to have been an accumulation of grievances, not the least of which was the fact that the fur trade was passing the Nuu'chah'nulth chief by; his lavish potlatch of that year was not to be repeated.[29] The most successful of all Amerindian attacks on vessels was against the *Tonquin* in 1811, which was blown up and left no survivors.[30]

From about 1806, crews began to winter on the coast; year-round trade developed as a result, and eventually posts were built; in 1827 Fort Langley was established on the Fraser River, about 50 kilometres inland from its mouth. Amerindian bands clustered around forts, but for different reasons than the 'homeguards' of the Northeast. When forts were built in their territory, tribal nations assumed they had the right to control access to these new centres for trade. Thus, when Fort Simpson was moved from the Nass River to the Tsimshian Peninsula in 1834, nine bands of Tsimshian lost no time in setting up camp about the new establishment; similarly, four bands of Kwakwaka'wakw converged on Fort Rupert soon after its contruction on the northern end of Vancouver Island in 1849. These bands were far more interested in controlling the trade these forts would engender than they were in hunting and providing services for them, as was the rule in the boreal forest. This had been the reason behind the annoyed reaction of the Nisga'a of the Nass River when Fort Simpson had been moved into Tsimshian territory.[31] On the other hand, if the Amerindians saw little advantage in having a fort in their midst and were reluctant to trade, there was no point in trying to maintain it. An attempt to establish a fort among the Chilcotin in 1829 met with this kind of a reaction and closed after 15 years.[32] Others were shorter-lived. In either case the Company had no alternative but to accept the situation; the wisest course was to go along with it. In the words of James Douglas (1803–77),[33] at that time chief factor at Fort Victoria (he would be named governor of Vancouver Island in 1851, and of the BC mainland in 1858, posts he would hold until his retirement in 1864), relying on the Amerindians to bring in the furs 'may prove in the end the safest and the least expensive way of improving the important territory in question.'[34] The Company never did establish the complete control it would have liked in New Caledonia, although it did eventually establish interior posts. The Nor'Westers had been the first on the scene, arriving overland across the Continental Divide to establish Fort McLeod on McLeod Lake in 1805, soon to be followed by others. The Hudson's Bay Company became active in the area about 1824, following its amalgamation with the Nor'Westers three years earlier.

However, when coastal traders sought to extend their commerce up the rivers, particularly toward the north, they found themselves facing stiff competition from Amerindian entrepreneurs. The extent of these networks surprised early traders when they found trade goods from the coast as far east as the Sekani of the Finlay and Parsnip rivers.[35] The situation was reminiscent of that faced by Cartier nearly three centuries earlier, when the Stadaconans had sought to protect their upriver trade monopoly against the Frenchman's plan to explore the river. Cartier had gone ahead anyway, but eventually the Stadaconans had been able to enforce their monopoly, which had lasted for 40 years until the disappearance of the St Lawrence Iroquois. In the Far Northwest, the Tsimshian and Tlingit were particularly aggressive in protecting their trade networks, and chiefs such as Legaic (Legex, Legaix) of the Tsimshian, who ran a strict monopoly over the Gitksan on the Upper Skeena, and the Nisga'a Wiiseaks (Shakes) on the Nass made it clear to whom they thought the trading rights on those rivers belonged.[36] When the HBC sent combative ex-Nor'Wester Peter Skene Ogden (1790–1854) in 1834 to establish a post on the Stikine River, he backed down in the face of a threatened trade war.[37] Here again, the

Pictograph at Skeena estuary proclaiming Legaic's trade monopoly in the area. Note the coppers at the left, indicating Legaic's wealth.
(© Canadian Museum of Civilization, photo Harlan I. Smith, 1925, 64381)

Company soon learned that in the short run at least it was wiser to co-operate with Amerindian networks rather than to compete with them, a policy that paid off as the maritime trade declined and that between the coast and the interior stepped up. Still, HBC officers were not pleased when they learned of Kwakwaka'wakw traders buying furs at higher prices than the Company was paying and reselling them to Yankee traders. Some groups of Amerindians were obviously more difficult to control than others.

Furs were not the only reason for the activity on the Northwest Coast. Fort Rupert, for example, was constructed with an eye on the potential of nearby coalfields that the Kwakwaka' wakw had shown the Euro-Canadians in 1835. The intention of the Kwakwaka'wakw had been to work the mines themselves and sell the coal to the HBC.[38]

Social Consequences

As elsewhere in the Americas, the social consequences of all this could be drastic. European diseases seem to have been slower in appearing than on the east coast, and the resultant population drops, while severe, appear to have been proportionately somewhat less than those in other regions of the hemisphere, which had drops in some cases of up to 95 per cent. The Northwest Coast population would reach its nadir in 1929, when it touched 22,605;[39] since then, it has been recovering. The connection between material wealth and rank, manifested in the potlatch, placed a premium on the control of trading networks. Chiefs who were well-placed in this regard, such as Legaic or 'Kwah of the Wet'suwet'en (Carrier) (c. 1755–1840), both of whom had large interior networks, expanded their spheres of influence and became very powerful.[40] Others who depended mainly on the sea otter, such as Muquinna, were able to do well for a while but then found their positions undercut as the trade passed them by. In the boreal forests, material wealth was not a consideration in selecting peace chiefs, nor were these chiefs concerned with trading. Trading chiefs had been a creation of the fur trade, a response to the penchant of the European traders to deal with chiefs, and had little, if any, connection with the general problems of leadership with which the peace chiefs were involved. Back in New Caledonia, one of the consequences of the increasing tempo of upriver trade was the spread of coastal cultures into the interior, reaching as far as the Wet'suwet'en on the interior plateau. Athapaskans around Atlin and Teslin lakes in the North were so affected by these trends they became known as 'interior Tlingit'. Counterbalancing these were influences being brought in by the fur brigades coming from the East; canoemen were often Iroquois, some of whom reached the coast (and even Hawaii), but most settled in Oregon and northwestern Alberta.

In the midst of all this, Northwest Coast cultures flourished, expressing themselves in the growing lavishness of ceremonies, but above all in their arts, by which they represented their mystical vision of the world and its powers. Their passion for carving, sculpting, painting, and weaving and for decoration generally overflowed onto the most utilitarian of objects; even such items as halibut fish hooks would be adorned with carvings. If the people were 'art intoxicated', the condition was catching, as visitors immediately succumbed and collected all they could.

As the coastal fur trade dwindled, enterprising artisans took to producing objects for this new market. The Haida of the Queen Charlotte Islands discovered a use for the slate deposits in their territory; they mined the soft stone, carved it into miniature totem poles, pipes, and other objects, polished the result to a shining black, and a new art form was born for which there was an instant demand, and which is still flourishing today. A leader in this development was the Haida chief Charles Edenshaw (Tahayghen, 'Noise in the housepit'; Nòngkwigetkla_s, 'They gave ten potlatches for him'; successor to the chiefly title of Eda'nsa, c. 1839–1920), a master sculptor who worked in many media. Today his great-grandson Robert Davidson follows in his footsteps. Argillite carving is only one of the new ways in which coastal artists channelled their creative geniuses in response to new challenges. Amerindian artists and artisans of the Atlantic coast had not been so fortunate in the sixteenth and seventeenth centuries: European tastes during those periods did not acknowledge 'primitive' arts and crafts; what little was collected was as curiosities, and practically nothing of that has survived. The results of these attitudes are evident in museums: where Northwest Coast art is probably the most heavily represented of any of the tribal arts of the world, there is practically nothing to give us a glimpse of the once-flourishing cultures of the Maritimes.

The absence of colonial rivalry during the process of settlement was not an unmixed blessing for the Natives of the Pacific coast. For one thing, once the trade receded into the background there was no common ground on which Indians and Europeans could interrelate; no alliances developed, such as the French–Abenaki partnership that had had such an effect on Canada's early history. Even though agriculture could not take over as it had in other parts of Canada, there was still no role for Amerindians in European settlements, except as wage labour in the fisheries and lumber camps.[41] Apart from the treaties negotiated by James Douglas, which will be considered later, there were no negotiations for the lands the settlers appropriated for themselves. The idea that Amerindians had neither sovereign nor proprietary rights prevailed. The problems that resulted from such attitudes became acute with the discovery of gold on the Fraser and Thompson rivers in 1857. Before that happened, the last of the colonial wars was fought in central Canada and in the United States—the War of 1812.

Part IV

Towards New Horizons

Chapter 15

Turntable of 1812–14

The terms of the Peace of Paris of 1783 that concluded the American War of Independence, particularly its cession of the Ohio Valley to the United States, caused stunned surprise among western Indians. As had happened with the Mi'kmaq and Wuastukwiuk in the Treaty of Utrecht, their lands had been ceded without any mention of Aboriginal inhabitants, allies or otherwise. The dream of pan-Indian unity that earlier in the century had inspired the Abenaki's Nescambiouit and the Fox's Kiala in their failed attempts to forge chains of alliances from the Great Lakes to the Atlantic was now an urgent political goal. Thirty-five nations assembled at Sandusky, in Ohio's Wyandot country (scene of one of the last battles in the recent war), in the first of a series of councils to consider the matter. Joseph Brant of the Mohawks lobbied hard for a confederation on the model of the Six Nations, which was further than most of the delegates were willing to go; but, realizing all too clearly the need for unity, some of them coalesced into a loose confederacy. Sir John Johnson (1741–1830), son of Sir William, who had succeeded his father as superintendent of Indians

for the Northern Department,[1] assured the delegates that the Paris peace in no way extinguished their rights to lands northwest of the Ohio River. Spurred by this 'Tomahawk Speech', as it has been called, the council agreed to hold to the line that had been established by the Treaty of Fort Stanwyx in 1768, the Ohio River, as the boundary beyond which European settlement was not to spread. Settlers and even governments showed little inclination to respect Amerindian rights; in 1783 North Carolina confiscated all Indian lands within the state. This was in line with the assumption of the American government that in winning independence it had automatically acquired title to all territories east of the Mississippi, whether or not Indians were living on them.[2] Outcries were such that by 1786 the right of Amerindians to land was acknowledged and a policy of purchase was in place. Not only was it poorly honoured in practice, but the Indians often simply did not want to sell. In the battles that inevitably erupted, Amerindians twice defeated the Americans. The latter rallied a larger military expedition than ever and destroyed the coalition in the

TIMELINE

1783	North Carolina confiscates all Indian lands; outcries lead to policy of purchase three years later.
1791	Miami chief Michikinakoua, with allied tribes, routes Americans on Miami River: the over 900 American casualties represent the largest numerical defeat by Amerindians of Americans.
1794	American military forces defeat Amerindian alliance in Battle of Fallen Timbers; British fail to help Natives and close doors of Fort Miami to them.
1795	Treaty of Greenville demands huge land cessions to Americans, opens Ohio Valley to settlers.
1807	Death of Joseph Brant, Mohawk war chief, and subsequent rise to pan-Indian leadership of Tecumseh, part Shawnee, part Creek, and his brother, Tenskwatawa, 'the Shawnee Prophet'.
1808	Tenskwatawa founds Prophetown.
1811	William Henry Harrison, Indiana governor, attacks Prophetown when Tecumseh is away on pan-Indian mission.
1812	17 July: Michilimackinac falls to Amerindians and British, following strategy devised by Tecumseh and other Amerindian chiefs.

	15 August: Fort Dearborn (Chicago) falls to massacre by Main Poc's Potawatomi.
	16 August: US General William Hull surrenders Fort Detroit after ruse concocted by Tecumseh.
	13 October: Battle of Queenston Heights, led by Mohawks John Brant and Major John Norton; British victory tempered by loss of General Isaac Brock, who had taken Fort Detroit with his friend, Tecumseh.
1813	24 June: Battle of Beaver Dams an Iroquoian-led victory for British.
	10 September: American naval victory on Lake Erie cuts British supply line to west.
	5 October: At Moraviantown in southern Ontario, Tecumseh and his Indian allies save General Henry Procter, who flees; Tecumseh, severely wounded, fights to death.
1814	5 July: Battle of Chippewa, in which American Iroquois, led by Red Jacket, fight against Canadian Iroquois under Major Norton. Treaty of Ghent ends hostilities between British and Americans

Battle of Fallen Timbers, 1794; not only did the British not come to the aid of their allies, they also closed the doors of Fort Miami, their nearest fort to the scene of battle. The battle effectively broke indigenous resistance to the western advance of non-Aboriginal settlement, as was only too evident in the land cessions demanded in the Treaty of Greenville in 1795. The continual loss of territory, even when compensated for by cash payments, was causing growing worry and resentment.[3]

Changing World

This was a period of profound changes in the Western world. In Europe, the French Revolution of 1789 led to the Napoleonic Wars (1800–1815), another in the long series of Anglo–French conflicts, which drained manpower from such peacetime activities as the fur trade and cut off markets. By 1808 the fur trade was in a depression. Without other economic resources, tribal nations dependent on the trade suffered severe hardships and turned to their British allies for help. The British, caught in unresolved antagonisms in the wake of American independence, and by this time more aware of the usefulness of Amerindian allies to preserve their colonies in the event of future hostilities, were only too willing to comply. Between 1784 and 1788 they spent £20,000 annually on Indian gift distributions, an expense with which the fur barons of Montreal willingly helped. As Montreal merchant James McGill (1744–1813) wrote to the governor: 'The Indians are the only Allies who can aught avail in the defence of the Canadas. They have the same interest as us, and alike are objects of American subjugation, if not extermination.'[4]

It was an ironic switch for the British. During the French and Indian War, they had complained bitterly about French maintenance and use of Amerindian allies, and when victorious the British had sought to discontinue the practice with disastrous results (Chapter 12). Now, 20 years later, they found themselves using the same tactics vis-à-vis the Americans.[5] In 1807, convinced by the *Chesapeake* affair[6] that a conflict was inevitable, London instructed Sir James Craig (1748–1812), newly appointed governor-in-chief of Canada, to ensure the loyalty of western Indians. After much weighing of the pros and cons of the situation, and remembering the support they had received from the Iroquois (particularly the Mohawk) during the recent war with the Americans, the British had concluded that Amerindian support was vital to the preservation of Britain's remaining North American colonies.[7] The very people whose pleas for help Britain had ignored at the Battle of Fallen Timbers in 1794, she now sought to win over to her cause. Amerindians, for their part, needed all the help they could get in their efforts to preserve their territories; in the early post-independence period in the United States, even the wavering British appeared preferable to the aggressively

expansionist Americans. Tecumseh sided with the British, not because he liked them particularly but because he saw them as the lesser of two evils. Others had more immediate needs in mind: as a Seneca chief pointed out, if his people were to support the British, it would be necessary for them to be kept well supplied with goods and arms.[8]

The death of Brant in 1807 opened the way for Tecumseh ('Shooting Star', 'Panther Crouching in Wait', *c.* 1768–1813), part Shawnee, part Creek, to move onto centre stage. Having lost his father and a brother to the Americans in the ongoing US frontier wars, he had become an advocate of pan-Indianism and had refused to participate in the Treaty of Greenville, which had opened the Ohio Valley for American settlement. As with Pontiac, Tecumseh was linked with a prophet, in his case a brother, Tenskwatawa ('Open Door', Lalawethika, 1775–1836). More widely known as the Shawnee Prophet, Tenskwatawa took his name from the saying of Jesus, 'I am the door'.[9] His nativistic religious revival prepared the way for Tecumseh's inter-tribal movement, with its doctrine that land did not belong to particular tribal nations but to Amerindians as a whole. Consequently, he argued, no single tribe had the right to cede land on its own, which should only be done by all the tribal nations of the region in council.[10] This was an Amerindian answer to the Proclamation of 1763, which held that Native lands could only be ceded to the British Crown; it was also a challenge to the policy of divide and rule.

Tecumseh as Leader

Tecumseh is widely regarded as the greatest of all Amerindian leaders during the period of resistance to European settlement. Although no authentic portrait of him exists, there are verbal descriptions of his appearance. Apparently he cut a striking figure, combining a fine physique with a great sense of style. He dressed in the manner of his people, but with a flair that drew the admiration of both Amerindians and non-Amerindians. His personality was equally impressive: Tecumseh combined a passionate concern for his people with a genius for strategy. As his friend General Isaac Brock (1769–1812) observed, if he had been British he would have been a great general.[11] During the War of 1812–14, warriors of more than 30 tribal nations fought under him.

Tecumseh challenged the cessions of territory the Americans were obtaining, particularly those wrung from Amerindians by William Henry Harrison, governor of Indiana Territory from 1800 to 1812. He set out to visit as many tribal nations as he could, trying to convince them to unite to prevent further encroachment. His proposal was a radical departure from traditional inter-tribal politics, yet Tecumseh made remarkable headway towards realizing his vision of an Amerindian alliance from Lake Michigan southward; he does not seem to have got further south than Alabama.[12]

As the influence of Tecumseh and Tenskwatawa spread, the British became interested, and the Americans, apprehensive. In his journeys, Tecumseh gained the support of the Potawatomi (principally through Chief Main Poc, until he defected), Ojibwa, Shawnee, Odawa, Winnebagos, Kickapoo; he had less, but some, success with the Delaware, Wyandot, Menominee, Miami, and Piankeshaw, among others. Creeks, who had been such strong supporters of the British in the recent war, felt particularly betrayed by the peace (their first reaction to the news had been to call it a 'Virginia lie'[13]), so very few joined. Tecumseh's appeal was to the younger warriors; older chiefs tended to oppose him on the grounds that his proposed inter-tribal council would undermine their authority. One of these opponents was the Miami chief Michikinakoua (Little Turtle, *c.* 1750–1812), who with allied tribes had routed the

Tecumseh, one of the greatest Indian leaders, came close to uniting Indians against European encroachments. He was killed in the War of 1812. *(Library and Archives Canada, C-3809)*

Americans under General Arthur St Clair (1734–1818) on the Miami River in 1791, inflicting over 900 casualties. As an Amerindian victory, it ranked second to that over Braddock in 1755; in terms of casualties, it was the worst defeat ever for Americans by Amerindians. However, it did not become the subject of popular legend as did a later Amerindian victory, the Battle of Little Bighorn (1876). Although Michikinakoua agreed that the future lay in negotiation rather than warfare, he thought that each tribal nation could do so on its own.

Despite such opposition, other factors came to Tecumseh's aid, such as the depression in the fur trade after 1808. The loss of markets for furs caused hardship among those who had adapted to the trade, a situation aggravated among Great Lakes Amerindians by two successive crop failures and the disappearance of game because of drought. Turning to the British for help, more than 5,000 converged on Amherstburg, seeking alliances with Britain. Amherstburg had already become a major centre for 'gift' distributions, as the British concentrated on providing equipment to obtain food, such as nets, traps, and snares, and, of course, guns and ammunition. The Americans were convinced the Amerindians were being armed for war. In the matter of gift diplomacy, the British had made a complete about-face since 1763; with chiefs they perceived to be influential, such as Tecumseh, they were especially generous. The problem was now rather the reverse of the earlier parsimony, as various administrators and officers vied with each other, especially in the distribution of rum.[14] This in turn contributed to other problems, as when supplies ran out, the situation could be worrisome in the extreme.[15]

The British by this time had developed a cadre of trader/agents who had learned how to deal with Amerindians, following the example of the French. Among these was the Irishman Matthew Elliott (c. 1739–1814), who had lived with the Shawnee for many years, married among them, and was so assimilated to the Amerindian way that he was not completely trusted by the British. Once dismissed from Indian Affairs on unproven charges of corruption, he was called back in 1808 as superintendent at Amherstburg because of his connection with the strategically located Shawnee; one of

his first actions was to arrange a council at Amherstburg in 1808, which attracted 5,000 Amerindians. Another influential figure was the Scot, Robert Dickson (c. 1765–1823), whose flaming red hair and beard became part of western folklore, earning him the Dakota name of Mascotopah; he was a brother-in-law of Yanktonai Dakota chief Red Thunder. A long-time trader, Dickson was British agent for the tribes west of Lake Huron; his was a hard-headed approach that earned him the reputation of being tough but fair, tempered by a strong streak of generosity, although his reputation in this regard was clouded by his tendency to favour the various Siouan peoples. Nevertheless, he played a major role rallying the western Indians to the British cause, to which they remained loyal during the war.[16] Other notable Amerindian agents included the mixed-blood Colonel Alexander McKee, superintendent general of Indian Affairs, 1794–9, married to a Shawnee, and influential in the Amerindian stand on the Ohio River as boundary between Euro-American and Amerindian territories, and interpreter Simon Girty (1741–1818), who as a boy had been captured and adopted by the Senecas and who was so accepted by Amerindians that he was admitted to their councils at the Glaize in 1792.[17] Even though he worked for the British, like Matthew Elliott, he was distrusted by them because he identified so completely with Amerindians; Americans regarded Girty as a traitor on all counts. The interests of the British and the Amerindians coincided in their opposition to the Americans.

The British were more interested in fostering trade than in provoking war. For one thing, on account of the deadly struggle with Napoleon on the European continent, they had neither the troops nor the resources for more military campaigns. Even Harrison admitted as much: in a report to Washington in 1811, he wrote that 'Candour obliges me to inform you that from two Indians of different tribes I have received information that the British agent absolutely dissuaded them from going to war against the United States.' But tensions were mounting, particularly between Harrison and Tecumseh. The Indiana governor was especially annoyed when Tecumseh moved to prevent land surveys. Biding his time, he seized the moment in 1811 when the Shawnee chief was away rallying southern tribes to his cause. Harrison attacked Prophetown, which Tenskwatawa had established in 1808 at the confluence of the Wabash and Tippecanoe rivers. The ensuing battle was less a victory for the Americans than it was a personal defeat for Tenskwatawa; his influence had been slipping, and this bloodshed accentuated the trend. For Tecumseh, the attack ended his plan to delay military action until Amerindians and British could gather sufficient forces to deal a decisive blow to the Americans. For the British, it confirmed their suspicions that the Canadian border was not safe from American aggression.

War of 1812–14

The last of the colonial wars in North America, the War of 1812–14 has been classed as a continuation of the American War of Independence. For Britain and the US it was an inconclusive contest that left important matters, such as those relating to Amerindians, as unresolved as they had been before the fighting; for the Amerindians, it was a turning point, as it was the last conflict in northeastern North America in which their participation was important and even decisive. The Indian allies were the major factor in Great Britain's successful defence of Upper Canada.[18] In the west, it was largely an Amerindian war. For instance, the fall of Michilimackinac on 17 July 1812 to British and Amerindian forces was an Amerindian victory; its strategy had been that of surprise and had been worked out by Tecumseh and other Amerindian chiefs. In the

account that follows, only some of the battles of this war are touched upon, mainly ones that relate in some way to Canada.

The psychological effect of the Michilimackinac victory was enormous, well beyond its broader military significance. Tribes now flocked unreservedly to the British flag; Elliott and Dickson had no trouble raising 4,000 warriors. It also had an impact on General William Hull (1753–1825), US commander at Detroit, whose fear of Amerindians was well known. He proclaimed that 'no white man found fighting by the side of an Indian will be taken prisoner.'[19] By a ruse that led him to believe that British forces on his flank included 5,000 Amerindians, which Tecumseh reinforced by means of the old trick of marching his warriors again and again past a vantage point in full view of the Americans, Hull was convinced that his situation was hopeless. When Tecumseh cut American communication lines, Hull surrendered on 16 August without firing a shot. Tecumseh and General Brock rode together into the fallen fort; it was a victory without casualties.[20] When Hull learned what had happened the day before at Fort Dearborn (Chicago), when most of the garrison had been massacred by Main Poc's Potawatomi, he probably felt justified. American officials saw no alleviating circumstances for General Hull, however, and he was court-martialled.

These successes, especially the fall of Detroit, encouraged the Six Nations, previously set on neutrality, to join British forces. They were to be a major factor in the British success at Queenston Heights on 13 October, when they appeared at a critical moment on the field of battle led by the Mohawk Major John Norton (Teyoninhokarawen, *fl.* 1784–1825) and John Brant ('Tekarihogen', Ahyonwaeghs, 1794–1832), the youngest son of Joseph Brant.[21] Again, the American fear of Amerindians had its effect and the invasion was repelled, with the Americans fleeing precipitously across the river. The cost was high for the British, as they lost Brock.[22]

Major John Norton (Teyoninhokarawen), who played an important role in leading Six Nations forces into battle on the British side during the War of 1812–14.
(© Canadian War Museum [CWM], 19950096-001)

John Brant, son of Joseph Brant. With Major John Norton, he led the Iroquois forces to victory during the Battle of Queenston Heights, 1812. John was elected to the Upper Canadian House of Assembly in 1830 but lost his seat on the charge of irregular voter practices.
(Metropolitan Toronto Reference Library, J. Ross Robertson Collection, T-15499)

Tecumseh began to lose the initiative in the north, despite the fact that he cut an American force to pieces near Fort Meigs, Indiana, on 5 May 1813.[23] However, he was able to get some Creeks to open war in the south, but their confederacy was split to the point of civil war; eventually the Americans under Andrew Jackson (1767–1845, later to become President of the US) destroyed what was left of their league in 1814.[24] In the meantime, the American naval victory on Lake Erie, 10 September 1813, cut the British supply line to Fort Malden (Amherstburg), thus endangering Amerindian alliances in the west, as this was the principal British centre for gift distribution.

The Battle of Beaver Dams, on 24 June 1813, was an Amerindian victory; Iroquoian, to be exact. According to Norton's much quoted remark, 'The Cognauguaga [Caughnawaga] Indians fought the battle, the Mohawks got the plunder and [Lieutenant James] Fitzgibbon [1780–1863] got the credit.'[25] At Queenston Heights, Roger Sheaffe (1763–1851), who had taken over as commander when General Isaac Brock was killed on the battlefield, had received the laurels.

The British general who succeeded Brock, Henry A. Procter (1763–1822), did not attract the admiration of Tecumseh, who compared him to a dog running off with its tail between its legs. His frustration with the British general was all the more understandable in that the Shawnee chief had by this time assembled one of the largest Indian 'armies' the Great Lakes had ever seen, variously estimated at between 2,000 and 3,000 warriors or even higher. The contrast with the British force was glaring—it counted only about 800 men. When Proctor finally made a stand at Moraviantown in southern Ontario on 5 October 1813, Tecumseh and his Indians did the fighting, saving the general's life. Tecumseh, severely wounded, fought until his death; Procter fled. What happened to the Indian leader's body is not known, any more than who killed him; some say he was buried near the scene of battle, others say that souvenir hunters soon rendered the Amerindian leader's body unrecognizable.[26] Among the many stories about Tecumseh's fate is an Ojibwa account recorded a century later, which claims that the Shawnee leader was wounded but did not die because he carried 'medicine'.[27]

After Tecumseh

The effect of the loss of Tecumseh would be hard to overestimate. No leader could fill his role as a catalyst for pan-Indian action. With his passing also went the tattered remains of Tenskwatawa's nativistic movement. However, it is going too far to maintain, as some have, that effective Amerindian participation in the war came to an end with the defeat at Moraviantown.[28] Warriors continued fighting until the end of the war, sometimes in large numbers, but the underlying unity of purpose that Tecumseh had evoked was fatally weakened, and eventually dead. The British cause was too ambiguous to fill the role, although in certain areas such as the upper reaches of Lake Huron and in Wisconsin, where Dickson continued to give out large quantities of presents, British influence continued to be strong. The British sought to compensate for this ambiguity by trying to enshrine Tecumseh's memory as an icon: they gave Tecumseh's son, Paukeesaa, a commission in the British army; his brother, the Shawnee Prophet, received a sword and pistols as gifts of the Prince Regent and was named principal chief of the Western Nations; and his sister, Tecumpease, was heaped with gifts of condolence. While such measures honoured ceremonial protocol, they could not transform a memory into a new Tecumseh or disguise the fact that Britain was not fully committed to the war, locked as she was in her struggle with Napoleon. Her wooing of the Amerindians in this particular case sprang not so much from humanist or ideological conviction as it did from the need to avail herself of all means possible to maintain and preserve her positions in two different theatres at once.

Americans moved to take advantage of the situation and to turn the Amerindians away from the British to their side of the fighting. Some Amerindians were persuaded, and a contingent of American Iroquois, largely Senecas under Red Jacket, fought on the American side at the Battle of Chippewa, 5 July 1814, against British forces that included 200 men of the Six Nations and 100 western Amerindians under Major Norton. So Iroquois were once more pitted against Iroquois, as had happened in the American War of Independence. In this battle the Canadian Amerindians incurred their heaviest losses of the war, although their role was not decisive. The list counted 87 killed and 5 taken prisoners, against 9 American Indians killed, 4 wounded, and 10 missing. The Amerindians were shocked by these casualties, incurred in fighting what was now a white man's quarrel.[29] The American Iroquois sent a deputation to discuss with the Canadian Six

Nations a new, and more inclusive, policy of neutrality. As a result, only a few warriors remained to fight the battle of Lundy's Lane, although other Amerindians continued to fight in other theatres.

Status Quo Ante Bellum

During the negotiations for the Treaty of Ghent, 1814, which formally ended the war, the British, having learned their lesson from the Treaty of Paris of 1783, tried to bargain for the establishment of an Amerindian territory, the boundaries of which would follow those fixed at the Treaty of Greenville (1795). This the Americans absolutely refused to agree to; the most they would accept was to recognize Amerindian lands as they had been before hostilities; in legal parlance, the status quo ante bellum. To suggest that this was a disappointment for Amerindians in the US is to put it mildly; it meant that despite all their battles, very often successful in individual cases, they had not been able to regain lost territories. Despite the assurances of the Treaty of Ghent— 'The Treaty of Omissions', as a French diplomat called it[30]—Indians continued to lose land. Métis communities that had developed in the Great Lakes area were overwhelmed and even occupied militarily.[31] Three years after the death of Tecumseh and five years after Tippecanoe, Indiana became a state. By 1817, forced removal of Amerindians from their traditional lands began to be implemented in the Ohio Valley, a policy that would culminate with the Trail of Tears for the Cherokee in the 1830s. In some instances Amerindians themselves decided to migrate, as the Potawatomi did in 1835–40 when they left their Great Lakes homelands to settle in central and southern Ontario, where they are today.[32] The 'undefended border' between Canada and the United States had become a reality in 1817 with the signing of the Rush-Bagot Convention.

For Canadian Amerindians, the War of 1812–14 was also the end of an era.[33] As long as the colonial wars had lasted, they had been able to maintain their positions in return for their war services. With the loss of that bargaining tool they were placed at a serious disadvantage. This was reflected in governmental reorganization: in 1830, Indian administration was shifted to the civilian arm. Settler expansion was dramatic—the population rose threefold from approximately 750,000 in 1821 to 2.3 million by 1851; in Upper Canada alone it rose by a factor of 10, to reach 952,000. Included in the influx were some Oneida of the Six Nations who, although they had sided with the Americans during the War of Independence, had been deprived of most of their lands in New York state. They settled around Muncey, Ontario, about 1840.

By this time, Amerindians east of the Great Lakes were already a minority in their own lands. It has been estimated that by 1812 they formed only better than 10 per cent of the population of Upper Canada.[34] In the midst of this agricultural expansion the fur trade continued for most of the century as a major economic activity, ensuring a common ground for peaceful interaction between Amerindians and Europeans. But even there, the end was in sight; as sociologist Denys Delâge put it, the time for the ancient way of life had passed; new conditions demanded new adaptations.[35] Adaptation, of course, had always been the key to Amerindian survival; the circumstances might have changed, but the requirement to work out satisfactory life patterns under prevailing conditions remained the same. Traditional values, instead of disappearing, would find new life and new forms in rising to these challenges.

Chapter 16

Canadian Aboriginal World in the Early Nineteenth Century

The imperial civil administration for British North America was dominated by two ideas concerning Amerindians in 1830: that as a people they were disappearing, and that those who remained should either be removed to communities isolated from Euro-Canadians or else be assimilated. In the midst of a rash of studies, commissions of various sorts, and recommendations as to what to do about Amerindians, the official position stabilized on its perceived duty to 'civilize' migrating Natives by settling them down as farmers.[1] Although there were those who wondered at the equation of farming with civilization, for all practical purposes it remained a guiding principle in Amerindian administration during the nineteenth century.[2] 'Civilization' was to be achieved by education, which was to be entrusted to missionaries. In the words of Lord Glenelg (Charles Grant, colonial secretary, 1835–9), the aim was 'to protect and cherish this helpless Race . . . [and] raise them in the Scale of Humanity'.[3] The administration of British North America remained based in London until 1860, when its civil arm was turned over to the colonies.

The funds for this program would come from the invested proceeds from the sale of lands acquired from the Amerindians. In other words, they would pay their own way into civilization. The working out of details was left mainly, but not entirely, in the hands of colonial governors. It should be remembered that at this juncture each colony (Nova Scotia, Prince Edward Island, New Brunswick, Lower Canada [Quebec], and Upper Canada [Ontario]) had separate administrations. (The two Canadas would be united in 1841, following the rebellions of 1837–8.) Rupert's Land and the west coast were administered by the Hudson's Bay Company. Another point to keep in mind is that this was the era of Utopian experiments—attempts to create communities that would reflect Victorian ideals of the good life. For Amerindians, these model villages would become an instrument for the inculcation of Euro-Canadian values. The initiative was not all on the non-Amerindian side, however; people such as the Mississaugas, recognizing that the old ways were no longer applicable, actively sought to work out their own accommodation to the new.[4]

TIMELINE

1637	First Amerindian 'reserve', at Sillery, near Quebec City.
1765	Moravian missionary Jens Haven intercedes to ease conflict between Labrador Inuit and Europeans, which had forced Inuit up the Labrador coast.
1769	Moravians receive land grant on northern Labrador coast.
1771	Haven founds first mission at Nain, which includes trading post.
1784	New Brunswick separated from Nova Scotia; refuses to recognize the only land grant to Amerindians previously made in the colony.
1812	Selkirk colony for white settlers established at Red River, site of the largest Métis settlement in the West.
1820	Whalers operating on east side of Baffin Island.
1824	Indigenous population of Canadas: 18,000.
1825	Miramichi fire in northern New Brunswick destroys 6,000 square miles of prime forest, the resource base of subsistence for countless Amerindians.
	Britain grants land along Credit River to Métis Methodist minister Peter Jones and his Mississauga converts.
1827	Grape Island settlement of Ojibwa in Bay of Quinte founded by American Methodist missionary William Case.
1830	Aboriginal population of New Brunswick less than 1,000.
1830s–40s	Upper Canada administration, over Iroquois protests, gives Grand River Navigation Company Six Nations' funds and land, and the company floods more Six Nations territory before going bankrupt. (Iroquois ultimately lose a 1948 court decision over the matter.)
1832	Hannah Bay massacre: starving Cree raid HBC outpost and kill eight Amerindians and Métis post master. They are caught and seven males are convicted and hanged.
1835	Indian Affairs agent T.G. Anderson begins Ojibwa settlement project at Manitowaning on Manitoulin Island; project eventually deemed a failure, but Ojibwa remain, founding village of Little Current.
1836	Grape Island project relocated to Rice Lake at Alderville, Ont.
	Anglican Herbert Beaver the first permanent west coast missionary, at Fort Vancouver.
	Sir Francis Bond Head, lieutenant-governor of Upper Canada, arranges large land surrenders by Ojibwa in Manitoulin chain and on Bruce Peninsula (the Saugeen tract).
1838	Only 1,425 Mi'kmaq, in wretched condition, listed as living in Nova Scotia.
1840s	HBC establishes posts in Far Northwest.
1841	First book, a hymnal, printed using Cree syllabary developed by Methodist missionary James Evans.
1842	Nova Scotia Act to provide for the Instruction and Permanent Settlement of the Indians.
1843	Cree prophet Abishabis killed by his own people as a windigo after leading short-lived religious movement.
1844	New Brunswick Act for the Management and Disposal of the Indian Reserves.
	Indigenous population of Canadas: 12,000.
1845–7	Fatal expedition, led by Sir John Franklin, to find Northwest Passage.

1847	Mississauga join Six Nations to establish New Credit, near Hagersville, Ont.
1850	Gunboat diplomacy begins on Pacific coast.
1850–4	Governor James Douglas, recognizing Aboriginal title, signs 14 treaties with Coast Salish on Vancouver Island.
1856	Ojibwa band settles on Christian Island in Georgian Bay.

1859	An Act Concerning Indian Reserves passed in Nova Scotia.
1862	Utopian experiment of lay Anglican William Duncan begins at Tsimshian village of Metlakatla with support of Tsimshian chief Paul Legaic.
1887	Duncan and 600 followers establish New Metlakatla in Alaska; Legaic and others stay behind.
1888	Warship sails Skeena River to quell Gitksan uprising.

A Moravian missionary who may be Jens Haven (1724–96) is shown speaking to Inuit at Nain, Labrador. After Maria Spilsbury (1777–1820).
(Library and Archives Canada, C-124432)

Mikak, as portrayed by John Russell (1744–1806) in 1769 during her visit to London.
(Photo courtesy Institut und Sammlung für Völkerkunde der Universität Göttingen)

Arctic and Subarctic

For the Inuit, there were two principal arenas for association with Euro-Canadians—the comparatively mild Labrador coast since the sixteenth century and the central and western Arctic since early in the nineteenth.[5] The hostilities between the Labrador coast Inuit and Europeans, which had carried over from the French regime, had resulted in the Inuit being driven northward. In 1765 the conflict was eased, although not terminated, through the efforts of Moravian missionary Jens Haven (1724–96), known to the Inuit as Ingoak (Inuit friend).[6] In 1769, the Moravians received a land grant of 100,000 acres (40,469 hectares), which enabled Haven two years later to launch his first mission (including a trading post and

workshop) at Nain. In winning this support he had been greatly assisted by an influential Inuk woman, Mikak (Micoc, *c*. 1740–95), who had been sent to London by Governor Palliser to impress her with English might in the hope that she would influence her people to stop harassing English fishing operations.[7] Three other land grants followed as the Moravians expanded their operations. When they combined trading with their missionary work, they found themselves in competition with the Hudson's Bay Company, a situation that peaked in the latter half of the nineteenth century. The Moravians never did successfully reconcile the contradictions between their evangelical and commercial interests, which eventually led to their abandonment of trade to the HBC in 1926.[8]

In the central and western Arctic whaling was the attraction, at first mainly for British and Scottish, although Dutch and others were also present in Davis Strait. By 1820 whalers were operating on the east side of Baffin Island and were moving westward; by shortly after mid-century, Americans dominated whaling off the west coast of Hudson Bay as well as in the western Arctic, usually staying for two years and wintering at Repulse Bay, just north of Southampton Island at the top of Hudson Bay, and later at Pauline Cove on Herschel Island in the Beaufort Sea, while the British predominated in Davis Strait and especially Cumberland Sound. Principal target of this hunt was the bowhead whale, sought for its oil but especially for its baleen ('whalebone'), much in demand to create the tightly corseted feminine silhouette then so fashionable.[9]

Individual enterprise was the order of the day, particularly in the western Arctic; there was no systematic organization of whaling operations, no government supervision.[10] For the Inuit, the association could be a profitable one in the short run as they hired out to the whalers; they also benefited from the debris (such as wood and metal) the latter left behind. In the long run, the adoption of the gun and trade goods (including foods such as flour, sugar, and tea)[11] led to loss of incentive to maintain ancient hunting skills and a consequent lessening of self-sufficiency. Introduced diseases compounded the situation; the combined effects of these factors would become severe later in the century. The massive attack on whale populations, started in the Strait of Belle Isle in the sixteenth century and fanning northward, had begun to affect the availability of the sea mammals for Native subsistence. Although whale meat was only one item of diet (walrus, for example, was used much more),[12] obtaining it was the ultimate challenge for the hunter. More importantly, the commercial slaughter of whales and walrus, at its peak from 1868 to 1883 (at the time the bison herds were being decimated on the prairies), resulted in widespread starvation.[13] By 1900 the original Inuvialuit of the western Arctic had disappeared, to be replaced by Alaskan Inuit who came with the American whalers.[14] This was but one indication of the dislocations resulting from contact that would eventually be more widespread.[15]

The British were still preoccupied with their centuries-old search for the Northwest Passage and the first half of the nineteenth century saw several attempts, including the most famous of them all, the lost expedition of Sir John Franklin (1786–1847) of 1845–7. Since no one except Inuit was interested in permanently settling in the Arctic, the question of land was not raised, and the Inuit did not sign any treaties until the Inuvialuit agreement of 1984. They were left to pursue their own lives in their own ways. Non-Native intrusions were few and scattered, such as the Moravian and Grenfell missions on the Labrador coast during the eighteenth and nineteenth centuries and the later ones in the Northwest Territories and Beaufort Sea via the Pacific. The HBC did not establish a permanent post in the High Arctic

until early in the twentieth century, although it had long operated Subarctic posts. A few Inuit worked for the company as hunters and interpreters; probably the best known, at least to non-Natives, was Ooligbuck (Oullibuck, Ullabuck, among other spellings, d. 1852), who at one point hunted for Franklin.

During the 1840s, the Hudson's Bay Company began establishing posts in the Far Northwest, despite serious doubts that its charter extended into those regions. The first was Peel River Post, which would later become Fort McPherson in the Northwest Territories. As the Company pushed westward into the Yukon,[16] evidence became stronger of trade with the Pacific coast, both Amerindian and Russian. While local Natives were pleased to have access to the new trade goods, coastal traders such as the Tlingit did not take kindly to this double invasion of their trading domains.[17] When the HBC established Fort Selkirk where the Pelly and Yukon rivers meet, in the homeland of the northern Tutchone, the Tlingit defended their commercial interests by wrecking the post and defying both British and Russians. In the midst of that three-cornered fight, the missionaries arrived—the Anglicans in 1861, with the Roman Catholics hard on their heels a year later.[18]

The Maritimes

Since the last known Beothuk died in 1829, there were no officially recognized Aboriginal peoples left in Newfoundland. Mi'kmaq who had migrated to the Bay St George area since the fall of New France were not accorded status until 1984, when the only reserve was established at Conne River. A suit for recognition brought by the other communities through the Federation of Newfoundland Indians (FNI) led to an Agreement-in-Principle in late 2007. In a 29 March 2008 ratification vote, 90 per cent of more than 3,200 Mi'kmaq who cast ballots voted for the agreement. The new Qalipu Mi'kmaq

First Nations band, which is to be a landless band, is expected to become official in 2010 and will represent Newfoundland Mi'kmaq who previously had no Indian Act status.[19] The province of Newfoundland and Labrador still has not recognized Aboriginal title.[20]

In Nova Scotia, anti-Amerindian sentiment, which was at least partly a legacy of the 150 years of the Mi'kmaq War, continued strong. Mi'kmaq were listed in 1838 as numbering 1,425, in wretched condition, and declining so rapidly they were expected to disappear altogether in about 40 years. Since no Aboriginal territorial rights as such had been recognized for them, apart from the right to hunt and fish 'at the pleasure of the sovereign' (Chapters 6, 11), if individual Mi'kmaq wanted land they were expected to apply for grants like anyone else. What they received, however, were licences of occupation 'during pleasure', and the lands in question were not surveyed.[21] About 20,050 acres (8,114 hectares) had been set aside for this purpose by Order-in-Council but neither lands nor locations were good, with none near Halifax, once a favoured hunting ground.[22] These lands were not reserved for specific bands; as legal historian Douglas Sanders has pointed out, all Amerindians were equally entitled to all reserves, a system that remained in effect until 1960.[23] Even so, they were continually invaded by non-Native squatters whom the government was unable (or unwilling) to control; what was even worse, homesteaders' tickets of location sometimes overlapped reserves.[24] Some chiefs, such as Andrew Meuse (fl. 1821–50, chief near the Gut of Annapolis Royal) and Charles Glode (Glower, d. 1852), lobbied hard for their people with some results. Meuse won the right for his people to pursue their traditional hunt of the porpoise.[25] Glode, a successful farmer in the same region, was one of the few Mi'kmaq to be granted freehold land, a break with Aboriginal landholding practice that did not sit well with his fellow tribesmen.

Nova Scotia's Act to provide for the Instruction and Permanent Settlement of the Indians of 1842 created the post of Indian Commissioner to supervise the reserves and to see that chiefs were publicly acknowledged by being made militia captains and provided with plans of their reserve surveys in order to organize distribution of lands among their people. The first holder of the new post, which was unpaid, was Joseph Howe (1804–73), who would later make his mark in Canadian history by opposing Confederation. Frustrated in his good intentions by lack of public support and by anti-Amerindian sentiment, he did not last in the position for much more than a year. Potato blight in 1846–8 added to both the colony's and the Amerindians' woes. It was not until 1859 that a determined effort was made to get the situation in hand by passing An Act Concerning Indian Reserves. Established squatters were to be allowed to buy the lands they had appropriated and the proceeds were to be placed in a fund for Amerindian relief; future squatters were to be ejected. Surveys were to be regularized and plots allocated to individual Amerindians. Soon it was announced that the boundaries of the reserves had been established beyond dispute; by 1866 reserves totalled 20,730 acres (8,389 hectares) for 637 Amerindian families. However, very few of the squatters paid anything for their lands, and none paid in full.[26] At the same time, not many Mi'kmaq had become farmers, which, according to their own myths, their ancestors had once been; further, they stubbornly held to their tribal custom of holding lands in common and objected to the division of reserves into individual holdings.

In 1830, New Brunswick counted an even smaller Aboriginal population than Nova Scotia: less than 1,000 Mi'kmaq, Wuastukawiuk, and Abenaki. Those of the white pine stands of the Miramichi had been devastated by the disastrous fire of 1825 that destroyed

6,000 square miles (15,540 square kilometres) of prime forest, along with their subsistence base. When New Brunswick was separated from Nova Scotia and became a colony in 1784, it refused to recognize the only land grant that had been made by the previous administration, 20,000 acres (8,094 hectares) along the Miramichi River to John Julian and his band. By the time the grant was confirmed in 1808, it had been reduced by half.[27]

As in Nova Scotia, the uncontrolled influx of Loyalists aroused resentment; in this case, troops had to be called in. Indian administration was as haphazard as in Nova Scotia, with lands being granted on an ad hoc basis and with such posts as Indian commissioners being unpaid. When lands set aside for Amerindians were finally listed, in 1838, 61,293 acres (24,804 hectares) were counted, divided among 15 reserves. Here, also, there was difficulty with squatters who refused to budge from Indian lands.[28] The situation was complicated by a border dispute with the United States, in which both sides called on Aboriginals to testify on their behalf. The colony resorted to gift distributions to gain the Amerindians' friendship, and the Natives were rewarded during the War of 1812 when they declared neutrality.

Sir Edmund Head, lieutenant-governor of New Brunswick, 1848–54, urged that Amerindians be treated as children, an idea widely prevalent at the time, thereby limiting their legal discretion and capacity for dealing with their own affairs. Moses H. Perley, Special Commissioner for Indian Affairs, 1841–8, reporting on the severe attrition of Amerindian lands,[29] tried hard to get a better deal for them but with no result. He played a major role in drafting the 1844 Act for the Management and Disposal of the Indian Reserves in the Province, but by the time it was passed it was so altered that his efforts to protect Amerindian wishes and interests were aborted. Reserves were to be re-allotted on the basis of 50 acres (20 hectares) per

An eighteenth-century depiction of whaling off the coast of Greenland. The skin umiaks of the Inuit could hold as many as 50 men and women. Inuit donned their best outfits for the occasion, in the belief that whales hated 'dirty habits'. From Hans Egede, *Description et histoire naturelle du Groënland*, tr. D.R.D.P., Copenhagen and Geneva, Frère Philibert, 1763.
(Photo courtesy The Newberry Library, Chicago)

family and the surplus was to be sold 'for the benefit of the Indians'. By 1867, although Amerindian holdings had been theoretically boosted to 66,096 acres (26,748 hectares), in fact, 16 per cent of that acreage had been sold, usually at ridiculously low prices, and 10,000 acres (4,047 hectares) were still occupied by squatters. As historian Leslie Upton (1931–80) pointed out, the only thing that saved Amerindians from total dispossession was the fact that much of New Brunswick was not suitable for agriculture, and most Amerindian lands were at best marginal.[30]

The indigenous situation was even worse in Prince Edward Island, which in 1767 had been divided among 66 absentee British proprietors, with nothing left for its Aboriginal inhabitants. For that matter, nothing had been left for the government, which consequently had been deprived of a major source of revenue. Numerous petitions gave rise to much debate, in which it was pointed out that although the Mi'kmaq had once raised the tomahawk against the British, they had put it down upon being promised fair treatment. 'They promised to leave us some of our land—but they did not—they drove us from place to place like wild beasts—that was not just.'[31] The colony's first official recognition of Amerindians was the passage of a law in 1856 providing for the appointment of a commissioner to look after Amerindian affairs. In 1859, 204 acres (83 hectares) on the Morell River were set aside for Amerindians, the only such successful transaction on the island.[32] Eventually, the offshore Lennox Island, 1,400 acres (567 hectares) in extent, was purchased for the Natives through the efforts of interested individuals in the colony and the Aborigines' Protection Society, founded in 1838. Funds for the project were raised in Britain and the sale was completed in 1870. Money was provided to settle seven Amerindian families. Four years later, almost 90 acres (36 hectares) were under cultivation.

The Canadas

The estimated indigenous population in Upper and Lower Canada (as Ontario and Quebec had been respectively designated in the Constitutional Act of 1791) in 1824 was about 18,000, a figure that did not include 'wild' Amerindians of the boreal forest. Twenty years later it had dropped to 12,000, lending credence to the popular belief of the 'vanishing Amerindian'; in contrast, between 1818 and 1828, the non-Native population doubled. As we have seen, the Proclamation of 1763 applied only to Upper Canada. In Lower Canada, village lands set aside for Amerindians during the French regime had been confirmed by the Montreal Capitulations of 1760. In Upper Canada, land-cession treaties had begun to be signed in 1764 and were continuing (Chapters 12, 17).

Wholesale changes radically altered Indian administration in the Canadas between 1828 and 1845 (Chapter 17). In 1828 Sir John Johnson retired, ending 80 years of dominance by the Johnson family. By this time it appeared to some influential persons, such as Sir George Ramsay, Earl of Dalhousie, governor-general, 1819–28, that a special branch for Aboriginals was superfluous, and he urged its devolution. This was successfully opposed by Major-General H.C. Darling, Indian Affairs' chief superintendent, 1828–30, in his 1828 report on Indian conditions, the first such for the Canadas. He advocated establishing model farms and villages, in effect a system of reserves, as the best means of civilizing Amerindians, a process in which the department would have a vital role relocating and re-establishing its charges. The recently established and thriving Mississauga farming village on the Credit River proclaimed the potentialities for such a project. This report has been called the founding document of the British civilizing program. In the meantime, the administration of Indian affairs in Lower Canada was hived off from that of Upper Canada to form a separate unit. What this meant in practice was that most of the experienced personnel stayed in Upper Canada; the branch already had a tradition of sons following in their fathers' footsteps in the service, quite apart from the Johnsons. There was some effort to recruit Amerindians as interpreters and clerks, but there were none employed at the policy-making level. With the Act of Union of 1841, Upper Canada became Canada West and Lower Canada became Canada East. With Confederation in 1867, the administrative apparatus of Canada West would be transferred to the new Dominion, absorbing the administrations from the other colonies.

In Canada East, the Amerindian villages of Odanak (St Francis), Bécancour, Caughnawaga (Sault St Louis, today's Kahnawake), St Regis (Akwesasne), Oka (Lake of Two Mountains, Kanesatake), and Lorette had been established long before the Conquest; in fact, the first 'reserve' in Canada, that of Sillery, had been set up near Quebec City two centuries earlier, in 1637, on the site of a Montagnais summer fishing station.[33] Inspired by the reserves that had been organized by the Jesuits in Brazil, the French were not trying to compensate Natives for lost territories; quite the contrary, the French King was setting aside land he considered to be French for Amerindian use under certain conditions.[34] In the case of Sillery, although it was established specifically for the benefit of Natives, its title rested with the Jesuits until 1651, when it was temporarily transferred to the Amerindians under the direction of the Jesuits.[35] The unusual gesture had been inspired by the need to ensure the loyalty of the Natives (most of whom were Huron) in the intensifying colonial wars. In the 1640s it counted about 40 Christian families and many more traditionalists. Most lived in bark wigwams; only the 'principal' Amerindians lived in European-style houses built for them.[36] It was, in effect, a residential mission to introduce agriculture to indigenes whose lands had been overhunted and overtrapped, and so had lost their traditional subsistence bases. However, restrictive regulations (for one thing, Indians were not permitted to hunt or fish without permission from either the Jesuits or a Christian captain),[37] compounded by problems associated with war, disease, and alcohol, dampened early enthusiasm; final blows were an Iroquois raid in 1655 and later a fire that destroyed most of the buildings. Title was returned to the Jesuits, the ethics of which have been questioned.[38] The transfer allowed

the missionaries during the latter part of the 1660s to begin opening up the reserve to European settlers, on the grounds that the Amerindians were not using it.[39] This trend was temporarily counterbalanced during the 1670s with the arrival of refugees from the Abenaki wars in the English colonies; however, the establishment of an Abenaki village, Saint François de Sales, on the Chaudière River drew the refugees away from Sillery. By 1688, Sillery was all but denuded of Amerindians.[40]

Reserves in the modern sense (lands set aside for Amerindians' continued use upon surrender of most of their territory)[41] did not appear until after the Proclamation; under the French regime, which did not recognize Aboriginal title, lands for Amerindian communities had been granted to missionaries 'for the benefit of the Amerindians'. This meant that Aboriginals, such as the Cree and Ojibwa in the North, were powerless to act when their lands were invaded by loggers and settlers without a by-your-leave, as were the Mi'kmaq of Restigouche with respect to their fishing grounds. Although their problems were not a priority with the new English government, involved as it was confronting the French, the Natives won their point in one case. In 1761, when the Jesuits took the stand that as the seigneurs of Caughnawaga they had the right to sell portions of its lands, the Iroquois complained to General Thomas Gage, military governor of Montreal from 1760 to 1763. Remembering that the Iroquois had been allies of the British in the recent war, the soldier governor saw to it that the Jesuits were deprived of all interest in the reserve, which was turned over to the Amerindians; as well, an agent was appointed to see that the rents of the ceded portions were accounted to the Iroquois.[42] This was ratified in 1764 by James Murray, governor of Quebec, 1763–6. Gage's action would stand Kahnawake in good stead in the future.

Sir John Colborne, lieutenant-governor for

Upper Canada, suggested in 1829 that the best way of financing the civilizing of Amerindians would be through leasing and sale of their lands. Sir James Kempt, governor of Lower Canada, 1828–30, agreed, and also supported the idea of model villages. Above all, Amerindians must become self-supporting citizens within the cultural framework of colonial life; the old hunting ways were doomed. Throughout the nineteenth century, this perceived need for Amerindians to march to the white man's drum would be a dominant administrative theme. In the meantime, the gift distributions were still continuing—the lesson of 1763 had not been forgotten, even though there was no more need for Amerindian military services, at least not until the disturbances of 1837–8. Those episodes prolonged the life of the distributions, even as the cost became steadily more unacceptable; finally, in 1858, they were brought to an end. The turning point can be dated to 1827, when the Ojibwa of Chenail Ecarte and Lower St Clair surrendered extensive tracts in the London and western districts for annuities and four reserves. In the meantime, the model village idea gained enough official support that it was able to proceed.[43] These experiments were all in Canada West, but they drew much of their inspiration from the long-established Amerindian villages of Canada East. The inhabitants of these earlier villages all were officially Christian and living sedentary lives, an achievement the British hoped to emulate in Canada West with its shorter history of contact.[44] In fact, they already had the examples in Canada West of two successful Christian Amerindian-inspired villages, one on the Credit River and the other at Grape Island, near Belleville, of which more later.

Another precursor of the model Amerindian village had been established by the Moravian Brothers on the Thames River near the future international border in 1792 for refugee Delawares. Although they called it Fairfield, it became popularly known as Moraviantown. Not only had it been successful (for one reason, Delaware were traditionally agriculturalists), it had even been more prosperous than surrounding colonial settlements. Looted and burned by the Americans in the War of 1812, the town had been rebuilt as New Fairfield in 1815 but never fully recovered. Beset by the usual problems of settler encroachments, which became steadily more serious, many of the Amerindians left for the American Middle West. There was also reluctance on the part of colonial authorities to grant the Delaware clear title to the land. In the end, in 1903, New Fairfield would be turned over to the Canadian Methodist Episcopal Church, a move resented by the Delaware.

A Mississauga-Welsh Métis who had become a Methodist minister, Peter Jones (Kahkewaquonaby, 'Sacred Feathers', 1802–56), was very successful converting his people to Methodism.[45] Although officials would have preferred it if Jones had been an Anglican (Anglicanism, as the established church of Great Britain, had received that same status in the Canadas), in 1825 they were impressed enough to offer to build a village of 20 houses on the west bank of the Credit River for the converts and to help them get started in their new lives as farmers on 1,619 hectares (4,000 acres) of land. Within 10 years the ex-hunters had cleared 344 hectares (850 acres), despite difficulties on all sides: the transition to farming life was not easy, despite determined effort. The Mississauga had been under heavy pressures to make the change and looked to Jones and his brother to help them find their way into this strange new world; Jones was selected chief at the age of 27, an unusual honour. He had to cope with officialdom's wish that his people would switch to Anglicanism, a move they resisted as they did not relate to that faith's structured institutionalism. That did not relieve the government's continuing suspicions of the

American ties of Methodism. When the band applied for a deed to its reserve, it was eventually refused on the grounds that title deeds could not be given to Amerindian bands. Moreover, the Mississauga were deemed not capable of handling such responsibility.[46] There was even an attempt to move the settlement to Manitoulin Island, presumably to distance it from American influence, a move the people were able to prevent. Eventually, at the invitation of the Six Nations, the Mississauga in 1847 established New Credit with them near Hagersville, Ontario, where they still are.

An American-born Methodist missionary, William Case (1780–1855), using American funds, in 1827 established a village on Grape Island in the Bay of Quinte, 10 kilometres east of Belleville. Since the island was only four hectares (10 acres), and the village counted 200 Ojibwa inhabitants, another island one kilometre away had to be used for planting crops and still a third for collecting firewood. Case ran the project like an army camp, and for a while it worked. In 1836 the project was re-established at a more suitable location at Alderville, on Rice Lake, where each household was provided with a 20-hectare (50-acre) farm. By 1848 the community had a school.

Two settlements launched under Indian Affairs auspices, at Coldwater and the Narrows (near Orillia) in 1829, had shorter lives. They were both under the direction of former fur trader and War of 1812 veteran Captain Thomas G. Anderson (1779–1875), Indian Affairs agent. Anderson was an authoritarian figure who, while genuinely concerned for the people he was working with—mostly Ojibwa, Odawa, and some Potawatomi refugees from the United States—still regarded them as minors whose interests were secondary to those of settlers.[47] In spite of this, chiefs co-operated; among these were Musquakie (Mayawassino, Waisowindebay, also known as William Yellowhead, d. 1864), who participated in making a

Peter Jones, as photographed during a visit to Edinburgh, 1845. This is believed to be the earliest camera study of a Canadian Aboriginal. *(National Galleries of Scotland)*

major land surrender to the British and whose family had been influential in keeping the Ojibwa of Lake Simcoe loyal to the British during the War of 1812. Another was John Aisance (Ascance, Essens, *c.* 1790–1847), who had fought with the British during that same war and who would rally a group of Ojibwa warriors into government service during the Rebellion of 1837.[48] Aisance, less compliant than Musquakie and frequently at odds with Anderson, still saw co-operation with white authorities as the way of the future. They and other chiefs, such as William Snake, helped the projects get off to a promising enough start that the department agreed to an extension of funding in 1833. By 1837, however, financial problems had become acute, and both settlements were abandoned. According to Aisance, fraud was involved. A number of years later, in 1856, his band moved to Christian Island, where it still is.

The department tried again with Anderson at Manitowaning on Manitoulin Island, in 1835. Funding was improved but problems developed between warring missionary sects, compounded by the paternalism of Anderson's administration. A report in 1858 called it a failure because it counted only 44 families and a total population of 170. As an official project, it was dead by 1862; but as a settlement, Manitowaning continued. A group of Ojibwa, acting on their own, established a village at Little Current, which also continues. A mission successfully launched by the Jesuits, Wikwemikong, is still on the island.

The ambiguities in the fates of these model villages arose as much out of the contradictions in official policy and administration as they did out of the indigenous factors involved. That such enterprises had the potential for success had been amply demonstrated in French Canada and Spanish America. The Indians who participated were perhaps the most committed of all to their success: fully aware that adaptation was the key to survival, as it had always been, and faced with the alarming drops in their numbers as well as the disappearance of their hunting subsistence bases, they did their best to make the projects work. This was particularly true of their educational aspects: both Natives and officialdom saw schooling as the key to the future. But where Indians viewed education as a tool for adaptation as Indians, administrators saw it as a tool for assimilation. Official goals were not always realistic, which, combined with a profound pessimism about Amerindian capabilities 'to rise to civilization', made it easy to see failure when difficulties arose. The fact that the survival rate of these projects was as good as it was speaks volumes for the determined efforts of

the Indians to make the best of a very difficult situation.

In his biography of Peter Jones, *Sacred Feathers*, historian Donald B. Smith has shown how the Methodist minister personified this struggle. In Smith's words, this remarkable man had

> lived in a period of oppression for Canada's native peoples. . . . For three decades Peter Jones fought back: to obtain a secure title to the reserves, a viable economic land base for each band, a first-class system of education, and Indian self-government. The white politicians largely ignored him . . . others today fight the political battles that Peter Jones began.[49]

Jones represented one response of the Ojibwa to the new pressures; another, more deeply rooted in pre-contact traditions, was the rise of Midewiwin, or Grand Medicine Society. Its ceremonies became central to Ojibwa life, with elaborate initiation rituals, ranked membership, and an organized 'priesthood' whose initiates were specialists in curing and prophesying. As with other nativistic spiritual movements, it was a cultural reaffirmation in the face of strange new forces.[50]

Attacking a Sinful History

At least one high official saw model villages as a waste of time. Sir Francis Bond Head, lieutenant-governor of Upper Canada from 1836 to 1838, had developed an interest in Amerindians as a consequence of having lived in Argentina and Peru; he was distressed at the 'fate of the red inhabitants of America, the real proprietors of its soil', which in his view was 'the most sinful story recorded in the history of the human race'. He reasoned that since hunters showed little if any inclination to become farmers and since model villages implanted more vices than they eradicated, it followed that the 'greatest kindness we can perform towards these Intelligent, simple-minded people is to remove and fortify them as much as possible from all Communication with the Whites.' He thought Manitoulin Island and its surrounding region would make a satisfactory refuge, as it was 'totally separated' from non-Natives.[51] Manitoulin, at 100 miles (161 km) in length and half again as wide, is the world's largest freshwater island.

Undeterred by the opposition of missionaries and later of the Aborigines' Protection Society, Bond Head took advantage of a gift distribution at Manitoulin Island in 1836 to arrange two major land cessions. He convinced a number of Ojibwa leaders to sign over 'the twenty-three thousand islands' of the Manitoulin chain on the promise that the region would be protected by the Crown as Amerindian territory. Further, Natives who took up residence there would be assisted in their new mode of life. The second agreement (1854) was with the Saugeen Ojibwas of the Bruce Peninsula. After warning them that the government could not control squatters moving into their territory, he promised that if they would move either to the Manitoulin Island region or the northern end of Bruce Peninsula above Owen Sound, the government would provide them with housing and equipment and see that they were properly settled. Overwhelmed by the pressures that followed an initial refusal, the Ojibwa signed over 1.5 million acres (607,028 hectares), the Saugeen tract, and were left with 'the granite rocks and bog land' of the remainder. However, few took advantage of the Manitoulin Island offer. Bond Head would have preferred to have obtained the whole of the Bruce Peninsula but had settled for what he thought he could get without argument. Using similar tactics, he proceeded to obtain other surrenders to the south.

The imperial government was greatly impressed with these huge, peaceful surrenders.

The Aborigines' Protection Society had another view: they saw the deals as an exchange of 3 million acres (1,214,057 hectares) of rich lands for '23,000 barren islands, rocks of granite, dignified by the name of Manitoulin Islands'. The Natives' attitude was ultimately one of helplessness in the face of the settler juggernaut, as their attempts at asserting their rights in the end availed them little, despite a Royal Declaration in 1847 acknowledging the Saugeen Ojibwa title to their aquatic territory and traditional fishing grounds around the Saugeen Peninsula, upon which they depended for their livelihood. Another proclamation in 1851 protected Indian lands from trespass, including islands within seven miles of the Saugeen Peninsula. It wasn't long, however, before the Indians were persuaded to grant leases to commercial fishing enterprises. As non-Aboriginal interests increased, the colonial government came to regard the Ojibwa's aquatic territory as public waters and to favour non-Aboriginal interests over those of the Indians.[52] The Saugeen Ojibwa, their best efforts to protect their concerns unavailing, observed that 'they were ruined. From their angle, it was no use to say anything more, as their Great Father was determined to have their land (not distinguishing between land and water as Europeans did, but regarding them as complementary parts of a whole)—that they were poor and weak and must submit, and that if they did not let him have his own way, they would lose it altogether.' Their discontent reached the point of passing the wampum belt to take up the hatchet. Warned that they could not prevail against the Euro-Canadians, they replied: 'We know that very well; but don't you see that we are all doomed to die; all our land is taken from us, and we think that if we kill a few of the white people they will come and kill us off, and then there will be an end of us.'[53]

The outbreak of the troubles of 1837–8 reminded officials that the days of the military usefulness of Amerindians in eastern British North America might not be entirely over. Indeed, in spite of their difficulties, some Ojibwa volunteered to fight with the government forces, but in Upper Canada the need never developed. In the meantime, Sir Francis Bond Head submitted his resignation, which Whitehall happily accepted.

Grand River Navigation Company

During this period the Six Nations along the Grand River found themselves embroiled in a different sort of problem. Faced in the 1820s with a scheme to open the Grand River for navigation, they did their best to oppose it on the grounds that parts of their lands would be flooded and their fisheries ruined.[54] In spite of this, the lieutenant-governor of Upper Canada agreed to help the Grand River Navigation Company by using Six Nations funds to purchase stock. Between 1834 and 1847, the Upper Canadian administration (and after 1840 that of the Union of the Canadas) aided the company to the tune of $160,000 from band funds without the consent of the Iroquois. Not only that, but 369 acres (149 hectares) of Iroquois land were granted to the company, again without band consent; this land was apart from the areas that were flooded. In the 1830s and 1840s five dams, five locks, and a towpath were built in the lower Grand River to a growing chorus of protest from the Iroquois. The company, unable to compete with the rage for railways then gathering momentum, went bankrupt, and the Iroquois found themselves holding worthless stock they had never wanted to purchase in the first place. Their attempts at obtaining restitution got nowhere: the imperial government in England maintained that the investment had been made at the suggestion of the colonial legislature and Canada maintained that Whitehall was responsible, as the lieutenant-governor who had originally approved it had been an

imperial appointee. The impasse continued after Confederation when the Canadian government refused to accept responsibility on the grounds that Canada did not have responsible government at the time of the debacle (responsible government had not been achieved until 1848). The Iroquois persisted through the years, but each fresh attempt met fresh obstacles; when the case finally came before the Exchequer Court (*Frank Miller v. The King*), the decision in 1948 went in favour of the Crown, as the British North America Act had made no provision for Canada to accept liability for events that had occurred before the Act of Union. The Supreme Court of Canada, on appeal, found that since the actual investment had not been completed until after 1840, there were grounds for restitution on that count if the statute of limitations had not taken effect.[55] An attempt to settle out of court proved fruitless, and there the matter stands today.

The Mississauga of the Credit River also had financial claims against the government, arising out of the management of monies received before Confederation by the Province of Canada from the sale of surrendered lands. The Mississauga finally won their case in 1905, in large part because of the work of a young lawyer, Andrew G. Chisholm, who would spend close to 50 years working on Indian claims, mostly in southern Ontario, until his death in 1943.[56]

Signs of Change

On the prairies, the buffalo-hunting way of life was in full swing during the first half of the century, although indications of things to come were becoming increasingly portentous: the fur trade was receding in importance, and the ultimate fate of the buffalo herds was not in doubt.[57] They could still impede travellers on occasion,[58] but already in the 1830s shortages had begun in certain areas, and for two years in

Indian fishing weir, Nicola, BC, late nineteenth century.
(Library and Archives Canada, PA-37999)

a row (1848–9) these shortages were increasingly serious. Cree told the Palliser expedition in the mid-nineteenth century that bison were becoming scarcer and scarcer, and they hoped that they would be provided with spades, hoes, and ploughs so they could get started at agriculture.[59] They were not the first; as early as the beginning of the nineteenth century the Saulteaux, on their own initiative, had begun to take up agriculture, and there were similar reports from Prince Albert, Saskatchewan.[60] However, despite overhunting[61] and such intrusions as the Selkirk colony at Red River in 1812, the tra-

ditional way of life was still essentially intact. Shortly after the arrival of the settlers, another agent for change appeared in the form of missionaries (1818: Joseph-Norbert Provencher [1787–1853], Catholic, who would become bishop of St Boniface in 1847; 1820: John West [d. 1845], Anglican; 1840: Robert Terrill Rundle [1811–96], Methodist; 1845: the Oblates and Grey Nuns, Catholic religious orders; 1851: John Black [1818–82], Presbyterian). Their direct attack on Amerindian and fur trade practices accentuated old social divisions and created new ones. As the 'custom of the country'

Paul Kane's view of a Métis encampment. Note the cattle and Red River carts.
(With permission of the Royal Ontario Museum © ROM, 912.1.25)

gave way to European mores, such chiefs as Peguis (Begouais, Pegouisse, 'Destroyer', 'Little Chip', baptized William King, 1774–1864) of the Saulteaux at Red River became actively aware that the treaty they had signed with Selkirk in 1817 had been with the non-Natives' interests in mind, not those of the Amerindians. In spite of his initial assistance to the colonists and his subsequent efforts to manage the situation to his people's advantage, Peguis realized the necessity of some adaptation to the newcomers' ways.[62] The Métis also were becoming uneasy about their land rights.

This mixture of cultures was matched by a confusion of laws. Three systems were in effect: Canadian, as a result of the Canada Jurisdiction Act of 1803, which was replaced in 1821 by An Act for Regulating the Fur Trade and establishing a Criminal and Civil Jurisdiction within certain parts of North America;[63] British, in those areas that came under the HBC charter of 1670; and Amerindian, usually expressed as 'custom of the country'. The Act for Regulating the Fur Trade had arisen out of the amalgamation of the Hudson's Bay Company and the North West Company; by its terms the HBC was granted a 21-year monopoly for 'trading with the Indians in all such parts of North America, not being part of the lands or territories hitherto granted to the said Governor and Company of Adventurers of England trading to Hudson's Bay, and not being part of any of His Majesty's Provinces in North America'.[64] The lack of clarity in this wording gave rise to uncertainty and disputes; for one thing, opinions differed whether it applied west of the Rockies.[65] There was no doubt about the status of Red River, which came under British (HBC) jurisdiction and in 1834 was reorganized as the District of Assiniboia, with an appointive council.

Syllabics and Prophets

In the meantime, a major cultural change was occurring among the northern Cree as they adopted a form of writing in the syllabary devised by Methodist missionary James Evans (1801–46) at Norway House, on Lake Winnipeg. The syllabic system developed by Evans drew on shorthand as well as on symbols already in use among the Cree; his genius was to adapt these to the language. In the eighteenth century, Abbé Pierre-Simon Maillard had earlier adapted Mi'kmaq symbols, but his system never achieved the wide acceptance of that of Evans. Evans printed his first book, a hymnal, in syllabics at Norway House in 1841, using type made from the lead lining of tea chests after first being moulded in clay, paper of inner birchbark, and ink concocted from sturgeon oil and soot. A fur press served for the printing and elk hide for the volume's covers. The use of the syllabary spread with amazing rapidity throughout the Cree-speaking North, so that by the end of the nineteenth century and the early part of the twentieth the Cree had one of the highest literacy rates in the world.[66] The system is adaptable to other Algonkian languages, such as Ojibwa and Montagnais, both closely related to Cree; it has also proved adaptable to the needs of such an unrelated language as Inuktitut and is now widely used by the Inuit. In those language areas in the North, the use of syllabics is flourishing in schools today. The system has not been generally adopted by speakers of Athapaskan languages, although in 1883 two Chipewyan chiefs of the eastern Athabasca district used it to write to Ottawa;[67] nor has it been adopted by peoples of the Pacific coast. Interestingly enough, when it came to signing treaties, officials expected Amerindians to sign an X, even though some signees could write in syllabics. When Cree chiefs prepared their acceptance speeches for Treaty Nine, they used syllabics.[68]

The spread of the system coincided with a religious movement that swept through the Hudson Bay Cree between the Churchill and Albany rivers in 1842–3. In the opinion of historian Jennifer S.H. Brown, syllabics probably played a special role 'along with the spreading impact of Evans' preaching'.[69] The movement, which combined Christian and traditional Native elements, gave rise to the prophet Abishabis ('Small Eyes', d. 1843) and his associate Wasiteck ('The Light'), who claimed they could provide their people with the knowledge to find the road to heaven, since they had been there themselves; they even provided a sketch map. In the end Abishabis was killed by his own people as a windigo (a being with an overweening appetite who preyed on humans) because of his increasingly unacceptable behaviour, up to and including murder. His movement was a reaction to the presence and teachings of non-Natives—as Brown has pointed out, the interaction had been going on for 170 years by that time—but it also vividly illustrated the creative response of Native religions in synthesizing the new teachings with their own beliefs. The rise of Native prophets in response to outside pressures was widespread among Amerindians, in both time and place. Neolin, who was associated with Pontiac, has already been noted, as has Tenskwatawa, who added a mystic element to Tecumseh's campaign. The prophet movement has continued, its most recent manifestation being among the Athapaskan Dene Dháa (Beavers) of the Northwest.[70]

An incident that may have been associated with messianism, although this is far from clear, was the Hannah Bay massacre of 1832. What is clear is that the perpetrators were starving, had asked the post personnel for help, and had found what they were offered to be inadequate. They were a Cree family who would later claim they had been ordered by the 'Spirit above' to kill the offenders—nine persons, all

Amerindians except the post master, who was a mixed blood. The family was tracked down and all its adult males executed, seven all told. One was 15 years old.[71] In the Cree view, the post officials had not honoured their trading alliance by fully sharing provisions in a time of need. In a later instance, Natives would recall that an Amerindian family starved to death because 'White people refused to share their shelter and food, as we had shared with them.'[72]

On to the West Coast

The tides of change took another form on the west coast. By 1852 there were 500 settlers on Vancouver Island; although the Proclamation of 1763 was not deemed to apply beyond the mountains, James Douglas at first sought to deal with the land question by means of treaties in what has been described by political scientist Paul Tennant as an 'unequivocal recognition of Aboriginal title'.[73] Between 1850 and 1854, he signed 14 treaties with Coast Salish bands on Vancouver Island, paying in blankets and other goods rather than cash for surrenders. He also, on Amerindian insistence, stopped settlers from enclosing unpaid-for lands. The land area involved in the treaties was limited (a total of 358 square miles—927 square kilometres), about 3 per cent of the island's area), as settlement was slow; by 1855, there were only 774 non-Natives living on Vancouver Island, clustered around Fort Victoria and Nanaimo.[74] When Douglas ran out of funds, none were forthcoming from either the colony's House of Assembly or the imperial Colonial Office. Both paid lip service to Amerindian title but neither would accept the financial responsibility for buying it out, despite repeated appeals by Douglas, backed by popular support among the settlers worried about an Amerindian backlash. Douglas did the next best thing and had reserves surveyed for Amerindians that included their village sites and burial grounds, as well as their cultivated fields and 'favorite places of resort', such as fishing stations. They were small, averaging about 10 acres (a little over four hectares) per family.

These reserves, although small by central Canadian standards (west coast Natives, being non-agricultural and largely dependent on the sea, were not seen as needing much land), took Amerindian wishes into account to some extent. When allotments proved to be insufficient, Douglas saw to it that they were increased. On one occasion, when Amerindians at Langley wanted to relocate their village, a new reserve was surveyed for them.[75] In addition, partly in compensation for the small size of the reserves, Douglas allowed Amerindians to pre-empt and purchase Crown lands on the same conditions that applied to non-Native settlers.[76] He managed this despite Colonial Office instructions that non-Native settlement was to be given priority. In other words, Douglas was as concerned about Amerindian rights as he was about those of settlers, and he sought to balance the two; this was a far cry from always acceding to Amerindian wishes, as some historians have assumed.[77] In fact, at one point he maintained that Amerindians did not need more than 10 acres per family (the amount the Indians usually asked for), a position he later modified by saying that 10 acres was a minimum figure.

From this, and from the fact that no more treaties were signed after 1854, Tennant argues that Douglas had changed his mind about the nature of Amerindian title and had come to accept the position that if the Amerindians were not actively using land in the European sense, they had no valid claims to it. In that case, neither negotiation nor compensation was necessary to open such lands for settlement. This implies that Douglas had come to regard treaties as no longer necessary.[78] These conflicting interpretations reflect the fact that the governor had to deal with incompatible claims while hampered by lack of funds; that he managed to keep the peace as well as he did speaks for his sense of fair play and justice.[79] The weakness of Douglas's policy, according to historian Robin Fisher, lay in its dependence 'on his own personal magnanimity and that it was never codified in any legislative enactment'.[80] The consequences of this would soon be evident with the governor's retirement in 1864, when subsequent provincial governments would argue that Douglas's arrangements had not been an acknowledgement of Indian title but simply an attempt to secure friendly relations with the Natives.[81] The Colonial Office's concern that settlers' interests be given priority would now be realized at the expense of Amerindians.

Even during Douglas's day, relations between settlers and Amerindians were uneasy. Violence had erupted early: in 1844, when Cowichans, Songhees, and Klallum killed livestock belonging to Fort Victoria, then attacked the fort itself when trade was suspended, it took a show of force to restore peace. In 1850, the period of coastal 'gunboat diplomacy' was launched in Canada (it was already being practised in other parts of the British Empire)[82] in response to the killing of three runaway sailors by the Newitty, a branch of the Kwakwaka'-wakw. A warship was sent, which destroyed a village and 20 canoes; the following year, another warship, another village. There were no arguments about financing punitive expeditions as there were concerning payment to Indians for land.[83] In 1852, an HBC shepherd was killed; Douglas persuaded Cowichan and Nanaimo chiefs to give up the persons involved. He empanelled a jury, and the murderer and his accomplice were tried and hanged in 1853, the first such criminal trial in the West.

Tensions mounted as settlers, alarmed at the continuing frontier wars in the United States, feared an Amerindian uprising against their settlements. The outbreak of the Crimean War (1853–6) compounded the situation; the sudden appearance of a group of peaceful Amerindians was enough to send settlers fleeing, convinced they were being attacked. When a non-Native settler was murdered in 1856, 400 sailors and marines equipped with two field pieces were sent out to capture the guilty Cowichan. The discovery of placer gold on the Fraser and Thompson rivers in 1857 added to the Amerindians' difficulties, as will be seen in Chapter 18.

The best known of the episodes involving gunboat diplomacy occurred in 1888 on the Skeena. Discontent had been bubbling in the region for a number of years, concerning land as well as social issues; Joseph W. Trutch, BC commissioner for Crown lands, 1864–71, until named the province's first lieutenant-governor, expressed official sentiment when he told a Kitkatla delegation in 1872, 'the days are past when your heathenish ideas can be tolerated in this land.'[84] Reports of an uprising on the Skeena were reaching Victoria in 1888. A Gitksan chief known as Kitwancool Jim (Kamalmuk) had followed Indian custom by killing a medicine man believed to have caused the death of several people, including the chief's child. The chief's brother had married the medicine man's widow, and as far as the Natives were concerned the matter was settled. Not so in the eyes of the authorities; attempting to arrest Jim, they killed him instead. The outraged reaction of the Indians aroused fears of an attack, and a gunboat and additional police were sent to the scene, accompanied by a 'war correspondent' from the Victoria *Daily Colonist*.[85] The presence of the warship so far upriver impressed the people, who had never seen such a vessel before. A series of meetings with the chiefs of the area emphasized the point that British law was to prevail; the chiefs agreed to abide by the new order of things. After 1890, gunboats were not used any more for this purpose.

Legaic presiding over a pole-raising ceremony while standing on the stairway leading to the entrance of his residence; the elevated position of the doorway signalled that it was a 'skyhouse', indicating Legaic's lofty position. The stairway symbolized the World Tree, the channel between underworld, earth, and sky. Two attendants hold coppers, thus displaying Legaic's wealth. Drawing by Fredee Alexcee.
(Photo © Canadian Museum of Civilization)

The Saga of Duncan and Legaic

A permanent missionary presence did not develop on the west coast until 1836, when the HBC appointed Herbert Beaver (1800–58) as Anglican chaplain at Fort Vancouver. He found much to censure in trader–Amerindian relations and was particularly critical of the Company; not surprisingly, he was transferred two years later.[86] Roman Catholics François-Norbert Blanchet (1795–1883) and Modeste

Demers (1809–71), both from Lower Canada, appeared in 1838; eventually, both would become bishops. The single most famous west coast missionary endeavour of the nineteenth century was launched in 1862 in the Tsimshian village of Metlakatla, 29 kilometres south of Fort Simpson. In fact, it is probably the best known of all the Canadian Utopian experiments involving Amerindians. It was the project of William Duncan (1832–1918), an Anglican schoolmaster who had never taken holy orders and who had come out under the auspices of the Church Missionary Society. He had arrived at Fort Simpson[87] in 1857, in the van of the Fraser River gold rush, an event that inspired him to establish his mission far enough away from outside influences that its converts could work out their own destinies with a minimum of interference.

Impressed by the enterprising Tsimshian, wealthy traders who were challenging the HBC monopoly, Duncan learned their language and cultivated the friendship of the influential Paul Legaic (d. 1894), third Tsimshian Eagle clan chief to hold that title.[88] By this time the new order ushered in by the fur trade was affecting the social equilibrium of the Tsimshian, which in 1862 was compounded when a severe smallpox epidemic struck the west coast. Legaic led 200 of his people who had settled near the fort back to Metlakatla; there he was baptized and adopted the name of Paul, thereby converting the title 'Legaic' into a surname. He helped Duncan transform Metlakatla into a mission village, blending the traditional with the new. In this Duncan was greatly aided, as historian Jean Friesen observed, by 'the natural adaptability of Tsimshian society to the type of Christianity he wanted to introduce'.[89] Government was by a council of chiefs (including Duncan) and 10 elected councillors; public order was maintained by Native constables selected from the ranks of house chiefs and headed by Legaic.

Eastern portion of Metlakatla, BC, with Anglican church in background and cannery buildings on left.
(Image HP-55799 courtesy of Royal BC Museum, BC Archives)

Initially supported by the HBC, the community became self-sufficient within four years by establishing a store as well as other enterprises, including a fish cannery. The neatly laid out community quickly became regarded as a model, 'reflecting light and radiating heat to all the spiritually dark and dead masses of humanity around us'. Dignitaries visiting the west coast included Metlakatla in their itineraries (the Governor-General himself came by in 1876)[90], and their reports were glowing. In its heyday, it counted up to 2,000 residents.

The mission lasted from 1862 until 1887. Duncan's authoritarian ways complicated his relationship with Legaic, and his unorthodox approach to religious matters led to the parting of the ways with the Church Missionary So-ciety. On the political front, confrontations with government over land led to a commission of inquiry in 1884, which recommended an immediate survey, under protection of a gunboat if necessary. Under those conditions, the survey was completed in 1886. The following year Duncan left for Annette Island, Alaska, where he re-established his village with 600 followers. Legaic stayed behind in the original Metlakatla and also maintained a residence at Fort Simpson to be near his daughter, who had married an HBC official. Today, both Metlakatlas still survive; the last known holder of the Legaic title died in 1938. A Methodist mission that had been established in 1873 at Fort Simpson by Thomas Crosby (1840–1914) was partly modelled on Duncan's enterprise.[91]

During the first half of the nineteenth century, the situation of Canada's Amerindians varied considerably from coast to coast, as this survey makes evident. With the ending of the colonial wars and the diminishing importance of the fur trade, the era of partnership between Indians and Europeans had come to an end. If adaptation had been the key to Native survival in the past, it now became the password that would allow Amerindians entry into the future.

Chapter 17

Pre-Confederation Administration in the Canadas

During the 1830s an extensive British parliamentary inquiry into the conditions of Aboriginal peoples was held throughout the empire. It was widely recognized that Amerindians, as well as other tribal peoples, were being unfairly deprived of their lands, but it was not generally agreed what should be done about it—or even acknowledged that anything should be done at all. The 15-member Select Committee on Aborigines, after 10 months of investigating the problems, issued its 1,000-page report in 1836–7. Its message was unequivocal: unregulated frontier expansion was disastrous for Native peoples, who almost without exception lost their lands.[1] Trespass was only part of the problem, however; the other was alienation by Amerindians, particularly in the form of leasing.[2] Curbing settlers was difficult politically, particularly in areas where defence needs seemed to require their presence. In an attempt to correct this situation, the Crown Lands Protection Act was passed in 1839, declaring Indian lands to be Crown lands. Because Indians held their land in common (apart from some individuals who had accepted the non-Native way), making the Crown the guardian of their lands in effect excluded most Amerindians from political rights based on individual property qualifications.[3] This endorsed the popular belief that Amerindians were to be regarded as children, in need of paternal protection.[4] In popular imagination during the nineteenth century, this was romanticized into the White Man's Burden.[5]

By 1830, the British Indian branch was 75 years old, operating as an adjunct of the military except for an experimental period, 1795–1816, which had resulted from charges of ineffectiveness in protecting Amerindian interests. Less idealistically, it could also be pointed out that during those years, Britain was preoccupied elsewhere with the Napoleonic Wars. Under the military, the emphasis had been on maintaining the Amerindians as allies instead of on controlling the settlers. However, the priorities of war quickly reasserted themselves, prompting the reversion of Amerindian administration to military control.[6] One Indian superintendent had been Joseph Brant's son, John.[7] Indian administration was practically a one-man operation, and desperately underfunded; easily, its principal interest was the

TIMELINE

1836–7	Select Committee on Aborigines of British Parliament issues 1,000-page report.	1850–1	Legislation passed to protect lands of Indians in the Canadas.
1839	Crown Lands Protection Act declares Indian lands to be Crown lands.	1857	An Act to encourage the Gradual Civilization of the Indian Tribes of the Canadas is ushered through legislature by John A. Macdonald.
1841	Act of Union of Upper and Lower Canada.	1859	Act for Civilizing and Enfranchising Indians passed in United Canadas.
1842–4	Bagot Commission examines Indian administration.	1860	Amerindian administration passed from British Colonial Office to the colonies.
1850	Commissioner of Lands position created in United Canadas.	1862	Manitoulin Island cession.
	Robinson Superior and Robinson Huron treaties: lands surrendered twice the area of all previous land cession treaties in Canada West.		

acquisition of land, and from 1839 that was handled by the Crown lands department. In fact, so little attention was paid to Indian affairs that the Act of Union (1841) forgot to make provision for it or for the payment of annuities for earlier land cessions, an oversight that was not corrected until 1844.

Although transferred to the civil arm in 1830, the Indian policy of the two Canadas continued, in principle, to be administered from London until 1860, through the lieutenant-governor of Upper Canada, who was also Superintendent-General of Indian Affairs. The position of Superintendent-General was in turn double-barrelled, as the holder was expected to act both for the Crown and for the Amerindians. Inevitably, there were occasions when it was impossible to reconcile the two roles.[8] In practice, colonial legislatures had considerable autonomy. In Upper Canada, control was exercised through the lieutenant-governor; in Lower Canada, through the military secretary, an arrangement that lasted until the reorganization of 1845, following the Act of Union. Funding for Amerindian administra-

tion was by allocation from five different sources and was uncertain, to say the least, reflecting the lack of importance now accorded Indian affairs, an attitude that would deepen until well into the twentieth century. Although control of Indian affairs was transferred to Canada in 1860, it would take two years before a single administration was set up, and even then unification was not complete.[9]

Herman Merivale, permanent undersecretary of the Colonial Office in London, 1847–60, developed the concept of regional approaches rather than an overarching policy applying to all.[10] This meant almost as many policies as there were colonies: in the Maritimes, it was one of 'insulation' of the Amerindians; in the Canadas, 'amalgamation'; in Rupert's Land and on the Northwest Coast, support of HBC administration, which in the latter case was tempered by Douglas's concern for Amerindian rights. In other words, in spite of good intentions, centralized imperial administration was not coping very well with the myriad local problems of colonial government. Neither did goals always synchronize: where

Three Huron chiefs of Jeune Lorette, 1825. From left: Michel Tsioui (Tracheandale), war chief; Stanislas Coska (Aharathaha), second chief of the Council; and André Romain (Tsouhahissen), chief of the Council.
(Metropolitan Reference Library, J. Ross Robertson Collection, T-14868)

the Colonial Office was concerned with rationalizing imperial administration in economic terms, in the colonies it was all too evident that Indians no longer fitted into imperial plans and that programs to ameliorate their situations would be costly. Attempts at enforced change were not getting very far, and the voices of the Natives themselves either were not being heard or were being ignored.

In the meantime, reports were pouring in from other investigations into Aboriginal affairs (there were three between 1839 and 1857). The most important from Canada was that of the Bagot Commission of 1842–4, named after chief commissioner Sir Charles Bagot (1781–1843), who had negotiated the international border between the United States and Canada in 1817.[11] Its recommendations revealed the existing lack of direction in Indian administration. Among other points it urged centralized control for the British North American colonies, the opposite of what was being practised by the Colonial Office, and it reaffirmed the Proclamation's position that Amerindians had possessory rights in regard to land, including the right to compensation for surrenders. The fact that the commission found it necessary to reiterate these points indicates that they were not always being honoured, as indeed they were not. It also recommended that reserves be surveyed and boundaries publicly announced; that a system of timber licensing be instituted for reserves; that all title deeds be registered and considered binding; that Indians be taught European techniques of land management (the report had described Indians as 'an untaught, unwary race among a population ready and able to take every advantage of them');[12] and, once all this had been done, that Indians be provided with livestock, agricultural implements, furniture, and the like in lieu of presents, so they could get started on the road to self-sufficiency in their new lives. The commissioners also thought that indigenous bands should be allowed to buy and sell land, at least between themselves, a measure they believed would encourage them to adopt individual freehold ownership in lieu of their traditional communal ownership, which they considered to be an 'uncivilized state'.[13] Finally, they urged that banks be established on reserves and that more schools for Natives be established, with the co-operation of various religious denominations.

Identifying goals was one thing; doing something about them proved to be something else again. Easiest to achieve were the department's reorganization and centralization under the civil secretary as Superintendent-General for Indian Affairs and the measures to improve the protection of Amerindian lands. More controversial was the gradual discontinuance of gift distributions, which Amerindians resisted. In their view, it was important to maintain the ceremonial renewal of their alliances with Great Britain each year, in which the distributions played an essential part. Thomas Anderson was one administrator who was against their discontinuance, although his reasons were quite different: such a move would result in serious deprivation.[14] Instead, he urged a more active program of education and evangelization. Budgetary considerations prevailed, and gift distributions were ended in 1858. Amerindian opposition to individualized land-ownership was not surprising, not only because of their entrenched customs but also because of the considerable land losses that invariably followed its imposition. Some Indian leaders, such as Peter Jones, advocated individual ownership within band-owned reservations.[15]

Only a few years after the Bagot Commission's report, in 1850, Lord Grey (Henry George Grey, secretary for the colonies from 1846 to 1852) told Lord Elgin (James Bruce, Governor-General of Canada, 1846–54) 'that less has been accomplished toward the civilization and improvement of Indians in Canada in proportion to the expense incurred than has been done for the native tribes in any of our other colonies.' Earl Grey has been described as the last of the colonial secretaries to give high priority to Aboriginal affairs.[16] At that time the Amerindian population was dropping fast.

Consequences of the Bagot Commission

In 1850 and 1851 two land acts were approved by the Canadian legislature, incorporating some of the Bagot Commission's recommendations as well as ideas of Governors Murray, Kempt, and Colborne: in 1850, An Act for the Protection of the Indians of Upper Canada from Imposition, and the Property Occupied and Enjoyed by Them from Trespass and Injury, and in 1851, An Act for the Better Protection of the Lands and Property of the Indians of Lower Canada. Hurriedly passed because loggers had been invading reserved lands in the Temiskaming and Abitibi regions, as well as in the Ottawa Valley, these measures strengthened the 1839 Protection Act, making it an offence for private individuals to deal with Amerindians concerning their lands. They also excluded Aboriginal lands from taxation, freed them from seizure for non-payment of debt, and provided for damages from such public works activities as railroad construction. The nature of Amerindian tenure was not elaborated, so it was unclear what 'Indian title' actually meant. In 1850, the post of Commissioner of Indian Lands was created, followed the next year in Lower Canada by the setting aside of 93,079 hectares (230,000 acres) for the creation of Amerindian reserves and the distribution of up to £1,000 annually. However, only 68,801 hectares (170,012 acres) were actually granted.[17] The land was vested in the Commissioner, who had control over leasing and rentals; Amerindians had no say in the matter. Today, Quebec counts 27 Amerindian reserves occupying 74,881 hectares.[18]

In the meantime, the amount of property involved, as well as other legal considerations, made it necessary to define the term 'Indian'. The 1851 Act for Lower Canada undertook the task without consulting Amerindians and came up with these criteria:

- all persons of Indian blood reputed to belong to the particular body or tribe of Indians interested in Indian lands or their descendants;

- all persons intermarried with any such Indians and residing amongst them, and all descendants of such persons;
- all persons residing among such Indians, whose parents on either side were or are Indians of such body or tribe, or entitled to be considered as such; and
- all persons adopted in infancy by any such Indians, and residing in the village or upon the lands of such tribes or bodies of Indians and their descendants.

It was quickly decided that this was too inclusive, so that same year the definition was revised, once more without Native input. This time non-Indians living among Amerindians were excluded, as well as non-Indians married to Amerindian women. 'Status' Indians, those who were officially registered, were differentiated from 'non-status' Indians, those not so registered.[19] Amerindian women married to non-Indians kept their status, but their descendants were not granted the right to claim it. Retained was the provision allowing non-Indian women married to registered Indians to acquire such status and to pass it on to their children. Ancestry was determined through the male line.[20] After Confederation, a 'blood quantum' proviso would be added to the definition of an Indian (Chapter 18).

Concerned about charges of lack of results for its civilizing program, the Canadian government named two commissioners to report on how policy goals were being realized. Their investigations resulted in John A. Macdonald (co-premier of the Canadas with Étienne-Paschal Taché, 1856–7, and with George-Étienne Cartier, 1857–62) piloting through An Act to encourage the Gradual Civilization of the Indian Tribes of the Canadas in 1857. It introduced the idea of enfranchisement for Amerindians, which Macdonald envisioned as a sought-after honour even though it involved dropping Amerindian status, and established the procedures by which it was to be achieved, most of which would stay on the books until 1960. Eligible were males 21 years of age and over, literate in English or French, minimally educated, and 'of good moral character and free from debt', who had passed a three-year probation. By those standards, a good proportion of the Euro-Canadian community would not have been eligible for the vote.[21] The successful indigenous candidate would receive 20 hectares of reserve land in fee simple on which he would pay taxes; it was hoped that this would lead to a cutting, or at least a loosening, of tribal ties.

Amerindians rallied in rejecting the Act; by 1876, only a single candidate had been enfranchised under its provisions. Even if some individuals were willing to take the step, bands stubbornly refused to allot the required land. They correctly saw the measure as an attempt to destroy Native communities and their way of life at the same time as it would break up their reserves, allotment by allotment; when all Indians became enfranchised, there would be no more land left in common and reserves would have disappeared. Not only did the measure displease Natives, it was also at cross-purposes with imperial policy. As pointed out by historian John Milloy, this provision changed the intent of the British program for the civilization of Amerindians and threatened the Proclamation of 1763, which had envisioned Indians secure on their reserves under the protection of the British imperial government.[22] Two years later, in 1859, the Act for Civilizing and Enfranchising Indians, while still encouraging enfranchisement and consolidating previous legislation pertaining to Aboriginals, dodged the issue of reserves. Even as it sought to bring Natives into the fold of Euro-Canadian society, it extended Canada West's ban on the sale of liquor to Amerindians to Canada East; after Confederation it was extended to the whole Dominion. The ban would stay on the books until 1951.

Much of this negative Amerindian reaction could have been avoided if more attention had been paid to the advice of Peter Jones, the Mississauga chief, who realized that the fundamental challenge was to make the Indians feel that they were being incorporated as full partners in the new order that would be Canada. As he pinpointed during the 1840s, this would involve such measures as security of ownership of reserve lands and equality of civil rights with Euro-Canadians.[23] Unfortunately, acknowledging Indians as equal partners while they still retained their own cultural identity proved a difficult step for mainstream Canada to take, and so this would be worked out very slowly. The next step, the passing of the Enfranchisement Act in 1869, will be discussed in Chapter 18.

In 1860, Canada took over Amerindian administration from Britain's Colonial Office by means of the Management of Indian Lands and Properties Act. The Commissioner of Crown Lands became Chief Superintendent of Indian Affairs in formal title, but the actual job was done by the deputy superintendent. Although Indian Affairs would not be elevated to a full department until 1880, its first full-time head was named in 1862. He was William Prosperous Spragge, who that same year had assisted William McDougall (1822–1905, Commissioner of Crown Lands, 1862–4) in negotiating the Manitoulin Island surrender. Spragge held his post until his death in 1874. As obvious from such an appointment, Amerindians had not been consulted. For them, these administrative changes did not represent an improvement, as settler interests were as opposed to Amerindian interests in the Canadas as they were elsewhere in British North America, and colonial governments were all under settler control. As for reserves, which were set aside by legislative act, they were for Indian use in common, although individual allotments could be made by chiefs or

Jacques-Pierre Peminuit Paul (Sa'k Piel Saqmow) of Shubenacadie, third from left, on the occasion of his installation as Grand Chief at St Mary's Cathedral, Halifax, 1856. He wears a medal presented to him on the occasion by Pope Pius IX. The man at far left is unidentified; next to him is Judge Christopher Paul (with white hair and goatee), cousin of the Grand Chief; at far right, John Noel, the grand chief's adopted son. The ladies are not identified.

(Public Archives of Nova Scotia, N-5488)

simply be appropriated by band members. While not recognized by the Crown, such allotments could be disposed of to other members of the band, but they could not be passed on to non-Amerindians. Non-Indians who sought to obtain such properties were subject to penalties.[24] A legal consequence of communal ownership was that Amerindians on reserves had no rights of action against their fellow tenants. It could be argued, of course, that this aided harmony and prevented discord.

When the public school system was set up during the 1850s, Amerindians were not included, as their administration was separate. The difficulties of Amerindians who sought to come to terms with the dominant society were illustrated by the case of Francis Assiginack ('Blackbird', 1824–63), son of Jean-Baptiste Assiginack (c. 1768–1865), an influential Odawa chief who had fought for the British in the War of 1812, had made large land cessions, and was an esteemed public servant. Francis, educated at Upper Canada College, would have liked to have continued to become a doctor but was twice refused support, the last time on the grounds that using Amerindian funds for such a purpose would not return benefits to the community commensurate with the expense involved.[25] Francis ended up being an interpreter and frustrated schoolmaster. In other words, after being given the benefits of a superior education, he was not allowed to define his own role in life. Not only did the dominant society demand assimilation, it reserved to itself the right to dictate the terms by which it could proceed.

Robinson Superior and Robinson Huron Treaties

In the meantime, tensions were increasing over diminishing resources to maintain the traditional Amerindian way of life. As overexploitation progressed, the concept of family hunting territories took on a new importance, and the custom of asking permission to hunt on another's territory crystallized into an enforced requirement. In northern Ontario, Pic River band members killed 14 Natives they found trespassing on their lands. The discovery of mineral deposits north of Lake Superior led the colonial government to authorize mining activities without consideration of Amerindian interests; when Chief Shingwaukonse (Little Pine, 1773–1854) of Garden River, near Sault Ste Marie, and other Ojibwa leaders went to Toronto and demanded that the revenues from the mining leases be paid to them as the owners of the region, they got nowhere.[26] Three years later, in 1849, another request, this time for a land settlement, again drew no response. The Ojibwa took matters into their own hands and moved to close the Quebec and Lake Superior Mining Company operation at Mica Bay by force. Within three weeks troops were on the scene to quell the 'rebellion', sometimes called the Michipicoten War.[27]

One of the two commissioners sent to investigate the situation was Thomas Anderson, of the Upper Canadian model village experiments, who had become Chief Superintendent for Indian Affairs in 1845, a post he held until 1858. The commissioners found the Ojibwa eager to formalize their relationship with the government by means of a treaty, even to the extent of being willing to leave the amount of compensation for the government to decide. Despite their expressed confidence in the 'wisdom and justice of their Great Father', and their obvious goodwill, they were clear-sighted about their objectives; the negotiations did not promise to be simple. Out of these negotiations would arise the practice of including in the treaties provisions for Amerindian reserves; in this, the Robinson treaties would set the pattern for the future. Amerindians had long had this idea, but earlier attempts to realize it had not resulted in an established procedure;

setting aside lands for Amerindians had been done on an ad hoc basis at the pleasure of the various colonial assemblies. Bond Head, in arranging land surrenders, had also included land provisions for Amerindians,[28] but this was not always honoured. Indian initiative in this regard was not encouraged; the Mississauga of Credit River, for example, tried unsuccessfully several times to obtain reserved locations. In the Amerindian view, reserves were not granted, they were simply lands that had not been shared with the newcomers.[29] This was how the matter was arranged in the Robinson treaties; later, under the numbered treaties, Amerindians surrendered the entire tract under negotiation on the promise of the Crown to reserve sections for their use.[30] Reserves were described as 'the cradle of the Indian civilizing effort—and the means of securing the white man's freedom to exploit the vast riches of a young dominion.'[31] Establishing large reserves in isolated areas came to be regarded as counter-productive; rather, to achieve the 'civilizing' goal, reserves should be small and, where feasible, placed near Euro-Canadian settlements. The theory was that such proximity would familiarize Amerindians with Euro-Canadian ways and encourage their adoption.[32] (An earlier version of this in the French regime had officials sending French families to live in Indian villages.)

Chief negotiator for the treaties was ex-fur trader William Benjamin Robinson (1797–1873), a younger brother of John Beverley Robinson of Family Compact fame; he had previously negotiated land settlements with Musquakie. His mandate was to obtain rights to as much land as possible for as little as possible from Penetanguishine along the north shore of Lake Huron and across to Batchawana Bay on the eastern shore of Lake Superior and down to Pigeon River. Payment was to be by annuities, and each band would be permitted to select a site for its own reserve; hunting and fishing rights would continue over the entire surren-

dered area. There were to be no gift distributions (even though this custom was still in practice and would not be abolished until eight years later), but as Amerindian etiquette required an exchange of gifts on such occasions, Robinson had to compromise on this. He was ably assisted in the negotiations by Jean-Baptiste Assiginack, at that point an interpreter in the service of Indian Affairs.

Chief Peau de Chat ('Cat Pelt', L'Avocat, fl. 1814–1850) and the Lake Superior chiefs signed on 7 September 1850, and two days later, Chief Shingwaukonse and leaders from Lake Huron, after holding out for better terms, also signed. Some of the chiefs were to claim later they had been pressured into signing and threatened to appeal to London. Each group was to receive a cash payment of £2,000, in addition to annuities, which for the Lake Superior group were set at £500 and for those from Lake Huron at £600, in both cases to be divided among band members. Lists of selected reserves were appended to each treaty;[33] sales of reserve lands and mineral rights were to be conducted by the government for the 'sole use and benefit' of the Indians. Proceeds of mineral rights that had been leased before the treaties were to be turned over to the Amerindians. Both treaties contained escalator annuity clauses. If the Amerindian population dropped below two-thirds of its treaty level, annuities were to be proportionately decreased; on the other hand, they could be increased at the Crown's pleasure if sales from surrendered lands permitted the government to do this at no additional expense from its general revenue. At the time of the signings, 1,943 souls were enumerated for the Lake Superior group and 1,458 for Lake Huron.

The lands surrendered amounted in area to twice that which had already been given up in all previous treaties combined in Canada West, extending north as they did to the height of land separating Rupert's Land from Canada; by now virtually all of Canada West was cleared of Amerindian title. The two Robinson treaties confirmed the pattern that had been developing since the Proclamation:

- negotiations were to be at open and public meetings, according to procedures laid down by the Proclamation of 1763;
- lands should be 'surrendered' only to the Crown;
- annexed to each treaty was to be a schedule of reserves to be held in common;
- annuities were to be paid each member of the signing band;
- finally, Amerindians were to retain 'full and free privilege to hunt over the territory now ceded by them and to fish in the waters thereof as they have heretofore been in the habit of doing', except for those portions that would be sold to private individuals or set aside by the government for specific uses.

One of the points that bothered the dissident chiefs was the small size of their annuities compared to those being accorded in southern Ontario. The answer, according to Robinson, lay in the fact that southern Ontario was already heavily settled because its lands were so good for agriculture, which had destroyed the hunting for the Amerindians of the region; in northern Ontario the lands were of little or no use for farming, which meant that the Amerindians would be able to continue to hunt in the foreseeable future. He did not refer to the ecological effects of mining in the mineral-rich region.

Another point that quickly drew attention was the nature of the 'surrender'. Since Amerindians did not claim absolute ownership of the lands, but only the right to their use, how could they surrender them to the Crown, or to anyone else for that matter? Another complication lay in the fact that since the Crown already claimed underlying title, what

was it accepting from the Amerindians? Such questions would give rise to a series of court cases, beginning with *St Catherine's Milling v. The Queen* (Chapter 23).

Manitoulin Island Cession

The influence of the Robinson treaties would soon be evident in the next major cession, that of Manitoulin Island. The region had been set aside as a reserve by the 1836 treaty with the Ojibwa, in the expectation that those living to the south would move there. But by 1860 only 1,000 people had moved in, and 3,000 acres (1,214 hectares) were under cultivation. Dissatisfied with this and under pressure to open more land for settlement, the government ended the project. William McDougall in 1862 successfully negotiated for 600,000 acres (242,811 hectares) of the reserve's land. His tactics were dubious to say the least and involved the use of liquor, despite an express governmental prohibition of such procedures. The deal was concluded for $700 in cash plus the proceeds from sales of the surrendered lands to homesteaders. All was not lost for the Amerindians: each head of family was allowed 100 acres (40 hectares), compared to the 25 acres (10 hectares) originally proposed, and single persons over the age of 21 received 50 acres (20 hectares) to be selected in such a way as to keep Indian communities intact. Also, they were granted fishing rights (earlier, there had been a move to exclude them from this activity). That there was even that much of a concession to the Amerindians was the result of the efforts of Assiginack, who had been of such help to Robinson and who had been one of the signatories to the 1836 treaty that had created the Manitoulin Island Reserve. Now, with all except two of the chiefs of the Catholic mission village of Wikwemikong, he resisted its dismemberment.

The treaties notwithstanding, the question of

protection for Amerindian lands remained essentially unsolved as settler encroachments continued in agriculturally attractive areas. A year before Confederation, An Act to Confirm title to Indian Lands in the Province of Canada sought once more to deal with this problem. At the same time, by its terms the government reserved to itself the right to sell reserved lands not being used by Amerindians, and to do so without consulting them. It was simply not considered necessary to get the agreement of the Natives in such a case. With Confederation, the three participating provinces that became four (Nova Scotia, New Brunswick, Quebec, Ontario) were allowed to keep control of Crown lands within their borders, as were Prince Edward Island and British Columbia when they joined a few years later. The prairie provinces, after they were created, were not granted that control until 1930.

Neither were Amerindians included when Confederation of British North America was agreed to in 1867; the question of their partnership was not even raised. Similarly, no one had thought to consult or even inform the Inuit before Privy Council issued a proclamation in 1880 transferring Britain's Arctic territories to the Dominion, and when Newfoundland joined in 1949 no mention was made of either the Inuit of Labrador or Amerindians of St George's Bay and other regions. The right to self-government, which the colonies had so vigorously and successfully claimed for themselves, was not being extended to its indigenous peoples. Marginalization of Amerindians was well underway in Ontario; among the Native communities, there was sadness, bitterness, and to some extent even resignation.

Chapter 18

The Many Fronts within Confederation

When the Dominion of Canada was created in 1867, Amerindians were declared a federal responsibility in the section of the British North America Act, 91(24), on 'Indians, and Lands reserved for Indians', the only reference in the Act to Canada's Aboriginal peoples. This separated their administration from that of Crown lands. Amerindians continued in a distinct legal category, that of wardship, from which they could, if they chose, step out to become as other Canadians, but the price was high. As matters stood, they at least had the advantage of protected lands; in Douglas Sanders's view, reserves were the main institution inherited by the Dominion from colonial administrations.[1] In the Amerindian view, the main inheritance was the tradition of the treaties to regulate relations between Indians and settlers, principally in connection with land. Euro-Canadians confidently expected that Indians would eventually be assimilated, as there was nothing in their way of life that was worth preserving; as Sir John A. Macdonald (Prime Minister of Canada, 1867–73, 1878–91) observed in 1887, 'the great aim of our legislation has been to do away with the tribal system and assimilate the Indian people in all respects with the other inhabitants of the Dominion as speedily as they are fit to change.'[2]

The low esteem for Indian culture was reflected in a disregard for Indian arts and crafts. The few Canadians who sought to collect Amerindian objects for museum display received only grudging help from the government, if any at all. Most collectors were Europeans, although there were also some Americans, so that a great deal of early Canadian Amerindian materials ended up outside the country. Not even the records of Indian Affairs were considered worth saving; besides, they were taking up storage space. As a consequence, there is little left in some series for the 1930s and 1940s. George Stanley and other interested scholars persuaded the department to save its records instead of destroying them.

Canada, originally consisting of Ontario, Quebec, Nova Scotia, and New Brunswick, acquired Rupert's Land[3] and the North-Western Territory in 1870; Manitoba became the fifth province that same year. British Columbia joined Confederation in 1871, and Prince Edward Island became the seventh province in

TIMELINE

1816	Cuthbert Grant leads Métis in Battle of Seven Oaks after Métis unrest and hardship following export embargo.
1845	Métis sign petition asking for definition of their status.
1847	Métis petition London for recognition of rights, declaration of colony free of HBC control.
1851	Métis again petition for colony, just as Vancouver Island had become colony in 1849.
1857	Palliser scientific expedition to report on conditions for living, settlement in Plains region.
	Fraser River gold strike.
1858	'Fraser River War' as Salish outraged by invasion of their territory by 25,000 gold-seekers.
1862	Sioux uprising in Minnesota; many escape to Assiniboia (Red River) District, but white settlers drug and return to US two Sioux leaders, who are among those executed in largest mass execution in US history.
1864	Retirement of Governor Douglas a blow to BC Indians: reserve sizes reduced; Amerindians viewed as having no rights.
	Chilcotin War: after raids and killings, five Amerindians sentenced and hanged.
1867	Confederation of Canada: Amerindians declared a federal responsibility by British North America Act.
1868	Thomas Spence, a Scottish businessman, elected president of self-governing council at Portage la Prairie, sets up Republic of Manitobah with own tax structure. Republic dies in flurry of revolver shots.
	Drought and crop failures on prairies; buffalo hunt in precipitous decline.
1869	An Act for the gradual enfranchisement of Indians . . . defines 'Indian' as at least one-quarter Indian blood and introduces three-year elective system for band leadership.
1869–70	First Riel Rebellion, led by Louis Riel, takes control of Red River and establishes provisional Métis-led government, to the dismay of Canada Firsters from Ontario.
1870	Canada acquires Rupert's Land and North-Western Territory from Britain.
	Manitoba Act rushed through federal Parliament to create new province; Riel flees to US.
	Blackfoot defeat Cree at Battle of Belly River, the last purely Amerindian battle in Canada.
1871	British Columbia joins Confederation, retains control of its Crown lands.
1874	Ottawa disallows BC's Crown Lands Act because it made no provision for Amerindian reserves or rights. (The special problems of Aboriginal land claims in BC continue into the twenty-first century.)

1873. These expansions meant that in four years Canada's Amerindian population increased from 23,000 to more than 100,000 (estimates that may be low), from 0.7 per cent of the population to 2.5 per cent.[4] These acquisitions complicated administration, as each area had a separate history made up of a distinctive set of experiences. If there was a common denominator in all this, it was the habit of governments to legislate in the interests of the dominant society without consulting Amerindians. Later, David Laird, who as Minister of the Interior and Lieutenant-Governor of the NWT was Superintendent-General of Indian Affairs, 1873–9, would claim that he had consulted with some Ontario chiefs while framing the Indian Act and had modified its provisions in accord with their wishes, but he did not substantiate this.[5]

This pattern was in place in 1868 when the Department of Secretary of State was formed and given responsibility for Amerindians; when Joseph Howe was named Secretary of State for the provinces in 1869 he was also made Superintendent-General of Indian Affairs, a position he retained until 1873, when the Department of the Interior took over Native administration. 'Indian affairs' involved control of Amerindian lands and property (including resources), as well as Indian funds. High on the department's priority list was the consolidation of the various items of legislation that had been inherited from previous administrations.

The task of forging a uniform system for the diverse situations across the new country was a formidable one. It was comparatively simple for the federal authority to expand the administration already in place in Ontario to incorporate those of Quebec and the Maritimes. In those areas, governments had been dealing with Amerindians for some time; besides, the proportion of Native population had become too low to be an important political consideration. On the prairies and in British Columbia, however, where Amerindians still were in the majority, settlers viewed them with apprehension and administrative networks were not fully developed. In both regions difficult problems would arise in connection with the Native peoples that would complicate the task of creating a dominion from sea to sea. The situation became even more diverse when Britain handed over her Arctic territories to the Dominion in 1880, adding the Inuit to Canada's administrative responsibilities.

Indian Affairs began by building on existing legislation. The year following Confederation it strengthened the 1857 Act with a measure 'designed to lead the Indian people by degrees to mingle with the white race in ordinary avocations of life';[6] in effect, it continued the 'guardianship policy'. Penalties for trespass on Amerindian lands were increased. This was followed by an even stronger measure, 'An Act for the gradual enfranchisement of Indians . . . ', passed in 1869, which in addition changed the definition of an Amerindian by adding a 'blood quantum' proviso. To qualify, a person born after the passing of the Act must now have at least one-quarter Indian blood.[7]

The Act also introduced the three-year elective system for bands. Powers of chiefs were somewhat extended and band councils were empowered to make bylaws on minor matters relating to police and public health, although still subject to being overridden by Indian Affairs; chiefs or band councillors could be deposed if the cabinet saw fit. This Act was drawn up with the Six Nations and other peoples who had had a long history of contact with non-Natives in mind. The cabinet decided, upon the recommendation of the Superintendent-General, which bands were ready for the three-year elective system, a step that could be taken without the consent of the band.[8] Once more, individual landholdings carved out of reserves were used to reward enfranchisement, this time by means of 'location tickets' that carried with them rights of inheritance.[9] Although those who became enfranchised lost the right to be classed as Indians under the Act, that did not affect either their treaty rights (other than treaty payments) or their right to live on a reserve. They took on the legal status of ordinary citizens, which meant, among other things, that they could hold a business licence, buy liquor, and send their children to public school. It was confidently expected that these new provisions would undermine resistance to enfranchisement; however, up to 1920, only slightly more than 250 Amerindians would choose to enfranchise under the Act.[10] Later, more Amerindians would accept to vote as the

Act's requirements were eased; when the Act was amended to allow Amerindians living off reserves to be enfranchised without the required land, 500 accepted within two years.

In the event of marrying out, the 1869 Act expanded features of the 1851 legislation that differentiated between men and women. If a registered Amerindian man married a non-Indian woman, she acquired her husband's status, which was passed on to their children. In contrast, the Amerindian wife of a non-Indian lost her right to annuity payments, to be a member of a band, or even to be an Amerindian within the meaning of the Act. This was modified somewhat by the provision that anyone with one-quarter Aboriginal blood could be classified as an Indian; in that case, the one-quarter Amerindian wife of a non-Indian could continue to collect payments, but her children could not claim Amerindian status on any count. These measures aroused considerable opposition, and the General Council of Ontario and Quebec Indians lobbied hard for the rights of indigenous women, but nothing came of their efforts.[11] The Indian Act of 1876, essentially a consolidation of the legislation considered in this and the previous chapter, would retain this feature. The 1876 Act will be considered in Chapter 19.

The Acts of 1868 and 1869, particularly the second one, were designed to break down tribal forms of government on the grounds they were 'irresponsible'. The elected band council would be the instrument to achieve this.[12] It was hardly surprising that, with the exception of the Mohawk of the Bay of Quinte, Amerindians 'evinced no desire to identify themselves with the proposed new order of things, or to give effect to it by applying for authority to hold elections'. Superintendent-General Spragge made that remark in 1871.[13] The bands (including the Six Nations) resisted by refusing to exercise even the limited powers they were accorded.

The Lure of Gold

If white settlement was impinging on Native hegemony on the west coast, the discovery of gold overwhelmed it. A precursor was the mini-gold rush in 1850–3 on the Queen Charlottes, followed by another of similar proportions on the Stikine in 1862. Fortunately for the Aboriginals involved (Haida and Tsimshian, respectively), both proved to be of short duration; but even so, there had been confrontations that had led Governor Douglas to assert British authority with shows of force. When news spread of the gold deposits of the Fraser River in 1857, this time the strike was of major proportions. The hard-rock gold discoveries of the Cariboo in 1862 compounded the situation.

The Salish of the Fraser had been quietly mining the placer gold for years, which they traded instead of furs at HBC posts. When the diminishing returns of the California goldfields caused miners to cast about for new regions to exploit, the word was soon out. In 1858, 25,000 gold-seekers flooded into Victoria; in short order, 10,000 men were panning for gold along the Fraser between Fort Langley and Fort Yale. Outraged at this invasion of their territory, Salish chief Spintlum and his warriors confronted the miners; the ensuing 'Fraser River War' was reported by a hysterical press in Victoria as a massacre of miners; the actual tally was 30 Amerindians and two non-Natives killed. Again, Douglas asserted British hegemony, announcing that British law applied to all, Amerindians as well as miners. He sought to win Aboriginal co-operation by appointing some of their leaders as magistrates, which did nothing to alleviate the havoc being wreaked upon the indigenous subsistence base.

The mining operations needed to extract the gold of the Cariboo strike, deep in the interior, meant the building of roads for the transport of equipment and supplies. Proceeding with all possible haste and no consideration for the damage to the Aboriginal hunting-and-gathering economy, the invaders interfered with Native salmon weirs, raided villages, and even looted graves. No protection was provided against the marauding newcomers; and when the Natives asked the road gangs for food, none was forthcoming. As the Amerindians saw it, since the non-Natives were destroying their subsistence base, it was up to them to replace it. On top of all this, the year of the strike, 1862, had also seen the outbreak of smallpox among the Chilcotins.

BC Refuses To Acknowledge Amerindian Title

The touch of Governor Douglas was sorely missed; retiring in 1864, he was replaced by Frederick Seymour (1820–69), who would hold the office until 1869. A new Commissioner of Crown Lands, Joseph W. Trutch (1826–1904), also appointed in 1864, considered Amerindians had no more rights to land 'than a panther or a bear' (to use a journalistic expression of the period); in Trutch's view, not only did Amerindians have no rights to the lands they claimed, they were 'of no actual value or utility to them, and I cannot see why they should either retain these lands to the prejudice of the general interest of the Colony, or be allowed to make a market of them either to the Government or to Individuals.'[14] His reductions of reserve sizes for the benefit of settlers have left a continuing legacy of litigation.

Matters quickly came to a head as the Chilcotins, the principal victims of these developments, sent out war parties to attack road gangs; the Chilcotin War of 1864 was on. After several bloody encounters in which 13 non-Natives were killed, eight of the insurgents, including chiefs Tellot, Alexis, and Klatsassin, were tricked into surrendering. British Columbia's celebrated outspoken judge, Matthew Baillie Begbie (1819–94), sentenced five of them

to hang, which was quickly carried out en masse, and one to life imprisonment.[15] The judge acknowledged that the treatment they had received from the usurpers had provoked their vengeance. The following year an ordinance was passed against the looting of Amerindian graves. Despite the apprehension of the Euro-Canadians, no generalized Amerindian war developed, but fear of what might happen was present in the province as late as 1900.

Where Douglas had accepted Indian requests for as much as 200 acres (81 hectares) per Indian householder, Trutch set the figure at a maximum of 10 acres (4 hectares).[16] (On the prairies, Amerindians were being allowed 160 acres—65 hectares.) Beginning in 1865, Trutch, in a program of 'adjustments', took away much of the reserve land that had been set aside for Amerindians, and the following year he issued an ordinance preventing them from pre-empting land without written permission from the governor.[17] Eventually, Amerindians lost the right to pre-empt altogether with the passing of the Pre-emption Act in 1870; what was left was the right of individuals to purchase lands from non-Amerindians. Since the Amerindians regarded the land as theirs already, this was not a 'right' they appreciated. At that time, non-Natives were allowed to pre-empt 65 hectares and purchase an additional 480 acres (194 hectares). Predictably, there was rising resentment among Amerindians at this sort of treatment. Non-Natives, uneasily aware of this even as they persisted in their actions, became more apprehensive than ever about an Amerindian uprising. One ray of light came in 1867, when British Columbia Indians were granted the right to give unsworn testimony in civil court actions, inquests, and official inquiries. The federal Indian Act of 1876 extended this to all Indians and to criminal cases as well.[18]

When British Columbia entered Confederation in 1871, it retained control of its Crown lands, the only western province granted this privilege up to that time. Indicating the importance Ottawa attached to its entry, this did not bode well for the Amerindians, even though Article 13 of the agreement gave Ottawa the responsibility for Amerindian administration and provided for the necessary transfer of lands to the federal authority. Again, the Natives had not been consulted, although they still outnumbered the newcomers at the time and would continue to do so until the mid-1880s.[19] With the exception of the adhesion to Treaty Eight in its northeastern corner, no post-Confederation treaties were signed in the province. One of the first acts of the new member of Confederation was to deprive Indians of the provincial franchise, which they did not regain until 1949 (in Quebec, Amerindians did not get the provincial vote until 1968). British Columbia did not create a ministry of Native Affairs until 1988.

Ottawa and British Columbia were locked almost immediately in a battle over the question of setting aside lands for reserves. Trutch expressed his province's view to the Prime Minister:

> The Canadian system, as I understand it, will hardly work here—we have never bought out any Indian claims to lands nor do they expect we should—but we reserve for their use and benefit from time to time tracts of sufficient extent to fulfill all their reasonable requirements for cultivation or grazing.[20]

At issue was the size of the allocations to be set aside for Amerindians. The federal government thought that 80 acres (32 hectares) would be required for a family of five, but BC did not see that any more than four hectares would be needed. Israel Wood Powell, the Dominion's first Indian superintendent in BC (1872–90), in 1873 negotiated a compromise of 20 acres (8 hectares) per family, regardless of size. This pleased no one; Ottawa soon had the occasion to express its views, which it did in 1874 when it disallowed BC's Crown Lands Act because it did not make provision for Amerindian reserves. That was the action of the Liberal government of Alexander Mackenzie (in office from 1873 to 1878); Sir John A. Macdonald was much more conciliatory to the province and was less concerned about protecting Amerindian rights.[21] British Columbia continued its policy of doling out lands to Amerindians in minimal lots; by the last decades of the century, the 90 reserves established for the Kwakwaka'wakw totalled 16,500 acres (6,680 hectares), an average of 183 acres (74 hectares) per reserve.[22]

The Challenge of the Métis

Hardly had Confederation been accomplished than the federal government came face to face with a situation that had been brewing for a long time in the Northwest: the demands of the Métis for recognition.

By this time there was a strong movement among the Métis of Red River to regard themselves as a 'New Nation', neither Amerindian nor white but a distinctive blend of both, that incorporated farming, buffalo hunting, and the fur trade. They even had their own national bard—Pierre Falcon (1793–1876), who was born and lived within the fur trade, and whose ballads became favourites with voyageurs while paddling as well as around their campfires. The Métis way of life had developed under the economic umbrella of the trade and in the isolation of the Northwest. They built their log cabins where they fancied, usually along riverbanks, for the most part without formal arrangements with the HBC—in fact, often without the Company's knowledge. As Sir George Simpson, governor of the HBC from 1826 to 1860, observed, 'We point out the situations where they may squat, we do not give them titles unless they make some arrangement for payment. . . . The majority have settled where they liked and we could not prevent them.'[23] At Red River, in the District of Assiniboia, a Métis sense of identity had crystallized with the troubles that developed after the coming of the Selkirk settlers in 1812—in the clash of cultures but above all in the rivalries of opposing fur-trading interests. The amalgamation of the North West Company and Hudson's Bay Company made the Métis the largest element in Red River's population; the 1871 census counted 9,800 Métis, of whom 5,720 were French-speaking and roughly 4,000 were English-speaking, out of a total population of 11,400. The remaining 1,600 were non-Natives; Amerindians had not been counted. In 1886, by which time Manitoba had been a province for a decade and a half and Red River had become Winnipeg, the provincial capital, the population picture had changed drastically. By then, Métis made up 1.6 per cent of Winnipeg's population; by 1901, the proportion had dropped to 0.3 per cent. However, together with Amerindians, they made up 6.4 per cent of the province's population.[24]

If the idea of a 'New Nation' can be traced to a single event, it would be the Battle of Seven Oaks in 1816, although it had received considerable impetus with the curtailing of the export of products of the hunt from the colony two years earlier. The War of 1812 had interrupted Red River's supply lines; as food shortages developed, Assiniboia governor Miles Macdonell (in office 1811–15) imposed an embargo on the export of provisions without a special licence—the Pemmican Proclamation of 1814. This greatly disturbed the Métis, for whom the export of pemmican was an important economic activity. They reacted by conducting a series of raids against the colony. In the spring of 1816, after a winter of starvation during which people died, the Métis Nor'Wester captain Cuthbert Grant (c. 1793–1854) assembled 60 buffalo hunters and attacked an HBC brigade bringing down pemmican, then captured and ransacked Brandon House, an HBC post. The Métis took the pemmican to Red River; at Seven Oaks they were challenged by Robert Semple (1777–1816, governor-in-chief of Rupert's Land since 1815) and 21 settlers; when the smoke cleared, Semple and all his men were dead, and one Métis had been killed. Grant's prestige among his people soared; at a meeting of Métis leaders at Qu'Appelle Valley that same year he was named 'Captain General of all the Half-Breeds'. He remained their leader until the rise of Louis Riel senior (1817–64) in the 1840s.[25]

As the buffalo herds diminished and receded and farming loomed ever closer as an alternative to the fur trade, both the hunt and traditional communal values began to give way to those of the individual. As more Métis became wage labourers, their relative position within the fur trade hierarchy declined: most now tended to find themselves at the level of menial labour rather than at that of the officer class, where some had been earlier. Mounting frustrations sometimes led to bizarre actions, such as joining General James Dickson's 'Indian Liberating Army' in 1836. Dickson (fl. 1835–7), a flamboyant figure of obscure origins, had come up from the United States to raise an army to assist Texas against Mexico, or perhaps to attack Santa Fe in order to set up a 'truly American' Utopia in which only Amerindians would be allowed to hold property.[26] While the movement had a brief life in the north, the fact that it attracted attention and even a few recruits says something about the level of discontent among the Métis, especially sons of HBC officers.

The prospect of the government encouraging white settlement spurred the Métis (particularly those who were French-speaking) to become more militant about expressing their concerns. In 1845, 977 of them signed a petition asking Alexander Christie, governor of Red River and Assiniboia, 1833–9, and of Assiniboia, 1844–9, to define their status. They claimed special rights by virtue of their

Amerindian blood; the governor held they had no more rights than those enjoyed by all British subjects. The Métis saw the HBC monopoly as leading to the 'utter impoverishment, if not the ruin, of the natives', whose welfare so little concerned them that they had not provided sufficient schools to prepare Native children for the changes everyone could see were coming. They were also upset at the appointment of a francophobe, Adam Thom (1802–90), as recorder (a judgeship) for Assiniboia; they had asked that a bilingual person be appointed to the post. Two years later, in 1847, they took their petition to England through the intercession of a London lawyer, Alexander Kennedy Isbister (1822–83), one-quarter Amerindian, who had been born at Cumberland House, the grandson of chief factor Alexander Kennedy and Aggathas, a Cree.[27] This time the Métis asked that the HBC charter be declared invalid; even if the charter was to be upheld, its jurisdiction did not extend beyond territories surrounding the Bay. As well, they claimed that Red River (reorganized into the District of Assiniboia in 1836) was beyond its range of authority and should be declared a colony.

This petition gave rise to spirited exchanges in the British Parliament. Powerful forces opposed monopolies in principle, but equally powerful forces saw the dangers of competition as outweighing those of monopoly and held that the Hudson's Bay Company provided the best means available to govern Rupert's Land. Colonial Secretary Merivale could not conceive of Native self-government; colonial status should only be granted to those regions where there were sufficient white settlers to ensure they would have control. Losing out in Parliament, the Métis could have appealed to the Privy Council, but only at their own expense. Their lobbying had already strained their meagre resources, so in 1850 the issue was dropped. Other petitions followed, however, including one in 1851 again demanding that

Red River be made a colony, as Vancouver Island had been in 1849.

That year, 1849, the Company in effect lost the power to enforce its monopoly when the sentence of Pierre-Guillaume Sayer (fl. 1796–1849) for free-trading was suspended. The Métis kept up their campaign against Adam Thom; eventually, HBC Governor Simpson withdrew him from office in 1851 but kept him on the payroll; he also gave in to demands that the Métis have a wider representation on the Assiniboia Council, but managed to fudge its execution. As HBC control eroded, a Canada West (Ontario) group that would later call itself Canada First began a campaign for the annexation of Red River to Canada. With Confederation it became strident, adding yet another challenge to the fundamentals of the old order of the 'custom of the country', with its elements of Amerindian law. The Métis were divided on the issue: William Kennedy (1814–90), a mixed-blood cousin of Isbister who had led one of the expeditions the British had sent to the Arctic in search of Franklin (in which he had insisted that the crew wear Native clothing), was an active exponent for the building of a transcontinental railway and annexation.

As the Métis were waging their war of words with the HBC and London for recognition of their claims, they continued actual hostilities in the field against their traditional enemies, the Sioux.[28] A confrontation with a much larger body of Sioux in 1851, the Battle of Grand Coteau, from which they emerged victorious, proved to be of even greater importance than Seven Oaks in encouraging their sense of identity. More problematic was the international border. At first, US officials had been inclined to listen to their arguments that they had rights to cross the border in pursuit of buffalo by virtue of their Amerindian blood; now, however, the American attitude was stiffening, and the Métis were finding themselves excluded from hunting south of the border.

The clamour became such that the British Parliament established a select committee in 1857 to examine British policy in the Northwest and to determine if the region (particularly the prairies) had potential for anything other than the fur trade or its provisioning. To be as completely informed as possible, the British Royal Geographical Society also sent out a scientific expedition under Captain John Palliser (1817–87) to report on the region. Canada West, not to be outdone, organized its own, under Toronto professor Henry Youle Hind (1823–1908) and engineer S.J. Dawson (1820–1902). The Canadian expedition, far from having a dispassionate assessment of regional potentialities on its mind, was to determine the best route for transportation and communication in order to facilitate annexation.

The upshot of all this was that mainland British Columbia was separated from HBC administration and became a Crown colony in 1858. Red River, with its predominantly mixed-blood population, was not deemed ready for such a status; as Merivale saw it, Natives could not be included 'in the arrangement of a regular community'. Besides, in the region as a whole, Amerindians predominated, and they were 'too self-sufficient and satisfied with their own way of life to adopt any other'.[29] Apparently, Crown colony status would only be granted if the European lifestyle was being followed. Since that was not the case, the best administration was that of the HBC, which should continue. Not surprisingly, the select committee did not think it advisable to test the validity of the HBC's charter. The disappointment in Red River was profound; as for the Amerindians, their fears for the future had not been allayed. Already, they wanted a treaty.

Natives and Confederation

Increasing immigration did nothing to relieve tensions at Red River. Even Peguis, the local Ojibwa chief who had tried so hard to come to terms with the non-Aboriginals as long as they were not too numerous, became worried as engulfment became a real prospect. He now claimed that the Selkirk Treaty had not properly extinguished Amerindian title, as the four chiefs who had signed it had not had the required powers. The land involved had been a strip a little over three kilometres long on each side of the Red and Assiniboine rivers. The ensuing controversy engendered more heat than light and would culminate with the Peguis band's loss of St Peter's Reserve in 1916 (Chapter 22): the HBC, for its part, never emulated Selkirk's action dealing with Aboriginal rights. When Confederation became a reality, four western Cree and Saulteaux chiefs were reported to have agreed among themselves about the extent and limits of their land claims in preparation for the negotiations they foresaw in the not-too-distant future. They worried about the intentions of the Canadian government in respect to their lands, particularly when troops were sent to Red River.[30] A Saulteaux band in Assiniboia allowed settlers onto their lands only on the condition that a permanent agreement be negotiated in three years.[31]

In Red River, the tensions of the political scene were exacerbated by those of changing social mores as Victorian standards, replacing those of the frontier, led to a series of sex scandals. These in turn erupted into open defiance of the HBC's established authority, which was experiencing increasing difficulty in having its voice heard.[32] As the Euro-Canadians were at each others' throats, the balance of power fell to the Métis, who in any event were the settlement's largest armed force.[33] The Sioux uprising in Minnesota in 1862 had its repercussions in Red River as refugees (largely Dakota) drifted in from the fighting, most of them in a deplorable state. In the spring of 1863, 600 of them appeared, ragged and starving, bringing the medals they had received from the British for their active alliance in the War of 1812.[34] Sioux had been fleeing in small numbers into Canada since the 1820s, but now the problem became acute as the people of Red River found themselves in the anomalous position of providing for their former enemies. When the HBC, as a representative of the British, pledged amity with the Sioux, Peguis (who would die in 1864 at the age of 90) and his people felt betrayed; that same year, 1864, a group of Ojibwa attacked a refugee Sioux encampment. Non-Native settlers behaved no better: frightened at the prospect of vengeful Americans invading their territory, they took it upon themselves to drug two of the Sioux chiefs, Shak'pay ('Little Six') and Wakanozhan, also known as Medicine Bottle, and hand them over to American agents.[35] The two were among those tried at Fort Snelling and executed for murder. Eventually most of the refugees were persuaded to settle at White Horse Plain, west of Fort Garry; in 1869, an estimated 500 were wintering there.

In the midst of these swirling tides of change, Red River's isolation from Canada became more evident than ever. Although this was the era of railroad-building, none was immediately foreseen for the Northwest; an application in 1851 to charter the Lake Superior and Pacific Railway was rejected by Canada's Standing Committee on Railways as both Amerindian and HBC land titles stood in the way. An irregular postal service with Canada was established in 1860: it operated by steamship, canoe, dogsled, and courier, depending on the season. The HBC was less than enthusiastic about this new service, as it competed with its own via York Factory. By either route, communication was slow; once the American transcontinental railroad reached the Mississippi in the 1850s, it was faster and easier to communicate via the United States.

As was only too obvious, the HBC could no longer effectively control the reins of power,

and voices began to be raised in favour of a provisional government with an elective council as 'a temporary government formed by the people themselves for the time being until the British Government shall see fit to take the place in its own hands'. In 1851, Rev. William Cockran (d. 1865) organized a self-governing council at Portage la Prairie, outside the District of Assiniboia, which began well with limited goals. But in 1868 a Scottish businessman, Thomas Spence (1832–1900), was elected president; he had much grander ideas and set up the community as the Republic of Manitobah, complete with its own tax structure. The Colonial Office, upon being informed of this enterprise, told the people that while they were within their rights to establish a council at the municipal level, no higher government exercising authority over British subjects might be formed without express permission from the Crown. In the meantime, some citizens of Manitobah were not at all sure they liked the idea of taxes and refused to pay; the republic died aborning, in a flurry of revolver shots. Meanwhile, in 1864, the Oblate Albert Lacombe (1827–1916), who was one-eighth Amerindian but who did not regard himself as Métis, established a self-governing community at Big Lake (St Albert). Even in the face of these initiatives, the Colonial Office steadfastly refused to undertake the responsibility of ending the Company's regime and setting up a Crown colony. John A. Macdonald, in London in 1865 to negotiate the terms of Confederation, reluctantly agreed to negotiate for the purchase of Rupert's Land and to extinguish Amerindian land rights once the region was under Canadian control. He had hoped the HBC would undertake this task before the transfer.

These were difficult years as well in aspects other than the political. Drought and grasshopper plagues brought crop failures; the buffalo hunt was declining and becoming more distant; the fisheries were at low ebb; in 1868, even the rabbits were at the bottom of their cycle. That was the year Ontario decided to build a road from the northwest angle of Lake of the Woods to Fort Garry in Red River as engineer Dawson of the Hind expedition had recommended in 1858. The project proceeded with more haste than foresight: Amerindian title was not always cleared, and their claims to fees for rights of passage and for timber being used were rarely heeded. In some cases Amerindians sold land that the Métis claimed. Troubles soon developed over wages, as Métis claimed they were being paid less than Euro-Canadians; in addition, wages were paid in scrip, which could only be redeemed at the store owned by Dr John Christian Schultz (1840–96), leader of the Canada Firsters. All this, plus the fact that the road had no legal mandate in the first place, as Red River was outside of Ontario's jurisdiction, brought the project temporarily to a halt. The Dawson Road, as it came to be called, eventually connected Red River to Fort William.

In spite of all these difficulties, a land rush was obviously developing. Settlers were already staking claims to land without regard to Amerindian rights. The poet and author Charles Mair (1838–1927), who had been paymaster for the Dawson Road, informed the Amerindians of Rat Creek that the influx of settlers was 'like the march of the sun, it could not be stopped'. The rush for land threatened the settlement pattern that had spontaneously developed among the fur-trade families of Red River, which mirrored that of the old regime of Quebec: river frontage farms with long thin ribbons of land stretching back into woodlots, assuring each holder of access to the river, the principal transportation route. Throughout all this, there was no official effort to inform the people of Red River as to what was going on; there was no attempt either to find out where they stood or to reassure them.

South of the border, Minnesota was a very interested spectator of Red River's troubles; its offer of $10 million for HBC lands was not accepted. In 1868, the state protested the impending transfer of HBC lands to Canada without a vote of the settlers (Amerindians, who were in the vast majority, were not mentioned), and passed a resolution favouring annexation to the United States. That same year Britain passed An Act for the Temporary Government of Rupert's Land, providing for a lieutenant-governor and an appointed council. All laws currently in force in Rupert's Land that were not in conflict with British law were to be retained. William McDougall, who as Commissioner of Crown Lands had negotiated the Manitoulin Island surrender of 1862 and who was actively working for the annexation of the Northwest to Canada, was appointed first lieutenant-governor in 1869. According to his instructions, he was to 'report upon the state of the Indian tribes now in the Territories, their numbers, wants, and claims', and how the HBC was dealing with them; he was also to make suggestions as to how the tribes could best be protected and 'improved'.[36]

Ottawa continued to be oblivious to the situation in Red River. When the new North-West Council was appointed, it was English and Protestant in composition, without representation of the region's French-language element. Even the English-language settlers protested this. In the meantime, another figure had reappeared on the scene: Louis Riel (1844–85), one-eighth Amerindian,[37] who had attended the Collège de Montréal for several years. A natural leader, with a strong sense that the Métis of Red River were indeed a 'New Nation', he represented the opposing force to Canada First. When in 1869 the English-language Métis William Dease (fl. 1855–70) had organized a meeting demanding that the payment for Rupert's Land be made to Amerindians and Métis as rightful owners of the land, not to the HBC, he had attended as an observer. Riel was

Louis Riel (seated, centre) and his councillors, 1869–70. In front, left to right, are Bob O'Lone and Paul Prue. Seated: Pierre Poitras, John Bruce, Riel, W.B. O'Donoghue, François Dauphinais. Standing in the rear: Le Roc, Pierre de Lorme, Thomas Bunn, Xavier Page, André Beauchemin, Baptiste Tereaux, and Thomas Spence. *(William John Topley; Library and Archives Canada, PA-12854)*

already a member of the Comité National des Métis, which had been organized to defend Métis rights with the active support of Abbé Joseph-Noël Ritchot (1825–1905) of St Norbert.

Red River Takes a Stand

The transfer of lands and authority from the HBC to Canada was scheduled for 1 December 1869, still without official consultation with the people of the Northwest. When word reached Red River that McDougall and his entourage were coming to the Northwest before the scheduled date of transfer, Riel and the Comité acted to defend their interests: they set up a blockade at the border on the Pembina Trail by which the official party must travel, and on 31 October refused to let them enter Assiniboia. This action had an added edge in

that McDougall's reputation as the negotiator of the infamous Manitoulin Island surrender had preceded him. McDougall had been warned of what would happen but had not believed that matters would come to that. The new Dominion had finally come face to face with the new nation whose existence it had steadily refused to acknowledge.

The Métis were not the only ones who viewed the transfer with apprehension and mistrust. Resident HBC officers, no more than the Métis, had not been consulted on the terms of the transfer, and no provision had been made for any claims they might have had. They resented English indifference to their fate, and they wondered about Canada's ability to maintain the union, especially in view of the US purchase of Alaska in 1867. Trade was flourishing between Red River and points south of the border, particularly St Paul and St Louis;[38] in the American view, it was only natural that the Northwest should become part of the United States, joining it with Alaska. The English-speaking settlers, while unhappy at what was happening, were not prepared to go as far as the Comité Nationale had carried matters.

The day after McDougall was turned back, a roll call revealed 402 men, all bearing arms, prepared to support Riel. Later that day, another 100 men were reported to come in. Discipline was strict: no alcohol. Two days later, 2 November, Louis Riel informed the HBC officer at Fort Garry that the fort was under the protection of his men, a move that forestalled a Canada First plan to take over. It also ensured the Comité's control over Red River at least until federal troops arrived, which could not be before spring.

McDougall, cooling his heels in Pembina, compounded his errors. In a snowstorm on 1 December, the day originally scheduled for the formal transfer of Rupert's Land to Canada, he crossed the border into Canada and read the proclamation that was to have put this in effect. Thus was HBC authority formally ended without any effective official authority to take its place. McDougall sought to correct this by commissioning John S. Dennis (1820–85), surveyor and militia officer, as 'lieutenant and conservator of the peace', authorizing him in the Queen's name to put down the Métis by force. The Canada Firsters greeted this with enthusiasm; the English-language settlers were skeptical and refused to co-operate. A group of Saulteaux at Lower Fort Garry under Chief Henry Prince (Mis-kou-kee-new, 'Red Eagle', son of Peguis) felt quite otherwise; they announced they were prepared to fight for the Queen; some Sioux also joined the Canada Firsters. A week later, on 8 December, Riel issued the 'Declaration of the People of Rupert's Land and the Northwest', stating that 'a people, when it has no government, is free to adopt one form of Government in preference to another, to give or to refuse allegiance to that which is proposed.' On 10 December the Métis flag was hoisted, and on the 27th, the first provisional government was established, with Riel elected president. Riel and his Métis were in control of Red River without having shed a drop of blood.

Back in Ottawa, Prime Minister Macdonald's immediate reaction on learning—on 25 November—of the Métis blockade had been to advise his representative in London not to complete the transaction with the HBC until Canada could be assured peaceful possession of the Northwest. He had then sent a message to McDougall, warning him that he was in effect approaching a foreign country under HBC control and that he could not force his way in. When McDougall chose to follow the line of the Canada Firsters and to go ahead anyway, he in effect created a political vacuum in Red River. Macdonald saw the consequences, both nationally and internationally, all too clearly:

> it is quite open by the Law of Nations for the inhabitants to form a Government ex necessitate for the protection of life and property, and such a government has certain sovereign rights by jus gentium which might be very convenient for the United States but very inconvenient for you. The temptation to an acknowledgement of such a Government by the United States would be very great and ought not to be lightly risked.[39]

And indeed, the Americans were observing events with a keenly interested eye. Macdonald sent the vicar-general of St Boniface, Jean-Baptiste Thibault (1810–79), and Colonel Charles René de Salaberry (1820–82) to reassure the Métis about government intentions; in December 1869, Macdonald appointed Donald A. Smith (1820–1914, named first Baron Strathcona in 1897) as special commissioner to investigate and calm the situation.

Subsequent events are etched in Canadian historical lore. McDougall never did gain entry to Assiniboia and had to return to Ottawa; Riel formed a second provisional government on 8 February 1870, which was more broadly representative of Assiniboia's community than the first had been. In the meantime, the rowdy behaviour of some Canada Firsters led to arrests, and on 4 March 1870 to the execution by court martial of Orangeman Thomas Scott, who had refused to keep the peace and who had insulted Métis sensibilities.[40] This inflamed racial passions between English-language Protestants and French-language Catholics; Quebec, which had remained aloof as it had regarded the Métis as 'savages', now came to their defence. Macdonald moved quickly to meet with a Red River delegation, not as representatives of its provisional government but as representatives of its organizing convention; terms were agreed upon and the Manitoba Act creating the province of Manitoba was rushed through Parliament, getting royal assent on 12 May. The name of the new province had been suggested by Riel: 'Spirit Strait' of the Crees, 'Lake of the Prairies' of the Assiniboines, the name stood for self-government and was already in use for the region. Macdonald made the 'postage stamp' province as small as possible, 28,490 square kilometres (11,000 square miles); official equality of French and English was guaranteed and a separate school system provided for. Crown lands were to be under Dominion control, with 1.4 million acres (566,560 hectares) being reserved for the unmarried children of the Métis, an area close to the size of Prince Edward Island. All existing occupancies and titles were to be respected, including those of Amerindians, a principle more easily stated than honoured, as events would prove.

McDougall fought hard to have the bill rejected. He was on good legal grounds: there were no provisions in the BNA Act for the inclusion of territories that had not previously been

Ambroise-Dydime Lépine (1840–1923), photographed in 1884. Lépine presided over the court martial that sentenced Thomas Scott to death, 3 March 1870. The sentence was carried out the next day. In 1874, Lépine was tried and convicted for the killing of Scott, but on the intervention of the Governor-General his sentence was commuted to two years' imprisonment and loss of civil rights. Seven years before his death, Lépine's rights were restored.
(Glenbow Archives, NA-2631-3)

organized as colonies. The Act had to be amended hastily to make the new province constitutional. Apart from the Selkirk Treaty, neither had Amerindian title to lands been extinguished. This pushed the federal government into negotiating the first of the numbered treaties of the West in 1871 and 1872.

In a move to forestall a filibustering raid from Ontario, Macdonald sent a military expedition to Red River in 1870 under Colonel G.J. Wolseley (1833–1913). The newly appointed A.G. Archibald, lieutenant-governor, 1870–3, was supposed to arrive ahead of the troops, which the Métis were counting on; unfortunately, it happened the other way around. Despite the unfinished state of both the Dawson Road and the transcontinental railway, and the necessity to negotiate rights of passage with the Ojibwa through whose territory the expedition had to pass,[41] the military expedition arrived first. Riel, forewarned, went into hiding.[42] The behaviour of the troops in the settlement did more damage than all the previous months of uncertainty. During the 10 months of the resistance, the Métis had served when needed as volunteers, even to providing their own arms and ammunition. Their conduct had been exemplary; now they were subjected to verbal and physical abuse, in two instances, to the point of being killed. Wolseley's expedition was Britain's last official military action in present-day Canada. Oddly enough, 1870 was also the year when the last purely Amerindian battle was fought in Canada when the Blackfoot defeated the Cree, inflicting heavy losses, in the Battle of Belly (Oldman) River.

Canada remained divided on the subject of Riel, as Ontario demanded that he be brought to justice and Quebec responded in his defence. Macdonald was able to announce in all truth that he had no idea as to the Métis leader's whereabouts, which he hoped would calm the situation. The Fenians, who were conducting sporadic raids from across the border, hoped for Métis help, particularly as one of them, William B. O'Donoghue (d. 1878), had been one of Riel's principal aides. The Métis leader refused, however, and in 1871 Archibald publicly shook his hand in thanks, a gesture that cost the lieutenant-governor his office. Riel was twice elected to Parliament for the constituency of Provencher, at first by acclamation in a by-election in 1873 and then the following year by defeating his Liberal opponent. Although he was never able to take his seat, he did slip into Ottawa long enough to sign the parliamentary oaths book, a gesture that led to his formal expulsion from the House.

The Red River crisis of 1869–70 and the subsequent question of amnesty were the first serious racial controversies to be faced by the Dominion. Although the English–French confrontation took centre stage, the underlying Amerindian–Métis–non-Native division had been the major factor. Great Britain might have lobbied for the creation of an Amerindian buffer state in the US during the negotiations for the Treaty of Ghent in 1814, but when it came to creating a Métis domain within her own colonies, she had not been up to the challenge.

Ironically, an ultimate result of the confrontations was to split the Métis into two groups: those of Red River and Rupert's Land (the 'New Nation') who had stood up for their rights, and the 'others' in the rest of the country who had not made such a stand.[43]

Chapter 19

First Numbered Treaties, Police, and the Indian Act

At Confederation, 123 treaties and land surrenders had already been negotiated in British North America with Amerindians. By the time of the James Bay Agreement in 1975, the number had approached 500.[1] An important period had been between 1860 and 1930, when 66 treaties were signed. Between 1931 and 1973 no new treaties were negotiated because of legislation prohibiting the use of band funds for land claim actions.[2] In acquiring Rupert's Land, to which the terms of the Proclamation of 1763 had not extended, the Canadian government had promised, on behalf of the imperial monarch, to negotiate with its Amerindians for the extinguishment of their title and the setting aside of reserves for their exclusive use. An imperial Order-in-Council of 15 July 1870 emphasized the point: 'any claims of Indians to compensation for lands required for purposes of settlement shall be disposed of by the Canadian government in communication with the Imperial government.'[3] It will be remembered that Indian title, although undefined, was considered to be usufructuary, the right to use the land for such purposes as hunting and fishing; it was not considered to include either sovereignty or ownership in fee simple. Even such limited rights were not universally acknowledged; the idea, developed in the sixteenth century, that Amerindians had no land rights at all was still alive, as officials made clear during negotiations. In this view, treaties were a moral, not a legal, obligation;[4] in practical terms, they were viewed as a means of avoiding conflict. In any event, Canada's promise to Britain to honour the provisions of the Proclamation of 1763 led directly to the numbered treaties, which began with Treaty One in 1871 and ended with Treaty Eleven in 1921, although adhesions continued to be signed until the 1950s. Subsequent treaties had proper names; a move to substitute the term 'agreement' for 'treaty' did not gain general acceptance, and the term 'treaty' has continued to be used. Within a space of 50 years a little more than half of Canada's Amerindians were covered by these arrangements.

In fulfilling its obligation the federal government was pragmatic: it moved to clear an area of Amerindian title only when it was found to have significant value or when political considerations were involved. Thus, when

TIMELINE

1871	Treaty One (Stone Fort Treaty) with Saulteaux (Ojibwa), Swampy Cree, and others in southern Manitoba.			Influx into Canada of Sioux fearing reprisals after Battle of Little Big Horn; by 1880, only 500 of these Sioux remained north of the border.
	Treaty Two (Manitoba Post Treaty) with Saulteaux, Cree, and other bands in central Manitoba.			Indian Act passed, a consolidation and revamping of pre-Confederation legislation from the Canadas.
1873	Treaty Three (Northwest Angle Treaty) with Ojibwa of northwestern Ontario and southeastern Manitoba.		1877	Treaty Seven, signed at Blackfoot Crossing, covers southern Alberta and opens lands for completion of transcontinental railway.
	North West Mounted Police force created.			
	Cypress Hills Massacre: American wolfers cross border after some horses were stolen and slay 20–30 Assiniboine encamped at sacred Amerindian meeting place.		1880	Amerindian administration becomes a separate department within Department of the Interior.
			1884	Potlatch feasts of Northwest Coast groups banned.
1874	Treaty Four with bands in southern Saskatchewan.		1885	Franchise Bill introduced by Macdonald with aim of Amerindian assimilation.
1875	Treaty Five with bands in northern Manitoba.			
1876	Treaty Six with Plains Indians of central Saskatchewan and Alberta includes provision of a 'medicine chest' that becomes the legal basis for free health care for all Amerindians.		1890s	Ghost Dance spiritual movement of American Sioux, which anticipates disappearance of white man, appears on Siouan reserves in Saskatchewan and Manitoba.
			1895	Thirst dances (sun dances) of Plains Amerindians banned. Like the potlatches, these continue secretively.

Manitoba became a province and settlers were already moving in, it was important to extinguish Indian title quickly to avoid possible confrontations. Canada was not in a financial position to repeat the costly frontier wars of the United States.

There were also mounting demands from Amerindians for treaties. As previously noted, it was due to such pressures that the Robinson Huron and Robinson Superior treaties had been negotiated in 1850; similar agitations were now developing in the West. When Archibald had taken over as lieutenant-governor of Manitoba and the North-Western Territory in 1870, he had been immediately faced with Amerindian insistence on treaties. Apparently he had studied the Ontario treaties and was also familiar with some of the American ones.[5] His response had been to send out a representative to investigate the Amerindian position. However, the first attempt to reach an accord in Manitoba, in 1870, ended in failure.

What Were the Treaties?

By this time treaties had become the federal government's tool for extinguishing Indian land rights; it regarded them as the final, once-and-for-all means of opening up Indian lands for settlement and development. This was missed by Amerindians at first because, by their custom, agreements were not necessarily

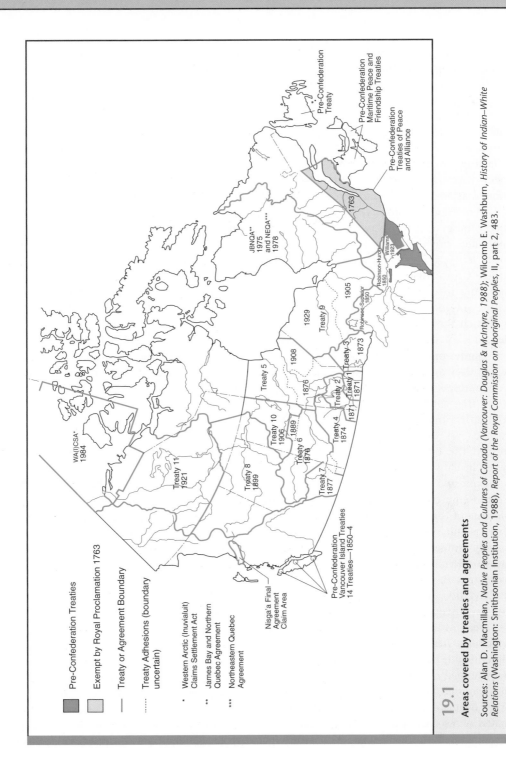

19.1

Areas covered by treaties and agreements

Pre-Confederation Treaties

Exempt by Royal Proclamation 1763

Treaty or Agreement Boundary

Treaty Adhesions (boundary uncertain)

* Western Arctic (Inuvialuit) Claims Settlement Act

** James Bay and Northern Quebec Agreement

*** Northeastern Quebec Agreement

Pre-Confederation Treaty

Pre-Confederation Maritime Peace and Friendship Treaties

Pre-Confederation Treaties of Peace and Alliance

Pre-Confederation Vancouver Island Treaties 14 Treaties—1850–4

Nisga'a Final Agreement Claim Area

WA(I)CSA* 1984

Treaty 11 1921

Treaty 8 1899

Treaty 10 1906

Treaty 7 1877

Treaty 6 1876

Treaty 5

Treaty 4 1874

1876

1908

1929

Treaty 9

1905

1873

Treaty 3

Treaty 2 1871

Treaty 1 1871

1871

JBNQA** 1975 and NEQA*** 1978

Robinson-Huron 1850

Robinson-Superior 1850

Williams 1923

1763

Sources: Alan D. Macmillan, *Native Peoples and Cultures of Canada* (Vancouver: Douglas & McIntyre, 1988); Wilcomb E. Washburn, *History of Indian–White Relations* (Washington: Smithsonian Institution, 1988), *Report of the Royal Commission on Aboriginal Peoples*, II, part 2, 483.

considered permanent, subject as they were to changing conditions that could call for renegotiation and renewal. Even pacts of peace and friendship undertaken to last forever had to be renewed from time to time with appropriate ceremonies to keep them 'alive'. This made provision for changing contexts, rather than reflecting on the permanence of the agreements themselves. Government representatives soon mastered Amerindian figures of speech for negotiations, appropriating (among others) such phrases as 'as long as the sun shines and the water flows'. When these were used in treaty language, Natives expected non-Natives to live up to their word.[6] In the Amerindian view, the treaties they were now negotiating with the Canadian government were a means by which they would be able to adapt to the demands of the contemporary world within the framework of their own traditions. In return they agreed to be loyal subjects of the Crown, respecting its laws and customs.

In the context of Indian–Euro-Canadian relations, a treaty has been defined as a compact or set of fundamental principles that formed the basis for future negotiations between Indians and non-Indians.[7] As John Long has expressed it, in the government view the treaties granted privileges to be enjoyed at the pleasure of the Crown; in the indigenous view they safeguarded rights.[8] The government was heavily influenced by the fact that in some areas settlement had preceded treaties. As can be imagined, in such cases settler reaction to Indian land rights was guarded, to say the least, and usually openly hostile.

Several of the treaties were modified by later adhesions. Treaty Six, for instance, had over 15, all to include bands that lived in the treaty area but who had not been dealt with in the original negotiations; the last was signed in 1956. Three other treaties had their areas extended. In the matter of reserves, the basis for calculation was one square mile (2.59 square kilometres) per

family of five in seven of the treaties; Treaty Eight was given the additional option of land in severalty, using the same formula as for the reserves. Treaties One, Two, and Five were allowed 160 acres (65 hectares) per family of five.

In the case of Manitoba, the federal government gave surprisingly little thought to the terms of the expected surrenders; officials seem to have regarded the exercise as little more than a formality. Accordingly, they paid much attention to the panoply and ceremony that would surround the negotiations, in the expectation that this would overawe the Amerindians and thus reduce their demands. Treaties One and Two were negotiated by Archibald and revised by Alexander Morris (1826–89), at that time Chief Justice of the Manitoba Court of Queen's Bench but who later was lieutenant-governor of the North-West Territories, from 1872 to 1876 (the spelling 'Northwest' was adopted in 1905). He succeeded Archibald as lieutenant-governor of Manitoba in 1873. Morris was responsible for negotiating Treaties Four, Five, and Six, and David Laird for Treaty Seven. Laird was also one of the commissioners for Treaty Eight. Missionaries were prominent in a number of these negotiations, sometimes as agents of the government, at others as mediators. In general they viewed the treaties as being in the best interests of the Amerindians and urged them to sign; they were equally insistent, however, that the government live up to the resultant obligations.

As the government had already experienced, negotiations were far from being either simple or easy. As Dawson described it:

> Any one who, in negotiating with these Indians, should suppose he had mere children to deal with, would find himself mistaken. In their manner of expressing themselves they make use of a great deal of allegory, and their illustration may at time appear childish enough, but in their actual dealings they are

Negotiations for Treaty One, as represented by the *Canadian Illustrated News*, 1871.
(Glenbow Archives, NA-1406-72)

shrewd and sufficiently awake to their own interests, and, if the matter should be one of importance, affecting the general interests of the tribe, they neither reply to a proposition, nor make one themselves, until it is fully dis-

cussed and deliberated upon in Council by all the Chiefs.

What was more, added Dawson, extreme caution had to be exercised as to what was said, as 'there are always those present who are charged with keeping every word in mind.'[9] He illustrated his point with the actions of a Fort Frances chief, who repeated to him, verbatim, what Dawson had said two years previously. The language difficulties that had plagued negotiations from the first arrival of Europeans continued to be an unsolved problem, compounded by the fact that now interpreters were usually government representatives.

It has often been assumed by historians that because more generous terms were offered in subsequent treaties, Indians must have improved their negotiating techniques and were driving harder bargains. An examination of the negotiations for Treaty One by historian David J. Hall has revealed that the government was ill-prepared and that the Indians forced major changes in the government's offerings.[10] During these discussions they raised most of the issues that appeared in subsequent treaties. That they were as successful as they were is a measure of their skill in negotiating, as they were at a serious disadvantage vis-à-vis the government, which could, and did, impose a 'take-it-or-leave-it' approach that meant that in the final analysis the Indians had little choice.[11] In two instances, those of Treaty Nine signed in 1905–6 and the Williams treaties of 1923, the Ontario and Canadian governments had worked out the terms before opening negotiations with the Natives.[12] There were holdouts among the Amerindians, in some cases until mid-twentieth century.

Stone Fort and Manitoba Post Treaties

Treaty One, called the Stone Fort Treaty because it was negotiated at Lower Fort Garry, which was built of stone, was signed on 3 August 1871; it was with the Saulteaux (Ojibwa), Swampy Cree, and others in southern Manitoba around Portage la Prairie and Winnipeg and included the area covered by the Selkirk Treaty of 1817, a total of 16,700 square miles (43,253 square kilometres). Treaty Two, called the Manitoba Post Treaty, was signed on 21 August 1871 with Saulteaux, Cree, and other bands in central Manitoba. The government was not only justifying its creation of Manitoba, it was preparing the way for white settlement; the Amerindians were interested in preserving as much of their way of life as possible and, alternatively, in putting themselves in a position to prepare for the changes that would become inevitable. Because of the difficulties that had developed with the Selkirk Treaty, which the Natives claimed had been signed by chiefs not properly selected to represent their people, the area it covered was included in Treaty One.

The question of delegates became a concern during the negotiations for Treaty One when a chief complained he could 'scarcely hear the Queen's words'. The impediment to his hearing had been caused by the HBC imprisonment of four Amerindians for breach of a service contract. Their release and attendance at the meeting improved the chief's hearing.[13]

The Indians opened negotiations by claiming enormous reserves, amounting to about two-thirds of Manitoba, a position Archibald and Wemyss Simpson, Indian Commissioner from 1871 to 1873, termed 'preposterous'. They were prepared to offer 160 acres (65 hectares) per family of five, and an annuity of $12, and they threatened the Natives with being swamped by settlers without any compensation if they did not agree. The chiefs were disturbed; they could not see that the government's offer would be of benefit to their children. One chief raised a point that had never even remotely occurred to the Euro-Canadians: what would happen if Indians had more children after they settled down? Archibald's reply was to the effect that they would be provided for from lands further west, forgetting that those lands already had their complement of

Aboriginal occupants. Was it really fair, another Indian asked, to allow the same amount of land for Indians as for non-Indians, considering the differences in their circumstances and ways of life? And what about assistance in getting started in this new life? The government promised schools and schoolmasters, ploughs and harrows. The Amerindians thought there should be more: clothing twice a year for the children and a fully furnished house for each settled indigenous family, besides cattle and equipment. They got the impression that the government negotiators agreed.

The terms for Treaties One and Two were similar. In return for the regions surrendered, which included the Selkirk lands, the government gave each Indian a present of $3 and an annuity of $15 per family of five, prorated for families of different size, payable in goods or cash. It stood firm on its offer of 160 acres per family of five, which the Indians reluctantly accepted. It agreed to maintain a school on each reserve and said it would prohibit the sale of liquor on reserves. The hunting and fishing rights promised by Archibald in his opening speech were omitted in the treaty's final draft. Neither was there any provision for the agricultural implements, livestock, and clothing that had been agreed to verbally. Even so, the terms accepted by Ottawa had exceeded original instructions. Upon receiving Amerindian complaints that verbal promises made during negotiations were not being honoured, Ottawa's first reaction was to say that the treaties could not be reopened. Archibald cautioned Ottawa about the Indians' extraordinary memory as to what was said during negotiations. The government finally agreed to provide livestock and agricultural implements, particularly as the Indians were expected to take up farming, but it refused to do anything about houses or medical aid. The Indians practically accused the Canadian government of having obtained their agreement to the treaties under false pretenses.

Eventually, in 1875, the government undertook to revise the two treaties. Annuities were brought into line with those of Treaty Three: $5 per head. The government also agreed to provide buggies, livestock, and farming implements, as well as distinctive suits of clothing for chiefs and headmen. The animals were to remain government property, but Indians were to have the use of them. Although the revision in favour of the Amerindians was substantial, it still did not give all that had been promised. After that, officials were much more careful about what was said during negotiations.

Northwest Angle Treaty

Treaty Three, the Northwest Angle Treaty, was signed 3 October 1873 with the Saulteaux of the Lake of the Woods district; most of the 55,000 square miles (142,450 square kilometres) it dealt with were in Ontario, except for a small portion in southeastern Manitoba. It finally cleared title to the Dawson Road and also provided for the railroad right-of-way. The Ojibwa were well aware that theirs was 'a rich country'. As Chief Mawedopenais of Fort Francis put it, 'the rustling of the gold is under my feet where I stand.'[14] Making the point that it was 'the Great Spirit who gave us this; where we stand upon is the Indians' property, and belongs to them', he observed that they had already been 'robbed' of lands by non-Indians, 'and we don't wish to give them up again without getting something in their place.'[15]

After prolonged and difficult negotiations, and several refusals by the Indians to sign, its final terms were more generous than those of the previous two treaties. For example, it provided for reserves based on 640 acres (259 hectares) for a family of five, a gratuity of $12, and annuity of $5 per capita. Besides a suit of clothing every three years, chiefs were to receive $25 each per annum and subordinate officers in each band, $15. Each chief was also to receive a flag and a medal. This time provision was made for the continuation of hunting and fishing rights, to the point of providing $1,500 annually for ammunition and twine for fishing nets. An array of agricultural equipment and supplies was included, including seeds and livestock. Schools were to be established, and the sale of liquor was to be prohibited on reserves. A request by the Amerindians that they be granted free passes on the Canadian Pacific Railway was rejected out of hand.[16]

The Métis had been influential in the negotiations; this was the first of the numbered treaties specifically to include them, which was done after some official hesitation at the request of Mawedopenais.[17] Similarly, during the bargaining for Treaties Four and Six, the Indians requested that their 'cousins' be included. At first this was accepted, and land was set aside for the Métis of Rainy River; however, as a consequence of the Red River troubles, Ottawa changed its mind and amended the Indian Act in 1880, excluding 'halfbreeds' from both the provisions of the Act as well as from treaties.[18] In spite of this, the Métis continued to be influential in the negotiations; according to Dufferin, they were 'the ambassadors between East and West'.[19] The Ojibwa of Treaty Three agreed. They told Morris, 'you owe much to the half-breeds.'[20] This contrasts with later representations of Métis as inferior people, lazy, improvident, untrustworthy.[21]

The better terms of Treaty Three reflected the greater familiarity of the Amerindians of the area with the governmental negotiating process and their greater political assertiveness. Perhaps as a result of the Robinson treaties, they had made it clear as early as 1859 that 'the country is theirs, and they do not abandon any of their rights by permitting the government surveyors to pass.'[22] They were the ones with whom rights-of-way had been negotiated for Wolseley's troops in 1870 and for whites in general the following year. It took

Morris four attempts over three years before they agreed to sign. In contrast, Treaty Five (1875) was signed speedily, even though the benefits were less.[23] At the conclusion of the Treaty Three negotiations, Mawedopenais borrowed from Euro-Canadian rhetoric: 'I take off my glove and in giving you my hand I deliver my birthright and lands; and in taking your hand, I hold fast all the promises you have made, and I hope they will last as long as the sun goes round and the water flows.'[24] The whites would have plenty of occasion to reflect on the implications of the rhetoric they used so freely during negotiations.

In the meantime, Treaty Three set precedents for subsequent treaties, particularly where agricultural equipment and livestock were concerned, as well as in its provisions for hunting and fishing rights in unsettled areas, although there was some improvement in terms in subsequent treaties. A major exception would be the 'medicine chest' clause of Treaty Six in 1876.

Eventually, in 1881, the boundaries of Manitoba were extended to include essentially those areas ceded by Treaties One, Two, and Three. In the case of Treaty Three, this would lead to a confrontation with Ontario and to Canada's first court case involving Aboriginal rights (a phrase that came into popular usage in the 1960s), *St Catherine's Milling v. The Queen* (Chapter 23); others would soon follow.

Police Head West

Ottawa was well aware of the growing instability in the West as the bison receded, as the transcontinental railroad was inching its way from sea to sea, as the HBC government was losing control, and as settlers were exerting more and more pressure on Amerindian and Métis lands. The possibility of the extension of the frontier wars of the United States into Canada, rather like what had happened in Nova Scotia

(Chapters 6, 7, 11), filled Ottawa with alarm: for one thing, Canada did not have at her disposal the resources for such a costly and ultimately wasteful procedure. Since the BNA Act stipulated that law enforcement was a provincial responsibility, however, a federal force would only be able to operate in those areas not yet organized into provinces; alternatively, it could come to an agreement with those provinces that did not have their own police.

Not long before, in the 1820s, Britain had created the Royal Irish Constabulary, a different kind of force from the usual decentralized British law enforcement agencies. For one thing, it was armed, which ordinary British police were not, and organized along military lines under centralized control. This was the model the British followed when they organized police forces in their colonies, such as India. Macdonald decided on the India variation for Canada. His original plan was to use Métis for at least half of the rank and file, under British officers. The troubles of 1869–70, in particular Ontario's violent reaction to the Métis initiative, led him to drop the idea. The North West Mounted Police that was created after enabling legislation was passed in 1873 was all white.[25]

Almost immediately, an incident brought the new force into action. The Cypress Hills, near the international border where the Alberta/Saskatchewan border would eventually be drawn, was a sacred area for Amerindians, where hostile tribes could camp in peace. It had become a favourite resort for American traders, men whose stock-in-trade was liquor, as well as for hunters/trappers called 'wolfers' because of the skins they usually obtained. A group of these wolfers at Fort Benton, Montana, had some horses stolen; their search for those they considered guilty brought them to the Cypress Hills, where they attacked an Assiniboine encampment, killing between 20 and 30 people (the accounts vary). In the charges and countercharges that followed, it was never established that the Assiniboines were indeed the culprits; in fact, the weight of evidence was to the contrary, and later it would be established that Crees had been the culprits.[26] What was clear at the time was the need for a law enforcement agency in the region; that year, nearly 100 Amerindians were killed in drunken brawls.[27]

Canada promptly sent out 150 North West Mounted Police to confront traders and wolfers, whose forts were reputed to be bristling with cannons. The trip was fraught with difficulties, not the least of which was the heavy mortality in the livestock that formed part of the equipment train. At one point the expedition was quite lost; the best known of the local guides who came to their rescue was Jerry Potts (Ky-yo-kosi, 'Bear Child', 1840–96), a Métis.[28] The Mounties finally arrived at Fort Whoop-Up, a trading post, to find only one trader there. He invited the police in to dinner.

Until 1885, the main tasks of the Mounties were the suppression of the liquor trade and the establishment of good relations with the Amerindians. They were successful on both counts. Canada at that point was on good terms with the Cree, an inheritance from the HBC. The attitude of the Blackfoot Confederacy, however, was uncertain; Superintendent James F. Macleod (1836–94) set about cultivating one of its chiefs, Crowfoot (Isapo-Muxika, 'Crow Indian's Big Foot', c. 1830–90), and soon became a personal friend.[29] The arrival of the police proved to be a boon for the Confederacy, which had suffered much from the whisky trade; in 1872–3 alone, 70 Blood were known to have died in drunken quarrels between themselves, this among a people who in precontact days had a very low incidence of violence within their own communities.

Treaty Six, signed in two ceremonies at Forts Carlton and Pitt in 1876, included the famous provision to maintain a 'medicine chest' for the

Sitting Bull, chief of the Hunkpapa Sioux, who came to Canada with 4,000 followers after they defeated the Americans in the Battle of the Little Bighorn, 1876. Their arrival at a time when the buffalo herds were diminishing made for an uneasy stay, and the Sioux soon began drifting back to the United States. Sitting Bull finally surrendered to the Americans in 1881. The contradictions in his reputation were such that he has been called the greatest Indian enigma of his time.
(Library and Archives Canada, C-20038)

benefit of the Amerindians; it became the basis for free health care for all Amerindians.[30] It also provided for rations in case of famine, important now that buffalo had become so scarce.

Treaty Seven, signed the following year at Blackfoot Crossing, near Gleichen, Alberta, attracted Canada's last great gathering of independent Plains Amerindians. It cleared the way for the construction of the railroad, among other items. Crowfoot had agreed to sign on the advice of a shaman, who had said the treaty would change his life and that of his people: 'What you will eat from this money will have your people buried all over these hills. You will be tied down, you will not wander the plains; the whites will take your land and fill it.'[31] But in spite of these consequences, there was no alternative. Crowfoot refused a Sioux proposal to wipe out the NWMP. With the signing of this treaty, the Canadian government had gained its immediate object of securing its western settlement frontier. Treaty Eight, involving today's northern Alberta, northwestern Saskatchewan, northeastern British Columbia, and parts of the Yukon and Northwest Territories, would not be signed until 1899, under pressure from the Klondike gold rush (Chapter 25). These treaties cleared title to most of the land that would be included in Alberta when it became a province in 1905.

An unexpected problem for the police was the influx of Sioux into Canada following the Battle of Little Big Horn in the United States in 1876. Instead of being a regional problem, as a similar situation had been in Red River a few years earlier, this time the question of the Sioux refugees was national because of changes in jurisdiction as a result of Confederation. Tatanka-I-yotank (Sitting Bull, *c.* 1836–90), chief of the Hunkpapa Sioux, and 4,000 of his followers streamed north into the Cypress Hills area at a time when northern buffalo hunters were heading south into the region in pursuit of the remaining herds. Not only were the food resources inadequate for so many people, but once more there was fear of an American invasion when the United States demanded that the refugees be forced to return. Most of them were persuaded by one means or another to do so; even Sitting Bull gave up after his last request for a reserve was refused. By 1880, only 500 remained.

Meanwhile, Ottawa recognized that it had inherited an obligation towards the Sioux, who had been allies of the British in the colonial wars, and in 1874 passed an Order-in-Council authorizing the setting aside of 12,000 acres

Crowfoot with his family, 1884.
(Glenbow Archives, NA-1480-31)

(4,856 hectares) for them at two sites in Saskatchewan, on the basis of 80 acres (32 hectares) per family of five. Eventually other reserves were created, the last in 1913, at Wood Mountain in Manitoba. All Sioux reserves today are in prairie parklands, more or less similar to ancestral Dakota homelands.[32]

Sioux have never been included in Canada's treaties, as they did not cede lands in this country. They are registered, however, and so are entitled to the benefits given to status Amerindians except for annuities in payment for land. Once they accepted the fact that buffalo hunting could no longer provide for their subsistence, they settled down to their ancient way of life, farming. But readjustments were not always smooth, and life could be very hard; until the end of the nineteenth century, the death rate exceeded the birth rate, so that by 1899 only 897 Sioux were listed for Canada. One of the few who took part in the 1885 troubles was Wapahaska ('White Cap', 'White Warbonnet'), who was briefly a member of Riel's council—'Exovidate'—in 1885. He was tried for participating in the rebellion but was acquitted on the grounds that he had been forced to join.[33]

The Indian Act

In response to the special administrative problems of the West, separate boards were set up in

1873 to deal with Amerindian affairs in Manitoba, the North-West Territories, and British Columbia. It was soon decided, however, that Confederation called for more centralization, so in 1875 the boards were abolished in favour of the superintendency system developed in central Canada over the previous century or more. This, in turn, called for centralized legislation. Amerindians, already the most regulated of peoples in Canada (later to be joined by the Inuit), would become even more so; their lives would be interfered with at every turn, down to, and including, the personal level.

The Indian Act of 1876 consolidated and revamped pre-Confederation legislation of the Canadas into a nationwide framework that is still fundamentally in place today, despite amendments that began almost as soon as it was passed—there were 28 by the time of the major revision in 1951. Its original goal of encouraging assimilation without forcing the issue, which would be lost sight of in the repression that would follow the 1885 troubles, was recovered in 1951. But the Act's fundamental purpose—to assimilate Amerindians—has remained a constant. The declared policy of Superintendent-General Laird was to legislate according to the views of the Amerindians, 'at least as far as their rights to property were concerned'.[34] In 1899, Clifford Sifton, Minister of the Interior and Superintendent-General for Indian Affairs from 1896 to 1905, agreed that Amerindian views should be considered, but immediately qualified that position by stating that 'the right of Indians to control the actions of the Department' would not be recognized 'under any circumstances'.[35]

Attempts were made to accommodate differences between bands' social structures, such as those of the East with their longer histories of association with whites and those of the West with their much shorter acquaintance with the new order. However, many of the provisions of the earlier Acts, which had been devised for

Amerindians rather than with them, were preserved intact. For example, measures for protection of reserve lands and resources were taken directly from the 1850–1 Acts, although somewhat strengthened, and the enfranchisement provisions of 1857 were retained and expanded. Now offered: any Amerindian who got a university degree qualifying him as a minister, lawyer, teacher, or doctor could become enfranchised and get a location ticket without going through the otherwise mandatory three-year probation. As previously noted, the regulation depriving Amerindian women married to non-Indians of their Indian status was retained.

One measure that came in for revision was the definition of an Amerindian. He was now described as 'a person who pursuant of this Act is registered as an Indian, or is entitled to be registered as an Indian'; also, a person of Amerindian blood reputed to belong to a band and entitled to use its lands.[36] Incidentally, a person could be registered without having signed a treaty. It also defined other terms for the first time, such as 'band', 'member of a band', and 'reserve'. According to the Act, a band is a body of Amerindians for whom the government has set aside lands for their common use and benefit; for whom the government is holding monies for their common use and benefit; or who have been declared a band by the governor-in-council for the purposes of the Act. A member of a band is a person whose name appears on a band list or who is entitled to have his/her name appear on such a list. A reserve, within the meaning of the Act, is a tract of land, the legal title to which is vested in the Crown, that has been set aside for the use and benefit of a band.

The 1869 provisions for local government by elected chiefs and band councils were revised to give Amerindians more control.[37] The elective system, not being traditional among Amerindians, had met with considerable resistance from some groups; the government's goal was administrative uniformity, but it also wanted to hasten assimilation by eliminating tribal systems. The measure was also opposed by officials such as Hayter Reed, Indian commissioner, 1888–95, and from 1893 deputy superintendent-general of Indian Affairs, who foresaw that Indians would use the system to elect traditional leaders, very few of whom he regarded as competent. Although the Superintendent-General could depose a chief he considered unsatisfactory, the reaction of the Amerindians was usually to re-elect him.

If Reed had had his way, he would have eliminated chiefs and band councils, thus almost totally suppressing Amerindian political activity, at least on the prairies. According to the Act of 1876, there was to be one chief for every band of 30 members, or in the case of larger bands, in the proportion of one chief and two second chiefs for every 200 people. No band was allowed more than six chiefs and 12 second chiefs and councillors. The chief's period of office was for three years, but he could be removed at any time for 'dishonesty, intemperance, or immorality' at the discretion of Indian Affairs. The responsibilities of the chief and council included, among other items, public health, maintenance of roads, bridges, ditches, and fences, construction and maintenance of schools and other public buildings, and granting of reserve lots and their registration. However, the Indian Affairs agent paid the bills, as the branch controlled the band funds. He was obviously in a position of power.

The imposition of the elective system and the accompanying overriding powers of the Superintendent-General were strongly opposed by the Six Nations because of its obvious interference with autonomous choice for forms of government. Imposing the electoral system was not an original idea—the French had done as much when the Jesuits had introduced the system under their supervision at Sillery in 1640. Their accounts do not mention encountering opposition.[38] In this early attempt to get Amerindians to govern themselves European-style, the problem had been to prevent them from being too severe, both in regulating and in punishing. The Sillery experiment was essentially over by 1660, despite some later Abenaki arrivals.[39] In the nineteenth century, however, Indians had become more openly assertive; the resistance reached the point that in 1880 an amendment strengthened the Superintendent-General's position. It confirmed his power to impose the elective system whenever he thought a band was ready for it, whether it wanted it or not; it also prohibited hereditary chiefs from exercising power unless they had been elected.

Lands held in trust by the Crown for the benefit of indigenous peoples could not be taxed, mortgaged, or seized in lieu of debt by any person other than an Indian or a band. The effect of this has been to reduce severely access to development capital, despite a modification that made some property other than land open to seizure.[40] However, an Indian could be taxed if he held property under lease or outside of the reserve. In Manitoba, the North-West Territories, and Keewatin District, Natives who had signed treaty were forbidden from acquiring lands by homestead or pre-emption; this was to prevent them from claiming both a share of a reserve and a homestead. (In British Columbia, it will be remembered, Indians were similarly excluded from acquiring homesteads, but without the protection of treaty.) The Superintendent-General retained the right to grant allotments on reserve lands in fee simple as a reward for enfranchisement. Most bands resisted the measure and refused to approve location tickets or to alienate lands, even for a limited period. This meant that persons holding location tickets could not lease their lands. Procedures for enfranchisement at first excluded western Amerindians, but this was amended in 1880 to include them. Annuities could be refused to convicted criminals or family deserters.[41]

As can be seen from the foregoing, the Indian Act is something of a 'total institution'; with the treaties, it touches on almost all aspects of the lives of status Indians. Both the treaties and the Indian Act place them in a separate category from other Canadians, but in different ways. From the Indian point of view, the two are at cross purposes; as they see it, the Act is designed to restrict and control, whereas the treaties aim at accommodation through mutual agreement. To Indians, the Act's goal to remake them, through education and social programs, into contributing members of what has become an industrialized and technological society is a violation of their treaties. For non-Aboriginals, the basic purpose of the Act has been the protection of Indians while setting the stage for their 'advancement'. Although the Act's immediate effect has been to put Indians into a separate legal category, they see it as paving the way for Indians to become fully participating members of a society based on the liberal democratic traditions of individual initiative supported by equal rights for all. As this is an ongoing process, the result has been a stream of amendments and revisions that have been necessary to keep the Act abreast of an evolving situation.[42] In theory, this should end with the Act legislating itself out of existence.

Upward Spiral of Regulation

Amerindian administration did not become a separate department until 1880, although even then it continued to be with the Department of the Interior, where it remained until 1936. The Minister of Interior was also Superintendent-General of Indian Affairs; however, effective power lay with the deputy superintendent-general. To the Superintendent's power to impose the elective system whenever he thought a band was ready for it was added the power to designate only elected officials as band spokesmen. Traditional leaders were not to be recognized, at least not when it came to dealing with the government. By imposing the Canadian political system, it was hoped that Amerindians would be led to adopt other aspects of the Canadian way of life.

In 1884 the elaborate feasts of the Northwest Coast Amerindians, known under the general label 'potlatch', were banned,[43] along with dances associated with tamawanas (religious, supernatural) rituals. This was done under pressure from both missionaries and government agents. In the case of the potlatches, the argument was that their 'giveaway' aspect was incompatible with Western economic practices and inimical to the concept of private property.[44] In the case of tamanawas rituals, dancing was against the religious convictions of some missionaries. The irony, of course, was that Amerindians, in common with many other peoples, considered music and dance to have been the gift of the gods— or perhaps stolen from them. Towards the end of the nineteenth century and into the twentieth century, missionaries were also campaigning to remove totem poles as symbols of an undesirable belief system and way of life. Their presence was regarded as encouraging resistance to the adoption of Christianity.

Eleven years later, in 1895, the thirst dances ('sun dances') of prairie Amerindians were in effect prohibited because of their ceremonial endurance features, which authorities did not consider acceptable.[45] Since the Natives regarded these as essential elements of the rituals, the result was to drive the dances underground, even though the prohibition could not be effectively enforced. The one attempt to do so with the potlatch before the sweep of 1921 was dismissed by the judge. In the meantime the Indians, with the help of their lawyers, became adept at taking advantage of legal technicalities that made it possible for them to hold their banned ceremonies without being arrested.[46] On 21 February 1896 a petition signed by three elders of the Na'as band asking for the restitution of their customs was published in *The Daily Colonist*, Victoria:

> If we wish to perform an act moral in its nature, with no injury or damage, and pay for it, no law in equity can divest us of such right.
>
> We see the Salvation Army parade through the streets of your town with music and drum, enchanting the town. . . . We are puzzled to know whether in the estimation of civilization we are human or fish on the tributaries of the Na'as River, that the felicities of our ancestors should be denied us.[47]

At this time the Ghost Dance was being performed on Siouan reserves such as the Wahpeton at Round Plain, Saskatchewan, and Wood Mountain, Manitoba, having made its way into Canada from the United States where it had originated in the 1890s. The exhausting dance was soon modified and incorporated into the Dakota Medicine Feast and became known as 'New Tidings'. Millenarianism was another type of mystical movement that also appeared from time to time; in 1904, for example, southern Saskatchewan was swept with rumours that 'the end of the world for the white people was coming, that only real Indians living in teepees would be spared and would then have all the world to themselves, and lots of buffalo to hunt.'[48] These movements worried officials because they strengthened the peoples' inner resources to withstand the intensifying onslaughts on their culture. The traditional way, far from disappearing as officials hoped, was reincarnating in different disguises.

An Act for conferring certain privileges on the more advanced bands of Indians of Canada, with the view of training them for the exercise of Municipal Affairs—the official name

of the Indian Advancement Act—sought to transform tribal regulations into municipal laws. Passed in 1884, it granted tribal councils limited powers of taxation, subject to the approval of the department; responsibility for public health; and the power to punish transgressions of bylaws. It also reduced the number of band councillors to six, a measure that Dr Peter Edmund Jones (1843–1909, son of Sacred Feathers and chief of the Port Credit band) thought unwise, as traditionally Amerindians were used to large councils. Reducing the number to six, he said, would 'be more like plunging them into municipal work than training them'.[49] The Act replaced the three-year election system, in effect since 1869, with annual elections, considered necessary for the municipal type of government the Act was preparing the bands for. Taking as few chances as it could, the Act also provided that chiefs deposed by the governor-in-council on grounds of dishonesty, intemperance, or immorality could not be immediately re-elected. Bands considered not advanced enough for this system were mostly in the West; the decision as to who qualified rested with the governor-in-council. In effect, the powers of the Superintendent-General, or his designated agent, to direct the band's affairs had been greatly increased: he could call for and supervise elections, and he could summon and preside over band meetings.[50] Amerindians, no matter where they were located, reacted to these new measures by considering them as just another attempt 'to force white ideas on the red men'.[51] Ironically, the first bands to express willingness to accept the proposed new order (The Pas, Birch River, and Cumberland House) were in the North-West Territories; but the first actually to put the annual election system into effect were in British Columbia. The Cowichans led the way, soon followed by the Kincolith of Nass River, then Metlakatla and Port Simpson. In all, only nine bands adopted the new system, some of

Mi'kmaq delegation meeting Lord Lorne, Governor-General of Canada, 1878–83.
(Library and Archives Canada, C-2295)

them under pressure. By 1906, what remained of the Indian Advancement Act was incorporated into the Indian Act. Further modifications of the Act will be discussed in Chapter 22.

In the meantime, on the prairies, the growing unrest among Amerindians, as buffalo became fewer and fewer, and the unhappiness of the Métis about their land situation turned governmental attention in other directions, and the Indian Act was amended once again, this time to make incitement of Indians to riot an offence.[52] Further, the Superintendent-General was authorized to prohibit the sale or gift of 'fixed ammunition' or 'ball cartridge' to Indians in Manitoba and the North-West Territories. Obviously, the government had

clear warnings of what was to come.

Still pursuing the integration of Amerindians, Macdonald introduced the Franchise Bill into Parliament in March of 1885, four days before the outbreak of the North-West Rebellion. With Amerindians east of the Great Lakes in mind, Macdonald proposed Dominion franchise for all males who were British subjects and who met certain minimum property qualifications, whether or not they were holding lands in severalty. Amerindians of Ontario and Quebec, he said, may not be contributing to the general assessment of the country:

> but they have their own assessment and their own system of taxation in their own bridges

and roads; they build their own school houses; they carry on the whole system in their own way, but it is in the Indian way, and it is an efficient way. They carry out all the obligations of civilized men . . . in every respect they have a right to be considered as equal with the whites.[53]

He added, however, that the Amerindians of the North-West Territories and Keewatin, Manitoba, and 'perhaps' British Columbia were not yet ready for the measure and should be excluded unless as individuals they were occupying separate tracts of land. The bill aroused vociferous opposition on the grounds that Amerindians in general were not paying taxes and that as wards of the government they were not entitled to be on the same footing as other citizens. The cry went up that it would allow the 'wild hordes' of western Amerindians led by the likes of Big Bear and Poundmaker to go 'from a scalping party to the polls'.[54] It speaks volumes for Macdonald's political expertise that he was able to get the bill passed; but the Liberals revoked it in 1898, claiming 'It is a derogation to the dignity of the people and an insult to free white people in the country to place them on a level with pagan and barbarian Indians.'[55]

Clearly, the country was not prepared to accept Amerindians on an equal footing, despite all the rhetoric about defending their rights. There was no question that when it became a matter of choosing between Amerindians and Euro-Canadians, the interest of the latter usually would be provided for. In the situation brewing in the West, the conflict of interests was moving steadily towards violence. It would be amazing how little violence there was, and of what short duration. Canada has much to be thankful for in the forbearance of her Aboriginal peoples.

Part V

Into the Contemporary World

Chapter 20

As the Old Way Fades, the New Looks Bleak

As it was becoming more and more evident that the bounty of nature had its limits—the bison, once 'countless' because they were so many, were rapidly becoming 'countless' because there were none left—so it was increasingly difficult for Amerindians and Métis to pursue their accustomed ways of life.[1] While all who depended on bison were affected, the problem was particularly acute for Amerindians, not so much because of unwillingness to adapt to changing conditions (after all, adaptability had been the key to their survival in the Americas for thousands of years), but because of the suddenness with which it was occurring.[2]

The decline of the herds did not manifest itself uniformly; the areas exploited by the Cree were among the first to be affected. The Cree, alarmed, held a series of councils in the Qu'-Appelle region in 1859 in which they voiced objections to the Métis winter hunt and maintained that the pursuit of bison should be restricted to Amerindians. They viewed the HBC expansion onto the prairies as part of the problem, and while they wanted trade, they did not like to see their lands invaded by strangers—

both whites and Métis—who also hunted there, which the Cree maintained they had no right to do. If the newcomers wanted meat, pemmican, or hides, they should purchase them from the Indians.[3] The scope of the Métis hunt is indicated by the size of Red River's two annual summer hunts; in 1849, just one of these, that of White Horse Plains, counted 700 Métis, 200 Indians, 603 carts, 600 horses, 200 oxen, 400 dogs, and one cat.[4] Realizing that restricting these massive hunts would be difficult, if not impossible, to enforce, the Cree approached government agents to get Ottawa to help out,[5] but with no result. Finally, in 1871, after the Battle of Belly River, they concluded a treaty with the Blackfoot that allowed them to hunt in Blackfoot territory, where the herds were still comparatively plentiful.[6]

For many Métis, agricultural or wage-earning options were already accepted into their lifestyle, but other problems arose so that the transition for them, too, became painful, if not quite as drastic as it would be for Amerindians. The fur trade, dominant for 200 years, had in many aspects reinforced the cultural and economic positions of Indians and Métis,

TIMELINE

1859	Cree hold series of councils in Qu'Appelle region over dwindling bison herds and massive Métis involvement in hunt.
1870s	Groups of Métis leave Red River to form new settlements to north and west.
1871	Cree conclude treaty with Blackfoot to allow them to hunt in Blackfoot territory.
1872	St Laurent founded along South Saskatchewan River by Gabriel Dumont and other Métis.
	Batoche, another Métis settlement, founded near St Laurent.
1878	John Norquay elected as Manitoba's first and only Métis premier, though he identified with his Orkney heritage.
1880	Riel is instrumental in getting Montana Amerindians to allow Canadian Plains Indians to hunt on their reservations; Canadian Natives raid horses of their traditional southern enemies, which breaks brief alliance.
1881–8	Edgar Dewdney, lieutenant-governor of North-West Territories, seeks to divide Indians just as Cree chief Big Bear seeks to unite them.
1882	Big Bear, leader of largest band of Plains Cree, forced finally to sign Treaty Six in order to get rations for his starving people after he has tried to form Amerindian alliances against white intrusion. He is made to take an isolated reserve.
	US military sent to confiscate horses and equipment of Canadian Natives hunting south of the border; border crossings restricted.
1884	Big Bear calls a thirst dance on Poundmaker's reserve—more than 2,000 participate. Dumont and other Métis ride south to Montana on 4 June to ask their spiritual leader, Riel, to return and help them in gaining rights that have been often promised but never given.

particularly in the West; the rapidity of its decline inevitably entailed a strong backlash.

The Métis: Their Trials Continue

The disregard of incoming settlers for Métis or Amerindian land claims quickly stirred a Native backlash. In 1872, the Métis asked Lieutenant-Governor Archibald to let them know 'what steps they should adopt to secure to themselves the right to prohibit people of other nationalities from settling in the lands occupied by them, without the consent of the Community.' Archibald had previously rejected their proposal that a block of land be reserved for their use, as was being done for Amer-

indians who signed treaty. The federal government was also opposed to the idea, claiming that the Métis should apply for land on an individual basis, as white settlers did. What could happen in such a case was illustrated in Manitoba, where most of the land set aside for 'children of the half-breed heads of families' had been acquired by speculators for only a fraction of its value. It has been estimated that not more than a quarter was actually occupied and improved by Métis, in spite of additional grants made in 1874.[7]

It is not clear that the Métis were informed about Ottawa's position concerning treating them as individuals rather than as communities; in any event, groups scattered from Red

River to establish independent settlements, a pattern that had been in effect for some time (see Chapter 18). The principal difference was that now farming was replacing buffalo hunting as the main subsistence base. The best known of these groups was one led by the perennial buffalo-hunt captain, Gabriel Dumont (1838–1906), reputed to speak six Native languages, besides French and English. In 1872 he led his group north to colonize an area about 45 to 50 kilometres long and some 10 kilometres wide, including a stretch of the South Saskatchewan River and Duck Lake; its southern boundary was Fish Creek.[8] One of the reasons for choosing this site was that it already had a mission, St Laurent, founded in 1871 by Oblate Alexis André (1833–93). Each family had a 'ribbon' lot with river frontage of about 200 metres, following the Red River pattern. Nearby were two other missions, St Louis and St Antoine de Padoue. The settlement connected with the latter dated to 1872 and was called Batoche after its founder, trader François-Xavier Letendre *dit* Batoche (*c.* 1841–1901), whose home was reputed to be the finest in the West. Batoche was the commercial centre for the cluster of Métis settlements, referred to collectively as South Branch, straddling the Carlton Trail (the main route to Edmonton) as well as the South Saskatchewan. The largest Métis settlement at that time in the West, St Albert, was not far from Fort Edmonton.

Ottawa in the meantime had already decided on the square survey as the settlement pattern for the West; however, anyone who had settled in the region prior to 1870 was entitled to a special survey to maintain original boundaries. In the case of the Métis this was important, as their 'ribbon' lots obviously did not conform to the square survey. After 1870, settlers had no legal right to special consideration, although surveyors were instructed to accommodate special claims as best they could. Usually this was done to the satisfaction of both parties. But at South Branch this did not happen, some say in error. Neither could the Métis get recognition of their land claims on the basis of Aboriginal right, as that had already been denied, nor on the basis of prior settlers' rights, as they were considered to be squatters. On the other side of the picture, the Métis were negligent about filing claims for patent.[9]

On 10 December 1873, Dumont called the St Laurent Métis together to discuss setting up a governing body. At that point the settlement counted about 322 people; later, its population would swell to 1,500. Dumont was unanimously elected president, and eight councillors were selected. They took the oath of office before Father André and proceeded to enact 28 basic laws modelled on those that governed the buffalo hunt, with the added right to levy taxes. Households were to be taxed for public services, besides providing labour for *corvées* (public works parties) as needed. The council was to meet once a month to settle such matters as failure to meet obligations or to follow regulations, such as that of obeying the captain while on a buffalo hunt. Disputes were to be settled as far as possible by arbitration, and contracts made on Sundays were to be considered null and void. Penalties (mostly fines) were to be levied for lighting fires after 1 August, for failure to restrain wandering horses or dogs that killed foals, as well as for defaming the characters of members of the community or for dishonouring girls and then refusing to marry them. The regulations did not mention theft (apart from horses) or violent crimes such as assault, manslaughter, or murder, all of which were extremely rare among the Métis at that time. On the positive side, there were regulations for conditions of labour and employment, and ferries were enjoined to transport people to and from church on Sundays without charge.

St Laurent was off to a promising start. Dumont, encouraged, visited other South Branch communities suggesting that they do likewise.

He seems to have hoped that they could eventually get together and work out a self-governing plan at least for South Branch and perhaps for the whole Northwest until the time when the North-West Council established by Canada would actually be ready to govern. When that happened, the St Laurent council assured federal officials, it would resign in favour of Ottawa's authority. However, the other communities were not well enough organized to rise to the challenge. In the meantime, the decrease of buffalo caused the St Laurent council to tighten its regulations and to petition the North-West Council to adopt its measures for the whole region. And then, other events intervened.

That summer, 1874, a party of 'free hunters' after buffalo arrived in the area the St Laurent settlers considered to be theirs. Dumont and his men, including some Crees, confronted the intruders and told them they were trespassing and breaking local laws. When the hunters refused to accept this, the Métis levied fines against them and exacted payment by confiscating their equipment and supplies to the required amount. The hunting party proceeded to the nearest HBC post, Fort Carlton, where they complained to the chief factor, Lawrence Clarke (1832–90). Clarke then reported the incident to Lieutenant-Governor Morris as an unwarranted attack; to Clarke, it looked like an open revolt against Canada.[10] The HBC, for its part, had been uneasy about St Laurent from the beginning, particularly after its recent experience at Red River, in which Dumont had offered his services to Riel during a visit in 1870.[11] The press did not improve matters: 'Another Stand Against Canadian Government Authority in the Northwest', headlines screamed. Ten thousand Crees were reported to be on the warpath; Fort Carlton was said to have fallen and six members of the North-West Mounted Police killed. Clarke seems to have been the origin of at least some of this misinformation; in any event, a detach-

Gabriel Dumont, buffalo hunt captain who was Louis Riel's military leader during the North-West Rebellion of 1885.
(Glenbow Archives, NA-1063-1)

ment of the NWMP under Superintendent Leif Crozier (1847–1901) was sent out, and the matter was thrashed out with the St Laurent council on 20 August 1875.

On examining the council's laws, Crozier expressed the opinion that they were eminently sensible for prevailing conditions. Neither did Edward Blake, federal Minister of Justice, 1875–7, see anything objectionable in them; he observed that the very fact they had been necessary pointed to the need for establishing a properly constituted government on the prairies. The council agreed to disband as a formal body, and the police said they would have no objections to the buffalo hunt being regulated along the suggested lines. It was 1877 before the North-West Council enacted hunting laws, too little and too late to save the herds.

In spite of everything, St Laurent and the Métis on the prairies generally were prospering because of the buffalo robe trade with the US, which on the northern Plains peaked during the 1870s.[12] Manufacture of pemmican was no longer the only, or even the principal, *raison d'être* of the buffalo hunt. The robe trade prized the winter hides of cows, encouraging selective killing that increased pressure on the herds. Short-term profits obscured long-term considerations; for example, the only asset possessed by a Saulteaux called Little Dog in 1873 was his hunting ability, when he hired out as a hunter; two years later he owned a train of six carts. Amerindian and Métis alike shared in this quick prosperity, and during the late 1860s and early 1870s the slaughter of the herds reached its greatest intensity.[13]

Deprived of their own council and thus of the ability to act on their own, the Métis petitioned for schools, or at least for help in getting them established. Ottawa, as usual, was slow, but eventually agreed to help. The Métis also asked for two representatives on the North-West Territories Council; Pascal Breland (d. 1896), long-time member of the Assiniboia council, was appointed. Lieutenant-Governor Morris was deeply disturbed, as Breland had no prestige in the Métis community; he called the appointment 'unjust' and predicted trouble. In 1878, Manitoba elected its only Métis premier, English-speaking John Norquay (1841–89); by that time the flood of immigration was changing Manitoba into an Ontarian community, a transition capped by the language legislation of 1890, which transformed Manitoba from the bilingual province that had been established in 1870 in accordance with Riel's dream into a unilingual English province. Premier Norquay, who identified with his Orkney rather than his Cree background, had initiated the process.

Land title continued to be a problem. There was no agreement among the Métis communities as to how it should be solved: some, such as the communities at Cypress Hills and Fort Qu'Appelle, petitioned on the basis of Aboriginal right; others wanted land grants such as had been awarded under the Manitoba Act and sought help in changing over to farming, as the Amerindians were being helped. Such a petition in 1877, the year of the Blackfoot Treaty, had 275 signatures of Métis in the region. St Laurent in its petitions did not mention relationship with Amerindians but did specify that it wanted its river-lot system to be recognized by the surveyors; officials said this was not necessary, that the Métis themselves could easily divide the square survey into the desired river lots. To the Métis, this was not satisfactory, as they wanted government recognition of their system, not an ad hoc adaptation. Also, if they did it themselves, they could not have official pegs to indicate their boundaries. To add to the confusion, survey maps were slow in appearing; until they did, the Métis could not make legal claims. David Mills, Minister of the Interior from 1876 to 1878, assured them that procedures would be hastened but did not specify on what basis grants would be made; however, his outspoken view was that the Métis should be considered the same as white settlers. In 1884 a government inspector came out, but he arrived at no solution the Métis could accept.

The Métis of Manitoba were no better off, despite the huge land grant of the Manitoba Act. Not only was the grant made before Amerindian title had been extinguished (that did not happen until Treaty One in 1871),[14] but, as we have already seen, its implementation had been plagued by delays, speculation, and outright theft. Even established river lots had not been secure: at Rat River, Manitoba, out of 93 Métis claims, 84 were rejected out of hand because of insufficient cultivation. Five claimants who had houses considered to be adequate and who had cultivated at least 5 acres received 40-acre (16-hectare) grants; 4 who had cultivated 10 acres received 80 acres (32 hectares).[15] In 1874, 'half-breed' heads of families were offered $160 in scrip that could be used to purchase Crown land, but its distribution was limited to what are now the three prairie provinces, the Mackenzie Valley, and the Northwest Territories.[16] Two years later, grants to children were increased to 240 acres (97 hectares). That same year, 1876, grants took the form of scrip, with most Métis taking money rather than land; scrip became an item of speculation even before it was issued. By 1880, 3,186 claims had been settled; it would be 1919 before all of the grant was distributed. Ninety per cent of the land ended up in the hands of persons other than Métis.[17]

Nothing seemed to work for the Métis, least of all getting Ottawa to listen. The efforts of such leaders as Dumont and Charles Nolin (1823–1902), a former Conservative cabinet minister in Manitoba, brought no results.[18] A vague amendment in 1878 to the Dominion Lands Act that appeared to recognize Métis rights had not been followed up. When they had been ignored before, during the political vacuum created by the passing of the Hudson's Bay Company government, they had got results by taking matters into their own hands. Now, in the midst of a world economic crisis (1883), they met once more to consider their course of action.

At St Laurent, on 30 March 1884, 30 Métis met at Abraham Montour's house. They recalled that Lord Lorne (John Douglas Sutherland Campbell, Governor-General, 1878–83), during his 1881 tour of the West, had promised to bring the Métis situation to the attention of the government. But nothing had happened. The Métis cry was similar to that of the Amerindians: 'the government stole our land, and now is laughing at us.' A few weeks later, at another meeting, it was decided to invite Riel back from his Montana refuge, where he was teaching school, so on 4 June 1884 Dumont and some companions rode south to get their leader.

This Is Our Life, This Is Our Land

Amerindians in the Canadian West are estimated to have numbered about 35,000 in 1870 (a figure considered by some to be too high); the Métis, about 10,000–12,000; non-Aboriginals, fewer than 2,000. Epidemics (an especially severe one in the 1870s hit the Cree hard) and swelling waves of immigration were changing these proportions: by 1883, whites heavily outnumbered Amerindians.[19]

For the Indians, there were two principal ways of life, Plains buffalo-based and woodland game-based, with the gathering of plant foods, such as berries and roots, being essential to both; the ancient pattern of the woodlands would last longer than that of the Plains. Indian population on the Plains was highest during the summer, when buffalo herds were at their largest. Bison did not have definite migratory movements, congregating where the feeding was most attractive.[20] This behaviour heightened the ceremonial aspect of hunting buffalo; as the herds diminished, shamans able to call the animals gained in importance and consequently in prestige. Bison were central to the ceremonial life of Plains Amerindians; the disappearance of the herds involved not only the loss of a subsistence base but also the dislocation of their cultures.[21] It was a major factor in the rise of the Ghost Dance.

Bison were not the first fauna of the region to show the effects of over-exploitation. In the parklands that marked the eastern borders of the Plains, caribou all but disappeared by early in the nineteenth century and moose had become noticeably fewer; this, along with the retreat of the buffalo, meant that the Saulteaux of the region were growing more dependent on small game or else were migrating to the

Maskepetoon, or Broken Arm, as sketched by
Gustavus Sohon.
(Glenbow Archives, NA-4169-1)

Plains.[22] For those who continued to trap, it became steadily more difficult to combine fur-gathering with the winter buffalo hunt. This reached the point that the HBC in some districts (such as Riding Mountain) began to import pemmican for hunters to keep them trapping furs. By the 1860s some hunters were taking part-time employment as canoemen, cart-drivers, and labourers in the fur trade.

An outstanding figure of this period was Maskepetoon ('Broken Arm', *c.* 1807–69), a Cree chief, probably the best known of the western converts to Methodism. Of wide-ranging intellect, he was one of the first on the Plains to learn the syllabic script, which he used with great proficiency and which may have aided his activities as a roving diplomat. In his efforts to calm the increasing tensions, in

1869 he entered a Blackfoot camp, traditional enemies of the Cree, with his son and a small party. They were all killed, signalling the eruption of warfare from the Missouri to Fort Edmonton. This was the setting for the last major battle between Cree and Blackfoot the following year, 1870, at Belly (later, Oldman) River, near today's Lethbridge. As many as 300 Cree and perhaps 40 Blackfoot died, according to traders who visited the scene shortly afterward.[23] This may have been mute testimony to uneven distribution of firearms between the two sides. As previously noted, the conflict was followed by the treaty of 1871, in which the Blackfoot allowed the Cree access to bison herds on their territory.

The transfer of HBC lands to Canada in 1870 increased Amerindian militancy. Abraham Wikaskokiseyin ('Sweetgrass', d. 1877),[24] chief of the Fort Pitt Crees and leading Amerindian spokesman during the Treaty Six negotiations, told officials: 'We hear our lands were sold and we do not like it; we don't want to sell our lands; it is our property, and no one has the right to sell them.'[25] Other chiefs were of the opinion that the land had been borrowed, as it could not be bought. In any event, Sweetgrass had signed the treaty and as a consequence had been killed by his own people, who felt that their lands had been signed away without them being properly consulted.[26]

Paskwaw (Pasquah, d. 1889), a Cree who headed a band of Plains Saulteaux, observed that if the sale had really happened, the Plains people should receive the money. Paskwaw was one of those who had opposed the entry of surveyors onto the Plains to plot the course for telegraph lines; as he saw it, the survey indicated subordination to the newcomers. He was a principal negotiator for Treaty Four, Qu'Appelle Treaty, which took two years to be hammered out and had resulted in more concessions (in the form of implements and seed to start farming) than the federal government had wished

(Above, left) Sweetgrass (Abraham Wikaskokiseyin), chief of the Fort Pitt Crees.
(Glenbow Archives, NA-1677-10)

(Above, right) Piapot (Payipwat, Kisikawasan, *c.* 1816–1908), in 1885. One of the major leaders of the Plains Cree at the time of the treaty signings on the prairies, he remained loyal to the Crown during the 1885 troubles. This contrasted with his long record of fighting for better treaty terms and the right to choose the location of his reserve, as well as for the right to practise traditional religious rituals in spite of Ottawa's 1895 ban. Twice arrested and imprisoned for his persistent efforts, he was finally deposed as chief by Ottawa in 1902. His followers remained loyal, however, and refused to select a successor until his death.
(Glenbow Archives, NA-532-1)

to make. Paskwaw eventually took a reserve five miles west of Fort Qu'Appelle. A year later Piapot (Payipwat, d. 1908), who had a larger following than Paskwaw, also signed the treaty, apparently in the mistaken belief that it had

been revised. Treaty Four was the first to recognize trapping as a feature of Amerindian life.

The year of the Cypress Hills Massacre, 1873, the most famous and influential of the Plains chiefs, Mistahimaskwa ('Big Bear', *c.* 1825–88), clashed with Gabriel Dumont when the Métis leader sought to direct the hunt on the High Plains.[27] Half Ojibwa, half Cree, Big Bear led the largest band of Cree on the Plains at that time, about 2,000 souls. As a young man he had been noted for his ability to shoot accurately under the neck of his horse while riding at full tilt. Of impressive presence, with a full, rich voice, he did not like dealing with non-Aboriginals. Like Tecumseh and Nescambiouit before him, he worked for pan-Amerindianism, as he saw that unless the people united in the face of non-Native settlement, they were lost. Refusing official gifts being distributed prior to Treaty Six negotiations, he said he did not want to be baited so that the government could put a rope around his neck. This has been widely interpreted as expressing fear of hanging; however, as historian Hugh Dempsey has demonstrated, the reference was not to death but to loss of freedom.[28] Big Bear did not like the terms being offered for Treaty Six, in particular the provision that Canadian law would become the law of the land; as he perceived it, the treaty would forfeit his people's autonomy. Accordingly, he refused to sign in 1876 but eventually was forced to do so in 1882, at Fort Walsh, to get rations for his people; by then, it was too late for him to have any impact on the treaty's terms, as they were already set. Big Bear was reduced to 247 followers and was in no position to argue when offered a remote reserve at Fort Pitt, well to the north.

Big Bear's campaign to unite Amerindians and to get better treaty terms had seriously alarmed Ottawa, causing officials to redouble their efforts to find chiefs, such as Mistawasis ('Big Child') and Ahchacoosacootacoopits ('Starblanket'), willing to negotiate. Of those who did, only Sweetgrass and Minahikosis ('Little Pine', c. 1830–85) had reputations that came close to that of Big Bear. Little Pine, the half Blackfoot, half Cree brother-in-law of Piapot, held out for three years but was finally persuaded by his starving people and signed in 1879. Another holdout had been Kamiyistowesit ('Beardy', c. 1828–89) of the Parklands People. In common with other dissenting chiefs, he maintained that since the Europeans had caused the buffalo to disappear, it was now their responsibility to provide for Indians. Beardy carried his objections to the point of threatening to seize the trading post at Duck Lake, in his band's hunting territory, if his demands for support were not met. Authorities responded by sending an NWMP detachment to reinforce the threatened post. Throughout these difficult times, withholding rations had been Ottawa's principal weapon for bringing the people into line. The NWMP fed 7,000 from its own rations, an act Ottawa considered to be encouraging the holdouts.

A Plains Cree chief who got along reasonably well with Euro-Canadians, in contrast to Big Bear, was Pitikwahanapiwiyin ('Poundmaker', c. 1842–86), nephew of Mistawasis and adopted son of Crowfoot, leading Blackfoot chief.[29] He inherited his name from his father, a shaman renowned for building pounds. Poundmaker could still argue for his people, however. Faced with government reluctance to go beyond the short term (in fact, it considered the Amerindian concern for their children and grandchildren to be little more than a smoke-screen), he observed, 'From what I can hear and see now, I cannot understand that I shall be able to clothe my children as long as the sun shines and water runs.' In the end, he was one of those who signed in 1876, although he continued to hunt and did not accept a reserve until 1879, about 64 kilometres west of Battleford. By then all in the Treaty Six area except Big Bear had bowed to the inevitable, but all had not accepted reserves. In the final accounting, the signers of Treaty Six did better than those of Treaty Four, winning such concessions as the 'medicine chest' clause (it would be 1930 before there was an on-reserve nursing station, at Fisher River, Manitoba) and also the promise of relief in the event of famine or pestilence. But the price had been an enormous area of land, 315,000 square miles (815,850 square kilometres).

There were also chiefs who got along so well with Euro-Canadians that they earned the mistrust of their people. One such was Mimiy ('Pigeon', Gabriel Coté, d. 1884), who headed a band of Saulteaux in the Swan River area. His relationship with the HBC was such that he is remembered as a 'Company chief'. He was one of the signers of Treaty Four.[30]

Looming Preventable Disaster

By 1876, the only place in Canada where there were enough bison left to pursue the old way of life was the Cypress Hills; there were larger herds in Montana, but they were kept from moving north by firing the grass along the border. Canadian Plains tribes converged on the Cypress Hills, a movement that peaked in 1877–9. In 1879 the NWMP had its first casualty, when an officer was killed by an unknown assailant.[31] Although most of the bands had selected reserves and some were getting started in their new way of life with government assistance, there were delays in surveying sites and in providing needed supplies and equipment. It was a standoff: as long as there were buffalo around, and the Amerindians wanted to hunt them, why move faster with the new program? The warnings of the NWMP, missionaries, and settlers of a looming but preventable disaster produced no results. As early as 1877 there were complaints that needed equipment was not arriving; those Amerindians who wanted to get started in their new way of life, and there were many, were more often than not frustrated by misguided bureaucratic paternalism, compounded by ineptitude. As anthropologist Ted Brasser has written, it has been easy, with hindsight, to criticize the government's han-

The Plains Cree chief Poundmaker saw clearly the change coming to his land and his people. The bison were fast disappearing from the prairies; soon settlers would follow the Mounted Police and the treaty negotiators. He reluctantly signed Treaty Six, but sought humane accommodation for his people: 'I cannot understand that I shall be able to clothe my children as long as the sun shines and water runs.'
(Library and Archives Canada, C-001875)

dling of the situation, for which it had no precedent.[32] The fact remains, however, that when Indians objected to the mismanagement, as in the case of Big Bear, they were blamed for the problems.[33] Similarly in the western Arctic, there were those who attributed the widespread starvation that followed the decimation of the whale and walrus herds to the effects of alcohol on the Inuit, claiming that it incapacitated the hunters.[34]

Long before the demise of the buffalo herds —in the very early days of the fur trade, in fact—some Amerindians, particularly those in the parklands, had already successfully taken up farming. Geographers D. Wayne Moodie and Barry Kaye hold that within a century of the establishment of the fur trade, Amerindian small-scale farming had expanded 200 miles to the north; the 'three sisters', corn, beans, and squash, were being grown up to 49° 10' N, their northern limit. This was in response to the needs of the posts for provisioning.[35]

Old hostilities went into abeyance as Blackfoot, Plains Cree, and Sioux consulted on measures to regulate the hunt. In 1880, Big Bear and Little Pine headed south to the remaining buffalo range on the Milk and Missouri rivers, where they met with Riel. The Métis leader was instrumental in persuading the Montana Amerindians—southern Assiniboine, Blackfeet, Crow, and Gros Ventre—to allow the northerners to hunt on their reservations. The alliance was broken when the Canadian Amerindians did not resist the temptation to raid the horses of their hosts, who after all were still traditional enemies. The US government lost patience and in 1882 sent out military expeditions to confiscate the horses and equipment of the Canadian Amerindians and to send them back north of the border. From then on, border crossings were restricted.

Meanwhile, Big Bear and other Plains Cree chiefs had been discussing a plan to select contiguous reserves, which would have resulted in a de facto Amerindian territory. They almost succeeded; the reserves they selected comprised much of what is now southern Alberta and southern Saskatchewan, from Gleichen to Swift Current and south to the international border. Ottawa, waking up to what was going on, moved to prevent it, even though it meant violating treaty provisions for freedom to select reserve locations. It also meant uprooting already established Indian farmers.[36] As already

noted, when Big Bear was finally forced to take a reserve in 1882, authorities made sure it was in an isolated location. Big Bear did not give up so easily; with other chiefs, he continued to try to get reserves as close together as possible in the region of Battleford. Oddly enough, the argument that Amerindian reserves should be concentrated rather than scattered would later be made by the Anglican bishop of Saskatchewan in 1907. His interest was administrative efficiency in such matters as providing the Indians with farm instructors and schools.[37]

Since 1880 Ottawa had been enforcing a policy of work for rations, except for the orphaned, sick, or aged. The famine clause of Treaty Six was interpreted to mean that only a 'general' famine warranted free rations. Per diem allowance for individuals was 13 oz. (383 grams) of flour, 3 oz. (99 grams) of bacon, 6 oz. (170 grams) of beef. This was ordered reduced by Lawrence Vankoughnet, deputy superintendent-general of Indian Affairs, 1874–93, and such agents as Hayter Reed, who succeeded Vankoughnet, 1893–7. Reed, in his reports, did not mention that Amerindians were starving, perhaps because he saw it as a result of laziness and moral turpitude. Reed was very much a man of the Victorian era; to the Cree, he was 'Iron Heart'.

Mounting food shortages led to desperate actions, and Amerindians began to kill the cattle that were supposed to get them started as farmers and ranchers. Even government agents realized that stopping rations of offenders would not solve the problem. Fines were used instead. In 1883, three Cree chiefs, Sehkosowayanew ('Ermineskin'), his brother Keskayiwew ('Bobtail'), and Samson (inheritor of the mantle of Maskepetoon), wrote to Sir John A. Macdonald, who as well as being Prime Minister held the Interior portfolio and thus was Superintendent-General:

> if no attention is paid to our case now we shall conclude that the treaty made with us six

A nineteenth-century textbook illustration, showing Amerindians begging for food while settlers clear the land. From *Lovell's Advanced Geography*, Montreal, 1880.
(Glenbow Archives, NA-1374-2)

years ago was a meaningless matter of form and that the white man has doomed us to annihilation little by little. But the motto of the Indian is, 'If we must die by violence, let us do it quickly.'[38]

Even Poundmaker, who had co-operated at first, became disgruntled and consulted with Big Bear, who for his part thought it would be a good idea to go to Ottawa to see if someone really was in charge of Amerindian affairs, and if so, to deal with him directly. Despite his reputation among Euro-Canadians as a troublemaker, the record indicates that Big Bear opposed violence and even prevented it on occasion; he recognized that negotiation was the route to working out constructive measures. But first the Amerindians had to get together and agree among themselves.

In 1884 Big Bear called a thirst dance to be held on Poundmaker's reserve; more than 2,000 participated, the largest united effort managed by the Cree. Authorities had been unable to stop it, despite frantic efforts (they had been able to forestall others in the recent past). Big Bear's aim was to get Amerindians to select a single representative for a term of four years who would speak for all; he also wanted the Cree to join in obtaining a single large reserve on the North Saskatchewan. He argued that Treaty Six had been unilaterally changed in Ottawa from what had been agreed to during negotiations: 'half the sweet thing taken out and lots of sour things left in'. A new treaty was needed, as well as a new concept for establishing reserves.

As Big Bear laboured to unite Amerindians, Edgar Dewdney, lieutenant-governor of the North-West Territories, 1881–8, worked to divide them. He did this by the differential distribution of rations, using food as an instrument to keep the people quiet whenever a situation threatened to get out of hand. In 1884 he invited Crowfoot to visit Regina and Winnipeg, where the Blackfoot chief was given a royal reception and, on seeing the size of the settlements, became all the more convinced of the futility of violence. Dewdney also obtained an amendment to the Indian Act that provided for the arrest of any Amerindian found on a reserve not his own without official approval; he was determined that never again would Big Bear or any other chief convoke a large assembly. That this violated the law, not to mention basic human rights, was overlooked in the fear of an Amerindian war. The police view simplified the situation: 'the government would not permit armed bodies of men, whether Indians or whites, to roam the country at large.'[39]

Although confrontations were increasing, up to this point there had been remarkably little violence. As some observers noted, Amerindians under starvation conditions were acting with far more restraint than whites would have done under the same circumstances; historian R.C. Macleod has pointed to the rarity of instances of starving Amerindians killing settlers' cattle.[40] At the time, this was not appreciated, and Ottawa persisted in the view that the situation in the West was really not its responsibility, in contrast to the Amerindian view that non-Amerindians should pay the piper for having provoked disaster.

Chapter 21

Time of Troubles, Time of Repression

The first Métis resistance, in 1869–70, occurred with the passing of the HBC as governing power in the Northwest and the transfer of its lands to Canada. The second resistance, this time an uprising, occurred with the passing of the buffalo as subsistence base and coincided with the completion of the Canadian Pacific Railway, which would bring in settlers in greater numbers than ever. (The first telegraph message between Toronto and Hamilton had been sent in 1846; by 1885, there were telephone lines in the West.)

In 1869–70, the HBC had possessed no effective police or military to enforce its decisions; in 1885, the NWMP was very much a presence on the northwestern Plains. In 1869–70, Wolseley's troops did not arrive until after the passing of the Manitoba Act, 1870; in 1885, troops arrived at Qu'Appelle a week after Riel set up his provisional government. In 1869–70, Riel and the Catholic Church worked closely together; in 1885 there was estrangement, particularly when Riel proposed reforming the Church and creating Ignace Bourget, bishop of Montreal, 1840–76, as 'Pope of the World'. In 1869–70, Métis had held the balance of power

in Red River and were the settlement's effective armed force; in 1885, Métis were heavily outnumbered by Euro-Canadian settlers.

Two years of poor crops (1883, frost; 1884, wet harvest) meant that the winter of 1884–5 had been hard. Ottawa appeared to lose its sense of direction, and it disarmed the North-West Territories militia; in 1884, Hector-Louis Langevin, Minister of Public Works, 1869–73, 1879–91, on touring the West, cancelled a scheduled visit to Prince Albert without telling the people. Big Bear was having his own problems as his war chiefs gained influence at his expense; his son Ayimasis (Imases, Little Bad Man, 1851–1921) was one of these; another was Kapapamahchakwew (Wandering Spirit, c. 1845–85). They advocated violence as the only way of regaining independence.[1] Big Bear recognized the futility of such a course of action but had been so involved trying to develop pan-Indianism that he had lost touch with his own people. Conditions were so obviously unsettled that Ottawa amended the Indian Act in 1884 to prohibit the sale or gift of 'fixed ammunition' or 'ball cartridges' to Indians of Manitoba and the North-West Territories.[2] That

TIMELINE

1884	Ottawa amends Indian Act to cut off sale or gift of ammunition to Indians in Manitoba and North-West Territories.
	Big Bear losing influence to Cree war chiefs who advocate violence to regain independence.
	16 December: Riel petitions Ottawa for all people of West—white, Indian, Métis—to be treated with full dignity as British subjects.
1884–5	Hard winter due to two straight years of poor crops for Plains Indians and Métis.
1885	Ottawa acknowledges Riel petition, but is only prepared to set up a commission.
	8 February: Riel replies: 'In 40 days they will have my answer.'
	8 March: Riel announces intention to set up provisional government.
	18 March: Métis seize Indian agent and other officials and occupy church at Batoche, cut telegraph lines from Regina to Prince Albert.
	19 March: Riel proclaims provisional government.
	26 March: Métis attack NWMP sortie at Duck Lake, killing 12. Riel, armed with crucifix, stops pursuit of routed police.
	end of March: Poundmaker's and Little Pine's people leave reserves, head towards Battleford.

	2 April: Big Bear's war chiefs pillage HBC stores at Frog Lake, killing nine. Big Bear stops onslaught in time to save HBC representative as well as other settlers who had sought refuge at fort.
	15 April: Big Bear takes NWMP's Fort Pitt in peaceful surrender.
	24 April: Métis ambush Canadian militia, led by F.D. Middleton, at Fish Creek.
	2 May: Poundmaker's sleeping camp attacked, and Poundmaker halts pursuit of fleeing militia.
	9–12 May: Middleton and militia defeat entrenched Métis, who run out of ammunition, at Batoche.
	15 May: Riel surrenders.
	26 May: Poundmaker surrenders.
	2 July: Big Bear walks into Fort Carlton to surrender.
	16 November: Riel, convicted of treason, is hanged at Regina.
	17 November: Eight Indians hanged at Battleford. Poundmaker, Big Bear, One Arrow sent to prison; all die soon after release.
	Pass system introduced to restrict Natives to their own reserves.
1906	Ban on sun dances is extended to all Amerindian dances.

this contravened the treaties was either over-looked or brushed aside.

Confrontation

In spite of all this uncertainty and unrest, Riel's return in 1884, while widely welcomed, did not trigger a call for violence. Riel himself repeatedly stressed his pacific intentions even

as he maintained that the North-West Territories should be a self-governing province and that Amerindians should be better treated. He also said that white settlers were being charged too much for land. The Métis wanted Riel to be appointed to the North-West Council, replacing Pascal Breland, whom they felt was not effectively representing their interests. The settlers, however, were not so sure, as they were

Big Bear (centre) trading at Fort Pitt, an HBC post on the North Saskatchewan River, 1884. In the same year the post was taken over by the North West Mounted Police. In April 1885, in the course of the uprising, Big Bear's band attacked the fort, which they evacuated and then burned.
(Library and Archives Canada, PA-118768)

worried about Riel's relations with Amerindians; although Big Bear did not join up with him, the Cree chief told Riel he was confident the Métis leader would not forget Indians in his fight for Métis rights. Vankoughnet, deeply suspicious of Big Bear, ordered a reduction of his band's rations.

The people were becoming hungrier and hungrier; even co-operative chiefs such as Mistawasis (Big Child) and Starblanket were complaining.[3] Not only were rations at issue but also the quality of agents and farm instructors Ottawa had sent out. Although there were exceptions, in general these men had little or no knowledge of Amerindians and little, if any, sympathy for them; they usually tried to enforce regulations by the book without consideration for particular situations.[4] Ottawa's policy was to transform Amerindians into small-scale farmers, but even that goal was so mired in regulations that there was little prospect of success.

As Riel pointed out in his petition to Ottawa on 16 December 1884, the people of the West had every right to be treated with the full dignity of British subjects, which was not happening. In his listing of complaints, he included those of Métis, Amerindians, and non-Natives. This time Ottawa acknowledged receipt of the petition; the Métis were so jubilant that on New Year's Day 1885 they honoured Riel at a banquet and presented him with a house, some money, and an illuminated address thanking him for his efforts on their behalf.

The optimism was premature. The most that Ottawa was prepared to do at the time was to establish a commission to list Métis who were resident in the Northwest in 1870 and their claims; it was not initially empowered to do anything about them. Dewdney, realizing this was too little too late, modified the message before relaying it to the Métis. The ploy did not work; on 8 February Riel replied, 'in 40 days they will have my answer.' The religious implications of that response were obvious, as the seasonal Lenten fast, which occurred at this time of year, lasted 40 days, and reflected the 40 days Jesus spent fasting in the wilderness at the beginning of his ministry. Riel's relations with Father Alexis André were already strained, and he was beginning to set himself up as a prophet. Aware of the anomaly of his position as an American citizen, he offered to return to the US and leave the Métis to work out their own problems. They refused to let him go, and at a secret meeting agreed to take up arms if necessary 'to save our country'.

On 8 March Riel announced his intention to set up a provisional government and presented a 10-point Bill of Rights. In it he maintained that the Métis of the North-West Territories should have the same rights to land grants as those of Manitoba; that they should be issued patents to their lands; and that the districts of Alberta and Saskatchewan should be created provinces, with legislatures elected on the basis of representation according to population, 'so that the people may be no longer subject to the despotism of Mr. Dewdney'.[5] He also asked for better provision for Amerindians and for respect for the 'lawful customs and usages' of the Métis. Two days later, the Métis began a novena;[6] Riel by this time had broken with Father André. Both novena and Riel's '40 days' ended on the 18th of March. The Métis seized the Indian agent and other officials, and occupied the church of St Antoine de Padoue at Batoche. They cut the telegraph lines from Regina to Prince Albert but left those to Battleford intact (Battleford had been the capital of the North-West Territories from 1877 to 1883, when Regina had taken over). The next day was St Joseph's Day, St Joseph being the patron saint of the Métis. Riel proclaimed his provisional government and the people armed themselves.

Kapeyakwaskonam ('One Arrow', c. 1815–86), chief of the Willow Crees whose reserve was the closest to South Branch, butchered all the cattle on his reserve and joined the Métis. Later, he would claim that he had been threatened by Dumont and forced into his action. Riel, emulating events of 1869–70, sent a summons to Fort Carlton on 21 March, calling upon it to surrender. Five days later, on 26 March, Superintendent Leif Crozier attempted a sortie from the fort with 100 Mounties and volunteers to seize a strategic supply point. He was met by the Métis at Duck Lake, a place chosen by the Métis; within 15 minutes, 12 of Crozier's men were dead and 11 wounded, a casualty rate of nearly 25 per cent. Five Métis and one Amerindian were killed (later it would be claimed that the Indian was there by mistake). Riel, armed with a crucifix, stopped the pursuit of the routed police, preventing an even worse massacre. As the defeated column returned to the fort, reinforcements of 100 men arrived. With this protection, the fort was evacuated to Prince Albert; thanks to Riel's restraint, there was no further action at this point.

Hard on the heels of these events, Poundmaker's and Little Pine's people left their reserves and headed for Battleford, headquarters for distributing supplies. Settlers took fright and fled into the fort; two of them were killed by Stoneys (Assiniboines). The Cree plundered the abandoned houses and stores during the last two days of March. Little Pine died just afterward.[7]

Big Bear's war chiefs took matters into their own hands and pillaged HBC stores at Frog Lake

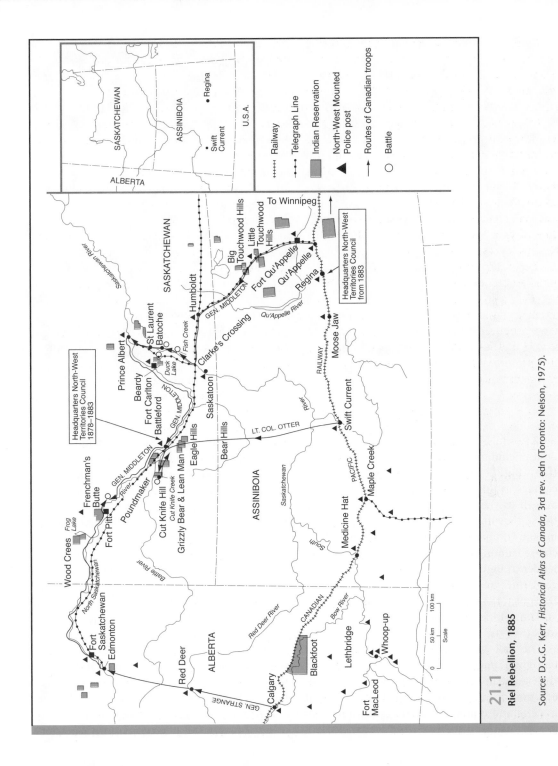

21.1
Riel Rebellion, 1885

Source: D.G.G. Kerr, *Historical Atlas of Canada*, 3rd rev. edn (Toronto: Nelson, 1975).

Men of the Winnipeg Field Battery asleep in a special railway car taking Louis Riel from Swift Current to Regina to stand trial for treason, 22 May 1885.
(Photograph by O.B. Buell. Saskatchewan Archives Board, R-B2298)

on 2 April. Nine people were killed in the incident, including the agent, two priests, and settlers. Big Bear succeeded in stopping the carnage in time to save the HBC representative, as well as the women and children.[8] Most of the settlers in the area were able to take refuge in Fort Pitt, an NWMP garrison, but after taking council among themselves they decided to surrender to Big Bear. The chief allowed the fort's garrison, under Inspector Francis Jeffrey Dickens (1844–86, son of novelist Charles Dickens), to leave without any problems, then took over the fort on 15 April.

The call to arms raised by these events brought a quick response across Canada. Since the Canadian Pacific Railway was not completed, transporting troops and supplies meant loading and unloading 16 times before reaching Regina. Even so, by 6 April Frederick Dob-

son Middleton (1825–98), commander of the Canadian militia, and his troops were marching north to Batoche from Qu'Appelle, armed with field guns and two Gatling guns, which had been developed during the US Civil War. From Swift Current, Colonel William Dillon Otter (1843–1929) headed for Battleford on 13 April, and from Calgary, Major-General Thomas Bland Strange (1831–1925) set off for Edmonton, where he arrived on 1 May. The sternwheeler *Northcote*, with armed men aboard, proceeded up the Saskatchewan River with the intention of acting as support for the ground troops; but it ran into a ferry cable the Métis had strung across the river and lost its stacks and masts. Its crew did not like being targets for Métis sharpshooters, so its brief career as a warship was ended.

On 24 April, Middleton ran into Dumont's

The surrender of Poundmaker to General Frederick Dobson Middleton, commander of the Canadian militia during the North-West Rebellion, 1885.
(Manitoba Archives)

ambush at Fish Creek, the southern boundary of the territory South Branch considered its own. Middleton was saved by premature firing of the Métis on his scouts. To the west on 2 May, Colonel Otter attacked Poundmaker's sleeping camp at Cut Knife Hill and was saved from rout by Poundmaker refusing to allow his warriors to go off in pursuit. The following week, 9–12 May, Middleton and 850 men confronted entrenched Métis, about 350 strong, at Batoche. After three days the Métis ran out of ammunition. It was the only clear defeat of the Métis during the uprising, but it was decisive. When the Canadian forces burned and pillaged after the battle, the clergy, including Riel's opponent, Father André, made an indignant protest.[9]

Riel surrendered on 15 May, Poundmaker on 26 May. On 28 May there was a brief skirmish near Frenchman's Butte, when Strange interrupted a thirst dance being held by Big Bear's band. The warriors quickly entrenched themselves; the two-day engagement was inconclusive. The hunt was on for Big Bear, and the military fanned out in all directions in his pursuit. On 2 July, Big Bear, accompanied by his youngest son, Horse Child, walked into Fort Carlton to surrender to a startled sentry. The rebellion's toll: 53 non-Natives killed, 118 wounded; about 35 Indians and Métis killed.

According to historian A. Blair Stonechild, less that 5 per cent of the Amerindian population of the Northwest was involved.[10] The financial cost to Canada: about $5,000,000.

Immediate Consequences

While the troubles were going on, the residents of Wolseley, Manitoba, passed a motion to send to Ottawa:

> It is now time for the Government to take decisive action, and that their first shall be that orders be issued to hang Riel to the first tree when he is caught; but, if there must be delay, that it shall only be long enough to capture Dewdney and hang the two together.[11]

The anger of the government, however, was not turned against its own representatives as it was against those who had protested the treatment they had received. The government charged or considered charging more than 200 individuals, most for treason-felony against an empire that had conscripted Amerindians and Métis into its orbit without consulting them and, in the case of Amerindians, without granting them citizenship. In the end 84 trials were held, 71 of which were for treason-felony, 12 for murder, and one (Riel's) for high treason; of the 129 individuals who were jailed, there were:

- 46 Métis, of whom 19 were convicted, 1 hanged, and 7 conditionally discharged; the remainder were either unconditionally discharged or not brought to trial;
- 81 Amerindians, of whom 44 were convicted and 8 hanged for murder; there was no plea bargaining for them;
- two Euro-Canadians, both charged with treason-felony, of whom both were acquitted, one on the grounds of insanity.[12]

Of the 19 Métis convicted, Riel was charged with treason under Edward III's Statute of Treasons (1352) and hanged on 16 November 1885.[13] Riel, who had become an American citizen during his sojourn in the US, was charged under the British doctrine that a person born a British subject could not lose that status through later naturalization in another country.[14] His hanging resulted in a mass protest meeting, 22 November, on the Champ de Mars, opposite Montreal's city hall, up to that point the largest such meeting in Canada's history. Most of the other Métis prisoners were convicted on the lesser charge of treason-felony, 11 being sentenced to seven years; three to three years; and four to one year each.

Most of the Amerindians (all Cree except for two Stoneys) were charged with treason-felony, but some were tried for murder as well as other offences. As the law stood at the time, a person charged with a criminal offence was not allowed to testify on his own behalf; a 'dock statement' was allowed, but this did not have the weight of testimony. Eleven of the Indians were sentenced to hang, of which three had their sentences commuted to life imprisonment; the other eight were hanged together at Battleford on 17 November, one of the two largest mass-hangings in Canada's history.[15] Prison sentences ranged up to 20 years for manslaughter and 14 years for arson.

Prison terms were virtual death sentences: of three leading chiefs sentenced to three years each, all had to be released before their terms were up and died within the year. The chiefs were Big Bear, Poundmaker, and One Arrow. Big Bear pleaded for amnesty for his band, many of whose members were hiding in the woods; if the government did not help before winter set in they would perish from want. (Some of Big Bear's followers went to Onion Lake, where they were fed at government expense until relocated on a new reserve in 1887.) Big Bear served a year and a half of his sentence before

Big Bear and Poundmaker in detention. Big Bear has had his hair shorn, an indignity that Poundmaker was spared through the intercession of his adoptive father, Crowfoot.
(Glenbow Archives, NA-1315-18)

his health broke; he died within months of his release, abandoned even by most of his own family, who had fled south. Eventually all of the Amerindians convicted of treason-felony were pardoned before their sentences were up.

Poundmaker had protested in court:

> The bad things they have said against me here are not true. I have worked only at trying to keep the peace. This spring, when my Indians, the halfbreeds and the white men fought, I prevented further killing. As soon as I heard what had happened at Batoche I led my people and went to the white man and gave myself up. If I had not done so, there would have been plenty of bloodshed. For this reason I am here . . . I will not excuse myself for saving the lives of so many people even if I must suffer for it now.[16]

He was at least spared one indignity as a prisoner: through the intercession of his adoptive father, Crowfoot, his hair was not cut. One Arrow had originally opposed signing Treaty Six but had finally signed five days after the general signing. As already noted, his band had joined Riel the day hostilities broke out; however, as he was at least 70 years old at the time, it is highly unlikely that he took an active part in the fighting. As with the other two chiefs, his trial was a near travesty: One Arrow spoke no English, the language of most of the proceedings, and very little was interpreted for him. His claim that he had not shot anyone and had had no intention of doing so was not listened to, and he was sentenced to three years. Released after seven months, he was not even able to walk and soon died. His reserve was considered to be the most unprogressive in Treaty Six.

Postscript to the Conflict

The South Branch Métis, particularly those of St Laurent, had fought to be recognized as a colony, but with special status that would acknowledge their Aboriginal right as well as their distinctive lifestyle, a blend of Amerindian and European customs. Although they shared grievances with both Amerindians and whites, the Métis considered themselves to be separate. With few individual exceptions, neither the Métis nor the Cree considered themselves to be fighting for each other; each group was fighting for itself, even as it sympathized with the other. They had a common enemy, a distant and uncomprehending bureaucracy. One of the ironies of the conflict was that it undid the decade during which Big Bear and other chiefs had worked for the autonomy and self-government of their people. Neither Indian Affairs nor the Ottawa administration in general saw that they had any responsibility for the 'prairie fire'. As for Ottawa's attitude, it can best be summed up in the observation that the hostility of those in power towards those whom they regarded as inferior—because they were 'others', strangers—has been a historical constant. In the ambience of 1885, the notion of accommodation with 'savages' was unthinkable, at least in the realm of practical politics. In the rough and tumble of building nation-states and extending them into empires, unity and conformity were the social and political ideals. Much as Amerindians might have been appreciated on their own merits in philosophic or artistic circles, in the political arena they were expected to conform to the prevailing ethos as exemplified by the dominant power. The idea of a cultural mosaic within the borders of a single nation-state was not yet taken seriously, if considered at all. That would come at a later period, but even then it would initially take little notice of Canada's Aboriginal peoples. For the Métis, such attitudes diminished and even precluded the role in which they could have excelled, as mediators between Amerindians and Euro-Canadians. Dufferin was one of the few who appreciated this; he attributed Canada's comparative rarity of frontier wars to the influence of the Métis, without whom 'it would have been impossible to establish' the generally peaceful relations.[17]

Controversy over the personality of Riel and, above all, over the roles of the government and the Métis in the confrontation is still very much alive. Riel's declaration of rights, labelled revolutionary at the time, seems mild today: he was asking for more liberal treatment for Amerindians and non-Native settlers as well as for the Métis. More heated is the argument over whether the government provoked the uprising in order to solve its problems in constructing the transcontinental railway. Political scientist Thomas Flanagan maintains that 'Métis grievances were at least partly of their own making; that the government was on the verge of resolving them when the Rebellion broke out.'[18] The conspiratorial thesis is upheld by historian Doug Sprague, who says that the uprising 'was not the result of some tragic misunderstanding, but of the government's manipulation of the Manitoba Métis since 1869' for reasons of political expediency.[19] The jury is still out. What there is no doubt about, as historian John E. Foster has observed, is that the defeat at Batoche ended for half a century the Métis struggle for corporate recognition.[20] And it would be a century before it regained a momentum even approximating that of the days of Riel.

The North-West Territories gained representation in the House of Commons, with Assiniboia getting two members and the regions that would become Saskatchewan and Alberta one each. In 1887, the Territories got two members in the Senate. Land transfers were made more flexible, and registration of deeds simplified.

The buffalo had provided food, shelter, and clothing to those who hunted it, and no part of the animal was wasted. Now it was gone, and the Amerindians and Métis who had depended on it were left without skins to make tents. This photograph illustrates the depths to which the once-affluent hunters were reduced.
(Provincial Archives of Alberta, B-772)

More Consequences for the Cree . . .

Deprived as they were of their leadership, with Big Bear and Poundmaker in prison and Little Pine dead, the Cree now found that even their remaining chiefs were under attack: Ottawa wanted all those who had not given unwavering support to the government to be deposed. Others could remain in office until their deaths, but they were not to be replaced. The goal was the destruction of tribal forms of gov-ernment, the atomization of Amerindian com-munities. The numbers of Indian agents were heavily increased and the NWMP was strength-ened. The once friendly relations between police and Amerindian cooled as attitudes hardened. Blair Stonechild makes the point that Macdonald, despite holding the portfolio of Superintendent-General of Indian Affairs from 1879 to 1887, never visited the Plains Amerindians during those critical years.[21]

Cree horses, guns, and carts were impound-ed, and those who were implicated in the uprising had their annuities discontinued for five years.[22] A pass system was introduced to restrain western Amerindians to their reserves, on the argument that those who had rebelled had violated their treaty rights and thus had lost them.[23] Ten years later the NWMP was reporting that Amerindians 'found wandering aimlessly about the prairie have been induced to return to their respective reserves.'[24] Indian presence in towns was discouraged under the vagrancy stipulations of the Criminal Code. Macdonald, while recognizing that the pass system could not be enforced in law, allowed it to be enforced with threats of deprivation of rations 'and other similar privileges'. Anti-Indian sentiment among cattlemen who feared for their stock (wealthy stockraisers had a powerful lobby in Ottawa) and what amounted to hysteria among settlers contributed to the repressions. In 1906, the ban on certain sun dance practices, previously noted, was extended to include all types of Amerindian dancing. These bans proved to be as difficult to enforce as the one against potlatches; the dances continued, but in hiding. Restrictions on the movements and customs of Natives remained until well into the twentieth century, and not just on the prairies, although that was the principal scene of action. In Dawson (Yukon), Indians were subjected to a curfew, and in 1923 a permit system was established for those who wished to move into the city. Although recognized as illegal, such measures were justified as necessary to protect the indigenes from evil non-Aboriginal influences.[25]

For the decade following 1885 these growing repressions were accepted without violence. When it did erupt, it was on the part of individuals: between 1895 and 1897, Charcoal, a Blood (Si'k-okskitsis, literally 'Black Wood Ashes', 1856–97), and Almighty Voice, a Cree (Kah-kee-say-mane-too-wayo, 'Voice of the Great Spirit', grandson of One Arrow, 1874–97), between them killed five policemen. The death toll was the result of the police trying to track them down, in separate pursuits.[26]

In 1896, a group of Tsuu T'ina defied police attempts to get them to leave Calgary. Police had become steadily more uncomfortable with the task of restricting Amerindian movements; as early as 1893, a police commissioner had issued a circular warning about sending Amerindians back to their reserves without legal justification. As the police withdrew their co-operation, passes became more of a monitoring device; however, some Indian agents continued to enforce them until the mid-1940s. The system has been described by historian F. Laurie Barron as a form of selectively applied administrative tyranny.[27]

. . . and for the Métis

Many Métis changed their names because of fear. Others fled to the US, particularly Montana, where they became known as 'Canadian Cree'; some of them actually joined the Cree under Big Bear's son, Ayimasis, who had also fled south, and were admitted to reserves. Still others fled north, particularly to the Mackenzie River area.

The two major dispersions, from Red River in 1870 and from South Branch in 1885, should not be allowed to obscure the fact that the Métis had long been scattered throughout the Northwest. The majority had settled in their own communities, although many assimilated with Euro-Canadians and others with Amerindians. There had been some success stories; an outstanding example was James McKay (1828–79), who became wealthy as a fur trader and politician. In the latter capacity his posts included serving as a member of the first council appointed by Manitoba's lieutenant-governor and as provincial Minister of Agriculture, 1874–5. Other prominent Canadians who counted Amerindians among their ancestors include Louis-François Laflèche, bishop of

Trois-Rivières (coadjutor, 1867–70; titular, 1870–98); Sir Edward Clouston (1849–1912), a first vice-president of the Bank of Montreal at the turn of the century; Dr S.F. Tolmie, Premier of British Columbia, 1928–33; Dr Norman Bethune (1890–1939), the Montreal physician who became a hero of China's Maoist revolution; Maurice Duplessis, Premier of Quebec, 1936–9 and 1944–59; and Peter Lougheed, Premier of Alberta, 1971–85.[28]

Land title remained a tortured question. Métis land claims were not dealt with by negotiation, as in the case of Amerindians, but by unilateral government action and Orders-in-Council. It was widely recognized that where Amerindians acquired special status through the treaties that extinguished their Aboriginal rights, the Métis did not gain long-term benefits with the settlement of their claims. Of the 566,560 hectares set aside in Manitoba for the Métis, only 242,811 had been distributed to them by 1882.[29] The scrip that Ottawa had introduced in 1874 to settle with the Métis provided for either a specified amount of alienable land or its equivalent in cash (land scrip or money scrip), a far cry from the long-term benefits extending through the generations that were granted the Amerindians, not the least of which was reserved land that could not be alienated. The great majority of the Métis insisted on scrip rather than treaty; as historian Diane Payment sees it, this did not reflect a lack of interest in land (on the contrary, title to their lands had been a major concern in their confrontations with Ottawa) but resistance to the increasingly stringent regulations that hampered their attempts to obtain title.[30] Politically, many Métis felt that they were a separate people.[31]

Their dilemma was that if they took treaty, they became legally Amerindian; if they took scrip, they moved into the non-Amerindian camp. Acceptance of scrip meant loss of entitlement to be registered as an Indian and exclusion from the Indian Act. Culturally, the line between the two classifications was far from clear-cut, but the distinction in legal consequences was enormous. For one obvious point, responsibility for status Indians was (and is) solely that of the federal authority, whereas the Métis, even though now constitutionally recognized as an Aboriginal people, are classed as ordinary citizens and so come under provincial jurisdiction in matters of property and civil rights. Non-status Indians are in the same legal category as the Métis.

The troubles of 1885 galvanized Ottawa into action on Métis land claims. Four days after the encounter at Duck Lake, on 30 March, the first of a series of commissions was empowered to extinguish Métis land claims; the last one would sit in 1921, after which claims were dealt with on an individual basis. Some of the commissions were held in conjunction with treaty negotiations, such as those for Treaty Eight (1899), or with adhesions, such as the one in 1889 for Treaty Six. In those areas where Amerindian title had been extinguished, allotments were to be in money or land scrip worth 65 hectares for Métis heads of households. A few weeks later an Order-in-Council provided that Métis in bona fide occupation of a river lot of 40 acres (16 hectares) would be able to purchase that land at one dollar an acre, then select 160 acres of land (65 hectares) for homestead. Two years were allowed for payment, with the patent withheld until payment was completed. In 1885, 1,815 claims were considered, of which 1,678 were allowed, valued at $279,000 in money scrip and 55,260 acres (22,263 hectares) in land scrip. In 1889, Métis living outside of areas ceded by treaty were allowed to apply for scrip.[32] Treaty Nine (1905–6) was not accompanied by a Half-Breed Claims Commission, whereas for Treaties Ten (1906) and Eleven (1921) the same negotiations dealt with both Amerindians and Métis. In the case of Treaty Eleven, the Métis of the

Scrip Commission meeting, 1899, in central Alberta at Hudson's Bay Company post at Lesser Slave Lake, held in conjunction with Treaty Eight negotiations.
(Glenbow Archives, NA-949-18)

Mackenzie River District each received $240 in cash because of the lack of suitable farmland.[33]

After all the confrontations over land, when it came to making a choice between cash in hand or an acreage, the overwhelming majority of Métis chose the money.[34] Land presented problems for many Métis because they often lived in regions that were marginal for agriculture, if farming could be practised at all; and their locations often were remote from land offices. For such people, it appeared more beneficial to sell their scrip. This was often done for a song; there are records of scrip being sold to speculators for as little as half its face value. Fortunes were made at the expense of the Métis—'half-breed scrip millionaires', in the parlance of the time.[35] In some cases, accepting scrip left Métis poorer than before, after a brief orgy of spending. Official attempts to make scrip non-transferable had incited such an uproar (mainly on the part of land speculators, according to some) that the government had retreated.[36]

The land claims commissions were under instructions to encourage Métis who had taken treaty and who were living on reserves to withdraw and take scrip. The Indian Act had been amended in 1879 for this purpose, but it required that the withdrawing Métis refund money received under treaty. Since few Métis had the funds to do this, the Act was changed in 1884 to remove the requirement for a refund. As a result of this liberalization, the second commission reported that 52 per cent of the 1,159 certificates granted were to Métis leaving treaty to take scrip. This was at least partly due to difficult conditions on reserves, where the Natives were living on meagre government handouts.

A backlash to this policy developed as settlers became alarmed at the influx of Métis into their communities, many so ill-equipped for this new lifestyle that they ended up as public charges. That made the government more cautious about encouraging Métis who were 'living like Indians' to withdraw from treaty; but those who were willing to adopt the mainstream lifestyle were still encouraged to do so.

The Klondike gold strike of 1896 dramatically changed the political scene in the North, catapulting Amerindian and Métis affairs to centre stage. The confrontations of the Fraser gold strike were replicated as fortune hunters flooded into the Yukon, intent on their personal quests and without regard for the rights of Amerindians or Métis. As the government hurriedly prepared to negotiate Treaty Eight, it was proposed that Métis be included with Amerindians. Most of the Métis were against the suggestion so two commissions were established, one to negotiate treaty with the Amerindians, the other to work out scrip for the Métis.[37] Still intent on encouraging as many as possible to enter treaty—some of those who identified as Amerindian had more non-Amerindian admixture than some who identified as Métis—the government first negotiated the treaty. It took two years to hammer out terms with Beaver, Cree, Chipewyan, Sekani, and others.[38] For the Métis, the offer was for $240 in cash or 240 acres (97 hectares) of land. When it came to issuing scrip, officials sought to avoid a repeat of the cut-price sales in Manitoba and once more tried not to make the scrip payable to the bearer on demand but requiring a legal assignment. The speculators who had come expecting to make a killing refused to accept such scrip. The Métis then also refused to accept it and threatened to influence Amerindians against taking treaty. Officials knuckled under and offered scrip payable on demand. Similarly, when officials sought to postdate scrip issued to children until their age of maturity, parents insisted that it be payable immediately. The first $240 scrip was sold for $75, and soon the price dropped even lower. In the end, the average price was well below that realized in Manitoba in 1885.

During the summer of 1899, the commission issued 1,195 money scrips worth $286,000 and 48 land scrips for 11,500 acres (6,070 hectares), about half of them at Lesser Slave Lake and others at Fort Vermilion, Fort Chipewyan, and Peace River Crossing.[39] Only a fraction of the benefits went to the Métis. In 1900, two new commissions dealt with the Métis of Saskatchewan and those parts of Manitoba that had not been included in its original boundaries. In its final report on this project in 1929, the year before Crown lands reverted to the provinces, Ottawa issued a statement that 24,000 claims had been recognized in the Northwest Territories, involving 2.6 million acres (1,052,183 hectares) in land scrip and 2.8 million acres (1,133,120 hectares) in money scrip. Later, the situation reversed itself, and during the 1920s and 1930s there were so many applications for reclassification into treaty status that in 1942 the department investigated its band lists and discharged 663 individuals. An inquiry by Alberta District Court Justice W.A. Macdonald led to the reinstatement of 129 of those who had been deleted.[40]

Chapter 22

Leading to an Administrative Shift

A consequence of the 1885 confrontations was to increase even further the centralizing tendencies of the Department of Indian Affairs, a process that would continue until 1951. The department assumed more and more control over the lives of Amerindians, until they did not have a free hand even in such personal matters as writing a will or, in the West, selling their own grain or root crops.[1]

As the power of the agents grew, it became steadily more arbitrary. Their duties accrued until they were expected to direct farming operations; administer relief in times of necessity; inspect schools and health conditions on reserves; ensure that department rules and provisions were complied with; and preside over band council meetings and, in effect, direct the political life of the band. Although agents did not have a vote at those meetings, they could, and did, influence proceedings. For example, when a deadlock developed at a council meeting of the Cowessess band in 1910, the agent cast the deciding vote. That was definitely against the rules, but the loophole that allowed such an action was not corrected until 1936. Some agents were also justices of the peace.

The principal problems facing the administration were a continuation of old ones: liquor, trespass, poaching, and unauthorized exploitation of reserve resources such as timber. In 1890, Manitoba and North-West Territories game laws were declared applicable to Amerindians, superseding treaties that guaranteed hunting and fishing rights on Crown lands in perpetuity. This would give rise to a series of court cases.

The idea of model villages had not died, and in fact attained what was hailed as its most notable success in the File Hills Colony, established in 1901 on 19,000 acres (7,689 hectares) on the Peepeekisis Reserve (named after the chief, 'Little Hawk') in the Qu'Appelle agency near Indian Head. It was the special project of W.M. Graham, the resident agent, who would later be Indian commissioner for the prairies, 1920–32. His idea was to extend the training received by young Indians at government schools in the Northwest,[2] ensuring that they would not 'regress' to their Native ways by returning to their own families and communities. Individual lots of 80 acres (32 hectares) each were assigned, with a portion of the

TIMELINE

1880s–90s	Rapid expansion of church-run residential schools for Native children.
1884, 1894	Superintendent-General of Indian Affairs empowered to lease undeveloped reserve lands without surrender or band consent.
1890	Indian agents empowered to enforce anti-vagrancy laws.
	Manitoba and North-West Territories game laws declared applicable to Amerindians.
1895	Band council elections made mandatory for many bands in eastern Canada.
1901	File Hills Colony, a 'model village', established on Peepeekisis Reserve in Qu'Appelle agency.
1908	BC refuses to lay out any more reserves.
1911	Amendment to Indian Act allows appropriation of reserve lands for public purposes; almost half of Blackfoot Reserve is sold.
1913	Nisga'a petition Judicial Committee of the Privy Council in London re Aboriginal right.
1914	Amerindians forbidden to perform traditional dances in Native garb at fairs and stampedes.
1914–18	About 4,000 Amerindians serve in Canadian Expeditionary Force during World War I.
1916	Royal Commission in BC recommends 'cutting off' parts of reserves and replacing them with lands of lesser value: some reserves thus eliminated, and 36,000 acres of reserve lands are lost. Allied Tribes of British Columbia is formed to fight government action, but united group has little success.
1918	Mohawk war veteran Fred Loft tries, unsuccessfully, to found pan-Canadian League of Indians.
1920	Indian Act amendment leads to enfranchisement (and loss of Indian status) of nearly 500 Amerindians in less than two years.
1923	Ontario settles claims filed by Ojibwa and Mississauga in 1869.
1936	Department of Mines and Resources absorbs Indian administration.
1938	BC fulfills obligation taken on when it joined Canada by conveying reserve lands to federal authority.
1951	Major changes to Indian Act, granting women the vote in band council elections, allowing secret ballot, limited but greater Native control of band affairs, less sweeping ministerial powers.
1958	Tyendinaga Reserve on Lake Ontario first to gain complete control of band funds.
	James Gladstone first Amerindian appointed to Canadian Senate.
1970	Supreme Court rules in *Drybones* that Aboriginals have right to drink alcohol in public.
	Blue Quills, near St Paul, Alberta, is the first Canadian school controlled by Amerindian band.
1979	Aboriginal Women's Walk from Oka to Ottawa in protest against discrimination of Indian Act against Native women.
1985	Indian Act amendments and Bill C-31 grant Indian women rights and status equal to those of men.

colony being left unsurveyed to allow for hunting and community pasture. As the colonists established their farms, some were able to handle as many as six or seven lots, while others who found that the farming life was not for them picked up and left. Those who remained were controlled to the point of even having their marriage partners selected for them. Visits between households were strictly limited, and such gatherings as powwows or dancing of any kind were forbidden (which did not mean that there were no such occasions, but that they were held secretly).

If Graham did not remove every vestige of tribal life, he still succeeded in creating a successful colony that attracted high-placed admiration; Earl Grey (Albert Henry George Grey, Governor-General 1904–11) paid an annual visit, handing out awards to those who excelled in various branches of farming.[3] Graham could not have achieved this without the co-operation of the colonists, even as they found some of his rules severe. After its initial burst of enthusiasm that lasted about 20 years, it settled into a stable pattern; in the 1930s, however, it began to lose its younger population. Although it was widely admired, the experiment was never repeated; for one thing, it was too costly for the budget-minded department. In more recent years the File Hills boarding school has been one of those named in connection with charges of student abuse, in this case leading to death.[4]

Elective versus Traditional Selection of Chiefs

Confrontations continued over the imposition of the elective form of government; in 1895 the government made elections mandatory for 42 bands in Ontario, six in Quebec, and seven in New Brunswick.[5] Four years later, all bands in Ontario, Quebec, New Brunswick, Nova Scotia, and Prince Edward Island were told to hold elections every three years; strong Amerindian resistance had made it impractical to insist on the one-year system. It was soon evident that such a sweeping order could not be implemented immediately in some cases, and in others not at all. Two bands illustrate the type of difficulties that arose, the Cowessess (named after the Plains Cree and Saulteaux chief, Kiwisance, 'Little Child', d. 1886, who signed

Treaty Four at Fort Qu'Appelle) and the Iroquoian St Regis, south of Cornwall at the intersection of the international border with the boundary between Ontario and Quebec.

At its own request, Cowessess went on the three-year elective system in 1887; however, Hayter Reed, the agent from 1881 to 1893, did not approve of the chief who was elected a few years later, an avowed advocate of traditional ways.[6] In 1894, Reed, now deputy superintendent-general of Indian Affairs, denied the band the right to hold another election on the grounds that Treaty Four had granted them the right to have chiefs and councillors but did not specify how they were to be selected; in the past, Cowessess had been allowed elections as a courtesy only. In the end, the Amerindians' persistence won out and Cowessess was finally allowed its elections.

In St Regis, a struggle developed between adherents to the traditional hereditary system of selecting chiefs and those who supported elections.[7] In 1889, after three chiefs were deposed by Order-in-Council following complaints from band members that they had misappropriated funds, the elective system was officially brought in. When elections were held in 1891, the five chiefs who won were all found guilty of dispensing liquor to gain votes. The election was disallowed and a new one was held the following year. Two of the newly elected chiefs quickly ran afoul of the department when they leased land it had already leased, and they were deposed on the grounds that their actions had been illegal. Claiming that the new system was creating disharmony, in contrast to the peace and friendship that had prevailed with the traditional way, St Regis asked in 1894 for a return of the hereditary system. The request was refused, and three subsequent attempts to hold elections in 1898 and 1899 ended in failure. It would be 1908 before the influence of the hereditary chiefs had faded sufficiently for elections to be held.[8] The struggle between the two systems was even more virulent on the Six Nations Reserve, 1894–1924, until finally the one-year elective system was imposed. The divisions arising from these struggles on the two reserves still exist today, with the hereditary factions being the principal advocates for reserve autonomy; indeed, they claim sovereignty, as will be seen later. Some bands, mainly on the prairies, were allowed to continue selecting their chiefs by their traditional methods. The department, in approving the chiefs so selected, regarded them as appointees.

As resistance against government by imposition intensified and bands refused to exercise their police and public health powers or to expend band funds for these purposes, the Superintendent-General was empowered to carry out these functions and appropriate the required band funds. By 1900, there were four systems of band government: the three-year elective (Indian Act), the one-year elective (Advancement Act), hereditary (Yukon, NWT, and in varying numbers in the provinces), and appointment (mainly on the prairies). On the heels of all this, in a move to discourage the traditional hunting and gathering way of life, the Manitoba and North-West Territories game laws were deemed to apply to Amerindians within those jurisdictions. A few years later, in 1922, provincial laws of general application were also declared applicable to reserves.[9]

Battle over Reserved Lands

Concomitant with reserving lands for Amerindians were provisions for their surrender, either temporarily by leasing or permanently by sale. In theory, reserve lands could only be surrendered by a majority of male reserve residents over the age of 21 at a meeting specially called for the purpose. Resistance of band councils to leasing lands even for a limited period led, in 1879, to power to allot reserve lands being taken from the band and given to the Superintendent-General. In 1884 and again in 1894, the Superintendent-General was empowered to lease undeveloped reserve lands without taking a surrender or obtaining band consent.[10] The one exception was land held by location ticket, in which case permission of the holder had to be obtained.

As band councils continued to oppose imposed regulations, the administration responded in 1898 by granting the Superintendent-General overriding powers. Frank Oliver, Minister of the Interior and Superintendent-General of Indian Affairs, 1905–11, soon followed this with another measure, which became known as the Oliver Act, that permitted Amerindians to be removed from any reserves next to or partly within a town of 8,000 inhabitants or more if the Exchequer Court so ruled. In effect, this abolished the reserves in question, which was what happened to the St Clair Ojibwa Reserve at Sarnia, Ontario, and to the Songhees Reserve at Victoria, BC. So died the policy of hastening assimilation by establishing reserves as close as possible to Euro-Canadian settlements; the lands had become so valuable that the policy took second place. Instead, more comments were being heard about the desirability of removing Indians to more remote areas.

Immigration policies also led to more and more pressure on Indian lands. As settlers flooded in, their increasing demands, along with those of developers and railway companies, influenced Indian Affairs to reconsider the size of reserves, many of which were regarded as already too large for the number of Indians living on them and becoming more so because of the prevalent decline in Native populations at that time. Reserve lands beyond immediate requirements came to be regarded as 'surplus' and thus open to negotiations for surrender to the Crown. The argument for such deals held that they benefited the Indians by providing them with ready cash to get started

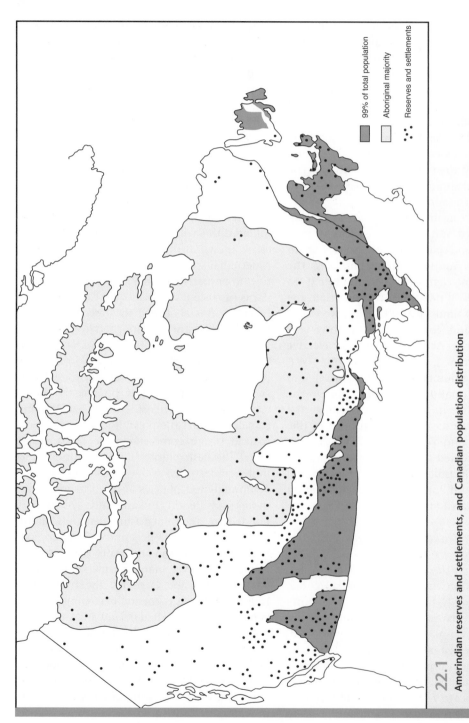

22.1

Amerindian reserves and settlements, and Canadian population distribution

Source: *Report of the Royal Commission on Aboriginal Peoples,* II, part 2, 450; adapted from Russel Lawrence Barsh, 'Canada's Aboriginal Peoples: Social Integration or Disintegration?', *Canadian Journal of Native Studies* 14, 1 (1994), and used with the permission of Brandon University, Brandon, Manitoba.

in their new way of life as farmers or ranchers. The other side of the picture was the income the department received when it resold the surrendered lands to the public. In spite of the cash inducement, Indians were seldom either eager or unanimous about surrendering; far more often, they had to be persuaded, reluctantly, to accept a deal. In Ontario, such deals took off after the War of 1812, when the Crown acquired some 2.8 million hectares of Indian lands from seven surrenders.[11] As the tide of immigration moved westward, the prairie provinces became the major scene for such activity; by the early years of the twentieth century, well over 785,000 acres (318,000 hectares) of their reserve lands, more than half of them in Saskatchewan, had been transferred to the Crown. The period between 1896 and 1911 saw 21 per cent—more than one-fifth—of reserve lands on the prairies thus surrendered.[12] Oliver was able to inform the House that between 1 July 1896 and 31 March 1909 the department sold 725,517 acres (293,606 hectares) of surrendered reserve lands for a total of $2,156,353. In 1910–11, almost half of the Blackfoot reserve in Alberta was sold for more than a million dollars.

Matters did not stop there. In 1911 Oliver won a further amendment to the Indian Act that allowed portions of reserves to be expropriated without surrender by municipalities or companies for roads, railways, or other public purposes. However, the consent of the governor-in-council was needed. David Laird, Indian commissioner for the prairies (1898–1909), justified the measure:

> The locking up of vast tracts which the Indians could not make use of was neither in their own nor in the public interest. Yet the Indians were in many cases averse to parting with any. The amendment in the new law which permits of fifty percent of the money derived from the sale of surrendered lands to

be immediately used, and the investment of the returns in outfitting Indians for work and enabling them to improve the conditions in which they live, has led many of the Indians to make surrenders. And thus with the proceeds of land that could only lie idle and unremunerative, they are being put in a position to make use of that which they still hold.[13]

Unfortunately, the surrender initiative did not yield the expected benefits for the Indians, which encouraged the resisters. In addition, some Indian Affairs officials had also opposed it; when their gloomy predictions turned out to be only too accurate, some Natives were moved to try action. In two instances, at St Peter's (Manitoba) and with the Peigan (Alberta), bands publicly called for the overturning of surrenders that had been taken. They were unsuccessful. There were other Indian protests as well, especially if expected terms were not fulfilled. Clifford Sifton, as Superintendent-General of Indian Affairs, 1896–1905, was ambivalent about the situation. While saying that the consent of the Indians concerned was necessary, he appears to have done little if anything to ensure that proper procedures were followed.[14] The result of all this was the eventual phasing out of surrenders in favour of leases.

Continuing Deadlock

In British Columbia, the continuing deadlock between the province and Ottawa on the question of Amerindian land gave rise to the Joint Commission for the Settlement of Indian Reserves in the Province of British Columbia to investigate and act on the problem, which it did, off and on, from 1876 to 1910.[15] Other initiatives included a Squamish delegation to Edward VII in London (1906), a petition to the Canadian government (1909),[16] another petition, which elicited Prime Minister Sir Wilfrid

Laurier's promise of help (1910),[17] a Royal Commission (1913–16),[18] and a petition by the Nisga'a to the Judicial Committee of the Privy Council in London (1913). The action of the Nisga'a had been spurred by BC's adamant refusal to discuss Aboriginal right or to allow the Royal Commission to consider the issue; in 1908, the province had refused to lay out any more reserves.[19] The Privy Council, in turn, said it could only consider such an appeal if it came from the courts of Canada. The findings of the Royal Commission, published in 1916, recommended the 'cutting off' of specified reserve lands[20] and their substitution with larger areas of lesser value. The measure cost the Indians 36,000 acres (14,569 hectares), including the elimination of entire reserves from the province's total of 871.[21]

While leading to an increase in the sizes of reserves, if not their land value, the cut-offs were bitterly opposed by Amerindians, especially as their opinions had not been heard.[22] In this case the problem was not that Amerindians were being ignored but that they had refused to appear before the Commission because, they claimed, its mandate was too narrow—it had not been empowered to consider Aboriginal right. They now (1916) organized into the Allied Tribes of British Columbia to fight the Commission's recommendations and to assert Aboriginal right as a priority. In spite of the spirited resistance of Allied Tribes leaders, Squamish chief Andrew Paull (1892–1959) and Haida Rev. Peter Kelly (1885–1966), among others, the Commission's report was approved by BC in 1923 and by Ottawa a year later.[23] In 1927, a Special Joint Committee of the Senate and House of Commons issued a 'final settlement' in which it held that BC's Amerindians had 'not established any claim to the lands of British Columbia based on Aboriginal or other title'. Such claims, the committee said, were 'more or less fictitious' and had been whipped up by designing Euro-Canadians more concerned with stirring mischief than with human rights.[24] It recommended that the Amerindians be granted $100,000 annually as compensation for the lack of treaty rights. At the same time the committee opposed allowing BC Amerindians to resort to the courts because that would cast doubt on all land titles in the province. All this had been preceded in 1859 by the denial of the provincial vote to Amerindians, along with Chinese and Japanese, a situation that remained until 1949.

The government used the direct method to curb mounting Indian protests: in 1910 it amended the Act to prohibit Amerindians from using band funds for land claim actions without the approval of the department, which it strengthened three days before the Allied Tribes hearings began in 1927. It did this by prohibiting Indians from soliciting for outside funds without special permission, a measure that remained in law until 1951.[25] Finally, in 1938, British Columbia fulfilled the terms of Clause 13 of its Act of Union by conveying 592,297 acres (239,694 hectares) to the federal authority. Today, there are 1,678 reserves in BC, out of 2,633 in all of Canada. Comparatively speaking, they are small; British Columbia, with Canada's second largest Native population (Ontario's is the largest), has the fourth highest allotment of land on a per capita basis.[26] Alberta, with only 96 reserves (eight of which are Métis settlements), has by far the highest allotment. The national per capita figure has dropped sharply in recent years as populations expand and the land area remains the same. Three of the largest reserves are around Calgary—those of the Blood, Blackfoot, and Peigan. By 1999, Amerindians held about 2,995,490 hectares of reserve lands, an average of 4.5 hectares per head, far below the standard set by the treaties and steadily dropping, as noted above. Reserves account for a little over 0.3 per cent of Canada's land area, but recent pacts have substantially increased the amount of land under Aboriginal control. Only one-third of the reserved land is suitable for agriculture and another one-sixth for raising livestock.[27]

If British Columbia held something of a record in the length of time it had taken—67 years—to fulfill its Confederation obligation to transfer Amerindian reserve lands to the federal authority, other provinces did not move much faster. For instance, it took Ontario 54 years to settle Ojibwa and Mississauga claims, first filed in 1869 and not settled until 1923, even though the claims had long been recognized as valid. The last component of the Manitoulin Island treaty of 1862 took a final step towards settlement with the agreement-in-principle involving 90,000 acres (36,422 hectares) that was signed in 1990. Administrative muddles characterized the process across the land; by comparison, Nova Scotia did not look so bad to be still transferring reserve lands to the federal jurisdiction during the last decade of the nineteenth century. In other provinces and territories, claims dating well back into the eighteenth century have still not been settled.[28] In almost all cases, the resolution of such claims owed more to Amerindian persistence than to government acknowledgement of responsibility.

One of the best-known cases of Amerindians being displaced from reserved lands desired by Euro-Canadians was that of St Peter's Reserve, near Selkirk, Manitoba, home of the Peguis band of Saulteaux. A long and bitter controversy over conflicting claims to the reserve's land between the band and non-Indians had resulted in a proposal that the Saulteaux surrender their reserve. The case was resolved, without consulting the Indians involved, by passing St Peter's Reserve Act in 1916. It confirmed individual patents to reserve land held by Amerindians, as well as those held by non-Indians who were prepared to pay an additional dollar an acre. Monies so raised were to be credited to the band. This 'solution', of course, involved the breakup of the reserve and the relocation of the band on the upper Fisher River, about 105 kilometres to the north on the shores of Lake Winnipeg. This was justified on the grounds that the new reserve was better suited to the Amerindians' lifestyle. Band members who did not hold patents and who refused to leave the old reserve were evicted by the RNWMP, under orders from the department, a process that involved the conviction of several of them for trespassing. The only thing left to them on the old site was a 53-hectare fishing station. The principle of prior rights had not protected the Saulteaux.

An earlier surrender of a reserve—in fact, the first in the West—was that of the Pahpahstayo (Passpasschase) band, established under Treaty Six; it involved what is today the southeast portion of the city of Edmonton. This was an early example of settlers—some of whom were squatters on the contested lands—not only objecting to the proximity of a reserve to a city, but also to rich farmlands in the hands of a people popularly believed to be uninterested in farming. Under intense pressure, most of the band members agreed to withdraw from treaty and accept instead the immediate benefits of scrip; by 1886, the reserve counted only 13 families remaining. When they agreed to join the Enoch band to the west of Edmonton, the surrender was declared complete, nine years after the original survey in 1880. Today, descendants of the disbanded group are seeking reinstatement as a band and a settlement for their lost lands, now swallowed in the urban sprawl of south Edmonton.[29]

Fortunately, there has been some change in attitudes. Today, more than 70 years later, the Kwanlin Dün band of Tutchone at Whitehorse, after having had their reserve relocated several times, finally asked to have it established atop a bluff at the edge of the city, a choice location. Their request was granted.[30]

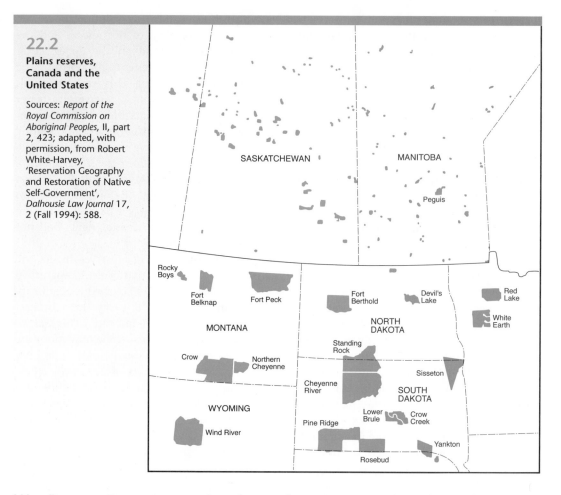

22.2

Plains reserves, Canada and the United States

Sources: *Report of the Royal Commission on Aboriginal Peoples*, II, part 2, 423; adapted, with permission, from Robert White-Harvey, 'Reservation Geography and Restoration of Native Self-Government', *Dalhousie Law Journal* 17, 2 (Fall 1994): 588.

War Renews Presssures on Lands

World War I saw a renewed wave of pressures on Amerindian lands. Once more the Indian Act was amended to appropriate or lease reserve lands for war production needs without band permission. Commissioner Graham established three of these 'Greater Production Farms' on Amerindian lands, totalling 62,128 acres (25,142 hectares). In addition, the program was financed out of band funds, also without permission, and to add even more insult to injury, the Amerindians in question were at the bottom of the priority list for using the equipment purchased for the projects. The Bloods of southern Alberta led the protests, but without result.[31]

In spite of the fact that they were not legally bound to enlist, Canada's Amerindians volunteered at a rate exceeding that of non-Indians. Approximately 4,000 served in the Canadian Expeditionary Force, about 35 per cent of those who were of eligible age for service.[32] They did this in spite of the fact that the government had not expected them to volunteer, and indeed had at first discouraged them from doing so on the grounds that if taken prisoner they might be refused the privileges of 'civilized warfare' because of the still-prevalent stereotype that they were 'savages'. A group of Indians from Cape Croker, Ontario, applied to four different recruiting centres and were rejected by each one.[33] However, such incidents apart, the policy was not strictly enforced, and was cancelled late in 1915. An Ojibwa from the Parry Island band in Ontario, Francis Pegahmagabow (1891–1952), one of the original members of the 1st Canadian Infantry Battalion, saw active service for nearly the entire war. He became legendary as a scout and sniper in such battles as Passchendaele, Ypres, and Amiens. Back home, he became chief of his band, and later a councillor. He is commemorated in the Canadian Indian Hall of Fame.[34]

Amerindians across the land also contributed in other ways, as historian Hugh Dempsey has pointed out in the case of the Bloods. They raised substantial amounts for the Red Cross despite the poverty on the reserves.[35] As veterans, however, Amerindians soon discovered that they were not getting the same benefits as non-Amerindians. In the words of one official: 'These returned Indian soldiers are subject to the provisions of the Indian Act and are in the same position as they were before enlisting.'[36] The equal treatment they had received in the armed forces (including the right to vote) would not be extended into civilian life, a situation that still prevailed until after World War II despite some improvement.[37]

Tightening the Reins

As the police pulled back from being used to enforce the pass system restricting the movements of western Amerindians, a measure clearly in contravention of basic human rights, the department moved to strengthen the other means that had already been called into play to achieve the purpose. In 1890, Indian agents were empowered as justices of the peace to enforce the Criminal Code's anti-vagrancy pro-

Corporal Francis Pegahmagabow was Canada's most highly decorated Indian in World War I. An Ojibwa of the Parry Island band in Ontario, he joined the 1st Battalion (Western Ontario Regiment) in 1914, and served as a scout and sniper. Reputed to be the greatest sniper on the Western Front, his exploits won him a Military Medal and two bars. *(Photo courtesy Fred Gaffen,* Forgotten Soldiers, *Penticton, BC, Theytus Books, 1985)*

visions. Similarly, in 1914, the bans on 'giveaway' ceremonies central to the potlatch (1884) and the endurance rituals of the thirst dance (1895) were strengthened with prohibitions against Amerindians appearing in Aboriginal garb and performing their traditional dances at fairs and stampedes; finally, such dances were prohibited in any type of dress unless the department had given prior approval in writing. This was a direct blow to Amerindian community cohesion. As anthropologist Michael Asch has pointed out for the Dene of the Northwest, dances in their various forms with their accompanying songs symbolically emphasized reciprocity and co-operation, fundamental for creating a sense of community.[38] This was not appreciated by the department, however, and a fit of enforcement of the bans developed during the 1920s, encouraged by missionaries outraged that Amerindians were continuing their ceremonies, either in secret or by evading the ban on technicalities. The RCMP conducted raids and confiscated ritual paraphernalia, some of which was sidetracked and sold for private gain by unscrupulous agents. Today the government is attempting to correct such injustices by helping Native groups set up their own museums to house returned objects, as in the cases of the Nyumbalees and Umista peoples on the west coast. Another such is the Kwagiulth Museum and Cultural Centre on Quadra Island. Much of the illegally sold material went to institutions in the United States, which are now contesting its return on the grounds that their purchases were in good faith.

The dismal record of enfranchisement stirred the government in 1917 to yet another amendment of the Indian Act, this time to allow Amerindians living off reserves to be granted the vote without property requirements. This resulted in the enfranchisement of nearly 500 people within two years. In 1921, a jubilant Duncan Campbell Scott, deputy superintendent-general, 1913–32, compared that figure with the 102 Amerindians who had been enfranchised in the preceding 53 years.[39] The government eased the way for Métis who had taken treaty to get the vote; it also paved the way for Amerindian women married to non-Indians to give up entirely their Indian status. Another aspect of this 1920s drive towards assimilation was the empowerment of the Superintendent-General to enfranchise Amerindians he considered qualified, whether they wanted it or not. As well, such individuals were to be given title to reserve lands they occupied and their share of band money.

Although these measures were designed with Indians east of the Great Lakes in mind, the alarm and hostility they aroused spread from coast to coast, and there was wide support for the Six Nations when it petitioned the Governor-General against them. The department's purpose was clear enough: as enunciated by Scott, it was 'to continue until there is not a single Indian in Canada that has not been absorbed into the body politic and there is no Indian question, and no Indian Department.'[40] In other words, as one observer put it, the extinction of Indians as Indians.[41] The 1920 amendment lasted only two years but was revived in a modified form in 1933, with the proviso that enfranchisement could not be imposed in violation of treaty promises. This was retained until the 1951 revision of the Indian Act. Old attitudes died hard, however, as was evident in the statement of Walter E. Harris, who as Minister of Citizenship and Immigration was responsible for Indian Affairs from 1950 to 1954, when he expressed the hope that the Act, even when revised, would be only temporary, as the 'ultimate goal of our Indian policy is the integration of the Indian into the general life and economy of the country.'[42]

That there was frustration on all sides is only too clear. The government's approach of treating the Amerindians as minors to be assimilated had led to resistance and defiance, both covert and open. As the government became more arbitrary, Indians reacted by refusing to co-operate, even to the point of creating hardships for themselves. Time and again they demonstrated they were prepared to endure deprivation and even misery rather than be treated like children. The government paid lip service to consultation, but in practice it could not bring itself to listen and actually take into account what the Natives were saying.[43] The old idea that Indians were human in form only and were not possessed of reason may have gone underground, and perhaps even taken on new forms, but in its essence it was alive and well.

Indians Move to Organize Themselves

Meanwhile, the process of more and stiffer regulations continued. The department had always looked askance at Indian attempts to organize politically and had barely tolerated the first successful effort, the Grand Indian Council of Ontario and Quebec, launched by Iroquois and Ojibwa in 1870. Eventually the department forced its dissolution by cutting off its funds.[44] The onset of the decade-long Great Depression in 1929 shifted official attention to other areas, particularly those of business and economics; plummeting prices for primary products such as fur and fish put Indian producers on welfare rolls.[45] Indian Affairs drifted into a state of flux and ad hoc decisions, in contrast to the directed policies that had marked the period from Confederation through the 1920s.

In 1936, Indian administration was absorbed by the Department of Mines and Resources, which was far more concerned with industrial development than with the social problems of the Natives. In fact, in the Far North, economic considerations overtook the civilizing program, and it went into reverse. On the premise that industrialization left them ill-equipped to earn a living, northern Amerindians were now encouraged in their traditional hunting and trapping activities, as these enabled them to be self-sufficient instead of becoming a burden on the public purse.[46] This move was spurred by the growing complexity of mechanization, which militated against the small-scale farming that many Indians had

Fred Loft, as painted by Toronto artist A.R. Hughes.
(Woodland Cultural Centre; gift of Affa Loft Matteson)

taken up in their attempts to cope with their changing world. Even if they could afford to acquire the new and larger machinery, which was rarely the case, their farms usually were too small to make effective use of it. This situation became acute after World War II. The result was that many Indians gave up farming.

In 1918 an Ontario provincial civil servant who was also a veteran of World War I, Frederick Ogilvie Loft (1861–1934), a Mohawk, tried to organize Amerindians into a national group he called the League of Indians.[47] His proposals included giving Indians the vote without losing their special status and allowing them greater control over band properties and funds, which in any event should be better managed and accounted for. Above all, he sought better standards of education for Amer-indian children. The department branded him an agitator, placed him under police surveil-lance, and sought to nullify his efforts by attempting to enfranchise him against his will. The League came to nought, but the need for a pan-Indian organization was recognized. The effective beginning of Indian activism in Canadian politics has been traced to a trip to Ottawa in 1943 by Andrew Paull and Dan Assu of the Native Brotherhood of BC to protest tax-ation of British Columbia's Indian fishermen as well as the placing of a ceiling price on sockeye salmon.[48] The trip triggered a chain of events that eventually contributed to the formation of the National Indian Brotherhood. Originally it was only for treaty Indians, but soon after its founding in 1968 it expanded to act on behalf of Native groups across Canada. It lasted until 1982, when the still-existing Assembly of First Nations emerged as the national Native voice.[49] Its membership consists of the chiefs of all the bands in Canada. In the meantime, in 1966, the Federation of Saskatchewan Indians under Walter Dieter had become the first Native organization to receive a federal grant to organ-ize its own community programs.

Shift in Attitudes

The new social scene that was a consequence of World War II brought with it a new change of attitude. Amerindians, despite the fact they were not citizens, had enlisted in proportionately higher numbers than did any other segment of the general population, repeating a pattern that had already been evident during World War I. It has been estimated that Native enlistments in World War II numbered up to 6,000. An unex-pected area in which they proved to have a unique advantage in the war effort was that of language. Indian languages were particularly useful for transmitting sensitive information: codes can be broken, but languages have to be learned. Canadian 'code talkers' used Cree; Americans used Navajo and Comanche.

When Indians returned to civilian life, the restrictions and inequities of their lot on reserves became so glaringly evident that veter-ans' organizations and church groups mounted a campaign that resulted in the establishment of a Joint Senate and House of Commons Com-mittee on the Indian Act, which held hearings from 1946 to 1948.[50] Amerindians were highly critical of the first draft of the proposed revi-sions. Led by James Gladstone of the Blood (Akay-na-muka, 'Many Guns', 1887–1971, Canada's first Native senator, named in 1958), they claimed that the draft, instead of entrench-ing Indians' special rights, particularly those relating to their treaties, in effect would only erode them even more than was already the case. Faced with such protests, the government set about revising the revisions. This time Indian witnesses were heard, the first time for such consultations at that level.[51] Although unanimity was far from being achieved, the psychological importance of allowing some Native input would be difficult to overestimate. Treaties and treaty rights concerned the Indians most, and they wanted these left in place, but with the freedom to govern themselves; land claims were not far behind. For the govern-ment, the goal continued to be assimilation, or as it was worded, transformation from the sta-tus of wards to that of full citizenship, but by encouragement as the original Act of 1876 had aimed for rather than the compulsion that characterized the amendments between 1880 and 1951. The revised Act of 1951 can hardly be called revolutionary, but it still heralded the dawn of a new era. For one illustration, a com-panion piece of legislation, passed the follow-ing year, provided for a universal old age pension for all Canadians over 70 years of age. Previously, regulations had been such that few Indians had benefited when the pension had been introduced in 1927. Another benefit extended to Indians in 1952 was their inclusion in the provisions of the Blind Persons Act.

Not since the first Indian Act was the minister's power as limited as it became in 1951; in some aspects it was reduced to a supervisory role, albeit with veto power. While the new Act did not allow bands to establish their own forms of government, it did increase their measure of self-control, as well as allow them to incorporate as municipalities. The secret ballot was introduced, and women were granted the vote in band council elections. Within two years 263 bands were holding elections; by 1980, the number had risen to 349.[52] By 2007, the total number of band elections had reached to 853, including by-elections.[53] There are approximately 255 First Nations that conduct their elections in accordance with the provisions of the Indian Act and the Indian band election regulations. The remaining First Nations conduct elections according to their own customary codes. They have their own set of procedures and rules governing their leadership selection and are thus not subject to the election provisions of the Indian Act.[54] Another 1951 recommendation was that health and education be turned over to the provinces. There would be some action on this, so that by the time of the White Paper in 1969 some of these services were already being delivered by the provinces and Amerindians were working to gain control of those programs that affected them.

Areas where the bands acquired authority under the new Act concerned the management of reserve lands, band funds, and the administration of bylaws. With a few exceptions, the band could now spend capital and revenue monies, which before could only be done by the governor-in-council or the minister. In fact, the band could now spend its monies for anything deemed to be in its general interest, unless the governor-in-council expressed reservations. This meant, for example, that the band could now fund lawsuits to advance claims. It

A new recruit received a blessing in 1942 during World War II.
(Department of National Defence/ Library and Archives Canada, PA-129070)

would be 1958, however, before any bands obtained complete control over their funds; by 1966, 36 were exercising such powers.

Anti-potlatch and anti-dance measures were repealed, leading to a renaissance of 'give-aways' in various forms from coast to coast.[55] Compulsory enfranchisement and restrictions

(Above, left) Lieut. David Greyeyes of Leask, Sask. (1914–1996), was the first Native to be commissioned from Canadian Army ranks during World War II. He joined the Saskatchewan Light Infantry in 1940 and served in the Italian campaign. His gallantry in action was recognized by the Greek government with the award of the Greek Military Cross, Class III. After the war he became chief of the Muskeg Lake Cree band, and was the first Amerindian to be appointed regional director of Indian Affairs. In 1977 he was named Member of the Order of Canada.
(Canapress Photo Service)

(Above, right) Cpl Huron Eldon Brant, a Mohawk from Deseronto, Ont., served with the Hastings and Prince Edward Regiment during World War II. He received the Military Medal for courage in action during the Sicilian campaign, which he is seen receiving from General Bernard Montgomery. One year later (1944), he was killed during an attack on Rimini, Italy.
(Library and Archives Canada, PA-130065)

on political organizations were dropped, both of which had become inoperative in any event; political organizations, such as the Allied Tribes of British Columbia, had been functioning since early in the century.[56] It took a case that was fought all the way to the Supreme Court in 1970 for Indians to win the right to drink in public. Joe Drybones, a Dene, was charged in Yellowknife with being drunk off a reserve, fined $10, and sentenced to three days in jail. Judge William Morrow reversed the decision as a violation of civil rights, a verdict the Supreme Court upheld, and the Indian Act was amended accordingly.

The Feminine Factor

Women's rights were slower in being dealt with, although voices such as those of Mary Two-Axe Earley (1911–96) of Kahnawake and Nellie Carlson of Saddle Lake had been raised since the 1950s in protest against discriminatory provisions of the Indian Act. Particularly galling was the Act's provision linking a woman's status to that of her husband. In practice, this meant that a white woman acquired Indian status upon marrying a status Indian; conversely, a status Indian woman lost hers when she married a non-Indian. In 1979 an Aboriginal Women's Walk from Oka to Ottawa's Parliament Hill drew national attention; rallies and sit-ins of band offices emphasized their point.[57] In 1981, as a result of a complaint by Sandra Lovelace of Tobique Reserve in New Brunswick, the United Nations Human Rights Committee found the Indian Act in breach of human rights. The Canadian government quickly moved to shift responsibility to the bands by granting them the power to decide whether or not a woman would lose status upon marrying a non-Indian.[58] Not until 1985, however, were the sections of the Act dealing with Amerindian women's rights (12.1.b) and federal control of band membership repealed (Bill C-31), granting women the right to retain their status upon marrying non-Indians and to pass it on to their children. Also reinstated were persons who had lost their status through such actions as enfranchisement or having obtained a university degree.[59] In the five years after the legislative changes, the number of status Amerindians grew by 19 per cent; with natural increase, the figure is 33 per cent.[60] In effect, Bill C-31 sounded the death knell of the official policy of assimilation. Incidentally, the 1999 court decision in *Corbière v. Canada* allowing off-reserve band members to vote in band elections has particularly affected reinstated Indian women, as so many of them live off-reserve.

Pauline Johnson (Tekahionwake; 1861–1913) became an international celebrity reading her poetry in theatrical productions. Born on the Six Nations Reserve, Ontario, of an English mother and a Mohawk father, she grew up with a foot in both cultures. This was later reflected in her public readings, for which she wore a specially designed 'Indian' dress for the first part and a European-style evening gown for the second part. As her career progressed, she became more passionate in her defence of Indian ways against the insensitivities of white society. Her death in Vancouver was marked by a funeral service in Christ Church Cathedral and burial in Stanley Park, where a monument was later erected in her honour.
(Library and Archives Canada, C-14141)

The bands were given until 20 November 2000 to implement the decision; a request by the Assembly of First Nations and treaty chiefs across the nation that they be allowed more time was turned down by the Supreme Court. The first band council election under the new regulations was held by the Ojibwa reserve in Manitoba called 'Ebb and Flow'.[61]

It had been estimated that about 50,000

James Gladstone, of the Blood Reserve, Alberta, was
the first treaty Indian to be appointed to the Senate,
in 1958. His daughter, Mrs Pauline Dempsey, adjusts
his headdress while his wife, Janie, looks on. The
occasion was his retirement, at age 83, in 1971.
(Canapress Photo Service)

Jenny Margetts (1936–91, left) of Edmonton and
Monica Turner of Geraldton, Ont., both of Indian
Rights for Indian Women, speak to reporters during
a demonstration in front of the Parliament
buildings, 1973. Jenny fought a lifelong battle
against sex discrimination in Indian band
membership and also worked for the establishment
of Indian language and cultural courses in schools
with a significant number of Native children.
(Canapress Photo Service)

persons would be eligible for reinstatement but
that fewer than 20 per cent would apply; a year
later, 42,000 had applied, far exceeding expectations. By 1991, a parliamentary study revealed that 69,593 individuals had regained
their status.[62] By July of 2003, the number was
reported to have reached well over 100,000.[63]
Regaining federal status has not meant acceptance back on reserves; only 6,834, or 2.4 per
cent, have returned. Yukon has the highest rate
of acceptance, 9.8 per cent, followed by Quebec
at 4.3 per cent; Alberta has the lowest rate, at
1.4 per cent. Crowded conditions on reserves
have been a limiting factor, but the prevailing
sentiment among Amerindians is that the legislation was imposed on them. The original

injustice had not been of their making, any
more than the law aimed at its correction. In
view of this position, the department redefined
Indians into two categories, one for those who
are registered federally and one for those whom
bands have accepted as members. By the end of
1995, 240 bands had adopted membership
codes; as these do not have to be published,

applicants are often unaware of the reasons for the decisions in their cases.[64]

Although the 1951 Act moved towards self-government, it did not go nearly far enough to satisfy such groups as the Six Nations, who claim sovereignty as actively as ever. Even those who are more moderate in their demands are still critical of the revised Act. As they put it, if its aim was to make full citizens of Amerindians, how could that be accomplished if they were not going to be allowed the attendant responsibilities? There is also the fact that with all the legislation piled on legislation over the past century, the administrative process has become very complex, which in itself encourages resistance. But there has been progress. One area where this has been evident is in the increased willingness of bands to exercise their powers to pass bylaws; between 1966 and 1978, the number of councils to pass bylaws tripled.[65] The gradual integration of Amerindians into provincial programs has resulted from the 1951 overhaul, particularly in regard to education, child welfare, and, in some cases, social assistance. Slowly, it is being acknowledged that being Amerindian is not incompatible with being Canadian, and that perhaps the First Nations might even have a dimension to add to the country's cultural riches.

A second joint committee for the review of Indian Affairs policy sat from 1959 to 1961. This time land claims surged to the forefront, and the committee responded by repeating a recommendation of the first joint committee in 1951, that a claims commission be established. That would not happen until 1969 (see Chapter 23).

Education for Amerindians: From Social Engineering to Aboriginal Control

When Amerindians had asked for schools during treaty negotiations, they had envisioned them as a means of preparing their children for the new way of life that lay ahead. They saw educational facilities as a right guaranteed by treaty, by which the government had promised 'to preserve Indian life, values, and Indian government authority'.[66] The final draft of Treaty One had stated that the government would 'maintain a school on each reserve hereby made, whenever the Indians of the reserve should desire it.'[67] Treaty Six negotiators Mistawasis and Ahchacoosacootacoopits tied the need for education to the disappearance of the buffalo. In 1881, Standing Buffalo (Tatanka-Najin, c. 1820–70) of Qu'Appelle reminded a visiting dignitary that his band was waiting for the day school that they had been promised.[68] What they foresaw was a partnership with the newcomers as they worked out their own adaptations.[69] Officials and others of the majority society, however, saw another purpose for schools: their use as instruments for assimilation. According to the BNA Act, education was a provincial responsibility, but Amerindians came within the purview of the federal authority. The treaties had committed the federal government to providing and maintaining schools and teachers on reserves, so that in practice Indian children were to be educated in schools run by the department, although some found their way into those run by the provinces. Education would become the single most expensive component of Indian administration. When the government in 1879 commissioned Nicholas Flood Davin, a lawyer and journalist who would later become the first MP for Assiniboia West, to recommend a course of action for western Amerindian education, administrators advised him not to use the schools in the East as a yardstick.[70]

Government had already started schooling in the Canadas—day and boarding schools—within a couple of decades of the War of 1812. As would be the case with their western counterparts later on, the Amerindian people took initiative towards education. In 1833, Chief Shawahnahness of the St Clair River Ojibwa wanted his children to learn to read and write so that white traders would not be able to cheat them. Chief Shingwaukonse (Little Pine) was so convinced of the importance of a school at Garden River that he postponed harvesting to go fundraising in southern Ontario. Prominent converts like George Copway (Kahgegagahbowh, 1818–69) and the Reverends John Sunday (Shahwundais, 1795–1875), Henry Bird Steinhauer (Sowengisik, 1818–69), and Peter Jones also were active in promoting education within their communities.[71]

But when Jones toured England in the 1830s and 1840s to raise money, he had in mind schools run by Aboriginal people and producing 'men and women able to compete with the white people, able to defend their rights in English, under English law'.[72] In 1846, Ojibwa Chief John Aisance from Beausoleil Island, who had fought with the British during the War of 1812, asked Captain Thomas G. Anderson, a former fur trader and veteran of the same war, for a local school during treaty negotiations, but noted that his band had moved 'four times, and I am too old to remove again.'[73] At this meeting, Anderson expressed the expectation that Amerindians would be running their schools within 25 years, and the chiefs pledged a fourth of their annuities to cover the cost of education during that time period. Within a decade, many would believe that the Amerindians were not getting their money's worth. In setting up schools, the government turned to those who had experience and independent sources of income, and could muster people willing to work in remote areas for low pay: the churches.

Like the government, mission-minded churches had not been idle in the eighteenth century and even earlier. New France, after all, had made abortive attempts at boarding schools as part of its assimilation policy. Then, in 1787, the New England Company, a non-sectarian Protestant organization, founded several schools, including an 'Indian college' at Sussex Vale, New Brunswick. Its original aim was to teach useful trades to Amerindian children through apprenticeship, but instead, the children ended up as a cheap source of labour for local farms and businesses. By 1826, the Reverend John West (d. 1845), who worked for both the Anglican Christian Missionary Society and the Hudson's Bay Company, was able to say, 'little or no good has accrued to the Natives from the Establishment of Sussex Vale.'[74]

Undaunted, the New England Company blamed the Amerindians, claiming that a more 'advanced' group would do better. To prove its point, it moved its operation to the Six Nations Reserve at Grand River and several other communities, such as at Bay of Quinte and Garden River, where the Company financed existing Anglican and Methodist stations.[75]

A network of schools was already in place, then, when colonial governments were ready to address the education issue.[76] The advantages of a partnership with the missionaries, who could raise funds independently and provided the labour, were obvious. The administration favoured residential schools over day schools, as it believed they speeded the process of assimilation.[77] There were two types of residential schools. Boarding schools were usually located on reserves and catered to students between the ages of eight and 14 years. Industrial schools, off reserves, had more elaborate programs and took in students until the age of 18. Curricula combined basic subjects with a half-day of 'practical' training. For boys, this involved agriculture, crafts, and some trades, and for girls, the domestic arts. Both aimed at preparing students for life in the lower fringes of the dominant society.

A school for Amerindian children had existed for some time near Brantford, not far from the Grand River Reserve, amid opposition mainly from among the 20 per cent of reserve residents who followed the Longhouse religion of Seneca chief Ganiodaio (Shanyadariyoh, 'Handsome Lake', d. 1815), which combined elements of the Christian religion and the traditional Iroquois belief system.[78] By 1829, it had become a 'mechanic's institution', known as the Mohawk Institute. More successful in attracting children than many of the other schools, by 1867 the Mohawk Institute had 90 students. In 1869, it would hire its first Aboriginal teacher, Isaac Barefoot, and send five of its students to Helmuth College in Brantford for further education.[79] But this success would not last.

From the beginning, many reserve parents refused to send their children away to school, and most of the students who enrolled were either orphans or from destitute families, whose needs were great. To counter parental resistance, the New England Company put three Amerindian people on the school's board of directors, but conditions did not improve. As time went on, funding dropped, and in 1898 the New England Company withdrew all support. As conditions deteriorated, parental resistance increased, prompting deputy superintendent-general Hayter Reed to blame the problems on the fact that the children were spending too much time on academic work and were being allowed to go home for vacations. A later school administrator overworked the children in an attempt to save money. Frederick Ogilvie Loft said of his time at the Institute, 'I recall the times when working in the fields, I was actually too hungry to be able to walk, let alone work.'[80]

Rebellion against the schools took many forms. On 19 April 1903, Institute residents set fire to the main building. Later, they burned barns and the playhouse. The government rebuilt the school, and Amerindians responded by creating the Indians' Rights Association, which succeeded in getting public curriculum taught in reserve day schools.[81] In 1913, a father sued the Mohawk Institute over the treatment his daughter had received at the hands of the principal. He won only a partial victory in court, but the principal was later fired. Other New England Company schools fared even worse.[82]

Any improvements to physical and sanitary conditions at the schools, however, would go only part way towards helping them gain acceptance in Aboriginal communities. Separation from family was a major issue; 'outing'—the practice of hiring students out as servants or manual labourers, with the schools collecting pay—was another; curriculum, yet another. Although students in industrial schools were supposed to spend a half-day at schooling and a half-day learning a useful trade, lack of funding meant that residents spent most of their time at manual labour. As well, to keep numbers—and grants—up, schools often admitted children who were too young to learn a trade.[83]

All of this, Davin dutifully ignored, and he consulted with no Aboriginal people before completing his report. The administration had seen potential for industrial schools in Ontario because, in their view, the Aboriginal population was 'advanced' enough to benefit from them. Now, in 1879, Davin recommended the same structure as beneficial to the 'warlike' Indians in the West.[84]

Despite the lack of success already seen in the East, Ottawa quickly decided it would be more economical to develop the already existing educational facilities of the missionary branches of various churches than it would be to create its own educational infrastructure. This arrangement would last until 1969, when society's growing secularization and separation of church and state diminished its effectiveness. In practice, in the West as in the East, the 'half-day' system of schoolwork plus 'useful' labour resulted in students spending much more time working on school farms or in household duties than in the classroom; according to Eleanor Brass, who grew up in the File Hills Colony, a boy who was in such a school for 10 years spent only four in the classroom.[85] In their heyday (1931 is reported to have been their peak year), there were more than 80 residential schools for Indians in Canada.[86]

An 1883 Order-in-Council marked the beginning of the first three industrial schools to open on the prairies: at Battleford and Qu'Appelle in the North-West, and at High River in the southern portion of what would become Alberta. The money came from the existing Indian budget, which reduced the amount available for relief—at a time when hunger was widespread across the prairies. Before the turn of the century, seven more schools would open, repeating the same story that had been told in the East.

Almost from the start, the school at Battleford was plagued by lack of funding, truancy, and low staff morale. As local parents refused to send their children, the Department of Indian Affairs recommended that the school start with 'orphans and children who have no natural protectors'.[87] When the Northwest Rebellion broke out, the students were scattered. By the late 1880s, opposition to the school had grown to the point where its viability was being questioned. Dunbow School at High River, which Oblate Father Albert Lacombe left in 1885 after a brief and unsuccessful tenure, did not fare much better.[88]

Qu'Appelle was the most successful of the initial three, in part because of its distance from the Rebellion and in part because of the tireless efforts of its first principal, Father Joseph Hugonnard (1848–1917), to wrest funding from the government.[89] Even so, throughout the lifespan of the industrial schools, Amerindian parents criticized them and resisted sending their children. At a meeting at the Muskowpetung Reserve in northern Saskatchewan early in the twentieth century, parents protested the secrecy surrounding sickness at the Regina school, its use of pupils as labourers,

and the breakup of home circles.[90] The children resisted by running away, stealing—often food—and, finally, committing arson. Parents refused to send their children to the point where the government started using the pass system to prevent parents from using their time off the reserves to interfere with their children's schooling. One mother attacked Father Hugonnard with a knife to give her children time to escape into the woods.[91]

By 1900, out of a total Amerindian population of about 20,000 between the ages of 6 and 15, 3,285 children were enrolled in 22 industrial and 39 boarding schools, and another 6,349 were in 226 day schools.[92] At first, schooling was not compulsory; however, agents could and did apply pressure on parents, usually in the form of withholding rations, to persuade them to part with their children. A day pupil of the 1890s reported that 'to ensure attendance the next day, each child was given biscuit of hardtack before leaving.' He could not remember any book learning being required. School attendance was not made compulsory until 1894, when Hayter Reed had the Indian Act amended to that effect.

In 1910, parents from the Beardy and Okemasis reserves filed a complaint against St Michael's Industrial School at Duck Lake. In particular, they protested the school's practice of 'outing' students to the community. The parents argued that the school should send graduates back to their families. The Indian agent agreed, calling the practice 'slavery'. That same year he reported that half the children who attended St Michael's died, usually from tuberculosis, before reaching the age of 18.[93] But the Oblates who ran the school fought the parents' petition for a day school, and St Michael's remained open.

Further west, Amerindians had been in the majority in British Columbia through much of the nineteenth century, and Governor James Douglas had more or less left them alone. By

Aboriginal parents camp by a residential school at Birtle, Manitoba, in 1904 in order to visit their children.
(Provincial Archives of Manitoba, N-10264)

the 1870s, however, the white population was growing, and the government started encouraging missionaries to found schools. Eventually, the size of the Aboriginal population, combined with furious competition among the Christian denominations, would see the creation of more industrial schools in BC than anywhere else in Canada, most run by the Roman Catholic Oblates, who already had a strong presence in the West.

Like industrial schools elsewhere, BC institutions were plagued by overcrowding and underfunding, which often led them to abandon their stated purpose: to teach young Amerindians a trade. Methodist-run Coqualeetza (St Paul) School near Chilliwack took children out of classes to do drudge work when it was short-staffed. Most of the graduates of the Anglican-

run school at Lytton ended up as unskilled farm labourers.[94]

Nonetheless, there were some success stories, often the result of exceptional individuals. James Gladstone remarked:

> Over the years I have been grateful for the education I received, and I have always been impressed about St Paul's mission and Calgary Industrial School. In those days, we had dedicated teachers . . . even today you can tell the Indians who went to those schools before 1905. They have been the backbone of our reserves.[95]

Mike Mountain Horse, who attended Calgary Industrial School at the same time as Gladstone and later became prominent in the

Indian League of Canada, agreed. Most, however, disagreed with this assessment.

In 1888, the Indian agent at Alert Bay, BC, noted that parents disliked the local school because it meant 'the downfall of all their most cherished customs', and the principal at Alert Bay cited the elders as the reason for low school attendance. As one historian has noted, 'Respect for other cultures was not included in the training of the nineteenth-century missionary.'[96] The practice of changing students' names served to strip them of their identity, and some schools referred to students by number. A boy who attended Qu'Appelle Industrial School later recalled having his braids cut off without explanation, leaving him wondering if his mother had died because, in the Assiniboine tradition, haircutting is associated with mourning.[97]

The decades of the 1880s and 1890s saw rapid expansion of industrial schools; increasing costs, however, soon gave rise to second thoughts. Between 1888 and 1889, the cost per pupil at Battleford rose from $329 to $400. Although Hayter Reed insisted that graduates not be allowed to return to reserves but instead sent to live in the general community, Clifford Sifton, who had become Minister of the Interior and Superintendent-General in 1896, did not see that Indians had 'the physical, mental or moral get-up' to compete with non-Indians on equal terms.[98] Accordingly, he considered industrial schooling for Indians a waste of time and effort. He did not mention that it was often difficult for Amerindians to find jobs, as many whites refused to work beside them. A 1902 report stated that out of 2,752 graduated students, only 599 were doing well.[99] Eleanor Brass, who as a Cree in the File Hills Colony had first-hand experience with the system, is of the opinion that the schools served a purpose for about one generation, during the transition from hunting to an agricultural way of life; after that they 'became the undoing of what had been previously taught' as graduates

usually did not get the opportunity to exercise what they had learned.[100]

By the turn of the century, enthusiasm for industrial schools had waned; rising costs and poor administration, including charges of abuse to students, led to a gradual phasing out of the program, which, as already indicated, would continue for most of the twentieth century. Metlakatla was closed by 1907, followed by the school in High River, Alberta, in 1922, among others during that 15-year period. From then on, Indian Affairs would concentrate on boarding and day schools. Even there, however, problems developed, particularly in relation to health. One of the statistics that came to light in investigations of 1907–9 was that of all the students who had attended Sarcee Boarding School between 1894 and 1908, 28 per cent had died, mostly from tuberculosis.[101] A comprehensive plan to deal with the situation was shelved because of the cost, but also because it would have undermined the authority of the churches running the schools. New regulations led to some improvement; also, new financing arrangements gave more responsibility to Indian Affairs, with the churches now principally providing personnel.[102] Still, charges of student abuse continued to surface from time to time (after the Oka standoff in 1990, these became widespread and received previously unaccustomed media coverage). As Titley has pointed out, up until a few decades ago the system had the backing of society in general.[103] These administrative problems brought day schools back into favour. Jenness observed in 1920:

> In many parts of Canada the Indians had no schools at all; in others only elementary mission schools in which the standard of teaching was exceedingly low. A few mission boarding-schools, subsidized by the government, accepted Indian children when very young, raised them to the age of sixteen, then sent

them back to their people, well indoctrinated in the Christian faith, but totally unfitted for life in an Indian community and, of course, not acceptable in any white one.[104]

The year of compulsory enfranchisement, 1920, was also the year for strengthening compulsory school attendance to ensure the compliance of all Amerindian children between the ages of 7 and 15. Ten years later, regulations were stiffened still more; by this time, Amerindian children could be committed to boarding schools and kept there until the age of 18 on the authority of the Indian agent, a measure far in excess of anything applied to non-Natives. These regulations might have been responsible for statistics reported by Duncan Campbell Scott, indicating that the number of Amerindian students had risen from 878 in 1918–19 to 2,228 in 1928–9. By 1932, the year of Scott's retirement, the number was reported at 17,163. In his final report, Scott said that attendance had risen from 64.29 per cent in 1920 to 74.51 per cent in 1930. This was mostly due to residential schools. To Scott, these figures were proof that Amerindians were on their way to becoming 'civilized'.[105]

Other statistics tell a different story. In 1930, three-quarters of Native pupils across Canada were in grades one to three; only three in 100 went past grade six. By mid-century, the proportion of Amerindian students beyond grade six had risen to 10 per cent, an improvement, but only one-third of the comparable level of Euro-Canadian children. Such figures could be explained at least partly by the type of curricula Amerindians were subjected to: the emphasis on the 'practical' was such that an Amerindian was lucky to reach grade five by the age of 18. As late as 1951, eight out of every 20 Indians over the age of five were reported to be without formal schooling, in spite of regulations for enforced attendance. Still, many Amerindian parents did what they could to encourage their children to go to school. According to the Royal Commission on Aboriginal Peoples, it has not been possible to determine the actual number of Aboriginal children who attended these schools because of incomplete records, although attempts have been made.[106]

Throughout all this, Amerindians had not been allowed to contribute to the content of studies or to exercise any control over schools, although some petitioned to have more emphasis on classwork and less on 'practical' training such as farming. Use of Native languages and the practice of traditional religions were forbidden. Despite their efforts to transform Indians, educators became aware that Indians were using the system to obtain 'the best that the white man had to teach' and were 'endeavoring to work out their own plans and their own self-determination'.[107] The vast majority remained distinctly Indian; as one official observed, the 'most promising pupils are found to have retrograded and to have become leaders in the pagan life of their reserves.' Officials were relearning in the nineteenth and twentieth centuries what had already been clearly evident in New France in the seventeenth, that the modal personality of a particular culture is by its very nature highly resistant to change.[108] Even when there was success and an individual moved into the labour market, this did not always suit the dominant society. To quote Oliver, 'we are educating these Indians to compete industrially with our own peoples, which seems to me a very undesirable use of public money.'[109] When Amerindians proved they were as adept as whites at their own game, the result could be hostility and rejection instead of acceptance.

Amerindians, of course, had another view of the influence of school:

When an Indian comes out of these places it is like being put between two walls in a room and left hanging in the middle. On one side are all the things he learned from his people and their way of life that was being wiped out, and on the other are the white man's way which he could never fully understand since he never had the right amount of education and could not be part of it. There he is, hanging in the middle of the two cultures and he is not a white man and he is not an Indian. They washed away practically everything an Indian needed to help himself, to think the way a human person should in order to survive.[110]

Amerindians' lively sense of humour continued to stand them in good stead, as Basil Johnston's *Indian School Days* illustrates.[111] In the Far North, at least one residential school struck a positive note as it included instruction in Native traditional skills in its curriculum. The Anglican school at Shingle Point, Yukon, had two Inuit hunters on staff to teach the boys hunting and fishing techniques; the girls received lessons in the domestic arts within the framework of Arctic conditions. Such concessions were rare; Gwich'in John Nerysoo of Tuktoyaktuk, when asked in 1981 what he had learned at school, replied, 'mostly about God and being good'.[112]

The parliamentary investigations that preceded the 1951 revision of the Indian Act rejected Indian Affairs education policy as it then was and proposed instead that Amerindian children be integrated into public schools. Ten years later, out of the 38,000 young Amerindians in school, almost one-fourth were attending provincially controlled institutions and the total proportion of Amerindian pupils beyond grade six had doubled.[113] By this time, however, there were those who were advocating autonomous Amerindian schools, separate from those of the dominant society. Indeed, such voices had been raised since the nineteenth century. One of these was that of Anglican missionary-educator Edward F.

Wilson (1844–1915): why, he asked, should Amerindians be denied independent communities? 'Would it not be pleasanter, and even safer for us, to have living in our midst a contented, well-to-do, self-respecting, thriving community of Indians, rather than a set of dependent, dissatisfied, half-educated and half-Anglicized paupers?'[114] Three-quarters of a century later, anthropologist Jacques Rousseau (1905–70) raised a similar point in Quebec when he argued against trying to transform Inuit into French Canadians.[115]

The last of the federal residential schools closed in 1996. The sense of hurt they left in their wake eventually came to be expressed in lawsuits by former students seeking damages for their compulsory school attendance and the treatment some had received. As of 2000, the Anglican Church was reported to be facing about 1,600 such lawsuits involving 26 of the residential schools it had once run in co-operation with the federal government. It was not alone: Roman Catholic, Presbyterian, Methodist, and United churches were among those that faced similar chilling prospects. Apologies on the part of the churches met with a cool reception.[116] However, on 11 March 2003, then minister Ralph Goodale, who was responsible for a resolution of the Indian residential schools issues, and the leaders of the Anglican Church across Canada ratified an agreement to compensate victims with valid claims of sexual and physical abuse at Anglican-run residential schools. They both agreed that the federal government would pay 70 per cent of the compensation and the Anglican Church would pay 30 per cent, to a maximum of $25 million.[117] In September 2007, the federal government finally announced an Indian residential schools settlement agreement (see Chapter 29).[118] There is a certain irony in the situation when one considers that there was a positive side to the residential school experience; a study of the Walpole Island First Nation's experience has revealed that a majority of its former students judged their education favourably, with the women in general reacting more positively than the men. More local studies need to be done to balance out the picture as a whole.[119]

Blue Quills, near St Paul, Alberta, became the first school in Canada to be controlled by an Amerindian band, in 1970.[120] Its success encouraged others to follow its example; in 1973 the Métis community at Ile à la Crosse in northern Saskatchewan took over the local school.[121] The following year the Ojibwa of Sabaskong Bay in northern Ontario defied the department and began the process of taking over their elementary school; three years later, in 1977, they were also running the secondary school.[122] Today, Indian Affairs encourages bands to take over full or partial administration of reserve schools, although its funding policy is not always consistent with this goal. By the early 1980s, 450 of the then 577 Indian bands in Canada had done so. Out of those, 187 bands were fully operating their own schools by 1984, almost half of them in British Columbia and most of the remainder on the prairies.[123] Two school districts have also come under Native control, the Nisga'a in British Columbia and the James Bay Cree in Quebec. In 1983–4, a fifth of Indian students were in band-operated schools. In many provinces, programs have been initiated to encourage indigenous cultural and language content; in 1990 the department signed an agreement with the Assembly of Manitoba Chiefs that allows them to administer their own education system on reserves. By 1999, Canada counted 466 schools being operated by Indian bands, an increase of 66.4 per cent over the previous 10 years.[124]

As to be expected, the influence of the old regime carries over, even as the new regime copes with such problems as the reluctance of Indian Affairs to allow a level of funding for band-operated schools comparable to that of provincially operated schools. Another problem is the transfer of authority: that of Indians is still limited except in the case of special agreements, as in Manitoba. In other words, old attitudes have not been eliminated; however, 'aggressive assimilation' is no longer the order of the day, and some Indian-run schools are chalking up good records.[125] That the growing flexibility is working both ways was illustrated by the election of Mohawk Doug Maracle as chairman of the Hastings County Board of Education in southern Ontario in 1990, and, in Edmonton, by the presentation of $500,000 from Canative Housing Corporation to the University of Alberta's Native Student Services in a ceremony in December 2000. This is the largest donation the university has received from an Aboriginal organization for its Native Studies program.[126]

Still, according to 1986 census figures, non-Indians are three times more likely than Indians to attend university and seven times more likely to earn a degree.[127] Of those Indians who undertake university studies, about one-quarter earn a degree, compared to more than one-half of non-Indian students. Although the earning power of Indians who obtain a degree increases substantially, the gap between that of similarly qualified non-Indians does not decrease—Indians at all levels of education earn about two-thirds that of non-Indians. Incidentally, the Mohawks of Kahnawake have one of the highest per family annual incomes ($30,000 average) of Native communities anywhere in Canada.[128] In 1991, the Public Service Commission reported that Natives leave government service at double the rate of other employees because of lack of advancement and challenge and an inability to aid their communities from within the bureaucracy.[129]

The intensity and duration of the campaign to capture Indian minds and hearts reflects the importance accorded to this aspect of nation-building. Control of education goes to the heart of the movement for self-government, a battle Canada fought with Great Britain in the nineteenth century, as Amerindians are waging it with Canada today.

A closely related phenomenon that temporarily gained strength as residential schools fell into disfavour was the practice of placing 'neglected' or disadvantaged Native children with white families, either as adoptees or in foster care. The 'Sixties Scoop', as it was popularly known, took off in Canada in the 1950s and reached its maximum intensity during the 1960s and early 1970s; in all, it has been estimated that 15,000 Native children were adopted into non-Native families, 3,000 of them from Manitoba alone. By the end of the 1960s, 30 to 40 per cent of all legal wards were Aboriginal, even though they made up less than 4 per cent of the national population.[130] These children were scattered far and wide after being removed from their families, many of them ending up in the United States and some even further afield. Their isolation was far greater than if they had been sent to residential school, which was usually located not far from their homes so that contact was not entirely cut off. The 'scoop' was justified on the grounds that most of the children were being rescued from extreme poverty and would have a better chance in life if raised in the more comfortable circumstances of the dominant culture. The practice was paralleled with the Aborigines of Australia; in the United States, the rule after 1978 was that Indian children could not be removed from their tribal areas, so that Indian children who became wards of the state were placed with Indian families. In Canada, the movement began to taper off in the 1980s, as it became apparent that instead of creating a homogeneous society, the practice was producing individuals who were neither white nor Indian, whose loss of cultural identity led to social dysfunction and was becoming a tradition in itself as it was passed on to the next generation.

Chapter 23

Canadian Courts and Aboriginal Rights

Canada's first Aboriginal rights case, *St Catherine's Milling v. The Queen* on the information of the Attorney General of Ontario (1885–9, also known as The Indian Title Case and The Ontario Lands Case), gave rise to two statements that set legal precedents in Canada, one concerning Aboriginal rights, the other, provincial rights. At the time, provincial rights aroused the greater passion; indeed, Aboriginal rights were considered almost incidental, although they were at the very heart of the dispute.

The case arose from the long-standing dispute between Ontario and the federal government over the location of the province's northwestern boundary. When Canada had purchased Rupert's Land its boundaries had been undefined. When Ottawa extinguished Amerindian title to the region with Treaty Three it assigned the newly opened territories to Manitoba, as Crown lands in that province were under federal jurisdiction. Ontario, where Crown lands were provincially controlled, charged Ottawa with trying to pare down the size of the older province and thus the area of the jurisdiction in which Ontario

was autonomous. Ottawa viewed the situation from a reverse perspective and saw Ontario attempting to encroach on federal prerogatives. In the words of Sir John A. Macdonald, 'there is not one stick of timber, one acre of land, or one lump of lead, iron or gold that does not belong to the Dominion, or to the people who purchased from the Dominion Government.'[1] The Indians whose lands were concerned were neither consulted nor brought to the witness stand. The issue regarding Ontario's northwestern boundary went to the Judicial Committee of the Privy Council in London, at that time Canada's supreme court of appeal, which in 1884 decided in favour of Ontario.

The Prime Minister was not so easily defeated, and delayed enacting the enabling legislation to put the decision into effect; Ontario responded by filing in the Chancery Division of the High Court of Ontario against the federally licensed St Catherine's Milling and Lumber Company for illegal logging on provincial lands. The company was caught between two warring levels of government. The case was first heard in 1885, the year of

TIMELINE

1717	Louis XV grants seigneury at Oka (Kanesatake) to Seminary of St Sulpice as Amerindian mission.
1721	Nearly 900 Indians move to area of Sulpician mission.
1841	British confirm seminary's title at Oka.
1868	Iroquois and Algonquins, citing Oka seminary's tyranny and oppression, unsuccessfully petition Ottawa for clear title to the land and their village.
1875	Sulpicians obtain court order to dismantle Methodist church at Oka.
1877	Natives burn Catholic church at Oka.
1885–9	*St Catherine's Milling v. The Queen:* Judicial Committee of the Privy Council, in complex jurisdictional case between Ontario and Ottawa, upholds validity of Proclamation of 1763 but claims that British, by setting foot in North America, gained title to all Indian lands.
1912	Privy Council upholds Oka seminary title in ongoing land dispute.
1936	Sulpicians sell most of Oka land to Belgian real estate company, which begins to sell parcels of land.
1961	Kanesatake Natives' request that land be formally declared a reserve gets no response.
1969–77	Indian Claims Commission headed by Dr Lloyd Barber.
1970	Federal Fisheries Act restricts Aboriginal right.
1973	Supreme Court split decision on Nisga'a land claim case (*Calder*) opens way for greater recognition of Aboriginal rights, although Nisga'a technically lose in court.

1975	Comprehensive claim by Kanesatake residents for Aboriginal title rejected by Ottawa.
1985	Supreme Court rules in *Simon v. the Queen* that only federal legislation can restrict Aboriginal hunting and fishing rights.
1986	Specific claim to land title at Kanesatake rejected.
1990	78-day standoff at Oka leads to the death of a Quebec police officer and, eventually, to the arrest of over 40 Mohawks. Two Warriors received jail terms; all others were acquitted or had charges dropped.
1991	Indian Claims Commission reinstituted.
1999	Supreme Court rules in favour of Mi'kmaq Donald Marshall Jr (the same man who had been wrongfully convicted of murder many years earlier) in case involving Native right to fish out of season.
2000	Nisga'a Final Agreement Act ratified by federal Parliament.
	Mi'kmaq lobster fishermen at Burnt Church, NB, emboldened by *Marshall* decision, set their own regulations for lobster fishery and become embroiled in violent confrontations with white lobstermen and Department of Fisheries and Oceans officials.
	Land governance deal signed by Natives of Kanesatake and federal government on 21 December. Chippewa claim for 1,030 hectares of land in Sarnia, Ont., rejected by Ontario Court of Appeal.

the Northwest Rebellion, by the Chancellor of Ontario, John Alexander Boyd (1837–1916). When rebellion had broken out, two of the judge's sons had immediately volunteered against Riel.[2]

Whose Land, Whose Title?

The argument had boiled down to exactly what the Dominion had obtained from the Amerindians in Treaty Three. D'Alton McCarthy

(1836–98), acting for the lumber company and hence for Ottawa, based his case on section 91(24) of the BNA Act, which specified that the Dominion was to bear responsibility for 'Indians, and Lands reserved for Indians'.[3] By virtue of that section the Dominion had undertaken to extinguish Amerindian title by means of treaties. Before the purchase, the federal argument went, Amerindians had been owners of the land, in fee simple, but subject to the restriction that they could only sell to the Canadian government. Neither provinces nor individuals had the right to buy lands from Amerindians. The Proclamation of 1763 had specifically referred to 'lands reserved for Indians'; certainly, the Treaty Three territory in question had been in that category at the time of Confederation. Because of the wording of the Proclamation, treaties were an essential prerequisite for the expansion of colonial settlement in British North America, and only the federal authority could engage in that activity.

McCarthy sought to demonstrate that the Crown had historically acquired land title from Amerindians through purchase rather than conquest. In support of that assertion, he described a long string of treaties with Amerindians, going back to the first days of the Thirteen Colonies. McCarthy's argument was that these treaties proved recognition on the part of the European colonizers that Aboriginal communities possessed a real estate in their ancestral lands, which included 'rights to occupy the land, to cut timber and to claim the mines and minerals from the land'. What was more, these rights were hereditary. The Dominion had purchased these rights in Treaty Three; thus it had acted within its proper jurisdiction when it had granted a timber-cutting licence to St Catherine's Milling and Lumber Company.

McCarthy called on only one witness, Alexander Morris, the former lieutenant-governor of the North-West Territories and chairman of the commission that had negotiated Treaty

Three. Recalling the negotiations, Morris said that the government had made two previous attempts before the successful third round; even so, it had taken 14 days of hard bargaining.

Oliver Mowat (1820–1903), Premier of Ontario, appeared for the plaintiffs. He was blunt: 'We say there is no Indian title in law or in equity. The claim of the Indians is simply moral and no more.' Property, so the argument went, could only be regarded as a 'creature of law', capable of being sustained only as long as the law that created it exists. Since Amerindians had no rules or regulations that could be considered laws, they had no title to their ancestral territories that could be recognized by the Crown. There could be no such thing as Indian title independent of the Crown's law. During the course of the province's arguments, Indians were described as an 'inferior race . . . in an inferior state of civilization' who had 'no government and no organization, and cannot be regarded as a nation capable of holding lands'.

Mowat's arguments referred back to Calvin's Case (1608) in England, a famous controversy during the course of which the prerogatives of the King were defined. Whenever the Crown conquered a non-Christian people, the Crown's law immediately replaced any laws the pagans might have recognized among themselves. Mowat widened the argument to include the 'discovery' by Christian kings of territories where pagans dwelt:

> At the time of the discovery of America, and long after, it was an accepted rule that heathen and infidel nations were perpetual enemies, and that the Christian prince or people first discovering and taking possession of the country became its absolute proprietor, and could deal with the land as such.[4]

As for the Proclamation of 1763, Mowat called it 'a provisional arrangement' that had been expressly repealed by the Quebec Act of 1774. In any event, it did not recognize pre-existing title but the source of whatever title Amerindians might possess, which was entirely at the pleasure of the Crown. The Proclamation had reserved lands for Amerindians only 'for the present', a temporary provision that had been pre-empted by the Quebec Act. As for Treaty Three, since Indians had never owned the land in fee simple, they had nothing to convey to the federal government. Mowat concluded by saying that since Ontario had been granted jurisdiction of its Crown lands under the terms of Confederation and since the disputed territory was geographically within Ontario, then the clearing of its Indian title was in favour of the Crown by right of Ontario. According to Mowat's reasoning, federal jurisdiction over 'lands reserved for Indians', as provided for at Confederation, applied only to lands that had been specifically reserved for Natives at the signing of the land-cession treaties.

Three weeks after the first hearing, on 10 June, Chancellor Boyd presented his decision, in a statement on Amerindian rights that set a precedent for Canadian courts in its thoroughness. By that date, the Northwest Rebellion was effectively over. Poundmaker had surrendered and only Big Bear was still at large. Boyd described Amerindians as characteristically being without fixed abode, moving about as the exigencies of life demanded. 'As heathens and barbarians it was not thought that they had any proprietary title to the soil, nor any claim thereto as to interfere with the plantations, and the general prosecution of colonization.'[5] As legal ownership of the land had never been attributed to them, he held that Treaty Three Indians had not conveyed any such rights to the federal government. The Dominion government had exceeded its rights in granting a licence to St Catherine's Milling Company, which was therefore invalid. According to Boyd, in legal terms Treaty Three was also meaningless; if they so chose, Amer-

indians could treat with the Crown for the extinction of their primitive right of occupancy. If they refused to do so, the government was not hampered but had perfect liberty to proceed with settlement and development of the country, displacing the Aboriginal peoples if necessary. He agreed with Ontario that the Proclamation of 1763 had been superseded by the Quebec Act of 1774 and was obsolete. Boyd's judgment continued:

> Before the appropriation of reserves the Indians have no claim except upon the bounty and benevolence of the Crown. After the appropriation, they become invested with a legally recognized tenure of defined lands; in which they have a present right as to the exclusive and absolute usufruct, and a potential right of becoming individual owners in fee after enfranchisement.[6]

Boyd's decision was maintained through three appeals, one to the Ontario Court of Appeal (heard one month after the hanging of Riel), the second to the Supreme Court of Canada (judgment, 20 June 1887, with two lengthy dissenting opinions), and finally to the Judicial Committee of the Privy Council (1888). The Privy Council, however, did not accept Ontario's argument that the Proclamation of 1763 was obsolete and upheld its legality. In its view, that did not alter the fact that title to the soil had rested with the Crown even before Treaty Three: 'The Crown has all along had a present proprietary estate in the land, upon which the Indian title is a mere burden.' In other words, as frequently had been pointed out, the British, by simply setting foot in North America, had acquired title to Indian lands. One of the lords, however, did hold that Indians had held a right of occupancy before Treaty Three, but it was 'a personal and usufructuary right, dependant upon the good will of the Sovereign'.[7] Another of the dissenting opinions disagreed with Ontario's narrow definition of 'reserves'. The *St Catherine's Milling* decision still remains in effect, despite some monumental legal battles since. Lawyer Bruce A. Clark noted in 1987 that of the four North American judges who up to that point had written off Amerindian title for ideological reasons, three were Canadian.[8] Since then, Justice Allan McEachern has joined the group (see later in this chapter).

Ottawa had not called an Amerindian witness from the Treaty Three area to stand as evidence of the Ojibwa's own conception of their land rights, even though it was on record in Morris's account of the treaty negotiations. During those negotiations, Mawedopenais, Fort Francis chief, had repeated a sentiment that Amerindians had been expressing in various terms ever since the first arrival of Europeans in North America: 'This is what we think, that the Great Spirit has planted us on this ground where we are, as you were where you came from. We think where we are is our property.' He added that the Great Spirit had provided the Amerindians with the rules 'that we should follow to govern us rightly'.[9] There was plenty of other such evidence available, as historian Donald Smith has pointed out. Peter Jones of the Mississauga had written: 'Each tribe or body of Indians has its own range of country, and sometimes each family its own hunting grounds, marked out by certain natural divisions . . . all the game within these bounds are considered their property. . . . It is at the peril of an intruder to trespass on the hunting grounds of another.'[10] Mississauga George Copway (1818–69) was even more categoric: 'The hunting grounds of the Indians were secured by right, a law and custom among themselves. No one was allowed to hunt on another's land, without invitation or permission.' Repeated offences could result in banishment from the tribe.[11]

As for the Amerindians of Treaty Three, they did not fare well. Ottawa and Ontario could not agree on the promised selection, location, and extent of reserves. For some it would be a generation, or even several generations, before their reserves were confirmed; for others, the process is still going on. Neither has the exact nature of Amerindian interest in reserve lands been fully defined, although, according to Indian and Northern Affairs Canada, the current working definition for 'reserve' is a '[t]ract of land, the legal title to which is held by the Crown, set apart for the use and benefit of an Indian band'.[12] As might be expected, differing interpretations have arisen out of different cases. One of the most influential has been *Attorney General of Quebec v. Attorney General of Canada*, usually referred to as *Star Chrome Mining*, 1920. It took the position that the Amerindian interest was usufructuary 'under the superintendence and management of the Commissioner of Indian lands'. However, the Commissioner could not dispose of such lands without the consent of the band, even though such a requirement was not in the legislation.[13]

Nearly Three Centuries of Confrontation at Oka

An even older but still only partially resolved case that maintained the position on Amerindian title upheld by *St Catherine's Milling v. The Queen* was that of the Amerindians of Oka against the Seminary of St Sulpice.[14] It dated from Louis XV's 1717 grant of a seigneury to the Seminary of St Sulpice on the Ottawa River where it meets the St Lawrence, about 30 kilometres west of Montreal, on the condition that it would be used as an Amerindian mission. The grant had been made at the order's request; according to one account, had 'they asked it for themselves, they would not have got it.'[15] Should the Amerindians abandon the mission, the land was to return to the Crown.[16] It was thought wiser to make the grant to the seminary rather than to the Amerindians, as the latter were considered to be incapable of conserving the property for themselves. It left unresolved the question of whether the Sulpicians were the sole proprietors or trustees, a point that would become more tortured as the potentialities of the region were developed.[17]

France, as we have seen, never recognized Aboriginal title and so never considered it necessary to negotiate with the Indians before granting lands to French subjects. In this case, the grant was to provide the seminary with a land base for its mission for Indians—principally Huron, Algonquin, and Iroquois, but also including Nipissings, Pawnee, Fox, and even some Sioux—who had been dislocated by war and other factors and who had gathered at Sault-aux-Récollets, near Montreal. In 1721 nearly 900 Indians moved to the new location at Lake of Two Mountains, with funds provided by a private benefactor, a Sulpician missionary who later became superior of the order in New France, François Vachon de Belmont (1645–1732). He is reported to have sunk a fortune into the project. The seminary also claimed to have incurred heavy expenses.[18] The site was chosen because it was far enough away to provide some protection from the temptations of the settlement at Montreal and close enough that the Indians could be quickly called on for military service in case of war.[19] As far as the Natives were concerned (particularly the Iroquois, who eventually predominated), this was their territory.

The British, in line with their stand that the French had extinguished whatever title the Amerindians might have had, recognized the grant as clear title for the seminary and even enlarged it. When the Indians went to court in 1781 to prove their proprietorship on the evidence of the 'Two-Dog Wampum' belt (the dogs, at each end of the belt, were the protectors of their land, represented by 27 beads), their claim was rejected.[20] The Indians of Kane-satake did not have the advantage of a sympathetic governor as did those of Kahnawake with Governor Gage in 1762; nor did they have the protection of a special treaty, as did the Huron of Lorette.[21] That the Iroquois position at Oka aroused concern, however, was evident in the fact that the British felt it necessary to issue a special ordinance in 1841 confirming the seminary's title. The gesture also had another purpose: it rewarded the seminary for its support of the government during the troubles of 1837–8. Encouraged by this support and now much less enthusiastic about its missionary role, especially as the Iroquois were deserting Catholicism in favour of Methodism, the seminary used economic means to pressure the Natives to leave and, whenever they did so, brought in French-Canadian settlers in their stead.[22]

In 1853 and 1854, the department sought to ease the situation for the Amerindians by setting aside lands for the Algonquin at Maniwaki, Quebec, and for the Iroquois at Doncaster, Ontario. Some accepted the compromise and moved to the new locations, but most rejected it. As the Commissioners' Report of 1858 observed, the 'attachment of the Indians to the parts of the country where they have been born and brought up is extreme.'[23] They continued to assert their claims to the land at Kanesatake by selling wood and staking out lots, actions for which some of them were imprisoned, as the seminary claimed right to the trees.[24] The situation again boiled over in 1868, when both the Algonquin and Iroquois, led by new Iroquois chief Joseph Onasakenarat (Sosé, Joseph Akirwirente, 1845–81), petitioned Ottawa.[25] Accusing the seminary of tyranny and oppression, they sought clear title to the land and to their village, Kanesatake. The result was the arrest and jailing of three chiefs, including Joseph (who would end up in jail eight times on charges involving land-related issues), and an Order-in-Council in 1869 reaffirming once more the seminary's seigneurial title.

Escalating violence, including the dismantling of the Methodist church by the Sulpicians with the authority of a court order in 1875, a raid two years later in the dead of night by provincial police, and the burning of the Catholic church, resulted in 14 Natives being charged with arson. One trial after another produced only hung juries; finally, in the sixth, the accused were acquitted by an English-speaking jury.[26] Another inquiry in 1878 held firm to the idea that Amerindians had no rights to land and found that the seigneury was the property of the seminary.[27] Faced with the Indians' stubborn refusal to accept this decision, the department arranged for the seminary to purchase 25,500 acres (10,320 hectares) in the Township of Gibson, Ontario, as compensation for the Natives and as a 'final solution' to the problem. Although the seminary built houses on the newly acquired lands and offered lots of 100 acres (40 hectares) (or more if required) for each family, as well as compensation to the Indians for improvements they had made at Oka, few finally agreed to the move. For one thing, they had not been consulted as to the location of the new reserve; for another, they considered the compensation offered to be inadequate.[28] This rejection led to still another report, in 1883, in which it was observed that there was a deep-seated public conviction that 'although the Indians may not have a legal claim to the lands, as owners thereof, they are nevertheless entitled to compensation for the loss of lands which they had been led to suppose were set apart for their benefit.'[29] In the meantime, not all was confrontation; between 1886 and 1910, Mohawks and Euro-Canadians collaborated on a reforestation project to stabilize the region's sandy soil. It became a model for other such efforts in the province.[30]

Since neither side would budge on the land issue, however, confrontations continued, and the case was eventually fought out in the courts, with Ottawa agreeing to pay the expenses of both sides. It wended its way to the Privy Council, which in 1912 decided in favour of the seminary but suggested that there might be a charitable trust for the Indians that could be enforced.[31] The implication was that Amerindian rights in the case could be dealt with outside the judicial system. No action resulted, either in or out of the courts, until the seminary, faced with a financial crisis in 1936, sold the major part of its seigneury, including the forest at Oka, to a Belgian real estate company.[32] A sawmill operation was set up, and after World War II the company began to sell off parcels of land for agricultural development. All this upset the Amerindians so much that in 1945 the alarmed department purchased the seminary's unsold lands, except those used for religious purposes, plus an additional 500 acres (202 hectares) of woodland for fuel, and assumed responsibility for the Natives.[33] The newly acquired land was administered as if it were a reserve, but without granting it that status. All this was done without consulting the residents of Kanesatake, who, far from considering this a final solution of the problem as the department had hoped, continued to press their claims, which included a forested area that was not part of the department's deal. Their request in 1961 that the land in question be formally declared a reserve brought no response. This was followed in 1975 with a comprehensive claim asserting Aboriginal title, which was rejected by the department. When the Amerindians riposted two years later with a specific claim, it, too, was eventually rejected in 1986. The Iroquois, for their part, continued to spurn proposals that they settle on nearby federal lands. In the meantime the Warrior movement was steadily gaining ground.

That the problem was not only unresolved but had intensified became dramatically evident in the summer of 1990 when the town of Oka announced that it was going to expand a

An unidentified Mohawk has his crossbow ready as he peers through the pine forest during the standoff at Kanesatake in 1990.
(The Canadian Press/Tom Hanson)

nine-hole golf course, built in the 1950s, into the disputed area. Oka took this stand after months of fruitless negotiations; the Iroquois responded by barricading the location. Quebec police, in a move eerily reminiscent of the events of more than a century earlier, attempted to storm the barricade, failed, and one policeman was killed.[34] Kahnawake residents, about 30 kilometres away, came to the support of their kin by blocking highways crossing their reserve, as well as Mercier Bridge, a popular commuter link into Montreal; the standoff at Kanesatake lasted for 78 days. Quebec tried

to cut off food supplies to the holdouts, a move circumvented by the Amerindians with the aid of the Red Cross. In the end the province asked Ottawa to send in the army, a move that alone cost $83 million; for the province, the bill has come to over $112 million. The total cost of the standoff came to well over $200 million.[35] In the trials that followed, two Mohawks were found guilty of 29 of 56 charges: Ronald Cross (known as 'Lasagna') was sentenced to four years and four months and Gordon ('Noriega') Lazore to 23 months. A third, Roger Lazore, was acquitted of all 12 charges that had been brought against him. Of 39 Mohawks brought to trial a few months later, five were freed for lack of evidence, and the remaining 34 were acquitted on all 88 counts against them. The trial, the biggest of its kind in Canadian history, had also been marked by the longest jury selection process.[36]

A decade later there was still no agreement on what had been learned from Oka. 'Oka: 10 years later. Change comes grudgingly, if at all' one headline proclaimed, in contrast to another, which held that 'Peace Reigns in Oka: Oka Wrote a New, Radical Chapter in the History of Aboriginal Canadians 10 Years Ago. The Scars Remain but Both Sides Say They've Moved On'. A third gloomed: 'Finding Peace Amid Oka's Ashes: Horrors of Decade-Old Crisis Still Resonate in Divided Community'. A fourth was more cautious: 'Dix ans après: Pas de leçon claire à tirer d'Oka' ('Ten years after: No clear lesson to be drawn from Oka').[37]

The old arguments that Amerindians have no rights to the land they have lived on for thousands of years, unless they have been asserted by special arrangements, are not only still alive but in some cases are more entrenched than ever. Unsolved problems, unlike old soldiers, have a habit of staying and growing instead of fading away.[38] On the positive side, the crisis has heightened public interest in the situation of Aboriginal peoples in general,

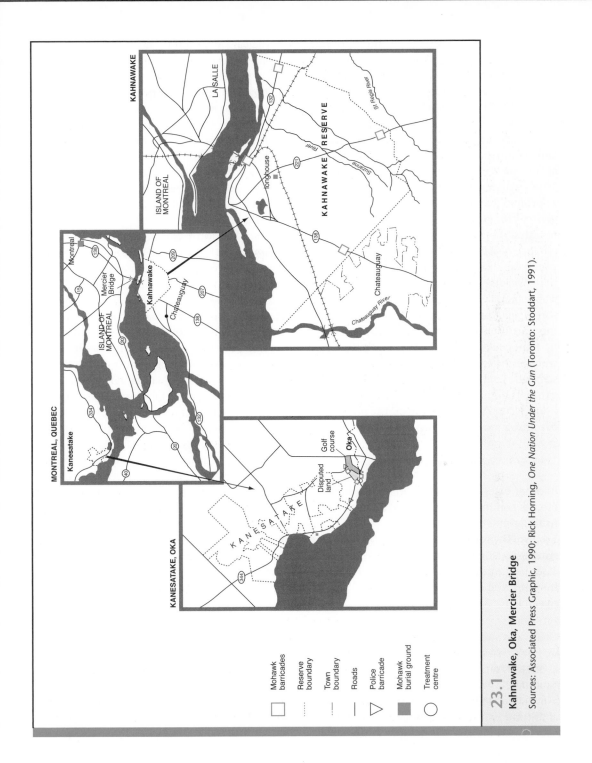

23.1

Kahnawake, Oka, Mercier Bridge

Sources: Associated Press Graphic, 1990; Rick Horning, *One Nation Under the Gun* (Toronto: Stoddart, 1991).

as witnessed by today's greater news coverage of their activities. Another positive development has been Ottawa's increase in funding for land claim settlements, which has had the salutary effect of somewhat speeding up a still all-too-slow process.[39] More specifically, the federal government continued an already launched policy of buying land in the disputed area to prevent another confrontation. Finally, 10 years after the crisis, it signed an agreement-in-principle with the Mohawks in June 2000, giving them legal jurisdiction over 960 hectares. After further negotiation, a land governance deal was signed on 21 December 2000, which was hailed by some as a step towards self-government. Still, for most Mohawks, it was a bittersweet victory: as far as they were concerned, the land has always been theirs.[40] In the meantime, an annual powwow, launched by Kanesatake the year after the crisis to encourage the easing of tensions inflamed by the standoff, held its tenth performance with the aid of the Kahurangi Maori Dance Company from New Zealand. Indigenous politics are becoming more and more international.

Some Other Arenas

In other cases before the courts, there has been more accommodation in regard to hunting and fishing rights than in the matter of land rights. Even so, the record has been by no means consistent. In Nova Scotia, for instance, a series of cases beginning in the 1920s all found against hunting and fishing rights, on the grounds that the 1752 treaty guaranteeing those rights was:

> a mere agreement made by the Governor and council with a handful of Indians giving them in return for good behaviour food, presents, and the right to hunt and fish as usual. . . . The savages' rights of sovereignty, even of ownership, was [sic] never recognized. Nova Scotia

had passed to Great Britain not by gift or purchase from or even by conquest of the Indians but by treaty with France, which had acquired it by priority of discovery and ancient possession; and the Indians passed with it.[41]

Such an agreement, the court ruled, could be terminated at will by either the provincial or federal government. Since Amerindian sovereignty had never been recognized, the 1752 agreement could not be classed as an international treaty.

That decision was upheld in 1958 in *Regina v. Simon* and again in 1969 in *Francis v. The Queen*; however, in the latter case, it was ruled that the treaties of 1725, 1752, and 1779 were still valid unless they had been changed by legislation 'properly enacted under the powers granted to the Government of Canada by Section 91 of the British North America Act'.[42] The federal Fisheries Act did just that in the following year, 1970. That situation remained until 1985, when the Supreme Court of Canada ruled in *Simon v. The Queen* that the 1752 agreement was still valid and only could be superseded by federal legislation, not provincial. In the eyes of the Mi'kmaq, the new decision meant that their rights were neither outmoded nor set aside.[43] Although the validity of the 1752 treaty has been upheld, its status as an international treaty was not. In the words of the ruling, an 'Indian treaty is unique: it is an agreement *sui generis* which is neither created nor terminated according to the rules of international law.'[44] Presumably, the same principle applies to other Amerindian treaties.

Similarly, usufructuary rights have been upheld in general by other provincial courts. In British Columbia, these were confirmed on appeal in *Regina v. White and Bob*, in 1965, on the basis they had existed since 'time immemorial'. The case had concerned the Saalequun tribe on Vancouver Island, which had ceded land to Governor Douglas in 1854 (see Chapter

16) but had reserved hunting rights for its members in those areas that remained unoccupied. In 1964 tribal members had been charged with possession of six deer carcasses outside of the hunting season as legislated by the British Columbia Game Act of 1960 (Amerindians had been under provincial hunting and trapping regulation since 1915); on appeal, it was ruled that treaty rights prevailed over provincial game laws.[45] The lawyer for the Amerindians was Thomas Berger, who would head the Mackenzie Valley Pipeline Inquiry of 1974–7. The decision was upheld by the Supreme Court, but on the basis of treaty rights; Aboriginal rights were not mentioned. Similar judgments have come down in other provinces. A major exception has been Quebec. Since it had no treaties to override its legislation, it has claimed the right to regulate hunting and fishing. Indian resistance in 1981 led to 400 heavily armed provincial police, backed by bulldozers and helicopters, raiding the Restigouche Reserve community and confiscating 250 kilograms of salmon and more than 75 nets. A second raid followed two days later, in which tear gas was used and the bridge linking the reserve to Campbellton, New Brunswick, was blocked. The Amerindians in their turn blockaded the four roads leading into their reserve. After the police left the reserve an agreement on fishing rights was reached.[46]

Federal game laws, on the other hand, have been held to prevail over treaties. The Migratory Birds Convention Act of 1960 was challenged in a series of cases, of which the following can be considered to be representative: *Regina v. Sikyea*, 1964 and 1965; *The Queen v. George*, 1966; and *Regina v. Cooper*, 1969.[47] In all of these cases the judgments confirmed the principle of the primacy of federal legislation over treaty provisions. Other cases, such as that of *Daniels v. the Queen*, 1968, and subsequent ones, have supported this position.

In other aspects of Aboriginal rights, the courts displayed less tolerance of Amerindian claims. For example, in British Columbia in 1969, Frank Calder, founder and president (1955–74) of the Nisga'a Tribal Council (now the Nisga'a Nation),[48] maintained that his people's Aboriginal title had never been extinguished and that none of their territory had been ceded to Britain. In *Calder v. Attorney General* he repeated what another spokesman had told a Royal Commission in 1888:

> What we don't like about the government is their saying this: 'We will give you this much land.' How can they give it when it is our own? We cannot understand it. They have never bought it from us or our forefathers. They have never fought or conquered our people and taken the land in that way, and yet they say now that they will give us so much land—our own land. . . . It has been ours for a thousand years.[49]

Consequently, Calder argued, provincial land legislation was invalid.

The BC Supreme Court ruled that whatever rights Indians might have possessed at time of contact had been overruled by the mere enactment of white man's law, in spite of the fact that none of the legislation so stated. In 1973, the Supreme Court of Canada upheld the ruling (on a vote of four to three) on a technicality.[50] Six of the bench felt that Aboriginal right existed but that it was 'dependent upon the goodwill of the Sovereign'; however, there was no agreement as to the present state of Nisga'a rights. The split had not been over the existence of Aboriginal rights as such but how they were to be interpreted and dealt with. As Justice J. Judson put it, 'The fact is that when the settlers came the Indians were there, organized in societies and occupying the land as their forefathers had done for centuries. This is what Indian title means.'[51] Justice Emmett Hall went further, stating that if possession were nine points of the law then the Nisga'a had undoubted possession of their lands in the Nass Valley and that the sole authority to extinguish their title was that of the federal government.

Pierre Trudeau, Prime Minister, 1968–79 and 1980–4, assessing this judgment, decided there was a legal case for Aboriginal rights, in spite of his earlier rejection of the concept.[52] Conceding that Amerindians might have more rights than he had recognized in the White Paper of 1969, he entrenched them without definition in the Constitution Act of 1982, despite a determined assault by the provincial premiers to prevent it. This partial constitutional victory for Aboriginal rights did not entail acceptance by the courts, as the *Bear Island* case illustrates.

The Bear Island Case

By far the most exhaustive legal examination to that time of Aboriginal rights occurred in *Attorney General of Ontario v. Bear Island Foundation*, 1984. At issue was the legal nature of the continuing interest of the Teme-agama Anishnabay (Bear Island people) in their ancestral lands, about 10,360 square kilometres (4,000 square miles) in and around Lake Temagami, against a provincial government that wished to open up the area for resource and tourist development. It had taken 20 years for the Teme-agama claim to reach the negotiating table, only to have discussion break down almost immediately and come before the court. The trial lasted 120 days; dozens of witnesses appeared and 3,000 exhibits were filed. The Teme-agama argued that not only was their identity deeply rooted in the region, but no representative of their people had signed the Robinson treaties.

Justice Donald Steele responded with a 284-page decision reiterating Judge Boyd's position from the *St Catherine's Milling* case—that the British Crown was the only ultimate source of legitimate authority in Canada and that whatever rights Amerindians possess stem from the Proclamation of 1763. In other words, in his view, the Proclamation is the source of Aboriginal rights in British territories, not a confirmation of pre-existing rights. He expanded this: 'Aboriginal rights exist at the pleasure of the Crown, and they can be extinguished by treaty, legislation, or administrative acts.'

In Judge Steele's view, the British Crown had acquired its rights in Canada by conquest, first against the French (he did not explain how that related to Amerindian title) and then against Pontiac in 1763. He made no mention of the Amerindian allies who had fought for the British on those occasions. The primitive level of Amerindian social organization, the judge wrote, meant that 'the Indian occupation could not be considered true and legal, and that the Europeans were lawfully entitled to take possession of the land and settle it with colonies.'[53] In his view, the only law is statutory law, that which has been legislated by an organized state; according to this interpretation, common law could not be deemed law unless enshrined in a court decision. Judge Steele's decision was upheld in 1989 on the basis of new evidence to the effect that during the Robinson negotiations the Teme-agama had sold their land for $25.

As historian Anthony J. Hall has pointed out, a legal problem that underlay this trial, as well as that in *St Catherine's Milling*, relates to the BNA Act of 1867. According to its terms, Ottawa was given responsibility for 'Indians, and Lands reserved for Indians'. However, section 109 stipulated that 'all Lands, Mines, Minerals and Royalties' from the land were to be the proprietary interest of the four provinces that first made up Confederation. (The prairie provinces obtained control of their natural resources in 1930.) This separation of powers has meant that the provinces have a vested interest in opposing Aboriginal land claims.[54]

British law has not always been as intransigent towards Aboriginal land rights as it has been in Canada. For instance, in *Queen v. Symonds* (1847), in New Zealand, the presiding judge stated:

> Whatever may be the opinion of jurists as to the strength or weakness of Native title . . . it cannot be too solemnly asserted that it is to be respected, and that it cannot be extinguished (at least in times of peace) otherwise than by the free consent of the Native occupiers.[55]

Political philosopher John Locke (1632–1704) argued that when Amerindians signed treaties with non-Amerindians the bonds they established were for specific purposes rather than being a comprehensive subordination of Amerindians to the will of non-Amerindians. That was an argument Big Bear would have understood; unfortunately, he was not able to cite the British authority. Locke called this the principle of contractual treaty of commonwealth. Thus, British law implicitly recognized existing rights of Native government. It also recognized Amerindian proprietary rights, as witnessed by its policy of compensation for the acquisition of Amerindian lands.

Inadequacy of Systems

In the meantime, there were (and are) serious concerns as to the adequacy of existing systems—whether by direct negotiation with the government or through the courts—to deal with Amerindian claims. Amerindians have long been convinced of this,[56] but alternatives have not been easy to work out. In 1890 formal arbitration was attempted with the establishment of a board to deal with disputes between Canada, Ontario, and Quebec. Amerindians were allowed little opportunity to participate, and in only one case were they even permitted to select their own lawyers. During its decade of existence (it lasted until the early 1900s), the board heard about 20 cases dealing with disputes over financial matters as well as grievances concerning lands. It succeeded in settling only three of these cases; two others of its decisions were later reversed by the courts. In short, it had been ineffective in dealing with Amerindian claims.

Legislation to establish an Indian Claims Commission began to be seriously considered in 1961; three years later, a conference to study the question was organized by the National Indian Council (formed in 1960) and funded by the department. An avalanche of submissions—about 300—was the result; on the whole, Indians were doubtful about the efficacy of the proposal. Eventually, in 1969, in the wake of the White Paper, Dr Lloyd Barber, vice-president of the University of Saskatchewan, was appointed Indian Claims Commissioner, with a mandate to receive and study grievances and to suggest the processes by which particular claims could best be adjudicated. The mandate excluded Aboriginal rights, reflecting Trudeau's personal rejection of the concept at that time, and so was greeted with suspicion on the part of Indians. The first hint of a change in Trudeau's position came during the Commission's second year, when its terms of reference were broadened to include comprehensive claims (claims arising in non-treaty areas), which opened the door for Dr Barber to consider Aboriginal rights. Although government policy did not officially change until after the Nisga'a (*Calder*) decision in 1973 and the Commission's life was short (it lasted until 1977), Dr Barber won high praise from Indian rights activist Harold Cardinal because of his even-handed approach and willingness to listen to all sides, which helped to narrow the gap between the government and the Amerindians.[57]

In his final report, Barber observed that claims could only be dealt with satisfactorily when Natives established their position through research. In other words, it was up to the Amerindians themselves to establish their claims, rather than waiting for others to do the right thing by them. He did not resolve the basic principles by which claims could be evaluated or what kind of mechanism would be best for their resolution. A Joint National Indian Brotherhood/Cabinet Committee, established in 1975, lasted for only three years before the Amerindians withdrew, and a Canadian Indian Rights Commission did not endure much longer. Reconciling national and regional priorities had been a major difficulty. It would be 1991 before the present Indian Claims Commission was established.

The department has consistently considered the courts to be a last resort for dealing with claims. As far as the Amerindians are concerned, litigation presents hazards, not the least of which is cost. While restrictions against Amerindians raising funds for such a purpose were removed in 1951, departmental funds available to them for research cannot be used for litigation without departmental consent.[58] Other aspects of the problem are considered in Chapter 26.

Amerindian Concepts of Land and Land Rights

The pressure of non-Native claims to their territories has led Indians to develop traditional concepts in contemporary terms. Native cyclical and holistic ways of viewing the world translate into land being held as common property by the tribal nation as a whole. Tribal members have an undivided interest in the land; everyone, as a member of the group, has a right to the whole. Furthermore, rights to the use of land belong not only to the living but to those who have gone before as well as to those who will come; neither do they belong exclusively to humans, but to other living things as well—animals, plants, sometimes (under spe-

cial circumstances) even rocks. The social contract embraces all living things. This concept of sharing with other forms of life is, of course, alien to Judeo-Christian thought. So is the Amerindian position that the original recipients of the Creator's largesse retain their rights as long as they or their descendants inhabit the earth; not included was the right to give that up. As the Indians see it, absolute ownership was not granted by the Creator.

Sharing did not mean giving up one's rights. When Amerindians signed treaties, they could not give up absolute ownership of the land because they never claimed it for themselves. During the eighteenth century, when the Abenaki had sought to curb English settlement on the east coast by asserting their territorial rights (Chapter 7), they were not claiming absolute ownership but the right to control the use of the land's resources. Geographer Conrad Heidenreich, however, argues that in the case of agricultural people such as the Huron, this was tantamount in practice to individual ownership.[59] Not so, say the Indians; the Huron system, like that of other Amerindian agricultural communities, reflected a communal ideology of land use, not that of individual ownership. The Crown, to claim absolute title, would have to obtain surrenders from past generations as well as those of the future. As far as Amerindians are concerned, when they signed treaties, they were not alienating their lands but sharing them.[60] They were astonished at the idea that their hunting and fishing rights originated with the Proclamation of 1763; in their view, those rights had always existed. The treaties had confirmed an already existing situation, subject to limitation only in areas where settlement had occurred. A Gitksan–Carrier (Wet'suwet'en) declaration in 1977 wasted no words: 'Recognize our Sovereignty, recognize our rights, so that we may fully recognize yours.'[61]

It is interesting in this connection to compare

Canada's approach to that of the United States, as both countries developed their legal systems from a common British base. But where the courts in Canada saw state organization, sovereignty, and property rights as being inseparably linked, the American courts had no difficulty in recognizing sovereignty in common law, quite apart from the state. The decisions of Chief Justice John Marshall (1755–1835) in *Johnson v. McIntosh* (1823) and *Worcester v. Georgia* (1832) in this regard have become classic: while acknowledging that 'power, war, conquest, give rights, which, after possession, are conceded by the world', he did not see them as extending beyond the 'exclusive right to purchase'. While this exclusive right diminished the sovereignty of the original nations by limiting their independence of action in selling their lands, it did not eliminate it.[62] From this arose the American concept of domestic dependent nations, a concept Canada has not acknowledged, although the Nisga'a treaty indicates a trend in that direction (see below).

For a while there was some movement in the Canadian courts away from the position they have held since the *St Catherine's Milling* decision. The first of these was *Baker Lake v. Minister of Indian Affairs and Northern Development* in 1980, in which the court listed the conditions that had to be met for it to find an Aboriginal title to be valid. They were: the Natives had to establish that they and their ancestors lived within, and were members of, organized societies; these societies occupied the specific territory over which they were claiming Aboriginal title; their occupation was exclusive; and this occupation was in effect when England claimed sovereignty over the region. The people at Baker Lake met these conditions and so won their case.[63]

The pre-existence of Aboriginal right before colonization and its survival afterwards were again acknowledged in *Guerin v. The Queen* (1984, the Musqueam case), when it was found to be a 'burden on the radical or final title of the Sovereign'.[64] The *Guerin* case had the further significance of recognizing the federal government's fiduciary responsibility towards Amerindians, in its turn a direct consequence of the Crown reserving to itself the right to acquire Amerindian lands in the Proclamation of 1763. In assuming that role, the government had also implicitly assumed the responsibility of always acting in the best interest of the Indians. In *Guerin* the government had leased 65 hectares of the band's lands to a Vancouver golf club at a rental far below prevailing rates and then had misrepresented the situation to the band. When the Musqueam finally got their hands on a copy of the lease 12 years later, they lost no time in going to court, which found that Indian Affairs had failed in its duties as a trustee.[65]

On the other side of the picture, a consequence has been the Musqueam band's move to sharply raise its rents to bring them into line with prevailing real estate values, particularly where their lands are located in what has become a prime residential section of Vancouver. As a result, 73 non-Aboriginal leaseholders who had built homes in the area found their rents skyrocketing from around $375 a year to $20,000 and even higher. When they complained, the federal government ruled in the band's favour, a decision that was later overturned by the Supreme Court of Canada with a tight 5–4 majority when it assessed the Musqueam's land as being worth only half the market value because of 'the political uncertainty and potential unrest' it saw as being typical of Indian reserves. Consequently, it ruled, the band could not charge more than $10,000 for a leaseholder's annual rent. The ramifications of the decision will be felt nationally, particularly in Ontario, where a majority of the non-Native leaseholders are located. It is estimated that they number about 60,000. For Musqueam Chief Ernie Campbell it was 'a sad day for this country' that saw land value being determined by the race of the owner. He foresaw it as limiting the future development of First Nations. In the view of the leaseholders, the value of reserve land is governed by the fact that it cannot be owned outright, rather than by the racial factor.[66] In the meantime, consequences were already being felt by the band, as its move to raise its rents so drastically had not been unanimous. In fact, it had caused a split, because the decision was said to have been reached at a meeting when only a small minority of band members were in attendance.[67] Incidentally, another BC nation, the Katzie of Pitt Lake, announced that it would not renew current leases on its lands when they became due in 2004. Unlike the Musqueam, it was said that it was not renegotiating rents.[68]

Three other recent cases have been widely viewed as representing a turning point in the Canadian legal approach to Aboriginal right, a consequence of section 35 of the Constitution Act, 1982.[69] The first of these, *Sparrow v. R.* (1987), concerned a BC Native who had used a fishing net larger than that allowed by law. The Court found that Aboriginal fishing, land, and hunting rights for food, social, and ceremonial purposes had priority over later restrictive legislation, and Sparrow was acquitted.[70] This interpretation of Aboriginal right was supported in *R. v. Adams* (1996) when the Supreme Court of Canada ruled that George Weldon Adams, a Mohawk, had a right to fish for food in Lake St Francis, contrary to Quebec fishery regulations. Such fishing, it was found, was an Aboriginal custom integral to traditional Mohawk culture in that region.[71] In the *Sioui* case (1990), the Court ruled that a 230-year-old safe-conduct was in effect a treaty and so took precedence over later laws.[72] The rights in question in both these cases relate to self-government, a consequence of what Justice Bertha Wilson has referred to as 'the Indians' historic occupation and possession of their tribal lands'.[73]

This trend received a sharp check in March 1991 when Justice Allan McEachern, in *Delgamuukw v. British Columbia*, rejected the claim of the Gitksan and Wet'suwet'en to Aboriginal right over 58,000 square kilometres of traditional lands in northern British Columbia, a resource-rich area about the size of Nova Scotia. As with most of the province's territory, it had never been ceded by treaty, nor had the people been conquered. The case had been launched in the British Columbia Supreme Court in May 1987 by 48 Gitksan and Wet'suwet'en hereditary chiefs; more than 100 witnesses were heard over nearly four years, making it the longest such hearing in Canada so far. It was also the most expensive, estimated to have cost $25 million. The judge toured the area of the claim and is reported to have read 10,000 documents. His conclusion went further than that of the *St Catherine's Milling* decision, and denied the existence of Aboriginal rights of ownership and jurisdiction; what rights the Natives possess are those of sustenance, which are a continuing burden on the right of the Crown. According to the judge, 'it is part of the law of nations, which has become part of common law, that the discovery and occupation of lands of this continent by European nations, or occupation and settlement, gave rise to the right of sovereignty.' He found that in this case the Crown had extinguished Aboriginal right before Confederation. McEachern did concede, however, that Indians have the right to use unoccupied Crown lands for traditional purposes, such as hunting and berry-picking, as long as they are within prevailing provincial laws.[74] The judgment was upheld by the BC Court of Appeal,[75] but then, in 1997, was overturned by the Supreme Court of Canada with the argument that oral tradition had not been given sufficient weight. It ruled that since oral histories are often the only evidence available, they must be considered 'as a repository of historical knowledge for

Gitksan dance group performs outside the Supreme Court of Canada at the opening of the Gitksan–Wet'suwet'en land-claims appeal, 1997.
(The Canadian Press/Fred Chartrand)

a culture'. Justice Brian Dickson stated: 'Claims to aboriginal title are woven with history, legend, politics and moral obligations.' In the Supreme Court's opinion, the laws of evidence must be adapted to place oral history on an equal footing with other types of evidence accepted in law, instead of being classed as hearsay, as was the prevailing practice.[76] It recommended that the case be reheard.

That decision greatly speeded up the final negotiations for the Nisga'a Final Agreement Act (Nisga'a treaty), ratified by Parliament in 2000 after 22 years at the bargaining table and nearly 200 years of lobbying on the part of the Nisga'a. It gave them self-governing rights to 1,900 square kilometres of land (8 per cent of the area they originally claimed) in exchange for giving up their tax-free status under the Indian Act (for details, see Chapter 28). Hailed as a breakthrough marking 'a new understanding between cultures',[77] the basic land claim had been enormously strengthened by the Supreme Court's decision regarding oral evidence. In the meantime, however, it has met strong opposition from both Aboriginal and non-Aboriginal sources. The Aboriginal challenges come from both within and without the Nisga'a Nation. From without, they concern competing claims for the land assigned to the Nisga'a: a neighbouring nation, the Gitanyow, has already resorted to the courts to press its counterclaim. Another neighbour, the Gitksan,

Donald Marshall Jr, at a press conference in Dartmouth, NS, following his acquittal, 10 May 1983.
(The Canadian Press/Albert Lee)

is still negotiating. From within, the challenge concerns the authority of the Nisga'a Tribal Council, which tribal dissenters see as not acting in accord with Aboriginal law.[78] The non-Aboriginal challenge, by the provincial Liberal Party, claims that the treaty is in violation of the Constitution Act of 1982 on the grounds that the self-government powers the treaty grants the Nisga'a will effectively make the band a state within a state. It was defeated by the BC Supreme Court when it ruled that the self-government powers in question are limited, and that the treaty expressly provides that in the case of conflict between Nisga'a laws and federal or provincial laws, the latter will prevail.[79] The Liberals have announced they will appeal.

The Chippewas of Sarnia, Ontario, were not so fortunate in their suit to regain 1,030 hectares of the city's land, which had been improperly surrendered nearly 150 years ago. The Ontario Court of Appeal ruled that the social cost of returning the land would be unacceptably high, causing great havoc and hardship. An appeal to the Supreme Court of Canada is considered likely.[80] In the midst of this complex legal scene, the 3,000-member Squamish Nation in its turn reached an out-of-court settlement in an omnibus trust action they had filed with the British Columbia Supreme Court in 1977 against the federal government. At issue was the expropriation and sale over the past century of about 600 hectares of land that had been set aside for the Natives. Settlement was reached when the Squamish

Two Natives in a dory check out one of their boats that was rammed and sunk by a Department of Fisheries and Oceans boat, 29 August 2000. The clash occurred when Fisheries personnel sought to retrieve lobster traps set by Natives off the coast of the Burnt Church Reserve in northern New Brunswick.

(The Canadian Press/Jacques Boissinot)

accepted Ottawa's offer of $92.5 million to give up their claim to the reserved lands, which included 35 hectares at Kitsilano Point, as well as parcels in North Vancouver and other areas of prime real estate.[81]

A decision that had explosive consequences was reached in 1999, when the Supreme Court of Canada acquitted Donald Marshall Jr, a Mi'kmaq, of charges under the Fisheries Act concerning the taking and sale of fish as a treaty right outside of the regulated season. (This was the same Marshall who had been jailed for 11 years for a murder of which he was exonerated in 1983.) Although Marshall's case had concerned eels, the consequences

were felt on the lobster fishing grounds when non-Native fishermen reacted against the differential imposition of restrictions by destroying Native lobster traps in New Brunswick's Miramichi Bay. The confrontation escalated in spite of a clarification from the Supreme Court that 'the treaty right . . . can be contained by regulation', a qualification not accepted by the Burnt Church band. In this they are supported by the legal argument that fishing is an Aboriginal right and therefore cannot be 'granted' by treaty.[82] Besides, the Indians insist that the few traps they set, compared to those set by non-Natives, do not represent a threat to lobster stocks. The Court's original interpretation of the 1760–1 treaties had been based on the view that they allowed First Nations the right to engage freely in traditional activities to the extent required to provide a moderate livelihood. The question of regulation was not touched upon. Bob Rae, the former Premier of Ontario, called to mediate the increasingly bitter two-month tug-of-war, finally brokered an agreement by which the Burnt Church band agreed to stop fishing on 7 October 2000, more than three weeks earlier than they had planned. By then the lobsters had already started their seasonal migration to colder waters, making them more difficult to catch. Also by then, Native fishing gear had been seized, a Department of Fisheries and Oceans boat had rammed a Native boat broadside, demolishing it and hurling its Mi'kmaq occupants into the water, and several Natives had been arrested. There the matter rests, with both the Mi'kmaq and the Department of Fisheries and Oceans claiming the right to regulate the fishery. Something of the difficulties hindering an agreement was illustrated by the Shubenacadie Mi'kmaq when they decided to go ahead and take advantage of the next commercial lobster season on their own terms. In the meantime, however, a compromise agreement has been generally agreed upon.[83]

Across the continent, on Vancouver Island, a fisheries dispute reverses the point at issue: there, non-Native sports fishermen are seeking to overturn an injunction that bars them from fishing on a section of the Big Qualicum River that runs through the Qualicum First Nation reserve. The possibility that the injunction will lead to the loss of public access in other rivers as well has led the anglers to launch an appeal to the BC Supreme Court.[84]

Another landmark decision, this one applying to hunting, was that of the Ontario Court of Appeal, when it ruled early in 2001 that the Métis, as a distinct Aboriginal people, have the constitutional right to hunt for food out of sea-son and without a licence. The case at issue dated back to 1993, when Steve and Roddy Powley were charged under the Game and Fish Act with unlawful possession of a moose and hunting without a licence. The two men, as members of the Métis community at Sault Ste Marie, claimed Aboriginal hunting rights. In the legal battles that followed, the charges were finally dismissed by the Ontario Superior Court early in 2000. This was the decision that was upheld in 2001 by the Ontario Court of Appeal, the province's highest court. It gave Ontario a year to work out its accommodation to the ruling. As its last resort, the province appealed to the Supreme Court of Canada (see Chapter 29).

The jubilant reaction of the Métis had less to do with hunting than with the fact that this was the first time a Canadian appellate court has recognized the legal existence of the Métis nation. Its effects will be major, even though it stopped short of defining the Métis as a people. The prevalent practice of denying Métis Aboriginal rights on the grounds that they lack legal definition received short shrift from Justice Robert C. Sharpe. 'While I do not doubt there has been considerable uncertainty about the nature and scope of Métis rights, this is hardly a reason to deny their existence.' He added that in spite of their 1982 constitutional recognition, there has been no serious effort anywhere in Canada to deal with Métis rights.[85] The Ontario government had based its case against the Powleys on the argument that without a legal definition by the courts, the Métis did not exist as a distinct nation.[86]

While the appellate court's decision applies only to hunting, the feeling is that it has opened the door for acknowledging that Métis have Aboriginal rights in other aspects of resource harvesting.[87]

As all this indicates, attempts to keep contentious Indian Affairs issues out of court have had only limited success. As the high-profile lobster standoff and now the Métis decision illustrate only too clearly, long-range planning is needed to prevent future clashes. Land also looms large as a contentious issue, and promises to keep the courts busy for many years to come. The government estimated that it would spend nearly half a billion dollars on land claims alone in 2001.[88] That is not to say, however, that other issues, such as tax exemption for Aboriginal business projects, will not be intervening.[89]

Chapter 24

First Nations at Home and Abroad

Six Nations and the League of Nations

During the 1920s, the Six Nations formed the largest and wealthiest Native group in the country.[1] As noted in Chapter 12, their principal reserve in southern Ontario had been established in 1784 after they had lost most of their original homelands in northern New York as a result of siding with the British in the American War of Independence. Following their disruption by that war and the subsequent Peace of Paris of 1783, the Iroquois had experienced a nativistic religious revival with Christian overtones. The prophet was the Seneca chief Ganiodaio ('Handsome Lake'), half-brother of Cornplanter, who through a series of visions beginning in 1799 had received instructions as to how the Iroquois should conduct themselves in their changed circumstances.[2] A strict code of ethics that included the Christian belief in heaven and hell as well as traditional Iroquoian elements such as belief in witchcraft, it became known as the Longhouse religion and became a powerful force in restoring cultural self-confidence. It

did not re-establish the shattered unity of the League, however; the Iroquois, who were now divided between two countries, as well as being scattered on various reserves, were also divided as to religion—Christianity and Longhouse—and in politics between those who accepted the new order and the traditonalists. As far as the country at large was concerned, their main claim to fame during the nineteenth century was as rivermen; when the British needed canoemen for their expedition up the Nile to relieve Khartoum, they recruited principally at Kahnawake.[3]

Autonomy an Old Issue

The Six Nations have a long record of arguing for autonomy, on the grounds that they had been sovereign allies of the British, dating back to the mid-seventeenth century. They had fought in Britain's colonial wars, first against the French and then against the Americans. They had received the Six Nations Reserve—Haldimand's Grant—because they were 'His Majesty's Allies', which they were to 'enjoy forever' under the King's 'protection'. (Apparently they were

TIMELINE

1896	Land set aside in Alberta for exclusive use of Métis at Saint-Paul-des-Métis.	1934	Royal Commission Appointed to Investigate the Conditions of the Half-Breeds of Alberta (Ewing Commission).
1922	Armed confrontation between Iroquois and RCMP.		
1923–4	Iroquois take their claim to sovereignty to League of Nations; case is dropped after British intervention at League of Nations.	1938	Alberta's Métis Population Betterment Act leads to creation of 10 Métis colonies, of which eight still exist.
1924	Ludger Bastien first Native elected to Quebec legislature.	1979	Métis legal action for $500 million in oil and gas revenues leads to Alberta government raids on settlement offices.
1930	L'Association des Métis d'Alberta et des Territoires du Nord Ouest organized.		

unaware of the terms of the Treaty of Utrecht, 1713, by which Britain claimed the Five Nations [as the league was then] as her 'subjects'.) Once the colonial wars were ended, however, they became very much aware that their status had changed; in 1839, when they demanded that they be governed according to their own laws, the authorities of Upper Canada refused to consider such a possibility.

Not surprisingly, the restrictions imposed by the Indian Act of 1876, and particularly by its subsequent amendments, without any Amerindian input, were deeply resented. The Six Nations challenged their underlying assumptions and thus the very foundations of federal policy: they rejected the authority of the department and of the Act it administered. Principal advocates of self-government were the hereditary chiefs, who once again, in 1890, petitioned Ottawa for recognition of their autonomy and exemption from the Indian Act. Again, they were rebuffed.

An amendment that year empowered the department to implement an elective system without the approval of the Amerindians involved. Although the department was reluctant to do so without the consent of the peo-

ple, it still saw the elective system as a means of satisfying the Indian desire for self-government, at least at the municipal level. In the department's view, the hereditary form of government encouraged adherence to an outmoded system that was ill-adapted to the needs of the contemporary world. Among the Natives, supporters of the new system, called 'Dehorners',[4] tended to be younger individuals, mostly Christian. Traditionalists were mainly older individuals who followed the Longhouse religion. In 1907 the Dehorners tried to work up a petition asking for the electoral system but could muster only 300 signatures—about one-quarter of the adult male population. Some traditionalists under Levi General (1873–1925), who held the Cayuga title Deskaheh, countered with a demand for complete sovereignty, while a third group took a middle position and urged as much co-operation with the department as possible. In the ensuing power struggle, Deskaheh won the day.

With the close of World War I, the Six Nations established a committee to campaign for sovereignty. The government countered with an amendment to the Indian Act that abolished tribal governments. A Six Nations

Deskaheh (Levi General), who travelled on an Iroquois passport, gained support in Europe for Six Nations sovereignty, but London intervened to make his appeal to the League of Nations futile. Upon his return in early 1925 after more than a year in Geneva and London, he was denied entry to Canada and spent the few months before his death later that year at the Tuscarora Reservation near Niagara Falls, New York.
(#446 John Kahionhes Fadden/Deskaheh)

petition to get the Supreme Court of Canada to decide whether they were allies or subjects of the Crown got nowhere and aroused little public concern. When the Six Nations tried to take its case to London, the British referred it back to Ottawa. However, there was much more public sympathy for the Six Nations cause in Europe than in Canada.

An armed confrontation between Iroquois and the RCMP in 1922, in which shots were fired, led the Iroquois to look for means to bring their case before an international tribunal. At the newly formed League of Nations, the Netherlands agreed to act as intermediary. Canada was in an awkward position, as it was still not free of colonial status and consequently not a full-fledged member of the League (a status it would not attain until 1925). When the case came before the League's secretary-general in 1923, Canada argued that it was a domestic matter and thus beyond the League's jurisdiction. In the meantime, Deskaheh, waging an effective campaign in London, issued a pamphlet entitled 'The Redman's Appeal for Justice', in which he maintained that all the Iroquois were asking for was home rule, much as the colonies had done a century earlier. Forced to reply, Canada claimed that because the gradual transfer of power from London to Ottawa in the Constitutional Act of 1791, the Act of Union of 1840, and the BNA Act of 1867 had made no special provision for the Six Nations or any other Amerindians, they had been included in the general package. A group of nations (Estonia, Ireland, Panama, Persia) rallied to the Six Nations' cause; when they were joined by Norway, the Netherlands, and Albania, London intervened, charging that 'minor powers' were interfering in the British Empire's 'internal affairs'. The case was dropped in 1924. A direct appeal by Deskaheh to George V brought no result.

The Imposition of Elective Council

In the meantime, Canada had appointed an investigator to examine the question of government on reserves as well as charges of mismanagement of Six Nations trust funds. The investigator could find no virtue in tribal government and recommended the institution of an elective system at the earliest possible date; he did not suggest a referendum. The decision was implemented without delay, and in 1924 an elective council was imposed on the Six Nations and the hereditary council abolished, according to the provisions of the 1920 amendment to the Indian Act. The elective system did not accord women the vote; under the hereditary system, women had had an important voice in the selection of chiefs. Ironically, at this time, 1924, a chief of the Loretteville Hurons, Ludger Bastien, became the first Native to be elected to a provincial legislature, that of Quebec.[5]

The department's high-handed introduction of elections to the Six Nations drew criticism in Canada as well as in Europe, not only because it was considered to be autocratic but also because it violated the terms of both the Haldimand Grant and the Simcoe Deed. The Haldimand document simply granted the Grand River lands to the Amerindians 'to enjoy forever'. The Simcoe Deed had been more specific, granting:

> the full and entire possession, use, benefit and advantage of the said district or territory to be held and enjoyed by them in the most free and ample manner, and according to the several customs and usages of them the said chiefs, warriors, women, and people of the said Six Nations.[6]

Despite such phrases as 'entire possession' and 'free and ample manner', Duncan Campbell Scott, the investigator, took a restrictive view of the above passage, claiming that it only referred to Aboriginal customs of land tenure and transfer, not to governing practices. In his view, the Iroquois could only benefit from British laws, which were 'civilizing and protective under all circumstances'.[7] As for the international criticism, it was seen as meddling in domestic affairs. A latter-day development has been the rise of the traditional confederacy council. This council has been recognized by the federal government, in the context of the negotiations on the current Caledonia issue (see Chapter 29).

Deskaheh's untimely death in 1925 dealt a heavy blow to the Iroquois independence movement; police activity on the reserve increased. But the movement did not die; in fact, it developed, nurtured as it was by a sense of betrayal of a historic alliance. It erupted again in 1928, when the hereditary chiefs declared independence. With rhetoric borrowed from the American model, they renounced allegiance to Canada and the British Crown. Although not taken seriously in official circles, the declaration attracted considerable press coverage. The Six Nations followed it up with still another delegation to London in 1930. It did not capture public imagination as Deskaheh had done; running out of money, the delegation had to return home.

The fight for sovereignty was far from over, however. In 1942, Kahnawake requested that their tribal laws replace the Indian Act. When the Act was revised in 1951, Iroquois from various reserves mounted a campaign against the changes, claiming that they were dictatorial and would retard their progress as a nation. During that same decade, Kahnawake took the Canadian government to court over lands expropriated for the St Lawrence Seaway; despite their resistance, the Iroquois lost 526 hectares (1,300 acres), which meant that the reserve was deprived of its river frontage, a cultural and economic blow for a people famed for their river expertise.[8] The Mohawks finally won a $1.5 million settlement in 1963 after 17 years of bitter negotiations. At one point they petitioned the United Nations to prevent land confiscations 'by brute force'.[9] In the meantime, they are charging licence fees to duck hunters and fishermen along the six-mile section of the St Lawrence Seaway that passes through the reserve. Such a measure is, of course, reminiscent of the tolls charged for rights of passage in pre-contact days. After losing an island to Expo 67, the Iroquois moved against the Euro-Canadians living on the reserve and evicted about a thousand of them in 1973 on the grounds of overcrowding.[10]

The result of all this was the deterioration of the band's relationship with the Quebec provincial police, to the point that in 1969 it established its own police force, called Peace-keepers, which eventually became the official law enforcement agency on the reserve.[11] More recently the Warrior movement—described as the defence arm of the Longhouse but not universally accepted as such—has gained support among those who felt that the Peacekeepers did not take a strong enough stand.[12] When the RCMP raided Kahnawake's cigarette stores[13] in 1988, the Warriors rallied the Iroquois to block the south entrance to Mercier Bridge, located on reserve land and connecting the Island of Montreal with the south shore. The standoff lasted 27 hours, with armed Warriors patrolling the bridge, 'the first instance of armed native resistance in Canada's recent history'.[14] The RCMP responded by describing the Mohawk as 'violent'.[15] Sixteen persons were charged with smuggling. The stage was set for the 'Indian summer' of 1990, when Kahnawake would again block the bridge in support of Kanesatake in its confrontation at Oka. Although the blockade was of short duration, the standoff lasted 78 days, with the two besieged communities being virtually cut off from the outside world. The Canadian Police Association branded the Mohawk as 'terrorists'.[16] The behaviour of the Canadian government once more drew the censure of the international community.

The Iroquois, in the meantime, assert their independence from Canada by using their own passports when travelling abroad, which Cuba, for one country, formally recognized in 1958. The people of Kahnawake assert their independence from Quebec by defying the provincial language legislation, Bill 101, in contrast to the Huron and Iroquois of Loretteville, who speak French. This was dramatically highlighted when 41 Mohawks, charged with a variety of offences as a result of the Oka standoff, won the right to have their trial in English.

Previously, in the case of three other Mohawks also charged with offences arising out of the Oka confrontation, a court ruling had upheld the right of the prosecuting lawyers to present their case in French.[17] The Kahnawake Survival School, whose language of instruction is English, is solidly established on a $4 million campus.

Ewing Commission and Alberta Métis

The Royal Commission Appointed to Investigate the Conditions of the Half-Breeds of Alberta was established in 1934 with a mandate to hold hearings into the health, education, and general welfare of the province's Métis, to submit a report, and to make recommendations for the improvement of their situation.[18] It was a provincial initiative; the matter had been discussed with Ottawa, particularly as many of the destitute Métis were descendants of Amerindians who had taken treaty, but the federal authority did not see the Métis as coming under its jurisdiction.

The Commission accepted the definition of Métis given by the Métis Association of Alberta: 'anyone with any degree of Indian ancestry who lives the life ordinarily associated with the Métis'. The association would later extend its definition to include anyone who considered himself/herself a Métis and who was accepted by the community as such, a position supported by the Royal Commission on Aboriginal Peoples (RCAP).[19] Eventually, when Alberta amended its Métis Population Betterment Act in 1940, it defined a Métis as 'a person of mixed white and Indian ancestry having not less than one-quarter Indian blood' but did not include 'either an Indian or non-Treaty Indian as defined in the Indian Act'. This definition was designed to restrict the numbers of those who would be eligible for provincial benefits. More recently, the RCAP came out in support of

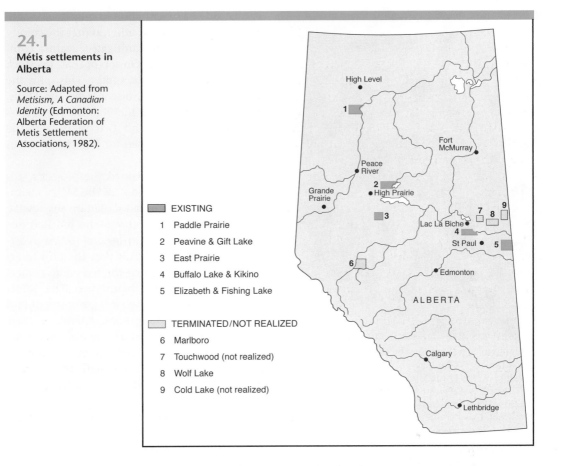

24.1

Métis settlements in Alberta

Source: Adapted from *Metisism, A Canadian Identity* (Edmonton: Alberta Federation of Metis Settlement Associations, 1982).

High Level

Fort McMurray

Peace River

1

Grande Prairie

2

High Prairie

3

Lac La Biche

4

St Paul

5

6

Edmonton

7   8   9

ALBERTA

Calgary

Lethbridge

EXISTING

1   Paddle Prairie

2   Peavine & Gift Lake

3   East Prairie

4   Buffalo Lake & Kikino

5   Elizabeth & Fishing Lake

TERMINATED/NOT REALIZED

6   Marlboro

7   Touchwood (not realized)

8   Wolf Lake

9   Cold Lake (not realized)

the view that Métis are in the same category as Indians under section 91(24) of the Constitution Act (BNA Act) of 1867, and has stated that their national culture was 'conceived in Quebec, gestated in Ontario, and born on the western plains'.[20]

As has already been noted, Métis considered that their Amerindian heritage had given them an unextinguishable right to land (Chapters 18, 20), and most of them did not accept that this right could be extinguished by treaty. As the West was settled by non-Aboriginals, the Métis became more and more scattered in small, impoverished bands. In 1895, Father Albert Lacombe approached Ottawa with a proposal to

establish a reserve for Métis where, under the guidance of the Catholic Church, they could be introduced to an agriculturally based mode of living. The government of Wilfrid Laurier (Liberal Prime Minister, 1896–1911) approved, seeing this as an alternative to scrip while also avoiding special status. However, it only contributed $2,000 to the project.

Saint-Paul-des-Métis was established the following year, 1896, the first time a tract of land was set aside for the exclusive use of the Métis. Four townships (92,160 acres, 37,296 hectares) near Saddle Lake Indian Reserve were leased for the project for 99 years at one dollar a year. Another four sections were set aside on

A Blackfoot delegation in 1886 in front of Earnscliffe, at that time the residence of Sir John A. Macdonald while he was Prime Minister. In front, left to right, North Axe, Peigan chief, and One Spot, a Blood subchief. Middle row: Three Bulls, half-brother of Crowfoot; Crowfoot, Blackfoot chief; and Red Cloud, Blood chief. Rear: Oblate Father Albert Lacombe and John L'Heureux, interpreter.
(Library and Archives Canada, PA-45666)

a separate lease for the site of a church, school, and priest's residence. The whole was under the direction of a syndicate that included the bishops of St Boniface, St Albert, and Prince Albert, as well as Father Lacombe, another cleric, and two laypersons. Each family was to receive 80 acres (32 hectares) as well as livestock and agricultural equipment and access to hay, grazing, and woodcutting.

The first year 30 families from across Alberta and Saskatchewan moved to St Paul; by 1897 there were 50 families, and two years later the Grey Nuns were operating a boarding school on the model of those for Amerindians.

Farmsteads had been allotted quickly enough, but far away from each other so that the colony was dispersed, which mitigated against community cohesiveness. On top of that, livestock and equipment did not appear. This, plus the general underfunding, discouraged the Métis, and they drifted away. In 1908, the Métis leases were terminated and two years later the reserve was thrown open for French-Canadian settlement.

The government blamed the project's failure on the lack of interest of the Métis, claiming that not enough had settled on the reserve to make it viable and those who did had not worked hard enough to become self-supporting. Undercapitalized as it was, the only alternative had been to open the reserve to settlers who could support themselves. The Métis claimed that even though the government had not fulfilled its obligations, many of their number had still succeeded; the real issue, they maintained, was the prospect of a Canadian Pacific Railway route through the region, which had enhanced the value of the land so that white settlers were clamouring to have it opened for general settlement. As the Métis saw it, church, government, and French Canadians had combined to ensure failure. A commission, set up to investigate Métis farmstead claims, disallowed 19 of the 63 that were presented, on account of non-residence.

Although some became successful farmers, most of the Métis drifted north, squatting on unsurveyed Crown lands where they could hunt, trap, and fish. The Métis settlements that sprang up tended to be on the fringes of white settlements: they were the 'road allowance people', living hand-to-mouth.[21] The province's Métis population at this time has been variously estimated at from 12,000 to 75,000. The onset of the Great Depression meant that Métis who had been barely eking out an existence now faced disaster. In 1930 they organized l'Association des Métis d'Alberta et des

Territoires du Nord Ouest; the first president was Joseph Dion (1888–1960), an enfranchised adopted nephew of Big Bear who was teaching on Keehewin Indian Reserve; his book, *My Tribe the Crees*, presented a Native view of the 1885 troubles. In 1940 the Association was reorganized and its title changed to the Métis Association of Alberta through the efforts of activists Malcolm Norris (1900–67) and James Brady (1908–67).[22] Since then the Association has grown from 50 to its present membership of about 3,000. Taking up the cause of land settlement projects for Métis, it reported that by the end of October 1933, 348 families had been resettled in northern Alberta. Impressive as this was, it was not catching up with the widespread misery. The Association's efforts caught the attention of the provincial government, at that time the reform-minded United Farmers of Alberta, which agreed to a public inquiry.

The Commission to investigate the Métis situation was set up in 1934 under the chairmanship of Alberta Supreme Court Judge Albert Freeman Ewing (1871–1946). One of the first arguments he heard was that the Métis were nomads by nature and not prepared to convert themselves into farmers; therefore there was no point in setting aside land for them. Northern Métis were confirmed hunters, trappers, and fishermen, capable of supporting themselves as long as their ecological base remained sound; some were even reported to be well off. It was soon revealed, however, that the situation was totally different in central and southern Alberta, where farming and ranching were widespread and oil exploration was spreading rapidly; all of these activities mitigated against game maintaining itself. There the Métis were without land and without a subsistence base; in fact, they were destitute, malnourished, and had severe health problems. Up to 80 per cent were illiterate.

In its final report, the Ewing Commission described the Métis condition as 'unfortunate'.

Those near Euro-Canadian settlements were living in shacks on road allowances, shunned and suspected by the non-Natives. Those in the north were better off, but precariously so. All were without education and health services. As the Commission saw it, the only way out of the situation was for the Métis to change their way of life to conform to that of the dominant society. It did not see that the government had a legal obligation to help them, as that had been extinguished with the issuance of scrip. But there were humanitarian considerations. Ewing opposed the granting of special status, as had happened with Amerindians, noting that a small group of Métis, mostly from the failed St Paul experiment, were successfully farming around Fishing Lake, although as squatters; they had petitioned for land in 1929 but without result. Rumour now had it that the government intended to open the region for general settlement, which would have repeated what had happened at Red River and St Laurent. Already the provincial government had before it a list of 11 proposed sites for Métis colonies presented by the Métis Association of Alberta. Taking its cue from this, the Commission proposed the establishment of farm colonies to be located on good agricultural land, near lakes with plentiful stocks of fish and with access to timber for building. These colonies should be so located as to be free from Euro-Canadian interference, and there should be provision for their expansion should that be called for.

Government-appointed supervisors would administer these colonies; there was no provision for self-government. Later, administrative responsibility was transferred to the Métis Rehabilitation Branch of the provincial Department of Welfare. A measure of self-government was agreed on in 1989 and confirmed the following year.

In the Commission's view, an allotment of land should be considered a privilege: 'no halfbreed would have an inherent right to join the colony and no half-breed would be compelled to join the colony, but if he did not join he could have no claim for public assistance.' The colonies were being recommended as a welfare measure, not as flowing from Aboriginal right. The Commission had recognized the Métis as a distinct socio-economic group that needed assistance but had stopped short of recognizing them as a unique cultural group with a right to preserve their distinctive character. Those in the colonies would not have special status, but neither would they be ordinary citizens. It was hoped that as the Métis became self-supporting farmers, the colonies would naturally dissolve into individual farms, a process that might take up to 50 years to work itself out.

The report also recommended that northern hunting and trapping Métis should each be granted 320 acres (130 hectares) of land to be held on the same basis as if they were in the colonies. Further, they should be allowed free hunting and fishing permits, as well as preference in acquiring them in areas where there was danger of game depletion.

Implementation of Recommendations

The Ewing Commission's recommendations were implemented in the Métis Population Betterment Act of 1938, at the time the most advanced legislation in Canada relating to the Métis. It was passed by Alberta's Social Credit government, the first in Canada, which had come into power with a large majority in 1935, defeating the previous government, the United Farmers of Alberta. The Act was also unusual in that it had been written in collaboration with Métis representatives; however, subsequent amendments have been unilateral on the government's part. These were not long in coming: in 1940 the definition of Métis was restricted, as mentioned above; in 1941 the lieutenant-governor in council was empowered

to create game preserves on the settlements, and the next year the minister was granted the power to levy an annual tax; other amendments concerned administration and related problems. In 1943 a Métis population betterment trust account was established, which was transformed into a fund in 1979.[23]

Initially, 12 locations were selected, of which 10 were opened for Métis settlement, all in central Alberta. Eventually, two of the colonies were closed so that today there are eight, comprising 539,446 hectares. The two closings, particularly that of Wolf Lake in 1960 over the protests of a dozen resident families, illustrated a principal weakness of the settlements: the Métis did not have underlying title and held their lands on leases. The largest of the settlements is Paddle Prairie, 724 kilometres north of Edmonton, which consists of 163,099 hectares; in 1984 it counted 644 souls. A 1995 estimate placed the population for all eight colonies at close to 6,000; off the settlements, lack of reliable figures means that Métis population estimates for the province vary wildly, between 55,000 and 110,000. The high figure is that of the Métis National Council, organized in 1983 as the voice for the five provincial organizations west of Quebec. It does not speak for either the Maritimes or the Northwest Territories.

Application for membership in an Alberta settlement goes through the Settlement Association Council. Once accepted, a Métis has 30 days to establish residence, 90 days to build a house, and a year to construct a livestock shelter. Today, 50 years later, the colonies, instead of disappearing, have become homelands for the Métis. It remains the only such program for the Métis in Canada. Incidentally, Alberta can also claim Canada's only Métis-specific welfare agency, the Métis Child and Family Services based in Edmonton.

Originally, each of the settlements dealt individually with the provincial government.

As this proved unsatisfactory, the Alberta Federation of Métis Settlement Associations was formed in 1975 to co-ordinate administration and also to prevent any more closures.[24] Problems continued, however; a legal action instituted by the Métis against the government for an estimated $500 million in oil and gas revenues from settlement lands culminated in 1979 with raids organized by the provincial Department of Social Services on six of the eight settlement offices, confiscating files pertaining to the suit. The provincial ombudsman adjudicated the dispute, deciding that some of the files were provincial property but that others should be returned to the settlements. The matter had been badly handled, and the Métis were owed an apology. The ombudsman urged that the Métis be given more control in running their own affairs and that more be hired in government service.[25]

In the meantime, responsibility for the Métis was transferred from Social Services to Municipal Affairs. With the Conservatives under Peter Lougheed forming the provincial government (he was Premier, 1971–85), a committee to review the Métis Betterment Act was set up under Grant MacEwan, who had been lieutenant-governor of the province from 1965 to 1974. Its report in 1984 strongly supported self-government and urged that title to Métis lands be transferred to the settlements.[26] The province partially implemented these recommendations when Conservative Premier Don Getty (in office, 1985–92) signed a pact in 1989 granting title to 512,000 hectares of land, an area about the size of Prince Edward Island, limited self-government, and a cash settlement of $310 million over a period of 17 years. It was hailed as setting a precedent.[27] It was not long, however, before residents were complaining of nepotism and financial mismanagement by settlement councils, in spite of the limitations on their newly acquired powers. The result was a provincial investigation of two of them,

Kikino and Buffalo Lake. In the meantime, a target date of 1997 was set for the settlements to assume full responsibility for their decisions.[28] Unfortunately, the failure of the Charlottetown Accord in 1992 took with it amendments that would have entrenched the constitutional position of Alberta's Métis settlements. Such a move would require joint action by the federal and Alberta governments.

All was not lost at the provincial level, however. The Métis Association of Alberta had entered into a special arrangement with the provincial government when it signed a framework agreement in 1987 calling for senior government officials and Association representatives to work out plans for the improvement of services and greater participation for the Métis in providing them. At first renewable annually, the agreement was renewed in 1989 for three years. In 1992 it was replaced with a tripartite agreement, carrying the process one step further. The Association, now officially named the Métis Nation of Alberta, culminated the series with a seven-year framework agreement that was signed in 1999 by its president, Audrey Poitras, and Ralph Klein, then Premier of the province. By its terms, the MNA received $1.5 million annually for the development of social services and special programs geared to the Métis community.[29] (A new seven-year framework agreement between the MNA and the provincial government was reached in 2008.) This was followed by an agreement between the Alberta Federation of Métis Settlement Associations and Ottawa for the federal government to provide $455,000 to set up community-based justice programs.[30] Ken Noskey, Métis Settlements president, observed that the accord was a major step for the Métis: 'When it comes to the justice system, we're moving from one place to another; from where justice made decisions about Métis to where justice is made by Métis.' The September 2003 Supreme Court decision in the

Powley case (in Ontario; see Chapter 29) appeared to have a positive effect on Alberta Métis hunting rights. As a result, on 28 September 2004 the Alberta Ministry of Aboriginal Affairs and Northern Development signed an Interim Harvesting Agreement that was ratified three days later by the Settlements General Council. The Agreement, however, does not 'affect, abrogate or derogate from, or recognize or affirm any constitutional or aboriginal rights'.[31]

On the economic front, the Settlement Sooniyaw Corporation ('sooniyaw' is the Cree word for money) was established with a $75,000 contribution from each of the eight settlements; and since then, the provincial Native Economic Development Program has agreed in principle to allot $4.2 million for an umbrella five-year development plan. Unresolved has been the matter of royalties from mineral rights, which currently go to Ottawa. There are 200 producing oil and gas wells on the settlements, estimated to have generated some $60 million in royalties since 1938.

Métis across Canada

Saskatchewan, Manitoba, and Quebec have undertaken rehabilitation projects that have been very successful in reclaiming over-exploited areas for the production of furs. While these projects are not specifically related to the Métis, they are obviously important for them because of their relevance to the hunting and trapping lifestyle. In the 1920s, registered traplines were introduced in British Columbia, a program that initially hurt Natives as it interfered with traditional allocations of territory. It was also seen as a treaty violation, one more in the growing number of regulations that were steadily restricting the Aboriginal way of life.[32] In British Columbia, the criticism was supported by a report that by 1956 only 10 per cent of its registered traplines were operated by

Natives. In spite of such difficulties, however, the system has been instrumental in controlling over-trapping and has integrated well with rehabilitation programs, thus making it possible to maintain the trapping way of life. It is now generally used throughout the North and in the Arctic; in Manitoba it was introduced in 1940, and six years later in Saskatchewan. Saskatchewan has combined its fur production program with farming assistance programs.

The number of Métis in Canada is difficult to estimate, as the many backgrounds of individuals of mixed ancestry have complicated the matter of identity.[33] According to Indian and Northern Affairs Canada, Métis people are 'those of mixed First Nation and European ancestry who identify themselves as Métis, as distinct from First Nations people, Inuit or non-Aboriginal people. The Métis have a unique culture that draws on their diverse ancestral origins, such as Scottish, French, Ojibway and Cree.'[34] Nonetheless, as ethnologist Trudy Nicks has made clear, there is considerable variation in both the use of the term and in material culture; there is no nationally agreed-upon definition. An exhibit mounted by Calgary's Glenbow Museum in 1985, entitled 'Métis' and marking the centennial of Riel's uprising, highlighted this problem rather than settling it.[35] The identification of Métis as Aboriginal in section 35(2) of the Constitution Act, 1982 has not solved the issue, as there was no attempt at definition. Since Aboriginal status carries with it certain privileges, the issue is a thorny one. This was illustrated in 1993, when two Métis hunters from Sault Ste Marie were acquitted of the charge of hunting and possessing moose out of season, an Aboriginal treaty right. Ontario unsuccessfully pursued the *Powley* case in higher courts, on the grounds that an 'ever-increasing' number of people calling themselves Métis has the potential of overwhelming conservation efforts across the country.[36]

In 1941, before the 'halfbreed' category was deleted from the census, 27,790 had been listed for the three prairie provinces, a figure that is almost certainly too low. Reluctance to identify as a half-breed may have been influenced by the pejorative connotations of the term. In 1981, when 'Métis' was introduced as a census category, 98,300 identified themselves as such across the country. However, the actual figure for those with some Amerindian admixture is still believed to be much higher; the Métis National Council considers 350,000 to be a more realistic estimate for Canada as a whole, still a very conservative estimate in the eyes of those who would push the figure to 16 per cent of the total population. The Council, analyzing statistics from the Aboriginal Peoples Survey of 1991, reported that 17 per cent of Métis over the age of 15 have less than grade nine education, compared with 13.9 per cent for the total population. Only 3.7 per cent of Métis had completed university education, compared to 5.1 per cent of Amerindians and 11.4 per cent of the general population. The unemployment rate for Métis more than 15 years old was 19 per cent, almost double the national average of 10.3 per cent, but still well below the 34 per cent reported in 1981. Of those employed, 60 per cent earn $10,000 a year or less. These figures may help to explain why Métis are more likely to be entrepreneurs than any other group in Canada.[37] On the basis of these figures, Métis share with Amerindians in being an economically underdeveloped segment among Canada's peoples.[38]

On the other side of the picture, Yvon Dumont, at the time president of the Métis National Council and a supporter of the Charlottetown Accord, was named lieutenant-governor of Manitoba in 1993, a position he held until 1999.

Chapter 25

Development Heads North

As it happened in the southwestern regions of Canada, so it happened in the Northwest: Canadian jurisdiction was extended through the fur trade, followed by missionaries and later the police. After its amalgamation with the North West Company, the Hudson's Bay Company founded posts all over the Subarctic northwest of British North America, an expansion that continued after the Company's surrender of Rupert's Land to Britain in 1869 and its transfer to Canada in 1870; however, by 1893 the Company had closed its last post in the Yukon, in the face of competition from Americans following their purchase of Alaska and also from whalers.[1] Missionaries (mostly from Britain, France, and Belgium) began to arrive in the middle of the century. The High Arctic did not come under Canadian jurisdiction until 1880, when it was transferred from Britain. Canada's title was not without its challengers—Denmark and Norway as well as others had claims, but they did not press their cases.[2] A census in 1857, conducted in connection with the British parliamentary inquiry into its policy in the Northwest, placed the population of the region (excluding the High Arctic) at 147,000 Amerindians (Cree and various branches of Athapaskans or Dene, such as Chipewyan, Dene Dháa, Inland Tlingit, Gwich'in, Slavey, and others), of which 4,000 were 'Esquimaux' (at that time Inuit were often referred to as 'Eskimaux Indians'). More realistic estimates of Inuit in the 1880s placed the figure at 10,000; by that time, however, epidemics had had their effect.[3] The 2006 census counted 50,480 Inuit.

At first the Canadian government was not at all anxious to assume responsibility for the northern Natives; whatever steps were necessary were taken through the medium of the fur traders and the missionaries. Consequently, the appearance of non-Natives did not at first radically alter subsistence patterns, although changes did occur with the emphasis on fur hunting in the boreal forest and whaling in the Arctic, and the concomitant availability of trade goods. Metal goods, such as knives, kettles, and axes, soon proved useful, as did nets and twine and, of course, guns. Even as they traded for these items, which in effect were tools of production, Amerindians retained a large degree of self-sufficiency. For some tribes, trade was for

TIMELINE

1860s	Inuk shaman, Qitdlarssuaq, leads four-year trek to find isolated Polar Inuit.
1868	More southerly route to Northwest bypasses Methye Portage.
1880	Jurisdiction of High Arctic transferred to Canada by Britain.
1880s	Steamships introduced on rivers—Athabasca, Slave, Mackenzie—into Northwest.
1883	Railway reaches Calgary.
1891	Railway reaches Edmonton.
1892	Sir Wilfred Grenfell begins medical missionary work on Labrador coast.
1893	HBC closes last Yukon post.
1895	NWMP establish first permanent post in Far North, in Yukon.
1898	Yukon becomes separate territory—just in time for Klondike gold rush.
1899	Treaty Eight, covering northern Alberta, northwest Saskatchewan, northeast BC, and parts of Yukon and NWT, is signed as a result of the Klondike gold rush.
1900s	Collapse of Arctic whaling industry.
1902	Entire band of Sadlermiut, perhaps the last remnant of earlier Dorset culture, perishes on Southampton Island.
1903	*Neptune* plies eastern Arctic waters to establish Canadian jurisdiction.

1905–6	Treaty Nine (James Bay Treaty), covering northern Ontario, and Treaty Ten in northern Saskatchewan, which clears the way for settlement with creation of province of Saskatchewan.
1911	HBC opens post at Chesterfield Inlet to meet growing demand for white fox skins.
1917	Northwest Game Act.
1918	Migratory Birds Convention Act.
1920	Dogribs refuse Treaty Eight payments because of attempts in recent legislation to restrict their hunting and fishing rights.
	Major oil strike at Norman Wells, NWT.
1921	Treaty Eleven, covering much of NWT.
1921–6	'Baby bounties' used to stop infanticide among Inuit.
1924	Two Inuit found guilty and hanged on Herschel Island for 1921 murder of police officer, five others.
	Indian Act amended to include Inuit (later to be excluded by 1951 revisions).
1939	Supreme Court rules that all Inuit are a federal responsibility.
1945	Alaska Highway is completed, further opening Northwest to white settlement.
1974	First NWT reserve, at Hay River.

acquiring items that Europeans regarded as luxuries but for Amerindians could have ceremonial or mystical significance. The Athapaskan Gwich'in of the Mackenzie River basin, for instance, were only interested in acquiring blue beads (beads being in the form of berries, believed to have curative qualities). But with time, as industrialization slowly invaded the North, the way of life was modified.

Opening the North

Changes initially occurred in transportation. Until 1856, all freight and travellers destined for the Athabasca-Mackenzie District followed the fur trade routes—either via York Factory on Hudson Bay or via Fort William at the western end of the St Lawrence system.[4] Between Lac La Loche and the Mackenzie River system, the

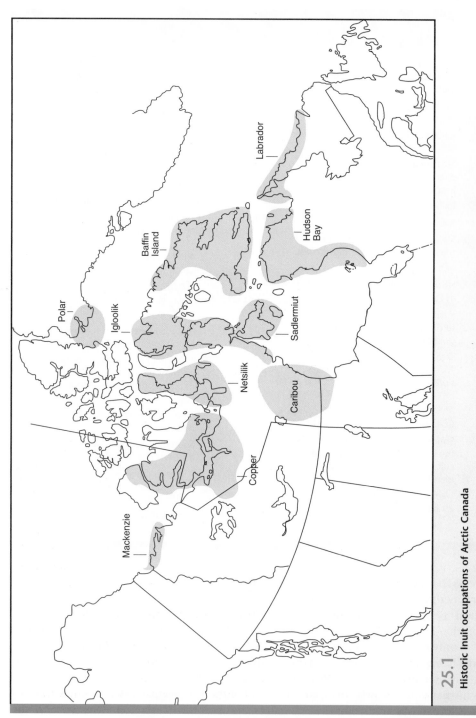

25.1

Historic Inuit occupations of Arctic Canada

Source: Adapted, with the permission of the Canadian Museum of Civilization, from Robert McGhee, *Canadian Arctic Prehistory* (Ottawa: Canadian Museum of Civilization, 1990).

Arctic life as depicted by an unknown Inuk artist, *c.* 1916. The sketch vividly portrays the Inuit's sense of relationship with their dogs and game in the Arctic vastness.
(With permission of the Royal Ontario Museum © ROM, Robert T. Flaherty Collection, 960.76.23)

12-mile Methye Portage in present-day northern Saskatchewan was the corridor through which all travellers passed. This had been the case since Amerindians had led Peter Pond to the portage in 1778. In 1868, at the initiative of Bishop Taché, an alternative route was developed along the North Saskatchewan to Fort Pitt, then overland to Lac La Biche, which drains into the Athabasca River. This more southerly route bypassed Methye Portage, which the HBC eventually abandoned in 1886. The completion of a wagon road from Edmonton to Athabasca Landing in the 1890s, a consequence of the Klondike gold rush, opened yet another route by which the once-isolated Northwest could be invaded from the south. Steamships on the Athabasca and Slave rivers in 1882, and three years later on the Mackenzie, emphasized the point. In the south, transportation was also being revolutionized: the railway reached Calgary in early 1883 and Edmonton in 1891. Voyages that had once taken weeks and months, even years, could now be accomplished in days.

Trappers and prospectors were quick to take advantage of the new situation. By 1894

Northern technology: deadfall trap of green spruce logs set for
wolverines by Billy Natkusiak, Kendall River, NWT, 1911.
(Library and Archives Canada, C-23634)

Fort McPherson, NWT, *c.* 1930: Anglican church on the left, Hudson Bay buildings in the distance.
(Library and Archives Canada, PA-102490)

An Inuit settlement, Prince Albert Sound, Victoria Island, NWT. It consists of a large snowhouse with four domes and two entrances.
(Archdeacon Webster, HBC Library, Winnipeg, A-33-4)

non-Native trappers were established at Fort Resolution, north of the sixtieth parallel; according to a Fort Chipewyan elder, there were 'white trappers all over the place, and we were on very friendly terms with them. I went trapping with them many times. . . . I would guide them and show them how to trap. They were very thankful for that as they took their pelts home.'[5]

Some non-Native trappers, however, introduced the use of poison, which was anathema to Amerindians;[6] their reaction was such that the government banned the practice. Enforcement was difficult, to say the least, and Amer-

indian resentment mounted as northern resources soon showed the effects of increased exploitation and fluctuations in wildlife cycles intensified.[7] To this, trade added the uncertainties of the marketplace, and subsistence in the North, never a matter to be taken for granted, began to become problematic. The winters of 1887–8 and 1888–9 saw people dying of starvation on such a scale that Ottawa was moved to provide relief through the HBC and the missions, a situation that would be repeated with increasing frequency. It would be 1938 before the Northwest Territories Council restricted trapping licences to residents of the territories.

An Inuk seal hunter demonstrates a harpoon.
(National Film Board of Canada. Photothèque/Library and Archives Canada/RD-002169)

At another level, the government had been providing assistance for mission schools at least in principle since 1873, although the specifications were such that few qualified, and even then it was a number of years before federal money actually arrived.[8] This association between government and missionaries would last until the 1940s, when schools for Natives, in the North as elsewhere, began to be secularized. Some medical care was also provided. Ottawa's official position, however, was that it had no responsibility towards people who had not signed treaty, and at the time it saw no rea-

son for one in those distant regions. When the North West Mounted Police arrived in the Yukon in 1895 to establish their first permanent post in the Far North (but south of the Arctic Circle), they were instructed 'not to give encouragement to the idea they [the Indians] will be received into treaty, and taken under the care of the government.'[9] Official conviction that Amerindians were waiting for the chance to live off government handouts did not take into account the deep psychological satisfaction of living off the land, despite its hardships and difficulties.[10] Such an attitude bolstered the conviction of those who saw the police as representing, in the words of author Hugh Brody, 'the fact that one nation was determined to include the vast Arctic hinterland, not only within its geographical frontiers, but within its moral and legal boundaries as well.'[11] The police posts would play a major role in this, not only through enforcing the law of the dominant society but also by performing such governmental functions as recording vital statistics, distributing mail, and collecting customs duties.

Two Views of Inuit/White Contacts

The police had come in response to missionary pressures, in particular the pleas of the Anglican missionary William Carpenter Bompas, bishop of Selkirk (Yukon) from 1891 until his death in 1906,[12] who, along with other missionaries, was deeply disturbed by the free flow of liquor and the freewheeling ways of both Inuit (or, more precisely, Inuvialuit, as the western Canadian Inuit call themselves) and whalers, who were largely American. The missionaries, already upset at the wife-lending practices of the Inuit,[13] were dismayed when this was willingly extended to the whalers, who were only too pleased to comply. Herschel Island, in the Beaufort Sea west of the mouth of the Mackenzie River, had been a wintering place for the western Arctic whaling fleet since 1888 and had become infamous in this regard.[14] The 'lawless frontier' ambience was more evident among western whalers than among those of the eastern waters; as one observer put it, 'the whalemen hung their consciences on Cape Horn as they passed into the Pacific.'[15] The police concurred that liquor was a problem but otherwise did not agree with the missionaries, especially Bompas, whom they regarded as being more concerned about the welfare of Aboriginal peoples than of non-Aboriginals.[16] Charles Constantine of the

NWMP (in the Yukon as inspector, 1894–7; as superintendent, 1897–1902) thought that Bompas exaggerated; neither he nor his fellow police officers could see that Inuit society was disintegrating as the missionaries claimed.[17] Self-help was still the rule, as illustrated in the eastern Arctic in the 1860s when an Inuk shaman, Qitdlarssuaq (d. 1875), led a four-year trek to find isolated Polar Inuit in need of help. On the Labrador coast Sir Wilfred Grenfell (1865–1940) began his medical missionary work in 1892, establishing a hospital at Battle Harbour the following year. He was soon operating a network of nursing stations, as well as an orphanage.

In the western Arctic more than 1,000 whalers were wintering at Herschel, occupying their off-season in living and trading with the Inuit. The Inuvialuit of the region numbered about 500; when gathered for trading some camped near the whalers, others on islands scattered along the coast. As with trading encounters between Europeans and Natives throughout the Americas, this was initially highly profitable for both sides, each within the terms of its own culture. For just one example, 100 primers (a device to detonate the main charge of a gun) that cost a total of 10 cents in New York traded in the Arctic for one musk-ox skin that sold in the south for $50. To the accusation that they overvalued their goods by as much as 20 times, traders pointed to their heavy costs;[18] even so, the trade built fortunes never before seen in the North. The Inuit also benefited through the acquisition of otherwise unavailable (or very rare) goods that eased the rigour of their lives, and they eagerly sought the new goods, not foreseeing, any more than did the non-Aboriginals, that their use would eventually contribute to dislocations in the ecological equilibrium as well as in Native social organization.[19]

The growing likelihood of violence and open disregard for authority finally persuaded Canada to act. The Yukon, stretching from the Subarctic

Inuit hunter Joshua Kango uses gas-line antifreeze to prevent his rifle from freezing on the nanniaq, the traditional hunt for polar bear on Frobisher Bay near Tonglait, Nunavut.
(The Canadian Press/Kevin Frayer)

into the Arctic, was organized into a district in 1895 and became a separate territory three years later, under a commissioner named by the federal Minister of Mines and Resources and an appointed council of up to six members.[20] In 1903, the year the Mounties arrived on Herschel Island, Canada sent Albert P. Low (director of the Geological Survey of Canada, 1906–13; first deputy minister of mines, 1907–13)[21] in the *Neptune* to establish Canadian jurisdiction and to report on the situation in the eastern Arctic;[22] other official trips to various Arctic regions followed. In the western Arctic the white population numbered about 500, drawn there by furs and minerals; Natives numbered about 2,600. Already there had been a severe decline in the Amerindian population, estimated to have been

about 8,000 at the beginning of the century. Police protests to the contrary, the missionaries' fears for the Inuit were realized—disease and the disruption of their lifestyle took their toll, and by 1920 there were no more of the original Inuvialuit in the Yukon, a situation that continues today.[23] Some survived around Tuktoyaktuk in the NWT, but most modern Inuvialuit moved in from Alaska. Local disappearances occurred in other areas as well, particularly where white whaling was active. For example, in 1902 an entire band of some 68 souls (Sadlermiut, believed by some to have been the last vestige of the Dorset)[24] perished of starvation and disease on Southampton Island, a consequence of dislocations that ultimately derived from whaling activities.[25] When whaling collapsed during the first decade of the twentieth century, triggered by a change in women's fashions and the increased use of petroleum products instead of whale oil, the Inuit were saved from immediate economic disaster by a new fashion, this time for white fox skins. The growing demand for this fur encouraged the HBC to open a post at Chesterfield Inlet in 1911, with others soon to follow in the general area.

Amerindians Seek Treaty

Amerindians in the North had been agitating for a treaty since the 1870s, despite their fear of the restrictions it could impose and their distrust of non-Amerindians. As the Cree headman Moostoos (c. 1850–1918, 'The Buffalo') would put it during Treaty Eight negotiations at Lesser Slave Lake, 'Our country is getting broken up. I see the White man coming in, and I want to be friends. I see what he does, but it is best that we should be friends.'[26]

The main Indian concern was for the protection of their hunting, fishing, and trapping rights; the danger they were in from white activities was all too evident.[27] Amerindians also hoped that treaty would provide a cushion against famine such as they had experienced in the late 1880s. Ottawa, however, held fast to its view that a treaty was unnecessary, as it saw little prospect of either industrial development or significant Euro-Canadian settlement north of the sixtieth parallel. On the prairies the government was pressuring Amerindians to take treaty and settle on reserves to clear the way for Euro-Canadian settlement it was actively encouraging (too quickly, according to some), but in the North during the 1890s it was doing the opposite because of the administrative and legal problems involved. For one thing, the Dominion Lands Act of 1872, under which settlement was being advanced, did not apply to territory where Indian title had not been extinguished. For another, the North's scattered population and migratory lifestyle made administration both difficult and expensive, although aid was provided in special cases. In the matter of treaties, Natives were caught in a circular bureaucratic argument they appeared to have no chance of winning. As far as the northern Natives were concerned, Canada had demonstrated it was more willing to show the flag than to accept the responsibilities that claiming sovereignty entailed, such as looking after the welfare of its subjects.[28]

It was not that the government was unaware of the North's rich resources. As early as 1793, Alexander Mackenzie had mentioned the tar and oil oozing from the banks of the Athabasca, and others had corroborated this.[29] In the 1870s and 1880s the government began to pay attention when its own geological surveys reported the same thing. In 1890–1, a geological survey estimated there were 4,700 million tons of tar in the region, as well as natural gas, bitumen, oil, and pitch.[30] Deposits of silver, copper, iron, asphaltum, and other minerals were also being mentioned. There were even reports of gold, but they attracted little attention as long as the British Columbia fields were producing. The remoteness of the Peace, Athabasca, and Mackenzie regions and difficulties of access and extraction put a damper on development enthusiasm.

There were also Amerindian factors to consider—as had happened at other times and places, Natives were not taking kindly to having their trading networks invaded. The Tlingit were particularly aggressive in this regard, controlling as they did the main routes between the coast and the interior, the Chilkoot, Chilkat, and Taku passes; they had long operated a trading monopoly in the region.[31] That was not a stance they could maintain when the 1896 strike at Rabbit Creek, later known as Bonanza Creek, set off the gold rush. Ironically, of the three persons who made the strike, two were Tagish—Skookum Jim and Dawson

(Tagish) Charlie—as was Kate, the wife of the third, George Carmack.[32] Whether they wanted it or not, the old way was gone forever as one of the most rapid migrations and economic expansions in history began.[33]

The first thing Canada did was to reassert its sovereignty, as Britain had done under similar circumstances in the Queen Charlotte Islands in 1852 and on the Fraser in 1857. In the Yukon, Canada did this by reinforcing its police force to nearly 300 men. The Indians, for their part, were becoming increasingly restive as they felt it was unjust 'that people who are not owners of the country are allowed to rob them of their living'.[34] Indian fish weirs were destroyed as miners rafted logs down the river, and Native villages were crowded out.[35] The influx of miners who were only too willing to take the law into their own hands added to the resentment already felt against non-Native trappers; as the situation threatened to go out of control, the police in 1897 instituted a system of patrols.[36]

On the whole, Amerindians regarded the patrols positively, except when the NWMP began to enforce regulations against hunting wood buffalo, in line with Ottawa's 1890 amendment to the Indian Act, which had empowered the governor-in-council to declare the game laws of Manitoba and the Northwest Territories to be applicable to Amerindians.[37] Enabling legislation was passed in the territories in 1894 (the Unorganized Territories' Game Preservation Act), and two years later enforcement began. This Act prohibited the use of poison and the running of game with dogs, among other provisions such as closed seasons on specified game. Wood bison, which Amerindians depended on for food, were included. Apparently this was the only such regulation applied to Amerindians at that time, but this turnabout on the part of the government from its repeated assurances that the Native way of life would not be interfered with reinforced doubts as to its good faith. Such regulation without regard for local conditions could also result in severe economic hardship, especially when game depletion reduced options.[38]

Treaty Eight (1899)

'The Trail of '98' saw the influx of gold-seekers reaching serious proportions; by the end of 1898, 860 prospectors had reached Fort Simpson. About 70 turned back, but the rest continued on and wintered on the banks of the Mackenzie.[39] The great majority of the miners were coming from the United States via the Pacific coast. Far from exhibiting any concern about Amerindian rights, they were contemptuous of them and openly shot the Natives' horses and dogs, interfered with traplines, and exploited fish and game resources at will; the police were too few and the area too large for them to cope adequately with the situation.[40] Several hundred alarmed Indians gathered at Fort St John in northeastern British Columbia and announced henceforth they would not allow anyone, even police, to pass through their territory until a treaty was signed. This time, June 1898, Ottawa agreed; the region delineated for negotiation included areas of known mineral wealth and possible farming value, as well as the all-Canadian routes to the goldfields, such as the northeastern corner of British Columbia, the southeastern corner of the Yukon, and the area north of Treaty Six. British Columbia did not object, as the portion of the province in question was of no particular interest to white settlers at that time, so in that area at least there was no conflict over land rights; as a result, the treaty was negotiated largely without consultation with the province.[41] It was not enough for Indians to ask for treaty to be included, even if they were suffering hardship, as illustrated by those of Ile à la Crosse, who were refused entry into Treaty Eight.[42]

The initial lack of militancy on the part of most of the Yukon Amerindians in defence of their rights—except for some groups in regard to trade, as previously noted, and the Dene of the Mackenzie Delta in the NWT—appears to have encouraged the government to exclude most of their territory from the negotiations. The argument was that the outlay required on the government's part could not be justified in face of the Yukon's comparatively limited potential.[43] The Oblate missionary turned historian, René Fumoleau, thought it more likely that 'Ottawa was afraid that the Indians would put too high a price on their rich land and decided to avoid the formality of a treaty.'[44] He speculated that what the Yukon lacked was a politically active Métis community, in contrast to the Lesser Slave Lake and Peace River regions, which had such communities and so were included.[45] According to historian William R. Morrison, the government was simply unwilling to undertake treaty obligations unless absolutely necessary; as the Amerindians of the Yukon were still successfully pursuing their traditional lifestyles, they would be encouraged to continue.[46] The government did compromise to the extent of setting aside small parcels of land for Amerindian use, which became known as 'residential reserves'. Because they were not protected by treaty or otherwise, these reserves could be moved to accommodate settler demands; one near Whitehorse was relocated four times between 1915 and 1923. There were occasions when the situation was reversed, and lands set aside for Amerindians were protected against non-Amerindian encroachment, as historian Kenneth Coates has pointed out. This happened at Tagish in 1898 and at Little Salmon in 1915.[47] Even without treaties, Yukon Amerindians still found themselves being directed by Ottawa—told how to live, how to run their affairs, where to send their children to school.

In the south, pressures mounted for the construction of the overland route to the goldfields from Edmonton via Peace River to Pelly Banks. By the spring of 1899, the North-West Territories government had constructed 350 miles of this route with the aid of a $15,000 grant from the Dominion.[48] Reports of gold at the eastern end of Great Slave Lake were luring prospectors up there even though the temperature hovered around 45 degrees below zero; the government expanded the territory it would include in the negotiation for Treaty Eight to take in the south shore of the lake. The result was the greatest area to be covered by treaty to that point, 324,900 square miles (841,491 square kilometres).

The treaty commissioners, headed by David Laird, were soon impressed with the 'keenness of intellect' and 'the practical sense' of the northerners in pressing their claims. 'They all wanted as liberal, if not more liberal terms, than were granted to the Indians on the plains', which warned the commissioners that the criteria used for the prairie treaties would not be acceptable in the North.[49] When commissioners tried to impose southern norms, the northerners reacted sharply: Moostoos observed that 'a Plains Indian turned loose in the bush would get lost and starve to death.'[50] The northerners, worried about the increasing frequency of famine, were unanimous in wanting assistance during such periods; they urged that the old and indigent who were no longer able to hunt and trap should be cared for by the government. The commissioners also noted, 'they seemed desirous of securing educational advantages for their children, but stipulated that in the matter of schools there should be no interference in their religious beliefs.' By this time most of the Natives had been converted to Catholicism.

By far the most important point the commissioners had to deal with was the Amerindians' fear that hunting and fishing rights —the commissioners called them 'privileges'—

would be curtailed, as was already happening in the case of the wood buffalo. They assured the people 'that only such laws as to hunting and fishing as were in the interest of the Indians and were found necessary in order to protect the fish and fur-bearing animals would be made, and that they would be as free to hunt and fish after treaty as they would be if they never entered it.' This was of vital importance for a people living in a land where agriculture, or even ranching, was not generally a viable alternative. Provision of ammunition and twine for making nets relieved Amerindian worries to some extent.

Another fear was that the people would be confined to reserves, as was happening in the south, which would have been inconsistent with the hunting life. Reserves, of course, were only feasible where a settled way of life was followed, such as farming or ranching. Accordingly, the matter of selecting reserved land was left for the future. 'It would have been impossible to have made a treaty if we had not assured them that there was no intention of confining them to reserves.'[51] At the time, reserves did not seem important. In the words of the commissioners, 'the great bulk of the Indians will continue to hunt and to trap.'[52] The people of Fort Chipewyan asked for a railway, which the commissioners said was beyond their powers to grant, but they assured the people they would make their wishes known to Ottawa. (At the time there was agitation in the south for a railway from Edmonton to the goldfields.) As has been remarked more than once, the Amerindians, not the government, were responsible for introducing most of the forward-looking parts of the treaty terms.

After two days of negotiations at Lesser Slave Lake the treaty was signed. Father Lacombe, repeating his earlier success with the Blackfoot, was a major influence in convincing the Amerindians of the government's good intentions and commitment to justice.[53] As only about half the Amerindians of the area had been present (2,217 initially accepted), it was necessary to follow up with adhesions, which involved nine meetings in 1899 and four in 1900. The government considered that the treaty not only extinguished Indian title, it also provided that Native usufructuary right would be 'subject to such regulation as may from time to time be made by the Government, and excepting such tracts as may be required for settlement, mining, lumbering, trading, or other purposes'.

The Aboriginal peoples had quite another view: they all held that the negotiators had guaranteed their rights to hunt, fish, and trap without restriction.[54] An elder later recalled:

> Moose is our main source of livelihood on this earth. Not like the white man, the King; he lived mainly on bread, he said. But the Indian lived on fish, ducks, anything. The King asked the Indian what he wanted for a livelihood. The Indian chose hunting and fishing not to be limited. As long as he lived.[55]

The Natives were not agreed, however, as to what they had given up in return for the recognition of this right. Some thought they had given up the land, while others believed they had agreed simply to share the land and its resources. None of them expressed concern about landownership, a topic that does not appear to have been clearly brought up during negotiations. In the eyes of one Native, 'the white man never bought the land. If he had bought it, there would have been very large sums of money involved.'[56] Finite boundaries and absolute ownership were unknown to the northern Indians. There does not appear to have been any discussion of sharing surface rights, such as those for timber and water, or subsurface rights, such as those for oil and minerals. Instead, the government, finding that the Indians acted as individuals rather than as a nation, offered 65-hectare allotments in severalty.

Another major area of difference between Amerindian understanding of the treaty and its actual provisions concerned health care and social services, including care of the aged. The Indians believe they had been assured of these, but they are not mentioned in the written document. Provisions that were included, such as aid to start farming where feasible, were not always honoured, at least not in the ways the Indians thought they should be.

This raises the difficult question of language and concepts. Anthropologist June Helm commented on the problems involved:

> How could anybody put in the Athapaskan language through a Métis interpreter to monolingual Athapaskan hearers the concept of relinquishing ownership of land, I don't know, of people who have never conceived of bounded property which can be transferred from one group to another. I don't know how they would be able to comprehend the import translated from English into a language which does not have those concepts, and certainly in any sense that Anglo-Saxon jurisprudence would understand.[57]

This problem of concepts bedevilled the Nelson Commission in 1959, which examined the unfulfilled provisions of Treaties Eight and Eleven in the Mackenzie District. It reported that it was 'impossible to make the Indians understand that it is possible to separate mineral rights or hunting rights from actual ownership of land.'[58]

To the Indians, Treaty Eight was essentially a peace and friendship treaty. In 1913–15, when the government moved to survey the Treaty Eight area, and particularly the individual allotments, the Natives reacted with mistrust and fear, seeing this as a threat to their liberty of movement. At Fort Resolution in 1920,

Dogribs refused to accept their treaty payments as they had become unhappy about attempts to restrict hunting and fishing. (In 1917, the Northwest Game Act had imposed closed seasons on moose, deer, caribou, and other animals essential to the economy of the Native people; in 1918, the Migratory Birds Convention Act signed by Canada and the United States had further restricted their hunting, as it had made no special provision for Amerindians.) They won recognition of their special position in a signed agreement and accepted the treaty payments. Then the document disappeared.[59] Similar problems were experienced at Fort Rae (the largest Indian settlement in the Northwest Territories) in 1928 and again at Fort Resolution in 1937. The courts have ruled that federal law prevails over treaty rights, but that of the provinces or territories does not.

Today, as industrialization and its accompanying non-Native settlement penetrate ever more deeply into the North and as the hunting way of life becomes secondary, reserves have assumed a different aspect for northern Amerindians.[60] In the Northwest Territories, the first reserve was created at Hay River in 1974; in British Columbia, one was established under Treaty Eight at Fort Nelson in 1961 (the province, however, as noted in Chapter 16, had been laying out reserves since the 1850s). In 1979, Ottawa set aside 18,000 acres (7,284 hectares) in Wood Buffalo National Park for the Fort Chipewyan Cree, following a breakdown of negotiations with Alberta; the Cree had requested 90,000 acres (36,422 hectares). The same band signed in 1986, when it received 12,280 acres (4,970 hectares) of reserve land with full mineral rights as well as hunting, fishing, and trapping rights, and $26.6 million in cash.

The Métis of the region could enter treaty at the time of signing, if they chose, or take scrip. In the latter case, they received either 240 acres (97 hectares) of land or $240 in cash.

An Indian encampment on the occasion of Treaty Nine payments in Ontario, 1929. Meat is placed high up on scaffolding to protect it from dogs.
(INAC collection, Library and Archives Canada, C-68950)

Treaties Nine, Ten (1905–6), and Eleven (1921)

The prospect of mining development and the need to clear railway right-of-way in northern Ontario finally influenced Ottawa to agree to Amerindian demands for a treaty, which had begun as far back as 1884.[61] The advent of the railroad had stepped up the rate of change in that part of the North, much to the concern of the Amerindians. Before negotiating with the northerners, Ottawa and Ontario worked out an agreement as to aims and responsibility for costs. Because of this, the request of Amerindians on the Quebec side of the interprovincial border to be included was refused. Treaty Nine (James Bay Treaty) involved 130,000 square miles (336,300 square kilometres); adhesions in 1929–30 covered territories included in Ontario when the province's final boundary was established in 1912. Treaty Ten, in northern Saskatchewan, was negotiated to clear land title for the province, created the year before, in 1905.

In the Northwest Territories, the years following the signing of Treaty Eight saw conditions go from bad to worse, particularly in the region north of Great Slave Lake and along the Mackenzie River. Even though it was not within

Chief Samson Beardy (standing) and Commissioners Walter C. Cain and Herbert N. Awrey (seated at table) during negotiation of Treaty Nine payments in Ontario, 1929. Seated in front row from left are Simeon and Jeremiah McKay, and Isaac Borkman. Johnny Anderson, Trout Lake, sits immediately to the left of Chief Beardy.
(Library and Archives Canada, PA-94969)

the jurisdiction of Treaty Eight, Indian Affairs opened an agency at Fort Simpson in 1911 'to distribute relief and to carry out experiments in farming', in co-operation with missionaries in the region. The agent arrived that summer with two horses, four oxen, and 10 tons of equipment and supplies. Local Amerindians, unforewarned, refused to shake hands with him 'as they thought he had come to take their country away from them.' Despite being so far north, the experiment went reasonably well and the suspicions of the Amerindians were allayed. Their lifestyle, however, remained unchanged, adapted as it was to northern conditions; not even such successful missionaries as Oblate Gabriel Breynat, bishop of the Mackenzie diocese, 1902–43, whose work was highly regarded, had been able to alter traditional patterns. This drew criticism: one observer wrote in 1913 that except for going to church, Amerindians had not changed their habits and were no better off.[62] There was now steamship service on the Mackenzie and other rivers during the summer, which opened the region to sport hunters, scientists, and others.[63]

In 1908, the HBC established its first permanent post north of the Arctic Circle; between 1910 and 1920, spurred by the growing presence of independent traders, in particular Revillon Frères, it opened 14 more.[64] The years 1915–20, a period of international tension, war, and revolution, saw the fur market peaking in value at the same time as the old barter system was replaced with the use of currency. Amerindians and Inuit, having no experience with this new form of buying and selling, were easily cheated. The post-World War I influenza epidemic hit the North hard, particularly the Inuit.

Two things happened in 1920: the fur market crashed, and the first oil gusher came in at Norman Wells, Northwest Territories: 'Biggest Oil Field in the World', newspapers reported. The first producing well yielded 1,000 barrels an hour. Ottawa was stirred into expanding its Council of Northwest Territories and establishing a Northwest Territories and Yukon branch of the Department of the Interior, headed by O.S. Finnie, formerly mining recorder for the Yukon; it would only last until 1931 as the oil boom never materialized.[65] An ordinance was quickly passed forbidding anyone from going to the District of Mackenzie, unless the police were satisfied that he or she was 'mentally and physically able, and properly equipped and outfitted'. The ordinance only lasted a year, but it gave the Royal Canadian Mounted Police, as the force was now named, at least some time to prepare for what was to come. According to one of its officers, 'any attempt to start an oil boom in Fort Norman oil shares or leases should be, if possible, discouraged.' For one thing, transportation was still not developed enough to handle a heavy increase in traffic. It was during this period that air travel was introduced to the North;[66] the *Edmonton Journal* of 18 January 1921 reported that a 36-hour dirigible passenger service was being proposed at a round-trip cost per passenger of $1,500. More practical at that stage was river transport, the price of which for a round trip was $200. Although such prices were a restraining factor, by themselves they were not enough. Extensive newspaper coverage on oil developments indicated only too clearly where public interest lay; while it was recognized that a treaty was now urgent, the coverage of this aspect of the situation was cursory.

With Treaty Eleven, as with Treaty Eight, Amerindians agreed to sign only after they had been assured of complete freedom to hunt, trap, and fish, and they had been reassured by Bishop Breynat that the government's word was good. They remember that they were told that the 'land shall be as it is, you shall keep on living on it as before.' For the Dene, the treaty was one of peace and friendship; land had not been at issue, although the territory involved was immense: 372,000 square miles (963,480 square kilometres). The negotiators had assured them this was their land. 'You can do whatever you want,' they told the Amerindians, 'we are not going to stop you.' When the government failed to live up to its word, the disenchanted Breynat publicly campaigned against the way the northern Amerindians were being treated, a campaign that has been carried on by Father Fumoleau.[67]

In 1973 the Dene filed a caveat in Alberta claiming Treaties Eight and Eleven were fraudulent; with the aid of retroactive legislation, the right to file the caveat was later denied.

The isolation that had been a protective shield for so long for the North had long since been broken; the final blow had come during World War II with the construction of the Alaska Highway, completed in 1945. Yukon Amerindians had helped to lay out its route and in so doing had opened up their territories to non-Native settlement.[68] By the 1950s, Amerindians were no longer free to hunt and fish as they pleased, and in some regions they had to register their traplines.[69]

What To Do about the Inuit?

Although non-Natives had been present in the eastern Arctic, off and on, since the eleventh century, and with increasing frequency since the seventeenth, the first permanent official presence had occurred in the western Arctic when Canada sent the NWMP in 1903 to establish posts at Herschel Island and Fort McPherson; the Eastern Arctic Patrol was not instituted on a regular basis until 1922, although there had been occasional government voyages since the late nineteenth century. For most Inuit, first experiences with the

Inuit children dancing, Igloolik, nineteenth century. From Captain William Edward Parry, *Voyage: Journal of a Second Voyage for the Discovery of the Northwest Passage from the Atlantic to the Pacific*, London, 1824.
(Photo courtesy The Newberry Library, Chicago)

new order were through the police, who represented the government until the mid-1950s, when the Department of Northern Affairs and Natural Resources took over. In the Arctic, problems of first contact were worked out in terms of the Criminal Code rather than of land, as had occurred to the south. Jenness calculated that in 1939 Ottawa spent $17 per Inuk to police the Arctic.[70] A neighbouring Arctic power, Denmark, maintained no police at all in Greenland. The Canadian officers were under orders not to meddle with Native customs as long as they were 'consistent with the general law'. Certain customs were to be discouraged, however, such as infanticide; an attempt in the Coronation Gulf area to stop this by a system of 'baby bounties' (issues of equipment, clothing, etc.) lasted only five years, 1921–6, partly because of difficulties in finding the families

scattered over a very large landscape.[71] More profoundly, the campaign had not taken into consideration the cultural and practical ramifications of the practice.[72] A major factor in its disappearance was the introduction of family allowances in 1945.

Canadian justice was also tempered by cultural considerations when other killings came to official attention, such as when two Oblate missionaries were killed in 1913 near Bloody Falls on the Coppermine River. The two Inuit involved, Uluksuk and Sinnisiak, believed they were acting in self-defence when the priests made threatening gestures during an altercation. After being found innocent in the first trial, both were sentenced to be hanged, but this was commuted to life imprisonment. They were released after two years and became guides and special helpers to the police.[73]

Dance of the 'Tlingit Esquimaux' at Fort McPherson, as sketched by Emile Petitot in *Les Grands Esquimaux*, Paris, Librairie Plon, 1887. Dancing and singing were favourite pastimes.

However, when a police officer fell victim in 1921, along with another non-Native and four Inuit, it was felt that an example was needed. A trial was held at Herschel Island and the two Inuit found guilty were hanged in 1924; one of them was about 16 years old. This was the first hanging in the Arctic.[74] It dramatically illustrated the Euro-Canadian emphasis on the offence and punishing the offender; in the Inuit way, the focus was to preserve the equilibrium of the community. Circumstances surrounding the offence were important, and above all, the penalty should not worsen an already bad situation.[75]

Insisting that the Inuit abide by Canadian law led to what was widely recognized as social injustice; by 1945 there were those who were convinced that the Criminal Code should not be applied to the Inuit, but no one could agree on an alternative, and so the situation remained. It was eased by the pliancy of the Inuit before the law officers; Diamond Jenness, in commenting on this, thought that the Natives were overawed by the self-assurance of the Euro-Canadians.[76] This should not be taken to imply that Inuit accepted second place; on the contrary, as one field officer reported, they met non-Natives 'of any official or social standing on an equal footing without the least embarrassment'.[77] Perhaps this contributed to the expressed preference of the police for the Inuit over the Indians, although after the killing of the officer there was less agreement about this.[78] The Amerindians, on the other hand, had their misgivings about the lawmen: at Churchill, rather than viewing them as protectors, they referred to them as 'the imprisoners'.[79] The police did not help their relations with the Natives when they were dilatory in engaging interpreters, as happened all too frequently.

Who should administer Inuit affairs? When it was realized that the ad hoc approach was unsatisfactory, official reaction was to lump Inuit with Amerindians. The first mention of Inuit in Canadian legislation occurred in 1924, when the Indian Act was amended to include them. This drew the comment from Arthur Meighen, who was in between his two terms as Prime Minister (1920–1 and 1926): 'I should not like to see the same policy precisely applied to the Eskimos as we have applied to the Indian. . . . After seventy-five years of tutelage and nursing . . . [the Indians] are still helpless on our hands.'[80]

Perhaps it was due to such sentiments that the Act had not been applied to Inuit when the Arctic Archipelago came under Canada's flag. The Inuit were brought under Canadian jurisdiction as ordinary citizens, as no treaties had been signed with them; neither were they wards, as Amerindians were. This had quickly caused administrative confusion, especially where liquor was concerned. The police treated the Inuit the same way they did the Amerindians in this regard, arguing that they were 'morally' the wards of Indian Affairs, if not legally so.[81] Doubts about the wisdom of such an approach were expressed by Finnie, who agreed with Meighen when he held that the Inuit 'will not be developed to the best advantage by the adoption of the methods . . . used in dealing with Indians.'[82] The Danish anthropologist Knud Rasmussen (1879–1933), who was one-quarter Inuit and who had spent much time in the Canadian Arctic, when asked for his opinion by Ottawa in 1925, said that the top priorities were wildlife conservation, health, and education.[83]

In 1927, Inuit affairs were transferred to the Northwest Territories. But the problem was not to be so easily resolved, particularly when the people starved as game diminished. When Quebec took Ottawa to court to get it to accept responsibility for the Inuit within its provincial borders, the federals tried to prove that the latter were not Indians—an anthropologically sound position, but only up to a certain point (Inuit and Amerindians are genetically distinct, except for Athapaskan-speakers of the Northwest).[84] Historically and politically, however, Inuit had been habitually classed as Indian, as Quebec proved in court. Its *coup de grâce* was to produce official correspondence, dated in 1879, in which Inuit were referred to as 'Indians'.[85] In 1939, the Supreme Court of Canada ruled that, for administrative purposes, the Inuit were Indians and therefore a federal responsibility; in 1950, the year the Inuit got the vote, an Order-in-Council vested authority for the Inuit in the Minister of Resources and Development. Administration of Inuit was kept separate from that of Amerindians; for example, there is no national registry for Inuit as there is for Indians, and the Inuit were specifically excluded from the Indian Act when it was revised in 1951. In other words, the status of Inuit as ordinary citizens has never been altered. Ironically, Quebec experienced a change of attitude in 1960 and began actively claiming jurisdiction over the Inuit within its borders, a process that was formalized with the establishment of a provincial ministry, Direction générale du Nouveau Québec, in 1962.[86] At one point federal and provincial authorities were even building rival schools.[87]

In the meantime, the problem of maintaining wildlife resources so that the Inuit could continue, at least to some extent, to live off the land had become critical. Officials remained convinced that Natives must be encouraged to maintain their traditional way of life, as otherwise they would degenerate.[88] In 1923, two huge game preserves were established for exclusive Native use, one in the Back and Thelon river basins, the other on Victoria and Banks islands. The latter became transformed into the Arctic Islands Game Preserve in 1926 when Finnie, in response to Rasmussen's recommendation, extended it to cover all Arctic islands.[89] Another recommendation, this one by a Royal Commission in 1922, that reindeer herds be established in the Canadian Arctic, was under consideration. Alaska had successfully introduced reindeer in the 1890s, which suggested that the same thing could be done in Canada.

Chapter 26

Social Fact and Developmental Theory

The centennial of Canada's Confederation in 1967 presented too good an opportunity to miss: at Expo in Montreal, Amerindians, with the support of Indian Affairs, erected a pavilion in which they publicly expressed, for the first time on a national scale, dissatisfaction with their lot.[1] The general public reacted with stunned disbelief that people in Canada were being treated in such a manner. Surely, people thought, Amerindians were exaggerating. Weren't they just being ungrateful for the many good things that had been done for them? Most Canadians had no way of knowing what was happening on the reserves and in the North. For Amerindians, it was an unheard-of opportunity to present grievances that dated back 300 years or more. As Lloyd Barber observed, the original peoples of this country had never been in a position 'to make their case and insist on rights that the rest of us would tend to take for granted'.[2] Canada, in celebrating the centennial of its Confederation, had simply not thought to include First Nations as founding members.

Ottawa's centralized administration was managed in what Louis St Laurent, Prime Minister from 1948 to 1957, referred to in 1954 as 'an almost continuous state of absence of mind'.[3] The disastrous decline in prices that marked the Great Depression of the 1930s found the people unprepared; for producers such as the northern fur trappers, there were no economic safety nets, apart from direct government handouts, to offset the drop in cash incomes. The results were starvation and widespread deprivation. According to historian Morris Zaslow, 'Canada did not awaken to the importance of the Canadian North until the establishment in 1953 of the federal Department of Northern Affairs and National Resources.'[4] The slowness of development of the North has been largely due to its nature: the Far North is not hospitable to uncontrolled free enterprise. The costs are so high that projects are effectively limited to large corporations and consortiums that have the co-operation of the state.[5]

The obviously marginalized position of Amerindians, in the North as elsewhere, spurred the federal government in 1963 to appoint anthropologist Harry B. Hawthorn to investigate their social, educational, and

TIMELINE

1930s	Reindeer herd introduced in western Arctic.	1969	Federal government White Paper proposes end of Indian Act, termination of treaties, that Aboriginals be treated equally with all other Canadians.
1933	Cree Lubicon band in northern Alberta, missed in Treaty Eight signing, applies for land settlement.		
1934	Failed relocations of Inuit to more suitable communities and hunting and fishing grounds begun in Arctic.	1971	Concerted Amerindian protest succeeds in retraction by Ottawa of White Paper proposals.
1940–79	Reserve site established for Cree Lubicon, but resource explorations and provincial road on Lubicon land create problems still unresolved.	1974	Gull Bay band of Ojibwa organizes reserve police force.
		1983	Mi'kmaq Donald Marshall Jr exonerated after spending 11 years in jail for murder he did not commit.
1953	Forced relocation of Inuit from Arctic Quebec and northern Baffin Island to Ellesmere Island in High Arctic.	1989–90	Woodland Cree break from Lubicon band, gain band status, and cut lucrative deal with federal and provincial governments.
1966	Hawthorn Report criticizes centuries-old policy of assimilation and presents view of Amerindians as 'citizens plus' because of their original inhabitancy.	1991	Loon River people break from Lubicon band, gain band status.
		1999	Loon River band signs land settlement agreement.
1967	Amerindian pavilion at Expo 67 brings plight of Canadian Aboriginals to public consciousness.		
	Abe Okpik first Inuk appointed to Northwest Territories Council.		

economic conditions. His report, which appeared in 1966, listed 151 recommendations, the underlying themes of which were that an Amerindian should not be forced to 'acquire those values of the majority society he does not hold, or wish to acquire', and that the department should assume a more active role as advocate for Indian interests, both in government and in society as a whole.[6] The report supported the continuation of the Indian Act but in modified form. It emphasized that Aboriginals were not taking advantage of even the limited opportunities for self-government allowed them by the Indian Act and revealed that their average per capita annual income was $600, compared to $1,400 for white Canadians, that their schooling was far below the national average, with a dropout rate of 94 per cent prior to high school graduation. The report urged that Indians have available to them the opportunity of being taught in their own languages. School texts were often not only inaccurate on the subject of Amerindians, they were usually insulting.[7]

Concerning self-government, Hawthorn noted that between 1951 and 1964, 118 bands (out of 577 at that time) had passed a total of 338 bylaws, an average of about three per band; only 23 per cent of all bands in Canada had passed at least one bylaw. This reflected the veto over any band decision that could be exercised by the governor-in-council. Once started, however, a band could become active; out of those 118 bands, 54 per cent had passed three or more bylaws. When it came to money by-laws, fewer than 50 bands had been deemed 'advanced' enough to exercise this power. The first band to receive such authority was that of Tyendinaga, an Iroquois reserve on the north shore of Lake Ontario, in 1958.

Amerindian trust funds, which began with the proceeds from surrendered lands, by the mid-1960s included capitalized annuities and monies derived from other assets. Major sources of income were from leases on Amerindian reserve lands, timber sales, leasing oil and gas exploration rights, sale of gravel, etc. Size of trust funds varied widely from band to band across Canada, some having considerable assets and others none at all. The degree of a band's autonomy was directly proportional to its control of its revenues; the Six Nations, which had that control, had what resembled municipal government. Its relationship with the federal authority continued to be difficult, particularly when Ottawa interfered with enforcement of bylaws, as happened from time to time. Lack of clear authority encouraged defiance of bylaws by opponents of the elective system, further complicating the situation. In other cases, Hawthorn pointed out, band councils were not passing bylaws because they were expected to follow the pattern set by Ottawa; far better, he suggested, to let them develop their own patterns.

In other words, the exercise of authority from without was flourishing on the reserves. According to Hawthorn, Amerindians reacted by orienting themselves primarily to family, extended kinship, and other groupings that did not necessarily relate to the reserve community as defined by Ottawa. Band councils persisted, not because they were perceived as responding to important local government needs but because the government insisted on dealing through them. This meant that local government failed on some reserves, particularly those in rural or isolated areas where the

agency system continued (it lasted until 1969). By complying with the system, bands assured themselves of more generous welfare grants; the price was that they were not responsible for decisions affecting their lives. This pattern of dependency took such root that in some cases bands actually voted against local autonomy. Even some urbanized bands took that stand, such as the one at Lorette, outside of Quebec City. Another consequence of the acceptance of welfare was the weakening of communal activities; welfare cheques have encouraged individualism and dependence on outside sources, and these factors have worked against community solidarity. This was a trend that had begun with the fur trade, with its emphasis on individual reward for individual effort.[8]

The Hawthorn Report was well received by the Amerindian community, which was quick to pick up on its 'citizens plus' concept. As the report explained this, 'in addition to the normal rights and duties of citizenship, Indians possess certain additional rights as charter members of the Canadian community.'[9] A major influence in the further easing of the Indian Act, the report also led to the White Paper of 1969, which Amerindians flatly rejected, as it did not include Hawthorn's recommended measures.

The 1969 White Paper and Some Consequences

In 1969 Ottawa came up with what has been described as a 'breathtaking governmental recipe for equality'. This was the White Paper, a proposal designed to break 'the pattern of 200 years' and to abolish the existing framework of Amerindian administration, widely criticized for setting Amerindians apart and hindering their development.[10] In part, the White Paper was a response to the American Indian Movement (AIM, or 'Red Power') that had arisen in Minnesota in 1968 and was spreading into

Canada, challenging the administration to allow Amerindians a greater say in running their own affairs. The movement was an off-shoot of the demands of prison populations for the right to conduct their own religious ceremonies, just as Christians had the right to theirs. In the case of the White Paper, the government announced it was going 'to enable the Indian people to be free—free to develop Indian cultures in an environment of legal, social and economic equality with other Canadians'.[11] To this end the BNA Act would be amended to terminate the legal distinction between Amerindians and other Canadians, the Indian Act would be repealed, and Amerindians would gradually take control of their reserves, subject to provincial laws. Indian Affairs would be phased out over a period of years, and services that had previously been provided on a special basis would be taken over by the federal and provincial agencies that serve the general public. Instead of Hawthorn's 'citizens plus', Amerindians were to become like all other Canadians; their special status would cease. This reflected Prime Minister Pierre Trudeau's belief that special status for a special group was fundamentally wrong in a democratic society. Aboriginal rights were not recognized, and the significance of treaties was challenged.

In effect, treaties would be terminated. According to the White Paper:

> A plain reading of the words reveals the limited and minimal promises which were included in them. . . . The significance of the treaties in meeting the economic, educational, health, and welfare needs of the Indian people has always been limited and will continue to decline. . . . once Indian lands are securely within Indian control, the anomaly of treaties between groups in a society and the government of that society will require that these treaties be reviewed to see how they can be equitably ended.

To help Amerindians adjust to this new situation, Ottawa said it would make $50 million available over five years for their economic development.

At the same time, the government proposed establishing an Indian Claims Commission as an advisory body. Ottawa made it clear it was not accepting Aboriginal rights in principle: 'These are so general and undefined that it is not realistic to think of them as specific claims capable of remedy except through a policy and program that will end injustice to Indians as members of the Canadian community.'

The issue could be seen as a question of individual rights versus collective rights. By the cancellation of the Indian Act and the treaties, Amerindians would be treated as individuals instead of as communities. In losing their special status, they would also lose compensation for the surrender of their ancestral lands. Canadians were following in the footsteps of two American initiatives: the 1952 termination program of the US Bureau of Indian Affairs, which pauperized the once affluent Menominees and Klamaths before it was halted in 1970; and the General Allotment Act (Dawes Act, 1887), which had resulted in severe attrition of American Indian lands before the Act was repealed in 1934.[12]

In formulating the White Paper, Ottawa had not involved Amerindians in any significant way. The result was that when the policy was announced, it hit a solid wall of opposition. Amerindians achieved something approaching unanimity for the first time since the arrival of Europeans, and probably for the first time ever. The National Indian Brotherhood (NIB) said flatly that the proposals were not acceptable: 'We view this as a policy designed to divest us of our aboriginal, residual, and statutory rights. If we accept this policy, and in the process lose our rights and our lands, we become willing partners in culture genocide. This we cannot do.'[13]

The government's proposal to transfer services to the provinces was interpreted as a move not only to sever federal links of responsibility and accountability towards Amerindians, but also to convert Amerindian reserves into a form of municipality. In the words of Dave Courchene (Neeghani Binehse, 'Leading Thunderbird'), president of the Manitoba Indian Brotherhood from 1967 to 1974:

> Once again the future of Indian people has been dealt with in a high-handed and arbitrary manner. We have not been consulted, we have been advised of decisions already taken. I feel like a man who has been told he must die and am now to be consulted on the methods of implementing that decision.[14]

When Barber was named commissioner for Indian land claims later that same year, the NIB rejected his office as an outgrowth of the White Paper, viewing it as an attempt to force the policy on Amerindians. He would not be authorized to deal with Aboriginal rights; rather, he would simply be adjudicating claims arising from treaties and settling grievances, most of which concerned lands and money. This reflected Prime Minister Trudeau's personal rejection of the concept of Aboriginal right at that time.

The government, in its attempts to answer these criticisms and to promote its policies, in 1970 hired a Cree lawyer from Calgary, William I.C. Wuttunee. A former chief of the National Indian Council of Canada who once had urged the establishment of a separate Amerindian state,[15] Wuttenee by then was advocating active Indian participation in white society and supported the White Paper. Instead of easing the opposition, as the government had hoped, the appointment inflamed it; Wuttenee was banned from several reserves, including his own, Red Pheasant.[16] Quickly resigning his new post, he wrote *Ruffled Feathers*, in which he observed that Amerindians should do more than 'cry about broken promises and broken treaties' and actively develop programs to improve their lot. He did not see that such a course of action would endanger Amerindian identity or the goal of self-government.[17] Native Senator James Gladstone was also sympathetic to the White Paper's goal of equality for all: as he had said on an earlier occasion, Amerindians 'are the only ethnic group in Canada with a special act.' He felt that the Indian Act was a hindrance for Amerindians rather than a help.[18] Other Amerindian voices upheld this position, particularly in British Columbia.[19]

An immediate effect of the White Paper was an enormous increase in research into Indian affairs, not only by academics, government officials, and concerned individuals but also by Amerindians themselves. Among the myriad reports and papers that resulted, the one written by the Indian Association of Alberta, *Citizens Plus* (known as the 'Red Paper'), was adopted as the official Amerindian response. Rejecting wardship, it still advocated special status, but as defined by the treaties.[20] The White Paper spurred the formation of the Union of BC Chiefs in 1969, but political cohesion did not develop, and the Union died in 1975. Eventually, the force of the opposition led Trudeau to concede that the government had been 'very naive . . . too theoretical . . . too abstract . . . not pragmatic enough or understanding enough'. He assured an Amerindian delegation, 'we won't force any solution on you, because we are not looking for any particular solution.' The White Paper was formally retracted on 17 March 1971.

The idea of devolving responsibility for Amerindian administration from Ottawa to the provinces, far from being dead, reappeared in 1986 in the Ministerial Task Force on Program Review (Nielsen Report), which couched the notion in financial terms, recommending that

In this photo, from June 1970, Harold Cardinal,
president of the Indian Association of Alberta, tells
Prime Minister Trudeau and cabinet members
that treaty claims should be handled by a 'truly
impartial' commission.
(The Canadian Press)

the cost of Amerindian programs be shared
with the provinces. It met the same fate as the
White Paper.[21]

Motivating Forces

Rising administrative costs had been at the
heart of this government initiative. There had
been a doubling in parliamentary appropria-
tions for Indian Affairs in less than a decade,
with an Amerindian population explosion of
almost equal proportions. There were then
2,428,114 hectares of reserve land, some in territory never surrendered by Indians. In addition, the school system for the Natives had
failed, and there was a growing need for massive social services. Countering these developments, bands were taking more control of their

own affairs, particularly since the 1980s. In
some cases, agents were being asked to leave
reserves, a step that Walpole Island First Nation
had initiated in 1965.

A side effect of the White Paper was to pop-
ularize the term 'Aboriginal rights', just coming
into general use at that time. The term 'aborigine' derives from the Latin *ab* ('from') and *origo*
('origin'), and was first defined in international
law in 1918:

> Aborigines are members of uncivilized tribes
> which inhabit a region at the time a civilized
> State extends its sovereignty over the region,
> and which have so inhabited from time imme-
> morial; and also the uncivilized descendants
> of such persons dwelling in a region.[22]

Contemporary Natives, of course, unanimously and quite rightly reject the notion that they
are 'uncivilized descendants' of 'uncivilized
tribes'; however, they have found the term useful because it takes in Amerindians, Métis, and
Inuit, and so has been adopted by all three. An
alternative is 'indigene', which does not carry
the connotation of 'uncivilized'. 'Aborigine'
was being used in Canada by early in the nineteenth century;[23] 'Aboriginal right' had made
an appearance by the end of the century. In
Canadian case law, we find the term in *Regina
v. White and Bob*, 1965, a case involving hunting and fishing rights (Chapter 23). As previously noted, 'Indian title' had been the term
used in the *St Catherine's Milling* case. As originally used, 'Aboriginal rights' referred only to
land; in 1972 it was defined as 'those property
rights which inure to Native peoples by virtue
of their occupation upon certain lands from
time immemorial'. Today, most Native speakers
use the term to include rights to self-determination and self-government. The terms 'specific claims' and 'comprehensive claims' came
into use in 1973 following the Nisga'a decision,
when Ottawa issued its policy on Amerindians

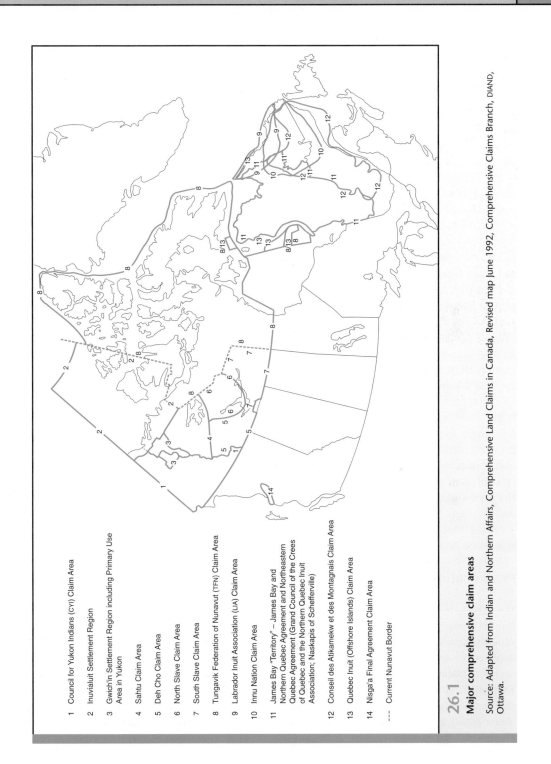

26.1

Major comprehensive claim areas

Source: Adapted from Indian and Northern Affairs, Comprehensive Land Claims in Canada, Revised map June 1992, Comprehensive Claims Branch, DIAND, Ottawa.

1 Council for Yukon Indians (CYI) Claim Area

2 Inuvialuit Settlement Region

3 Gwich'in Settlement Region including Primary Use Area in Yukon

4 Sahtu Claim Area

5 Deh Cho Claim Area

6 North Slave Claim Area

7 South Slave Claim Area

8 Tungavik Federation of Nunavut (TFN) Claim Area

9 Labrador Inuit Association (LIA) Claim Area

10 Innu Nation Claim Area

11 James Bay "Territory" – James Bay and Northern Quebec Agreement and Northeastern Quebec Agreement (Grand Council of the Crees of Quebec and the Northern Quebec Inuit Association; Naskapis of Schefferville)

12 Conseil des Atikamekw et des Montagnais Claim Area

13 Quebec Inuit (Offshore Islands) Claim Area

14 Nisga'a Final Agreement Claim Area

- - - Current Nunavut Border

and Inuit land claims. 'Specific claims' are those that concern obligations arising out of the treaties, the Indian Act, or regulations; 'comprehensive claims' are those arising in areas where rights of traditional use and occupancy have not been extinguished by treaty or superseded by law.[24] The first comprehensive claim Ottawa accepted for negotiation was that of the Council for Yukon Indians, a claim that was not resolved until 1993.[25] Details of the final agreement are dealt with in Chapter 27.

The withdrawal of the White Paper has meant that the Indian Act is still in effect; currently, the government still has the legal right to make unilateral decisions, even to the point of terminating treaties. As early as 1971, however, it was funding Native political organizations to act as forums for policy discussions.[26] This, of course, was a complete turnabout from its 1920s move to curb such organizations by cutting their funding. In other areas, such as social assistance programs, Amerindians are no longer expected to assimilate to Euro-Canadian ways. Reserves, instead of being regarded as temporary expedients for easing Amerindians into mainstream society, are now seen as homelands that Amerindians have a right to control. But it will take a long time to rectify the poor social conditions that have developed on so many of them.[27] It is now generally accepted that settling land claims is a key to economic development.

Proliferating Claims

The great increase in Aboriginal claims in recent years reflects the freedom of action Amerindians now possess. In the past, rules of application that were not a serious hindrance for non-Indians were severe handicaps for Natives. This was the case with the regulation that required governmental approval before a claim could be launched against the Crown. The special status of Indians meant that practically all their dealings were with the government, so that before the rule was repealed in 1951 it was difficult for them to get their cases heard. This was further complicated by their status as wards of the government—wards were not believed to have the legal right to challenge their guardians. In the words of Arthur Meighen in 1916, in connection with the surrender of St Peter's Reserve near Winnipeg: 'The Government of Canada represents the Indians; the Indians are our wards, and we are making the settlement as their guardians.'[28] There was no shortage of critics to point out that the arbitrary removal of the reserve to another location was hardly the behaviour of a guardian. Other reserves have suffered similar treatment; for instance, when agricultural settlement expanded into the Peace and Rainy River districts during the 1920s, reserves were subdivided for farms.[29] The ambivalence of the government's position at the political level led to vacillation between authoritarianism and accommodation on the practical level. On the one hand the government prevented the development of claims, but on the other it encouraged and funded them by means of loans. This ambivalence has been encouraged by the high stakes involved—in Ontario alone, about 87 per cent of the land and waters are still held by the Crown.

In general, there was more concern with settling issues than with finding effective mechanisms to determine the validity for claims. Under the circumstances, it was far easier for the claims to be created than to be resolved. The comment of Ellen Fairclough, Minister of Citizenship and Immigration, 1958–62, to the Department of Justice in 1961 was indicative of official attitudes: 'Knowing the history of Indian claims one may well ask whether, even if adjudicated, they will ever be permanently settled as far as the Indians are concerned.'[30]

One of the best-known and longest-standing claims that is still unresolved is that of the

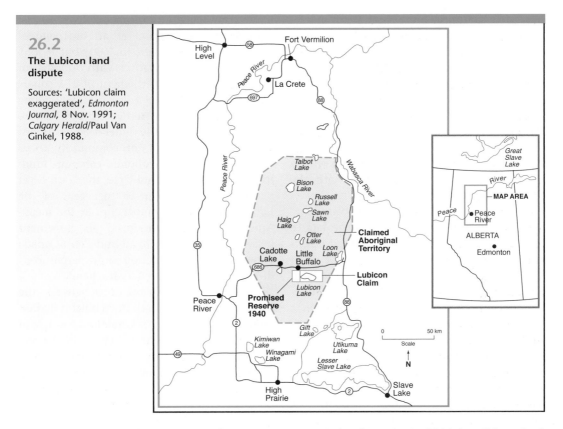

26.2

The Lubicon land dispute

Sources: 'Lubicon claim exaggerated', *Edmonton Journal*, 8 Nov. 1991; *Calgary Herald*/Paul Van Ginkel, 1988.

Cree Lubicon band of the Treaty Eight area in oil-rich northern Alberta.[31] One of the groups that had been missed at the treaty signing, it was not until 1933 that the band applied for a land settlement. The move had been spurred by fears that the Great Depression would drive hordes of whites into the bush, even those regions as remote as that of the Lubicon; in fact, that was already happening in some areas. Ottawa, responding in 1939, promised the band a reserve. On the basis of a band count of 127 members, and according to the terms of Treaty Eight, a site of 25.4 square miles (65 square kilometres) was selected in 1940 at the western end of Lubicon Lake and approved by both federal and provincial governments. However, the site was never surveyed. Disputes had arisen about band lists, which blossomed into a judicial inquiry in 1944 that did not lead to a settlement acceptable to the band. There matters lay until 1952, when mining and oil explorations expanded into the Lubicon's area. By then the situation was much more complex, particularly after 1979, when a provincial road provided easy access to the previously remote region. The band's attempts to prevent the road construction had failed. By 1982 there were 400 oil wells within a 24-kilometre radius of the Lubicon band community,[32] whose main settlement was called 'Little Buffalo'. Alberta's approval for a pulp mill in the general region, while not directly affecting lands claimed by the Lubicon, has not simplified the situation either.[33] In the meantime, in 1978, a chief named Bernard Ominayak, who is still in office, had taken over the band's leadership.

Court hearings, more judicial inquiries (including one by former Justice Minister Davie Fulton in 1985–6), a vigorous public relations campaign that involved road blockades, and an attempt to boycott an exhibition, 'The Spirit Sings', held at Calgary's Glenbow Museum in 1988 in conjunction with the Fifteenth Olympic Winter Games still have not resulted in a settlement. At one point in 1988 it looked as though the cycle would be broken when an agreement was reached with the province. But the deal fell apart when Ottawa objected to 60 of the names on the band list.[34] Another sticking point has been the band's insistence on compensation for what it claims is irreparable damage to its way of life, a point that neither the courts nor Ottawa has been willing to grant. The band, once a self-sustaining hunting community, now depends on a combination of wage work and transfer payments to supplement hunting, which has been reduced to part-time because of the erosion of the wildlife base. This situation, of course, is not unique to the Lubicon but has become prevalent throughout the North. In spite of this changing pattern in the basic lifestyle, cultural identity remains strong; for one thing, the Lubicon still retain Cree as their first language.

In 1989, 350 of its members broke away and won Ottawa's recognition as a separate band, 'Woodland Cree'. Within a year the Woodland Cree reached an agreement-in-principle with federal and provincial governments, by which they received a reserve of 142 square kilometres, $35.1 million for the construction of a new community, plus $13 million for socio-economic development and $512,000 in cash.[35] What the Woodland Cree gave up in return was not announced; what was clear was that the department's policy of taking advantage of divisions among the people themselves was working, as the Treaty Eight chiefs have unanimously refused to recognize the new

band. Another group, the Loon River people, won federal recognition as an independent band under Treaty Eight in 1991, but it took eight years of negotiation with Alberta for them to win a land settlement of 181 square kilometres (70 square miles) in 1999 along with a provincial cash settlement of $7.5 million. In addition, the federal government provided $44 million for community infrastructure and socio-economic catch-up funding. With the Woodland Cree, the Loon River people represent about 30 per cent of the Lubicon's claimed membership. In the meantime, Ominayak announced an agreement between the Lubicon band and Petro-Canada allowing for oil exploration under certain conditions on lands claimed by the band.

At present, the negotiations between the federal government and the Lubicon nation remain unresolved, a consequence, perhaps, of the Lubicon's appearance before the United Nations Human Rights Committee in 2005 to press the Canadian government to settle the long-standing claim. As of June 2008, negotiations between both parties had been broken off for several years.[36]

Another confrontation that also came into the national spotlight, but for a much shorter period, was that of the Ojibwa of Kenora, Ontario, about 160 kilometres east of Winnipeg and 480 kilometres west of Thunder Bay. The town had become a gathering point for dislocated Amerindians as their hunting way of life had become steadily less viable. The good relations that had been enjoyed by non-Aboriginals and Amerindians during the economic partnership of fur-trade days slowly gave way to recrimination and bitterness; Natives found little place in the wage-earning economy that took over and were seen as being a useless drain on public resources. By the 1960s, social division and discrimination were entrenched; by 1964 the Indians had had enough and organized a march of protest on Ottawa. The first such event in Canada, it involved 400 Indians and six reserves.

As usual on such occasions, agitators were blamed; if anything, the prejudices of the whites were intensified. Since peaceful measures had not worked, the Natives organized themselves in the Ojibway Warriors Society, under the leadership of Louis Cameron, and barricaded themselves in an armed camp in Anishinabe Park, on land they claimed as rightfully theirs. The land, purchased by Indian Affairs as a camping area for Indians, had been sold without consultation with the Natives to the town, which had developed it into a tourist area. The four-week stand-off was deplored by many of the Indians themselves; the Warriors Society did not enjoy the support of many of those who had participated in the 1964 march. They felt that such tactics were too much reflective of the confrontational approach of the American Indian Movement, which would be more successful in encouraging backlash than in finding solutions. In effect, that is what happened.[37]

At the close of 1990, between 500 and 600 specific land claims were outstanding, some of them for 15 years or more. Of these, about 100 have been settled. The present Indian Specific Claims Commission, with increased funding to speed up the process, was established in 1991 in response to the Oka crisis. Despite some success, it has also met with frustrations. Its cost during its first five years of operation totalled $23 million.[38]

A complicating factor in all these cases is the administrative complexity of the Canadian federation, particularly the division of powers between Ottawa and the provinces. Indians are a federal responsibility, while land and social programs come under provincial authority. Lengthy negotiations, sometimes lasting for years, are the result. For just one example, there is no end in sight for settling land claims that have already been brought forward, let alone those that have yet to be made.

Across the Border in Alaska

In 1971, on the heels of the failed White Paper, both Canadian Amerindians and the government were keenly aware of the agreement reached by the United States and the Native peoples of Alaska. Alaskan Amerindians, Inuit, Kupik and Inupiat Eskimos, and Aleut had laid claims to most of Alaska; when oil and gas exploration continued, they had been able to obtain a land freeze in 1966 until their claims were settled. The Alaska Native Claims Settlement Act of 1971 marked a radical departure from any previous Native land settlement policy in the US or elsewhere. It was the first time that subsurface rights were included in a Native claims settlement; in Canada, Amerindians would not obtain such rights until the James Bay Agreement of 1975.

The Act entitled Alaskan Natives to 40 million acres (16,189,424 hectares) divided among 220 villages and 12 regional corporations; the entitlement comprised about 15 per cent of the state's area. The villages have the surface estate to 22 million acres (8,903,083 hectares) while the corporations (which are under Native control) hold all subsurface rights plus full title to 16 million acres (6,474,970 hectares). The remaining 2 million acres (809,371 hectares) are for sundry purposes, including cemeteries and historic sites. Units can be allotted from this land, not exceeding 160 acres (65 hectares) per capita, to Natives living outside of villages. A land-use commission was also established, of which at least one member must be a Native; its role is advisory, not regulatory. The whole project was financed by a grant of a half-billion dollars from the US treasury over a period of 11 years, as well as by another half-billion from mineral resources from lands conveyed to the state. In this way, the state shared in the settlement of Native claims. The rationale behind this settlement was that it should not only satisfy legal and moral claims but should also provide a foundation for the social and economic advancement of Native peoples.

Although it has not been smooth sailing for the Alaska solution, which encountered unexpected difficulties,[39] the present outcome is positive. For one thing, the Permanent Fund, established after the oil strike at Prudhoe Bay, has been sharing resultant revenues with residents on an annual basis. In 1996, this meant that 543,000 Alaskans each received a cheque for $1,130.68.[40] For another, the 12 Alaska Native regional corporations, established under the Alaska Native Claims Settlement Act, saw their revenues grow by 250 per cent over the past decade. Profits grew by 98 per cent and shareholder equity doubled.

A Declaration of First Nations

In 1973 the Canadian government, responding to a claim by the Natives of the Yukon, as well as to claims in British Columbia and Quebec, reaffirmed its continuing responsibility for Indians and Inuit under the BNA Act; it also referred to the Proclamation of 1763 as 'a basic declaration of the Indian people's interests in land in this country'. It recognized the loss of traditional use and occupancy of lands in BC, northern Quebec, Yukon, and the Northwest Territories in areas where 'Indian title was never extinguished by treaty or superseded by law.' For those areas, the government offered to negotiate and enshrine in legislation a settlement involving compensation or benefits in return for relinquishment of the Native interest. There was the qualifier that while Ottawa could negotiate for the two northern areas, elsewhere provincial governments were involved. By now, however, Natives were more interested in entrenchment of their rights than in extinguishment. They relied on a statement made by the Queen in Calgary in 1973: 'You may be assured that my government of Canada recognizes the importance of full compliance with the spirit and terms of your treaties.'

In the midst of these developments, 'A Declaration of First Nations' was adopted by the Joint Council of Chiefs and Elders:

> We, the original peoples of this land know the Creator put us here.
> The Creator gave us laws that govern all our relationships to live in harmony with nature and mankind.
> The laws of the Creator defined our rights and responsibilities.
> The Creator gave us our spiritual beliefs, our languages, our culture, and a place on Mother Earth which provided us with all our needs.
> We have maintained our freedom, our languages, and our traditions from time immemorial.
> We continue to exercise the rights and fulfill the responsibilities and obligations given to us by the Creator for the land upon which we were placed.
> The Creator has given us the right to govern ourselves and the right to self-determination.
> The rights and responsibilities given to us by the Creator cannot be altered or taken away by any other Nation.

These views have roots that go deep into Amerindian traditions, even though expressed in contemporary terms. Both Pontiac and Tecumseh would have been comfortable with its fundamental premises. Pontiac, reminding the British that 'This country was given by God to the Indians', added that it was the role of the British to preserve it for their joint use.[41] The British, of course, were already convinced the country was theirs, by right of their recent conquest of the French and also by settlement.

Today, the Canadian public, in general, is supportive of—or at least does not strongly oppose—the Amerindian position, particularly in regard to land claims.[42] There has also been a growing public awareness that the justice system has not served Aboriginals well; they are three times more likely to be jailed than non-Aboriginals. This was dramatically illustrated by the Donald Marshall case in Nova Scotia. Marshall, a Mi'kmaq, was convicted in 1971 for a murder he did not commit and was jailed for 11 years before being exonerated in 1983. A subsequent investigation pilloried the justice system for failing Marshall at every turn.[43] Similarly in Alberta, a Royal Commission headed by Justice Allan Cawsey found that 'Systemic discrimination exists in the criminal justice system. There is no doubt that aboriginal people are over-represented in this system and that, at best, the equal application of the law has unequal results.'[44] Former Indian Affairs Minister Tom Siddon (in office, 1990–3) agreed that Canadian justice in general has displayed 'inadequate sensitivity' to the particular needs of the Natives.[45] On the other side of the picture, the first Justice of the Territorial Court of the Northwest Territories (from 1955 to 1965), Jack Sissons, became known for his efforts to apply the law in terms that the people understood.[46] This was carried a step further on 6 October 2000 with the opening of Canada's first Aboriginal court on the Tsuu T'ina reserve just west of Calgary. With an Aboriginal judge, Aboriginal prosecutors, and Aboriginal peacemakers, it is geared to recognize Native traditions and values, as well as languages and customs. Chief Roy Whitney sees it as 'providing the opportunity to create our own system of justice'. Expected to cost about $250,000 annually, the court is financed by the Alberta Justice Department.[47]

Another promising development was pioneered earlier by Ontario's Gull Bay band (Ojibwa) when it organized its own reserve police force in 1974, a first for Canada. Others have followed suit, with encouraging results: a drop in the crime rate on reserves serviced by their own police. Kanesatake recently took this step when it signed an agreement with the federal and provincial governments. It was hailed as a breakthrough in easing relations with the Sûreté du Québec (the Quebec police), which had remained strained ever since the Oka/Kanesatake crisis six years earlier. Called Peacekeepers, as is the already established force at Kahnawake, the 12-man force is maintaining the general law of the land as well as that of Kanesatake.[48]

The Emerging Arctic

The introduction of a reindeer herd into Canada's western Arctic in the 1930s was an event of epic proportions. Officials, concerned about providing the Inuit with a stable subsistence base as wildlife diminished and impressed with Alaska's success with a herd imported in the 1890s, decided to follow suit. Earlier failures with similar projects made them cautious.[49] They hired Arctic expert A.E. Porsild, later to become chief botanist of the National Museum of Canada, 1946–7, and his brother, Robert T., to assess the feasibility of such a project. Acting on their report that the area between the Mackenzie and Coppermine rivers and between Great Bear Lake and the Arctic Ocean was capable of supporting 500,000 animals, the federal government purchased an Alaskan herd of about 3,000 animals in 1929.[50] The drive was entrusted to Lapp herders under the direction of Andrew Bahr, who was in his sixties. The story of their progress over 3,200 kilometres (2,000 miles) across 'the roof of the world' was eagerly followed by the press; finally, in 1935, 2,370 animals (fewer than 700 of which were among those who had left Nome five years earlier) arrived at Kittigazuit in the eastern Mackenzie Delta. There the herd was maintained for 40 years under government management until being sold to private interests in 1974. Since then the herd has flourished; it now numbers some 16,000 animals, although it still has not reached the size envisioned by the Porsilds. Neither has the government's vision of turning

Inuit hunters into herders been more than partially realized.[51] It has, however, supplied the region with meat, hides, and antlers for export to Korea, and its promise is high for the future. Two other herds of about 800 animals each have been started further east.[52] In August 2007, an international network of scientists began to examine caribou and wild reindeer herds across the Arctic, from Alaska and Yukon to Greenland and Russia. The four-year, $4 million International Polar Year project aims to gather data across the region on those herds, how they are changing, and how that affects people who depend on the animals for survival.[53]

Other efforts were less successful, from all points of view. These included attempts at introducing sheep and pigs, and experimentations with grasses, potatoes, and other crops. According to historian Richard Diubaldo, most of these attempts were characterized by haste and lack of proper research.[54]

The destruction of the natural subsistence base in the Far North was proceeding faster than replacements, although there were successes, such as the programs to rehabilitate beaver and muskrat in trapped-out areas.[55] The collapse of the white fox market, 1948–50, when the rest of Canada was experiencing an economic boom, was another manifestation of the widespread and complex changes sweeping the Far North. The difficulties of the trapping industry increased even more with the campaign of the anti-fur lobby; in the 1990s, it was again in a severe depression.

A turning point in official evaluation of the Arctic was reached during and after World War II, when its strategic importance in world geopolitics became glaringly evident. The crucial roles of its weather stations and the Distant Early Warning radar line to military operations caused authorities to take another look at the land and its people. Not that there was an immediate change in attitude: when family allowances and old age pensions were intro-

duced, for instance, there was hesitation about including northern Natives; in the end they were not sent cheques, but credit was arranged at HBC posts for designated food supplies.[56] In the case of family allowances, the requirement that the children attend school led to the government undertaking the construction of the necessary buildings in the forties, and thus to the end of the old reliance on missions.

Throughout this period the policy of 'encouraging' Inuit to relocate in areas selected by the government was in full force; as Jenness remarked, permanent villages were not within the Inuit experience before the arrival of whites, and not one that has been developed since has been on a site selected by them.[57] At first the relocations were co-ordinated with the fur trade; the HBC was informed in 1934 that if it wished to continue its operation in the North, it must assume responsibility for Native welfare without expense to the department.[58] That failures resulted is hardly surprising; the considerations that guided the selections did not always match with the conditions needed by the Inuit for survival. This was illustrated by a series of attempts that began in 1934 when 22 Inuit from Cape Dorset, 18 from Pond Inlet, and 12 from Pangnirtung were transported to Dundas Harbour. What had appeared to officials to be a suitable location, accessible by sea, abounding in marine life, and with good prospects for furs, turned out to have ice conditions in winter that impeded both hunting and dog-team travel needed to maintain traplines. After two years the Inuit had to be evacuated, some to go back to their home bases but others to try life in still another location. In the succeeding years Inuit were transported to one site after another (Croker Bay, Arctic Bay, Fort Ross, Spence Bay), each one of which proved to be unsuitable for the hunting and trapping way of life that officials were convinced must be preserved.[59]

This shifting of the Inuit population in a

Voisey sisters, Repulse Bay, NWT, modelling their lavishly decorated parkas, 1940.
(Reproduced with the permission of Natural Resources Canada 2008, courtesy of the Geological Survey of Canada, photo #86759 by D.A. Nichols)

frantic search for locations where they could combine traditional lifestyles with trapping reached its peak from 1958 to 1962 but continued at least to the end of the seventies.[60] Game continued to diminish, and Inuit continued to die of starvation and disease as they were shuttled back and forth. Harassed officials, on receiving reports that there were plenty of fish in the lakes, issued gill nets to a group near Baker Lake, either ignorant of or disregarding a taboo of the Inuit of the region against eating fish harvested by drowning. The Inuit had no objections to fish caught by methods that did

not involve drowning, however. By the mid-fifties and early sixties the Inuit had the highest rate of tuberculosis in the world, an ironic situation at a time when an elaborate health-care system was being established in the Arctic. According to anthropologist Robert Williamson, by 1964 more than 70 per cent of Keewatin Inuit had been in sanatoria for periods ranging from three months to nine years.[61] Those sent 'outside' for treatment often vanished without a trace as far as their families and relatives were concerned; sometimes, in the case of children, they were adopted by southern families without their parents being informed.[62]

Still convinced of the need to relocate, the government considered, and rejected, a plan to move the Inuit to the south. The North needed its people, above all those who knew how to cope with its rigorous demands. A new reason had also emerged to reinforce the argument for more balanced use of natural resources: the need for settlement to support Canada's claims to sovereignty. Spurred by this imperative of international politics, the government began in 1953 to move Inuit from Inukjuak (Port Harrison) in Arctic Quebec, where the population had grown too large for living off the land, to Ellesmere Island, in the High Arctic, where game resources were untouched. As well, Inuit were brought in from Pond Inlet, northern Baffin Island. In all, nearly 90 Inuit were relocated to Grise Fiord and Resolute Bay in a forced move to which they did not become reconciled. Now living side by side at Grise Fiord, the two Inuit communities still have not integrated with each other; those at Resolute Bay have done better. Not only that, but the game resources available were not what the new arrivals were used to; the social and community ramifications of this sudden switch are only now becoming appreciated. As anthropologist Milton Freeman has made clear, integrity of food supply and cultural identity are fundamentally linked for Arctic hunters.[63]

Although the second generation has managed somewhat better, and the government has regarded Grise Fiord as a showplace it is proud to display to important visitors, basic problems such as the control of local game resources have not yet been resolved. Older Inuit have drifted back to their original homes and have asked for $10 million in compensation, plus expenses for their return. When the Aboriginal Affairs Committee of the House of Commons came out in favour of compensation, the government offered $200,000 plus a plaque recognizing the role of the Inuit in establishing Canada's claims to those distant regions.[64] Since then the government has claimed that its principal purpose in the relocations had been to improve the lot of the Inuit, a claim that has been disputed by historian Shelagh Grant.[65] In Grant's view, concern about its sovereignty in the Arctic had been Canada's principal motivation for the resettlement policy, which she termed a 'misadventure'. The Inuit put it more strongly: as they see it, they have been the subjects of a social and political experiment.[66]

In the opinion of anthropologist Milton Freeman, 'long-term viability of a small artificial community such as Grise Fiord has always been in doubt.'[67] An Inuk voice on the problems of the new communities was that of Abe Okpik, who in 1967 was the first Inuk to be appointed to the Northwest Territories Council. He had come to official attention through his successful campaign to abolish the system of identifying Inuit with numbered fibre discs worn around the neck instead of names for such purposes as census-taking and welfare distribution.[68] In his view, poverty had no place in the traditional lifestyle; it began 'when a person is bewildered and has no way to impose his ways in a completely new environment'.[69]

A strikingly different impression of the resettlement programs was reported by Gordon Robertson, deputy minister of resources and development and commissioner for the Northwest Territories when he visited Resolute Bay in 1960; on a second visit, in 1976, he was secretary to the cabinet for federal–provincial relations. In his recently published *Memoirs of a Very Civil Servant*, he said he never heard a word of complaint. 'Nor did I ever, from 1953 to 1963, receive any request by any Inuit or family to move back to their former home. I did receive requests from some of the people of Resolute and Grise Fiord to have friends from Inukjuak come to join them because the hunting at the new settlements was so much better than on the "hungry coast".[70]

The accusation of the slaughter of Inuit sled dogs may remain outstanding for some Inuit to this day. Inuit elders alleged the RCMP were responsible for a mass culling of sled dogs in Nunavik and Nunavut between 1950 and 1970, carried out either at the direction of the government or on the RCMP's own initiative. In May 2006, the Royal Canadian Mounted Police presented its *Final Report* on the matter to the Minister of Public Safety, Stockwell Day. The review did not uncover any evidence to support the allegations and pointed out that the length of time between when such actions were said to have been taken and when complaints 'first came public in 1999–2000' created difficulty in determining truth. The allegations were linked to the government aim at the time to settle Inuit in communities, and the *Report* suggested that they may have reflected a lament for the loss of a way of life, noting that dialogue and understanding are now necessary. The *Report*, however, did find evidence that some Inuit sled dogs were destroyed by members of the RCMP. This was said to have been undertaken for public health and safety reasons, in accordance with the law, for the purpose of containing canine epidemics or at the request of dog owners.[71]

As the Inuit became 'one of the most heavily assisted, administered, and studied groups on earth',[72] the advice of Canadian explorer Vilhjalmur Stefansson (1879–1962)[73] began to seem more attractive: allow the Inuit to work out their own solutions to the dramatic changes in their circumstances, but support them when necessary. Stefansson maintained the difficulties of living in the Arctic had been exaggerated; in his famous phrase, it was actually a 'friendly' place.[74] Instead of keeping Inuit away from non-Native settlements, as the government had been trying with increasing desperation to do, allow them to come in and provide as many jobs as possible. The government acceded to this fundamental reorientation of policy, which was announced in the Northwest Territories Legislative Council by deputy minister Gordon Robertson in 1958.[75]

Co-operatives, designed to bring the control of renewable resources into the regions, made their appearance the following year, 1959, when two were set up in the Ungava Bay district. They quickly spread throughout the Arctic and into the Northwest Territories. Initially concerned with the harvesting of such resources as fish, fur, and game, they soon expanded into handicrafts and the arts, as well as into managing housing projects, retail stores, and other commercial ventures. They have proven to be a major aid to the Inuit in their leap into the market economy, which in turn created a new set of problems.[76] For one example, the move of the Inuit into permanent communities led to a housing crisis, which Ottawa made worse by decreeing that houses should be uniformly built, thereby denying thousands of years of traditional ecological knowledge. The program got underway in the 1950s but never managed to catch up with the need; in 1991 there were reports of 16 people living in one inadequate house, and Nellie Cournoyea, territorial government leader, 1991–5, estimated that immediate needs called for 2,000 more units, without taking into account the forecast of a doubled population within 30 years.[77]

In May 1959 the first Canadian Inuk to speak in an official capacity addressed the Eskimo Affairs Committee meeting in Parliament's East Block in Ottawa. John Diefenbaker, Conservative Prime Minister, 1957–63, was among those present. George Koneak of Fort Chimo (Kuujjuaq, Nunavik) had just returned from a visit to Greenland, where he had been impressed with the prosperity of the Inuit, who were 'working and making money—as fishermen, farmers, working in different factories', who owned 'a lot of boats, a lot of houses'. In Koneak's view, 'the Eskimos don't want to go back to the old days any more.' What they wanted was help to join in the technological world that had engulfed them.[78]

As if that were not challenge enough, the Arctic is facing an even more profound change: global warming, the effects of which are first manifesting themselves in those ice-bound regions. As the warming climate modifies the environment, the wildlife also changes, with new forms appearing and established ones fading away. For one obvious example, as ice floes melt, seals, a traditional Inuit food source, disappear. As well, later seasonal freeze-ups and earlier breakups shorten the hunting season. Insects, birds, and fish are all adapting their ranges to the changing circumstances. Thunder and lightning, once unknown in those regions, now characterize the summers. (For more on climate change and global warming, see Chapter 29.)

Deeply disturbing is the growing gap between traditional ecological knowledge and the situation as it has become today. Fiercely debated is the role of human industry in encouraging these developments and to what extent they can be controlled. A video made at Sachs Harbour, a fishing village on the shores of Banks Island in Canada's western Arctic, tells what has happened so far in that area. It was shown to delegates of 170 countries at a global warming conference in The Hague.[79]

Chapter 27

Rocky Road to Self-Government

The legal position of Amerindians in Canada is determined not only by the Indian Act but also by the Constitution and the treaties. Despite the Canadian Charter of Rights and Freedoms, which in theory overrides all other statutes, the Indian Act continues to define Amerindian rights even as 'it reflects so little faith in the Indians.'[1] Far from viewing Amerindians as equals, its goals of protection and assimilation have led to an emphasis on control rather than development.[2] Initiative and enterprise have been stifled, ensuring a high degree of poverty and underachievement. In the words of Native spokesman Harold Cardinal, it has 'subjugated to colonial rule the very people whose rights it was supposed to protect'.[3] This was not fundamentally altered when Amerindians were granted the federal vote in 1960 without compromising their special status. By that time, Amerindian veterans had the vote, as well as individuals living off reserves and those on reserves who had accepted taxation; Inuit had had the vote since 1950. Even with enfranchisement, Amerindians, whether veterans or otherwise, did not have access to equality of opportunity and social benefits. Max Yalden, head of the Canadian Human Rights Commission, 1987–96, joined those who again raised the cry of the 1969 White Paper, that the Department of Indian and Northern Affairs should be scrapped and the 'outdated and paternalistic' Indian Act replaced with new policies.[4]

Developing technology has been turning more industrial attention to northern resources; in 1957, Diefenbaker led the Conservatives to an overwhelming victory with his vision of the 'New North'. His model was a colonial one: improved transportation to the North, so that people and industrial know-how could be brought in to exploit northern resources and ship the benefits south. This attitude was also reflected in changes in federal procedure; in 1966, Indian administration and northern resources management were combined in the Department of Indian Affairs and Northern Development, which is how matters stand today, except that the name has been shortened to Indian and Northern Affairs. Industrialization has continued in the earlier pattern, with little consideration for the cultural milieu of the North or the needs of its peoples.

TIMELINE

1960	Amerindians enfranchised without compromising their unique status.
1961	Highway from Edmonton completed to Yellowknife.
1966	Indian administration and northern resources management combined in Department of Indian Affairs and Northern Development (today called Department of Indian and Northern Affairs).
1968	Smallboy's Camp, a traditionalist encampment on Crown land in southern Alberta, is established by hereditary Cree chief Johnny Bob Smallboy.
1969	Chief John Tetlichi of Fort McPherson first Indian named to Northwest Territories Council.
1970	Mercury pollution of English–Wabigoon River system in northwestern Ontario, which devastated Grassy Narrows and Whitedog reserves since 1950s, is traced to Reed Paper Company mill at Dryden, Ontario.
1971	Inuit Tapirisat of Canada formed in response to announcement of Quebec's proposed James Bay hydroelectric project.
1972	Cree and Inuit of northern Quebec get injunction to stop James Bay Project, but it is suspended on appeal.
1974–7	Mackenzie Valley Pipeline Inquiry (Berger Inquiry) sets new standard for listening to and accounting for Aboriginal concerns about development projects.
1975	James Bay and Northern Quebec Agreement reached between governments and Inuit and Cree of northern Quebec falls short of entrenching Native rights.
1976–7	Len Marchand first Amerindian federal cabinet minister.

1978	Northeastern Quebec Agreement signed by Innu and Hydro-Québec and provincial and federal governments extends area of James Bay Agreement.
1982	Patriation of Canadian Constitution; Constitution Act, 1982 recognizes and affirms 'existing aboriginal and treaty rights'.
1983	Report of the Special Parliamentary Committee on Indian Self-Government (Penner Report) urges distinct form of Aboriginal self-government.
1983–7	Three First Ministers' Conferences on Aboriginal rights, mandated in Constitution Act, 1982, accomplish little.
1984	Cree-Naskapi Act of Quebec, hailed as the first self-government legislation for Natives, replaces Indian Act for regions it covers.
	Western Arctic Claim Agreement extinguishes Inuvialuit Aboriginal title in exchange for $55 million and ownership of 96,000 square kilometres.
1988	Ethel Blondin, a Dene, elected as the first Native woman MP.
1989	Labrador Innu protest low-flying NATO planes from Goose Bay.
1990	Manitoba MLA Elijah Harper, an Oji-Cree chief, withholds vote on ratification of Meech Lake Accord, effectively killing agreement that would have given Quebec special status while ignoring Amerindians.
1994	Mary Simon, an Inuk, appointed Circumpolar Ambassador.
1999	Nunavut, a new territory hived off from NWT in eastern Arctic, is officially founded on 1 April.

Diefenbaker's first project, a road system launched in the late 1950s, took more than a decade to complete. A highway from Edmonton reached Hay River in 1960 and Yellowknife the following year. When finally finished in the early 1970s, the Dempster Highway linked Dawson City and Inuvik.[5] Its purpose was not to serve northern communities so much as to facilitate southern exploitation of northern resources. Fortunately, it did not have the deadly impact of the Alaska Highway, the construction of which had been followed by waves of epidemics among the Native populations. During the winter of 1942–3, one small community, Teslin, Yukon, suffered outbreaks of six different diseases in eight epidemics.[6]

The Ojibwa of the Grassy Narrows and Whitedog reserves, 90 kilometres north of Kenora, Ontario, in the area of Treaty Three, experienced a different aspect of what could happen as a result of uncontrolled industrial activity. In the 1950s the reserves' water supplies showed signs of mercury pollution, but it was 1970 before it was discovered that the Reed Paper Company, a subsidiary of the British multinational, Reed International, was dumping methyl-mercury into the English–Wabigoon River system. The mill, 170 kilometres upstream at Dryden, Ontario, built in 1911, had been purchased by Reed in 1961. The contamination forced the reserves to close their commercial fisheries; still, government reaction was slow, even in the face of growing health problems in the two communities. Eventually, the Ojibwa took matters into their own hands and invited Japanese specialists from Minamata, Japan, where a similar situation had occurred, to assess what was happening. They confirmed the presence of 'Minamata disease', a motor and nervous disorder caused by mercury poisoning. Treaty assurances proved to be of little protection; when Reed announced plans for a new mill in 1974 the people had to prepare

their own case on land use and forest management. In the midst of the public scandal, an agreement for the new mill, containing some provision for environmental protection, was signed in 1976. Although contamination levels have been slowly reduced so that they are 'no longer way out of whack with other systems', the people must restrict their intake of fish to avoid unacceptable levels of methyl-mercury in their systems, as the case of a three-year-old girl illustrated.[7] Still not resolved are the possible effects of logging operations on the traditional subsistence base of wild rice harvesting, not to mention fishing, trapping, and hunting.[8]

An out-of-court settlement for $8.7 million, reached in 1985, has paved the way for the reserves to develop a program encouraging environmentally friendly industries.

Pipelines and Hydro Projects

The discovery of oil at Prudhoe Bay, Alaska, in 1968, seven years after oil exploration had begun in the Canadian High Arctic, led to a proposal for a pipeline running south down the Mackenzie Valley for 3,800 kilometres (2,400 miles) to connect into existing pipeline systems, crossing regions covered by Treaties Eight and Eleven. Three years later, in 1971, Quebec announced its intentions of developing James Bay as a gigantic hydroelectric project in a region where no treaties had been signed. In neither case was thought given to consulting the peoples of the regions involved;[9] after all, in the past, railways had been built and dams constructed without any such consultations, even though whole villages had to be relocated and local subsistence bases were ruined without compensation (this had happened in the 1960s at Manicouagan, Quebec, and in British Columbia when the W.A.C. Bennett Dam flooded the Parsnip River system; and in the 1970s at South Indian Lake, Manitoba, with the damming of the Churchill

River). The priority of development over local community well-being had never been seriously questioned, no matter what the degree of social disruption.[10]

But times had changed. Now even the churches, traditional instruments for assimilation and upholders of government policy, were questioning the high social price of economic development undertaken without regard to local situations. Anglicans had expressed their concerns in a pamphlet titled *Beyond Traplines*;[11] the Catholics in *Northern Development: At What Cost?*[12] In 1986, the General Council of the United Church of Canada publicly apologized to the Native peoples of Canada for seeking to impose on them 'our civilization as a condition of accepting the Gospel', an attempt that had left everyone involved the poorer. Recognizing that an apology in itself was not enough, the General Council in 1988 established an All Native Circle Conference as a forum of Aboriginal self-government within the church. What this meant in practice, according to Sam Bull (1947–96) of Goodfish Lake Reserve, was that Natives could now sit as equals in church assemblies dealing with Native issues. That same year Rev. Charles Arthurson, a Cree, was elected suffragan (assistant) bishop in the Anglican diocese of Saskatchewan, a first for that church.[13] Three years later, the Canadian Council of Churches convened at the Nayo-Skan Development Centre on the Hobbema Reserve outside of Edmonton to hear Nelson Okeymaw talk on Cree spiritual beliefs, with their stress on respect for Mother Earth. Such an interfaith event would have been unheard of as recently as a few decades ago.[14] Later that summer, during the annual pilgrimage to Lac Ste Anne, northwest of Edmonton, the Canadian Oblates apologized for 'the hurts caused to some of the Aboriginal peoples by the residential schools', and expressed a desire to be 'part of the healing process wherever necessary'.[15]

On the industrial front, the James Bay Project was launched without prior consultation with the Indians and Inuit who would be affected and without any intention to do so. On 30 April 1971, Robert Bourassa, Liberal Premier of Quebec from 1970 to 1976 and again from 1986 to 1994, announced the immediate start of the project, which would reconfigure the region's water and land, the largest such undertaking in North America. The Inuit reacted by forming themselves into a number of associations,[16] which were then co-ordinated by Tagak Curley (grandson of a whaler) and Meeka Wilson in 1971 under a new blanket organization, Inuit Tapirisat of Canada. It became a major voice for Inuit across the Arctic, working to 'gain political and economic control and to preserve the culture, identity, and way of life of the Inuit and to help them find their role in a changing society.' For example, the teaching of Inuktitut in Quebec classrooms, started in 1965, had made very little progress; now, however, the project took on new life and became a regular part of school curricula. Regional Inuit groups have blossomed; in northern Quebec, some of these are co-operating with the Grand Council of the Crees for the settlement of land claims that have been outstanding since the northward expansion of Quebec's boundaries in 1898 and again in 1912. A condition of these extensions was that the province would recognize and obtain surrender of Amerindian land rights, an obligation that had not been fulfilled. The last adjustment to Quebec's boundaries occurred in 1927, when the Labrador border was redrawn, transferring lands inhabited by Innu, Cree, and Inuit to Newfoundland's jurisdiction. Once again, Natives had not been consulted in these territorial adjustments. In the meantime, Inuit Tapirisat elected a young woman, Okalik Eegeesiak, as leader in 1997.

Quebec already had a record of refusing to delay development projects pending the

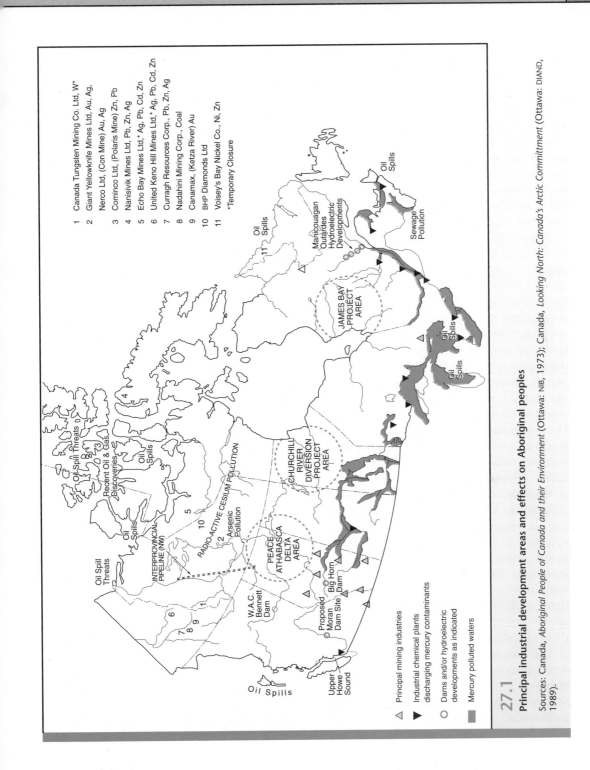

27.1

Principal industrial development areas and effects on Aboriginal peoples

Sources: Canada, *Aboriginal People of Canada and their Environment* (Ottawa: NIB, 1973); Canada, *Looking North: Canada's Arctic Committment* (Ottawa: DIAND, 1989).

Legend contents in figure:

1 Canada Tungsten Mining Co. Ltd, W*
2 Giant Yellowknife Mines Ltd, Au, Ag,
   Nerco Ltd, (Con Mine) Au, Ag
3 Cominco Ltd, (Polaris Mine) Zn, Pb
4 Nanisivik Mines Ltd, Pb, Zn, Ag
5 Echo Bay Mines Ltd,* Ag, Pb, Cd, Zn
6 United Keno Hill Mines Ltd,* Ag, Pb, Cd, Zn
7 Curragh Resources Corp., Pb, Zn, Ag
8 Nadahini Mining Corp., Coal
9 Canamax, (Ketza River) Au
10 BHP Diamonds Ltd
11 Voisey's Bay Nickel Co., Ni, Zn
*Temporary Closure

△ Principal mining industries
▲ Industrial chemical plants
   discharging mercury contaminants
○ Dams and/or hydroelectric
   developments as indicated
▨ Mercury polluted waters

resolution of Native claims. In 1972, the application for an injunction to halt the James Bay hydroelectric project on the part of the Grand Council of the Crees (Quebec) and the Northern Quebec Inuit Association was granted by Judge Albert Malouf, only to be suspended on appeal one week later. The Quebec Court of Appeals eventually ruled that Aboriginal rights in the territory had been extinguished by the Hudson's Bay Company charter of 1670. It did not explain on what basis such a unilateral action on the part of an overseas monarch was recognized in international law.

Going Public

The uproar stirred by the Inuit and Cree was unprecedented; besides the usual speeches, meetings, and public demonstrations in Ottawa, Montreal, and Quebec City, among other places, theatrical evenings were held in which Natives put on performances that ranged from the traditional to the contemporary; and the James Bay Cree publicly burned a Quebec government communiqué that had been written in the wrong Cree dialect for the region to which it was sent. All of this was widely reported in newspapers and on radio and television; films were made and books rushed into print. The Natives, realizing that they must negotiate rather than simply oppose, based their case on the need for reciprocity. After an agreement was reached, Billy Diamond, chief of the Waskaganish band of James Bay Cree, observed: 'It has been a tough fight, and our people are still very much opposed to the project, but they realize that they must share their resources.'[17]

The James Bay and Northern Quebec Agreement of 1975—the term 'treaty' was temporarily out of fashion—has been described as the last of the old-time treaties, although it did break some new ground.[18] It has also been called the first modern Aboriginal claims settlement in Canada, as it left the Inuit and Cree communities of Quebec with substantial control of their own political, economic, and social affairs, although the final say still rested with the government.[19] It created programs for hunter income support, for environmental protection, and for sharing wildlife management. Besides compensation of $232.5 million over 21 years and special economic development assistance, Natives maintained ownership of 2,140 square miles (5,543 square kilometres) around their communities and hunting and fishing rights in other areas. Mineral and subsurface rights remained with Quebec, but Natives won a veto over the province's use of those rights, as well as compensation in the case of development. A second land category counted 24,000 square miles (62,160 square kilometres) where the Cree have the exclusive right to hunt, fish, and trap; these lands are administered jointly by Cree and the non-Native municipality of James Bay. A third category, by far the largest, was surrendered by the Cree to the province, but with the understanding they would have special consideration for their traditional activities. The Northeastern Quebec Agreement with the Innu (Naskapi) of Schefferville in 1978, signed by Hydro-Québec and the provincial and federal governments, confirmed and extended the regions to which the James Bay Agreement applied.

More generous than the numbered treaties, the accord still fell far short of entrenching Native rights, and as far as the Natives are concerned the expectations to which it gave rise have not been met.[20] Critics have pointed to the price: the flooding of 10,500 square kilometres of once productive hunting land by the James Bay hydroelectric project without consideration of wildlife factors. Their point was dramatically reinforced in 1984, when Hydro-Québec inadvertently drowned 10,000 caribou by releasing a large volume of water out of the Caniapiscau Reservoir during the migration of the George's River caribou herd. On top of everything else, expected contracts for hydroelectric power did not materialize. Concerted lobbying efforts in New York state by the Cree, led by Matthew Coon Come and supported by the Sierra Club and other environmental organizations, resulted in New York, in 1992, cancelling two contracts for electricity supply valued at $17.6 billion. This effectively killed the second phase of the James Bay Project. At the time, natural gas—transmitted by pipeline from western Canada—was a cheaper source of energy.[21] Soon after, in 1994, the second phase (Great Whale) was put on indefinite hold; as far as the Cree are concerned, it is dead.

Of the project's three originally planned phases, the first (La Grande) was completed in 1985, with nine major dams and 37 generating stations, not to mention extensive transmission lines. This represents 67 per cent of the area originally projected to be flooded and 57 per cent of the projected power generation. The 2002 Paix des Braves, an extensive agreement between the Cree and the Quebec government, cleared the way for the third phase (Eastmain and Rupert) to begin early in the twenty-first century. This involves diversion of the waters of the Eastmain and Rupert rivers to the La Grande system, as well as a power station and large reservoir, completed in 2006, on the Eastmain River. Notably, this project has involved greater consideration for environmental consequences, including clearing of brush and trees prior to flooding so that methyl mercury pollution of the waters is reduced.[22]

Negotiations for self-government for Nunavik (Inuit territory of northern Quebec), underway since 1993, as well as those with the province's Cree and Innu, are continuing. Nunavik is expected to have a regional governance structure by 2011 or 2012 (see Chapter 29). For the Cree, the Paix des Braves, which provides $3.4 billion for community and economic development over the next 50 years, was

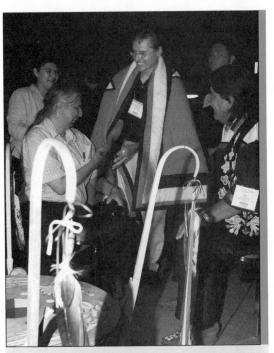

Matthew Coon Come, a northern Quebec Cree, is said to be one of the 'least assimilated' of Aboriginal leaders. As a young man he saw how the James Bay Agreement both hurt and helped his people, and as Grand Chief of the Hudson Bay Cree he was instrumental in stopping Hydro-Québec's Great Whale River project. As AFN National Chief, he aimed to get Ottawa to act on the recommendations of the Royal Commission on Aboriginal Peoples.
(The Canadian Press/Jonathan Hayward)

followed in 2007 by an agreement with the federal government providing an additional $1.4 billion over 20 years in compensation for aspects of the James Bay and Northern Quebec Agreement that Ottawa had failed to meet.[23] These agreements, as well as the Sanarrutik Agreement signed by the Quebec Inuit and the provincial government in April 2002,[24] have set the stage for the transfer of responsibility for justice and social and economic development, as well as self-government, to the Aboriginal peoples. Despite the large sums of money and

Isaiah Awashish, Indoh-hoh-sou (a Mistissini Cree traditional hunter), balloting during the ratification of the the James Bay and Northern Quebec Agreement, 1976.
(© 2008 Harvey Feit)

the devolution of powers to Native groups, however, some critics have seen such agreements as the thin edge of the wedge that inevitably draws the people away from their own cultures. Of particular concern to the Natives have been forestry practices, such as clear-cutting, which have a detrimental effect on their way of life, and, in the political arena, talk of Quebec secession without taking the interests of the First Nations into account.[25]

Like the James Bay Project, the Mackenzie Valley Pipeline Inquiry of 1974–7 also quickly developed a high public profile. The chiefs of the Mackenzie Valley Amerindian bands had started things off by filing a caveat on about one-third of the Northwest Territories. Although their right to issue such a caveat was denied on appeal in 1975 on technical grounds, Justice William Morrow's judgment raised doubts as to whether the treaties had extinguished Aboriginal right. In 1974, Prime Minister Trudeau, with a minority government, was pressured by the New Democratic Party to appoint Justice Thomas Berger to chair a board of inquiry into the matter. In carrying out his mandate, Berger not only decided to consult the people directly, he broke with tradition by seeing to it that the media were kept informed and could cover the hearings. The resultant publicity outdid even that of James Bay; public interest was intense, as southern Canadians learned about life in the North, many of them for the first time. They were reminded that northerners, too, had a way of life to protect:

> I wonder how people in Toronto would react if the people of Old Crow went down to Toronto and said, 'Well, look, we are going to knock down all those skyscrapers and high rises . . . blast a few holes to make lakes for muskrat trapping, and you people are just going to have to move out and stop driving cars and move into cabins.[26]

Another witness was more blunt:

> Your nation is destroying our nation. . . . We are a nation. We have our own land, our own ways, and our own civilization. We do not want to destroy you and your land. . . . your Prime Minister is willing to say that Louis Riel was not all wrong. He is willing to say that, a hundred years later, but is he willing to change the approach that destroyed Louis Riel?[27]

When Berger's report appeared in 1977, it became a best-seller.[28]

His recommendation that the pipeline be put on hold for 10 years to allow time for

Native concerns to be considered was a shocker to many Canadians, accustomed as they were to development being given top priority. In the most thorough official study of the northern Native subsistence base to that time, Berger demonstrated its economic importance. More emotionally, the people had spoken eloquently about the North as their homeland; it was not just an adjunct of the south, to be developed for southern profit. Eventually, the pipeline as originally envisaged became unnecessary, at least in the short run, as large quantities of natural gas were discovered in Alberta and British Columbia, providing more easily available sources of fuel. In other words, if the pipeline as originally envisaged had been built, it would have become a white elephant.[29] In 1985, an oil pipeline running about half the length of the Mackenzie Valley, from Norman Wells to northern Alberta, was completed, two years before Thomas Berger's moratorium was to end.

The lapsing of the moratorium revived interest in the original proposal, but with a difference: this time, the First Nations, instead of opposing it, have sought a share of the action. This change, in part, can be explained by the fact that land claim agreements, except for the Deh Cho, have been achieved in the Mackenzie Delta and Mackenzie Valley in the years since the Berger Inquiry. Stephen Kakfwi, Premier of the Northwest Territories from 2000 to 2003, indicated support of the proposal, provided that the Natives are major participants. To this end, Ron Jamieson, senior vice-president of the Bank of Montreal's Aboriginal banking unit, worked with Aboriginal leaders to map out a strategy. Consequently, an Aboriginal Pipeline Group, with the promise of a one-third stake in the 1,220-kilometre pipeline that would extend from the Arctic coast across the Mackenzie Delta and down the Mackenzie Valley to link up with a transcontinental line in northern Alberta, joined the Producer Group in this northern megaproject, the total cost of which was estimated in 2006 at over $16 billion. Whether the Aboriginal Pipeline Group, even with land claim settlements, is able to secure enough funding to participate remains to be seen. By mid-2008, the proposal had passed through the various stages of assessment and awaited ministerial approval. This turnabout has been influenced by dramatic price increases that by the end of the 1990s had boosted the estimated value of natural gas reserves in the High Arctic to more than $200 billion. As might be expected, nearly a decade later this estimated value has more than doubled. The Inuvialuit of the western Arctic, whose land claim had been settled in 1984, lost no time in taking advantage of this favourable turn of the market and negotiated four oil and gas concessions that netted them $75.5 million.[30]

Two other commissions that have been influential in the development of Native claims were those of law professor Kenneth Lysyk to study a Yukon pipeline route as an alternative to the one proposed for the Mackenzie Valley and that of Justice Patrick Hartt to study the environment of northern Ontario.[31] The Ontario commission was established in 1978 to facilitate negotiations between the province, Ottawa, and the Amerindians.

Most recently, with the discovery of diamonds in the Lac de Gras region of the Northwest Territories in 1991, the first diamond mine in the NWT, Etaki, began production in 1998 on a profitable note, and a second mine, Diavik, signed an environmental agreement with five neighbouring Aboriginal groups that enabled it to begin production in 2003. Another mine, Jericho, opened just across the border in Nunavut in 2006, but ceased production early in 2008, while another NWT diamond mine, Snap Lake, began production in 2008.[32] Thus, the industrial development of the Northwest Territories, with diamond mining leading the way, is proceeding with environmental and local community concerns in mind. This is a break with previous practice, which in general around the world has placed economic concerns first and foremost, with only incidental attention being paid to environmental and human consequences, if any such attention was paid at all.

Indeed, a lack of concern for human health and the environment has been the case in regard to the development of the oil sands in northern Alberta, which has affected numerous First Nations. Extraction of bitumen from the sands requires 2–4.5 cubic metres of water, drawn from the Athabasca River, for each cubic metre of oil. Vast tailings ponds are created to hold the fouled water used in the process, and water levels in the river and downstream, at Lake Athabasca, have dropped precipitously, having a negative effect on Native subsistence and commercial fishing and on fish stocks and entire ecosystems. In March 2007, the Athabasca Chipewyan First Nation and the Miskew Cree First Nation joined with the University of Alberta's Pembina Institute in proclaiming the province's water management strategy for the river a failure. As Pat Marcell of the Athabasca Chipewyan First Nation stated, 'We're talking about the survival of the Athabasca River, but more than that this is about the survival of our people.'[33] In addition, doctors at Fort Chipewyan have encountered a large cluster of rare cancers and other diseases, very possibly the result of pollution from the tar sands operations. Upstream, in the area of extraction, the Lubicon Cree, still without a land claim settlement, have had their territory exploited for commercial profit from the oil sands just as happened earlier when their land was logged.[34]

On the other side of the ledger, First Nations increasingly are participating in the world of business. Branching out from such traditional sectors as fishing, farming, and setting up arts and crafts outlets, First Nations have turned to resource development—oil and gas, forestry, and mining, for three obvious examples. There are now 1,600 active wells on Aboriginal lands and at least 12 band-owned oil and gas companies, not to mention a myriad of service contractors. In forestry, a half-dozen mills are owned by Native bands. In mining, Alberta's Siksika Reserve is contemplating reactivating three coal mines that were closed in the late 1960s. Aboriginal Business Canada, an arm of Industry Canada, estimates that there are now more than 20,000 Aboriginal-owned businesses across the land. Although they account for only 1 per cent of Canada's businesses, their growth rate has easily led the field; between 1981 and 1996, it was 170 per cent.[35]

Such activity is not without its problems. For example, in the mid-1990s the Stoney Nation of Morley, Alberta, taking advantage of stricter forestry regulations introduced in British Columbia, which meant that BC mills were undersupplied with cut timber, engaged in extensive clear-cutting on the Stoney Reserve with the permission of the Department of Indian Affairs. Some band members protested against this rapacious economic endeavour, and the Rocky Mountain Eco-system Coalition, a non-Native environmental group, pressured Indian Affairs to stop the activity. Following a CTV report on the clear-cutting and its environmental impact, the work was finally halted in February 1995, but only after a wide swath had been cut in the foothills between Calgary and Banff.[36]

Even successful Aboriginal development corporations experience failures: with government support, the Kitsaki Management Limited Partnership, the business arm of the Lac La Ronge Indian band, joined with Weyerhaeuser Canada and two other northern Saskatchewan Cree First Nations in building a $22.5 million sawmill. The mill, for a short time, employed 45 workers, but the softwood lumber dispute between Canada and the United States led to significantly lower prices for the mill, which closed in 2002. Nonetheless, Kitsaki, by 2006, employed over 500 people and had up to 1,000 seasonal workers, with gross revenues over $70 million.[37] On its own and in partnership with other, smaller First Nations and non-Aboriginal businesses, this successful Cree business corporation is involved in diverse enterprises that include trucking, a golf course, catering, a hotel, mining, contracting, insurance, food processing, and environmental consultancy.[38]

A major issue stems from the tax-free status of reserves. This was highlighted when the Blood Tribe at Standoff, Alberta, near Lethbridge, reached a deal for the replacement of lands absorbed into one of the province's parks. The land involved is the site of the Bowden oil refinery, a $200 million a year operation, which the Blood offered to purchase for $50 million while asking that the deal be tax-free. A possible consequence could be more and more companies seeking joint ventures with First Nations in order to profit from the tax-free position of reserves.[39] In March 2005 the federal government announced that $887,500 in federal funding would be made to assist the Blood Tribe in taking a historic first step into the oil and gas drilling business through the acquisition of a 50 per cent interest in an oil and gas drilling rig. This joint venture with Western Lakota Energy Services in a $7.4 million project is expected to create 15 direct jobs for the First Nation and up to 70 indirect jobs, as well as training opportunities and expanded business expertise.[40]

On the Political Front

The period between the rejection of the 1969 White Paper and the patriation of the British North America Act in 1982 was marked by protest and confrontation, bureaucratic dissension, and policy confusion.[41] This was epitomized in a 1974 clash between west coast

A worker for Northern Lights Foods, one of many enterprises of Kitsaki, the business arm of the Lac La Ronge Indian band, harvests wild organic chanterelle mushrooms.
(Northern Lights Foods)

Amerindians and an RCMP riot squad in Ottawa that disrupted the opening of Parliament. About 200 Natives had come from Vancouver —'Native Peoples' Caravan'—in what was supposed to have been a peaceful protest against poor living conditions. Nervous authorities called out the riot squad and then brought out the military; this was the first time that such measures were taken against Native demonstrators.[42] A few years later, the negotiations that preceded the adoption of the Canadian Constitution saw considerable Native unrest. As a Dene leader observed to Michael Asch, 'While others are trying to negotiate their way out of Confederation, we are trying to negotiate our way in.'[43]

Amerindians, Inuit, and Métis, concerned that Aboriginal rights be enshrined in the new Constitution and convinced they were not being given a fair hearing in Canada, sent delegation after delegation to Britain and continental Europe to press their cause on the international scene. The reasoning was that since Canada was a signatory to international covenants obliging her to protect and promote the rights of her first peoples, then international pressure could be influential not only in getting her to live up to the commitment but in convincing Canadians that it would be in their best interests to do so. At one point 300 Amerindians went to Britain to present their case to the Queen; at the request of the short-lived Tory government of Joe Clark (1979–80), they were denied an audience.

Eventually, when the constitutional patriation was accomplished in 1982, Native peoples won recognition of 'existing' Aboriginal rights, but without a definition of the term; however, there was provision that such rights could not be adversely affected by anything in the Charter of Rights and Freedoms.[44] Its recognition of Métis as Aboriginals was a consequence of their earlier recognition by the Manitoba Act of 1870. As a sop for Natives having been excluded from the constitutional negotiations, provision was made for three conferences with first ministers the year after patriation. What these conferences, held in the mid-1980s, made clear was that as matters stand in constitutional affairs, the Aboriginal role is at best advisory. Whatever the justification for Aboriginal self-government, it rests at the local level. When it comes to constitutional issues that concern the country as a whole, the final say rests essentially with the federal Parliament and provincial legislatures.

The term 'constitution' as used here is a Western political concept. It provides 'a set of rationally conceived and formalized rules for the exercise of political powers and, equally important, for the restraint of political power.'[45] For Indians, the Constitution embodies not only the internal sovereignty of the tribe but also symbolizes the aspiration for self-determination for the people. By this time the term 'Aboriginal rights' was being applied to far more than just land issues; as far as Amer-

indians were concerned, it also included self-government. Cree lawyer Delia Opekokew elaborated: Aboriginal right, she wrote, 'recognizes our ownership over lands we have traditionally occupied and used and our control and ownership over the resources of the land—water, minerals, timber, wildlife and fisheries.'[46] What was more, she added, such a right 'recognizes our Indian government's sovereignty over our people, lands and resources.'

As sociologist J. Rick Ponting has commented, Amerindians are not seeking to be granted self-government so much as to win recognition that viable Indian governments existed long before the arrival of Europeans;[47] in other words, they seek recognition of their inherent right to govern themselves. Tribal governments ranged from the ostensibly simplest types of band leadership of the Arctic and Subarctic hunters to the hierarchical chiefdoms of the west coast and the paramount chiefdoms of the east coast, to the Iroquoian confederacies with their interlocking systems of village, tribal, and intertribal councils. By the middle of the twentieth century, these traditional forms of self-government had been to some extent supplanted by the elective forms imposed by Indian Affairs; the process, however, was by no means complete. Although badly battered, the movement for self-government had not died, and some non-Indian voices had been raised in its defence. One of these was that of the Anglican missionary Edward F. Wilson, previously noted in Chapter 19. In 1891, the Canadian Research and Aid Society, in its journal *The Canadian Indian*, published a series of articles supporting Amerindian control over their own affairs. The articles maintained that Natives had a right to an 'independent Indian community' with powers to make their own laws and held that this would not be a threat to Canada.[48]

In 1983 this position received a powerful impetus from publication of the Report of the

Special Parliamentary Committee on Indian Self-Government, known as the Penner Report after the committee's chairman, Keith Penner, Liberal MP for Kenora (1968–88). Acknowledging that Amerindians would rather have self-government than representation in Parliament, the report urged that they be allowed to establish their own level of government, distinct from those of the municipality and the Indian Act. Such changes, it stated, should be entrenched in legislation, which would involve a fundamental restructuring of the relationship between Amerindians and the federal government, including the phasing out of the Indian Act and the Department of Indian Affairs, a process seen as taking about five years. A major result would be the reinforcement of Aboriginal rights.

Hopes had been high at the launching of the first of the three constitutionally mandated First Ministers' Conferences on Aboriginal affairs in 1983. In the words of Prime Minister Trudeau, 'we are not here to consider whether there should be institutions of self-government, but how these institutions should be brought into being . . . [and] how they fit into the interlocking system of jurisdictions by which Canada is governed.' Or, as the ebullient Inuit delegate Zebedee Nungak put it, 'We're here to do constructive damage to the status quo.'[49] That was just what some of the provincial premiers feared; the ideas to be explored and perhaps put into practice were largely untried in the realm of practical politics. As has so often been the case in human history, the prevailing tolerance was for the known evils, not for those unknown. On top of that, Brian Mulroney, Conservative Prime Minister, 1984–93, at first apparently enthusiastic about resolving the question of Aboriginal rights, pulled back, so that the third and last of the conferences, in 1987, was even more frustrating than the first two.

Not many weeks after the failure of the third conference, the Meech Lake Accord, recognizing Quebec as a distinct society and granting special status, was signed by Mulroney and the provincial premiers, to be ratified within three years. The disillusionment among the Amerindians and Inuit was profound: what had been denied to them was now being given to Quebec. Amerindians and Inuit rallied, and when the opportunity presented itself to kill the Accord by legislative means, they took it. The occasion was when the provincial legislatures had to ratify the agreement, requiring a unanimous vote. Elijah Harper, an Oji-Cree chief from Red Sucker Lake and the only Native member of the Manitoba legislature (NDP, Rupertsland),[50] withheld his vote, on the grounds that procedural rules were not being followed. The Speaker of the House agreed, observing that the Accord was too important 'to open the door for some future legal challenge because all the rules weren't obeyed'. Time was of the essence, as the matter had been introduced to the legislature at the last minute. Harper's delaying tactics meant that the deadline of 23 June could not be met, and so the Accord died.[51] Harper, incidentally, had been one of the chiefs who had gone to London in 1980 to lobby the Queen for fair treatment of Aboriginals in the patriation of the Canadian Constitution; at the royal signing of the Constitution in Ottawa in 1982, he had refused an invitation to attend.[52]

It was not that Indians were opposed to recognizing Quebec as a distinct society, as Phil Fontaine, then in the midst of his term as head of the Assembly of Manitoba Chiefs, 1989–97, pointed out. Quite the contrary: 'We recognize that and support that. But if Quebec is distinct, we are even more distinct. That's the recognition we want, and will settle for nothing less.' In a letter to Bourassa, the Manitoba chiefs wrote in terms familiar to Quebecers:

We, the original people of this country, have

Elijah Harper, at that time NDP member of the Manitoba legislature for Rupertsland, holds an eagle feather for spiritual strength as he uses delaying tactics to prevent the Meech Lake Accord from being ratified, 1990.
(The Canadian Press/Winnipeg Free Press/Wayne Glowacki)

inherited through the original traditions of our forefathers 55 distinct original languages. Fifty-two of these original languages of Canada are now on the brink of extinction. Unlike you, we cannot retrieve these languages from our mother country. Our mother country is Canada.[53]

Fontaine equated recognition with power: 'Like Quebec, we want to be recognized as a distinct society, because recognition means power.' The power Amerindians are seeking is that of self-government, 'the ability to make laws that will govern our communities and we want a justice system that is more compatible with the traditions of our people.'[54]

Inching Towards Political Control

The stalling of Aboriginal rights at the constitutional level has to some extent been counterbalanced by an inching towards recognition at local levels, a movement that began well before the Penner Report but which has been encouraged by it.[55] Native organizations were becoming more effective, Native arts (expressing Native identity) were attracting international attention, and new ways of handling political issues were being worked out. For example, between 1913 and 1954, the three districts of Keewatin, Mackenzie, and Franklin in the Northwest Territories were governed by the deputy minister of the Department of the Interior and a council consisting of Anglican and Roman Catholic missionaries, an HBC trade commissioner, and an RCMP commissioner. Following epidemics that swept through the Dene and Inuit, political control was transferred to the Department of Indian Affairs and Northern Development. A more representative NWT government was formed in 1967, when its administrative base was moved to Yellowknife from Ottawa. Since then there has been a steady move towards more local responsibility.[56]

Yukon, which has had an elective council since 1908, has been going in a similar direction; its capital was transferred first to Dawson and then, in 1953, to Whitehorse. If anything, it is further along the road than the Northwest Territories.[57] In both cases, power formally resides with a commissioner appointed by Ottawa, but in practice he acts only on the advice of an executive council appointed by the elected legislative assembly. However, more local control can only be effective to the extent that individuals participate in public affairs. In 1969, Chief John Tetlichi of Fort McPherson became the first Indian to be named to the Northwest Territories Council; in 1970, Louis Rabesca of Fort Rae was the first elected Indian member. For the Inuit, Simonie Michael was elected in 1967, the same year that Abe Okpik had been appointed. Nick Sibbeston, part Slavey from Fort Simpson, carried the flag for the Métis on the council in 1970; later, he would become government leader.

The Northwest Territories government has seen a dramatic increase in Native participation since it became fully elective in 1975. This has influenced the character of the Legislative Council, which has eschewed the party system in favour of indigenous consensus politics that accords an important role to local councils. In other words, the move is towards decentralization. This contrasts with the Yukon, whose government has begun to look more like that of a province since its introduction of party politics and, consequently, more centralization.[58]

Louis Riel's example of taking part in Canada's political life has been followed by a growing number of Natives. This began in provincial governments, as already noted with the election of the Huron chief Ludger Bastien to the Quebec legislature in 1924.[59] It gained impetus when Nisga'a chief Frank Calder was elected to British Columbia's legislature in 1949. It should be remembered, however, that at least one Indian, John Brant, had been elected during the colonial period, but he was disqualified.[60] Federally, the first Amerindian elected to Parliament since Confederation was Len Marchand, who served as the Liberal representative for Kamloops–Cariboo from 1968 to 1979; he was also Canada's first Amerindian federal cabinet minister, serving as Minister of State for Small Business, 1976–7, and as Minister of State for the Environment, 1977–9; his last posting was in the Senate, where he served from 1984 to 1998. (James Gladstone's appointment in 1958 as Canada's first Amerindian senator has already been noted.) Wilton Littlechild became the first treaty Amerindian member of Parliament when he was elected as Progressive Conservative member for Wetaskiwin in 1988, the same year that Ethel Blondin-

Andrew became the pioneer Native woman MP (Liberal, Western Arctic). Littlechild quit politics in 1993, the year that Blondin was appointed Secretary of State (Training and Youth). She became Secretary of State (Children and Youth) in 1997. Ralph Goodale (Liberal, Wascana) was named Minister of Natural Resources and Minister Responsible for the Canadian Wheat Board in 1999. He also served as Federal Interlocutor for Métis and Non-status Indians. That same year, Métis Robert Nault (Liberal, Kenora–Rainy River) was named Minister of Indian Affairs. The first Inuk member of Parliament, Peter Freuchen Ittinuar (NDP, Nunatsiaq), grandson of the explorer, won his seat in 1979; in 1982 he crossed the floor to join the Liberals, and in 1984 he was defeated in the wake of financial troubles.

At the provincial level, Mike Cardinal was elected to the Alberta legislature under the Conservative banner in 1989 and served as Social Services Minister from 1992 to 1996, when he quit politics. Most recently, in 2000, British Columbia Premier Uijal Dosanjh took the highly unusual step of appointing an unelected Indian chief to the BC cabinet when he named Ed John, former Grand Chief of the First Nations Summit of British Columbia, as the province's Minister of Children and Families.[61]

The number of Natives appointed to public office is steadily increasing, both federally and provincially, as are those in the civil service. In 1974, an Amerindian became a lieutenant-governor when Ralph Steinhauer (1905–87) was named for Alberta, serving until 1979.

Inuk Willie Adams was named to the Senate in 1971, Inuk Charlie Watt in 1984, and Métis Thelma Chalifoux in 1997. When Mulroney packed the Senate with eight extra members in 1990 in the battle over the passage of the Goods and Services Tax, Walter Twinn, chief of the Sawridge band of Alberta (d. 1997), was one of them, bringing the number of Natives who had been named to the Senate to five. Later, Twinn was reported to be considering resigning in view of Amerindian opposition to the tax, but he did not take the step.[62] In 1994, Mary Simon of Nunavik, in 2008 the president of Inuit Tapiriit Kanatami, became the first Inuk to be appointed to an ambassadorial position when she was named Circumpolar Ambassador. In 1992, Dan Goodleaf of Kahnawake became the first Indian deputy minister in the federal service when he was appointed to that post in Indian Affairs. He held it until 1995, when he was named ambassador to Costa Rica. Another ambassadorial appointment was that of Jim Bartleman to the European Union in 2000. Formerly ambassador to NATO, Cuba, and Israel, among other postings, he was also foreign policy adviser to Jean Chrétien. Bartleman is a Chippewa from Rama First Nation of Ontario.

On an organizational level, the Cree-Naskapi Act of Quebec, 1984, was a result of the Penner Report, as well as being a consequence of the James Bay and Northern Quebec Agreement (JBNQA) and its related accords of 1975–8. Hailed as the first self-government legislation for Natives in Canada, the Cree-Naskapi Act has replaced the Indian Act for the regions it serves and establishes the communities as corporate entities, over and above their members' legal existence as individual persons.[63] It applies to the first category of lands created by the JBNQA, which were transferred by Quebec to Ottawa for the exclusive use and benefit of the James Bay Cree, and to Naskapi lands of the same designation. Its legal priority is second to that of the James Bay and Northern Quebec Native Claims Settlement Act, the federal statute that gave effect to the JBNQA. It has priority over all other legislation. However, depending on the set of figures used, there was disagreement as to the extent to which Ottawa had implemented the agreed-upon funding formula. The government maintained it had effected 80 per cent of its commitments. Chief Henry Mianscum of the Mistassini band took an opposite view: 'probably 70 per cent of that Agreement hasn't been implemented.'[64] As noted earlier, a 2007 agreement that included a $1.4 billion payout from the federal government to the Cree was meant, finally, to rectify Ottawa's failed commitments in this regard. In the opinion of anthropologist Sally Weaver, the Cree-Naskapi case as 'a prototype experience with self-government . . . [did] not inspire confidence in the [Mulroney] Conservative government's commitment to self-government or in the Treasury Board's willingness to provide the resources to a First Nation group once they are legally bound to a self-governing course.'[65] Clearly, as the *Report of the Cree-Naskapi Commission, 1988*, recommended, those involved 'should establish a common fiscal statement stating the costs of implementation'. Other essential needs to be provided are comprehensive justice services and a locally administered economic development plan.[66]

The Western Arctic Claim Agreement (Inuvialuit Final Agreement) was also reached in 1984.[67] It extinguished Inuvialuit Aboriginal title to the western Arctic in return for ownership of 96,000 square kilometres stretching up to Banks Island, along with payments of $45 million in benefits and $10 million for economic development. The administration of all this came under the umbrella Inuvialuit Regional Corporation (IRC), organized the following year; its concerns include wildlife conservation and management, as is generally the case in these northern agreements. Nellie Cournoyea, formerly government leader for the Northwest Territories, became the IRC chairperson early in 1996. Its business arm, the Inuvialuit Development Corporation, purchased a transportation firm for $27 million with a virtual monopoly on barge transportation in the Canadian Arctic; another of its projects has been the establishment of the Inuvialuit Renewable Resources Development Corporation, which is working on creating international and domestic markets for musk-ox meat and wool. The Inuvialuit are exclusive owners of the government-set muskox quotas for their region.[68] This by no means exhausts the list of their enterprises, which include the largest regional airline in the western Arctic, energy, real estate, and participation as a member of the Aboriginal Pipeline Group; IRC branches maintain offices in several cities. On top of all that, the IRC has paid Inuvialuit elders a minimum of $1,000 each annually since 1986 (one year they got $2,500); in 1990, the IRC distributed $100 to every Inuvialuit over 18 years of age. These distributions come out of its profits. By 2008, out of the Corporation's net income of $35.2 million, a total distribution of more than $3.8 million was made to 3,812 Inuvialuit beneficiaries, with each person receiving $1,001.09.[69]

In Yukon, after nearly two decades of negotiation, an Umbrella Final Agreement was signed in 1993 whereby the territory's 14 Amerindian bands retain ownership of 44,000 square kilometres and receive compensation of $260 million while avoiding complete extinguishment of Aboriginal title. Besides protection for wildlife, the agreement also creates a constitutional obligation to negotiate self-government.[70]

That entrenchment of Aboriginal rights as a feature of land claim settlements is still far from being conceded by the federal government was dramatically illustrated by the cancellation of the Dene/Métis Western Arctic Land Claim agreement late in 1990.[71] The agreement, reached after 14 years of negotiation, would have given the Dene/Métis surface title to 181,230 square kilometres of land (a region for which the Dene adopted the name of 'Denendeh' in 1981) and subsurface rights to 10,000 square kilometres, as well as $500 million in cash and special hunting and fishing rights.[72] The point at issue was the Dene/Métis demand to renegotiate a clause in the preliminary agreement that required the surrender of Aboriginal and treaty rights in return for the settlement. As the Dene see it, 'Our laws from the Creator do not allow us to cede, release, surrender or extinguish our inherent rights.'[73] Two of the claim's five regions had already split from the umbrella 12,000-member Dene Nation and 3,000-member Métis Association over the issue; the federal government moved to take advantage of the situation and announced it would start talks with the breakaway councils of the Mackenzie Delta Gwich'in and the Sahtu Dene/Métis. Despite the protests of the umbrella Dene/Métis, the talks resulted six months later (in 1991) in the Gwich'in accepting 22,332 square kilometres straddling the Yukon–NWT border, plus subsurface rights to 93 square kilometres and a compensation of $75 million over 15 years.[74] In return for giving up their Aboriginal claim, the Gwich'in received title to their assigned land in fee simple. The deal received royal approval in 1992, and that of the Sahtu was proclaimed in 1994. The Gwich'in Tribal Council used $1 million of its settlement to develop Tl'oondik Healing Camp on the Peel River, a short distance from Fort McPherson.[75]

Nunavut ('Our Land') Is Born

The creation of the territory of Nunavut out of the Northwest Territories on 1 April 1999 was a dramatic moment for the country. Indeed, it aroused international attention, as illustrated by the visit of Jacques Chirac, the President of France, when the fledgling territory was five months old.[76] Comprising more than 2.2 million square kilometres, better than a fifth of Canada's entire surface, Nunavut is the largest land claim settlement in the country's history. The agreement involved the surrender of Aboriginal title on the part of the Inuit (who, according to the 2006 census, numbered 24,635 in Nunavut out of a total population of 29,474[77]), but gave them ownership in fee simple of 350,000 square kilometres, an area half the size of Saskatchewan.[78] In effect, this is the largest private landholding in North America. As well, the Inuit receive $1.17 billion in cash over 14 years. These transformations of Aboriginal title involved the Inuit acknowledging an underlying Crown title, a step seen by some as possibly preparing the way for the eventual breakup of their traditional territories.[79] Nunavut's official languages are English, French, and Inuktitut, although the Nunavut government recently has put forth legislation to give priority to Inuktitut (see Chapter 29); the territorial flag depicts a red inukshuk with a blue North Star.

A thorny problem had been the negotiation of a boundary between Nunavut to the east, with its population of Inuit, and Denendeh to the west, with its Dene/Métis, splitting the Northwest Territories into two and involving a cash settlement of $701 million. After 20 years of often bitter negotiations, John Parker, commissioner for the Northwest Territories, 1979–89, was named as arbitrator in January 1991. His recommendation, accepted by Ottawa in April of that year, was for a boundary running north from the Manitoba–Saskatchewan border to the centre of the Thelon Game Sanctuary, then jogging northwest to the Inuvialuit border near Paulatuk. This arrangement did not satisfy the Dene, who lost out in the contested area of Contwoyto Lake in the central Arctic.[80] The boundary was settled in favour of Nunavut in 1993.

The idea for the creation of a northern jurisdiction administered in co-operation with the Inuit developed after World War II and came under active consideration beginning in 1978 as a result of a proposal by Inuit Tapirisat (now named Inuit Tapiriit Kanatami).[81] The concept received a major boost in 1985 when it was supported by the Royal Commission on the Economic Union and Development Prospects for Canada (the Macdonald Commission) on the grounds that regional governments adapted to particular circumstances, cultural and otherwise, would better meet the needs of the Canadian North. That same year, 1985, the project received unexpected outside support when the United States sent the *Polar Sea* through the Northwest Passage without permission from Canada. This was the second such infringement on the part of the Americans (the first was the voyage of the *Manhattan* in 1971), who wanted those waters to be declared international. Since the Inuit have been in the region for more than a thousand years and represent about 85 per cent of its present population, the creation of a self-governing territory was seen as the best possible demonstration of effective occupation, thus enormously strengthening Canada's claim to Arctic sovereignty. The Northwest Territories endorsed the idea by a margin of 54 to 46 per cent in a plebiscite held in 1992, which led to an accord being signed that same year for the creation of the new territory.[82]

The project took final shape in 1993 with the Nunavut Land Claim Settlement and finally with the federal Nunavut Act. The territory was given a new style of 'public government', more or less on the elective provincial model but with greater decentralization.[83] In one major aspect it differs from the party-oriented governments to the south in that in some areas it follows the Inuit practice of reaching decisions by consensus. Native traditions have influenced the justice system, worked out in co-operation with the Royal Canadian Mounted Police.[84] Also different is the court system, which has been simplified by combining the usual two levels (superior and territorial) into one. A consequence of all this has been a need to address the territory's acute shortage of lawyers, which led to the opening of a school of law in 2001. Akitsiraq Law School, open only to Inuit, will initially offer a four-year program, taught through the University of Victoria.

Performers and Inuit Junior Rangers carrying the flags of Canada's ten provinces and three territories during the celebration marking the founding of Nunavut as Canada's newest territory, 1 April 1999. The ceremony was held in Iqaluit, capital of the new territory.
(The Canadian Press/Shaun Best)

The new territory is not entirely Inuit, however. Non-Natives are participating; four of the first Legislative Assembly's 19 members were not Inuit. The first Premier, chosen by the elected members of the Legislative Assembly, was 34-year-old Paul Okalik. As of 2008, Okalik, a southern-trained lawyer who sees the co-operation of the two peoples as essential to the new territory's success, was the longest-serving Premier in Canada. A major challenge is training Native personnel as administrators. However, the Nunavut government faces many new challenges, including creating job opportunities for a large workforce of young people. Approximately, 56 per cent of Nunavut's population is under the age of 25, and the median age of the total population is 23 years old (for the Inuit population, the median age is only 20.1).[85] Other challenges that face the territory are how to increase residents' income and education levels, and finding ways to cope with a cost of living that is two to three times higher than that of southern Canadians. As well, Nunavut residents, through their government, are in charge of education, health, social services, and many other provincial-type responsibilities. The government helps stimulate the regional economy by creating government jobs as well as spinoff jobs in the private sector.

Another challenge is financial: as matters stood when Finance Minister Kelvin Ng presented the territory's third budget, a $12 million deficit was forecast for the upcoming fiscal year. During the territory's first two years, federal

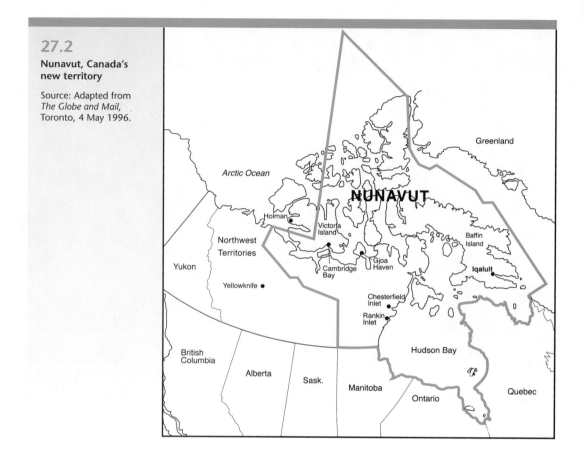

27.2

Nunavut, Canada's new territory

Source: Adapted from *The Globe and Mail*, Toronto, 4 May 1996.

transfers averaging $581 million a year accounted for 90 per cent of its total budget. At first, keeping spending in line with available funds was comparatively simple. But as programs developed, costs inevitably rose. This was particularly the case with housing, of which there was a serious shortage. In Ng's view, an active program to deal with this situation had been the direct cause for the predicted shortfall.[86] Lack of housing, while eased, remained a problem that has been compounded by new difficulties such as rising costs, particularly of fuel and transportation.[87] Widespread poverty and high unemployment show no signs of easing. According to the most recent census, about 12 per cent of houses in First Nation communities are overcrowded, compared to 1 per cent elsewhere in Canada. As of 31 March 2005, of the almost 96,800 houses in First Nation communities, more than 21,200 (21.9 per cent) were judged to be in need of major repairs and about 5,500 (5.7 per cent) needed to be replaced.[88] Added to all this is growing labour unrest. Still, for Inuit elder Nancy Karetak-Lindell, the first elected MP for Nunavut, the creation of the territory has given her people the incentive to tackle such problems. As she sees it, it has given them back their lives—literally, when one considers the challenge of dealing with its current suicide rate among the young, the highest in the world.[89]

At the other end of the spectrum is the

Prime Minister Jean Chrétien and French President Jacques Chirac are greeted by Paul Okalik, right, government leader of Nunavut, and other leaders upon arrival at Iqaluit, capital of Nunavut, 5 September 1999.

(The Canadian Press/Paul Chiasson)

question of time zones. The territory straddles three: Mountain, Central, and Eastern. The initial decision to place the entire territory on Central Time proved highly unpopular, as in some areas it meant that the sun set at 1 p.m. The solution has been a compromise, that of eliminating daylight saving time. As a result, Nunavut's first six months of the year are now on Central Time, and the second six months on Eastern Time.

In the view of the Royal Commission on Aboriginal Peoples, the Inuit have made the most progress towards self-government of all of Canada's Aboriginal peoples. In its words, 'Only the Inuit are well advanced in the pro-

cess of political reform.' Sociologist Maybelle Mitchell attributes this to their adaptability, which has always been a prime requirement for survival in the Arctic.[90]

Ottawa, meanwhile, has been extending self-government at the municipal level to some Amerindian bands, in line with the long-held legal opinion that if Indians have the national vote they should be allowed to run their own affairs at the local level. In 1986, the 650-member Sechelt band assumed legal and political control in fee simple of a reserve of 10 square miles (26 square kilometres), 50 kilometres north of Vancouver, after a decade of effort on their part. The deal involved compensation of

$54 million but no general land claim settlement. For many Indians, this represented a compromise with their claim to an inherent right to self-government at the national level. As of 1981, band councils were administering 60 per cent of Amerindian program funds, amounting to about $600 million; for the most part, however, this had to be done within guidelines laid down by the department. Since Sechelt, Alberta's tiny but wealthy Sawridge band has negotiated a self-government agreement, and, more recently, other such agreements have been made (see Chapter 29) and still others are in process.

The reorganization of Canada's federalism, much discussed since the failure of Meech Lake, must make new provision for Amerindians, delegates agreed at the three-day Self-Determination Symposium held by the Assembly of First Nations at the University of Toronto in October 1990. Dene Georges Erasmus, the Assembly's National Chief (1985–91), described the Amerindian vision of the new order of things as one of 'sharing, recognition, and affirmation'.[91] He pointed to the American model: 'The United States is comfortable with recognizing that tribal peoples . . . have the right to govern themselves in many areas. . . . We have problems getting the government to even mouth the words "nation to nation".'[92] The alternative of civil disobedience was raised by Chief Ben Michel of the Innu. He argued that 'an attack on the economic base of Canada' would not be an insurrection, since Canada uses its economic power to suppress Native sovereignty. Rather, he said, it would be an exercise in sovereignty, at least for the Innu, who have never surrendered it.[93]

Hunters, Bombers, and a Breakaway

On another front, the Innu of Labrador, after a year of campaigning, won an injunction in 1989 to prevent the military from continuing its low-flying exercises over their terrain. The injunction was later overturned. The judge who had been sympathetic to the Innu appeal was an Inuk, James Igloliorte; in his judgment he observed that the lands in question had not been covered by treaties: 'none of their people ever gave away rights to the land to Canada, and this is an honest belief each person holds.'[94] His reasoning is worth considering in some detail:

> The provincial and federal statutes do not include as third parties or signatories any Innu people. I am satisfied that the four [appellants] believe their ancestors predate any Canadian claims to ancestry on this land. Since the concept of land as property is a concept foreign to original people the Court must not assume that a 'reasonable' belief be founded on English and hence Canadian law standards. The Innu must be allowed to express their understanding of a foreign concept on their terms, or simply to express what they believe.

The Innu, Igloliorte went on, do not believe that their rights were affected either by the Proclamation of 1763 or by 'the present occupation'.

> All of the legal reasonings are based on the premise that somehow the Crown acquired magically by its own declaration of title to the fee a consequent fiduciary obligation to the original people. It is time this premise based on 17th century reasoning be questioned in the light of 21st century reality. . . . The [recent] history of these Innu people is a glaring reminder that integration or assimilation alone will not make them a healthy community.

The judge concluded that criminalizing the Innu for their stand implies that 'the Court will have been unable to recognize the fundamental right of all persons to be treated equally before the law.'

As the government dragged its feet, public support for the Innu in their campaign grew. Walks to Ottawa in 1990—one starting in Halifax, the other in Windsor, Ontario—culminated in rallies on Parliament Hill and in a demonstration that ended with the arrest of 116 individuals. The Innu, who number about 12,000, claimed that Canadian and other pilots of the North Atlantic Treaty Organization make about 7,000 flights a year over their lands, sometimes zooming within a few metres of the ground. The Innu said this frightens the game, which has diminished as a result, and consequently this has threatened their lifestyle. A revealing look at the attitude of the military, which regards the Labrador interior as an empty land, is presented in the National Film Board production by Hugh Brody, *Hunters and Bombers*. As of August 2000, the Innu had called a truce in their campaign to stop the low-level flights in Labrador. The Department of National Defence had agreed to call off the high-speed flights, while the Innu had agreed to drop their court case.[95]

In 1968, Johnny Bob (Robert) Smallboy (Apitchitchiw, 1898–1984), a hereditary chief of the Ermineskin band at Hobbema, Alberta, left the reserve and with 143 followers set up camp on an old Indian hunting ground on the shores of Lake Muskiki, 65 kilometres northwest of Nordegg. For some time the chief had been worried about overcrowding on the reserve; but even more, he was concerned about the loss of traditional values under the stresses of today's technology-dominated ethos. According to the Indians, the inspiration for this gesture of reaffirmation came from Lazarus Roan (1903–78), an elder who had had a vision of a future catastrophe awaiting humans unless they followed the spirits' instructions. To avoid disaster, Lazarus and his people should leave the reserve, camp in a place designated by the spirits, and follow the old way of life.

In carrying out this directive, Smallboy not only confronted the government, as he and his followers camped on Crown lands, but he also split with many of his people who did not share Lazarus's vision. According to Randall J. Brown, a Native counselling specialist with Employment Canada who spent some time at the camp, the initial impetus to revivify traditional customs soon modified, and in two or three years members of the camp were living in log cabins (and later frame houses) instead of tents, had radio and television, and were no longer trying to live solely off the land. Economically, the camp survived because of oil royalties its people receive as members of the Hobbema bands. But in other aspects tradition has remained strong, as in the celebration of the sun dance and the observance of shaking tent rituals. That there was considerable public sympathy for the Crees' gesture was indicated in 1979 when Smallboy was awarded the Order of Canada. His camp is still on Kootenay Flats[96] and has developed a wilderness program for the rehabilitation of problem youths, 'the best of the worst from streets and reserves, society's rejects', in the words of Wayne Roan, president of the Nihtuskinan Society, which is in charge of the project.[97]

A counterbalancing trend was manifested in the launching of the World Council of Indigenous Peoples, an affiliate of the United Nations, in 1975 at Port Alberni, BC. Present were representatives from both of the Americas, Eurasia, and Scandinavia. Shuswap Chief George Manuel (1921–89), head of the National Indian Brotherhood (1970–6), was a key figure.

Chapter 28

Coercion, Standoffs, an Agreement, and a Royal Commission

A consequence of the Oka crisis was Prime Minister Mulroney's announcement of the setting up in 1991 of the Royal Commission on Aboriginal Peoples (RCAP) to investigate and report on the situation of Aboriginal peoples across the country, which the Prime Minister characterized as being second only in national importance to the current constitutional crisis. Seven commissioners were appointed; of the four who were Aboriginal, none represented the western numbered treaties. Of the two co-chairs, Georges Erasmus was formerly president of the Dene Nation, Northwest Territories, and more recently National Chief of the Assembly of First Nations, and René Dussault was a judge of the Quebec Appeals Court. The Commission's report was to be presented in 1994; instead, it did not appear until late in 1996. Not only was it the longest sitting for such a Commission in Canada's history, it was also the most expensive, even in terms of its initial budget of $42 million; that figure eventually ballooned to $58 million. The next most expensive was the Royal Commission on Reproductive Technology, which cost about $27 million.

The historical significance of the RCAP was pointed out by Peter Russell, professor of political science at the University of Toronto: 'This is the first time in modern history that the non-Aboriginal people have sat down with Aboriginal people and together . . . reviewed where they've been together and tried to chart a course on where they want to go.'[1] It would be the most thorough official investigation ever undertaken of Aboriginal life in Canada.[2]

While RCAP Listened, Problems Continued

In the meantime, the ending of the Oka standoff did not mean the end of tensions and demonstrations, as Aboriginal leaders continued their arguments for a larger constitutional role for their people.[3] That unsolved problems were continuing to fester as the RCAP set about its investigations became starkly evident in January 1993 when six children on the Innu reserve at Davis Inlet, Labrador, tried to commit suicide after sniffing gas fumes. The incident quickly blew up into an international scandal: 'Tragedy at Davis Inlet. The near-suicides of six

TIMELINE

1967	Newfoundland moves caribou-hunting Innu to island community of Davis Inlet, after a previous move on the mainland in 1948.	1996	Agreement reached to relocate Innu from Davis Inlet.
		1997	First Nations Bank of Canada begins operations in Saskatoon; five branches now open.
1991–6	Royal Commission on Aboriginal Peoples concludes with five-volume, 3,537-page report including 440 specific recommendations.	1998	Formal government regret expressed for residential school abuses and $350 million healing fund established.
1995	Confrontation between RCMP and dissident Shuswap Traditionalists encamped on private land at Gustafsen Lake, BC.	2000	Matthew Coon Come, Grand Chief of the Hudson Bay Cree, is elected National Chief of the Assembly of First Nations.
	Standoff over disputed land on shore of Lake Huron between Kettle and Stoney Point First Nation (Chippewa) and Ontario Provincial Police results in shooting death of Native activist Dudley George.		Deal reached to allow the Innu to have the final say concerning their children.
		2003	Davis Inlet Innu relocate to Natuashish.

teens display the hollowness of government promises to improve the community', according to a headline in *The Gazette*, Montreal.[4]

The story of Davis Inlet, an Innu community of about 500, is one of forced relocation, an all too familiar occurrence for Native settlements in the face of advancing agricultural and industrial frontiers. In the case of Davis Inlet, the process started in 1948 when the Newfoundland government decided that the caribou-hunting Innu, who have never been covered by the Indian Act, would be better off as fishermen and woodcutters at a location 240 kilometres distant from their traditional territory. The deaths of 70 of the Innu over the next two years led the community's survivors to seek their own remedy—they walked back to their old homeland. Again, they were not allowed to stay; less than 20 years later, in 1967, they were moved again, this time from their mainland site to an island in Davis Inlet. Once more, it was a move that made it impossible for them to continue their traditional

caribou-hunting way of life. The government's expressed reason: the new location was better suited for building housing and sewage systems. For the Innu, the sense of powerlessness at being once more involuntarily cut off from their customary pursuits led to a spiral of welfare dependency, alcoholism, gasoline sniffing, and suicide. The six rescued children were not alone in their suicide attempt: in one year, 25 per cent of the Innu adults were reported to have tried the same thing. In the wake of the publicity following their rescue, the six children were brought to Saddle Lake Reserve, outside of Edmonton, where they spent six months in a drug and alcohol treatment centre run by Poundmaker's Lodge and the Nechi Institute. At the same time, a group of Nechi counsellors went to Davis Inlet to work with the community itself.[5] As Colin Samson writes, however, '[w]ithin months of their return, the children returned to their gas-sniffing' because the causes of substance abuse—poverty and despair in the community—had not been

In the newly built village of Natuashish, the technologies of two very different worlds adorn the outside of a house.
(Photo by Dominick Tyler)

adequately addressed.[6] The difficulties proved not to be quickly resolved as long as the basic problem remained, which became clearly evident when some teenagers went on a New Year's Eve rampage and severely damaged a school.[7] It was not until late in 1996 that a relocation agreement was finally reached, this time to a site that the community accepted.[8] As of December 2000, however, the planned relocation had exceeded its original budget by $30 million, the Innu remained excluded from the Indian Act, and conflict with the federal government continued over how to effect the needed change. As Davis Inlet Chief Simeon

Tshakapesh said, 'unless meaningful changes occur, we are facing extinction. . . . They still want to control everything. That's going to be a big stumbling block in our healing plan.' And indeed, when the government moved to take over the finances of the two Labrador communities (Davis Inlet and Sheshatshiu) because of their operating deficits, the protests were loud.[9]

The gas-sniffing problem continued in other Innu communities, such as Sheshatshiu, which counts a population of 1,200, and became a major national news story in late 2000. If anything, the problem got worse as children, some as young as six, openly sniffed gasoline in the streets. In Chief Paul Rich's words: 'You see kids with a green garbage bag or a plastic shopping bag. They carry them around with gas inside and they sniff all day.' Unable to cope with the situation, Chief Rich took the unprecedented step of calling upon the Newfoundland government to send child protection officials to remove as many as 39 children and take them into care. In supporting the move, Peter Penashue, president of the Innu Nation, observed that 'this is the first time that I know of . . . that we've asked the government to take children en masse.' The government, after some hesitation because of the highly charged issue of removing Aboriginal children from their families, sent 12 of the troubled young people to a detoxification centre on a military base at Goose Bay as a 'temporary' measure. The location was chosen because of its high security; an earlier attempt to use a centre in Sheshatshiu failed because of its lack of facilities to control the comings and goings of the children. On 13 December 2000, federal Health Minister Alan Rock and Industry Minister Brian Tobin (who two months earlier had been the Newfoundland Premier) announced a deal that would allow the Innu to have the final say in the treatment of their children and families. One significant step in this regard was the creation of the Tshikapisk

Foundation, the goal of which is to reconnect young Innu to the traditional knowledge and country lifeways of their people through experience on the land.[10] In the meantime, Aboriginal communities across Canada have rallied to work out a healing program within a Native context. As they have assessed the situation, many more children are involved in the gas-sniffing syndrome than has been reported.

As for Davis Inlet and its squalid conditions, finally, in 2003, the building of the new community of Natuashish on the mainland near Davis Inlet, with a new sewer and water system and improved access to caribou herds, had been completed at a cost of more than $150 million, and the 680 residents of Davis Inlet had been relocated. This was a beginning, and by 2008 the school at Natuashish had awarded diplomas to its first two high school graduates, enrolment in adult education programs had increased dramatically, and kindergarten enrolment had nearly doubled from the previous year.[11]

Apart from the Davis Inlet episode, the most publicized of the forced relocations were those of the Inuit, whose experiences were stepped into high gear during the 1930s and lasted until the 1970s (Chapter 26). However, other groups across the land suffered similar treatment.[12] The reasons for the moves were various, such as the need to make room for one form or another of industrial or agricultural development, which inevitably diminished wildlife resources upon which the Natives depended. In the case of the Inuit, the official desire was to make it possible for them to maintain their traditional way of life in new areas where wildlife was comparatively abundant, when living off the land became steadily more difficult in their old locations. This policy was born of the then current belief that the Arctic's development potential would not be sufficient to support alternative lifestyles. Sometimes, as with the relocation of the Innu to Davis Inlet, the motivation was simply administrative convenience. Another

example of this was when Indian Affairs moved to centralize Mi'kmaq settlements in Nova Scotia. A combination of factors, complicated by the Depression of the 1930s, had led the department to conclude that such a program would make administrative sense. Between 1942 and 1949, residents of 20 small reserves were pressured into relocating to Eskasoni, on Cape Breton Island, and to Shubenacadie, on the Nova Scotia mainland. The result was that by the 1980s these two reserves were seriously overcrowded and in the throes of increased, instead of diminished, welfare dependence, not to mention soaring rates of substance abuse and suicide.[13] Others who experienced similar relocations include various bands of Amerindians in northern Manitoba, Yukon, and British Columbia, as well as the Labrador Inuit.

Once More, Confrontation

During the years immediately following Oka, protests in various forms, such as occupations of land or offices, or the erection of barricades at strategic places, erupted sporadically across the land. In 1995, two drew considerable national attention: the land occupations at Gustafsen Lake, British Columbia, and at Ipperwash, Ontario.

The Gustafsen Lake episode concerned a privately owned ranch that contained a site used by neighbouring reserve residents for sun dance ceremonies. An outside group of Natives from other parts of the country as well as from the United States continued camping on the site after the ceremonies, refusing rancher Lyle James's request to leave. They argued that this was unceded Indian land, as indeed it was, since there had been no treaties in the area, and besides, they claimed, the land was sacred as it was used for the sun dance. They called themselves Defenders of the Shuswap Nation and/or Shuswap Traditionalists. As they armed themselves, the Royal Canadian Mounted

Police, who had been called in to dislodge the dissident campers, reinforced their presence until more than 200 were on the site. The occupiers' leader, Jones William ('Wolverine') Ignace of Chase, BC, announced that defending Amerindian title was worth dying for and rejected conciliatory overtures by AFN National Chief Ovide Mercredi, who had come to act as mediator. However, Ignace and his defiant defenders not only did not have the support of the regional chiefs, they were condemned by many of them. Eventually, after an occupation of about four months and a shootout with police, they were persuaded by Stoney medicine man John Stevens of Morley, Alberta, to give themselves up and face the inevitable police charges. Several of the group, including Ignace, already had criminal records. The episode was reported to have cost the Canadian taxpayers $5.5 million.

As to be expected, the Gustafsen Lake standoff invited comparisons with Oka. At Oka, the land in question had deep historical significance for the Mohawks, and their grievances concerning its ownership went back two and a half centuries. Aboriginal peoples across the land rallied to their cause, doing everything they could to help. At Gustafsen Lake, regional chiefs disclaimed historical significance for the land at issue, observing that its use for sun dances was a recent development.[14] At Oka, a policeman had been killed; at Gustafsen Lake, two police wearing bulletproof vests were struck. A postscript to the latter episode concerned one of the protestors who had fired on the policemen. James Pitawanakwat was on day parole one year into a three-year sentence for mischief when he became involved at Gustafsen Lake. After the shooting, he fled to the United States, whereupon Canada launched extradition proceedings to get him back to serve the rest of his sentence. Oregon District Court Judge Janice Stewart denied the application on the grounds that the Gustafsen Lake confronta-

tion had been an attempt 'by indigenous people to overthrow an occupying government in an effort to achieve self-rule'. As she saw it, the uprising had been part of a general Native protest against the European takeover of their lands that began in 1492. An immediate consequence of the ruling is that Pitawanakwat, because of his Native heritage, is free to live in the United States as a resident alien. In the meantime, the US State Department has downgraded the Gustafsen Lake standoff to the status of a 'land dispute', far short of the uprising of a people seeking to regain a lost heritage.[15]

The standoff at Ipperwash was of a different order. The land in question was part of the Stoney Point Reserve on the shore of Lake Huron and had been appropriated from the Kettle and Stoney Point First Nation (Chippewa, a branch of Ojibwa) by the federal government in 1942 under the War Measures Act for use as a military training base. The Chippewa received about $50,000 in compensation and were told the land would be returned after World War II when it was no longer needed. Despite a confirmation of this by an Order-in-Council in 1981, the military continued to use it as a summer cadet training camp and as a recreation facility. In 1982 the federal government agreed to pay the Chippewa $2.4 million in compensation for the use of the land, but further delayed its return pending an environmental assessment and cleanup necessary after 40 years of military use. Finally, in 1993, a group of Chippewa, impatient at the seemingly endless delays, set up camp in the disputed territory.

The occupation's peaceful beginning did not last as the influence of radical activists, such as members of the American Indian Movement, took effect. Escalating violence through the summer of 1995 finally led to the withdrawal of the military from the camp.[16] A Memorandum of Understanding quickly followed, laying out the terms of the transfer. It was agreed that the all-important cleanup of

Jones William ('Wolverine') Ignace walks past masked guards at the protestors' camp at Gustafsen Lake, BC, during the four-month occupation, 1995. The protesting Amerindians claimed the area as unceded sacred land.
(Canapress Photo Service)

the site would be a joint operation by the federal government and the Kettle and Stoney Point First Nation. A Mohawk lawyer, Ralph Brant, was named negotiator; most recently before that, he had been director in Atlantic Canada for Indian Affairs.

Hard upon the heels of this settlement, a group of Chippewa calling themselves Stoney Pointers began an occupation of the adjoining Ipperwash Provincial Park. It also had once been part of the reserve, but more importantly, it contains an ancient burial ground the Chippewa wanted returned. In this dispute, they were dealing with the province, which mobilized the Ontario Provincial Police to remove the protestors. In the ensuing confrontation, Dudley George, a Chippewa, was killed, Canada's first Amerindian casualty in a land-claim standoff.[17] An Ontario provincial court found the police officer involved, Sergeant Kenneth Deane, guilty of criminal negligence causing death.[18] However, his sentence did not include a prison term.

A third occupation during 1995, this one comparatively peaceful and consequently eclipsed in the news, was that of Ontario's Serpent Mounds Provincial Park by the 400-member Hiawatha First Nation. The band won its claim against the federal government for improperly leasing the reserve land to Ontario for a provincial park, and received $2.8 million in compensation for loss of the use of the land. Ontario, for its part, turned the operation of the park over to the band, which is now running the show.[19]

BC's First Land Claim Agreement: The Nisga'a Treaty

British Columbia's position in relation to its Native peoples was for a long time unique in Canada. For one thing, apart from the 14 small treaties on Vancouver Island negotiated by Governor James Douglas, 1850–4, and the overlap of Treaty Eight into its northeastern corner in 1899, the province had not negotiated treaties with its First Nations. Not recognizing Aboriginal rights, it denied having any outstanding obligations that could be settled by way of land claims. It maintained this position until 1990, when it finally yielded to the combination of court rulings, federal pressure, and a change in public attitude, and agreed to open talks. Two years later, the newly formed New Democratic government promised to resolve the claims, of which there were 47, covering most of the province. This raised the hopes of Amerindian leaders, whose demands soared to encompass more than 110 per cent of the province's land. The government responded by announcing that only 5 per cent would be available for settling claims.[20]

The Nisga'a were the first of BC's claimants to have their case heard (Chapter 23). A nation of 5,500 in the Nass Valley and spreading to the northwest, they had initially filed their claim 70 years earlier.[21] Originally, it involved 24,000 square kilometres of the northern part of the province; finally, after intensive negotiations (behind closed doors for the final two years), the Nisga'a agreed to accept 1,900 square kilometres. Other terms included $190 million in

compensation, municipal-style self-government, exclusive rights to their territory's pine-forest mushroom harvest, shares in the Nass River's salmon run and forest industries, and the return of listed Nisga'a artifacts held by the Canadian Museum of Civilization and the Royal British Columbia Museum.[22] This agreement-in-principle reflected flexibility on all sides. Even though only preliminary, it still set a precedent, as illustrated by its provisions concerning taxation: the Nisga'a accepted phasing out of tax exemption for their people after a transitional period of eight years for sales taxes and 12 years for income taxes. The land being turned over to the Nisga'a, to be communally owned in fee simple, is valued at $100 million. Still, it is a fraction of what was once theirs. Chief Joe Gosnell, who led the campaign, has been elected the first president of the Nisga'a Nation's new government.

Thus the persistence of the Nisga'a has paid off, and their treaty was ratified by Parliament in 2000. The *Calder* case of 1973 (Chapter 23) set the scene: although that decision had gone against the Nisga'a on a technicality, the judges had agreed that the First Nation did indeed have Aboriginal title to its ancestral lands. From there the Nisga'a never stopped pressing, first the federal government, then, after 1990, the provincial government as well. The discussions were neither simple nor easy: at one point they were broken off entirely when the two governments could not agree on either the values at stake or the sharing of responsibilities. It took a tragedy to break the deadlock: the shooting of Dudley George at Ipperwash. The prospect of spreading violence very quickly brought the negotiators back to the table, and the terms of British Columbia's first preliminary agreement on a land claim were soon settled.[23] Not surprisingly, in view of its past policies, BC faces the largest roster of unsettled comprehensive claims of any of the provinces. As of 2008, according to INAC figures, 20 comprehensive claims, covering 40 per cent of Canada's land mass, have been settled.[24] Across the country, 1,297 specific claims are in process in various categories.[25]

The RCAP Report

The commissioners' five-volume, 3,537-page report, when it finally appeared, was stunning in its magnitude and the scope of its proposals for Canada and Canadians, involving as it did a fundamental reorganization of the country's social and political institutions in relation to Aboriginal peoples. In the commissioners' words:

> We advocate recognition of Aboriginal nations within Canada as political entities through which Aboriginal people can express their distinctive identity within the context of Canadian citizenship. . . . At the heart of our recommendations is the recognition that Aboriginal peoples are peoples, that they form collectives of unique character, and that they have a right to governmental autonomy.[26]

In other words, the relationship between Aboriginal and non-Aboriginal people is a central facet of Canada's heritage. With this in mind, the commissioners identified four key issues: the need for a new relationship between Aboriginal and non-Aboriginal peoples, self-determination through self-government, economic self-sufficiency, and healing for Aboriginal peoples and communities. They made 440 recommendations detailing specific measures to achieve these goals. Among the more significant and far-reaching were the following:

- The Queen and Parliament should issue a new royal proclamation confirming and supplementing the Proclamation of 1763, along with new legislation providing for the implementation of existing treaty rights and guidelines for the negotiation of new treaties. This would involve the establishment of a national Crown Treaty Office as well as provincial treaty offices. The new proclamation should also acknowledge and express regret 'for policies that deprived Aboriginal peoples of their lands and interfered with their customs'. With reconciliation, Aboriginal peoples could 'embrace their Aboriginal and Canadian citizenship without reservation'.

- The creation of an Aboriginal parliament, to be known as the House of First Peoples, as a third order of government in addition to the federal Parliament and the provincial legislatures. Its function would be to advise these houses on matters relating to Aboriginal peoples. The new house would be elected by First Nations at the same time as the federal elections. Aboriginal voters would be enumerated in the national enumeration.

- The right to self-determination to be vested in Aboriginal nations rather than in small local communities. An Aboriginal nation is defined as a sizable body of Aboriginal people with a shared sense of national identity occupying a certain territory or group of territories. This would mean merging 1,000 or more separate bands, Inuit villages, and Métis settlements into 60 to 80 Aboriginal nations entitled to self-government.

- Negotiations to be undertaken with federal, provincial, and territorial governments to provide First Nations with lands sufficient to foster Aboriginal economic self-reliance, as well as cultural and political autonomy. As matters stand, reserves would not provide a sufficient base; looking south of the border, the United States has reserved for Aboriginal use 30 per cent more land in proportion to its population than has Canada. H. Anthony Reynolds, RCAP executive director, observed that up to 15 per cent of Canada's lands could be set aside for its Aboriginal nations, in line with what has been suggested for Alaska. Particular attention should be paid to the needs of the Métis; at present, Alberta is the only province where they have a land base (Chapter 24).

- Aboriginal nations to develop their own system of taxation, which would include personal income taxes. Federal, provincial, and Aboriginal governments to co-ordinate their fiscal arrangements, which would include extending the system of equalization payments for the provinces to Aboriginal nations.
- Abolition of the Department of Indian Affairs and the creation of two new departments in its stead: a Department of Aboriginal Relations and a Department of Indian and Inuit Services, each to be headed by its own minister. In the case of the Department of Aboriginal Relations, this would be a senior post.
- Other recommended appointments include a permanent treaty commission and the replacement of the Indian Claims Commission with an Aboriginal Land and Treaties Tribunal, whose decisions would be final and not subject to court review. These two bodies would be inde-pendent, to avoid the present situation in negotiations whereby 'federal officials act as both judge and jury'.
- The enactment of an Aboriginal Nations Recognition and Government Act to establish criteria for the recognition of Aboriginal nations and to complete a cit-izenship that is consistent with interna-tional norms of human rights and with the Canadian Charter of Rights and Freedoms. In their commentary, the com-missioners observed that 'Aboriginal

nations are not racial groups; rather they are organic political and cultural entities . . . they often have mixed genetic her-itages and include individuals of varied ancestry.'[27]

- That every person who identifies as Métis and is accepted by the Métis nation should be recognized as a member of that nation, and that this be acknowledged by the Canadian government.
- Aboriginal peoples should be recognized as possessing a unique form of dual citi-zenship, as citizens both of an Aboriginal nation and of Canada.
- Canada should support the 1993 Draft Declaration of the Rights of Indigenous Peoples, which is being considered by the United Nations.
- The Crown has a special fiduciary obliga-tion to protect the interests of the Aboriginal people, including Aboriginal title.
- Federal and provincial governments should enter into long-term development deals with Aboriginal nations to provide funding for economic development.
- A national Aboriginal bank should be established, staffed, and controlled by Aboriginal people, to provide support for large-scale projects and to raise capital for economic development. This recommen-dation recalls a proposal made a century and a half ago by the Bagot Commission, to the effect that a bank be established on each reserve. However, the idea at that time was to facilitate financial services, rather than to allow for Aboriginal con-trol. In the meantime, the Bank of Mon-treal early in the 1990s established a system of branches catering specifically to First Nations' needs. According to Ron Jamieson, senior vice-president of Abor-iginal banking for the Bank of Montreal, the aim of the program is to facilitate

Aboriginal participation in the nation's economic life. By the late 1990s, the program included 16 branches, 11 of them on reserves.[28]

- Federal and provincial governments should fund a major 10-year initiative for employment development and training.
- Aboriginal communities should be allowed to make innovative use of social assistance funds for employment and social development.
- All Canadian governments are called upon to support a holistic approach to social assistance, which would integrate social and economic development with Aboriginal traditions and values.
- Canada should acknowledge a fiduciary responsibility to support Aboriginal nations and their communities in restoring Aboriginal families to a state of health and wholeness. This would include amending legislation to recognize Aboriginal family law in areas such as divorce, child custody, and adoption.
- Governments and other organizations should collaborate in developing a system of healing centres and lodges under Aboriginal control but also fully supported by mainstream health and social services. This network of healing centres should be available to Amerindian, Inuit, and Métis communities in both rural and urban settings on an equitable basis.
- Governments must supplement resources available to Aboriginal people to meet their needs for housing, water, and sanitation services. Acute risks to health and safety should be treated as emergencies and targeted for immediate action.
- Federal, provincial, and territorial governments should promptly acknowledge that education is of central importance to Aboriginal self-government, and that the Crown has an obligation to support a full range of education services, including continuance of post-secondary education assistance as provided for by the numbered treaties. The teaching of Aboriginal languages should be accorded priority, and to this end the federal government should provide an annual grant of $10 million for five years to support an Aboriginal language foundation. The Métis language Michif was noted as needing help to be saved from extinction.
- The creation of an Aboriginal Peoples' International University is recommended to promote traditional knowledge and Aboriginal research.
- Women should be assured full and equal participation in all stages of discussion leading to the development of self-government, as well as being included in governing bodies for Aboriginal health, healing, and educational institutions. There should also be provision made for the active participation of elders, youth, and persons with disabilities.
- An Aboriginal Arts Council should be established to foster visual and performing arts as well as literature.
- Aboriginal representatives should be involved in all planning for future constitutional conferences, and have a role in the amending process and a veto over any changes that affect Aboriginal rights.
- Perhaps most controversial of all, at least in the short run, has been the commissioners' recommendation of additional spending of $1.5 to $2 billion annually by Indian Affairs on top of its present budget for the next 15 years to jump-start welfare-dependent Aboriginal communities on the road to economic self-sufficiency.

The list goes on from there, dealing with such matters as co-management of wildlife resources, keeping Aboriginal customary usage in mind when establishing national parks, the issue of ownership and management of cultural historic sites, and even a proposal for the establishment of an electronic worldwide information clearing office. A cautionary note was sounded in connection with the current mining development at Voisey's Bay in Labrador: that it must not be allowed to repeat the experiences of the past, such as those already noted for the Davis Inlet Innu.

In the view of the RCAP, there are four dimensions to social change in reference to Natives: healing, improving economic opportunity, developing human resources as well as Aboriginal institutions, and adapting mainstream institutions to Aboriginal as well as non-Aboriginal needs.[29] On the subject of self-government, the commissioners had some interesting thoughts about urban Natives. They proposed what they called 'Community of Interest Government'. Such a government would operate on the basis of voluntary membership within municipal boundaries. Its powers would be delegated from Aboriginal national governments and/or provincial governments.[30] The Commission tossed a bouquet to Quebec for its hunter income support programs, which were developed as part of its northern land claim agreements. These are not matched anywhere else in Canada.[31]

Even as the commissioners were hammering out their recommendations, some of them had already been realized, at least in part, and others were in the process. Three examples are the northern Quebec community of Oujé-Bougoumou, the establishment of Canada's first Aboriginal bank, and the restructuring of the Indian Act.

Climbing Out from Under

Today Oujé-Bougoumou, counting 709 souls, is one of the nine northern Quebec bands listed under the James Bay and Northern Quebec Agreement of 1975. Their village has been recognized by the United Nations as one of 50 world-class models, integrating as it does traditional concepts with contemporary engineering techniques and architectural designs. It was not always thus: for years the group was disorganized and without effective leadership, not recognized as a separate band by either federal or provincial governments, but as 'strays' from the Mistassini Cree; they were originally known as Chibougamou Cree. There was no government help forthcoming as their hunting and gathering way of life was disrupted by industrial development in one location after another. Living conditions went from bad to worse, until they matched 'the worst in the developed world'.

The Oujé-Bougoumou's troubles had started in the 1920s, when their territory became the focus of mining development. There followed a period during which the Crees were displaced time and again as they got in the way of mining interests. It would take years of persistent effort on the part of individuals such as former chief Jimmy Mianscum, but eventually, in the 1980s, they won recognition as a band and renamed themselves the Oujé-Bougoumou Cree Nation. After still more administrative battles, and now with a new chief, Abel Bosum, they selected a site at Lake Opémisca, engaged the services of one of Canada's leading architects, Douglas Cardinal, a Blackfoot from Alberta, and set about building yet another village. When negotiations with the federal and provincial governments collapsed, they declared jurisdiction over their territory of 10,000 square kilometres. As Native leaders across the country rallied to their cause, deals were finally signed with Quebec (1989) and, in 1991, with Ottawa.

As the Nisga'a would also do, the Oujé-Bougoumou had not allowed themselves to become trapped in the role of victim but kept their gaze determinedly on the future. Their hopes are high for their new village: they see it

Amerindians in ceremonial dress took part in the opening ritual that launched the First Nations Bank, 1996. The ceremony was held in Toronto, but the first branch to go into operation was in Saskatoon. The Toronto-Dominion Bank is helping the all-Native financial institution get started.

(Andy Clark; Reuters)

as a healing centre, a place of learning, physical sustenance, and spiritual renewal. In the words of Bosum, from 'the very beginning, our objective has been to build a place and an environment that produces healthy, secure, confident and optimistic people.'[32] Oujé-Bougoumou gives every indication that it is well on the way to realizing this vision.

First Nations Bank of Canada

Within three weeks of the RCAP report, one of its recommendations was realized when Canada's first Aboriginal bank was ceremonially launched in Toronto by Prime Minister Jean Chrétien and Native leaders. Using Toronto-Dominion Bank facilities to provide services to both Native and non-Native customers, the First Nations Bank of Canada began operations in Saskatoon in 1997. It is a co-operative enterprise, involving the Saskatchewan Federation of Indian Nations and the Saskatchewan Indian Equity Foundation besides Toronto-Dominion. The latter provided $8 million of the start-up capital, 80 per cent of the total. Besides servicing a Native clientele, the bank is seeking to attract the investment of land claim settlement monies paid to Indian bands across the country. Off to a flying start, it now has five branches in operation, in Saskatoon, Chisasibi (James Bay region of Quebec), Walpole Island (Ontario), Whitehorse, and Winnipeg.[33]

Noting that the bank 'will be a piece of Canadian history' that was nearly four years in the making, Saskatchewan Federation chief Blaine Favel observed:

> The road to political self-determination, the road to self-government, is directly linked to the role of economic development. If we are to have strong self-government, if we are to have a strong political direction, we have to have a strong economic base.[34]

When the bank was founded, National Chief Matthew Coon Come of the Assembly of First Nations, who is on the bank's board, saw it as part of an Aboriginal economic development that is steadily gaining momentum. He remarked that the First Nations were 'already involved in aviation, co-distribution, oil and gas, they have all kinds of construction companies and I think it is just a step toward self-sufficiency.'[35] He added that the benefits will include a greater degree of Native economic control and greater sensitivity to needs of First Nation communities and businesses, as well as an opportunity to share in the profits.

Amending the Indian Act, Again

On the political front, an initiative of Ronald Irwin (Indian Affairs Minister, 1993–7) to amend the Indian Act to give Aboriginal nations more control over their own affairs met with an angry reception on the part of Indian leaders, who felt that the proposed measures did not go far enough and that the Act should be abolished. Irwin defended the proposed amendments on the grounds that they would strip away some of the archaic ministerial power of Indian Affairs, removing governmental interference with daily decisions on reserves. Those bands that have agreed to the new measures would be able to manage their own lands and resources, on condition that

they develop a land code and hold a referendum beforehand. Environmental standards and penalties would have to be reconciled with federal and provincial laws. For the first time in federal legislation, the proposed changes included an assurance that they would not affect existing Aboriginal rights or those arising from treaties. Those bands accepting this new law, which would be entirely voluntary, would no longer be subject to the Indian Act; once the decision was put into effect, however, it would be irreversible.

The vast majority of the bands contacted beforehand about these proposals did not respond; of those who did, 14 agreed to participate. The opposition stemmed from the legislation's piecemeal approach, which did not follow the RCAP recommendation to abolish the Indian Act and totally restructure the administrative relationship of Natives and government. Much as the First Nations have criticized and even denounced the Act in the past, its partial dismantling is seen as avoiding getting at what they see as the root of the problem: its 'paternalism'. However, as Native input was requested before the revised Act was introduced to Parliament, and as participation would be voluntary, the argument in this case seems to have been about procedure rather than paternalism as such. The critics also held that the land proposals could lead to reserve lands being open to seizure for debt. On top of everything, they saw Irwin's action as a way of getting around the RCAP recommendations without dealing with them directly.[36] Only too keenly aware of Ottawa's record for shelving commission reports, National Chief Ovide Mercredi moved quickly to warn Ottawa that implementing the RCAP recommendations was its 'last best chance' to improve the lot of marginalized Aboriginal peoples, thus avoiding rising remedial expenditures for social and economic ills, not to mention the possibility of violence. Georges Erasmus, RCAP co-chair, expressed the Aboriginal position succinctly: 'if the reality is that once more people's hopes have been dashed, and that this was all for nothing, then what we say is that people will resort to other things.'[37] In the meantime, the bill died on the order paper when a federal election was called for 2 June 1997.

The idea behind the bill remained very much alive, however. In January 2001, Robert Nault, Irwin's successor as Minister of Indian Affairs, proposed supplementing the Indian Act with a First Nations Governance Act. Besides transferring the supervision of band votes to Elections Canada, the proposed Act would have given bands increased powers to levy taxes on reserves, as well as the right to garnishee wages and seize assets. Along with this would go increased band accountability to band members. Nault saw the proposed measure as a step towards self-government. The reaction of the Indians was predictable: unless they are involved in working out the new format, it will not get the support it needs to succeed.[38] The aftermath of the proposed First Nations Governance Act is discussed in Chapter 29.

Concerns, Hopes, and Fears

It has surprised no one that the RCAP report was hailed by Aboriginal leaders as an 'inspiring road map to the future', all the more because it so clearly expressed the Aboriginal position. An early criticism of the RCAP was that it 'listens only to Indians'.[39] This was denied by Erasmus, who said that the Commission was neither an Aboriginal organization nor an advocacy group. He saw it as 'walking a middle line'.[40] As for Irwin, even as he rejected the Commission's call for a huge leap in short-term spending as a political non-starter,[41] he found that its proposal that Aboriginal peoples be organized into nations for the purpose of self-government was 'a good idea'. As he expressed it, with larger groupings 'you can get better services'.[42] At the time of writing, Indian Affairs had reached 30 self-government final agreements across Canada; as well, '81 self-government negotiation tables representing 384 Aboriginal communities' were ongoing in the summer of 2008.[43]

In general, Indian Affairs acknowledges that it needs to build a new partnership with Aboriginal peoples, as well as to strengthen their communities to enable them to govern themselves. It also acknowledges that 'the inherent right of self-government is an existing Aboriginal and treaty right.'[44] This right to govern themselves is accepted in relation to matters internal to their communities, integral to their particular cultures, languages, and institutions, and with respect to their special relationship to their land and resources. Further, federal authorities say they are prepared to give Aboriginal peoples the tools necessary to achieve this.

A step towards this new approach was taken early in 1998, when Jane Stewart, Minister of Indian Affairs and Northern Development, 1997–9, officially expressed the government's regret for the residential school abuses and announced a $350 million healing fund to help those who had suffered. At the same time Stewart announced an action plan called 'Gathering Strength' to develop a partnership with the First Nations to carry out needed reforms in general administration. This was in response to the frequent complaint that, in the past, policy changes involving First Nations were usually undertaken without prior consultation with the peoples involved. While the reaction of Native leaders was mixed, to say the least, particularly as the statement of regret had been made by the Minister of Indian Affairs rather than the Prime Minister,[45] the department was still able to report a year later that an agenda to correct the situation had been developed with the Assembly of First Nations and that, in fact, it was already in operation at national, regional, and community levels.

Aboriginal mood of the nineties: a masked warrior looking through barbed wire exemplifies the confrontations that marked the decade.

(Andy Clark; Reuters)

Matthew Coon Come, however, who replaced Phil Fontaine as National Chief of the Assembly of First Nations in 2000, did not accepted the apology as good enough. Chief Coon Come wanted a national Truth and Reconciliation Commission to be established by Order-in-Council to act as a national forum for venting feelings and working out problems caused by the residential school experience.[46] As discussed in the next chapter, a formal apology from the Prime Minister for the residential schools was finally made in June 2008, and Chief Coon

Come's call for a Truth and Reconciliation Commission also had been met.

On the matter of self-government, everyone agrees that there is no question of trying to implement the 'one size fits all' paradigm.[47] Practical arrangements have to take into account the differing circumstances of each case. Fiscal restraint means that federal funding must be achieved through reallocation of existing resources, which involves taking the interests of other Canadians into account. Where their jurisdictions or interests are affected, provincial or territorial governments must be included in negotiations. In general, tripartite (federal, provincial, Aboriginal) processes have been found to be the most effective. Whatever the approach, easy answers are not to be expected, nor are any in sight.

Admittedly, the report presents some difficult challenges. On the negative side there is the argument that Canada already has a multiplicity of levels of government, and adding another could only complicate an already complex situation. There is also the fear that such a move, in combination with the other RCAP proposals, would separate Aboriginal peoples even more than they are now from the general body of Canadian citizens. Despite the commissioners' denial that the Aboriginal nations are racially defined, it is difficult to see how that could be avoided in view of band membership requirements. On the positive side, the country has been presented with its first thoroughly thought-out blueprint for incorporating its First Nations as full partners in the Canadian confederation. That said, it is striking how similar many of the RCAP proposals are to those of two previous reports: *Indian Self-Government in Canada* (Penner Report, 1983) and *A Survey of the Contemporary Indians of Canada: Economic, Political, Educational Needs and Policies* (Hawthorn Report, 1966). In neither of these cases was the government response more than partial at best, when it responded at all.

However, the need for action does not all lie on one side. Amerindian leadership must also accept its share of responsibility in mapping out the future, National Chief Coon Come said at an Aboriginal health conference held in early 2001 in Ottawa. In a speech entitled 'Our Voice, Our Decisions, Our Responsibility', he made the point that solutions to the social ills that plague the Amerindian community cannot all come from outside. 'We are the ones who have to do something. We must act.' High on his list of priorities was leadership accountability, all too frequently lacking in present band administrations. In his words, 'we need to clean up our own act.' Perry Bellegarde, an Assembly of First Nations regional chief, agreed: 'We as leaders have to show the way and be good role models for our youth.'[48]

Reactions to these calls for action will profoundly affect Canada's future as a nation.

Some Background

The population of status Indians in Canada on and off reserves stood at 659,890 in 1999.[49] According to projections, that population would have reached 798,211 in 2008.[50] A study concluded in 1995 reported the Cree forming the largest linguistic group at 31 per cent, followed by the Ojibwa at about 22 per cent.[51] The majority are members of 612 bands on 2,633 reserves. As of 1993, 70 per cent of the bands had less than 1,000 members, while 10 per cent had more than 2,000. According to the Aboriginal Peoples Survey done in conjunction with the census of 1996, Canada's total population reporting Aboriginal ancestry stood at 1,101,960, a figure that includes 720,740 Métis and 41,800 Inuit. The most recent figures, from the 2006 census, indicate a total Aboriginal identity population of 1,172,785. Of these, 698,025 identified as Indian, while Métis totalled 389,780 and Inuit numbered 50,480.[52] The total Amerindian population at Confedera-

tion has been estimated at between 100,000 and 125,000, dropping to its low point in the 1920s. Since then the population has multiplied 10 times, with the rate of growth taking a strong upward turn during the 1960s to surpass that of the Canadian population as a whole. Where Amerindians had represented 1.1 per cent of the population in 1961, 20 years later the proportion had increased to 1.5 per cent. In 1996 the figure was 3.0 per cent; today, it is 3.8 per cent and still growing. In Manitoba, the proportion is 15.5 per cent, in Saskatchewan, 14.9 per cent. It rises sharply in the North, to 25.1 per cent in the Yukon and 50.3 per cent in the Northwest Territories. In Nunavut, the Aboriginal identity population, almost all of whom are Inuit, accounts for 85 per cent of the total population.[53] The average age of Amerindians is younger than in the national population: according to the 1996 census, 53 per cent are under 24 years of age, compared to 33 per cent of all Canadians. By 1999, life expectancy for Amerindian women was 76 years, and for men, 69 years. For Canadians at large, the figures were 80.9 years for women and 74.6 for men. In its 1996 report, the RCAP noted information from the Native Physicians Association that there were 51 self-identified Aboriginal physicians at that time.[54] The Amerindian birth rate (3.15 births per woman) was almost twice that of non-Amerindians (1.7 births per woman). Between 1991 and 1996, the Inuit population grew at an average annual rate of 2.3 per cent, twice the average national rate. If maintained, that means the Inuit population will have doubled in 35 years.[55] On the other hand, the suicide rate among Natives is six times that of the nation as a whole.[56] For individuals under 25, it is the highest in the world. In 1996, more than 33 per cent of Canada's once self-sustaining and independent Indians were on welfare; on reserves, the figure was 45 per cent. The unemployment rate within the Native labour force was more than double that of the population as a whole. At the same time, however, Aboriginal entrepreneurship has been exploding, from 6,000 Aboriginal-owned businesses in 1989 to 20,000 in 1998. About 45 per cent of the total Aboriginal population lives in cities.

The 1998–9 federal expenditure for Aboriginal and Northern Affairs programs for the period ending 31 March 1999 was $4.9 billion, down from the $6.2 billion reported for 1995–6. Most of this was for education, social services, and health care, which are provided for Canadians in general by provincial and municipal governments. When these factors are considered, as well as the differences in the growth rate between the Aboriginal and general populations, the rate does not vary widely from that for program spending by all Canadian governments combined.[57] As of 2000, 29 per cent of the employees of the Department of Indian and Northern Affairs were Native; three years earlier, in 1997, it had been 25 per cent. By far the greatest number are in Ottawa, with the fewest in the Atlantic region. The comparable figure reported for the Bureau of Indian Affairs in the United States, as of 1992, was 90 per cent.

Chapter 29

We Are Sorry

Introduction

On 11 June 2008, the Prime Minister of Canada rose in the House of Commons and made history with three words: 'We are sorry.' His statement, and others that day by the leaders of the other parties in Parliament, and the responses by the leaders of five national Aboriginal organizations, may have been a historic watershed in Canada's Aboriginal history, marking a new beginning in the relationship between Aboriginal people and the federal government in Canada. The apology was for the many harms wrought on stolen children by the residential schools since the nineteenth century. Quite apart from the apology, which was a promise fulfilled, however, there was nothing new attached to the words: 'We are sorry.' As many Aboriginal people said that day, the real work to heal their relationship with Canada was only about to begin, and whether it would change thereafter remained a question mark in the early twenty-first century. In this century there are indeed plenty of questions.

An April 2008 *Globe and Mail* article, headlined 'Natives threaten Olympic disruptions', quoted the Assembly of First Nations National Chief, Phil Fontaine, as stating that 'The situation here is compelling enough to convince Canadians that while it is okay and right to express outrage with the Chinese government's position against Tibet and the Tibetans, they should be just as outraged, if not more so, about our situation here.'[1] Most Canadians reading that headline would be shocked that we would be compared with the human rights abuses of China against Tibet. Such is still the broad lack of understanding of Aboriginal issues in Canada. What are the legacies of the past relations between Canada's founding peoples and later settlers for Canadians in 2008, and why are these issues still with us? All of the many issues cannot be covered in a single chapter (they are covered and updated elsewhere in this book), but some of them are highlighted here. We need a stock-taking—on the most significant of these issues, perhaps a new ledger drawn by the experiences and actions of indigenous people—for our needs in the twenty-first century. A regional and local perspective has long been the strength of First Nations and their survival, rather than the

TIMELINE

2003 Phil Fontaine, an Ojibwa from Sagkeeng First Nation, is elected as National Chief of the Assembly of First Nations.

In September, with the decision in *Powley*, the Supreme Court of Canada affirms that Métis have rights that are recognized in and protected by Canada's Constitution.

Thomas King is the first Aboriginal person to give the Massey Lectures.

2005 In October, high E. coli levels found in the Kashechewan Reserve water treatment plant and its drinking water system in northern Ontario.

In October, Henco Industries decides to develop the Douglas Creek Estates adjacent to the Six Nations Reserve in Caledonia, which later causes clashes between residents of Caledonia and the Six Nations; the issue remains in negotiation.

In November, Prime Minister Paul Martin announces landmark Kelowna Accord.

2006 Kelowna Accord scrapped by the newly elected Conservative government of Stephen Harper.

2007 Ipperwash Inquiry Final Report released on 31 May.

In June, Harper announces Land Rights Action Plan in response to the National Day of Protests.

In July, Ontario Ministry of Aboriginal Affairs is established in response to the Ipperwash Final Report.

In September, the international community adopts the United Nations Declaration on the Rights of Indigenous Peoples, despite opposition from Canada and three other countries.

On 19 September, a landmark compensation deal is announced by the federal government for an estimated 80,000 former residential school students from designated schools, who are to receive in total an estimated $1.9 billion.

Federal legislation introduced to the House of Commons establishing an independent Specific Land Claims Tribunal. As of June 2008 it had yet to receive third reading and royal assent.

Late in 2007, Michael Bryant, Ontario's new Minister of Aboriginal Affairs, promises to return Ipperwash Provincial Park to the Kettle and Stoney Point First Nation.

Inuk activist Sheila Watt-Cloutier nominated, along with former US Vice-President Al Gore, for the Nobel Peace Prize for her work as an environmental activist.

2008 In January the federal government approves the landmark Indian Residential Schools Settlement Agreement and payments begin. As part of this agreement a Truth and Reconciliation Commission is to be appointed.

On 16 February, the first indigenous (Cree) opera, *The Journey* (*Pimooteewin*), receives its world premiere in Toronto: written by Tomson Highway; composer Melissa Hui; director/choreographer Michael Greyeyes.

In a free vote in the House of Commons on 8 April, the UN Declaration on the Rights of Indigenous Peoples accepted by a majority of members. The minority Conservative government votes en bloc against the motion. The Canadian media fail to report this event.

On 29 May a second National Day of Action is held peacefully on the issues of Aboriginal children, poverty, and other economic issues.

In June, the Truth and Reconciliation Commission, chaired by Justice Harry S. LaForme, begins its examination of residential schools issues. This Commission will last for five years and will cost $60 million.

On 11 June the Prime Minister makes a statement of apology to former students of Indian residential schools in the House of Commons.

outmoded, nineteenth-century nation-building approach of Canada's politicians. As a place on Turtle Island (the Earth), Canada fundamentally has been a product of a treaty process; it is to that process we are returning.

Much of the 'action' and press attention in recent years has been in Ontario, and our focus will be on events in that province. The same issues, shaped by unique local and regional circumstances, continue across the country.

Beverley Jacobs, Head of the Native Women's Association of Canada, and Phil Fontaine, Assembly of First Nations Chief, shown here in the House of Commons on 11 June 2008 alongside former residential school students, await Prime Minister Stephen Harper's official apology. *(The Canadian Press/Fred Chartrand)*

'Picasso of the North' Norval Morrisseau preserved traditional indigenous culture
through his colourful and influential works of art.
(Graham Bezant/The Toronto Star)

A good place to begin drawing this new ledger, and an important person with whom to begin, is Norval Morrisseau, the Ojibwa visual artist who was one of Canada's most prominent artists of the twentieth century. Morrisseau died on 4 December 2007 after a long battle with Parkinson's disease; he was *about* 75 years old.[2] His achievements included both commercial and critical acclaim for his work, as well as awards such as the Order of Canada. He became the only First Nations artist to date to have an independent show at the National Gallery of Canada.[3] Recognized as spearheading a cultural renaissance in First Nations arts and culture since the 1960s, Morrisseau had an impact on many Aboriginal artists across Canada, who aspired to have the courage that he possessed in bringing traditional indige-nous knowledge to the forefront and thereby overcoming a long-standing government policy of assimilation.[4]

Ruth Phillips, the art historian, wrote that he 'blazed a path that many young artists followed. He was a great role model for younger artists. His courage, in confronting the oppression, the attempt by government policy which began in the nineteenth century to silence and hasten the end of traditional indigenous knowledge, it took great courage to confront that. He was an extraordinary man.'[5] The head of the Canadian collection at the Art Gallery of Ontario, Gerald McMaster, has said that Morrisseau's work was influential because it had come at a time when First Nations art did not yet exist in its present form: 'Morrisseau's presence woke people up.

He was the torchbearer' and he 'had enormous power and influence over several generations of artists.'[6]

By 2008, Morrisseau and others—First Nations artists of the Woodland school that he effectively created by his example; numerous Inuit sculptors, printmakers, and painters; and popular musicians such as Kashtin, Susan Aglukark, Buffy Sainte-Marie, and Robbie Robertson—had achieved great success in their professions and had become inspirations and been recognized both within their own communities and in the wider society. Often, they had to walk a tightrope to overcome tremendous obstacles. They would face many of the same problems that other indigenous people face today in terms of racism and stereotyping by non-Aboriginal people.[7] These courageous individuals leave a tremendous legacy for the present and future generations, to the extent that today the primary shapers of Canada's indigenous history are indigenous persons themselves. They have shaped the new ledger for Canada in their own terms. Nowhere is this truer than in international and sovereignty issues.[8]

International and Sovereignty Issues

The current federal Conservative government recently denied indigenous rights in the international sphere. It was not always so. Domestically, such rights are part and parcel of Canada's Constitution Act (1982), in section 35(1), which states that 'The existing aboriginal and treaty rights of the aboriginal peoples of Canada are hereby recognized and reaffirmed.' These peoples, as has been seen throughout this book, are 'the Indian, Inuit and Métis peoples of Canada' (s. 35[2]).[9] At the same time, the Indian Act (since 1876, as revised) is still on the books, and this federal legislation is racist and colonial, and takes away the rights of those Aboriginal Canadian citizens for whom the nation-state recognizes the same rights under its Constitution. The legislative consequences of all of this history, which Amerindians must still live with and work through today, prevail in spite of the many initiatives taken by Canada's Aboriginal peoples to change the policies and the processes of the federal government as well as to resist the implementation of current national policies on a day-to-day basis.

The fundamental issue is one of indigenous sovereignty. The same is true on the international stage. On 13 September 2007, the United Nations General Assembly adopted the Declaration on the Rights of Indigenous Peoples by an overwhelming majority: 143 votes in favour, 4 negative votes (Canada, Australia, New Zealand, and the United States), and 11 abstentions. Les Malezer, chair of the International Indigenous Peoples' Caucus, welcomed the adoption of the Declaration in a statement to the General Assembly:

> The Declaration does not represent solely the viewpoint of the United Nations, nor does it represent solely the viewpoint of the Indigenous Peoples. It is a Declaration which combines our views and interests and which set the framework for the future. It is a tool for peace and justice, based upon mutual recognition and mutual respect.

The Declaration 'calls on nations with Aboriginal peoples to give them more control over their lands and resources' but 'is not binding'. Governments are urged, however, 'to introduce laws to underpin its provisions'. In June 2007 it was reported that a 'Canadian delegate has told the council it will have "no legal effect in his country" and that "several of the articles would violate the national constitution or even prevent the country's armed forces from taking measures necessary for its defence."' However,

'Indigenous coalition representatives say they believe the big power opposition was largely driven by concern over the potential loss of state control over how natural resources like oil, gas and timber, are exploited.'[10] Canada's negative vote on the Declaration, it should be noted, was after previous Canadian governments had been instrumental at the UN in initiating and drafting the document.

On 8 April 2008, as reported in the American *Indian Country Today* but not in any Canadian newspapers or in electronic media, at the urging of Canada's First Nations, the House of Commons 'passed a resolution to endorse the declaration as adopted by the UN General Assembly and called on the government of Canada to "fully implement the standards contained therein."' Mary Simon, currently president of the Inuit Tapiriit Kanatami, stated that 'The UN Declaration on the Rights of Indigenous Peoples provides a road map for the reconciliation of indigenous and non-indigenous peoples in Canada and around the world.' The House voted 148–113, with the Liberals, NDP, and Bloc Québécois voting in favour as a direct response to requests made to them by national Aboriginal organizations. The federal Conservatives continued with their opposition to this declaration: 'This government's latest arguments against the declaration show just how ridiculous their position has become', said Chief Wilton Littlechild, international chief for Treaty Six, in a release. 'The UN declaration explicitly states that treaties and other agreements with indigenous peoples are to be honoured and respected.' Tellingly, this *Indian Country Today* report states that 'The Harper government's arguments are belied by briefing notes from legal advisers to the departments of Foreign Affairs, Indian Affairs and National Defence to government ministers', and even the federal government's 'legal advisers had recommended that Canada endorse the UN declaration and support its adoption.'[11] This human rights issue is now joined in Canada both at the international and domestic levels.

What accounts for these differences in Canadian Amerindian policies and the reality of indigenous existence in Canada? The answer lies in the issue of sovereignty and the disparate histories of indigenous and non-indigenous people in Canada. The primary objective of the former is spiritual—one of peace and protection of the land (Mother Earth) and the waters of Turtle Island. This is a sacred trust. The continuity and integrity of their lands are important to the survival of the First Nations as an indigenous people. Generations of First Nation members have used the land and have shared in its bounty and its uses. Moreover, they will continue to use this land and teach their children about the Creator and the land. Thus, this relationship between the people and the natural world is all-important if they are to survive culturally. It is both simple and profound.[12] Today, the larger business of the Constitution and the treaty-making process, through various land rights policies, still remains incomplete and unfulfilled. It is currently being defined on an issue-by-issue basis by the courts.

Canada's Aboriginal policies, through a long process of denial, have created institutional racism and corresponding resistance movements that have culminated in violence and death. The events of the Temagami blockades (1988–90) in northern Ontario, of the summer of 1990 centred on Oka, Quebec, of Ipperwash (1995) and Caledonia (2006) in southern Ontario, and of Gustafsen Lake in British Columbia and Burnt Church in New Brunswick will not be erased from history or memory. Nor will the ongoing problems of the Innu of Labrador, the Deh Cho of the Northwest Territories, the Lubicon Cree of northern Alberta and of the many other outstanding claims be solved by inaction and denial. The initiative for change in recent Aboriginal history has almost always come from the Aboriginal people. At the same time, federal and provincial government policies have often been characterized by reaction, crisis management, and denial.

In the early twenty-first century the prominent issues arising for Canada's Aboriginal policies remain outstanding and unresolved. Ultimately, these issues are 'all about the land', as was recently observed by Alex Neve, secretary-general for Amnesty International Canada, and Murray Klippenstein, counsel for the George family during the Ipperwash Inquiry. They stated: 'Return of these lands [Ipperwash] now would offer powerful redress to Dudley George's family, as his death came about due to his efforts to assert the rights of his people. What better way to evidence the dawn of a new approach than to ensure redress of the land rights violations at the heart of the Ipperwash tragedy.'[13] Sovereignty and land rights cannot be separated. They are central to indigenous rights in Canada. In this sense, Canada's Aboriginal policies have been a wholesale failure in the face of the resistance to them by Aboriginal citizens. And these policies, made with little or no consultation, have led directly to the denial by the federal government of Aboriginal rights in Canada and on the international stage. Of note, the federal government has failed to replace the Indian Act by 2008. Instead, it proposed a glorified form of municipal-style governance created by federal legislation. The clear alternative lies in the recognition and development of the inherent right of Aboriginal governance made by and for indigenous people in Canada. This alternative has been proposed to be included in Canada's Constitution Act, 1982 as a new part of section 35 since the 1980s. If such a change were made, the Indian Act would become redundant.

Governance and Land Rights Issues: The Proposed First Nations Governance Act of 2002 and the Legacies of the Indian Act

Early in the twenty-first century the federal government attempted, but failed, to do away with the Indian Act. The First Nations Governance Act (FNGA), first proposed in January 2002 by the federal Department of Indian Affairs, was to amend the original Indian Act (1876). Introduced by former Liberal Indian Affairs Minister Robert Nault as Bill C-7, it created much discussion on the issue of Aboriginal governance. The proposed legislation, which died when then Prime Minister Paul Martin ended the parliamentary session in 2004, set forth a wave of debate between the federal government and many Aboriginal groups across Canada. Many First Nations leaders opposed the legislation because it did not recognize the inherent right of self-government and also was seen as an attack on existing Aboriginal and treaty rights. The federal government claimed that its goals of self-government would increase the accountability of both First Nations and their governments. However, the stated federal goals of improving issues such as education, poverty, health care, housing, and, more specifically, how these issues were to be addressed under this proposed Act, revealed obvious disagreements about how to achieve the ends.

The main principles of the Act included the development of a system by First Nations to choose their own leaders and develop clear rules on financial spending and accountability. First Nations wished to have their form of governance based on their customs, laws, and cultures as well as on their Aboriginal and treaty rights. The major opposition to this Act concerned the process under which the proposed Act would come into existence, and great concern was expressed over the lack of prior consultation. The opposition over the proposed

On 14 June 2002, Matthew Coon Come, National Chief of the Assembly of First Nations, tore up a copy of the newly introduced First Nations Governance Act in support of a pledge by the Federation of Saskatchewan Indians to fight the legislation. Native leaders rejected the proposed bill because it dictated how First Nations must govern themselves and ignored the diversity among Aboriginal groups. Coon Come said the legislation demonstrates the 'utter contempt' of the government towards First Nations.

(The Canadian Press/Fred Chartrand)

FNGA proved that a tremendous amount of mistrust and discontent among many Aboriginal groups still is directed towards the federal government, heightened considerably by the plethora of outstanding residential school issues and the previous reluctance to apologize to First Nations for them.

The Indian Act can no longer accommo-date the existing governance structures in that it fails to address some major issues, such as the ability of First Nations' councils to manage their own financial affairs without appropriate funding (as is most often the case with treaty Indians except for those few First Nations who happen to have been fortunate enough to have reserve or ancestral lands where valuable minerals and fossil fuels are found and who have established impact and benefit agreements with industry); the separation of issues concerning these councils and that of administration in terms of economic development and sustainability; and the ability of councils to delegate authority.[14] (These issues have been dealt with in regard to the Inuit in Canada's North, where development corporations to handle the funds from claims settlements have been established as separate from their democratic governance structures. Some treaty bands, e.g., the Lac La Ronge band in northern Saskatchewan, also have established ambitious and successful development agencies.) In 2002 Nault stated that the First Nations Governance Act:

> would enable First Nations people to create community governance systems designed to reflect their needs. The proposed Act would give communities the modern tools they need to operate effective, responsible and accountable governance structures, the solid basis needed for future development.

In addition, it would also 'be a part of the Government's overall agenda to improve the lives of Aboriginal people by providing tools for greater self-sufficiency and economic development.'[15] The latter eventually became part of the Kelowna Accord of 2005, an attempt to give First Nations some equity in Canada, but as discussed below, this agreement fell by the wayside with the election of a minority Conservative government in early 2006.

The proposed FNGA represented how First Nations are classified in Canada in terms of differentiated citizenship under the Indian Act, and it created an ongoing divisive problem for Nault. Throughout the spring, summer, and fall of 2003, First Nations across Canada participated in community meetings, information sessions, and discussion groups; they also pro-vided written proposals in their submissions to the minister. Over 10,000 First Nations people participated in the process and discussed their views on the matter of how Bill C-7 could be implemented to improve the lives of Aboriginal peoples across Canada. As well, a joint Ministerial Advisory Committee, which included First Nations representatives and government officials, was formed to provide expert advice and guidance on the legislative options, which was presented in its report to Nault in March of 2004.[16]

The federal government's initiative sought to bring together what it regarded as all of the indigenous leaders from across Canada in an effort to consult them on the proposed legislation. This could not be achieved; for one thing, it presupposed who the leaders were. For some, this effort at consultation was a replay of the White Paper of 1969, which ironically brought some change, including an increased politicization and the enhanced organizational power of Canada's Aboriginal peoples and, indirectly, the Charter of Rights and Freedoms and the entrenchment of Aboriginal rights in the Constitution.

The opposition to the proposed FNGA rose steadily, and included many non-Aboriginal groups. As the former Chief of the Assembly of First Nations, Matthew Coon Come, stated in condemning the proposed legislation: 'This will leave us a legacy of shame, a legacy of despair and a legacy of colonialism when we are looking for a legacy of hope for our future generations.' Joining Coon Come were Amnesty International, and the United, Anglican, and Catholic churches of Canada.[17] The increasing numbers of opposition groups posed problems for Nault. He did not have public opinion on his side, causing him to push the proposed legislation back in terms of the government's agenda. It also illustrated the ongoing lack of communication between the First Nations and the federal government.

Opposition to the FNGA focused on the vague nature of the proposed legislation and, especially, on the fact that it failed to address the issue of an inherent right to self-government, which had not been included in section 35 of the Constitution Act, 1982. Under Bill C-7, the government did not explicitly specify who actually possesses this right, such as 'certain bands under the Indian Act' or 'signatories to treaty rights'.[18] In the end, Bill C-7 raised issues that were not inherent; it didn't touch on constitutional rights; and it related only to federal legislation and policy matters. Its aim was federal housekeeping, not a new deal for Canada's Amerindians. Through a lack of consultation and by not providing for a process to recognize the inherent right of Aboriginal governance, Nault was unsuccessful. To this day, however, the federal government is effectively implementing this failed bill in a piecemeal fashion as if it were federal legislation.[19]

The debate over the inherent right of self-government is complicated, dating back much earlier than the Constitution Act of 1982, which does not affirm this inherent right. One legal observer has argued that 'Recognition of the inherent right is based on the view that the Aboriginal peoples of Canada have the right to govern themselves in relation to matters that are internal to their communities, integral to their unique cultures, identities, traditions, languages and institutions and with respect to their special relationship to their land and their resources.'[20] Many of these First Nations have different methods of governance and distinct values as to how to govern themselves. To use a 'one-size-fits-all' solution will simply not work.[21]

Many First Nations leaders, such as former Six Nations Chief Roberta Jamieson, argued that Bill C-7 was unconstitutional. Jamieson spelled it out succinctly: 'I think the process is flawed, the bill is flawed and the arrogance and the colonial approach that continues to be taken by this government and now through the committee to ram this through, in spite of our opposition, is really just deteriorating the relationship between our people and the government.' The federal government responded to Jamieson's attack by stating that she had simply refused to engage in the process of possibly amending and improving the piece of legislation. However, Jamieson unequivocally rejected the proposed Act: 'We take that position on a legal basis, constitutional basis and on a moral basis. We believe it cannot be amended and we adamantly reject it. We have been very clear that we oppose it at this stage and if it is passed, we will oppose it then.'[22] Many Aboriginal leaders became increasingly resistant to the possible ramifications of the Act on their own communities.

The proposed implementation of Bill C-7 also highlighted the variety of distinctions of indigenous and Canadian citizenships and the relationship between Aboriginal groups and leaders and the federal government. Aside from the 21 First Nations currently operating under four self-government agreements, the 330 remaining First Nations under the Indian Act at present choose their leadership outside the Act in a manner according to the different customs of their respective communities. This applies to the 196 that were never moved into the Indian Act system, but also to more than 100 First Nations that had been under the Indian Act but reverted by request to a customary governance model.[23] These statistics suggest that a policy issue such as self-governance cannot be simply implemented broadly on so many different communities. Legislation needs to focus on the distinctive needs of each Aboriginal community, as has been the case with comprehensive agreements (e.g., Nisga'a Final Agreement Act, Yukon First Nations Land Claims Settlement Act, Nunavut Land Claims Agreement Act), and not simply on a broad federal-wide initiative that fails to address such immediate issues as health care, education, poverty, and housing.[24] An accord, however, was reached at Kelowna with the federal government in the fall of 2005 to provide over $5 billion for First Nations to meet their specific needs. The current Conservative government failed to live up to that agreement after gaining power in the federal election of January 2006.[25]

When he was Prime Minister, Paul Martin argued that the fundamentals of Bill C-7 were necessary for good government, financial administration, and electoral codes. However, Nault, despite the mounting opposition from many groups and First Nations leaders, was rather confused by the opposition to Bill C-7: 'What is it exactly that people would like to consult and review before we move on to put in place more modern principles of governance and enable First Nations so they can have more responsive institutions for their people? I'm confident that this debate will conclude with improvements to First Nations governance. Under the Indian Act there is none and we all know that there is a need to have these modern tools.'[26] Nevertheless, although there is no question that the Indian Act needs to be revised or, better yet, eliminated, it will take many years to find a proper and just solution that meets the diverse needs of different First Nations for Aboriginal governance.[27]

This innovation would come from Aboriginal people and their communities. By 2008, various models of Aboriginal governance had taken shape. Recently established self-governance agreements with the Kwanlin Dün First Nation in Yukon, First Nations in Manitoba, and the Anishinabek Nation in Ontario provide a basis for new government-to-government relationships based on partnership and respect.[28] Another approach—public government as opposed to ethnic government—has been established in Nunavut,

where Inuit make up 85 per cent of the population and the territorial government is responsible to and for all citizens of Nunavut, including the non-Inuit (Qallunaat or 'white people'). In effect, of course, the government is controlled by the majority Aboriginal population. An agreement-in-principle has been signed for a similar public (but chiefly Inuit) government, the Nunavik Regional Government, in northern Quebec. Once this Nunavik government is established in the next few years, it remains to be seen whether such a regional governance structure within a province might serve as a model for types of self-government in the northern reaches of some other provinces.[29]

The issues that self-government agreements address include land, funding, economic development, and wildlife, forestry, and heritage resource management. Many outstanding, diverse issues are of importance to Aboriginal communities. Stumbling blocks can involve such issues as unique cultures, identities, traditions, languages, and the institutions concerned with the special relationship Aboriginal communities have towards their land and resources.[30] In a number of instances over the past two decades, from coastal British Columbia to the northern tip of Labrador, and from northern Yukon through Nunavut, some of these issues have been resolved with the establishment of national parks and national park reserves within traditional homelands. These are co-managed by the local Aboriginal community and Parks Canada. Besides providing some employment opportunities for Aboriginal communities, such areas can allow for hunting and harvesting exclusive to the indigenous people while maintaining their status as protected from resource exploitation. Once again, however, those groups that never were party to a historic treaty and that achieve comprehensive land claim agreements, as many in the territorial North have, are in a better position in this regard than the treaty Indians to the south, whose specific claims relate to the disposition of the parcels of land they received through the treaty process.[31]

The goals and aspirations of self-government for many First Nations citizens may depend on their geographic proximity to large urban centres in southern Canada. For example, Yukon and the Northwest Territories have vastly different resources from those of Ontario, and the issues surrounding self-government may vary. The federal government recognizes the uniqueness of the North and that public government should play a prominent role in order to address the distinctive features of the region, where, demographically, many communities are of mixed ethnicity and others have a majority of Aboriginal Canadians.[32] As an example, the significance of a negotiated settlement will allow for the Kwanlin Dün First Nation to enact its own laws to address the use of control, management, and protection of the land, which includes the protection of fish, wildlife, and habitat, administration of justice, and taxation. In terms of its citizens the First Nation will have legal authority concerning many social issues, such as marriage, programs and services related to both language and culture, and social and welfare services. The purpose of these initiatives is to ensure a better quality of life for all of the citizens of the Kwanlin Dün First Nation in order to address their specific needs and increase the self-reliance of this community within and near Whitehorse, Yukon.[33]

On 16 February 2007, the then Minister of Indian Affairs, Jim Prentice, announced that the Anishinabek Nation and its Grand Council Chief had signed an agreement-in-principle to establish a framework for the Anishinabek Nation, represented in negotiations by the Union of Ontario Indians, in assuming greater control over its own institutions of government. Chief John Beaucage

stated that the 'purpose of the AIP is to work toward eliminating the Indian Act and in reasserting jurisdiction and re-establishing our own forms of government.'[34] The implementation of self-government, according to Beaucage, would provide practical and effective ways to improve the overall living conditions of the people of the more than 40 First Nations in the Lake Huron, Georgian Bay, and Lake Superior region represented by the Anishinabek Nation. For the federal government, these types of agreements are viewed as a way of replacing the outdated provisions of the Indian Act with a modern legislative framework for First Nations' governance. The main purpose of this agreement is to strengthen the internal governance and solidify the political and financial accountability of First Nations governments to their citizens, while operating within Canada's constitutional framework.[35]

Thus, there have been some steps towards First Nations achieving self-government in the early twenty-first century, but many conflicts remain with respect to Canada's Constitution. In November 2007, an Ontario court ruled against the attempt of the Mississaugas of Scugog Island First Nation to enact a law prohibiting strikes at a popular casino near Port Perry, Ontario, operated by this First Nation. The ruling stated that they did not have the constitutional right to enact their own labour code on reserve lands. The Mississaugas had intended to use their treaty rights to regulate the work activities and control access to their land. However, in order for that principle to be accepted, they would have had to show that they had a constitutionally protected right related to their traditions. They did not do so.[36] For many years, at least since 1965 when the Walpole Island (Bkejwanong) First Nation—50 kilometres northeast of Windsor at the mouth of the St Clair River—kicked out its Indian agent, many indigenous communities have practised their own form of governance.[37] It is imperative that such practical models of indigenous governance continue to be developed by First Nations in the twenty-first century.[38]

The Métis Nation and the Steve Powley Case

On 19 September 2003, a landmark decision was made in favour of the Métis in the hunting rights case of *R. v. Powley*.[39] The decision rendered by the Supreme Court of Canada recognized the Aboriginal right to hunt of the Métis community at Sault Ste Marie. The case involved both Steve and Roddy Powley, who had been hunting just outside of Sault Ste Marie, Ontario, in 1993. They had killed a bull moose and carded the moose with a Métis card, issued from the Métis Nation of Ontario, that read 'harvesting my meat for winter'. Both of them were reported for cutting up the moose meat by neighbours under the Crime Stoppers program and were arrested for hunting moose without a licence and unlawful possession of a moose.[40]

The initial *Powley* case lasted for over five years, until 1998 when the trial judge ruled in favour of the Powleys and their right to hunt as Métis under s. 35 of the Constitution Act, 1982. The Crown (Ontario) appealed to the Ontario Court of Appeal but the trial decision was upheld. Subsequently, the Supreme Court of Canada, in a unanimous decision, ruled in favour of the Powleys.[41] Jean Teillet, a great-grandniece of Louis Riel, was the most prominent legal counsel representing the Powleys in the case. The protection of Métis hunting rights is historically important to many aspects of the traditional Métis culture and life. The Métis communities must be recognized and protected similarly to other Aboriginal communities, such as other First Nations and the Inuit.[42]

The Supreme Court decision in September 2003 was declared to be a victory for Ontario Métis. The interim president and spokesperson for the Métis National Council, Audrey Poitras, stated:

> The highest court of this land has finally done what Parliament and the provincial governments have refused to do and have delivered justice to the Métis people. This decision is a great victory for the Métis Nation. The federal and provincial governments can no longer refuse to negotiate with the Métis Nation and treat us as though we don't have any Aboriginal rights. Those days are over.[43]

The Métis had made another step in their long journey to be recognized as distinctive people since the time of the Red River resistance movement and the hanging of Louis Riel.

The *Powley* decision reaffirmed Métis rights under Canada's Constitution. However, while Métis people registered with the Métis Nation of Ontario believe they have the 'right' to hunt or catch fish for social, ceremonial, and personal use, there had been legal disagreement on the implications of this judgment. Consequently, many unresolved issues pertaining to the Métis and their right to hunt and fish across Canada remained unresolved.

In October 2005, Jim McLay, a fisherman and the president of the Saguingue (Southampton) Métis on the Bruce Peninsula in southwestern Ontario, had his gill nets and the fish in them seized by Ontario Ministry of Natural Resources (OMNR) conservation officers. McLay was not arrested or charged with any crime for commercial fishing. Two years later, in the fall of 2007, OMNR returned the nets to McLay, but not the fish (the latter were literally given away). He demanded an apology from the OMNR staff, who refused to do so. This issue involves the relationship between the *Powley* decision and the existing law and policy of the province, as well as the agreement (flowing from *Powley*) between the Métis of Ontario and the province in July 2004, which recognized the Métis right to hunt and fish in Ontario.

The OMNR interpreted *Powley* as being applicable only north of the French River.[44] A legal ruling in June 2007 clarified this issue and the agreement was found to apply across Ontario. McLay believed that he was owed an apology since 'the recent ruling proves he was doing nothing wrong when conservation officers seized his fishing equipment. He said he was fishing for his own consumption and for ceremonial food, which was to be served to about 30 people at the Saguingue Métis Nation's annual fall banquet.' He explained further that the fish 'weren't just for myself, they were for our citizens, children and elders.'[45] To date, McLay and the Métis have never received an apology. He also has not fished for over two years because the OMNR had threatened to seize his boat if he did so.

In retrospect, McLay believes that the OMNR had immediately reneged on the 2004 agreement with the Métis Nation of Ontario and that he had done nothing wrong. The OMNR tried to justify its arbitrary action towards McLay, which was made contrary to its own agreement:

> The ministry acted correctly in this situation. We were acting on the laws that were in place at that point in time [and if] you've got a net set that is a quarter of a mile long, usually a guy is setting for commercial purposes. Are you going to be using 1,000 pounds of fish for personal use? These were some of the questions that were going through some of our heads. That's why the nets were seized at that point in time.[46]

McLay believes that he will now be allowed to resume his traditional fishing, thereby allowing Ontario Métis to hunt and fish for ceremonial purposes.[47]

The Ipperwash Inquiry and Final Report

The Ipperwash Inquiry was established by Ontario on 12 November 2003, under the Public Inquiries Act. Its mandate was to inquire and report on events surrounding the death of Dudley George, who was shot, and later died, in September 1995 during a First Nation protest at Ipperwash Provincial Park (see Chapter 28). For eight years, both the federal and provincial governments failed to call for any inquiry into the death of George or the events at Ipperwash. After the provincial Liberals were elected, this was one of the first things the new government acted on. The Inquiry was asked to make recommendations that would avoid violence in similar circumstances in the future. Justice Sidney B. Linden was appointed commissioner. The Commission's final, four-volume report, covering over 1,500 pages, was made public on 31 May 2007. The provincial government immediately accepted all of the report's recommendations and has proceeded to implement them.[48]

Ipperwash is an example of the repeated failures of the provincial and federal governments to resolve long-standing land issues with many First Nations across Canada. These events, such as those that occurred at Temagami, Oka, Ipperwash, and Caledonia, could have been prevented had both levels of government been active in seeking solutions to unresolved land disputes, which have led to much resistance on the part of frustrated Aboriginal groups. The case of the Stoney Point Reserve in Ontario has evolved like any other land rights issue in Canada—the federal government takes literally decades to resolve these issues. The Stoney Point Reserve was taken by the federal government in 1942 and still today has not been returned on the basis of the original agreement. These issues are reflected in the final report of the Ipperwash Inquiry.

The final report revealed the disconnections and miscommunications between the OPP and the Aboriginal protestors who had been occupying the provincial park. However, there had been many instances of inappropriate and culturally insensitive remarks made by OPP officers towards Aboriginal people. These were revealed during the Inquiry in tape-recorded conversations and radio transmissions from 5–6 September 1995. On numerous occasions racist remarks had been made by the OPP, and the final report stated that the conduct among members of the police contributed to the lack of a timely, peaceful resolution to the occupation of the park by the protestors.[49] There is little doubt that the police neither respected nor understood the protestors' objective in occupying the park.

The final report stated that on 6 September, Premier Mike Harris had sought an injunction to remove the protestors from the park within 24 hours. This approach was far more aggressive and drastic than that suggested by the Attorney General, who had wanted a slow and cautious approach in resolving the matter.[50] Harris's actions came under question during the Inquiry. Commissioner Linden wrote unequivocally: 'To maintain police independence, the government cannot direct when and how to enforce the law. Neither the Premier, the responsible Minister, nor anyone in government should attempt to specify a time period, such as twenty-four hours, for the occupiers to be removed from the Park.'[51] The sudden actions of the OPP and their tactical units in storming the park led to a confrontation between the police and the First Nations' occupiers. There appeared to be miscommunication on both sides. During the confrontation, in which no firearms had been found on any of the occupiers of the park, Dudley George was shot three times by one of the officers, who erroneously claimed that Dudley had a rifle.[52]

No evidence from the Inquiry suggested

Native protestor Dudley George at what is believed to be the site of the sacred Indian burial ground that ignited the 6 September 1995 land claims standoff in Ipperwash Provincial Park.
(*The Canadian Press/Port Huron Times Herald/Tony Pitts*)

that Dudley George had a rifle, or in fact that any of the occupiers of the park had any firearms whatsoever. Many of the officers who testified at the Inquiry corroborated this evidence. The Inquiry also revealed that the police and tactical units were not trained to deal with Aboriginal protests. They had treated the protestors as if they were a soccer crowd or another form of unruly protest, such as wildcat strikers. From the beginning of the occupation, the provincial authorities, from the Premier down to the OPP, appeared to be rather insensitive and unaccustomed to Aboriginal issues, in spite of the lessons that should have been learned from the events of the Temagami blockades and in northern Ontario in support of Oka several years earlier. The final report found that the death of Dudley George and the confrontation between the OPP and the occupiers of the park could have been prevented if the government and OPP had taken a more cautious and understanding approach towards resolving the matter peacefully.

The Ipperwash report included numerous recommendations regarding federal or provincial policy issues and policing matters. Specifically, it immediately led to the creation of a stand-alone provincial Ministry of Aboriginal Affairs. Some of these key policy issues and findings are outlined below.[53]

Policing and the OPP

The Inquiry closely examined the role the police played in this tragic event. Its recommendations in this policy area included the following:

- The OPP should develop a strategy to restore relationships with both Aboriginal and non-Aboriginal communities after an Aboriginal occupation or protest. The provincial, federal, and municipal governments should support and participate in this strategy. This strategy should be distributed to interested parties and posted on the OPP website.
- Police planning for responding to an Aboriginal occupation or protest should include:
  a) A communication strategy for important messages that ought to be conveyed to the occupiers;
  b) The technical aspects of how police would communicate with the occupiers; and
  c) Specified people outside the police service who could effectively communicate with the occupiers.

- All telephone calls to and from the command post should be recorded and minutes should be kept of all meetings of the Incident Commander. Incident Commanders should continue to be accountable for keeping accurate, detailed notes at the time of events.

Provincial and Federal Policies

Too often, because 'Indians, and Lands reserved for the Indians' are a federal responsibility under the Constitution, the federal and provincial levels of government in Canada's federal system have failed to co-ordinate or even to understand each other's policies regarding Aboriginal peoples. At Ipperwash, for example, reserve land had been taken by the federal government for a military base during World War II, and right next to the base was a provincial park, also on reserve land. All the while, the people—whose ancestral land this was and is—had been left in the lurch. The Ipperwash Inquiry final report made several recommendations regarding federal and provincial responsibilities.

- The provincial government should invite the federal government to participate in interministerial 'blockade' committees to inform and co-ordinate governmental responses to Aboriginal occupations and protests when a potential federal interest is engaged.
- The Ontario Secretariat for Aboriginal Affairs, in consultation with Aboriginal organizations, should compile a list of available negotiators, and facilitators could assist the government to quickly and peacefully resolve issues that emerge.
- The provincial government should commit sufficient resources to the Ministry of Aboriginal Affairs to enable it to carry out its responsibilities. The budget for the

ministry should include funding for a revitalized land claims process in Ontario, for the Ontario Aboriginal Reconciliation Fund, and for programs to improve Aboriginal/non-Aboriginal relations in Ontario.

- The provincial government and Ministry of Aboriginal Affairs should create mechanisms for obtaining input from Aboriginal communities on planning, policy, legislation, and programs affecting Aboriginal interests.

- The federal government should issue a public apology with appropriate compensation to the Kettle and Stoney Point First Nation for the failure of the federal government for more than 60 years to honour its promise to return the lands to the First Nation.

- The provincial government should establish a permanent, independent, and impartial agency to facilitate and oversee the settling of land and treaty claims in Ontario. The agency should be called the Treaty Commission of Ontario.

- The provincial government should make every reasonable effort to establish the Treaty Commission of Ontario with the full co-operation of the federal government. If that is not possible, the provincial government should establish the Treaty Commission on its own in co-operation with First Nations in Ontario.

- The provincial government should prepare public education materials regarding Aboriginal burial and heritage sites.

- The provincial government should improve public education about its land claim policies.

By the fall of 2007, the Ministry of Aboriginal Affairs and its new minister, Michael Bryant, had accepted and undertaken to implement the recommendations of the Ipperwash Inquiry to resolve other long-standing land rights disputes. However, both the provincial and federal governments will need to implement these recommendations to bring about a policy of justice and fairness for First Nations.

On 21 December 2007, Bryant announced that Ipperwash Provincial Park would be returned to the Chippewas of Kettle and Stoney Point First Nation: 'we are sending a clear signal that the McGuinty government is acting on the Premier's ambitious agenda on Aboriginal affairs.'[54] In the interim, the land and the park are to be co-managed by the community, government, and the First Nation, after which it would be transferred to the First Nation permanently. Sam George, Dudley's brother, applauded the decision by Bryant to return the land: 'It shows it's like a game of hockey. We can all play on the same forward line together.'[55] This initial step by the Ontario government is important in addressing the key land rights issues that have plagued both the provincial and federal governments for many years. The events at Ipperwash would be echoed at Caledonia with the Six Nations resistance on their land issues.[56]

Caledonia and Federal Specific Claims Policies

Despite having a specific claims policy since 1973 and first establishing an Office of Native Claims in 1974 (since reorganized), the federal government has resolved relatively few such claims relating to its failure to administer reserves and treaties properly. Canada's commitment to reform the specific claims process has been long overdue; issues such as Oka and Caledonia arise because of the inaction on behalf of the federal government in the overall process it has been using in settling specific claims across Canada. It has been estimated that more than a thousand unresolved claims are on the books today. A more efficient and fair process will ensure benefits to all Canadians. The events at Caledonia, near Hamilton and Brantford in southern Ontario, continue at a tremendous cost to the Six Nations Reserve, the residents of Caledonia, and the Ontario government, which has borne the financial burden in resolving this issue. An accelerated and more efficient process would go a long way towards bringing some resolution to historic injustices between the federal government and First Nations.[57]

After a quarter-century of non-negotiations, the issue over an unresolved land issue in the small town of Caledonia came to the forefront when, in the fall of 2005, Henco Industries began development of the Douglas Creek Estates subdivision on land called the Plank Road (which had been leased, but not sold, by the Six Nations in the 1830s) adjacent to the Six Nations Reserve. The land has been in dispute since the mid-nineteenth century. The situation deteriorated, during the late winter and spring of 2006, into clashes between Six Nations protestors who had occupied the area and many of the residents of Caledonia, who resented the occupation of the land. As the situation in Caledonia dragged on and became volatile, it signified, as had Ipperwash, the failure of the federal and provincial governments to initiate a more efficient process in settling land rights disputes.

In the case of Caledonia, a small town on the Grand (formerly the Bear) River, a group of Six Nations protestors had occupied the unfinished Douglas Creek Estates housing development on 28 February 2006. The protestors from the Six Nations claimed that the land belonged to them, under the Haldimand Grant of 1784, which was to be six miles on each side of the river, and including the river, from its mouth on Lake Erie to its source. The federal government believed that the land had been surrendered in 1841 in order for a highway to be built.[58]

The Six Nations of the Grand River is a community with which Canada and Ontario are negotiating in respect to a number of issues, including those arising out of the Caledonia situation. Between 1976 and 1994, the Six Nations had filed 29 claims with Canada, only one of which has been settled. In 1994 the Six Nations brought a claim in court against Canada and Ontario for an accounting of all transactions involving Six Nations lands and the proceeds of their disposition. Of those claims, 14 currently are in litigation against Canada.[59] As of 2006, the Douglas Creek Estates had been one of those claims in the process of litigation. The Chief of the Six Nations, David General, concerned about the possible ramifications of the construction on the land, had warned Henco Industries about going ahead with the development.[60]

The events in Caledonia became national news when the group of Six Nations protestors moved onto the construction site, erecting tents, a teepee, and a wooden building. On 10 March, Henco Industries obtained an injunction ordering the protestors off the site, but without result.[61] Another injunction followed on 28 March—the protestors would be facing criminal as well as civil contempt charges if they did not agree to leave the area. This only seemed to infuriate and further empower the protestors, and the situation escalated into clashes between non-Aboriginal residents of Caledonia and the Six Nations. On 20 April approximately 100 police were called in, and later that day they conducted a raid on the protestors occupying the housing project, arresting 16 people.[62]

The divide between the communities was becoming increasingly hostile, and on 25 April the issue of racism became apparent when Haldimand County Mayor Trainer told the CBC that the Caledonia residents 'have to go to work to support their families and if they don't go to work, they don't get paid.' She further

Blockade set up by Six Nations protestors at Caledonia, Ontario.
(John Brooks photo)

stated: 'They don't have money coming in automatically every month, they've got to work and the natives have got to realize that.'[63] Following these comments, the county council voted to replace her with the deputy mayor. Racism, both overt and implicit, had long been part of land rights issues.[64]

By April of 2006, the Ontario government was secretly negotiating with Henco Industries to purchase the disputed land, and eventually purchased the Douglas Creek Estates property for $21.1 million; on 29 March 2007 the federal government contributed $15.8 million towards Ontario's purchase of the property.[65] This purchase was an effort to set the stage for

negotiating long-term solutions in regard to the various specific claims the Haudenosaunee/Six Nations had filed over the previous three decades, beginning in 1976. The negotiations had been ongoing between the Six Nations and the federal government, with little input from Ontario and the local municipalities, when the issues were first formally raised with Ontario in 1981.[66]

In June of 2007, Prime Minister Stephen Harper recognized that the negotiation and settlement process for specific claims across the country had been ineffective and slow by announcing that the federal government would be spending millions of dollars to expedite the process by establishing an independent tribunal. The process of settling specific claims has taken an average of 13 years. The federal government planned to streamline the settlement process by increasing funding to approximately $250 million a year.[67] At the current pace of negotiations, the Assembly of First Nations has said that it would take about 130 years to resolve all of the outstanding claims.

Despite the federal announcement, many First Nations groups decided to proceed with the planned National Day of Action on 29 June 2007. The First Nations groups came together and protested the inaction of the federal government pertaining to racism, poverty, and outstanding unresolved land claims on that day. The announcement made on behalf of the federal government was also widely believed to be an effort to prevent any large-scale disruptions during the National Day of Action, which included the blocking of railway lines and the shutdown of major highways.[68] Indigenous people once again had to rely on their own agency.

Harper's plan to address these ongoing grievances, according to the federal Department of Indian Affairs, would ensure impartiality and fairness, greater transparency, faster processing, and better access to mediation. There are four key elements to this plan:

1. the creation of an independent tribunal to bring greater fairness to the process;
2. more transparent arrangements for financial compensation through dedicated funding for settlements;
3. practical measures to remove bottlenecks and ensure faster processing of claims;
4. focusing the work of the current Indian Claims Commission to make greater use of its services in dispute resolutions once the new tribunal is in place.

This latter point would aim at easing the existing problems and the backlog of claims in the future. However, as of the summer of 2008, these proposed changes have not yet been put into place.[69]

On 27 November 2007, the Conservative Minister of Indian Affairs, Chuck Strahl, introduced the Specific Claims Tribunal Act in the House of Commons, which would create an independent tribunal to help resolve the specific claims of First Nations. The introduction of the legislation was greeted warmly by AFN leader Phil Fontaine, who praised the introduction of an independent tribunal that will ensure greater fairness in the way specific claims are handled. While negotiation will remain the first priority in settling specific land claims, the purpose of the tribunal would be to make binding decisions where negotiations over a three-year period have been rejected by one party or have led nowhere. The independent tribunal would be made up of six sitting superior court judges.[70]

While the Caledonia land dispute remains primarily a federal matter, some of the Six Nations claims are against both Canada and Ontario. Negotiation still is the best option for a relatively peaceful end to the ongoing situation in Caledonia. The provincial government had learned from the deadly confrontation of Ipperwash and went back to the pre-Mike Harris policies, during the Temagami and Oka blockades of 1988–90, to find a more reasonable response to peaceful indigenous actions and protests.[71] At the end of May 2007, the federal government offered $125 million to the Haudenosaunee/Six Nations to settle four of the 28 outstanding claims. Negotiations between the two parties continue.[72] Following the Ontario provincial election in October of 2007, which returned a majority Liberal government, Premier Dalton McGuinty announced that former Attorney General Michael Bryant had been named the new Minister of Aboriginal Affairs. Then, on 26 November, Bryant visited the occupation site and was met with angry protestors from both sides, who were still frustrated over the slow pace of the negotiations between the Six Nations and the federal government.[73]

In December of 2007, progress was reported on settling one of the Six Nations claims with an offer of $26 million to compensate for the loss of 970 hectares of land flooded many years earlier for the Welland Canal project. Bryant told the Canadian Press he was a little more hopeful that a settlement can be reached: 'The Six Nations have deemed this latest offer to be worth considering and that might give the talks some momentum.'[74]

At the federal level, Harper shuffled his cabinet in August 2007, replacing the outgoing minister, Jim Prentice, with Chuck Stahl as the new Minister of Indian Affairs. Whether this and other changes at the federal level will have a significant impact on the specific claims process remains to be seen. Many First Nations groups are becoming increasingly frustrated by the current process, especially in the province of BC, which has approximately half of the outstanding land claims—both specific and comprehensive—in Canada. The new specific claims legislation had not seen the light of day by the summer of 2008. As a result, the AFN held another peaceful National Day of Action on 29 May; more actions of peace were surely to follow.[75] We can expect these will escalate, especially in Ontario, where various Aboriginal leaders were jailed in the fall of 2007 (and released by the courts in the spring of 2008) as a result of protests against the province's antiquated mining legislation, and against mining companies pursuing exploration on Crown (read 'Aboriginal') lands in eastern and northern Ontario.[76]

Comprehensive Claims: The Tsawwassen Agreement of 2007

A historic agreement in the BC treaty process (for comprehensive claims) was reached between the Tsawwassen First Nation and both the federal and provincial governments late in 2007. The Tsawwassen First Nation is located approximately 25 km south of Vancouver, on the southern side of the Lower Mainland, and has about 358 citizens. This agreement will allow for the ownership of their land in fee simple (rather than as an Indian reserve). The Tsawwassen government will become a member of the Greater Vancouver Regional District.[77] The process began in 1993 when the Tsawwassen First Nation entered into the six-stage treaty process with the British Columbia Treaty Commission.

Tsawwassen First Nation Chief Kim Baird, who negotiated the agreement on behalf of her people, believes it will be beneficial to her community because of the new recognition of the First Nation as an independent and active participant in its political region. Chief Baird stated that this treaty, 'the first in the Lower Mainland, abolishes the Indian Act through self-government—not assimilation. It gives us the tools to build a healthy community and the opportunity to participate fully in the Canadian economy.'[78] The economic benefits of the agreement include more integration with the local economy and the First Nation's right to such resources as fish and land. As well, the Tsawwassen are to receive approximately 700 hectares of valuable waterfront area close to an expanding port development, and the capital transfer is close to $14 million over a 10-year span.[79]

The Tsawwassen agreement was the first to be negotiated and ratified for the Lower Mainland under the BC treaty process and was also the first to involve a First Nation in an urban context. It did not, however, meet with universal approval from other BC First Nations. In October 2007, when the agreement was introduced in the BC legislature, the Union of BC Indian Chiefs, led by Chief Stewart Philip, protested. In Philip's view, many Aboriginal people opposed the treaty because it is designed to extinguish Aboriginal title, terminate Aboriginal rights, and enfranchise First Nations' citizens merely for the sake of business and industry.[80] In November 2007, the BC legislature ratified the agreement and it was sent to the House of Commons in Ottawa for first reading. Once the legislation is approved by the federal House of Commons and Senate, the agreement will come into effect.

The significance and impact of the Tsawwassen agreement, in the final analysis, may be negligible as First Nations struggle to deal with many of the pertinent grassroots, community issues (such as self-government, Aboriginal title, and land claims) in the early part of the twenty-first century. If many First Nations oppose similar agreements such as the Tsawwassen agreement and, instead, reject them, the future may be much different for the BC treaty process. For example, the Lheidli T'enneh near and within Prince George, in a March 2007 ratification vote, rejected an agreement that their leaders had achieved. As has already been argued, there needs to be a bottom-up approach that comes from within First Nations rather than solutions imposed by governments or simply by an Aboriginal elite. The BC treaty process, clearly, is still in flux, and the Tsawwassen deal may well be insignificant except in regard to that First Nation's specific community needs. In the end, such negotiations are about communication (or lack thereof) between leaders and First Nation members; about giving up, forever, statutory (Indian Act) and constitutional (s. 35) rights and privileges; about taxation; about much of the financial compensation of an agreement going to pay legal fees; about losing ancestral lands that, with enactment of the federal enabling legislation, are gone forever. Treaty rights also remain a huge issue for First Nations right across Canada.

Economic Development and Education: The Kelowna Accord

On 25 November 2005 Prime Minister Paul Martin announced in Kelowna, BC, that an accord (effectively what was regarded by some Aboriginal people as a national treaty) had been reached whereby more than $5 billion over a five-year period would be provided by the federal government in an effort to improve the daily lives of Aboriginal Canadians in terms of housing, health care, education, and economic opportunities. The Kelowna Accord was seen by some to be a belated attempt by the federal government to begin to meet at least some of the social equity issues raised by the recommendations of RCAP in 1996. The historic occasion was concluded by federal and provincial first ministers and Aboriginal leaders, who had set the course for a plan that would improve the lives of all the Aboriginal people and their communities across Canada. Prime Minister Martin stated that 'Our plan is built on a foundation of respect, accountability and shared responsibility.'[81] The Accord had five-year targets within a 10-year plan to ensure that actions would remain focused and accountable. The first ministers and Aboriginal leaders both agreed that broad indicators would be used to assess progress, while more specific measures and targets would be developed at regional and sub-regional levels.[82]

Aboriginal people and communities significantly trail behind other Canadians in many different areas, including health, education, and economic well-being, and the Kelowna Accord aimed to begin to address these inequities. In regard to education, 44 per cent of Aboriginal people ages 20–4 have less than a high school education; among the rest of Canadians, 19 per cent have not completed high school. By 2001, only 23 per cent of Aboriginal people ages 18–29 had completed any of various forms of post-secondary education, compared to 43 per cent in the rest of Canada.[83] The federal government pledged to address these issues in the Kelowna Accord by increasing the number of Aboriginal students in post-secondary education programs through the provision of bursaries, scholarships, and apprenticeships. The federal government had also pledged a review to identify how the overall gap and disparity in post-secondary education might be closed.

Another issue was improvement in health care. Infant mortality, youth suicide, childhood obesity, and diabetes all are approximately 20 per cent higher for Aboriginals than for the rest of the population. The government pledged to double the number of health professionals serving Aboriginal communities in 10 years from the present level of 150 physicians and 1,200 nurses.[84] The goal of this initiative was to match the statistics for other Canadians in the course of a five- to 10-year period. Phil Fontaine stated that 'All of the targets we've set are achievable. We're driving this process and we're forcing government to respond to our plan.'[85]

The main obstacle to the Kelowna Accord came when Paul Martin's minority government fell and the ensuing federal election of 23 January 2006 brought Stephen Harper's Conservative Party to power with another minority government. Martin had repeatedly stated during the election campaign that the Kelowna Accord would never be brought before the House of Commons with a Conservative government led by Harper. Unfortunately for Aboriginal people, he was right and another opportunity was missed.

Many Aboriginal leaders expressed their concerns over the newly elected Conservative government and whether it would honour the Accord. The Conservatives did not make it an election priority, and their first budget did not indicate a commitment to the agreement.[86] Instead, the Harper government offered only

On 25 November 2005, at the first Ministers and National Aboriginal Leaders meeting in Kelowna, BC, Prime Minister Paul Martin announced an agreement to improve social programs for Aboriginal Canadians. *(The Canadian Press/Adrian Wyld)*

$150 million in 2006 and $300 million in 2007 to improve education programs, provide clean water, upgrade mostly off-reserve housing, and close the socio-economic gap between Aboriginal people and the rest of Canada's population. As Canada's military budget grew and its overseas involvement in Afghanistan increased in scope, the severe reduction in funding for Aboriginal socio-economic problems drew criticism from many First Nations leaders. Fontaine stated that the 'Kelowna Accord was designed to eradicate poverty in First Nations communities and make Canada a better place. This budget suggests to me that we won't be able to move ahead on those commitments.'[87] He was correct.

The only response from the Conservative government came from then Indian Affairs Minister Jim Prentice, who questioned the validity of the agreement. He believed that the first ministers had actually not reached a written agreement and questioned whether Quebec had been properly engaged in the political process, noting that its Aboriginal leadership apparently did not take part. In fact, the Accord had been endorsed by the Prime Minister and all of the Premiers and it had the approval of the Assembly of First Nations (including Quebec) and its leader, Phil Fontaine. By 2007, the Kelowna Accord and its promises of money and investment in Aboriginal communities across Canada appeared to be dead.

The failure to implement the Kelowna Accord was a clear indication that the federal government was not prepared to offer the financial support needed to improve the many First Nation communities and citizens who continue to live far below the standards of the rest of Canada. The unemployment rate on reserves is about 29 per cent and off-reserve it is 19 per cent, while the national rate is 7 per cent. The median employment income for Aboriginal Canadians is $16,000, while the average for other Canadians is close to $25,000.[88] The Kelowna Accord was supposed to help close this gap in five years. As of early 2008, the federal government had not extended or announced any plan of financial support to First Nation citizens akin to the Kelowna Accord, either on- or off-reserve.

The Residential Schools Settlement Agreement, 2007

An agreement to compensate the estimated 80,000 recognized survivors of designated Indian residential schools was ratified by the federal government on 19 September 2007. This agreement was only for those who attended and who survived in designated schools; it is estimated that many students did not survive their time in residential schools and, of course, many others have died since residential schools in Canada date to the late nineteenth century. The issues surrounding the profound damage to individuals, communities, and cultures will be the subject of the Indian Residential Schools Truth and Reconciliation Commission, headed by Ontario Court of Appeal Justice Harry S. LaForme of the Mississauga of New Credit First Nation, who was appointed to head the Commission in May 2008 and whose work began in June 2008.[89]

The September 2007 agreement with the federal government was to provide at least $1.9 billion to residential school survivors. The last federally run residential school had been closed in 1996 in Saskatchewan.[90] There have been many painful stories and memories from indigenous persons of a legacy of physical and sexual abuse. The path to a settlement agreement with the federal government and the Canadian churches who also ran these schools took over 10 years, from the time in January 1998 when the federal government announced an Aboriginal Action Plan, which called for a renewed partnership with many Aboriginal people and the community to recognize the past mistakes and injustices.[91]

With many lawsuits related to the residential schools still pending, the federal government proposed payments for all former residential school students who were alive as of 30 May 2005. The proposal included an initial payout of $10,000 plus $3,000 for each year they attended the school. However, the proposal included a provision that the acceptance of such an offer would release the government and the involved churches of all further liability relating to the Indian residential school experience, except in serious cases of sexual abuse or any physical abuse. For this purpose, an Independent Assessment Process (IAP) was set up to address these serious cases of abuse.[92] Furthermore, there have also been issues related to non-Aboriginal lawyers who have been seen to be getting rich off these claims.[93]

Cree children from the Lac La Ronge band at an Anglican Church mission school in Saskatchewan, March 1945. On the blackboard at left is the admonition 'Thou shalt not tell lies.'
(Bud Glunz/Library and Archives Canada, PA-134110)

In the current deal, each eligible person who attended a designated residential school is expected to receive approximately $28,000. Not everyone, however, was happy with this agreement or its payment, and legal actions remain outstanding. The former students who decided to take the settlement money will not be able to sue the government, the churches, or any other defendant in a class action lawsuit, the government stated.[94] As of the summer of 2008, it was not known how many residential school survivors would accept the offer of the federal government, or continue by way of litigation. The process of payments began late in 2007. While the Indian residential schools settlement brought some closure for the federal government and the churches accused in the lawsuits, financial compensation can never replace the suffering and anguish. Perhaps even the work of a Truth and Reconciliation Commission over five years will not suffice. The long-term damages to First Nation individuals, families, and communities are incalculable.

Demographic Issues and Urbanization

In January 2008, Statistics Canada released its latest census report on Aboriginal people, based on data from the 2006 census. The total number of Canadians who self-identified as

Aboriginal surpassed a million—1,172,790 people. That number represents approximately 3.8 per cent of the total population.[95] Perhaps the most interesting aspect of the Aboriginal population today is that its growth rate is six times higher than that of the non-Aboriginal population of Canada. In fact, between 1996 and 2006 Canada's Aboriginal population grew by a remarkable 45 per cent. Much of the rapid growth has been in the Métis and Inuit populations. The population of the Métis between 1996 and 2006 nearly doubled, to a total estimated figure of 389,785; the Inuit population rose by 26 per cent, to 50,485.[96] Among other factors, over the past decade the Aboriginal fertility rate was nearly 30 births per 1,000 people, compared to a national rate of 13 per 1,000.[97] This has resulted in a significantly more youthful Aboriginal population.

It may be, given Canada's history and evidence of non-reporting as a result of racism in Canadian society, that many more indigenous people reside in Canada than census statistics indicate—perhaps over double the census figures of 2006, or somewhere between two and three million people, which would represent about 10 per cent of the Canadian population and would be the second highest number in the world behind New Zealand, where 15 per cent of the population is indigenous. For example, the Kitchener–Waterloo area (which was originally part of the Six Nations Reserve dating back to 1784 and was, as well, Mississauga territory before and after that date) is a place of Métis residence dating at least to the mid-eighteenth century, and indigenous people in this area today number over 10,000, while the 2006 census report listed only 4,650.[98]

The growth and identification of the Métis in Ontario are one cause of the dramatic increase in Aboriginal population. The Métis population now represents 33 per cent of Canada's total Aboriginal population. First Nations peoples still represent the majority of this population, at 63 per cent, while the Inuit, who have the youngest population, comprise 4 per cent.[99] The Inuit population especially is a result of a high fertility rate, with the median age of the Inuit at 22 years, while the median age for the non-Aboriginal population is 40 and for the First Nation population it is 25.[100]

The 2006 census shows the continuing trend in the urbanization of Canada's Aboriginal people, which reached 54 per cent in 2006. The highest urban concentration of Aboriginal people remained in Winnipeg, with 68,380, or about 10 per cent of that city's population.[101] In comparison, the census statistics show Toronto with an Aboriginal population of 26,575, or about 0.5 per cent of the total population. As Aboriginal urbanization increases steadily, particular cities have become magnets for this migration, notably Winnipeg, Vancouver, Saskatoon, Prince Albert, Edmonton, and Calgary.[102] This change will reshape the face of Canada and its cities in the twenty-first century. An estimated 40 per cent of First Nations people live on reserves. The off-reserve population, as a percentage of the total First Nations population, has increased by 2 per cent since 1996.[103] Many status Indians divide their time between their jobs in the city and their homes on reserve.[104] Such changes, as more Aboriginal people move to urban environments, will have a significant impact on the Indian Act and how Aboriginal people are identified and counted by themselves (and others) in the future, thereby influencing federal and provincial policies.

In sum, the Aboriginal population remains younger and is growing at a far more rapid pace than the non-Aboriginal population of Canada. Three factors account for this rapid growth: a high birth rate, an increase in those who identify themselves as Aboriginal, and the increasing participation of Indian reserves in the census—in 2001, 30 reserves were not enumerated; in 2006, this number had dropped to

22. These demographic trends will continue for many years to come.[105]

Environmental and Health Issues: The Kashechewan Water Crisis

The ongoing environmental struggle for many Aboriginal communities across Canada came to the fore once again in October 2005. High E. coli levels were found in the Kashechewan Reserve water treatment plant and its drinking water system. The poor water conditions at Kashechewan became news just before the First Nations chiefs gathered to discuss the upcoming November 2005 Kelowna conference with the Prime Minister and the premiers. The First Nations meeting, which was set to discuss such issues as poverty, housing, and self-government, was overshadowed by the events at Kashechewan, where many of the residents had to be airlifted off the reserve due to the poor quality of water after flooding.[106] Kashechewan is a Cree First Nation community of approximately 1,900 people located on the Albany River near James Bay in northern Ontario. The closest urban centre is Timmins, about 450 kilometres to the south.[107]

By 2005, there had already been two evacuations as a result of flooding. In 1995 a new water treatment plant had been built to replace the existing one; however, the new water treatment plant was reported to be too small to handle the expansion that the reserve had undergone. As a result, the tides from James Bay pushed the dirty water back and across the intake of the plant. In April 2005, about 200 people had been flown off the reserve after flooding had damaged several basements of homes with raw sewage and contaminated water. Flooding also had damaged the pump house, which was eventually shut down. The E. coli in the drinking water caused worsening skin conditions for people on the reserve, such as scabies and impetigo.[108] The problem, how-

ever, was and is not limited to Kashechewan. Recurring problems of the lack of clean water have been the experience of many First Nations communities across Canada; in British Columbia, for example, the Kwicksutaineuk First Nation had a boil-water advisory in effect for about nine years.[109]

The situation in Kashechewan became a national embarrassment for the federal government in its failure to provide clean water on this northern reserve for nearly two years. According to Indian and Northern Affairs Canada, the leaders of a First Nation community, typically a band's chief and council, are responsible for the operation and maintenance of water treatment facilities and for the delivery of safe drinking water to its residents. The federal Department of Indian Affairs provides the funding to each First Nation to support these services and also for the training of treatment facility operators. In October 2005, the federal Liberal government said that the Kashechewan Reserve would be relocated to higher ground within a period of 10 years. However, following the defeat of the Liberals in the January 2006 federal election, this plan was circumvented.

The 2005 budget of $1.6 billion for a water management strategy on reserves did not appear to be adequate. The new Conservative government had pledged to increase funding to implement regulatory testing for all reserves.[110] By June 2006, then Indian Affairs Minister Jim Prentice had appointed a former Ontario provincial Tory cabinet colleague, Alan Pope, as the special federal representative on this issue to develop a solution to the crisis in Kashechewan. Prentice stated on 6 June 2006 that 'The current situation in Kashechewan is unacceptable and the Government is committed to finding a long-term solution for the community. The answer involves more than geography; we need to focus on providing the best possible future for the families and children of Kashechewan.'[111] By the end of 2006 Pope had concluded his work and had more than 50 recommendations for the minister to review.

Soon, the federal Department of Indian and Northern Affairs had come up with a five-step plan to deal not just with the Kashechewan crisis but also with the broader issue of potable water on reserves. This plan proposed:

1. To work with 21 First Nations communities, the most at risk, that currently had high-risk water systems and drinking water advisories in place.
2. To ensure that certified operators oversee all treatment plant facilities by the end of the year and require that treatment plant operators complete necessary training programs.
3. To implement the protocol for safe drinking water for First Nations communities. The protocol establishes clear standards for the design, construction, operation, maintenance, and monitoring of treatment facilities and sets out clear roles and responsibilities for all those accountable.
4. To assemble a panel of experts to provide options for a regulatory framework, including new legislation.
5. To deliver regular reports on progress.[112]

This plan was introduced in the House of Commons late in 2007. However, over 170 First Nation communities in Canada are considered to have high-risk water systems, and one must wonder, given the federal government's handling of the Kelowna Accord, where funding will be found to address the problem across Canada. There is no question that the federal government will have its hands full to come up with a viable solution to this issue, as well as to meet the need for legislated standards for water quality for reserves and other Aboriginal communities.

As for Kashechewan, despite a proposal to relocate the community near Timmins, the residents of this reserve chose to return to their homeland. On 30 July 2007, the federal government, represented by Prentice and Health Minister Tony Clement, and the Kashechewan First Nation, represented by Chief Jonathon Solomon, signed an agreement to redevelop a healthy and sustainable community in its present location. Prentice stated: 'The decision to rebuild on the current site respects the wishes of residents to stay on their traditional land, and makes use of existing infrastructure.'[113] The redevelopment process will address priority areas such as skill development, on-reserve housing; socio-economic sustainability, health programs, public safety, infrastructure development, and maintenance.

Quite apart from a fouled water supply, the community of Kashechewan had experienced problems common to many reserves in Canada: high unemployment, lack of housing, and lack of infrastructure. With this new promise and new plan moving forward, Chief Solomon saw the water crisis of 2005 as in the past, and an opportunity for his people to move forward: 'We have faced a number of challenges and uncertainties in the past. Working in partnership with the Government of Canada to create a safe and stable environment, we can now look ahead to a brighter future.'[114] Kashechewan, however, could be a case of the squeaky wheel getting the grease. The commitment of the federal government towards initiating long-term reform on reserves across Canada remains to be seen, and the water crisis in Kashechewan was an example of how dire the conditions remain in many First Nations communities.[115]

Arctic Sovereignty and the North

The development of Canada's northern communities, specifically those of the Inuit people, has become increasingly popularized in southern Canada and has become a vital aspect of Canadian sovereignty in the early twenty-first century. The political issues surrounding Canadian Arctic sovereignty have been well documented since the effects of climate change have renewed debate over the possible future use of the Northwest Passage for shipping between Pacific Asia and Europe, a route that would be several thousand kilometres shorter than the current shipping routes (chiefly using the Panama Canal).

The sovereignty issue came under close scrutiny in the summer of 2007, when Russia sent a naval ship to the North Pole to plant a Russian flag in a titanium capsule on the ocean floor. Such events have caused the dispute over the Arctic to become increasingly apparent at the international level, in particular with Canada having repeatedly failed in the past to assert its sovereignty in this area. However, the recent dispute goes beyond Canada and Russia and is considered an international issue under international law. The United States, Denmark, and Norway also have made claims to portions of the Arctic Ocean seabed—an issue centred on future oil and gas exploration and revenues, and many shipping nations would like to see the Northwest Passage as an international shipping route, although the most likely routes come close to land inhabited by Canada's Inuit.[116] Clearly, Canadian Arctic sovereignty relates to complex issues concerning the regulation of shipping activities, environmental degradation, and the Inuit.[117]

The major obstacle that the Canadian government has faced in the Arctic has been the difficulty in terms of the regulation and surveillance of the vast geographic area. For many years the federal government had pledged to increase its military presence in the region, but this never amounted to much more than political posturing. In July of 2007, Prime Minister Harper announced that Canada would add six to eight patrol vessels that would be in operation for seasonal northern duty by 2013 or 2014.[118] Many critics believe that Harper's announcement was nothing more than a political ploy, and a plan for greater military spending, but not a true attempt to address the issue of national sovereignty and security in the Far North.

The Inuit see their territory as integral to their economy of fishing, trapping, and hunting. They also spend a great amount of time working and living on or adjacent to the ice, which in effect turns it into an extension of the land.[119] The area has been gaining increasing attention for the exploration of resources such as oil, gas, diamonds, gold, and other minerals. According to a US geological survey, the Arctic contains approximately one-quarter of the world's undiscovered energy resources.[120] This exploration continues to be a threat not only to the traditional way of life for many of the Inuit, but to their territory as well.

As a result of these issues of sovereignty, late in 2007 the federal government announced 'The Northern Dimension of Canada's Foreign Policy' and its four objectives:[121]

1. To enhance the security and prosperity of all Canadians, especially northerners and Aboriginal peoples.
2. To assert and ensure the preservation of Canada's sovereignty in the North.
3. To establish the circumpolar region as a vibrant geopolitical entity integrated into a rules-based international system.
4. To promote the human security of northerners and the sustainable development of the Arctic.

Given this policy initiative, Canada's Aboriginal and Inuit inhabitants of the North will continue to play a prominent role in the twenty-first century.

Over the past decade, the federal and the

territorial governments have been working with the many Aboriginal communities located in Yukon, the Northwest Territories, and Nunavut concerning these emerging issues. In 1999, a co-ordinated Northern Development Strategy was created to carry out scientific research and development among all government agencies.[122] By 2006, the federal Department of Indian and Northern Affairs had developed a strategic economic development plan for Canada's northern territories. The plan called for the federal government to work with northern communities and their municipal governments to strengthen their economies and businesses. The targeted investment program called for approximately $90 million spread over the three territories over a five-year period.[123] The strategy aimed to address the specific economic needs of each of the three territories.

As we saw above, the Aboriginal population in Canada's North has been increasing rapidly over the past decade, as the 2006 census clearly shows. The future of the North and of Canada's Arctic sovereignty will depend on the willingness of the federal government to commit the resources necessary. Continued investment in the natural resources, sustainable development, and environmental protection of the North must be a high priority in the twenty-first century.

The Inuit and Climate Change in the North

By early 2008, according to Environment Canada, the top weather story was climate change in the North: 'At the top of the world, the dramatic disappearance of Arctic sea ice . . . was so shocking that it quickly became our No. 1 weather story.'[124] The continued melting of the polar ice cap and vastly larger expanses of ice-free waters during the late summer in the Arctic Ocean, and especially overall climate

change, became one of the most prominent political issues confronting the Inuit in their homeland.

Climate change dominated political discussions pertaining to the environment in the first decade of the twenty-first century in Canada. The Conservative government had backed out of the Kyoto Protocol, deeming its targets to be unrealistic. Global warming and climate change, especially in the Arctic, became a hot-button issue with the release of Al Gore's Academy Award-winning documentary, *An Inconvenient Truth*. In Canada, an Inuk activist, Sheila Watt-Cloutier, was prominent for being nominated, along with former US Vice-President Gore, for the Nobel Peace Prize in 2007—which Gore ultimately won—for their work as environmental activists.[125] On environmental issues, Watt-Cloutier represents approximately 150,000 Inuit across Canada, Alaska, and Greenland.

Watt-Cloutier has worked for the past decade as an activist for the traditional Inuit way of life in the North. Her homeland, the Arctic, has been getting increasingly warmer, which causes a direct threat to the Inuit. For Watt-Cloutier, this is a human rights issue because of the challenges to the traditional Inuit culture of hunting, fishing, health, and security.[126] In one of her many appearances in 2007, Watt-Cloutier appeared before an international commission on human rights in the US, lobbying them to monitor the link between climate change and the traditional Inuit way of life:

> They wanted to hear the legal aspects, the broader issues of the connection between human rights and climate change, so we were able to testify on the broader larger picture of climate change and human rights, not just for Inuit but for vulnerable peoples of the world, most people have not made that connection and I think unless you're living in that situation

where you see that automatic connection of an erosion or a destruction of your way of life it's hard to see that connection. But today I think they learned a lot more from us.[127]

Watt-Cloutier had been the first to develop a link between human rights and climate change in 2003.

In June of 2007, Prime Minister Harper declared that Canada would not be able to meet its Kyoto targets in regard to lowering greenhouse gas emissions. The main reason for the failure to live up to this commitment, put simply, is the negative short-term impact it would have on the Canadian economy.[128] However, years of inaction on behalf of all levels of government have helped to create the current climate change crisis. A growing awareness of climate change and global warming has become increasingly apparent across Canada. According to a recent poll conducted for CTV and the *Globe and Mail*, 'the environment topped a list of concerns for people across Canada. About 36 per cent of people named climate change as the world's biggest threat.'[129] Yet, rhetoric and public opinion will not solve the issue of global warming; there must be action by governments at all levels across the globe, not only in Canada or in the Arctic.

Sheila Watt-Cloutier, as one Inuk woman, has embodied the aphorism of the environmental movement to 'think globally, act locally.' As she has explained, she tries 'to bring with me the best of the sound judgment and wisdom and focus and reflection that a hunter does, because my people expect me to come home with something that helps to alleviate the challenges we are facing.'[130] Watt-Cloutier is

Inuk environmental activist Sheila Watt-Cloutier on an offshore barrier in Iqaluit, NU, 12 October 2007. *(The Canadian Press/Chris Windeyer)*

a hero for the Inuit in their homeland. For the Inuit in the North, awareness of climate and of changing conditions has always been central to survival and part of indigenous knowledge, however overlooked such knowledge often has been in the course of Canada's history. No longer—on many issues—can this disregard continue to be the case, not only for the sake of Canada's founding peoples, but for the sake of all Canadians.

Epilogue

If any one theme can be traced throughout the history of Canada's Amerindians, it is the persistence of their identity. The confident expectation of Europeans in the nineteenth century that Indians were a vanishing people, the remnants of whom would finally be absorbed by the dominant society, has not happened.[1] The 2006 census clearly states otherwise. If anything, Indians (along with Inuit and the Métis) are more prominent in the collective conscience of the nation than they have ever been, and if anyone is doing the absorbing it is the Amerindians. Adaptability has always been the key to their survival; it is the strongest of Amerindian traditions. Just as the dominant society has learned from the Indians, so the Indians have absorbed much from the dominant society, but they have done it in their own way. In other words, Aboriginal people have survived as themselves, and have preferred to remain as such even at the cost of social and economic inequality.[2]

In the Canadian multicultural mosaic, the Aboriginal peoples have been reported to be the least happy with their lot.[3] In part, this is a reaction to cultural loss, particularly evident in the realm of language. Of the 50 or so Aboriginal tongues spoken in Canada at the time of contact, several are now extinct (Beothuk, Huron, Neutral) and most of the others are endangered, some seriously. Cree, Ojibwa, and Inuktitut appear to have the best chances of survival,[4] although even the survival of Inuktitut is in some doubt. Two language bills—the Inuit Languages Protection Act and the Official Languages Act—have passed first and second readings in the Nunavut legislature and, as of 2008, were at the committee stage of examination. These bills are not as stringent as Quebec's famous language law, but the hope is that they will help to protect Inuktitut as the language of life and work in Nunavut. The Inuit concern regarding the possible loss of their language is reflected in census data, where 64 per cent of Canadian Inuit in 2006 reported Inuktitut as their mother tongue, down from 68 per cent 10 years earlier, and 'the number of Inuit who speak Inuktitut at home has fallen from 58 per cent in 1996 to 50 per cent' in 2006.[5]

On the other hand, Aboriginal spiritual beliefs have displayed a remarkable vitality and indeed have been enjoying a renaissance. An expression of this has been the introduction of Aboriginal elements into Roman Catholic ritual, a movement that began in the prairie West, particularly in Edmonton. Recently there has been a convergence of Aboriginal and science-based knowledge that holds exciting promise for both the Aboriginal and non-Aboriginal communities. All this has gone hand in hand with the rise of political activism and the campaign for land and treaty rights and natural resources, self-determination and self-government. This is the opposite of a separatist movement; what Indians are asking for is full and equal participation in the Canada of today and of the future; this was the clear message of the *Report of the Royal Commission on Aboriginal Peoples*. This movement is not without its problems, as the old ways are widely held by Natives to be the best expression of their identity, and there is resistance to the party politics of representative democracy, which is regarded by some as an imposition. 'Self-government' is interpreted by many Natives to mean participation on their own terms.[6] On the other side of the coin, change is the very essence of Aboriginal tradition. It recognizes that the cycle of life is one of constant motion; while basic patterns can be detected, there is no guarantee that they will be repeated in exactly the same way. No society today is the same as it was a century ago, even though there is continuity in many of its elements. Living traditions, like living societies, also change; what worked in one set of circumstances may not work in another. Indigenous identities are fluid and complex issues.[7] Survival, and its concomitant adaptation, continues to be the key.

The reaffirmation of Aboriginal identity has not been a sudden development; Amerindians have always had a clear idea of who they are. What is new is the demand for recognition of this identity by the dominant society. In the early twenty-first century Canada's founding

Tomson Highway is a Cree from Brochet, in northern Manitoba. He hit a high point in his writing career during the 1980s with his award-winning plays, *The Rez Sisters* and *Dry Lips Oughta Move to Kapuskasing*. He holds several honorary degrees and is a member of the Order of Canada. His most recent work, *The Journey (Pimooteewin)*, with composer Melissa Hui, is the first Aboriginal opera and premiered in Toronto in 2008.
(Michael Cooper Photographic)

peoples are demanding fairness. Several factors have contributed to this development, some of them of comparatively long standing and others very recent.

First of all, there has been the growing international recognition of Native art, especially since World War II. West coast art has long been appreciated—dating back to the days of first meetings in the eighteenth century, in fact—but that of other regions has been slower in gaining acknowledgement. In the 1940s, largely through the efforts of Toronto artist James A. Houston, Inuit learned printmaking. Carving in soapstone and ivory and

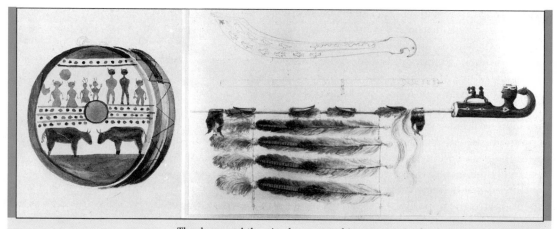

The drum and the pipe have central importance in the Amerindian way of life.
These drawings are from Paul Kane's sketchbook.
(With permission of the Royal Ontario Museum © ROM, 946.15.31 and 946.15.33)

the creation of tapestries were also encouraged; with the support of the Canadian government, the Hudson's Bay Company, and the Canadian Handicrafts Guild and the development of co-operatives to handle production and marketing, Inuit art became known worldwide. Another success story that developed somewhat later, that of Eastern Woodlands art, favours painting over printmaking, although both forms are practised.[8] Crafts such as porcupine quill work, beading, embroidery, and leather work have also come into their own and are much in demand. This flowering of Native arts and crafts illustrates very well the Aboriginal capacity to use new techniques to bring traditional arts, whose antiquity approaches those of Europe, Africa, and Australia,[9] into the contemporary world. In the literary, musical, and theatrical arts, as well as hockey, Canada's national game, Native expression is winning respectful attention. The message is clear: Canada's first peoples, far from being interesting relics of the past, are a vital part of Canada's persona, both present and future. The life of the Copper Thunderbird, Norval Morrisseau, speaks eloquently to that fact.

It was only a matter of time for this growing cultural self-confidence to express itself, and to be listened to, in other arenas as well. A key area is education, and Natives have demonstrated their effectiveness in taking control of the schooling of their children. The justice system has been slower to respond, but there, too, the Native input is becoming more evident as Aboriginal self-confidence grows. If one were to pinpoint the moment of truth for this cultural momentum, it would be when Elijah Harper said 'No' to the Meech Lake Accord. The occasion could not have been more appropriate: not only was the whole nation watching and listening, but a good part of the world as well. Harper rose to the occasion, withstood the pressures mounted to bring him into line, and spoke for himself and his people. He even took himself by surprise: 'I never realized that I would have such an impact on this country.'[10] Canada's Natives had finally caught the attention not only of their fellow Canadians but of the international world as well. And they had fundamentally altered the nation's course of events. The standoffs at Temagami, Oka, Ipperwash, and Caledonia followed, as

Amerindians took determined positions against ancient wrongs.[11] The point was emphasized when 300 indigenous leaders held a summit of their own concurrently with the Summit of the Americas, at Quebec City in April 2001. Then AFN National Chief Coon Come was invited to attend the general summit, but without provision for him to meet with the top leaders from the Americas.[12] Still, this set a precedent indicating that the message is being heard: no longer will Aboriginal people stand meekly by as others run things to suit themselves, without taking into serious account the people who were on the scene first. As the case of Canada so well illustrates, its confederation may be young, but it has components that are ancient.

The early twenty-first century included new challenges for Aboriginal people across Canada, as well as unresolved problems from the past. The federal Conservative government elected in early 2006 wasted no time undoing the efforts of its predecessors by immediately scrapping the Kelowna Accord and by its refusal in 2007, as only one of four nations in the world, to accept the United Nations Declaration of Indigenous Rights. On 8 April 2008, the opposition parties put that right by passing a resolution in the House of Commons endorsing the Declaration. The Tories opposed it. The new century also brought some closure to other issues, such as the release of the final report of the Ipperwash Inquiry into the death of Dudley George, along with the Ontario government's pledge to return the provincial park to the Stoney and Kettle Point First Nation. The residential schools settlement provided some of the Aboriginal survivors of designated residential schools at least some compensation for their tragic experiences of assimilation over the course of the twentieth century. However, the pain of all of these experiences can never be taken back, and many Aboriginal people, individually and collectively, will never recover what they lost.

While there remains hope that the twenty-first century will bring positive change for all Aboriginal people across Canada, many of the issues now confronting them are dramatically evident. There is still a significant gap in the standard of living compared to the rest of Canada, in terms of economic development, housing, education, and health care. Unresolved land rights issues, which have always posed a tremendous strain on the relationship with the federal and provincial governments, continue to be a central issue. The federal government introduced legislation in the fall of 2007 to speed up the specific claims process through the establishment of an independent tribunal. By the summer of 2008 that legislation still had not been passed. The slow pace of negotiations has created a deep mistrust on the part of First Nations people towards the federal and provincial governments and their commitment to resolve long-standing disputes.

The foreign policy stance on indigenous rights by the federal government was a startling reminder that Canada's policy on Aboriginal rights—as human rights—always has been one of denial, and thus a failure.[13] Kenneth Deer, a Mohawk from Kahnawake and editor of *The Eastern Door*, reflected on Canada's failure at the UN Commission on Human Rights in 2007, noting that the influence and image of Canada as an advocate for human rights abroad has been severely damaged. Canada, after all, had played a central role at the United Nations over the previous decade in the initiation and framing of this document. Deer noted that Louise Arbour, a former Canadian Supreme Court justice and the UN High Commissioner for Human Rights, stated that many Canadians cling to an "'unduly romantic vision" of their country as an international peacemaker and honest broker on the world scene—a vision largely rooted in the achievements of former Liberal Prime Minister Lester Pearson and the Nobel Peace Prize he won more than half a century ago. "I think Canadians have an image of themselves that is now pretty dated, that is not reflective of the contemporary position."[14] Nevertheless, to many Aboriginal people in Canada, the recent decision has come as no surprise, and the federal government stance at the UN has become all too familiar. In the early twenty-first century one of many unanswered questions relating to the future of Aboriginal peoples in Canada is whether they can become partners in building a more equitable nation of nations, or if they will be forced, by governments and by the indifference of public opinion, to focus exclusively, in piecemeal fashion, on their own often desperate needs. Many questions still remain in spite of the words: 'We are sorry.'

Appendix: National Historic Sites of Canada Commemorating Aboriginal History

ALBERTA

64. **Blackfoot Crossing**
    Traditional meeting place on Blackfoot reserves

63. **British Block, Cairn & Suffield Tipi Rings**
    Aboriginal site on CFB Suffield

65. **Earthlodge Village**
    Remains of Aboriginal village

62. **Frog Lake Massacre (Parks Canada administered)**
    Site of Cree uprising, 1885

68. **Head-Smashed-In Buffalo Jump**
    World Heritage Site—Aboriginal bison drive

67. **Old Women's Buffalo Jump**
    Aboriginal bison drive in use for 1,500 years

66. **Treaty Seven Signing Site**
    Treaty signed in 1877 with Blackfoot Nation

BRITISH COLUMBIA

72. **Kiix?in Village and Fortress**
    Archaeological sites of First Nations village and fortress with significant architectural remains

82. **Kitselas Canyon Area**
    Remains of two Aboriginal villages and petroglyphs

84. **Kitwanga Fort (Parks Canada administered)**
    Tsimshian village

83. **Kitwanga Totem Poles**
    Totem poles record families of Kitwanga Fort

85. **Kitwankul**
    Gitksan village

79. **Kiusta Village**
    Former Haïda village

70. **Marpole Midden**
    Site of midden, excavated in 1892

81. **Metlakatla Pass Area Indian Site**
    Site of winter villages of Tsimshian

75. **Nan Sdins (Parks Canada administered)**
    Remains of Haida longhouses and totem poles

78. **New Gold Harbour Area**
    Site of Haida village

77. **Skedans**
    Former Haida village

76. **Tanu**
    Former Haida village

71. **Weir's (Taylor's) Beach Earthworks Site**
    Pre-contact site on Vancouver Island

74. **Whaler's Shrine Site**
    Aboriginal ritual site

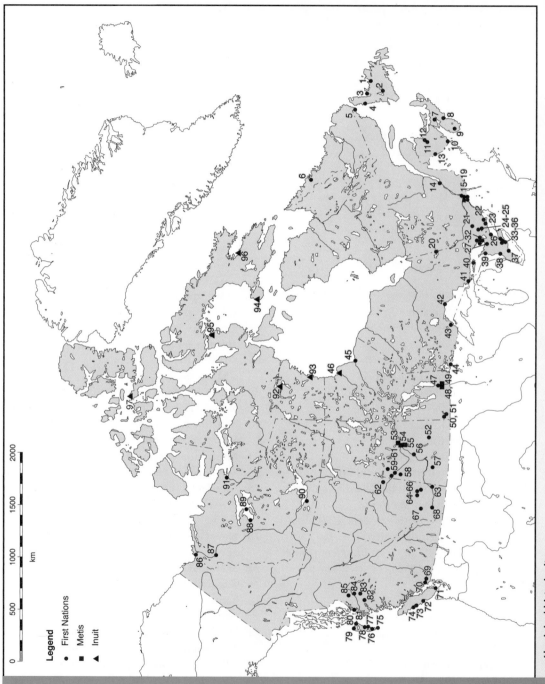

Aboriginal historic sites

Legend

• First Nations
■ Metis
▲ Inuit

69. **Xa:ytem/Hatzic Rock**
    Habitation site of Stó:lo peoples
80. **Yan Village Indian Site**
    Former Haida village
73. **Yuquot**
    Spanish settlement site, 1789–95

MANITOBA

48. **Battle of Seven Oaks**
    Conflict between Métis and Red River settlers, 1816
50. **Brockinton Indian Sites**
    Late prehistoric site, Blackduck phase
51. **Linear Mounds** (Parks Canada administered)
    Aboriginal burial mounds, AD 1000–1200
49. **Riel House** (Parks Canada administered)
    Family home of Métis leader Louis Riel
46. **Sea Horse Gully Remains**
    Large Dorset and Pre-Dorset site
47. **The Forks** (Parks Canada administered)
    Historic meeting place, junction of the Red and Assinboine rivers
45. **York Factory** (Parks Canada administered)
    Hudson's Bay Company's principal fur trade depot from 1684–1870s

NEW BRUNSWICK

11 **Augustine Mound Site**
    Pre-contact burial mound
13. **Meductic Indian Village/Fort Meductic**
    Principal Maliseet settlement
10. **Minister's Island Pre-contact Sites**
    Pre-contact shell midden, 500 BC–AD 1500
12. **Oxbow Sites**
    Well-preserved, 3,000-year archaeological record

NEWFOUNDLAND & LABRADOR

1. **Beothuk Site**
    Major archaeological site for Beothuk history
3. **Fleur de Lys Soapstone Quarries**
    Resource extraction by Dorset culture

2. **Indian Point**
    Well-documented Beothuk site
5. **L'Anse Amour Burial**
    Burial site, Maritime Archaic culture
6. **Okak**
    Archaeological site, several cultures occupied
4. **Port au Choix** (Parks Canada administered)
    Pre-contact burial and habitation sites

NORTHWEST TERRITORIES

88. **Déline Fishery/Franklin's Fort**
    Wintering quarters of Sir John Franklin and his second expedition
89. **Grizzly Bear Mountain and Scented Grass Hills**
    Expression of cultural values through the interrelationship between landscape, oral histories, graves, and cultural resources
90. **Hay River Mission Sites**
    Mission buildings, significant to Dene community
86. **Kittigazuit Archaeological Sites**
    Beluga hunting, Kittegaryumiut and Mackenzie Delta
87. **Nagwichoonjik (Mackenzie River)**
    Flows through Gwichya Gwich'in traditional homeland and continues to be culturally, socially, and spiritually significant

NOVA SCOTIA

8. **Bedford Petroglyphs**
    Spiritually significant petroglyph site
7. **Debert Paleo-Indian Site**
    Archaeological remains of Aboriginal caribou hunting
9. **Kejimkujik** (Parks Canada administered)
    Important Mi'kmaq cultural landscape

NUNAVUT

93. **Arvia'juaq and Qikiqtaarjuk**
    Inuit summer occupation sites with rich history and surviving in situ resources
96. **Blacklead Island Whaling Station**
    Aboriginal and European bowhead whaling

91. **Bloody Falls**
Pre-contact hunting and fishing sites

92. **Fall Caribou Crossing**
Site of critical importance to the historical survival of Inuit community

95. **Igloolik Island Archaeological Sites**
Archaeological sequence, 2000 BC–AD 1000

94. **Inuksuk**
Inuit complex of 100 stone landmarks

97. **Port Refuge**
Pre-contact occupations, trade with Norse colonies

ONTARIO

26. **Bead Hill**
Remains of seventeenth-century Seneca village

23. **Carrying Place of the Bay of Quinte**
Site of 1787 treaty between British and Mississauga

36. **Chiefswood**
Italianate-style birthplace of poet Pauline Johnson

22. **Christ Church Royal Chapel**
Historic royal chapel linked with establishment of Mohawk in Ontario

43. **Cummins Pre-contact Site**
Extensive late Paleo-Indian stone quarry

39. **Donaldson Site**
Aboriginal site, 500 BC–AD 300

31. **Etharita Site**
Main village of Wolf Tribe of Petun, 1647–9

30. **Fort Sainte Marie II**
Jesuit mission to Hurons, 1649–50

33. **Her Majesty's/St Paul's Chapel of the Mohawks**
First Protestant church in Upper Canada, 1785

44. **Manitou Mounds**
Religious and ceremonial site for 2,000 years; Rainy River Mounds

21. **Mazinaw Pictograph Site**
Largest Algonkian pictograph site in Canada

34. **Middleport Site**
Archaeological site, Middle Ontario Iroquois

29. **Mnjikaning Fish Weirs** (Parks Canada administered)
Aboriginal fishing site

28. **Ossossane Sites**
Principal village of Bear clan of Hurons

38. **Parkhill Site**
Paleo-Indian habitation site, c. 8000 BC

24. **Peterborough Petroglyphs**
Algonkian petroglyph site

42. **Pic River Site**
Complex of pre-contact Woodland culture sites

27. **Saint-Louis Mission** (Parks Canada administered)
Site of Huron village destroyed by Iroquois in 1649

32. **Sainte-Marie Among the Hurons Mission**
Headquarters of Jesuit mission to Hurons, 1639–49

25. **Serpent Mounds Complex**
Aboriginal peninsula site, 60 BC–AD 300

40. **Sheguiandah**
Site of pre-contact stone quarry

37. **Southwold Earthworks** (Parks Canada administered)
Site of Attiwandaronk Indian village, c. AD 1500

35. **Walker Site**
Large Iroquoian site, historical Attiwandaronk tribe

41. **Whitefish Island**
Ojibwa historic site

QUEBEC

19. **Battle of the Lake of Two Mountains**
Site of defeat of Iroquois by French, 1689

15. **Caughnawaga Mission/Mission of St Francis Xavier**
Jesuit mission to Mohawks established 1647

16. **Caughnawaga Presbytery**
Oldest surviving building at mission, eighteenth century

17. **Fort St-Louis**
    Built in 1725 for protection of Christian Iroquois

18. **Hochelaga**
    Iroquois village visited in 1535 by Jacques Cartier

14. **Notre-Dame-de-Lorette Church**
    Mission church to the Hurons with seventeenth-century art objects, 1865

20. **Pointe Abitibi**
    Traditional summering area and sacred place for the Algonquin

SASKATCHEWAN

54. **Batoche** (Parks Canada administered)
    Métis village; site of 1885 Battle of Batoche

58. **Battle of Cut Knife Hill**
    Cree repulse Canadian attack, 1885

53. **Battle of Duck Lake**
    First battle of 1885 North-West Rebellion

55. **Battle of Fish Creek** (Parks Canada administered)
    Site of battle between Métis and Canadian forces, 1885

60. **Fort Pitt**
    Site of Hudson's Bay Company post, signing of Treaty Six

52. **Fort Qu'Appelle**
    Hudson's Bay Company post, negotiation of Treaty Four

59. **Frenchman Butte** (Parks Canada administered)
    Site of 1885 battle, Cree and Canadian troops

57. **Gray Burial Site**
    One of the oldest burial sites on Plains, c. 3000 BC

61. **Steele Narrows**
    Last engagement of North-West Rebellion, 1885

56. **Wanuskewin**
    Complex of Plains Indian cultural sites

Notes

Introduction

1. On 18 June 1936, William Lyon Mackenzie King, Liberal Prime Minister of Canada (1921–6, 1926–30, 1935–48), observed in the House of Commons 'that if some countries have too much history, we have too much geography.' John Robert Colombo, ed., *Colombo's Canadian Quotations* (Edmonton, 1974), 306.
2. Harold A. Innis, *The Fur Trade in Canada* (Toronto, 1962), 392.
3. Izumi Shimada and John F. Merkel, 'Copper Alloy Metallurgy in Ancient Peru', *Scientific American* 265, 1 (July 1991): 80–6.
4. Ian Hodder, *Reading the Past* (Cambridge, 1986), 102, 147–70.
5. 'Professor warns of native rift', *Edmonton Journal*, 19 Oct. 1990; 'Oka standoff sparked fears of IRA-type crisis, Ciaccia says', *Globe and Mail*, 15 Jan. 1991; Sarah Schmidt, 'New-Age Warriors', *Saturday Night*, 14 Oct. 2000, 22–9.
6. See Ives Goddard's discussion of the subject in David Damas, ed., *Handbook of North American Indians, 5: Arctic* (Washington, 1984), 5–7.
7. Denys Delâge, 'Les Iroquois chrétiens des "réductions", 1667–1770. I—Migration et rapports avec les Français', *Recherches amérindiennes au Québec* 20, 1 and 2 (1991): 64.
8. I.S. MacLaren, 'Samuel Hearne's Accounts of the Massacre at Bloody Falls, 17 July 1771', *Ariel: A Review of English Literature* 22, 1 (1991): 25–51; MacLaren, '"I came to rite thare portraits": Paul Kane's Journal of his Western Travels, 1846–1848', *American Art Journal* 21, 2 (1989): 6–88.

Chapter 1

1. See the introduction for an explanation of 'BP'.
2. Cultures have been described as symbolic structures that provide the means for human satisfaction once survival has been assured. See David Rindos, 'The Evolution of the Capacity for Culture: Sociobiology, Structuralism, and Cultural Evolution', *Current Anthropology* 27, 4 (1986): 326.
3. Tom D. Dillehay, 'The Great Debate on the First Americans', *Anthropology Today* 7, 4 (1991): 13. The oldest skeleton found so far (in Texas) has been dated to 11,600 years ago. 'Hemisphere's oldest remains identified, geologist says', *Toronto Star*, 1 Nov. 1992.
4. Brian M. Fagan, *The Great Journey* (London, 1987), 26.
5. See, for example, Jeffrey Goodman, *American Genesis* (New York, 1981). Some of the various approaches to the study of early man in the Americas are found in William S. Laughlin and Albert B. Harper, eds, *The First Americans: Origins, Affinities and Adaptation* (New York and Stuttgart, 1979).
6. Knut R. Fladmark demonstrates the complementarity of myth and scientific discourse by using legends to amplify his text in *British Columbia Prehistory* (Ottawa, 1986).
7. Norval Morrisseau, *Legends of My People the Great Ojibway* (Toronto, 1965), 15; Mircea Eliade, *Gods, Goddesses, and Myths of Creation* (New York, 1974), 135–6.
8. A variation of this myth is found among the Athapaskan Wet'suwet'en of the Cordilleran

plateau. See A.G. Morice, *Au pays de l'ours noir* (Paris, 1897), 76–8.

9. A survey of types of creation myths and their distribution in North America is that of Anna Birgitta Rooth, 'The Creation Myths of the North American Indians', *Anthropos* 52 (1957): 497–508.

10. For one, 'The Origin of Gitxawn Group at Kitsumkalem', in Marius Barbeau and William Beynon, coll., *Tsimshian Narratives 2* (Ottawa, 1987), 1–4. Others are in Marius Barbeau, *Tsimshian Myths* (Ottawa, 1961).

11. Joseph de Acosta, *The Natural and Morall History of the East and West Indies*, tr. E.G., 2 vols (London, 1880; reprint of 1604 edition), I, 57–61; first published in Latin in 1590. A current joke among Indians illustrative of their attitude towards the Bering Strait migration route has it that the reason why their people wound up in the Americas instead of staying in Asia was that 'they couldn't get their bearings straight.'

12. 'What the Stone Tools Tell Us', *Archaeology* 49, 6 (1996): 61.

13. Steven B. Young, 'Beringia: An Ice-Age View', in William W. Fitzhugh and Aron Crowell, eds, *Crossroads of Continents: Cultures of Siberia and Alaska* (Washington, 1988), 106–10.

14. Robert E. Ackerman, 'A Siberian Journey: Research Travel in the USSR, July 20–August 20, 1990', an unpublished report to the National Endowment for the Humanities and Washington State University, 25 Sept. 1990.

15. Anthropologist Alan L. Bryan, personal communication. The view that Siberia was not peopled before 20,000 years ago is maintained by Nikolai N. Dikov, 'On the Road to America', *Natural History* 97, 1 (1988): 14.

16. Virginia Morell, 'Confusion in Earliest America', *Science* 248 (1990): 441.

17. Carl Ortwin Sauer, *Land and Life*, ed. John Leighly (Berkeley, 1969), 300–12.

18. Peter Schledermann, *Crossroads to Greenland: 3000 Years of Prehistory in the Eastern High Arctic* (Calgary, 1990), 314–15. Four possible ways by which the Arctic could have been peopled are presented in schematized form by Robert McGhee in *Canadian Arctic Prehistory* (Scarborough, Ont., 1978), 18–21.

19. Knut R. Fladmark, 'The Feasibility of the Northwest Coast as a Migration Route for Early Man', in Alan Lyle Bryan, ed., *Early Man in America from a Circum-Pacific Perspective* (Edmonton, 1978), 119–28.

20. Knut R. Fladmark, 'Times and Places: Environmental Correlates of Mid-to-Late Wisconsinan Human Population Expansion in North America', in Richard Shutler Jr, ed., *Early Man in the New World* (Beverly Hills, Calif., 1983), 27. See also Margaret Munro, 'Underwater world of B.C. could be missing link in early man's travels', *Edmonton Journal*, 9 Aug. 1993.

21. See Richard Shutler Jr, 'The Australian Parallel to the Peopling of the New World', in Shutler, ed., *Early Man in the New World*, 43–5.

22. Ruth Gruhn, 'Linguistic Evidence in Support of the Coastal Route of Earliest Entry into the New World', *Man* new series 23, 2 (1988): 77–100.

23. Joseph H. Greenberg, *Language in the Americas* (Stanford, Calif., 1987), 331–7; Greenberg, 'Linguistic Origins of Native Americans', *Scientific American* (Nov. 1992): 94–9. Greenberg espouses the classification of all the languages of the world into 15 basic stocks, to which a number of isolated languages would have to be added. His ultimate goal is to relate them all in a single language family. Some of the pros and cons of Greenberg's theories are discussed by Jared M. Diamond, 'The Talk of the Americas', *Nature* 344 (1990): 589–90. It is estimated that if present trends continue, 90 per cent of the world's surviving 6,000 languages will disappear in the next hundred years.

24. N. Guidon and G. Delibrias, 'Carbon-14 dates point to man in the Americas 32,000 years ago', *Nature* 321 (1986): 769–71. Also, 'American visitors 32,000 years ago', *The Times*, London, 8 Aug. 1986.

25. Nième Guidon, 'Cliff Notes', *Natural History* 96, 8 (1987): 8. Carbonized hearth remains from Santa Rosa Island off the southern California coast have yielded 30,000-year-old dates, but these are vigorously disputed. See L.S. Cressman, *Prehistory of the Far West: Homes of Vanquished Peoples* (Salt Lake City, 1977), 69–70; William J. Wallace, 'Post-Pleistocene Archaeology, 9000 to 2000 B.C.', in Robert F. Heizer, ed., *Handbook of North American Indians, 8: California* (Washington, 1978), 30.

26. 'Relics suggest that humans came to New World 36,000 years ago', *Edmonton Journal*, 2 May 1991.

27. William N. Irving, 'The First Americans: New Dates for Old Bones', *Natural History* 96, 2 (1987): 8–13. Irving and paleobiologist Richard Harrington claim that a campsite at Old Crow River dates back 150,000 years. See Barry Estabrook, 'Bone Age Man', *Equinox* 1, 2 (1982): 84–96.

28. Jacques Cinq-Mars, 'La place des grottes du Poisson-Bleu dans la préhistoire beringienne', *Revista de Arqueología Americana* 1 (1990): 9–32. See also Catharine McClellan, *Part of the Land,*

Part of the Water: A History of the Yukon Indians (Vancouver, 1987), 50–1. On the debate about pre-Clovis sites, see Eliot Marshall, 'Clovis Counterrevolution', *Science* 249 (1990): 738–41.

29. McClellan, *Part of the Land*, 49–50.

30. Knut R. Fladmark, 'The First Americans: Getting One's Berings', *Natural History* (Nov. 1986): 8–19. For the view that the corridor could have been used for migrations, see N.W. Rutter, 'Late Pleistocene History of the Western Canadian Ice-Free Corridor', *Canadian Journal of Anthropology* 1, 1 (1980): 1–8. This entire issue of *CJA* is devoted to studies of the corridor.

31. D. Wayne Moodie, Kerry Abel, and Alan Catchpole, 'Northern Athapaskan Oral Traditions and the White River Volcanic Eruption', paper presented at 'Aboriginal Resource Use in Canada: Historical and Legal Aspects' conference, University of Manitoba, 1988. See also McClellan, *Part of the Land*, 54–5.

32. See, for example, Douglas C. Wallace, Katherine Garrison, and William Knowles, 'Dramatic Founder Effects in Amerindian Mitochondrial DNAs', *American Journal of Physical Anthropology* 68 (1985): 149–55.

33. Two surveys of current thinking on the subject, both with the title 'Who Were the First Americans?', indicate the high level of popular interest in the question. The first article, by Sharon Begley and Andrew Murr, appeared in *Newsweek* 133, 17 (26 Apr. 1999): 50–8; the other, by Sasha Nemecek, appeared in *Scientific American* 283, 3 (Sept. 2000): 80–7. Newspaper reports are so numerous that only a sampling can be given here: 'First settlers may have arrived from Europe', *National Post*, 2 Nov. 1999; Frank X. Mullen Jr, 'After 10,000 Years, Dispute Remains: Clan of the Cave Man May Predate Indians', *USA Today*, 2 Aug. 2000, 10D; Tracey Ober, 'Brazilian skull suggests early Americans predated Asian arrival', *Globe and Mail*, 21 Sept. 1999; Faye Flam, 'Prehistoric Melting Pot: Recent Archaeological Discoveries Have Scientists Speculating That Early People Migrated to the Americas from Many Places and Directions, Not Just from Asia Via the Bering Strait,' *The Gazette*, Montreal, 28 Nov. 1999, C4.

34. Russell Thornton, *American Indian Holocaust and Survival: A Population History Since 1492* (Norman, Okla., 1987), 15–41; Henry F. Dobyns, *Their Number Become Thinned: Native American Population Dynamics in Eastern North America* (Knoxville, Tenn., 1983), 34–45. See also Pierre Chaunu, *L'Amérique et les Amériques* (Paris, 1964), 21.

35. Bruce G. Trigger and William R. Swagerty, 'Entertaining Strangers: North America in the Sixteenth Century', in Trigger and Wilcomb Washburn, eds, *The Cambridge History of the Peoples of the Americas* (Cambridge, 1996), I, part 1, 362–3.

36. Dobyns, *Their Number Become Thinned*, 42; Thornton, *American Indian Holocaust*, 25–33.

37. Pre-Columbian population estimates were beginning to be revised early in the twentieth century. In 1913, for instance, the US Bureau of Ethnology calculated that the Amerindian population of the United States had declined 65 per cent since the arrival of Europeans. Joseph K. Dixon, *The Vanishing Race: The Last Great Indian Council* (Garden City, NY, 1913), 6.

   A recent study points to the danger of assuming that early epidemics alone caused the catastrophic population drops. In northern Manitoba, despite heavy death rates during the influenza epidemic following World War I, population recovery could be swift if other factors did not intervene. Ann Herring, 'The 1918 Flu Epidemic in Manitoba Aboriginal Communities: Implications for Depopulation Theory in the Americas', paper presented to the American Society for Ethnohistory, Toronto, 1990.

38. James Brooke, 'Melting ice yields ancient artifacts', *Globe and Mail*, 5 Oct. 1999.

39. Theodore G. Schurr et al., 'Amerindian Mitochondrial DNA Have Rare Asian Mutations at High Frequencies, Suggesting They Derived from Four Primary Maternal Lineages', *American Journal of Human Genetics* 46 (1990): 613–23. For a different interpretation of the evidence, see Milford H. Wolpoff's article in Erik Trinkaus, ed., *Emergence of Modern Humans: Biocultural Adaptations in the Late Pleistocene* (Cambridge, 1989).

40. J.H. Greenberg, C.G. Turner II, and S.L. Zegura, 'The Settlement of the Americas: A Comparison of the Linguistic, Dental, and Genetic Evidence', *Current Anthropology* 27, 4 (1986): 477–97.

41. One population estimate for the entire neolithic world of 10,000 years ago sets it at 75 million, organized into something like 150,000 tribal nations. John H. Bodley, ed., *Tribal Peoples and Development Issues: A Global Overview* (Mountain View, Calif., 1988), 1. Today, the number of tribal peoples still in existence may be as many as 200 million (ibid., iii).

42. Schledermann, *Crossroads to Greenland*, 319.

43. Paul S. Martin, 'Prehistoric Overkill', in Martin and H.E. Wright Jr, eds, *Pleistocene Extinctions: The Search for a Cause* (New Haven, 1967), 75–105. Also Martin, 'The Pattern and Meaning of

Holarctic Mammoth Extinctions', in David M. Hopkins et al., eds, *Paleoecology of Beringia* (New York, 1982), 399–408.

44. William H. Hodge, *The First Americans Then and Now* (New York, 1981), 15–16.

45. The Siberian find, at a site near Magadan Oblast, has been radiocarbon dated to 8,300 years ago. 'Discovery raises questions over settling of New World', *Globe and Mail*, 2 Aug. 1996. On fluted points in Canada, see R. Cole Harris, ed., *Historical Atlas of Canada*, I (Toronto, 1987), plate 2.

46. Ibid., plates 5 and 6.

47. Fagan, *The Great Journey*, 8.

48. Sauer, *Land and Life*, 237–40; W.C. Boyd, *Genetics and the Races of Man: An Introduction to Modern Physical Anthropology* (Boston, 1950), 227.

49. Michael Brown, *The Search for Eve* (New York, 1990), 315.

50. Sauer, *Land and Life*, 239.

51. Christy G. Turner II, 'Ancient Peoples of the North Pacific Rim', in Fitzhugh and Crowell, eds, *Crossroads of Continents*, 113–15. Amerindians share with Asiatics the conformity of their incisors, which are scooped out at the back, 'shovel-shaped'. Turner believes that this feature, combined with genetic evidence, suggests three basic groups for original Amerindians: Amerind, Na-Dene, and Aleut-Inuit.

52. Emöke J.E. Szathmary, 'Human Biology of the Arctic', in David Damas, ed., *Handbook of North American Indians, 5: Arctic* (Washington, 1984), 70–1.

53. This section has been drawn, in part, from my article, 'A Historical Reconstruction for the Northwestern Plains', *Prairie Forum* 5, 1 (1980): 19–27.

54. Although the Inca were skilled metallurgists, they used their craft largely, although not entirely, for ceremonial purposes. However, it is now known that copper alloy metallurgy was more important than previously thought and was used for mundane purposes. See Izumi Shamada and John F. Merkel, 'Copper Alloy Metallurgy in Ancient Peru', *Scientific American* 265, 1 (1991): 80–6. Inca architecture, roads, and engineering projects were based on Stone Age technology. This technology, of course, was no more confined to stone than that of the Bronze Age was to bronze, or the Iron Age to iron. It may well be that bone and wood were just as important as stone, or even more so; their perishability, however, particularly that of wood, has made it highly unlikely that this can ever be determined with any precision. As stone and bone technology gave way to that of metals,

some tribal peoples came to regard stone tools as thunderbolts. See C.J.M.R. Gullick, *Myths of a Minority* (Assen, 1985), 25.

55. Alan L. Bryan, 'An Overview of Paleo-American Prehistory from a Circum-Pacific Perspective', in Bryan, ed., *Early Man in America*, 306–27. The oldest stone tools known so far, crafted more than 2.5 million years ago, have been found in Ethiopia. 'Oldest known stone tools found, but makers remain anonymous', *Ottawa Citizen*, 23 Jan. 1997.

56. J.Z. Young et al., *The Emergence of Man* (London, 1981), 207–8. Similarly, red, the colour of life, was very early attributed high symbolic significance. Red ochre was thus prized by tribal peoples around the world.

57. Archery was practised at least 10,000 years ago in Japan. See Fumiko Ikawa-Smith, 'Late Pleistocene and Early Holocene Technologies', in Richard Pearson, ed., *Windows on the Japanese: Studies in Archaeology and Prehistory* (Ann Arbor, 1986), 212.

58. *Lost Visions, Forgotten Dreams*, exhibit guide, Canadian Museum of the American Indian (1996), n.p.

59. Brian O.K. Reeves, 'Communal Bison Hunters of the Northern Plains', in L.B. Davis and Reeves, eds, *Hunters of the Recent Past* (London, 1990), 170–1.

60. Sauer, *Land and Life*, 284.

61. Ibid., 175. The recent discovery of a 6,000-year-old wooden walkway buried in a peat bog in England has pointed to the existence of very early stable communities. See John M. Coles, 'The World's Oldest Road', *Scientific American* 201, 5 (1989): 100–6. On the difficulties of interpreting archaeological data, see Ian Hodder, *Reading the Past* (Cambridge, 1986).

62. Bill Scanlon, 'Fires Uncover New Anasazi Sites', Scripps Howard News Service, 25 July 2000.

63. Fladmark, 'Times and Places', 41.

64. A map of historic trade systems between Siberia and North America probably also indicates earlier routes. See Fitzhugh and Crowell, eds, *Crossroads of Continents*, 236–7.

Chapter 2

1. 'Increase in carbon dioxide spurred farming, article says', *Globe and Mail*, 9 Oct. 1995; 'Earliest Agriculture in the New World', *Archaeology* 50, 4 (July–Aug. 1997): 11. Also Kenneth M. Ames, 'Myth of the Hunter-Gatherer', *Archaeology* 52, 5 (Sept.–Oct. 1999): 45–9.

2. Carl Ortwin Sauer, *Land and Life*, ed. John Leighly (Berkeley, 1971), 178. Archaeologist Norman

Clermont has observed that in the St Lawrence Valley, early agricultural communities developed in conjunction with fishing sites. He theorizes that a series of hard winters about AD 1000 encouraged farming as a means of obtaining enough food to store for the cold months. See Clermont, 'Why Did the St. Lawrence Iroquois Become Agriculturalists?', *Man in the Northeast* 40 (1990): 75–9.

3. Barry Kaye and D.W. Moodie, 'The Psoralea Food Resource of the Northern Plains', *Plains Anthropologist* 23, 82, pt. 1 (1978): 329–36. Use of the wild turnip as a food resource intensified with the growth of population that followed the advent of the horse. Prairie turnip flour is a good source of vitamin C.

4. Henry T. Lewis and Theresa A. Ferguson, 'Yards, Corridors, and Mosaics: How to Burn a Boreal Forest', *Human Ecology* 16, 1 (1988): 57–77. Fire, of course, had many more uses than those pertaining to agriculture and game management. See 'Our Grandfather Fire: Fire and the American Indian', in Stephen J. Pyne, *Fire in America* (Princeton, NJ, 1982), 71–83.

5. The section on agriculture is partly adapted from Olive Patricia Dickason, '"For Every Plant There Is a Use": The Botanical World of Mexica and Iroquoians', in *Aboriginal Resource Use in Canada: Legal and Historical Aspects* (Winnipeg, 1991), 11–34. My thanks to Dr Walter Moser, University of Alberta, for providing the Latin names.

6. S.G. Stephens, 'Some Problems of Interpreting Transoceanic Dispersal of the New World Cottons', in Carroll L. Riley et al., eds, *Man Across the Sea: Problems of Pre-Columbian Contacts* (Austin, Texas, 1971), 401–5.

7. J.B. Hutchinson, R.A. Silow, and S.G. Stephens, *The Evolution of Gossypium and Differentiation of the Cultivated Cottons* (London, 1947), 74–80. For the argument that the two New World species were developed in the Americas with plants that came from Africa, see Stuart J. Fiedel, *Prehistory of the Americas* (Cambridge, 1987), 161. For the case that cotton was domesticated from naturally hybridized plants growing wild in the Americas, see Joseph Needham and Lu Gwei-Djen, *Trans-Pacific Echoes and Resonances: Listening Once Again* (Singapore and Philadelphia, 1985), 62. See also Chapter 3 below.

8. On the contributions of Amerindian farmers to world agriculture, see Earl J. Hamilton, 'What the New World Gave to the Economy of the Old', in Fredi Chiapelli, ed., *First Images of America: The Impact of the New World on the Old*, 2 vols (Berkeley, 1976), II, 853–84; Barrie Kavash, *Native Harvests* (New York, 1979); Jack Weatherford, *Indian Givers: How the Indians of the Americas Transformed the World* (New York, 1988). Maize is also used as raw material for a wide variety of industrial products. It has been estimated that maize as a crop is worth more each year than all the gold and silver taken out of the Americas by the conquistadors. See Arturo Warman, 'Corn as Organizing Principle', *Northeast Indian Quarterly* 6, 1 and 2 (1989): 22. Maize, incidentally, was the staple for the transatlantic slave trade, as it prevented scurvy.

9. Peter McFarlane and Wayne Haimila, *Ancient Land, Ancient Sky: Following Canada's Native Canoe Routes* (Toronto, 1999), 120.

10. Only 20 per cent of Andean crops reproduce readily above 2,700 metres. On the distribution of maize as a crop, see Victor A. Shnirelman, 'Origin and Early History of Maize', *European Review of Native American Studies* 3, 2 (1989): 23–8, particularly the map on page 25.

11. Corn requires 60 to 70 days to produce a crop; rice requires 120–40 days. Pierre Chaunu, *L'Amérique et les Amériques* (Paris, 1964), 19. In Europe at the time of contact, the standard yield of Old World cereals was six units of seed collected for each unit of seed planted, a rate that under favourable circumstances could increase to 10:1. The standard for corn was 150:1; in bad years, the yield could drop to 70:1. Warman, 'Corn as Organizing Principle', 21.

12. There has been spirited debate about the origin of corn as a cultigen and, consequently, an extensive list of publications. Among the articles (being shorter and perhaps more readable) are: Steve Connor, 'Stone Age People Modified Crops', *The Independent*, 18 Mar. 1999, 12; Paul C. Mangelsdorf, 'Mystery of Corn', *Scientific American* 183, 1 (1950): 20–4; Mangelsdorf, 'Mystery of Corn: New Perspectives', *Proceedings of the American Philosophical Society* 127, 4 (1983): 215–47; Mangelsdorf, 'The Origin of Corn', *Scientific American* 255, 2 (1986): 80–6; George W. Beadle, 'The Ancestry of Corn', *Scientific American* 242, 2 (1980): 112–19; Walton C. Galinat, 'The Origin of Maize', *Annual Review of Genetics* 5 (1971): 447–78; J.M.J. de Wet and J.R. Harlan, 'Origin of Maize: The Tripartite Hypothesis', *Euphytica* 21 (1972); James H. Kempton, 'Maize as a Measure of Indian Skill', *Symposium on Prehistoric Agriculture*, University of New Mexico (Millwood, NY, 1977); Louis Werner, 'Caught in a maize of genes', *Américas* 52, 3 (May–June 2000):

6–17. For an archaeological report on the subject, see Douglas S. Byers and Richard S. MacNeish, eds, *The Prehistory of Teohuacan Valley*, 5 vols (Austin, Texas, 1967–72). Early research on the domestication of corn was done by the Soviet botanist V.I. Vavilov, whose findings were reported in 'Mexica i Tsentralnaia Amerika kak osnovnoi tsentr proiskoozhdenia kulturnykh rasternii', *Trudy po prikladnoi botanike, genetike i selektsii* 26, 3 (1931); and in Vavilov, 'Velikiye zemledeltsheskie kultury dokolumbovoi Ameriki i ikh vzaimootnosheniia', *Izvestiia Gosudarstvennogo Geografocheskogo Obshchestva* 71, 10 (1939).

13. Chili peppers, first domesticated on the Gulf coast, made their way to India, where they now form part of the traditional cuisine. India is also the leading grower of peanuts, another New World crop.

14. Stephen Lewandowski, 'Three Sisters—An Iroquoian Cultural Complex', *Northeast Indian Quarterly* 6, 1 and 2 (1989): 45. The story of O-na-tah, spirit of corn, tells how corn became separated from her sister plants in modern agriculture. ('O-na-tah Spirit of Corn', ibid., 40.)

15. Patricia S. Bridges, 'Changes in Activities with the Shift to Agriculture in the Southeastern United States', *Current Anthropology* 30, 3 (1989): 385–94. Skeletal studies also indicate changes in the division of labour between men and women as a result of the shift to maize agriculture. An increase in the variety of chores is indicated for women; men show fewer changes.

16. For an overview of subsistence patterns, see Harold E. Driver, *Indians of North America* (Chicago, 1970), 53–83.

17. Carl Ortwin Sauer, *Sixteenth-Century North America: The Land and People As Seen by the Europeans* (Berkeley, 1971), 181.

18. Despite their usefulness, dogs were regarded by some northern peoples as fundamentally hostile to humans and were associated with evil and witchcraft. See Catharine McClellan, *My Old People Say: An Ethnographic Survey of Southern Yukon Territory*, 2 vols (Ottawa, 1975), I, 161–7. Others had a much different view, not only demonstrating considerable respect, but in the case of some groups, such as the Dogrib, believing they were descended from a dog. Kerry Abel, *Drum Songs* (Montreal and Kingston, 1993), 131.

19. Sauer, *Sixteenth-Century North America*, 239, 293. The use of dogs as packers predates their use for traction. In southern Yukon, for example, dog teams pulling toboggans did not appear until the nineteenth century. (McClellan, *My Old People Say*, I, 162.)

20. Chrestien Le Clercq, *New Relation of Gaspesia*, ed. William F. Ganong (Toronto, 1910), 296. See also Reuben Gold Thwaites, ed., *Jesuit Relations and Allied Documents*, 73 vols (Cleveland, 1896–1901), XXII, 293.

21. Virgil J. Vogel, *American Indian Medicine* (Norman, Okla., 1970), 9; Daniel E. Moermon, *Medicinal Plants of Native America*, 2 vols (Ann Arbor, 1986); Charles H. Talbot, 'America and the European Drug Trade', *First Images* 2: 813–32. Early settlers soon learned to appreciate Amerindian medical lore and incorporated it into their own practice. See Alfred Goldsworthy Bailey, *The Conflict of European and Eastern Algonkian Cultures 1504–1700* (Toronto, 1969), 120–1.

22. Brian Swarbrick, 'A 9,000-year-old housing project', *Alberta Report* 18, 34 (1991): 50–1.

23. R. Cole Harris, ed., *Historical Atlas of Canada*, I (Toronto, 1987), plates 8 and 14.

24. Brian O.K. Reeves, *Culture Change in the Northern Plains 1000 B.C.–A.D. 1000* (Edmonton, 1983), 156, 190–3.

25. Richard G. Forbis, 'Alberta', in Warren W. Caldwell, ed., *The Northwestern Plains: A Symposium* (Billings, Mont., 1968), 44. An earth village described by Peter Fidler (1769–1822), who was in Saskatchewan late in the eighteenth century, has not been located. See Thomas F. Kehoe and Alice Kehoe, 'Saskatchewan', ibid., 32.

26. John R. Topic, 'The Ostra Site: The Earliest Fortified Site in the New World', in Diana Claire Tkaczuk and Brian C. Vivian, eds, *Cultures in Conflict: Current Archaeological Perspectives* (Calgary, 1989), 215–27.

27. The processes by which this can occur are examined by Kenneth M. Ames, 'The Evolution of Social Ranking on the Northwest Coast of North America', *American Antiquity* 46, 4 (1981): 789–805. Using the example of the Pacific Northwest Coast, he suggests that the conjunction of subsistence specialization, circumscribed environment, and population growth may have led to the development of ranking as a system for maximizing use of resources. Warfare may also have been a factor. Another theory stresses the economics of production: where there is a substantial time lapse between the input of labour and the realization of its results, then social mechanisms become necessary to ensure that those who did the work reap at least some of the benefits. See Ron Brunton, 'The Cultural Instability of Egalitarian Societies', *Man* 24, 4 (1989): 673–4.

28. Brunton, 'Cultural Instability', 673.

29. The Cree word for leader, of which 'okima' is one form, contains the root 'to give away'. See Colin Scott, 'Hunting Territories, Hunting Bosses and Communal Production among Coastal James Bay Cree', *Anthropologica* 28, 1 and 2 (1986): 171 n2. On what was expected of Montagnais chiefs, see Thwaites, ed., *Jesuit Relations*, XXVI, 155–63.

30. Chrestien Le Clercq, *Nouvelle relation de la Gaspésie*, 2 vols (Paris, 1691), I, 379–81.

31. Thwaites, ed., *Jesuit Relations*, VI, 243.

32. One study goes so far as to say the chief's authority was 'absolute' within certain spheres but in practice was constrained by the well-being of the community. See Arthur E. Hippler and Stephen Conn, *Traditional Athabascan Law Ways and Their Relationship to Contemporary Problems of 'Bush Justice'* (Fairbanks, 1972). This would accord, at least in part, with the observation of HBC Captain Zachariah Gillam (1636 o.s.–1682) that Amerindians had 'some chief persons that are above the rest, yet working with them'. Cited by Toby Morantz, 'Old Texts, Old Questions—Another Look at the Issue of Continuity and the Early Fur Trade Period', paper presented to the American Society for Ethnohistory, Chicago, 1989.

33. Thomas Jefferys, *The Natural and Civil History of the French Dominions in North and South America. I: A Description of Canada and Louisiana* (London, 1760), 67.

34. Thwaites, ed., *Jesuit Relations*, IX, 235.

35. Le Clercq, *Nouvelle relation*, I, 381–6.

36. Concerning the Plains Amerindians in this regard, see Chapters 4 and 13.

37. Torture as practised in Europe was part of the judicial system rather than that of warfare. At a time when nation-states were consolidating their positions, it was used as a means of control of certain elements within their own societies that for various reasons were considered undesirable. The majority of Amerindians who followed the practice (most prevalent in the East) belonged to non-state societies and used torture of outside enemies to demonstrate their community solidarity and superiority over hostile alien forces. They did not torture those within their own communities. See Olive Patricia Dickason, *The Myth of the Savage and the Beginnings of French Colonialism in the Americas* (Edmonton, 1984), xi; Dickason, 'Louisbourg and the Indians: A Study in Imperial Race Relations, 1713–1760', *History and Archaeology* 6 (1976): 91–2.

38. Maurice Godelier, 'Infrastructures, societies and history', *Current Anthropology* 19, 4 (1978): 763–

71. Godelier argues that force came into play once inequalities had been established.

39. Miguel Leon-Portilla, '"Men of Maize', in Alvin M. Josephy Jr, ed., *America in 1492: The World of the Indian Peoples before the Arrival of Columbus* (New York, 1992), 159.

40. Fiedel, *Prehistory of the Americas*, 137.

41. For a description of the Cahokia site, see Melvin Fowler, *The Cahokia Atlas* (Springfield, Ill., 1989). A comprehensive study is Thomas E. Emerson and R. Barry Lewis, eds, *Cahokia and the Hinterlands* (Urbana, Ill., 1990).

42. Robert McGhee, 'Labrador's Mysterious Burial Mound', *Canadian Heritage* (Dec. 1981): 11–13; McGhee, 'The Burial Mound Builders', in *Ancient Canada* (Ottawa, 1989): 47–54; James A. Tuck and Robert J. McGhee, 'An Archaic Indian Burial Mound in Labrador', *Scientific American* 225, 5 (1976): 122–9.

43. Warman, 'Corn as Organizing Principle', 21.

Chapter 3

1. R. Cole Harris, ed., *Historical Atlas of Canada*, I (Toronto, 1987), plate 8.

2. Julian H. Steward advocates multilinear evolution in *Theory of Culture Change* (Urbana, Ill., 1976).

3. Bob Connolly and Robin Anderson, *New Guinea Highlanders Encounter the Outside World* (London, 1988).

4. Stephen H. Lekson, Thomas C. Windes, John R. Stein, and W. James Judge, 'The Chaco Canyon Community', *Scientific American* 259, 1 (1988): 100–9.

5. Thor Heyerdahl, *Early Man and the Ocean: A Search for the Beginnings of Navigation and Seaborne Civilizations* (New York, 1980), 3–26.

6. Peter Caley, 'Canada's Chinese Columbus', *Beaver* Outfit 313, 4 (1983): 5.

7. The most thorough study of Beothuk canoe design to date is that by Ingeborg Constanze Luise Marshall, *Beothuk Bark Canoes: An Analysis and Comparative Study* (Ottawa, 1985).

8. Ingeborg Marshall makes the point that Beothuk canoes are only known today through models. No one has made a full-size copy to test it for seaworthiness. Marshall, *The Red Ochre People* (Vancouver, 1982), 12.

9. Marshall, *Beothuk Bark Canoes*, vi, 128–9.

10. E.F. Greenman, 'Upper Paleolithic in the New World', *Current Anthropology* 3 (1962): 61. See also Edwin Tappen Adney and Howard I. Chapelle, *The Bark Canoes and Skin Boats of North America* (Washington, 1964), 94–8; Alice B. Kehoe, 'Small

Boats Upon the North Atlantic', in Carrol Riley et al., eds, *Man Across the Sea: Problems of Pre-Columbian Contacts* (Austin, Texas, 1971), 275–92.

11. John Barber, 'Oriental Enigma', *Equinox* 49 (1990): 92.

12. Kuang-chih Chang, 'Radiocarbon dates from China: Some initial interpretations', *Current Anthropology* 14, 5 (1973): 525–8.

13. On the white-bone, white-meat variety, see George F. Carter, 'Pre-Columbian Chickens in America', in Riley et al., eds, *Man Across the Sea*, 178–218; Carter, 'Chinese Contacts with America: Fu Sang Again', *Anthropological Journal of Canada* 14, 1 (1976): 10–24. On the black-boned, dark-meated 'melanotic' chicken, found in Mexico, Mesoamerica, and Guatemala, see Carl L. Johannessen, 'Folk Medicine Uses of Melanotic Asiatic Chickens as Evidence of Early Diffusion to the New World', *Social Science and Medicine* 15D (1981): 427–34; Johannessen, 'Melanotic Chicken Use and Chinese Traits in Guatemala', *Revista de Historia de América* 93 (1982): 73–89. Melanotic chickens were not eaten but used in magical and curing rituals by both Mayans and Chinese.

14. Caley, 'Canada's Chinese Columbus', 8–9. Although living in China, Hwui Shan was an Afghan and apparently spoke Chinese imperfectly, which did not help his credibility upon his return. Still, his story was officially recorded, although in condensed form. From this skimpy evidence, it has been inferred that he arrived at the Aleutian Islands before heading south to Fu-Sang, held by some to be Mexico.

15. John R. Swanton, 'The First Description of an Indian Tribe in the Territory of the Present United States', in Nathaniel M. Caffee and Thomas A. Kirby, eds, *Studies for William A. Read* (Baton Rouge, La, 1940), 326–38.

16. Japanese pottery dates from before 12,000 BP: Fumiko Iwaka-Smith, 'Late Pleistocene and Early Holocene Technologies', *Windows on the Japanese: Studies in Archaeology and Prehistory* (Ann Arbor, 1986), 199–216. Childe called pottery 'the earliest conscious utilization by man of a chemical change'. V.G. Childe, *Man Makes Himself* (New York, 1951), 76. Earliest pottery is associated with cooking.

17. Kehoe, 'Small Boats', 288–9; Stuart J. Fiedel, *Prehistory of the Americas* (Cambridge, 1987), 109.

18. Terry Grieder, *Art and Archaeology in Pashash* (Austin, Texas, 1979), maintains there is evidence of the potter's wheel having been used to produce Recuay ceramics, AD 290–360.

19. Blow guns were developed in areas where bamboo was found. They were the precursors of the gun barrel. On a possible Japanese connection, see Nancy Yaw Davis, *The Zuni Enigma* (New York, 2000).

20. *Sweat of the Sun: Gold of Peru* (Edinburgh, 1990). This is the catalogue for the exhibition of the same name.

21. Catharine McClellan, *Part of the Land, Part of the Water: A History of the Yukon Indians* (Vancouver, 1987), 55–6. The Beothuk of Newfoundland also appear to have done this with iron. See Chapter 5.

22. Stephen Jett, 'Trans-oceanic Contacts', in Jesse D. Jennings, ed., *Ancient Native Americans* (San Francisco, [1978]), 623.

23. See Gordon F. Ekholm, 'A Possible Focus of Asiatic Influence in the Late Classic Cultures of Meso-america', in Jesse D. Jennings, ed., *Memoirs of the Society for American Archaeology*, 9, supplement to *American Antiquity* 18, 3, part 2 (1953): 72–97.

24. The case for the Indian origin of New World cotton, both as a crop and its manufacture into textiles, is presented by J.B. Hutchinson, R.A. Silow, and S.G. Stephens, *The Evolution of Gossypium and Differentiation of the Cultivated Cottons* (London, 1947), 79–80, 136–9.

25. Jett, 'Trans-oceanic Contacts', 636; Barber, 'Oriental Enigma', 86. See also M.D.W. Jeffreys, 'Pre-Columbian Maize in Asia', in Riley et al., eds, *Man Across the Sea*, 376–400; Hugh C. Cutler and Leonard W. Blake, 'Travels of Corn and Squash', ibid., 367–75.

26. It is not known how long amaranth has been cultivated in such Chinese provinces as Yunan and Kwaichow. In western China, amaranth seeds are popped, dipped in syrup, and eaten as candy. Joseph Needham and Lu Gwei-Djen, *Trans-Pacific Echoes and Resonances: Listening Once Again* (Singapore and Philadelphia, 1985), 62–3.

27. A detailed description of these correlations is in Barber, 'Oriental Enigma', 82–95. See also B.J. Meggers, 'The Trans-Pacific Origin of Meso-American Civilization: A Preliminary Review of the Evidence and Its Theoretical Implications', *American Anthropologist* 77 (1975): 1–27.

28. Heyerdahl, *Early Man and the Ocean*, 376–7.

29. A reasoned assessment of Fell's strengths and failings is David H. Kelley's 'Proto-Tifinagh and Proto-Ogham in the Americas', *Review of Archaeology* 11, 1 (1990): 1–10. Kelley concludes: 'We need to ask not only what Fell has done wrong in his epigraphy, but also where we have gone wrong as archaeologists.'

30. David H. Kelley, 'Diffusion: Evidence and Process', in Riley et al., eds, *Man Across the Sea*, 60–5; Marc K. Stengel, 'The Diffusionists Have Landed', *Atlantic Monthly* (Jan. 2000): 35–48.

31. Nigel Davies, *Voyagers to the New World* (Albuquerque, NM, 1979).

32. Ibid., 253.

33. John Howland Rowe, 'Diffusionism and Archaeology', *American Antiquity* 31, 3, part 1 (1966): 334–7.

34. Jared Diamond, *Guns, Germs, and Steel* (New York, 1999), 217–38. Diamond observes that the task of developing writing was so difficult that it occurred comparatively late in human cultural development. It may also have been invented independently in Egypt by 3000 BC and in China by 1300 BC, but this is less certain. Once invented, it spread rapidly, diversifying as it went. According to Diamond, one of the reasons that hunting and gathering societies neither developed nor adopted writing was their lack of institutional needs for its use. When Spaniards arrived in the sixteenth century, they found 18 different writing systems in Mesoamerica. See Alice B. Kehoe, *North American Indians, A Comprehensive Account* (Englewood Cliffs, NJ, 1981), 41.

35. Heyerdahl, *Early Man and the Ocean*, 84–91.

36. An earthenware shard, found on Saturna Island, has been identified as Oriental in origin and dated to about AD 300. Unfortunately, it was out of context by the time it came to the attention of museum authorities. See Caley, 'Canada's Chinese Columbus', 10.

37. Anna Birgitta Rooth, 'The Creation Myths of the North American Indians', *Anthropos* 52 (1957): 508.

38. Michael H. Brown, *The Search for Eve* (New York, 1990), 315. Polynesians, in their turn, are genetically similar to Chinese and Indonesians.

39. Needham and Lu, *Trans-Pacific Echoes*, 64.

Chapter 4

1. Canada's ecology, subsistence bases, and population distribution for 1500 are mapped in R. Cole Harris, ed., *Historical Atlas of Canada*, I (Toronto, 1987), plates 17, 17A, 18. Seasonal Algonkian and Iroquoian cycles are schematized in plate 34.

2. Robin Ridington, 'Technology, world view, and adaptive strategy in a northern hunting society', *Canadian Review of Sociology and Anthropology* 19, 4 (1982): 469–81.

3. Ethnologist June Helm, University of Iowa, divides the Subarctic into the shield with associated Hudson Bay lowlands and Mackenzie borderlands, the cordillera, the Alaska plateau, and the region south of the Alaska range. The first division, that of the Subarctic shield and borderlands, covers approximately three-quarters of the land mass of the Arctic. June Helm, ed., *Handbook of North American Indians, 6: Subarctic* (Washington, 1981), 1.

4. Russell Thornton, *American Indian Holocaust and Survival: A Population History Since 1492* (Norman, Okla., 1987), 32.

5. Robert T. Boyd, 'Demographic History, 1774–1874', in Wayne Suttles, ed., *Handbook of North American Indians, 7: Northwest Coast* (Washington, 1990), 135. Richard Inglis, curator of ethnology, Royal British Columbia Museum, estimates the pre-contact population for the west coast from California to Alaska at 500,000. (*Vancouver Sun*, 21 Nov. 1987.)

6. Harris, ed., *Historical Atlas of Canada*, plate 9.

7. Cited by Ruth Gruhn, 'Linguistic Evidence in Support of the Coastal Route of Earliest Entry into the New World', *Man* new series 23, 2 (1988): 77–9. Amerindian languages, besides being complex, used a wider variety of sounds and ways of making sounds than did European languages. As a result, during the early days of contact, it was simpler for an Indian to learn a European language than for a European to learn an Indian one.

8. See Harris, ed., *Historical Atlas of Canada*, plate 66, on linguistic evidence indicating extremely ancient habitation of the Northwest Coast. The discovery of a longhouse dated to 9,000 years ago near Mission, BC, appears to be an archaeological breakthrough. See *Alberta Report* 18, 34 (1991): 50–1.

9. This is still a living tradition today. See, for instance, the report of the Union of British Columbia Indian Chiefs of their conference held in Vancouver, 23–6 February 2000, 'Protecting Knowledge: Traditional Resource Rights in the New Millennium'. Recently in the United States, the Hopi Nation asked a man to stop telling non-Indians about sacred Hopi prophecies because they are secret and should be controlled only by Hopis.

10. There is some evidence that chiefdoms had appeared among some of the Iroquois. See William C. Noble, 'Tsouharissen's Chiefdom: An Early Historic 17th Century Neutral Iroquoian Ranked Society', *Canadian Journal of Archaeology* 9, 2 (1985): 131–46.

11. An offshoot of the sexual division of labour and responsibility was that it prevented celibacy. See

Reuben Gold Thwaites, ed., *Jesuit Relations and Allied Documents*, 73 vols (Cleveland, 1896–1901), XVI, 163. Another consequence was the clear definition of roles, a major factor in the harmony that prevailed in the encampments. (Ibid., VI, 233–4.)

12. Ibid., VI, 243; V, 195.

13. Miguel León-Portilla, *Aztec Thought and Culture* (Norman, Okla., 1963), 71–9.

14. Thwaites, ed., *Jesuit Relations*, IX, 59–61; XII, 9–11, 225.

15. Ames, 'Evolution of Social Ranking', 797.

16. 'Moiety': half. This division of a community into two halves was for ceremonial purposes.

17. Descriptions of various aspects of potlatch ceremonialism are found in Stuart Piddocke, 'The Potlatch System of the Southern Kwakiutl: A New Perspective', *Southwestern Journal of Anthropology* 21 (1965): 244–64; Helen Coderre, *Fighting with Property: A Study of Kwakiutl Potlatching and Warfare, 1792–1930* (New York, 1950); Frederica de Laguna, 'Potlatch Ceremonialism on the Northwest Coast', in William W. Fitzhugh and Aron Crowell, eds, *Crossroads of Continents: Cultures of Siberia and Alaska* (Washington, 1988), 271–80.

18. Ernest S. Burch Jr, 'War and Trade', in Fitzhugh and Crowell, eds, *Crossroads of Continents*, 231–2.

19. Gary Coupland, 'Warfare and Social Complexity on the Northwest Coast', in Diana Claire Tkaczuk and Brian C. Vivian, eds, *Cultures in Conflict* (Calgary, 1989), 205–14. The Quinault have a more peaceful explanation: they see social distinctions arising from the fact that wealth tended to concentrate with certain families or groups of families, who were thus favoured for providing chiefs; continuing through many generations, a class was born. See Pauline K. Capoeman, ed., *Land of the Quinault* (Taholah, Wash., 1990), 73–4.

20. Victor P. Lytwyn, 'Waterworld: The Aquatic Territory of the Great Lakes First Nations', in *Gin Das Winan: Documenting Aboriginal History in Ontario* (Toronto, 1996), 14. Gilles Havard, in *La grande paix de Montréal de 1701* (Québec, 1992), 132–5, lists 27 Great Lakes nations.

21. Iroquoian languages are related to Siouan and Caddoan. The Caddo, of the US Southwest, were organized into hierarchical chiefdoms at the time of European contact; the Sioux had been connected earlier with the Mississippian Mound Builders.

22. Harris, ed., *Historical Atlas of Canada*, plate 12.

23. Succotash, an Amerindian dish that was adopted by early settlers, was made with corn and beans boiled with fish or meat.

24. A description of Huronia as first seen by Europeans is in Thwaites, ed., *Jesuit Relations*, XVI, 225–37.

25. On the possible Basque origin of the word 'Iroquois', see Peter Bakker, 'A Basque Etymology for the Word Iroquois', *Man in the Northeast* 40 (1990): 89–93. He postulates that the word derives from two Basque elements that together mean 'killer people'. An earlier explanation for the term is that it is of Algonkian origin and signifies 'snake'. The Ojibwa referred to both Hurons and Five Nations as 'Nahdoways', snakes. Peter Jones, *History of the Ojebway Indians* (London, 1861), 111.

26. They called themselves Wendat, People of the Peninsula, and their land Wendake. 'Wendat' could also refer to the confederacy. The name 'Huron' was given them by the French because of the coiffures of the warriors, which reminded them of the bristles on the spine of a boar. Diamond Jenness, *Indians of Canada* (Ottawa, 1932), 82. Odawa men affected a similar hairstyle. Apparently the term 'huron' also referred to manner of dress, implying rusticity.

27. Gabriel Sagard, *The Long Journey to the Country of the Hurons*, tr. H.H. Langton (Toronto, 1939), 104.

28. Gabriel Sagard, *Histoire du Canada, et voyages que les frères mineurs Recollects y ont faicts pour la conversion des infidelles*, 4 vols (Paris, 1636), III, 728.

29. The 30,000 estimate for the Hurons was made by Champlain, who spent a winter in Huronia. Geographer Conrad Heidenreich believes it is probably about one-third too large; he uses the figure 20,000. Heidenreich, *Huronia: A History and Geography of the Huron Indians 1600–1650* (Toronto, 1971), 96–103.

30. The Arendarhonons, 'the People of the Rock', had the second largest population among the Huron confederates. They may have joined about 1590, long after the two founding tribes confederated, perhaps early in the fifteenth century. Their late date of joining raises the question whether the Arendarhonons came from Stadacona.

31. Thwaites, ed., *Jesuit Relations*, X, 279–317; Bruce G. Trigger, *Children of Aataentsic*, 2 vols (Montreal and Kingston, 1976), I, 85–90; Jenness, *Indians of Canada*, 293.

32. Trigger, *Children of Aataentsic*, I, 197.

33. According to the Huron historian Margaret Vincent Tehariolina, the Huron were an offshoot of the Seneca and thus essentially the same people. Tehariolina, *La nation huronne, son histoire, sa culture, son esprit* (Québec, 1984), 96–7.

34. 'Oka and Its Inhabitants', in *The Life of Rev.*

Amand Parent, the first French-Canadian ordained by the Methodist Church (Toronto, 1887), 167.

35. Hiawatha has been identified as an Onondaga by birth and a Mohawk by adoption, and also as a Huron. Some of the versions of the origins of the league are told by Christopher Vecsey, 'The Story of the Iroquois Confederacy', *Journal of the American Academy of Religion* 54, 1 (1986): 79–106. Indian historian Bernard Assiniwi gives his version in *Histoire des Indiens du haut et du bas Canada: moeurs et coutumes des Algonkins et des Iroquois*, 3 vols (Québec, 1973), I, 111–24.

36. Alice Beck Kehoe, *The Ghost Dance* (Toronto, 1989), 115. Hiawatha's name, 'One Who Combs', was earned because he combed the snakes out of Thadodaho's hair. There are several versions of the story, one of which is recounted by Paul A.W. Wallace, *The White Roots of Peace* (Port Washington, NY, 1968), 11–17.

37. Daniel K. Richter, 'War, Peace, and Politics in Seventeenth Century Huronia', in Tkaczuk and Vivian, eds, *Culture and Conflict*, 285–6.

38. A report in the *Jesuit Relations* says that the Onondaga alternated men and women as head sachems (XXI, 201).

39. Nathaniel Knowles, 'The Torture of Captives by the Indians of Eastern North America', *Proceedings of the American Philosophical Society* 82, 2 (Mar. 1940), reprinted in *Scalping and Torture: Warfare Practices among North American Indians* (Ohsweken, Ont., 1985).

40. 'Anishinabe' (plural, Anishinabeg) means 'the people'. 'Ojibwa' translates as 'the talk of the robin'. The subsistence basis of the Odawa was dealt with by William Newbigging, 'The Ottawa Settlement of Detroit', paper presented to the Canadian Historical Association, 1992. In the seventeenth century, the closely related Ojibwa, Odawa, and Algonquin were loosely confederated into the Council of Three Fires. Today they are more or less merged as Ojibwa (Anishinabe), a process that took off during the nineteenth century. Nipissings, Saulteaux, and Mississauga are among others who are included.

41. A detailed study of the exploitation of wild rice and its cultural ramifications is that of Thomas Vennum, *Wild Rice and the Ojibway People* (St Paul, Minn., 1988). See also Kathi Avery and Thomas Pawlick, 'Last Stand in Wild Rice Country', *Harrowsmith* 3, 7 (May 1979): 32–47, 107.

42. Sagard, *Histoire du Canada*, IV, 846.

43. Catharine McClellan, verbal communication.

44. An early description of them is that of Jesuit Pierre Biard (1567?–1622) in Thwaites, ed., *Jesuit Relations*, II, 73–81. At Quebec, Jesuit Paul Le Jeune was vividly impressed with the facial painting of Amerindians, as well as by their general appearance when he saw a group of 600 warriors, 'tall, powerful', wearing, among other skins, those of elk, bear, and beaver. Thwaites, ed., *Jesuit Relations*, V, 23; VI, 25.

45. Alan D. McMillan, *Native Peoples and Cultures in Canada: An Anthropological Overview* (Vancouver, 1988), 246.

46. Samuel Hearne, *A Journey from Prince of Wales's Fort in Hudson's Bay to the Northern Ocean in the Years 1769 · 1770 · 1771 · 1772*, ed. J.B. Tyrrell (Toronto, 1911), 163.

47. J. Garth Taylor, 'The Case of the Invisible Inuit: Reconsidering Archaeology, History and Oral Tradition in the Gulf of St. Lawrence', in Allen P. McCarney, ed., *Thule Eskimo Culture: An Anthropological Perspective* (Ottawa, 1979). For the earlier view that the Inuit had reached the Gulf of St Lawrence, see Diamond Jenness, *Eskimo Administration: II: Canada* (Montreal, 1972; reprint), 7. This volume is part of a five-volume series on Inuit administration from Alaska to Greenland, published by the Arctic Institute in 1962–8.

48. The expression is borrowed from the Navajo's Blessingway ceremony.

49. Anthropologists once argued that the Great Plains could not have been inhabited to any extent before the advent of the horse and the gun. Clark Wissler wrote in 1906, 'the peopling of the plains proper was a recent phenomenon due in part to the introduction of the horse and the displacement of tribes by white settlement.' Wissler, 'Diffusion of Culture in the Plains of North America', *International Congress of Americanists*, 15th session (Quebec, 1906), 39–52. Although Wissler later modified his position, A.L. Kroeber in 1939 was still arguing that the Plains had developed culturally 'only since the taking over of the horse from Europeans'. Kroeber, *Cultural and Natural Areas of Native North America* (Berkeley, 1939), 76.

50. Thomas F. Kehoe, 'Corralling Life', in Mary LeCron Foster and Lucy Jane Botscharow, eds, *The Life of Symbols* (Boulder, Colo., 1990), 175–93.

51. Head-Smashed-In has been named a World Heritage Site by UNESCO.

52. Eleanor Verbicky-Todd, *Communal Buffalo Hunting among the Plains Amerindians: An Ethnographic and Historic Review* (Edmonton, 1984), 25–32. At a later date an offender risked being flogged or even (among the Kiowa) having his horse shot.

53. Richard G. Forbis, *A Review of Alberta Archaeology to 1964* (Ottawa, 1970), 27.

54. Harris, ed., *Historical Atlas of Canada*, plate 15. See also Brian O.K. Reeves, *Culture Change in the Northern Plains: 1000 B.C.–A.D. 1000* (Edmonton, 1983); H.M. Wormington and Richard G. Forbis, *An Introduction to the Archaeology of Alberta, Canada* (Denver, 1965), particularly the summary and conclusion, 183–201.

55. Jack Brink and Bob Dawe, *Final Report of the 1985 and 1986 Field Season at Head-Smashed-In Buffalo Jump* (Edmonton, 1989), 298–303.

56. Thwaites, ed., *Jesuit Relations*, X, 225.

57. On the importance of reciprocity, see Chrestien Le Clercq, *Nouvelle Relation de la Gaspésie*, 2 vols (Paris, 1691), I, 324. Europeans, not appreciating the principle of 'I give to you that you might give to me', quickly denigrated it as 'Indian giving', particularly when Amerindians, perceiving that the Europeans did not reciprocate, asked for their gifts back.

58. Chrestien Le Clercq, *First Establishment of the Faith in New France*, 2 vols, tr. John Gilmary Shea (New York, 1881), I, 124.

59. Knut R. Fladmark, *British Columbia Prehistory* (Ottawa, 1986), 50. In other words, trade in the region is at least 10,000 years old.

60. Recent research by historian Laurier Turgeon has revealed that copper, particularly in the form of kettles, was important in early Indian–Basque trade. See Turgeon, 'Basque–Amerindian Trade in the Saint-Lawrence during the Sixteenth Century: New Documents, New Perspectives', *Man in the Northeast* 40 (1990): 81–7.

61. Richter, 'War, Peace, and Politics', 286.

62. Harris, ed., *Historical Atlas of Canada*, plate 14.

63. Pierre de Lancre, *Tableau de l'inconstance des mauvais anges et démons, ou il est amplement traicté des sorciers et de la sorcellerie . . .* (Paris, 1612), 30; Lope de Isasti, *Compendio Historial de la M.N.Y.M.L. Provincia de la Guipúzcoa* (San Sebastian, 1850), 164. An early eighteenth-century observer reported that Inuktitut resembled Basque. See Nicolas Jérémie, *Twenty Years at York Factory, 1694–1714* (Ottawa, 1926), 17. He had a point: Basque is an agglomerative language, as are those of Amerindians and Inuit. The most authoritative work to date on Basques in America is Selma Huxley, ed., *Los vascos en el marco Atlantico Norte Siglos XVI y XVII* (San Sebastian, 1988).

64. Personal communication. The word 'adesquidex' is reported in Thwaites, ed., *Jesuit Relations*, III, 81. For other words, see Bakker's 'Two Basque Loanwords in Micmac', *International Journal of American Linguistics* 55, 2 (1989): 258–60. Another possible indication of Basque–Amerindian association is the presence of the 'lauburu' design motif among the Mi'kmaq and other Amerindian peoples, as well as among the Basques. The Basques consider the motif as a sort of national symbol and believe that it originated with them. See Peter Bakker, 'The Mysterious Link between Basque and Micmac Art', *European Review of Native American Studies* 5, 1 (1991): 21–4.

65. Elliott Coues, ed., *New Light on the Early History of the Great Northwest 1799–1814*, 3 vols (New York, 1897), I, 383.

66. *The Canadian Encyclopedia*, 4 vols (Edmonton, 1988), I, s.v. 'Chinook Jargon'; Geographic Board, Canada, *Handbook of Indians in Canada* (Ottawa, 1913), 94; Harold E. Driver, *Indians of North America* (Chicago, 1970), 213. An early study of Chinook is that of anthropologist Franz Boas, 'Chinook Songs', *Journal of American Folk-Lore* 1 (1888): 220–6; see also Robert L. Reid, 'The Chinook Jargon and British Columbia', *British Columbia Historical Quarterly* 6, 1 (1942): 1–11. George Woodcock describes the Chinook lingua franca as a simplification of Chinook proper, a Wakashan language, but with other elements added. Woodcock, *A Social History of Canada* (Toronto, 1989), 20–2.

67. A.I. Hallowell, 'Some Psychological Characteristics of the Northeastern Indians', in Frederick Johnson, ed., *Man in Northeastern North America* (Andover, Mass., 1940), 25. Amerindians much admired emotional control, giving rise to the European stereotype of the 'haughty Indian'.

68. Peter Caley, 'Canada's Chinese Columbus', *The Beaver* Outfit 313, 4 (1983): 4.

69. Thwaites, ed., *Jesuit Relations*, VI, 233. Later, Le Jeune referred to the Montagnais as 'real buffoons' (ibid., 243).

70. Le Clercq made the remark in reference to the Mi'kmaq (*Nouvelle Relation*, 388); however, hospitality is characteristic of tribal societies generally. It was also practised in pre-Renaissance Europe. Unfortunately, Europeans forgot their own traditions and did not generally reciprocate Amerindian hospitality. As a result, Amerindians continued the custom among themselves, but with Europeans they soon began to demand payment, much to the latter's disgust. Chrestien Le Clercq, *New Relation of Gaspesia*, ed. William F. Ganong (Toronto, 1910), 246.

71. *An Account of the Customs and Manners of the Micmakis and Maricheets, Savage Nations, Now Dependent on the Government of Cape Breton*

(London, 1758), 4.

72. Jay Miller, 'People, Berdaches, and Left-handed Bears', *Journal of Anthropological Research* 38, 3 (1982): 274–87. See also Colin Scott, 'Knowledge Construction among Cree Hunters: Metaphors and Literal Understanding', *Journal de la Société des Américanistes* 75 (1989): 193–208, particularly 194–5. Stephen A. McNeary discusses these beliefs as expressed by the Tsimshian in 'Image and Illusion in Tsimshian Mythology', in Jay Miller and Carol M. Eastman, eds, *Tsimshian and Their Neighbors of the North Pacific Coast* (Seattle, 1984). See also the description of the Amerindian estimation of the reasoning capacity of beavers in *Nouveaux Voyages de Mr. le Baron de Lahontan dans l'Amérique septentrionale*, 2 vols (The Hague, 1703), 155–9. The Jesuits observed that Amerindians considered all souls—minds—to be immortal, whether human or otherwise. (Thwaites, ed., *Jesuit Relations*, VI, 175–7.)

73. A. Irving Hallowell, 'Ojibway Ontology, Behavior and World View', in Hallowell, *Contributions to Anthropology* (Chicago, 1976). See also Catharine McClellan, *My Old People Say: An Ethnographic Survey of Southern Yukon Territory*, 2 vols (Ottawa, 1975), 86–8; Brian Swarbrick, 'A 9,000-year-old housing project', *Alberta Report* 18, 34 (1991): 50–1, concerning the belief of the Sto:Lo of British Columbia (a subgroup of the Coast Salish) that certain 'transformer' rocks were actually 'men of stone'. The Indians believed that being turned into stone was the fate of chiefs who did not share their wealth with their people.

74. Claude Lévi-Strauss has explored the general nature of these myths in *The Jealous Potter*, tr. Bénédict Chorier (Chicago, 1988). A study of the myths of a particular group, the Ojibwa of Big Trout Lake in Canada's Subarctic, showing their relationship to Amerindian myths as a whole, is that of Emmanual Désveaux, *Sous le signe de l'ours* (Paris, 1988). Nicolas Denys describes Indian love for storytelling in *The Description and Natural History of the Coasts of North America (Acadia)*, ed. William F. Ganong (Toronto, 1908), 418–19.

75. Jenness, *The Indians of Canada*, 173.

76. Le Clercq, *Nouvelle Relation*, 89.

77. For a general study of the phenomenon, see Tkaczuk and Vivian, eds, *Cultures in Conflict*.

78. By the end of the seventeenth century, a French officer would observe that northeastern Indians were 'never rash in declaring war; they hold frequent Councils before they resolve upon it.' R.G. Thwaites, ed., *New Voyages to North America by Baron de Lahontan*, 2 vols (Chicago, 1905), II, 507.

Le Clercq agreed: war, he wrote, was never declared except as a last resort on the advice of Old Men. (Le Clercq, *New Relation*, 269.) By mid-eighteenth century Thomas Jefferys expressed a different view: Indians, he wrote, rarely 'refuse to engage in a war to which they have been invited by their allies: on the contrary, they seldom wait till they are called to take up arms, the least motif being sufficient to determine them to it.' Jefferys, *The Natural and Civil History of the French Dominions in North and South America. I: A Description of Canada and Louisiana* (London, 1760), 53, 68. Le Jeune observed that even in wars 'some order' was maintained, and they were not undertaken 'without reason; and the commonest reason for their taking arms is when some Nation refuses to give satisfaction for the death of someone, and to furnish the presents required by the agreements made between them.' (Thwaites, ed., *Jesuit Relations*, X, 225.)

79. Daniel K. Richter, 'War and Culture: The Iroquois Experience', *William and Mary Quarterly* 40, 4 (1982): 528–59.

80. This is also true for tribal societies around the world. See Bruce Trigger, *The Indian and the Heroic Age of New France* (Ottawa, 1970), 4.

81. Erland Nordenskiöld, *Origin of the Indian Civilizations in South America* (Götenborg, 1931), 6–11, 74–6. A particularly interesting case of this 'leapfrogging' is that of the distinctive kayak-like Kutenai canoe; the only other place where such a river craft is found is on the Amur River, on the Chinese–Siberian border.

82. John Webster Grant, *Moon of Wintertime: Missionaries and the Indians of Canada in Encounter since 1534* (Toronto, 1984), 24. Grant points out that the ultimate religious symbol of the Indians is the circle, representing the circuit of the heavens, and adds that for the Christians the symbol might well be the arrow flying from creation to the final apocalypse.

83. For example, in the *Jesuit Relations* there is a chapter devoted to the differences between Europeans and Amerindians (XLIV, 277–309), but little, if any, mention is made of resemblances.

84. Le Clercq, *Nouvelle Relation*, 379–81.

85. Thwaites, ed., *Jesuit Relations*, III, 91. Although Biard was speaking about the Mi'kmaq, this was reported for other Amerindian societies as well. For example, see George Henry Loskiel, *History of the Missions of the United Brethren among the Indians in North America*, tr. C.I. LaTrobe (London, 1794), 132; Nicolas Perrot (1644–1718), *Mémoire sur les moeurs, coustumes et relligion des sauvages de*

l'Amérique Septentrionale (Leipzig and Paris, 1864; Johnson Reprint, 1968), 78.

86. A variant of this story appeared in the *Christian Science Monitor*, 19 Oct. 1989, 10.

Chapter 5

1. This chapter was developed from my 'Three Worlds, One Focus: Europeans Meet Inuit and Amerindians in the Far North', in Richard C. Davis, ed., *Rupert's Land: A Cultural Tapestry* (Calgary, 1988), 51–78. The term 'Inuit', meaning 'human beings' ('Inuk' in the singular), widely used among the people for themselves, was adopted by the Inuit Circumpolar Conference in 1977 for all the people formerly referred to as 'Eskimo'. People of the western Arctic are called Inuvialuit; other regional terms include 'Inuinait' and 'Inumagit'. (Bishop John R. Sperry, Yellowknife, in a letter published in *Arctic* 40, 4 [1987]: 364.) 'Inuit' has been officially adopted in Canada. See José Mailhot, 'L'Etymologie de "Esquimau": Revue et Corrigée', *Études/Inuit/Studies* 2, 2 (1978): 59–69; Yvon Csonka, *Collections arctiques* (Neuchâtel, Switzerland, 1988), 11, 18. On the question of first contacts with Europeans, see Robert McGhee, *Canada Rediscovered* (Hull, Que., 1991).

2. William R. Morrison, *Under the Flag: Canadian Sovereignty and the Native People in Northern Canada* (Ottawa, 1984), 97.

3. Ibid., 100.

4. Urs Bitterli, *Cultures in Conflict: Encounters between European and Non-European Cultures, 1492–1800*, tr. Ritchie Robertson (London, 1989).

5. This is the thesis of Tryggvi J. Oleson, *Early Voyages and Northern Approaches* (Toronto, 1963), 9.

6. Kaj Birket-Smith, *Eskimos* (Copenhagen, 1971), 13. An account of the first meeting of Greenland Skraelings with Norsemen is reproduced, ibid., 28–9. See also L.H. Neatby, 'Exploration and History of the Canadian Arctic', *Handbook of North American Indians, 5*, 337–90.

7. Wendell H. Oswalt, *Eskimos and Explorers* (Novato, Calif., 1979), 11.

8. Miller Christy, *The Voyages of Captain Luke Foxe of Hull, and Captain Thomas James of Bristol, in search of a North-West Passage, in 1631–32*, 2 vols (London, 1894), I, 104–5, 'Plefkins on Greenland'.

9. 'Arctic "little people" reported sighted', *Edmonton Journal*, 4 Nov. 1990.

10. For example, French cosmographer André Thevet (*c.* 1517–92) reported that Amerindians at first honoured Spaniards as prophets and even as gods. Thevet, *Les singularitez de la France Antarctique*, ed. Paul Gaffarel (Paris, 1878), 139–40.

11. Pierre Margry, *Découvertes et établissements dans l'ouest et dans le sud de l'Amérique septentrionale (1614–1754)*, 6 vols (Paris, 1976–86), VI, 181–2, extrait d'une lettre du sieur de Bienville au ministre, 10 avril 1706.

12. Nathaniel Wachtel, *The Vision of the Vanquished: The Spanish Conquest of Peru through Indian Eyes, 1530–1570* (London, 1977), 13–24; Bernardino de Sahagún (d. 1590), *Florentine Codex: General History of the Things of New Spain*, eds Arthur J.O. Anderson and Charles E. Dibble, 12 vols (Santa Fe, NM, 1970–5), XII, 4; Albert Garcia, *La découverte et la conquête du Pérou d'après les sources originales* (Paris, 1975), 68, 102, 125. The myth of the returning hero is far from dead. In Peru, for example, myth has it that the head of Inca Ri exists and is growing a body toward the feet. When his body is complete, the Inca will return. The Inca in this context is the 'originating principle of every being' and is reconstructing itself in the Andean underworld.

13. Bob Connolly and Robin Anderson, *First Contact: New Guinea Highlanders Encounter the Outside World* (New York, 1988), 34–55. Explorers visiting South Sea islands for the first time were taken for spirits (or gods, as it is often put); Captain James Cook (1728–79) experienced this reaction in Hawaii in 1778.

14. Charlotte M. Gradie, 'Spanish Jesuits in Virginia: The Mission That Failed', *Virginia Magazine of History and Biography* 96, 2 (1988): 144, 148.

15. On the English appreciation of Indian trade, see Peter Wraxall, *An Abridgement of the Indian Affairs Contained in Four Folio Volumes transacted in the Colony of New York, from the Year 1678 to the Year 1751*, ed. C.H. McIlwain (Cambridge, Mass., 1915), xxiii–xxvii.

16. R. Cole Harris, ed., *Historical Atlas of Canada*, I (Toronto, 1987), plate 16; Joel Berglund, 'The Decline of the Norse Settlements in Greenland', *Arctic Anthropology* 23, 142 (1986): 109–35.

17. See temperature graph in Harris, ed., *Historical Atlas of Canada*, plate 16.

18. The argument that the Norse communities did not adapt either culturally or technologically to changing conditions is presented by Thomas H. McGovern, 'The economics of extinction in Norse Greenland', in T.M. Wigley, M.J. Ingram, and G. Farmer, eds, *Climate and History* (Cambridge, 1981), 404–33. For example, they never adopted Inuit sea-mammal hunting technology (the most advanced in the world at that time) or skin boats, despite the unavailability of timber.

Culturally, they concentrated on bigger and more elaborate churches and the latest in European fashion and dress.

19. By the eighteenth century sentiments had changed, and when the celebrated explorer Louis-Antoine de Bougainville (1729–1811) brought a Tahitian to Paris, he was severely criticized for snatching a young man from the security of his native home to expose him to the corrupting influences of a European metropolis. In vain, Bougainville protested that the Tahitian had come voluntarily. The young man died on the return voyage, 1771.

20. W.A. Kenyon, *Tokens of Possession* (Toronto, 1975), 41, 121.

21. William C. Sturtevant and David Beers Quinn, 'This New Prey: Eskimos in Europe in 1567, 1576, and 1577', in Christian F. Feest, ed., *Indians and Europe* (Aachen, 1987), 80.

22. The term 'Qallunaat' or 'Kabloona' is thought to have originated from the Inuktitut term meaning 'people who pamper their eyebrows', perhaps a variation of 'qallunaaraaluit', which refers to materialism, interference with nature, and greed. See Minnie Aodla Freeman, *Life among the Qalunaat* (Edmonton, 1978), after the Foreword. Another translation that has been proposed is 'people with bushy eyebrows'.

23. Charles Francis Hall, *Arctic Researches and Life among the Esquimaux* (New York, 1865), 251, 290, 385.

24. Christy, *Voyages*, I, 90–1.

25. Ibid., I, 50ff.; Nicholas Jérémie, *Twenty Years at York Factory, 1694–1714* (Ottawa, 1926), 16.

26. This technology was used by the Thule of the eastern Arctic as well as the Punuk of the west, and had been adopted by the whalers of the west coast, such as the Nuu'chah'nulth (Nootka) of Vancouver Island. See Jean-Loup Rousselot, William W. Fitzhugh, and Aron Crowell, 'Maritime Economics of the North Pacific Rim', in Fitzhugh and Crowell, eds, *Crossroads of Continents: Cultures of Siberia and Alaska* (Washington, 1988), 163–72. A toggling harpoon found at L'Anse Amour Mound in Labrador, dating back to 7500 BP, may be the oldest such weapon in the world. See James A. Tuck and Robert McGhee, 'Archaic Cultures in the Strait of Belle Isle Region, Labrador', *Arctic Anthropology* 12, 2 (1975): 76–91. For a general description of Inuit whaling technology, see J. Garth Taylor, 'Inuit Whaling Technology in Eastern Canada and Greenland', in Allen P. McCartney, ed., *Thule Eskimo Culture: An Anthropological Perspective*

(Ottawa, 1979), 292–300.

27. Robert McGhee, *Ancient People of the Arctic* (Vancouver, 1996), 201–2, 221.

28. If an 'e' is substituted for the second 'o', Oupeeshepow becomes Oupeeshepew, which means 'always busy', according to Reg Louttit, chief of the Attawapiskat Cree north of Moose Factory. (Personal communication.)

29. Glyndwr Williams, ed., *Andrew Graham's Observations on Hudson's Bay 1767–91* (London, 1969), 204.

30. Toby Morantz, 'Oral and Recorded History in James Bay', in William Cowan, ed., *Papers of the Fifteenth Algonquian Conference* (Ottawa, 1984), 181–2.

31. Christy, *Voyages*, I, 137.

32. John S. Long, 'Narratives of Early Encounters between Europeans and the Cree of Western James Bay', *Ontario History* 80, 3 (1988): 230.

33. Clifford G. Hickey, 'An Examination of Processes of Cultural Change among Nineteenth Century Copper Inuit', *Études/Inuit/Studies* 8, 1 (1984): 13–35. Hickey also hypothesizes that the rich and varied cultural development among Alaskan Inuit testifies to the efficiency of their traditional trade with Siberia. Its roots go deep into the prehistory of Beringia and its environs. See Hickey, 'The Historic Beringian Trade Network: Its Nature and Origins', in McCartney, ed., *Thule Eskimo Culture*, 411–34.

34. Harris, ed., *Historical Atlas of Canada*, plate 23.

35. Colonial Office 194/27, 263, Palliser to the Secretary of the Admiralty, 25 Aug. 1766. Cited by W.H. Whiteley, 'The Establishment of the Moravian Mission in Labrador and British Policy, 1763–83', *Canadian Historical Review* 45, 1 (1964): 31, 39–40.

36. Jean Alfonce (Jean Fonteneau), *Les Voyages avantureux du Capitaine Ian Alfonce, Sainctongeois* (Poitiers, 1559), 27v; Giovanni Battista Ramusio, *Navigations et Voyages (XVI siècle)*, tr. Général Langlois and M.J. Simon (Paris, 1933), 111.

37. J. Callum Thomson, 'Cornered: Cultures in Conflict in Newfoundland and Labrador', in Diana Claire Tkacuzk and Brian C. Vivian, eds, *Cultures in Conflict: Current Archaeological Perspectives* (Calgary, 1989), 199. See above, Chapter 3, for a similar tradition among the southern Tutchone of the Yukon.

38. Sir Richard Whitbourne, *A Discourse and Discovery of New-found-land, with many reasons to prove how worthy and beneficiall a Plantation may there be made, after a far better manner than now is* (London, 1620), 2–4.

39. See George W. Brown, David M. Hayne, and Frances G. Halpenny, eds, *Dictionary of Canadian Biography* (Toronto, 1966), VI, s.v. 'Shawnadithit'. Harold Horwood, 'The people who were murdered for fun', *Maclean's,* 10 Oct. 1959, 27–43.

40. Ramsay Cook, ed., *The Voyages of Jacques Cartier* (Toronto, 1993), xxxiii–xxxiv.

Chapter 6

1. H.P. Biggar, ed., *The Voyages of Jacques Cartier* (Ottawa, 1924), 61–2. For an Indian view of 'an adventurer called Jacques Cartier' on the St Lawrence, see Bernard Assiniwi, *Histoire des Indiens du haut et du bas Canada: moeurs et coutumes des Algonkins et des Iroquois,* 3 vols (Québec, 1973), II, 29–81.

2. The generally accepted version of the origin of the name 'Canada' is that it derived from the Iroquoian 'ka-na-ta', meaning village. A good argument can be made, however, that it comes from the Montagnais 'ka-na-dun', meaning clean land. During the sixteenth century, the term 'Canadian' referred to the people of the North Shore, today's Montagnais, closely related to Cree and speaking a variation of the same language. These people were among the first trading partners of the French, which the Iroquois were not.

3. Olive Patricia Dickason, 'Concepts of Sovereignty at the Time of First Contacts', in L.C. Green and Olive P. Dickason, *The Law of Nations and the New World* (Edmonton, 1989), 223–4.

4. François de Belleforest and Sebastian Münster, *La Cosmographie universelle de tout le monde . . . ,* 2 vols (Paris, 1575), II, 2190–2.

5. Biggar, ed., *Voyages of Jacques Cartier,* 264; H.P. Biggar, ed., *A Collection of Documents Relating to Jacques Cartier and the Sieur de Roberval* (Ottawa, 1930), 463.

6. Marcel Trudel, *Histoire de la Nouvelle-France I: Les vaines tentatives, 1524–1603* (Montréal, 1963), 151–75; Antoine de Montchrestien, *Traicté de l'oeconomie politique . . . ,* S.l., s.d., 214.

7. Bruce G. Trigger and James F. Pendergast, 'Saint Lawrence Iroquoians', in Trigger, ed., *Handbook of North American Indians, 15: Northeast* (Washington, 1978), 358–9.

8. Biggar, ed., *Voyages of Jacques Cartier,* 158. It should be remembered that Cartier only spent a day at Hochelaga.

9. Belleforest and Münster, *La Cosmographie,* II, 2190–2.

10. Reuben Gold Thwaites, ed., *Jesuit Relations and Allied Documents,* 73 vols (Cleveland, 1896–1901), I, 105.

11. H.P. Biggar, ed., *The Works of Samuel de Champlain,* 6 vols (Toronto, 1922–36), V, 78.

12. Bruce G. Trigger, *Natives and Newcomers: Canada's 'Heroic Age' Reconsidered* (Montreal and Kingston, 1985), 146. In general, I am following Trigger, who discusses the question of the Laurentian Iroquoians in detail, 144–8.

13. Christopher Carlile's report in Richard Hakluyt, *The Principal Navigations, Voyages, Traffiques and Discoveries of the English Nation,* 12 vols (Glasgow, 1903–5), VIII, 145–6; Pierre-François-Xavier de Charlevoix, *Histoire et description générale de la Nouvelle France,* 3 vols (Paris, 1744), I, 21.

14. John Witthoft, 'Archaeology as a Key to the Colonial Fur Trade', in *Aspects of the Fur Trade* (St Paul, Minn., 1967), 57.

15. Biggar, ed., *Works of Samuel de Champlain,* II, 96.

16. Trigger, *Natives and Newcomers,* 96–100, 105–8.

17. Biggar, ed., *Voyages of Cartier,* 177–8. See also Trigger, *Natives and Newcomers,* 137, 147. Although Cartier's is a second-hand account and should therefore be treated with caution, there is archaeological evidence of large-scale warfare, as Trigger points out.

18. Trigger, *Natives and Newcomers,* 106–8. See also J.B. Jamieson, 'Trade and Warfare: Disappearance of the St. Lawrence Iroquoians', *Man in the Northeast* 39 (1990): 79–86. Jamieson argues that the dynamics of the St Lawrence Iroquois disappearance had nothing to do with European trade.

19. Alfred Goldsworthy Bailey, *The Conflict of European and Eastern Algonkian Cultures 1504–1700* (Toronto, 1969), xviii.

20. Biggar, ed., *Voyages of Cartier,* 76.

21. Charles A. Martijn, 'Innu (Montagnais) in Newfoundland', in William Cowan, ed., *Papers of the Twenty-first Algonquian Conference* (Ottawa, 1990), 227–64.

22. Thwaites, ed., *Jesuit Relations,* VI, 233.

23. Biggar, ed., *Works of Samuel de Champlain,* I, 98–102.

24. Bruce G. Trigger, *Indians and the Heroic Age of New France* (Ottawa, 1970), 10–11.

25. Eleanor Burke Leacock and Nancy Oestreich Lurie, eds, *North American Indians in Historical Perspective* (New York, 1971), 351.

26. Jan Kupp, 'Could the Dutch Commercial Empire Have Influenced the Canadian Economy during the First Half of the Eighteenth Century?', *Canadian Historical Review* 52, 4 (1971): 367–88.

27. Richard Glover, ed., *David Thompson's Narrative 1784–1812* (Toronto, 1962), 45. Thompson, Canada's greatest geographer, was apprenticed to

the Hudson's Bay Company in 1784 at the age of 14, serving with that company until 1797, when he defected to the North West Company.

28. Thwaites, ed., *Jesuit Relations*, V, 97.

29. Ibid., XXVI, 155–63; XVIII, 205; Pierre d'Avity, Seigneur de Montmartin, *Description générale de l'Amérique, troisième partie du Monde* . . . (Paris, 1660), 42–3. See also Trigger, *Natives and Newcomers*, 204–5.

30. See, for example, Bruce G. Trigger, 'Champlain Judged by His Indian Policy: A Different View of Early Canadian History', *Anthropologica* 13 (1971): 94–100. This was a special issue devoted to essays in honour of anthropologist Diamond Jenness.

31. Thwaites, ed., *Jesuit Relations*, VI, 7–19; Marcel Trudel, *Histoire de la Nouvelle France III: La seigneurie des Cent-Associés, 1627–1663* (Montréal, 1979), 128.

32. Trigger, *Indians and the Heroic Age*, 15; Denys Delâge, *Le pays renversé* (Montréal, 1985), 108.

33. Gabriel Sagard, *Histoire du Canada et voyages que les frères mineurs Recollects y ont faicts pour la conversion des infidelles*, 4 vols (Paris, 1636), II, 512.

34. Gabriel Sagard, *The Long Journey to the Country of the Hurons*, tr. H.H. Langton (Toronto, 1939), 45–6, 268.

35. Chrestien LeClercq, *First Establishment of the Faith in New France*, 2 vols, tr. John Gilmary Shea (New York, 1881), I, 136. See also Marc Lescarbot, *The History of New France*, ed. W.L. Grant, 3 vols (Toronto, 1907–14), III, 25–6; Nicolas Denys, *The Description and Natural History of the Coasts of North America (Acadia)*, ed. William F. Ganong (Toronto, 1908), 447–8; Thwaites, ed., *Jesuit Relations*, III, 81.

36. Charlevoix, *Histoire et description* III, 87–8.

37. J.B. Tyrrell, ed., *David Thompson's Narrative of His Explorations in Western America, 1784–1812* (Toronto, 1916), 206.

38. Claude C. Le Roy *dit* Bacqueville de la Potherie (1663–1736), *Histoire de l'Amérique septentrionale*, 4 vols (Paris, 1722), III, 176–7; Louis Armand de Lom d'Arce de Lahontan, *New Voyages to North America by Baron de Lahontan*, ed. R.G. Thwaites, 2 vols (Chicago, 1905), I, 82. There are reports of wasteful hunting for food as well. See, for example, Glyndwr Williams, ed., *Andrew Graham's Observations on Hudson's Bay 1767–91* (London, 1969), 154, 280.

39. Charlevoix, *Histoire et description*, I, 126.

40. Johannes de Laet, *L'Histoire du Nouveau Monde, ou Description des Indes occidentales* . . . (Leyden, 1640), 36.

41. Bernard G. Hoffman, *Cabot to Cartier* (Toronto, 1961); David Sanger, 'Culture Change as an Adaptative Process in the Maine–Maritimes Region', *Arctic Anthropology* 12, 2 (1975): 60–75. Sanger writes of the 'staggering' quantity of swordfish remains found on Monhegan Island, 12 miles offshore from Pemaquid, Maine. See Alice B. Kehoe, *North American Indians, A Comprehensive Account* (Englewood Cliffs, NJ, 1981), 212–13. A Penobscot whale hunt is described in 'A True Relation of the Voyage of Captaine George Waymouth, 1605, by James Rosier', in Henry Sweetser Burrage, ed., *Early English and French Voyages, Chiefly from Hakluyt, 1534–1608* (New York, 1952), 392. Pierre-Antoine-Simon Maillard mentioned whale fat and seal oil as principal features of a Mi'kmaq feast: 'Lettre de M l'Abbé Maillard sur les missions de l'Acadie, et particulièrement sur les missions Micmaques', *Soirées canadiennes* 3 (1863): 303. Seal oil was basic in early Mi'kmaq diet. Abbé J.A. Maurault (1819–70) makes the point that all the Natives of Acadia and New England shared a similar culture and lived in much the same manner. Maurault, *Histoire des Abenakis depuis 1605 jusqu'à nos jours* (Sorel, Québec, 1866), 9.

42. Thwaites, ed., *Jesuit Relations*, XLVII, 223; Denys, *Description and Natural History*, 196; D.B. Quinn, ed., *New American World: A Documentary History of North America to 1612*, 5 vols (New York, 1979), III, 348; Lescarbot, *History of New France*, II, 309.

43. 'Mi'kmaq' is widely accepted as meaning 'allies' (Jenness, *Indians of Canada*, 267), although this is not entirely certain. The term the Mi'kmaq used for themselves was 'El'nu', 'true men'. They were probably the Toudamans of Cartier and were certainly the Souriquois of Lescarbot; they were also called Tarratines, a reference to their trading proclivities. Wuastukwiuk (Maliseets) were known to Champlain and the early Jesuits as Etchemin or Eteminquois. The language of the Mi'kmaq shares certain characteristics with Cree, the most widespread of the Algonkian group, as well as with Arapaho of the central Plains.

44. Lescarbot, *History of New France*, III, 358–9.

45. Ibid., 312–13.

46. E.B. O'Callaghan and J.R. Brodhead, eds, *Documents Relative to the Colonial History of the State of New York*, 15 vols (Albany, NY, 1853–87), IX, 161.

47. Denys, *Description and Natural History*, 446–9.

48. Charlevoix, *Histoire et description*, I, 128; Denys, *Description and Natural History*, 195–6.

49. Archives de la Marine, Series B3, vol. IX, Sieur de Narp to Minister of the Marine, 23 Sept. 1671,

f.374. Cited by Cornelius J. Jaenen, *Friend and Foe: Aspects of French–Amerindian Cultural Contact in the Sixteenth and Seventeenth Centuries* (Toronto, 1976), 123.

50. Virginia Miller, 'Social and Political Complexity on the East Coast: The Micmac Case', in Ronald J. Nash, ed., *The Evolution of Maritime Cultures on the Northeast and Northwest Coasts of America* (Burnaby, BC, 1983), 51. In another article, Nash argues that the Mi'kmaq at the time of contact were on their way to becoming organized into chiefdoms. Ronald J. Nash, 'An Alternative History: Uninterrupted Views of Micmac Society', in Diana Claire Tkaczuk and Brian C. Vivian, eds, *Cultures in Conflict: Current Archaeological Perspectives* (Calgary, 1989), 187–94.

51. LAC, AC, C¹¹B 10:4–5, lettre de Joseph de Monbeton de Brouillan *dit* Saint-Ovide (governor of Ile Royale 1718–39), le 13 septembre 1727 en délibération du conseil, le 17 février 1728. Similar episodes occurred in the Caribbean. See Gullick, *Myth of a Minority*, 25.

52. Ellice B. Gonzalez, *Changing Economic Role for Micmac Men and Women: An Ethnohistorical Analysis* (Ottawa, 1981), 63, 87–8.

53. The remaining section of this chapter is based on my article, 'Amerindians between French and English in Nova Scotia, 1713–1763', *American Indian Culture and Research Journal* 20, 4 (1986): 31–56.

54. See, for example, the French King's permission to Pierre-Charles Le Sueur (1657–1704), a *coureur de bois*, to explore the possibility of developing copper and lead deposits in the Mississippi region. The document contains no hint that there might be Amerindian title to consider. Pierre Margry, *Découvertes et établissements dans l'ouest et dans le sud de l'Amérique septentrionale (1614–1754)*, 6 vols (Paris, 1976–86), VI, 62, extrait d'une lettre du Ministre de la Marine à Champigny, 27 avril 1697.

55. Article 17 reads: 'Les Sauvages qui seront amenés à la foi et en feront profession seront censés et réputés naturels français, quand bon leur semblera, et y acquérir, tester, succéder et accepter donations et legs, tous ainsi que les vrais régnicoles et originaires français, sans être tenus de prendre aucune lettre de déclaration ni de naturalité.' *Edits, ordonnances royaux, déclarations et arrêts du Conseil d'état du roi concernant le Canada*, 3 vols (Québec, 1854–6), I, 10.

56. *Collection de documents inédits sur le Canada et l'Amérique publiées par le Canada Français*, 3 vols (Québec, 1888–90), I, 196.

57. *Collection de manuscrits contenant lettres, mémoires et autres documents historiques relatifs à la Nouvelle-France*, 4 vols (Québec, 1883–5), I, 175, Instructions pour le Sieur de Courcelle au sujet des indiens. See also Dickason, 'Louisbourg and the Indians', 38, 109–25.

58. Similarly, when France was defeated in 1760, southern tribes refused to recognize the British takeover, as they had never given up their lands. See Jack M. Sosin, *Whitehall and the Wilderness* (Lincoln, Neb., 1961), 66.

59. The Dutch purchase of Manhattan Island (8,094 hectares; 20,000 acres) from the Canarsee Algonquians for 60 guilders ($24) in trade goods has become legendary in colonial lore.

60. 'Memorial for the Motives of the Savages, called Mickmakis and Maricheets for continuing the war with England since the last peace', in *An Account of the Customs and Manners of the Micmakis and Maricheets, Savage Nations, Now Dependent on the Government of Cape Breton* (London, 1758), 62–72. This is a translation, with one short paragraph missing, of one of the documents reproduced in *Les derniers jours de l'Acadie (1748–1758)*, ed. Gaston Du Boscq de Beaumont (Paris, 1899), 248–53.

61. This was the opinion of Sir Edward Coke (1552–1634), England's influential Chief Justice of the Common Pleas. See W.S. Holdsworth, *A History of English Law* (London, 1944), IX, 83–4; also, Robert A. Williams, *The American Indian in Western Legal Thought* (New York, 1990), 269–70.

62. 'Les sauvages sont peu de chose, étant nos alliées, mais pourraient devenir quelque chose de considérable, étant nos ennemis.' (LAC, AC, C¹¹B 4:251–6, 17 nov. 1719.)

63. LAC, AC, C¹¹B 12:37v, Saint-Ovide à Maurepas, 25 nov. 1731. See also *Account of the Customs and Manners*, 85, 'Letter from Mons. de la Varenne'. A major work on French missionary activity in Acadia is Lucien Campeau's compilation of documents, *Monumenta Novae Franciae I: La première mission d'Acadie (1602–1616)* (Québec, 1967). A second volume, *Monumenta Novae Franciae II: Etablissement à Québec (1616–1634)*, appeared in 1979.

64. LAC, Nova Scotia A 32:222, Maillard to Peregrine Hopson (governor of Nova Scotia, 1752–5), 11 Sept. 1748.

65. Thomas Pichon, *Lettres et Mémoires pour servir à l'histoire Naturelle, Civile et Politique du Cap Breton* (La Haye and London, 1760; Johnson Reprint, 1966), 101–2.

66. Thomas B. Akins, ed., *Selections from the Public*

Documents of the Province of Nova Scotia (Halifax, 1869), 178–9, Cornwallis to Captain Sylvanus Cobb, 13 Jan. 1749.

67. LAC, AC, C¹¹B, vol. 31:63, Raymond to minister, 19 nov. 1751. On French concern that the Mi'kmaq (as well as their other allies) had no causes for complaint about gift distributions, see LAC, AC, B, vol. 45/2:260–6 [122–9]; ibid., 267–73 [129–34].

68. Dickason, 'Louisbourg and the Indians', 111–14.

69. Thwaites, ed., *Jesuit Relations*, I, 177. There were also reports of them having lived to great ages in past times. Denys told of one Mi'kmaq said to have reached the age of 160 years. He attributed such long life to the Mi'kmaq habit of drinking 'only good soup, very fat'. He also reported that some Mi'kmaq could recite their genealogies back for 20 generations. Denys, *Description and Natural History*, 400, 403, 410.

70. LAC, AC, C¹¹A, vol. 122:13, 30 sept. 1705.

Chapter 7

1. Later, they were referred to as 'Canibas', wolves.

2. This chapter is a revision and extension of Olive P. Dickason, 'The French and the Abenaki: A Study in Frontier Politics', *Vermont History* 58, 2 (1990): 82–98.

3. Margaret Vincent Tehariolina, *La nation huronne, son histoire, sa culture, son esprit* (Québec, 1984), 94.

4. Dean R. Snow, *The Archaeology of New England* (New York, 1980), 38; Reuben Gold Thwaites, ed., *Jesuit Relations and Allied Documents*, 73 vols (Cleveland, 1896–1901), III, 111.

5. Marc Lescarbot, 'La Deffaite des Sauvages Armouchiquois', *History of New France*, ed. W.L. Grant, 3 vols (Toronto, 1907–14), III, 497–508. An English version of the poem, translated by Thomas Goetz, is in William Cowan, ed., *Papers of the Sixth Algonquian Conference, 1974* (Ottawa, 1975), 159–77. See also Pauline MacDougall Seeber, 'The European Influence on Abenaki Economics Before 1615', in William Cowan, ed., *Papers of the Fifteenth Algonquian Conference* (Ottawa, 1984), 203–14; Neal Salisbury, *Manitou and Providence: Indians, Europeans, and the Making of New England, 1500–1643* (Oxford, 1982), 68–70.

6. Pierre-Victor-Palma Cayet (1525–1610), *Chronologie septenaire de l'Histoire de la Paix entre les Roys de France et d'Espagne*, 2 vols (Paris, 1605), II, 423. This description was repeated by Lescarbot, *History of New France*, II, 169. He at first attributed it to Champlain but later said that Champlain had admitted that it was 'fabulous' and that the

Armouchiquois really were 'as good looking men . . . as ourselves, well built and agile'. (Ibid., 172.) Interestingly enough, Tartars were described as similarly deformed.

7. Henry P. Biggar, ed., *The Works of Samuel de Champlain*, 6 vols (Toronto, 1922–36), I, 356–7. Marc Lescarbot expresses the same sentiments in *History of New France*, II, 327. The suspicion of cannibalism is found in Thomas Corneille, *Dictionnaire universel, géographique et historique . . .*, 3 vols (Paris, 1708), I, s.v. 'Armouchiquois'; and Thwaites, ed., *Jesuit Relations*, II, 73.

8. Seeber, 'European Influence', 210.

9. In 1613, it was reported that there 'has always been war . . . between the Souriquois [Mi'kmaq] and Iroquois'. Thwaites, ed., *Jesuit Relations*, I, 105.

10. Asticou (*fl.* 1608–16) was a Penobscot sagamo, as Aguigueou presumably was also.

11. Thwaites, ed., *Jesuit Relations*, III, 71.

12. Biggar, ed., *Works of Champlain*, I, 103, 109; V, 313–16; P-André Sévigny, *Les Abénaquis habitat et migrations (17e et 18e siècles)* (Montréal, 1976), 64–5.

13. Thwaites, ed., *Jesuit Relations*, XII, 187; XXXIV, 57; XXXVIII, 41.

14. Gordon M. Day, 'Western Abenaki', in Bruce G. Trigger, ed., *Handbook of North American Indians, 15: Northeast* (Washington, 1978), 150. See also Thwaites, ed., *Jesuit Relations*, XXIV, 183–5; XXXVI, 103.

15. Native settlement patterns for 1625–1800 are mapped in R. Cole Harris, ed., *Historical Atlas of Canada*, I (Toronto, 1987), plate 47.

16. The phrase is used by Gordon Day, 'English–Indian Contacts in New England', *Ethnohistory* 9 (1962): 28.

17. Thomas Charland, *Histoire des Abénakis d'Odanak (1675–1937)* (Montréal, 1964), 44, 75–6; Jean Lunn, 'The Illegal Fur Trade Out of New France, 1713–60', *Canadian Historical Association Annual Report 1939*, 61–76.

18. *An Account of the Customs and Manners of the Micmakis and Maricheets, Savage Nations, Now Dependent on the Government of Cape Breton* (London, 1758), 89, 'Letter from Mons. de la Varenne'.

19. Abbé Joseph A. Maurault held that intermarriage in New France was at its peak during the first three-quarters of the seventeenth century. Maurault, *Histoire des Abenakis depuis 1606 jusqu'à nos jours* (Sorel, Québec, 1866; reprint 1969), 75.

20. *Documentary History of the State of Maine, Baxter Manuscripts* (Portland, Maine, 1916), XXIII, 56,

Conference with five of the Eastern Indians, Boston, 11 Jan. 1713.

21. E.B. O'Callaghan and J.R. Brodhead, eds, *Documents Relative to the Colonial History of the State of New York*, 15 vols (Albany, NY, 1853–87), IX, 871, M. de Vaudreuil to the Duke of Orleans, 1716; LAC, CO 217/1:364–6, 'Answer of Indians of Penobscot to the Commissioners', Apr. 1714; LAC, AC, C¹¹B 1:340v–42, lettre de Bégon, 25 sept. 1715, dans les déliberations de Conseil; 28 mars 1716, ibid., lettre de Costebelle, 7 sept. 1715, 335–6; Pierre-François-Xavier de Charlevoix, 'Mémoire sur les limites de l'Acadie', *Collection de manuscrits contenant lettres, mémoires et autres documents historiques relatifs à la Nouvelle-France*, 4 vols (Québec, 1833–85), III, 50–1. Also Charlevoix, *Histoire et description générale de la Nouvelle France*, 3 vols (Paris, 1744), II, 377.

22. *Journal of the Honorable House of Representatives of His Majesty's Province of Massachusetts-Bay in New-England* (Boston, 1744), 57, William Shirley to the General Court, 18 July 1744.

23. *Rapport de l'Archiviste de la Province de Québec*, 1947–8, 269, Vaudreuil au ministre, Québec, 16 sept. 1714.

24. O'Callaghan and Brodhead, eds, *Documents*, IX, 940, 'Memoir on the Present Condition of the Abenaquis, 1724'.

25. Olive Patricia Dickason, 'Louisbourg and the Indians: A Study in Imperial Race Relations, 1713–1760', *History and Archaeology* 6 (1976): 66–9. See also the warning of Jesuit Pierre de La Chasse (1670–1749) concerning what the Abenaki reaction to such a proposition would be, in *Collection de manuscrits*, III, 51, Memoire sur les limites de l'Acadie.

26. LAC, AC, B, vol. 47:1263–4 [279], 16 juin 1724; ibid., C¹¹B, vol. 7, 191–193v, 10 déc. 1725.

27. Sévigny, *Les Abénaquis*, 160–1.

28. LAC, AC, C¹¹B, vol. 5:187–187v, Saint-Ovide to minister, 5 sept. 1720.

29. O'Callaghan and Brodhead, eds, *Documents*, IX, 902, Vaudreuil to Governor William Burnett, 11 July 1721.

30. Dickason, 'Louisbourg and the Indians', 111–14; Victor Morin, *Les médailles décernées aux Indiens: Etude historique et numismatique des colonisations européennes en Amérique* (Ottawa, 1916).

31. Charlevoix, *Histoire et description*, I, 541; II, 404; Thwaites, ed., *Jesuit Relations*, LXVII, 121, letter from Jesuit Jean-Baptiste Loyard (1678–1731), written in 1721.

32. O'Callaghan and Brodhead, eds, *Documents*, IX, 948–9, Abstract of M. de Vaudreuil's Despatch;

ibid., 939–40, Memoir on the Present Condition of the Abenaquis, 1724.

33. An overview of Amerindian contributions to the establishment of New France is that of John H. Dickinson, 'Les Amérindiens et les débuts de la Nouvelle-France', *6e Convegno Internazionale di studi canadesi* (Selva di Fasano, 1985), Sezione III, 87–108.

34. The town had developed as a consequence of a mission founded by Sébastian Rale at Norridgewock (today's Old Point, South Madison, Maine) in 1694. Both he and Mog were killed there in 1724.

35. *Massachusetts Historical Society Collections*, 2nd ser. 8 (1826): 260, Eastern Indians' letter to the Governor, 27 July 1721.

36. Kenneth M. Morrison, *The Embattled Northeast: The Elusive Ideal of Alliance in Abenaki–Euramerican Relations* (Berkeley, 1984), 155–93; *Dictionary of Canadian Biography*, II, s.v. 'Rale, Sébastien'.

37. R.O. MacFarlane, 'British Policy in Nova Scotia to 1760', *Canadian Historical Review* 19, 2 (1938): 160.

38. Morrison, *Embattled Northeast*, 182–3.

39. For one such episode, see Charland, *Histoire*, 83.

40. *Dictionary of Canadian Biography*, III, s.v. 'Atecouando'. This chief is not to be confused with the earlier one of the same name, *fl.* 1701–26. Chiefs were referred to by their titles rather than their personal names.

41. *Dictionary of Canadian Biography*, III, s.v. 'Nodogawerrimet'.

42. Early accounts of the two military expeditions are to be found in Maurault, *Histoire des Abenakis*, 178–84, 186–93; however, the episodes are regularly included in histories of New France. Le Febvre de La Barre (1622–88) was governor-general of New France, 1682–5.

43. *Collection de manuscrits*, II, 54, Mémoire sur les limites de l'Acadie.

44. Colin G. Calloway, *Western Abenaki of Vermont, 1600–1800* (Norman, Okla., 1990), 248–51.

Chapter 8

1. Reuben Gold Thwaites, ed., *Jesuit Relations and Allied Documents*, 73 vols (Cleveland, 1896–1901), XVI, 231; XXXIX, 49. The leader of the French was Samuel de Champlain (*c.* 1570–1635), who is thus the Father of New France although he was never named governor.

2. Thwaites, ed., *Jesuit Relations*, XVI, 229; XXXIX, 49. There is a possibility that Hurons had met French

earlier, perhaps in 1600. See Bruce G. Trigger, *The Children of Aataentsic: A History of the Huron People to 1660*, 2 vols (Montreal and Kingston, 1976), I, 246.

3. Ibid., I, 30. Thwaites, ed., *Jesuit Relations*, XVI, 227–9.

4. Trigger, *Children of Aataentsic*, I, 226–7. Hochelagan refugees may even have joined the Abenaki and Five Nations. (Thwaites, ed., *Jesuit Relations*, XXII, 215.)

5. Trigger, *Children of Aataentsic*, I, 244; Thwaites, ed., *Jesuit Relations*, XVI, 227–9. Huron settlement patterns and missions are mapped in R. Cole Harris, ed., *Historical Atlas of Canada*, I (Toronto, 1987), plate 34. A good, short overview of the Huron is Conrad E. Heidenreich, 'Huron', in Bruce G. Trigger, ed., *Handbook of North American Indians, 15: Northeast* (Washington, 1987), 368–88.

6. Trigger, *Children of Aataentsic*, I, 30. Trigger has pointed to the fact that the Ataronchronon were not listed by the Jesuits in their description of the Huron Confederacy. See Thwaites, ed., *Jesuit Relations*, XVI, 227–9.

7. Trigger, *Children of Aataentsic*, I, 220–1. For sixteenth-century patterns of trade and warfare in the St Lawrence Valley, see Harris, ed., *Historical Atlas of Canada*, plate 33.

8. Gabriel Sagard, *Histoire du Canada, et voyages que les frères mineurs Recollects y ont faicts pour la conversion des infidelles*, 4 vols (Paris, 1636), I, 170.

9. Thwaites, ed., *Jesuit Relations*, XXV, 27.

10. Ibid., XX, 221.

11. Montmagny's name, referring to a mountain, suggested to the Iroquois their term for the French governor, 'Onontio', which means mountain. From then on, that was their name/title for New France's top official. Champlain, often referred to as New France's first governor, was never so named officially.

12. There were three Huron chiefs of that name recorded during the seventeenth century. The other two were both baptized: Jean Baptiste Atironta (d. 1650) and Pierre Atironta (d. 1672). See *Dictionary of Canadian Biography*, I.

13. Allumette Island is today's Morrison Island, near Pembroke, Ontario.

14. Of two other known chiefs with the name Tessouat, one met Champlain in 1603; his successor, also known as Le Borgne de l'Isle, died in 1636. See *Dictionary of Canadian Biography*, I.

15. Trigger gives a detailed account of Champlain's dealings with Tessouat in *Children of Aataentsic*, I, 281–6.

16. Ibid., 311. Biggar's identification of the village as Onondaga has been discounted by Trigger.

17. Thwaites, ed., *Jesuit Relations*, XXI, 203–5.

18. Ibid., XI, 207–9.

19. Trigger, *Children of Aataentsic*, II, 473–6. Brûlé had apparently retained more of his French connections than previously believed. See Lucien Campeau, *Monumenta Novae Franciae II: Etablissement à Québec (1616–1634)* (Québec, 1979), 808–9.

20. Thwaites, ed., *Jesuit Relations*, I, 103–7.

21. It should be noted, however, that Champlain's weapons and equipment were reputed to be the latest and best.

22. Charlevoix describes the clash in *Histoire et description générale de la Nouvelle France*, 3 vols (Paris, 1744), I, 150–2.

23. Ibid., 142. See also Trigger, *Children of Aataentsic*, I, 220.

24. A description of beaver, its living habits, how it was hunted, and how its pelts were processed for the fur trade is in Charlevoix, *Histoire et description*, III, 94–107. See also J.B. Tyrrell, ed., *David Thompson's Narrative of His Explorations in Western America* (Toronto, 1916), 1–4, 10–11, 198–200; Harold A. Innis, *The Fur Trade in Canada* (New Haven, 1930). The Huron trade is examined in detail in Conrad Heidenreich, *Huronia: A History and Geography of the Huron Indians 1600–1650* (Toronto, 1971), 242–99.

25. Thwaites, ed., *Jesuit Relations*, IV, 207; VIII, 57; Trigger, *Children of Aataentsic*, I, 336–7; Heidenreich, *Huronia*, 250.

26. Thwaites, ed., *Jesuit Relations*, V, 239; for 1645 and 1646, XXVII, 85, and XXVIII, 235. See also Trigger, *Children of Aataentsic*, II, 479; Heidenreich, *Huronia*, 280.

27. Thwaites, ed., *Jesuit Relations*, XXVII, 89–91; Trigger, *Children of Aataentsic*, II, 604–5. Also, George T. Hunt, *The Wars of the Iroquois* (Madison, Wis., 1960), 81–2, 87–104.

28. Philippe Jacquin, *Les indiens blancs* (Paris, 1989), 251 n37.

29. W.J. Eccles, *France in America* (New York, 1972), 57.

30. Thwaites, ed., *Jesuit Relations*, V, 263–5.

31. Ibid., X, 77.

32. In Acadia there had been confrontations between Jesuits and traders. See Marc Lescarbot, *The History of New France*, ed. W.L. Grant, 3 vols (Toronto, 1907–14), III, 48, 53.

33. The first missionary in Canada was the secular priest Jessé Fleché (d. ?1611), who spent a few weeks in Acadia in 1610, during which he baptized the

paramount Mi'kmaq chief Membertou, his family, and members of his band, for a total of 21 individuals. He was followed by the Jesuits, who arrived the following year, in 1611, and were incensed to find a Mi'kmaq with eight wives who considered himself a Christian. (Thwaites, ed., *Jesuit Relations*, I, 109–13.) The first two Jesuits to work in Canada were Pierre Biard (1567–1622) and Enemond Massé (1575–1646). The latter, trying to live Amerindian-style during the winter of 1611–12, lost so much weight that his host, Louis Membertou (son of the famous chief), feared he would die and that the French would accuse the Mi'kmaq of having killed him. (Lescarbot, *History of New France*, III, 56.)

34. The Recollects were naturally unhappy about this. For their views on the Jesuits, see Pierre Margry, *Découvertes et établissements dans l'ouest et dans le sud de l'Amérique septentrionale (1614–1754)*, 6 vols (Paris, 1976–86), I, 5–15.

35. *Treizième tome du Mercure François* (Paris, 1629), 32; Thwaites, ed., *Jesuit Relations*, VI, 25; Lescarbot, *History of New France*, I, 184. Also, Olive Patricia Dickason, *The Myth of the Savage and the Beginnings of French Colonialism in the Americas* (Edmonton, 1984), 251.

36. Thwaites, ed., *Jesuit Relations*, VI, 25.

37. Sagard's dictionary is reproduced in Sagard, *Histoire du Canada*, IV. On Le Caron, see Chrestien Le Clercq, *First Establishment of the Faith in New France*, tr. John Gilmary Shea, 2 vols (New York, 1881), I, 248–50. Brébeuf's translation into Huron of Ledesma's catechism is reproduced by Margaret Vincent Tehariolina, *La nation huronne, son histoire, sa culture, son esprit* (Québec, 1984), 436–50.

38. Cornelius J. Jaenen, *Friend and Foe: Aspects of French–Amerindian Cultural Contact in the Sixteenth and Seventeenth Centuries* (Toronto, 1976), 75.

39. Thwaites, ed., *Jesuit Relations*, VI, 147; XXV, 113.

40. Ibid., XI, 1472.

41. Sagard, *Histoire du Canada*, I, 165: '. . . le sang me gelle quand je r'entre en moy-mesme, & considere qu'ils faisoient plus d'estat d'un castor que du salut d'un peuple . . .' An article denying the Jesuit involvement in the fur trade is that of Patrick J. Lomasney, 'The Canadian Jesuits and the Fur Trade', *Mid-America* 15 (new ser., vol. 4), 3 (1933): 139–50.

42. Thwaites, ed., *Jesuit Relations*, V, 83; IX, 171–3; VI, 80–2. See also Jacquin, *Les Indiens blancs*, 74–5.

43. Thwaites, ed., *Jesuit Relations*, IX, 53.

44. Ibid., XVI, 53–5; IX, 239.

45. Trigger, *Children of Aataentsic*, I, 429–33; Gabriel Sagard, *The Long Journey to the Country of the Hurons*, ed. George M. Wrong (Toronto, 1939), 118, 183. Floppy-eared dogs would later fascinate Amerindians in British Columbia. On the French reaction to the Hurons' dogs, see Thwaites, ed., *Jesuit Relations*, VII, 43–5.

46. Thwaites, ed., *Jesuit Relations*, VIII, 109–13; Trigger, *Children of Aataentsic*, II, 495. The Jesuits did not make much use of their mill, as they found that sagamité was better when made from corn pounded in a wooden mortar, after the manner of the Hurons.

47. Apparently the Hurons had a more restrained reaction and refused to eat salted foods because they said they smelled bad. See Sagard, *Long Journey*, 118. The belief developed among the Amerindians that the reason Europeans were able to resist their witchcraft was because they ate so much salt.

48. Thwaites, ed., *Jesuit Relations*, V, 237; VIII, 119; XIII, 171. Biard reported a similar reaction on the part of the Mi'kmaq. Ibid., III, 123, cited by Dickason, *Myth of the Savage*, 276.

49. Cornelius J. Jaenen, 'Amerindian Views of French Culture in the Seventeenth Century', *Canadian Historical Review* 55, 3 (1974): 261–91.

50. Thwaites, ed., *Jesuit Relations*, XV, 163.

51. Ibid., XXVIII, 41.

52. Ibid., VIII, 43; XV, 113. At one point, Hurons rejected French kettles as possible sources of contagion. Thwaites, ed., *Jesuit Relations*, XV, 21.

53. Ibid., XIII, 147.

54. Ibid., XXXI, 121; XIX, 197–9; XX, 29.

55. Bruce G. Trigger, 'Early Iroquoian Contacts with Europeans', in Trigger, ed., *Handbook of North American Indians, 15: Northeast*, 352; Karl H. Schlesier, 'Epidemics and Indian Middlemen: Rethinking the Wars of the Iroquois, 1609–1653', *Ethnohistory* 23, 2 (1976): 129–45.

56. Denys Delâge, *Le pays renversé: Amérindiens et européens en Amérique du nord-est 1600–1664* (Québec, 1985), 106.

57. *Dictionary of Canadian Biography*, I, s.v. 'Oumasasikweie'.

58. Henry P. Biggar, ed., *The Works of Samuel de Champlain*, 6 vols (Toronto, 1922–36), VI, 379. Champlain, in his letter to Richelieu, 18 Aug. 1634, wrote: 'Pour les vaincre et réduire en l'obéissance de Sa Majesté, six-vingt hommes de France bien équipés avec les sauvages nos alliés suffiraient pour les exterminer ou les faire venir à la raison.'

59. Thwaites, ed., *Jesuit Relations*, XXVII, 89–91; XXVIII, 47.

60. See below, Chapter 10.

61. Guy Laflèche, *Les saints martyrs canadiens*, 2 vols (Québec, 1988), I, 32.

62. Thwaites, ed., *Jesuit Relations*, XXXII, 99.

63. José António Brandão, *Your Fyre Shall Burn No More* (Lincoln, Neb., 1998), 98–9. See also Roland Viau, *Enfants du néant et mangeurs d'âmes: guerre, culture et sociétés en Iroquoisie ancienne* (Montréal, 1997), 40–4.

64. The two were Brébeuf and Gabriel Lalement (1610–49). They were canonized in 1930, along with six others, all Jesuits except Jean de la Lande, a *donné*. See Laflèche, *Les saints martyrs*, I, 33, 299.

65. Tehariolina, *La nation huronne*, 47.

66. *Dictionary of Canadian Biography*, III, s.v. 'Orontony'.

67. Thwaites, ed., *Jesuit Relations*, XLIII, 265.

68. Denys Delâge, 'Les Iroquois chrétiens des "réductions", 1667–1770. I—Migration et rapports avec les Français', *Recherches amérindiennes au Québec* 20, 1–2 (1991): 64.

69. Ibid., 59–70.

70. Tehariolina, *La nation huronne*, 306–9; *Dictionary of Canadian Biography*, II. Kondiaronk was 'Adario' in Lahontan's dialogues.

71. LAC, MG 8: Documents relatifs à la Nouvelle-France et au Québec (XVIIe–XXe siècles), E1, f60, James Murray, *Report of the Government of Quebec and dependencies thereof, c.* 1762. The promise contained in the document was defined by the Supreme Court of Canada as a treaty. See John Thompson, 'The Treaties of 1760', *The Beaver* 76, 2 (1996): 23–8.

72. '230-year-old treaty guaranteeing Hurons' rights is valid: top court', *The Gazette*, Montreal, 25 May 1990, A5. For the historical background, see Georges Sioui, *Pour une autohistoire amérindienne* (Québec, 1989), 111–30. The Hurons had been arrested for cutting saplings in a provincial park north of Quebec City to build a sweat lodge. See also Chapter 23.

73. John Webster Grant, *Moon of Wintertime: Missionaries and the Indians of Canada in Encounter since 1534* (Toronto, 1984), 45–6.

74. Thwaites, ed., *Jesuit Relations*, XVIII, 103–7. Jesuit historian Lucien Campeau challenges this, on the grounds that the Amerindian tradition of tolerance allowed Christians and non-Christians to live in peace. Campeau, *La Mission des Jésuites chez les Hurons 1634–1650* (Montréal, 1987), 276–8.

75. Thwaites, ed., *Jesuit Relations*, LII, 179; Henry Warner Bowden, *American Indians and Christian Missions* (Chicago, 1981), 88; Trigger, *Natives and Newcomers*, 255.

76. Thwaites, ed., *Jesuit Relations*, XVI, 33; Trigger, *Children of Aataentsic*, II, 547, 700; Trigger, *Natives and Newcomers*, 254–5; Bowden, *American Indians and Christian Missions*, 87–8. Converts denied commercial reasons for their actions. (Thwaites, ed., *Jesuit Relations*, XX, 288.)

77. Grant, *Moon of Wintertime*, 42; Thwaites, ed., *Jesuit Relations*, XVII, 47–9. Chihwatenha was killed in 1640, reportedly by the Seneca. Bruce Trigger, however, maintains that it was the deed of his fellow villagers, who believed he was a sorcerer and had turned against them. See Trigger, *Natives and Newcomers*, 249. See also Thwaites, ed., *Jesuit Relations*, XIX, 151–7; XXIII, 195.

78. LAC, MG 1, AC, C¹¹C, vol. 16:4 (seconde pièce, Mémoire sur l'Ile Royale, 1750: '. . . il y a lieu de croire qu'ils [the Indians] n'Embrassent la religion Catholique que par Interest . . . ils la pratique en Apparence, en font les Exercices, vont même à confesse, mai ils s'y presentent faux honte d'avouer leur turpitude, d'ou il est apparent qu'ils en sortent sans repentir de leurs fautes.'

79. John S. Long makes this point in connection with the Cree and Montagnais of James Bay, in 'Manitu, Power, Books and Wiihtikow: Some Factors in the Adoption of Christianity by Nineteenth-Century Western James Bay Cree', *Native Studies Review* 3, 1 (1987): 1–30.

80. Thwaites, ed., *Jesuit Relations*, V, 153–5.

81. Such behaviour has been observed among northern Amerindians. See Jean-Guy Goulet, 'Religious Dualism among Athapaskan Catholics', *Canadian Journal of Anthropology* 3, 1 (1982): 1–18.

82. Thwaites, ed., *Jesuit Relations*, XXII, 73. See also ibid., XVII, 211.

83. Ibid., XXXIV, 123.

84. Ibid., 105, 217. At times Jesuits were allowed to address councils, as Brébeuf did in 1638 at a meeting that had been especially convoked to hear him. (Ibid., XV, 113–15.)

85. Ibid., XXII, 179, 307, concerning the number of guns among the Hurons; Elizabeth Tooker, 'The Iroquois Defeat of the Huron: A Review of Causes', *Pennsylvania Archaeologist* 33, 1–2 (1963): 115–23. On the reasons why the Iroquois adopted firearms despite their inefficiency at that period, see Thomas B. Abler, 'European Technology and the Art of War in Iroquoia', in Diana Claire Tkaczuk and Brian C. Vivian, eds, *Cultures in Conflict: Current Archaeological Perspectives* (Calgary, 1989), 173–282. Some French officials were under the impression that the Iroquois were the first Amerindians to use guns. (LAC, AC, C¹¹A, 122:202–3.)

86. Campeau, *La Mission des Jésuites*, 345–59.

87. See W.J. Eccles, *The Canadian Frontier 1534–1760* (Toronto, 1969), ch. 6.

88. Thwaites, ed., *Jesuit Relations*, XL, 215.

89. For a study of the factors that led to the 1701 peace, see Gilles Havard, *La grande paix de Montréal de 1701* (Montréal, 1992).

Chapter 9

1. Much of the material for this chapter has been drawn from Olive Patricia Dickason, 'Three Worlds, One Focus: Europeans Meet Inuit and Amerindians in the Far North', in Richard C. Davis, ed., *Rupert's Land: A Cultural Tapestry* (Calgary, 1988), 51–78.

2. On the prehistoric trade of the Huron, see Bruce G. Trigger, *The Children of Aataentsic: A History of the Huron People to 1660*, 2 vols (Montreal and Kingston, 1976), I, 176–86; on its development after the arrival of the French, ibid., II, 608–12.

3. Reuben Gold Thwaites, ed., *Jesuit Relations and Allied Documents*, 73 vols (Cleveland, 1896–1901), I, 101.

4. Five northern routes, some of them said to be ancient, were described by the Jesuits, with the comment that they were 'more difficult to travel than the high road from Paris to Orleans'. The fifth route was for peoples north and west of Lake Superior. Thwaites, ed., *Jesuit Relations*, XLIV, 239–45; LVI, 203. See also Toby Morantz, 'The Fur Trade and the Cree of James Bay', in Carol M. Judd and A.J. Ray, eds, *Old Trails and New Directions: Papers of the Third North American Fur Trade Conference* (Toronto, 1980), 23–4.

5. Alice Beck Kehoe, *The Ghost Dance* (Toronto, 1989), 115.

6. James W. VanStone, 'Northern Athapaskans: People of the Deer', in William H. Fitzhugh and Aron Crowell, eds, *Crossroads of Continents: Cultures of Siberia and Alaska* (Washington, 1988), 68. The increase in famine manifested itself very early. In 1635, starving Amerindians of the Gaspé allegedly killed and ate a young boy whom the Basques had left with them to learn their language. (Thwaites, ed., *Jesuit Relations*, VIII, 29.) Pierre-François-Xavier Charlevoix would later observe that although Amerindians knew how to endure hunger, they still died from it. See Charlevoix, *Histoire et description générale de la Nouvelle France*, 3 vols (Paris, 1744), III, 338.

7. Nicholas Denys, *The Description and Natural History of the Coasts of North America (Acadia)*, ed. William F. Ganong (Toronto, 1908), 440–1.

8. Missionaries and traders soon noted how much the northerners prized tobacco. Thwaites, ed., *Jesuit Relations*, LVI, 189.

9. Christopher L. Miller and George R. Hamell, 'A New Perspective on Indian–White Contact: Cultural Symbols and Colonial Trade', *Journal of American History* 73, 3 (1986): 311–28.

10. Pierre Margry, *Découvertes et établissements dans l'ouest et dans le sud de l'Amérique septentrionale (1614–1754)*, 6 vols (Paris, 1976–86), I, 119. On the dangers of the rivers, ibid., 164–5.

11. Ibid., VI, 482, extrait des lettres de Sieur de Fabry à l'occasion du voyage à Santa Fé. Experienced travellers took rolls of birchbark with them, not only for the repair of canoes but also for the construction of shelters. Ibid., I, 120, Récit de ce qui c'est passé de plus remarquable dans le voyage de MM Dollier et Galinée, 1669–70.

12. Ibid., I, 118. See also Henry Sweetser Burrage, ed., *Early English and French Voyages, Chiefly from Hakluyt* (New York, 1952), 368.

13. Hudson's Bay Official London Correspondence Book Outwards, 1679–1741, A.6/1:86–86v, HBC Archives. See also Arthur J. Ray, *Indians in the Fur Trade: Their Role as Trappers, Hunters, and Middlemen in the Lands Southwest of Hudson Bay 1660–1870* (Toronto, 1974), 75–9. Some historians maintain that the gun was initially of very limited usefulness. See Morantz, 'The Fur Trade and the Cree of James Bay', 41; Arthur J. Ray, 'Indians as Consumers', in Judd and Ray, eds, *Old Trails and New Directions*, 261.

14. Samuel Hearne, *A Journey from Prince of Wales's Fort in Hudson's Bay to the Northern Ocean in the Years 1769 · 1770 · 1771 · 1772*, ed. J.B. Tyrell (Toronto, 1911), 310.

15. Rolf Knight, *Ecological Factors in Changing Economy and Social Organization among the Rupert House Cree* (Ottawa, 1968), 20.

16. Daniel Francis and Toby Morantz, *Partners in Furs: A History of the Fur Trade in Eastern James Bay 1600–1870* (Montreal and Kingston, 1983), 61–3, 86, 170. John M. Cooper describes early trapping techniques in *Snares, Deadfalls, and Other Traps of the Northern Algonquians and Northern Athapaskans* (Washington, 1938).

17. Toby Morantz, 'Old Texts, Old Questions—Another Look at the Issue of Continuity and the Early Fur Trade Period', paper presented to the American Society for Ethnohistory, Chicago, 1989.

18. Arthur Dobbs, *An Account of the Countries adjoining to Hudson's Bay* (London, 1744; reprint New York, 1967), 59.

19. J.B. Tyrrell, ed., *David Thompson's Narrative of His*

Explorations in Western America, 1784–1812 (Toronto, 1916), 164. A summary of early accounts of this event is in Ray, *Indians in the Fur Trade*, 4–11.

20. Peter A. Cumming and Neil H. Mickenberg, eds, *Native Rights in Canada* (Toronto, 1972), 142.

21. HBC Official London Correspondence Book Outwards 1679–1741, A.6/1.6, HBC Archives; E.E. Rich, ed., *Letters Outward 1679–1694* (Toronto, 1948), 9; Cumming and Mickenberg, eds, *Native Rights in Canada*, 142 n36; Francis and Morantz, *Partners in Furs*, 23. These instructions were repeated to Nixon's successor, Henry Sergeant, in 1683. See A.6/1:30v, HBC Archives.

22. John Oldmixon, *The History of Hudson's-Bay, Containing an Account of its Discovery and Settlement, the Progress of It, and the Present State; of the Indians, Trade and Everything Else Relating to It*, in J.B. Tyrrell, ed., *Documents Relating to the Early History of Hudson Bay* (Toronto, 1931), 400–1. See also Arthur J. Ray and Donald Freeman, *'Give Us Good Measure': An Economic Analysis of Relations between the Indians and the Hudson's Bay Company before 1763* (Toronto, 1978), 60–1; E.E. Rich, 'Trade Habits and Economic Motivation among the Indians of North America', *Canadian Journal of Economics and Political Science* 26 (1960): 35–53 (reprinted, with illustrations added, under the title 'The Indian Traders' in *The Beaver* Outfit 301 [1970]: 5–20); A. Rotstein, 'Trade and Politics: An Institutional Approach', *Western Canadian Journal of Anthropology* 3, 1 (1972): 1–28.

23. Francis and Morantz, *Partners in Furs*, 213–24; Edwin Thompson Denig, *Five Indian Tribes of the Upper Missouri*, ed. John C. Ewers (Norman, Okla., 1961), 112.

24. Mary Black-Rogers, 'Varieties of "Starving": Semantics and Survival in the Subarctic Fur Trade, 1750–1850', *Ethnohistory* 33, 4 (1986): 368; Bruce M. White, '"Give Us a Little Milk": The Social and Cultural Significance of Gift Giving in the Lake Superior Fur Trade', in T.C. Buckley, ed., *Rendezvous: Selected Papers of the Fur Trade Conference 1981* (St Paul, Minn., 1984), 187.

25. The French had earlier experienced difficulty in this regard. Galinée reported that even in his day (the second half of the seventeenth century) they had not yet mastered the techniques of fishing in the northern rivers. Margry, *Découvertes et établissements*, I, 163–4.

26. Carol M. Judd, 'Sakie, Esquawenoe, and the Foundation of a Dual-Native Tradition at Moose Factory', in Shepard Krech III, ed., *The Subarctic Fur Trade* (Vancouver, 1984), 87.

27. For details, see Chapter 16, pp. 209–10.

28. Hearne, *Journey to the Northern Ocean*, 185n. For a similar reaction on the part of the Inuit at a later period, see Charles Francis Hall, *Arctic Researches and Life among the Esquimaux* (New York, 1865), 297. Jesuits reported in 1646 that when Amerindians killed animals, 'they eat the meat of these without bread, without salt, and without other sauce than the appetite.' (Thwaites, ed., *Jesuit Relations*, XXIX, 75.) 'Appetite supplies the place of all sauces . . . they dined without bread and without wine.' (Ibid., XXXII, 265.)

29. HBC Archives, 1742, B.135/a/11:67, Moose Fort Journal, 1742, cited by Francis and Morantz, *Partners in Furs*, 58–9.

30. Hearne, *Journey to the Northern Ocean*, 306.

31. Dobbs, *An Account*, 42.

32. Hearne, *Journey to the Northern Ocean*, 85–6n.

33. Sylvia Van Kirk, 'Thanadelthur', *The Beaver* Outfit 304, 4 (1974): 40–5; Keith Crowe, *A History of the Original Peoples of Northern Canada* (Montreal and Kingston, 1991), 76–8. James Houston, *Running West* (Toronto, 1989), is a historical novel detailing Thanadelthur's life.

34. The French had long since learned the truth of this. Gabriel Sagard said the French should never go into the woods without an experienced guide, as even such travel aids as a compass could fail. He told of Étienne Brûlé, an experienced *coureur de bois*, who had once lost his way and mistakenly wandered into an Iroquois village, where he escaped torture and death only by a lucky happenstance. Sagard, *Histoire du Canada, et voyages que les frères mineurs Recollects y ont faicts pour la conversion des infidelles*, 4 vols (Paris, 1636), I, 466–7; II, 429–30. Champlain had got lost in Huronia. See Marcel Trudel, *Histoire de la Nouvelle France II: Le comptoir: 1604–1627* (Montréal, 1966), 221. A young Amerindian lad, raised by the French and christened Bonaventure, died as a result of being lost in the woods following an accident. (Thwaites, ed., *Jesuit Relations*, IX, 221.) There has never been a study of the economic value of Amerindian contributions to European voyages of discovery in the interior of the Americas, if such would be possible. It must have been considerable.

35. Richard Glover, ed., *David Thompson's Narrative 1784–1812* (Toronto, 1962), 90.

36. Actually, the French had encountered bison in 'Florida' much earlier, as attested by an engraving of bison-hunting in André Thevet's *La Cosmographie Universelle*, 2 vols (Paris, 1575), II, 1007v.

37. When Hearne returned from his voyage, his

guides Matonabbee and Idotlyazee provided a map of the lands they had visited. June Helm's study of the chart revealed how it co-ordinates with modern maps. See Helm, 'Matonabbee's Map', *Arctic Anthropology* 26, 2 (1989): 28–47. For other Amerindian maps, see R. Cole Harris, ed., *Historical Atlas of Canada*, I (Toronto, 1987), plate 59. Arctic explorer Sir John Franklin (1786–1847) availed himself of Amerindian and Inuit sketch maps. See Charles Mair, *Through Mackenzie's Basin* (Toronto, 1908), 96–7. About 100 Inuit maps drawn on paper for explorers have survived. Among themselves, Inuit either gave verbal instructions or drew maps on sand or snow. See David F. Pelly, 'How the Inuit Find Their Way in the Trackless Arctic', *Canadian Geographic* 3, 4 (1991): 58–64.

38. Bob Beal, 'French Reap Reward from Western Posts', *Edmonton Journal*, 24 Sept. 1986, E1.

39. Bruce G. Trigger, *Natives and Newcomers: Canada's 'Heroic Age' Reconsidered* (Montreal and Kingston, 1985), 184–94. For the varying effects of the trade on northern Native societies and economies, see Krech III, ed., *Subarctic Fur Trade*.

40. For a nineteenth-century observation of this characteristic, see Arthur J. Ray, *The Canadian Fur Trade and the Industrial Age* (Toronto, 1990), 91. It is still evident today.

41. HBC Archives, B.135/a/11:69, cited by Francis and Morantz, *Partners in Furs*, 59.

42. HBC Archives, B.135/a/31:27v–29v, Moose Fort Journal 1758–9.

43. HBC Archives, A.6/4:86v, cited by Francis and Morantz, *Partners in Furs*, 91.

44. John S. Long, 'Manitu, Power, Books and Wiihtikow: Some Factors in the Adoption of Christianity by Nineteenth-Century Western James Bay Cree', *Native Studies Review* 3, 1 (1987): 8–9.

45. Eric Ross, *Beyond the River and the Bay* (Toronto, 1970), 29–31.

46. Ibid., 31.

47. Daniel Will Harmon, *Sixteen Years in the Indian Country*, ed. W. Kaye Lamb (Toronto, 1957), 55.

48. Charles Bishop, 'The Henley House Massacres', *The Beaver* Outfit 307 (1976): 36–41; Sylvia Van Kirk, *Many Tender Ties: Women in Fur-Trade Society 1670–1870* (Norman, Okla., 1983), 43–4. Marcel Giraud wrote that the *coureurs de bois* instigated the massacre: *The Métis in the Canadian West*, tr. George Woodcock, 2 vols (Edmonton, 1986), I, 141.

49. Nicolas Perrot (*c.* 1644–1717), *Mémoire sur les moeurs, coustumes et relligion des sauvages de l'Amérique septentrionale*, ed. J. Tailhan (Montréal, 1973), 126–8, 292–4; Thwaites, ed., *Jesuit Relations*, LV, 105–15; Margry, *Découvertes et établissements*, I, 96–9.

50. William W. Warren, *History of the Ojibway People* (St Paul, Minn., 1984), 131.

51. Ibid., 131–2.

52. 'Ainsy cette nation peut connoistre qu'on prétend d'en demeurer le maistre.' (Margry, *Découvertes et établissements*, I, 89, second extrait de 'l'addition au mémoire de Jean Talon au Roy', 10 nov. 1670.) Voyages of exploration were usually undertaken for the purpose of territorial expansion; for example, La Vérendrye on his western voyage left a trail of lead plaques indicating that the region was claimed by France (ibid., VI, 609), as did Galinée and Dollier de Casson, whose ostensible mission was the spreading of the faith.

53. Thwaites, ed., *Jesuit Relations*, LXVIII, 283.

54. Donald B. Smith, 'Who Are the Mississauga?', *Ontario History* 67, 4 (1975): 211–23; Leroy V. Eid, 'The Ojibway–Iroquois War: The War the Five Nations Did Not Win', *Ethnohistory* 17, 4 (1979): 297–324.

55. James G.E. Smith, 'The Western Woods Cree: Anthropological Myth and Historical Reality', *American Ethnologist* 14 (1987): 434–48.

56. L.J. Burpee, ed., *Journals and Letters by Pierre Gaulthier de Varennes et de La Vérendrye* (Toronto, 1927), 25.

57. John S. Milloy, *The Plains Cree: Trade, Diplomacy and War, 1790–1870* (Winnipeg, 1988), 41–66, 119–20.

Chapter 10

1. There is an enormous body of literature on the Iroquois wars. Besides George T. Hunt's *The Wars of the Iroquois* (Madison, Wis., 1967), see W.J. Eccles, *Canada Under Louis XIV 1663–1701* (Toronto, 1964), especially chs 7–10; Eccles, *Frontenac the Courtier Governor* (Toronto, 1959), especially chs 8–10; Francis Jennings, *The Ambiguous Iroquois Empire* (New York, 1984). A detailed account of the war to 1646 is Leo-Paul Desrosier's *Iroquoisie* (Montréal, 1947). Bruce G. Trigger deals with aspects of Iroquoian conflicts in *Natives and Newcomers* (Montreal and Kingston, 1985). Among articles not cited in the bibliography are Keith F. Otterbein, 'Why the Iroquois Won: An Analysis of Iroquois Military Tactics', *Ethnohistory* 11 (1964): 56–63; and Otterbein, 'Huron vs. Iroquois: A Case Study of Intertribal Warfare', *Ethnohistory* 26, 2 (1979): 141–52.

2. *Dictionary of Canadian Biography*, I, s.v. 'Pieskaret';

Claude C. Le Roy *dit* Bacqueville de la Potherie, *Histoire de l'Amérique septentrionale*, 4 vols (Paris, 1722), I, 297–303. See also Guy Laflèche, *Les saints martyrs canadiens*, 2 vols (Québec, 1988), II, 159–60, 162–3.

3. Desrosiers, *Iroquoisie*, 304.

4. Pierre-François-Xavier de Charlevoix, *Histoire et description générale de la Nouvelle France*, 3 vols (Paris, 1744), II, 160–1.

5. François Dollier de Casson, *A History of Montreal 1640–1672*, tr. and ed. Ralph Flenley (London, 1928), 131; originally published in Montreal, 1868, from a copy of a Paris manuscript brought to Canada by Louis-Joseph Papineau, leader of the 1837–8 rebellions in Lower Canada. The manuscript does not bear Dollier de Casson's name but has been attributed to him on the strength of internal evidence.

6. Ibid., 117–18, 139.

7. LAC, MG 7, 1a, 10, Collection Moreau, vol. 841:251v, d'Endemare à François de la Vie, Fort Richelieu, 2 sept. 1644.

8. Bibliothèque Nationale, Paris, Fonds Français, vol. 10204, ff. 203–4.

9. Reuben Gold Thwaites, ed., *Jesuit Relations and Allied Documents*, 73 vols (Cleveland, 1896–1901), XXVIII, 57.

10. Cited by William Kip, *The Early Jesuit Missions in North America* (New York, 1846), 54. These observations would be repeated almost exactly by the British in Australia during the nineteenth century as they settled in lands the Aborigines considered theirs. See, for example, Henry Reynolds, *Frontier* (Sydney and London, 1987), 3–57.

11. Thwaites, ed., *Jesuit Relations*, XXXIII, 229–49; Trigger, *Natives and Newcomers*, 265.

12. Dollier de Casson, *History of Montreal*, 127, 143, 155.

13. John A. Dickinson, 'La guerre iroquoise et la mortalité en Nouvelle-France, 1608–1666', *Revue d'histoire de l'Amérique française* 36, 1 (1982): 31–47; Bruce G. Trigger, 'Early Iroquoian Contacts with Europeans', in Trigger, ed., *Handbook of North American Indians, 15: Northeast* (Washington, 1978), 352.

14. LAC, AC, C¹¹G, vol. 6:69–70v, Mémoire sur les compagnies sauvages proposées par le Sieur de La Motte envoyé à Monseigneur en 1708; ibid., C¹¹A, vol. 122:10–42, unsigned letter from Quebec, 30 sept. 1705. On chiefs receiving commissions, see LAC, AC, C¹¹B, vol. 23:28v, Du Quesnel to Maurepas, 19 oct. 1741; ibid., vol. 29:63v, Des Herbiers to Rouillé, 27 nov. 1750; ibid., 68, Des Herbiers to Rouillé, 6 déc. 1750.

15. E.B. O'Callaghan and J.R. Brodhead, eds, *Documents Relative to the Colonial History of the State of New York*, 15 vols (Albany, NY, 1853–87), IX, 363.

16. Pierre Margry, *Découvertes et établissements dans l'ouest et dans le sud de l'Amérique septentrionale (1614–1754)*, 6 vols (Paris, 1976–86), I, 141, Récit de ce qui c'est passé de plus remarquable dans le voyage de MM. Dollier et Galinée, 1669–70.

17. O'Callaghan and Brodhead, eds, *Documents*, IX, 95, Journal of Count de Frontenac's Voyage to Lake Ontario in 1673.

18. For a detailed account of this expedition and the factors leading up to it, see Eccles, *Frontenac the Courtier*, 161–72.

19. Louis Armand de Lom d'Arce de Lahontan was one French officer who saw advantages in the Amerindian style of warfare: Lahontan, *Nouveaux voyages de Mr. le Baron de Lahontan dans l'Amérique septentrionale*, 2 vols (The Hague, 1703), I, 238–9.

20. Bacqueville de la Potherie says that 40 Iroquois were taken. *Histoire de l'Amérique septentrionale*, I, 332–3.

21. Daniel K. Richter, 'War and Culture: The Iroquois Experience', *William and Mary Quarterly* 40, 4 (1982): 548–53.

22. Yves F. Zoltvany, 'New France and the West, 1701–1713', *Canadian Historical Review* 46, 4 (1965): 304.

23. Richter, 'War and Culture', 549.

24. Anthony F.C. Wallace, *Death and Rebirth of the Seneca* (New York, 1969), 111–14; Wallace, 'Origins of Iroquois Neutrality: The Grand Settlement of 1701', *Pennsylvania History* 24 (1957): 223–35. See also Gilles Havard, *La Grande paix de Montréal de 1701* (Montréal, 1992).

25. Zoltvany, 'New France and the West', 302–5.

26. The Iroquois claimed they had conquered lands from the Appalachians to the Kentucky River and then by the Ohio River and Mississippi to the Great Lakes and the Ottawa River. This included long-past conquests being disputed rather than only territory actually occupied. Jack M. Sosin, *Whitehall and the Wilderness: The Middle West in British Colonial Policy, 1760–1775* (Lincoln, Neb., 1961), 74 n58.

27. Ibid., 551.

28. Lahontan, *Nouveaux voyages*, II, 84–9.

29. A detailed description is by Thomas Jefferys, *The Natural and Civil History of the French Dominions in North and South America I: A Description of Canada and Louisiana* (London, 1760), I, 62–3. The practice of adopting war captives was not unique to the Iroquois.

30. Bacqueville de la Potherie, *Histoire de l'Amérique septentrionale*, I, 346–64. He wrote that their Catholic faith was the only common ground between the newcomers and the French.

31. Henri Béchard, *The Original Caughnawaga Indians* (Montreal, 1976), 57–65; Denys Delâge, 'Les Iroquois chrétiens des "réductions", 1667–1770. I—Migration et rapports avec les Français', *Recherches amérindiennes au Québec* 21, 1–2 (1991): 62. Havard, *La grande paix de Montréal de 1701*, 79, 85. Ateriata later fell out of favour with the French for unknown reasons, but he still remained loyal to them.

32. Daniel K. Richter, 'Iroquois versus Iroquois: Jesuit Missions and Christianity in Village Politics, 1642–1686', *Ethnohistory* 32, 1 (1985): 1–16; *Dictionary of Canadian Biography*, I, s.v. 'Garakontié'.

33. Milo Milton Quaife, ed., *The Western Country in the 17th Century: The Memoirs of Antoine Lamothe Cadillac and Pierre Liette* (New York, 1962), 67–8.

34. On Chabert de Joncaire in another context, see below, Chapter 11.

35. Eldest son of Nicolas-Antoine de Villiers, who led the winter raid at Grand Pré against the English in 1749.

36. An account of the last phase of the Fox War is by Joseph L. Peyser, 'The Fate of the Fox Survivors: A Dark Chapter in the History of the French in the Upper Country, 1726–1737', *Wisconsin Magazine of History* 73, 2 (1989–90): 93.

37. Louise Phelps Kellogg, *The Fox Indians during the French Regime*, reprinted from *Proceedings of the State Historical Society of Wisconsin 1907* (Madison, Wis., 1908), 178.

38. Thomas B. Akins, ed., *Selections from the Public Documents of the Province of Nova Scotia* (Halifax, 1869), 486, General Edward Whitmore to Lawrence, Louisbourg, 20 June 1760. See also John Stewart McLellan, *Louisbourg from its Foundation to its Fall, 1713–1758* (London, 1918); Olive Patricia Dickason, 'Louisbourg and the Indians: A Study in Imperial Race Relations, 1713–1760', *History and Archaeology* 6 (1976): 72–9.

39. The texts of these treaties are in Cumming and Mickenberg, eds, *Native Rights in Canada*, 300–6; William Daugherty, *Maritime Indian Treaties in Perspective* (Ottawa, 1983), 75–8; Canada, *Indian Treaties and Surrenders*, 3 vols (Toronto, 1971), II, 199–204. On Treaty No. 239, see Chapter 12, p. 148.

40. LAC, AC, B 49/2:705–7, de Maurepas, 28 mai 1726, and B 8:34–8v, 18 sept. 1726. The charge was in a letter from Longueuil and Bégon, 31 oct. 1725

(*Collection de manuscrits*, III, 126).

41. LAC, AC, C¹¹B 35:125, Chevalier Augustin Boschenry de Drucour (governor of Ile Royale, 1754–8), au ministre, 18 nov. 1755.

42. LAC, MG 18, E29, vol. 2, section 4, Discours fait aux sauvages du Canada par M. de Saint-Ovide, gouverneur de l'Acadie avec les Responses que les sauvages on faites. On French attempts to curb Mi'kmaq raids, see LAC, AC, C¹¹B, vol. 28:75–8, Des Herbiers to Rouillé, 9 aug. 1749.

43. There are two versions of this declaration. The earlier one is reproduced in *Report Concerning Canadian Archives, 1905*, 3 vols, 1906, 2: App. A, pt. III, in 'Acadian Genealogy and Notes' by Placide Gaudet, 239. The later one is in *Collection de documents inédits sur le Canada et l'Amérique publiées par le Canada français*, 3 vols (Québec, 1888–90), I, 17–19.

44. Akins, ed., *Public Documents of Nova Scotia*, 581, Council aboard the *Beaufort*, 1 Oct. 1749; ibid., 581–2, Proclamation of Governor Cornwallis, Oct. 1749.

45. LAC, Nova Scotia A 17:129–32; Nova Scotia B 1:53–5.

46. Dickason, 'Louisbourg and the Indians', 99–100. 'Humanity cries out against such things', a contemporary observer wrote, 'which should cause a just horror.' LAC, AC, C¹¹C, vol. 8:88v, Couagne to Acaron, directeur de Bureau des Colonies, 4 nov. 1760. The proclamation authorizing the bounty still remains on Nova Scotia's books, although such bounties are prohibited by the Criminal Code. According to newspaper accounts, the government fears that revoking the law and apologizing for it would precipitate a rash of lawsuits. Richard Foot, 'Colonial bounty on Mi'kmaq scalps still on the books', *National Post*, 5 Jan. 2000, A1, A2.

47. J.B. Brebner, 'Subsidized Intermarriage with the Indians', *Canadian Historical Review* 6, 1 (1925): 33–6.

48. LAC, AC, C¹¹B, vol. 31:62–3.

49. LAC, AC, C¹¹B, vol. 32:163–6, Prevost à Antoine Louis Rouillé, Comte de Joüy (minister of the marine, 1749–54), 10 sept. 1752; ibid., vol. 33:159v, Prevost à Rouillé, 12 mai 1753; Akins, ed., *Public Documents of Nova Scotia*, 672–4, Council minutes, Halifax, 16 Sept. 1752.

50. LAC, CO 217/18:277–4, Ceremonials at Concluding a Peace . . . , 25 June 1761.

51. LAC, AC, C¹², vol. 1:3v, Mémoire du Roy pour servir d'instruction au Sr. Dangeac nommé au gouvernement des Iles St. Pierre et de Miquelon, 23 fév. 1763.

52. Denis A. Bartels and Olaf Uwe Janzen, 'Micmac Migration to Western Newfoundland', paper presented to the Canadian Historical Association, Victoria, 1990.

53. W.A. Kenyon and J.R. Turnbull, *The Battle for the Bay 1686* (Toronto, 1971); Arthur S. Morton, *A History of the Canadian West to 1870–71*, ed. Lewis G. Thomas (Toronto, 1973), 92–103.

54. C.S. Mackinnon, 'The 1958 Government Policy Reversal in Keewatin', in Kenneth S. Coates and William R. Morrison, eds, *For Purposes of Dominion* (Toronto, 1989), 159.

Chapter 11

1. This section follows Olive Patricia Dickason, 'Louisbourg and the Indians: A Study in Imperial Race Relations, 1713–1760', *History and Archaeology* 6 (1976): 39–41, with additions and some changes.

2. A thorough study on French dealings with Amerindians in Canada is by Cornelius J. Jaenen, *The French Relationship with the Native People of New France and Acadia* (Ottawa, 1984).

3. E.B. O'Callaghan and J.R. Brodhead, eds, *Documents Relative to the Colonial History of the State of New York*, 15 vols (Albany, NY, 1853–87), IV, 206–11, London Documents 10, 'Mr. Nelson's Memorial about the state of the Northern Colonies in America', 24 Sept. 1696.

4. Ibid. The English quickly followed suit. One of the most famous of these episodes occurred in 1710, when four Iroquois sachems were brought to London and presented to Queen Anne as kings of the League of Five Nations. See John G. Garratt, *The Four Indian Kings* (Ottawa, 1985).

5. LAC, AC, B, vol. 57/1:639 [139], Maurepas à Beauharnois, 8 avr. 1732.

6. O'Callaghan and Brodhead, eds, *Documents*, IV, 206–11.

7. Thomas Pichon, *Lettres et mémoires pour servir à l'histoire naturelle, civile et politique du Cap Breton* (La Haye and London, 1760; reprint, 1966), 140.

8. In his words, 'heureux celui qui en sçait monter les ressorts pour les faire jouer à Sa Volonté, depuis tout ce tems je n'ai encore pu parvenir à ce point de Science.' LAC, CO, Nova Scotia A, vol. 32:232, Maillard to Hopson, 11 Sept. 1748.

9. Nicholas Perrot, *Mémoire sur les moeurs, coustumes et relligion des sauvages de l'Amérique septentrionale*, ed. J. Tailhan (Montréal, 1973), 78.

10. Thomas C. Haliburton, *An Historical and Statistical Account of Nova Scotia*, 2 vols (Halifax, 1829), I, 101.

11. O'Callaghan and Brodhead, eds, *Documents*, X, 14, Paris Documents 9, Beauharnois and Hocquart to Maurepas, 12 Sept. 1745.

12. Francis Parkman, *The Jesuits in North America in the Seventeenth Century* (Toronto, 1907), 44.

13. *Collection de manuscrits contenant lettres, mémoires et autres documents historiques relatifs à la Nouvelle France*, 4 vols (Québec, 1833–35), I, 175, 'Instructions pour le Sieur de Courcelle au sujet des indiens', 1665.

14. Olive Patricia Dickason, *The Myth of the Savage and the Beginnings of French Colonialism in the Americas* (Edmonton, 1984), 217–20.

15. Reuben Gold Thwaites, ed., *Jesuit Relations and Allied Documents*, 73 vols (Cleveland, 1896–1901), V, 145; VI, 85; VII, 227; IX, 105; XI, 53.

16. Dickason, *Myth of the Savage*, 219–20. On the subject of the program's failure, particularly with the Montagnais Pierre Pastedechouan (*fl.* 1620–36), see Thwaites, ed., *Jesuit Relations*, VI, 85–9.

17. These efforts are summarized by Cornelius J. Jaenen, *The Role of the Church in New France* (Toronto, 1976), ch. 2; Jaenen, 'Education for Francization: The Case of New France in the Seventeenth Century', in Jean Barman, Yvonne Hébert, and Don McCaskill, eds, *Indian Education in Canada*, 2 vols (Vancouver, 1986), I, 45–63; Bruce G. Trigger, *The Children of Aataentsic: A History of the Huron People to 1660*, 2 vols (Montreal and Kingston, 1976).

18. Dickason, *Myth of the Savage*, 258–62.

19. The following account follows that in Dickason, 'Louisbourg and the Indians', 26–7.

20. Henry P. Biggar, ed., *The Works of Samuel de Champlain*, 6 vols (Toronto, 1922–36), V, 66–8, 76, 103–7; *Dictionary of Canadian Biography*, I, s.v. 'Cherououny'; Marcel Trudel, *Histoire de la Nouvelle France II: Le comptoir 1604–1627* (Montréal, 1966), 359–60.

21. *Jugements et délibérations du Conseil Souverain de la Nouvelle France*, 7 vols (Québec, 1885–91), I, 129–30, 174–5. See also W.J. Eccles, *The Canadian Frontier 1534–1760* (Toronto, 1969), 77–9.

22. LAC, AC, F³, article 95, 35, Reglements faits par les chefs sauvages de l'Ile Royale, de Nartigonneiche, et de Chikpenakady et de Monsieur de Bienville dans le conseil tenu au Port Toulouse pour la distribution des presents, 9 juil. 1739. The text is written in French and twice in Mi'kmaq, in script and ideograms. See also LAC, AC, C¹¹B, vol. 22:118–24, Bourville à Maurepas, 26 oct. 1740.

23. Antonio de Ulloa (1716–95), *A Voyage to South America . . .*, 2 vols, tr. John Adams (London, 1806), II, 376–7.

24. Eccles, *Canadian Frontier*, 78.

25. Denys Delâge, 'Les Iroquois chrétiens des "réductions", 1667–1770. I—Migration et rapports avec les Français', *Recherches amérindiennes au Québec* 21, 1–2 (1991): 65.

26. Jean Lunn, 'The Illegal Fur Trade out of New France, 1713–60', Canadian Historical Association *Historical Papers* (1939): 61–76. Delâge says he has found only one instance of an Indian being charged with smuggling.

27. *An Account of the Customs and Manners of the Micmakis and Maricheets, Savage Nations, Now Dependent on the Government of Cape Breton* (London, 1758), 88–9.

28. This reached such proportions that the Maliseet were reputed to be descendants of Malouins: Philippe Jacquin, *Les Indiens blancs* (Paris, 1989), 32. This comes from Joseph A. Maurault, *Histoire des Abenakis depuis 1606 jusqu'à nos jours* (Sorel, Québec, 1866), 6 n3. Maurault claimed the Abenaki called the mixed-bloods Maliseets because most of the fathers came from St Malo.

29. Thwaites, ed., *Jesuit Relations*, V, 211; X, 26.

30. Chrestien Le Clercq, *First Establishment of the Faith in New France*, tr. John Gilmary Shea, 2 vols (New York, 1881), I, 74–7, 'Brief of Pope Paul V for the Canada mission, 1618'.

31. Dickason, *Myth of the Savage*, 241.

32. See, for example, Biard's ruminations on the subject. He concluded that the reasons for Canada's severe climate were the presence of so much water and the fact that the land had not been cleared and cultivated. (Thwaites, ed., *Jesuit Relations*, III, 55–61.)

33. Amerindians who depended on hunting and gathering did not generally use salt, which they claimed shortened life, and some even regarded it as poisonous (agricultural peoples, however, valued it, and used it as an item of trade). See Dickason, *Myth of the Savage*, 325 n50; Thwaites, ed., *Jesuit Relations*, V, 103. 'French snow'—sugar—was also seen in the same light (ibid., XIV, 51). Diets, imposed by different ways of life, influenced salt preferences.

34. Dom Guy Oury, *Marie de l'Incarnation (1599–1672) Correspondance* (Solesmes, 1971), 112, lettre du 4 sept. 1640. Nearly three-quarters of a century later, similar sentiments were expressed by Father Pierre-Gabriel Marest (1662–1714): '. . . the horror of our forests, those vast uninhabited Regions in which I would certainly perish if I were abandoned, presented themselves to my mind and took away nearly all my courage.' Thwaites, ed., *Jesuit Relations*, LXVI, 269. See also

Trudel, *Histoire de la Nouvelle France II: Le comptoir*, 384–6. My thanks to Claire Gourdeau, Laval University, for these references.

35. See Jennifer S.H. Brown, *Strangers in Blood: Fur Trade Company Families in Indian Country* (Vancouver, 1980); Sylvia Van Kirk, *Many Tender Ties: Women in Fur Trade Society 1670–1870* (Norman, Okla., 1983).

36. Claude C. Le Roy *dit* Bacqueville de la Potherie, *Histoire de l'Amérique septentrionale*, 4 vols (Paris, 1722), IV, 180–1.

37. Peter N. Moogk, 'Les Petits Sauvages: The Children of Eighteenth-Century New France', in Joy Parr, ed., *Childhood and Family in Canadian History* (Toronto, 1982), 27.

38. Pierre Chaunu, *L'Amérique et les Amériques* (Paris, 1964), 109.

39. Trigger, *Children of Aataentsic*, I, 325.

40. Dickason, *Myth of the Savage*, 144–7; Biggar, ed., *Works of Champlain*, II, 48. Le Jeune shared this belief: 'Their natural color is like that of those French beggars who are half-roasted in the Sun, and I have no doubt the Savages would be very white if they were well covered.' (Thwaites, ed., *Jesuit Relations*, V, 23.) Some even extended this belief to Africans: 'The children of this country are born white, and change their colour in two days to a perfect black.' E.G. Ravenstein, ed., *The Strange Adventures of Andrew Battell of Leigh in Angola and the Adjoining Regions* (London, 1901; reprint, 1967), 49.

41. Thwaites, ed., *Jesuit Relations*, IX, 219.

42. Ibid., VIII, 49; X, 27; XIV, 19. The Jesuits were very conscious of the need to establish schools for the French, otherwise they 'would become Savages, and have less instruction than the Savages themselves.' Ibid., XXXVI, 175.

43. Chrestien Le Clercq, *Nouvelle relation de la Gaspésie*, 2 vols (Paris, 1691), 285–6; Gabriel Sagard, *Histoire du Canada, et voyages que les frères mineurs Recollects y ont faicts pour la conversion des infidelles*, 4 vols (Paris, 1636), I, 166–7; Thwaites, ed., *Jesuit Relations*, VIII, 5–59.

44. Thwaites, ed., *Jesuit Relations*, XXVIII, 49–65.

45. Ibid.

46. Ibid., XXI, 45.

47. Sagard, *Histoire du Canada*, I, 166. See also Daniel A. Scalberg, 'Seventeenth and Early Eighteenth-Century Perceptions of Coureurs-de-Bois Religious Life', *Proceedings of the Annual Meeting of the Western Society for French History* 17 (1990): 82–95.

48. Sagard, *Histoire du Canada*, II, 457.

49. Thwaites, ed., *Jesuit Relations*, XIV, 19–21.

50. Ibid., III, 105.

51. Ibid., XLVII, 203. For a discussion of these problems, see Olive Patricia Dickason, 'From "One Nation" in the Northeast to "New Nation" in the Northwest: A Look at the Emergence of the Metis', *American Indian Culture and Research Journal* 6, 2 (1982): 1–21.

52. Abbé H.R. Casgrain, 'Coup d'oeil sur l'Acadie', *Le Canada Français* 1 (1888): 116–17.

53. *Account of the Customs and Manners*, 89–90. The letter has been attributed to Abbé Pierre Maillard.

54. Ibid., 101–2.

55. Gaston du Boscq de Beaumont, comp. and ed., *Les derniers jours de l'Acadie (1748–1758)* (Paris, 1899), 85.

56. Lisa Poirier, 'J'étions un Métis', *L'Actualité* (juillet 2000): 39–40.

57. Pierre Margry, *Découvertes et établissements dans l'ouest et dans le sud de l'Amérique septentrionale (1614–1754)*, 6 vols (Paris, 1976–86), V, 146, Lamothe Cadillac, mémoire adressée au Maurepas.

58. Sieur de Diéreville, *Relation of the Voyage to Port Royal in Acadia or New France*, ed. John C. Webster (Toronto, 1933), 187.

59. Standard works in this regard are Brown's *Strangers in Blood* and Van Kirk's *Many Tender Ties*.

60. Margry, *Découvertes et établissements*, V, 120, Nations habitans dans le gouvernement de Lamothe Cadillac; ibid., 107, Usages des sauvages. See also Louis Armand de Lom d'Arce de Lahontan, *Nouveaux voyages de Mr. le Baron de Lahontan dans l'Amérique septentrionale*, 2 vols (The Hague, 1703), II, 143, in which Amerindian women are described as being mistresses of their own bodies.

61. Robert-Lionel Séguin, *La vie libertine en Nouvelle-France au XVIIe siècle*, 2 vols (Montréal, 1972), I, 47. Several members of the Chabert de Joncaire and Le Moyne families followed this path. See LAC, AC, C¹¹A 18:82, 147–8; Marcel Giraud, *The Métis in the Canadian West*, tr. George Woodcock, 2 vols (Edmonton, 1986), I, 232–4. Biographies of members of the Chabert de Joncaire family are in *Dictionary of Canadian Biography*, II, III, IV; for Le Moyne de Maricourt and his brother Charles Le Moyne de Longueuil, II. See also, O'Callaghan and Brodhead, eds, *Documents*, IX, 580. The *Documents* index lists Philippe-Thomas Chabert de Joncaire (1707–c. 1766) as a French Indian.

62. Pierre-François-Xavier de Charlevoix, *Histoire et description générale de la Nouvelle France*, 3 vols (Paris, 1744), III, 89.

63. Thwaites, ed., *Jesuit Relations*, XIV, 261–3; XVI, 263; XXI, 137–9.

64. LAC, AC, F¹A, Fonds des Colonies, I–X; O'Callaghan and Brodhead, eds, *Documents*, IX, 207, La Barre to Seignelay, 4 nov. 1683; ibid., 269–71.

65. Marriage 'à la gaumine' also appeared in the colony, an import from France. The contracting couple, wishing to avoid the required formalities, would attend mass and raise their hands together as the officiating priest blessed the worshippers, thus inadvertently sanctifying the union.

66. Thwaites, ed., *Jesuit Relations*, LXV, 69, 263. See also the Michilimackinac table of marriages, 1698–1765, in Jacqueline Peterson, 'A Social Portrait of the Great Lakes Métis', *Ethnohistory* 25, 1 (1978): 50; Marcel Giraud, *Histoire de la Louisianne française*, 2 vols (Paris, 1953–8), I, 315–16; Louise Phelps Kellogg, *The French Régime in Wisconsin and the Northwest* (New York, 1968), 386–405; Natalie Maree Belting, *Kaskaskia under the French Regime* (New Orleans, 1975), 13–16.

67. For some French objections to intermarriage, see Margry, *Découvertes et établissements*, V, 158–9, Lamothe Cadillac, rapports des débats qui ont eu lieu à propos de son projet dans l'assemblée ordonnée par le roi et dans sa conférence avec M. de Callières.

68. LAC, AC, C¹³A 3:819–24, Duclos au ministre, 25 déc. 1715.

69. An interesting example of such an envoy was 'Colonel Louis Cook' (Atiatoharongwen, *c.* 1740–1814) of the American army, a half-Abenaki from Caughnawaga, who served as go-between to the Oneida during the American War of Independence. His father was black. See *Dictionary of Canadian Biography*, V, s.v. 'Atiatoharongwen'; F.B. Hough, *A History of St. Lawrence and Franklin Counties, New York, from their Earliest Period to the Present Time* (Albany, NY, 1853), 182.

70. LAC, AC, C¹¹C, vol. 16, pièce 28, unsigned letter, 6 July 1746.

71. Belting, *Kaskaskia*, 74–5; Cornelius J. Jaenen, *Friend and Foe: Aspects of French–Amerindian Cultural Contact in the Sixteenth and Seventeenth Centuries* (Toronto, 1976), 164–5.

72. Peter Bakker, 'Canadian Fur Trade and the Absence of Creoles', *The Carrier Pidgin* 16, 3 (1988): 1–3.

73. See above, Chapter 4 and note 66.

74. George Lang, 'Voyageur Discourse and the Absence of Fur Trade Pidgin', paper presented to the American Society for Ethnohistory, Toronto, 1990; in *Canadian Literature* 133 (Winter, 1992): 51–63.

75. Peter Bakker, 'The Genesis of Michif: A First Hypothesis', in William Cowan, ed., *Papers of the Twenty-first Algonquian Conference* (Ottawa, 1990), 12–35; Bakker, 'Relexification: The Case of the Métif (French Cree)', in N. Baretzy, W. Enninger, and T. Stolz, eds, *Sprachkontakt. Beiträge zum s. Essener Kolloquium über Grammatikalisierung: Naturlichkeit un System Okonomie*, 2 vols (Bochum, 1989). See also Sarah Grey Thomason and Terrence Kaufman, *Language Contact, Creolization, and Genetic Linguistics* (Berkeley, 1988), 228–33. Patline Laverdure and Ida Rose Allard have compiled *The Michif Dictionary: Turtle Mountain Chippewa Cree*, ed. John C. Crawford (Winnipeg, 1983).

76. Thomason and Kaufman, *Language Contact*, 232–3.

77. Robert A. Papen, 'Le Métif: Le ne plus ultra des grammaires en contact', *Revue québecoise de linguistique théorique et appliquée* 6, 2 (1987): 57–70.

78. A study by Peter Bakker of Aarhus University, Denmark, has been acclaimed as 'an analytical breakthrough'. Bakker, *A Language of Our Own* (New York, 1997). See also 'A dying language: French dominates tongue spoken by Manitoba Metis', *The Gazette*, Montreal, 15 Mar. 1991.

79. Charlevoix, *Histoire et description*, III, 322.

80. 'La relation dernière de Marc Lescarbot, Paris, 1612', in Lucien Campeau, ed., *Monumenta Novae Franciae I: La première mission d'Acadie (1602–1616)* (Québec, 1967), 184: 'On ne peut arracher tout d'un coup les coutumes et façons de faire invétérées d'un peuple quel que soit.'

Chapter 12

1. Olive Patricia Dickason, 'Concepts of Sovereignty at the Time of First Contact', in L.C. Green and Olive P. Dickason, *The Law of Nations and the New World* (Edmonton, 1989), 221.

2. Reuben Gold Thwaites, ed., *Jesuit Relations and Allied Documents*, 73 vols (Cleveland, 1896–1901), XXXVI, 250–1.

3. Antoine de Montchrestien, *Traicté de l'oeconomie politique* . . . , s.l., n.d., 218.

4. [Claude Razilly], 'Mémoire du Chevalier de Razilly', *Revue de Géographie* 19 (1886): 374–83, 453–64. Similar sentiments were later expressed by Antoine Biet, *Voyage de la France Equinoxiale en l'ile de Cayenne, entrepris par les Français en l'année 1652* (Paris, 1664), preface.

5. Dorothy V. Jones, 'British Colonial Indian Treaties', in Wilcomb Washburn, ed., *Handbook of North American Indians, 4: History of Indian–White Relations* (Washington, 1988), 185.

6. Maurice Torrelli, 'Les Indiens du Canada et le droit des traités dans la jurisprudence canadienne', *Annuaire Français de Droit International* 20 (1974): 227–49.

7. The text of the treaty is in Peter A. Cumming and Neil H. Mickenberg, eds, *Native Rights in Canada* (Toronto, 1972), 296–8. In the Amerindian view, this guarantee was for pre-existing rights. See *Indian Treaty Rights*, Federation of Saskatchewan Indians, n.d.

8. See above, Chapter 10, p. 131. For a Wuastukwiuk view of the two 1725 treaties, see Andrea Bear Nicholas, 'Maliseet Aboriginal Rights and Mascarene's Treaty, not Dummer's Treaty', in William Cowan, ed., *Actes du dix-septième Congrès des Algonquinistes* (Ottawa, 1986), 215–29.

9. The text is in Cumming and Mickenberg, eds, *Native Rights in Canada*, 302–6.

10. David L. Ghere, 'Mistranslations and Misinformation: Diplomacy on the Maine Frontier, 1725 to 1755', *American Indian Culture and Research Journal* 8, 4 (1984): 3–26.

11. Gabriel Sagard, *Histoire du Canada, et voyages que les frères mineurs Recollects y ont faicts pour la conversion des infidelles*, 4 vols (Paris, 1636), II, 444: '. . . Truchemens, qui souvent ne rapportent pas fidellement les choses qu'on leur dit, ou par ignorance ou par mespris, qui est une chose fort dangereuse, & de laquelle on a souvent vue arriver de grands accidents.'

12. Pierre-Antoine-Simon Maillard, 'Lettre de M. l'Abbé Maillard sur les missions de l'Acadie et particulièrement sur les missions Micmaques', *Soirées canadiennes* 3 (1863): 358–9. As he reported on one occasion, circumlocution was the only answer: 'Je leur fis voir qu'il était impossible de conserver en français le sens de ce qu'ils voulaient dire, en le rendant de mot à mot; que le tour que j'avais pris, était le véritable; qu'il était au-dessus d'eux d'exprimer aussi fidèlement en français de pareilles phrases mikmaques.' Similarly, explaining scripture was not always easy (ibid., 409–10).

13. William Daugherty, *Maritime Indian Treaties in Perspective* (Ottawa, 1983), 69, 77, 83. This ratification followed the 1744 declaration of war by William Shirley (governor of Massachusetts, 1741–9 and 1753–6) against the Wuastukwiuk of St John River and the Mi'kmaq of Cape Sable. Charles Henry Lincoln, ed., *The Correspondence of William Shirley*, 2 vols (New York, 1912), I, 150–1, Shirley to the Lords of Trade, 16 Oct. 1744.

14. Thomas B. Akins, ed., *Selections from the Public Documents of the Province of Nova Scotia* (Halifax,

1869), 682–5; Daugherty, *Maritime Indian Treaties*, 50–1, 84–5; Cumming and Mickenberg, eds, *Native Rights in Canada*, 307–9.

15. Akins, ed., *Public Documents of Nova Scotia*, 671, Council minutes, Halifax, 14 Sept. 1752. Amerindian resistance to land surveys had long been troubling the British. Ibid., Council minutes, Halifax, 4 Sept. 1732.

16. Max Savelle, *The Diplomatic History of the Canadian Boundary 1749–1763* (New Haven, 1940), 147.

17. Article 40 reads: 'The savages or Indian Allies of His Most Christian Majesty shall be maintained in the lands they inhabit, if they choose to reside there; they shall not be molested on any pretense whatsoever, for having carried arms and served His Most Christian Majesty; they shall have, as well as the French, liberty of religion, and shall keep their missionaries.' See also Torrelli, 'Les Indiens du Canada', 236.

18. James Sullivan, Alexander C. Flick, and Milton W. Hamilton, eds, *The Papers of Sir William Johnson*, 14 vols (Albany, NY, 1921–65), VII, 785.

19. English watchdog sloops reported that 'the French . . . are very busy carrying on a trade with the Indians.' MG 12: Great Britain, Admiralty 106, vol. 1123:369, letter from Jacob Hurd.

20. See, for instance, the complaints of the Seneca: Anthony F.C. Wallace, *Death and Rebirth of the Seneca* (New York, 1969), 114–15.

21. Johnson's Journal of Indian Affairs, 9–12 Dec. 1758, in *Papers of Sir William Johnson*, X, 69, 73. Amerindian complaints in this regard were long-standing, and they had frequently requested authorities to ban the sale of liquor. See, for example, the plea in 1722 of the Mahican to William Burnett, governor-in-chief of New York and New Jersey, 1720–8. E.B. O'Callaghan and J.R. Brodhead, eds, *Documents Relative to the Colonial History of the State of New York*, 15 vols (Albany, NY, 1853–87), V, 663–4.

22. The governor of Virginia reported this to the Board of Trade in 1756. See Jack M. Sosin, *Whitehall and the Wilderness: The Middle West in British Colonial Policy, 1760–1775* (Lincoln, Neb., 1961), 30.

23. Peter Wraxall, *An Abridgement of Indian Affairs . . . Transacted in the Colony of New York for the Year 1678 to the Year 1751*, ed. Charles H. McIlwain (Cambridge, Mass., 1915), ix, 153 n2.

24. David A. Armour, ed., *Attack at Michilimackinac 1763* (Mackinac Island, Mich., 1988), 25. This is a reproduction of Alexander Henry's *Travels and Adventures in Canada and the Indian Territories*

between the Years 1760 and 1764 (New York, 1809).

25. Sosin, *Whitehall and the Wilderness*, 31.

26. Gordon M. Day and Bruce G. Trigger, 'Algonquin', in Trigger, ed., *Handbook of North American Indians, 15: Northeast* (Washington, 1978), 795; Robert J. Surtees, 'The Iroquois in Canada', in Francis Jennings, ed., *The History and Culture of Iroquois Diplomacy* (Syracuse, NY, 1985), 70.

27. Denys Delâge, 'Les Iroquois chrétiens des "réductions", 1667–1770. I—Migration et rapports avec les Français', *Recherches amérindiennes au Québec* 21, 3 (1991).

28. *Papers of Sir William Johnson*, III, 965. The spelling of this citation has been corrected; Croghan's is so bad it interferes with reading.

29. The question of Pontiac's origins is unresolved. Howard H. Peckham discusses the evidence in *Pontiac and the Indian Uprising* (Chicago, 1947), 15–16 n2. Contemporary reports inform us that he was of better than medium height and not handsome. Ibid., 28–9.

30. Ibid., 29.

31. Robert Rogers, *Concise Account of North America* . . . (London, 1765), 240, 243. An extract is reprinted in Peckham, *Pontiac*, 59–62 n8.

32. *Dictionary of Canadian Biography*, III, s.v., 'Pontiac'. The other 'Delaware Prophet' had a religious message.

33. Carl F. Klinck, ed., *Tecumseh, Fact and Fiction in Early Records* (Englewood Cliffs, NJ, 1961), 184–5. See also Colin Calloway, *Crown and Calumet: British–Indian Relations, 1783–1815* (Norman, Okla., 1987), 217.

34. Helen Hornbeck Tanner, ed., *Atlas of Great Lakes Indian History* (Norman, Okla., 1987), 48. For a detailed account of the uprising, see 48–53. See also Peckham, *Pontiac*, 99–100.

35. For a contrary view, see Wilbur R. Jacobs, 'The Indian Frontier of 1763', *Western Pennsylvania Historical Magazine* 34, 3 (1951): 185–98.

36. Peckham, *Pontiac*, 316.

37. At the time the fort was built, the Dakota–Ojibwa War had been going on for something like a century. During a temporary peace in 1787 the combatants agreed to recognize the British King. Clayton W. McCall, 'The Peace of Michilimackinack', *Michigan History Magazine* 28, 3 (1944): 367–83.

38. Mary 'Molly' Brant, consort of Sir William Johnson, superintendent of Northern Indian Affairs who had died in 1774, was a more powerful figure among the matrilineal Mohawk than her famous younger brother. On her importance among her people, it was reported that 'one word

from her goes farther with them than a thousand from any white Man without Exception who in general must purchase their Interest at a high rate.' The Iroquois did not regard Joseph as their leading war chief; that honour was accorded the Seneca Kaien?kwaahto'n (Sayenqueraghta, d. 1786), who also fought for the British. See Barbara Graymont, *The Iroquois in the American Revolution* (Syracuse, NY, 1972), 159.

39. Red Jacket took part in a council that removed Brant from office in 1805, but Brant managed to stay on another two years. Red Jacket, employed as a runner for the British during the American War of Independence, had been rewarded for his services with a richly embroidered red jacket. He later threw in his lot with the Americans, although he would have preferred neutrality. See Mary H. Eastman, *The American Aboriginal Portfolio* (Philadelphia, 1853), 9–13.

40. On the participation of the Six Nations in the American War of Independence, see George F.G. Stanley, 'The Six Nations and the American Revolution', *Ontario History* 56, 4 (1964): 217–32.

41. George F.G. Stanley, *The War of 1812: Land Operations* (Toronto, 1983), 13–14.

42. A.L. Burt, 'A New Approach to the Problem of the Western Posts', *Canadian Historical Association Report* (1931): 61–95.

43. John Leslie discusses the treaty and its background in *The Treaty of Amity, Commerce and Navigation, 1794–1796: The Jay Treaty* (Ottawa, 1979).

44. The texts of the proclamations of 1761 and 1762 and excerpts from that of 1763 are reproduced in Cumming and Mickenberg, eds, *Native Rights in Canada*, 285–92. See also Bradford W. Morse, ed., *Aboriginal Peoples and the Law: Indian, Metis, and Inuit Rights in Canada* (Ottawa, 1985), 52–4, 191–6.

45. For a detailed study of the Proclamation, see Jack Stagg, 'Anglo–Indian Relations in North America to 1763 and an Analysis of the Royal Proclamation of 7 October 1763', Ottawa, 1981.

46. Jones, 'British Colonial Indian Treaties', 189–90.

47. Robert J. Surtees, 'Canadian Indian Treaties', in Washburn, ed., *Handbook of North American Indians, 4: History of Indian–White Relations*, 202.

48. Stagg, 'Anglo–Indian Relations', 386.

49. Torrelli, 'Les Indiens du Canada', 237–9.

50. Surtees, 'Canadian Indian Treaties', 202.

51. Lisa Patterson, 'Errant Peace Treaty', *The Archivist* 16, 6 (1989): 15.

52. Donald B. Smith, 'The Dispossession of the Mississauga Indians: A Missing Chapter in the Early History of Upper Canada', *Ontario History* 73, 2 (1981): 72. Wabakinine was a signatory to several land-cession treaties. See *Dictionary of Canadian Biography*, IV.

53. Canada, *Indian Treaties and Surrenders*, 3 vols (Toronto, 1971), I, 42ff.

54. Lillian F. Gates, *Land Policies of Upper Canada* (Toronto, 1968), 49, 51. According to historian Robert J. Surtees, the average price was four pence an acre. Surtees, 'Canadian Indian Treaties', 204.

55. The importance of Amerindians in colonial policy was indicated by the wish of John Graves Simcoe, first lieutenant-governor of Upper Canada, 1791–6, to establish the capital on the site of London, to be near the Amerindian allies. See R.J. Surtees, 'The Changing Image of the Canadian Indian: An Historical Approach', in D.A. Muise, ed., *Approaches to Native History in Canada: Papers of a conference held at the National Museum of Man* (Ottawa, 1977), 121.

56. The text of the grant is reproduced in Isabel Thompson Kelsay, *Joseph Brant, 1743–1807: Man of Two Worlds* (Syracuse, NY, 1984), 363. See also Gates, *Land Policies*, 14–15.

57. Charles M. Johnston, ed., *The Valley of the Six Nations: A Collection of Documents on the Indian Lands of the Grand River* (Toronto, 1964), 52. See also Kelsay, *Joseph Brant*, 370.

58. Gates, *Land Policies*, 49. On Brant's struggle with the administration, see Charles M. Johnston, 'Joseph Brant, the Grand River Lands and the Northwest Crisis', *Ontario History* 55 (1963): 267–82.

59. A later court case that involved Brant's leasing activities was *Sheldon v. Ramsay*, 1852. The issue was whether or not lands believed to belong to a certain Mallory (not a Native) would be forfeited for treason. It developed that the lands in question had been leased by Brant; the court ruled that the Mohawk chief had had no authority for such an action, as neither he nor the Six Nations had possessed title in fee simple. See Bruce A. Clark, *Native Liberty, Crown Sovereignty* (Montreal and Kingston, 1990), 19 and n15.

60. Surtees, 'The Iroquois in Canada', 76. An outline of Brant's real estate dealings is in Johnston, ed., *Valley of Six Nations*, xlii–liv. For a study of the legal dissensions that ensued, see Sidney L. Harring, *White Man's Law* (Toronto, 1998), ch. 2.

61. Kelsay, *Joseph Brant*, 555–6. Interestingly enough, Brant had initially maintained that the purchase from the Mississauga had not been necessary, as these had been Iroquois lands from time

immemorial. Later he became land agent for the Mississauga, indicating a de facto acknowledgement of their title.

62. Stewart Bell, 'One-member B.C. band jumps on the land-claims bandwagon', *The Gazette*, Montreal, 5 Oct. 1995; 'The littlest band in the land', *Globe and Mail*, 14 Oct. 1995. See also <vancouver.ca/commsvcs/socialplanning/initiatives/aboriginal/storyscapes/story04.htm>. Larrabee grew up in Vancouver's Chinatown and only learned of her Aboriginal heritage, from her mother, when she was 24 years old. Her mother, a full Aboriginal who had been traumatized by her Indian residential school experience, had married a man of Chinese descent and passed as Asian herself rather than admit her Native heritage for fear of added discrimination and hurt. Rhonda Larrabee's grandparents were among the last people to leave the reserve. A 2003 documentary film, *A Tribe of One*, was made about Chief Larrabee.

63. Surtees, 'Canadian Indian Treaties', 203; Boyce Richardson, 'Kind Hearts or Forked Tongues?', *The Beaver* Outfit 67, 1 (1987): 16.

64. Canada, *Indian Treaties and Surrenders*, I, 47. Musquakie's band eventually settled in Rama Township in 1839, after several moves. Muskoka, a region north of Toronto, may have had its name derived from that of the chief.

65. R.A. Humphreys, 'Governor Murray's Views . . .', *Canadian Historical Review* 16 (1935): 166–9.

Chapter 13

1. This chapter is an adaptation of my paper, 'A Historical Reconstruction for the Northwestern Plains', *Prairie Forum* 5, 1 (1980): 19–37.

2. Joseph Jablow, *The Cheyenne in Plains Indian Trade Relations 1795–1840*, Monographs of the American Ethnological Society, 19 (Seattle, 1950), 14; Robert H. Lowie, *Indians of the Plains* (New York, 1963), 45.

3. William Duncan Strong, 'The Plains Culture Area in the Light of Archaeology', *American Anthropologist* 23, 2 (1933): 271–87, held that horse nomadism represented no more than a 'thin and strikingly uniform veneer' on earlier cultural manifestations. On the lack of specific rites among the Plains Cree for the increase of horses even though they were the symbol of wealth, see David G. Mandelbaum, *The Plains Cree* (Regina, 1979), 63.

4. LAC, RG 10, Indian Affairs Records, Headquarters, microfilm reel no. C-12030, vol. 7727, file 23,040-

1A, James W. Daley, Indian Agent, Walpole Island, to the Secretary, federal Department of Indian Affairs, Ottawa, 10 Dec. 1940.

5. F.G. Roe, *The Indian and the Horse* (Norman, Okla., 1951), 54.

6. John C. Ewers, *The Horse in Blackfoot Indian Culture* (Washington, 1955), 2–3.

7. Roe, *Indian and Horse*, 74–5.

8. John Price, *Indians of Canada: Cultural Dynamics* (Scarborough, Ont., 1979), 176.

9. Dolores A. Gunnerson, 'Man and Bison on the Plains in the Protohistoric Period', *Plains Anthropologist* 17, 55 (1972): 2. It has been theorized that the custom of burning altered the ecology of river valleys so that the subsistence base of the communities was undermined. The average life of a Plains farming village has been estimated at about 30 years.

10. T.H. Lewis, ed., 'The Narrative of the Expedition of Hernando de Soto by the Gentleman of Elvas', in Frederick W. Hodge, ed., *Spanish Explorers in the Southern United States 1528–1543* (New York, 1907), 213.

11. Henry Kelsey, *The Kelsey Papers* (Ottawa, 1929), 13, cited by Eleanor Verbicky-Todd, *Communal Buffalo Hunting among the Plains Indians: An Ethnographic and Historic Review* (Edmonton, 1984), 134.

12. George W. Arthur, *An Introduction to the Ecology of Early Historic Communal Bison Hunting among the Northern Plains Indians* (Ottawa, 1975), 72.

13. Oscar Lewis, *The Effects of White Contact upon Blackfoot Culture with Special References to the Fur Trade*, Monographs of the American Ethnological Society, 6 (New York, 1942), 38–40.

14. Elliott Coues, ed., *New Light on the Early History of the Great Northwest 1799–1814*, 3 vols (New York, 1897), II, 526.

15. Ibid., I, 352; II, 526.

16. Bernard Mishkin, *Rank and Warfare among Plains Indians*, Monographs of the American Ethnological Society, 3 (Seattle, 1940), 10; Richard Glover, ed., *David Thompson's Narrative 1784–1812* (Toronto, 1962), 267–8. For other such raids, see A.S. Morton, ed., *The Journal of Duncan M'Gillivray of the Northwest Company at Fort George on the Saskatchewan, 1794–1795* (Toronto, 1979), 27.

17. John McDougall, *Wa-pee Moostooch or White Buffalo* (Calgary, 1908), 132–50.

18. Glover, ed., *David Thompson's Narrative*, 241–2; Frank Raymond Secoy, *Changing Military Patterns on the Great Plains*, Monographs of the American Ethnological Society, 21 (Seattle, 1953), 33;

Lewis, *Effects of White Contact*, 11; George E. Hyde, *Indians of the High Plains* (Norman, Okla., 1959), 121, 133–4. See also R. Cole Harris, ed., *Historical Atlas of Canada*, I (Toronto, 1987), plate 57, for a schematic diagram of the diffusion of horses.

19. James Teit, 'The Salishan Tribes of the Western Plateau', 45th Annual Report, US Bureau of Ethnology (1927–8) (Washington, 1930), 109–10; Mishkin, *Rank and Warfare*, 9.

20. Secoy, *Military Patterns*, 36–8.

21. Glover, ed., *David Thompson's Narrative*, 240–4.

22. John C. Ewers, 'Was There a Northwestern Plains Subculture? An Ethnographic Appraisal', in Warren W. Caldwell, ed., *The Northwestern Plains: A Symposium* (Billings, Mont., 1968), 71. See also Hugh A. Dempsey, *Indian Tribes of Alberta* (Calgary, 1986).

23. John C. Ewers, *The Blackfeet* (Norman, Okla., 1958), 6–7; Lewis, *Effects of White Contact*, 7–9.

24. 'Gros Ventre' translates as 'Big Bellies', an appellation said to have been earned because of their big appetites. They called themselves Willow People. F.W. Hodge, *Handbook of Indians of Canada* (Ottawa, 1913), 51–2.

25. Ewers, 'Ethnographic Appraisal', 73. 'Atsina' was the Blackfoot term for these people and 'Gros Ventre' the French. Another name for them was 'Haaninin', 'chalk men' or 'men of soft white stone'.

26. Ewers, *Blackfeet*, 24–5.

27. Graded societies had different levels of membership, each with its particular functions and honours.

28. Regina Flannery, *The Gros Ventres of Montana, Part I: Social Life*, Anthropological Series #15 (Washington, 1953), 5; Alfred L. Kroeber, *Ethnology of the Gros Ventre* (New York, 1908), 145. Another fur trader, however, found them to be lazy and 'good only at stealing horses'. Morton, ed., *Duncan M'Gillivray*, 26–7, 73–4.

29. Cf. James Henri Howard, *The Plains-Ojibwa or Bungi, Hunters and Warriors of the Northern Prairie* (Vermillion, SD, 1965). Edwin Thompson Denig says that the Ojibwa and Cree were so intermingled as to be difficult to distinguish. See John C. Ewers, ed., *Five Indian Tribes of the Upper Missouri* (Norman, Okla., 1961), 100.

30. Coues, ed., *New Light*, II, 713–14. For a Spanish governor's ingenious argument in favour of providing guns to *indios barbaros* in order to make them less formidable, see Max L. Moorhead, *The Apache Frontier* (Norman, Okla., 1968), 127–8.

31. A Cree tradition from the Churchill River area has

it that the first time they met non-Aboriginals they were presented with a gun, but without live ammunition. Once they obtained ammunition, the Cree found the gun to be 'a good hunting weapon'. John S. Long, 'Narratives of Early Encounters between Europeans and the Cree of Western James Bay', *Ontario History* 80, 2 (1968): 230, 231.

32. Secoy, *Military Patterns*, 52.

33. Brian J. Smith, 'How Great an Influence was the Gun in Historic Northern Plains Ethnic Movements?', in Diana Claire Tkaczuk and Brian C. Vivian, eds, *Cultures in Conflict: Current Archaeological Perspectives* (Calgary, 1989), 253–61. Diamond Jenness, for his part, had no doubts that the gun disturbed the equilibrium not only between humans and the animals they hunted, but also between human groups. Jenness, *Eskimo Administration: II: Canada* (Montreal, 1972), 7.

34. Delegates to a Peigan–Salish (Flathead) peace council vividly described the effect that guns could have. See Glover, ed., *David Thompson's Narrative*, 390–1.

35. Ibid., 393.

36. Ibid., 207, 240. The Shoshoni were doubly unfortunate, as they were also confronted by Sioux armed with guns who pushed them westward into the mountains and sagebrush desert.

37. Hyde, *High Plains*, 164–5.

38. Coues, ed., *New Light*, II, 726.

39. Peter Fidler's Journal, HBC Archives, E 3/2:19, 31 Dec. 1792. See also F.W. Howay, 'David Thompson's Account of His First Attempt to Cross the Rockies', *Queen's Quarterly* 40 (1933): 337. A touching account of the Blackfoot's first encounter with non-Aboriginals is told by George Bird Grinnell, *The Story of the Indians* (New York, 1911), 224–40.

40. Various voyages into the interior are described by Arthur S. Morton, *A History of the Canadian West to 1870–71*, ed. Lewis G. Thomas (Toronto, 1973), 263–90.

41. Glyndwr Williams, 'The Puzzle of Anthony Henday's Journal, 1754–55', *The Beaver* Outfit 309, 3 (1978): 53.

42. Lewis, *Effects of White Contact*, 17–18.

43. Morton, ed., *Duncan M'Gillivray*, 31. That there might have been some grounds for the Blackfoot suspicions is indicated by French practices in the Huron trade, in which preferential treatment was accorded to converts. See Chapter 8 above.

44. E.E. Rich, *The Fur Trade in the Northwest to 1857* (Toronto, 1967), 158. It should be noted that

Amerindians regularly used fire to control vegetation, which in turn influenced the movements of the herds.

45. Howay, 'David Thompson's Account', 335; Glover, ed., *David Thompson's Narrative*, 272–9, 389.

46. Lewis, *Effects of White Contact*, 23.

47. J.B. Tyrrell, ed., *David Thompson's Narrative of His Explorations in Western America, 1784–1812* (Toronto, 1916), xc. For a different version, see J.E.A. Macleod, 'Peigan Post and the Blackfoot Trade', *Canadian Historical Review* 24, 3 (1943): 273–9.

48. Lewis, *Effects of White Contact*, 24.

49. Glover, ed., *David Thompson's Narrative*, 229. Thompson, of course, was repeating hearsay.

50. Ibid., 392–4. He called the intruders 'French Canadians'.

51. Pemmican was made from dried, pounded buffalo meat mixed with buffalo fat, about five parts meat to four parts fat, to which berries were sometimes added. One kilogram of pemmican had the food value of four to eight kilograms of fresh meat or fish. The development of its manufacture, believed to have occurred about 3000 BC, was a major factor in the emergence of the classic period of the Northern Plains Bison Hunting Culture. Brian O.K. Reeves, 'Communal Bison Hunters of the Northern Plains', in L.B. Davis and Reeves, eds, *Hunters of the Recent Past* (London, 1990), 169–70.

52. Lewis, *Effects of White Contact*, 35–6.

53. David G. Mandelbaum, *The Plains Cree* (New York, 1940), 246. Lewis says that among the Blackfoot, the third or fourth wife had such an inferior status that she was referred to as a 'slave'. Lewis, *Effects of White Contact*, 38–40.

54. Mandelbaum, *Plains Cree*, 57.

55. Daniel Williams Harmon, *Sixteen Years in the Indian Country: The Journals of Williams Harmon*, ed. W. Kaye Lamb (Toronto, 1957), 69.

56. Glover, ed., *David Thompson's Narrative*, 177–8.

57. David G. Mandelbaum, *Anthropology and People: The World of the Plains Cree* (Saskatoon, 1967), 6.

58. Ibid.

59. Coues, ed., *New Light*, I, 292–3; II, 498–9; Morton, *History of the Canadian West to 1870–71*, 253; Alexander Mackenzie, *Voyages from Montreal on the River St. Lawrence Through the Continent of America* (London, 1801), xiii–xiv. Mackenzie's work is reported to have been ghost-written. See Franz Montgomery, 'Alexander Mackenzie's Literary Assistant', *Canadian Historical Review* 18, 3 (1937): 301–4.

Chapter 14

1. Stephen Hume, 'Was B.C. discovered by Francis Drake?', *Ottawa Citizen*, 6 Aug. 2000, A5. According to the research of BC geographer Samuel Bawlf, Drake, while circumnavigating the globe, 1578–80, reached the mouth of the Stikine River where it cuts through the Alaska panhandle. The visit was kept secret to hide it from the Spaniards, who were claiming the entire North American west coast.

2. W.J. Eccles, 'The Fur Trade in the Colonial Northeast', in Wilcomb Washburn, ed., *Handbook of North American Indians, 4: History of Indian–White Relations* (Washington, 1988), 332.

3. John Witthoft, 'Archaeology as a Key to the Colonial Fur Trade', *Aspects of the Fur Trade* (St Paul, Minn., 1967), 56–7.

4. Samuel Hearne, *A Journey to the Northern Ocean in the Years 1769 · 1770 · 1771 · 1772*, ed. J.B. Tyrrell (Toronto, 1911), 330n. Archaeologist Clifford Hickey speculates that these beads could have been of Russian origin; Hearne thought they might be Danish from Davis Strait.

5. For a detailed account of these hostilities, see Kerry Abel, *Drum Songs* (Montreal and Kingston, 1993), ch. 5.

6. Trudy Nicks, 'The Iroquois and the Fur Trade in Western Canada', in Carol M. Judd and A.J. Ray, eds, *Old Trails and New Directions: Papers of the Third North American Fur Trade Conference* (Toronto, 1980), 86. See also Nicks, 'Origins of the Alberta Métis: Land Claims Research Project 1978–1979', workpaper for the Métis Association of Alberta.

7. HBC Archives, B 60/e/3, Edmonton District Report for 1819; cited by Nicks, 'Origins of Alberta Métis', 20.

8. Trudy Nicks, 'Mary Anne's Dilemma: The Ethnohistory of an Ambivalent Identity', *Canadian Ethnic Studies* 17, 2 (1985): 106.

9. Trudy Nicks and Kenneth Morgan, 'Grand Cache: The Historic Development of an Indigenous Alberta Métis Population', in Jacqueline Peterson and Jennifer S.H. Brown, eds, *The New Peoples: Being and Becoming Métis in North America* (Winnipeg, 1985), 163–81.

10. Methye Portage was also known as Portage La Loche. 'Methye' is the Cree word for a freshwater fish, the burbot.

11. E.E. Rich, 'Trade Habits, Economic Motivation, among the Indians of North America', *Canadian Journal of Economics and Political Science* 26, 1 (1960): 35–53. This article was reprinted, with illustrations added, under the title 'The Indian

Traders', *The Beaver* Outfit 301 (1970): 5–20.

12. Richard Glover, ed., *David Thompson's Narrative 1784–1812* (Toronto, 1962), 273–4.

13. W.A. Sloan, 'The Columbia link—native trade, warfare, and European penetration of the Kootenays', paper presented to the Orkney–Rupert's Land Colloquium, Orkney Islands, 1990.

14. Arthur S. Morton, ed., *The Journal of Duncan M'Gillivray of the Northwest Company at Fort George on the Saskatchewan* (Toronto, 1979), 56.

15. Glover, ed., *David Thompson's Narrative*, 305–6; Elliott Coues, ed., *New Light on the Early History of the Great Northwest 1799–1814*, 3 vols (New York, 1897), II, 713.

16. Alice Beck Kehoe, *The Ghost Dance* (Toronto, 1989), 100.

17. L.F.S. Upton, 'Contact and Conflict on the Atlantic and Pacific Coasts of Canada', *B.C. Studies* 45 (1980): 103–15. See also R. Cole Harris, ed., *Historical Atlas of Canada*, I (Toronto, 1987), plate 66.

18. Robert T. Boyd, 'Demographic History, 1774–1784', in Wayne Suttles, ed., *Handbook of North American Indians, 7: Northwest Coast* (Washington, 1990), 135.

19. F.W. Howay, 'An Outline Sketch of the Maritime Fur Trade', *Canadian Historical Association Report* (1932): 5–14.

20. Robin Fisher, *Contact and Conflict* (Vancouver, 1977), 3; F.W. Howay, 'Early Days of the Maritime Trade on the Northwest Coast', *Canadian Historical Review* 4 (1923): 26–44.

21. Upton, 'Contact and Conflict on the Atlantic and Pacific Coasts of Canada', 103–15.

22. Made Beaver was a beaver pelt cleaned, stretched, and dried for the trade.

23. 'Muquinna' was a chiefly title of the Mochat band and was held by several chiefs. The holder of the title referred to here not only controlled the trade of his own people, but also that of the Kwakwaka'wakw of the Nimkish River.

24. Arrell Morgan Gibson, *The American Indian: Prehistory to the Present* (Lexington, Mass., 1980), 177.

25. Fisher, *Contact and Conflict*, 16. See also F.W. Howay, 'Indian Attacks upon Maritime Traders of the Northwest Coast, 1785–1805', *Canadian Historical Review* 6, 4 (1925): 287–309.

26. *Dictionary of Canadian Biography*, IV, s.v. 'Koyah'.

27. Fisher, *Contact and Conflict*, 15. Various versions of the incident are given by F.W. Howay, 'The Ballad of the Bold Northwestman: An Incident in the Life of Captain John Kendrick', *Washington Historical Quarterly* 20 (1929): 114–23.

28. One of the survivors was John Jewitt, who published his experiences in *A Journal Kept at Nootka Sound . . .* (Boston, 1807).

29. Possible motivations are discussed in Fisher, *Contact and Conflict*, 16.

30. Gabriel Franchère, *Journal of a Voyage to the Northwest Coast of North America during the Years 1811, 1812, 1813 and 1814*, ed. W. Kaye Lamb (Toronto, 1969), 124–7.

31. Fisher, *Contact and Conflict*, 30.

32. Ibid., 35.

33. Douglas had been born in British Guiana, the son of a Scots trader and 'a free colored woman'.

34. PABC, Correspondence Inward, Douglas to McLoughlin, Fort Vancouver, 10 Oct. 1840; cited by Fisher, *Contact and Conflict*, 32.

35. Fisher, *Contact and Conflict*, 31.

36. Both 'Legaic' and 'Wiiseaks' were chiefly titles by which the incumbents were known. For example, there were five recorded Legaics, a title held by the Eagle clan. The first known holder of the title built a trade empire during the second half of the eighteenth century, which the second Legaic expanded by establishing a trading relationship with the HBC, which was cemented in 1832 by the marriage of his daughter to Dr John Frederick Kennedy, an official with the Company. See Michael P. Robinson, *Sea Otter Chiefs* (Vancouver, [1978]), 61–87; *Dictionary of Canadian Biography*, XII, s.v. 'Legaic, Paul'. Tsimshian stories of Legaic and Wiiseaks are in Marius Barbeau and William Beynon, coll., *Tsimshian Narratives 2* (Ottawa, 1987).

37. Fisher, *Contact and Conflict*, 32.

38. E.E. Rich, ed., *The Letters of John McLaughlin from Fort Vancouver to the Governor and Committee*, First series, 1825–38 (London, 1941), IV, app. A, Duncan Finlayson to John McLaughlin, 334–5.

39. Some estimates place the pre-contact population much lower, and the nadir at 10,000. See Thomas Berger, *Fragile Freedoms: Human Rights and Dissent in Canada* (Toronto, 1981), 229.

40. On Kwah, see Charles A. Bishop, 'Kwah: A Carrier Chief', in Judd and Ray, eds, *Old Trails and New Directions*, 191–204. Kwah is remembered mainly for a confrontation with Douglas, in which he spared the latter's life.

41. See Rolf Knight, *Indians at Work: An Informal History of Native Indian Labour in British Columbia 1858–1930* (Vancouver, 1978).

Chapter 15

1. For purposes of administration, the English colonies were divided into two departments, the northern and the southern.

2. Reginald Horsman, *Expansion and American Indian Policy, 1783–1812* (East Lansing, Mich., 1967), 171.

3. On the intolerance of American frontiersmen to Amerindian rights, see Robert L. Fisher, 'The Western Prologue to the War of 1812', *Missouri Historical Review* 30, 3 (1936): 272.

4. LAC, RG 8, series C, vol. 257:31, McGill to Prevost, Montreal, 19 Dec. 1812; George F.G. Stanley, 'The Indians in the War of 1812', *Canadian Historical Review* 31, 2 (1950): 152–3.

5. George F.G. Stanley, *The War of 1812: Land Operations* (Toronto, 1983), 64–5.

6. Britain, in its pursuit of the Napoleonic Wars, had insisted on its right to stop neutral vessels on the high seas in search of contraband and British deserters. In 1807, when the American *Chesapeake* refused to allow the British to take off suspected runaways, the British HMS *Leopard* fired on her, killing three of her men. The Americans retaliated with economic sanctions against Britain, though these were ineffective. See John Sugden, *Tecumseh's Last Stand* (Norman, Okla., 1985), 20.

7. Stanley, 'Indians in the War of 1812'; Stanley, 'The Significance of the Six Nations' Participation in the War of 1812', *Ontario History* 55, 4 (1963): 215–31.

8. Haldimand Papers 21783: 276–7, Seneca chief to council, Detroit, 1 Dec. 1782; cited by Colin Calloway, *Crown and Calumet: British–Indian Relations, 1783–1815* (Norman, Okla., 1987), 61.

9. John 10:9. See R. David Edmunds, *The Shawnee Prophet* (Lincoln, Neb., 1983), 28–41.

10. For a reaction to this policy, see 'Tecumseh's Claims: An American View', in Carl F. Klinck, ed., *Tecumseh* (Englewood Cliffs, NJ, 1961), 75.

11. Apparently the admiration was mutual. See 'Brock and Tecumseh', ibid., 138.

12. R. David Edmunds, *Tecumseh and the Quest for Indian Leadership* (Boston, 1984), 148–53.

13. Calloway, *Crown and Calumet*, 11.

14. Haldimand Papers 21763: 225–6, Brigadier General Allen Maclean to Haldimand, 8 Aug. 1783, cited ibid., 62.

15. Ibid., 69.

16. *Dictionary of Canadian Biography*, VI. The Dakota call the War of 1812 Pahinshashawacikiya, 'when the Redhead begged for our help'. Peter Douglas Elias, *The Dakota of the Canadian Northwest: Lessons for Survival* (Winnipeg, 1988), 8.

17. Walter Lowrie and Matthew St Clair Clarke, eds, *American State Papers. Class II. Indian Affairs, 1789–1827*, 2 vols (Washington, 1832–4), I, 322; Calloway, *Crown and Calumet*, 116–20.

18. Robert S. Allen, *His Majesty's Indian Allies: British Indian Policy in the Defence of Canada, 1774–1815* (Toronto, 1992), 120. See also George F.G. Stanley, 'The Indians in the War of 1812', in Morris Zaslow, ed., *The Defended Border: Upper Canada and the War of 1812* (Toronto, 1964), 174–88.

19. Stanley, *War of 1812*, 95–6.

20. A description of the battle is in Edmunds, *Tecumseh and the Quest for Indian Leadership*, 180.

21. 'Tekarihogen' was the name of a chieftainship of the Six Nations (alleged by the Mohawks to be the primary one), hereditary in Brant's mother's clan. *Dictionary of Canadian Biography*, VI, s.v. 'Tekarihogen'.

22. Stanley, *War of 1812*, 65–6, 122, 128–31.

23. Edmunds, *Tecumseh and the Quest for Indian Leadership*, 192–3.

24. Reginald Horsman, *The Frontier in the Formative Years, 1783–1815* (New York, 1970), 179–83.

25. Calloway, *Crown and Calumet*, 202–3; Stanley, *War of 1812*, 196–9.

26. Matthew Elliott's description of the battle is in Calloway, *Crown and Calumet*, 236–7; another version is in Stanley, *War of 1812*, 211–12. On the reported desecration of Tecumseh's body, see Sugden, *Tecumseh's Last Stand*, 136–81.

27. Edwin Seaborn, *The March of Medicine in Western Ontario* (Toronto, 1944), 9–10. For other versions, see Klinck, ed., *Tecumseh*, 200–19.

28. Sugden is particularly emphatic on this point: *Tecumseh's Last Stand*, 193–5. See also the list of battles in which Amerindians took part, and the percentage of their participation, in Helen Hornbeck Tanner, ed., *Atlas of Great Lakes Indian History* (Norman, Okla., 1987), 108–15. More than a third of these battles were fought after Moraviantown.

29. Many more Indians than whites fought in the war, with a number of the battles involving only Indians. As a consequence, apart from a few specific battles, there are no statistics available for Indian casualties.

30. Stanley, *War of 1812*, 394.

31. Kerry A. Trask, 'Settlement in a Half-Savage Land: Life and Loss in the Métis Community of La Baye', *Michigan Historical Review* 15 (1989): 1–27.

32. Robert S. Allen, *Her Majesty's Indian Allies* (Toronto, 1993), 197–8; Edward S. Rogers and Donald B. Smith, eds, *Aboriginal Ontario* (Toronto, 1994), 123–4.

33. John F. Leslie, 'Buried Hatchet', *Horizon Canada* 4, 40 (1985): 944–9.

34. Robert J. Surtees, 'Canadian Indian Treaties', in

Wilcomb E. Washburn, ed., *Handbook of North American Indians, 4: History of Indian–White Relations* (Washington, 1988), 204.

35. Denys Delâge, *Le pays renversé: Amérindiens et européens en Amérique du nord-est, 1600–1664* (Montréal, 1985), 339–47.

Chapter 16

1. Later, ranching would be advocated, as the 'work suits the Indians better'. Not only that, but ranching could be co-ordinated with hunting. In the view of the NWMP, 'Farming is too steady and monotonous work for them, although some have fine fields.' (Canada, *N.W.M.P. Report, 1895*, 5.)

2. As Alexandre Taché (bishop of St Boniface, Man., 1853–71, archbishop, 1871–94) acidly observed, farming, 'although so desirable, is not the sole condition in the state of civilization'. Canada, *Sessional Papers 1885*, No. 116, 'Papers . . . in connection with the extinguishment of the Indian title preferred by Half-breeds resident in the North-West Territories', 85, Taché to Col. J.S. Dennis, deputy minister of the interior, 29 Jan. 1879.

3. Cited by L.F.S. Upton, 'The Origins of Canadian Indian Policy', *Journal of Canadian Studies* 10, 4 (1973): 59.

4. Donald B. Smith, *Sacred Feathers* (Toronto, 1987). This is a biography of Rev. Peter Jones (KahKewaquonaby), who devoted his life to leading his people into the new world.

5. J. Garth Taylor, *Labrador Eskimo Settlements of the Early Contact Period* (Ottawa, 1974); W. Gillies Ross, *Whaling and Eskimos: Hudson Bay 1860–1915* (Ottawa, 1975).

6. *Dictionary of Canadian Biography*, IV, s.v. 'Haven, Jens'. See also Diamond Jenness, *Eskimo Administration: II: Canada* (Montreal, 1972), 9–10. The Moravian Brethren, also known as *Unitas Fratrum*, was a pietist Protestant missionary group founded in 1727 by Count Nikolaus Ludwig von Zinzendorf (1700–60). They already had missions in Greenland when they were invited by the British to establish in Labrador.

7. *Dictionary of Canadian Biography*, IV, s.v. 'Mikak'.

8. Barnett Richling, 'Without Compromise: Hudson's Bay Company and Moravian Trade Rivalry in Nineteenth Century Labrador', in Bruce G. Trigger, Toby Morantz, and Louise Dechêne, eds, *Le Castor Fait Tout* (Montreal, 1987), 456–84.

9. An adult whale would have as much as 2,000 pounds of baleen in its jaws; in 1883, baleen brought $4.75 a pound.

10. Ross, *Whaling and Eskimos*, 138.

11. On adaptation to Euro-Canadian foods, see Morris Zaslow, *The Northward Expansion of Canada 1914–1967* (Toronto, 1988), 153.

12. John R. Bockstoce, *Whales, Ice, and Men: The History of Whaling in the Western Arctic* (Seattle, 1986), 130, 136.

13. Ibid., 135–42.

14. Morris Zaslow, *The Opening of the Canadian North 1870–1914* (Toronto, 1971), 258.

15. On the effects of the change of diet, see William Morrison, *Under the Flag: Canadian Sovereignty and the Native People in Northern Canada* (Ottawa, 1984), 74–6.

16. The name 'Yukon' (Youcon, Ou-kun-ah) derives from an Indian word, probably Gwich'in, meaning great river or white water river. If the Bering Strait migration hypothesis is correct, then the Yukon, with Alaska, is North America's oldest inhabited region. Kenneth S. Coates and William R. Morrison, *Land of the Midnight Sun: A History of the Yukon* (Edmonton, 1988), 2, 5.

17. Ibid., 13, 25, 50.

18. Catharine McClellan, *Part of the Land, Part of the Water: A History of the Yukon* (Vancouver, 1987), 67–70, 75–84; Coates and Morrison, *Land of the Midnight Sun*, 23–30.

19. Federation of Newfoundland Indians, at: <www.qalipu.com/w_press.html>.

20. David T. McNab, 'The Mi'kmaq Nation of Newfoundland and Section 35 of the Charter of Rights and Freedoms', in Rick Riewe and Jill Oakes, eds, *Aboriginal Connections to Race, Environment and Traditions* (Winnipeg, 2006), 27–35; e-mail, Brendan Sheppard to David T. McNab, 18 Sept. 2007.

21. L.F.S. Upton, *Micmacs and Colonists: Indian–White Relations in the Maritimes, 1713–1867* (Vancouver, 1979), 82–7.

22. Ibid., 91.

23. Douglas Sanders, 'Government Indian Agencies in Canada', in Wilcomb E. Washburn, ed., *Handbook of North American Indians, 4: History of Indian–White Relations* (Washington, 1988), 279.

24. Upton, *Micmacs and Colonists*, 95.

25. During the nineteenth century the porpoise was particularly valued for its oil, which was used in the manufacture and maintenance of fine watches. A bill before the Nova Scotia House of Assembly to ban the shooting of porpoises in the bay had passed two readings when Meuse made his plea that resulted in the bill's defeat.

26. Upton, *Micmacs and Colonists*, 96.

27. Ibid., 99; Peter A. Cumming and Neil H. Mickenberg, eds, *Native Rights in Canada* (Toronto, 1972), 308–9.

28. Upton, *Micmacs and Colonists*, 99–100.

29. Cumming and Mickenberg, eds, *Native Rights*, 102.

30. Upton, *Micmacs and Colonists*, 112.

31. Journals of the Legislative Assembly of Prince Edward Island, 7 Jan. 1812, 11–12, cited by Upton, *Micmacs and Colonists*, 115.

32. Ibid., 118.

33. Reuben Gold Thwaites, ed., *Jesuit Relations and Allied Documents*, 73 vols (Cleveland, 1896–1901), VI, 151; Lucien Campeau, 'Roman Catholic Missions', in Washburn, ed., *Handbook of North American Indians, 4: History of Indian–White Relations*, 465–8. See also James P. Ronda, 'The Sillery Experiment: A Jesuit–Indian Village in New France, 1637–1663', *American Indian Culture and Research Journal* 3, 1 (1979): 1–18.

34. William Henderson, *Canada's Indian Reserves: Pre-Confederation* (Ottawa, 1980), 2–5.

35. George Stanley, 'The First Indian "Reserves" in Canada', *Revue d'histoire de l'Amérique française* 4 (1950): 178; Thwaites, ed., *Jesuit Relations*, LXVI, 43.

36. Thwaites, ed., *Jesuit Relations*, XXIII, 303; LX, 131.

37. Stanley, 'First Indian "Reserves"', 185.

38. Léon Gérin, 'La Seigneurie de Sillery et les Hurons', *Mémoires de la Société Royale du Canada*, ser. 2, vol. 6 (1900): sec. 1, 75–115. See also Georges E. Sioui, *Pour une autohistoire amérindienne: Essai sur les fondements d'une morale sociale* (Québec, 1989), 124–5.

39. Thwaites, ed., *Jesuit Relations*, XLVII, 263, 299; LXVI, 43–7; Henderson, *Canada's Indian Reserves*, 3. On Sillery's religious and social failure as far as the Montagnais were concerned, see Kenneth M. Morrison, 'Baptism and Alliance: The Symbolic Mediations of Religious Syncretism', *Ethnohistory* 37, 4 (1990): 416–37.

40. Stanley, 'First Indian "Reserves"', 186–7; Richard H. Bartlett, *Indian Reserves in Quebec* (Saskatoon, 1984), 2 n6.

41. More precisely, a reserve is 'a tract of land in which the aboriginal interest is permanently preserved for a particular group of native people'. Jack Woodward, *Native Law* (Toronto, 1989), 222. See also Brian Slattery, 'Understanding Aboriginal Rights', *Canadian Bar Review* 66 (1987): 743–4, 769–71. A Cree term applied to reserves is 'iskonikun', what is left over, scraps. This refers to the fact that many reserves are ill-suited for agriculture and have long since become useless for hunting and trapping. See Eleanor Brass, *I Walk in Two Worlds* (Calgary, 1987), 71.

42. Henderson, *Canada's Indian Reserves*, 4–5.

43. The Sarnia, Kettle Point, and Stoney Point reserves and Moore Township. Henderson, *Canada's Indian Reserves*, 10 and n56.

44. Boyce Richardson, 'Kind Hearts or Forked Tongues?', *The Beaver* Outfit 67, 1 (1987): 18.

45. Smith, *Sacred Feathers*, chs 6, 7. Other Amerindian clerics, all Methodists, included George Copway (Kahgegagahbowh, 'He Who Stands Forever', 1818–69); Peter Jacobs (Pahtahsaga, 'One Who Makes the World Brighter', *c.* 1807–94); and War of 1812 veteran John Sunday (Shah-wun-dais, 'Sultry Heat', *c.* 1795–1875). Two of these, Copway and Jacobs, ran into funding difficulties that resulted in their expulsion from their ministries.

46. John F. Leslie and Ron Maguire, *The Historical Development of the Indian Act* (Ottawa, 1978), 18–19.

47. Peter S. Schmaltz, *The History of the Saugeen Indians* (Ottawa, 1977), 82–4. 'Saugeen' is Ojibwa for 'mouth of the river'.

48. *Dictionary of Canadian Biography*, IX, s.v. 'Musquakie'; VIII, s.v. 'Aisance'. For more on Aisance, see Smith, *Sacred Feathers*, 212–13.

49. Smith, *Sacred Feathers*, 349.

50. On such movements in general, see Anthony F.C. Wallace, 'Revitalization Movements: Some Theoretical Considerations for Their Comparative Study', *American Anthropologist* 58, 2 (1956): 264–81. See also Selwyn Dewdney, *The Sacred Scrolls of the Southern Ojibway* (Toronto, 1975); Ruth Landes, *Ojibwa Religion and Midéwiwin* (Madison, Wis., 1968).

51. Francis Bond Head, *A Narrative*, 2nd edn (London, 1839), app. A, 'Memorandum on the Aborigines of North America'. This memorandum is reproduced in part in Adam Shortt and Arthur G. Doughty, eds, *Canada and Its Provinces*, 23 vols (Toronto, 1914–17), V, 337–9. Sir Francis had been knighted in 1831, reportedly because of his demonstration of the military usefulness of the lasso.

52. Peggy J. Blair, 'The Supreme Court of Canada's "Historic" Decision in *Nikal* and *Lewis*: Why Crown Fishing Policy in Upper Canada Makes Bad Law', Master's thesis (University of Ottawa, 1998), 52–9. See also Victor P. Lytwyn, 'Waterworld: The Aquatic Territory of the Great Lakes First Nations', in Dale Standen and David McNab, eds, *Gin Das Winan: Documenting Aboriginal History in Ontario* (Toronto, 1996), 14–28.

53. Smith, *Sacred Feathers*, 163–4; Schmalz, *History of the Saugeen Indians*, 56–148.

54. B.E. Hill, 'The Grand River Navigation Company and the Six Nations Indians', *Ontario History* 63, 1 (1971): 31–40; Richard C. Daniel, *A History of Native Claims Processes in Canada 1867–1979* (Ottawa, 1980), 122–30.

55. Sidney L. Harring, *White Man's Law: Native People in Nineteenth-Century Canadian Jurisprudence* (Toronto, 1998), 58, 148.

56. According to Daniel, Chisholm was the most active of the lawyers who worked on Amerindian cases. Others included R.V. Sinclair of Ottawa and Walter O'Meara in British Columbia. Daniel, *History of Native Claims*, 198.

57. Maurice F.V. Doll, Robert S. Kidd, and John P. Day, *The Buffalo Lake Métis Site: A Late Nineteenth Century Settlement in the Parkland of Central Alberta* (Edmonton, 1988), 13–14.

58. Paul Kane, *Wanderings of an Artist* (Edmonton, 1968; first published 1859), 89.

59. Irene M. Spry, *The Palliser Expedition: An Account of John Palliser's British North American Expedition 1857–1860* (Toronto, 1963), 60.

60. F.G. Roe, 'Early Agriculture in Western Canada in Relation to Climatic Stability', *Agricultural History* 26, 3 (1952): 109. On pre-contact agriculture in the Red River area, see *Prehistory of the Lockport Site* (Winnipeg, 1985), 11. Willingness to take up agriculture was also noted by John Leonard Taylor, 'Development of an Indian Policy for the Canadian North-West, 1869–79', Ph.D. thesis (Queen's University, 1976), 188, 242–3.

61. The Nor'Westers alone regularly prepared 30 to 50 tons of pemmican each season for the company's fur brigades. A.S. Morton, *History of Prairie Settlement and Dominion Lands Policy* (Toronto, 1938), 208.

62. Laura L. Peers, 'Rich Man, Poor Man, Beggarman, Chief: Saulteaux in the Red River Settlement, 1812–1833', in William Cowan, ed., *Papers of the Eighteenth Algonquian Conference* (Ottawa, 1987), 265–9.

63. Both the Jurisdiction Act of 1803 and the Fur Trade Act of 1821 were concerned with extending the Canadian court system into the Northwest. The 1803 Act had been inspired by the Louisiana Purchase of the same year.

64. Arthur S. Morton, *A History of the Canadian West to 1870–71*, ed. Lewis G. Thomas (Toronto, 1973), 628.

65. Hamar Foster, 'Long-Distance Justice: The Criminal Jurisdiction of Canadian Courts West of the Canadas, 1763–1859', *American Journal of Legal History* 34, 1 (1990): 6.

66. J.A.H. Bennett and J.W. Berry, 'The Future of Cree Syllabic Literacy in Northern Canada', paper presented at the Fifteenth Algonquian Conference, Winnipeg, 1986.

67. A page of the letter is reproduced in René Fumoleau, *As Long As This Land Shall Last* (Toronto, 1973), 33.

68. Duncan Campbell Scott, 'The Last of the Indian Treaties', *Scribner's Magazine* 40, 5 (1906): 581–2. Among those who applauded Evans's achievement during his lifetime was William Case, who established the model village at Grape Island. See Fred Landon, *Selections from the Papers of James Evans, Missionary to the Indians* (Toronto, 1930), 6–7.

69. Jennifer S.H. Brown, 'The Track to Heaven: The Hudson Bay Cree Religious Movement of 1842–1843', in William Cowan, ed., *Papers of the Thirteenth Algonquian Conference* (Ottawa, 1982), 59. See also *Dictionary of Canadian Biography*, I, s.v. 'Abishabis'; John S. Long, 'The Cree Prophets: Oral and Documentary Accounts', *Journal of the Canadian Church Historical Society* 31, 1 (1989): 3–13.

70. See, for example, Pat Moore and Angela Wheelock, eds, *Wolverine Myths and Visions: Dene Traditions from Northern Alberta* (Edmonton, 1990). Compiled by the Dene Wodih Society, this work deals with Dene prophets, particularly Nógha ('Wolverine', *fl.* 1920s) of the Dene Dháa, and recounts wolverine stories as told by the people. On northern shamanism, see Catharine McClellan, *My Old People Say: An Ethnographic Survey of Southern Yukon Territory*, 2 vols (Ottawa, 1975), II, 529–75.

71. Daniel Francis and Toby Morantz, *Partners in Furs: A History of the Fur Trade in Eastern James Bay 1600–1870* (Montreal and Kingston, 1983), 158–60; Cecil Chabot, 'Merging Cree and Non-Cree Understandings of the 1832 Washaw Conflict', MA thesis (University of Montreal, 2002).

72. John S. Long, '"No Basis for Argument"? The Signing of Treaty Nine in Northern Ontario, 1905–1906', *Native Studies Review* 5, 2 (1989): 38. A less violent example of Amerindian reaction to a non-Native transgression of Native trading protocol is told by McClellan, *My Old People Say*, II, 507–8. In this case the Chilkats felt that their trading privileges had been violated.

73. Paul Tennant, *Aboriginal Peoples and Politics* (Vancouver, 1990), 20.

74. Rolf Knight, *Indians at Work: An Informal History*

of Native Indian Labour in British Columbia 1858–1930 (Vancouver, 1978), 236.

75. Robin Fisher, *Contact and Conflict: Indian–European Relations in British Columbia 1774–1890* (Vancouver, 1977), 154–6.

76. Tennant, *Aboriginal Peoples and Politics*, 21–38.

77. For example, according to Robert Cail, 'So long as Douglas was governor, the Indians had only to ask to receive additional land.' Cail, *Land, Man, and the Law: The Disposal of Crown Lands in British Columbia, 1871–1913* (Vancouver, 1974), 179.

78. Tennant, *Aboriginal Peoples and Politics*, 30–8.

79. Cumming and Mickenberg, eds, *Native Rights in Canada*, 176–80; Fisher, *Contact and Conflict*, 153–6; Wilson Duff, *The Indian History of British Columbia*, vol. 1, *The Impact of the White Man* (Victoria, 1964), 61.

80. Fisher, *Contact and Conflict*, 156.

81. Dennis Madill, *British Columbia Treaties in Historical Perspective* (Ottawa, 1981), 31.

82. Barry M. Gough, *Gunboat Frontier: British Maritime Authority and Northwest Coast Indians, 1846–1890* (Vancouver, 1984).

83. J.E. Michael Kew, 'History of Coastal British Columbia Since 1846', in Wayne Suttles, ed., *Handbook of North American Indians, 7: Northwest Coast* (Washington, 1990), 159.

84. Fisher, *Contact and Conflict*, 208.

85. Gough, *Gunboat Frontier*, 205–8.

86. Beaver's criticisms continued even after his departure. A letter he wrote in 1892 on the subject is reproduced in Nellie B. Pipes, 'Indian Conditions in 1836–38', *Oregon Historical Quarterly* 32, 4 (1931): 332–42.

87. Fort Simpson has been labelled the 'London of the Northwest Coast' because it was the largest settlement in the region and was the hub for trading activity.

88. The most complete work on Duncan is Jean Usher's *William Duncan of Metlakatla* (Ottawa, 1974). See Usher, 'Duncan of Metlakatla: The Victorian Origins of a Model Indian Community', in W.L. Morton, ed., *The Shield of Achilles: Aspects of Canada in the Victorian Age* (Toronto, 1968), 286–310; Fisher, *Contact and Conflict*, 125–36; John Webster Grant, *Moon of Wintertime: Missionaries and the Indians of Canada in Encounter since 1534* (Toronto, 1984), 129–32. On Legaic, see *Dictionary of Canadian Biography*, XII, s.v. 'Legaic, Paul'; Michael P. Robinson, *Sea Otter Chiefs* (Vancouver, c. 1978).

89. Usher, *William Duncan of Metlakatla*, 135. Jean Friesen was formerly Jean Usher.

90. Frederick Temple Blackwood, 1st Marquess of Dufferin and Ava, governor-general of Canada, 1872–8.

91. Thomas Crosby, *Up and Down the Pacific Coast by Canoe and Mission Ship* (Toronto, 1914), 65–6.

Chapter 17

1. John H. Bodley, ed., *Tribal Peoples and Development Issues: A Global Overview* (Mountain View, Calif., 1988), 63–9.

2. Some of these problems are still continuing. For example, the community of Shannonville, Ontario, occupies lands that were leased by the Iroquois of Tyendinaga early in the nineteenth century to a certain Turton Penn for 999 years. William Henderson, *Canada's Indian Reserves: Pre-Confederation* (Ottawa, 1980), 38 n48.

3. John Leslie and Ron Maguire, *The Historical Development of the Indian Act* (Ottawa, 1978), 11.

4. A clear exposition of this position is that of Herman Merivale, 'Policy of Colonial Governments towards Native Tribes, as Regards Their Protection and Their Civilization', in Bodley, ed., *Tribal Peoples*, 95–104.

5. The phrase 'white man's burden' owes its origin to Rudyard Kipling, who used it in reference to Amerindians in the US.

6. Leslie and Maguire, *Historical Development*, 12. See also Robert S. Allen, 'The British Department and the Frontier in North America, 1755–1830', *Occasional Papers in Archaeology and History*, No. 14 (Ottawa, 1975).

7. John Brant was elected to Upper Canada's House of Assembly by the riding of Haldimand in 1830. His victory was challenged, however, on the grounds of voting irregularities, and he lost his seat the following year. It is widely believed in the Six Nations that the real reason Brant lost out was because he was an Indian.

8. Dennis Madill, 'Band Council Powers', in *Indian Government under Indian Act Legislation 1868–1951* (Ottawa, 1980).

9. John E. Hodgetts, *Pioneer Public Service: An Administrative History of the United Canadas, 1841–1867* (Toronto, 1955), 223.

10. David McNab, 'The Colonial Office and the Prairies in the Mid-Nineteenth Century', *Prairie Forum* 3, 1 (1978): 21–38.

11. It was published in two parts, in *Journals of the Legislative Assembly of the Province of Canada*, 1844–5, app. EEE; and ibid., 1847, app. T.

12. Cited by Boyce Richardson, 'Kind Hearts or Forked Tongues?', *The Beaver* Outfit 67, 1 (1987): 23. The commissioners appear to have considered

that Amerindian loss of lands was in large part due to alienation by the Amerindians themselves. Such a view would have been reinforced by the lack of Amerindian action in launching suits against trespass or for the recovery of lost lands.

13. *Journals of the Legislative Assembly of the Province of Canada*, 1847, app. T.

14. Leslie and Maguire, *Historical Development*, 21.

15. Donald B. Smith, *Sacred Feathers* (Toronto, 1987), 184.

16. Robin Fisher, *Contact and Conflict: Indian–European Relations in British Columbia 1774–1890* (Vancouver, 1977), 86.

17. Toby Morantz, 'Aboriginal Land Claims in Quebec', in Ken Coates, ed., *Aboriginal Land Claims in Canada* (Toronto, 1992), 107.

18. *Schedule of Indian Bands, Reserves and Settlements* (Ottawa, 1987), 11–17. Amerindian settlements, of which there are about a dozen, are not included, as they do not have lands specifically set aside for them.

19. Some reserve the term 'Indian' for those who are registered. See, for example, J. Rick Ponting and Roger Gibbins, *Out of Irrelevance* (Toronto, 1980), xv.

20. For later developments on this, see Chapter 18.

21. John L. Tobias, 'Protection, Civilization, Assimilation: An Outline History of Canada's Indian Policy', *Western Canadian Journal of Anthropology* 6, 2 (1976): 16. This article was reprinted in A.L. Getty and Antoine S. Lussier, eds, *As Long As the Sun Shines and Water Flows* (Vancouver, 1983), 39–55.

22. John S. Milloy, 'The Early Indian Acts: Developmental Strategy and Constitutional Change', in Getty and Lussier, eds, *As Long As the Sun Shines and Water Flows*, 59.

23. Smith, *Sacred Feathers*, 238–9.

24. Henderson, *Canada's Indian Reserves*, 15.

25. *Dictionary of Canadian Biography*, IX, s.v. 'Assikinack, Francis'.

26. For a study of the long Ojibwa struggle with the mining companies, see Janet E. Chute, *The Legacy of Shingwaukonse: A Century of Native Leadership* (Toronto, 1998).

27. Douglas Leighton, 'The Historical Significance of the Robinson Treaties of 1850', paper presented to the Canadian Historical Association, Ottawa, 1982; Richardson, 'Kind Hearts or Forked Tongues?', 24–7; George Brown and Ron Maguire, eds, *Indian Treaties in Historical Perspective* (Ottawa, 1979), 26.

28. Robert J. Surtees, 'Canada's Indian Treaties', in Wilcomb E. Washburn, ed., *Handbook of North American Indians, 4: History of Indian–White*

Relations (Washington, 1988), 203, 206.

29. This view is expressed in a pamphlet issued by the Federation of Saskatchewan Indians, *Indian Treaty Rights*, n.d., n.p.

30. Jack Woodward, *Native Law* (Toronto, 1989), 236. See also Richard Bartlett, 'The Establishment of Indian Reserves on the Prairies', *Canadian Native Law Reporter* 3 (1980): 3–56.

31. Allen G. Harper, 'Canada's Indian Administration: Basic Concepts and Objectives', *América Indigena* 5, 2 (1945): 132. See also Roger Gibbins and J. Rick Ponting, 'Historical Overview and Background', in Ponting, ed., *Arduous Journey: Canadian Indians and Decolonization* (Toronto, 1986), 25.

32. Hodgetts, *Pioneer Public Service*, 209–10.

33. A rule of thumb for determining their size was to allow 80 acres (32 hectares) per family; however, there was considerable variation in practice.

Chapter 18

1. Douglas Sanders, 'Government Indian Agencies', in Wilcomb E. Washburn, ed., *Handbook of North American Indians, 4: History of Indian–White Relations* (Washington, 1988), 279.

2. Malcolm Montgomery, 'The Six Nations Indians and the Macdonald Franchise', *Ontario History* 56 (1964): 13.

3. The price was $1.5 million, or about one penny for every three hectares.

4. *Census of Canada*, 1871, I, 332–3; 1881, I, 300–1; 1941, 684–91.

5. Wayne Daugherty, 'The Elective System', in *Indian Government under Indian Act Legislation, 1868–1951* (Ottawa, 1980), 4.

6. Cited by Boyce Richardson, 'Kind Hearts or Forked Tongues?', *The Beaver* Outfit 67, 1 (1987): 31.

7. On current legal meanings of 'Indian', see Jack Woodward, *Native Law* (Toronto, 1989), 5–12.

8. Daugherty, 'The Elective System', 3.

9. John L. Tobias, 'Protection, Civilization, Assimilation: An Outline History of Canada's Indian Policy', *Western Canadian Journal of Anthropology* 6, 2 (1976): 17–18.

10. Ibid., 22–3.

11. Kathleen Jamieson, *Indian Women and the Law in Canada: Citizens Minus* (Ottawa, 1978), 69–73.

12. Dennis Madill, 'Band Council Powers', in *Indian Government under Indian Act Legislation, 1868–1951*, 2.

13. Daugherty, 'The Elective System', 2.

14. Thomas Berger, *Fragile Freedoms: Human Rights*

and Dissent in Canada (Toronto, 1981), 222.

15. N.L. Barlee, 'The Chilcotin War of 1864', *Canada West Magazine* 6, 4 (1976): 13–23. Another version of Klatsassin's behaviour has it that his people had been decimated by smallpox in 1862, and when a Euro-Canadian threatened him with a return of the disease he went on his rampage. See *Dictionary of Canadian Biography*, IX, s.v. 'Klatsassin'.

16. Robin Fisher, 'Joseph Trutch and Indian Land Policy', *B.C. Studies* 12 (1971–2): 17.

17. 'Ordinance further to define the law regulating acquisition of Land in British Columbia'.

18. CP Canada Statutes 39 vic. cap. 18, clauses 74–8. These provisions were later dropped from the Indian Act when the right to testify by affirmation became general.

19. J.E. Michael Kew, 'History of Coastal British Columbia Since 1849', in Wayne Suttles, ed., *Handbook of North American Indians, 7: Northwest Coast* (Washington, 1990), 159.

20. LAC, MG 26A, Macdonald Papers, vol. 278, 127650–1, Trutch to Macdonald, 14 Oct. 1872, cited by John F. Leslie and Ron Maguire, eds, *The Historical Development of the Indian Act* (Ottawa, 1978), 58.

21. Berger, *Fragile Freedoms*, 228.

22. *Report of the Royal Commission on Aboriginal Peoples*, 5 vols (Ottawa, 1996), II, part 2, 784.

23. Cited by A.S. Morton, *A History of Prairie Settlement and Dominion Lands Policy* (Toronto, 1938), 214. Earlier, Simpson was governor of the HBC's Northern Department, 1821–6.

24. Nathalie J. Kermoal, 'Le "Temps de Cayoge": La vie quotidienne des femmes métisses au Manitoba de 1850 à 1900', Ph.D. thesis (University of Ottawa, 1996), xliii n23, 40.

25. For the story of Grant, see Margaret MacLeod and W.L. Morton, *Cuthbert Grant of Grantown* (Toronto, 1974).

26. M. Elizabeth Arthur, 'General Dickson and the Indian Liberating Army in the North', *Ontario History* 62, 3 (1970): 151–62; *Dictionary of Canadian Biography*, VII, s.v. 'Dickson, James'. There is some speculation that Dickson might have been connected with Robert Dickson and his Sioux wife.

27. Barry Cooper, 'Alexander Kennedy Isbister: A Respectable Victorian', *Canadian Ethnic Studies* 17, 2 (1985): 44–63; *Dictionary of Canadian Biography*, XI, s.v. 'Isbister, Alexander Kennedy'. He had gone to England at the age of 20. His portrait hangs in the National Portrait Gallery, London.

28. Most of the Métis of Red River were of Cree descent and so had inherited the animosity that existed betweeen Cree and Sioux.

29. For some of the colonial secretary's views, see Herman Merivale, 'Policy of Colonial Governments towards Native Tribes, as Regards Their Protection and Their Civilization', in John H. Bodley, ed., *Tribal Peoples and Development Issues: A Global Overview* (Mountain View, Calif., 1988), 95–204; David T. McNab, 'Herman Merivale and Colonial Office Indian Policy in the Mid-Nineteenth Century', in Ian A.L. Getty and Antoine S. Lussier, eds, *As Long As the Sun Shines and Water Flows* (Vancouver, 1983), 85–103.

30. Alexander Morris, *The Treaties of Canada with the Indians* (Toronto, 1880; reprint, 1971), 169.

31. LAC, RG 6, C–1, vol. 316, file 995, William McDougall to Secretary of State for the Provinces, 5 Nov. 1869; 'Copy of the Indian Agreement', *The Globe*, Toronto, 4 Sept. 1869, 3. Both references cited by Richard C. Daniel, *History of Native Land Claims Processes in Canada 1867–1979* (Ottawa, 1980), 3.

32. For details of these troubles, see Frits Pannekoek, *A Snug Little Flock: The Social Origins of the Riel Resistance of 1869–70* (Winnipeg, 1991).

33. Although the French language predominated among Red River Métis, in biological fact they were more mixed than that would indicate. Historian Diane Payment has illustrated this with names: MacGillis (Magillice), Bruce (Brousse), Sayer (Serre), McKay (Macaille), and McDougall (McDoub). Payment, *Batoche (1870–1970)* (St Boniface, Man., 1983), 1.

34. Their story is told by Peter Douglas Elias, *The Dakota of the Canadian Northwest: Lessons for Survival* (Winnipeg, 1988). See also James H. Howard, *The Canadian Sioux* (Lincoln, Neb., 1984); Roy W. Meyer, 'The Canadian Sioux Refugees from Minnesota', *Minnesota History* 41, 1 (1968): 13–28; George F.G. Stanley, 'Displaced Red Men: The Sioux in Canada', in Ian A.L. Getty and Donald B. Smith, eds, *One Century Later* (Vancouver, 1978), 55–81.

35. According to Elias, the pair were taken by Americans in a raid: *The Dakota of the Canadian Northwest*, 23. See also Howard, *The Canadian Sioux*, 28.

36. Daniel, *History of Native Land Claims*, 4, citing John Leonard Taylor, 'The Development of an Indian Policy for the Canadian North-West, 1869–70', Ph.D. thesis (Queen's University, 1975), 28.

37. He was the grandson of Jean-Baptiste Lagimodière (1778–1855) and Marie Anne Gaboury (1780–1875), first non-Aboriginal woman in the

West. During the winter of 1816–17, Jean-Baptiste and a companion had travelled by foot from Red River to Montreal (17 Oct. 1816–10 Mar. 1817) to inform Lord Selkirk about the Battle of Seven Oaks. Riel's parents were farmers and did not participate in either the fur trade or the buffalo hunt.

38. On the St Paul trade, see Rhoda R. Gilman, Carolyn Gilman, and Deborah M. Stultz, *The Red River Trails: Oxcart Routes between St. Paul and the Selkirk Settlement 1820–1870* (St. Paul, 1979).

39. LAC, Macdonald Papers, vol. 516, Macdonald to McDougall, 27 Nov. 1869; cited by Donald Creighton, *John A. Macdonald*, 2 vols (Toronto, 1966; first published 1955), II, 51.

40. Ontario was particularly enraged because the court martial that had condemned Scott had been made up of Métis and Amerindians. See Arthur Silver, 'French Quebec and the Métis Question, 1869–1885', in Carl Berger and Ramsay Cook, eds, *The West and the Nation* (Toronto, 1976), 91–113.

41. George F.G. Stanley, *The Birth of Western Canada: A History of the Riel Rebellion* (Toronto, 1960; first published 1936), 129, 135–6.

42. In 1872 Macdonald sent $1,000, via Archbishop Taché, for both Riel and Ambroise-Dydime Lépine (1834–1923) to stay out of the country. Riel took advantage of the offer, but Lépine, who had headed the court martial that had condemned Scott, came back.

43. *Report of the Royal Commission on Aboriginal Peoples*, 5 vols (Ottawa, 1996), IV, ch. 5, 'Métis Perspectives', 199–384.

Chapter 19

1. As noted in Chapter 12, there are 483 agreements listed in Canada, *Indian Treaties and Surrenders from 1680 to 1902*, 3 vols (Ottawa, 1891–1912; facsimile, 1971). Since then a few have been added.

2. Regarding legislation restricting use of band funds for land claims, see Chapter 22, p. 301.

3. George Brown and Ron Maguire, eds, *Indian Treaties in Historical Perspective* (Ottawa, 1979), 32.

4. Richard C. Daniel, 'Indian Rights and Hinterland Provinces: The Case of Northern Alberta', MA thesis (University of Alberta, 1977), ch. 2.

5. John Leonard Taylor, 'The Development of an Indian Policy for the Canadian North-West, 1869–70', Ph.D. thesis (Queen's University, 1975), 45–6.

6. The *Report of the Royal Commission on Aboriginal Peoples*, 5 vols (Ottawa, 1996), while acknowledging that Aboriginal treaties were kept 'alive' through periodic renegotiations to adapt them to changing circumstances (II, part 1, 11), later observed that 'their central feature makes them irrevocable' (19).

7. The United States stopped making treaties with Amerindians in 1871, the year that Canada signed the first of its 11 numbered treaties.

8. John S. Long, '"No Basis for Argument?" The Signing of Treaty Nine in Northern Ontario, 1905–1906', *Native Studies Review* 5, 2 (1989): 36.

9. Canada, Parliament, *Sessional Papers*, 1867–8, no. 81, 18; 1869, no. 42, 20–1.

10. For an examination of the negotiations for Treaty One, see David J. Hall, '"A Serene Atmosphere"? Treaty 1 Revisited', *Canadian Journal of Native Studies* 4, 2 (1984): 321–58.

11. Harold Cardinal, *The Unjust Society: The Tragedy of Canada's Indians* (Edmonton, 1969), 36.

12. Richard C. Daniel, *A History of Native Claims Processes in Canada 1867–1979* (Ottawa, 1980), 12. Canada had agreed, in 1894, that any future treaties within Ontario would require the province's concurrence. Similarly, later adhesions presented little, if any, opportunity for negotiations. The territories involved could be considerable—in Treaty Nine, for instance, most of northern Ontario was involved in the adhesion of 1929.

13. Hall, '"A Serene Atmosphere"? Treaty 1 Revisited', 325.

14. Alexander Morris, *Treaties of Canada with the Indians* (Toronto, 1880; reprint, 1971), 62.

15. Ibid.

16. The idea of train passes was not out of line, of course. The railways handed them out to privileged customers, such as persons in certain professions. In the United States, Amerindians were allowed free rides on western railroads but were not entitled to free seats; they could ride in boxcars.

17. Morris, *Treaties*, 69.

18. John S. Long, 'Treaty No. 9 and Fur Trade Company Families: Northeastern Ontario's Half-breeds, Indians, Petitioners and Métis', in Jacqueline Peterson and Jennifer S.H. Brown, eds, *The New Peoples: Being and Becoming Métis in North America* (Winnipeg, 1985), 145; *Report of the Royal Commission on Aboriginal Peoples*, IV, 261.

19. Morris, *Treaties*, 293–5. George F.G. Stanley referred to 'the invaluable assistance of the half-breeds' in maintaining comparative peace on Canada's frontier. Stanley, *The Birth of Western*

Canada: A History of the Riel Rebellion (Toronto, 1960), 214. See also Grant MacEwan, *Métis Makers of History* (Saskatoon, 1981).

20. Jean Friesen, 'Magnificent Gifts: The Treaties of Canada with the Indians of the Northwest 1869–70', *Transactions of the Royal Society of Canada* ser. 5, 1 (1986): 47–8. See also Stanley, *Birth of Western Canada*, 214–15. Another view, claiming that the Métis were more than facilitators, but also negotiators, interpreters, reporters, and witnesses on their own behalf, is David T. McNab, 'Hearty Co-operation and Efficient Aid: The Metis and Treaty #3', *Canadian Journal of Native Studies* 3, 1 (1983): 131–49.

21. Diane Payment, *Batoche (1870–1970)* (St Boniface, Man., 1983), 2–3; Marcel Giraud, *The Métis in the Canadian West*, tr. George Woodcock, 2 vols (Edmonton, 1986), II, 253–78. Giraud's work is permeated with a pejorative view of Métis and concludes that only absorption by Euro-Canadians will save them.

22. Boyce Richardson, 'Kind Hearts or Forked Tongues?', *The Beaver* Outfit 67, 1 (1987): 28.

23. Taylor, 'Development of an Indian Policy', 191.

24. Ibid., 29.

25. In 1904 the force was renamed the Royal North-West Mounted Police; in 1920, it became the Royal Canadian Mounted Police, which is still its designation today. On the NWMP, see R.C. Macleod, *The NWMP and Law Enforcement 1873–1905* (Toronto, 1976).

26. Philip Goldring, *Whiskey, Horses and Death: The Cypress Hills Massacre and Its Sequel*, Occasional Papers in Archaeology and History No. 21 (Ottawa, 1973).

27. Paul F. Sharp, 'Massacre at Cypress Hills', *Saskatchewan History* 7 (1954): 81–99; Morris Zaslow, *The Opening of the Canadian North* (Toronto, 1971), 15–17.

28. B.D. Fardy, *Jerry Potts, Paladin of the Plains* (Langley, BC, 1984).

29. A biography is by Hugh A. Dempsey, *Crowfoot: Chief of the Blackfeet* (Edmonton, 1972). Dempsey points out (pp. 93–107) that Crowfoot was not the head chief of the Blackfoot Confederacy, as generally believed by non-Natives, but one of the chiefs of the Blackfoot proper. The other members of the Confederacy, the Blood, Tsuu T'ina, and Peigan, each had their own chiefs, and they all participated in the treaty negotiations. Crowfoot, however, was particularly highly regarded by the Euro-Canadians, and this increased his influence among his fellow chiefs in treaty matters.

30. John F. Leslie and Ron Maguire, eds, *The Historical Development of the Indian Act* (Ottawa, 1978), 59. See also Peter A. Cumming and Neil H. Mickenberg, eds, *Native Rights in Canada* (Toronto, 1972), 125.

31. Dempsey, *Crowfoot*, 102.

32. Roy W. Meyer, 'The Canadian Sioux Refugees from Minnesota', *Minnesota History* 41, 1 (1968): 13–28; Alice B. Kehoe, 'The Dakotas in Saskatchewan', in Ethel Nurge, ed., *The Modern Sioux* (Lincoln, Neb., 1970), 148–82.

33. Peter Douglas Elias, *The Dakota of the Canadian Northwest: Lessons for Survival* (Winnipeg, 1988), 172. A closer look at White Cap's trial is in Bob Beal and Rod Macleod, *Prairie Fire: The 1885 North-West Rebellion* (Edmonton, 1984), 327–30.

34. Leslie and Maguire, eds, *Historical Development*, 60.

35. Ibid., 100.

36. The 'Indian Register' is a list maintained by the government; it consists of Band Lists and General Lists. Those who are registered and subject to the Indian Act are 'status' Amerindians.

37. Leslie and Maguire, eds, *Historical Development*, 65.

38. Reuben Gold Thwaites, ed., *Jesuit Relations and Allied Documents*, 73 vols (Cleveland, 1896–1901), XVIII, 101–6.

39. Ibid., XX, 143–53.

40. *Report of the Royal Commission on Aboriginal Peoples*, II, part 2, 809.

41. Leslie and Maguire, eds, *Historical Development*, 67.

42. On the role of the Indian Act, see John F. Leslie, *A Historical Survey of Indian–Government Relations, 1940–1970* (Ottawa, 1993), esp. 12–19.

43. The term 'potlatch' included several different types of feasts, of which the 'giveaway' was one. Jay Miller described feasts as 'knots holding together the . . . social fabric'. Miller, 'Feasting with the Southern Tsimshian', in Margaret Seguin, ed., *The Tsimshian. Images of the Past: Views for the Present* (Vancouver, 1984), 27–39.

44. For a contemporary view of the matter, see A.G. Morice, *Au pays de l'ours noir* (Paris, 1897), 146–61.

45. Edward Ahenakew, *Voices of the Plains Cree* (Toronto, 1973), 182.

46. George Manuel and Michael Posluns, *The Fourth World: An Indian Reality* (Don Mills, Ont., 1974), 78–9.

47. Cited by Cody Poulton, 'Songs from the Gods: "Hearing the Voice" in the Ascetic Rituals of West Coast Indians and Japanese Liturgic Drama',

paper presented to the Thirty-third International Congress of Asian and North African Studies, University of Toronto, 1991.

48. Alice Beck Kehoe, *The Ghost Dance* (Toronto, 1989), 129–34; F.L. Barron, 'The Indian Pass System in the Canadian West, 1882–1935', *Prairie Forum* 13, 1 (1988): 31.

49. LAC, RG 10, vol. 2116, file 22:155, letter to Sir John A. Macdonald from Chief Peter Jones, 11 Feb. 1884, cited by Wayne Daugherty, 'The Elective System', *Indian Government under Indian Act Legislation, 1868–1951* (Ottawa, 1980), 14.

50. John L. Tobias, 'Protection, Civilization, Assimilation: An Outline History of Canada's Indian Policy', *Western Canadian Journal of Anthropology* 6, 2 (1976): 19–20.

51. Leslie and Maguire, eds, *Historical Development*, 77, 85–6.

52. Ibid., 81.

53. Ibid., 87.

54. This cry was raised by David Mills, who under Prime Minister Alexander Mackenzie had been Minister of the Interior, 1876–8. *House of Commons Debates*, 1885, vol. 2, 1580: The Franchise Bill, 4 May 1885, cited by Leslie and Maguire, eds, *Historical Development*, 86.

55. Malcolm Montgomery, 'The Six Nations Indians and the Macdonald Franchise', *Ontario History* 56 (1964): 20.

Chapter 20

1. At the same time a similar situation was being experienced in the western Arctic with the whale and walrus populations, and for similar economic reasons. See John R. Bockstoce, *Whales, Ice, and Men: The History of Whaling in the Western Arctic* (Seattle, 1986), chs 7, 8. There the similarity ends, as the decimation of the sea mammals did not have side benefits, such as the freeing of land for agricultural settlement.

2. John L. Tobias, 'Indian Reserves in Western Canada: Indian Homelands or Devices for Assimilation', in D.A. Muise, ed., *Approaches to Native History in Canada* (Ottawa, 1977), 89–103.

3. Henry Youle Hind, *Narrative of the Canadian Red River Exploring Expedition of 1857 and of the Assiniboine and Saskatchewan Exploring Expedition of 1858*, 2 vols (Edmonton, 1971), I, 360–1; John S. Milloy, *The Plains Cree: Trade, Diplomacy and War, 1790–1870* (Winnipeg, 1988), 107–8.

4. Hind, *Narrative*, II, 110.

5. House of Commons, *Sessional Papers*, 10, 7 (1877), Special app. A (No. 11): xxxv–xxxvi.

6. Sarah Carter, *Lost Harvests: Prairie Indian Reserve Farmers and Government Policy* (Montreal and Kingston, 1990), 36.

7. Arthur S. Morton, *History of Prairie Settlement and Dominion Lands Policy* (Toronto, 1938), 236–8.

8. Bob Beal and Rod Macleod, *Prairie Fire: The 1885 North-West Rebellion* (Edmonton, 1984), 41. Dumont had become buffalo-hunt captain at the age of 25.

9. Thomas Flanagan has analyzed the situation in detail in *Riel and the Rebellion: 1885 Reconsidered* (Saskatoon, 1983).

10. Some hold that Clarke was an *agent provocateur* for Macdonald, actively fomenting trouble as a way out of solving financial difficulties that were plaguing the construction of the Canadian Pacific Railway. See Don McLean, *Home from the Hill: A History of the Metis in Western Canada* (Regina, 1987).

11. George Woodcock, *Gabriel Dumont* (Edmonton, 1975), 81–4.

12. In the south, where transportation facilities were better, the buffalo robe trade had been active since the second half of the eighteenth century.

13. Frank Gilbert Roe, *The North American Buffalo* (Toronto, 1970), 467ff.

14. Currently the Manitoba Métis have initiated court action against Ottawa on the grounds that they were defrauded out of most of their grant. Amerindians of Treaties One and Three, for their part, have filed against the Métis claim, on the grounds that their title was not extinguished at the time the Manitoba Act was passed.

15. *Report of the Royal Commission on Aboriginal Peoples*, 5 vols (Ottawa, 1996), IV, 352.

16. Donald Purich, *The Metis* (Toronto, 1968), 74.

17. *Report of the Royal Commission on Aboriginal Peoples*, IV, 339, figure. Earlier (p. 334) the report gives 1900 as the completion date for the children's grants.

18. Nolin's support of the Métis cause appears to have been dubious, to say the least. Having fallen out with his Métis colleagues, he appeared as a Crown witness at the trials that followed the uprising. Later, he was appointed a magistrate. Purich, *The Metis*, 102–3.

19. P.R. Mailhot and D.M. Sprague, 'Persistent Settlers: The Dispersal and Resettlement of the Red River Metis, 1870–1885', *Canadian Journal of Ethnic Studies* 17 (1985): 1–30.

20. D.W. Moodie and Arthur J. Ray make the point that hunters understood the factors that influenced bison behaviour, so they knew where to look for the herds. See Moodie and Ray, 'Buffalo

Migrations in the Canadian Plains', *Plains Anthropologist* 21, 71 (1976): 45–51.

21. Eleanor Verbicky-Todd, *Communal Buffalo Hunting among the Plains Indians: An Ethnographic and Historic Review* (Edmonton, 1984), 243–5.

22. Hind, *Narrative*, I, 311.

23. Alexander Johnston, comp., *The Battle at Belly River: Stories of the Last Great Indian Battle* (Lethbridge, Alta, 1966). Belly River became the Oldman in 1890.

24. Sweetgrass had become a chief by achieving what Maskepetoon had failed to do: he entered a Blackfoot camp alone, killed a warrior, and captured 40 horses. By 1870 he had become principal chief of the River Cree; in the meantime, in 1865, he had adopted the name Abraham when he had been converted by Father Albert Lacombe. The HBC dubbed him 'Chief of the Country'. See *Dictionary of Canadian Biography*, X, s.v. 'Wikaskokiseyin'.

25. Arthur J. Ray, *Indians and the Fur Trade: Their Role as Trappers, Hunters, and Middlemen in the Lands Southwest of Hudson Bay 1660–1870* (Toronto, 1974), 228.

26. Hugh A. Dempsey, *Big Bear: The End of Freedom* (Vancouver, 1984), 77–8.

27. Ibid.; R.S. Allen, 'Big Bear', *Saskatchewan History* 25, 1 (1972): 1–17; William B. Fraser, 'Big Bear, Indian Patriot', *Alberta Historical Review* 14, 2 (1966): 1–13; *Dictionary of Canadian Biography*, XI, s.v. 'Mistahimaskwa'.

28. Dempsey, *Big Bear*, 74, 80. See also Alexander Morris, *The Treaties of Canada with the Indians* (Toronto, 1880; reprint, 1971), 240; John L. Tobias, 'Canada's Subjugation of the Plains Cree, 1879–1885', *Canadian Historical Review* 64, 4 (1983): 524.

29. Before contact, there were not the clear distinctions between 'tribes' that were later imposed by Europeans. Thus, even though the Blackfoot and Cree considered each other enemies, Crowfoot saw nothing anomalous in adopting Poundmaker because of his striking resemblance to a son he had lost.

30. *Dictionary of Canadian Biography*, XI, s.v. 'Mimiy'.

31. A Blood, Kukatosi-poka (Starchild, Kucka-toosi-nah, *c.* 1860–89), was tried for the murder but acquitted for lack of evidence. *Dictionary of Canadian Biography*, XI, s.v. Kukatosi-poka.

32. T.J. Brasser, *Blackfoot* (Ottawa, n.d.), 3.

33. Carter, *Lost Harvests*, 30. This carefully documented study imputes the failure of the agricultural programs to government policy rather than to the supposed inability of Amerindians to become farmers.

34. Bockstoce, *Whales, Ice, and Men*, 139.

35. D.W. Moodie and Barry Kaye, 'Indian Agriculture in the Fur Trade Northwest', *Prairie Forum* 11, 2 (1986): 171–84; Moodie and Kaye, 'The Northern Limit of Indian Agriculture in North America', *Geographical Review* 59, 4 (1969): 513–29. Archaeological evidence that farming was practised in southern Manitoba during the Late Woodland Period (AD 800–1700) has been found at the Lockport site. It appears to have been discouraged by climatic changes around 1500. *Prehistory of the Lockport Site* (Winnipeg, 1985), 16.

36. Carter, *Lost Harvests*, 112.

37. Saskatchewan Archives Board, Campbell Innes Papers, 5, Rev. J.A. Mackay Papers, box 5, Indian Schools, 1907–8, cited by Carter, *Lost Harvests*, 246.

38. Cited by Beal and Macleod, *Prairie Fire*, 74.

39. *Report of the Commissioner of the North-West Mounted Police Force, 1884*: Commissioner A.G. Irvine, 8.

40. R.C. Macleod, *The North-West Mounted Police and Law Enforcement 1873–1905* (Toronto, 1976), 29.

Chapter 21

1. John L. Tobias, 'The Subjugation of the Plains Cree, 1879–1885', *Canadian Historical Review* 64, 4 (1983): 539; *Dictionary of Canadian Biography*, XI, s.v. 'Kapapamahchakwew'.

2. John F. Leslie and Ron Maguire, eds, *Historical Development of the Indian Act* (Ottawa, 1978), 81.

3. Bob Beal and Rod Macleod, *Prairie Fire: The 1885 North-West Rebellion* (Edmonton, 1984), 63, 115–16, 120; Isabel Andrews, 'Indian Protest against Starvation: The Yellow Calf Incident of 1884', *Saskatchewan History* 28, 2 (1975): 41–51. Mistawasis was Poundmaker's uncle and was renowned as a hunter.

4. One of the exceptions was Robert Jefferson, a farm agent in the Battlefords during the 1880s who was sympathetic to the Amerindians. He was with Poundmaker's band during the troubles and assembled his observations into a slim volume: *Fifty Years on the Saskatchewan: Being a history of the Cree in Canadian domestic life and the difficulties which led to the serious agitation and conflict of 1885 in the Battleford locality* (Battleford, Sask., 1929).

5. The Métis Declaration of Rights is reproduced in full in Beal and Macleod, *Prairie Fire*, 136.

6. In the Roman Catholic Church, a novena is a

series of devotions made on nine successive days for some special purpose.

7. Pihew-kamihkosit ('Red Pheasant'), whose reserve was also in the region, had died just before the sortie began.

8. A Cree Anglican clergyman's view of the event is that of Dr Edward Ahenakew, 'An Opinion of the Frog Lake Massacre', *Alberta Historical Review* 8, 3 (1966): 9–15. Another Cree view, this time by a descendant of Big Bear, is Joseph F. Dion, *My Tribe the Crees* (Calgary, 1979). Contemporary accounts were compiled and edited by Rudy Wiebe and Bob Beal in *War in the West: Voices of the 1885 Rebellion* (Toronto, 1985). The sensationalized press accounts that contributed to public hysteria at the time are described by Sarah Carter, *Aboriginal People and Colonizers of Western Canada to 1900* (Toronto, 1999), 159ff.

9. Diane Payment, *Batoche (1870–1970)* (St Boniface, Man., 1983), 61–2. Despite the defeat and subsequent difficulties, Batoche expanded and prospered in later years. Ibid., 136.

10. A. Blair Stonechild, 'The Indian View of the 1885 Uprising', in J.R. Miller, ed., *Sweet Promises* (Toronto, 1991), 259–76. Gabriel Dumont's account of the rebellion was translated by George F.G. Stanley and published in the *Canadian Historical Review* 30, 3 (Sept. 1949): 249–69.

11. *Manitoba Free Press*, 7 Apr. 1885, front page.

12. Will Jackson (1861–1952), one-time secretary to Riel, was acquitted as insane. The two had parted ways over the question of Aboriginal rights. The other was Tom Scott, the non-Native leader of the English-language Métis.

13. This was the same statute under which eight men had been hanged in Burlington Heights, Ontario, in 1814 for high treason during the War of 1812. See William R. Riddell, *The Ancaster 'Bloody Assize' of 1814* (Toronto, 1923; reprinted from *Ontario Historical Society Papers and Records* 20 [1922]: 107–25). Wandering Spirit was one of those hanged at North Battleford.

14. D.H. Brown, 'The Meaning of Treason in 1885', *Saskatchewan History* 28, 2 (1975): 65–73.

15. The other occasion has been mentioned in note 13, above. In neither case do the consequences compare with those of the Sioux uprising of 1862–3 in the United States. Of 303 Sioux who were condemned to death, 38 were executed at Fort Snelling, Minnesota, the largest mass hanging in American history.

16. Norma Sluman, *Poundmaker* (Toronto, 1967), 270. See also Donald C. Barnett, *Poundmaker* (Don Mills, Ont., 1976).

17. Alexander Morris, *The Treaties of Canada with the Indians* (Toronto, 1880; reprint, 1971), 294.

18. Thomas Flanagan, *Riel and the Rebellion: 1885 Reconsidered* (Saskatoon, 1983), viii. See also Flanagan's study of Riel's millennialism, *Louis 'David' Riel, Prophet of the New World* (Toronto, 1979).

19. D.N. Sprague, *Canada and the Metis, 1869–1885* (Waterloo, Ont., 1988), 184.

20. John E. Foster, 'The Plains Metis', in R. Bruce Morrison and C. Roderick Wilson, eds, *Native Peoples: The Canadian Experience*, 2nd edn (Toronto, 1995), 435.

21. Stonechild, 'Indian View', 275.

22. Tobias, 'Subjugation of the Plains Cree', 547–8.

23. F.L. Barron, 'The Indian Pass System in the Canadian West, 1882–1935', *Prairie Forum* 13, 1 (1988): 28; Sarah A. Carter, 'Controlling Indian Movement: The Pass System', *NeWest Review* (May 1985): 8–9. The system lasted until 1941, but some northern reserves reported that it was still being enforced during the 1960s. Although only 28 reserves were officially designated as disloyal during the disturbances, the system was generally applied in the prairie West.

24. *Annual Report of the North-West Mounted Police, 1895*, app. B, Superintendent W.B. Steele, 45.

25. Kenneth S. Coates and William R. Morrison, *Land of the Midnight Sun: A History of the Yukon* (Edmonton, 1988), 206–7.

26. Hugh A. Dempsey, *Charcoal's World* (Saskatoon, 1978); Frank W. Anderson, *Almighty Voice* (Aldergrove, BC, 1971). On Almighty Voice, see also Carter, *Aboriginal People and Colonizers*, 174–5.

27. Barron, 'Indian Pass System', 39. In 1902, a delegation from South Africa came to study the Canadian pass system as a method of social control.

28. Most of the names listed were provided by Dr Donald B. Smith, University of Calgary.

29. See Sprague, *Canada and the Metis*, 104–5, 124. The question of the distribution of lands set aside for the Métis when Manitoba was created a province is currently before the courts. Thomas Berger is acting on behalf of the Métis.

30. Payment, *Batoche*, 73–4.

31. Joanne Overvold sees the role of women as being central to the struggle of the Métis to maintain a separate identity. She depicts the Métis of the Northwest Territories in *Our Metis Heritage . . . a portrayal* (n.p., 1976). Her comment on the role of women is on p. 103.

32. See Chapter 25.

33. René Fumoleau, *As Long As This Land Shall Last* (Toronto, 1973), 207–8; Richard C. Daniel, *A History of Native Claims Processes in Canada 1867–1979* (Ottawa, 1980), 24.

34. Fumoleau, *As Long As This Land Shall Last*, 76.

35. Marcel Giraud, 'The Western Metis after the Insurrection', *Saskatchewan History* 9, 1 (1956): 5.

36. A detailed study of the situation is that of Paul L.A.H. Chartrand, *Manitoba's Métis Settlement Scheme of 1870* (Saskatoon, 1991).

37. A readable contemporary account of the two commissions is Charles Mair, *Through the Mackenzie Basin* (Toronto, 1908).

38. On Treaty Eight, see Chapter 25.

39. Morris Zaslow, *The Opening of the Canadian North* (Toronto, 1971), 225–6.

40. Daniel, *Native Claims*, 25.

Chapter 22

1. Government control over the sale of Amerindian crops was officially described as a 'kindly supervision' to ensure that Amerindians were 'getting a fair deal'. See Edward Ahenakew, *Voices of the Plains Cree* (Toronto, 1973), 147. This book is an eloquent depiction of Plains Cree life before and after contact.

2. Eleanor Brass, 'The File Hills Ex-Pupil Colony', *Saskatchewan History* 6, 2 (1953): 66. Mrs Brass is the daughter of Fred Dieter, one of the colony's outstanding farmers who was awarded a silver shield. Born and raised in the colony, she reminisces about her life in her autobiography, *I Walk in Two Worlds* (Calgary, 1987). See also E. Brian Titley, *A Narrow Vision* (Vancouver, 1986), 18–19; Titley, 'W.M. Graham: Indian Agent Extraordinaire', *Prairie Forum* 1 (1983): 25–41; 'Indian students forced into marriage, farm life', *Globe and Mail*, 10 Dec. 1990.

3. Earl Grey's sister, Lady Minto, claimed that she and her brother were descended from Pocahontas. See Donald B. Smith, *From the Land of Shadows: The Making of Grey Owl* (Saskatoon, 1990), 227 n15.

4. 'Assault, death common at schools, natives say', *Globe and Mail*, 11 Dec. 1990. Complaints about mission-run schools had been voiced at least since the 1940s.

5. Wayne Daugherty, 'The Elective System', in *Indian Government under Indian Act Legislation, 1868–1951* (Ottawa, 1980), 6.

6. The Cowessess band's election problems have been dealt with in detail by Daugherty, 'The Elective System', 28–35.

7. Ibid., 39–45.

8. Thomas Stone, 'Legal Mobilization and Legal Penetration: The Department of Indian Affairs and the Canada Party at St. Regis, 1876–1918', *Ethnohistory* 22, 4 (1975): 381.

9. John L. Tobias, 'Protection, Civilization, Assimilation: An Outline History of Canada's Indian Policy', *Western Canadian Journal of Anthropology* 6, 2 (1976): 21, 24.

10. Ibid., 21.

11. Robert J. Surtees, 'Indian Land Sessions in Upper Canada, 1815–1830', in Ian A.L. Getty and Antoine S. Lussier, eds, *As Long As the Sun Shines and Water Flows* (Vancouver, 1983), 66; Peggy Martin-McGuire, *First Nation Land Surrenders on the Prairies, 1896–1911* (Ottawa, 1998), xiii. This is a detailed study of 25 surrenders, prepared for the Indian Claims Commission.

12. Richard H. Bartlett, *Indian Reserves and Aboriginal Lands in Canada: A Homeland* (Saskatoon, 1990), 26. See also Stewart Raby, 'Indian Land Surrenders in Southern Saskatchewan', *Canadian Geographer* 17, 1 (Spring 1973), 36–52; Sarah Carter, 'The Push for Land Surrender', in Carter, *Lost Harvests* (Montreal and Kingston, 1990), 244–9.

13. Canada, Indian Affairs, *Report, 1910–11*, 196, cited by Morris Zaslow, *The Opening of the Canadian North* (Toronto, 1971), 232–3. From 1909 to 1914, Laird was adviser to Indian Affairs in Ottawa.

14. Martin-McGuire, *First Nation Land Surrenders on the Prairies*, 461–2. See also D.J. Hall, 'Clifford Sifton and Canadian Indian Administration 1896–1905', in Getty and Lussier, eds, *As Long As the Sun Shines and Water Flows*, 120–44.

15. Heading the Commission were Gilbert Malcolm Sproat (1876–9, for the first two years in office, as co-commissioner with Alexander C. Anderson and Archibald McKinley), Peter O'Reilly (1880–98), and A.W. Vowell (1899–1910). By 1892, the Commission was granting reserves that ranged in size from seven to 230 acres (three to 93 hectares) per capita, depending on the region. Complaints from non-Native settlers concerning these amounts led the province to refuse to sanction any more, leading to the dissolution of the Commission in 1910.

16. The delegation of 1906 was led by Chief Joe Capilano of the North Vancouver Squamish and other chiefs. They were listened to politely but did not get any action. See Peter A. Cumming and Neil H. Mickenberg, eds, *Native Rights in Canada* (Toronto, 1972), 188; G.E. Shankel, 'The Development of Indian Policy in British

Columbia', Ph.D. thesis (University of Washington, 1945), 193–4.

17. Cumming and Mickenberg, eds, *Native Rights*, 188–9.

18. Usually called the McKenna-McBride Commission, after J.A.J. McKenna, assistant Amerindian commissioner for the Northwest, 1901–9, and Richard McBride, Premier of BC, 1903–15. McBride did not actually serve on the Commission.

19. Thomas Berger, *Fragile Freedoms: Human Rights and Dissent in Canada* (Toronto, 1981), 231. During this time also, commercial fishing licences were not being issued to west coast Indians; in 1923 they were allowed to apply for them. See E.E. Laviolette, *The Struggle for Survival* (Toronto, 1973), 138.

20. These were described by Lloyd Barber as 'prime development land'. Barber, 'The Implications of Indian Claims for Canada', address given at the Banff School of Advanced Management, Banff, Alberta, 9 Mar. 1978.

21. Reuben Ware, *The Lands We Lost: A History of Cut-Off Lands and Land Losses from Indian Reserves in British Columbia* (Vancouver, 1974), 1; J.E. Michael Kew, 'History of Coastal British Columbia Since 1849', in Wayne Suttles, ed., *Handbook of North American Indians, 7: Northwest Coast* (Washington, 1990), 160.

22. The text of the Commission's report is reproduced in Ware, *Lands We Lost*, 179–98, along with the texts of the Commission's 98 interim reports proposing land alienations for a variety of reasons, pp. 114–77. A study that takes a sympathetic view of British Columbia's position on the land question is Robert E. Cail, *Land, Man, and the Law: The Disposal of Crown Lands in British Columbia, 1871– 1913* (Vancouver, 1974), chs 11, 12, 13.

23. The story of the political adaptation of British Columbia Indians to non-Native pressures and the development of Native organizations in the province is told by Paul Tennant, 'Native Political Organization in British Columbia, 1900–1960: A Response to Internal Colonialism', *B.C. Studies* 55 (1982): 3–49. The Allied Tribes lasted until 1927; its battles would be picked up by the Native Indian Brotherhood in 1931.

24. Richard C. Daniel, *A History of Native Claims Processes in Canada, 1867–1979* (Ottawa, 1980), 50–2. See also Wilson Duff, *The Indian History of British Columbia*, vol. 1, *The Impact of the White Man* (Victoria, 1964), 69–70; Cail, *Land, Man, and the Law*, 243.

25. James S. Frideres, *Native Peoples in Canada: Contemporary Conflicts* (Scarborough, Ont., 1983), 233–66; Leslie and Maguire, eds, *Historical Development of the Indian Act*, 120. Anthropologist. Peter Kulchyski thinks that the measure may have contributed to the breakup of the Allied Tribes of BC in 1927. Kulchyski, 'Headwaters: A new history', *The Press Independent* 21, 27 (12 July 1991): 5.

26. The land issue became a factor in the saga of British Columbia's most famous outlaw, Peter Simon Gunanoot (*c.* 1874–1933), who eluded police for 13 years, from 1906 to 1919. Gunanoot ('Little Bear that Walks up a Tree'), a prosperous Gitksan trapper and storekeeper of Hazelton (Gitenmaks), BC, upon being wanted for murder, took to the woods with his family. Their success in evading capture was at least partly due to the complicity of the Amerindians of the region, who were agitating for an extension of their reserve and for payment for lands occupied by non-Aboriginals. Gunanoot eventually voluntarily surrendered, was tried, and acquitted. See David R. Williams, *Simon Peter Gunanoot: Trapper Outlaw* (Victoria, 1982); Thomas P. Kelley, *Run Indian Run* (Markham, Ont., 1972).

27. The relatively small size of Canadian reserves compared with those of the United States is analyzed by Robert White-Harvey in 'Reservation Geography and the Restoration of Native Self-Government', *Dalhousie Law Journal* 17, 2 (Fall 1994): 527.

28. For example, the Walpole Island dispute. In that case, a framework agreement was finally reached in 1989. David T. McNab, 'Exchanging Time and the Ojibwa: An Exploration of the Notions of Time and Territoriality', paper presented to the American Ethnohistory Society, Toronto, 1990.

29. 'South Edmonton claimed by Pahpahstayo First Nation', *Windspeaker* 14, 4 (1996): 8; 'Papaschase wants to re-establish land base', ibid., 12, 14 (1994): 5; 'Indians lured into giving up rich lands', *Edmonton Journal*, 2 Apr. 1983. See also Kenneth James Tyler, 'A Tax-eating Proposition: The History of the Passpasschase Indian Reserve', MA thesis (University of Alberta, 1979).

30. Kenneth S. Coates and William R. Morrison, *Land of the Midnight Sun: A History of the Yukon* (Edmonton, 1988), 289.

31. Hugh A. Dempsey, *The Gentle Persuader* (Saskatoon, 1986), 50–2.

32. James Dempsey, 'Problems of Western Canadian Indian War Veterans after World War One', *Native Studies Review* 5, 2 (1989): 1.

33. James St G. Walker, 'Race and Recruitment in World War I: Enlistment of Visible Minorities in the Canadian Expeditionary Force', *Canadian Historical Review* 70, 1 (1989): 5.

34. *Native Soldiers, Foreign Battlefields* (Ottawa: Minister of Supply and Services, 1993), 9–11.

35. Dempsey, *The Gentle Persuader*, 49. Similarly, the Inuit, even those in remote communities, raised money for famine relief for Ethiopia in 1984. See 'Northern Generosity Snowballs', *Globe and Mail*, 29 Nov. 1984. See also Fred Gaffen, *Forgotten Soldiers* (Penticton, BC, 1985); Terry Lusty, *Metis, Social-Political Movement* (Calgary, 1973).

36. Cited by Dempsey, 'Problems of Western Canadian Indian War Veterans', 5, 6.

37. Peter S. Schmalz, *The Ojibwa of Southern Ontario* (Toronto, 1991), 233–4; Gaffen, *Forgotten Soldiers*, 70–2.

38. Michael Asch, *Kinship and the Drum Dance in a Northern Dene Community* (Edmonton, 1988), 89–97.

39. Morris Zaslow, *The Northward Expansion of Canada 1914–1967* (Toronto, 1988), 162.

40. E. Brian Titley, *A Narrow Vision: Duncan Campbell Scott and the Administration of Indian Affairs in Canada* (Vancouver, 1986), 50.

41. Allan G. Harper, 'Canada's Indian Administration: Basic Concepts and Objectives', *América Indígena* 5, 2 (1945): 127.

42. John F. Leslie and Ron Maguire, eds, *The Historical Development of the Indian Act* (Ottawa, 1978), 191.

43. A documentary novel vividly portraying the incomprehension and frustration of Euro-Canadians who very much want to help Amerindians, but who think they can do it by telling them what to do, is by Alan Fry, *How a People Die* (Toronto, 1970). The view that the administration was really concerned with non-Aboriginal goals and not with those of Amerindians is expressed by Shelagh D. Grant in 'Indian Affairs under Duncan Campbell Scott: The Plains Cree of Saskatchewan, 1913–1931', *Journal of Canadian Studies* 18, 3 (1983): 21–39.

44. Titley, *A Narrow Vision*, 96.

45. Canada, *Annual Report of Indian Affairs Branch, 1937*.

46. For an example of this policy, see Kenneth S. Coates, 'Best Left as Indians: The Federal Government and the Indians of the Yukon, 1894–1950', *Canadian Journal of Native Studies* 4, 2 (1984): 179–204.

47. Peter Kulchyski, '"A Considerable Unrest": F.O. Loft and the League of Indians', *Native Studies Review* 4, 1–2 (1988): 95–113; Stan Cuthand, 'The

Native Peoples of the Prairie Provinces in the 1920's and 1930's', in Ian A.L. Getty and Donald B. Smith, eds, *One Century Later: Western Canadian Reserve Indians Since Treaty 7* (Vancouver, 1978), 31–5; Titley, *A Narrow Vision*, 102–9; Zaslow, *Northward Expansion*, 165–6.

48. John F. Leslie, *A Historical Survey of Indian–Government Relations, 1940–1970* (Ottawa, 1993), 3–4.

49. A detailed history of the National Indian Brotherhood and analysis of its operations is in Ponting and Gibbins, *Out of Irrelevance*, 195–279. A dated but still useful compilation of Indian organizations is that of Don Whiteside, *Historical Development of Aboriginal Political Associations in Canada: Documentation* (Ottawa, 1973); see also Whiteside, *Aboriginal People: A Selected Bibliography Concerning Canada's First People* (Ottawa, 1973).

50. Years later the lot of Amerindian war veterans was still giving rise to complaints and investigations. See, for example, 'Indian war veterans mistreated: report', *Globe and Mail*, 7 June 1984. The joint committee, during its three years of existence, heard 122 witnesses and studied 411 written briefs. Zaslow, *Northward Expansion*, 298. Particularly irritating was the practice of awarding the traplines of registered Indians to non-Aboriginal veterans.

51. There were exceptions. For one, in 1920, Indian spokespersons had been invited to attend House of Commons hearings on amendments to the Indian Act that proposed compulsory enfranchisement. In spite of their opposition, however, the bill was passed.

52. *Indian Conditions: A Survey* (Ottawa, 1980), 84.

53. E-mail correspondence, Marc Boivin, band governance, Indian and Northern Affairs Canada, re 'Election Results Report 2007', to Paul-Emile McNab, 2 Oct. 2007.

54. Indian and Northern Affairs Canada, at: <www.ainc-inac.gc.ca/ps/lts/nelts/ele/index_e.html>.

55. See, for example, Alice B. Kehoe, 'The Giveaway Ceremony of Blackfoot and Plains Cree', *Plains Anthropologist* 25, 87 (1980): 17–26.

56. E. Palmer Patterson II, *The Canadian Indian: A History Since 1500* (Toronto, 1972), 171–2.

57. Janet Silman, *Enough Is Enough: Aboriginal Women Speak Out* (Toronto, 1994; first published 1987), 149–72.

58. The best known of the cases contesting Amerindian women's loss of status when they married non-Amerindians was that of *Attorney General of Canada v. Lavell* (1974). Jeannette

Lavell, an Ojibwa, fought the issue all the way to the Supreme Court of Canada, where the decision finally went against her, as well as against Yvonne Bedard in a companion case that was heard at the same time. See Kathleen Jamieson, *Indian Women and the Law in Canada: Citizens Minus* (Ottawa, 1978), 79–88; Silman, *Enough Is Enough*, 13–14; Pauline Comeau and Aldo Santin, *The First Canadians* (Toronto, 1990), 32–3. See also *Report of the Royal Commission on Aboriginal Peoples*, 5 vols (Ottawa, 1996), IV, 32.

59. For the criticism that Bill C-31 has substituted one form of inequality for another, see the report prepared for the Assembly of First Nations by Stewart Clatworthy and Anthony H. Smith, 'Population Implications of the 1985 Amendment to the Indian Act', 1992.

60. *Report of the Royal Commission on Aboriginal Peoples*, IV, 35.

61. Thomas Isaac, *Aboriginal Law Cases, Materials, and Commentary* (Saskatoon, 1995), 429–30; 'Supreme Court dismisses delay in off-reserve voting', *Ottawa Citizen*, 4 Nov. 2000; 'First "Off Reserve" Votes in Manitoba Band Election', CBC News World Online, 24 Nov. 2000. The Assembly of First Nations voiced its objections in a flyer entitled 'The Corbière Decision'.

62. 'Few reinstated status Indians return to reserves in province', *Edmonton Journal*, 15 Apr. 1991.

63. Indian and Northern Affairs Canada, at: <www.ainc-inac.gc.ca/2002-templates/ssi/print_e.asp>. Also see Bill Tremblay, 'Status or non-status—that is the cultural question', *Wawatay News* 24, 22 (6 Nov. 1997): 4.

64. *Report of the Royal Commission on Aboriginal Peoples*, IV, 46–7.

65. *Indian Conditions*, 85.

66. *Indian Treaty Rights*, Federation of Saskatchewan Indians, undated pamphlet. See also Suzanne Fournier and Ernie Crey, *Stolen from Our Embrace: The Abduction of First Nations Children and the Restoration of Aboriginal Communities* (Vancouver, 1997), 54.

67. Alexander Morris, *The Treaties of Canada with the Indians* (Toronto, 1880; reprint, 1971), 315.

68. J.R. Miller, *Shingwauk's Vision: A History of Native Residential Schools* (Toronto, 1996), 98–100.

69. Federation of Saskatchewan Indians, *Indian Treaty Rights*, undated pamphlet. See also Suzanne Fournier and Ernie Crey, *Stolen from Our Embrace: The Abduction of First Nations Children and the Restoration of Aboriginal Communities* (Vancouver, 1997), 4.

70. Jennifer Lorretta Pettit, 'To Chistianize and

Civilize', Ph.D. thesis (University of Calgary, 1997), 56.

71. Miller, *Shingwauk's Vision*, 76–80.

72. Donald B. Smith, *Sacred Feathers: The Reverend Peter Jones and the Mississauga Indians* (Toronto, 1987), 160.

73. Minutes of the General Council of Indian Chiefs and Principal Men held at Orillia, Lake Simcoe Narrows, on Thursday, the 30th, and Friday, the 31st, July, 1846, on the proposed removal of the smaller gommunities [*sic*] and the establishment of manual labour schools (Orillia, Ont., 1846), 20–1. At: <www.canadiana.org>.

74. Cited in Pettit, 'To Christianize and Civilize', 26–7.

75. Ibid., 22.

76. In 1820, West used the opportunity given to him as HBC chaplain to attempt evangelizing and schooling on behalf of the Anglican Church Missionary Society. In his journal, he noted that Saulteaux chief Peguis questioned him very closely but, in the end, did not hand over his children. West, *The Substance of a Journal During a Residence at the Red River Colony, British North America* (London, 1824).

77. Federation of Saskatchewan Indians, *Indian Treaty Rights*. See also Fournier and Crey, *Stolen from Our Embrace*, 56.

78. Handsome Lake's story is told in Alice B. Kehoe, *The Ghost Dance* (Toronto, 1989), 116–23. The standard work on the prophet is Anthony F.C. Wallace, *Death and Rebirth of the Seneca* (New York, 1969).

79. Pettit, 'To Christianize and Civilize', 25–6.

80. Ibid., 51–2.

81. Ibid., 68.

82. Ibid., 36–40.

83. Two of the most recent studies of residential schools are Miller's *Shingwauk's Vision* and John Sheridan Milloy, *A National Crime: The Canadian Government and the Residential School System* (Winnipeg, 1999). There are many published eyewitness accounts of the industrial and residential schools.

84. N.F. Davin, 'Report on Industrial Schools for Indians and Halfbreeds', 14 Mar. 1879, LAC, RG 10, vol. 6001, file 1–1–1, pt. 1, 10.

85. Brass, *I Walk in Two Worlds*, 45.

86. Fournier and Crey, *Stolen from Our Embrace*, 50, 61. According to *Windspeaker* (May 1998) in a special section entitled 'Classroom Edition', 4, the number of residential schools peaked at 88. Geoffrey York writes about some of these schools in *The Dispossessed: Life and Death in Native Canada* (London, 1990).

87. Department of Indian Affairs (DIA), *Annual Report, 1883*, CSP (No. 4) 1884, xi, cited in Miller, *Shingwauk's Vision*, 106.

88. Father Albert Lacombe complained that his Blackfoot students were too big and too 'well acquainted with the Indian fashion' to accept institutionalization. He also created controversy by hiring Jean L'Hereaux, a local man rumoured to be a pedophile, as a recruiter. When he stepped down in 1885, Father Lacombe left behind a school with only three students. His successor resigned after three years as principal, claiming that only two of 25 graduates had enough education and skill to succeed. DIA, *Annual Report, 1884*, 89, cited in Pettit, 'To Christianize and Civilize', 109. For a description of the Dunbow School, see Raymond J.A. Huel, *Proclaiming the Gospel to the Indians and Métis* (Edmonton, 1996), 128–31. The author claims that the Oblates were aware of the allegations concerning L'Hereaux.

89. Success was relative; by Father Hugonnard's statistics, about 20 per cent of students died under his care. Milloy, *National Crime*, 92.

90. Miller, *Shingwauk's Vision*, 350.

91. Huel, *Proclaiming the Gospel*, 151.

92. DIA, *Annual Report, 1900*, 26–45; *Census of Canada*, 1941, I, 684–91, cited by Jean Barman, Yvonne Hébert, and Don McCaskill, 'The Legacy of the Past: An Overview', in Barman et al., eds, *Indian Education in Canada*, 2 vols (Vancouver, 1986), I, 7.

93. Cited in Arlene Roberta Greyeyes, 'St. Michael's Indian Residential School, 1894–1926', MA thesis (Carleton University, 1995), 129, 138.

94. For a description of the Lytton, BC, school, see Miller, *Shingwauk's Vision*, 318–19.

95. James Gladstone, 'Indian School Days', *Alberta Historical Review* 15, 1: 24, cited in Pettit, 'To Christianize and Civilize', 17.

96. Historian Robert Choquette, cited in Pettit, 'To Christianize and Civilize', 17.

97. Greyeyes, 'St. Michael's Indian Residential School', 66.

98. Hall, 'Clifford Sifton and Canadian Indian Administration', 126.

99. Titley, *A Narrow Vision*, 78–80.

100. Brass, *I Walk in Two Worlds*, 45. A much more critical look at the effects of residential schooling is that of Linda R. Bull, 'Indian Residential Schooling: The Native Perspective', M.Ed. thesis (University of Alberta, 1991).

101. One estimate places the total number of deaths among students in all residential schools in Canada at 50,000. See the letter of Rev. Kevin D. Annett, Ganges, BC, in the *Guardian Weekly*, 6–12 July 2000, 13.

102. Titley, *A Narrow Vision*, 82–7.

103. *The fifth estate*, CBC-TV, 8 Jan. 1991.

104. Cited by Barman, Hébert, and McCaskill, 'Legacy of the Past', 9.

105. Titley, *A Narrow Vision*, 91, 93.

106. *Report of the Royal Commission on Aboriginal Peoples*, I, 388–9 n15.

107. Barman, Hébert, and McCaskill, 'Legacy of the Past', 7.

108. A. Irving Hallowell, *Culture and Experience* (Philadelphia, 1955), 308. The French in the seventeenth century had made determined efforts at transforming Amerindians into Frenchmen and had experienced equally discouraging results. See Olive Patricia Dickason, *The Myth of the Savage and the Beginnings of French Colonialism in the Americas* (Edmonton, 1984), 217–21, 251–70.

109. Hall, 'Clifford Sifton and Canadian Indian Administration', 126.

110. Norma Sluman and Jean Goodwill, *John Tootoosis* (Ottawa, 1982), 109, cited by Barman, Hébert, and McCaskill, 'Legacy of the Past', 11. On residential schools in British Columbia, see Celia Haig-Brown, *Resistance and Renewal: Surviving the Indian Residential School* (Vancouver, 1988).

111. (Toronto, 1988). Also, 'Indian School "wasn't all bad"—ex-student', *Edmonton Journal*, 11 June 1991.

112. Coates and Morrison, *Land of the Midnight Sun*, 141–2; Shelagh D. Grant, *Sovereignty or Security? Government Policy in the Canadian North, 1936–1950* (Vancouver, 1988), 33–4 n37.

113. Barman, Hébert, and McCaskill, 'Legacy of the Past', 13.

114. J. Donald Wilson, '"No Blanket To Be Worn in School": The Education of Indians in Nineteenth-Century Ontario', in Barman et al., eds, *Indian Education in Canada*, I, 82.

115. Jacques Rousseau, 'The Northern Québec Eskimo Problem and the Ottawa–Québec Struggle', *Anthropological Journal of Canada* 7, 2 (1968): 2–21.

116. Catherine Ford, 'Apology does not mean instant forgiveness', *Calgary Herald*, 9 Sept. 2000, O7. See also James Brooke, 'Facing ruin from lawsuits, Anglicans in Canada slash budgets', *New York Times*, 23 Aug. 2000; Rick Mofina, 'Churches have no easy exit from native lawsuits', *National Post*, 18 Sept. 2000; Ben

McIntyre, 'Canadian church faces ruin over sex cases', *The Times*, London, 24 Aug. 2000; 'Catholic order says lawsuits could bankrupt it', *National Post*, 22 May 2000.

117. CBC News, at: <www.cbc.ca/canada/story/2007/08/20/aboriginal-settlement.html>.

118. CBC News, at: <www.cbc.ca/canada/story/2007/09/19/residential-schools.html>.

119. James Miller and Edmund Danziger Jr, '"In the Care of Strangers": Walpole Island First Nation's Experiences with Residential Schools after the First World War', *Ontario History* 92, 1 (Spring 2000): 71–88. See also Janet Steffenhagen, 'Minister traces activism to residential school', *Vancouver Sun*, 3 Nov. 2000, A12. Another such graduate, although from a different school, is Matthew Coon Come, former National Chief of the Assembly of First Nations. For a profile on Coon Come, see Graham Fraser, 'Chief hunter', *Toronto Star*, 16 Dec. 2000, J1, J4.

120. The story of the Amerindian takeover of the school is told by Diane Persson, 'The Changing Experience of Indian Residential Schooling: Blue Quills, 1931–1970', in Barman et al., eds, *Indian Education in Canada*, I, 150–67.

121. Howard Adams, *Prison of Grass: Canada from the Native Point of View* (Toronto, 1975), 213–14.

122. 'A lesson in misery: Canadian Indians look back in anger at residential school days', *Globe and Mail*, 2 Dec. 1989. This is an excerpt from York's *The Dispossessed*.

123. *Recent Development in Native Education* (Toronto, 1984), 14, cited by Barman, Hébert, and McCaskill, 'The Legacy of the Past', 16.

124. Canada, Department of Indian Affairs and Northern Development, *Basic Departmental Data 1999*, 36. An early example of indigenous curriculum development was the Cree Way Project of Rupert House during the 1970s. See Richard Preston, 'The Cree Way Project: an experiment in grass-roots curriculum development', in William Cowan, ed., *Papers of the Tenth Algonquian Conference* (Ottawa, 1979), 92–101.

125. See, for example, 'Sweet success for native school', *Edmonton Journal*, 1 Oct. 1990; 'Bias absent in all-native school', ibid., 25 Nov. 1989.

126. Terry Lusty, in *Alberta Sweetgrass* (Jan. 2001): 12.

127. Robin Armstrong, Jeff Kennedy, and Peter R. Oberle, *University Education and Economic Well-Being: Indian Achievement and Prospects* (Ottawa, 1990), vii.

128. Gerald R. Alfred, *Heeding the Voices of Our Ancestors: Kahnawake Mohawk Politics and the Rise of Native Nationalism* (Toronto, 1995), 2.

129. 'Racism forcing natives from civil service: report', *Ottawa Citizen*, 12 Feb. 1991. Earlier, the Assembly of Manitoba Chiefs filed complaints against 28 federal departments and agencies, charging discrimination on the job against Amerindians. 'Natives file job bias complaints against federal government', *Edmonton Journal*, 4 Dec. 1990.

130. Fournier and Crey, *Stolen from Our Embrace*, 81–114; Jason Clayworth, '"Stolen" native wants family, culture back', *Ottawa Citizen*, 10 Oct. 2000 (reprint from *Des Moines Register*); Brad Evenson, 'Native adoption policy—a Canadian tragedy', *Edmonton Journal*, 19 Apr. 1999; 'Indian boy returned to adoptive kin in U.S.', *The Gazette*, Montreal, 21 Mar. 1999.

Chapter 23

1. Donald B. Smith, 'Aboriginal Rights a Century Ago', *The Beaver* 67, 1 (1987): 7. Also Anthony J. Hall, 'The St. Catherine's Milling and Lumber Company vs. The Queen: A Study in the Relationship of Indian Land Rights to Federal–Provincial Relations in Nineteenth-Century Canada', unpublished manuscript, 10. See also Bradford W. Morse, ed., *Aboriginal Peoples and the Law: Indian, Metis, and Inuit Rights in Canada* (Ottawa, 1985), 57–9; Morris Zaslow, *The Opening of the Canadian North* (Toronto, 1971), 150–1.

2. For Boyd's background, see Smith, 'Aboriginal Rights', 7–10. One of Boyd's professors at the University of Toronto had been Sir Daniel Wilson (1816–85), a well-known ethnologist who was the author of *Prehistoric Man: Researches into the Origin of Civilisation in the Old and the New World* (Cambridge and Edinburgh, 1862). See *Dictionary of Canadian Biography*, XII, s.v. 'Wilson, Sir Daniel'.

3. The legal argument follows Hall, 'St. Catherine's Milling', 10–15.

4. *Reports of the Supreme Court of Canada*, vol. 13, 1887, 596–7.

5. Smith, 'Aboriginal Rights', 12.

6. *Ontario Reports, 1885*, 231.

7. Smith, 'Aboriginal Rights', 15.

8. Bruce A. Clark, *Indian Title in Canada* (Toronto, 1987), 113. The Canadian judges are Boyd, Henri-Elzéar Taschereau, and Donald Steele.

9. Alexander Morris, *The Treaties of Canada with the Indians* (Toronto, 1880), 59. On Treaty Three, 'The North-West Angle Treaty', see 44–76.

10. Peter Jones, *History of the Ojebway Indians* (London, 1861), 71.

11. George Copway, *Life, History and Travels of Kah-ge-ga-gah-bowh* (Philadelphia, 1847), 20.

12. Indian and Northern Affairs Canada, at: <www.ainc-inac.gc.ca/pr/info/tln_e.html >.

13. Richard H. Bartlett, *Indian Reserves and Aboriginal Lands in Canada: A Homeland* (Saskatoon, 1990), ch. 6. See also *Metisism, A Canadian Identity* (Edmonton, 1982), 58–60.

14. This account follows Richard C. Daniel, *A History of Native Claims Processes in Canada 1867–1979* (Ottawa, 1980), 77–83. Donald Smith compiled the most complete bibliography on pre-1990 Oka in *Le Sauvage. The Native People in Quebec: Historical Writing on the Heroic Period (1534–1663) of New France* (Ottawa, 1974), 129–31. For a post-1990 bibliography, see Geoffrey York and Loreen Pindera, *People of the Pines* (Toronto, 1991).

15. 'Oka and Its Inhabitants', in *The Life of Rev. Amand Parent, the first French Canadian ordained by the Methodist Church* (Toronto, 1887), 186. See also Beta (pseud.), *A Contribution to a Proper Understanding of the Oka Question; and a Help to its Equitable and Speedy Settlement* (Montreal, 1879), 8.

16. George F.G. Stanley, 'The First Indian "Reserves" in Canada', *Revue d'histoire de l'Amérique française* 4 (1950): 206–7. The 1718 deed, in English translation, as well as other documents pertaining to the case are reproduced in Beta (pseud.), *Contribution*, 77–92.

17. In the words of Philippe de Vaudreuil, governor-general of New France, 1703–25, the Amerindians 'ne sont point capable de conserver les choses qui leur sont les plus nécessaires.' Stanley, 'First Indian "Reserves"', 206.

18. Jean Lacan, *An Historical Notice on the Difficulties Arisen Between the Seminary of St. Sulpice of Montreal and Certain Indians, at Oka, Lake of Two Mountains: A Mere Case of Right of Property* (Montreal, 1876), 14–17. On François Vachon de Belmont, see *Dictionary of Canadian Biography* II, s.v. 'Vachon'.

19. LAC, C¹¹A, 106:422–4, Arrêt du Conseil sur le changement proposé pour la Mission du Sault-aux-Récollets, 31 mars 1716. Oka Amerindians fought with Canadians at the Battle of Chateauguay, 1812. ('Oka and Its Inhabitants', 188–90.)

20. Jan Grabowski, 'Mohawk Crisis at Kanesatake and Kahnawake', *European Review of Native American Studies* 5, 1 (1991): 12.

21. On Kahnawake, see Chapter 16; on Lorette, Chapter 8.

22. 'Oka and Its Inhabitants', 190–1, 193; Beta (pseud.), *Contribution*, 14–15. In 1870, Parent reported 110 Amerindian Methodists at Oka.

23. Cited by Rev. William Scott, *Report Relating to the Affairs of the Oka Indians, made to the Superintendent General of Indian Affairs* (Ottawa, [1883]), 53.

24. Ibid., 29; 'Oka and Its Inhabitants', 191, 202, 235.

25. In 1874, Chief Joseph became an assistant to Amand Parent. He translated the four gospels into Iroquois. For more on the chief, see *Dictionary of Canadian Biography*, XI; John MacLean, *Vanguards of Canada* (Toronto, 1918), 167–79.

26. Albert R. Hassard, 'When the Oka Seminary Went Up in Flames', *Famous Canadian Trials* (Toronto, 1924), 106–23.

27. 'Oka and Its Inhabitants', 205–18; Beta (pseud.), *Contribution*, 15.

28. Scott, *Report Relating to the Affairs of the Oka Indians*, 53–4.

29. Ibid., 59.

30. Michel F. Girard, 'La crise d'Oka à la lumière de l'ecologie historique', *NHSG Newsletter* (Oct. 1990): 4–8. The Native History Study Group is part of the Canadian Historical Association.

31. *Privy Council, Angus Corinthe and Others . . . Plaintiffs, and Ecclesiastics of the Seminary of St. Sulpice of Montreal, Defendants*, in Canadian Indian Rights Commission Library, box 85 (1). Also, Daniel, *History of Native Claims*, 79–82.

32. Registration office, district of Two Mountains, Acte de vente entre La Compagnie de Saint-Sulpice et la Compagnie immobilière Belgo, 21 oct. 1936, cited by Michel F. Girard, *Étude historique sur la forêt du village d'Oka* (Québec, 1990).

33. Department of Indian and Northern Affairs, Miscellaneous Correspondence, Oka, 1945–1953, vol. 1, file 0/121–1–5, Order-in-Council of 2 Apr. 1945.

34. The events leading up to the raid, and the raid itself, are described by Loreen Pindera, 'The Making of a Warrior', *Saturday Night* 106, 3 (1990): 30–9.

35. 'The high cost of Oka', *Edmonton Journal*, 6 May 1991; 'Tories reverse position, agree to Oka enquiry', *Globe and Mail*, 29 Nov. 1990; 'Quebec deeper in red', *Calgary Herald*, 29 Nov. 1990.

36. Rene Laurent, 'Two Mohawks get prison terms for Oka violence', *The Gazette*, Montreal, 20 Feb. 1992, A1–2; Catherine Buckie, 'Jury-selection process ends in trial of Mohawks', ibid., 30 Apr. 1992; Rene Laurent, '5 Mohawks freed for lack of evidence', ibid., 11 June 1992, A4; Rene Laurent, 'Jury acquits all defendants in Oka trial', ibid., 4

July 1992, A1, A5; 'Quebec says it won't appeal jury's acquittal of Mohawks', ibid., 25 July 1992.

37. *Windspeaker* 18, 3 (July 2000): 2–3; *Calgary Herald*, 11 July 2000, A3; *Ottawa Sun*, 15 July 2000, 8; *Le Droit*, 12 juil. 2000, 28.

38. 'Oka still confounds us', *Edmonton Journal*, 9 May 1991. Quebec's Parti Québécois, at its 1991 convention, resolved that a sovereign Quebec state would recognize autonomous Native nations within its borders. According to the resolution, drafted with the help of Aboriginals, Native laws would take precedence over Quebec laws in specific areas where agreement had been reached by both parties. 'Delegates agreed on allowing native autonomy', *Globe and Mail*, 28 Jan. 1991. The project has been only partially realized.

39. British Columbia's Hartley Bay band (near Prince Rupert), frustrated with the slow progress of settlements, has started signing its own deals with industry, environmental groups, and other First Nations. 'Fed up, B.C. Indian band goes it alone in signing deals', *The Gazette*, Montreal, 22 July 2000, A15.

40. 'Mohawks sign historic land deal', *Ottawa Citizen*, 22 June 2000; 'Mohawks to get land near Oka', *Globe and Mail*, 21 June 2000; Mike Blanchfield, 'Oka Mohawks sign "milestone" land deal', *National Post*, 22 Dec. 2000, A7.

41. Peter A. Cumming and Neil H. Mickenberg, eds, *Native Rights in Canada* (Toronto, 1972), 98. The case was *Rex v. Syliboy*, [1929] 1 D.L.R. 307, (1928), 50 C.C.C. 389 (NS Cty Ct).

42. Cumming and Mickenberg, eds, *Native Rights in Canada*, 99.

43. *The Mi'kmaq Treaty Handbook* (Sydney and Truro, NS, 1987), 13. Also Donald Marshall Sr, Alexander Denny, and Putus Simon Marshall, 'The Covenant Chain', in Boyce Richardson, ed., *Drum Beat: Anger and Renewal in Indian Country* (Ottawa, 1989), 71–104.

44. *Simon v. The Queen*, [1985] 2 S.C.R. 387 at 404.

45. Cumming and Mickenberg, eds, *Native Rights in Canada*, 210.

46. See National Indian Brotherhood, *Inquiry into the Invasion of Restigouche*, Preliminary Report, 15 July 1981.

47. Cumming and Mickenberg, eds, *Native Rights in Canada*, 216–20.

48. Calder graduated from the Anglican Theological College of the University of British Columbia and in 1949 was elected to the BC legislature, where he served for 26 years, first for the New Democratic Party, then for Social Credit. He was Minister without Portfolio, 1972–3. In 1996, he

received the National Aboriginal Achievement Award.

49. The original statement had been made by David McKay, a Greenville chief, to the Joint Reserves Allotment Commission that had been established in 1876. See David Raunet, *Without Surrender, Without Consent: A History of the Nishga Land Claims* (Vancouver, 1984), 90.

50. The case had been brought to the Supreme Court without provincial authorization.

51. David W. Elliott, 'Aboriginal Title', in Morse, ed., *Aboriginal Peoples and the Law*, 74.

52. See Cumming and Mickenberg, eds, *Native Rights in Canada*, 331–2; Thomas R. Berger, 'Native History, Native Claims and Self-Determination', *B.C. Studies* 57 (1983): 16.

53. 'The Bear Island Decision', *Ontario Reports* (2nd ser.), 49, part 7, 17 May 1985: 353–490. A review of the issues at stake, particularly those of forestry management, is by Bruce W. Hodgins and Jamie Benidickson, *The Temagami Experience* (Toronto, 1989). The Indian view is presented by Gary Potts, 'Last-Ditch Defence of a Priceless Homeland', in Richardson, ed., *Drum Beat*, 203–28.

54. Anthony J. Hall, 'The Ontario Supreme Court on Trial: Justice Donald Steele and Aboriginal Right', unpublished manuscript, 2.

55. H.F. Von Haast, ed., *New Zealand Privy Council Cases 1840–1932* (Wellington, 1938), 390, *The Queen (or the Prosecution of C.H. McIntosh) v. Symonds*.

56. See, for instance, Harold Cardinal's views on the subject in *The Rebirth of Canada's Indians* (Edmonton, 1977), 159–62.

57. Ibid., 164–5.

58. Daniel, *History of Native Claims*, 237–8.

59. Conrad Heidenreich, *Huronia: A History and Geography of the Huron Indians 1600–1650* (Toronto, 1971), 168–71.

60. For the example of the Ojibwa's misunderstanding in this regard, see Donald B. Smith, *Sacred Feathers: The Reverend Peter Jones and the Mississauga Indians* (Toronto, 1987), 24–5.

61. 'Gitksan–Carrier Declaration', in Don Monet and Skanu'u (Ardythe Wilson), *Colonialism on Trial* (Philadelphia and Gabriola Island, BC, 1992), 15.

62. Cumming and Mickenberg, eds, *Native Rights in Canada*, 17–19; Bruce A. Clark, *Native Liberty, Crown Sovereignty* (Montreal and Kingston, 1990), 13–19.

63. Donald Purich, *Our Land: Native Rights in Canada* (Toronto, 1986), 57.

64. Clark, *Native Liberty*, 31.

65. The question of the Crown's responsibility to act in the best interests of the Indians is dealt with extensively by Leonard Ian Rotman in *Parallel Paths: Fiduciary Doctrine and the Crown–Native Relationship in Canada* (Toronto, 1996). See also Purich, *Our Land*, 58–9; J.R. Miller, *Skyscrapers Hide the Heavens* (Toronto, 1989), 263.

66. Kirk Makin and Robert Matas, 'Reserve land worth half of market value: court', *Globe and Mail*, 10 Nov. 2000, A5; 'Native real estate worth less, Supreme Court rules', *Ottawa Citizen*, 10 Nov. 2000, A10; 'Leaseholders on native land win battle over rents', *National Post*, 10 Nov. 2000, A3.

67. Barbara Yaffe, 'Musqueam factions engage in battle of petitions', *Vancouver Sun*, 27 July 2000, A13.

68. Scott Simpson, 'Leaseholders on Indian Lands at Pitt Lake Upset over Ouster', ibid., 2 Mar. 2000, A1; 'Aboriginal Landlords Act at Cross-Purposes', ibid., 3 Mar. 2000, A14; Byron Churchill, 'Katzie Indians "Within Rights" to Vote Against Lease Renewals: About 56 Non-Natives Have Cabins on Rented Land', ibid., 8 Mar. 2000, B1.

69. On the Constitution's adoption, see Chapter 27.

70. Jack Woodward, *Native Law* (Toronto, 1989), 66–7.

71. 'George Weldon Adams (Appellant) v. Her Majesty the Queen (Respondent) and the Attorney General of Canada (Intervenor)', *Canadian Native Law Reporter* 4 (1996): 1–26. On the question of commercial fishing, however, the courts have ruled that Aboriginal right can be subjected to regulation.

72. For details of the *Sioui* case, see Chapter 8; also 'Confrontation gets natives into land talks', *Edmonton Journal*, 20 Aug. 1990.

73. Clark, *Native Liberty*, 31.

74. 'Land claim dismissed', *Edmonton Journal*, 8 Mar. 1991; 'Judge heard 100 witnesses, read 10,000 documents', ibid., 17 Mar. 1991; 'Natives hit another dead end', ibid., 17 Mar. 1991; 'A stunning blow to native rights', *The Gazette*, Montreal, 13 Mar. 1991; Ronald Sutherland, '"The white man's law" wins again', *Globe and Mail*, 2 Aug. 1992. Some saw the verdict as a partial victory for the hereditary chiefs. See Greg Joyce, 'Court backs Indians' right to major land claim in BC', *The Gazette*, Montreal, 26 June 1993.

75. The Indian position is presented by Neil J. Sterritt, 'Unflinching Resistance to an Implacable Invader', in Richardson, ed., *Drum Beat*, 265–94. Sterritt was president of the Gitksan-Wet'suwet'en Tribal Council, 1981–7. For an Indian view of the proceedings, see Monet and Skanu'u, *Colonialism on Trial*. On the decision of the hereditary chiefs not to appeal to the Supreme Court of Canada, see Jeffrey Simpson, 'Aboriginal rights are different things to judges and politicians', *Globe and Mail*, 4 Sept. 1996; Barbara McLintock, 'B.C. treaty talk brings on rights ruling', *Edmonton Journal*, 3 Feb. 1996, 135.

76. 'Supreme Court: Accept oral history as evidence', *Globe and Mail*, 15 Dec. 1997, A25.

77. 'Nisga'a ceremony seals historic deal', *Globe and Mail*, 5 Aug. 1998. Tom Molloy, chief negotiator, and Donald Ward tell the story of the making of the treaty in *The World Is Our Witness: The Historic Journey of the Nisga'a into Canada* (Calgary, 2000).

78. Concerning Aboriginal challenges from without the Nisga'a Nation, see Neil Sterritt, 'The Nisga'a Treaty: Competing Claims Ignored!', *B.C. Studies* 120 (Winter 1998–9): 73–97; Rick Mofina, 'B.C. Band challenges Nisga'a deal', *Ottawa Citizen*, 8 Nov. 1999; 'Nisga'a Treaty Leaves Issues Unresolved for Gitanyow', *Vancouver Sun*, 22 May 2000, A9. Concerning challenges from within the Nisga'a Nation, see Neil Seeman, 'Nisga'a land claim challenged by band dissidents', *National Post*, 23 Mar. 2000.

79. Mark Hume, 'Nisga'a treaty survives B.C. Liberals' challenge', *National Post*, 25 July 2000, A2; Rod Mickleburgh, 'Court rejects legal challenge to Nisga'a Treaty', *Globe and Mail*, 25 July 2000, A5.

80. Kirk Makin, 'Chippewa lose bid for Ontario land', *Globe and Mail*, 22 Dec. 2000.

81. Glenn Bohn, 'Squamish leaders agree to forfeit claims to former reserves', *National Post*, 9 June 2000. The agreement was accepted by the membership in a vote a little over a month later. (Robert Matas, 'Squamish support land-claims settlement', *Globe and Mail*, 25 July 2000, A1, A5.) Also, 'Squamish Approve $92.5 Million Deal to Settle Claims', *Vancouver Sun*, 25 July 2000, B5.

82. Peggy Blair, 'Taken for "Granted": Aboriginal Title and Public Fishing Rights in Upper Canada', *Ontario History* 92, 1 (Spring 2000): 31–55.

83. Kevin Cox, 'Native lobster fishery ends but dispute doesn't', *Globe and Mail*, 7 Oct. 2000, A7; Graeme Hamilton, 'Burnt Church votes to end fall fishery early', *National Post*, 20 Sept. 2000; 'Nova Scotia tribe to fish for lobster despite lack of agreement with Ottawa', Associated Press, 20 Nov. 2000. For the Mi'kmaq view of the dispute, see Paul Barnsley, 'Anger mounts', *Windspeaker* Oct. 2000, 1, 11; for the lobster situation, see Kevin Cox, 'The real lobster problem', *Globe and Mail*, 2 Sept. 2000; 'Ottawa, natives reach compromise on fishing', *Globe and Mail*, 23 Apr. 2001, A4.

84. Scott Simpson, 'Coho dispute pits anglers against Indians', *Vancouver Sun*, 3 Nov. 2000, A6.

85. This was a situation that Aboriginal people across the board were keenly aware of. Rick Mofina, 'Government ignores rights rulings, natives say', *Ottawa Citizen*, 28 Feb. 2001, A3.

86. Mark Holmes, 'So just who is a Métis?' *Globe and Mail*, 1 Mar. 2001, A13.

87. Kirk Makin, 'Court recognizes Métis as a distinct people', *Globe and Mail*, 24 Feb. 2001, A1, A15; Jennifer Prittie, 'Court orders Ontario to recognize Métis and their right to hunt', *National Post*, 24 Feb. 2001, A4.

88. Mark MacKinnon, 'Expense of Indian claims soaring', *Globe and Mail*, 28 Feb. 2001, A4.

89. Rick Mofina, 'More native conflicts feared: memo', *Ottawa Citizen*, 17 Jan. 2001, A5; Therese Tedesco and Carol Howse, 'Natives make refinery bid', *National Post*, 23 Jan. 2001; 'Even competitors mum on tax-free zone for the Blood Tribe', ibid.

Chapter 24

1. This section owes a special debt to E. Brian Titley, *A Narrow Vision: Duncan Campbell Scott and the Administration of Indian Affairs in Canada* (Vancouver, 1986), 110–34; Joëlle Rostkowski, 'The Redman's Appeal for Justice: Deskaheh and the League of Nations', in Christian Feest, ed., *Indians and Europe* (Aachen, 1987), 435–53; Ann Charney, 'The Last Indian War', *The Idler* 29 (July–Aug. 1990): 14–22.

2. See Alice B. Kehoe, *The Ghost Dance* (Toronto, 1989), 116–23; Anthony F.C. Wallace, *Death and Rebirth of the Seneca* (New York, 1969).

3. C.P. Stacey, 'Canada and the Nile Expedition of 1884–1885', *Canadian Historical Review* 33 (1952): 319–40; Louis Jackson, *Our Caughnawagas in Egypt* (Montreal, 1885). Jackson, leader of the Caughnawaga (Kahnawake) canoemen, recounts the adventures of the Iroquois as non-combatants in the expeditionary force. A brief excerpt is reproduced in Penny Petrone, ed., *First People, First Voices* (Toronto, 1983), 136–8.

4. Traditionally, horns (deer antlers, buffalo horns) were considered to be instruments of power and were worn by shamans and leaders. The 'Dehorners' opposed the traditional power structure.

5. Margaret Vincent Tehariolina, *La nation huronne, son histoire, sa culture, son esprit* (Québec, 1984), 317–18.

6. Titley, *A Narrow Vision*, 133.

7. Ibid.

8. The original grant to the seigneury of Sault St Louis was for 44,000 acres (17,806 hectares); Kahnawake today comprises 13,000 acres (5,261 hectares).

9. Toby Morantz, 'Aboriginal Land Claims in Quebec', in Ken Coates, ed., *Aboriginal Land Claims in Canada* (Toronto, 1992), 105.

10. Charney, 'The Last Indian War', 14, 17.

11. Ibid., 16.

12. The Iroquoian term that translates into English as 'warrior' is more nearly equivalent to 'young man'. The meaning of the term and the role of the Warriors in Iroquois society are discussed in *Akwesasne Notes* 22, 4 (1990): 6. The Mohawk *Akwesasne Notes*, which began publication in 1969, is published in the New York section of St Regis Reserve. The 'ideological father' of the current Warrior movement was Louis Hall of Kahnawake (1916–1993).

13. Because of an Indian Act provision that no taxes be paid on goods owned or used by Amerindians on Amerindian land, cigarettes can be sold more cheaply on reserves than elsewhere. The cigarette trade has become an important source of revenue for some reserves, particularly those near the international border. See Charney, 'The Last Indian War', 17–18.

14. Ibid., 14.

15. '"Armed, violent" poster stuns fugitive Mohawks', *Edmonton Journal*, 20 Oct. 1988.

16. 'Police call Mohawks "terrorists" in national ad', *Edmonton Journal*, 19 Sept. 1990. The advertisement, headed 'We Oppose Terrorism', ran that same day in newspapers across Canada. The role of the Warriors in the 1990 standoff is discussed in *Akwesasne Notes* 22, 4 (1990): 8.

17. 'Language issue raised anew at Mohawks' trial', *The Gazette*, Montreal, 23 Apr. 1991; 'Quebec Mohawks have right to English at trial, court rules', *Edmonton Journal*, 3 May 1991; 'Right to English trial granted: Judge contradicts earlier ruling in parallel Mohawk case', *Globe and Mail*, 2 May 1991.

18. Sources for this section are Judith Hill, 'The Ewing Commission, 1935: A Case Study of Metis Government Relations', MA thesis (University of Alberta, 1977); The Metis Association of Alberta et al., *Metis Land Rights in Alberta: A Political History* (Edmonton, 1981).

19. *Report of the Royal Commission on Aboriginal Peoples*, 5 vols (Ottawa, 1996), IV, 203.

20. Ibid., 209, 258.

21. See Maria Campbell's classic *Halfbreed* (Toronto,

1973).

22. Their story is told by Murray Dobbin, *The One-and-a-Half Men* (Vancouver, 1981). Both Norris and Brady were veterans of World War II, Norris having served in the RCAF and Brady with the Royal Canadian Artillery. Dr Adam Cuthand, who had seen service with the Canadian army, became the founding president of the Manitoba Metis Federation in 1968.

23. Donald Purich, *The Metis* (Toronto, 1968), 144.

24. Trudy Nicks, 'Mary Anne's Dilemma: The Ethnohistory of an Ambivalent Identity', *Canadian Ethnic Studies* 17, 2 (1985): 110.

25. Purich, *The Metis*, 148–9.

26. For a discussion of the Métis and Aboriginal right, see *Metisism: A Canadian Identity* (Edmonton, 1982).

27. 'Pact makes history: "It's our land," Metis say as Getty signs', *Edmonton Journal*, 2 July 1989, 1; also, 'Historic vote on Metis deal known today', ibid., 21 June 1989.

28. Dan Smith, *The Seventh Fire* (Toronto, 1993), 187–8.

29. Marie Burke, 'Métis sign provincial agreement', *Alberta Sweetgrass* 6, 4 (May 1999): 3.

30. 'Deal allows Alberta Metis to create justice programs', *Edmonton Journal*, 9 Nov. 1999.

31. Canadian Aboriginal Issues Database, University of Alberta, at: <www.ualberta.ca/~walld/metistime.html>.

32. For instance, in 1949 in the Northwest Territories, Oblate missionaries noted that Indians did not want registered traplines but asked instead that they be allocated a large territory they could use in common. Oblate Archives, St Albert, Alberta, Fort Good Hope file #1, vol. 5: 28.

33. A personal statement on being Métis is by Dorothy Daniels, 'Metis Identity: A Personal Perspective', *Native Studies Review* 3, 2 (1987): 7–15. See also Duke Redbird, *We Are Metis: A Metis View of the Development of a Native Canadian People* (Willowdale, Ont., 1980).

34. Indian and Northern Affairs Canada, at: <www.ainc.inac.gc.ca/pr/info/tln_e.html>.

35. See the critique by Trudy Nicks, 'Metis: A Glenbow Museum Exhibition', *Muse* 3, 4 (1986): 52–8. The catalogue for the exhibition, Julia Harrison, *Metis* (Vancouver, 1985), gives a good short history of western Métis.

36. James McCarten, 'Any hunting rights must await Métis definition, Ontario says', *Globe and Mail,* 1 Nov. 2000. On the Acadians currently rediscovering their Aboriginal heritage, see Chapter 11.

37. James S. Frideres briefly surveys the Métis situation in *Native Peoples in Canada: Contemporary Conflicts* (Scarborough, Ont., 1983), 267–92.

38. Jon M. Gerrard, Secretary of State for Science, Research and Development, and Western Economic Diversification, addressing the annual meeting of the Métis National Council, Ottawa, 14 Feb. 1996.

Chapter 25

1. William R. Morrison, *Under the Flag: Canadian Sovereignty and the Native People in Northern Canada* (Ottawa, 1984), 32–4; Kenneth S. Coates and William R. Morrison, *Land of the Midnight Sun: A History of the Yukon* (Edmonton, 1988), 43–7; Arthur S. Morton, *A History of the Canadian West to 1870–71*, ed. Lewis G. Thomas (Toronto, 1973), 708–9. Concerning whalers as traders, see John R. Bockstoce, *Whales, Ice, and Men: The History of Whaling in the Western Arctic* (Seattle, 1986), 192–4.

2. Morrison, *Under the Flag*, 31–41. On the process by which Canada acquired the Arctic Archipelago, see Morris Zaslow, *The Opening of the Canadian North* (Toronto, 1971), 88–100; W. Gillies Ross, 'Whaling, Inuit, and the Arctic Islands', in Morris Zaslow, ed., *A Century of Canada's Arctic Islands 1880–1980* (Ottawa, 1981), 33–50.

3. Zaslow, *Opening of the Canadian North*, 93–4.

4. René Fumoleau, *As Long As This Land Shall Last* (Toronto, 1973), 27–30; Zaslow, *Opening of the Canadian North*, 88–100.

5. Interview with Felix Gibot recorded by Richard Lightning, Treaty and Aboriginal Rights Research of the Indian Association of Alberta, 5 Feb. 1974, in Richard Price, ed., *The Spirit of the Alberta Indian Treaties* (Edmonton, 1987), 157.

6. *Report of the North-West Mounted Police 1898*, Part II, Patrol Report, Fort Saskatchewan to Fort Simpson, inspector W.H. Routledge, 96.

7. A fine study of the relationship between the northern Cree and the animals upon which they depend is by Robert Brightman, *Grateful Prey* (Berkeley, 1993).

8. Kerry Abel, '"Matters are growing worse": Government and Mackenzie Missions, 1870–1921', in Kenneth S. Coates and William R. Morrison, eds, *For Purposes of Dominion* (Toronto, 1989), 75. The Yukon's first Indian residential school was established at Carcross in 1901 by Anglican bishop W.C. Bompas.

9. Department of Indian Affairs, vol. 1115, Deputy Superintendent's Letterbook, Hayter Reed to Charles Constantine, commander of the first

Yukon police contingent, 29 May 1894, cited by Kenneth S. Coates, 'Best Left As Indians: The Federal Government and the Indians of the Yukon, 1884–1950', *Canadian Journal of Native Studies* 4, 2 (1984): 181. This article is drawn from Coates, 'Best Left as Indians: Native–White Relations in Yukon Territory, 1840–1950', Ph.D. thesis (University of British Columbia, 1984).

10. For example, John Tetso, *Trapping is My Life* (Toronto, 1970); Maxwell Paupanekis, 'The Trapper', in Malvina Bolus, ed., *People and Pelts* (Winnipeg, 1972), 137–43.

11. Hugh Brody, *The People's Land: Eskimos and Whites in the Eastern Arctic* (Harmondsworth, England, 1975), 29.

12. Bompas had been bishop of Athabasca, 1874–84, and bishop of Mackenzie, 1884–91. He had been in the North since 1865, a record for nineteenth-century missionaries. An associate of his who would become a leading voice on behalf of the Amerindians was I.O. Stringer, who arrived in the North in 1894 and succeeded Bompas as bishop of Selkirk (Yukon).

13. 'Wife-lending' would be more appropriately called 'spouse-sharing'. When whaling captains shared Inuit partners' wives, the latter thought of themselves as sharing the captains with their far-away wives.

14. Morrison, *Under the Flag*, 45–6; Diamond Jenness, *Eskimo Administration: II: Canada* (Montreal, 1972), 14; Abel, '"Matters are growing worse"', 76; Bockstoce, *Whales, Ice, and Men*, 276–9. As Thomas Stone points out, the whalers, constrained by their highly structured lives aboard ship, did not develop public mechanisms for dealing with conflict within the broader community as did the miners in the Yukon. Stone, 'Atomistic Order and Frontier Violence: Miners and Whalemen in the Nineteenth-Century Yukon', *Ethnology* 22, 4 (1983): 327–39. See also Stone, 'Flux and Authority in a Subarctic Society: The Yukon Miners in the Nineteenth Century', *Ethnohistory* 30, 4 (1983): 203–16. By the time the police arrived, most whalers were wintering at Baillie Island, 483 kilometres to the east.

15. Ernest Beaglehole, *Social Change in the South Pacific: Rarotonga and Aitutaki* (Aberdeen, Scotland, 1957), 70, cited by W. Gillies Ross, *Whaling and Eskimos: Hudson Bay 1860–1915* (Ottawa, 1975), 138. See also Bockstoce, *Whales, Ice, and Men*.

16. Coates and Morrison, *Land of the Midnight Sun*, 112–13.

17. Richard Diubaldo, *The Government of Canada and the Inuit, 1900–1967* (Ottawa, 1985), 13–14.

18. Morrison, *Under the Flag*, 87.

19. A film, Barry Greenwald's *Between Two Worlds*, tells the story of Joseph Idlout of Pond Inlet and Resolute Bay, a leading hunter who embraced the Euro-Canadian way. He was successful enough that he and his family were the subject of a National Film Board classic, *Land of the Long Day*, directed by Doug Wilkinson in 1951; the family also adorned the back of the Canadian $2 bill. Idlout ended up as a barfly, surviving on handout jobs. On 2 June 1968 he died in an accident. *Between Two Worlds* is reviewed in the *Edmonton Journal*, 11 Sept. 1990. The happier story of another hunter who made the same transition is *I, Nuligak*, ed. and tr. Maurice Metayer (Toronto, 1966).

20. Gurston Dacks, *A Choice of Futures: Politics in the Canadian North* (Toronto, 1981), 90; David R. Morrison, *The Politics of the Yukon Territory, 1898–1909* (Toronto, 1968), ch. 3.

21. Low, who had done much to explore Labrador, in 1903 had commanded the Government Expedition to Hudson Bay and Northward. F.J. Alcock, 'Albert Peter Low', in William C. Wonders, ed., *Canada's Changing North* (Toronto, 1976), 76–81.

22. W. Gillies Ross, 'Canadian Sovereignty in the Arctic: The *Neptune* Expedition of 1903–04', *Arctic* 29, 2 (1976): 87–104.

23. Catharine McClellan, *Part of the Land, Part of the Water: A History of Yukon Indians* (Vancouver, 1987), 43. Jenness says that by 1930 not more than a dozen—if that—could claim descent from the western Arctic's original inhabitants. (*Eskimo Administration: II*, 14.)

24. Alan D. McMillan, *Native Peoples and Cultures of Canada* (Vancouver, 1988), 246.

25. Jenness, *Eskimo Administration: II*, 11 and n1. According to one report, four children survived.

26. Charles Mair, *Through the Mackenzie Basin* (Toronto, 1908), 60. The speech has also been attributed to Wahpeehayo ('White Partridge'), who was also in attendance.

27. John S. Long, *Treaty No. 9: The Indian Petition, 1889–1927* (Cobalt, Ont., 1978); James Morrison, *Treaty Nine (1905–06): The James Bay Treaty* (Ottawa, 1986).

28. Government of Nunavut, at: <www.gov.nu.ca/Nunavut/English/about/ourland.pdf>.

29. Jenness was strong on this point, and highly critical of Canada's performance. *Eskimo Administration: II*, 17.

30. Richard C. Daniel, 'Spirit and Terms of Treaty Eight', in Price, ed., *Spirit of the Alberta Indian*

Treaties, 58.

31. R.B. McConnell, *Report on a Portion of the District of Athabasca Comprising the Country between the Peace River and the Athabasca River North of Lesser Slave Lake* (Ottawa, 1893), cited by René Fumoleau, *As Long As This Land Shall Last* (Toronto, 1973), 39; Daniel, 'Spirit and Terms of Treaty Eight', 58–9.

32. Julie Cruikshank and Jim Robb, *Their Own Yukon* (Whitehorse, 1975), 2.

33. Their sudden wealth did not make life better for Skookum Jim Mason or Dawson Charlie, Kate's brothers. The latter fell off a bridge in 1908 and was drowned; Skookum Jim retired to his home grounds at Carcross, where he died in 1916. Kate Carmack was abandoned by her husband, who went to California and remarried; Kate stayed at Carcross, where she became something of a tourist attraction. See Zaslow, *Opening of the Canadian North*, 145.

34. H.A. Innis, 'Settlement and the Mining Frontier', in W.A. Mackintosh and W.L.G. Joerg, eds, *Canadian Frontiers of Settlement*, IX, Part II (Toronto, 1936), 183.

35. *Report of the Commissioner of the North-West Mounted Police*, Northern Patrol 1897, 170. The observation was made in connection with the custom of non-Native trappers to use poison bait.

36. For some Indian memories about what happened on the Klondike River, see Cruikshank and Robb, *Their Own Yukon*, 13–15.

37. Fumoleau, *As Long As This Land Shall Last*, 58; Daniel, 'Spirit and Terms of Treaty Eight', 63. The story of the 'lost patrol', 1910–11, when four policemen died, is one of the many reminders of the dangers of overconfidence in the North. The patrol, headed by Inspector F.J. Fitzgerald, was to go from Dawson to Fort McPherson; Fitzgerald not only did not take along a Native guide, he had refused help when it had been offered. The story has been the subject of a CBC television drama. See Dick North, *The Lost Patrol* (Vancouver, 1995).

38. John L. Tobias, 'Protection, Civilization, Assimilation: An Outline History of Canada's Indian Policy', *Western Canadian Journal of Anthropology* 6, 2 (1976): 21; Zaslow, *Opening of the Canadian North*, 96–7. The Métis also were upset about the regulation. Mair, *Through the Mackenzie Basin*, 92.

39. The problem as it applied in the North in general is touched upon by Arthur J. Ray, *The Canadian Fur Trade and the Industrial Age* (Toronto, 1990), 197–221.

40. Fumoleau, *As Long As This Land Shall Last*, 47. See also J.G. MacGregor, *The Klondike Rush through Edmonton 1897–1898* (Toronto, 1970).

41. Mair, *Through the Mackenzie Basin*, 23–4.

42. Dennis Madill, *B.C. Indian Treaties in Historical Perspective* (Ottawa, 1981), 63.

43. Daniel, 'Spirit and Terms of Treaty Eight', 58.

44. Fumoleau, *As Long As This Land Shall Last*, 59.

45. Ibid., 51.

46. Ibid., 60.

47. Morrison, *Under the Flag*, 52.

48. Coates, 'Best Left As Indians', 184. Coates maintains that Ottawa's reluctance to assign reserves was due to the worry that gold might later be discovered on them.

49. Daniel, 'Spirit and Terms of Treaty Eight', 65.

50. Official report of Treaty Eight Commission, 1899, in Fumoleau, *As Long As This Land Shall Last*, 84. The account that follows is drawn from this report.

51. Ibid., 74, citing a sworn affidavit by James K. Cornwall ('Peace River Jim'), 1937, on his recollections of the treaty negotiations. Cornwall was involved in transportation projects.

52. Fumoleau, *As Long As This Land Shall Last*, 86.

53. Ibid.

54. Mair, *Through the Mackenzie Basin*, 63.

55. Price, ed., *Spirit of Alberta Indian Treaties*, 106.

56. Daniel, 'Spirit and Terms of Treaty Eight', 82.

57. Interview with Felix Gibot in Price, ed., *Spirit of Alberta Indian Treaties*, 159.

58. Cited ibid., 95. The case in which the comment was made was *Paulette et al.*, Supreme Court of Northwest Territories, 1973–7.

59. Daniel, 'Spirit and Terms of Treaty Eight', 95–6.

60. Fumoleau, *As Long As This Land Shall Last*, 192–6.

61. Daniel, 'Spirit and Terms of Treaty Eight', 96–7.

62. John S. Long, '"No Basis for Agreement"? The Signing of Treaty Nine in Northern Ontario, 1905–1906', *Native Studies Review* 5, 2 (1989): 26.

63. Fumoleau, *As Long As This Land Shall Last*, 142.

64. Zaslow, *Opening of the Canadian North*, 90–1.

65. Jenness, *Eskimo Administration: II*, 23. See also Ray, *Canadian Fur Trade in the Industrial Age*; Morris Zaslow, *The Northward Expansion of Canada 1914–1967* (Toronto, 1988).

66. Shelagh D. Grant, *Sovereignty or Security? Government Policy in the Canadian North, 1936–1950* (Vancouver, 1988), 14–19.

67. Kerry Abel, *Drum Songs* (Montreal and Kingston, 1993), 205–6; Zaslow, *The Northward Expansion of Canada*, 177–81.

68. Abel, '"Matters are growing worse"', 82. A typescript copy, dated 5 June 1938, of Breynat's memorandum denouncing government treatment of

Indians is in the Alberta Provincial Archives, 17.220, item 994, box 25. A marginal note says the memorandum was published in the *Toronto Star* towards the end of June and in *Le Soleil* (Quebec), 3 July 1938.

69. McClellan, *Part of the Land*, 90.

70. On some of the problems of the trapping life today, see James W. VanStone, 'Changing Patterns of Indian Trapping in the Canadian Subarctic', in Wonders, ed., *Canada's Changing North*, 170–86.

71. Keith J. Crowe, *A History of the Original Peoples of Northern Canada* (Montreal and Kingston, 1974), 163.

72. Diubaldo, *Government of Canada and the Inuit*, 17–18.

73. Milton Freeman has linked the practice among the Netsilik Inuit to the need to maintain existing cultural balances in sex roles. Freeman, 'Ethos, Economics and Prestige, a Re-Examination of Netsilik Eskimo Infanticide', *Vernhandlungen des XXXVIII. Internationalen Amerikanistenkongresses II* (Stuttgart-München, 1968).

74. R.G. Moyles, *British Law and Arctic Men* (Saskatoon, 1979); Gaston Carrière, *Dictionnaire biographique* (Ottawa, 1979), VIII, 141.

75. For details of this and other cases about the same time, see Diubaldo, *Government of Canada and the Inuit*, 15–17. A detailed study of the first murder trial in the Arctic, in 1917, in which the two Inuit charged were found guilty but granted clemency, is Moyles, *British Law and Arctic Men*.

76. *The Inuit Way: A Guide to Inuit Culture* (Ottawa, [1990]), 6. A less idealized version, as practised by the Copper Inuit, is described by Diamond Jenness, *Report of the Canadian Arctic Expedition 1913–18. Vol. 12: The Life of the Copper Eskimos* (Ottawa, 1922), 94–6. Oddly enough, the pre-gold rush mining communities in the Yukon developed a system of justice that had certain resemblances to that of the Inuit. Not only was the offence itself judged, but also the character of the accused and what he was likely to do in the future. This was called 'forward-looking justice'. See Coates and Morrison, *Land of the Midnight Sun*, 60–1.

77. Jenness, *Life of the Copper Eskimos*, 232.

78. Diubaldo, *Government of Canada and the Inuit*, 36. The comment was as revealing about the officer's attitude as about the Inuit's.

79. Morrison, *Under the Flag*, 127–30.

80. Ibid., 94.

81. John F. Leslie and Ron Maguire, eds, *The Historical Development of the Indian Act* (Ottawa, 1978), 119.

82. Jenness, *Eskimo Adminstration: II*, ch. 2.

83. Diubaldo, *Government of Canada and the Inuit*, 32.

84. C.S. Mackinnon, 'The 1958 Government Policy Reversal in Keewatin', in Coates and Morrison, eds, *For Purposes of Dominion*, 160.

85. On the distinction, see Michael H. Brown, *The Search for Eve: Have Scientists Found the Mother of Us All?* (New York, 1990), 315. On the genetic links with Athapaskan-speakers, see Emöke J.E. Szathmary, 'Human Biology in the Arctic', in David Damas, ed., *Handbook of North American Indians, 5: Arctic* (Washington, 1984), 70–1; Richard J. Diubaldo, 'The Absurd Little Mouse: When Eskimos Became Indians', *Journal of Canadian Studies* 16, 2 (1981): 34–40.

86. The letters are reproduced in Diubaldo, *Government of Canada and the Inuit*, 46–7. The practice of classifying 'Esquimaux' as Amerindian endured until well into the twentieth century. See, for example, the 1934 edition of *Webster's International Dictionary* (cited ibid., 45).

87. Louis-Edmond Hamelin, *Canadian Nordicity: It's Your North Too*, tr. W. Barr (Montreal, 1979), ch. 6.

88. The fuss over the legal status of Inuit is examined by Frank James Tester and Peter Kulchyski in *Tammarniit (Mistakes)* (Vancouver, 1994), 13–42.

89. Mackinnon, 'Government Policy Reversal', 161.

90. Diubaldo, *Government of Canada and the Inuit*, 57. See also Constance Hunt, 'The Development and Decline of Northern Conservation Reserves', *Contact* 8, 4 (1976).

Chapter 26

1. Little of this is reflected in the pamphlet, *Indians of Canada Pavilion*, given to visitors, although it presented a spectrum of Amerindian views. Its general approach is expressed in the statement: 'I see an Indian, tall and strong in the pride of his heritage. He stands with your sons, a man among men.' Such romanticism was more effective in literature than in politics.

2. Lloyd Barber, 'The Implication of Indian Claims for Canada', address given at the Banff School of Advanced Management, Banff, Alberta, 9 Mar. 1978. Officially, there had been a reluctance to allow Amerindians to argue their case.

3. *House of Commons Debates*, 8 Dec. 1953, 698. The expression had first been used by Sir John Robert Seeley, professor of modern history at Cambridge, referring to the expansion of the British Empire during the period 1688–1815. Seeley, *The Expansion of England* (London, 1883).

4. Morris Zaslow, *The Opening of the Canadian North* (Toronto, 1971), 278.

5. Hugh Brody, *The People's Land: Eskimos and Whites in the Eastern Arctic* (Harmondsworth, England, 1975), 220.

6. H.B. Hawthorn, *A Survey of the Contemporary Indians of Canada: Economic, Political, Educational Needs and Policies*, 2 vols (Ottawa, 1966–7), I, 6.

7. A seminal article on historians' approach to Amerindians is James W. St G. Walker, 'The Canadian Indian in Historical Writing', Canadian Historical Association, *Historical Papers* (1971): 21–51. A follow-up report, also by Walker, 'The Indian in Canadian Historical Writing, 1971–1981', appeared in Ian A.L. Getty and Antoine S. Lussier, eds, *As Long As the Sun Shines and Water Flows* (Vancouver, 1983), 340–57.

8. The social dislocations that have resulted from these shifts in values and circumstances were the subject of a special report, 'A Canadian Tragedy', *Maclean's* 99, 28 (14 July 1986): 12–25.

9. Hawthorn, *A Survey of Contemporary Indians*, I, 13.

10. R.W. Dunning, 'Indian Policy—A Proposal for Autonomy', *Canadian Forum* 49 (Dec. 1969): 206–7. A detailed analysis of the birth of the White Paper is Sally Weaver, *Making Canadian Indian Policy: The Hidden Agenda 1968–1970* (Toronto, 1981). See also J. Rick Ponting and Roger Gibbins, *Out of Irrelevance* (Toronto, 1980), 25–9.

11. *Statement of the Government of Canada on Indian Policy, 1969*, 3. See also Bradford W. Morse, 'The Resolution of Land Claims', in Morse, ed., *Aboriginal Peoples and the Law: Indian, Metis and Inuit Rights in Canada* (Ottawa, 1985), 618–21.

12. Arrel Morgan Gibson, *The American Indian: Prehistory to the Present* (Lexington, Mass., 1980), 486–512, 550–5.

13. 'Statement of National Indian Brotherhood', in *Recent Statements by the Indians of Canada*, Anglican Church of Canada General Synod Action 1969, Bulletin 201, 1970, 28.

14. Cited by Weaver, *Making Canadian Indian Policy*, 174. See also Marie Smallface Marule, 'The Canadian Government's Termination Policy: From 1969 to the Present Day', in Ian A.L. Getty and Donald B. Smith, eds, *One Century Later: Western Canadian Reserve Indians Since Treaty 7* (Vancouver, 1978), 103–16.

15. Ponting and Gibbins, *Out of Irrelevance*, 197.

16. 'Wuttunee termed "traitorous", barred from his home reserve', *Globe and Mail*, 4 May 1970.

17. William I.C. Wuttunee, *Ruffled Feathers* (Calgary, 1971), 136–41.

18. Hugh Dempsey, *The Gentle Persuader: A Biography of James Gladstone, Indian Senator* (Saskatoon, 1986), 204–6.

19. At an Amerindian conference at Kamloops in Nov. 1969, some expressed regret at the complete rejection of the White Paper. See Paul Tennant, *Aboriginal Peoples and Politics: The Indian Land Question in British Columbia, 1849–1989* (Vancouver, 1990), 153.

20. The text of *Citizens Plus* was reproduced in *The First Citizen* 7 (June 1970). Other Amerindian responses appear ibid. 8 (July 1970).

21. Menno Boldt, *Surviving as Indians* (Toronto, 1993), 46, 66.

22. Alpheus Henry Snow, *The Question of Aborigines in the Law and Practice of Nations* (Washington, 1919), 7.

23. A circular published by the Society for Converting and Civilizing the Indians of Upper Canada, 20 Oct. 1830, read, in part: '. . . it must be a matter of deep concern to reflect that there exist in this Province a very great number of Aborigines in this Country, the original possessors of the soil on which we are now living, and enjoying the blessings of civilized life, to whom the glad tidings of Salvation, as published in the gospel of Jesus Christ, are still altogether unknown.' (Metropolitan Toronto Reference Library, History, H-1830.)

24. Some cases involving Aboriginal right in the English-speaking world are surveyed in Brian Slattery, *Ancestral Lands, Alien Laws: Judicial Perspectives on Aboriginal Title* (Saskatoon, 1983), 44–5.

25. W.R. Morrison, *A Survey of the History and Claims of the Native Peoples of Northern Canada* (Ottawa, 1983), 44–53; 'Siddon says Yukon land claim deal won't mean Indian self-government', *Edmonton Journal*, 22 Oct. 1990. The agreement provides for 41,440 square kilometres (over 8 per cent of Yukon's land mass) to be retained by the Natives, who also were to receive $242.7 million (in 1989 dollars) in compensation. See Indian and Northern Affairs Canada, at: <www.ainc-inac.ga.ca/pr/agr/umb/index_e.html>.

26. Douglas Sanders, 'Government Agencies in Canada', in Wilcomb E. Washburn, ed., *Handbook of North American Indians, 4: History of Indian–White Relations* (Washington, 1988), 282.

27. See, for example, Heather Robertson, *Reservations Are for Indians* (Toronto, 1970).

28. Richard C. Daniel, *A History of Native Claims Processes in Canada, 1867–1979* (Ottawa, 1980), 118–21.

29. Morris Zaslow, *The Northward Expansion of Canada 1914–1967* (Toronto, 1988), 151.

30. DINA file 1/3-11, vol. 1, E. Fairclough to E.D.

Fulton, 9 Nov. 1961, cited by Daniel, *History of Native Claims*, 217.

31. This account is based on Darlene Abreu Ferreira, 'Need Not Greed: The Lubicon Lake Cree Band Claim in Historical Perspective', MA thesis (University of Alberta, 1990). See also Naila Clerici, 'The Spirit Still Sings at Lubicon Lake: Indian Rights in Canada, a Case Study', *Proceedings of the 7th International Convention of Canadian Studies*, Catania, Italy, 1988; Boyce Richardson, 'Wrestling with the Canadian System: A Decade of Lubicon Frustration', in Richardson, ed., *Drum Beat: Anger and Renewal in Indian Country* (Ottawa, 1989), 231–64.

32. Ferreira, 'Need Not Greed', 93.

33. 'Lubicon Cree Defy Japanese Logging Plans', *Akwesasne Notes* 22, 6 (1991): 10–19.

34. Jack Danylchuk, '"Fresh start" sought on land claim talks', *Edmonton Journal*, 23 May 1995, A7.

35. 'Cree sign land-claim agreement', *Edmonton Journal*, 20 Dec. 1990, 1.

36. Friends of the Lubicon, at: <www.tao.ca/~fol/pa/neg.htm>.

37. Anastasia M. Shkilnyk, *A Poison Stronger Than Love: The Destruction of an Ojibwa Community* (New Haven, 1985), 123–32.

38. 'Land claims office getting no results', *Edmonton Journal*, 26 May 1996, A3. A more positive picture is presented by the *Report of the Royal Commission on Aboriginal Peoples*, 5 vols (Ottawa, 1996), II, part 2, 547.

39. On the difficulties, see J. Rick Ponting, ed., *Arduous Journey: Canadian Indians and Decolonization* (Toronto, 1986), 299. For Thomas R. Berger's impression, see *Village Journey* (New York, 1985).

40. 'They're actually giving money away in Alaska', *Ottawa Citizen*, 12 Oct. 1996.

41. Howard H. Peckham, *Pontiac and the Indian Uprising* (Chicago, 1947), 66.

42. Ponting and Gibbins, *Out of Irrelevance*, 81.

43. The findings of the Royal Commission into the Donald Marshall Jr prosecution were reported in *Globe and Mail*, 27 Jan. 1990, A9.

44. 'Justice on trial', *Edmonton Journal*, 30 Mar. 1991, H1, H3.

45. 'Justice system falls short, Siddon says', *Edmonton Journal*, 27 Mar. 1991.

46. Sissons published his memoirs under the title *Judge of the Far North* (Toronto, 1968).

47. Shelley Knapp, 'Country's first aboriginal court opens today', *Calgary Herald*, 6 Oct. 2000, B7.

48. 'A breakthrough in Kanesatake', *The Gazette*, Montreal, 27 Dec. 1996.

49. Richard Diubaldo, *Stefansson and the Canadian Arctic* (Montreal and Kingston, 1978), 145–60.

50. Richard Diubaldo, *The Government of Canada and the Inuit, 1900–1967* (Ottawa, 1985), 74. See also R.M. Hill, 'Reindeer Resource in the Mackenzie Delta—1968', in Wonders, ed., *Canada's Changing North*, 225–9.

51. Canada, Department of Mines and Resources, *Report of the Department for the Fiscal Year Ended March 31, 1944* (Ottawa, 1944), 70. See also J.K. Stager, 'Reindeer herding as private enterprise in Canada', *Polar Record* 22, 137 (1984): 127–36. A fictionalized re-creation of the drive is by Allen Roy Evans, *Reindeer Trek* (Toronto, 1946).

52. Zaslow, *Northward Expansion*, 145.

53. CBC News, at: <www.cbc.ca/canada/north/story/2007/08/28/north-caribou.html>.

54. Diubaldo, *Government of Canada and the Inuit*, 130–1.

55. Zaslow, *Northward Expansion*, 145–6.

56. C.S. Mackinnon, 'The 1958 Government Policy Reversal in Keewatin', in Kenneth S. Coates and William R. Morrison, eds, *For Purposes of Dominion* (Toronto, 1989), 162.

57. Diamond Jenness, *Eskimo Administration: II. Canada* (Montreal, 1972), 9.

58. Diubaldo, *Government of Canada and the Inuit*, 118.

59. Jenness, *Eskimo Administration: II*, 59–64; Zaslow, *Northward Expansion*, 168–73. See also 'Displaced Inuit wait six years for a new village', *Globe and Mail*, 14 Aug. 1984; E. Lyall, *An Arctic Man* (Edmonton, 1979).

60. Diubaldo, *Government of Canada and the Inuit*, 118–30; Mackinnon, 'Government Policy Reversal', 166–7. One observer likened the northern service officers who were placed in charge of these villages to the agents on Amerindian reserves.

61. Robert G. Williamson, *Eskimo Underground: Socio-Cultural Change in the Canadian Central Arctic* (Uppsala, 1974), 82. See also David E. Young, ed., *Health Care Issues in the Canadian North* (Edmonton, 1988); P.G. Nixon, 'Early Administrative Developments in Fighting Tuberculosis among Canadian Inuit: Bringing State Institutions Back In', *Northern Review* 2 (1988): 67. Widespread adoption of the foods, clothing, and housing of non-Natives has been seen as injurious to Native health. Zaslow, *Northward Expansion*, 153.

62. 'Decades later, Inuit far from home', *Toronto Star*, 27 Dec. 1988; 'Lost Inuk's family found, N.W.T. brings him home', *Edmonton Journal*, 5 Jan. 1989; 'Families still search for Inuit sent south in '40s

and '50s', ibid., 23 Jan. 1989; 'Inuit unlock mystery of 1950s epidemic', ibid., 23 Jan. 1989; 'Inuit teen finds his family—at last', ibid., 6 July 1989; 'Burial locations bring peace of mind', ibid., 24 June 1990.

63. Milton M.R. Freeman, 'Tradition and Change: Problems and Persistence in the Inuit Diet', in I. de Garine and G.A. Harrison, eds, *Coping with Uncertainty in Food Supply* (Oxford, 1988), 166.

64. 'Ottawa must pay Inuit for relocation: report', *The Gazette*, Montreal, 20 June 1990, B4. For background information, see Milton M.R. Freeman, 'The Grise Fiord Project', in David Damas, ed., *Handbook of North American Indians, 5: Arctic* (Washington, 1984), 676–82.

65. 'No apology from the federal government to uprooted Inuit', *Edmonton Journal*, 20 Nov. 1990; 'Ottawa uprooted Inuit for Arctic "sovereignty"', ibid., 26 June 1991; 'Study disputes Inuit relocation', ibid.

66. The Inuit relocations of 1939–63 are studied by Frank James Tester and Peter Kulchyski, *Tammarniit (Mistakes)* (Vancouver, 1994). See also *Report of the Royal Commission on Aboriginal Peoples*, I, 411ff., and the three-volume interim report issued in 1994 under the general title, *The High Arctic Relocation*.

67. Freeman, 'The Grise Fiord Project', 682. Also Freeman, 'Patrons, Leaders and Values in an Eskimo Settlement', paper presented at the symposium, The Contemporary Cultural Situation of the Northern Forest Indians of North America and the Eskimo of North America and Greenland, in *Verhandlungen des XXXVIII. Internationalen Amerikanistenkongresses* (Stuttgart-München, 1968).

68. Traditionally, Inuit did not have family names. This, of course, was characteristic of tribal peoples everywhere. The disc system was introduced in 1941 and was discontinued in 1971 when Inuit were persuaded to adopt surnames.

69. Abe Okpik, 'Bewildered Hunters in the 20th Century', *North* 13, 4 (1966): 48–50.

70. Gordon Robertson, *Memoirs of a Very Civil Servant* (Toronto, 2000), cited by Andrew Duffy and Paul Gessell, 'Retired Trudeau "chose to destroy"', *Ottawa Citizen*, 8 Oct. 2000, A2.

71. *Final Report: RCMP Review of Allegations Concerning Inuit Sled Dogs*, at: <www.rcmp-grc.gc.ca/ccaps/sled_dogs_final_e.htm>.

72. Zaslow, *Northward Expansion*, 301.

73. Stefansson had led the science-oriented Canadian Arctic Expedition, 1913–18, which among other things mapped and carried out geological studies.

But see Jennifer Niven, *The Ice Master: The Doomed 1913 Voyage of the Karluk* (New York, 2000), a historical account of the start of the expedition, which Stefansson apparently abandoned when their ship, the *Karluk*, became trapped in the ice north of Alaska. For a review, see Richard Martyn, 'Voyage of the damned', *Toronto Star*, 17 Dec. 2000, D12, D13.

74. Vilhjalmur Stefansson, *The Friendly Arctic: The Story of Five Years in Polar Regions* (New York, 1943). See also William R. Morrison, *Under the Flag: Canadian Sovereignty and the Native People in Northern Canada* (Ottawa, 1984), 74–7.

75. Mackinnon, 'Government Policy Reversal', 166–7.

76. Zaslow, *Northward Expansion*, 277–9. Marybelle Mitchell, *From Talking Chief to a Native Corporate Elite* (Montreal and Kingston, 1996), 160ff.

77. 'Prescription for North begins with better housing', *Edmonton Journal*, 19 May 1991. Nellie Cournoyea, the daughter of a Norwegian trapper and an Inuvialuit mother, grew up on a trapline in the Mackenzie Delta.

78. Diubaldo, *Government of Canada and the Inuit*, 1–7. See also Diubaldo, 'You Can't Keep the Native Native', in Coates and Morrison, eds, *For Purposes of Dominion*, 171–85.

79. Alanna Mitchell, 'Rumbles from the Arctic', *Ottawa Citizen*, 15 Nov. 2000, A1, A4; Kate Jaimet, 'Inuit woman travels to The Hague to warn world of climate crisis', ibid.

Chapter 27

1. Allan G. Harper, 'Canada's Indian Administration: The Indian Act', *América Indígena* 5, 3 (1946): 313.

2. J. Rick Ponting and Roger Gibbins, *Out of Irrelevance: A Socio-Political Introduction to Indian Affairs in Canada* (Toronto, 1980), 100; Gurston Dacks, *A Choice of Futures: Politics in the Canadian North* (Toronto, 1981), 199.

3. Harold Cardinal, *The Unjust Society: The Tragedy of Canada's Indians* (Edmonton, 1969), 44.

4. 'Indian Affairs' $2.5-billion buys a lot of red tape', *Edmonton Journal*, 24 Nov. 1980. See also 'Scrap Indian Affairs, report urges', ibid., 22 Nov. 1990; 'Scrap the Indian Act', ibid., 23 Nov. 1990.

5. Kenneth S. Coates and William R. Morrison, *Land of the Midnight Sun: A History of the Yukon* (Edmonton, 1988), 281–2.

6. J.F. Marchand, 'Tribal Epidemics in Yukon', *Journal of the American Medical Association* 123 (1943): 1019–20.

7. 'Indians eating contaminated fish', *Globe and Mail*, 5 Nov. 1990, A4.

8. Colin De'Ath and Gregory Michalenko, 'High Technology and Original Peoples: The Case of Deforestation in Papua New Guinea and Canada', in John H. Bodley, ed., *Tribal Peoples and Developmental Issues: A Global Overview* (Mountain View, Calif., 1988), 177–8; A.M.A. Shkilnyk, *A Poison Stronger Than Love: The Destruction of an Ojibway Community* (New Haven, 1985); George Hutchison and Dick Wallace, *Grassy Narrows* (Toronto, 1977); Sherri Aikenhead, 'Tough Struggle Back', *Maclean's* 99, 28 (14 July 1986): 19.

9. Dacks, *A Choice of Futures*, 148. One-third of the world's fresh water is found in Canada, half of which is in Quebec.

10. However, there was concern in some quarters. See Paul Charest, 'Les barrages hydro-électriques en territoires montagnais et leurs effets sur les communautés amérindiennes', *Recherches amérindiennes au Québec* 9, 4 (1980): 323–37; 'Southern Indian Lake and Hydro Development', edited proceedings of Manitoba Environmental Council, Winnipeg, 19 Jan. 1973.

11. Charles E. Hendry, *Beyond Traplines: Assessment of the Work of the Anglican Church of Canada with Canada's Native Peoples* (Toronto, 1969). See also Hugh and Karmel McCullum, *This Land Is Not for Sale* (Toronto, 1975). An earlier examination of the issue was John Melling's *Right to a Future: The Native Peoples of Canada* (Toronto, 1967).

12. The Catholic statement, by the administrative board of the Canadian Conference of Catholic Bishops, first appeared in *The Catholic Register*, 11 Oct. 1975, and has since been published as a pamphlet.

13. 'New role in church could aid self-government, natives say', *Edmonton Journal*, 18 Aug. 1988; 'Anglicans choose first native bishop', ibid., 5 Nov. 1988.

14. 'Investigating a different faith', *Globe and Mail*, 18 May 1991.

15. *Catholic New Times*, 8 Sept. 1991, 1.

16. Outstanding among these was the Committee for Original People's Entitlement (COPE), founded in 1969 by Agnes Semmler, a Gwich'in Métis who became its first president, and Nellie Cournoyea. With headquarters in Ottawa, it became the voice of the Inuvialuit.

17. Cited by Colin Scott, 'Ideology of Reciprocity between the James Bay Cree and the Whiteman State', in Peter Skalník, ed., *Outwitting the State* (New Brunswick, NJ, 1989), 103.

18. The agreement was signed by the government of Quebec, three Quebec Crown corporations, the Grand Council of the Crees (of Quebec), the Northern Quebec Inuit Association, and the government of Canada. It involved 6,650 Cree living in eight communities and 4,386 Inuit in 15 communities.

19. Harvey Feit, 'Legitimation and Autonomy in James Bay Cree Responses to Hydro-Electric Development', in Noel Dyck, ed., *Indigenous Peoples and the Nation-State: 'Fourth World' Politics in Canada, Australia and Norway* (St John's, 1985), 28–9. For an overview of the treaty's impact, see James F. Hornig, ed., *Social and Environmental Impacts of the James Bay Hydroelectric Project* (Montreal and Kingston, 1999).

20. *James Bay and Northern Quebec Agreement Implementation Review February 1982* (Ottawa, 1982).

21. Robert M. Bone, *The Geography of the Canadian North: Issues and Challenges*, 3rd edn (Toronto, 2009), ch. 6.

22. Ibid., chs 6, 8; Stanley Warner and Raymond Coppinger, 'Hydroelectric Power Development at James Bay: Establishing a Frame of Reference', in Hornig, ed., *Social and Environmental Impacts*, 19–38; Philip Authier and Graeme Hamilton, 'Quebec shelves Great Whale', *The Gazette*, Montreal, 19 Nov. 1994, A1, A8.

23. Jeff Heinrich, '$1.4B Deal Gives Cree Promise of Nationhood', *National Post*, 17 July 2007, A4; Bone, *Geography of the Canadian North*, ch. 8.

24. Jane George, 'Nunavik Leaders Celebrate First Quebec Payout', *Nunatsiaq News*, 21 June 2002, at: <www.nunatsiaq.com/archives/nunavut0206 21/news/nunavik/20621_1.html>, cited in Bone, *Geography of the Canadian North*, ch. 8.

25. Peter Kulchyski, *Unjust Relations: Aboriginal Rights in Canadian Courts* (Toronto, 1994), 121; Rhéal Séguin, 'Innu, Quebec, Ottawa set key negotiation terms', *Globe and Mail,* 27 Mar. 2000; Allison Lampert, 'Avalanche warning unheeded: Coroner. Quebec must develop prevention plans, report says', *The Gazette*, Montreal, 19 Apr. 2000; 'Quebec Cree Expand Anti-Logging Campaign', *CBC Newsworld Online*, 19 May 2000; Jim Bronskill, 'Quebec natives should have say in secession: paper', *National Post*, 19 June 2000.

26. Berger Community Hearings, Rainer Genelli, Whitehorse, vol. 23, 2374–5, cited by Robert Page, *Northern Development: The Canadian Dilemma* (Toronto, 1986), 212.

27. Berger Community Hearings, Philip Blake, Fort McPherson, vol. 12, 1081, cited by Page, *Northern*

Development, 213.

28. Thomas R. Berger, *Northern Frontier, Northern Homeland*, 2 vols (Ottawa, 1977). See also Martin O'Malley, *The Past and Future Land* (Toronto, 1976); Hugh and Karmel McCullum and John Olthuis, *Moratorium: Justice, Energy, the North, and the Native People* (Toronto, 1977).

29. Peter Foster, 'Exploring Mackenzie', *National Post*, 4 Mar. 2000, D1, D8.

30. Bone, *Geography of the Canadian North*, ch. 6 and Figure 6.9; Carol Howes, 'N.W.T. gives conditional support to Mackenzie Valley pipeline', *National Post*, 11 April 2000; Steven Chase, 'NWT natives push for big role in Mackenzie Valley pipeline', *Globe and Mail*, 19 July 2000, B1, B4; Dan Westell, 'Ownership dispute clogs plans for northern pipeline', *Financial Times*, London, 2 Aug. 2000, 34; 'Oil block sale nets Inuvialuit $75 million', *Edmonton Sun*, 3 May 2000, 39.

31. Richard C. Daniel, *A History of Native Claims Processes in Canada 1867–1979* (Ottawa, 1980), 226.

32. Robert M. Bone, *The Regional Geography of Canada*, 4th edn (Toronto, 2008), 496–7; Bone, *Geography of the Canadian North*, ch. 5; Allan Robinson, 'NWT mine makes Dia Met profit shine', *Globe and Mail*, 4 May 2000; Keith Damsell, 'Diavik clears environmental hurdle', *National Post*, 9 Mar. 2000, C03.

33. Tar Sands Watch, 'Pembina Institute Press Release', 22 Mar. 2007, at: <www/tarsandswatch.org/pembina-institute-press-release-0>.

34. Julie Graham, 'Like Oil and Water: The True Cost of the Tar Sands', Kairos: Canadian Ecumenical Justice Initiatives, at: <www.kairoscanada.org/e/action/LikeOil&Water_AlbertaStory.pdf>.

35. Carol Howes, 'The new native tycoon', *National Post*, 27 Jan. 2001, D5.

36. Greg Poelzer, 'Aboriginal People and Environmental Policy in Canada: No Longer at the Margins', in Debora L. VanNijnatten and Robert Boardman, eds, *Canadian Environmental Policy: Context and Cases in a New Century*, 2nd edn (Toronto, 2002), 100–4.

37. Bone, *Geography of the Canadian North*, ch. 8.

38. Kitsaki Management Limited Partnership, at: <www.kitsaki.com/companies.html>.

39. Theresa Tedesco and Carol Howes, 'Natives make refinery bid', *National Post*, 23 Jan. 2001, A1, C8.

40. Indian and Northern Affairs Canada, at: <www.ainc-inac.gc.ca/nr/prs/j-a2005/2-02160_e.html>.

41. J. Rick Ponting, ed., *Arduous Journey: Canadian Indians and Decolonization* (Toronto, 1986), 34–41. Also, David Alan Long, 'Trials of the Spirit: The Native Social Movement in Canada', in Long and Olive Patricia Dickason, eds, *Visions of the Heart* (Toronto, 1996), 377–96.

42. 'Status Indians number half a million', *Globe and Mail*, 30 Aug. 1990, A5.

43. Michael Asch, *Home and Native Land: Aboriginal Rights and the Canadian Constitution* (Toronto, 1984), 105.

44. On possible legal implications of the constitutional provisions, see Brian Slattery, 'The Constitutional Guarantee of Aboriginal and Treaty Rights', *Queen's Law Journal* 8, 1–2 (1982): 232–73.

45. J. Anthony Long, Leroy Little Bear, and Menno Boldt, 'Federal Indian Policy and Indian Self-government in Canada: An Analysis of a Current Proposal', *Canadian Public Policy* 8, 2 (1982): 194.

46. Delia Opekokew, *The First Nations: Indian Government and the Canadian Confederation* (Saskatoon, 1980).

47. Ponting, ed., *Arduous Journey*, 318. A study of the legal aspects involved is Brian Schwartz, *First Principles: Constitutional Reform with Respect to the Aboriginal Peoples of Canada, 1982–1984* (Kingston, Ont., 1985).

48. David A. Nock, *A Victorian Missionary and Canadian Indian Policy: Cultural Synthesis v. Cultural Replacement* (Waterloo, Ont., 1988), 136–7. The articles, written under the pseudonym 'Fair Play', have been attributed to E.F. Wilson (1844–1915), Church of England missionary who was an advocate of self-government for Native peoples.

49. Ponting, ed., *Arduous Journey*, 321. Nungak was president of Makivik Corporation, the business arm of the Quebec Inuit, until he resigned for personal reasons in mid-1998. See *Nunatsiaq News*, at: <www.nunatsiaq.com/archives/nunavik 981120/nun80925_01.html>. With Eugene Arima, he co-authored *Eskimo stories—unikkaatuat* (Ottawa, 1969). The tales are illustrated with photographs of Inuit carvings.

50. Harper, a treaty Amerindian, was the provincial Minister for Northern Affairs, 1986–8. Ovide Mercredi, a Cree of Grand Rapids, Manitoba, at that time Manitoba regional chief of the Assembly of First Nations, and Phil Fontaine, Ojibwa grand chief of the Assembly of Manitoba Chiefs, were Harper's advisers on Meech Lake. Both Mercredi and then Fontaine were later elected National Chief of the Assembly of First Nations.

51. 'Foes stall accord again', *Edmonton Journal*, 15 June 1990.

52. 'Elijah Harper: one man, one feather', *The Gazette*, Montreal, 23 June 1990.

53. 'Native leaders turn tables on Quebec', ibid., 18 June 1990.

54. 'Give us a government of first nations', ibid., 1990.

55. A study on Indian self-government has been prepared by the Institute for Research and Public Policy: Frank Cassidy and Robert L. Bish, *Indian Government: Its Meaning in Practice* (Halifax and Lantzville, BC, 1989).

56. On the need for local control for such matters as health care, see Nancy Gibson, 'Northern Medicine in Transition', in David E. Young, ed., *Health Care Issues in the Canadian North* (Edmonton, 1989), 110–21. For the early struggles for responsible government, see Lewis H. Thomas, *The Struggle for Responsible Government in the North-West Territories 1870–97* (Toronto, 1978), 234–63.

57. Dacks, *A Choice of Futures*, 92–3; Kenneth Coates and Judith Powell, *The Modern North: People, Politics, and the Rejection of Colonialism* (Toronto, 1989).

58. Kerry Abel, *Drum Songs* (Montreal and Kingston, 1993), 258–61.

59. Margaret Vincent Tehariolina, *La nation huronne, son histoire, sa culture, son esprit* (Québec, 1984), 317–18.

60. See Chapter 17, n7.

61. Kim Lunman, 'Native chief named to B.C. Cabinet', *Globe and Mail*, 2 Nov. 2000, A4. Besides resigning as head of the First Nations Summit, Chief John also stepped down as chief negotiator for his own band, the Tl'azt'en nation in northwestern BC, in order to accept the cabinet post.

62. 'Alberta native senator considered quitting over GST', *Edmonton Journal*, 5 Jan. 1991.

63. *Report of the Cree-Naskapi Commission, 1988*, 10.

64. Ibid., 45.

65. Sally Weaver, 'Indian Policy in the New Conservative Government, Part II: The Nielsen Task Force in the Context of Recent Policy Initiatives', *Native Studies Review* 2, 2 (1986): 23. The case was *Guerin v. The Queen*.

66. *Report of the Cree-Naskapi Commission, 1988*, 45–7.

67. The agreement was signed by the government of Canada with COPE representing the Inuvialuit.

68. 'Gourmets from New York to Tokyo feast on North's Guerin woolly musk-ox', *Edmonton Journal*, 21 May 1991. Muskox meat was awarded a gold medal by the Chefs of America; the wool, eight times warmer by weight than sheep's wool, competes with cashmere.

69. Inuvialuit Regional Corporation, '2008 Distribution Payments', at: <www.inuvialuit.com/beneficiaries/2006payments.html>.

70. *Report of the Royal Commission on Aboriginal Peoples*, 5 vols (Ottawa, 1996), IV, 420.

71. In this matter, the government has not followed the report of its Task Force to Review Comprehensive Claims Policy (Coolican Report), which urged that extinguishment of all Aboriginal rights be abandoned as a requirement for a claim settlement. See *Living Treaties: Lasting Agreements* (Ottawa, 1985), 43.

72. 'Dene-Metis land deal dead, Siddon says', *Edmonton Journal* 8 Nov. 1990; 'Land claims back to square one', ibid., 24 Nov. 1990.

73. Deh Cho First Nation, *Declaration of Rights*, 1993, 1. See also *Report of the Royal Commission on Aboriginal Peoples*, IV, 427.

74. 'Indians reach regional deal', *Edmonton Journal*, 14 July 1991; 'Gwich'in Indians back $75M land-claims deal', ibid., 22 Sept. 1991. Also, *Report of the Royal Commission on Aboriginal Peoples*, IV, 426.

75. Ibid., III, 245.

76. Jill Mahoney, 'On a frosty northern night, Nunavut is born', *Globe and Mail*, 1 Apr. 1999, A1, A6; Janice Tibbetts, 'Pomp, partying and a holiday greet the birth of Inuit homeland', *Ottawa Citizen*, 1 Apr. 1999, A1, A2; Shawn Ohler, 'Nunavut born with high hopes, big challenges', *National Post*, 1 Apr. 1999, A1, A5; Robert Perkins, 'A promised land for Inuits', *Boston Globe*, 1 Apr. 1999, A23; Ruth Walker, 'A new territory that became a reality on April 1 may set an example', *Christian Science Monitor*, 5 Apr. 1999; Richard Wagamese, 'Lines on the land: Nunavut ignores the ancient native concept of "territory"', *Ottawa Citizen*, 21 Apr. 1999; Jules Richer, 'Chirac visite le Nunavut en compagnie de Chrétien', *Le Droit*, 6 Sept. 1999.

77. Statistics Canada, 'Aboriginal Peoples: Highlight Tables, 2006 Census', 15 Jan. 2008, at: <www12.statcan.ca/english/census06/data/highlights/Aboriginal/index.cfm?Lang=E>.

78. Keith Watt, 'Uneasy Partners', *The Globe and Mail Report on Business Magazine* (Sept. 1990): 46–7; 'Inuit, gov't strike land deal' and 'Inuit dream carries high price tag', *Edmonton Journal*, 17 Dec. 1991.

79. Walter Rudnicki, 'The Politics of Aggression: Indian Termination in the 1980s', *Native Studies Review* 3, 1 (1987): 83–4.

80. 'Dene feel cheated by government deal with

Inuit', *Edmonton Journal*, 20 June 1991.

81. The pros and cons of the Nunavut proposal are discussed in John Merrit et al., *Nunavut Political Choices and Manifest Destiny* (Ottawa, 1989). See also Jacques M. Shore, 'A toast to Nunavut's birth', *Globe and Mail*, 1 Apr. 1999, A2.

82. 'N.W.T. residents narrowly approve Nunavut', *The Gazette*, Montreal, 5 May 1992; 'Accord signed to create Nunavut by '99', *Edmonton Journal*, 31 Oct. 1992. See also E. Quinn Duffy, *The Road to Nunavut: The Progress of the Eastern Arctic Inuit since the Second World War* (Montreal and Kingston, 1988).

83. *Report of the Royal Commission on Aboriginal Peoples*, II, part 1, 149.

84. Relations between the Inuit and the RCMP had been strained ever since the latter's campaign in the 1950s and 1960s to kill Inuit sled dogs on the grounds that they spread diseases and were a danger to the communities. The Inuit considered the dogs an important part of their lifestyle. The RCMP later changed its tactics and apologized to the Natives. In 1998 the dispute boiled over again when dogs killed a six-year-old girl in Iqaluit. This time a compromise was worked out, with the dogs being banned from certain areas. Janice Tibbetts, 'When Mounties shot down sled dogs', *Ottawa Citizen*, 30 Mar. 1999; Adrian Humphries, 'New compromise may save Iqaluit's dog sled tradition', *National Post*, 25 Jan. 2001, A2. For more on this subject, see Chapter 26, p. 385.

85. Statistics Canada, 'Aboriginal Peoples: Highlight Tables, 2006 Census'.

86. Andrew Duffy, 'Nunavut finances in a mess', *Ottawa Citizen*, 28 Feb. 2001, A1, A2; Andrew Duffy, 'Nunavut facing financial crisis', *National Post*, 28 Feb. 2001, A12.

87. Luiza Chwialkowsa, 'Nunavut facing 25% rise for fuel', *National Post*, 21 Sept. 2000; Rob Weber, 'New government, old problem: Shivering in Nunavut', *Toronto Star*, 8 Apr. 2000, K4.

88. Indian and Northern Affairs Canada, at: <www.ainc-inac.gc.ca/pr/info/info104_e.html>.

89. Jennifer Pritchett, 'Nunavut MP faces the future', and Nick Forster, 'It will give us back our lives', both in *Ottawa Citizen*, 1 Apr. 1999.

90. *Report of the Royal Commission on Aboriginal Peoples*, V, 2; Marybelle Mitchell, *From Talking Chief to Native Corporate Elite* (Montreal and Kingston, 1996), esp. ch. 6.

91. *Self-determination Symposium Summary Report* (Ottawa, 1990), 60. Erasmus was president of the Dene Nation, Northwest Territories, 1976–83.

92. *Christian Science Monitor*, 18 Oct. 1990, 11.

93. 'Innu chief warns government', *Globe and Mail*, 2 Oct. 1990. A survey of various Amerindian priorities is in Boyce Richardson, ed., *Drum Beat: Anger and Renewal in Indian Country* (Ottawa, 1989). See also J. Anthony Long and Menno Boldt, eds, *Governments in Conflict? Provinces and Indian Nations in Canada* (Toronto, 1988); Leroy Little Bear, Menno Boldt, and J. Anthony Long, eds, *Pathways to Self-Determination: Canadian Indians and the Canadian State* (Toronto, 1984).

94. Judgment of Igloliorte, P.C.J., in *Regina v. Daniel Ashini et al.*, Provincial Court of Newfoundland, District of Happy Valley/Goose Bay, Labrador, 18 Apr. 1989. See also Daniel Ashini, 'David Confronts Goliath: The Innu of Ungava versus the NATO Alliance', in Richardson, ed., *Drum Beat*, 45–70.

95. CBC News, at: <www.cbc.ca/news/story/2000/08/18/nf_innu000818.html/>.

96. Randall J. Brown, 'Smallboy's Camp: A Contemporary Example of a Revitalization Movement', unpublished manuscript. The event received wide press coverage; for example, 'Here we are, here we stay, chief says: Smallboy's squatters look to old ways', *Edmonton Journal*, 30 May 1975; 'I'd trade my award for more real estate', ibid., 17 Jan. 1980; 'Cree leader: "I'll hang before moving"', *Akwesasne Notes* 3, 4 (1971): 1.

97. 'Smallboy's Camp seeks support', *Edmonton Journal*, 13 Oct. 1991.

Chapter 28

1. Quoted by Rudy Platiel, 'Vast changes sought to aid natives', *Globe and Mail*, 22 Nov. 1996, 1.

2. Gilles Gauthier, 'Le départ d'"un long débat"', *La Presse*, 22 nov. 1996, B1; Dan Smith, 'New deal urged for First Nations', *Toronto Star*, 22 Nov. 1996; Jean Dion, 'Audace sur le front de l'autonomie', *Le Devoir*, 22 nov. 1996, A2; 'On propose la création d'un parlement autochtone', *Le Journal de Montréal*, 22 nov. 1996; Jack Aubry, 'Aboriginals offer "last chance"', *The Gazette*, Montreal, 22 Nov. 1996, A1; 'Paying the price: How a report plays on two reserves', *Maclean's* 109, 49 (2 Dec. 1996): 16–19; Scott Feschuk, 'Cost of reforms $30-billion, report on Aboriginals says', *Globe and Mail*, 22 Nov. 1996; Marty Logan, 'Last chance for Canada—report', *Windspeaker* 14, 9 (Jan. 1997): 1.

3. *People to People, Nation to Nation: Highlights from the Report of the Royal Commission on Aboriginal Peoples* (Ottawa, 1996), ix. Also issued in French, Cree, and Inuktitut.

4. *The Gazette*, Montreal, 4 Feb. 1993. Also see 'Moved far from their homes, natives seek a deadly escape', *Globe and Mail*, 6 Feb. 1996.

5. 'A salute to Saddle Lake, Poundmaker's and Nechi', *Edmonton Journal*, 7 Sept. 1993, A8; 'The mending of young lives', ibid., 28 June 1993.

6. Colin Samson, *A Way of Life That Does Not Exist: Canada and the Extinguishment of the Innu* (St John's and London, 2003), 280.

7. 'Destruction of school at Davis Inlet isn't an isolated incident: ex-chief', *The Gazette*, Montreal, 4 Jan. 1997; Stephen Thorne, 'Young Davis Inlet natives charged in school vandalism', *Globe and Mail*, 4 Jan. 1997, A4.

8. '$85M deal sends Innu to new home', *Edmonton Journal*, 10 July 1996.

9. Tonda MacCharles, 'Ottawa moves to help addicted Innu children', *Toronto Star*, 14 Dec. 2000, A2; 'Innu Nation president condemns Ottawa for taking over', *National Post*, 25 Jan. 2001, A10.

10. Adrian Humphreys, 'Take our kids, desperate Innu plead', *National Post*, 17 Nov. 2000, A3; 'Innu ask officials to remove gas-sniffing children from town', *Ottawa Citizen*, 17 Nov. 2000, A3; Kevin Cox, 'Gas-sniffing Innu youths taken to detox barracks', *Globe and Mail*, 22 Nov. 2000, A2; MacCharles, 'Ottawa moves to help addicted Innu children'. The Tshikapisk Foundation, which was a direct result of the troubles of the Mushuau Innu of Davis Inlet, is headed by a board of directors that includes Innu leaders and hunters, as well as academic researchers who have worked with and for the Innu, such as the British sociologist Colin Samson. See <www.tshikapisk.ca/home/10>.

11. 'Innu of Davis Inlet residents feel deserted: Last families face months in ghost town', Turning Point: Natives and Newcomers Online, at: <www.turning-point.ca/?q=node/191>; CBC News, 'Small graduating class marks Natuashish milestone', 6 June 2008, at: <www.cbc.ca/canada/newfoundland-labrador/story/2008/06/06/natuashish-school.html>.

12. The story of one of these is told by Deborah Wilson, 'Natives seek compensation for land: Lheit-Lit'en claim Prince George site was wrongfully seized 80 years ago', *Globe and Mail*, 1 May 1992, A7.

13. *Report of the Royal Commission on Aboriginal Peoples*, 5 vols (Ottawa, 1996), I, 417–22. Chapter 11 deals with relocations in general.

14. Rudy Platiel, 'Significant differences seen between native standoffs', *Globe and Mail*, 29 Aug. 1996, A4.

15. Kirk Makin, 'U.S. judge won't extradite Canadian native activist', *Globe and Mail*, 23 Nov. 2000, A1, A5.

16. Peter Moon, 'A long story of occupation', *Globe and Mail*, 8 Sept. 1995.

17. A detailed account of the incident, based on official documents, is by Peter Edwards, 'Death in the dark: What happened at Ipperwash', *Toronto Star*, 24 Nov. 1996, F1, F6.

18. Michael Grange, 'Officer guilty in Ipperwash Killing', *Globe and Mail*, 29 Apr. 1997; 'Ipperwash: un agent reconnu coupable', *Le Droit*, Ottawa, 29 avril 1997; Peter Edwards, 'OPP officer guilty in Indian's death', *Toronto Star*, 29 Apr. 1997.

19. Rudy Platiel, 'Band's claim for park land settled', *Globe and Mail*, 22 Jan. 1997.

20. Ross Howard, 'A terrible territorial tangle', *Globe and Mail*, 29 May 1995. The figure of 110 per cent was the apparent result of different bands laying overlapping claims.

21. For an account of the early phase of the Nisga'a claim, see Kristin Jackson, 'Drawing the line: B.C. Indians claim a rich chunk of the province', *Pacific (Seattle Times/Seattle Post-Intelligencer)*, 2 Oct. 1988.

22. *Nisga'a Treaty Negotiations Agreement-in-Principle*, issued jointly by the Government of Canada, the Province of British Columbia, and the Nisga'a Tribal Council, 15 Feb. 1996. The agreement involved the return of almost 200 artifacts held by the Canadian Museum of Civilization. Buzz Bourdon, 'Nisga'a artifacts heading home', *Ottawa Citizen*, 19 Nov. 1999.

23. Ross Howard, 'Native standoffs heat up BC talks', *Globe and Mail*, 13 Sept. 1995; Art Wilson, 'Nisga'a sign historic treaty with B.C., federal governments', *Native Network News* (Feb. 1996): 1. For a negative view of the agreement, see Foster J.K. Griezic, 'The Nisga'a agreement: a great deal or a great steal?', *Globe and Mail*, 5 Mar. 1996.

24. Indian and Northern Affairs Canada, at: <www.ainc-inac.gc.ca/ps/clm/gbn/gbn_e.pdf>.

25. Indian and Northern Affairs Canada, at: <www.ainc-inac.gc.ca/ps/clm/fct2-eng.asp>.

26. *Report of the Royal Commission on Aboriginal Peoples*, V, 1.

27. Ibid., V, 154–5.

28. Jamie Monastyrski, 'New banking branch tailor-made for Aboriginal needs', *Wawatay News*, Anishinini edition, 6 Nov. 1997, 2.

29. *Report of the Royal Commission on Aboriginal Peoples*, V, 12.

30. Ibid., II, part 1, 154–6; *People to People, Nation to Nation*, 29.

31. *Report of the Royal Commission on Aboriginal Peoples*, IV, 478.

32. Quoted by John Goddard, 'In from the cold', *Canadian Geographic* 114, 4 (1994): 36–47. This account is based on his article. See also *Report of the Royal Commission on Aboriginal Peoples*, III, 396, 419.

33. The First Nations Bank of Canada at: <www.firstnationsbank.com/branches.jsp>.

34. John Ibbitson, 'First native bank a Canadian first', *The Gazette*, Montreal, 10 Dec. 1996.

35. Rudy Platiel, 'First native bank to open next year', *Globe and Mail*, 10 Dec. 1996.

36. Huguette Young, 'Irwin se contente de demi-mesures', *Le Droit*, Ottawa, 13 déc. 1996; Rudy Platiel, 'Battle escalates over Indian Act', *Globe and Mail*, 13 Dec. 1996; ibid., 'Changing the Indian Act', 16 Dec. 1996; 'Block changes to Indian Act, national chief tells Chrétien', *The Gazette*, Montreal, 8 Dec. 1996.

37. Scott Feschuk and Rudy Platiel, 'Natives warn Ottawa not to ignore report', *Globe and Mail*, 22 Nov. 1996, A8. See also Maurice Champagne, 'Autochtones: "notre" dernière chance: Le rapport Erasmus-Dussault nous arrive comme un baume civilisateur', *La Presse*, 5 déc. 1996, B3.

38. Brian Laghi, 'New law to reform native voting', *Globe and Mail*, 16 Jan. 2001, A1; Brian Laghi, 'Natives seek role in Nault initiative', ibid., 17 Jan. 2001, A4.

39. Michelle Lalonde, 'Aboriginals panel listens only to Indians' supporters: MP', *The Gazette*, Montreal, 8 May 1993, A4.

40. 'Commission staff divided on advocacy for natives', *Edmonton Journal*, 9 Mar. 1995.

41. Reinforcing this reaction was the report of the failure of a five-year $1 billion federal economic development program to make an appreciable dent in Aboriginal poverty. See Murray Brewster, 'Billion-dollar fund spent on Indian poverty had little effect: study', *The Gazette*, Montreal, 16 Dec. 1996. Anticipating a negative response, the commissioners included a detailed cost analysis in their report to support their case. (*Report of the Royal Commission on Aboriginal Peoples*, V, 23–54.)

42. Dan Smith, 'Concept of Aboriginal "nations" is one that Ottawa can embrace', *Toronto Star*, 23 Nov. 1996, A12.

43. E-mail correspondence, Nathalie Bérubé, analyst/coordinator, Treaties and Aboriginal Government, Indian and Northern Affairs Canada, to Paul-Emile McNab, 17 June 2008.

44. The government's position was presented by Allan MacDonald, senior policy adviser, Indian and Northern Affairs Canada, at a conference on archaeological resource management in a land claims context held by Parks Canada, Ottawa, 20–2 Jan. 1997.

45. The mixed reaction was reflected in newspaper reports. Some examples: Erin Anderssen and Edward Greenspon, 'Federal apology fails to mollify native leaders', *Globe and Mail*, 8 Jan. 1998, A4; Jack Aubry, 'Reconciliation divides native groups', *Ottawa Citizen*, 8 Jan. 1998, A3; Jack Aubry, 'Native leaders disappointed, but some see reason for hope', *Edmonton Journal*, 8 Jan. 1998, A3; Laura Eggertson, 'An Apology, at long last', *Toronto Star*, 13 Feb. 1998, A20; Tod Mohamed, 'The politics of saying sorry', *Ottawa Citizen*, 1 Mar. 1998. Even the Inuit, who were not involved, had a comment, in the person of Zebedee Nungak, 'Apology to Indians soothes and jars', *The Gazette*, Montreal, 28 Jan. 1998.

46. Lorna Dueck, 'Sorry isn't good enough', *Globe and Mail*, 31 Oct. 2000.

47. Something of the complexity of the current Aboriginal scene is caught in Ron F. Laliberte et al., eds, *Expressions in Canadian Native Studies* (Saskatoon, 2000).

48. 'Coon Come tells native leaders to sober up', *National Post*, 28 Feb. 2001, A7; 'Coon Come's Call', *Ottawa Citizen*, 1 Mar. 2001, A14; 'Mr Coon Come steps into line of fire', *Globe and Mail*, 2 Mar. 2001, A12; Rick Mofina, 'Chiefs aren't all drunkards, natives insist', *Ottawa Citizen*, 1 Mar. 2001, A4.

49. Indian Affairs and Northern Development, *Registered Indian Population by Sex and Residence 1999* (Ottawa, 2000), xx.

50. Indian Affairs and Northern Development, *Basic Departmental Data 1999* (Ottawa, Feb. 2000), 5.

51. A survey of Indians' legal position in Canada is by Paul Williams, 'Canada's Laws about Aboriginal Peoples: A Brief Overview', *Law and Anthropology* 1 (1986): 93–120. This is an international yearbook published by the University of Vienna.

52. Statistics Canada, 'Aboriginal Peoples: Highlight Tables, 2006 Census', 15 Jan. 2008, at: <www12.statcan.ca/english/census06/data/highlights/Aboriginal/index.cfm?Lang=E>.

53. Calculated from ibid.

54. *Report of the Royal Commission on Aboriginal Peoples*, III, 263.

55. In the United States, the prediction is that by 2050 the Native population will reach 4.4 million, nearly double what it is now. According to the Census Bureau, this is faster than whites or

African-Americans, but slower than Hispanics, Asians, or Pacific Islanders. Mark Fogarty, 'Census Bureau predicts Native American populations will double in 50 years', *Indian Country Today*, 17 Nov. 2000.

56. The RCAP issued a special report on Native suicides, *Choosing Life* (Ottawa, 1995). Some saw the responsibility of the high suicide rate as resting with the Amerindian communities themselves. See Stewart Bell, 'Accept blame for suicides, B.C. band told', *Edmonton Journal*, 29 Feb. 1996.

57. *Report of the Royal Commission on Aboriginal Peoples*, V, 34.

Chapter 29

I am indebted to Paul-Emile McNab, who acted as a research assistant in preparing this new chapter.

1. 'Natives threaten Olympic disruptions', *Globe and Mail*, 18 Apr. 2008, 1.

2. No one knows his year of birth, given variously as 1931 to 1933, since he was probably born in the bush south of Lake Nipigon: <www.thestar.com/printArticle/282555>.

3. *National Post*, 5 Dec. 2007, at: <www.national post.com/most_popular/Story.html?id=145224>.

4. Ibid.

5. Paul Gessell, 'Artist dies', *Ottawa Citizen*, 4 Dec. 2007, at: <www.canada.com/ottawacitizen/news/story.html?id=510196db-b058-44f4-a555-8e5405d239ed&k=46459>. 'Ruth Phillips, an art historian who is compiling a catalogue of all of Mr. Morrisseau's known works, called the artist's death a huge shock. "Norval Morrisseau bridged the historical tradition of his ancestors—which ranged from ritual arts used in Shamanism . . . to beautifully decorated clothing, painting on rocks—to a new form of modern art expressed in drawings and prints," she said. "He also took oral traditions and transformed them into modern visual art." Ms. Phillips remembers Mr. Morrisseau as a "spiritual, warm and engaging man."'

6. *National Post*, 4 Dec. 2007, at: <www.national post.com/news/story.html?id=144191>.

7. Ute Lischke and David T. McNab, eds, *Walking a Tightrope: Aboriginal People and Their Representations* (Waterloo, Ont., 2005), 1–18.

8. See, for example, the Métis scholar, Jennifer Welsh, *At Home in the World: Canada in the 21st Century* (Toronto, 2004); Ute Lischke and David T. McNab, eds, *The Long Journey of a Forgotten People: Métis Identities and Family Histories* (Waterloo, Ont., 2007).

9. David T. McNab, 'Visitors to Turtle Island: The Impact of Indigenous People and Places on the European Newcomers', work in progress.

10. 'UN council approves indigenous rights treaty', ABC News Online, 30 June 2006.

11. 'Endorsing their rights', *Indian Country Today*, 21 Apr. 2008, at: <www.indiancountry.com/content.cfm?id=1096417131>.

12. David T. McNab, 'The Spirit of *Delgamuukw* and Aboriginal Oral Traditions in Ontario', in Owen Lippert, ed., *Beyond the Nass Valley: National Implications of the Supreme Court's Delgamuukw Decision* (Vancouver, 2000), 273–83.

13. Alex Neve and Murray Klippenstein, 'Ipperwash is still all about the land', *Toronto Star*, 26 Aug. 2006, F5.

14. Indian and Northern Affairs Canada, Summary of the First Nations Governance Act (Ottawa, 2002), at: <www.fng-gpn.gc.ca>.

15. Robert D. Nault, Minister of Indian and Northern Affairs Canada, 'First Nations Governance', 9 Oct. 2002.

16. Indian and Northern Affairs Canada, Summary of the First Nations Governance Act.

17. Fred R. Fenwick, 'First Nations Governance Act', *Law Now* 27, 3 (Dec. 2003): 3, 4.

18. Paco Francoli, 'Showdown on Governance Act Expected', *Hill Times* 685 (5 May 2003): 3–4.

19. Ibid., 2; author's discussions with federal officials in the Ontario Regional Office of the federal Department of Indian and Northern Affairs, Nov. 2006.

20. Fenwick, 'First Nations Governance Act', 4–5.

21. Ibid.

22. Rana F. Abbas, 'We've heard it all before', *Windspeaker* 21, 3 (June 2003): 12–13.

23. Indian and Northern Affairs Canada, Summary of the First Nations Governance Act.

24. Francoli, 'Showdown on Governance Act Expected', 2–3.

25. Abbas, 'We've heard it all before', 12–13.

26. Paul Barnsley, 'Governance Act dead for now—Nault', *Windspeaker* 21, 8 (Nov. 2003): 18.

27. Wayne Warry, *Unfinished Dreams: Community Healing and the Reality of Aboriginal Self-Government* (Toronto, 1999).

28. Indian and Northern Affairs Canada, at: <www.ainc-inac.gc.ca/nr/spch/2007/ang_e.html>.

29. Robert M. Bone, *The Geography of the Canadian North: Issues and Challenges*, 3rd edn (Toronto, 2009), ch. 8.

30. Indian and Northern Affairs Canada, at: <www.ainc-inac.gc.ca/nr/spch/2007/ang_e.html>.

31. Philip Dearden and Steve Langdon, 'Aboriginal

Peoples and National Parks', in Dearden and Rick Rollins, eds, *Parks and Protected Areas in Canada*, 3rd edn (Toronto, 2009), ch. 14.

32. Indian and Northern Affairs Canada, at: <www.ainc-inac.gc.ca/nr/spch/2007/ang_e.html>.

33. Indian and Northern Affairs Canada, at: <www.ainc-inac.gc.ca/nr/prs/j-a2007/2-2845_e.html>.

34. Ibid.

35. Ibid.

36. Tracey Tyler, 'Native band can't enact labour code, court rules', *Toronto Star*, 28 Nov. 2007.

37. See David T. McNab, *Circles of Time: Aboriginal Land Rights and Resistance in Ontario* (Waterloo, Ont., 1999), 182.

38. Canadian Heritage, at: <www.pch.gc.ca/special/gouv-gov/section2/infobox4_e.cfm>.

39. Jean Teillet, 'The Winds of Change: Métis Rights after Powley, Taku and Haida', in Lischke and McNab, eds, *The Long Journey of a Forgotten People*, 55–78.

40. Métis Nation of Ontario, at: <www.metisnation.org/harvesting/Powley_Case/news01.html>.

41. Ibid.

42. Ibid.

43. Ibid.

44. Bill Henry, 'MNR returns seized nets', *Owen Sound Sun-Times*, 5 Jan. 2008, A1, A3; e-mail correspondence between David T. McNab, Patsy McArthur, and Jim McLay, 6 Jan. 2008. I am indebted to Patsy McArthur and Jim McLay for drawing this issue to my attention.

45. Henry, 'MNR returns seized nets'; e-mail correspondence between McNab, McArthur, and McLay.

46. Henry, 'MNR returns seized nets'; e-mail correspondence between McNab, McArthur, and McLay.

47. Henry, 'MNR returns seized nets'; e-mail correspondence between McNab, McArthur, and McLay.

48. Sidney B. Linden, *Report of the Ipperwash Inquiry*, 31 May 2007, at: <www.ipperwashinquiry.ca/>.

49. Sidney B. Linden, *Report of the Ipperwash Inquiry: Volume 4, Executive Summary* (Toronto, 2007), 29.

50. Ibid., 43.

51. Ibid., 44.

52. Ibid., 73.

53. See ibid., 95–112, for all of these recommendations and findings.

54. CBC News, at: <www.cbc.ca/canada/story/2007/12/20/ipperwash-ont.html>.

55. Ibid.

56. For a recent comparison, albeit superficial, of land rights in South Africa and Canada, see Joan G. Fairweather, *A Common Hunger: Land Rights in Canada and South Africa* (Calgary, 2006). Ipperwash is referred to on pp. 197–8.

57. Indian and Northern Affairs Canada, at: <www.ainc-inac.gc.ca>.

58. CTV News, at: <www.ctv.ca/servlet/ArticleNews/story/CTVNews/20060712/caledonia_protest_060712/20060712/>.

59. Ontario Ministry of Aboriginal Affairs, at: <www.aboriginalaffairs.osaa.gov.on.ca/english/caledonia/faq.htm>. The number of unresolved issues regarding the Six Nations is a result of the large size of the original Haldimand Grant, as well as the simple fact that the grant was made well over two centuries ago. Although the Six Nations presently are forced to seek redress on an issue-by-issue basis, they nonetheless are in an advantageous position, vis-à-vis many other treaty Indians, because of the size of the Haldimand Grant and its location in southern Ontario, where property and land values are high. The fact that Joseph Brant, the Six Nations leader of the late eighteenth and early nineteenth centuries, sold off significant portions of the grant has only complicated matters for modern-day negotiators.

60. CTV News, at: <www.ctv.ca/servlet/ArticleNews/story/CTVNews/20060712/caledonia_protest_060712/20060712/>.

61. CBC News, at: <www.cbc.ca/news/background/caledonia-landclaim/index.html>.

62. Ibid.

63. Ibid.

64. See Bruce W. Hodgins, Ute Lischke, and David T. McNab, eds, *Blockades and Resistance: Studies in Actions of Peace and the Temagami Blockades of 1988–89* (Waterloo, Ont., 2003), 1–10; McNab, *Circles of Time*, 1–10.

65. Ontario Ministry of Aboriginal Affairs, at: <www.aboriginalaffairs.osaa.gov.on.ca/english/caledonia/faq.htm>.

66. The author was present in 1981 when this event occurred. He was then working for the provincial government as the Senior Indian Land Claims Researcher in the former Office of Indian Resource Policy in the Ontario Ministry of Natural Resources.

67. CBC News, at: <www.cbc.ca.canada/story/2007/06/11/land-claims.html>.

68. Ibid.

69. Indian and Northern Affairs Canada, at: <www.ainc-inac.gc.ca>.

70. Indian and Northern Affairs Canada, at: <www.ainc-inac.gc.ca/nr/prs/s-d2007/2-2970-eng.asp>.

71. See David T. McNab and Ute Lischke, 'Actions of Peace: Introduction', in Hodgins et al., *Blockades*

and Resistance, 1–9; McNab, 'Remembering an Intellectual Wilderness: A Captivity Narrative at Queen's Park in 1988–89', ibid., 31–53.

72. Ontario Ministry of Aboriginal Affairs, at: <www.aboriginalaffairs.osaa.gov.on.ca/english/caledonia/faq.htm>.

73. Rob Ferguson, 'Caledonia protests greet Bryant', *Toronto Star*, 26 Nov. 2007, at: <www.thestar.com/News/Ontario/article/279946>.

74. CBC News, at: <www.cbc.ca/canada/toronto/story/2007/12/13/caledonia-offer.html>.

75. Lischke and McNab, 'Actions of Peace: Introduction', 1–9.

76. 'Rally to support Robert Lovelace and the KI 6', *Globe and Mail*, 8 Apr. 2008, at: <www.globeinvestor.com/servlet/story/CNW.20080408.C3741/GIStory>.

77. Government of British Columbia, at: <www.gov.bc.ca/arr/firstnation/tsawwassen/>.

78. BC Liberal Party, at: <www.bcliberals.com/EN/1341/9655?PHPSESSID=11a0a0416cbcd16cbd1c3cd6b0502c4c>.

79. Ibid.

80. CBC News, at: <www.cbc.ca/canada/british-columbia/story/2007/10/15/bc-legislaturetreaty.html>.

81. Government of Canada, Privy Council Office, at: <www.pco.gc.ca/index.asp?lang=eng&page=information&sub=publications&doc=sft-ddt/2004_1_e.htm>.

82. Ibid.

83. Ibid.

84. CBC News, at: <www.cbc.ca/news/background/aboriginals/undoing-kelowna.html>.

85. Ibid.

86. Ibid.

87. Ibid.

88. Government of Canada, Privy Council Office, at: <www.pco.gc.ca/index.asp?lang=eng&page=information&sub=publications&doc=sft-ddt/2004_1_e.htm>.

89. Linda Diebel, 'Seeking truth about lost children', *Toronto Star*, 29 May 2008, at <www.thestar.com/News/Canada/article/432707>.

90. Jane O'Hara with Patricia Treble, 'Residential Church School Scandal', *Maclean's*, 26 June 2000, at: <www.thecanadianencyclopedia.com/index.cfun?PgNm=TCE&Params=M1ARTM0012194>.

91. Ibid.

92. CBC News, at: <www.cbc.ca/news/background/aboriginals/timeline_residentialschools.html>.

93. Jonathon Gatehouse, 'Residential Schools Cash Draws Closer', *Maclean's*, 16 Apr. 2007, at: <www.macleans.ca/homepage/magazine/article.jsp?content=20070416_104189_104189>.

94. CBC News, at: <www.cbc.ca/canada/story/2007/08/20/aboriginal-settlement.html>.

95. Statistics Canada, 'Aboriginal Peoples in Canada in 2006: Inuit, Métis and First Nations, 2006 Census', *The Daily*, 15 Jan. 2008, at: <www.statcan.ca/Daily/English/080115/d080115a.htm>.

96. Ibid.

97. Robert M. Bone, *The Regional Geography of Canada*, 4th edn (Toronto, 2008), 170.

98. Statistics Canada, at: <www12.statcan.ca/english/census06/data/profiles/aboriginal/Details/Page.cfm?Lang=E&Geo1=CMA&Code1=541__&Geo2=PR&Code2=35&Data=Count&SearchText=Kitchener&SearchType=Begins&SearchPR=01&B1=All&GeoLevel=&GeoCode=541>. See also Jeff Outhit, 'Census shows region attracts natives', *Kitchener–Waterloo Record*, 16 Jan. 2008, B1–2. The author of this chapter has argued that there were many Métis in Ontario from an early date. See David T. McNab, 'Métis Participation in the Treaty-Making Process in Ontario: A Reconnaissance', *Native Studies Review* 1, 2 (1985): 57–79. For a personal account, in which the author traces his family through seven generations from northeastern Saskatchewan to the banks of the Grand River, also then known as the Bear River, see David T. McNab, 'Hiding in Plane View: Aboriginal Identities and a Fur Trade Company Family through Seven Generations', in David R. Newhouse, Cora J. Voyageur, and Dan Beavon, eds, *Hidden in Plain Sight: Contributions of Aboriginal Peoples to Canadian Identity and Culture* (Toronto, 2005), 295–308.

99. Statistics Canada, 'Aboriginal Peoples in Canada in 2006', *The Daily*, 15 Jan. 2008.

100. Ibid.

101. Statistics Canada, at: <www12.statcan.ca/english/census06/data/highlights/Aboriginal/index.cfm?Lang=E>.

102. Ibid.

103. Statistics Canada, 'Aboriginal Peoples in Canada in 2006', *The Daily*, 15 Jan. 2008.

104. Ibid.

105. Statistics Canada, at: <www12.statcan.ca/english/census06/analysis/aboriginal/surpass.cfm>.

106. CBC News, at: <www.cbc.ca/story/canada/national/2005/11/01/afn-regina051101.html>.

107. CBC News, at: <www.cbc.ca/news/background/aboriginals/kashechewan.html>.

108. Ibid.

109. Ibid.

110. Indian and Northern Affairs Canada, at: <www.ainc-inac.gc.ca/nr/prs/s-d2006/kfnp_e.html>.

111. Ibid.

112. Ibid.

113. Indian and Northern Affairs Canada, at: <www.ainc-inac.gc.ca/nr/prs/m-a2007/2-2915-eng.asp>.

114. Ibid.

115. For example, the Walpole Island (Bkejwanong) First Nation, situated south of the Chemical Valley on the St Clair River, recently constructed its very first water treatment plant, which was completed in 2007. It replaced, in part, the old Indian Affairs office, which was symbolically torn down.

116. CBC News, at: <www.cbc.ca/news/background/cdmilitary/arctic.html>.

117. Matthew Carnaghan and Allison Goody, *Canadian Arctic Sovereignty* (Ottawa, Jan. 2006), at: <www.parl.gc.ca/info/library/PRBpubs/prb0561-e.htm>.

118. James Travers, 'Arctic issues make for good politics', *Toronto Star*, 10 July 2007, at: <www.thestar.com/printArticle/234195>.

119. CBC News, at: <www.cbc.ca/news/background/cdmilitary/arctic.html>.

120. Carnaghan and Goody, *Canadian Arctic Sovereignty*.

121. Robert Dufresne, *Canada's Legal Claims Over Arctic Territory and Waters* (Ottawa, 6 Dec. 2007), at: <www.parl.gc.ca/information/library/PRBpubs/prb0739-e.htm>.

122. Indian and Northern Affairs Canada, at: <www.ainc-inac.gc.ca/pr/pub/indigen/tkin_e.html>.

123. Indian and Northern Affairs Canada, at: <www.ainc-inac.gc.ca/nr/prs/j-a2006/02759bk_e.html>.

124. CBC News, at: <www.cbc.ca/canada/story/2007/12/27/weather-list.html>.

125. 'Nation Builder 2007: Sheila Watt-Cloutier', *Globe and Mail*, 28 Dec. 2007, at: <www.theglobeandmail.com/servlet/story/RTGAM.20071227.wnationbuilderwattcloutier28/EmailBNStory/National/home>.

126. CTV News, at: <www.ctv.ca/servlet/ArticleNews/story/CTVNews/20070301/arctic_warming_070301?s_name=&no_ads=>.

127. Ibid.

128. CBC News, at: <www.cbc.ca/world/story/2007/06/04/harper-germany.html>.

129. CTV News, at: <www.ctv.ca/servlet/ArticleNews/story/CTVNews/20080102/environment_2007_080102/20080102?hub=SciTech>.

130. 'Nation Builder 2007: Sheila Watt-Cloutier'.

Epilogue

1. Even Diamond Jenness subscribed to the idea of the 'vanishing Indian'. In his words: 'Doubtless all the tribes will disappear. Some will endure only a few years longer, others, like the Eskimo, may last several centuries. Some will merge steadily with the white race, others will bequeath to future generations only an infinitesimal fraction of their blood.' In any event, he added, Indians had already contributed everything they had that was culturally valuable to the dominant civilization. Jenness, *The Indians of Canada* (Ottawa, 1958), 264.

2. Menno Boldt, 'Social Correlates of Nationalism: A Study of Native Indian Leaders in a Canadian Internal Colony', *Comparative Political Studies* 14, 2 (1981): 205–31.

3. Dave Brown, 'Measuring the happiness of Canada's ethnic groups: Aboriginals report least satisfaction with life, study finds', *Ottawa Citizen*, 18 Nov. 2000, C1.

4. Alan D. McMillan, *Native Peoples and Cultures of Canada* (Vancouver, 1988), 6.

5. Sara Minogue, 'People of Nunavut fight to save Inuktitut language', *Calgary Herald*, 20 Jan. 2008, at: <www.canada.com/calgaryherald/story.html?k=80163&id=0b8913d9-9ea1-48ee-b401-0366a1384195>.

6. *Report of the Royal Commission on Aboriginal Peoples*, 5 vols (Ottawa, 1996), V, 5.

7. See Ute Lischke and David T. McNab, eds, *Walking a Tightrope: Aboriginal People and Their Representations* (Waterloo, Ont., 2005), 1–18.

8. Selwyn Dewdney, 'Birth of a Cree–Ojibway Style of Contemporary Art', in Ian A.L. Getty and Donald B. Smith, eds, *One Century Later: Western Canadian Reserve Indians Since Treaty 7* (Vancouver, 1978), 117–25.

9. Niède Guidon, 'Cliff Notes', *Natural History* 96, 8 (1987): 10.

10. 'Harper speaks on Native Awareness', *Native Sports, News, and Culture* 2, 4 (1991): 26. See also Pauline Comeau, *Elijah: No Ordinary Hero* (Vancouver, 1993).

11. See Bruce W. Hodgins, Ute Lischke, and David T. McNab, eds, *Blockades and Resistance: Studies in Actions of Peace and the Temagami Blockades of 1988–89* (Waterloo, Ont., 2003), 1–9.

12. Rick Mofina, 'Coon Come invited to Quebec summit', *Ottawa Citizen*, 31 Mar. 2001, A6.

13. See David T. McNab, 'A Brief History of the Denial of Indigenous Rights in Canada', in Janet Miron, ed., *A History of Human Rights in Canada* (Toronto, 2009).

14. Kenneth Deer, 'Our Native Rights Stance Is a Foreign Policy Failure', *Embassy: Canada's Foreign Policy Newsweekly*, 21 Nov. 2007, at: <www.embassymag.ca/html/index.php?display=story&full_path=/2007/november/21/deer/>.

Bibliography

Manuscript Sources

Library and Archives Canada, Ottawa
 MG 1 Archives des Colonies.
  Série B. Lettres envoyées.
  Série C^{11}A. Correspondance générale, Canada.
  Série C^{11}B. Correspondance générale, Ile
   Royale.
  Série C^{11}C. Amérique du Nord.
  Série C^{11}G. Correspondance Raudot
   Pontchartrain, domaine de l'occident at Ile
   Royale.
  Série C^{12}. Correspondance générale, St Pierre et
   Miquelon.
  Série C^{13}A. Correspondance générale,
   Louisiane.
  Série F^{1}A. Fonds des Colonies.
  Série F^3. Collection Moreau de Saint-Méry.
 MG 2: Archives de la Marine.
  Série B^3. Lettres reçues.
 MG 7: Bibliothèques de Paris.
  Bibliothèque Nationale, Département de man-
   uscrits.
  1A, 2, Fonds français.
  1A, 10, Collection Moreau.
 MG 8: Documents relatifs à la Nouvelle France et
  au Québec (XVIIe–XXe siècles).
 MG 11: Colonial Office.
  Nova Scotia Papers.
  Nova Scotia A.
  Nova Scotia B.
 MG 18: Pre-Conquest Papers.
  E29, Pierre-François-Xavier Charlevoix Papers.
 MG 21: British Museum. Sloane and Additional
  Manuscripts.
  Haldimand Papers.

 MG 26A: Macdonald Papers.
 RG 6: Secretary of State.
 RG 10: Indian and Northern Affairs.
  Deputy Superintendent's Letterbook.
  Headquarters Files; Miscellaneous
   Correspondence, Oka.

Provincial Archives of Alberta
 Oblates de Marie Immaculate.

Oblate Archives, St Albert, Alberta

Provincial Archives of British Columbia
 Correspondence Inward.

Saskatchewan Archives Board
 Campbell Innes Papers.
 Rev. J.A. Mackay Papers.
 Indian Schools, 1907–8.

Hudson's Bay Company Archives, Winnipeg
 HBC Official Correspondence Book Outwards.
 Moose Fort Journal.
 Peter Fidler's Journal.

Provincial Court of Newfoundland, District of Happy
 Valley/Goose Bay, Labrador, Judgment of
  Igloliorte, PCJ, in *Regina v. Daniel Ashini et*
  al., 18 Apr. 1989, typescript.

Unpublished Theses, Papers, Manuscripts

Ackerman, Robert E. 'A Siberian Journey: Research Travel in the USSR, July 20–August 20, 1990', unpublished report to the National Endowment for the Humanities and Washington State University, 25 Sept. 1990.

Barber, Lloyd. 'The Implications of Indian Claims for Canada', address given at the Banff School of Advanced Management, Banff, Alberta, 9 Mar. 1978.

Bartels, Denis A., and Olaf Uwe Janzen. 'Micmac Migration to Western Newfoundland', paper presented to the Canadian Historical Association, Victoria, 1990.

Bennett, J.A.H., and J.W. Berry. 'The Future of Cree Syllabic Literacy in Northern Canada', paper presented at the Fifteenth Algonquian Conference, Winnipeg, 1986.

Blair, Peggy J. 'The Supreme Court of Canada's "Historic" Decisions in *Nikal* and *Lewis*; Why Crown Fishing Policy in Upper Canada Makes Bad Law', Master of Law thesis (University of Ottawa, 1998).

Brown, Randall J. 'Smallboy's Camp: A Contemporary Example of a Revitalization Movement', typescript.

Bull, Linda R. 'Indian Residential Schooling: The Native Perspective', M.Ed. thesis (University of Alberta, 1991).

Chabot, Cecil. 'Merging Cree and Non-Cree Understandings of the 1832 Washaw Conflict', MA thesis (University of Montreal, 2002).

Coates, Kenneth S. 'Best Left as Indians: Indian–White Relations in Yukon Territory, 1840–1950', Ph.D. thesis (University of British Columbia, 1984).

Daniel, Richard C. 'Indian Rights and Hinterland Provinces: The Case of Northern Alberta', MA thesis (University of Alberta, 1977).

Ferreira, Darlene Abreu. 'Need Not Greed: The Lubicon Lake Cree Band Claim in Historical Perspective', MA thesis (University of Alberta, 1990).

Greyeyes, Arlene Roberta. 'St. Michael's Indian Residential School, 1894–1926', MA thesis (Carleton University, 1995).

Hall, Anthony J. 'The St. Catherine's Milling and Lumber Company vs. The Queen: A Study in the Relationship of Indian Land Rights to Federal–Provincial Relations in Nineteenth-Century Canada', typescript.

———. 'The Ontario Supreme Court on Trial: Justice Donald Steele and Aboriginal Right', typescript.

Hamilton, John David. 'The Absent-Minded Revolution: A Political and Social History of the NWT, 1990', 385-page manuscript.

Hazell, Stephen, executive director, Canadian Arctic Resource Committee. Circular letter, n.d.

Herring, Ann. 'The 1918 Flu Epidemic in Manitoba Aboriginal Communities: Implications for Depopulation Theory in the Americas', paper presented to the American Society for Ethnohistory, Toronto, 1990.

Hill, Judith. 'The Ewing Commission, 1935: A Case Study of Metis Government Relations', MA thesis (University of Alberta, 1977).

Kerbiriou, Anne-Hélène. 'L'objectif de la foi. L'image des Amérindiens dans le corpus photographique des missionnaires Oblats, Nord-Ouest canadien, 1880–1930', Ph.D. thesis (Université Laval, 1994).

Kermoal, Nathalie J. 'Le "Temps de Cayoge": La vie quotidienne des femmes métisses au Manitoba de 1850 à 1900', Ph.D. thesis (University of Ottawa, 1996).

Leighton, Douglas. 'The Historical Significance of the Robinson Treaties of 1850', paper presented to the Canadian Historical Association, Ottawa, 1982.

McNab, David T. 'Exchanging Time and the Ojibwa: An Exploration of the Notions of Time and Territoriality', paper presented to the American Ethnohistory Society, Toronto, 1990.

Manitoba Environmental Council. 'Southern Indian Lake and Hydro Development', edited proceedings, Winnipeg, 19 Jan. 1973.

Martin-McGuire, Peggy. 'First Nation Land Surrenders on the Prairies, 1896–1911'. Ottawa: Prepared for the Indian Claims Commission, 1998.

Moodie, D. Wayne, Kerry Abel, and Alan Catchpole. 'Northern Athapaskan Oral Traditions and the White River Volcanic Eruption', paper presented at conference, Aboriginal Resource Use in Canada: Historical and Legal Aspects, University of Manitoba, 1988.

Morantz, Toby. 'Old Texts, Old Questions—Another Look at the Issue of Continuity and the Early Fur Trade Period', paper presented to the American Ethnohistory Society, Chicago, 1989.

Pettit, Jennifer Lorretta. 'To Chistianize and Civilize', Ph.D. thesis (University of Calgary, 1997).

Poulton, Cody. 'Songs from the Gods: "Hearing the Voice" in the Ascetic Rituals of West Coast Indians and Japanese Liturgic Drama', paper presented to the Thirty-third International Congress of Asian and North African Studies, University of Toronto, 1991.

Robson, Robert. 'The Indian Act: A Contemporary Perspective', University of Manitoba, typescript.

Shankel, G.E. 'The Development of Indian Policy in British Columbia', Ph.D. thesis (University of Washington, 1945).

Sloan, W.A. 'The Columbia link—native trade, warfare, and European penetration of the Kootenays', paper presented to the Orkney–Rupert's Land Colloquium, Orkney Islands, 1990.

Taylor, John Leonard. 'The Development of an Indian Policy for the Canadian North-West, 1869–70', Ph.D. thesis (Queen's University, 1975).

Printed Documents and Reports

Akins, Thomas B. *Selections from the Public Documents of the Province of Nova Scotia*. Halifax: Annand, 1869.

Bagot Commission Report. *Journals of the Legislative Assembly of the Province of Canada*, 1844–5, app. EEE; and 1847, app. T.

'The Bear Island Decision', *Ontario Reports* (2nd ser.), 49, part 7, 17 May 1985, 353–490.

Berger, Thomas R. *Northern Frontier, Northern Homeland*, 2 vols. Ottawa: Supply and Services Canada, 1977.

Berger Community Hearings.

Campeau, Lucien. *Monumenta Novae Franciae I: La première mission d'Acadie (1602–1616)*. Québec: Les Presses de l'Université Laval, 1967; and *II: Etablissement à Québec (1616–1634)*, 1979.

Canada. Department of Indian Affairs Annual Reports.

Canada. Department of Mines and Resources. *Report of the Department for the Fiscal Year Ended March 31, 1944*. Ottawa: King's Printer, 1944.

Canada. *Indian Treaties and Surrenders*, 3 vols. Ottawa: Brown Chamberlin, 1891–1912 (Coles Facsimile, 1971).

Canada. Parliament. *House of Commons Debates*.
———. *House of Commons Sessional Papers*.

Canada. North-West Mounted Police Reports.

Census of Canada. Various years.

Clatworthy, Stewart, and Anthony H. Smith. *Population Implications of the 1985 Amendment to the Indian Act*. Report prepared for the Assembly of First Nations, 1992.

Collection de documents inédits sur le Canada et l'Amérique publiées par le Canada français, 3 vols. Québec: Demers, 1888–90.

Collection de manuscrits contenant lettres, mémoires et autres documents historiques relatif à la Nouvelle-France, 4 vols. Québec: A. Coté, 1833–85.

A Collection of Documents Relating to Jacques Cartier and the Sieur de Roberval, ed. Henry P. Biggar. Ottawa: Public Archives of Canada, 1930.

Documents Relating to the Constitutional History of Canada, 1759–1771, eds Adam Shortt and Arthur G. Doughty. Ottawa, 1918.

Edits, ordonnances royaux, déclarations et arrêts du Conseil d'état du roi concernant le Canada, 3 vols. Québec: Fréchette, 1854–6.

Hawthorn, H.B. *A Survey of the Contemporary Indians of Canada: Economic, Political, Educational Needs and Policies*, 2 vols. Ottawa: Indian Affairs, 1966–7.

Indian Claims Commission Proceedings. Special Issue on Land Claims Reform. Ottawa: Minister of Supply and Services, 1995.

James Bay and Northern Quebec Agreement Implementation Review February 1982. Ottawa: Department of Indian Affairs and Northern Development, 1982.

Johnston, Charles M., ed. *The Valley of the Six Nations: A Collection of Documents on the Indian Lands of the Grand River*. Toronto, 1964.

Journals of the Honorable House of Representatives of His Majesty's Province of Massachusetts-Bay in New England. Boston, 1744.

Journals of the Legislative Assembly of Prince Edward Island.

Journals of the Legislative Assembly of the Province of Canada.

Jugements et délibérations du Conseil Souverain de la Nouvelle France, 7 vols. Québec: A. Coté, 1885–91.

Kelsey, Henry. *The Kelsey Papers*. Ottawa: Public Archives of Canada and the Public Record Office of Northern Ireland, 1929.

Lincoln, Charles Henry, ed. *The Correspondence of William Shirley*, 2 vols. New York: Macmillan, 1912.

Linden, Sidney B. *Report of the Ipperwash Inquiry*, 31 May 2007, at: <www.ipperwashinquiry.ca/>.
———. *Report of the Ipperwash Inquiry: Volume 4, Executive Summary*. Toronto: Ministry of the Attorney General, 2007.

Living Treaties: Lasting Agreements. Ottawa: Department of Indian Affairs and Northern Development, 1985.

Lowrie, Walter, and Matthew St Clair Clarke, eds. *American State Papers. Class II. Indian Affairs, 1789–1827*, 2 vols. Washington, 1832–4.

McConnell, R.B. *Report on a Portion of the District of Athabasca Comprising the Country between the Peace River and the Athabasca River North of Lesser Slave Lake*. Ottawa: Queen's Printer, 1983.

Maine Historical Society Collections.

Massachusetts Historical Society Collections.

Morris, Alexander. *The Treaties of Canada with the Indians*. Toronto: Belfords, Clarke, 1880 (Coles Reprint, 1971).

National Indian Brotherhood. *Inquiry into the Invasion of Restigouche*. Preliminary Report, 15 July 1981.

O'Callaghan, E.B., and J.R. Brodhead, eds. *Documents Relative to the Colonial History of the State of New York*, 15 vols. Albany, NY: Weed Parsons, 1853–87.

Ontario Reports.

People to People, Nation to Nation: Highlights of the Report of the Royal Commission on Aboriginal Peoples. Ottawa: Minister of Supply and Services, 1996.

Protecting Knowledge: Traditional Resource Rights in the New Millennium. Report of conference hosted by the Union of British Columbia Chiefs, Vancouver, 23–6 Feb. 2000.

Rapport de l'Archiviste de la Province de Québec, 1947–8.

Recent Development in Native Education. Toronto: Canadian Education Association, 1984.

Report Concerning Canadian Archives, 1905, 3 vols. 1906.

Report of the Royal Commission on Aboriginal Peoples, 5 vols. Ottawa: Minister of Supply and Services Canada, 1996.

Report of Treaty Eight Commission, 1899.

Reports of the Cree–Naskapi Commission. Ottawa, 1968, 1988.

Reports of the Supreme Court of Canada.

Rich, E.E., ed. *Letters Outward 1679–1694.* Toronto: The Champlain Society, 1948.

Royal Canadian Mounted Police. *Final Report: RCMP Review of Allegations Concerning Inuit Sled Dogs*, 2006, at: <www.rcmp-grc.gc.ca/ccaps/sled_dogs_final_e.htm>.

Self-Determination Symposium Report. Ottawa: Assembly of First Nations, 1990.

Statement of the Government of Canada on Indian Policy, 1969.

Statutes of Canada.

Sullivan, James, Alexander C. Flick, and Milton W. Hamilton, eds. *The Papers of Sir William Johnson*, 14 vols. Albany, NY: University of the State of New York, 1921–65.

Thwaites, Reuben Gold, ed. *Jesuit Relations and Allied Documents*, 73 vols. Cleveland: Burrows Bros, 1896–1901. Available on-line at: <puffin.creighton.edu/jesuit/relations>.

Tyrrell, J.B., ed. *Documents Relating to the Early History of Hudson Bay.* Toronto: The Champlain Society, 1931.

Media (Newspapers, Television)

Akwesasne Notes.
Alberta Sweetgrass.
Boston Globe.
Calgary Herald.
Catholic New Times.
The Catholic Register.
CBC Newsworld Online.
Christian Science Monitor.
Edmonton Journal.
the fifth estate, CBC-TV.
Financial Times, London
First Citizen.
The Gazette, Montreal.
Globe and Mail, Toronto.
Guardian Weekly.
Indian Country Today.
Le Droit, Ottawa-Hull.
Manitoba Free Press.
National Post.
Native Network News.
Native Sports, News, and Culture, Edmonton.
Nunatsiaq News.
Ottawa Citizen.
Owen Sound Sun-Times.
The Press Independent, Somba K'e, NWT.
Saturday Night.
The Times, London.
Toronto Star.
Treizième tome du Mercure François. Paris: Estienne Richer, 1629.
Vancouver Sun.
Wawatay News.
Windspeaker.

Internet Resources

British Columbia Liberal Party: www.bcliberals.com
Canadian Broadcasting Corporation: www.cbc.ca
CTV News: www.ctv.ca
Embassy: Canada's Foreign Policy Newsweekly: www.embassymag.ca
First Nations Bank: www.firstnationsbank.com
Friends of the Lubicon: www.tao.ca/~fol
Government of British Columbia: www.gov.bc.ca
Government of Canada, Privy Council Office: www.pco.gc.ca
Government of Nunavut: www.gov.nu.ca
Indian and Northern Affairs Canada: www.ainc-inac.gc.ca
Inuvialuit Regional Corporation: www.inuvialuit.com
Kairos: Canadian Ecumenical Justice Initiatives: www.kairoscanada.org
Kitsaki Management Limited Partnership: www.kitsaki.com
Library of Parliament, publications: www.parl.gc.ca/information/library/PRBpubs
Nunatsiaq News: www.nunatsiaq.com
Ontario Ministry of Aboriginal Affairs: www.aboriginalaffairs.osaa.gov.on.ca

Royal Canadian Mounted Police: www.rcmp-grc.gc.ca

Statistics Canada: www.statcan.ca and www12.stat can.ca

Tar Sands Watch: www/tarsandswatch.org

Turning Point: Natives and Newcomers Online: www.turning-point.ca

University of Alberta: www.ualberta.ca

Reference Works

The Canadian Encyclopedia, ed.-in-chief, James H. Marsh, 4 vols. Edmonton: Hurtig, 1988.

The Dictionary of Canadian Biography, general eds George W. Brown, David M. Hayne, Frances G. Halpenny, and Ramsay Cook, 14 vols (continuing). Toronto: University of Toronto Press, 1966–.

Dictionnaire universel, géographique et historique . . . , ed., Thomas Corneille, 3 vols. Paris: Jean-Baptiste Coignard, 1708.

Laverdure, Patline, and Ida Rose Allard. *The Michif Dictionary: Turtle Mountain Chippewa Cree*, ed. John C. Crawford. Winnipeg: Pemmican Publishers, 1983.

LeClaire, Nancy, and George Cardinal. *Alberta Elders' Cree Dictionary. alperta ohci kehtehayak nehiyaw otwestamâkewasinahikan,* ed. Earle Waugh. Edmonton: University of Alberta Press, 1998.

Whiteside, Don. *Aboriginal People: A Selected Bibliography Concerning Canada's First People.* Ottawa: National Indian Brotherhood, 1973.

———. *Historical Development of Aboriginal Political Association in Canada: Documentation.* Ottawa: National Indian Brotherhood, 1973.

Books and Articles

Abbas, Rana F. 'We've heard it all before', *Windspeaker* 21, 3 (June 2003): 12–13.

Abel, Kerry. *Drum Songs.* Montreal and Kingston: McGill-Queen's University Press, 1993.

——— and Jean Friesen, eds. *Aboriginal Resource Use in Canada: Historical and Legal Aspects.* Winnipeg: University of Manitoba Press, 1991.

Acosta, Joseph de. *The Natural and Morall History of the East and West Indies*, tr. E.G., 2 vols. London: Hakluyt Society, 1880. (Reprint of 1604 edn.)

Adams, Howard. *Prison of Grass: Canada from the Native Point of View.* Toronto: New Press, 1975. (Revised edn, Saskatoon: Fifth House Press, 1989.)

Adney, Edwin Tappen, and Howard I. Chapelle. *The Bark Canoes and Skin Boats of North America.* Washington: Smithsonian Institution, 1964.

Ahenakew, Edward. 'An Opinion of the Frog Lake Massacre', *Alberta Historical Review* 8, 3 (1966): 9–15.

———. *Voices of the Plains Cree.* Toronto: McClelland & Stewart, 1973.

Aikenhead, Sherri. 'Tough Struggle Back', *Maclean's* 99, 28 (1986): 19.

Alfonce, Jean (Jean Fonteneau). *Les Voyages avantureaux du Capitaine Ian Alfonce, Sainctongeois.* Poitiers: Ian le Marnef, 1559.

Alfred, Gerald R. *Heeding the Voices of Our Ancestors: Kahnawake Mohawk Politics and the Rise of Native Nationalism.* Toronto: Oxford University Press, 1995.

Alfred, Taiaiake. *Peace, Power, Righteousness: An Indigenous Manifesto.* Toronto: Oxford University Press, 1999.

Allen, R.S. 'Big Bear', *Saskatchewan History* 25, 1 (1972): 1–17.

———. 'The British Indian Department and the Frontier in North America, 1755–1830', *Occasional Papers in Archaeology and History* No. 14 (Ottawa: Canadian Historical Sites, 1975): 5–125.

———. *Her Majesty's Indian Allies.* Toronto: Dundurn Press, 1993.

Ames, Kenneth M. 'The Evolution of Social Ranking on the Northwest Coast of North America', *American Antiquity* 46, 4 (1981): 789–805.

An Account of the Customs and Manners of the Micmakis and Maricheets, Savage Nations, Now Dependent on the Government of Cape Breton. London, 1758.

Anderson, Frank W. *Almighty Voice.* Aldergrove, BC: Frontier Publishing, 1971.

Andrews, Isabel. 'Indian Protest against Starvation: The Yellow Calf Incident of 1884', *Saskatchewan History* 28, 2 (1975): 41–51.

Armour, David A., ed. *Attack at Michilimackinac 1763.* Mackinac Island, Mich.: Mackinac Island State Park Commission, 1988. This is a reproduction of Alexander Henry's *Travels and Adventures in Canada and the Indian Territories between the Years 1760 and 1764.* New York, 1809.

Armstrong, Robin, Jeff Kennedy, and Peter R. Oberle. *University Education and Economic Well-Being: Indian Achievement and Prospects.* Ottawa: Indian and Northern Affairs Canada, 1990.

Arthur, George W. *An Introduction to the Ecology of Early Historic Communal Bison Hunting among the Northern Plains Indians.* Ottawa: National Museums of Canada, 1975.

Arthur, M. Elizabeth. 'General Dickson and the Indian Liberating Army in the North', *Ontario History* 62, 3 (1970): 151–62.

Asch, Michael. *Home and Native Land: Aboriginal Rights and the Canadian Constitution.* Toronto: Methuen, 1984.

———. *Kinship and the Drum Dance in a Northern Dene*

Community. Edmonton: Boreal Institute for Northern Studies, 1988.

Assembly of First Nations. *Breaking the Silence*. Ottawa: First Nations Health Commission, 1994.

Assiniwi, Bernard. *Histoire des Indiens du haut et du bas Canada: moeurs et coutumes des Algonkins et des Iroquois*, 3 vols. Québec: Leméac, 1973.

Avery, Kathi, and Thomas Pawlick. 'Last Stand in Wild Rice Country', *Harrowsmith* 3, 7 (May 1979): 32–47.

Avity, Pierre d'. *Description générale de l'Amérique, troisième partie du Monde . . .* Paris: Claude Sonnius, 1660.

Axtell, James. *The Invasion Within: The Contest of Cultures in Colonial North America*. New York: Oxford University Press, 1985.

Bacqueville de la Potherie, Claude C. Le Roy *dit*. *Histoire de l'Amérique septentrionale*, 4 vols. Paris: J.L. Nion and F. Didot, 1722.

Bailey, Alfred Goldsworthy. *The Conflict of European and Eastern Algonkian Cultures 1504–1700*. Toronto: University of Toronto Press, 1969. (First published Saint John: New Brunswick Museum Monograph Series No. 2, 1937.)

Bakker, Peter. 'Canadian Fur Trade and the Absence of Creoles', *The Carrier Pidgin* 16, 3 (1988): 1–3.

———. 'Relexification: The case of the Métif (French Cree)', in N. Baretzy, W. Enninger, and Th. Stolz, eds, *Sprachkontakt. Beiträge zum s. Essener Kolloquium über Grammatikalisierung: Naturlichkeit un System Okonomie*, vol. 2. Bochum: Brockreyer, 1989.

———. 'Two Basque Loanwords in Micmac', *International Journal of American Linguistics* 55, 2 (1989): 258–60.

———. 'The Genesis of Michif: A First Hypothesis', in William Cowan, ed, *Papers of the Twenty-first Algonquian Conference*. Ottawa: Carleton University, 1990: 12–35.

———. 'A Basque Etymology for the Word Iroquois', *Man in the Northeast* 40 (1990): 89–93.

———. 'The Mysterious Link between Basque and Micmac Art', *European Review of Native American Studies* 5, 1 (1991): 21–4.

———. *A Language of Our Own*. New York: Oxford University Press, 1997.

Barbeau, Marius. *Tsimshian Myths*. Ottawa: National Museum of Canada Bulletin No. 174, 1961.

——— and William Beynon, coll. *Tsimshian Narratives 2*. Ottawa: Canadian Museum of Civilization Mercury Series Paper No. 3, 1987.

Barber, John. 'Oriental Enigma', *Equinox* 49 (1990): 83–95.

Barlee, N.L. 'The Chilcotin War of 1864', *Canada West Magazine* 6, 4 (1976): 13–23.

Barman, Jean, Yvonne Hébert, and Don McCaskill, eds. *Indian Education in Canada*, 2 vols. Vancouver: University of British Columbia Press, 1986.

Barnett, Donald C. *Poundmaker*. Don Mills, Ont.: Fitzhenry & Whiteside, 1976.

Barnsley, Paul. 'Governance Act dead for now—Nault', *Windspeaker* 21, 8 (Nov. 2003): 18.

Barron, F.L. 'The Indian Pass System in the Canadian West, 1882–1935', *Prairie Forum* 13, 1 (1988): 25–42.

——— and James B. Waldram, eds. *1885 and After: Native Society in Transition*. Regina: University of Regina, 1986.

Bartlett, Richard H. 'The Establishment of Indian Reserves on the Prairies', *Canadian Native Law Reporter* 3 (1980): 3–56.

———. *Indian Reserves in Quebec*. Saskatoon: University of Saskatchewan Native Law Centre, Studies in Aboriginal Rights No. 8, 1984.

———. *Indian Reserves and Aboriginal Lands in Canada: A Homeland*. Saskatoon: University of Saskatchewan Native Law Centre, 1990.

Beadle, George W. 'The Ancestry of Corn', *Scientific American* 242, 2 (1980): 112–19.

Beaglehole, Ernest. *Social Change in the South Pacific: Rarotonga and Aitutaki*. Aberdeen, Scotland: University Press, 1957.

Beal, Bob, and Rod Macleod. *Prairie Fire: The 1885 North-West Rebellion*. Edmonton: Hurtig, 1984.

Béchard, Henri. *The Original Caughnawaga Indians*. Montreal: International Publishers, 1976.

Belleforest, François de, and Sebastian Münster. *La Cosmographie universelle de tout le monde . . .*, 2 vols. Paris: Michel Sonnius, 1575.

Belting, Natalie Maree. *Kaskaskia under the French Regime*. New Orleans: Polyanthos, 1975.

Berger, Thomas R. *Fragile Freedoms: Human Rights and Dissent in Canada*. Toronto: Clarke, Irwin, 1981.

———. 'Native History, Native Claims and Self-Determination', *B.C. Studies* 57 (1983): 10–23.

———. *Village Journey*. New York: Hill and Wang, 1985.

Berglund, Joel. 'The Decline of the Norse Settlements in Greenland', *Arctic Anthropology* 23, 142 (1986): 109–35.

Beta (pseud.). *A Contribution to a Proper Understanding of the Oka Question; and a Help to its Equitable and Speedy Settlement*. Montreal, 1879.

Biet, Antoine. *Voyage de la France Equinoxiale en l'isle de Cayenne, entrepris par les Français en l'année 1652*. Paris: François Clouzier, 1664.

Biggar, Henry P., ed. *The Works of Samuel de Champlain*, 6 vols. Toronto: The Champlain Society, 1922–36.

———, ed. *The Voyages of Jacques Cartier*. Ottawa: Acland, 1924.

Birket-Smith, Kaj. *Eskimos*. Copenhagen: Rhodos, 1971.

Bishop, Charles. 'The Henley House Massacres', *The Beaver* Outfit 307 (1976): 36–41.

Bitterli, Urs. *Cultures in Conflict: Encounters between European and Non-European Cultures, 1492–1800*, tr. Ritchie Robertson. London: Polity Press, 1989. (First published in German, 1986.)

Black-Rogers, Mary. 'Varieties of "Starving": Semantics and Survival in the Subarctic Fur Trade, 1750–1850', *Ethnohistory* 33, 4 (1986): 353–83.

Blondin, George. *When the World Was New: Stories of the Sahtú Dene*. Yellowknife: Cutcrop, the Northern Publisher, 1990.

———. *Yamoria the Lawmaker: Stories of the Dene*. Edmonton: NeWest Press, 1991.

Boas, Franz. 'Chinook Songs', *Journal of American Folk-Lore* 1 (1888): 220–6.

Bockstoce, John R. *Whales, Ice, and Men: The History of Whaling in the Western Arctic*. Seattle: University of Washington Press, 1986.

Bodley, John H., ed. *Tribal Peoples and Development Issues: A Global Overview*. Mountain View, Calif.: Mayfield Publishers, 1988.

Boldt, Menno. 'Social Correlates of Nationalism: A Study of Native Indian Leaders in a Canadian Internal Colony', *Comparative Political Studies* 14, 2 (1981): 205–31.

———. *Surviving as Indians*. Toronto: University of Toronto Press, 1993.

Bolus, Malvina, ed. *People and Pelts: Selected Papers of the Second North American Fur Trade Conference*. Winnipeg: Peguis, 1972.

Bone, Robert M. *The Regional Geography of Canada*, 4th edn. Toronto: Oxford University Press, 2008.

———. *The Geography of the Canadian North: Issues and Challenges*, 3rd edn. Toronto: Oxford University Press, 2009.

Bowden, Henry Warner. *American Indians and Christian Missions*. Chicago: University of Chicago Press, 1981.

Boyd, W.C. *Genetics and the Races of Man: An Introduction to Modern Physical Anthropology*. Boston: Little, Brown, 1950.

Brass, Eleanor. 'The File Hills Ex-Pupil Colony', *Saskatchewan History* 6, 2 (1953): 66–9.

———. *I Walk in Two Worlds*. Calgary: Glenbow Museum, 1987.

Brasser, T.J. *Blackfoot*. Ottawa: National Museum of Canada, Canada's Visual History, vol. 46, n.d.

Brebner, J.B. 'Subsidized Intermarriage with the Indians', *Canadian Historical Review* 6, 1 (1925): 33–6.

Bridges, Patricia S. 'Changes in Activities with the Shift to Agriculture in the Southeastern United States', *Current Anthropology* 30, 3 (1989): 385–94.

Brightman, Robert. *Grateful Prey*. Berkeley: University of California Press, 1993.

Bringhurst, Robert. *A Story as Sharp as a Knife*. Vancouver: Douglas & McIntyre, 1999.

Brink, Jack, and Bob Dawe. *Final Report of the 1985 and 1986 Field Season at Head-Smashed-In Buffalo Jump*. Edmonton: Archaeological Survey of Alberta No. 16, 1989.

Brody, Hugh. *People's Land: Eskimos and Whites in the Eastern Arctic*. Harmondsworth, England: Penguin, 1975.

———. *Maps and Dreams*. Vancouver: Douglas & McIntyre, 1988. (First published 1981.)

Brown, D.H. 'The Meaning of Treason in 1885', *Saskatchewan History* 28, 2 (1975): 65–73.

Brown, George, and Ron Maguire, eds. *Indian Treaties in Historical Perspective*. Ottawa: Indian and Northern Affairs, 1979.

Brown, Jennifer S.H. *Strangers in Blood: Fur Trade Company Families in Indian Country*. Vancouver: University of British Columbia Press, 1980.

———. 'The Track to Heaven: The Hudson Bay Cree Religious Movement of 1842–1843', in William Cowan, ed., *Papers of the Thirteenth Algonquian Conference*. Ottawa: Carleton University, 1982.

Brown, Michael H. *The Search for Eve: Have Scientists Found the Mother of Us All?* New York: Harper & Row, 1990.

Brunton, Ron. 'The Cultural Instability of Egalitarian Societies', *Man* 24, 4 (1989): 673–81.

Bryan, Alan Lyle, ed. *Early Man in America from a Circum-Pacific Perspective*. Edmonton: Archaeological Researches International, 1978.

Buckley, T.C., ed. *Rendezvous: Selected Papers of the Fur Trade Conference 1981*. St Paul: Minnesota Historical Society, 1984.

Burpee, L.J., ed. *Journals and Letters by Pierre Gaulthier de Varennes et de La Vérendrye*. Toronto: The Champlain Society, 1927.

Burrage, Henry Sweetser, ed. *Early English and French Voyages, Chiefly from Hakluyt, 1534–1608*. New York: Barnes and Noble, 1952.

Burt, A.L. 'A New Approach to the Problems of the Western Posts', *Canadian Historical Association Report* (1931): 61–95.

Bussidor, Ila, and Üstün Bilgen-Reinart. *Night Spirits: The Story of the Relocation of the Sayisi Dene*. Winnipeg: University of Manitoba Press, 1997.

Byers, Douglas S., and Richard S. MacNeish, eds. *The Prehistory of Teohuacan Valley*, 5 vols. Austin: University of Texas Press, 1967–72.

Caffee, Nathaniel M., and Thomas A. Kirby, eds. *Studies for William A. Read*. Baton Rouge: Louisiana State University Press, 1940.

Cail, Robert. *Land, Man, and the Law: The Disposal of Crown Lands in British Columbia, 1871–1913*. Vancouver: University of British Columbia Press, 1974.

Cairns, Alan C. *Aboriginal Peoples and the Canadian State*. Vancouver: University of British Columbia Press, 2000.

Caldwell, Warren W., ed. *The Northwestern Plains: A Symposium*. Billings, Mont.: Center for Indian Studies, Rocky Mountain College, 1968.

Caley, Peter. 'Canada's Chinese Columbus', *The Beaver* Outfit 313, 4 (1983): 4–11.

Calloway, Colin G. *Crown and Calumet: British–Indian Relations, 1783–1815*. Norman: University of Oklahoma Press, 1987.

———. *The Western Abenakis of Vermont, 1600–1800*. Norman: University of Oklahoma Press, 1990.

Campbell, Maria. *Halfbreed*. Toronto: McClelland & Stewart, 1973.

Campeau, Lucien. *La Mission des Jésuites chez les Hurons 1634–1650*. Montréal: Bellarmin, 1987.

'A Canadian Tragedy', *Maclean's* 99, 28 (14 July 1986).

Capoeman, Pauline K., ed. *Land of the Quinault*. Taholah, Wash.: Quinault Indian Nation, 1990.

Cardinal, Harold. *The Unjust Society: The Tragedy of Canada's Indians*. Edmonton: Hurtig, 1969.

———. *The Rebirth of Canada's Indians*. Edmonton: Hurtig, 1977.

Carnaghan, Matthew, and Allison Goody. *Canadian Arctic Sovereignty*. Ottawa: Library of Parliament, Jan. 2006. At: <www.parl.gc.ca/info/library/PRB pubs/prb0561-e.htm>.

Carter, George F. 'Chinese Contacts with America: Fu Sang Again', *Anthropological Journal of Canada* 14, 1 (1976): 10–24.

Carter, Sarah A. 'Controlling Indian Movement: The Pass System', *NeWest Review* (May 1985): 8–9.

———. *Lost Harvests: Prairie Indian Reserve Farmers and Government Policy*. Montreal and Kingston: McGill-Queen's University Press, 1990.

———. *Aboriginal People and Colonizers of Western Canada to 1900*. Toronto: University of Toronto Press, 1999.

Casgrain, H.R. 'Coup d'oeil sur l'Acadie', *Le Canada Français* 1 (1888): 116–17.

Cassidy, Frank, ed. *Aboriginal Self-Determination: Proceedings of a conference held September 30–October 3, 1990*. Toronto: Oolichan Books and Institute for Research on Public Policy, 1991.

——— and Robert L. Bish. *Indian Government: Its Meaning in Practice*. Halifax and Lantzville, BC: Oolichan Books, 1989.

Cayet, Pierre-Victor. *Chronologie septenaire de l'Histoire de la Paix entre les Roys de France et d'Espagne*, 2 vols. Paris: J. Richer, 1605.

Chamberlin, J.E. *The Harrowing of Eden: White Attitudes toward North American Natives*. Toronto: Fitzhenry & Whiteside, 1975.

Chang, Kuang-chih. 'Radiocarbon Dates from China: Some Initial Interpretations', *Current Anthropology* 14, 5 (1973): 525–8.

Charest, Paul. 'Les barrages hydro-électriques en territories montagnais et leurs effets sur les communautés amérindiennes', *Recherches amérindiennes au Québec* 9, 4 (1980): 323–37.

Charland, Thomas. *Histoire des Abénakis d'Odanak (1675–1937)*. Montréal: Lévrier, 1964.

Charlevoix, Pierre-François-Xavier de. *Histoire et description générale de la Nouvelle France*, 3 vols. Paris: Giffart, 1744. (In English, 1866–72.)

Charney, Ann. 'The Last Indian War', *The Idler* No. 29 (July–Aug. 1990): 14–22.

Chartrand, Paul L.A.H. *Manitoba's Métis Settlement Scheme of 1870*. Saskatoon: Native Law Centre, University of Saskatchewan, 1991.

Chaunu, Pierre. *L'Amérique et les Amériques*. Paris: Armand Colin, 1964.

Chiapelli, Fredi, ed. *First Images of America: The Impact of the New World on the Old*, 2 vols. Berkeley: University of California Press, 1976.

Childe, V.G. *Man Makes Himself*. New York: Mentor Books, 1951. (First published, London, 1936.)

Christy, Miller. *The Voyages of Captain Luke Foxe of Hull, and Captain Thomas James of Bristol, in search of a North-West Passage, in 1631–32*, 2 vols. London: Hakluyt Society, 1894.

Chute, Janet. *The Legacy of Shingwakonse*. Toronto: University of Toronto Press, 1998.

Cinq-Mars, Jacques. 'La place des grottes du Poisson-Bleu dans la préhistoire beringienne', *Revista de Arqueología Americana* 1 (1990): 9–32.

Citizens Plus, text reproduced in *The First Citizen* 7 (June 1970).

Clark, Bruce A. *Indian Title in Canada*. Toronto: Carswell, 1987.

———. *Native Liberty, Crown Sovereignty*. Montreal and Kingston: McGill-Queen's University Press, 1990.

———. *Justice in Paradise*. Montreal and Kingston: McGill-Queen's University Press, 2000.

Clerici, Naila. 'The Spirit Still Sings at Lubicon Lake: Indian Rights in Canada, a Case Study', *Proceedings of the 7th International Convention of Canadian Studies*. Catania, Italy, 1988.

Clermont, Norman. 'Why Did the St. Lawrence Iroquois Become Agriculturalists?', *Man in the Northeast* 40 (1990): 75–9.

Coates, Kenneth S. 'Best Left as Indians: The Federal Government and the Indians of the Yukon, 1894–1950', *Canadian Journal of Native Studies/La revue canadienne des études autochtones* 4, 2 (1984): 179–204.

———. *Best Left as Indians: Native–White Relations in the Yukon Territory, 1840–1973.* Montreal and Kingston: McGill-Queen's University Press, 1993.

———, ed. *Aboriginal Land Claims in Canada.* Toronto: Copp Clark Pitman, 1992.

——— and William R. Morrison, eds. *Land of the Midnight Sun: A History of the Yukon.* Edmonton: Hurtig, 1988.

——— and ———, eds. *For Purposes of Dominion.* Toronto: Captus University Publications, 1989.

——— and Judith Powell. *The Modern North: People, Politics, and the Rejection of Colonialism.* Toronto: James Lorimer, 1989.

Coderre, Helen. *Fighting with Property: A Study of Kwakiutl Potlatching and Warfare, 1792–1930.* New York: Augustin, American Ethnological Society Monograph #18, 1950.

Coles, John M. 'The World's Oldest Road', *Scientific American* 201, 5 (1989): 100–6.

Comeau, Pauline. *Elijah: No Ordinary Hero.* Vancouver: Douglas & McIntyre, 1993.

——— and Aldo Santin. *The First Canadians: A Profile of Canada's Native People Today.* Toronto: James Lorimer, 1990.

Connolly, Bob, and Robin Anderson. *First Contact: New Guinea Highlanders Encounter the Outside World.* London: Penguin, 1988.

Cook, Ramsay, ed. *The Voyages of Jacques Cartier.* Toronto: University of Toronto Press, 1993.

Cooper, Barry. 'Alexander Kennedy Isbister: A Respectable Victorian', *Canadian Ethnic Studies/Études ethniques au Canada* 17, 2 (1985): 44–63.

Cooper, John M. *Snares, Deadfalls, and Other Traps of the Northern Algonquians and Northern Athapaskans.* Washington: Catholic University of America, 1938.

Copway, George. *Life, History and Travels of Kah-ge-ga-gah-bowh.* Philadelphia: James Harmstead, 1847.

———, or Kah-ge-ga-gah-bowh, chief of the Ojibway Nation. *The Traditional History and Characteristic Sketches of the Ojibway Nation.* London: Charles Gilpin, 1850.

Coues, Elliott, ed. *New Light on the Early History of the Great Northwest 1799–1814*, 3 vols. New York: Harper, 1897.

Creighton, Donald. *John A. Macdonald*, 2 vols. Toronto: Macmillan, 1966. (First published 1955.)

Crerar, Duff, and Jaroslav Petryshyn, eds. *Treaty 8 Revisited: Selected Papers on the 1999 Centennial Conference.* Grande Prairie, Alta: Lobstick Editorial Collective, 2000.

Cressman, L.S. *Prehistory of the Far West: Homes of Vanquished Peoples.* Salt Lake City: University of Utah Press, 1977.

Crosby, Thomas. *Up and Down the Pacific Coast by Canoe and Mission Ship.* Toronto: Missionary Society of the Methodist Church, 1914.

Crowe, Keith J. *A History of the Original Peoples of Northern Canada.* Montreal and Kingston: McGill-Queen's University Press, 1974.

Cruikshank, Julie. *Life Lived Like a Story: Life Stories of Three Yukon Elders.* Vancouver: University of British Columbia Press, 1990.

———. *Reading Voices: Dän Dhá Ts'edenintth'é. Oral and Written Interpretations of the Yukon's Past.* Vancouver: Douglas & McIntyre, 1991.

———. 'Oral Tradition and Oral History: Reviewing Some Issues', *Canadian Historical Review* 75, 3 (Sept. 1994).

——— and Jim Robb. *Their Own Yukon.* Whitehorse: Yukon Indian Cultural Education Society and Yukon Native Brotherhood, 1975.

Csonka, Yvon. *Collections arctiques.* Neuchâtel, Switzerland: Musée d'Ethnologie, 1988.

Culture Change in the Northern Plains: 1000 B.C.–A.D. 1000. Edmonton: Archaeological Survey of Alberta, Occasional Papers No. 20, 1983.

Cumming, Peter A., and Neil H. Mickenberg, eds. *Native Rights in Canada.* Toronto: General Publishing, 1972. (First published 1970.)

Dacks, Gurston. *A Choice of Futures: Politics in the Canadian North.* Toronto: Methuen, 1981.

Daniel, Richard C. *A History of Native Claims Processes in Canada 1867–1979.* Ottawa: Department of Indian and Northern Affairs, 1980.

Daniels, Dorothy. 'Metis Identity: A Personal Perspective', *Native Studies Review* 3, 2 (1987): 7–15.

Daugherty, Wayne E. *Maritime Indian Treaties in Perspective.* Ottawa: Indian and Northern Affairs Canada, 1983.

——— and Dennis Madill. *Indian Government under Indian Act Legislation 1868–1951.* Ottawa: Indian and Northern Affairs, 1980.

Davies, Nigel. *Voyagers to the New World.* Albuquerque: University of New Mexico Press, 1979.

Davis, L.B., and R.O.K. Reeves. *Hunters of the Recent Past.* London: Unwin Hyman, 1990.

Davis, Nancy Yaw. *The Zuni Enigma.* New York: Norton, 2000.

Davis, Richard C., ed. *Rupert's Land: A Cultural Tapestry.* Calgary: Calgary Institute for the Humanities, 1988.

Day, Gordon. 'English–Indian Contacts in New England', *Ethnohistory* 9 (1962): 24–40.

Dearden, Philip, and Steve Langdon. 'Aboriginal Peoples and National Parks', in Dearden and Rick Rollins, eds, *Parks and Protected Areas in Canada*, 3rd edn. Toronto: Oxford University Press, 2009: ch. 14.

De'Ath, Colin, and Gregory Michalenko. 'High Technology and Original Peoples: The Case of Deforestation in Papua New Guinea and Canada', in John H. Bodley, ed., *Tribal Peoples and Development Issues*. Mountain View, Calif.: Mayfield Publishing, 1988: 166–80.

Deer, Kenneth. 'Our Native Rights Stance Is a Foreign Policy Failure', *Embassy: Canada's Foreign Policy Newsweekly*, 21 Nov. 2007, at: <www.embassy-mag.ca/html/index.php?display=story&full_path=/2007/november/21/deer/>.

Delâge, Denys. *Le pays renversé: Amérindiens et européens en Amérique du nord-est, 1600–1664*. Montréal: Boréal Express, 1985. In English: *Bitter Feast: Amerindians and Europeans in Northeastern North America, 1600–64*, tr. Jane Brierly. Vancouver: University of British Columbia Press, 1993.

———. 'Les iroquois chrétiens des "réductions", 1667–1770. I—Migration et rapports avec les Français', *Recherches amérindiennes au Québec* 21, 1–2 (1991): 59–70.

Dempsey, Hugh A. *Crowfoot, Chief of the Blackfeet*. Edmonton: Hurtig, 1972.

———. *Charcoal's World*. Saskatoon: Western Producer, 1978.

———. *Big Bear: The End of Freedom*. Vancouver: Douglas & McIntyre, 1984.

———. *The Gentle Persuader: A Biography of James Gladstone, Indian Senator*. Saskatoon: Western Producer, 1986.

———. *Indian Tribes of Alberta*. Calgary: Glenbow-Alberta Institute, 1986. (1st edn, 1978.)

Dempsey, James. 'Problems of Western Canadian Indian War Veterans after World War One', *Native Studies Review* 5, 2 (1989): 1–18.

Denig, Edward Thompson. *Five Indian Tribes of the Upper Missouri*, ed. John C. Ewers. Norman: University of Oklahoma Press, 1961.

Denys, Nicholas. *The Description and Natural History of the Coasts of North America (Acadia)*, ed. William F. Ganong. Toronto: The Champlain Society, 1908.

Desrosier, Leo-Paul. *Iroquoisie*. Montréal: Les Études de l'Institut d'Histoire de l'Amérique Française, 1947.

Désveaux, Emmanuel. *Sous le signe de l'ours*. Paris: Éditions de la Maison des Sciences de l'Homme, 1988.

Dewdney, Selwyn. *The Sacred Scrolls of the Southern Ojibway*. Toronto: University of Toronto Press, 1975.

———. 'Birth of a Cree–Ojibway Style of Contemporary Art', in Getty and Smith, eds, *One Century Later*.

Diamond, Billy. 'Villages of the Dammed', *Arctic Circle* 1, 3 (1990): 24–30.

Diamond, Jared M. 'The Talk of the Americas', *Nature* 344 (1990): 589–90.

Diamond, Stanley, ed. *Culture in History*. New York: Columbia University Press, 1960.

Dickason, Olive Patricia. 'Louisbourg and the Indians: A Study in Imperial Race Relations, 1713–1760', *History and Archaeology* 6 (1976): 1–206.

———. 'A Historical Reconstruction for the Northwestern Plains', *Prairie Forum* 5, 1 (1980): 19–27.

———. 'From "One Nation" in the Northeast to "New Nation" in the Northwest: A Look at the Emergence of the Metis', *American Indian Culture and Research Journal* 6, 2 (1982): 1–21.

———. *The Myth of the Savage and the Beginnings of French Colonialism in the Americas*. Edmonton: University of Alberta Press, 1984.

———. 'Three Worlds, One Focus: Europeans and Amerindians in the Far North', in Richard C. Davis, ed., *Rupert's Land: A Cultural Tapestry*. Waterloo, Ont.: Wilfrid Laurier University Press for the Calgary Institute for the Humanities, 1986: 51–78.

———. 'Amerindians between French and English in Nova Scotia, 1713–1763', *American Indian Culture and Research Journal* 20, 4 (1986): 31–56.

———. 'The French and the Abenaki: A Study in Frontier Politics', *Vermont History* 58, 2 (1990): 82–98.

Dickinson, John A. 'La guerre iroquoise et la mortalité en Nouvelle-France, 1608–1666', *Revue d'histoire de l'Amérique française* 36, 1 (1982): 31–47.

———. 'Les Amérindiens et les débuts de la Nouvelle-France', *6e Convegno Internazionale di studi canadesi*. Selva di Fasano: Biblioteca della Ricerca Cultura Straniera 13, 1985. Sezione III.

Diéreville, Sieur de. *Relation of the Voyage to Port Royal in Acadia or New France*, ed. John C. Webster. Toronto: The Champlain Society, 1933.

Dikov, Nikolai N. 'On the Road to America', *Natural History* 97, 1 (1988): 10–14.

Dillehay, Tom D. 'The Great Debate on the First Americans', *Anthropology Today* 7, 4 (1991): 12–13.

Dion, Joseph F. *My Tribe the Crees*. Calgary: Glenbow Museum, 1979.

Diubaldo, Richard J. *Stefansson and the Canadian Arctic*. Montreal and Kingston: McGill-Queen's University Press, 1978.

———. 'The Absurd Little Mouse: When Eskimos Became Indians', *Journal of Canadian Studies* 16, 2 (1981): 34–40.

———. *The Government of Canada and the Inuit, 1900–1967*. Ottawa: Indian and Northern Affairs Canada, 1985.

Dixon, Joseph K. *The Vanishing Race: The Last Great Indian Council*. Garden City, NY: Doubleday, 1913.

Dobbin, Murray. *The One-and-a-Half Men*. Vancouver: New Star Books, 1981.

Dobbs, Arthur. *An Account of the Countries adjoining to Hudson's Bay*. London, 1744. (Reprint, New York: Johnson, 1967.)

Dobyns, Henry F. *Their Number Become Thinned: Native American Population Dynamics in Eastern North America*. Knoxville: University of Tennessee Press, 1983.

Doll, Maurice F.V., Robert S. Kidd, and John P. Day. *The Buffalo Lake Métis Site: A Late Nineteenth Century Settlement in the Parkland of Central Alberta*. Edmonton: Provincial Museum of Alberta, 1988.

Dollier de Casson, François. *A History of Montreal 1640–1672*, tr. and ed. Ralph Flenley. London: Dent, 1928. (First published 1868.)

Driver, Harold E. *Indians of North America*. Chicago: University of Chicago Press, 1970. (First published 1961; revised 1969.)

Du Boscq de Beaumont, Gaston, comp. and ed. *Les derniers jours de l'Acadie (1748–1758)*. Paris: E. Lechevalier, 1899.

Duff, Wilson. *The Indian History of British Columbia: vol. 1, The Impact of the White Man*. Victoria: Provincial Museum of Natural History and Anthropology, 1964.

Dufresne, Robert. *Canada's Legal Claims over Arctic Territory and Waters*. Ottawa: Library of Parliament, 6 Dec. 2007. At: <www.parl.gc.ca/information/library/PRBpubs/prb0739-e.htm>.

Dunning, R.W. 'Indian Policy—A Proposal for Autonomy', *Canadian Forum* 49 (Dec. 1969): 206–7.

Dyck, Noel, ed. *Indigenous Peoples and the Nation-State: 'Fourth World' Politics in Canada, Australia and Norway*. St John's: Memorial University of Newfoundland, 1985.

Eber, Dorothy. *People from Our Side: An Inuit Record of Seekooseelak—the Land of the People of Cape Dorset, Baffin Island*. Edmonton: Hurtig, 1973.

Eastman, Mary H. *The American Aboriginal Portfolio*. Philadelphia: Lippincott, 1853.

Eccles, W.J. *Frontenac the Courtier Governor*. Toronto: McClelland & Stewart, 1959.

———. *Canada under Louis XIV 1663–1701*. Toronto: McClelland & Stewart, 1964.

———. *The Canadian Frontier 1534–1760*. Toronto: Holt, Rinehart and Winston, 1969.

———. *France in America*. New York: Harper & Row, 1972.

Edmunds, R. David. *The Shawnee Prophet*. Lincoln: University of Nebraska Press, 1983.

———. *Tecumseh and the Quest for Indian Leadership*. Boston: Little, Brown, 1984.

Eid, Leroy V. 'The Ojibway–Iroquois War: The War the Five Nations Did Not Win', *Ethnohistory* 17, 4 (1979): 297–324.

Eliade, Mircea. *Gods, Goddesses, and Myths of Creation*. New York: Harper & Row, 1974.

Elias, Peter Douglas. *The Dakota of the Canadian Northwest: Lessons for Survival*. Winnipeg: University of Manitoba Press, 1988.

Elliott, David W. 'Aboriginal Title', in Morse, ed., *Aboriginal Peoples and the Law*.

Emerson, Thomas E., and R. Barry Lewis, eds. *Cahokia and the Hinterlands*. Urbana: University of Illinois Press, 1990.

Estabrook, Barry. 'Bone Age Man', *Equinox* 1, 2 (1982): 84–96.

Evans, Allen Roy. *Reindeer Trek*. Toronto: McClelland & Stewart, 1935.

Ewers, John C., ed. *The Horse in Blackfoot Indian Culture*. Washington: Smithsonian Institution, 1955.

———, ed. *Five Indian Tribes of the Upper Missouri*. Norman: University of Oklahoma Press, 1961.

Fagan, Brian M. *The Great Journey*. London: Thames and Hudson, 1987.

Fairweather, Joan G. *A Common Hunger: Land Rights in Canada and South Africa*. Calgary: University of Calgary Press, 2006.

Fardy, B.D. *Jerry Potts, Paladin of the Plains*. Langley, BC: Mr. Paperback, 1984.

Federation of Saskatchewan Indians. *Indian Treaty Rights*. n.d.

Feest, Christian, ed. *Indians and Europe*. Aachen: Rader Verlag, 1987.

Fenwick, Fred R. 'First Nations Governance Act', *Law Now* 27, 3 (Dec. 2003).

Fiedel, Stuart J. *Prehistory of the Americas*. Cambridge: Cambridge University Press, 1987.

Fisher, Robert L. 'The Western Prologue to the War of 1812', *Missouri Historical Review* 30, 3 (1936): 267–81.

Fisher, Robin. 'Joseph Trutch and Indian Land Policy', *B.C. Studies* 12 (1971–2): 3–33.

———. *Contact and Conflict: Indian–European Relations in British Columbia 1774–1890*. Vancouver:

University of British Columbia Press, 1977.

Fitzhugh, William W., and Aron Crowell, eds. *Crossroads of Continents: Cultures of Siberia and Alaska*. Washington: Smithsonian Institution, 1988.

Fladmark, Knut R. *British Columbia Prehistory*. Ottawa: National Museums of Canada, 1986.

———. 'The First Americans: Getting One's Berings', *Natural History* (Nov. 1986): 8–19.

Flanagan, Thomas. *Louis 'David' Riel, Prophet of the New World*. Toronto: University of Toronto Press, 1979.

———. *Riel and the Rebellion: 1885 Reconsidered*. Saskatoon: Western Producer Prairie Books, 1983.

———. *First Nations? Second Thoughts*. Montreal and Kingston: McGill-Queen's University Press, 2000.

Flannery, Regina. *The Gros Ventres of Montana. Part I: Social Life*. Anthropological Series #15. Washington: Catholic University of America Press, 1953.

Forbis, Richard G. *A Review of Alberta Archaeology to 1964*. Ottawa: National Museum of Canada, 1970.

Foster, Hamar. 'Long-Distance Justice: The Criminal Jurisdiction of Canadian Courts West of the Canadas, 1763–1859', *American Journal of Legal History* 34, 1 (1990): 1–48.

Foster, Mary LeCron, and Lucy Jane Botscharow, eds. *The Life of Symbols*. Boulder, Colo.: Westview Press, 1990.

Fournier, Suzanne, and Ernie Crey. *Stolen from Our Embrace: The Abduction of First Nations Children and the Restoration of Aboriginal Communities*. Vancouver: Douglas & McIntyre, 1997.

Fowler, Melvin. *The Cahokia Atlas*. Springfield, Ill.: Illinois Historic Preservation Agency, 1989.

Franchère, Gabriel. *Journal of a Voyage to the Northwest Coast of North America during the Years 1811, 1812, 1813, and 1814*, ed. W. Kaye Lamb. Toronto: The Champlain Society, 1969.

Francis, Daniel, and Toby Morantz. *Partners in Furs: A History of the Fur Trade in Eastern James Bay 1600–1870*. Montreal and Kingston: McGill-Queen's University Press, 1983.

Francis, R. Douglas, Richard Jones, and Donald B. Smith. *Origins: Canadian History to Confederation*, and *Destinies: Canadian History Since Confederation*. Toronto: Holt, Rinehart and Winston, 1988. (2nd edn, 1992.)

Francoli, Paco. 'Showdown on Governance Act Expected', *Hill Times* 685 (5 May 2003): 3–4.

Fraser, William B. 'Big Bear, Indian Patriot', *Alberta Historical Review* 14, 2 (1966): 1–13.

Freeman, Milton M.R. 'Ethos, Economics and Prestige, a Re-Examination of Netsilik Eskimo Infanticide', in *Vernhandlungen des XXXVIII. Internationalen Amerikanistenkongresses II*. Stuttgart-München, 1968.

———. 'Patrons, Leaders and Values in an Eskimo Settlement', paper presented at the symposium, The Contemporary Cultural Situation of the Northern Forest Indians of North America and the Eskimo of North America and Greenland, in *Vernhandlungen des XXXVIII. Internationalen Amerikanistenkongresses II*. Stuttgart-München, 1968.

———. 'Tradition and Change: Problems and Persistence in the Inuit Diet', in I. de Garine and G.A. Harrison, eds, *Coping with Uncertainty in Food Supply*. Oxford: Clarendon Press, 1988.

Freeman, Minnie Aodla. *Life among the Qalunaat*. Edmonton: Hurtig, 1978.

Frideres, James S. *Native People in Canada: Contemporary Conflicts*. Scarborough, Ont.: Prentice-Hall, 1983. (1st edn, 1974.)

Friesen, Gerald. *The Canadian Prairies: A History*. Toronto: University of Toronto Press, 1984.

Friesen, Jean. 'Magnificent Gifts: The Treaties of Canada with the Indians of the Northwest 1869–70', *Transactions of the Royal Society of Canada* ser. 5, 1 (1986): 41–51.

Fry, Alan. *How a People Die*. Toronto: Doubleday, 1970.

Fumoleau, René. *As Long As This Land Shall Last*. Toronto: McClelland & Stewart, 1973.

Gaffen, Fred. *Forgotten Soldiers*. Penticton, BC: Theytus Books, 1985.

Galinat, Walton C. 'The Origin of Maize', *Annual Review of Genetics* 5 (1971): 447–78.

Garcia, Albert. *La découverte et la conquête du Pérou d'après les sources originales*. Paris: Klincksieck, 1975.

Garratt, John G. *The Four Indian Kings*. Ottawa: Public Archives of Canada, 1985.

Gatehouse, Jonathon. 'Residential Schools Cash Draws Closer', *Maclean's*, 16 Apr. 2007, at: <www.macleans.ca/homepage/magazine/article.jsp?content=20070416_104189_104189>.

Gates, Lillian F. *Land Policies of Upper Canada*. Toronto: University of Toronto Press, 1968.

Geographic Board of Canada. *Handbook of Indians of Canada*. Ottawa, 1913.

George, Chief Dan, and Helmut Hirnschall. *My Heart Soars*. Vancouver: Hancock House, 1974.

George, Jane. 'Nunavik Leaders Celebrate First Quebec Payout', *Nunatsiaq News*, 21 June 2002, at: <www.nunatsiaq.com/archives/nunavut020621/news/nunavik/20621_1.html>.

Gérin, Léon. 'La Seigneurie de Sillery et les Hurons', *Mémoires de la Société Royale du Canada* ser. 2, 6 (1900): sec. 1, 75–115.

Gessell, Paul. 'Artist dies', *Ottawa Citizen*, 4 Dec. 2007, at: <www.canada.com/ottawacitizen/news/story.html?id=510196db-b058-44f4-a555-8e5405d239ed&k=46459>.

Getty, Ian A.L., and Antoine S. Lussier, eds. *As Long As the Sun Shines and Water Flows*. Vancouver: University of British Columbia Press, 1983.

——— and Donald B. Smith, eds. *One Century Later: Western Canadian Reserve Indians Since Treaty 7*. Vancouver: University of British Columbia Press, 1978.

Ghere, David L. 'Mistranslations and Misinformation: Diplomacy on the Maine Frontier, 1725 to 1755', *American Indian Culture and Research Journal* 8, 4 (1984): 3–26.

Gibson, Arrell Morgan. *The American Indian: Prehistory to the Present*. Lexington, Mass.: D.C. Heath, 1980.

Gilman, Rhoda R., Carolyn Gilman, and Deborah M. Stultz. *The Red River Trails: Oxcart Routes between St. Paul and the Selkirk Settlement 1820–1870*. St Paul: Minnesota Historical Society, 1979.

Girard, Michel F. *Étude historique sur la forêt du village d'Oka*. Québec: Ministère de l'environnement, 1990.

———. 'La crise d'Oka à la lumière de l'écologie historique', *NHSG Newsletter* (Oct. 1990): 4–8.

———. *Histoire de la Louisianne française*, 2 vols. Paris: Presses Universitaires de France, 1953–8.

———. 'The Western Metis after the Insurrection', *Saskatchewan History* 9, 1 (1956): 1–15.

———. *The Métis in the Canadian West*, 2 vols, tr. George Woodcock. Edmonton: University of Alberta Press, 1986.

Glover, Richard, ed. *David Thompson's Narrative 1784–1812*. Toronto: The Champlain Society, 1962.

Godelier, Maurice. 'Infrastructures, Societies and History', *Current Anthropology* 19, 4 (1978): 763–71.

Goldring, Philip. 'Whiskey, Horses and Death: The Cypress Hills Massacre and its Sequel', *Occasional Papers in Archaeology and History* No. 21. Ottawa: National Historic Sites Service, 1973.

Gonzalez, Ellice B. *Changing Economic Role for Micmac Men and Women: An Ethnohistorical Analysis*. Ottawa: National Museum of Man, 1981.

Gooderham, George H. 'The Gypsy Indians and the Last Treaty', *Alberta History* 34 (1980): 15–19.

Goodman, Jeffrey. *American Genesis*. New York: Summit Books, 1981.

Gough, Barry M. *Gunboat Frontier: British Maritime Authority and Northwest Coast Indians, 1846–1890*. Vancouver: University of British Columbia Press, 1984.

Goulet, Jean-Guy. 'Religious Dualism among Athapaskan Catholics', *Canadian Journal of Anthropology/Revue Canadienne d'Anthropologie* 3, 1 (1982): 1–18.

Grabowski, Jan. 'Mohawk Crisis at Kanesatake and Kahnawake', *European Review of Native American Studies* 5, 1 (1991): 11–14.

Gradie, Charlotte M. 'Spanish Jesuits in Virginia: The Mission That Failed', *Virginia Magazine of History and Biography* 96, 2 (1988): 131–56.

Grant, John Webster. *Moon of Wintertime: Missionaries and the Indians of Canada in Encounter since 1534*. Toronto: University of Toronto Press, 1984.

Grant, Shelagh D. 'Indian Affairs under Duncan Campbell Scott: The Plains Cree of Saskatchewan, 1913–1931', *Journal of Canadian Studies* 18, 3 (1983): 21–39.

———. *Sovereignty or Security? Government Policy in the Canadian North, 1936–1950*. Vancouver: University of British Columbia Press, 1988.

Graymont, Barbara. *The Iroquois in the American Revolution*. Syracuse, NY: Syracuse University Press, 1972.

Green, L.C., and Olive P. Dickason. *The Law of Nations and the New World*. Edmonton: University of Alberta Press, 1989.

Greenberg, Joseph H. *Language in the Americas*. Stanford, Calif.: Stanford University Press, 1987.

———, C.G. Turner II, and S.L. Zegura. 'The Settlement of the Americas: A Comparison of the Linguistic, Dental, and Genetic Evidence', *Current Anthropology* 27, 4 (1986): 477–97.

Greenman, E.F. 'Upper Paleolithic in the New World', *Current Anthropology* 3 (1962): 41–91.

Greenwald, Barry. *Between Two Worlds*. Ottawa: National Film Board, 1990.

Grieder, Terry. *Art and Archaeology in Pashash*. Austin: University of Texas Press, 1979.

Grinnell, George Bird. *The Story of the Indians*. New York: Appleton, 1911.

Gruhn, Ruth. 'Linguistic Evidence in Support of the Coastal Route of Earliest Entry into the New World', *Man* (new ser.) 23, 2 (1988): 77–100.

Guidon, Niède, 'Cliff Notes', *Natural History* 96, 8 (1987): 6–12.

——— and G. Delibrias. 'Carbon-14 Dates Point to Man in the Americas 32,000 Years Ago', *Nature* 321 (1986): 769–71.

Gullick, C.J.M.R. *Myths of a Minority*. Assen: Van Gorcum, 1985.

Gunnerson, Dolores A. 'Man and Bison on the Plains

in the Protohistoric Period', *Plains Anthropologist* 17, 55 (1972): 1–10.

Haig-Brown, Celia. *Resistance and Renewal: Surviving the Indian Residential School*. Vancouver: Tillacum Library, 1988.

Hakluyt, Richard. *The Principal Navigations, Voyages, Traffiques and Discoveries of the English Nation*, 12 vols. Glasgow: James MacLehose, 1903–5.

Haliburton, Thomas C. *An Historical and Statistical Account of Nova Scotia*, 2 vols. Halifax: Joseph Howe, 1829.

Hall, Charles Francis. *Arctic Researches and Life among the Esquimaux*. New York: Harper, 1865.

Hall, David J. '"A Serene Atmosphere"? Treaty 1 Revisited', *Canadian Journal of Native Studies* 4, 2 (1984): 321–58.

Hallowell, A. Irving. *Culture and Experience*. Philadelphia: University of Pennsylvania Press, 1975.

———. *Contributions to Anthropology*. Chicago: University of Chicago Press, 1976.

Hamelin, Louis-Edmond. *Canadian Nordicity: It's Your North Too*, tr. W. Barr. Montreal: Harvest House, 1979.

Hamell, George. 'Strawberries, Floating Islands, and Rabbit Captains: Mythical Realities and European Contact in the Northeast during the Sixteenth and Seventeenth Centuries', *Journal of Canadian Studies* 21, 4 (1987): 72–94.

Hamilton, John David. *Arctic Revolution*. Toronto: Dundurn Press, 1994.

Handbook of North American Indians, general ed., William C. Sturtevant, Washington: Smithsonian Institution, 1978–; vol. 4, *History of Indian–White Relations*, ed. Wilcomb E. Washburn, 1988; vol. 5, *Arctic*, ed. David Damas, 1984; vol. 6, *Subarctic*, ed. June Helm, 1981; vol. 7, *Northwest Coast*, ed. Wayne Suttles, 1990; vol. 8, *California*, ed. Robert F. Heizer, 1978; vol. 15, *Northeast*, ed. Bruce G. Trigger, 1978.

Harmon, Daniel Will. *Sixteen Years in the Indian Country: The Journals of William Harmon 1800–1816*, ed. W. Kaye Lamb. Toronto: Macmillan, 1957.

Harper, Alan G. 'Canada's Indian Administration: Basic Concepts and Objectives', *América Indigena* 5, 2 (1945): 119–32.

———. 'Canada's Indian Administration: The "Indian Act"', *América Indigena* 5, 3 (1946): 297–314.

Harris, R. Cole, ed. *Historical Atlas of Canada I*. Toronto: University of Toronto Press, 1987.

Harrison, Julia. *Metis*. Vancouver: Douglas & McIntyre, 1985.

Hassard, Albert R. 'When the Oka Seminary Went Up in Flames', *Famous Canadian Trials*. Toronto: Carswell, 1924.

Havard, Gilles. *La grande paix de Montréal de 1701*. Montréal: Recherches amérindiennes au Québec, 1992.

Head, Francis Bond. *A Narrative*. London: Murray, 1839. (First published 1838.) App. A: 'Memorandum on the Aborigines of North America'. This memorandum is reproduced in part in Adam Shortt and Arthur G. Doughty, eds, *Canada and Its Provinces*, 23 vols. Toronto: Glasgow, Brook and Company, 1914–17, v, 337–9.

Hearne, Samuel. *A Journey from Prince of Wales's Fort in Hudson's Bay to the Northern Ocean in the Years 1769·1770·1771·1772*, ed. J.B. Tyrrell. Toronto: The Champlain Society, 1911.

Heidenreich, Conrad. *Huronia: A History and Geography of the Huron Indians 1600–1650*. Toronto: McClelland & Stewart, 1971.

Helm, June. 'Matonabbee's Map', *Arctic Anthropology* 26, 2 (1989): 28–47.

Henderson, William. *Canada's Indian Reserves: Pre-Confederation*. Ottawa: Indian and Northern Affairs, 1980.

Hendry, Charles E. *Beyond Traplines: Assessment of the Work of the Anglican Church of Canada with Canada's Native Peoples*. Toronto: Anglican Church, 1969.

Hereditary Chiefs of the Gitksan and Wet'suwet'en People. *The Spirit of the Land. The Opening Statement of the Gitksan and Wet'suwet'en Hereditary Chiefs in the Supreme Court of British Columbia May 11, 1987*. Gabriola, BC: Reflections, 1989.

Heyerdahl, Thor. *Early Man and the Ocean: A Search for the Beginnings of Navigation and Seaborne Civilizations*. New York: Vintage Books, 1980.

Hickey, Clifford G. 'An Examination of Processes of Cultural Change among Nineteenth Century Copper Inuit', *Études/Inuit/Studies* 8, 1 (1984): 13–35.

Hildebrandt, Walter, Sarah Carter, and Dorothy First Rider. *The True Spirit and Original Intent of Treaty 7*. Montreal and Kingston: McGill-Queen's University Press, 1996.

Hill, B.E. 'The Grand River Navigation Company and the Six Nations Indians', *Ontario History* 63, 1 (1971): 31–40.

Hind, Henry Youle. *Narrative of the Canadian Red River Exploring Expedition of 1857, and of the Assiniboine and Saskatchewan Exploring Expedition of 1858*, 2 vols in one. Edmonton: Hurtig, 1971. (Originally published in London, 1860.)

Hippler, Arthur E., and Stephen Conn. *Traditional Athabascan Law Ways and Their Relationship to Contemporary Problems of 'Bush Justice'*. Fairbanks: University of Alaska, 1972.

Hodder, Ian. *Reading the Past*. Cambridge: Cambridge University Press, 1986.

Hodge, F.W. *Handbook of Indians of Canada*. Ottawa: King's Printer, 1913.

Hodge, William H. *The First Americans Then and Now*. New York: Holt, Rinehart and Winston, 1981.

Hodgetts, John E. *Pioneer Public Service: An Administrative History of the United Canadas, 1841–1867*. Toronto: University of Toronto Press, 1955.

Hodgins, Bruce W., and Jamie Benidickson. *The Temagami Experience*. Toronto: University of Toronto Press, 1989.

———, Ute Lischke, and David T. McNab, eds. *Blockades and Resistance: Studies in Actions of Peace and the Temagami Blockades of 1988–89*. Waterloo, Ont.: Wilfrid Laurier University Press, 2003.

Hoffman, Bernard G. *Cabot to Cartier*. Toronto: University of Toronto Press, 1961.

Holdsworth, W.S. *A History of English Law*, vol. 9. London: Methuen, 1944.

Hopkins, David M., et al., eds. *Paleoecology of Beringia*. New York: Academic Press, 1982.

Hornig, James F., ed. *Social and Environmental Impacts of the James Bay Hydroelectric Project*. Montreal and Kingston: McGill-Queen's University Press, 1999.

Horsman, Reginald. *Expansion and American Indian Policy, 1783–1812*. East Lansing: Michigan State University Press, 1967.

———. *The Frontier in the Formative Years, 1783–1815*. New York: Holt, Rinehart and Winston, 1970.

Horwood, Harold, 'The People Who Were Murdered for Fun', *Maclean's*, 10 Dec. 1959, 27–43.

Hough, F.B. *A History of St. Lawrence and Franklin Counties, New York, from their Earliest Period to the Present Time*. Albany, NY, 1853.

Houston, James. *Running West*. Toronto: McClelland & Stewart, 1989.

Howard, James H. *The Plains-Ojibwa or Bungi, Hunters and Warriors of the Northern Prairie*. Vermillion: South Dakota Museum, University of South Dakota, 1965.

Howard, James H. *The Canadian Sioux*. Lincoln: University of Nebraska Press, 1984.

Howay, F.W. 'Early Days of the Maritime Trade on the Northwest Coast', *Canadian Historical Review* 4, (1923): 26–44.

———. 'Indian Attacks upon Maritime Traders of the Northwest Coast, 1785–1805', *Canadian Historical Review* 6, 4 (1925): 287–309.

———. 'The Ballad of the Bold Northwestman: An Incident in the Life of Captain John Kendrick', *Washington Historical Quarterly* 20 (1929): 114–23.

———. 'An Outline Sketch of the Maritime Fur Trade', *Canadian Historical Association Report* (1932): 5–14.

———. 'David Thompson's Account of His First Attempt to Cross the Rockies', *Queen's Quarterly* 40 (1933): 333–56.

Howley, James P. *The Beothucks or Red Indians*. Toronto: Coles Facsimile, 1980. (1st edn, Cambridge University Press, 1915.)

Huel, Raymond J.A. *Proclaiming the Gospel to the Indians and Métis*. Edmonton: University of Alberta Press, 1996.

Humphreys, R.A. 'Governor Murray's Views . . .', *Canadian Historical Review* 16 (1935): 166–9.

Hunt, Constance. 'The Development and Decline of Northern Conservation Reserves', *Contact* 8, 4 (1976).

Hunt, George T. *The Wars of the Iroquois*. Madison: University of Wisconsin Press, 1967.

Hutchinson, J.B., R.A. Silow, and S.G. Stephens. *The Evolution of Gossypium and Differentiation of the Cultivated Cottons*. London: Oxford University Press, 1947.

Hutchison, George, and Dick Wallace. *Grassy Narrows*. Toronto: Van Nostrand Reinhold, 1977.

Huxley, Selma, ed. *Los vascos en el marco Atlantico Norte Siglos XVI y XVII*. San Sebastian: Eusko Kultur Egintza Etor S.A., 1988.

Hyde, George E. *Indians of the High Plains*. Norman: University of Oklahoma Press, 1959.

Indian Conditions: A Survey. Ottawa: Indian Affairs and Northern Development, 1980.

Indian Government under Indian Act Legislation, 1868–1951. Ottawa: Indian and Northern Affairs, 1980.

Indians of Canada Pavilion. DIAND pamphlet for Expo 67.

Innis, Harold A. *The Fur Trade in Canada*. New Haven: Yale University Press, 1930.

———. 'Settlement and the Mining Frontier', in W.A. Mackintosh and W.L.G. Joerg, eds, *Canadian Frontiers of Settlement*, vol. 9, part 2. Toronto: Macmillan, 1936.

The Inuit Way: A Guide to Inuit Culture. Ottawa and Pauktuutit: Inuit Women's Association, *c.* 1990.

Irvin, William N. 'The First Americans: New Dates for Old Bones', *Natural History* 96, 2 (1987): 8–13.

Isaac, Thomas. *Aboriginal Law: Cases, Materials, and Commentary*. Saskatoon: Purich, 1995.

Isasti, Lope de. *Compendio Historial de la M.N.Y.M.L. Provincia de la Guipúzcoa*. San Sebastian: Ignacio Ramon Baroja, 1850.

Jablow, Joseph. *The Cheyenne in Plains Indian Trade Relations 1795–1840*. Monograph of the American Ethnological Society, 19. Seattle: University of Washington Press, 1950.

Jackson, Louis. *Our Caughnawagas in Egypt*. Montreal:

Drysdale, 1885.

Jacobs, Wilbur R. 'The Indian Treaties of 1763', *Western Pennsylvania Historical Magazine* 34, 3 (1951): 185–98.

Jacquin, Philippe. *Les indiens blancs*. Paris: Payot, 1989.

Jaenen, Cornelius J. 'Amerindian Views of French Culture in the Seventeenth Century', *Canadian Historical Review* 55, 3 (1974): 261–91.

———. *Friend and Foe: Aspects of French–Amerindian Culture Contact in the Sixteenth and Seventeenth Centuries*. Toronto: McClelland & Stewart, 1976.

———. *The Role of the Church in New France*. Toronto: McGraw-Hill Ryerson, 1976.

———. *The French Relationship with the Native People of New France and Acadia*. Ottawa: Indian and Northern Affairs Canada, 1984.

Jamieson, J.B. 'Trade and Warfare: Disappearance of the St. Lawrence Iroquoians', *Man in the Northeast* 39 (1990): 79–86.

Jamieson, Kathleen. *Indian Women and the Law in Canada: Citizens Minus*. Ottawa: Minister of Supply and Services, 1978.

Jefferys, Thomas. *The Natural and Civil History of the French Dominions in North and South America I: A Description of Canada and Louisiana*. London, 1760.

Jenness, Diamond. *Report of the Canadian Arctic Expedition 1913–18*. Vol. 12: *The Life of the Copper Eskimos*. Ottawa: Acland, 1922.

———. *Indians of Canada*. Ottawa: Acland, 1932.

———. *Eskimo Administration: II. Canada*. Montreal: Arctic Institute of North America, 1972 (reprint). This volume is part of a five-volume series on Inuit administration from Alaska to Greenland published by the Arctic Institute, 1962–3.

Jennings, Francis. *The Ambiguous Iroquois Empire*. New York: Norton, 1984.

———, ed. *The History and Culture of Iroquois Diplomacy*. Syracuse, NY: Syracuse University Press, 1985.

Jennings, Jesse D., ed. *Memoirs of the Society for American Archaeology*, 9 supplement to *American Antiquity* 18, 3, part 2 (1953): 72–97.

———, ed. *Ancient Native Americans*. San Francisco: Freeman, *c.* 1978.

Jérémie, Nicholas. *Twenty Years at York Factory, 1694–1714*. Ottawa: Thorburn and Abbott, 1926.

Jewitt, John. *A Journal Kept at Nootka Sound . . .* Boston: J. Jewitt, 1807.

Johannessen, Carl L. 'Folk Medicine Uses of Melanotic Asiatic Chickens as Evidence of Early Diffusion to the New World', *Social Science and Medicine* 15D (1981): 427–34.

———. 'Melanotic Chicken Use and Chinese Traits in Guatemala', *Revista de Historia de América* 93 (1982): 73–89.

Johnson, Frederick, ed. *Man in Northeastern North America*. Andover, Mass.: Philips Academy, 1940.

Johnston, Alexander, comp. *The Battle of Belly River: Stories of the Last Great Indian Battle*. Lethbridge: Lethbridge Branch of the Historical Society of Alberta, 1966.

Johnston, Basil. *Indian School Days*. Toronto: Key Porter Books, 1988.

Johnston, Charles M. 'Joseph Brant, the Grand River Lands and the Northwest Crisis', *Ontario History* 55 (1963): 267–82.

Jones, Peter. *History of the Ojebway Indians; with Especial References to Their Conversion to Christianity*. London: A.W. Bennett, 1861.

Judd, Carol M., and A.J. Ray, eds. *Old Trails and New Directions: Papers of the Third North American Fur Trade Conference*. Toronto: University of Toronto Press, 1980.

Kane, Paul. *Wanderings of an Artist*. Edmonton: Hurtig, 1968. (First published 1859.)

Kavash, Barrie. *Native Harvests*. New York: Random House, 1979.

Kaye, Barry, and D.W. Moodie. 'The Psoralea Food Resource of the Northern Plains', *Plains Anthropologist* 23, 82, pt 1 (1978): 329–36.

Kegg, Maude. *Portage Lake: Memories of an Ojibwa Childhood*, ed. and transcribed by John D. Nichols. Edmonton: University of Alberta Press, 1991.

Kehoe, Alice B. 'The Dakotas in Saskatchewan', in Ethel Nurge, ed., *The Modern Sioux*. Lincoln: University of Nebraska Press, 1970.

———. 'The Giveaway Ceremony of Blackfoot and Plains Cree', *Plains Anthropologist* 25, 87 (1980): 17–26.

———. *North American Indians, A Comprehensive Account*. Englewood Cliffs, NJ: Prentice-Hall, 1981.

———. *The Ghost Dance*. Toronto: Holt, Rinehart and Winston, 1989.

Kelley, David H. 'Proto-Tifinagh and Proto-Ogham in the Americas', *Review of Archaeology* 11, 1 (1990): 1–10.

Kelley, Thomas. *Run Indian Run*. Markham, Ont.: Paperjacks, 1972.

Kellogg, Louise Phelps. *The Fox Indians during the French Regime*. Reprinted from *Proceedings of the State Historical Society of Wisconsin 1907*. Madison, 1908: 142–88.

———. *The French Régime in Wisconsin and the Northwest*. New York: Cooper Square, 1968.

Kelsay, Isabel Thompson. *Joseph Brant, 1743–1807:*

Man of Two Worlds. Syracuse, NY: Syracuse University Press, 1984.

Kempton, James H. 'Maize as a Measure of Indian Skill', *Symposium on Prehistoric Agriculture*, University of New Mexico. Millwood, NY: Kraus Reprint, 1977.

Kenyon, W.A. *Tokens of Possession*. Toronto: Royal Ontario Museum, 1975.

———— and J.R. Turnbull. *The Battle for the Bay 1686*. Toronto: Macmillan, 1971.

Kip, William. *The Early Jesuit Missions in North America*. New York: Wiley and Putnam, 1846.

Klinck, Carl F. *Tecumseh: Fact and Fiction in Early Records*. Englewood Cliffs, NJ: Prentice-Hall, 1961.

Knight, Rolf. *Ecological Factors in Changing Economy and Social Organization among the Rupert House Cree*. Ottawa: National Museum of Canada Anthropology Papers No. 15, 1968.

————. *Indians at Work: An Informal History of Native Indian Labour in British Columbia 1858–1930*. Vancouver: New Star Books, 1978.

Knowles, Nathaniel. 'The Torture of Captives by the Indians of Eastern North America', *Proceedings of the American Philosophical Society* 82, 2 (Mar. 1940). Reprinted in *Scalping and Torture: Warfare Practices among North American Indians*. Ohsweken, Ont.: Iroqrafts Reprints, 1985.

Knudtson, Knut, and David Suzuki. *Wisdom of the Elders*. Toronto: Stoddart, 1992.

Krech, Shepard, III, ed. *The Subarctic Fur Trade*. Vancouver: University of British Columbia Press, 1984.

Kroeber, Alfred L. *Ethnology of the Gros Ventre*. New York: Anthropological Papers of the American Museum of Natural History I, 1908.

————. *Cultural and Natural Areas of Native North America*. Berkeley: University of California Press, 1939.

Kulchyski, Peter. '"A Considerable Unrest": F.O. Loft and the League of Indians', *Native Studies Review* 4, 1–2 (1988): 95–113.

————. 'Headwaters. A new history', *The Press Independent* (Somba K'e, NWT) 21, 27 (12 July 1991): 5.

————. 1994. *Unjust Relations: Aboriginal Rights in Canadian Courts*. Toronto: Oxford University Press, 1994.

Kupp, Jan. 'Could the Dutch Commercial Empire Have Influenced the Canadian Economy during the First Half of the Eighteenth Century?', *Canadian Historical Review* 52, 4 (1971): 367–88.

Lacan, Jean. *An Historical Notice on the Difficulties Arisen Between the Seminary of St. Sulpice of Montreal and Certain Indians, at Oka, Lake of Two Mountains: A Mere Case of Right of Property*. Montreal: La Minerve, 1876.

Laet, Joannes de. *L'Histoire du Nouveau Monde, ou Description des Indes occidentales . . .* Leyden: B. & A. Elzevier, 1640.

Laflèche, Guy. *Les saints martyrs canadiens*, 2 vols. Québec: Singulier, 1988.

Laliberte, Ron F., Priscilla Settee, James B. Waldram, Rob Innes, Brenda Macdougall, Lesley McBain, and F. Laurie Barron, eds. *Expressions in Canadian Native Studies*. Saskatoon: University of Saskatchewan Extension Press, 2000.

Lahontan, Louis Armand de Lom d'Arce de. *Nouveaux Voyages de M. le Baron de Lahontan dans l'Amérique septentrionale*, 2 vols. The Hague: Honoré Frères, 1703.

————. *New Voyages to North America by Baron de Lahontan*, 2 vols, ed. R.G. Thwaites. Chicago: A.C. McClurg, 1905.

Lancre, Pierre de. *Tableau de l'inconstance des mauvais anges et démons, ou il est amplement traicté des sorciers et de la sorcellerie . . . .* Paris: A. Berjon, 1612.

Landes, Ruth. *Ojibwa Religion and Midéwiwin*. Madison: University of Wisconsin Press, 1968.

Landon, Fred. 'Selections from the Papers of James Evans, Missionary to the Indians', *Ontario Historical Society Papers and Records* 26 (1930): 6–7.

Lang, George. 'Voyageur Discourse and the Absence of Fur Trade Pidgin', *Canadian Literature* 133 (Winter, 1992).

Laughlin, William S., and Albert B. Harper, eds. *The First Americans: Origins, Affinities and Adaptation*. New York and Stuttgart: Gustav Fischer, 1979.

Laviolette, E.E. *The Struggle for Survival*. Toronto: University of Toronto Press, 1973.

Leacock, Eleanor Burke, and Nancy Oestreich Lurie, eds. *North American Indians in Historical Perspective*. New York: Random House, 1971.

Le Clercq, Chrestien. *Nouvelle relation de la Gaspésie*. Paris: Auroy, 1691.

———— (att.). *First Establishment of the Faith in New France*, 2 vols, tr. John Gilmary Shea. New York: John G. Shea, 1881. (First published in Paris, 1691.)

————. *New Relation of Gaspesia*, ed. William F. Ganong. Toronto: The Champlain Society, 1910.

Lekson, Stephen H., Thomas C. Windes, John R. Stein, and W. James Judge. 'The Chaco Canyon Community', *Scientific American* 259, 1 (1988): 100–9.

León-Portilla, Miguel. *Aztec Thought and Culture*. Norman: University of Oklahoma Press, 1963.

Lescarbot, Marc. *The History of New France*, 3 vols, ed.

W.L. Grant. Toronto: The Champlain Society, 1907–14. (Based on 3rd edn, 1618; first published 1609.)

———. 'La Deffaite des Sauvages Armouchiquois', tr. Thomas Goetz, in William Cowan, ed., *Papers of the Sixth Algonquian Conference*. Ottawa: National Museums of Canada, 1975: 159–77.

Leslie, John F. *The Treaty of Amity, Commerce and Navigation 1794–1796: The Jay Treaty*. Ottawa: Indian and Northern Affairs Canada, 1979.

———. 'Buried Hatchet', *Horizon Canada* 4, 40 (1985): 944–9.

——— and Ron Maguire. *The Historical Development of the Indian Act*. Ottawa: Indian and Northern Affairs, 1978.

Lévi-Strauss, Claude. *The Jealous Potter*, tr. Bénédicte Chorier. Chicago: University of Chicago Press, 1988. (*La potière jalouse*. Paris: Plon, 1985).

Lewandowski, Stephen. 'Three Sisters—An Iroquoian Cultural Complex', *Northeast Indian Quarterly* 6, 1–2 (1989): 41–5.

Lewis, Henry T., and Theresa A. Ferguson. 'Yards, Corridors, and Mosaics: How to Burn a Boreal Forest', *Human Ecology* 16, 1 (1988): 57–77.

Lewis, John C. *The Horse in Blackfoot Indian Culture*. Washington: Smithsonian Institution, 1955.

———. *The Blackfeet*. Norman: University of Oklahoma Press, 1958.

Lewis, Oscar. *The Effects of White Contact upon Blackfoot Culture with Special References to the Fur Trade*. Monographs of the American Ethnological Society #6. New York, 1942.

Lewis, T.H., ed. 'The Narrative of the Expedition of Hernando de Soto by the Gentlemen of Elvas', in Frederick W. Hodge, ed., *Spanish Explorers in the Southern United States 1528–1543*. New York: Scribner's, 1907.

The Life of Rev. Amand Parent, the first French-Canadian ordained by the Methodist Church. Toronto: Briggs, 1887.

Lischke, Ute, and David T. McNab, eds. *Walking a Tightrope: Aboriginal People and Their Representations*. Waterloo, Ont.: Wilfrid Laurier University Press, 2005.

——— and ———, eds. *The Long Journey of a Forgotten People: Métis Identities and Family Histories*. Waterloo, Ont.: Wilfrid Laurier University Press, 2007.

Little Bear, Leroy, Menno Boldt, and J. Anthony Long. *Pathways to Self-Determination: Canadian Indians and the Canadian State*. Toronto: University of Toronto Press, 1984.

Living Treaties: Lasting Agreements. Ottawa: Department of Indian Affairs and Northern Development, 1985.

Lomasney, Patrick J. 'The Canadian Jesuits and the Fur Trade', *Mid-America* 15 (new ser., vol. 4), 3 (1933): 139–50.

Long, David Alan, and Olive Patricia Dickason, eds. *Vision of the Heart*. Toronto: Harcourt Brace, 1996. (2nd edn, 2000.)

Long, John S. *Treaty No. 9: The Indian Petition, 1889–1927*. Cobalt, Ont.: Highway Book Shop, 1978.

———. 'Manitu, Power, Books and Wiihtikow: Some Factors in the Adoption of Christianity by Nineteenth-Century Western James Bay Cree', *Native Studies Review* 3, 1 (1987): 1–30.

———. 'Narratives of Early Encounters between Europeans and the Cree of Western James Bay', *Ontario History* 80, 3 (1988): 227–45.

———. 'The Cree Prophets: Oral and Documentary Accounts', *Journal of the Canadian Church Historical Society* 31, 1 (1989): 3–13.

———. '"No Basis for Argument"?: The Signing of Treaty Nine in Northern Ontario, 1905–1906', *Native Studies Review* 5, 2 (1989): 19–54.

Long, J. Anthony, and Menno Boldt, eds. *Governments in Conflict? Provinces and Indian Nations and the Canadian State*. Toronto: University of Toronto Press, 1988.

———, Leroy Little Bear, and Menno Boldt. 'Federal Indian Policy and Indian Self-government in Canada: An Analysis of a Current Proposal', *Canadian Public Policy/Analyse de Politiques* 8, 2 (1982): 188–94.

Loo, Tina. 'Don Cranmer's Potlatch: Law as Coercion, Symbol and Rhetoric in British Columbia, 1884–1951', *Canadian Historical Review* 73, 2 (1992): 125–65.

Loskiel, George Henry. *History of the Missions of the United Brethren among the Indians in North America*, tr. C.I. LaTrobe. London: The Brethren's Society for the Furtherance of the Gospel, 1794.

Lost Visions, Forgotten Dreams. Exhibition guide, Canadian Museum of Civilization, 1996.

Lowie, Robert H. *Indians of the Plains*. New York: American Museum of Natural History, 1963. (1st edn, 1954.)

Lunn, Jean. 'The Illegal Fur Trade Out of New France, 1713–60', *Canadian Historical Association Annual Report* (1939): 61–76.

Lusty, Terry. *Metis, Social-Political Movement*. Calgary: Metis Historical Society, 1973.

Lyall, E. *An Arctic Man*. Edmonton: Hurtig, 1979.

Lytwyn, Victor P. 'Waterworld: The Aquatic Territory of the Great Lakes First Nations', in Dale Standen and David McNab, eds, *Gin Das Winan:*

Documenting Aboriginal History in Ontario. Toronto: Champlain Society Occasional Papers No. 2, 1996: 14–28.

McCall, Clayton W. 'The Peace of Michilimackinack', *Michigan History Magazine* 28, 3 (1944): 367–83.

McCarthy, Martha. *From the Great River to the Ends of the Earth: Oblate Missions to the Dene, 1847–1921*. Edmonton: University of Alberta Press, 1995.

McCartney, Allen P., ed. *Thule Eskimo Culture: An Anthropological Perspective*. Ottawa: National Museum of Man Mercury Series, Archaeological Survey of Canada Paper No. 88, 1979.

McClellan, Catharine. *My Old People Say: An Ethnographic Survey of Southern Yukon Territory*, 2 vols. Ottawa: National Museum of Man, 1975.

——. *Part of the Land, Part of the Water: A History of the Yukon Indians*. Vancouver: Douglas & McIntyre, 1987.

McCullum, Hugh and Karmel. *This Land Is Not for Sale*. Toronto: Anglican Book Centre, 1975.

——, ——, and John Olthuis. *Moratorium: Justice, Energy, the North, and the Native People*. Toronto: Anglican Book Centre, 1977.

McDougall, John. *Wa-pee Moostooch or White Buffalo*. Calgary: Herald Job Printing, 1908.

MacEwan, Grant. *Métis Makers of History*. Saskatoon: Western Producer, 1981.

McFarlane, Peter, and Wayne Haimila. *Ancient Land, Ancient Sky*. Toronto: Alfred A. Knopf, 1999.

MacFarlane, R.O. 'British Policy in Nova Scotia to 1760', *Canadian Historical Review* 19, 2 (1938): 154–67.

McGhee, Robert. *Canadian Arctic Prehistory*. Toronto: Van Nostrand Reinhold, 1978.

——. 'Labrador's Mysterious Burial Mound', *Canadian Heritage* (Dec. 1981): 11–13.

——. *Ancient Canada*. Ottawa: Canadian Museum of Civilization, 1989.

——. *Canada Rediscovered*. Hull, Que.: Canadian Museum of Civilization, 1991.

McGovern, Thomas M. 'Contributions to the Paleo-economy of Norse Greenland', *Acta Archaeologica* (Copenhagen) 54 (1983): 73–122.

MacGregor, J.G. *The Klondike Rush through Edmonton 1897–1898*. Toronto: McClelland & Stewart, 1970.

Mackenzie, Alexander. *Voyages from Montreal on the River St. Lawrence through the Continent of America*. London, 1801.

Maclane, Craig, and Michael Baxendale. *This Land Is Our Land: The Mohawk Revolt at Oka*. Montreal and Toronto: Optimum Publishing International, 1990.

MacLaren, Ian S. '"I came to rite thare portraits": Paul Kane's Journal of His Western Travels, 1846–1848', *American Art Journal* 21, 2 (1989): 6–88.

——. 'Samuel Hearne's Accounts of the Massacre at Bloody Falls, 17 July 1771', *Ariel: A Review of English Literature* 22, 1 (1991): 25–51.

McLean, Don. *Home from the Hill: A History of the Metis in Western Canada*. Regina: Gabriel Dumont Institute of Native Studies and Applied Research, 1987.

MacLean, John. *Vanguards of Canada*. Toronto: Missionary Society of the Methodist Church, 1918.

McLellan, John Stewart. *Louisbourg from Its Foundation to Its Fall, 1713–1758*. London: Macmillan, 1918.

MacLeod, J.E.A. 'Peigan Post and the Blackfoot Trade', *Canadian Historical Review* 24, 3 (1943): 273–9.

MacLeod, Margaret, and W.L. Morton. *Cuthbert Grant of Grantown*. Toronto: McClelland & Stewart, 1974.

McMillan, Alan D. *Native Peoples and Cultures of Canada: An Anthropological Overview*. Vancouver: Douglas & McIntyre, 1988.

McNab, David T. 'The Colonial Office and the Prairies in the Mid-Nineteenth Century', *Prairie Forum* 3, 1 (1978): 21–38.

——. 'Hearty Co-operation and Efficient Aid: The Metis and Treaty #3', *Canadian Journal of Native Studies* 3, 1 (1983): 131–49.

——. 'Métis Participation in the Treaty-Making Process in Ontario: A Reconnaissance', *Native Studies Review* 1, 2 (1985): 57–79.

——. *Circles of Time: Aboriginal Land Rights and Resistance in Ontario*. Waterloo, Ont.: Wilfrid Laurier University Press, 1999.

——. 'The Spirit of *Delgamuukw* and Aboriginal Oral Traditions in Ontario', in Owen Lippert, ed., *Beyond the Nass Valley: National Implications of the Supreme Court's Delgamuukw Decision*. Vancouver: Fraser Institute, 2000: 273–83.

——. 'Hiding in Plane View: Aboriginal Identities and a Fur Trade Company Family through Seven Generations', in David R. Newhouse, Cora J. Voyageur, and Dan Beavon, eds, *Hidden in Plain Sight: Contributions of Aboriginal Peoples to Canadian Identity and Culture*. Toronto: University of Toronto Press, 2005: 295–308.

——. 'The Mi'kmaq Nation of Newfoundland and Section 35 of the Charter of Rights and Freedoms', in Rick Riewe and Jill Oakes, eds, *Aboriginal Connections to Race, Environment and Traditions*. Winnipeg: Aboriginal Issues Press, University of Manitoba, 2006: 27–35.

——. 'A Brief History of the Denial of Indigenous Rights in Canada', in Janet Miron, ed., *A History of Human Rights in Canada*. Toronto: Canadian Scholars' Press, 2009.

Madill, Dennis. *British Columbia Treaties in Historical Perspective*. Ottawa: Indian and Northern Affairs Canada, 1981.

Mailhot, José. 'L'Etymologie de "Esquimau": Revue et Corrigé', *Études/Inuit/Studies* 2, 2 (1978): 59–69.

Mailhot, P.R., and D.M. Sprague. 'Persistent Settlers: The Dispersal and Resettlement of the Red River Metis, 1870–1885', *Canadian Journal of Ethnic Studies* 17 (1985): 1–30.

Maillard, Pierre-Antoine-Simon. 'Lettre de M. l'Abbé Maillard sur les missions de l'Acadie, et particulièrement sur les missions Micmaques', *Soirées canadiennes* 3 (1863): 290–426.

Mair, Charles. *Through the Mackenzie Basin*. Toronto: William Briggs, 1908.

Mandelbaum, David G. *Anthropology and People: The World of the Plains Cree*. Saskatoon: University of Saskatchewan Lectures #12, 1967.

———. *The Plains Cree*. Regina: Canadian Plains Research Centre, 1979. (First published in the American Museum of Natural History Anthropological Papers #37, Pt 2, 1940.)

Mangelsdorf, Paul C. 'Mystery of Corn', *Scientific American* 183, 1 (1950): 20–4.

———. 'Mystery of Corn: New Perspectives', *Proceedings of the American Philosophical Society* 127, 4 (1983): 215–47.

———. 'The Origin of Corn', *Scientific American* 255, 2 (1986): 80–6.

Manuel, George, and Michael Posluns. *The Fourth World: An Indian Reality*. Don Mills, Ont.: Collier Macmillan Canada, 1974.

Marchand, J.F. 'Tribal Epidemics in Yukon', *Journal of the American Medical Association* 123 (1943): 1019–20.

Margry, Pierre. *Découvertes et établissements dans l'ouest et dans le sud de l'Amérique septentrionale (1614–1754)*, 6 vols. Paris: Jouaust, 1976–86. (First published 1880.)

Marshall, Eliot. 'Clovis Counterrevolution', *Science* 249 (1990): 738–41.

Marshall, Ingeborg Constanze Luise. *The Red Ochre People*. Vancouver: Douglas & McIntyre, 1982.

———. *Beothuk Bark Canoes: An Analysis and Comparative Study*. Ottawa: National Museum of Man Mercury Series Paper No. 102, 1985.

———. *A History and Ethnography of the Beothuk*. Montreal and Kingston: McGill-Queen's University Press, 1996.

Martijn, Charles A. 'Innu (Montagnais) in Newfoundland', in William Cowan, ed., *Papers of the Twenty-first Algonquian Conference*. Ottawa: Carleton University, 1990.

Martin, Paul S., and H.E. Wright Jr, eds. *Pleistocene Extinctions: The Search for a Cause*. New Haven: Yale University Press, 1967.

Maurault, Joseph A. *Histoire des Abenakis depuis 1606 jusquà nos jours*. Sorel, Qué.: Atelier Typographique de la Gazette de Sorel, 1866. (Reprint, SR Publishers, 1969.)

Meggers, B.J. 'The Trans-Pacific Origin of Meso-American Civilization: A Preliminary Review of the Evidence and Its Theoretical Implications', *American Anthropologist* 77 (1975): 1–27.

Meili, Dianne. *Those Who Know: Profiles of Alberta's Native Elders*. Edmonton: NeWest Press, 1991.

Melling, John. *Right to a Future: The Native Peoples of Canada*. Toronto: The Anglican Church of Canada and the United Church of Canada, 1967.

Mercredi, Ovide, and Mary Ellen Turpel. *In the Rapids: Navigating the Future of First Nations*. Toronto: Viking, 1993.

Merritt, John, et al. *Nunavut Political Choices and Manifest Destiny*. Ottawa: Canadian Arctic Resources Committee, 1989.

Metis Association of Alberta et al. *Metis Land Rights in Alberta: A Political History*. Edmonton: Metis Association of Alberta, 1981.

Metisism, A Canadian Identity. Edmonton: Alberta Federation of Metis Settlement Associations, 1982.

Meyer, Roy W. 'The Canadian Sioux Refugees from Minnesota', *Minnesota History* 41, 1 (1968): 13–28.

The Mi'kmaq Treaty Handbook. Sydney and Truro, NS: Native Communications Society of Nova Scotia, 1987.

Miller, Christopher L., and George R. Hamell. 'A New Perspective on Indian–White Contact: Cultural Symbols and Colonial Trade', *Journal of American History* 73, 3 (1986): 311–28.

Miller, J.R. *Skyscrapers Hide the Heavens*. Toronto: University of Toronto Press, 1989.

———. 'Owen Glendower, Hotspur, and Canadian Indian Policy', *Ethnohistory* 37, 4 (1990): 386–415.

———. *Shingwauk's Vision*. Toronto: University of Toronto Press, 1996.

Miller, Jay. 'People, Berdaches, and Left-handed Bears', *Journal of Anthropological Research* 38, 3 (1982): 274–87.

——— and Carol M. Eastman, eds. *Tsimshian and Their Neighbors of the North Pacific Coast*. Seattle: University of Washington Press, 1984.

Milloy, John S. *The Plains Cree: Trade, Diplomacy and War, 1790–1870*. Winnipeg: University of Manitoba Press, 1988.

————. *A National Crime: The Canadian Government and the Residential School System, 1879–1986*. Winnipeg: University of Manitoba Press, 1999.

Mishkin, Bernard, *Rank and Warfare among Plains Indians*. Monographs of the American Ethnological Society #3. Seattle: University of Washington Press, 1940.

Mitchell, Marybelle. *From Talking Chiefs to Corporate Elite*. Montreal and Kingston: McGill-Queen's University Press, 1996.

Moermon, Daniel E. *Medicinal Plants of Native America*, 2 vols. Ann Arbor: University of Michigan Museum of Anthropology Technical Report #19, 1986.

Molloy, Tom. *The World Is Our Witness: The Historic Journey of the Nisga'a into Canada*. Calgary: Fifth House, 2000.

Monet, Don, and Skanu'u (Ardythe Wilson). *Colonialism on Trial*. Philadelphia and Gabriola Island, BC: New Society Publishers, 1992.

Montchrestien, Antoine de. *Traicté de l'oeconomie politique . . . .* Paris: Funck-Brentano, 1889. (First published in Rouen and Paris, 1615.)

Montgomery, Franz. 'Alexander Mackenzie's Literary Assistant', *Canadian Historical Review* 18, 3 (1937): 301–4.

Montgomery, Malcolm. 'The Six Nations Indians and the Macdonald Franchise', *Ontario History* 56 (1964): 13–25.

Moodie, D. Wayne, and Barry Kaye. 'Indian Agriculture in the Fur Trade Northwest', *Prairie Forum* 11, 2 (1986): 171–84.

———— and ————. 'The Northern Limit of Indian Agriculture in North America', *Geographical Review* 59, 4 (1969): 513–29.

———— and Arthur J. Ray. 'Buffalo Migrations in the Canadian Plains', *Plains Anthropologist* 21, 71 (1976): 45–51.

Moogk, Peter N. 'Les Petits Sauvages: The Children of Eighteenth-Century New France', in Joy Parr, ed., *Childhood and Family in Canadian History*. Toronto: McClelland & Stewart, 1982.

Moore, Pat, and Angela Wheelock, eds. *Wolverine Myths and Visions: Dene Traditions from Northern Alberta*. Edmonton: University of Alberta Press, 1990.

Moorhead, Max L. *The Apache Frontier*. Norman: University of Oklahoma Press, 1968.

Morantz, Toby. 'Oral and Recorded History in James Bay', in William Cowan, ed., *Papers of the Fifteenth Algonquian Conference*. Ottawa: Carleton University, 1984: 171–91.

Morell, Virginia. 'Confusion in Earliest America', *Science* 248 (1990): 439–41.

Morice, A.G. *Au pays de l'ours noir*. Paris: Delhomme et Briguet, 1897.

Morin, Victor. *Les médailles décernées aux Indiens: Étude historique et numismatique des colonisations européennes en Amérique*. Ottawa, 1916.

Morris, Alexander. *The Treaties of Canada with the Indians*. Toronto, 1880; reprint, Coles Publishing, 1971.

Morrison, David R. *The Politics of the Yukon Territory, 1898–1909*. Toronto: University of Toronto Press, 1968.

Morrison, James. *Treaty Nine (1905–06): The James Bay Treaty*. Ottawa: Department of Indian Affairs, 1986.

Morrison, Kenneth M. *The Embattled Northeast: The Elusive Ideal of Alliance in Abenaki–Euramerican Relations*. Berkeley: University of California Press, 1984.

————. 'Baptism and Alliance: The Symbolic Mediations of Religious Syncretism', *Ethnohistory* 37, 4 (1990): 416–37.

Morrison, R. Bruce, and C. Roderick Wilson. *Native Peoples: The Canadian Experience*. Toronto: McClelland & Stewart, 1986. (2nd edn, 1995.)

Morrison, William R. *A Survey of the History and Claims of the Native Peoples of Northern Canada*. Ottawa: Treaties and Historical Research Centre, 1983.

————. *Under the Flag: Canadian Sovereignty and the Native People in Northern Canada*. Ottawa: Indian and Northern Affairs, 1984.

Morrisseau, Norval. *Legends of My People the Great Ojibway*. Toronto: Ryerson, 1965.

Morse, Bradford W., ed. *Aboriginal Peoples and the Law: Indian, Metis and Inuit Rights in Canada*. Ottawa: Carleton University Press, 1985.

Morton, Arthur S. *History of Prairie Settlement and Dominion Lands Policy*. Toronto: Macmillan, 1938.

————. *A History of the Canadian West to 1870–71*, ed. Lewis G. Thomas. Toronto: University of Toronto Press, 1973. (First published, 1939.)

————, ed. *The Journal of Duncan M'Gillivray of the Northwest Company at Fort George on the Saskatchewan, 1794–1795*. Toronto: Macmillan, 1979.

Moyles, R.G. *British Law and Arctic Men*. Saskatoon: Western Producer Prairie Books, 1979.

Muise, D.A. *Approaches to Native History in Canada*. Ottawa: National Museum of Man, 1977.

Nash, Ronald J., ed. *The Evolution of Maritime Cultures on the Northeast and Northwest Coasts of America*. Burnaby, BC: Simon Fraser University Archaeology Publication #11, 1983.

Native Soldiers, Foreign Battlefields. Ottawa: Minister of Supply and Services, 1993.

Needham, Joseph, and Lu Gwei-Djen. *Trans-Pacific Echoes and Resonances: Listening Once Again*. Singapore and Philadelphia: World Scientific, 1985.

Nicholas, Andrea Bear. 'Maliseet Aboriginal Rights and Mascarene's Treaty, Not Dummer's Treaty', in William Cowan, ed., *Actes du dix-septième Congrès des Algonquinistes*. Ottawa: Carleton University, 1986.

Nicks, Trudy. 'Mary Anne's Dilemma: The Ethnohistory of an Ambivalent Identity', *Canadian Ethnic Studies/Études ethniques au Canada* 17, 2 (1985): 103–14.

———. 'Metis: A Glenbow Museum Exhibition', *Muse* 3, 4 (1986): 52–8.

———. 'Origins of the Alberta Metis: Land Claims Research Project 1978–1979', workpaper for the Metis Association of Alberta.

Niven, Jennifer. *The Ice Master: The Doomed 1913 Voyage of the Karluk*. New York: Hyperion, 2000.

Nixon, P.G. 'Early Administrative Developments in Fighting Tuberculosis among Canadian Inuit: Bringing State Institutions Back In', *Northern Review* 2 (1988): 67–84.

Noble, William C. 'Tsouharissen's Chiefdom: An Early Historic 17th Century Neutral Iroquoian Ranked Society', *Canadian Journal of Archaeology* 9, 2 (1985): 131–46.

Nock, David A. *A Victorian Missionary and Canadian Indian Policy: Cultural Synthesis v. Replacement*. Waterloo, Ont.: Wilfrid Laurier University Press, 1988.

Nordenskiöld, Erland. *Origin of the Indian Civilizations in South America*. Göteborg: Elanders Boktryckeri Aktiebolag, 1931.

North, Dick. *The Lost Patrol*. Vancouver: Raincoast Books, 1995. (First published 1978, and reprinted eight times.)

'Northern Development: At What Cost?', *The Catholic Register*, 11 Oct. 1975.

Nuligak. *I, Nuligak*, ed. and tr. Maurice Metayer. Toronto: Peter Martin, 1966.

Nungak, Zebedee, and Eugene Arima. *Eskimo Stories— unikkaatuat*. Ottawa: National Museums of Canada, 1969.

'Oka and Its Inhabitants', in *The Life of Rev. Amand Parent, the first French-Canadian ordained by the Methodist Church*. Toronto: Briggs, 1887.

Okpik, Abe. 'Bewildered Hunters in the 20th Century', *North* 13, 4 (1966): 48–50.

Oldmixon, John. *The History of Hudson's-Bay, Containing an Account of its Discovery and Settlement, the Progress of It, and the Present State; of the Indians, Trade and Everything Else Relating to It*, in

J.B. Tyrrell, ed., *Documents Relating to the Early History of Hudson Bay*. Toronto: The Champlain Society, 1931.

Oleson, Trygvi. *Early Voyages and Northern Approaches*. Toronto: McClelland & Stewart, 1963.

O'Malley, Martin. *The Past and Future Land*. Toronto: Peter Martin, 1976.

'O-na-tah Spirit of Corn', *Northeast Indian Quarterly* 6, 1–2 (1989): 40.

Opekokew, Delia. *The First Nations: Indian Government and the Canadian Confederation*. Saskatoon: Federation of Saskatchewan Indians, 1980.

———. *The First Nations: Indian Governments in the Community of Man*. Regina: Federation of Saskatchewan Indians, 1982.

Oswalt, Wendell H. *Eskimos and Explorers*. Novato, Calif.: Chandler and Sharp, 1979.

Oury, Dom Guy. *Marie de l'Incarnation*, 2 vols. Québec: Presses de l'Université Laval, 1973.

Overholt, Thomas W., and J. Baird Callicott. *Clothed-in-Fur and Other Tales*. Lanham, Md: University Press of America, 1982.

Overold, Joanne. *Our Metis Heritage . . . a portrayal*. n.p.: Metis Association of the Northwest Territories, 1976.

Page, Robert. *Northern Development: The Canadian Dilemma*. Toronto: McClelland & Stewart, 1986.

Pannekoek, Frits. *A Snug Little Flock: The Social Origins of the Riel Resistance of 1869–70*. Winnipeg: Watson & Dwyer, 1991.

Papen, Robert A. 'Le Métif: Le nec plus ultra des grammaires en contact', *Revue québécoise de linguistique théorique et appliquée* 6, 2 (1987): 57–70.

Parkman, Francis. *The Jesuits in North America in the Seventeenth Century*. Toronto: Morang, 1907. (First published 1867.)

Patterson, E. Palmer, II. *The Canadian Indian: A History Since 1500*. Toronto: Collier-Macmillan Canada, 1972.

Patterson, Lisa. 'Errant Peace Treaty', *The Archivist* 16, 6 (1989).

Paul, Daniel N. *We Were Not the Savages: A Micmac Perspective on the Collision of European and Aboriginal Civilization*. Halifax: Nimbus, 1993.

Payment, Diane. *Batoche (1870–1970)*. St Boniface, Man.: Editions du Blé, 1983.

Pearson, Richard, ed. *Windows on the Japanese: Studies in Archaeology and Prehistory*. Ann Arbor: Center for Japanese Studies, University of Michigan, 1986.

Peckham, Howard H. *Pontiac and the Indian Uprising*. Chicago: University of Chicago Press, 1947.

Peers, Laura L. 'Rich Man, Poor Man, Beggarman, Chief: Saulteaux in the Red River Settlement,

1812–1833', in William Cowan, ed., *Papers of the Eighteenth Algonquian Conference*. Ottawa: Carleton University, 1987: 261–70.

Pelly, David F. 'How Inuit Find Their Way in the Trackless Arctic', *Canadian Geographic* 3, 4 (1991): 58–64.

Perrot, Nicholas (*c.* 1644–1717). *Mémoire sur les moeurs, coustumes et relligion des sauvages de l'Amérique septentrionale*, ed. J. Tailhan. Montréal: Editions Elysées, 1973. (First published 1864.)

Peterson, Jacqueline. 'A Social Portrait of the Great Lakes Métis', *Ethnohistory* 25, 1 (1978): 41–67.

—— and Jennifer S.H. Brown, eds. *The New Peoples: Being and Becoming Métis in North America*. Winnipeg: University of Manitoba Press, 1985.

Petrone, Penny, ed. *First Peoples, First Voices*. Toronto: University of Toronto Press, 1983.

——, ed. *Northern Voices: Inuit Writing in English*. Toronto: University of Toronto Press, 1988.

Pettipas, Katherine. *Severing the Ties that Bind*. Winnipeg: University of Manitoba Press, 1994.

Peyser, Joseph L. *Letters from New France*. South Bend, Ind.: Joseph L. Peyser, 1983; revised 1988.

——. 'The Fate of the Fox Survivors: A Dark Chapter in the History of the French in the Upper Country, 1726–1737', *Wisconsin Magazine of History* 73, 2 (1989–90): 82–110.

Pichon, Thomas. *Lettres et mémoires pour servir à l'histoire naturelle, civile et politique du Cap Breton*. La Haye and London, 1760. (Johnson Reprint, 1966.)

Piddocke, Stuart. 'The Potlatch System of the Southern Kwakiuktl: A New Perspective', *Southwestern Journal of Anthropology* 21 (1965): 244–64.

Pindera, Loreen. 'The Making of a Warrior', *Saturday Night* 106, 3 (1990): 30–9.

Pipes, Nellie B. 'Indian Conditions in 1836–38', *Oregon Historical Quarterly* 32, 4 (1931): 332–42.

Pitseolak, Peter, and Dorothy Harley Eber. *People from Our Side*, tr. Ann Hanson. Montreal and Kingston: McGill-Queen's University Press, 1993.

Poelzer, Greg. 'Aboriginal People and Environmental Policy in Canada: No Longer at the Margins', in Debora L. VanNijnatten and Robert Boardman, eds, *Canadian Environmental Policy: Context and Cases in a New Century*. Toronto: Oxford University Press, 2002.

Ponting, J. Rick, ed. *Arduous Journey: Canadian Indians and Decolonization*. Toronto: McClelland & Stewart, 1986.

—— and Roger Gibbins. *Out of Irrelevance: A Socio-Political Introduction to Indian Affairs in Canada*. Toronto: Butterworths, 1980.

Prehistory of the Lockport Site. Winnipeg: Manitoba Department of Cultural Affairs and Historic Resources, 1985.

Preston, Richard. 'The Cree Way Project: An Experiment in Grassroots Curriculum Development', in William Cowan, ed., *Papers of the Tenth Algonquian Conference*. Ottawa: Carleton University, 1979.

Price, John. *Indians of Canada: Cultural Dynamics*. Scarborough, Ont.: Prentice-Hall, 1979.

Price, Richard, ed. *The Spirit of Alberta Indian Treaties*. Edmonton: Pica Pica Press, 1987. (First published 1979.)

Purich, Donald. *The Metis*. Toronto: James Lorimer, 1968.

——. *Our Land: Native Rights in Canada*. Toronto: James Lorimer, 1986.

Pyne, Stephen J. *Fire in America*. Princeton, NJ: Princeton University Press, 1982.

Quaife, Milo Milton, ed. *The Western Country in the 17th Century: The Memoirs of Antoine Lamothe Cadillac and Pierre Liette*. New York: Citadel Press, 1962.

Quinn, D.B., ed. *New American World: A Documentary History of North America to 1612*, 5 vols. New York: Arno and Bye, 1979.

Raby, Stewart. 'Indian Land Surrenders in Southern Saskatchewan', *Canadian Geographer* 17, 1 (Spring 1973).

Ramusio, Giovanni Battista (1485–1557). *Navigations et Voyages (XVI siècle)*, tr. Général Langlois and M.J. Simon. Paris: Centre de Documentation 'André Thevet', 1933. (First published in three vols, 1554–1606.)

Raunet, David. *Without Surrender, Without Consent: A History of the Nishga Land Claims*. Vancouver: Douglas & McIntyre, 1984.

Ravenstein, E.G., ed. *The Strange Adventures of Andrew Battell of Leigh in Angola and the Adjoining Regions*. London: Hakluyt Society, 1901. (Kraus Reprint, 1967.)

Ray, Arthur J. *Indians in the Fur Trade: Their Role as Trappers, Hunters, and Middlemen in the Lands Southwest of Hudson Bay 1660–1870*. Toronto: University of Toronto Press, 1974.

——. *The Canadian Fur Trade and the Industrial Age*. Toronto: University of Toronto Press, 1990.

——. *I Have Lived Here Since the World Began*. Toronto: Lester Publishing and Key Porter Books, 1996.

—— and Donald Freeman. *'Give Us Good Measure': An Economic Analysis of Relations between the Indians and the Hudson's Bay Company before 1763*. Toronto: University of Toronto Press, 1978.

[Razilly, Claude]. 'Mémoire du Chevalier de Razilly',

Revue de Géographie 19 (1886): 374–83, 453–64.

Redbird, Duke. *We Are Metis: A Metis View of the Development of a Native Canadian People*. Willowdale, Ont.: Ontario Metis & Non-Status Indian Association, 1980.

Reeves, Brian O.K. *Culture Change in the Northern Plains 1000 B.C.–A.D. 1000*. Edmonton: Archaeological Survey of Alberta, Occasional Paper No. 20, 1983.

Reid, Robert L. 'The Chinook Jargon and British Columbia', *British Columbia Historical Quarterly* 6, 1 (1942): 1–11.

Reynolds, Henry. *Frontier*. Sydney and London: Allen & Unwin, 1987.

Rich, E.E. 'Trade Habits, Economic Motivation, among the Indians of North America', *Canadian Journal of Economics and Political Science* 26, 1 (1960): 35–53. This article was reprinted, with illustrations added, under the title 'The Indian Traders', *The Beaver* Outfit 301 (1970): 5–20.

———. *The Fur Trade in the Northwest to 1857*. Toronto: McClelland & Stewart, 1967.

———, ed. *The Letters of John McLaughlin from Fort Vancouver to the Governor and Committee*, 1st ser., 1825–38. London: The Hudson's Bay Record Society, 1941.

Richardson, Boyce. 'Kind Hearts or Forked Tongues?' *The Beaver* Outfit 67, 1 (1987): 16–41.

———, ed. *Drum Beat: Anger and Renewal in Indian Country*. Ottawa: Assembly of First Nations, 1989.

Richardson, John. *Wacousta; Or, The Prophecy: A Tale of Canada*, 3 vols. London and Edinburgh: Cadell and Blackwood, 1832.

Richter, Daniel K. 'War and Culture: The Iroquois Experience', *William and Mary Quarterly* 40, 4 (1982): 528–59.

———. 'Iroquois versus Iroquois: Jesuit Missions and Christianity in Village Politics, 1642–1686', *Ethnohistory* 32, 1 (1985): 1–16.

Riddell, William R. *The Ancaster 'Bloody Assize' of 1814*. Toronto, 1923. (Reprinted from *Ontario Historical Society Papers and Records* 20 [1923]: 107–25.)

Ridington, Robin. 'Technology, World View, and Adaptive Strategy in a Northern Hunting Society', *Canadian Review of Sociology and Anthropology* 19, 4 (1982): 469–81.

Riley, Carroll, et al., eds. *Man across the Sea: Problems of Pre-Columbian Contact*. Austin: University of Texas Press, 1971.

Rindos, David. 'The Evolution of the Capacity for Culture: Sociobiology, Structuralism, and Cultural Evolution', *Current Anthropology* 27, 4 (1986): 315–32.

Robertson, Gordon. *Memoirs of a Very Civil Servant*. Toronto: University of Toronto Press, 2000.

Robertson, Heather. *Reservations Are for Indians*. Toronto: Lewis and Samuel, 1970.

Robinson, Michael P. *Sea Otter Chiefs*. Vancouver: Friendly Cove Press, c. 1978.

Roe, Frank Gilbert. *The Indian and the Horse*. Norman: University of Oklahoma Press, 1951.

———. 'Early Agriculture in Western Canada in Relation to Climatic Stability', *Agricultural History* 26, 3 (1952): 104–23.

———. *The North American Buffalo*. Toronto: University of Toronto Press, 1970. (1st edn 1951.)

Rogers, Edward, and Donald B. Smith, eds. *Aboriginal Ontario*. Toronto: Ontario Historical Studies Series, 1994.

Rogers, Robert. *Concise Account of North America . . .* London: J. Millan, 1765.

Ronda, James P. 'The Sillery Experiment: A Jesuit–Indian Village in New France, 1637–1663', *American Indian Culture and Research Journal* 3, 1 (1979): 1–18.

Rooth, Anna Birgitta. 'The Creation Myths of the North American Indians', *Anthropos* 52 (1957): 497–508.

Ross, Eric. *Beyond the River and the Bay*. Toronto: University of Toronto Press, 1970.

———. *Returning to the Teachings: Exploring Aboriginal Justice*. Toronto: Penguin, 1996.

Ross, W. Gillies. *Whaling and Eskimos: Hudson Bay 1860–1915*. Ottawa: National Museums of Canada Publications in Ethnology No. 10, 1975.

———. 'Canadian Sovereignty in the Arctic: The Neptune Expedition of 1903–04', *Arctic* 29, 2 (1976): 87–104.

Rotman, Leonard Ian. *Parallel Paths: Fiduciary Doctrine and the Crown–Nation Relationship in Canada*. Toronto: University of Toronto Press, 1996.

Rotstein, A. 'Trade and Politics: An Institutional Approach', *Western Canadian Journal of Anthropology* 3, 1 (1972): 1–28.

Rousseau, Jacques. 'The Northern Québec Eskimo Problem and the Ottawa–Québec Struggle', *Anthropological Journal of Canada* 7, 2 (1968): 2–21.

Rowe, John Howland. 'Diffusionism and Archaeology', *American Antiquity* 31, 3, pt 1 (1966): 334–7.

Rudnicki, Walter. 'The Politics of Aggression: Indian Termination in the 1980s', *Native Studies Review* 3, 1 (1987): 81–93.

Rutter, N.W. 'Late Pleistocene History of the Western Canadian Ice-Free Corridor', *Canadian Journal of Anthropology* 1, 1 (1980): 1–8.

Sagard, Gabriel. *The Long Journey to the Country of the Hurons*, tr. H.H. Langton. Toronto: The

Champlain Society, 1939. (First published in Paris, 1632.)

———. *Histoire du Canada, et voyages que les frères mineurs Recollects y ont faicts pour la conversion des infidelles*, 4 vols. Paris: Sonnius, 1636.

Sahagún, Bernardino de (d. 1590). *Florentine Codex. General History of the Things of New Spain*, 12 vols, eds Arthur J.O. Anderson and Charles E. Dibble. Sante Fe, New Mexico: University of Utah and the School of American Research, 1970–5. (First published in Mexico in three vols, 1829–30.)

Salisbury, Neal. *Manitou and Providence: Indians, Europeans, and the Making of New England, 1500–1643*. Oxford: Oxford University Press, 1982.

Samson, Colin. *A Way of Life That Does Not Exist: Canada and the Extinguishment of the Innu*. St John's and London: ISER Books/Verso, 2003.

Sanger, David. 'Culture Change as an Adaptative Process in the Maine–Maritimes Region', *Arctic Anthropology* 12, 2 (1975): 60–75.

Sauer, Carl Ortwin. *Land and Life*, ed. John Leighly. Berkeley: University of California Press, 1969. (First published 1963.)

———. *Sixteenth Century North America: The Land and People as Seen by the Europeans*. Berkeley: University of California Press, 1971.

Savelle, Max. *The Diplomatic History of the Canadian Boundary 1749–1763*. New Haven: Yale University Press, 1940.

Scalberg, Daniel A. 'Seventeenth and Early Eighteenth-Century Perceptions of *Coureurs-de-Bois* Religious Life', *Proceedings of the Annual Meeting of the Western Society for French History* 17 (1990): 82–95.

Schedule of Indian Bands, Reserves and Settlements. Ottawa: Indian and Northern Affairs Canada, 1987.

Schledermann, Peter. *Crossroads to Greenland: 3000 Years of Prehistory in the Eastern High Arctic*. Calgary: Arctic Institute of North America, 1990.

Schlesier, Karl H. 'Epidemics and Indian Middlemen: Rethinking the Wars of the Iroquois, 1609–1653', *Ethnohistory* 23, 2 (1976): 129–45.

Schmaltz, Peter S. *The History of the Saugeen Indians*. Ottawa: Ontario Historical Society Research Publication No. 5, 1977.

———. *The Ojibwa of Southern Ontario*. Toronto: University of Toronto Press, 1991.

Schmidt, Sarah. 'New-Age Warriors', *Saturday Night*, 14 Oct. 2000, 22–9.

Schurr, Theodore, et al. 'Amerindian Mitochondrial DNA Have Rare Asian Mutations at High Frequencies, Suggesting They Derived from Four Primary Maternal Lineages', *American Journal of Human Genetics* 46 (1990): 613–23.

Schwartz, Brian. *First Principles: Constitutional Reform with Respect to the Aboriginal Peoples of Canada, 1982–1984*. Kingston, Ont.: Institute of Intergovernmental Relations, 1985.

Scott, Colin. 'Hunting Territories, Hunting Bosses and Communal Production among Coastal James Bay Cree', *Anthropologica* 28, 1–2 (1986): 163–73.

———. 'Ideology of Reciprocity between the James Bay Cree and the Whiteman State', in Peter Skalník, ed., *Outwitting the State*. New Brunswick, NJ: Transaction Publishers, 1989.

———. 'Knowledge Construction among Cree Hunters: Metaphors and Literal Understanding', *Journal de la Société des Américanistes* 75 (1989): 193–208.

Scott, Duncan Campbell. 'The Last of the Indian Treaties', *Scribner's Magazine* 40, 5 (1906): 573–83.

Scott, William. *Report Relating to the Affairs of the Oka Indians, made to the Superintendent General of Indian Affairs*. Ottawa, [1883].

Seaborn, Edwin. *The March of Medicine in Western Ontario*. Toronto: Ryerson, 1944.

Secoy, Frank Raymond. *Changing Military Patterns on the Great Plains*. Monographs of the American Ethnological Society 21. Seattle: University of Washington Press, 1953.

Seeber, Pauline MacDougall. 'The European Influence on Abenaki Economics before 1615', in William Cowan, ed., *Papers of the Fifteenth Algonquian Conference*. Ottawa: Carleton University 1984.

Seguin, Margaret, ed. *The Tsimshian. Images of the Past: Views for the Present*. Vancouver: University of British Columbia Press, 1984.

Séguin, Robert-Lionel. *La vie libertine en Nouvelle-France au XVIIe siècle*, 2 vols. Montréal: Leméac, 1972.

Sévigny, P-André. *Les Abénaquis habitat et migrations (17e et 18e siècles)*. Montréal: Bellarmin, 1976.

Sharp, Paul F. 'Massacre at Cypress Hills', *Saskatchewan History* 7 (1954): 81–99.

Shimada, Izumi, and John F. Merkel. 'Copper Alloy Metallurgy in Ancient Peru', *Scientific American* 265, 1 (1991): 80–6.

Shkilnyk, Anastasia M. *A Poison Stronger Than Love: The Destruction of an Ojibwa Community*. New Haven: Yale University Press, 1985.

Shnirelman, Victor A. 'Origin and Early History of Maize', *European Review of Native American Studies* 3, 2 (1989): 23–8.

Shorten, Lynda. *Without Reserve: Stories of Urban Natives*. Edmonton: NeWest Press, 1980.

Shortt, Adam, and Arthur G. Doughty, eds. *Canada and Its Provinces*, 23 vols. Toronto: Glasgow, Brook and Company, 1914–17.

Shutler, Richard, Jr, ed. *Early Man in the New World.* Beverly Hills, Calif.: Sage Publications, 1983.

Siggins, Maggie. *Riel: A Life of Revolution.* Toronto: HarperCollins, 1994.

Silman, Janet. *Enough Is Enough.* Toronto: Women's Press, 1994. (First published 1987.)

Silver, Arthur. 'French Quebec and the Métis Question, 1869–1885', in Carl Berger and Ramsay Cook, eds, *The West and the Nation.* Toronto: McClelland & Stewart, 1976: 91–113.

Sioui, Georges. *Pour une autohistoire amérindienne: Essai sur les fondements d'une morale sociale.* Québec: Les Presses de l'Université Laval, 1989. In English, *For an Amerindian Autohistory*, tr. Sheila Fischman. Montreal and Kingston: McGill-Queen's University Press, 1992.

———. *Les Wendats: Une civilisation méconnue.* Québec: Les Presses de l'Université Laval, 1994.

Sissons, Jack. *Judge of the Far North.* Toronto: McClelland & Stewart, 1968.

Slattery, Brian. 'The Constitutional Guarantee of Aboriginal and Treaty Rights', *Queen's Law Journal* 8, 1–2 (1982): 232–73.

———. *Ancestral Lands, Alien Laws: Judicial Perspectives on Aboriginal Title.* Saskatoon: University of Saskatchewan Law Centre, 1983.

———. 'Understanding Aboriginal Rights', *Canadian Bar Review* 66 (1987): 727–83.

Sluman, Norma. *Poundmaker.* Toronto: Ryerson Press, 1967.

——— and Jean Goodwill. *John Tootoosis.* Ottawa: Golden Dog Press, 1982.

Smith, Dan. *The Seventh Fire.* Toronto: Key Porter Books, 1993.

Smith, Donald B. *Le Sauvage. The Native People in Quebec: Historical Writing on the Heroic Period (1534–1663) of New France.* Ottawa: National Museums of Canada, 1974.

———. 'Who Are the Mississauga?', *Ontario History* 67, 4 (1975): 211–23.

———. 'The Dispossession of the Mississauga Indians: A Missing Chapter in the Early History of Upper Canada', *Ontario History* 73, 2 (1981): 67–87.

———. 'Aboriginal Rights a Century Ago', *The Beaver* 67, 1 (1987): 4–15.

———. *Sacred Feathers: The Reverend Peter Jones (Kahkewaquonaby) and the Mississauga Indians.* Toronto: University of Toronto Press, 1987.

———. *From the Land of Shadows: The Making of Grey Owl.* Saskatoon: Western Producer Prairie Books, 1990.

Smith, James G.E. 'The Western Woods Cree: Anthropological Myth and Historical Reality', *American Ethnologist* 14 (1987): 434–48.

Snow, Alpheus Henry. *The Question of Aborigines in the Law and Practice of Nations.* New York and Washington: Government Printing Office, 1919.

Snow, Dean R. *The Archaeology of New England.* New York: Academic Press, 1980.

Society for Converting and Civilizing the Indians of Upper Canada. Circular, 20 Oct. 1830, in Metropolitan Toronto Public Library, History, H-1830.

Sosin, Jack M. *Whitehall and the Wilderness: The Middle West in British Colonial Policy, 1760–1775.* Lincoln: University of Nebraska Press, 1961. (Reprinted 1980.)

Sperry, John R. Letter published in *Arctic* 40, 4 (1987): 364.

Sprague, D.N. *Canada and the Metis, 1869–1885.* Waterloo, Ont.: Wilfrid Laurier University Press, 1988.

——— and R.P. Frye, comps. *The Genealogy of the First Metis Nation.* Winnipeg: Pemmican, 1983.

Spry, Irene M. *The Palliser Expedition: An Account of John Palliser's British North American Expedition 1857–1860.* Toronto: Macmillan, 1963.

Stacey, C.P. 'Canada and the Nile Expedition of 1884–1885', *Canadian Historical Review* 33 (1952): 319–40.

Stager, J.K. 'Reindeer Herding as Private Enterprise in Canada', *Polar Record* 22, 137 (1984): 127–36.

Stagg, Jack. 'Anglo–Indian Relations in North America to 1763 and an Analysis of the Royal Proclamation of 7 October 1763'. Ottawa: Department of Indian Affairs and Northern Development, Research Branch, 1981.

Stanley, George F.G. 'The First Indian "Reserves" in Canada', *Revue d'histoire de l'Amérique française* 4 (1950): 178–209.

———. 'The Indians in the War of 1812', *Canadian Historical Review* 31, 2 (1950): 145–65. Reprinted in Morris Zaslow, ed., *The Defended Border: Upper Canada and the War of 1812.* Toronto: Macmillan, 1964.

———. *The Birth of Western Canada: A History of the Riel Rebellion.* Toronto: University of Toronto Press, 1960. (First published 1936.)

———. 'The Significance of the Six Nations' Participation in the War of 1812', *Ontario History* 55, 4 (1963): 215–31.

———. 'The Six Nations and the American Revolution', *Ontario History* 56, 4 (1964): 217–32.

———. *The War of 1812: Land Operations.* Toronto: Macmillan, 1983.

Stefansson, Vilhjalmur. *The Friendly Arctic: The Story of Five Years in Polar Regions.* New York: Macmillan, 1943.

Steward, Julian H. *Theory of Culture Change*. Urbana: University of Illinois Press, 1976.

Stone, Thomas. 'Legal Mobilization and Legal Penetration: The Department of Indian Affairs and the Canada Party at St. Regis, 1876–1918', *Ethnohistory* 22, 4 (1975): 375–408.

——. 'Atomistic Order and Frontier Violence: Miners and Whalemen in the Nineteenth Century Yukon', *Ethnology* 22, 4 (1983): 327–39.

——. 'Flux and Authority in a Subarctic Society: The Yukon Miners in the Nineteenth Century', *Ethnohistory* 30, 4 (1983): 203–16.

Stonechild, A. Blair. 'The Indian View of the 1885 Uprising', in J.R. Miller, ed., *Sweet Promises*. Toronto: University of Toronto Press, 1991: 259–76.

Strong, William Duncan. 'The Plains Culture Area in the Light of Archaeology', *American Anthropologist* 35, 2 (1933): 271–87.

Such, Peter. *Riverrun*. Toronto: Clark, Irwin, 1973.

——. *Vanished Peoples*. Toronto: NC Press, 1978.

Sugden, John. *Tecumseh's Last Stand*. Norman: University of Oklahoma Press, 1985.

Swarbrick, Brian. 'A 9,000-year-old Housing Project', *Alberta Report* 18, 34 (1991): 50–1.

Sweat of the Sun: Gold of Peru. Edinburgh: City of Edinburgh Museum and Art Gallery, 1990.

Tanner, Helen Hornbeck, ed. *Atlas of Great Lakes Indian History*. Norman: University of Oklahoma Press, 1987.

Taylor, J. Garth. *Labrador Eskimo Settlements of the Early Contact Period*. Ottawa: National Museums of Canada, 1974.

Tehariolina, Margaret Vincent. *La nation huronne, son histoire, sa culture, son esprit*. Québec: Editions du Pélican, 1984.

Teillet, Jean. 'The Winds of Change: Métis Rights after Powley, Taku and Haida', in Lischke and McNab, eds, *The Long Journey of a Forgotten People*, 55–78.

Teit, James. 'The Salishan Tribes of the Western Plateau', *45th Annual Report, U.S. Bureau of Ethnology (1927–1928)* (Washington, 1930), 28–396.

Tennant, Paul. 'Native Political Organization in British Columbia, 1900–1960: A Response to Internal Colonialism', *B.C. Studies* 55 (1982): 3–49.

——. *Aboriginal Peoples and Politics: The Indian Land Question in British Columbia, 1849–1989*. Vancouver: University of British Columbia Press, 1990.

Tester, Frank James, and Peter Kulchyski. *Tammarniit (Mistakes)*. Vancouver: University of British Columbia Press, 1994.

Testso, John. *Trapping Is My Life*. Toronto: Peter Martin, 1970.

Thevet, André. *La Cosmographie Universelle*, 2 vols. Paris: Chaudiere, 1575.

——. *Les singularitez de la France Antarctique*, ed. Paul Gaffarel. Paris: Maisonneuve, 1878. (Reprint of 1558 edition.)

Thistle, Paul C. *Indian–European Trade Relations in the Lower Saskatchewan River Region to 1840*. Winnipeg: University of Manitoba Press, 1986.

Thomas, Lewis H. *The Struggle for Responsible Government in the North-West Territories 1870–97*. Toronto: University of Toronto Press, 1978. (First published 1956.)

Thomason, Sarah Grey, and Terrence Kaufman. *Language Contact, Creolization, and Genetic Linguistics*. Berkeley: University of California Press, 1988.

Thornton, Russell. *American Indian Holocaust and Survival: A Population History Since 1492*. Norman: University of Oklahoma Press, 1987.

Titley, E. Brian. 'W.M. Graham: Indian Agent Extraordinaire', *Prairie Forum* 1 (1983): 25–41.

——. *A Narrow Vision: Duncan Campbell Scott and the Administration of Indian Affairs in Canada*. Vancouver: University of British Columbia Press, 1986.

Tkaczuk, Diana Claire, and Brian C. Vivian, eds. *Cultures in Conflict: Current Archaeological Perspectives*. Calgary: University of Calgary, 1989.

Tobias, John L. 'Protection, Civilization, Assimilation: An Outline History of Canada's Indian Policy', *Western Canadian Journal of Anthropology* 6, 2 (1976): 13–30.

——. 'The Subjugation of the Plains Cree, 1879–1885', *Canadian Historical Review* 64, 4 (1983): 519–48.

Tooker, Elizabeth. 'The Iroquois Defeat of the Huron: A Review of Causes', *Pennsylvania Archaeologist* 33, 1–2 (1963): 115–23.

Torrelli, Maurice. 'Les Indiens du Canada et le droit des traités dans la jurisprudence canadienne', *Annuaire Français de Droit International* 20 (1974): 227–49.

Trask, Kerry A. 'Settlement in a Half-Savage Land: Life and Loss in the Metis Community of La Baye', *Michigan Historical Review* 15 (1989): 1–27.

Trigger, Bruce G. *The Indian and the Heroic Age of New France*. Ottawa: Canadian Historical Association Booklet No. 30, 1970.

——. 'Champlain Judged by His Indian Policy: A Different View of Early Canadian History', *Anthropologica* 13 (1971): 85–114.

——. *The Children of Aataentsic: A History of the Huron People to 1660*, 2 vols. Montreal and Kingston: McGill-Queen's University Press, 1976.

——. *Natives and Newcomers: Canada's 'Heroic Age'*

Reconsidered. Montreal and Kingston: McGill-Queen's University Press, 1985.

———. 'Early Native North American Response to European Contact', *Journal of American History* 77, 4 (1991): 1195–1215.

———, Toby Morantz, and Louise Dechêne, eds. *Le Castor Fait Tout*. Montreal: Lake St Louis Historical Society, 1987.

——— and Wilcomb Washburn, eds. *Cambridge History of the Native Peoples of the Americas*. Cambridge: Cambridge University Press, 1996.

Trudel, Marcel. *Histoire de la Nouvelle-France I: Les vaines tentatives, 1524–1603*. Montréal: Fides, 1963.

———. *Histoire de la Nouvelle-France II: Le comptoir 1604–1627*. Montréal: Fides, 1966.

———. *Histoire de la Nouvelle-France III: La seigneurie des Cent-Associés, 1627–1663*. Montréal: Fides, 1979.

Tuck, James A., and Robert McGhee. 'Archaic Cultures in the Strait of Belle Isle Region, Labrador', *Arctic Anthropology* 12, 2 (1975): 76–91.

——— and ———. 'An Archaic Indian Burial Mound in Labrador', *Scientific American* 235, 5 (1976): 122–7.

Turgeon, Laurier. 'Basque–Amerindian Trade in the Saint-Lawrence during the Sixteenth Century: New Documents, New Perspectives', *Man in the Northeast* 40 (1990): 81–7.

Tyrrell, J.B., ed. *David Thompson's Narrative of His Explorations in Western America, 1784–1812*. Toronto: The Champlain Society, 1916.

Ulloa, Antonio de. *A Voyage to South America . . .* , 2 vols, tr. John Adams. London: J. Stockdale, 1806. (Published in Spanish, 1748; first English edn, 1758.)

Upton, Leslie F.S. 'The Origins of Canadian Indian Policy', *Journal of Canadian Studies* 10, 4 (1973): 51–61.

———. 'The Extermination of the Beothuks of Newfoundland', *Canadian Historical Review* 58, 2 (1977): 133–53.

———. *Micmacs and Colonists: Indian–White Relations in the Maritimes, 1713–1867*. Vancouver: University of British Columbia Press, 1979.

———. 'Contact and Conflict on the Atlantic and Pacific Coasts of Canada', *B.C. Studies* 45 (1980): 103–15.

Usher, Jean. 'Duncan of Metlakatla: The Victorian Origins of a Model Indian Community', in W.L. Morton, ed., *The Shield of Achilles: Aspects of Canada in the Victorian Age*. Toronto: McClelland & Stewart, 1968.

———. *William Duncan of Metlakatla*. Ottawa: National Museums of Canada, 1974.

Van Kirk, Sylvia. 'Thanadelthur', *The Beaver* Outfit 304, 4 (1974): 40–5.

———. *Many Tender Ties: Women in Fur-Trade Society 1670–1870*. Norman: University of Oklahoma Press, 1983. (First published in Winnipeg, 1980.)

Vavilov, V.I. 'Mexica i Tsentralnaia Amerika kak osnovnoi tsentr proiskoozhdenia kulturnykh rasternii', *Trudy po prikladnoi botanike, genetike i selektsii* 26, 3 (1931).

———. 'Velikiye zemledeltsheskie kultury dokolumbovoi Ameriki i ikh vzaimootnosheniia', *Izvestiia Gosudarstvennogo Geografocheskogo Obshchestva* 71, 10 (1939).

Vecsey, Christopher. 'The Story of the Iroquois Confederacy', *Journal of the American Academy of Religion* 54, 1 (1986): 79–106.

Vennum, Thomas. *Wild Rice and the Ojibway People*. St Paul: Minnesota Historical Society Press, 1988.

Verbicky-Todd, Eleanor. *Communal Buffalo Hunting Among the Plains Indians: An Ethnographic and Historical Review*. Edmonton: Archaeological Survey of Alberta Occasional Papers #24, 1984.

Vogel, Virgil J. *American Indian Medicine*. Norman: University of Oklahoma Press, [1970].

Von Haast, H.F., ed. *New Zealand Privy Council Cases 1840–1932*. Wellington: Butterworths, 1938.

Wachtel, Nathaniel. *The Vision of the Vanquished: The Spanish Conquest of Peru through Indian Eyes, 1530–1570*. London: Hassocks, 1977.

Walker, James W. St G. 'The Canadian Indian in Historical Writing', Canadian Historical Association, *Historical Papers* (1971): 21–51.

———. 'The Indian in Canadian Historical Writing, 1972–1982', in Getty and Lussier, eds, *As Long As the Sun Shines and Water Flows*, 340–61.

———. 'Race and Recruitment in World War I: Enlistment of Visible Minorities in the Canadian Expeditionary Force', *Canadian Historical Review* 70, 1 (1989): 1–26.

Wallace, Anthony F.C. 'Revitalization Movements: Some Theoretical Considerations for Their Comparative Study', *American Anthropologist* 58, 2 (1956): 264–81.

———. 'Origins of Iroquois Neutrality: The Grand Settlement of 1701', *Pennsylvania History* 24 (1957): 223–35.

———. *Death and Rebirth of the Seneca*. New York: Vintage Books, 1969.

Wallace, Douglas C., Katherine Garrison, and William Knowles. 'Dramatic Founder Effects in Amerindian Mitochondrial DNAs', *American Journal of Physical Anthropology* 68 (1985): 149–55.

Wallace, Paul A.W. *The White Roots of Peace*. Port

Washington, NY: Ira J. Friedman, 1968.

Ware, Reuben. *The Lands We Lost: A History of Cut-Off Lands and Land Losses from Indian Reserves in British Columbia*. Vancouver: Union of BC Chiefs Land Claims Research Centre, 1974.

Warman, Arturo. 'Corn as Organizing Principle', *Northeast Indian Quarterly* 6, 1–2 (1989): 20–7.

Warren, William W. *History of the Ojibway People*. St Paul: Minnesota Historical Society Press, 1984. (1st edn 1885.)

Warry, Wayne. *Unfinished Dreams: Community Healing and the Reality of Aboriginal Self-Government*. Toronto: University of Toronto Press, 1999.

Watt, Keith. 'Uneasy Partners', *The Globe and Mail Report on Business Magazine* (Sept. 1990): 42–9.

Weatherford, Jack. *Indian Givers: How the Indians Transformed the World*. New York: Crown Publishers, 1988.

Weaver, Sally. *Making Canadian Indian Policy: The Hidden Agenda 1968–1970*. Toronto: University of Toronto Press, 1981.

———. 'Indian Policy in the New Conservative Government, Part II: The Nielsen Task Force in the Context of Recent Policy Initiatives', *Native Studies Review* 2, 2 (1986): 1–84.

Welsh, Jennifer. *At Home in the World: Canada in the 21st Century*. Toronto: HarperCollins, 2004.

Werner, Louis. 'Caught in a Maize of Genes', *Americas* 52, 3 (May–June 2000): 6–17.

West, Reverend John. *The Substance of a Journal During a Residence at the Red River Colony, British North America*. London, 1824.

Wet, J.M.J. de, and J.R. Harlan. 'Origin of Maize: The Tripartite Hypothesis', *Euphytica* 21 (1972).

'What the Stones Tell Us', *Archaeology* 49, 6 (1996): 61.

Whitbourne, Sir Richard. *A Discourse and Discovery of New-found-land, with many reasons to prove how worthy and beneficiall a Plantation may there be made, after a far better manner than now is*. London: Felix Kyngston, 1620.

Whitehead, Ruth Holmes. *The Old Man Told Us: Excerpts from Micmac History 1500–1950*. Halifax: Nimbus, 1991.

Whiteley, W.H. 'The Establishment of the Moravian Mission in Labrador and British Policy, 1763–83', *Canadian Historical Review* 65, 1 (1964): 29–50.

Wiebe, Rudy, and Bob Beal. *War in the West: Voices of the 1885 Rebellion*. Toronto: McClelland & Stewart, 1985.

——— and Yvonne Johnson. *Stolen Life: The Journey of a Cree Woman*. Toronto: Alfred A. Knopf, 1998.

Wilkinson, Doug. *Land of the Long Day*. Ottawa: National Film Board, 1951.

Williams, David R. *Simon Peter Gunanoot: Trapper Outlaw*. Victoria: Sono Nis Press, 1982.

Williams, Glyndwr. 'The Puzzle of Anthony Henday's Journal, 1754–55', *The Beaver* Outfit 309, 3 (1978): 40–56.

———, ed. *Andrew Graham's Observations on Hudson's Bay 1767–91*. London: Hudson's Bay Record Society, 1969.

Williams, Paul. 'Canada's Laws about Aboriginal Peoples: A Brief Overview', *Law and Anthropology* 1 (1986): 93–120.

Williams, Robert A. *The American Indian in Western Legal Thought*. New York: Oxford University Press, 1990.

Williamson, Robert G. *Eskimo Underground: Socio-Cultural Change in the Canadian Central Arctic*. Uppsala: Institutionen för Allmän och Jämförande Etnografi Vid Uppsala Universitet, 1974.

Winter, Keith. *Shananditti*. Vancouver: J.J. Douglas, 1975.

Wissler, Clark. 'Diffusion of Culture in the Plains of North America', *International Congress of Americanists*, 15th session (Quebec, 1906): 39–52.

Witthoft, John. 'Archaeology as a Key to the Colonial Fur Trade', in *Aspects of the Fur Trade*. St Paul: Minnesota Historical Society, 1967.

Wonders, William C., ed. *Canada's Changing North*. Toronto: McClelland & Stewart, 1976.

Woodcock, George. *Gabriel Dumont*. Edmonton: Hurtig, 1975.

———. *A Social History of Canada*. Toronto: Penguin, 1989.

Woodward, Jack. *Native Law*. Toronto: Carswell, 1989.

Wormington, H.M., and Richard G. Forbis. *An Introduction to the Archaeology of Alberta, Canada*. Denver: Denver Museum of National History, 1965.

Wraxall, Peter. *An Abridgement of the Indian Affairs Contained in Four Folio Volumes transacted in the Colony of New York, from the Year 1678 to the Year 1751*, ed. C.H. McIlwain. Cambridge, Mass.: Harvard University Press, 1915.

Wuttunee, William I.C. *Ruffled Feathers*. Calgary: Bell Books, 1971.

York, Geoffrey. *The Dispossessed: Life and Death in Native Canada*. London: Vintage UK, 1990. (First published 1989.)

——— and Loreen Pindera. *People of the Pines: The Warriors and the Legacy of Oka*. Toronto: Little, Brown, 1991.

Young, David E., ed. *Health Care Issues in the Canadian North*. Edmonton: Boreal Institute for Northern Studies, 1989. (First published 1988.)

Young, J.Z., et al. *The Emergence of Man*. London: The

Royal Society and The British Academy, 1981.

Zaslow, Morris. *The Opening of the Canadian North*. Toronto: McClelland & Stewart, 1971.

———. *The Northward Expansion of Canada 1914–1967*. Toronto: McClelland & Stewart, 1988.

———, ed. *A Century of Canada's Arctic Islands*. Ottawa: Royal Society of Canada, 1981.

Zoltvany, Yves F. 'New France and the West, 1701–1713', *Canadian Historical Review* 46, 4 (1965): 301–22.

Index